T3-ANT-578

Digital MOS Integrated Circuits

OTHER IEEE PRESS BOOKS

Geometric Theory of Diffraction, *Edited by R. C. Hansen*
Modern Active Filter Design, *Edited by R. Schaumann, M. A. Soderstrand, and K. R. Laker*
Adjustable Speed AC Drive Systems, *Edited by B. K. Bose*
Optical Fiber Technology, II, *Edited by C. K. Kao*
Protective Relaying for Power Systems, *Edited by S. H. Horowitz*
Analog MOS Integrated Circuits, *Edited by P. R. Gray, D. A. Hodges, and R. W. Brodersen*
Interence Analysis of Communication Systems, *Edited by P. Stavroulakis*
Integrated Injection Logic, *Edited by J. E. Smith*
Sensory Aids for the Hearing Impaired, *Edited by H. Levitt, J. M. Pickett, and R. A. Houde*
Data Conversion Integrated Circuits, *Edited by Daniel J. Dooley*
Semiconductor Injection Lasers, *Edited by J. K. Butler*
Satellite Communications, *Edited by H. L. Van Trees*
Frequency-Response Methods in Control Systems, *Edited by A.G.J. MacFarlane*
Programs for Digital Signal Processing, *Edited by the Digital Signal Processing Committee*
Automatic Speech & Speaker Recognition, *Edited by N. R. Dixon and T. B. Martin*
Speech Analysis, *Edited by R. W. Schafer and J. D. Markel*
The Engineer in Transition to Management, *I. Gray*
Multidimensional Systems: Theory & Applications, *Edited by N. K. Bose*
Analog Integrated Circuits, *Edited by A. B. Grebene*
Integrated-Circuit Operational Amplifiers, *Edited by R. G. Meyer*
Modern Spectrum Analysis, *Edited by D. G. Childers*
Digital Image Processing for Remote Sensing, *Edited by R. Bernstein*
Reflector Antennas, *Edited by A. W. Love*
Phase-Locked Loops & Their Application, *Edited by W. C. Lindsey and M. K. Simon*
Digital Signal Computers and Processors, *Edited by A. C. Salazar*
Systems Engineering: Methodology and Applications, *Edited by A. P. Sage*
Modern Crystal and Mechanical Filters, *Edited by D. F. Sheahan and R. A. Johnson*
Electrical Noise: Fundamentals and Sources, *Edited by M. S. Gupta*
Computer Methods in Image Analysis, *Edited by J. K. Aggarwal, R. O. Duda, and A. Rosenfeld*
Microprocessors: Fundamentals and Applications, *Edited by W. C. Lin*
Machine Recognition of Patterns, *Edited by A. K. Agrawala*
Turning Points in American Electrical History, *Edited by J. E. Brittain*
Charge-Coupled Devices: Technology and Applications, *Edited by R. Melen and D. Buss*
Spread Spectrum Techniques, *Edited by R. C. Dixon*
Electronic Switching: Central Office Systems of the World, *Edited by A. E. Joel, Jr.*
Electromagnetic Horn Antennas, *Edited by A. W. Love*
Waveform Quantization and Coding, *Edited by N. S. Jayant*
Communication Satellite Systems: An Overview of the Technology, *Edited by R. G. Gould and Y. F. Lum*
Literature Survey of Communication Satellite Systems and Technology, *Edited by J. H. W. Unger*
Solar Cells, *Edited by C. E. Backus*
Computer Networking, *Edited by R. P. Blanc and I. W. Cotton*
Communications Channels: Characterization and Behavior, *Edited by B. Goldberg*
Large-Scale Networks: Theory and Design, *Edited by F. T. Boesch*
Optical Fiber Technology, *Edited by D. Gloge*
Selected Papers in Digital Signal Processing, II, *Edited by the Digital Signal Processing Committee*
A Guide for Better Technical Presentations, *Edited by R. M. Woelfle*
Career Management: A Guide to Combating Obsolescence, *Edited by H. G. Kaufman*
Energy and Man: Technical and Social Aspects of Energy, *Edited by M. G. Morgan*
Magnetic Bubble Technology: Integrated-Circuit Magnetics for Digital Storage and Processing, *Edited by H. Chang*
Frequency Synthesis: Techniques and Applications, *Edited by J. Gorski-Popiel*
Literature in Digital Processing: Author and Permuted Title Index (Revised and Expanded Edition), *Edited by H. D. Helms, J. F. Kaiser, and L. R. Rabiner*
Data Communications via Fading Channels, *Edited by K. Brayer*
Nonlinear Networks: Theory and Analysis, *Edited by A. N. Willson, Jr.*
Computer Communications, *Edited by P. E. Green, Jr. and R. W. Lucky*
Stability of Large Electric Power Systems, *Edited by R. T. Byerly and E. W. Kimbark*
Automatic Test Equipment: Hardware, Software, and Management, *Edited by F. Liguori*
Key Papers in the Development of Coding Theory, *Edited by E. R. Berkekamp*

Digital MOS Integrated Circuits

Edited by
Mohamed I. Elmasry
Associate Professor of
Electrical Engineering
University of Waterloo

A volume in the IEEE PRESS Selected Reprint Series,
prepared under the sponsorship of the
IEEE Solid-State Circuits Council.

The Institute of Electrical and Electronics Engineers, Inc., New York

IEEE PRESS

1981 Editorial Board

S. B. Weinstein, *Chairman*

J. M. Aein
R. W. Brodersen
J. K. Butler
R. E. Crochiere
P. H. Enslow, Jr.
E. W. Herold
A. W. Love
A. G. J. MacFarlane
M. G. Morgan
B. R. Myers
Norman Peach
P. M. Russo
Herbert Sherman

W. R. Crone, *Managing Editor*

Isabel Narea, *Production Manager*

Copyright © 1981 by
THE INSTITUTE OF ELECTRICAL AND ELECTRONICS ENGINEERS, INC.
345 East 47th Street, New York, NY 10017
All rights reserved.

PRINTED IN THE UNITED STATES OF AMERICA

Sole Worldwide Distributor (Exclusive of IEEE):

JOHN WILEY & SONS, INC.
605 Third Ave.
New York, NY 10016

Wiley Order Numbers: Clothbound: 0-471-86202-9
Paperbound: 0-471-86203-7

IEEE Order Numbers: Clothbound: PC01503
Paperbound: PP01511

Library of Congress Catalog Card Number 81-6522

Library of Congress Cataloging in Publication Data
Main entry under title:

Digital MOS integrated circuits.

(IEEE Press selected reprint series)
Bibliography: p.
Includes indexes.
1. Integrated circuits—Large scale integration—Addresses, essays, lectures.
2. Integrated circuits—Very large scale integration—Addresses, essays, lectures.
3. Metal oxide semiconductors—Addresses, essays, lectures. I. Elmasry, Mohamed I., 1943-
TK7874.D535 621.381'73 81-6522
ISBN 0-87942-151-7 AACR2
ISBN 0-87942-152-5 (pbk.)

This book is dedicated to all the men and women who have made the field of *Integrated Circuits* one of the most rewarding and enjoyable careers in recent years.

Acknowledgment

The editor would like to thank Professor D. A. Hodges of the University of California at Berkeley and Dr. W. D. Pricer and Dr. L. M. Terman of IBM for their valuable comments, interest, and encouragement. The research and the scientific atmosphere created at the University of Waterloo by my colleagues has provided the inspiration for this project.

During the challenging and enjoyable 1980–81 year I have spent at the Micro-components Organization of Burroughs Corporation in San Diego, I was able to complete this book and for that I would like to thank Steve Ou and Bob Gilberg.

Contents

Preface xi

Part I: MOS in Digital Circuit Design 1

Section 1.1: Digital MOS Integrated Circuits 3

Digital MOS Integrated Circuits: A Tutorial, *M.I. Elmasry* (March 1981) 4

Section 1.2: Depletion Loads 28

A High-Performance n-Channel MOS LSI Using Depletion-Type Load Elements, *T. Masuhara, M. Nagata, and N. Hashimoto* (*IEEE Journal of Solid-State Circuits*, June 1972) 29

Analysis and Characterization of the Depletion-Mode IGFET, *Y. A. El-Mansy* (*IEEE Journal of Solid-State Circuits*, June 1980) 37

Section 1.3: Circuit Techniques 46

Eliminating Threshold Losses in MOS Circuits by Bootstrapping Using Varactor Coupling, *R.E. Joynson, J.L. Mundy, J. F. Burgess, and C. Neugebauer* (*IEEE Journal of Solid-State Circuits*, June 1972) 47

A MOST Inverter with Improved Switching Speed, *J. Koomen and J. van Den Akker* (*IEEE Journal of Solid-State Circuits*, June 1972) 55

FET Logic Configuration, *E. M. Blaser and D. A. Conrad* (*IEEE International Solid State Circuits Conference*, 1978) 62

Section 1.4: Comparison of MOS Logic Gates 64

Comparison of MOSFET Logic Circuits, *P. W. Cook, D. L. Critchlow, and L. M. Terman* (*IEEE Journal of Solid-State Circuits*, October 1973) 65

Part II: Digital VLSI 73

Section 2.1: Scaling-Down MOSFETs 76

Design of Ion-Implanted MOSFETs with Very Small Physical Dimensions, *R. H. Dennard, F. H. Gaensslen, H-N Yu, V. L. Rideout, E. Bassous, and A. R. LeBlanc* (*IEEE Journal of Solid-State Circuits*, October 1974) 77

1μm MOSFET VLSI Technology: Part II—Device Designs and Characteristics for High-Performance Logic Applications, *R. H. Dennard, F. H. Gaensslen, E. J. Walker, and P. W. Cook* (*IEEE Journal of Solid-State Circuits*, April 1979) 89

Analytical Models of the Threshold Voltage and Breakdown Voltage of Short-Channel MOSFETs Derived from Two-Dimensional Analysis, *T. Toyabe and S. Asai* (*IEEE Journal of Solid-State Circuits*, April 1979) 97

Characteristics and Limitation of Scaled-Down MOSFETs Due to Two-Dimensional Field Effect, *H. Masuda, M. Nakai, and M. Kubo* (*IEEE Transactions on Electron Devices*, June 1979) 105

Generalized Guide for MOSFET Miniaturization, *J.R. Brews, W. Fichtner, E. H. Nicollian, and S. M. Sze* (*IEEE Electron Device Letters*, January 1980) 112

Performance Limits of E/D NMOS VLSI, *K. N. Ratnakumar, J. D. Meindl, and D. J. Bartelink* (*IEEE International Solid State Circuits Conference*, 1980) 115
On Scaling MOS Devices for VLSI, *Y. A. El-Mansy (IEEE International Conference on Circuits and Computers, 1980)* 118

Section 2.2: Processing Technologies 123

Scaling the Barriers to VLSI's Fine Lines, *J. Lyman* (*Electronics*, June 19, 1980) 124
HMOS II Static RAMs Overtake Bipolar Competition, *R.M. Jecmen, C–H Hui, A. V. Ebel, V. Kynett, and R. J. Smith* (*Electronics*, September 13, 1979) 136
C–MOSLSI: Comparing Second Generation Approaches, *D. L. Wollesen* (*Electronics*, September 13, 1979) 141
Twin-Tub CMOS–A Technology for VLSI Circuits, *L. C. Parrillo, R. S. Payne, R. E. Davis, G. W. Reutlinger, and R. L. Field* (*IEEE International Electron Devices Meeting*, 1980) 149
Silicon–Gate n–Well CMOS Process by Full Ion–Implantation Technology, *T. Ohzone, H. Shimura, K. Tsuji, and T. Hirao* (*IEEE Transactions on Electron Devices*, September 1980) 153
Comparison of Bulk Silicon and SOS for VLSI CMOS, *A. Aitken* (*IEEE International Electron Devices Meeting*, 1980) 160
1μm MOSFET VLSI Technology: Part 1—An Overview, *H-N Yu, A. Reisman, C. M. Osburn, and D. L. Critchlow* (*IEEE Journal of Solid–State Circuits*, April 1979) 164

Section 2.3: Novel Circuit Structures for VLSI 171

Single–Device–Well MOSFET's, *E. Z. Hamdy, M. I. Elmasry, and Y. A. El-Mansy* (*IEEE Transactions on Electron Devices*, March 1981) 172
A Quadruply Self–Aligned MOS (QSA MOS) A New Short Channel High-Speed High-Density MOSFET for VLSI, *K. Ohta, K. Yamada, K. Shimizu, and Y. Tarui* (*IEEE International Electron Devices Meeting*, 1979) 178
MOS Buried Load Logic, *Y. Sakai, T. Masuhara, O. Minato, and N. Hashimoto* (*IEEE International Solid–State Circuits Conference*, 1980) 182
One–Gate–Wide CMOS Inverter on Laser–Recrystallized Polysilicon, *J. F. Gibbons and K. F. Lee* (*IEEE Electron Device Letters*, June 1980) 184

Section 2.4: Circuit and System Design for VLSI 186

The Evolution of Digital Electronics Towards VLSI, *R. W. Keyes* (*IEEE Journal of Solid–State Circuits*, April 1979) 187
Cost and Performance of VLSI Computing Structures, *C. A. Mead and M. Rem* (*IEEE Journal of Solid–State Circuits*, April 1979) 196
The Design of Special–Purpose VLSI Chips, *M. J. Foster and H. T. Kung* (*IEEE Computer*, January 1980) 204
1μm MOSFET VLSI Technology: Part III—Logic Circuit Design Methodology and Applications, *P. W. Cook, S. E. Schuster, J. T. Parrish, V. Di Lonardo, and D. R. Freedman* (*IEEE Journal of Solid–State Circuits*, April 1979) 218
Delay–Time Optimization for Driving and Sensing of Signals on High–Capacitance Paths of VLSI Systems, *A. M. Mohsen and C. A. Mead* (*IEEE Journal of Solid–State Circuits*, April 1979) 231

Part III: MOS Memory Cells and Circuits 241

Section 3.1: Memory Circuits and Cells 242

MOSFET Memory Circuits, *L. M. Terman* (*Proceedings of the IEEE*, July 1971) 243
A Survey of High–Density Dynamic RAM Cell Concepts, *P. K. Chatterjee, G. W. Taylor, R. L. Easley, H-S Fu, and A. F. Tasch, Jr.* (*IEEE Transactions on Electron Devices*, June 1979) 258
One-Device Cells for Dynamic Random–Access Memories: A Tutorial, *V. Leo Rideout* (*IEEE Transactions on Electron Devices*, June 1979) 271
A 2K x 8-Bit Static MOS RAM with a New Memory Cell Structure, *T. Ohzone, T. Hirao, K. Tsuji, S. Horiuchi, and S. Takayanagi* (*IEEE Journal of Solid–State Circuits*, April 1980) 285
Variable Resistance Polysilicon for High Density CMOS RAM, *T. Iisuka, H. Nozawa, Y. Mizutani, H. Kaneko, and S. Kohyama* (*IEEE International Electron Devices Meeting*, 1979) 290
High Performance MOS EPROMs Using a Stacked–Gate Cell, *P. J. Salsbury, W. L. Morgan, G. Perlegos, and R. T. Simko* (*IEEE International Solid–State Circuits Conference*, 1977) 294
A Novel MOS PROM Using a Highly Resistive Poly-Si Resistor, *M. Tanimoto, J. Murota, Y. Ohmori, and N. Ieda* (*IEEE Transactions on Electron Devices*, March 1980) 296

Section 3.2: Peripheral Circuits . . . 300

The Design of MOS Dynamic RAMs, *R. C. Foss* (*IEEE International Solid-State Circuits Conference*, 1979) . . . 301

Peripheral Circuits for One-Transistor Cell MOS RAMs, *R. C. Foss and R. Harland*, (*IEEE Journal of Solid-State Circuits*, October 1975) . . . 303

Storage Array and Sense/Refresh Circuit for Single-Transistor Memory Cells, *K. U. Stein, A. Sihling, and E. Doering* (*IEEE Journal of Solid-State Circuits*, October 1972) . . . 310

Optimization of the Latching Pulse for Dynamic Flip-Flop Sensors, *W. T. Lynch and H. J. Boll* (*IEEE Journal of Solid-State Circuits*, April 1974) . . . 315

Cross-Coupled Charge-Transfer Sense Amplifier, *L. G. Heller* (*IEEE International Solid-State Circuits Conference*, 1979) . . . 321

Part IV: MOS Digital Circuit Applications . . . 323

Section 4.1: Programmable Logic Arrays . . . 325

High-Speed Static Programmable Logic Array in LOCMOS, *P. May and F. C. Schiereck* (*IEEE Journal of Solid-State Circuits*, June 1976) . . . 326

A Study in the Use of PLA-Based Macros, *P. W. Cook, C. W. Ho, and S. E. Schuster* (*IEEE Journal of Solid-State Circuits*, October 1979) . . . 331

Section 4.2: Digital Signal Processors . . . 338

LSI's for Digital Signal Processing, *N. Ohwada, T. Kimura, and M. Doken* (*IEEE Journal of Solid-State Circuits*, April 1979) . . . 339

A Single-Chip Digital Signal Processor for Voiceband Applications, *Y. Kawakami, T. Nishitani, E. Sugimoto, E. Yamauchi, and M. Suzuki* (*IEEE International Solid-State Circuits Conference*, 1980) . . . 346

A Digital Signal Processor for Telecommunications Applications, *J. R. Boddie, G. T. Daryanani, I. I. Eldumiati, R. N. Gadenz, J. S. Thompson, S. M. Walters, and R. A. Pedersen* (*IEEE International Solid-State Circuits Conference*, 1980) . . . 348

Section 4.3: Microprocessors . . . 350

Projecting VLSI's Impact on Microprocessors, *D. Queyssac* (*IEEE Spectrum*, May 1979) . . . 351

The Intel 8086 Microprocessor: A 16-bit Evolution of the 8080, *S. P. Morse, W. B. Pohlman, and B. W. Ravenel* (*IEEE Computer*, June 1978) . . . 355

A Microprocessor Architecture for a Changing World: The Motorola 68000, *E. Stritter and T. Gunter* (*IEEE Computer*, February 1979) . . . 364

Section 4.4: Static RAMs . . . 373

A High Performance Low Power 2048-Bit Memory Chip in MOSFET Technology and its Application, *R. Remshardt and U. G. Baitinger* (*IEEE Journal of Solid-State Circuits*, June 1976) . . . 374

A High Performance 4K Static RAM Fabricated with an Advanced MOS Technology, *R. D. Pashley, W. H. Owen, III, K. R. Kokkonen, R. M. Jecmen, A. V. Ebel, C. N. Ahlquist, and P. Schoen* (*IEEE International Solid-State Circuits Conference*, 1977) . . . 382

A 5 V-Only 4-K Static RAM, *V. G. McKenny* (*IEEE International Solid-State Circuits Conference*, 1977) . . . 385

A 25ns 4K Static RAM, *R. M. Jecmen, A. V. Ebel, R. J. Smith, V. Kynett, C-H Hui, and R. D. Pashley* (*IEEE International Solid-State Circuits Conference*, 1979) . . . 387

A 1K x 8-Bit 5V-Only Static RAM, *G. S. Leach, J. M. Hartman, K. L. Clark, and T. R. O'Connell* (*IEEE International Solid-State Circuits Conference*, 1978) . . . 390

A 16K x 1b Static RAM, *R. D. Pashley, S. S. Liu, W. H. Owen, III, J. M. Owen, J. Shappir, R. J. Smith, and R. M. Jecmen* (*IEEE International Solid-State Circuits Conference*, 1979) . . . 392

A High-Performance MOS Technology for 16K Static RAM, *S. S. Liu, R. J. Smith, R. D. Pashley, J. Shappir, C. H. Fu, and K. R. Kokkonen* (*IEEE International Electron Devices Meeting*, 1979) . . . 395

2K x 8b HCMOS Static RAMs, *T. Masuhara, O. Minato, T. Sasaki, H. Nakamura, Y. Sakai, T. Yasui, and K. Uchibori* (*IEEE International Solid-State Circuits Conference*, 1980) . . . 398

Fully Static 16Kb Bulk CMOS RAM, *T. Iizuka, K. Ochii, T. Ohtani, T. Kondo, and S. Kohyama (IEEE International Solid-State Circuits Conference, 1980)* . . . 401

A 64Kb Static RAM, *T. Ohzone, S. Kondo, K. Tsuji, T. Shiragasawa, T. Ishihara, and S. Horiuchi* (*IEEE International Solid-State Circuits Conference*, 1980) . . . 404

Section 4.5: Dynamic RAMs 406

Dynamic RAMs, *J. G. Posa* (*Electronics*, May 22, 1980) 407
A 16K x 1 Bit Dynamic RAM, *P. R. Schroeder and R. J. Proebsting* (*IEEE International Solid–State Circuits Conference*, 1977) 418
A 5V–Only 64K Dynamic RAM, *L. S. White, Jr., N. H. Hong, D. J. Redwine, and G. R. Mahan Rao* (*IEEE International Solid–State Circuits Conference*, 1980) 420
A Single 5V 64K Dynamic RAM, *K. Itoh, R. Hori, H. Masuda, Y. Kamigaki, H. Kawamoto, and H. Katto* (*IEEE International Solid–State Circuits Conference*, 1980) 422
A Fault–Tolerant 64K Dynamic Random–Access Memory, *R. P. Cenker, D. G. Clemons, W. R. Huber, J. B. Petrizzi, F. J. Procyk, and G. M. Trout* (*IEEE Transactions on Electron Devices*, June 1979) 424
A Silicon and Aluminum Dynamic Memory Technology, *R. A. Larsen* (*IBM Journal of Research and Development*, May 1980) 432
A 256 K Dynamic RAM, *S. Matsue, H. Yamamoto, K. Kobayashi, T. Wada, M. Tameda, T. Okuda, and Y. Inagaki* (*IEEE International Solid–State Circuits Conference*, 1980) 447
Automatic Refresh Dynamic Memory, *H. J. Boll, E. N. Fuls, J. T. Nelson, and L. D. Yau* (*IEEE International Solid–State Circuits Conference*, 1976) 449
A Self-Refreshing 4K RAM with Sub–mW Standby Power, *J. M. Caywood, J. C. Pathak, G. L. Van Buren, and S. W. Owen* (*IEEE International Solid–State Circuits Conference*, 1979) 452

Section 4.6: ROMs, PROMs, and EPROMs 455

High-Density CMOS ROM Arrays, *R. G. Stewart* (*IEEE Journal of Solid–State Circuits*, October 1977) 456
A 4Mb Full Wafer ROM, *Y. Kitano, S. Kohda, H. Kikuchi, and S. Sakai* (*IEEE International Solid–State Circuits Conference*, 1980) 461
A 16Kb Electrically Erasable Nonvolatile Memory, *W. S. Johnson, G. Perlegos, A. Renninger, G. Kuhn, and T. R. Ranganath* (*IEEE International Solid–State Circuits Conference*, 1980) 463
A 64K EPROM Using Scaled MOS Technology, *G. Perlegos, S. Pathak, A. Renninger, W. Johnson, M. Holler, J. Skupnak, M. Reitsma, and G. Kuhn* (*IEEE International Solid–State Circuits Conference*, 1980) 466

Bibliography 469

Author Index 483

Subject Index 485

Editor's Biography 489

Preface

Over the past two decades, the spectacular development of digital systems in the areas of data and signal processing has been a result of the development of integrated circuit technology. Today, we are constrained only by what it is possible to integrate *economically* on a single silicon chip.

The key to using a technology is in circuits—they are the link between a technology and the system elements. Each new generation of digital, data, or signal processing systems can be linked to an advance in a technology, with its appropriate set of circuit techniques, CAD tools, and system architectures.

In the early 1960's small scale integrated (SSI) bipolar chips with tens of transistors were available. The system's functional complexity was on the order of a flip-flop. About the same time, MOS devices were introduced. They offered advantages over existing digital bipolar logic families, mainly simpler fabrication process and smaller size. In about 1965, medium scaled integrated (MSI) bipolar chips with hundreds of transistors were introduced. The system's functional complexity was on the order of a counter. By 1970, large scale integrated (LSI) bipolar and MOS chips with thousands of transistors were being designed. For the first time, this allowed the integration of a subsystem on a chip—a complexity on the order of a microprocessor. At this point, integrated circuit designers found themselves facing new, interesting, and challenging frontiers by addressing themselves to such problems as system architecture, chip partitioning, and logic simulation. This trend continued and by 1980 very large scale integrated (VLSI) chips, mainly MOS, with tens of thousands of transistors, became the state–of–the–art. Today, complete systems can be integrated on a single silicon chip, and VLSI circuit design has become a most interesting and challenging career.

Will this trend continue? The experience of the semiconductor industry has been that requirements, once identified and stated, are met sooner or later, and it seems that barriers are more apparent than real. At this stage it would appear there are several problems looking for solutions: yield, testing, reliability, CAD tools, standardization, and educating a new generation of VLSI circuit designers. However, these problems, like the problems of the past, will be solved. For example, yields improve as production techniques develop, testing is fundamental to good engineering and rapid advances are being made in understanding the reliability of large systems and the physical factors affecting VLSI chip reliability. Progress is continually being made in developing CAD tools for VLSI chip design and in standardizing many VLSI chip parameters, e.g. a lower operating power supply than the 5V used today. A trend towards educating a new generation of VLSI circuit designers has developed in many universities and is supported by the industry. Textbooks have recently been written to emphasize this trend and this book is an attempt in that direction.

Part I covers the use of MOS devices in digital circuit design. Single-channel MOS and CMOS circuits are discussed. The use of different integrated load structures is analyzed. Some specific circuit techniques, eg. bootstrapping, are described. The dynamic-mode of operating a MOS circuit is discussed.

In Part II, progress in digital MOS VLSI is examined. More specifically, the device-based route to VLSI: scaling of MOSFETs is presented. Some of the state-of-the-art technologies are described. A circuit-based route to VLSI, eg. use of device merging, is also discussed. Finally, VLSI circuit and system design approaches are given.

In Part III, MOS memory cells and their peripherial circuits are examined.

In Part IV, some examples in logic and memory applications of digital MOS are given.

Finally, a selected bibliography with over 500 references, grouped in ten sections, is given.

In conclusion, let me state that a review of predictions made about semiconductor circuits in the past would indicate that those concerned with what was able to be done were usually more accurate than those concerned with what was not able to be done. Our experience has been that, providing there is a real requirement, the technology, in conjunction with circuit innovations, was developed to meet the need. Thus, if we wish to predict the future capability of digital integrated circuit technology, we must identify the future applications, and then confidently predict that techniques will be invented to meet them.

M. I. Elmasry
Waterloo, Ontario, Canada
July 1980
San Diego, California, U.S.A.
January 1981

Part I
MOS in Digital Circuit Design

This Part deals with the analysis and the design of MOS digital circuits. It is expected that the reader is familiar with basic MOS physical characteristics, modeling aspects, and general circuit techniques. An excellent treatment of the physical aspects of MOSFETs and semiconductor devices in general is given by Grove [1]. A reference book in this area is Sze [2]. The modeling aspects, are covered by Cobbold [3] and Richman [4]. An excellent treatment of the different aspects of integrated circuits (both bipolar and MOS) is given by Hamilton and Howard [5] and by Muller and Kamins [6]. MOS circuits is the topic of a classic text by Crawford [7], of texts by Penney and Lau [8], Carr and Mize [9], and of the recent system/layout oriented text by Mead and Conway [10].

Dealing with circuit design is different from dealing with circuit analysis. While circuit analysis is an engineering science, circuit design is a science and an art. The artistic aspects of circuit design are difficult to explain because they are not algorithmic. These artistic aspects can also differ from designer to designer with the only reasonable explanation that they are efficient and they work. One of these artistic related aspects is the use of circuit techniques. Most of these techniques are surprisingly universal. For example, the technique of merging different semiconductor devices to achieve VLSI structures is applicable to bipolar circuits (as in integrated injection logic [I^2L]), as well as MOS circuits (as in single device well [SDW] MOSFETs). SDW MOSFETs are explained in Section 2.3. In addition, Section 1.3 deals with a circuit technique which is more suitable to MOS than to bipolar circuits, namely bootstrapping.

Good circuit designers are not born, their skills are developed by gaining knowledge in a relatively *wide* spectrum of engineering sciences. For example, the study of bipolar circuits is recommended for MOS circuit designers. The text by Meyer, Lynn, and Hamilton [11] is a good source of information.

Section 1.1 is a tutorial paper which deals with basic concepts in MOS digital circuit design. NMOS as well as CMOS circuits are discussed. Both dc and transient analysis are presented. Basic building blocks, eg. inverters, logic gates, and flip-flops are explained. Static and dynamic mode of operation are studied.

Section 1.2 contains two papers on depletion type MOSFETs. The paper by Mashuhara *et al.* explains circuit design consideration for using depletion type MOSFETs as loads. Static and transient characteristics are included. Although the technology used to realize the experimental test structures is not the state–of–the–art (1980s), the circuit design approach is still basically the same. In a paper by El-Mansy the analysis and the characterization of depletion–type MOSFETs is presented. A model and its basic elements are given in terms of processing data.

Section 1.3 contains three papers on circuit techniques which are commonly used in MOS digital circuit design. The first two papers deal with a circuit technique which has been widely used and referred to as "bootstrapping." It provides a circuit-based solution to eliminate threshold losses in MOS circuits. The third paper presents a novel MOS circuit configuration which is similar to I^2L bipolar circuit structures, as it uses the same circuit partitioning technique. Thus, it proves the point that circuit techniques are more or less universal.

The last section deals with the comparison of MOS logic gates. The paper by Cook *et al.* compares four-phase dynamic logic circuits, CMOS, single channel static MOS logic circuits with linear (nonsaturated) and depletion-type loads. The parameters used for this comparison are power dissipation, delay, and silicon area. The comparison is done by using the early 1970's MOS technologies; doing a similar comparison using the early 1980's MOS technologies is left as a challenging project to the reader.

The reader is referred to Section 1 of the bibliography which contains references on the use of MOSFETs in digital circuit design.

References

[1] A. S. Grove, "Physics and Technology of Semiconductor Devices," John Wiley, 1976.

[2] S. M. Sze, "Physics of Semiconductor Devices," John Wiley, 1969.

[3] R. S. C. Cobbold, "The Theory and Applications of Field–Effect Transistors," Wiley–Interscience, 1970.

[4] P. Richman, "MOS Field-Effect Transistors and Integrated Circuits," John Wiley, 1973.

[5] D. J. Hamilton and W. G. Howard, "Basic Integrated Circuit Engineering," McGraw-Hill, 1975.

[6] R. S. Muller and T. I. Kamins, "Device Electronics for Integrated Circuits," John Wiley, 1977.

[7] R. H. Crawford, "MOSFET in Circuit Design," McGraw-Hill, 1967.

[8] W. M. Penney and L. Lau, "MOS Integrated Circuits," Van Nostrand Reinhold, 1972.

[9] W. N. Carr and J. P. Mize, "MOS/LSI Design and Application," McGraw-Hill, 1972.

[10] C. Mead and L. Conway, "Introduction to VLSI Systems," Addison-Wesley, 1980.

[11] C. S. Meyer, D. K. Lynn, and D. J. Hamilton, "Analysis and Design of Integrated Circuits," McGraw-Hill, 1968.

Section 1.1
Digital MOS Integrated Circuits

Digital MOS Integrated Circuits: A Tutorial

MOHAMED I. ELMASRY, SENIOR MEMBER IEEE

Abstract—**Basic digital NMOS and CMOS integrated circuits are analyzed. Dc and transient performance is studied using first-order design equations. Static and dynamic circuits are discussed. The effects of device parameters on circuit performance are explained.**

1. Introduction

The dual purpose of this tutorial paper is to review the main characteristics of MOS transistors as they are related to digital circuit design and to analyze basic static and dynamic NMOS digital circuits using first-order dc and transient design equations. The study of digital NMOS circuits is followed by a similar study of digital CMOS circuits, and the most basic digital circuit, the static inverter, is analyzed in detail. This is followed with an explanation of how the design of logic gates and flip-flops, both static and dynamic, is related to the design of the simple static inverter.

2. MOS Device Characteristics

Figure 1 shows a diagrammatic cross-section in a NMOS transistor [1]. It consists of two n^+ regions, introduced in a P substrate by diffusion or ion implantation. In circuit operation, the more positive region is called the drain while the other region is called a source. The surface region between the source and drain is called the channel. The conduction through this channel is controlled by the voltage on the gate, which is either metal or polysilicon. The gate is separated from the channel by a thin layer of a dielectric, usually silicon oxide.

If the voltage of the source terminal is taken as a reference, then V_{DS}, V_{GS}, and V_{BB} are the voltages of the drain, gate, and substrate respectively. V_{BB} is referred to as the back-gate bias. For NMOS digital circuits V_{BB} is an applied negative or zero voltage. The negative V_{BB} is either supplied from off-chip, or is generated on-chip from the available positive power supply V_{DD} (see Appendix A).

An applied positive V_{DS} allows electrons, when present in the channel, to drift from the source to the drain causing I_{DS} to flow from the drain to the source. In depletion-type NMOS

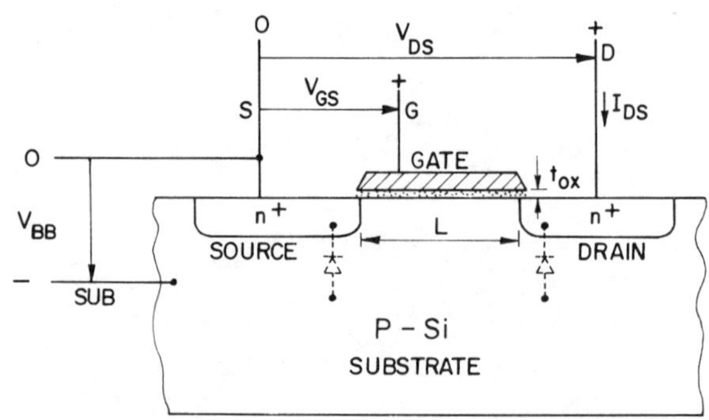

Fig. 1. Diagrammatic cross-section in an NMOS transistor showing parasitic diodes and terminal voltages.

devices, electrons are present in the channel even at $V_{GS} = 0$. This is achieved by ion implanting the surface channel with n-type material. An increase in V_{GS} increases I_{DS}. However, if V_{GS} is negative and larger than $|V_T|$, where V_T is the threshold voltage of the depletion-type device, the channel is depleted and I_{DS} is reduced to zero. In enhancement-type NMOS, electrons are only present at the surface if V_{GS} is positive and larger than V_T where V_T is the threshold voltage of the enhancement-type device. An increase in V_{GS} increases I_{DS}.

2.1 DC Characteristics

Two important dc characteristics of the NMOS transistor are shown in Fig. 2:

- the drain current I_{DS} vs. the drain voltage V_{DS} for different values of V_{GS} at a given substrate bias V_{BB}; and
- the drain current I_{DS} vs. the gate voltage V_{GS} at a given V_{BB}.

Three regions of operation can be distinguished on the I_{DS} vs. V_{DS} characteristic:

1. The off region, where

$$V_{GS} < V_T$$

$$I_{DS} \simeq 0$$

This region is also referred to as the subthreshold region where I_{DS} increases exponentially with V_{DS} and V_{GS} [1]. The value of I_{DS} in this region is much smaller than its value

Manuscript received April 28, 1981.

The author is with the Department of Electrical Engineering, University of Waterloo, Waterloo, Ontario, Canada N2L 3G1. This work is supported in part by NSERCC Grants A9334 and PRAI 7705.

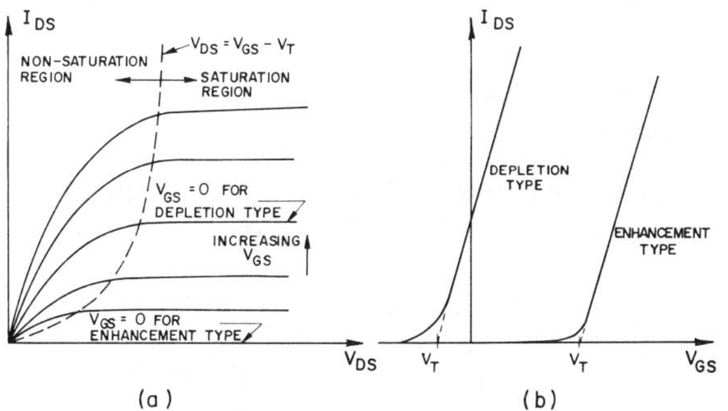

Fig. 2. (a) I_{DS} vs. V_{DS} and (b) I_{DS} vs. V_{GS} for a given V_{BB}. Note that V_T is positive for enhancement-type NMOS devices and negative for depletion-type.

when $V_{GS} > V_T$. Thus, in many NMOS circuits for $V_{GS} < V_T$, the transistor is considered off and $I_{DS} \simeq 0$. However, the small value of I_{DS} in this region could affect the circuit performance as in MOS dynamic memory circuits.

2. The nonsaturation region, where

$$V_{DS} < V_{GS} - V_T$$

$$I_{DS} = \beta[(V_{GS} - V_T)\, V_{DS} - \frac{1}{2} V_{DS}^2] \quad (1)$$

3. The saturation region, where

$$V_{DS} \geqslant V_{GS} - V_T$$

$$I_{DS} = \frac{\beta}{2}\,[V_{GS} - V_T]^2 \quad (2)$$

where

$$\beta = \frac{W}{L}\,\frac{\epsilon_{ox}\mu}{t_{ox}} = \frac{W}{L}K' \quad (3)$$

W = width of the MOS channel

L = length of the MOS channel (in the direction of current flow)

ϵ_{ox} = permittivity of the gate oxide

t_{ox} = thickness of the gate oxide

μ = average surface mobility of carriers (μ_n in the case of electrons in NMOS, and μ_p in the case of holes in PMOS)

V_T = threshold voltage

C_{ox} = gate capacitance per unit area = $\dfrac{\epsilon_{ox}}{t_{ox}}$

2.1.1 *The Conduction Factor K'*

The conduction factor K' ($\equiv \epsilon_{ox}\,\mu/t_{ox}$) is technology dependent and is specified for a given MOS process. Thus it is not a circuit design variable. For a t_{ox} range of 1000-500°A, it has a typical value of 12-25 $\mu A/V^2$ for NMOS devices and 5-10 $\mu A/V^2$ for PMOS. As the value of t_{ox} decreases with advances in technology, K' increases. The difference between K'_n and K'_p results from the fact that $\mu_n \sim 2.5\,\mu_p$.

K' is a function of temperature because of its dependency on μ:

$$\frac{K'}{K'_0} = \left(\frac{T}{T_0}\right)^{-3/2} \quad (4)$$

where K'_0 is the value of K' at room temperature (T_0 = 298°K) and T is the absolute temperature (°K).

2.1.2 *The Geometrical Ratio (W/L)*

This ratio is a circuit design parameter. The minimal value of L (L_{min}) is determined by the MOS fabrication process. L_{min} is determined mainly by the mask channel length, the tolerances on that length and the lateral diffusions of both the source and the drain regions. The minimum value of W is usually in the order of the minimum value of L. Increasing (W/L) will increase the drain current for a given set of operating voltages. However, increasing W increases the gate area and the source and the drain diffusion areas and hence increases the value of the capacitances associated with the gate and with the source-substrate and the drain-substance junctions.

2.1.3 *The Threshold Voltage V_T*

V_T is a function of the MOS processing parameters and the substrate bias V_{BB}. In general, it is also a function of V_{DS}. In order to highlight these different functional dependencies, V_T of an enhancement-type NMOS can be written as:

$$V_T = V_{TO} + \Delta V_T(V_{BB}) - \Delta V_T(V_{DS}) \quad (5)$$

where

$$V_{TO} = \left(\phi_{GS} - \frac{Q_{SS}}{C_{ox}}\right) + \gamma(2\phi_F)^{1/2} + 2\phi_F \quad (5a)$$

$$= V_{FB} + \gamma(2\phi_F)^{1/2} + 2\phi_F$$

$$\Delta V_T(V_{BB}) = \gamma[(|V_{BB}| + 2\phi_F)^{1/2} - (2\phi_F)^{1/2}] \quad (5b)$$

$$\Delta V_T(V_{DS}) = z(V_{DS} + 2|V_{BB}| + 2V_{Bi}) \quad (5c)$$

$$\gamma = \frac{(2\,\epsilon_{ox} q N_B)^{1/2}}{C_{ox}} \quad (5d)$$

$$z = \frac{\eta_0\,(x_j, N_B)}{C_{ox}\,L^n} \quad (5e)$$

ϕ_{GS} = gate voltage necessary to counter balance the gate-to-silicon work function difference.

Q_{SS}/C_{ox} = gate voltage necessary to counter balance the effect of the oxide surface charge Q_{SS}.

$V_{FB} = \phi_{GS} - \dfrac{Q_{SS}}{C_{ox}}$ = gate voltage necessary to cause the flat band condition at the silicon surface, hence the name "flat-band voltage". The flat band condition occurs when the energy bands in the substrate are flat at the surface [1]. In this condition, there is zero electric field at the silicon surface. If the gate voltage is more positive than V_{FB}, for P-type substrates, the silicon surface is in depletion, i.e., there are no mobile carriers at the surface. If the gate voltage is further increased the surface starts to "invert", i.e., electrons are attracted to the surface forming a conductive channel.

$\gamma(2\phi_F)^{1/2}$ = gate voltage necessary to counter balance the effect of the charge created by the exposed dopants at the surface. ϕ_F is the substrate Fermi potential at the surface, and is equal to $\dfrac{KT}{q}$ $\ell n \dfrac{N_B}{n_i}$, where $\dfrac{KT}{q}$ is the thermal voltage, n_i is the intrinsic concentration for silicon, n_i^2 = 1.5 X

$10^{33}\ T^3\ e^{-1.2q/KT}\ cm^{-6}$, N_B is the average substrate concentration at the silicon surface. Note that a surface implant at the MOS channel is usually used to influence N_B [2].

$2\phi_F$ = additional gate voltage, by definition necessary to produce a "strong inversion" condition at the silicon surface.

$\Delta V_T(V_{BB})$ = increase in the threshold voltage due to the reverse bias on the back-gate (substrate). If V_{BB} = 0 then $\Delta V_T(V_{BB}) = 0$.

$\Delta V_T(V_{DS})$ = decrease in the threshold voltage due to the short channel effect. For large L, $\Delta V_T(V_{DS})$ tends to zero.

$\eta_0(x_j, N_B)$ = factor which is a function of the source and drain junction depth x_j and N_B [3].

n = factor which ranges between 2.6 and 3.2 for $10^{15}\ cm^{-3} \leqslant N_B \leqslant 10^{16}\ cm^{-3}$, $1.5\ \mu m \leqslant x_j \leqslant 0.41\ \mu m$ [3].

V_{Bi} = source (or drain)-substrate built-in voltage = $\frac{KT}{q}\ \ell n \frac{N_B N}{n_i}$ where N is the average impurity concentration of the source and drain diffusions.

Examining equation (5) reveals the following:

1. V_{TO} is not a function of the operating voltages and is a function of temperature.
2. The sensitivity of the threshold voltage V_T to V_{BB}: $\Delta V_T(V_{BB})$ is determined by γ which is a function of $N_B^{1/2}\ C_{ox}^{-1}$. Increasing N_B or decreasing C_{ox}, i.e., increasing t_{ox}, will increase that sensitivity.
3. The sensitivity of the threshold voltage V_T to V_{DS}: $\Delta V_T(V_{DS})$ is determined by z which tends to zero for long channel devices. z is an empirical factor [3] which is proportional to x_j, $1/N_B$, $1/C_{ox}$ in addition to $1/L$. Decreasing x_j, increasing N_B or decreasing t_{ox} (hence increasing C_{ox}) reduces the sensitivity of V_T to V_{DS} in short channel devices.
4. In short channel and narrow channel devices. γ is a function of both L and W; a decrease in L decreases γ and a decrease in W increases γ. This dependency of γ on L and W affects V_{TO} and $\Delta V_T(V_{BB})$ and could be incorporated empirically in equation (5d). This effect should be considered in the design of digital circuits using MOS devices of small dimensions because a transistor having $W = W_{min}$, $L = L_{min}$ may have a different dc characteristic from one having $W = mW_{min}$ and $L = mL_{min}$, although (W/L) of the two transistors are the same.

Note that temperature affects both K' and V_T in such a way that the effects on I_{DS} could cancel each other. Thus, MOS transistors can be operated so that they exhibit positive, negative, or zero temperature coefficient [1].

2.2 Transient Characteristics

The transient performance of an MOS integrated circuit is a function of the total capacitance at the output node. This capacitance C_{out} is the summation of the parasitic output capacitance C_0 and the input gate capacitance(s) of the loading stage(s) C_{IN}.

The parasitic output capacitance C_0 is the summation of two capacitances:

1. C_J—the junction capacitance of the output diffusion(s). This capacitance varies with the junction voltage V_j:

$$\frac{C_J}{C_{JO}} = \left(1 - \frac{V_j}{V_{Bi}}\right)^n$$

where

C_J = junction capacitance at voltage V
C_{JO} = junction capacitance at zero voltage
V_j = junction voltage (negative for reverse-bias)
V_{Bi} = built-in junction potential
n = factor between 0.5 and 0.3 depending upon junction abruptness

2. C_{INT}—the interconnector capacitance associated with metal, polysilicon, or diffusion interconnection lines. C_{INT} is voltage independent and usually contributes to C_{out} in LSI circuits where complex interconnection patterns exist.

The input capacitance C_{IN} of an MOS transistor consists of the following components [1,4,5,6] as shown in Fig. 3(a).

C_{OS}, C_{OD}—the source and the drain overlap capacitances resulting from the overlap of the gate on the source and the drain diffusions: $C_{OS} = C_{ox}\ell_S W$, $C_{OD} = C_{ox}\ell_D W$ where ℓ_S and ℓ_D are the overlap lengths.

C_{GS}, C_{GD}— represent gate to channel capacitances lumped at the source and drain regions of the channel respectively:

$$C_{GS} = C_{ox}WL\ f_S(V),\ C_{GD} = C_{ox}WL\ f_D(V)$$

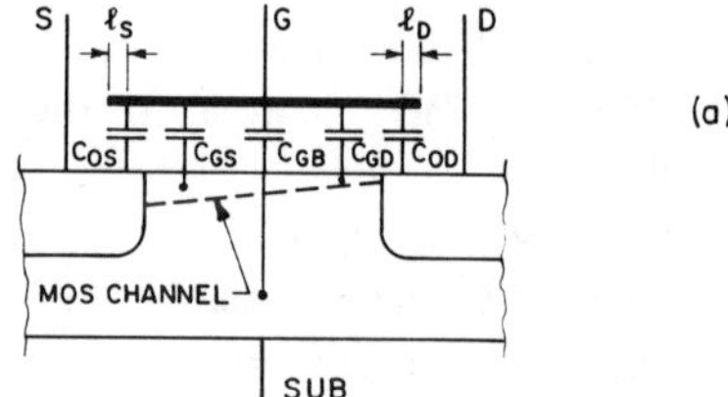

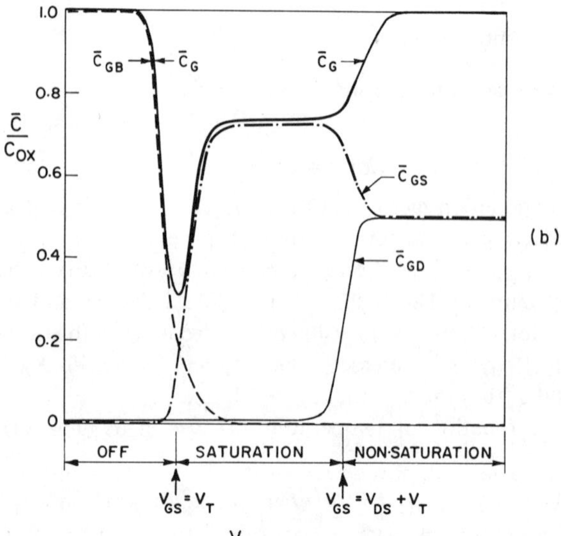

Fig. 3. (a) The different components of C_{IN}; (b) the voltage dependency of the capacitances per unit area: $\bar{C}_{GS}$, $\bar{C}_{GD}$, $\bar{C}_{GB}$, and $\bar{C}_G$ vs. V_{GS}.

C_{GB}—the gate-substrate capacitance:

$$C_{GB} = C_{ox} WL\, f_B(V)$$

where $f_S(V)$, $f_D(V)$ and $f_B(V)$ are voltage dependent functions. Figure 3(b) demonstrates the nature of the voltage dependency of the capacitances per unit areas: $\overline{C}_{GS}$, $\overline{C}_{GD}$, $\overline{C}_{GB}$, and $\overline{C}_G$ of an NMOS transistor vs. V_{GS} where $\overline{C}_G = \overline{C}_{GS} + \overline{C}_{GD} + \overline{C}_{GB}$. When the transistor is off, the only nonzero component is $\overline{C}_{GB}$. This component is due to the series combination of the surface depletion layer and gate oxide capacitances. As the transistor turns on $\overline{C}_{GB}$ reduces to zero because of the shielding effect of the inversion layer. In the nonsaturation region, the source and the drain regions of the MOS channel are inverted and $\overline{C}_{GS} \simeq \overline{C}_{GD} \simeq C_{ox}/2$. In the saturation region, where the drain region of the channel is pinched-off, $\overline{C}_{GD}$ reduces to zero from $C_{ox}/2$ and $\overline{C}_{GS}$ increases from that value to approximately 2/3 C_{ox}. Figure 3(b) shows that $\overline{C}_G$ vs. V_{GS} has a minimum just below $V_{GS} = V_T$.

2.3 Leakage and Breakdown

It is important to consider leakage currents in an MOS chip, especially if the circuit is operating in a dynamic mode and particularly in dynamic memories. The leakage currents are associated with the source and drain p-n junctions. The absolute values of these currents should be minimized, and their variation with temperature should be considered [1].

A potential source of parasitic current in MOS circuits is the current associated with the thick field oxide MOS transistors which have a thick (field) oxide. This current increases exponentially as the gate voltage approaches the threshold voltage of the field-oxide MOSFETs. The threshold voltage of the field-oxide MOSFETs can be increased by increasing the surface doping density under the field oxide.

In MOS circuits, breakdown can occur by different mechanisms. Avalanche breakdown can occur in the reverse-biased drain-substrate junction. Punch-through breakdown can also occur if the depletion region of the drain-substrate junction reaches the source-substrate junction. Either type of breakdown may predominate for a given MOS structure, e.g., punch-through breakdown could be the predominate for short channel MOSFETs. Although both types of breakdowns are related to the *p-n* junction characteristics, they are strongly affected by the presence of a gate oxide and a conducting gate [4].

3. The Static NMOS Inverter

The NMOS inverter, as shown in Fig. 4(a), consists of an enhancement type driver transistor and a load. The load is one of the following: (a) a saturated enhancement-type NMOS device, (b) a nonsaturated enhancement-type NMOS device, (c) a depletion-type NMOS device, or (d) a polysilicon resistor.

Figure 4(b) shows the load lines of the above four loads superimposed on the I_{DS} vs. V_{DS} of the driver. The intersection of the load line with the driver characteristic for $V_{GS} = V_{IN} = V_0$, gives $V_{DS} = V_{OUT} = V_1$ where V_0 is the low voltage level representing logical '0' (see Appendix B), $V_0 < V_{TD}$, V_{TD} is the threshold voltage of the driver and V_1 is the high voltage level representing logical '1'. Similarly, the intersection of the load line with the driver characteristics for $V_{GS} = V_{IN} = V_1$, gives $V_{DS} = V_{OUT} = V_0$.

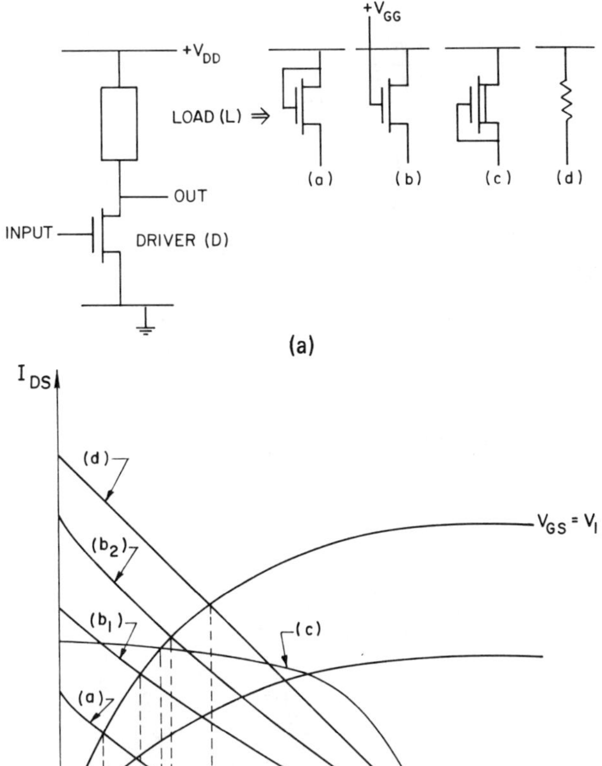

Fig. 4. (a) NMOS inverter with different loads; (b) load lines superimposed on the driver transistor I_{DS} vs. V_{DS} characteristic. V_{GG} for case $(b_2) > V_{GG}$ for case (b_1).

3.1 DC Analysis

3.1.1 *Saturated Enhancement-type Load*

The saturated enhancement-type load was used in the early digital MOS integrated circuits. Figure 5 shows an inverter using NMOS devices. The load device has its gate connected to its drain (i.e., $V_{DS} = V_{GS}$), and operates in the saturation region when it conducts, since $V_{DS} > (V_{GS} - V_{TL})$, where V_{TL} is the threshold voltage of the load device.

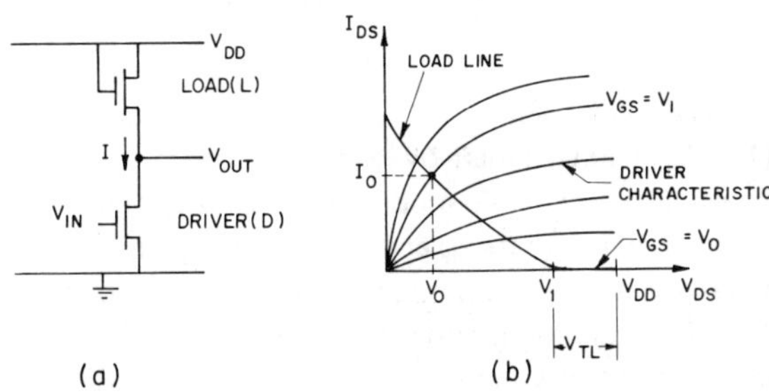

Fig. 5. (a) NMOS inverter with saturated enhancement-type load; (b) load line superimposed on the driver I_{DS} vs. V_{DS} characteristic, showing the operating current I_0 when $V_{OUT} = V_0$.

The dc circuit operation is explained as follows:

(a) when $V_{IN} = V_0$, $V_0 < V_{TD}$, the driver is off, $I \approx 0$ and

$$V_{OUT} = V_1 = V_{DD} - V_{TL} \qquad (6)$$

(b) when $V_{IN} = V_1$, $V_1 > V_{TD}$, the driver is operating in the nonsaturation region, the load device is in saturation and $I = I_0$ where:

$$I_0 = \frac{K'\left(\frac{W}{L}\right)_L}{2} [(V_{DD} - V_0) - V_{TL}]^2 \quad (7a)$$

$$= K'\left(\frac{W}{L}\right)_D [(V_1 - V_{TD}) V_0 - \frac{1}{2} V_0^2] \quad (7b)$$

If $V_0 << V_{DD}$ and $V_0 << V_1 - V_{TD}$ then (7) can be simplified:

$$I_0 \simeq \frac{K'\left(\frac{W}{L}\right)_L}{2} (V_{DD} - V_{TL})^2 = \frac{K'\left(\frac{W}{L}\right)_L}{2} V_1^2 \quad (8a)$$

$$\simeq K'\left(\frac{W}{L}\right)_D (V_1 - V_{TD})V_0 \quad (8b)$$

From (8) we obtain:

$$\frac{\left(\frac{W}{L}\right)_D}{\left(\frac{W}{L}\right)_L} \geqslant \frac{V_1}{2V_0} \quad (9)$$

and

$$V_0 \simeq \frac{I_0}{K'\left(\frac{W}{L}\right)_D (V_1 - V_{TD})} \quad (10)$$

Thus from (9) if V_1/V_0 is taken to be 10, $\left(\frac{W}{L}\right)_D / \left(\frac{W}{L}\right)_L$ should be $\geqslant 5$. Because the ratio of (W/L) of the driver to that of the load must be greater than unity, the circuit is referred to as "a ratioed circuit." To summarize: the voltage levels of the NMOS inverter V_1, V_0, V_t, where V_t is the logic threshold of the inverter (see Appendix B) and the dc power dissipation are given by:

$$V_1 = V_{DD} - V_{TL}$$

$$V_0 \cong \frac{I_0}{K'\left(\frac{W}{L}\right)_D (V_1 - V_{TD})}$$

$$V_t \geqslant V_{TD} \quad (11)$$

$$P_{DC}\ (@\ V_{OUT} = V_1) \simeq 0$$

$$P_{DC}\ (@\ V_{OUT} = V_0) = I_0\ V_{DD}$$

where I_0 is given by (8a).

In (11) I_0 is determined by transient considerations or by the allowable power dissipation. V_{DD} is usually fixed by subsystem design considerations and today it is typically = 5 V.

It is clear that V_1 increases as the power supply voltage V_{DD} increases. The maximum allowable V_{DD} must be less than the junction breakdown voltage of the drain-substrate junction. It should also be less than the voltage at which the parasitic field-oxide MOS transistors start to conduct.

Because the substrate-source junction of the load device is more reverse biased than the driver, V_{TL} is larger than V_{TD} due to the back-gate bias effect. The higher the V_{BB} value of the load, the higher the value of V_{TL}, and the lower the value of V_1. Because $V_1 \doteq V_{DD} - V_{TL}$, the saturated enhancement-type MOS load is said to introduce "threshold losses" in the value of V_1. As we explain in the following sections, depletion-type nonsaturated enhancement type and bootstrapped MOS loads do not introduce threshold losses.

The low logical voltage level, V_0, is a function of the operating current I_0. As I_0 increases, the dc power dissipation increases and the speed of operation also increases as we explain in 3.2. V_0 can be reduced (hence increasing the logic swing and the NM_o noise margin) by increasing the geometrical ratio $(W/L)_D$ of the driver transistor, hence increasing its size, with respect to $(W/L)_L$.

The threshold voltage V_t of the inverter (see Appendix B) is $\geqslant V_{TD}$. The higher the ratio $[(W/L)_D/(W/L)_L]$ is, the closer V_t to V_{TD} becomes. If the driver is replaced with a number of stacked transistors connected in a series, as in the case of an MOS NAND gate (see 4), then V_{TD} and hence V_T of the upper input transistors are higher than that of the lower transistors because of the back-gate bias effect. This is a drawback for using NAND gates in NMOS logic design.

3.1.2 *Nonsaturated Enhancement-type Load*

One drawback of using a saturated enhancement-type load is the threshold voltage losses caused by the load, resulting in $V_1 = V_{DD} - V_{TL}$.

This situation can be rectified if the load is operating in the nonsaturation region by connecting its gate to V_{GG} where $V_{GG} > (V_{DD} + V_{TL})$. In this case V_1 can be made close to V_{DD} by increasing V_{GG} as shown in Fig. 4(b). The inverter dc circuit operation is explained as follows:

(a) when $V_{IN} = V_0$, $V_0 < V_{TD}$, the driver is off, the load is nonsaturated and $V_{OUT} = V_1 = V_{DD} - V_{DS}|_{load}$ where $V_D|_{load}$ is the voltage drop across the load device. If the inverter is driving only MOS gates, which is usually the case with high input impedances, then $V_{DS}|_{load} \simeq 0$ and $V_1 \simeq V_{DD}$.

It should be noted that $V_{DS}|_{load}$ can be reduced for a given load current by increasing $(W/L)_L$ or $(V_{GG} - V_{TL})$ at the expense of increasing the gate power dissipation.

(b) when $V_{IN} = V_1$, $V_1 > V_{TD}$, the driver is operating in the nonsaturation region, the load is nonsaturated and $I = I_0$ where

$$I_0 = K'\left(\frac{W}{L}\right)_L [(V_{GG} - V_{TL} - V_0)(V_{DD} - V_0) - \frac{1}{2}(V_{DD} - V_0)^2] \quad (12a)$$

$$= K'\left(\frac{W}{L}\right)_D [(V_1 - V_{TD}) V_0 - \frac{1}{2} V_0^2] \quad (12b)$$

If $V_0 << V_{DD}$, $V_0 << V_1 - V_{TD}$, $V_{GG} - V_{TL} >> V_{DD}$ then (12) can be simplified:

$$I_0 \simeq K'\left(\frac{W}{L}\right)_L (V_{GG} - V_{TL})V_{DD} \quad (13a)$$

$$\simeq K'\left(\frac{W}{L}\right)_D (V_1 - V_{TD})V_0 \quad (13b)$$

From (13) we obtain

$$\frac{\left(\frac{W}{L}\right)_D}{\left(\frac{W}{L}\right)_L} \geqslant \frac{V_{GG} - V_{TL}}{V_0} \tag{14}$$

and

$$V_0 \simeq \frac{I_0}{K' \left(\frac{W}{L}\right)_D (V_1 - V_{TD})} \tag{15}$$

where I_0 is given by (13a).

In summary, using a nonsaturated enhancement-type load offers a higher V_1, and hence higher logic swing and higher noise margins. Moreover, it offers an improvement in transient performance, as shown in 3.2. This improved performance is obtained at the expense of adding the extra power supply V_{GG}.

3.1.3 *Depletion-type Load*

Depletion-type devices are widely used as loads in NMOS logic circuits. They offer a voltage logic level $V_1 \simeq V_{DD}$ as shown in Fig. 4(b). In addition, the constant current characteristic improves the transient performance of the circuit [7]. The inverter dc circuit operation is explained as follows:

(a) when $V_{IN} = V_0$, $V_0 < V_{TD}$, the driver is off, the load is nonsaturated and similar to the nonsaturated enhancement-type case:

$$V_{OUT} = V_1 = V_{DD} - V_{DS}|_{load} \simeq V_{DD}$$

It should be noted that $V_{DS}|_{load}$ can be reduced for a given load current by increasing $\left(\frac{W}{L}\right)_L$ or $|V_{TL}|$.

(b) when $V_{IN} = V_1$, $V_1 > V_{TD}$, the driver is operating in the nonsaturation region, the load is saturated and $I = I_0$ where

$$I_0 = \frac{K' \left(\frac{W}{L}\right)_L}{2} V_{TL}^2 \tag{16a}$$

$$= K' \left(\frac{W}{L}\right)_D [(V_1 - V_{TD}) V_0 - \frac{1}{2} V_0^2] \tag{16b}$$

If $V_0 << V_1 - V_{TD}$, then (16) can be simplified:

$$I_0 = \frac{K' \left(\frac{W}{L}\right)_L}{2} V_{TL}^2 \tag{17a}$$

$$\simeq K' \left(\frac{W}{L}\right)_D (V_1 - V_{TD}) V_0 \tag{17b}$$

From (17) we obtain:

$$\frac{\left(\frac{W}{L}\right)_D}{\left(\frac{W}{L}\right)_L} \geqslant \frac{V_{TL}^2}{2 V_0 (V_1 - V_{TD})} \tag{18}$$

$$V_0 \simeq \frac{I_0}{K' \left(\frac{W}{L}\right)_D (V_1 - V_{TD})} \tag{19}$$

where I_0 is given by (17a). It should be noted here that because of the back-gate bias effect on the depletion load, V_{TL}, and hence I_0, should be either taken as an average or a worse case value.

3.1.4 *Resistive Load*

Polyresistors have recently been used in the design of NMOS digital integrated circuits especially static memories. As shown in Fig. 4(b), a resistive load provides $V_1 \simeq V_{DD}$. In fact, the nonsaturated enhancement-type MOS load dc characteristic approaches that of a resistance when $V_{GG} >> V_{DD} + V_{TL}$ as shown in Fig. 4(b), case (b_2). The inverter dc circuit operation is explained as follows:

(a) when $V_{IN} = V_0$, $V_0 < V_{TD}$, the driver is off and similar to the nonsaturated enhancement-type case:

$$V_{OUT} = V_1 = V_{DD} - V|_{load} \simeq V_{DD}$$

Similarly $V|_{load}$ can be reduced for a given load current by decreasing the value of the load resistance R.

(b) when $V_{IN} = V_1$, $V_1 > V_{TD}$, the driver is operating in the nonsaturation and $I = I_0$ where

$$I_0 = \frac{V_{DD} - V_0}{R} \tag{20a}$$

$$= K' \left(\frac{W}{L}\right)_D [(V_1 - V_{TD}) V_0 - \frac{1}{2} V_0^2] \tag{20b}$$

If $V_0 << V_{DD}$, then (20) can be simplified

$$I_0 \simeq \frac{V_{DD}}{R} \tag{21a}$$

$$\simeq K' \left(\frac{W}{L}\right)_D (V_1 - V_{TD}) V_0 \tag{21b}$$

From (21) we obtain

$$RK' \left(\frac{W}{L}\right)_D \geqslant \frac{V_{DD}}{V_0 (V_1 - V_{TD})} \tag{22}$$

$$V_0 \simeq \frac{I_0}{K' \left(\frac{W}{L}\right)_D (V_1 - V_{TD})} \tag{23}$$

where I_0 is given by (21a).

3.2 Transient Analysis

The transient performance of an MOS inverter is a function of two times (see Fig. 6):

1. The discharging time t_{dis}, which is the time taken by the output node capacitance C_{out} to discharge through the driver transistor, from V_1 to V_0.
2. The charging time t_{ch}, which is the time taken by C_{out} to charge, through the load from V_0 to V_1.

In calculating t_{dis} and t_{ch} we will direct our attention to simplified expressions for the purpose of using them in the first phase of circuit design. The approach follows that of Crawford [8]. It is important to remember here that the time (t) taken by a capacitance (C) to change its voltage by ΔV, using a constant current (I), is given by the simple relation $t = C\,\Delta V/I$. In the following analysis we shall assume the input voltage to the MOS inverter is an ideal voltage step.

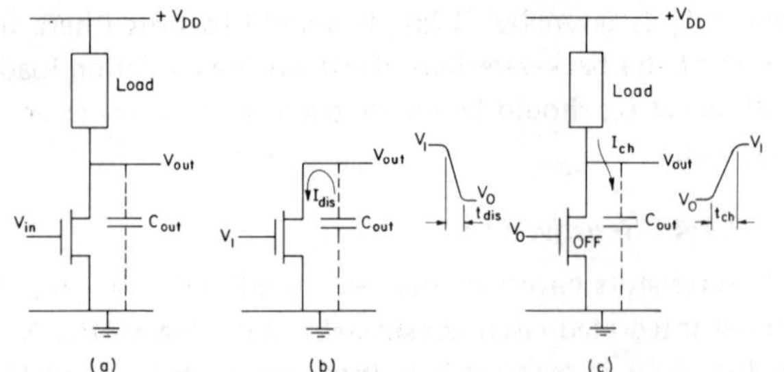

Fig. 6. (a) NMOS inverter showing output node capacitance; (b) simple circuit for discharging; (c) simple circuit for charging.

3.2.1 *The Discharging Time t_{dis}*

As shown in the dc analysis of the MOS inverter, the ratio of $\left(\frac{W}{L}\right)_D$ to $\left(\frac{W}{L}\right)_L$ is large, hence the on resistance of the driver transistor is much less than the on resistance of the load transistor. As a result, during the discharging of the output node capacitance, when $V_{IN} > V_{TD}$ and the driver is on, it is reasonable to neglect the current through the load [8]. Hence, the discharging circuit can be simplified, as shown in Fig. 6(b), to C_{out} with initial output voltage = V_1 and an on driver transistor with $V_{IN} = V_1$. The final output voltage = V_0.

During the discharging time, the driver is initially in the saturation region and the constant drain current:

$$I_D = \frac{\beta_D}{2}(V_1 - V_{TD})^2$$

will partially discharge C_{out} in a time given by

$$(t_{dis})_1 = \frac{C_{out}\Delta V}{I_D} \tag{24}$$

where

$$\Delta V = V_1 - V''_{OUT}$$

and V''_{OUT} is the output voltage at which the driver begins operating in the nonsaturation region (i.e., $V''_{OUT} = V_1 - V_{TD}$).

Equation (24) can be written in the form

$$(t_{dis})_1 = 2\frac{C_{out}}{g_{mD}}\frac{V_{TD}}{V_1 - V_{TD}} \tag{25}$$

where

$$g_{mD} = \beta_D(V_1 - V_{TD})$$

When the driver transistor begins to operate in the nonsaturation region at $V_{OUT} = V''_{OUT}$, the available current to discharge the output capacitance is not a constant and the discharging time $(t_{dis})_2$ for C_{out} to discharge from V''_{OUT} to V_0 can be obtained from the solution of the differential equation which results from equating the capacitance current through C_{out} to the current through the driver [8]:

$$C_{out}\frac{dV_{OUT}}{dt} = \beta_D(V_1 - V_{TD})V_{OUT} - \frac{\beta}{2}V_{OUT}^2$$

which gives

$$V_{OUT} = (V_1 - V_{TD})\frac{2e^{-t/\tau_D}}{1 + e^{-t/\tau_D}} \tag{26}$$

where

$$\tau_D = C_{out}/g_{mD}$$

$$g_{mD} = \beta_D(V_1 - V_{TD})$$

Solving (26) for $(t_{dis})_2$ as a difference between the time at which $V_{OUT} = V''_{OUT}$ and the time at which $V_{OUT} = V_0$ gives

$$(t_{dis})_2 = \tau_D \ln\left[\frac{2(V_1 - V_{TD})}{V_0} - 1\right] \tag{27}$$

From (19) and (21):

$$t_{dis} = \tau_D\left(\frac{2V_{TD}}{V_1 - V_{TD}} + \ln\left[\frac{2(V_1 - V_{TD})}{V_0} - 1\right]\right) \tag{28}$$

As shown from (28), t_{dis} is reduced if (V_1/V_{TD}) is increased, hence the higher the logical '1' voltage level, the lower the discharging time.

Because $(t_{dis})_2 >> (t_{dis})_1$, $V_1 >> V_{TD}$, and $V_1 >> V_0$, (28) can be simplified:

$$t_{dis} = \tau_D \ln\frac{2V_1}{V_0} \simeq \tau_D \ln\frac{V_1}{V_0} = \frac{C_{out}}{\beta_D(V_1 - V_{TD})}\ln\frac{V_1}{V_0} \tag{28a}$$

i.e., t_{dis} is linearly proportional to C_{out}, β_D^{-1} and $(V_1 - V_{TD})^{-1}$, and is logarithmically proportional to V_1/V_0. Thus, t_{dis} can be reduced, for a given C_{out}, by increasing $(W/L)_D$ or the driving voltage factor $(V_1 - V_{TD})$.

3.2.2 *The Charging Time t_{ch}*

During the charging time the driver is off and C_{out} will charge through the load as shown in Fig. 6(c).

Case 1: Saturated Enhancement-type Load

Equating the capacitive current through C_{out} to that through the load we obtain the differential equation for the output voltage V_{OUT}:

$$C_{out}\frac{dV_{OUT}}{dt} = \frac{\beta_D}{2}[V_{DD} - V_{OUT} - V_{TL}]^2$$

With the initial condition:

$$\text{at } t = 0,\ V_{OUT} = V_0$$

the solution is:

$$V_{OUT} = (V_1 - V_0)\frac{t/\tau_L}{2 + \frac{t}{\tau_L}} + V_0$$

hence

$$t_{ch} = \tau_L\left(\frac{V_1 - V_0}{V_0}\right) = \tau_L\left(\frac{V_1}{V_0} - 1\right) = \tau_L\frac{V_\ell}{V_0} \tag{29}$$

where

$$\tau_L = \frac{C_{out}}{g_{mL}}$$

$$g_{mL} = \beta_L(V_{DD} - V_{TL})$$

From (29) it is clear that the charging time is proportional to the time constant τ_L. Reducing C_{out}, increasing β_L (i.e., the size of the load device), or the voltage factor $(V_{DD} - V_{TL})$ will decrease t_{ch}. Moreover, reducing the logic swing V_ℓ (or reducing V_1/V_0), at the expense of reducing the noise margins, will also reduce t_{ch}. As the output voltage rises during t_{ch}, the substrate-source bias of the load increases and hence V_{TL} increases. Thus, in calculating g_{mL}, V_{TL} may be taken as an average value in the voltage range $V_0 \leqslant V_{OUT} \leqslant V_1$. However, a pessimistic value of t_{ch} can be obtained if V_{TL} is taken as the maximum value where $V_{OUT} = V_0$.

Case 2: Nonsaturated Enhancement-type Load

Similarly, the differential equation describing the output voltage V_{OUT} is given by:

$$C_{out}\frac{dV_{OUT}}{dt} = \frac{\beta_L V_{DD}^2}{2m}\left(1 - \frac{V_{OUT}}{V_{DD}}\right)\left(1 - m\frac{V_{OUT}}{V_{DD}}\right)$$

Calculating t_{ch} requires calculating

$$t_{ch} = \int_{t@V_{OUT} = V_0}^{t@V_{OUT} = V_1} dt$$

$$= C_{out}\frac{2m}{\beta_L V_{DD}}\int_{\frac{V_{OUT}}{V_{DD}} = \frac{V_0}{V_{DD}}}^{\frac{V_{OUT}}{V_{DD}} = \frac{V_1}{V_{DD}}} \frac{d(V_{OUT}/V_{DD})}{\left(1 - \frac{V_{OUT}}{V_{DD}}\right)\left(1 - m\frac{V_{OUT}}{V_{DD}}\right)}$$

which gives

$$t_{ch} = \tau_c \frac{1}{1-m}\ell n\left[\frac{\left(1 - m\frac{V_1}{V_{DD}}\right)\left(1 - \frac{V_0}{V_{DD}}\right)}{\left(1 - m\frac{V_0}{V_{DD}}\right)\left(1 - \frac{V_1}{V_{DD}}\right)}\right]$$

$$= 2\frac{C_{out}}{\beta_L V_{DD}}\frac{m}{1-m}\ell n\left[\frac{\left(1 - m\frac{V_1}{V_{DD}}\right)\left(1 - \frac{V_0}{V_{DD}}\right)}{\left(1 - m\frac{V_0}{V_{DD}}\right)\left(1 - \frac{V_1}{V_{DD}}\right)}\right]$$

$$0 \leqslant m < 1 \qquad (30)$$

where

$$m = \frac{V_{DD}}{2(V_{GG} - V_{TL}) - V_{DD}}$$

The factor m is a measure of the biasing conditions on the load [8]. If $V_{GG} >> V_{DD}$ and $V_{GG} >> V_{TL}$, m tends to zero and the MOS load transistor acts like a resistance. As m approaches unity, i.e., $(V_{GG} - V_{TL})$ approaches V_{DD}, the nonsaturated load approaches the saturated load. Note that (30) is not valid for $m = 1$.

It is clear that as m approaches zero, t_{ch} approaches zero. Reducing C_{out}, increasing β_L or increasing V_{DD} will decrease t_{ch}. Because of the back-gate bias effect during charging, in calculating m, V_{TL} may be taken as a pessimistic value as is done in Case 1 or can be taken as an average value for the voltage range $V_0 \leqslant V_{OUT} \leqslant V_1$. For example, it can be taken at:

$$V_{OUT} = \frac{V_1 + V_0}{2}.$$

Case 3: Depletion-type Load

Assuming that the load current is constant during the charging time as the output voltage rises from V_0 to V_1 then

$$t_{ch} = \frac{C_{out}V_\ell}{I_0} \qquad (31)$$

where I_0 is given by (16a) and an average value of V_{TL} is used. The charging time can be reduced by decreasing V_ℓ C_{out} or increasing I_0, where I_0 can be increased by increasing V_{TL} or β_L.

Case 4: Resistive Load

From the analysis of a simple RC circuit:

$$t_{ch} = R_L C_{out}\,\ell n\frac{V_{DD} - V_0}{V_{DD} - V_1} \qquad (32)$$

NMOS Transient Performance—In 3.2, the transient performance of the basic NMOS inverter has been analyzed. Let us now calculate from the simple relations (28a), (29), (30), (31), and (32), typical values for t_{ch} and t_{dis}. Assume $V_{DD} = 5$ V, $V_{TD} = 0.5$ V and $K' = 25\,\mu A/V^2$:

1. For $V_1 = 5$ V, $V_0 = 0.1$ V, (28a) gives: $t_{dis} \simeq 30$ nsec for $C_{out} = 1$ pF and $(W/L)_D = 1$
2. For $V_1 = V_{DD} - V_{TL} = 5 - 0.7 = 4.3$ V, $V_0 = 0.1$ V, (29) gives: $t_{ch} \simeq 400$ nsec for $C_{out} = 1$ pF and $(W/L)_L = 1$
3. For $V_1 = 4.9$ V, $V_0 = 0.1$ V, (3) gives: $t_{ch} \simeq 6.7$, 25.6, 259 nsec for $m = 0.1, 0.5, 0.9$ respectively, and $C_{out} = 1$ pF and $(W/L)_L = 1$
4. For $V_1 = 5$ V, $V_0 = 0.1$ V, $V_{TL} = -2.5$ V, (31) gives: t_{ch} = 62.7 nsec for $C_{out} = 1$ pF and $(W/L)_L = 1$
5. For $V_1 = 0.9\,V_{DD}$, $V_0 = 0.1\,V_{DD}$ (32) gives:
   $t_{ch} = 2.2\,R_L C_{out}$
   $= 2.2$ nsec for $C_{out} = 1$ pF and $R_L = 1K\Omega$.

Examining the above typical values shows that the charging time in the case of saturated enhancement-type load is relatively high. The nonsaturated enhancement-type load offers improvement, the lower the value of m is (i.e., $V_{GG} >> V_{DD}$) the lower t_{ch}. The depletion-type load also offers improvement. Because $(W/L)_D$ must be greater than $(W/L)_L$, $t_{ch} >> t_{dis}$. The resistive case with $R_L = 1K\Omega$ offers a reference time for t_{ch} for the different cases. For example, a non-saturated enhancement-type load, for $m = 0.1$, 0.5 and 0.9 resembles a resistive load with $R_L = 1$, 10, and 100 $K\Omega$ respectively.

Examining the above typical values show also that increasing $(W/L)_L$ (i.e., the device size) of the load improves t_{ch}. Similarly, increasing the size of the driving transistor improves t_{dis}. However, it should be noted that increasing the size of these transistors increases their input capacitances, i.e., their loading on the previous stages, and the overall delay may not improve. Moreover, increasing the size of these transistors adds more capacitance to C_{out} and again the overall delay may not improve. Thus, increasing the size of the driving and the load transistors should be considered in association with their effect on the overall delay of a digital MOS chip [14].

NMOS Delay-Power Tradeoffs—It has been shown previously that the NMOS static inverter consumes dc power only when the output voltage is low. Thus

$$P_{DC}|_{av} = \tfrac{1}{2} I_0 V_{DD} \qquad (33)$$

where I_0 is the inverter dc current when the output voltage is low. In addition to this component of power dissipation, there is a transient power component due to the switching of the output node capacitance C_{out}. This is given by:

$$P_t = C_{out}V_\ell^2 f \qquad (34)$$

where V_ℓ is the logic swing and f is the switching frequency. The maximum switching frequency is given by: $f_{max} = 1/(t_{ch} + t_{dis})$.

In order to *highlight* the tradeoff that exists in the design of MOS digital circuits between delay and power dissipation, let us consider the case of a static inverter with a depletion-type load and let us assume that $t_{dis} << t_{ch}$ and the inverter is on half of the time. Thus, the total power dissipation at the maximum switching frequency is given by:

$$P = \frac{1}{2} I_0 V_{DD} + (C_{out} V_\ell^2 / t_{ch})$$

and the inverter average delay time is given by:

$$\tau_D = \frac{t_{ch} + t_{dis}}{2} \simeq \frac{t_{ch}}{2} = \frac{C_{out} V_\ell}{2 I_0}$$

Thus, the delay-power product is given by:

$$\tau_D P = \frac{1}{4} C_{out} V_\ell V_{DD} + \frac{1}{2} C_{out} V_\ell^2 \simeq \frac{3}{4} C_{out} V_{DD}^2 \qquad (35)$$

This shows that the delay-power product is proportional to $C_{out} V_{DD}^2$.

NMOS Source-Followers and Push-Pull Drivers—In addition to the basic NMOS inverter discussed in 3.1 and 3.2, other circuit configurations are also used in the design of NMOS digital circuits. Two of these are the source-follower and the push-pull driver. Source-followers are used to reduce the capacitive loading on a given node while push-pull drivers are used to drive high capacitive loads, e.g., off-chip loads. Because of the close relationship between the two circuits, they are discussed here with the aid of Fig. 7.

The static inverter in Fig. 7 consists of a driving transistor Q and a load. The output node of that inverter (node 2) is driving the source-follower transistor Q_1. The load of that source-follower is the switchable transistor Q_2. The capacitive loading of node 2 is the gate-source and the gate-drain capacitances of Q_1, rather than C_{out}. Thus, Q_1 isolates node 2 from the loading capacitance C_{out}.

Q_1 and Q_2 are operating in the push-pull mode to charge and discharge C_{out}, thus the name "push-pull driver." As Q_1 is turned on, Q_2 is turned off and vice versa. It can be assumed that the circuit consists of a source-follower transistor Q_1 with a switchable load Q_2, or a driving transistor Q_2 with a switchable load Q_1. The push-pull operation allows high charging and discharging currents resulting in low switching times. The transistor Q_1 could be an enhancement or a depletion type. If it is an enhancement-type, the push-pull driver does not consume dc power since either Q_1 or Q_2 is on during the steady state. Thus, there is no dc requirement on the ratio $[(W/L)_2/(W/L)_1]$ and the circuit configuration is "ratioless." However, the voltage at node 3 suffers from threshold losses. In the case of a depletion-type load, threshold losses are eliminated at the expense of dc power consumption. The circuit in this case must be ratioed.

Bootstrapped Loads—It has been shown in 3.1 and 3.2 that when operating the NMOS load transistor in the nonsaturation region by tying its gate to V_{GG}, $V_{GG} > V_{DD} + V_{TL}$, threshold losses are eliminated and the transient performance is improved. These two results can be obtained without the need for the extra power supply, V_{GG}, by bootstrapping the load.

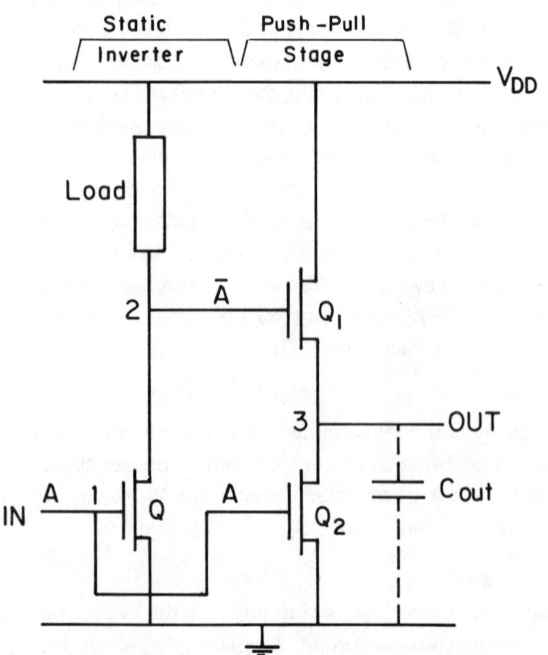

Fig. 7. NMOS push-pull driver.

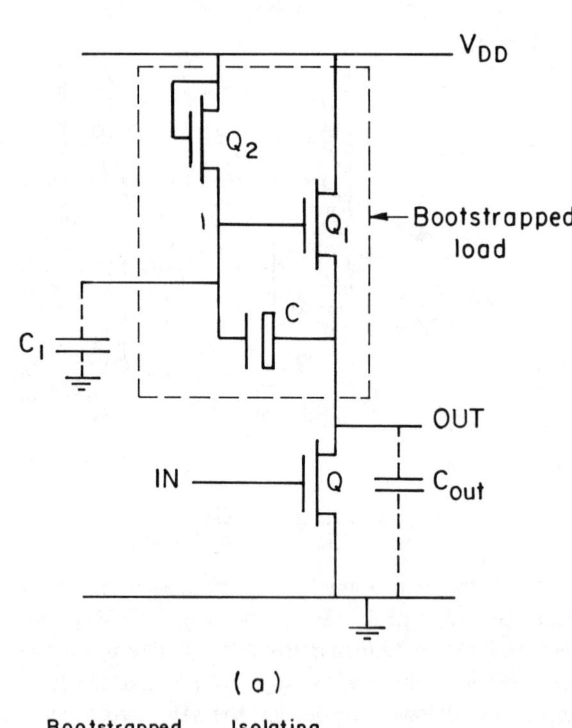

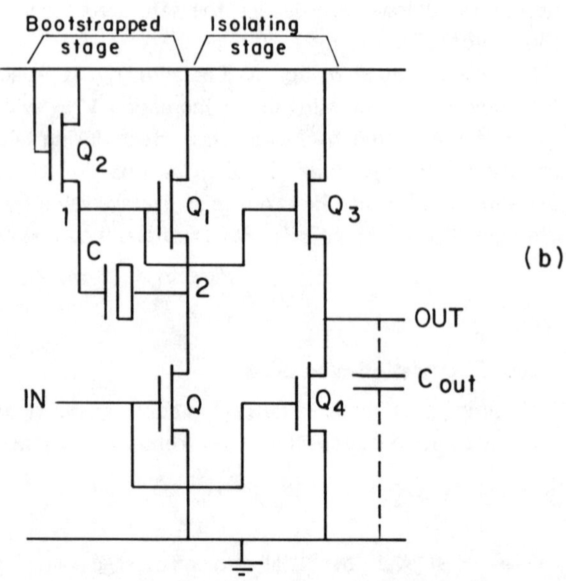

Fig. 8. (a) Bootstrapped load; (b) isolated bootstrapped load.

Bootstrapping allows the gate of the NMOS load transistor to rise above V_{DD} *during switching*, thus allowing the load to operate in the nonsaturation region. The basic circuit is shown in Fig. 8(a) and consists of the load transistor Q_1, a biasing transistor Q_2, and an MOS capacitor C. The biasing transistor Q_2 allows node 1 to float at $(V_{DD} - V_{T2})$, where V_{T2} is the threshold voltage of Q_2. As the input voltage drops, the output voltage rises by an amount $= \Delta V$. Because of the capacitive coupling, node 1 rises by an amount $= \Delta V'$: $\Delta V' = \Delta VC/C_1 + C$, i.e., if $C >> C_1$, where C_1 is the parasitic capacitance of node 1, then $\Delta V' \approx \Delta V$. In the limit $\Delta V = V_{DD}$, the voltage at node 1 can reach up to $(2V_{DD} - V_{T2})$ allowing Q_1 to operate in the nonsaturation region.

It should be noted that as node 1 rises above V_{DD}, Q_2 shuts off and isolates node 1 from the rest of the circuit [9].

It should also be noted that bootstrapping is a dynamic operation occurring when the output voltage switches. If the output node capacitance C_{out} is large and the output voltage rises slowly, then the bootstrap coupling between the output node and node 1 occurs at a slower rate. This can be resolved by isolating the output node capacitance C_{out} from the bootstrapped load using a source-follower as shown in Fig. 8(b). The isolating stage consists of a bootstrapped transistor Q_3 and a driver transistor Q_4. The output node is now isolated from the bootstrapped load.

NMOS Transmission Gates—The NMOS transmission gate is used in the design of static and dynamic NMOS digital circuits. It consists of a single transistor as shown in Fig. 9. The gate is simply a symmetrical switch controlled by the voltage on node 1. If that voltage is greater than V_T, then nodes 2 and 3 are connected through the on resistance of the NMOS device. If that voltage is less than V_T then the NMOS device is off and nodes 2 and 3 are separated by an open circuit. Thus, a transmission gate can be used as a two-input AND gate where the inputs are applied to node 1 and node 2 (or 3) and the output is at node 3 (or 2).

The back-gate bias effect should be considered in the design of NMOS transmission gates. Thus V_T is a function of the voltage on nodes 2 and 3. Nodes 2 and 3 take the role of a source or drain depending on the values of their respective voltages. The on resistance of the NMOS device can be reduced by increasing (W/L) or the voltage driving factor $[(V \text{ at node } 1) - V_T)]$.

Because of the capacitive coupling between node 1 and nodes 2 and 3, a feed-through voltage appears at nodes 2 and 3 as the voltage at node 1 changes. The effect of the feed-through voltages on the overall circuit performance where the transmission gate is used should be evaluated.

4. Static Logic Gates and Flip-Flops

To realize static MOS logic gates, the driver transistor of the inverter circuit is replaced with a number of MOS transistors. If they are connected in series, as shown in Fig. 10(a), a NAND gate results, since the output is low only if all the inputs are high, i.e., all the transistors are on. If the transistors are connected in parallel, as shown in Fig. 10(b), a NOR gate results, since the output is low if any of the inputs is high, i.e., any one transistor is on. The transistors can also be connected in series-parallel arrangements, such as shown in Fig. 10(c), to realize more complex logic functions.

The design of an m-input MOS logic gate usually follows that of an inverter. First, an inverter is designed to meet a given dc and transient performance and $(W/L)_D$ and $(W/L)_L$ are determined. Then $(W/L)_D$ of the parallel transistors in the case of the NOR gate and the series transistors in the case of the NAND are determined. In the case of a NOR gate, since a worse situation results if only one of the m parallel transistors

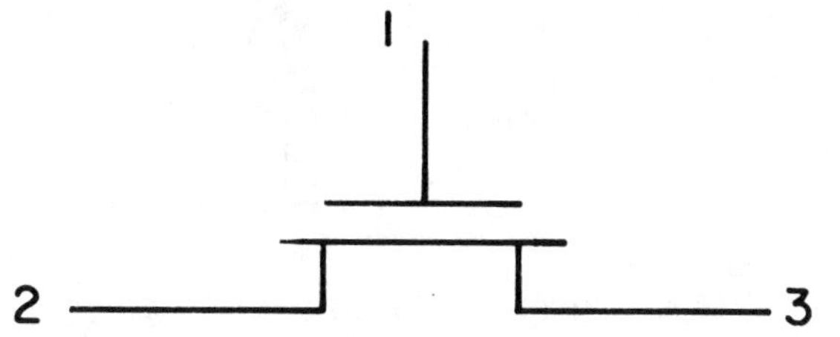

Fig. 9. NMOS transmission gate.

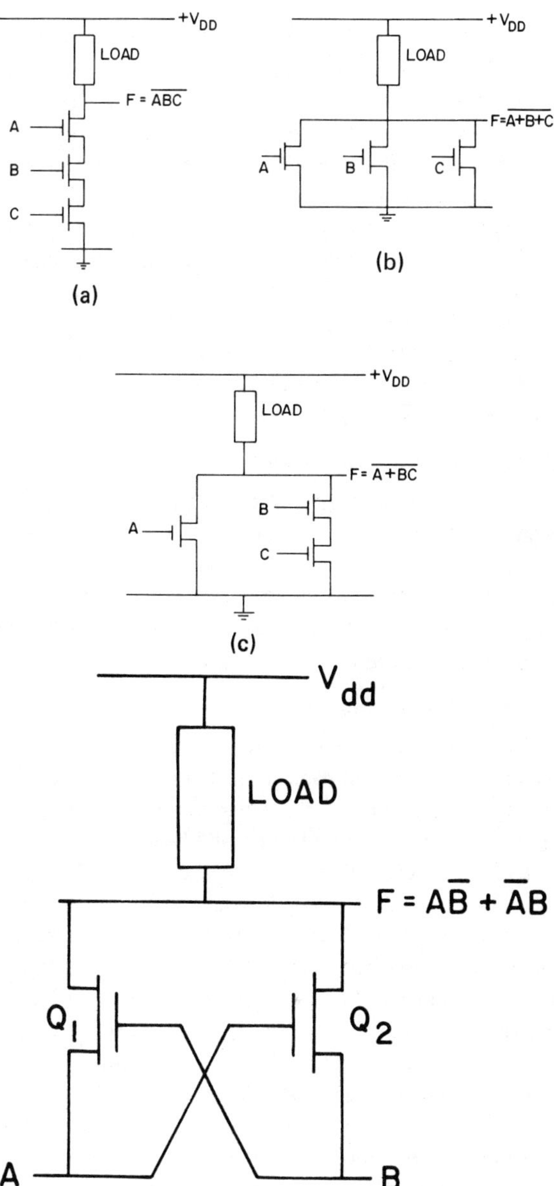

Fig. 10. (a) NMOS NAND gate; (b) NMOS NOR gate; (c) NMOS logic gate with series-parallel arrangement of driver transistors; (d) realization of an Exclusive-OR using two NMOS transistors and a load.

is on at a given time, $(W/L)_D$ of the NOR gate drivers is taken to be = $(W/L)_D$ of the inverter driver. However, in the case of a NAND gate, since the driver transistors are connected in series, the $(W/L)_D$ of the NAND gate drivers is taken to be m times $(W/L)_D$ of the inverter driver. As a result NAND MOS logic gates take more area than NOR gates.

In designing NOR gates, with $(W/L)_L$ and $(W/L)_D$ the same as that of an inverter, the logic levels V_0 and V_1 would be the same as that of an inverter. However, because the m parallel drivers contribute more capacitance to the output node than a single driver, the (W/L) of the load and the driver transistors of the NOR should be increased to obtain the same transient performance as that of the inverter.

4.1 Special Circuit Configurations

In addition to the NMOS logic gates shown in Fig. 10(a-c), innovative NMOS circuit configurations are sometimes used to efficiently realize specific complex logic functions. An example is shown in Fig. 10(d), where the circuit realizes the Exclusive-OR function F, $F = A\overline{B} + \overline{A}B$ by using both the gate and the drain of Q_1 and Q_2 as inputs.

4.2 NMOS Static Flip-Flops

Figure 11 shows a cross-coupled static flip-flop consisting of two inverters connected back to back, i.e., the output of one is connected to the input of the other, and two access transistors Q_3 and Q_4. The load structures could be polyresistors or MOS transistors. The circuit has two storage states: (1) V_A is low, V_B is high, Q_1 is on and Q_2 is off, (2) V_A is high, V_B is low, Q_1 is off and Q_2 is on. The state of the flip-flop can be changed by turning on the two access transistors (Q_3 and Q_4), and applying the input and its complement as shown in Fig. 11.

The dc logic levels at V_A and V_B nodes are determined by the loads and the driver transistors Q_1 and Q_2. The dc design procedure is similar to that of an inverter. In order to minimize the dc power dissipation (stand-by power) of the flip-flop, the load structures are chosen to have high value resistances, i.e., in the case of polyresistors high value resistors are chosen and in the case of MOS transistors, a low value of $(W/L)_L$ is chosen.

The transient performance of the flip-flop is determined by the internal node capacitances C_1 and C_2 and the charging and discharging currents available. Because the loads have high value resistances they supply small charging currents to the internal nodes and most of these currents are provided by the input circuits through the access transistors.

5. Dynamic MOS Circuits

The delays of static MOS circuits can be reduced by using advances in MOS technologies. However, it is possible to increase the throughput (the number of processed computations per unit time) of an MOS logic system by pipelining the circuit operation, where the delays of the system building blocks do not accumulate. The key feature of this approach is that the delay contribution of each block is with respect to a master clock, and that delay does not transfer from one block to another. Thus, the maximum frequency of operation of a pipelined system is determined by the delay of a *single*, although the slowest, block. Dynamic MOS logic circuits lead inherently to a pipeline operation, and can realize logic and arithmetic functions with a high throughput rate.

In dynamic MOS circuits, a master clock is used to generate different timing clocks, which are used to control the dynamic operation of the circuit. These clocks are referred to as multiphase clocks [2 phase (2ϕ), 3 phase (3ϕ), four phase (4ϕ), etc.]. Although in principle the number of clocks can be increased to any number, four clocks is a practical compromise [5, 10], and 4ϕ dynamic circuits are commonly used. However, first we shall study 2ϕ dynamic circuits since they are the simplest.

5.1 Two-Phase (2ϕ) Circuits

The basic operations in 2ϕ dynamic circuits are:

1. *Charging* a capacitance through an MOS transistor during a first time slot (precharge time).
2. *Logically discharging* that capacitance (discharging it or not depending on the logical state(s) of the input(s)) through input transistor(s) during a second time slot (evaluation time).
3. *Transferring* the logical state (the voltage level on the capacitance) to the input of the next gate during the proper time slot (sampling time).

Figure 12 shows two 2ϕ inverters connected in cascade. Each inverter consists of three transistors Q_1, Q_2 and Q_3. The charging transistor Q_1 permits the output capacitance C_{out} to charge. The input transistor Q_2 provides a discharging path for C_{out}. The transferring transistor Q_3 allows a charge transfer between C_{out} and the input capacitance C_i of the next stage.

The above three basic operations are performed under the control of two nonoverlapping clocks ϕ_1 and ϕ_2 as shown in the timing diagram of Fig. 13. We assume that the input sequence is logical '1' - '0' - '1'. The logical inputs are presented by voltage signals which maintain their levels during the ϕ_1

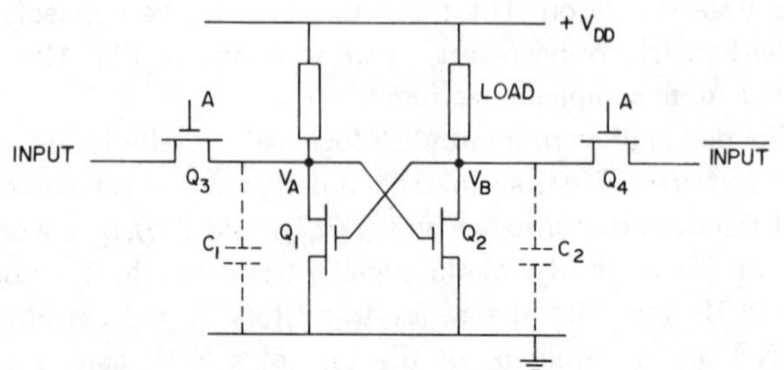

Fig. 11. NMOS static flip-flop with access transistors.

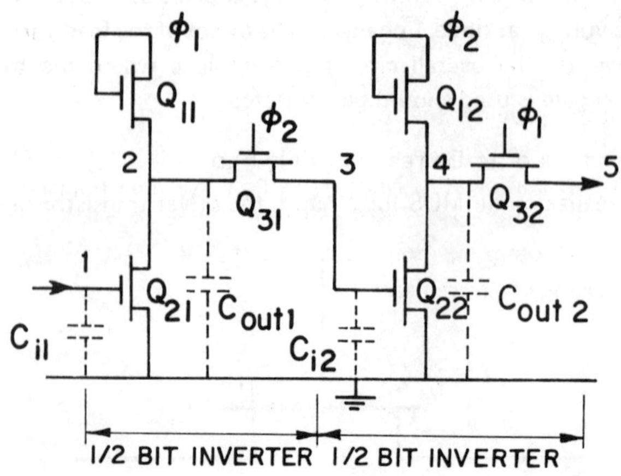

Fig. 12. Two 2ϕ inverters connected in cascade.

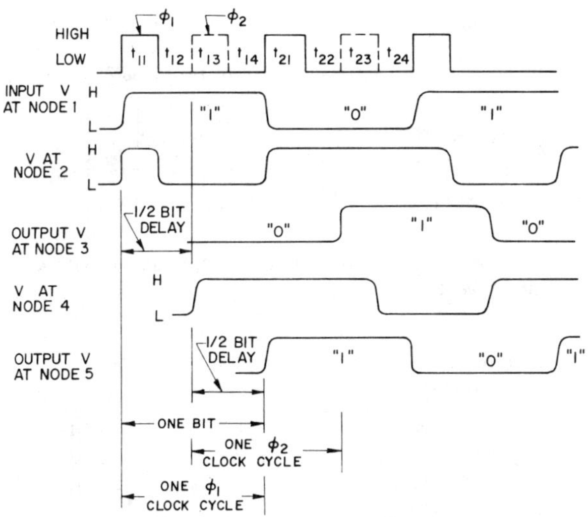

Fig. 13. Timing diagram of Fig. 12.

clock cycles. For the case when the input is '1' the following sequence of operations occurs.

During the time interval t_{11} (precharge time), C_{out1} is precharged through Q_{11}. During t_{12} (evaluation time), because the input is high, C_{out1} is discharged through Q_{21}. During t_{13} (sampling time), Q_{31} conducts and a charge sharing occurs between C_{out1} and C_{i2}. If $C_{out1} >> C_{i2}$ the voltage level at node 3 will be approximately the same as that of node 2: (V at node 3) = (V at node 2) ($C_{out1}/C_{out1} + C_{i2}$). Note that the input information which was available at node 1 during t_{11} has been inverted at node 3 and is available during t_{13}, i.e., the input information has been inverted with a half-bit delay (a half clock cycle).

During the same time interval t_{13}, C_{out2} it precharged through Q_{12}. During t_{14}, because the input at node 3 is low, node 4 stays high. During t_{21}, Q_{32} conducts and the input capacitance of the next stage shares the charge of C_{out2} and a high voltage results at node 5, i.e., the input information at node 3 has been inverted with another half-bit delay.

The sequence of operations for a logical '0' input at node 1 is shown in Fig. 13 and can be similarly explained.

Figure 14 shows a logic symbol of the two inverters of Fig. 12. The first inverter type (ϕ_1/ϕ_2) accepts input at ϕ_1 clock cycles and provides output at ϕ_2 clock cycles. The second inverter type (ϕ_2/ϕ_1) accepts input at ϕ_2 clock cycles and provides output at ϕ_1 clock cycles. As a result, two inverters of the same type cannot be successively connected.

Logic gates can be realized by replacing the input transistor Q_2 of a two-phase inverter with a combination of transistors. As before, parallel transistors provide the NOR function, serial transistors provide the NAND function and mixed serial/parallel arrangements provide complex logic functions. As in the case of static gates, NOR gates take less area than NAND gates. Flip-flops can be realized using such 2ϕ gates. Figure 15 shows some examples where 2ϕ AND, OR, NOR and noninverting gates are used.

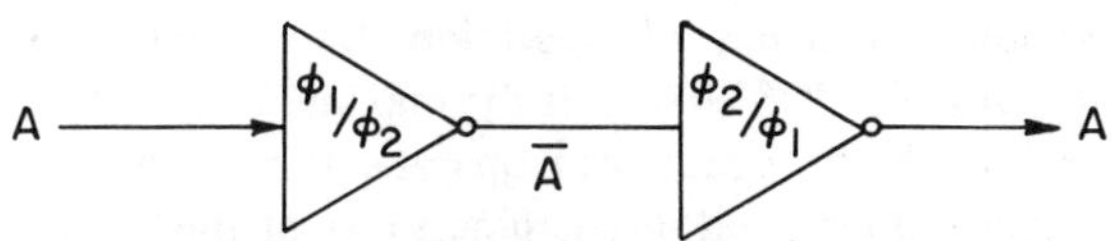

Fig. 14. Logic symbol of 2ϕ inverters.

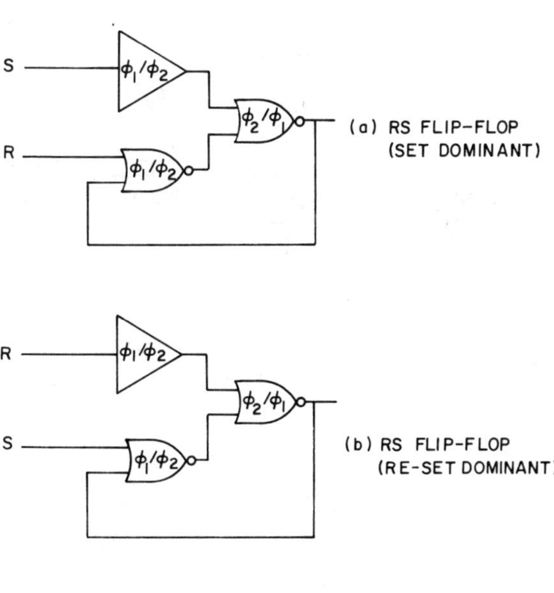

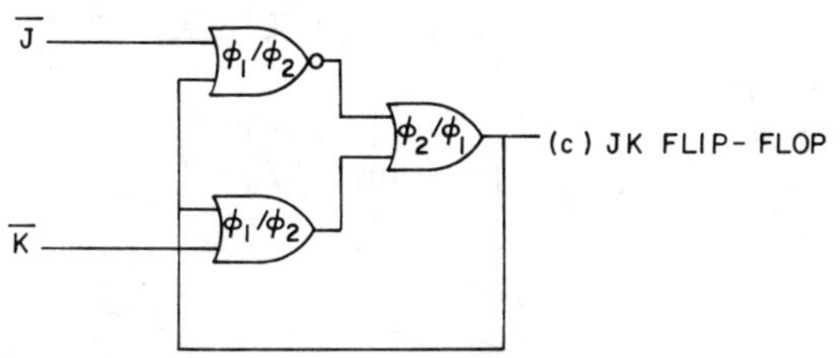

Fig. 15. Dynamic 2ϕ flip-flops.

With reference to Fig. 12, faning-out in 2ϕ circuits can be done at node 3. In this case the basic gate consists of Q_1 and Q_2 followed by the transferring transistor Q_3. The interconnection capacitances in this case are added to that of node 3. Alternatively, faning-out can be done at node 2. In this case the basic gate consists of a transferring transistor Q_3 followed by Q_1 and Q_2. Thus, for each input, a Q_3 and a Q_2 are required. The interconnection capacitances in this case are added to that of node 2. The advantage of this method of faning out is having $C_{out} > C_i$, because efficient charge sharing results during sampling times. However, the first method uses fewer transistors and fewer diffusion regions than the second method [11].

The basic 2ϕ circuit can be modified to meet different requirements. For example, Fig. 16(a) shows one configuration where Q_1 is operating from V_{DD}, while its gate is clocked with ϕ_1. The transferring transistor Q_3 is clocked with ϕ_2. The inverter (Q_1 and Q_2) consumes power when ϕ_1 is high. Its design is based on the static inverter design given in 3. Because in this configuration $(W/L)_D/(W/L)_L > 1$, to meet the dc requirements it is referred to as a ratioed configuration. Note that in the configuration of Fig. 12 both the gate and the drain of the load transistor are clocked with ϕ_1. This results in saving the power line V_{DD}. Again the design of the inverter is based on the static inverter design. The configuration is also a ratioed configuration.

In Fig. 16(b), both load and driver transistors are clocked using ϕ_1 and in this case no dc path exists. The power dissipation of the inverter is only a transient power given by $C_{out}V_\ell^2f$. Moreover, because of the absence of a dc path, the load and the driver transistors do not have to satisfy any dc requirements. As a result, there is no need for a ratio between $(W/L)_D$ and $(W/L)_L$. In this case the (W/L) of both transistors are determined from transient considerations: the charging time is

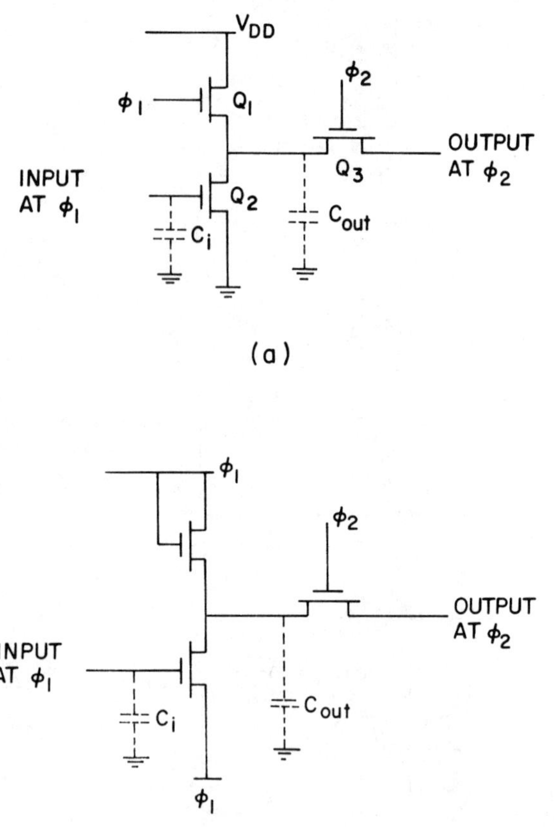

Fig. 16. Two other 2ϕ configurations: (a) ratioed configuration and (b) ratioless configuration with overlapping clocks.

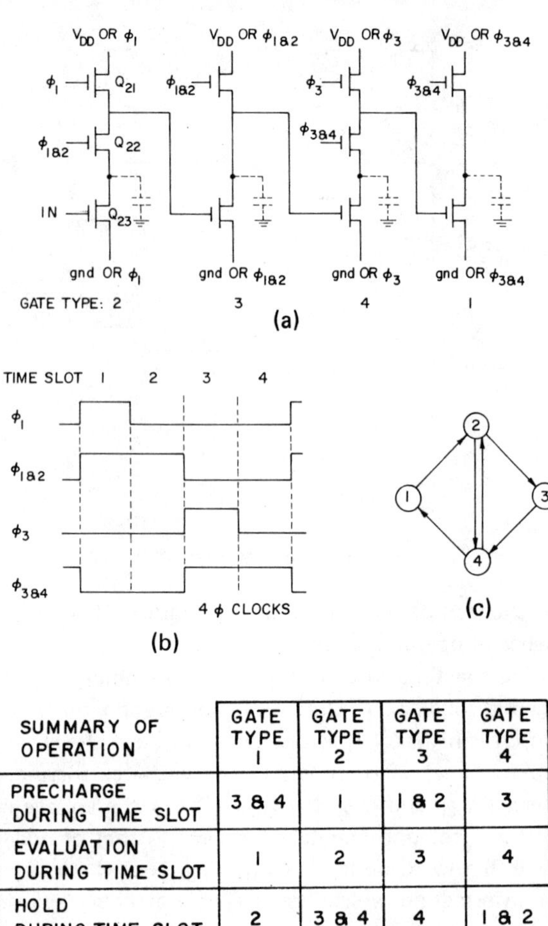

SUMMARY OF OPERATION	GATE TYPE 1	GATE TYPE 2	GATE TYPE 3	GATE TYPE 4
PRECHARGE DURING TIME SLOT	3 & 4	1	1 & 2	3
EVALUATION DURING TIME SLOT	1	2	3	4
HOLD DURING TIME SLOT	2	3 & 4	4	1 & 2

(d)

Fig. 17. Four 4ϕ inverters with overlapping clocks (a) circuit diagram; (b) timing diagram; (c) connection diagram; (d) summary of operation.

determined by $(W/L)_L$ and the discharging time is determined by $(W/L)_D$. Thus, this configuration is a ratioless configuration. It has the advantage of not using a V_{DD} or a ground line, no dc power dissipation, and using relatively small size devices for the load and the driver, compared to ratioed circuits for the same loading capacitance. However, it has the disadvantage of contributing large load capacitance to the clock lines.

5.2 Four-Phase (4ϕ) Circuits

One disadvantage of 2ϕ MOS dynamic circuits is the reduction of logic levels during the transfer operation through the transmission gate. This can be overcome by using more than two clocks to control the dynamic operation of the circuits. In this section we will discuss the operation of 4ϕ circuits using a given circuit configuration. The discussion can be easily extended to other circuit configurations.

Figure 17(a) shows four 4ϕ inverters connected in cascade. They are of four types and use 4ϕ overlapping clocks as shown in Fig. 17(b). Type 2 inverters operate under the control of the ϕ_1 and $\phi_{1\&2}$ clocks. With reference to the timing diagram of Fig. 17(b), the output capacitance of type 2 gates precharge during the time slot 1 (i.e., when both ϕ_1 and $\phi_{1\&2}$ are at high level). During time slot 2 the logic voltage level on the output capacitance is logically discharged through Q_{23} depending upon the logic input signal. In the same time slot, the output voltage logic level is transferred to the input capacitance of the next stage (Q_{22} is on). Thus, an inverting logic operation has been realized with a fourth-bit time delay. During time slots 3 and 4, the input node capacitance of the next stage will hold that logic level. This operation is summarized in the table of Fig. 17(d). It should be noted that in Fig. 17(a) each gate could be of the ratioed type or the ratioless type as we have explained in dealing with 2ϕ circuits. For example, for type 2 gates, the drain of Q_{21} can be connected to V_{DD} or ϕ_1 and the source of Q_{23} can be connected to ground or ϕ_1.

The operation of the other 4ϕ inverters of Fig. 17 can be similarly explained. The connection diagram of Fig. 17(c) shows, for example, that type 1 inverters can feed into type 2, while type 2 can feed into type 3 or type 4. The connection diagram can be easily obtained from a detailed timing diagram of the system.

Figure 18 shows another example of 4ϕ logic inverters along with the nonoverlapping clocks used. A connection diagram and a table for the summary of operation are left as an exercise for the reader.

Four-phase NOR gates are obtained by replacing the single input transistor of the inverter (e.g., Q_{23} in Fig. 17) with transistors connected in parallel. Four-phase flip-flops are realized using 4ϕ logic gates in a manner similar to the realization of 2ϕ flip-flops using 2ϕ logic gates.

Maximum Frequency of Operation—One important parameter in dynamic MOS circuits is the maximum clock frequency f_{max} at which the circuit can operate. If τ_1 and τ_2 are the worst case charging and discharging times of the output node capacitance then

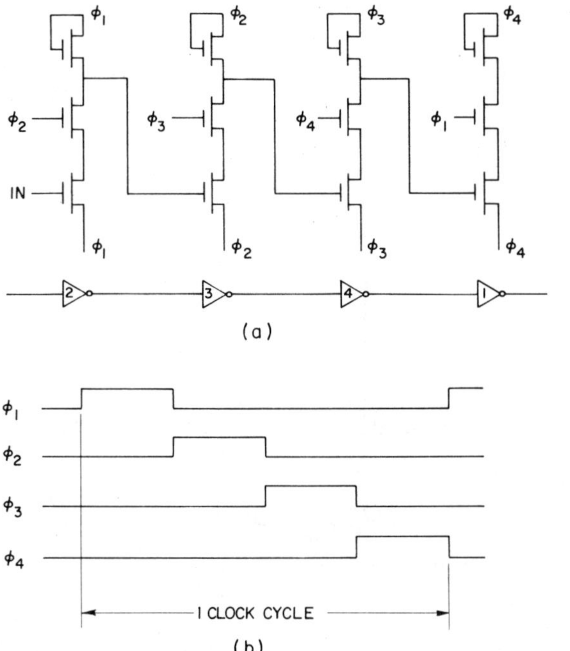

Fig. 18. Four 4ϕ inverters with nonoverlapping clocks (a) circuit diagram and (b) timing diagram.

$$f_{max} = \frac{1}{n(\tau_1 + \tau_2)}$$

where n is a factor which is a function of the clocking scheme used, e.g., in the two-phase nonoverlapping clocks of Fig. 12, $n = 2$.

Minimum Frequency of Operation—Because in dynamic MOS logic circuits the logic binary information is represented by a voltage level on a capacitance, the clock frequency has to be higher than a certain minimum f_{min} at which the stored charge of the capacitance starts to leak and the voltage level starts to deteriorate. The evaluation of f_{min} involves knowing the leakage currents of the MOS transistors under consideration. In a 2ϕ nonoverlapping logic system:

$$\frac{1}{2 f_{min}} = \frac{\Delta V.C}{I_\ell}$$

Where ΔV is the allowable deterioration in the high logic level, C is the total note capacitance, and I_ℓ is the leakage current associated with that node.

Clock Noise in Dynamic Circuits—Because of the capacitive coupling between the clock lines and the various nodes in a dynamic circuit, the nodes are subjected to changes in their voltages (noise) during the switching of the clocks. If the magnitude of these voltage changes is high enough, faulty operations could result. Computer simulation is used in these situations to assure that the circuit can tolerate this clock noise.

Clock Power Dissipation—In dynamic MOS circuits, the different clocks required by the circuits are generated on-chip and contribute to the total power dissipation. This clock power dissipation is a transient (dynamic) power given by $\Sigma C_\phi V_\phi^2 f_\phi$ where C_ϕ is the capacitive loading on the individual clock lines, V_ϕ is the clock voltage swing, and f_ϕ is the clock frequency.

6. Complementary MOS (CMOS) Circuits

The use of a p-channel MOS as a load for an n-channel MOS driver provides the basic complementary CMOS inverter, as shown in Fig. 19(a). Logic gates and flip-flops can be realized using the complementary pair. Today, CMOS is the only MOS logic family available realizing standard SSI, MSI, and LSI functions. The family offers many advantages, including high noise immunity, operation at a wide range of power supply voltages, low power dissipation, relatively high speed, and compatibility to other logic families. The main disadvantage of the family is the relatively high silicon area consumed because of the need of complementary MOS pairs for each added logic input as shown in 6.2.

CMOS circuits can be fabricated using P-well, N-well or twin-tub CMOS technologies [12]. In a P-well CMOS technology the starting material is N-silicon substrate and is used to fabricate the PMOS devices, while a diffused or ion implanted P-well is used to fabricate the NMOS devices. More recently an N-well CMOS technology has been introduced which is compatible with NMOS technologies where the starting material is a P-silicon substrate and is used to fabricate NMOS devices and

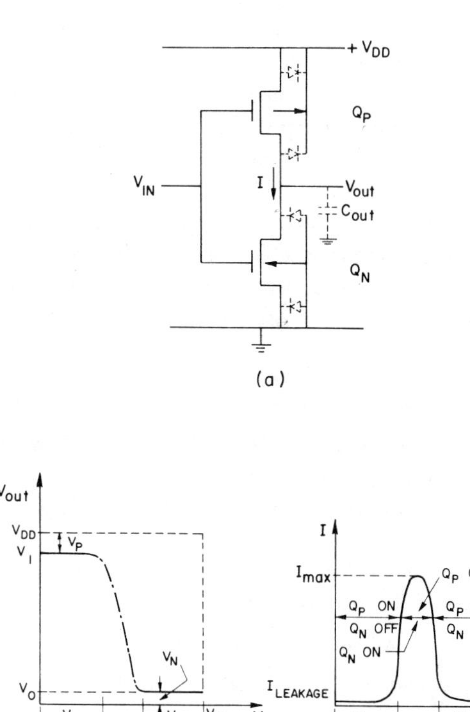

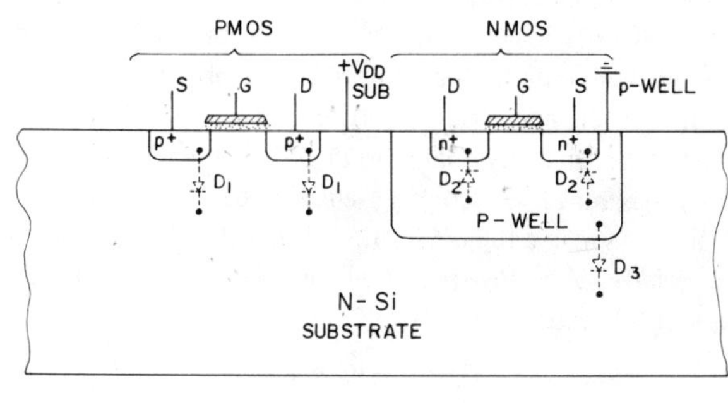

Fig. 19. CMOS inverter (a) circuit diagram; (b) transfer characteristic; (c) I vs. V_{IN}; (d) cross-section in a P-well CMOS technology.

an ion implanted N-well is used to fabricate the PMOS devices. In a twin-tub CMOS technology, the starting material is a high resistivity silicon and two ion implanted N and P tubs are used to fabricate the PMOS and NMOS devices respectively.

Figure 19(d) shows a cross-section in NMOS and PMOS devices in a P-well CMOS technology. The following parasitic diodes are shown: D_1 is the substrate-source/drain junction diode, D_2 is the well-source/drain junction diode, and D_3 is the well-substrate junction diode. The three diodes make up a three junction thyrister (SCR) and during circuit operation it may latch-up. Techniques are used to minimize this hazardous circuit operation [12].

6.1 The CMOS Static Inverter

The basic inverter operation can be best explained with the aid of the transfer characteristic of Fig. 19(b).

1. If V_{IN} is a logic '0' (i.e., $V_{IN} = V_0$, $V_0 < V_{TN}$, where V_{TN} is the threshold voltage of Q_N), Q_N is off. If $|V_0 - V_{DD}| > |V_{TP}|$, where V_{TP} is the threshold voltage of Q_P, then Q_P is on. The output voltage in this case is given by

$$V_{OUT} = V_1 = V_{DD} - V_P \tag{36}$$

where V_P is the voltage drop across Q_P and is given by

$$V_P = I_P R_P \simeq I_P \frac{1}{\beta_P[(V_{DD} - V_0) - |V_{TP}|]}$$

where I_P is the current supplied by Q_P to Q_N and to the loads. If the inverter is loaded with MOS gates, as is often the case, then I_P is negligible in the order of the leakage current of the substrate-source and drain junctions and $V_1 \simeq V_{DD}$. If I_P is not negligible, then by increasing β_P (i.e., the size of Q_P) it is possible to achieve $V_P << V_{DD}$ and, hence, $V_1 \approx V_{DD}$.

2. If V_{IN} is a logical '1' (i.e., $V_{IN} = V_1$, $V_1 > V_{TN}$) then Q_N is on. If $|V_1 - V_{DD}| < |V_{TP}|$ then Q_P is off. The output voltage in this case is given by

$$V_{OUT} = V_0 = V_N \tag{37}$$

where V_N is the voltage drop across Q_N and is given by

$$V_N = I_N R_N \simeq I_N \frac{1}{\beta_N(V_1 - V_{TN})}$$

where I_N is the current sunk by Q_N from Q_P and from the loads. If the loads are MOS gates then I_N is a leakage current and $V_N \approx 0$. However, if the loads are bipolar circuits (e.g., T^2L gates) then I_N could be considerable. In this case V_0 can be reduced by increasing β_N.

Thus, the logic levels of a CMOS inverter can be made close to V_{DD} and ground; and a logic swing V_ℓ of the order of V_{DD} results. This is a main feature of CMOS gates. The threshold voltage of CMOS logic gate V_t (see Appendix B for the definition of V_t) is close to $\frac{V_{DD}}{2}$ if symmetrical devices are used, i.e., $\beta_N = \beta_P$. The $\beta_N = \beta_P$ condition can be achieved if $\left[\left(\frac{W}{L}\right)_P / \left(\frac{W}{L}\right)_N\right] = \frac{\mu_N}{\mu_P} \approx 2.5$. Thus, equal noise margins result which are $\approx \frac{V_{DD}}{2}$. This is another feature of CMOS gates.

As shown in Fig. 19(c), the gate current I passes between V_{DD} and ground only when both Q_P and Q_N are on, i.e., during the transition region. During the two steady states, $I \approx I_{leakage}$ and the dc power dissipation of the gate is given by

$$P_{DC} = V_{DD} I_{leakage} \tag{38}$$

This power dissipation is a negligible component of the total power dissipation of the gate as will be explained.

From Fig. 19(b) it is clear that the minimum value of V_{DD} is given by:

$$V_{DD}|_{min} = V_{TN} + |V_{TP}| \tag{39}$$

If V_{DD} is lower than that value, the gate demonstrates a hysteresis transfer characteristic as shown in Fig. 20, and it can not be used as a logic gate.

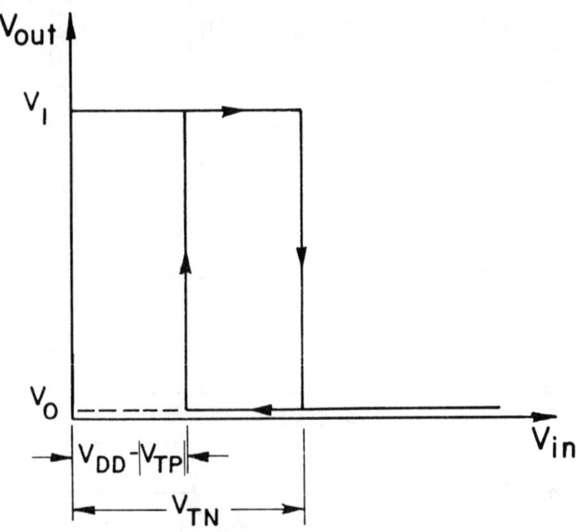

Fig. 20. Hysterises transfer characteristic of a CMOS inverter, $V_{DD} < (V_{TN} + |V_{TP}|)$.

Transient Analysis—If we consider a CMOS inverter with an ideal step input voltage from 0 to V_{DD}, the charging and discharging times can be calculated following the approach outlined in 3.2. The discharging time, t_{dis}, which is the time taken for the output capacitance C_{out} to discharge through Q_N from an output logic level of $V_1 \simeq V_{DD}$ to an output logic level of V_0, is given by:

$$t_{dis} = \tau_N \left[\frac{2}{\dfrac{V_{DD}}{V_{TN}} - 1} + \ell n \left(\frac{2(V_{DD} - V_{TN})}{V_0} - 1\right)\right] \tag{40}$$

where

$$\tau_N = \frac{C_{out}}{g_{mN}} = \frac{C_{out}}{\beta_N(V_{DD} - V_{TN})}$$

Equation (40) is similar to (28). Because of the symmetry of the problem, the charging time t_{ch} which is the time taken for C_{out} to charge through Q_P from V_0 to V_1 is given by:

$$t_{ch} = \tau_P \left[\frac{2}{\left(\dfrac{V_{DD}}{|V_{TP}|}\right) - 1} + \ell n \frac{2(V_{DD} - |V_{TP}|)}{V_{DD} - V_1} - 1\right] \tag{41}$$

where

$$\tau_P = \frac{C_{out}}{g_{mp}} = \frac{C_{out}}{\beta_P(V_{DD} - |V_{TP}|)}$$

It should be noted that (40) and (41) can be simplified as in (28a).

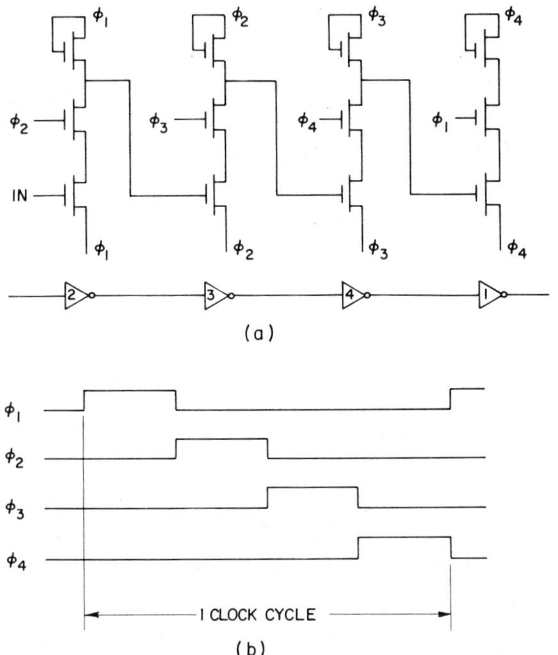

Fig. 18. Four 4ϕ inverters with nonoverlapping clocks (a) circuit diagram and (b) timing diagram.

$$f_{max} = \frac{1}{n(\tau_1 + \tau_2)}$$

where n is a factor which is a function of the clocking scheme used, e.g., in the two-phase nonoverlapping clocks of Fig. 12, $n = 2$.

Minimum Frequency of Operation—Because in dynamic MOS logic circuits the logic binary information is represented by a voltage level on a capacitance, the clock frequency has to be higher than a certain minimum f_{min} at which the stored charge of the capacitance starts to leak and the voltage level starts to deteriorate. The evaluation of f_{min} involves knowing the leakage currents of the MOS transistors under consideration. In a 2ϕ nonoverlapping logic system:

$$\frac{1}{2 f_{min}} = \frac{\Delta V.C}{I_{\ell}}$$

Where ΔV is the allowable deterioration in the high logic level, C is the total note capacitance, and I_{ℓ} is the leakage current associated with that node.

Clock Noise in Dynamic Circuits—Because of the capacitive coupling between the clock lines and the various nodes in a dynamic circuit, the nodes are subjected to changes in their voltages (noise) during the switching of the clocks. If the magnitude of these voltage changes is high enough, faulty operations could result. Computer simulation is used in these situations to assure that the circuit can tolerate this clock noise.

Clock Power Dissipation—In dynamic MOS circuits, the different clocks required by the circuits are generated on-chip and contribute to the total power dissipation. This clock power dissipation is a transient (dynamic) power given by $\Sigma C_{\phi} V_{\phi}^2 f_{\phi}$ where C_{ϕ} is the capacitive loading on the individual clock lines, V_{ϕ} is the clock voltage swing, and f_{ϕ} is the clock frequency.

6. Complementary MOS (CMOS) Circuits

The use of a p-channel MOS as a load for an n-channel MOS driver provides the basic complementary CMOS inverter, as shown in Fig. 19(a). Logic gates and flip-flops can be realized using the complementary pair. Today, CMOS is the only MOS logic family available realizing standard SSI, MSI, and LSI functions. The family offers many advantages, including high noise immunity, operation at a wide range of power supply voltages, low power dissipation, relatively high speed, and compatibility to other logic families. The main disadvantage of the family is the relatively high silicon area consumed because of the need of complementary MOS pairs for each added logic input as shown in 6.2.

CMOS circuits can be fabricated using P-well, N-well or twin-tub CMOS technologies [12]. In a P-well CMOS technology the starting material is N-silicon substrate and is used to fabricate the PMOS devices, while a diffused or ion implanted P-well is used to fabricate the NMOS devices. More recently an N-well CMOS technology has been introduced which is compatible with NMOS technologies where the starting material is a P-silicon substrate and is used to fabricate NMOS devices and

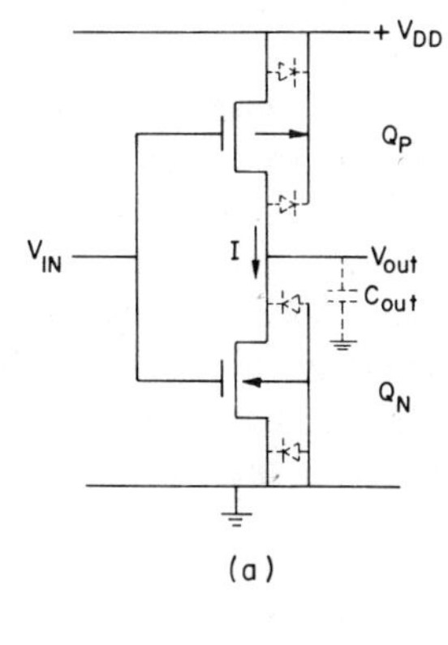

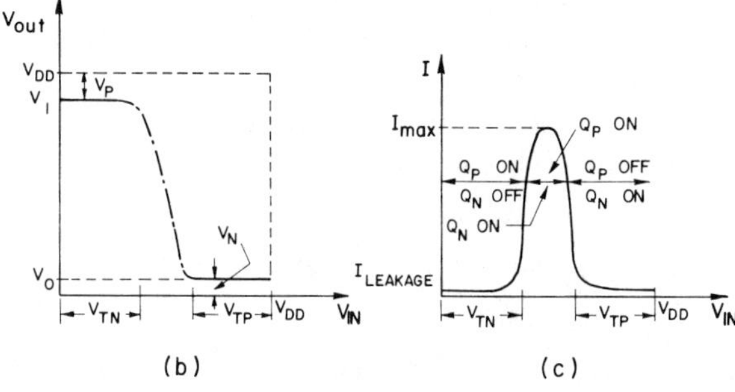

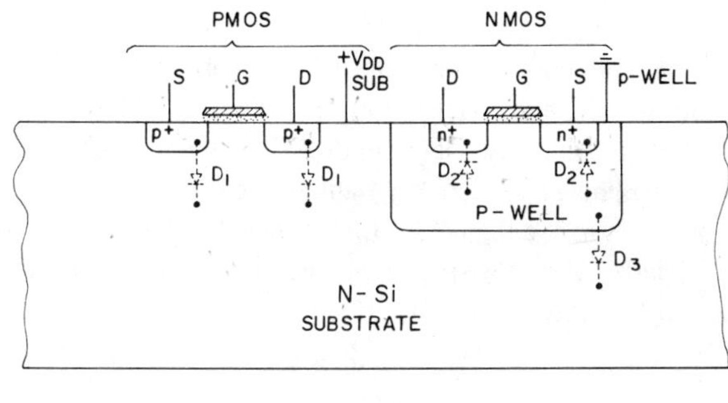

Fig. 19. CMOS inverter (a) circuit diagram; (b) transfer characteristic; (c) I vs. V_{IN}; (d) cross-section in a P-well CMOS technology.

an ion implanted N-well is used to fabricate the PMOS devices. In a twin-tub CMOS technology, the starting material is a high resistivity silicon and two ion implanted N and P tubs are used to fabricate the PMOS and NMOS devices respectively.

Figure 19(d) shows a cross-section in NMOS and PMOS devices in a P-well CMOS technology. The following parasitic diodes are shown: D_1 is the substrate-source/drain junction diode, D_2 is the well-source/drain junction diode, and D_3 is the well-substrate junction diode. The three diodes make up a three junction thyrister (SCR) and during circuit operation it may latch-up. Techniques are used to minimize this hazardous circuit operation [12].

6.1 The CMOS Static Inverter

The basic inverter operation can be best explained with the aid of the transfer characteristic of Fig. 19(b).

1. If V_{IN} is a logic '0' (i.e., $V_{IN} = V_0$, $V_0 < V_{TN}$, where V_{TN} is the threshold voltage of Q_N), Q_N is off. If $|V_0 - V_{DD}| > |V_{TP}|$, where V_{TP} is the threshold voltage of Q_P, then Q_P is on. The output voltage in this case is given by

$$V_{OUT} = V_1 = V_{DD} - V_P \tag{36}$$

where V_P is the voltage drop across Q_P and is given by

$$V_P = I_P R_P \simeq I_P \frac{1}{\beta_P[(V_{DD} - V_0) - |V_{TP}|]}$$

where I_P is the current supplied by Q_P to Q_N and to the loads. If the inverter is loaded with MOS gates, as is often the case, then I_P is negligible in the order of the leakage current of the substrate-source and drain junctions and $V_1 \simeq V_{DD}$. If I_P is not negligible, then by increasing β_P (i.e., the size of Q_P) it is possible to achieve $V_P << V_{DD}$ and, hence, $V_1 \approx V_{DD}$.

2. If V_{IN} is a logical '1' (i.e., $V_{IN} = V_1$, $V_1 > V_{TN}$) then Q_N is on. If $|V_1 - V_{DD}| < |V_{TP}|$ then Q_P is off. The output voltage in this case is given by

$$V_{OUT} = V_0 = V_N \tag{37}$$

where V_N is the voltage drop across Q_N and is given by

$$V_N = I_N R_N \simeq I_N \frac{1}{\beta_N (V_1 - V_{TN})}$$

where I_N is the current sunk by Q_N from Q_P and from the loads. If the loads are MOS gates then I_N is a leakage current and $V_N \approx 0$. However, if the loads are bipolar circuits (e.g., T^2L gates) then I_N could be considerable. In this case V_0 can be reduced by increasing β_N.

Thus, the logic levels of a CMOS inverter can be made close to V_{DD} and ground; and a logic swing V_ℓ of the order of V_{DD} results. This is a main feature of CMOS gates. The threshold voltage of CMOS logic gate V_t (see Appendix B for the definition of V_t) is close to $\frac{V_{DD}}{2}$ if symmetrical devices are used, i.e., $\beta_N = \beta_P$. The $\beta_N = \beta_P$ condition can be achieved if $\left[\left(\frac{W}{L}\right)_P \Big/ \left(\frac{W}{L}\right)_N\right] = \frac{\mu_N}{\mu_P} \approx 2.5$. Thus, equal noise margins result which are $\approx \frac{V_{DD}}{2}$. This is another feature of CMOS gates.

As shown in Fig. 19(c), the gate current I passes between V_{DD} and ground only when both Q_P and Q_N are on, i.e., during the transition region. During the two steady states, $I \approx I_{leakage}$ and the dc power dissipation of the gate is given by

$$P_{DC} = V_{DD}\, I_{leakage} \tag{38}$$

This power dissipation is a negligible component of the total power dissipation of the gate as will be explained.

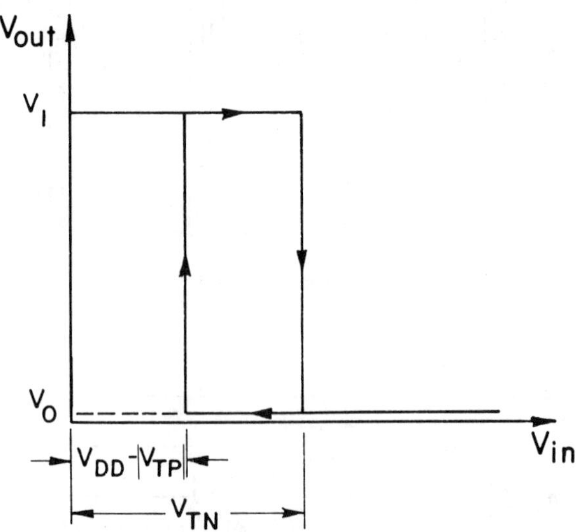

Fig. 20. Hysterises transfer characteristic of a CMOS inverter, $V_{DD} < (V_{TN} + |V_{TP}|)$.

From Fig. 19(b) it is clear that the minimum value of V_{DD} is given by:

$$V_{DD}|_{min} = V_{TN} + |V_{TP}| \tag{39}$$

If V_{DD} is lower than that value, the gate demonstrates a hysteresis transfer characteristic as shown in Fig. 20, and it can not be used as a logic gate.

Transient Analysis—If we consider a CMOS inverter with an ideal step input voltage from 0 to V_{DD}, the charging and discharging times can be calculated following the approach outlined in 3.2. The discharging time, t_{dis}, which is the time taken for the output capacitance C_{out} to discharge through Q_N from an output logic level of $V_1 \simeq V_{DD}$ to an output logic level of V_0, is given by:

$$t_{dis} = \tau_N \left[\frac{2}{\dfrac{V_{DD}}{V_{TN}} - 1} + \ell n \left(\frac{2(V_{DD} - V_{TN})}{V_0} - 1 \right) \right] \tag{40}$$

where

$$\tau_N = \frac{C_{out}}{g_{mN}} = \frac{C_{out}}{\beta_N (V_{DD} - V_{TN})}$$

Equation (40) is similar to (28). Because of the symmetry of the problem, the charging time t_{ch} which is the time taken for C_{out} to charge through Q_P from V_0 to V_1 is given by:

$$t_{ch} = \tau_P \left[\frac{2}{\left(\dfrac{V_{DD}}{|V_{TP}|}\right) - 1} + \ell n \, \frac{2(V_{DD} - |V_{TP}|)}{V_{DD} - V_1} - 1 \right] \tag{41}$$

where

$$\tau_P = \frac{C_{out}}{g_{mp}} = \frac{C_{out}}{\beta_p (V_{DD} - |V_{TP}|)}$$

It should be noted that (40) and (41) can be simplified as in (28a).

Another useful transient parameter is the delay through a CMOS inverter τ_D, defined as the delay time between the input and the output waveforms measured at the $\frac{V_{DD}}{2}$ points for a chain of CMOS inverters or a ring oscillator. This is given by [13]:

$$\tau_D \simeq \frac{0.9\,C_{out}}{V_{DD}\,\beta_N}\left[\frac{1}{\left(1-\frac{V_{TN}}{V_{DD}}\right)^2}+\frac{1}{\frac{\beta_P}{\beta_N}\left(1-\frac{|V_{TP}|}{V_{DD}}\right)^2}\right] \quad (42)$$

If $(V_{TN}/V_{DD}) \ll 1$ and $\frac{|V_{TP}|}{V_{DD}} \ll 1$ then:

$$\tau_D \simeq \frac{0.9\,C_{out}}{V_{DD}\,\beta_N}\left[1+\frac{\beta_N}{\beta_P}\right] \quad (42a)$$

i.e., under these conditions V_{TN} and V_{TP} have only a small effect on the delay time and τ_D is linearly proportional to (C_{out}/V_{DD}) and β_N^{-1} ($\beta_N = \beta_p$ by design). This result is demonstrated in Fig. 21.

For $V_{DD} = 5V$, $K' = 25\ \mu A/V^2$, $\beta_N = \beta_p$, the simplification of (40) and (41) give $t_{ch} = t_{dis} = 30$ nsec while (42a) gives $\tau_D = 14.4$ nsec for a $C_{out} = 1$ pF and a $\left(\frac{W}{L}\right)_N = 1$. This compares favorably with the corresponding transient performance of NMOS circuits.

Transient Power Dissipation—The transient power dissipation of a CMOS inverter has two components. The first results from charging and discharging the output capacitance through the finite on resistance of Q_N and Q_P. This component is given by:

$$P_{t1} = C_{out} V_\ell^2 f \quad (43)$$

where C_{out} is the total output-node capacitance including the capacitive effect of the interconnections, V_ℓ is the logic swing of the gate ($V_\ell = V_1 - V_0 \simeq V_{DD}$), and f is the frequency of switching. The second transient power dissipation component arises from the fact that the input (and hence the output) voltage waveforms have finite rise and fall times. The waveform of the current supplied by V_{DD} to a CMOS gate is shown in Fig. 22, and as a result a power dissipation P_{t2} occurs:

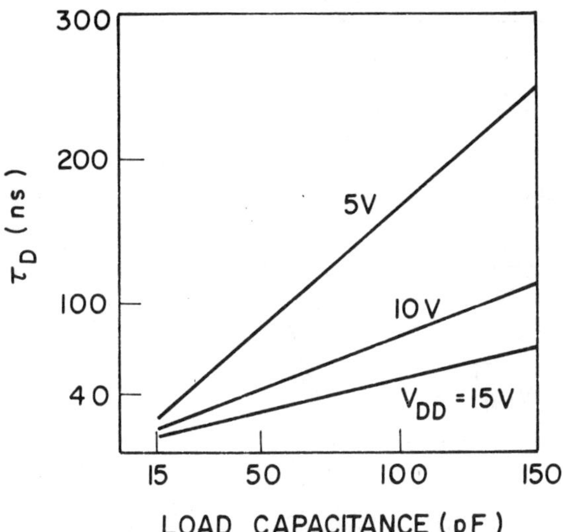

Fig. 21. Delay vs. load capacitance for different values of V_{DD} for a given CMOS inverter.

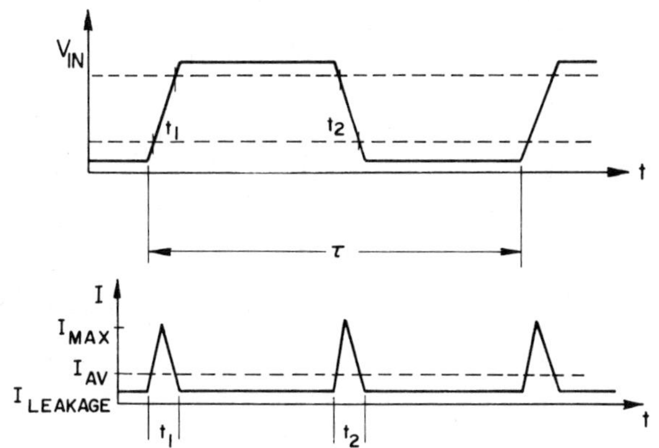

Fig. 22. Input voltage and current waveforms for a CMOS inverter.

$P_{t2} = V_{DD} I_{av}$,

$$I_{av} = \frac{1}{2} I_{max}\left[\frac{V_{DD} - (V_{TN} + |V_{TP}|)}{V_{DD}}\right]\left(\frac{t_1 + t_2}{\tau}\right) \quad (44)$$

where

$$I_{max} = \frac{V_{DD}}{R_N + R_P}$$

If t_1 and $t_2 \ll \tau$ then $P_{t2} \ll P_{t1}$.

CMOS Delay-Power Trade-offs—In CMOS circuits the main component of power dissipation is P_{t1}. Thus, the total power dissipation at the maximum frequency of operation is given by:

$$P \approx C_{out} V_\ell^2 / 2\tau_D \quad (45)$$

and the delay-power product is given by:

$$\tau_D P = 0.5\, C_{out} V_\ell^2 = 0.5\, C_{out} V_{DD}^2. \quad (46)$$

This shows that the delay-power product in CMOS digital circuits, as in the case of NMOS circuits, is proportional to $C_{out} V_{DD}^2$.

6.2 CMOS Static Gates

Logic gates (and hence flip-flops) can be realized using the complementary pairs. Figures 23(b) and (c) show a two-input NAND and a two-input NOR. Each input requires a complementary pair. In the case of the NAND gate the p-channel devices are connected in parallel while the n-channel devices are connected in series. But in the case of the NOR gate the n-channel devices are connected in parallel while the p-channel devices are connected in series.

In CMOS logic gates the standby dc current of the gate is ≈ 0 because there is no dc path between V_{DD} and ground for any logic combination of the input. For example, for the two-input NOR and NAND gates shown in Fig. 23 for any input logic combination ($x_1 x_2$ = 00, 01, 11 or 10) the dc current of the gate is zero.

The design of a CMOS logic gate follows that of an inverter. First, an inverter is designed to meet a given dc and transient performance, and $(W/L)_N$ and $(W/L)_p$ are determined. Then $(W/L)_N$ and $(W/L)_P$ of the devices of a logic gate are determined as follows. If a CMOS m-input NAND gate is to be designed to have the same dc and transient performance as that of the inverter, then for the same values of C_{out}: $(W/L)_P$ of the NAND gate devices should be $\geqslant (W/L)_P$ of the inverter while $(W/L)_N$ should be $\geqslant$ m $(W/L)_N$ of the inverter. On the

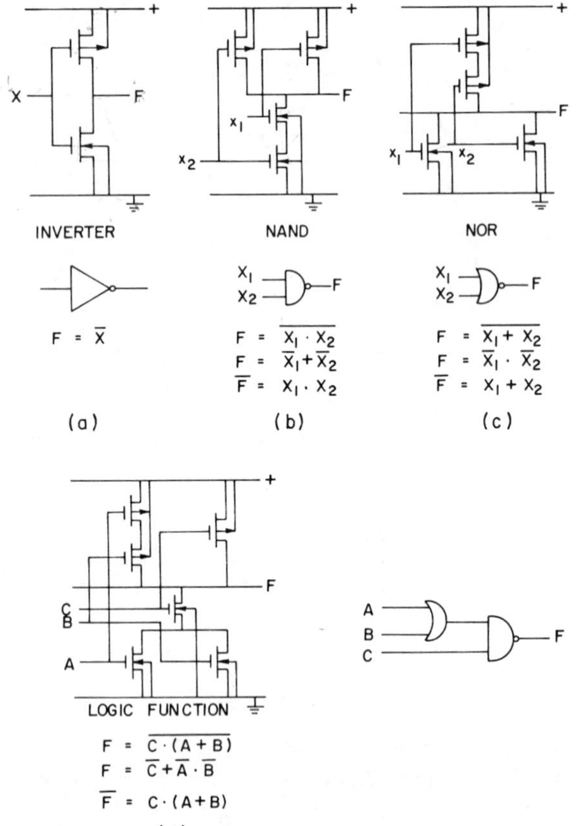

Fig. 23. CMOS logic gates (a) inverter; (b) two-input NAND; (c) two-input NOR; (d) a two-input complex logic gate.

other hand, if a CMOS m-input NOR gate is to be designed to have the same dc and transient performance as that of the inverter, then for the same values of C_{out}, $(W/L)_P$ of the NOR gates should be $\geqslant$ m $(W/L)_P$ of the inverter, while $(W/L)_N$ should be $\geqslant (W/L)_N$ of the inverter. Note that the increase in the size of the NMOS devices in the case of the NAND gate and the increase in the size of the PMOS devices in the case of the NOR gates allows the logic levels V_0 and V_1 to be the same as that of the inverter if the dc currents are nonzero. The size of these transistors should be further increased because C_{out} is larger than that of the inverter. Note also that for the same performance and for the same number of inputs the NAND gate consumes less silicon area than that of a NOR gate because of the smaller area taken by the NMOS devices. Hence, CMOS NAND gates are more widely used than NOR gates. This is the opposite of NMOS logic gates where NOR gates are more widely used.

It should be noted that the back-gate bias effect has to be taken into consideration in the design of the NMOS devices of the NAND gate and in the design of the PMOS devices of the NOR gate. In the case of a CMOS inverter, no back-gate bias effect has to be considered because the sources of the n- and p-channel devices are connected to their corresponding substrates.

CMOS Transmission Gates—As shown in Fig. 24, a CMOS transmission gate consists of a complementary pair connected in parallel. It acts as a switch, with the logical variable A as the control input. Let us assume that A is connected to the n-channel device and $\overline{A}$ is connected to the p-channel device. If A is high, the gate is on and acts as a switch with an on resistance of R_N and R_P in parallel. If A is low, the gate is off and

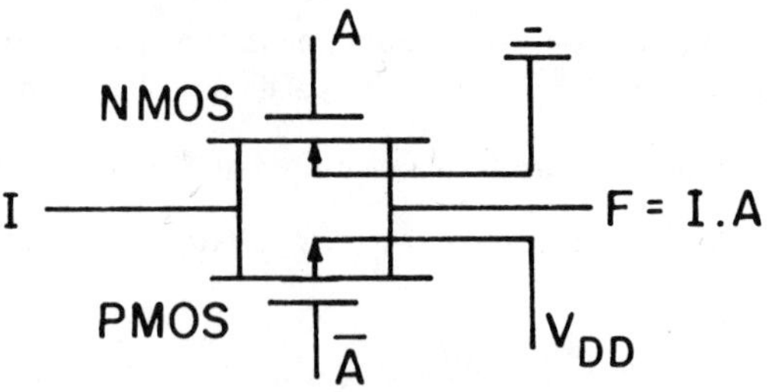

Fig. 24. CMOS transmission gate.

presents a high resistance between the terminals. It should be noted that in CMOS transmission gates the back-gate bias effect on both the NMOS and PMOS devices must be taken into account in designing CMOS transmission gates to meet specific dc and transient requirements.

The advantage of using a complementary pair, rather than a single NMOS or PMOS device, to realize a transmission gate in CMOS can be explained with the aid of Fig. 25. Although in Fig. 25 we assume that there is no time delay between A and $\overline{A}$, the conclusion of the following discussion is general. Figure 25 shows A and $\overline{A}$ waveforms and also shows the times at which the NMOS and PMOS devices turn on. Figure 25(a) shows these times for a reference case where the input logic

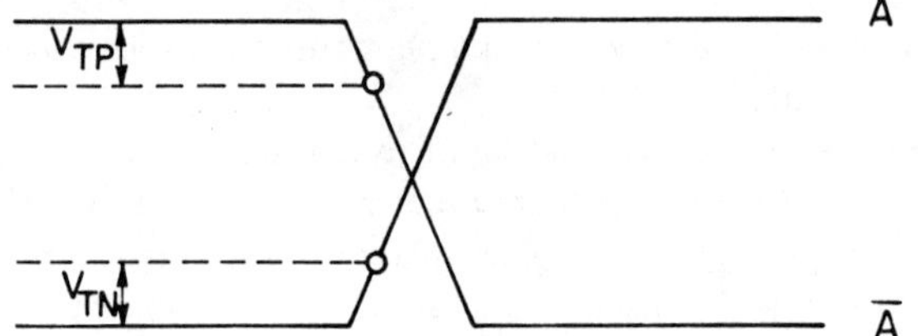

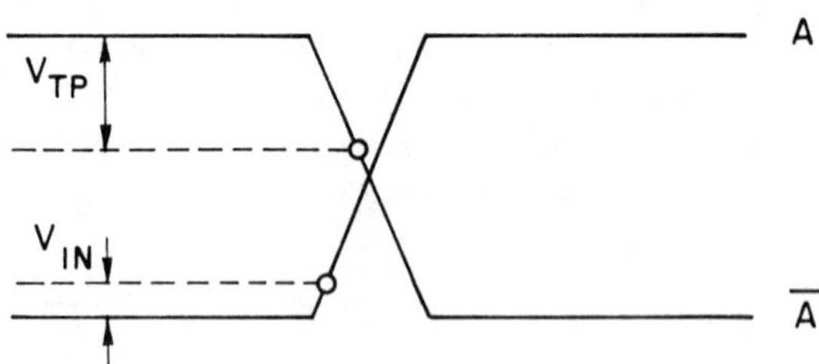

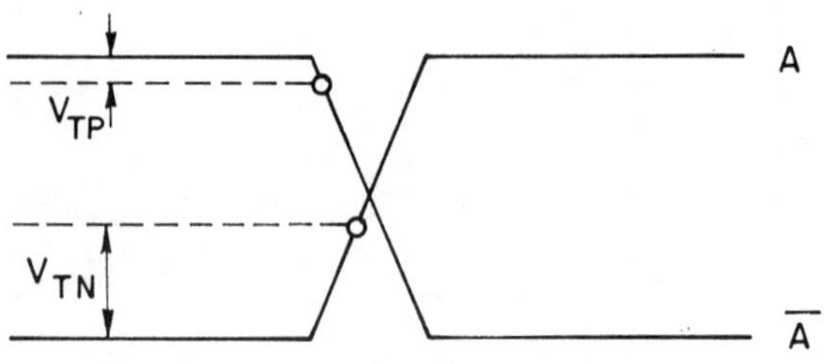

Fig. 25. CMOS transmission gate waveforms.

level is $\approx \frac{V_{DD}}{2}$, and as a result $V_{TN} \simeq |V_{TP}|$. In this case the two devices turn on at the same time. Figure 25(b) shows these times for the case where the input logic level ≈ 0, and $|V_{TP}| > V_{TN}$ because of the back-gate bias effect. In this case the NMOS device turns on before the PMOS and the transmission gate delay time between the input and the output is almost the same as in case (a). Similarly, if the input logic level $\approx V_{DD}$ and as a result $V_{TN} > |V_{TP}|$, as shown in Fig. 25(c), the delay time of the gate will be unaffected. In conclusion, independent of the voltage level of the input variable of the CMOS transmission gate, the gate delay time is approximately the same. It is easy to see that this is *not* the case when single-channel type is used in designing transmission gates.

A drawback of the CMOS transmission gate is that it consumes more area than a single-channel transmission gate. Thus, if the area is of prime concern, non-complementary n-channel transmission gates are used.

6.3 CMOS Static Flip-Flops

The basic building blocks of CMOS flip-flops are the CMOS inverter, logic gates, and transmission gates. Figure 26 shows a cross-coupled CMOS static flip-flop. In the storage mode where V_A is high, V_B is low, Q_1 and Q_4 are on while Q_2 and Q_3 are off. Similarly, in the storage mode where V_A is low, V_B is high, Q_1 and Q_4 are off while Q_2 and Q_3 are on. The standby power dissipation of the cell is very small. The state of the flip-flop is changed by using two CMOS transmission gates connected to V_A and V_B nodes as shown in Fig. 26.

Figure 27 shows a D-type CMOS master-slave static flip-flop. Each of the master and the slave requires the presence of the clock to latch up and store the information. Thus they differ from the basic cross-coupled configuration of Fig. 26. The transmission gates are represented with ideal switches: $(TG)_1$, $(TG)_2$, $(TG)_3$, and $(TG)_4$. The transmission gate $(TG)_1$ connects the master section to the input data (D) when the clock input (C) is low, while $(TG)_3$ connects the slave section to the output of the master section (node 1) when the clock input (C) is high. The gates $(TG)_2$ and $(TG)_4$ are identical to $(TG)_3$ and $(TG)_1$ respectively, and are used to latch the master and the slave sections during C and $\overline{C}$ time slots respectively. Figure 27(c) shows the flip-flop timing diagram.

6.4 CMOS Dynamic Flip-Flops

The D-type static flip-flop can be modified to obtain the dynamic one shown in Fig. 28. Although the term dynamic flip-flop is commonly used to refer to Fig. 28, each stage is basically a dynamic shift-register stage. Each stage consumes less area than its corresponding stage, Fig. 27, because of the absence of the latching paths. The information is stored on the output node capacitances of the two inverters. As in dynamic

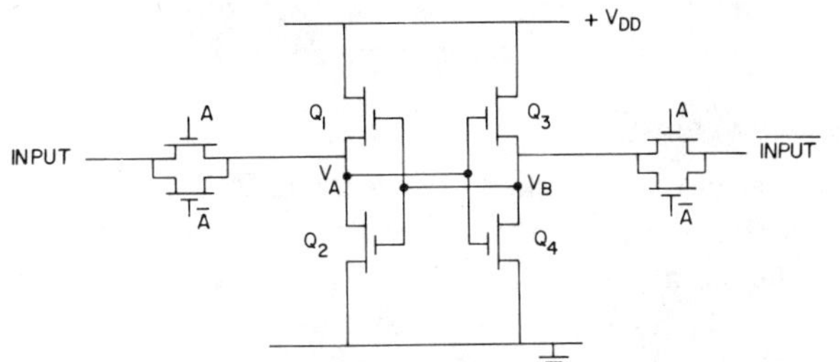

Fig. 26. CMOS cross-coupled static flip-flop.

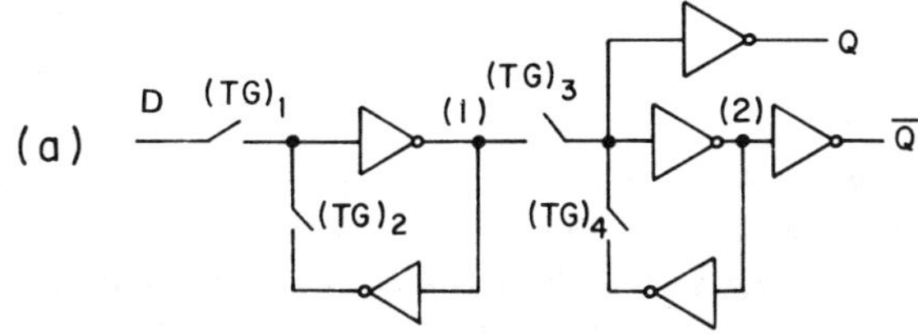

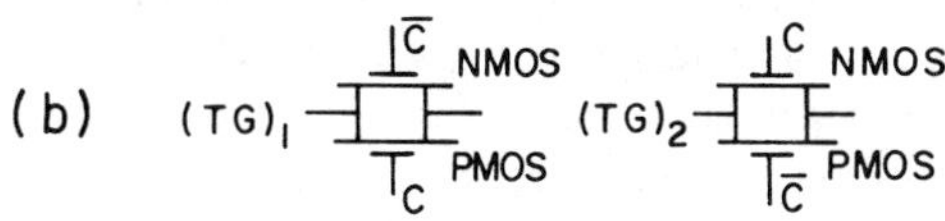

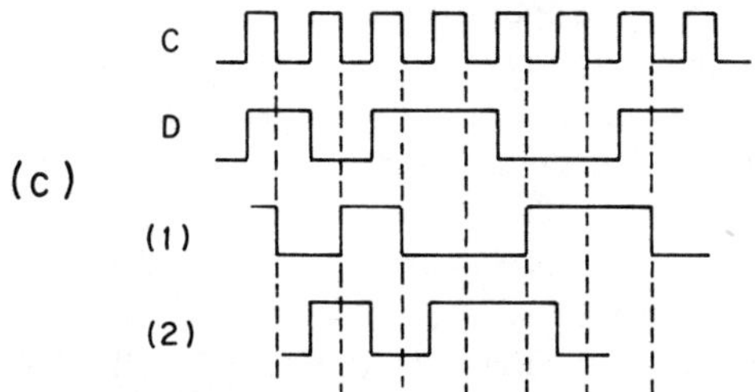

Fig. 27. CMOS Master-Slave static D-type flip-flop (a) circuit diagram; (b) transmission gate types; (c) timing diagram.

circuits, the minimum clock frequency is limited by the leakage paths at these output nodes.

The D-type CMOS flip-flop is the simplest to realize and it is advantageous to use it in LSI subsystem designs as a storage or shift register element. However, if other flip-flop types are required, e.g., JK- flip-flops, the D-type flip-flop can be modified to realize these types.

7. Comments and Discussion

In this paper a simple analysis of some basic NMOS and CMOS digital circuits is given. This analysis is useful in the first phase of circuit design. At a later phase, circuit analysis computer programs with adequate models are used to analyze and to aid in the design of MOS integrated circuits. It is suggested that the reader use these programs to compare the computed performance to that predicted by the simple analysis. We like to stress here that a simple circuit analysis, with reasonable approximations, is *always* possible even for the most complicated circuit configurations. It is hoped that the reader would develop such analysis for the proposed projects of Appendix C and for the circuit configurations covered in this book.

The following is a summary of some basic guidelines, based on the material covered in this paper, to be used in the design of digital MOS integrated circuits:

1. A simple digital model for an MOS transistor is that it is a switch, either on or off, which can be controlled by the gate voltage. The off resistance of this switch, between the

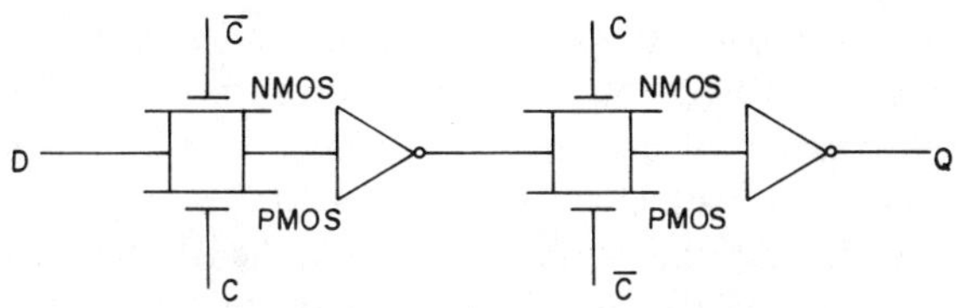

Fig. 28. CMOS Master-Slave dynamic D-type flip-flop.

drain and the source, is very high and is close to an open circuit. The on resistance can be reduced by increasing the (W/L) of the transistor or by increasing the gate voltage.

The gate voltage required to turn-on or turn-off the transistor is V_T and it is a function of process parameters, the substrate bias V_{BB}, and, in general, the drain-source potential $V_{DS} \cdot V_T$ can be controlled by ion implanting the MOS channel. Thus, the MOS circuit designer can choose from MOS transistors with different values of V_T. For example, an NMOS transistor could be enhancement-type, e.g., $V_T = 0.7$ v, weak-enhancement, $V_T = 0.3$ v, depletion-type, $V_T = -2$ v, weak-depletion, $V_T = -1$ or zero-V_T type, $V_T \approx 0$.

2. The drain current I_{DS} of an MOS transistor is a function of the operating voltages.

Below V_T, the MOS transistor allows a "small" I_{DS} to flow and in this region I_{DS} increases exponentially with V_{DS} and V_{GS}. This region of operation is called the subthreshold region, and the value of I_{DS} is much smaller than when V_{GS} is greater than V_T.

Above V_T, I_{DS} is a function of $(V_{GS} - V_T)$ and V_{DS}. At very low V_{DS} where $V_{DS} \ll (V_{GS} - V_T)$, I_{DS} is approximately linearly proportional to the product $(V_{GS} - V_T)\, V_{DS}$. As V_{DS} increases, I_{DS} becomes less dependent on V_{DS}, and I_{DS} approximately "saturates" for $V_{DS} \geqslant (V_{GS} - V_T)$, i.e., the rate of change of I_{DS} with respect to V_{DS} reduces. This is called the saturation region.

For the same V_T and the same operating voltages, I_{DS} is linearly proportional to (W/L).

3. It is useful to restate guideline 2 from another viewpoint—by considering the voltage drop across the gate-source terminals—V_{GS} required for a given I_{DS} (see Appendix C, project 5).

Above V_T, the required V_{GS} is the summation of V_T plus *current dependent* terms. These terms can be made small by increasing (W/L) or by reducing the operating current. For example, in the saturation region V_{GS} is given by:

$$V_{GS} = V_T + \left(\frac{2\, I_{DS}}{\beta}\right)^{1/2}$$

4. If an enhancement-type NMOS transistor has its gate connected to its drain, the resulting two terminal device conducts in one direction in a diode-like manner with a square-law I-V characteristic as shown in Fig. 29(a):

$$I = \frac{K'}{2}\left(\frac{W}{L}\right)(V - V_T)^2$$

Alternatively, if a depletion-type NMOS transistor has its gate connected to its source, the resulting two terminal device conducts in both directions as shown in Fig. 29(b). For positive small values of V, it acts as a modulated nonlinear resistance and for positive large values of V it acts as a current source. For negative values of V, it conducts in a diode-like manner with a square-law I-V characteristic similar to the enhancement-type case.

5. Although PMOS are currently used to fabricate a number of MOS products, in the state-of-the-art MOS chips, PMOS transistors are generally limited to CMOS circuits. Single-channel state-of-the-art chips use NMOS circuits.

6. During the operation of static digital MOS circuits, the output logic node is either pulled "up" towards V_{DD} through pull-up polyresistors or MOS load transistors, or pulled "down" towards ground through pull-down MOS drivers. In NMOS circuits, the pull-up MOS load transistors are either enhancement or depletion type while in CMOS circuits they are enhancement PMOS transistors. This MOS circuit configuration is referred to as the pull-up pull-down (PUD) configuration.

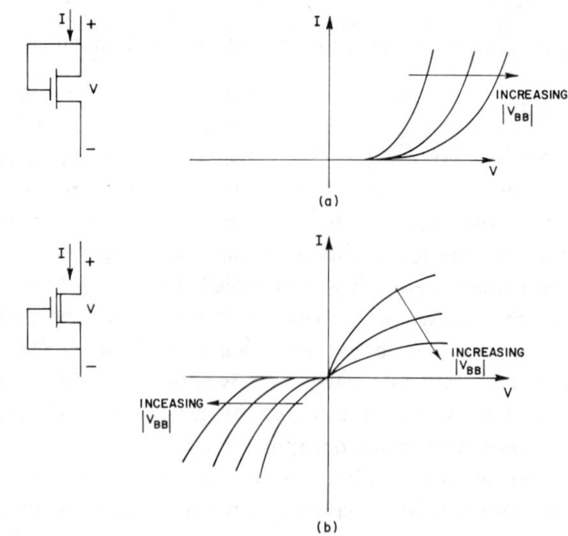

Fig. 29. (a) Two terminal enhancement-type NMOS; (b) two terminal depletion-type NMOS.

In NMOS circuits with depletion-type loads, the pull-down circuit path is "stronger" than the pull-up path, thus V_0 would have the range 0.1 to 0.05 V_{DD} while V_1 would be $\simeq V_{DD}$. However, in CMOS circuits the pull-down and the pull-up circuit "strengths" are usually the same and $V_0 \simeq 0$ and $V_1 \simeq V_{DD}$.

7. Not only do the pull-up and pull-down circuit paths in static MOS gates affect V_0 and V_1, but also they affect t_{ch} and t_{dis} by affecting the average available currents, $\bar{I}_{ch}$ and $\bar{I}_{dis}$, to charge and discharge the output node capacitance C_{out}. Because MOS transistors do not suffer from charge storage effects, as in bipolar transistors, t_{ch} and t_{dis} can be expressed simply by $V_\ell C_{out}/\bar{I}_{ch}$ and $V_\ell C_{out}/\bar{I}_{dis}$ respectively.

8. In addition to polyresistors, NMOS and PMOS transistors with various values of V_T, other circuit elements which may be available to MOS digital circuit designers in a given technology are MOS capacitances which are formed between gates and MOS channels and poly capacitances which are formed between two layers of poly or between poly and metal.

9. MOS transistors and capacitances can be arranged to realize NMOS or CMOS dynamic circuits which are controlled by multiphase clocks where information is stored on capacitances.

10. In MOS circuits, especially dynamic and CMOS circuits, a transient power dissipation, $CV_\ell^2 f$ can be an important component of the total power dissipation.

Acknowledgment

The author would like to thank Dr. L. M. Terman of IBM for his critical review of the manuscript and for his many valuable comments; and Dr. Y. A. El-Mansy of Intel Corporation and H. Tuan, L. Peterson, and D. Pearson of the Micro-components Organization, Burroughs Corporation, for useful discussions.

Feedback from students attending my integrated circuit classes at Waterloo has been extremely valuable.

Appendix A

Substrate Bias Generators

In many circuit applications it is desirable to reverse bias the substrate of an NMOS chip. Reverse biasing the substrate-source junctions, rather than zero biasing them, reduces the parasitic capacitances of these junctions and reduces the injected carriers from the source regions into the substrate. Reducing the parasitic capacitances enhances the performance of both static and dynamic NMOS digital circuits. Reducing the injected carriers is important in NMOS dynamic memories because these carriers contribute to the discharging of the storage nodes. Moreover, a substrate bias reduces the sensitivity of V_T on V_{BB} and increases the field-oxide threshold voltage.

From the system viewpoint, it is convenient to have the reverse bias of the substrate generated on-chip, saving a V_{BB} pin and eliminating the need for generating a negative power supply.

An on-chip substrate bias generator, as shown in Fig. A1, consists of an oscillator and a charge pumping circuit. The oscillator is either a ring or an RC type which consists of an odd number of inverters, usually 5 or 7. An advantage of the RC oscillator is that its frequency of oscillation is less sensitive to processing parameters. The R and C are integrated on chip, using a depletion-type NMOS as an R and an MOS capacitor as a C as shown in Fig. A2. The charge pumping circuit consists of an MOS capacitance C and two rectifying (diode-like connected) enhancement NMOS transistors Q_1 and Q_2. The output of the circuit, node 3, is connected to a pad which is connected, on the package, to the back of the chip (the substrate). Figure A1 shows the substrate parasitic diodes: D_1 is associated with node 2 while D_2 to D_m are associated with the different circuit nodes. These nodes are at different positive potentials and some of them are at $+V_{DD}$. These diodes represent leakage currents and parasitic capacitances as shown in Fig. A1. Also shown in Fig. A1 is a parasitic bipolar transistor associated with Q_1.

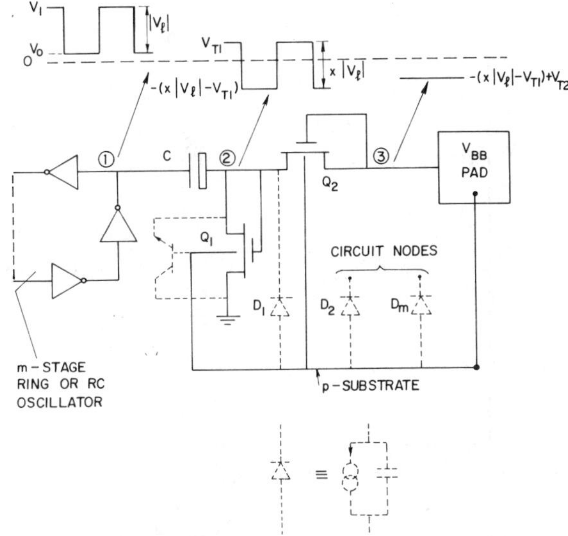

Fig. A1. Substrate bias generator: circuit diagram, waveforms, and substrate diode equivalent circuit.

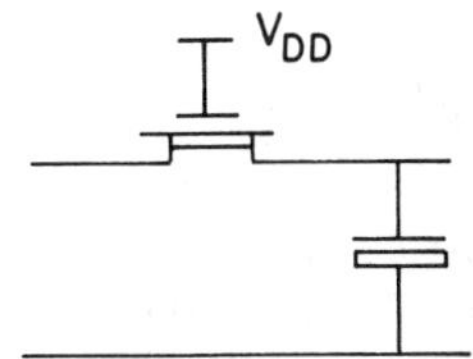

Fig. A2. RC network for RC oscillators.

The circuit operates as follows. The oscillator delivers a waveform at node 1, roughly a square wave with logic swing V_ℓ, from V_0 to V_1. The frequency of oscillation is typically 10 MHz, and V_0 and V_1 are typically 0.05 V_{DD} and 0.95 V_{DD} respectively. Neglecting leakage, C and Q_1 clamp the input wave form to a V_{T1} above ground, as shown at node 2, with a voltage swing of χV_ℓ where χ is determined by C and C_1 where C_1 is the parasitic capacitance at node 2: $\chi \simeq C/C_1 + C$ and approaches unity for $C \gg C_1$. Q_2 and the large capacitance at node 3 (the summation of the capacitances of D_2 to D_m) stabilize the voltage at node 3 to $[-(\chi|V_\ell| - V_{T1}) + V_{T2}]$.

Because Q_2 has less substrate bias than Q_1, $V_{T2} < V_{T1}$. Q_2 can be eliminated from the circuit and in this case D_1 and the large capacitance at node 3 stabilizes the voltage at node 3 to $[-(\chi|V_\ell| - V_{T1}) + V_j]$ where V_j is the turn-on voltage of D_1. Because V_{T2} can, by design, be made smaller than V_j, the value of V_{BB} is more negative in the case where Q_2 is used.

In the case of dc loading conditions when leakage currents pass through the substrate diodes, the output voltage V_{BB} at node 3 would be less negative than its open circuit value. The value of V_{BB} under loading conditions can be enhanced by the double pumping circuit shown in Fig. A3.

Because the substrate-drain junction of Q_1 is slightly forward biased by an amount $= V_{T2}$, a parasitic bipolar transistor results which makes the voltage at node 2 less negative. This bipolar action can be reduced by increasing the channel length of Q_1.

A drawback of using an on-chip substrate bias generator is the fact that the substrate terminal is not dc grounded, i.e., it floats. As the circuit nodes switch, because of the capacitive coupling between these nodes and the substrate, the substrate potential is pulsed around its dc value. The value of this pulse is proportional to $C_a/C_a + C_b$ where C_a is the capacitance associated with the switching nodes and C_b is the capacitance associated with the nonswitching nodes including V_{DD} (ac ground). Although usually $C_a \ll C_b$, in some chips where simultaneous switching is occurring at the same time, as in the case of dynamic memories where signal lines are precharged simultaneously, the effect of pulsing the substrate on the circuit performance should be evaluated.

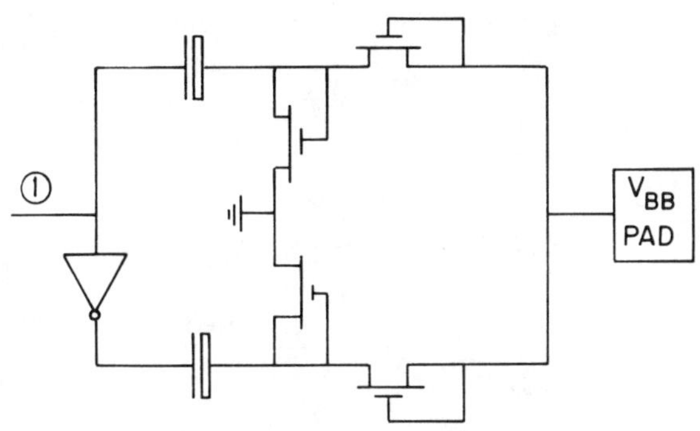

Fig. A3. Double pumping circuit.

Logic Levels and Noise Margins

The operation of a digital binary circuit is quite distinct from that of a linear circuit in that devices are intended to be either "on" or "off". The input and output voltages are at two levels, either "high" representing a logic '1', or "low" representing a logic '0'. These two levels are actually a band of voltages separated by a buffer voltage zone to ensure that the state of a device can be determined even in the presence of noise.

In a digital system, two basic operations are performed. The first operation is to realize a logic function, that is to determine a logic output variable in terms of input logic variables (e.g., NAND gate) or to determine a logic output variable in terms of the input logic variables and the previous state of the output (e.g., a flip-flop). The second operation performed in a digital system is transferring a logic signal from one logic block (logic source) to the input of another logic block(s) (logic detector(s)) through a transmission system (Fig. B1). This transmission system can be either on-chip (metal lines), or between chips (on a printed-circuit board). A logic block has usually more than one input and each output is used as an input for a number of other logic blocks. The number of inputs is called the *fan-in* and the number of blocks driven by one output is called the *fan-out.*

Ideally, at the input of a logic detector, the voltage signal is detected with respect to a *threshold voltage* V_t. Although in NMOS digital circuits V_t is related to the MOS device threshold voltage V_T, V_t is a parameter defined for any digital logic block: in ideal inverting logic blocks, if the input voltage is greater than V_t the output voltage will be at logical '0' and if the input voltage is less than V_t the output will be at logical '1'.

Signal distortion, due to attenuation or system noise, causes a reduction of the system reliability. Since distortion is primarily introduced by the noise in the system, it is conventional to refer to the margin allowed for distortion of the logic levels through the transmission system as the noise margins. Two *voltage noise margins* are defined (Fig. B1):

$$
\begin{aligned}
VNM_0 &\equiv \text{voltage noise margin for a logical '0'}\\
&\equiv V_{t\min} - V_{0\max}\\
VNM_1 &\equiv \text{voltage noise margin for a logical '1'}\\
&\equiv V_{1\min} - V_{t\max}
\end{aligned}
\qquad \text{(B1)}
$$

The difference between the two levels V_1 and V_0 is called the *logic swing* V_ℓ.

DC Transfer Characteristics

Noise margin definitions have been stated by considering the

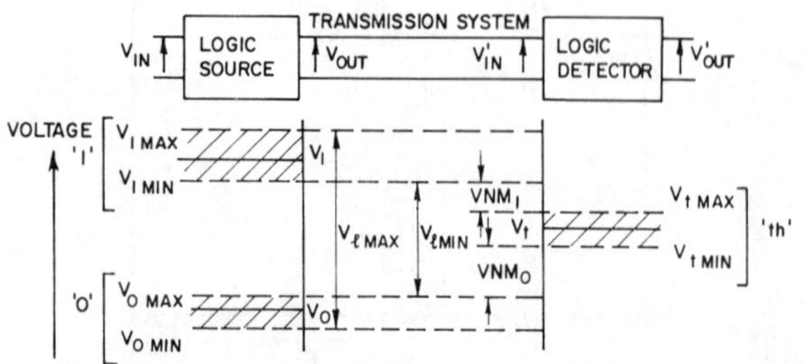

Fig. B1. System model for digital circuits, logic levels, and noise margins.

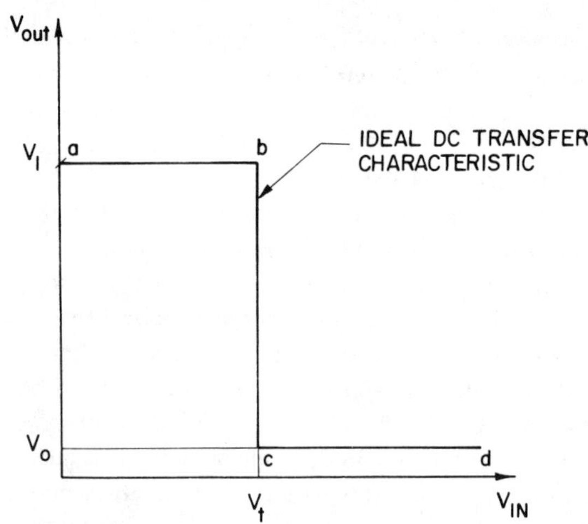

Fig. B2. Ideal dc transfer characteristic of an inverting digital circuit.

transmission system. Alternatively, the dc transfer characteristic (V_{OUT} vs. V_{IN}) of a logic gate also provides information regarding logic levels and noise margins. Figure B2 shows an ideal dc transfer characteristic of an inverting logic gate. It consists of three sections: two zero-gain (for steady-state operation) sections (ab and cd), where the output voltages are V_1 and V_0 respectively, and an infinite-gain transition section (bc) where the input voltage level is V_t. The noise margins of the circuit are the same as the ones given in Fig. B1.

Nonideal dc transfer characteristics, as shown in Fig. B3, have a finite gain in the transition region. Because the input and the output levels must be compatible, i.e., V_0 and V_1 must be the same for both input and output, in order to determine V_0 and V_1, V_{OUT} vs. V_{IN} is replotted (shown dotted) using the V_{OUT} axis as V_{IN} and the V_{IN} axis as V_{OUT}. This intersects the transfer characteristic at point (1) and (2), giving V_0 and V_1, and at the reference point (4). The line joining points (1) and (2) has a slope of −1 and intersects the transfer characteristic at point (3) where by definition $V_{IN} = V_t$. Two extra points on the transfer characteristic are of importance: (5) and (6) where the slopes are −1. Between these two points the gain is higher than unity.

In Fig. B3 the voltage noise margins (*VNM*) of the circuit are defined as the input voltage change required to cause the output to change from an operating point to the nearest unity gain

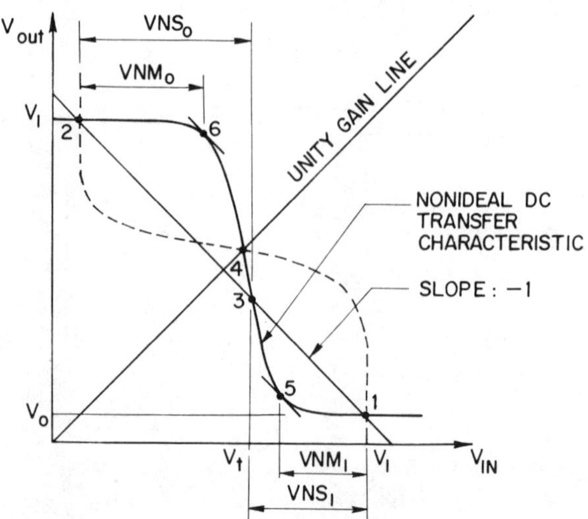

Fig. B3. Nonideal dc transfer characteristic of an inverting digital circuit.

point. Moreover, voltage noise sensitivities (*VNS*) are defined as the input voltage change required to cause the output voltage to change from an operating point to the threshold point. Note that if the dc transfer characteristic of Fig. B3 is approximated by an ideal one, then points 3, 4, 5, 6 coincide at $V_{IN} \equiv V_t$ and $VNM \equiv VNS$. The deviation of a transfer characteristic from an ideal one is measured by the voltage transition width: $VTW \equiv [V_{IN}@5 - V_{IN}@6]$. If VTW is small, the transfer characteristic can be approximated by an ideal one.

DC Transfer Characteristics: Examples

In this section we shall examine the transfer characteristics of an NMOS inverter with an enhancement-type NMOS driver transistor and one of the following types of loads:

(a) a resistive load
(b) a saturated enhancement-type NMOS load
(c) a nonsaturated enhancement-type NMOS load

The dc transfer characteristics are obtained analytically using two relations:

(i) the relationship between the driver current I_D and the input voltage V_{IN}:
if $V_{IN} - V_{TD} \leqslant V_{OUT}$, the driver is in saturation and

$$I_D = \frac{\beta_D}{2}(V_{IN} - V_{TD})^2 \quad \text{(B2)}$$

if $V_{IN} - V_{TD} > V_{OUT}$, the driver is in the nonsaturation region and

$$I_D = \beta_D[(V_{IN} - V_{TD})V_{OUT} - \tfrac{1}{2}V_{OUT}^2] \quad \text{(B3)}$$

(ii) the relationship between the load current I_L and the output voltage V_{OUT}:

(a) a resistive load:

$$I_L = \frac{V_{DD} - V_{OUT}}{R_L} \quad \text{(B4)}$$

(b) a saturated enhancement-type load:

$$I_L = \frac{\beta_L}{2}(V_{DD} - V_{OUT} - V_{TL})^2 \quad \text{(B5)}$$

(c) a nonsaturated enhacement-type load:

$$I_L = \beta_L[(V_{GG} - V_{OUT} - V_{TL})(V_{DD} - V_{OUT}) - \tfrac{1}{2}(V_{DD} - V_{OUT})^2] = \frac{\beta_L V_{DD}^2}{2m}\left(1 - \frac{V_{OUT}}{V_{DD}}\right)\left(1 - m\frac{V_{OUT}}{V_{DD}}\right) \quad \text{(B6)}$$

where

$$m = \frac{V_{DD}}{2(V_{GG} - V_{TL}) - V_{DD}} \quad \text{for } V_{GG} - V_{TL} > V_{DD} \quad \text{(B7)}$$

The parameter m [8] is a measure of the biasing conditions on the load. As $V_{GG} >> V_{DD}$ and $V_{GG} >> V_{TL}$, m tends to zero and the load approaches a resistance load characteristic. The inequality shown in (B7) demonstrates the fact that m and hence (B6) are only valid if the load is operating in the nonsaturation region.

In computing the dc transfer characteristics we shall assume that there is no dc load current at the output of the inverter, i.e., $I_D = I_L$ [8].

A Resistive Load

(i) $V_{IN} - V_{TD} \leqslant V_{OUT}$
Equating (B2) and (B4) we obtain (Fig. B4):

$$1 - V'_{OUT} = V_{DD}\frac{R_L\beta_D}{2}(V'_{IN} - V'_{TD})^2$$

where V'_{OUT}, V'_{IN}, V'_{TD} are normalized voltages with respect to the maximum value of the output voltage V_{DD}.

(ii) $V_{IN} - V_{TD} > V_{OUT}$
Equating (B3) and (B4) we obtain (Fig. B4):

$$1 - V'_{OUT} = V_{DD}R_L\beta_D[(V'_{IN} - V'_{TD})(V'_{OUT}) - \tfrac{1}{2}V'^{2}_{OUT}]$$

A Saturated Enhancement-type Load

(i) $V_{IN} - V_{TD} \leqslant V_{OUT}$
Equating (B2) and (B5) (Fig. B5):

$$(1 - V'_{OUT}) = \sqrt{\frac{\beta_D}{\beta_L}}(V'_{IN} - V'_{TD})$$

where V'_{OUT}, V'_{IN} and V'_{TD} are voltages normalized with respect to the maximum value of the output voltage $(V_{DD} - V_{TL})$.

(ii) $V_{IN} - V_{TD} > V_{OUT}$
Equating (B3) and (B5) (Fig. B5):

$$(1 - V'_{OUT}) = \sqrt{\frac{\beta_D}{\beta_L}}[2(V'_{IN} - V'_{TD})(V'_{OUT}) - V'^{2}_{OUT}]^{1/2}$$

A Nonsaturated Enhancement-type Load

(i) $V_{IN} - V_{TD} \leqslant V_{OUT}$
Equating (B2) and (B6) (Fig. B6):

$$(1 - V'_{OUT})^{1/2}(1 - mV'_{OUT})^{1/2} = \sqrt{m}\sqrt{\frac{\beta_D}{\beta_L}}(V'_{IN} - V'_{TD})$$

where V'_{OUT}, V'_{IN} and V'_{TD} are normalized with respect to the maximum value of the output voltage V_{DD}.

(ii) $V_{IN} - V_{TD} > V_{OUT}$
Equating (B3) and (B6) (Fig. B6):

$$(1 - V'_{OUT})^{1/2}(1 - mV'_{OUT})^{1/2} = \sqrt{m}\sqrt{\frac{\beta_D}{\beta_L}}\{2(V'_{IN} - V'_{TD})V'_{OUT} - V'^{2}_{OUT}\}^{1/2}$$

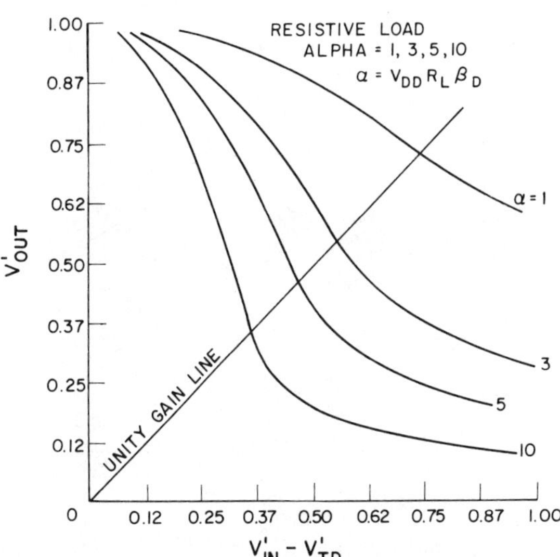

Fig. B4. DC transfer characteristic, resistive load.

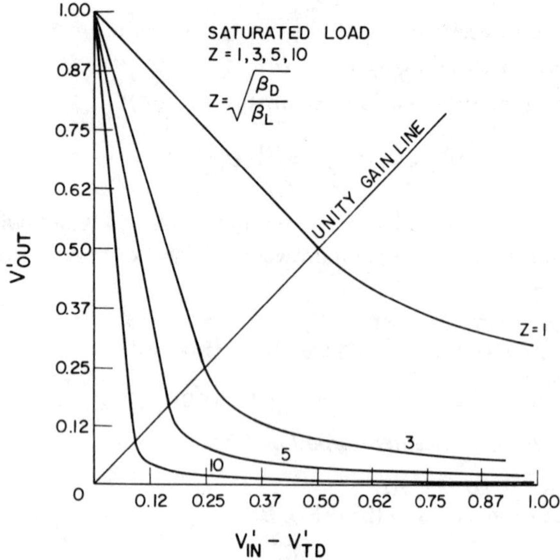

Fig. B5. DC transfer characteristic, saturated load.

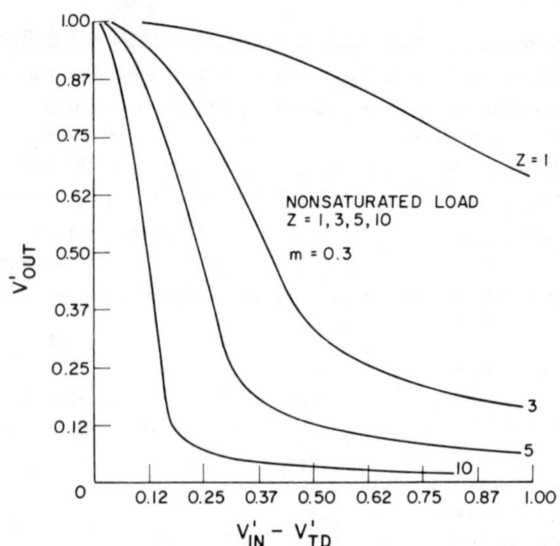

Fig. B6. (ii) DC transfer characteristic, nonsaturated load, $m = 0.3$.

Figures B4 to B6 show that the transition width V_{TW} of the transfer characteristic, and hence the gain of the inverter, is a function of the circuit parameters: V_{TW} can be reduced by increasing $R_L \beta_D$ in the case of resistive loads, by increasing $\sqrt{\beta_D/\beta_L}$ in the case of saturated loads and by increasing $\sqrt{\beta_D/\beta_L}$, or by increase m in the case of nonsaturated loads.

The threshold voltage of the inverter V_t is a function of V_{TD} and the circuit parameters. For example, in the case of a resistive load for $\alpha = 10$, $V_t \simeq V_{TD} + 0.4\ V_{DD}$, in the case of a saturated load for $(\beta_D/\beta_L) = 9$, $V_t \simeq V_{TD} + 0.25\,(V_{DD} - V_{TL})$, in the case of a nonsaturated load for $(\beta_D/\beta_L) = 9$, $m = 0.5$, $V_t \simeq V_{TD} + 0.4\ V_{DD}$ and in all cases the higher the value of (β_D/β_L), the lower the value of V_t.

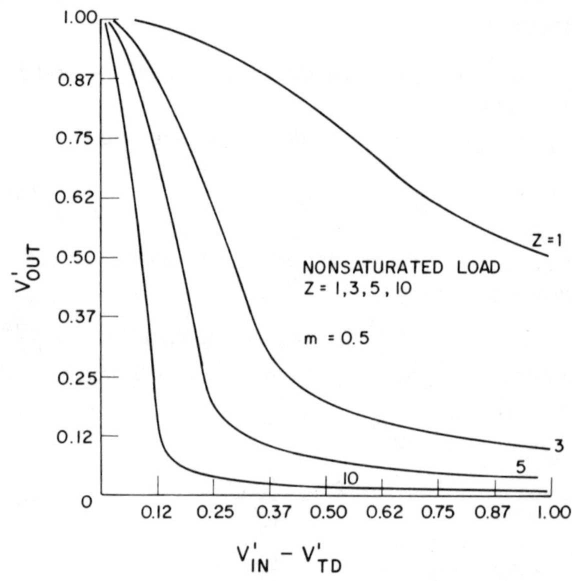

Fig. B6. (iii) DC transfer characteristic, nonsaturated load, $m = 0.5$.

Appendix C

Digital MOS Integrated Circuits Projects

In the following projects make any necessary, but reasonable assumptions, e.g., value of available power supply; layout design rules [14]; process parameters: V_{TO}, γ, z . . . , etc.; and system/circuit constraints: speed of operation, allowable power dissipation, operating temperatures . . . , etc. Use any

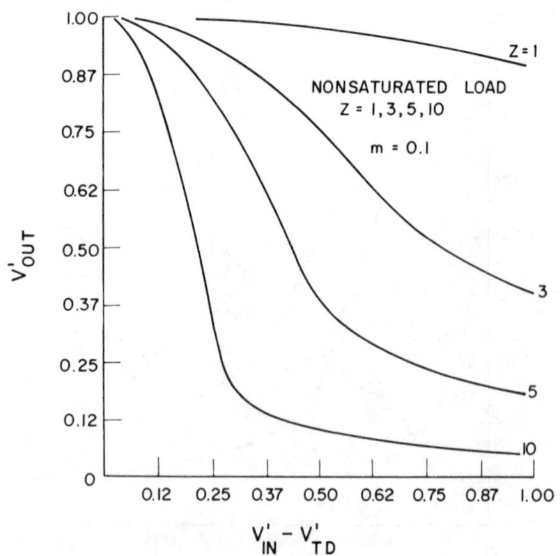

Fig. B6. (i) DC transfer characteristic, nonsaturated load, $m = 0.1$.

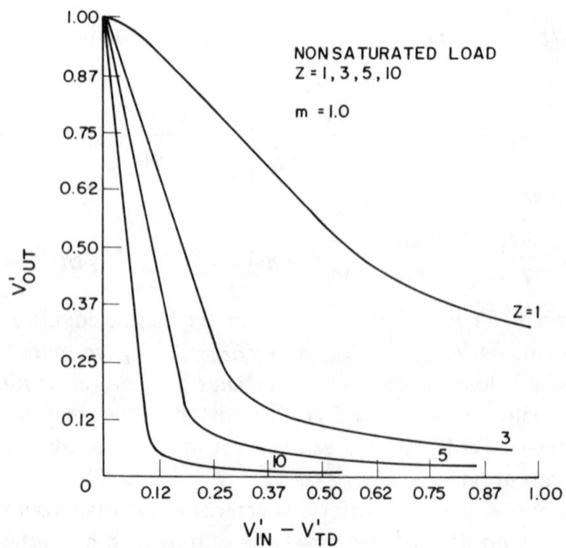

Fig. B6. (iv) DC transfer characteristic, nonsaturated load, $m = 1.0$.

level of analysis, first-order analytical equations and/or computer simulations. If integrated circuit fabrication facilities are available, layout, fabricate, test, and evaluate your design.

1. Compare static NMOS integrated inverters with different loads regarding V_1, V_0, V_t, VNMs, P_{DC}, t_{ch}, t_{dis}, delay-power product and area.
2. Compare static CMOS logic circuits to static E/D NMOS (NMOS circuits with depletion-type load) regarding area, delay times and speed-power product. Use different logic circuits with different complexity in the comparison, e.g., inverter, four-input NAND (or NOR), full-adder, and a multiplier cell.
3. Design multiphase dynamic CMOS logic circuits [15]. Compare this design to dynamic 2ϕ and 4ϕ NMOS logic circuits regarding area, maximum frequency of operation, and total power dissipation.
4. In CMOS digital circuits $V_{DD}|_{min} = V_{TN} + |V_{TP}|$. What is $V_D|_{min}$ in static NMOS digital circuits? Compare the operations of the two circuit types at $V_{DD}|_{min}$ regarding V_0, V_1, V_t, VNM, t_{dis} and t_{ch}.
5. In bipolar transistors, the base-emitter voltage V_{BE} is given by:

$$V_{BE} \simeq \frac{KT}{q} \ln \frac{I_c}{J_S h_{fe} A_c}$$

where I_c is the operating collector current, J_S is the saturation current density, a process parameter, h_{fe} is the transistor current gain, a process parameter, and A_c is the collector-base junction area, a layout design parameter. Obtain a similar expression for the V_{GS} of an NMOS transistor. Compare V_{BE} to V_{GS} regarding sensitivity to processing parameters, circuit design parameters, operating currents and voltages, and temperature.
6. Design CMOS circuits for CMOS/TTL and TTL/CMOS interfaces.
7. Design NMOS circuits for NMOS/TTL and TTL/NMOS interfaces [16]. Compare with the circuits of project 6 regarding area.
8. Design cross-coupled static flip-flops with minimum stand-by power dissipation using (a) poly resistor loads, (b) depletion loads, and (c) complementary loads. Compare regarding area, power dissipation and speed of operation.
9. Design JK CMOS static and dynamic flip-flops using the D-type flip-flop to operate at 10 MHz clock. Compute static and dynamic power dissipations and area.
10. Design a 4ϕ JK NMOS flip-flop to operate at 10 MHz. Compare to that of project 9 regarding area, static, and dynamic power dissipations.
11. Design an 8-bit shift register to operate at 10 MHz and to consume the minimum area. Choose the technology and the circuit configuration: static or dynamic NMOS, static or dynamic CMOS.
12. Use a multiplier cell to compare the area taken by static NMOS and CMOS circuits with the following interconnection systems:
(1) metal and poly; (2) metal, poly 1, and poly 2; and (3) poly 1, poly 2, and two layers of metal.
13. Design a substrate bias generator to have an open circuit voltage of −3 volts. Examine the design for loading conditions, capacitive coupling to the substrate, and power dissipation.
14. Design a static half-adder using (1) NMOS NOR gates, (2) NMOS single gate with series/parallel arrangement, (3) CMOS NAND gates, and (4) CMOS single gate with series/parallel arrangement to operate from V_{DD} = 5 V and to have a total t_D = 20 nsec, $V_0 \leqslant 0.1$ V and $V_1 \geqslant 4$ V. Compare the design regarding area, power dissipation, and VNMs.
15. Design a clock driver for dynamic circuits using (1) NMOS E/D and (2) CMOS. V_{DD} = 5 V, capacitive load = C_ϕ = 20 pF. Calculate and compare V_ϕ, f_{max}, and power dissipation. Redesign the circuits for V_ϕ = 7 V with V_{DD} = 5 V.

References

[1] R. S. C. Cobbold, *Theory and Applications of Field-Effect Transistors*, Wiley Interscience: 1970.

[2] T. W. Sigman and R. Swanson, "MOS threshold shifting by ion implantation," *Solid State Electronics*, vol. 16, pp. 1217–1232, 1973.

[3] H. Masuda et al., "Characteristics and limitation of scaled-down MOSFET's due to two-dimensional field effect," *IEEE Trans. on Electron Devices*, vol. ED-26, no. 5, pp. 980–986, June 1979.

[4] A. S. Grove, *Physics and Technology of Semiconductor Devices*, John Wiley: 1976.

[5] W. M. Penny and L. Lau, *MOS Integrated Circuits*, Van Nostrand Reinhold Company: 1972.

[6] Y. A. El-Mansy and A. R. Boothroyd, "A new approach to the theory and modeling of insulated-gate field-effect transistors," *IEEE Trans. on Electron Devices*, pp. 241–253, March 1977.

[7] M. I. Elmasry, *Digital MOS Integrated Circuits*, IEEE Press: 1981, Section 1.2.

[8] R. H. Crawford, *MOSFET in Circuit Design*, McGraw-Hill: 1967.

[9] M. I. Elmasry, *Digital MOS Integrated Circuits*, IEEE Press: 1981, Section 1.3.

[10] B. G. Watkins, A low-power multiphase circuit technique, *IEEE JSSC*, pp. 213–220, December 1967.

[11] M. I. Elmasry, "An optimal two-phase MOS-LSI logic system," *International EE Conference—Toronto*, pp. 136–137, October 1973.

[12] M. I. Elmasry, *Digital MOS Integrated Circuits*, IEEE Press: 1981, Section 2.2.

[13] J. R. Burns, "Switching response of complementary symmetry MOS transistor logic circuits," *RCA Review*, pp. 627–661, December 1964.

[14] C. Mead and L. Conway, *Introduction to VLSI Systems*, Addison Wesley: 1980.

[15] Y. Suzuji et al., "Clocked CMOS calculator circuitry," *IEEE JSSC*, pp. 462–469, December 1973.

[16] W. N. Carr and J. P. Mize, *MOS/LSI Design and Application*, McGraw-Hill: 1972.

Section 1.2
Depletion Loads

A High-Performance n-Channel MOS LSI Using Depletion-Type Load Elements

TOSHIAKI MASUHARA, MEMBER, IEEE, MINORU NAGATA, MEMBER, IEEE, AND NORIKAZU HASHIMOTO

Abstract—A design approach of the depletion-load inverter is given in which an attempt is made to obtain large noise margins. It is predicted that the circuit will operate with a 10–15 pJ/pF power-delay product at +5-V supply voltage.

Some experimental integrated circuits were designed and fabricated by making use of a novel n-channel MOS technology that utilizes both enhancement and depletion-type MOSFET on a chip. A fully decoded transistor–transistor logic (TTL)-compatible READ-ONLY memory was fabricated, resulting in 300 ns total access time at a +5-V single power supply.

Manuscript received April 1, 1971; revised July 2, 1971.
The authors are with the Central Research Laboratory, Hitachi Ltd., Kokubunji, Tokyo, Japan.

I. Introduction

IN THE conventional p-channel MOS integrated circuits, enhancement-type MOSFET are commonly used as the load elements because no additional processing steps are required for the fabrication of load elements. However, the switching speed can be improved with the use of depletion-type load MOSFET as it has been suggested earlier [1], [2]. Some device structures and processing techniques have already been proposed to realize both enhancement and depletion-type MOSFET on a chip; for example, ion-implanted channel structure

Reprinted from *IEEE J. Solid-State Circuits*, vol. SC–7, pp. 224–231, June 1972.

[3], double-diffused structure [4], and MNOS structure [1]. However, until very recently it has been impractical to make both types of MOSFET on the same chip. The design theory of the circuit also has been left undeveloped.

In this paper, a design approach will be given of an inverter configuration with a depletion-type load MOSFET whose gate electrode is connected to the output node. The largest problem in designing the integrated circuit is that the circuit must operate with sufficiently large noise margins. In this paper, the starting point of the design is based on this point of view. The switching performance and power-delay product of the circuit predicted by computer analyses also will be discussed.

The measured results will be shown for a single NOR gate and a 2048-bit READ-ONLY memory in the rest of the paper. These integrated circuits were realized in a monolithic form by making use of a newly developed n-channel structure that consists of both enhancement-type MOSFET with a gate insulator of SiO_2/Al_2O_3 double layer and depletion-type MOSFET with a gate insulator of SiO_2/phosphosilicate glass (PSG) double layer [8].

II. Design Considerations

A. Device Equations

For the purpose of simplifying the design, an n-channel MOSFET is considered throughout the paper and the design is based on the current equations derived from the simple gradual channel approximation of the MOSFET. In this model, drain current I is given as follows [5].

1) Cutoff region $V_G - V_S \leqq V_T$

$$I = 0. \tag{1}$$

2) Saturation region $0 < V_G - V_S - V_T \leqq V_D - V_S$

$$I = (\beta/2)(V_G - V_S - V_T)^2. \tag{2}$$

3) Nonsaturation region $V_D - V_S \leqq V_G - V_S - V_T$

$$I = \beta[(V_G - V_S - V_T)(V_D - V_S) - \tfrac{1}{2}(V_D - V_S)^2] \tag{3}$$

in which

$$\beta = \frac{W}{L}\frac{\epsilon_{ox}}{T_{ox}}\mu \tag{4}$$

where V_D, V_S, and V_G are drain, source, and gate voltage, respectively, V_T is the threshold voltage, T_{ox} and ϵ_{ox} are the thickness and dielectric constant of the gate insulator, W and L are the width and the length of the channel, and μ is carrier mobility in the channel. The term "pinch-off voltage" is commonly used for the depletion-type MOSFET, however, in this paper the name "threshold voltage" is used for both types of MOSFET, which has the same physical meaning.

Threshold voltage is modulated by positively biasing the source terminal, which is especially important for the load MOSFET. The modulated threshold is given by [6]

$$V_T = V_T(V_S = 0) + K[(V_S + 2\phi_F)^{1/2} - (2\phi_F)^{1/2}] \tag{5}$$

in which ϕ_F is Fermi potential, and K is the constant that represents the substrate bias effect given by

$$K = (T_{ox}/\epsilon_{ox})\,(2q\epsilon_S N)^{1/2} \tag{6}$$

where q is electron charge, N is the impurity concentration of the substrate, and ϵ_S is the dielectric constant of the substrate.

B. Static Characteristics

The depletion-load inverter configuration described here is shown in Fig. 1. The schematic dc-transfer characteristics of the circuit are illustrated in Fig. 2. Off level V_{OFF} is apparently equal to the supply voltage. Thus

$$V_{OFF} = V_{DD}. \tag{7}$$

Other circuit parameters, on level V_{ON} and circuit threshold V_{c1} and V_{c2} shown in Fig. 2 are approximated by using (2) and (3) for driver and load MOSFET as follows:

$$V_{ON} \simeq \frac{V_a^2}{2(V_{DD} - V_{TD})} \tag{8}$$

$$V_{c1} = \frac{V_a}{(1 + \beta_R)^{1/2}} + V_{TD} \tag{9}$$

$$V_{c2} = (4/3)^{1/2} V_a + V_{TD} \tag{10}$$

in which V_a is the characteristic voltage for the depletion-load configuration given by

$$V_a = (V_{TL}^2/\beta_R)^{1/2} \tag{11}$$

where V_{TD} and V_{TL} are the threshold of the driver and the load MOSFET, respectively, V_{DD} is the supply voltage, and β_R is the ratio of the channel conductance of the driver β_D and the load β_L. It should be noticed that V_a (V_{TL}) is a function of the output node voltage if $K \neq 0$, so that V_{c1} should be estimated by using the modulated value of $V_a(V_{TL})$ in (9).

Dividing (7)–(11) by V_{DD} and denoting the dimensionless voltage using a small character v, such as $v_{off} = V_{OFF}/V_{DD}$, the following expressions are obtained:

$$v_{off} = 1 \tag{12}$$

$$v_{on} \simeq v_a^2/[2(1 - v_{td})] \tag{13}$$

$$v_{c1} = v_a/(1 + \beta_R)^{1/2} + v_{td} \tag{14}$$

$$v_{c2} = (4/3)^{1/2} v_a + v_{td} \tag{15}$$

$$v_a = (v_{tl}^2/\beta_R)^{1/2}. \tag{16}$$

The two noise margins shown in Fig. 2 are given as follows:

$$V_{m1} = V_{c1} - V_{\mathrm{ON}} \tag{17}$$

$$V_{m2} = V_{DD} - V_{c2} \tag{18}$$

or in the dimensionless expressions,

$$v_{m1} = v_{c1} - v_{\mathrm{on}} \tag{19}$$

$$v_{m2} = 1 - v_{c2}. \tag{20}$$

In general, on level is designed to be small compared to the supply voltage, that is $v_{\mathrm{on}} \ll 1$. Therefore, the condition for the largest noise margins is approximately given by

$$v_{c1} + v_{c2} \simeq 1. \tag{21}$$

Since v_{c1} and v_{c2} are the functions of v_{td}, v_{tl}, and β_R, (21) indicates a relation between v_{td}, v_{tl}, and β_R necessary to obtain a circuit threshold of about one-half of the supply voltage. Fig. 3 illustrates this relation with β_R as a parameter. Hence, Fig. 3 shows the optimum combination of the threshold voltages at a given condition of supply voltage and β_R. For example, if the given condition is that the supply voltage is +5 V and $\beta_R = 1$, one optimum combination is $v_{td} = 0.2$ and $v_{tl} = -0.32$, which corresponds to $V_{TD} = 1$ V and $V_{TL} = -1.6$ V.

Although Fig. 3 may be used if the threshold voltage of the load is arbitrarily adjusted, it often happens that the values of the threshold and the supply voltage are given. In this case, a design diagram shown in Fig. 4 may be useful, in which the dependence of the circuit threshold v_{c1}, v_{c2} and on level v_{on} upon β_R are shown at the condition of $v_{td} = 0.2$, and $v_{tl} = -0.3$. It is clear in this figure that the optimum condition (21) for the design is satisfied at $\beta_R \simeq 1$.

Figs. 5–7 show the dc-transfer curves of the depletion-load inverter calculated by the computer analysis, which illustrate the influences of the three design parameters K, β_R, and V_{TL} upon dc-transfer curves. The values of the device parameters are chosen corresponding to the device structure described in Section III. A +5-V supply voltage is assumed here. The two characteristic features to be described of the depletion load compared with the enhancement load is apparent in these figures. First, circuit threshold V_{c1} decreases with increasing the value of K. This effect is due to the variation of the load curve resulting from the variation of V_{TL} when the output node voltage is high. Second, dc-transfer characteristics strongly depend on V_{TL}. Therefore, a consideration of the distribution of V_{TL} becomes important in designing the integrated circuit.

In summary, the depletion-load circuit has the following features about the dc characteristics.

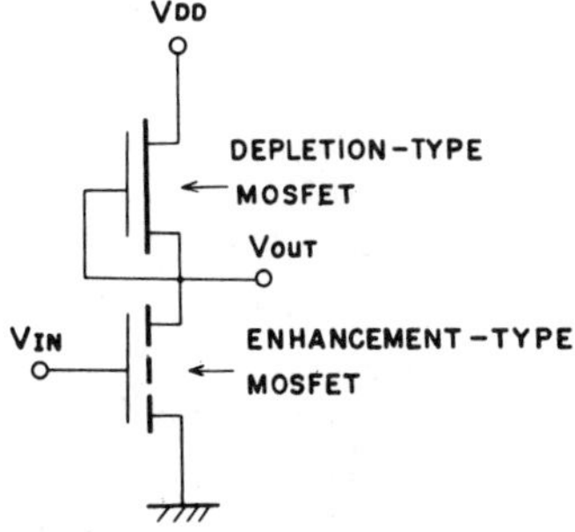

Fig. 1. Inverter circuit with a depletion-type load MOSFET.

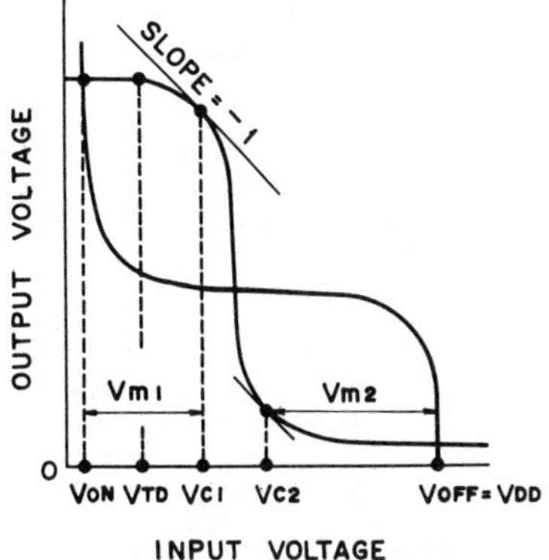

Fig. 2. Schematic dc-transfer characteristics of the inverter with a depletion-type load MOSFET

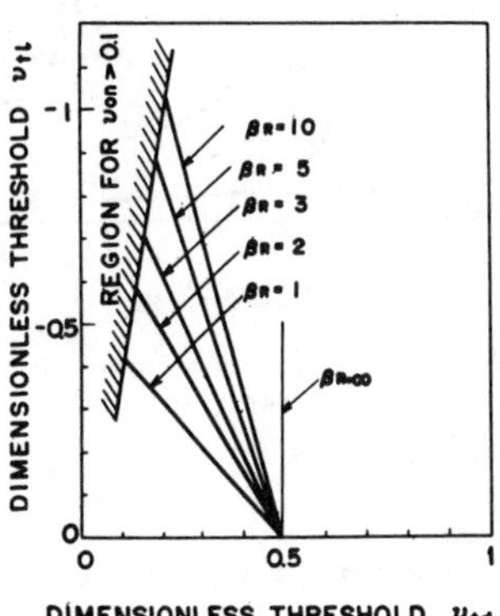

Fig. 3. Relations between v_{tl} and v_{td} necessary to obtain a circuit threshold of ½ V_{DD} at $K = 0$. The hatched region corresponds to $v_{\mathrm{on}} > 0.1$.

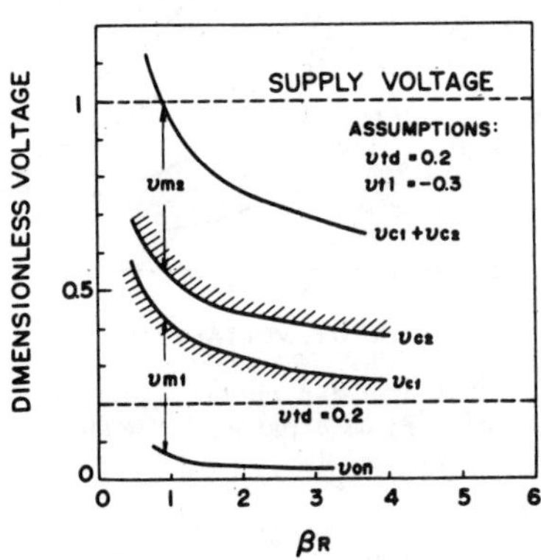

Fig. 4. Circuit threshold v_{c1}, v_{c2}, and on level v_{on} as a function of β_R when $v_{td} = 0.2$, $v_{tl} = -0.3$, and $K = 0$.

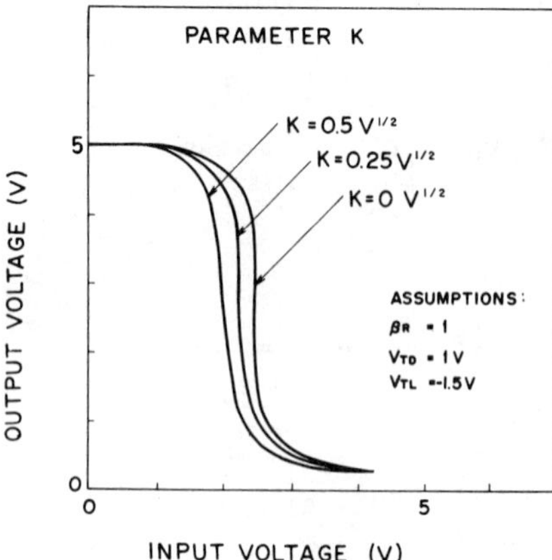

Fig. 5. Calculated dc-transfer characteristics of the depletion-load inverter with K as a parameter when $\beta_R = 1$, $V_{TD} = 1$ V, and $V_{TL} = -1.5$ V.

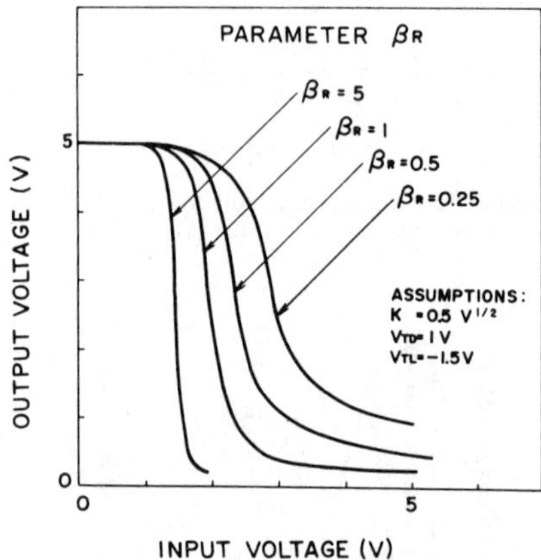

Fig. 6. Calculated dc-transfer characteristics of the depletion-load inverter with β_R as a parameter when $K = 0.5$ V$^{1/2}$, $V_{TD} =$ 1 V, and $V_{TL} = -1.5$ V.

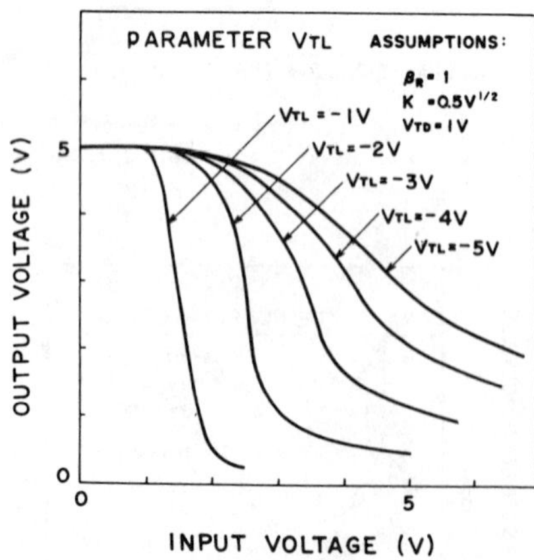

Fig. 7. Calculated dc-transfer characteristics of the depletion-load inverter with V_{TL} as a parameter when $\beta_R = 1$, $K = 0.5$ V$^{1/2}$, and $V_{TD} = 1$ V.

1) Off level is equal to the supply voltage.

2) The circuit threshold is higher than the threshold voltage of the driver MOSFET.

3) Both the combination of the threshold voltages and the geometries of both types of MOSFET can be adjusted to obtain large noise margins.

4) Not only the geometrical ratio of the driver and the load MOSFET, but also the threshold of the load MOSFET are the important design parameters.

5) The circuit threshold depends on the value of K.

C. Transient Characteristics and Power-Delay Product

It is well known that in the load MOSFET of the conventional enhancement-load inverter, current is proportional to V^2, whereas in the depletion-load configuration described in this paper, the load MOSFET exhibits a nearly constant-current-type current-voltage characteristic. For this reason, the depletion-load circuit has a relatively high turnoff switching speed compared with the enhancement-load circuit.

Let us make a rough comparison of the switching delay between the depletion load and the enhancement load when the driver MOSFET becomes OFF. The following assumptions are made in this comparison.

1) Both circuits are operated with the single power supplies, i.e., V_{GG} for the enhancement load and V_{DD} for the depletion load.

2) Off levels are equal for both circuits. Therefore, $V_{GG} = V_{DD} + V_T$.

3) On levels are equal for both circuits.

4) The driver MOSFET have the same channel geometry for both circuits.

In the depletion-load inverter a time $t_{1/2,D}$, necessary to pull up the voltage at the output node from the low state to one-half of the supply voltage, is approximated by

$$t_{1/2,D} \simeq \frac{C}{\beta_{L,D} v_{tl}^2 V_{DD}} \tag{22}$$

in which C is the capacitance at the output node and substrate bias effect is neglected $K = 0$. In the case of enhancement load operated in the saturation region $t_{1/2,E}$ is given by

$$t_{1/2,E} \simeq \frac{2C}{\beta_{L,E}(V_{GG} - V_T)} \tag{23}$$

where V_{GG} is the gate voltage of the load MOSFET. From the assumption (2) i.e., $V_{GG} = V_{DD} + V_T$, the ratio $t_{1/2,E}/t_{1/2,D}$ leads to

$$\frac{t_{1/2,E}}{t_{1/2,D}} \simeq 2v_{tl}^2\left(\frac{\beta_{R,E}}{\beta_{R,D}}\right) \tag{24}$$

in which $\beta_{R,D}$ and $\beta_{R,E}$ represent the β_R in the depletion load and enhancement load, respectively. To satisfy assumption (3), load currents should be equal for both circuits because the ON resistance of the driver MOSFET is equal. Therefore, $V_{TL}^2/\beta_{R,D} = V_{DD}^2/\beta_{R,E}$. Substituting this relation into (24) yields $t_{1/2,E}/t_{1/2,D} = 2$. This advantage in switching speed arises from the differences of the shape of load curves. If a comparison is made on the basis of equal power dissipation, much more advantage will be expected in the depletion-load circuit, because a higher power supply is required in the enhancement-load circuit.

In Figs. 8–10 the results of the detailed calculation of the turnoff characteristics of the depletion-load inverter circuit are shown in which the values of the three parameters K, β_R, and V_{TL} are used corresponding to Figs. 5–7. These results are obtained by the numerical integration of the load current through the depletion load to the output node. The following influences of two parameters K and V_{TL} that are characteristic in the depletion load should be noticed. First, the larger the value of K, the slower the switching speed becomes. This effect of K is due to the variation of the load curve caused by the variation of V_{TL} as described in the dc characteristics. Second, the transient characteristics strongly depend on the value of V_{TL}, so that the variation of V_{TL} directly leads to the variation of the switching speed. Therefore, the threshold of the load is again the important design parameter.

Power dissipation when the inverter is ON is given by

$$P_{\text{ON}} \simeq (\beta_L/2) v_{tl}^2 V_{DD}^3 \qquad (25)$$
$$= (\beta_L/2) V_{TL}^2 V_{DD}.$$

Therefore, power dissipation increases in proportion to V_{DD} if the specific circuit that has fixed β_R and V_{TL} is considered. However, power dissipation has V_{DD}^3 dependency if the dimensionless threshold voltages, v_{td} and v_{tl} can be held constant for any specified supply voltage by optimizing the value of V_{TD} and V_{TL}. In practical case, V_{TD} and V_{TL} are process dependent, so it is easier to adjust β_R rather than v_{td} and v_{tl} so that the circuit has good dc-transfer characteristics at any supply voltage. In this case also power dissipation varies approximately in proportion to V_{DD}^3, which will be shown in Fig. 11.

Combining (22) and (25), power-delay of the depletion-load circuit is given by

$$P_{\text{ON}} \times t_{1/2,D} \simeq (C/2) V_{DD}^2. \qquad (26)$$

Though (26) gives a rough estimation of power-delay product, it should accurately be estimated by using the delay time calculated from the circuit configuration of the cascaded inverters. The results of the calculation are shown in Figs. 11 and 12 as a function of the supply voltage. It is apparent from Fig. 11 that the circuit operates with a 10–15 pJ/pF power-delay product at +5 V, and an operation of 3 pJ/pF may be possible at +2 V. It should be noticed here that each point in these figures corresponds to the different values of β_R, for the circuit is designed to have a sufficient noise margin at any supply voltage.

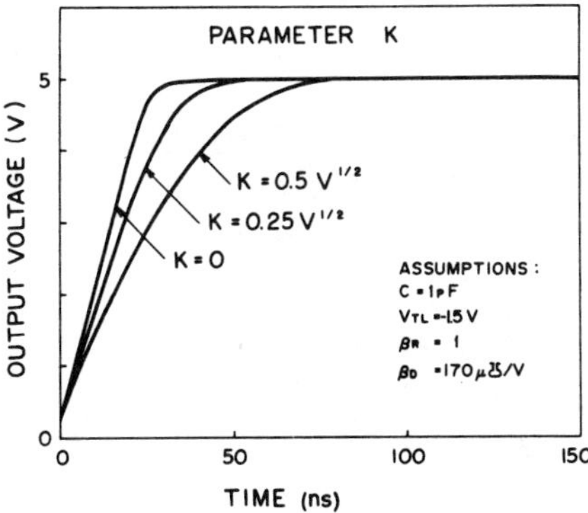

Fig. 8. Calculated turnoff responses of the depletion-load inverter with K as a parameter when $C = 1$ pF, $V_{TD} = 1$ V, $V_{TL} = -1.5$ V, $\beta_R = 1$, and $\beta_D = 170$ μ℧/V.

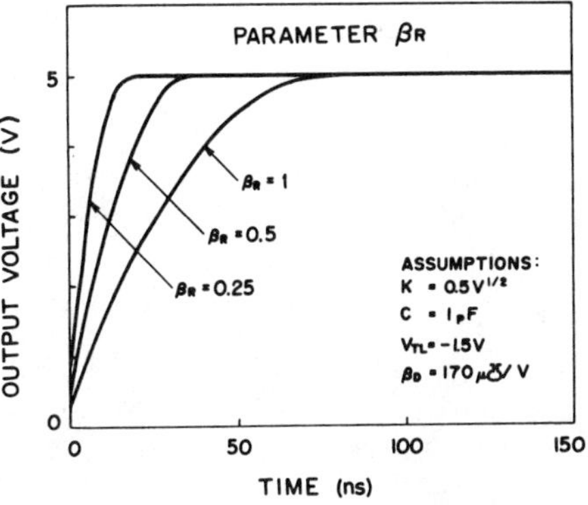

Fig. 9. Calculated turnoff responses of the depletion-load inverter with β_R as a parameter when $C = 1$ pF, $V_{TD} = 1$ V, $K = 0.5$ V$^{1/2}$, $V_{TL} = -1.5$ V, and $\beta_D = 170$ μ℧/V.

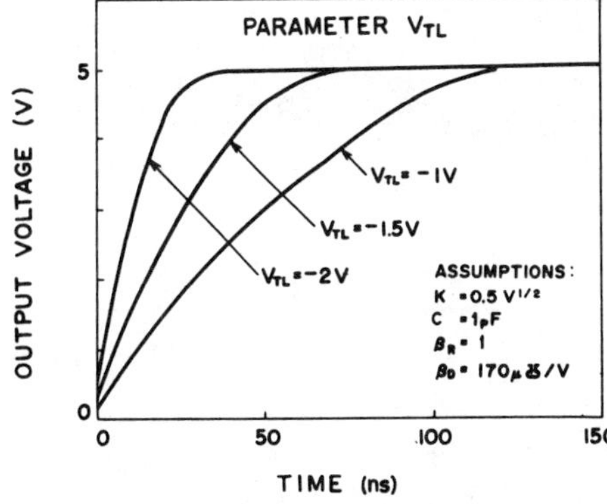

Fig. 10. Calculated turnoff responses of the depletion-load inverter with V_{TD} as a parameter when $C = 1$ pF, $V_{TD} = 1$ V, $K = 0.5$ V$^{1/2}$, $\beta_R = 1$, and $\beta_D = 170$ μ℧/V.

III. Experimental Results

Some test circuits are designed based on the design considerations described in Section II, and are fabricated in a monolithic form by making use of a newly developed n-channel technology. In Fig. 13 a cross section is shown of the integrated circuit described here. The substrate is

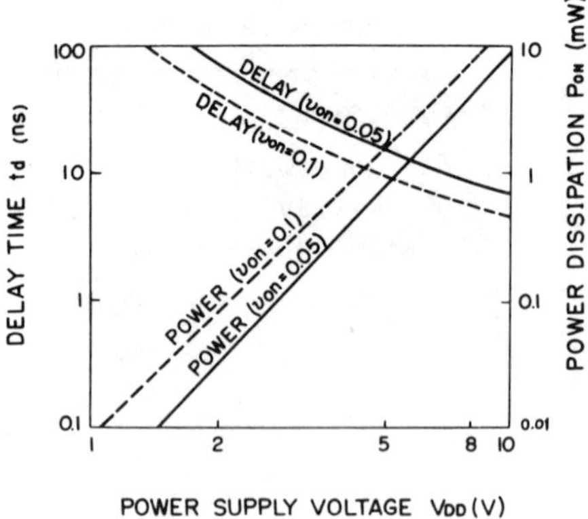

Fig. 11. Calculated delay time and power dissipation as a function of supply voltage when $V_{TD} = 1$ V, $V_{TL} = -1.5$ V, and $\beta_D = 170$ $\mu\mho$/V.

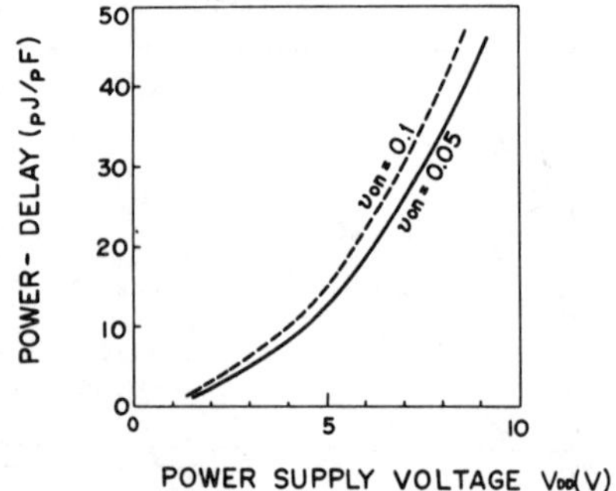

Fig. 12. Power-delay product calculated from Fig. 11 as a function of supply voltage.

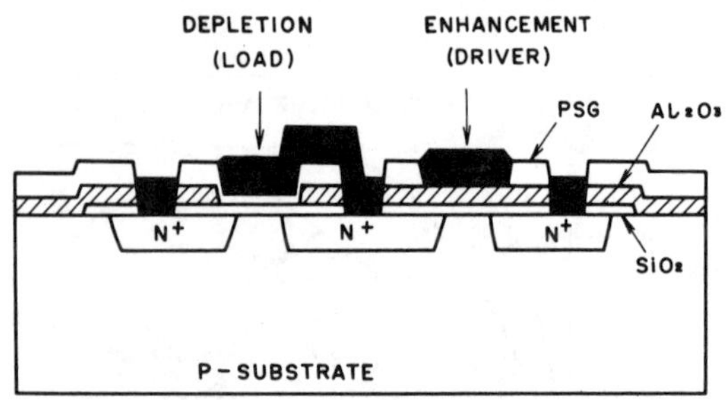

Fig. 13. Cross section of the n-channel MOS integrated circuit.

a 10-ohm·cm (100) p-type silicon wafer. Enhancement-type MOSFET have an Al_2O_3 layer over thermally grown SiO_2 as a gate insulator. The threshold voltage is controlled by varying the thickness ratio of an SiO_2/Al_2O_3 layer down to +1 V [7] to operate with a +5-V supply voltage. These enhancement-type MOSFET have an electron mobility of about 1000 $cm^2/V \cdot s$, that is, about five times greater than that of conventional p-channel MOSFET. Depletion-type MOSFET have an SiO_2 layer passivated with PSG as a gate insulator, and the threshold is about −1.5 V. At the isolation region, the field insulator of phosphosilicate glass over Al_2O_3 has a threshold voltage no less than +20 V (typically 50 V). Thus, each MOSFET becomes perfectly isolated. The details of the processing technology were already reported [8].

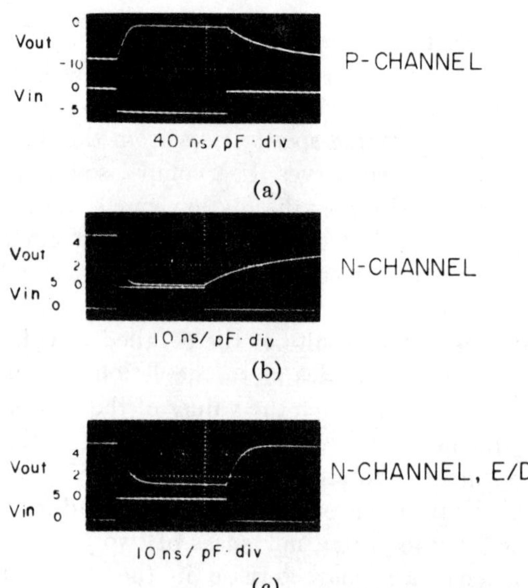

Fig. 14. Comparisons of the switching speeds. (a) p-channel enhancement load ($P_{ON} = 1.6$ mW). (b) n-channel enhancement load ($P_{ON} = 0.9$ mW). (c) n-channel depletion-load inverter ($P_{ON} = 3.0$ mW) with the driver MOSFET of the same geometry.

Fig. 14 shows the measured transient waveforms of a single NOR gate compared with the p-channel and n-channel enhancement-load circuit with the driver MOSFET of the same geometry. It is apparent that the n-channel depletion-load circuit shows almost an order-of-magnitude improvement in switching speed over the conventional p-channel circuit. The measured power-delay of the n-channel depletion-load circuit was 15 pJ/pF at +5-V supply voltage and 6 pJ/pF at +3 V. This improvement in switching speed and power-delay product arises because of the following.

1) Using depletion load, about 2–3 times improvement in power-x delay product is obtained.

2) High election mobility of the n-channel MOSFET enhances the switching speed.

3) Low voltage operation is possible because of the low threshold voltage of the driver MOSFET with an SiO_2/Al_2O_3 layer as a gate insulator.

The basic technology was applied to the large-scale array yielding a 2048-bit READ-ONLY memory. Fig. 15 shows the entire MOS LSI chip. The circuit diagram of the memory is illustrated in Fig. 16. The array consists essentially of five-stage cascades of the inverters, i.e., 2 input buffers, an address decoder, a memory array, and an output buffer. Each stage has a depletion-type load MOSFET. For this reason, this system is the best example to demonstrate the capability of the new technology. The design theory and optimization technique described in Section II can be directly applied to the system.

The input–output dc-transfer characteristics of the READ-ONLY memory is shown in Fig. 17. The circuit has a threshold of approximately 1.6 V and a low level of about 0.2 V independent of the supply voltage. The output buffer can sink about 3 mA when a low level is 0.4

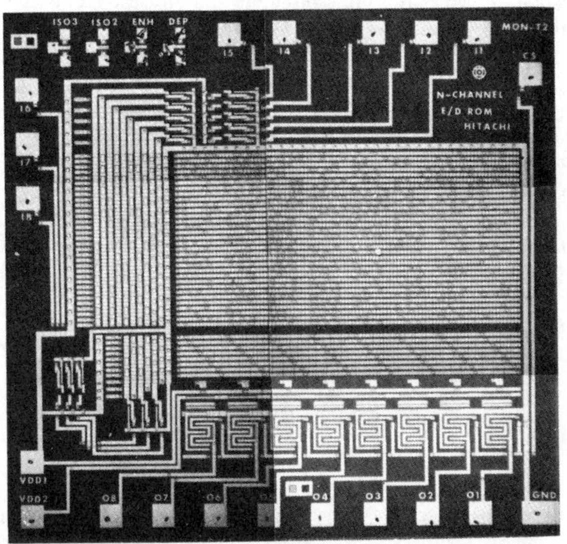

Fig. 15. Entire MOS LSI chip of the 2048-bit READ-ONLY memory. Actual size of the chip is 3.2 × 3.0 mm².

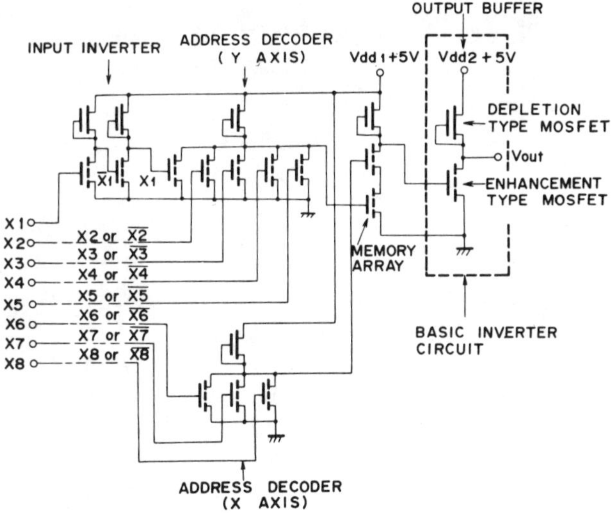

Fig. 16. Circuit diagram of 2048-bit n-channel READ-ONLY memory.

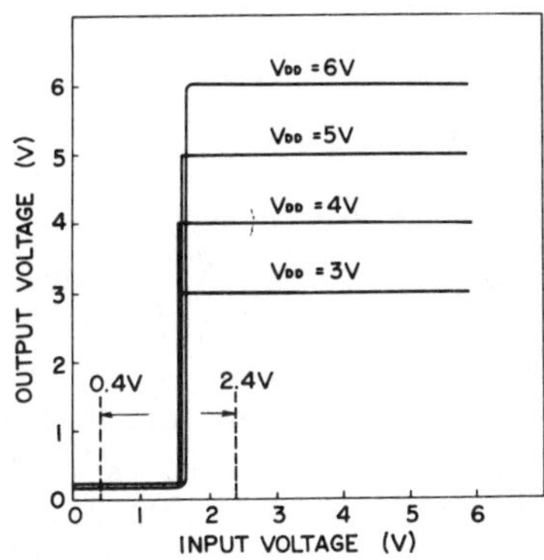

Fig. 17. Experimental dc-transfer characteristics of the READ-ONLY memory.

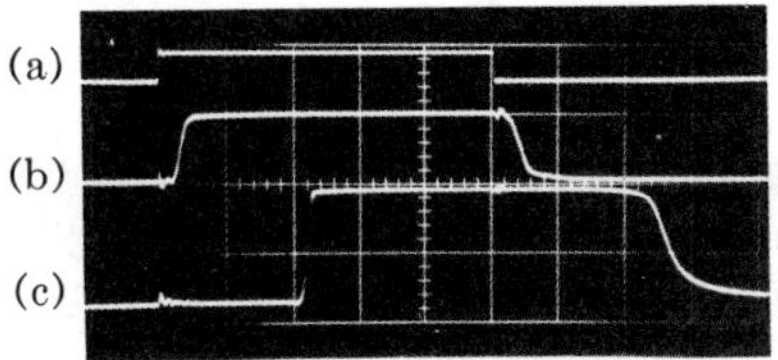

Fig. 18. (a) Input waveform. (b) Output waveform of the n-channel READ-ONLY memory (total power dissipation—100 mW) (c) Output waveform of the conventional p-channel READ-ONLY memory (total power dissipation—60 mW) with the same chip size and the same memory pattern. Vertical scale: 5 V/div for (b) and (c). Horizontal scale: 1 μs/div.

V. Therefore, the chip is fully TTL compatible both at the input and the output.

The measured output waveform of the chip is shown in Fig. 18 when a "1" address is read. Also shown here is the corresponding waveform of the p-channel READ-ONLY memory with the same chip size and the same memory pattern. A speed advantage by a factor of seven is obvious.

The main features achieved by the LSI chip are summarized as follows: 1) 2048-bits (256 words by 8 bits) fully decoded static READ-ONLY memory with output buffers, 2) 300-ns total access time, 3) +5-V single power supply, 4) TTL compatible both at the input and the output with no additional power supply and interfacing circuitry required, and 5) 100-mW total power dissipation with 8 output buffers.

IV. Conclusion

A design approach of the depletion-load inverter has been made from the point of view that the starting point of the design is to obtain sufficiently large noise margins. It was found that the optimum value of β_R is 1 at a +5-V supply voltage when $V_{TD} = 1$ V and $V_{TL} = -1.5$ V. Switching speed and power-delay product of the circuit were estimated with the result that the circuit can operate with a 10–15 pJ/pF power-delay product at +5 V.

Some experimental integrated circuits were designed based on the design theory described above and fabricated by making use of a novel n-channel device structure. The device structure consists of 1) enhancement-type MOSFET with a gate insulator of SiO_2/Al_2O_3 double layer, 2) depletion-type MOSFET with a gate insulator of SiO_2/PSG double layer, and 3) a field insulator of Al_2O_3/PSG double layer. The measured power-x delay product of a single NOR gate was 15 pJ/pF at +5 V, which is consistent with the predicted value. The 2048-bit READ-ONLY memory was fabricated to demonstrate the capability of the technology resulting in a 300-ns total access time with a +5-V single power supply.

It is felt that the application of this circuit and device technology to other arrays such as random-access memory or logic circuits would greatly increase the performance.

Acknowledgment

The authors wish to thank N. Kozuma and Y. Koga for their constant encouragement, and T. Tokuyama and S. Nishimatsu for their valuable discussions.

References

[1] H. C. Lin and C. J. Varker, "Normally-on load devices for IGFET switching circuit," *NEREM Rec.*, pp. 124–125, 1969.
[2] Y. Hayashi and T. Tarui, "EDT-MOS-IC," presented at the 1969 Nat. Conv. IECE, Japan.
[3] J. Macdougall and K. Manchester, *Electronics*, pp. 86–90, June 1970.
[4] Y. Tarui, Y. Hayashi, and T. Sekigawa, "DSA enhancement-depletion MOS-IC," presented at the Int. Electron Devices Meeting, Washington, D. C., Oct. 1970.
[5] S. R. Hofstein and F. P. Heiman, "The silicon insulated-gate field-effect transistor," *Proc. IEEE,* vol. 51, pp. 1190–1202, Sept. 1963.
[6] R. H. Crawford, *MOSFET in Circuit Design.* New York: McGraw-Hill, 1967, Chap. 2, 4.
[7] S. Nishimatsu and T. Tokuyama, "N-channel enhancement type MOSICs utilizing alumina film," presented at the 1st Conf. Solid-State Devices, Tokyo, Japan, 1969.
[8] M. Nagata, N. Hashimoto, and T. Masuhara, "Nanosecond n-channel monolithic integrated circuits with depletion-mode transistors as load devices," presented at the Int. Electron Devices Meeting, Washington, D. C., Oct. 1970.

Analysis and Characterization of the Depletion-Mode IGFET

YOUSSEF A. EL-MANSY, MEMBER, IEEE

Abstract—Using simple charge-voltage relationships, a four-terminal model is developed for the depletion-mode IGFET. Various conditions which can coexist at the surface, such as accumulation, depletion, and inversion, are taken into account. The implanted channel is approximated by a box profile. The basic model elements, namely, the source-drain transport current and the various charging currents, are explicitly given in terms of known processing data and implanted channel parameters. Device threshold voltage, drain saturation voltage, and conditions for surface inversion are explicitly given as a function of these parameters.

I. Introduction

DEPLETION-mode IGFET's are normally fabricated by introducing impurity ions of the opposite type to the starting substrate to form a shallow layer underneath the gate of the device. This layer can be achieved by ion implantation, diffusion, epitaxial growth, or otherwise. Ion implantation is the most commonly used method because exact control of the number of impurity atoms and their distribution is essential for reproducible device characteristics. To produce an n-channel depletion-mode device in a standard NMOS process, n-type impurities are selectively introduced into the p-type starting material. If an n-doped polysilicon gate is used, the resulting device will have a negative threshold voltage and is capable of conduction with zero voltage between the gate and the source.

The use of these devices was originally limited to load elements in enhancement-depletion logic in order to decrease the power-delay product [1], [2]. In such a case, the source and the gate are tied together and the device approximates a current source. Recently [3], [4], depletion-mode devices have become widely used in more general configurations to utilize their superior qualities such as high mobility and low surface generated $1/f$ noise. Also, the same device with appropriate implant conditions is the basic element in bulk-channel charge-coupled device technology. To account for these various modes of operation, a general model which is explicitly related to known processing information, device geometry, and properly handles the nonlinear dc and charging current components is essential.

Initially, the current behavior of the device was described by an enhancement surface device model with a threshold voltage shifted as a function of the number of impurities implanted in the channel. Such modeling is adequate for lightly doped shallow implanted channels where the devices are used as load elements. More accurate analysis to account for the finite thickness of the implanted channel has been performed by Edwards and Marr [5]. A simpler version of the analysis was carried out by Huang and Taylor [6] where the effects of the finite channel thickness are represented by an average semiconductor capacitance in series with the gate oxide capacitance. For a heavily implanted deep channel, the device cannot be turned off by applying a gate voltage due to the formation of a surface inversion layer which causes the gate to lose control over the channel. A device operating in this mode was described by Verbracken *et al.* [7] where the substrate is used as the input signal terminal to utilize the high gain obtainable for this configuration. More recently, accurate analysis has been presented by Haken [8] wherein simple measurements performed on an IGFET to determine the implanted layer properties relevant to buried-channel charge-coupled device applications were used. In all these analyses, charging currents in the device were mostly ignored and only experimental characterization and semiquantitative description of device capacitances were attempted [9], [10].

The present work therefore has the following objectives.

1) Development of a physical model that uses basic processing information and covers all regions of device operation except the subthreshold region.

2) Modeling the charging currents in the device in a manner that can be directly implemented in a circuit analysis program.

3) Using model parameters that are easily and systematically obtained from a simple and small number of measurements of device terminal parameters.

In Section II, the dc and charging current elements of the model are derived from basic charge densities in the device. This results in all the elements required for an equivalent circuit representation. Device terminal characteristics that are useful in defining the implanted region parameters are discussed in Section III. Finally, some of the experimental results and discussion of such results are given in Section IV.

II. Analysis

A. Charge Densities

Two cross sections of an n-channel device in the direction of channel current flow and in the lateral direction are shown schematically in Fig. 1 with basic coordinate and voltage definitions. The boundaries of the two space-charge regions which modulate the conducting channel are illustrated. The depletion width of the p-n junction formed by the channel and the substrate is controlled by the channel voltage. The conditions

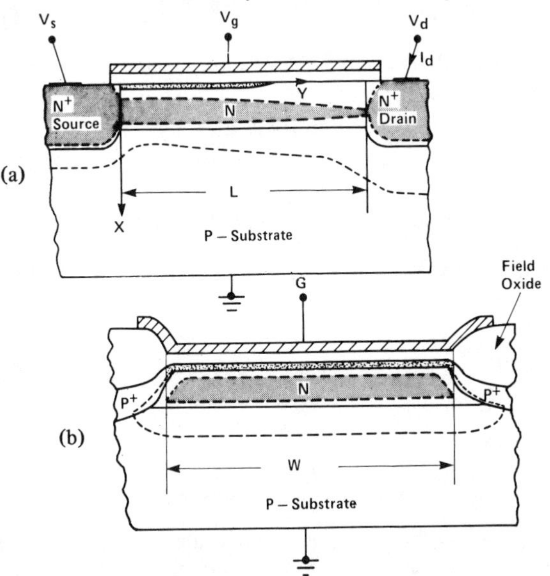

Fig. 1. Device cross sections showing coordinates, device dimensions, and voltage definitions (a) in the direction of current flow and (b) in the lateral direction.

Manuscript received June 20, 1979; revised December 12, 1979.

The author was with Bell-Northern Research, Ottawa, Ont., Canada. He is now with the Intel Corporation, Aloha, OR 97005.

Reprinted from *IEEE J. Solid-State Circuits*, vol. SC–15, pp. 331–340, June 1980.

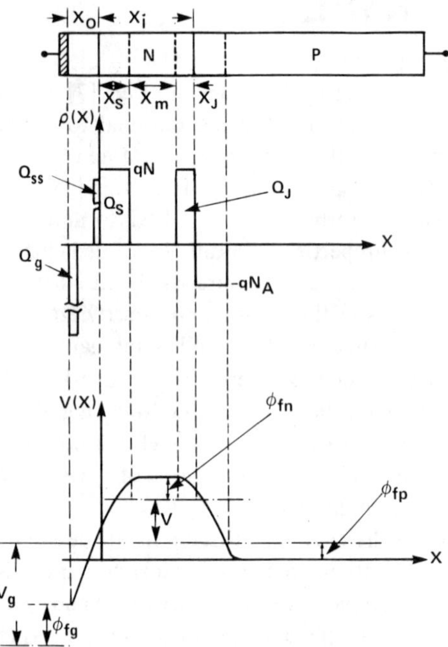

Fig. 2. An elemental section of the device at a position along the channel where the surface is depleted. Also shown is the charge and potential distribution in the direction normal to the surface.

in the surface space-charge region are due to the combined effects of the gate and channel voltages. These conditions range from accumulation of electrons at the surface for a positive gate voltage to the existence of a p-type surface inversion layer at a large negative gate voltage. Fig. 2 shows an elemental section of the device at a position y, together with the charge and potential distribution in the direction perpendicular to the surface.[1] The implanted layer is approximated by a rectangle of height N and width X_i. Later, we discuss a method for defining these parameters. Using the gradual channel approximation (GCA), we can write for the charge density Q_m in the channel

$$Q_m = -Q_i + Q_j + Q_s \tag{1}$$

where the various charge density (per unit surface area) components are defined as follows.

The implanted layer charge density is given by

$$Q_i = qNX_i. \tag{2}$$

The p-n junction space-charge density Q_j is given by

$$Q_j = qNX_j = K_E\sqrt{V_m} \tag{3}$$

where[2]

$$K_E = \sqrt{2\epsilon qN_E},$$

$$N_E = \frac{N_A \cdot N}{N_A + N},$$

[1] The distributions shown correspond to a position where the surface is not inverted.

[2] All voltages are with respect to the neutral substrate region. V_m is the electrostatic potential of the channel with respect to neutral substrate, while V is the corresponding voltage of the channel defined consistently with the externally applied voltages V_S, V_d, and V_g. Such a definition makes the gradients of both V_m and V equal, therefore causing the diffusion components of channel current to be zero.

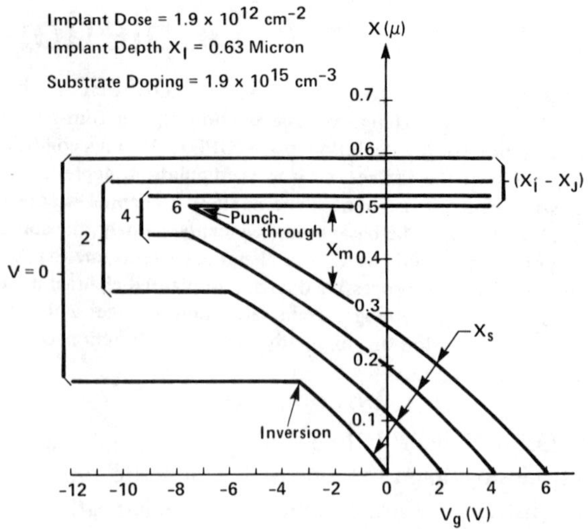

Fig. 3. Variation of surface and p-n junction space-charge region widths. A value $V_{fb} = 0$ is used.

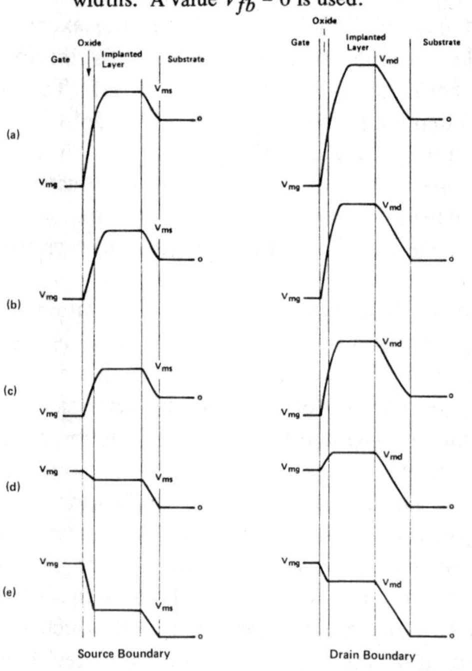

Fig. 4. Potential distributions in the gate, oxide, and semiconductor regions of the device at source and drain boundaries. In all the plots, source and drain voltages are kept constant, while the gate voltage is changed from a large negative value (a) to a large positive value (e).

ϵ is the permittivity of silicon, $V_m = V + \phi_B$, V is the channel voltage at any point between source and drain, and $\phi_B = \phi_{fn} + \phi_{fp}$ is the p-n junction equilibrium barrier height. V takes the values V_s and V_d, while V_m takes the values V_{ms} and V_{md} at the source and drain terminals, respectively. The component Q_s takes the following values depending on the relationship between the gate and channel electrostatic potentials:

$$Q_s = \left.\begin{cases} -C_0(V_{mg} - V_m) & V_{mg} > V_m \quad \text{accumulation} \\ = qNX_s & V_{TI} < V_{mg} \leqslant V_m \quad \text{depletion} \\ = qNX_{sm} & V_{mg} \leqslant V_{TI} \quad \text{inversion} \end{cases}\right\} \tag{4}$$

where[2] C_0 is the gate oxide capacitance per unit area,

$$V_{mg} = V_g - V_{fb} + \phi_B$$

where V_g is the applied gate voltage

$$V_{fb} = -\phi_{fg} + \phi_{fn} - \frac{Q_{SS}}{C_0},$$

and V_{TI} is the threshold for surface inversion given as

$$V_{TI} = -K_N \sqrt{V_m}/C_0$$

where

$$K_N = \sqrt{2\epsilon qN}.$$

The surface space-charge region thickness is given by

$$X_s = K_N(\sqrt{V_m - V_{mg} + V_C} - \sqrt{V_C})/qN \tag{5a}$$

where $V_C = qN\epsilon/(2C_0^2)$.

When inversion occurs at the surface, the space-charge region X_s attains a maximum value X_{sm} given by

$$X_{sm} = K_N \sqrt{V_m}/qN. \tag{5b}$$

It is implied here that once an inversion layer is formed at the surface, it is connected to the p-substrate and therefore has the same potential as the substrate.[3]

The set of equations (1)-(4) is valid at any point along the surface between the source and the drain. Whether all the conditions mentioned in (4) actually occur in a given device will depend on the number of impurities in the implanted layer, the thickness of that layer, and the channel voltage. As the gate voltage is reduced below the flat band value, the surface region becomes depleted and one of two conditions is encountered.

1) The value of Q_m in (1) becomes zero before the threshold for inversion is reached, and in this case the channel punches through and is cutoff or

2) Inversion occurs at the surface first and in this case the channel does not punch through.

To illustrate these points, the surface space-charge region thickness X_s and the lower channel boundary depth $(X_i - X_j)$ are plotted in Fig. 3 for a specified device. For channel voltages below 6 V, inversion conditions occur first, while for channel voltages greater than or equal to 6 V, the channel punches through. The channel voltage V can be any value along the channel including the source and drain boundaries. The above relations (1)-(5) can therefore be used at these boundaries to define basic device parameters.

Specifically, we now use the mobile charge density along the channel together with the source and drain boundary conditions to evaluate various device terminal parameters representative of performance characteristics and relevant to model formulation.

B. Channel Current and Conductances

Neglecting diffusion current, the channel (drain) current can be written as (refer to Fig. 1)

$$I_d = -\mu W Q_m \frac{dV_m}{dy} \tag{6}$$

integrating between source and drain

$$I_d = \frac{-\mu W}{L} \int_{V_{ms}}^{V_{md}} Q_m \, dV_m \tag{7}$$

where W and L are the width and the length of the device, respectively.

Substituting for Q_m from (1) into (7), we obtain

$$I_d = \frac{\mu W}{L} [Q_i(V_{md} - V_{ms}) - \tfrac{2}{3} K_E(V_{md}^{3/2} - V_{ms}^{3/2}) - F_S] \tag{8}$$

where $K_E = \sqrt{2\epsilon qN_E}$ and F_S is the contribution of the surface space-charge region to the current defined as

$$F_S = \int_{V_{ms}}^{V_{md}} Q_s \, dV_m. \tag{9}$$

The function F_S takes different values depending on the conditions existing at the surface; see Fig. 4. We now evaluate this function for the different situations ranging from inversion to accumulation (all along the surface), with reference to the conditions of (4).

1) Inversion Along the Entire Surface [Fig. 4(a)]: This condition exists for gate voltages satisfying the inequality $V_{mg} \leqslant -(K_N/C_0)\sqrt{V_{md}}$. In this case, Q_s comprises the positive ions existing within the surface depletion layer and is given by $Q_s = -K_N \sqrt{V_m}$ while

$$F_S = \tfrac{2}{3} K_N (V_{md}^{3/2} - V_{ms}^{3/2}). \tag{9a}$$

2) Inversion at Source, Depletion at Drain [Fig. 4(b)]: This condition exists for gate voltages in the range

$$-\left(\frac{K_N}{C_0}\right)\sqrt{V_{md}} < V_{mg} \leqslant -\left(\frac{K_N}{C_0}\right)\sqrt{V_{ms}}.$$

The surface in this case is inverted at the source end and up to a point along the surface where the potential is given by $V_m = V_{ID}$. Beyond this point and up to the drain, the surface is depleted. Therefore, Q_s is given by

$$\begin{aligned} Q_s &= K_N \sqrt{V_m} && V_{ms} < V_m \leqslant V_{ID} \\ &= K_N[\sqrt{(V_m - V_{mg}) + V_C} - \sqrt{V_C}] && V_{ID} < V_m \leqslant V_{md} \end{aligned}$$

where $V_{ID} = (-C_0 V_{mg}/K_N)^2$ is the potential of the point separating the inverted section from the depleted section and

$$\begin{aligned} F_S &= K_N \left[\int_{V_{ms}}^{V_{ID}} K_N \sqrt{V_m} \, dV_m + \int_{V_{ID}}^{V_{md}} (\sqrt{V_m - V_{mg} + V_C} - \sqrt{V_C}) \, dV_m \right] \\ &= \tfrac{2}{3} K_N [V_{ID}^{3/2} - V_{ms}^{3/2} + (V_{md} - V_{mg} + V_C)^{3/2} \\ &\quad - (V_{ID} - V_{mg} + V_C)^{3/2} - \sqrt{V_C}(V_{md} - V_{ID})]. \end{aligned} \tag{9b}$$

3) Depletion Along the Entire Surface [Fig. 4(c)]: In this case, the gate potential is in the range $-(K_N\sqrt{V_{ms}}/C_0) < V_{mg} \leqslant V_{ms}$. The charge Q_s is

$$Q_s = K_N(\sqrt{V_m - V_{mg} + V_C} - \sqrt{V_C})$$

and the function F_S is

[3] The inversion layer is connected to the substrate via the field region implant which results in frequency-independent characteristics up to high frequencies.

$$F_S = \tfrac{2}{3} K_N [(V_{md} - V_{mg} + V_C)^{3/2} - (V_{ms} - V_{mg} + V_C)^{3/2} - \sqrt{V_C}\,(V_{md} - V_{ms})]. \tag{9c}$$

4) Accumulation at Source, Depletion at Drain [Fig. 4(d)]: This condition exists for a gate potential, is in the range $V_{ms} < V_{mg} \leqslant V_{md}$, and Q_s is given by

$$\begin{aligned} Q_s &= C_0(V_m - V_{mg}) && V_{ms} \leqslant V_m \leqslant V_{mg} \\ &= K_N(\sqrt{V_m - V_{mg} + V_C} - \sqrt{V_C}) && V_{mg} < V_m \leqslant V_{md}. \end{aligned}$$

The function F_S is then given by

$$F_S = C_0 \frac{V_{mg}^2}{2} - C_0\left(\frac{V_{ms}^2}{2} - V_{ms}V_{mg}\right) + \tfrac{2}{3} K_N [(V_{md} - V_{mg} + V_C)^{3/2} - V_C^{3/2} - \sqrt{V_C}(V_{md} - V_{mg})]. \tag{9d}$$

5) Accumulation Along the Entire Surface [Fig. 4(e)]: The gate potential for this condition is always greater than V_{md}. The charge Q_s is then

$$Q_s = C_0(V_m - V_{mg})$$

and F_S is

$$F_S = C_0\left(\frac{V_{md}^2}{2} - V_{mg}V_{md}\right) - C_0\left(\frac{V_{ms}^2}{2} - V_{mg}V_{ms}\right). \tag{9e}$$

It should be noted that for terms arising from accumulation of electrons at the surface, i.e., those terms in (9d) and (9e) with a premultiplier C_0, a surface mobility value should be used in place of the bulk mobility. As will be shown later in the results, the surface mobility required to fit the measured values is about one-half the bulk value.

Depending on the parameters of the implanted region, some of the conditions outlined above may not be encountered. For example, for shallow implants, inversion may not occur at the surface, and in this case, the whole range of device currents is covered by conditions 3), 4), and 5) above. Such would be the case also if the surface region is completely isolated from the substrate.

Differentiating the drain current with respect to the terminal voltages results in four small-signal conductances corresponding to the four terminals. These are defined as drain conductance $g_d = \partial I_d/\partial V_d$, source conductance $g_s = \partial I_d/\partial V_s$, gate transconductance $g_m = \partial I_d/\partial V_g$, and substrate transconductance $g_{mb} = -(g_d + g_s + g_m)$.

C. Charging Current and Capacitance Components

To formulate the charging current model [11] of the device, we need only consider the charge components that give rise to gate and substrate charging currents. This is due to the overall charge neutrality of the device.

The charge density on the gate at any point along the channel is given by

$$\left.\begin{aligned} Q_g &= -Q_s = C_0(V_{mg} - V_m) && V_{mg} > V_m && \text{accumulation} \\ &= -Q_s = -qNX_s && V_{TI} < V_{mg} < V_m && \text{depletion} \\ &= C_0 V_g && V_{mg} \leqslant V_{TI} && \text{inversion} \end{aligned}\right\} \tag{10}$$

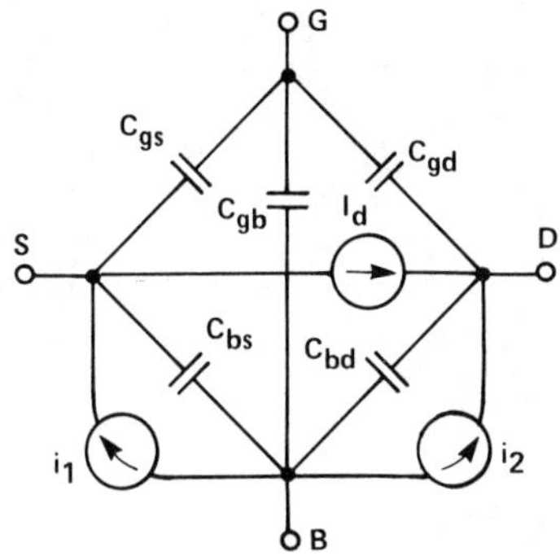

Fig. 5. Equivalent circuit of the device showing the transport current I_d and the various capacitance components.

and the charge density contributing to a substrate charging current is

$$\left.\begin{aligned} Q_b &= -Q_j && V_{mg} > V_m && \text{accumulation} \\ &= -Q_j && V_{TI} < V_{mg} < V_m && \text{depletion} \\ &= -Q_j - Q_s - Q_g && V_{mg} < V_{TI} && \text{inversion} \end{aligned}\right\}. \tag{11}$$

Using (6), the total gate and substrate charges are given by

$$Q_G = W\int_0^L Q_g\,dy = \frac{-\mu W^2}{I_d}\int_{V_{ms}}^{V_{md}} Q_g Q_m\,dV_m = \frac{-\mu W^2}{I_d}\cdot F_G \tag{12}$$

and

$$Q_B = \frac{-\mu W^2}{I_d}\int_{V_{ms}}^{V_{md}} Q_b Q_m\,dV_m = \frac{-\mu W^2}{I_d}\cdot F_B. \tag{13}$$

The gate and substrate charging current components can be written as

$$i_g = \frac{dQ_G}{dt} = C_{gs}\frac{d(V_g - V_s)}{dt} + C_{gd}\frac{d(V_g - V_d)}{dt} + C_{gb}\frac{dV_g}{dt} \tag{14}$$

and

$$i_b = \frac{dQ_B}{dt} = C_{bs}\frac{d(-V_s)}{dt} + C_{bd}\frac{d(-V_d)}{dt} + C_{bg}\frac{d(-V_g)}{dt} \tag{15}$$

where

$$C_{kj} = \frac{-\partial Q_k}{\partial V_j} = \frac{\mu W^2}{I_d^2}[I_d F_{kj} - F_k g_j] \tag{16a}$$

where the subscripts k and j refer to the device terminals b, d, s, and g and the function F_{kj} is defined as $F_{kj} = \partial F_k/\partial V_j$.

The six capacitance components provide all the information required to implement the charging currents in the device in a circuit analysis program. The configuration used is illustrated in Fig. 5 where the two capacitive current sources i_1 and i_2 represent the asymmetry of the gate and substrate regions of the device. These two sources are given by [11]

$$i_1 + i_2 = (C_{bg} - C_{gb})\frac{dV_g}{dt}. \tag{16b}$$

The division of the sources between source and drain terminals is carried out in proportion to a combination of the other four

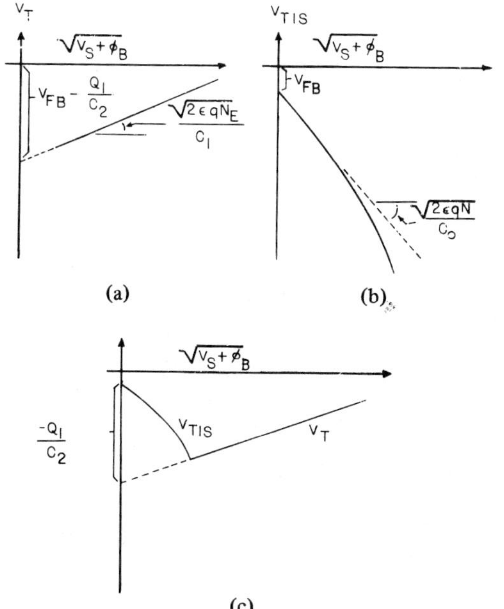

Fig. 6. Behavior of device threshold voltages as a function of source-substrate voltage. (a) Threshold for inversion. (b) Cutoff threshold. (c) Combined plot.

components in a manner similar to that for enhancement devices discussed in detail in [11].

To illustrate the simplicity of the approach, an example is given in the Appendix to derive all the model components for one of the regions of operation, namely, inversion along the surface. Other regions of operation can be treated in a similar manner to complete the model. Such a model has been derived and implemented in a circuit simulator.

III. Device Threshold and Saturation Voltages

Insight is provided into the dependence of the device characteristics upon the various processing parameters (e.g., implant dose, implant depth, oxide thickness) by considering the influence of these parameters on the gate threshold voltage and the saturation voltage.

1) Threshold Voltages: As discussed earlier, there exist two parameters; the gate voltage required to completely turn the device off is denoted as V_T and the threshold for surface inversion as V_{TIS}. The threshold voltage V_T is obtained by equating Q_m at the source end to zero to obtain (the source is taken as the reference terminal)

$$V_T = V_{fb} - \frac{N_E}{N} V_{ms} + \frac{\sqrt{2\epsilon q N_E V_{ms}}}{C_1} - \frac{Q_i}{C_2}. \tag{17}$$

The threshold for inversion at the source is

$$V_{TIS} = V_{fb} - \frac{\sqrt{2\epsilon q N V_{ms}}}{C_0} - V_{ms} \tag{18}$$

where $C_1 = C_0/(1 + C_0/C_i)$, $C_2 = C_0/(1 + (C_0/2C_i))$, and $C_i = \epsilon/X_i$.

Of course, the relevant threshold is used depending on the implanted layer parameters and bias conditions. If V_T is plotted as a function of $\sqrt{V_{ms}}$, a straight line is obtained as shown in Fig. 6(a). The slope and intercept of such a line provide the information on the implanted layer parameters and surface conditions (flat band voltage). The slope of the plot is a function of N_E and C_1 and both depend on the implanted region thickness X_i. Thus, knowledge of the starting material doping N_A and the oxide thickness X_o enables the extraction of X_i. The intercept of such a line gives the flat band voltage (since Q_i and C_2 are known). For heavy doses with a large X_i, the device cannot be turned off without the use of source-substrate voltage. In such a case, the slope of the V_{TIS} curve at $V_{ms} = 0$ gives the doping N, and the intercept is simply (V_{fb}); see Fig. 6(b).[4] In general, for heavy implanted devices, the two thresholds V_T and V_{TIS} are obtainable depending on the range of applied V_{ms}. In this case, shown in Fig. 6(c), enough information can be obtained to extract the dose Q_i and the substrate doping N.

As was mentioned earlier, the finite thickness of the implant changes the threshold equation in two ways. First, the substrate body coefficient is increased due to the smaller capacitance C_1 as compared to C_0 (note that N_E is reduced from N_A, but the net result is an increase of the term $\sqrt{N_E/C_1}$). Second, the threshold is shifted by an amount Q_i/C_2 which for a finite X_i is larger than Q_i/C_0. This could be seen more clearly by rewriting

$$\frac{Q_i}{C_2} = \frac{Q_i}{C_0}\left(1 + \frac{C_0}{2C_i}\right).$$

This shows that an implant thickness of about three times the oxide thickness would produce a 50 percent error if the simple Q_i/C_0 voltage shift is used instead of the exact value given above.

Two limiting cases of the threshold equation are of interest due to their simplicity and their practical significance.

a) Very shallow implants: $X_i \to 0$, $N \approx \infty$. In this case, $C_i \to \infty$ and $C_1 = C_2 = C_0$.

Thus, V_T becomes

$$V_T = V_{fb} + \frac{\sqrt{2\epsilon q N_A V_{ms}}}{C_0} - \frac{Q_i}{C_0} \tag{19}$$

which is the standard enhancement device threshold shifted by the implant contribution $(-Q_i/C_0)$. Note that in this case V_{fb} should be replaced by $(V'_{fb} + \phi_B)$ where V'_{fb} is the flat band voltage of the enhancement device, and ϕ_B would correspond to the usual $2\phi_f$ term in the enhancement device threshold expression.

b) Intrinsic substrates, $N_A \to 0$. For intrinsic substrates, the V_T expression reduces to

$$V_T = V_{fb} - \frac{Q_i}{C_0}\left(1 + \frac{C_0}{2C_i}\right). \tag{20}$$

This relation is useful for lightly doped substrates (>100 Ω · cm). It still shows that the effect of Q_i on V_T should be accounted for properly.

2) Device Saturation Voltage: This is defined as the drain voltage at which the drain current reaches its maximum value for a fixed gate voltage. For the one-dimensional treatment with no velocity saturation effects, this is equivalent to setting $Q_m = 0$ at the drain end of the channel. Using the expression

[4]If instead the substrate is taken as a reference, then a plot of the threshold for inversion $(V_{TIS} + V_s)$ versus $(V_s + \phi_B)^{1/2}$ would be a straight line.

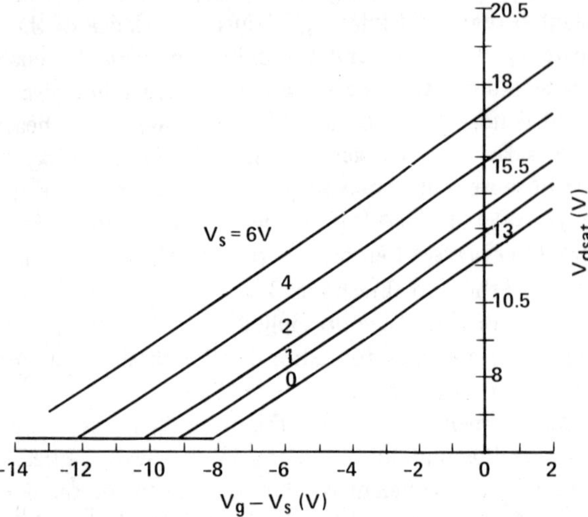

Fig. 7. Drain saturation voltage as a function of gate and source voltages. Device parameters used are the same as in Fig. 3.

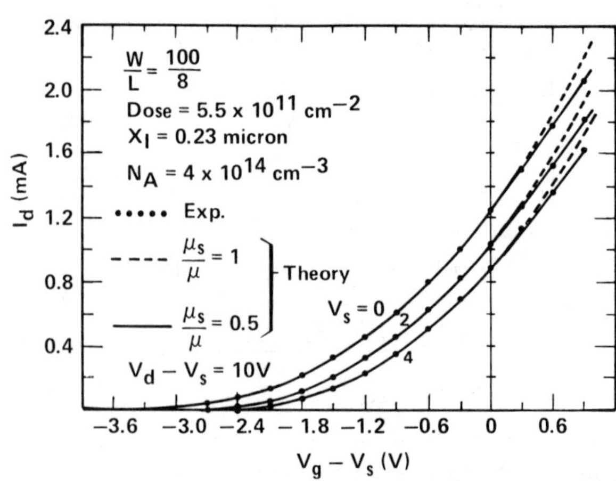

Fig. 8. The drain current-voltage characteristics of a lightly implanted device covering the depletion and accumulation regions. The need for using a surface mobility is illustrated.

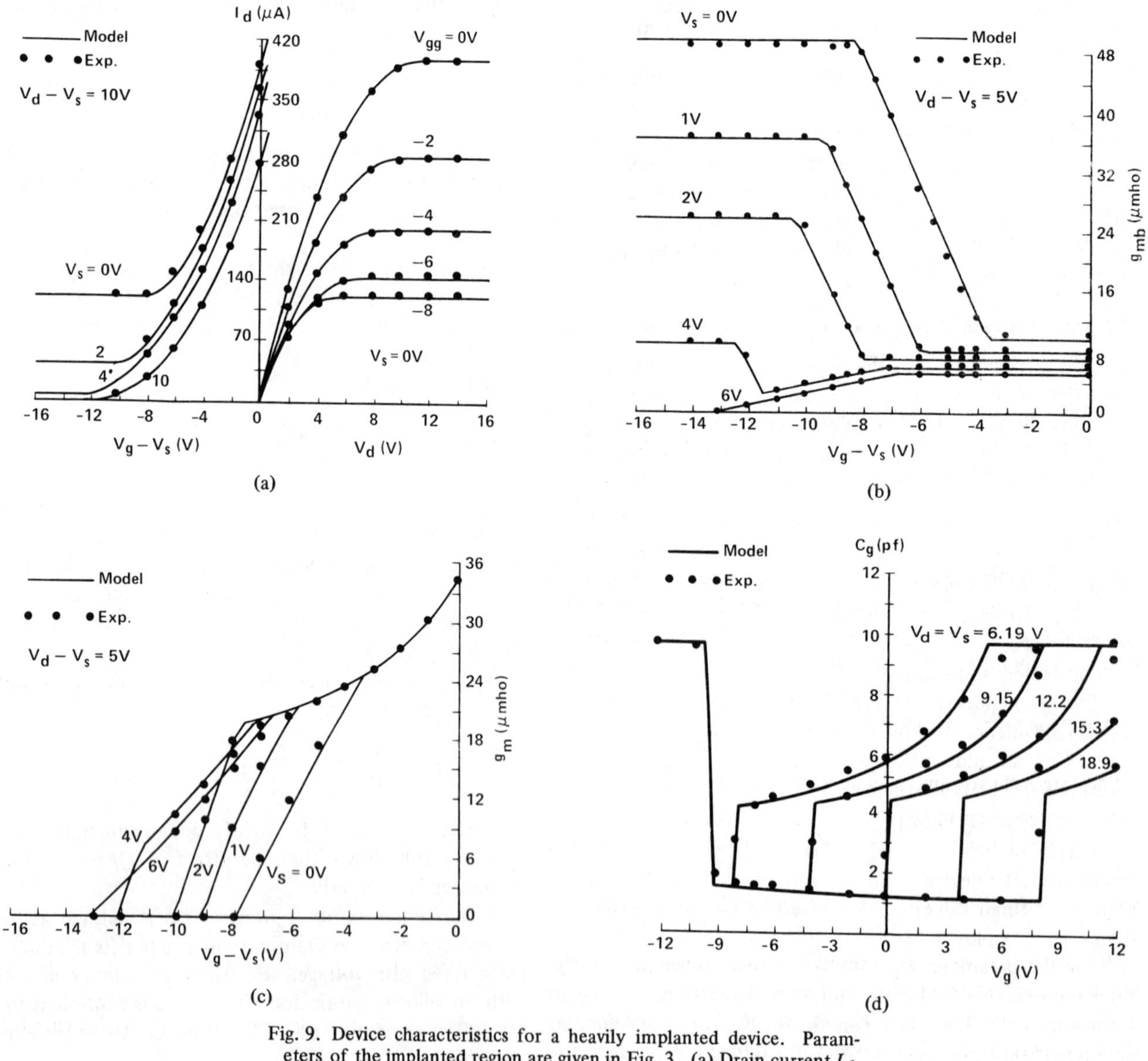

(a)

(b)

(c)

(d)

Fig. 9. Device characteristics for a heavily implanted device. Parameters of the implanted region are given in Fig. 3. (a) Drain current I_d. (b) Substrate transconductance g_{mb}. (c) Gate transconductance g_m. (d) Gate capacitance C_g.

of (1) for Q_m and replacing V_m by V_{mp}, we obtain

$$K_N [\sqrt{(V_{mp} - V_{mg}) + V_C} - \sqrt{V_C}] + K_E \sqrt{V_{mp}} = Q_i \quad (21)$$

where the drain saturation voltage is

$$V_{d\,\mathrm{sat}} = V_{mp} - \phi_B$$

which can be solved for V_{mp} as a function of V_{mg}. This produces an approximately linear relationship. Such a relation is valid as long as the surface region at the drain is depleted. If the region is accumulated, the device cannot be pinched off. If the drain end is inverted, then the alternate expression

$$K_N \sqrt{V_{mp}} + K_E \sqrt{V_{mp}} = Q_i \quad (22)$$

is used instead. In this case, the gate is screened from the channel by the inversion layer and V_{mp} becomes independent of the gate voltage. A typical behavior of $V_{d\mathrm{sat}}$ as a function of V_g and V_s is shown in Fig. 7 with the relevant process information as given in Fig. 3. In many situations, the linear part in the $V_{d\mathrm{sat}}$ curve can be expressed as

$$V_{d\mathrm{sat}} = V_g - V_T. \quad (23)$$

This becomes an exact relationship for the case of an intrinsic substrate and starts deviating from linearity as the substrate doping increases.

IV. Results and Discussion

Measurements were performed on devices with a wide range of implant conditions. Results from two representative devices are presented. The first has a light shallow implant which is typical of what can be obtained from an E/D NMOS process. The second uses a heavier implant dose, thereby covering the various regions of operation from inversion to accumulation at the surface.

1) Experimental Results: Results of comparing the drain current-gate voltage characteristics of the device with shallow implant to model prediction are illustrated in Fig. 8. As shown in the figure, for gate voltages higher than the source voltage, the surface is accumulated and a reasonable matching between model and experiment is achieved only by using a surface mobility value lower than the bulk channel value. In this particular case, a surface mobility of about 50 percent of the bulk value is required. The implanted region parameters were obtained following the procedure outlined in Section III. Even though this device is only 8 μm long, it has exhibited very little evidence of short channel effects.

A set of dc and small-signal characteristics of the heavily implanted device is shown in Fig. 9. The parameters for this device are as given in Fig. 3. In Fig. 9(a), the drain current as a function of both gate and drain voltages is illustrated. As can be seen, the device cannot be turned off by applying a gate voltage for small values of source to substrate voltages (up to 6 V). Thus, a plot of the type shown in Fig. 6(c) would characterize the parameter V_{TIS} up to a source voltage of 6 V than the parameter V_T for higher V_s values. The role played by the surface inversion layer in screening the channel from the gate or alternatively making the substrate terminal more effective in modulating the channel is illustrated in Fig. 9(b) and (c). The behavior of the substrate transconductance g_{mb} under various conditions depends strongly on whether an inversion layer exists at the surface and whether the device is operating in saturation. The following points can be made regarding the behavior of g_{mb} [refer to Fig. 9(b)].

a) If the surface is depleted or accumulated, then g_{mb} is independent of V_g since the signal applied to the substrate terminal does not affect the surface space-charge region.

b) As the gate voltage is decreased to cause inversion at the source end, the channel is now modulated from both sides and g_{mb} starts to increase. Further decrease of gate voltage causes the inversion layer to propagate towards the drain, thereby increasing g_{mb}. This continues until the whole length of the channel is inverted, at which point g_{mb} reaches a maximum value.

c) If the drain end is pinched off, the voltage at the drain end of the channel (V_{mp}) becomes a function of V_g and thus reduces as V_g is decreased (see Fig. 7). This results in a reduction of g_{mb} (e.g., the two curves corresponding to $V_s = 4, 6$ V) until the source end inverts ($V_s = 4$ V) where g_{mb} rises again or the device is cut off ($V_s = 6$ V).

Similar points can be made regarding the behavior of the gate transconductance g_m shown in Fig. 9(c). The difference here is that the inversion layer plays an opposite role, i.e., once it starts to form, it screens the channel from the signal on the gate and results in a sharp drop in g_m.

In Fig. 9(d), the total gate capacitance is shown as a function of gate-substrate voltage. This figure illustrates the various modes of operation for the device as the gate voltage is changed from a large negative voltage to a large positive voltage. Since the source and drain voltages are equal, the conditions existing at the surface are uniform from the source to the drain. At a large negative gate voltage, the implanted region is fully depleted all the way between the source and the drain, and the surface conditions are adequate for the creation of an inversion layer. Thus, the total gate capacitance is equal to the gate-to-substrate component which is the oxide capacitance. As the gate voltage increases, the inversion layer disappears and the gate-to-substrate capacitance is now the series combination of oxide capacitance, implanted layer capacitance, and p-n junction (formed by the implanted region and the substrate) capacitance. Further increase in the gate voltage causes the channel to start forming, which gives rise to the sudden increase in the capacitance due to the two capacitance components C_{gs} and C_{gd}. The channel starts widening as the gate voltage increases and the surface space-charge region thickness reduces, resulting in a gradual increase in C_{gs} and C_{gd}. Finally, the surface region thickness becomes zero and the surface becomes accumulated, in which case the sum of C_{gs} and C_{gd} reaches the oxide capacitance again.

2) Discussion: Some of the advantages of using a depletion-mode device as the load element in an inverter configuration are high channel mobility, low surface-generated noise, and close resemblance to a current source. In addition to these, the depletion-mode device contributes only small capacitance loading at the output node. This would be the case for proper matching of the process parameters and the voltage used. In Fig. 10(a), the various capacitance components contributed to the output node by a load device having a low implant dose are shown. It is obvious that as long as the device is operating in the saturation mode, it contributes less than 20 percent of the gate oxide capacitance. However, once in the linear region, the component C_{gd} increases rapidly towards half of the oxide capacitance. The same type of plot is shown in Fig. 10(b) for a larger implant dose and deeper channel. In this case, the device enters the linear region at relatively lower voltages and the loading of the output mode is more severe. To illustrate these advantages, Fig. 10(c) shows the contribution of a saturated enhancement device to the output node which is approximately 70 percent of the oxide capacitance of the device over most of the voltage range.

V. Conclusions

A nonlinear dc and charging current model for the depletion-mode IGFET has been presented. The model is defined in terms of basic processing related parameters which can be obtained from a simple set of terminal measurements. A systematic procedure for deriving the various capacitance components of the model has been presented which is computationally very efficient and directly usable in circuit simulation programs. The device model describes device operation in all voltage ranges and all surface conditions. Measurements are presented on various dc and small-signal parameters. Finally, it is shown that the contribution of the device capacitance to the output node capacitance is one of the important factors to be considered when designing a process to ensure that the load device is operating in the saturation mode over most of the voltage range covered by the output node.

Appendix

Derivation of Model Parameters

As an example to illustrate the systematic approach to deriving the various dc and capacitance parameters, we apply these formulas to some of the regions of operations. Consider the case where inversion exists along the whole surface where we have

$$Q_m = -Q_i + (K_E + K_N)\sqrt{V_m} \tag{A1}$$

$$Q_g = C_0 V_{mg} \tag{A2}$$

and

$$Q_b = -(K_E + K_N)\sqrt{V_m} - C_0 V_{mg}. \tag{A3}$$

Therefore,

$$I_d = \frac{\mu W}{L}\left[Q_i(V_{md} - V_{ms}) - \tfrac{2}{3}(K_E + K_N)(V_{md}^{3/2} - V_{ms}^{3/2})\right] \tag{A4}$$

$$F_G = -Q_i C_0 V_{mg}(V_{md} - V_{ms}) + \tfrac{2}{3} C_0 V_{mg}(K_E + K_N) \cdot (V_{md}^{3/2} - V_{ms}^{3/2}), \tag{A5}$$

$$F_B = \tfrac{2}{3} Q_i(K_E + K_N)(V_{md}^{3/2} - V_{ms}^{3/2}) - \tfrac{1}{2}(K_E + K_N)^2(V_{md}^2 - V_{ms}^2) - F_G. \tag{A6}$$

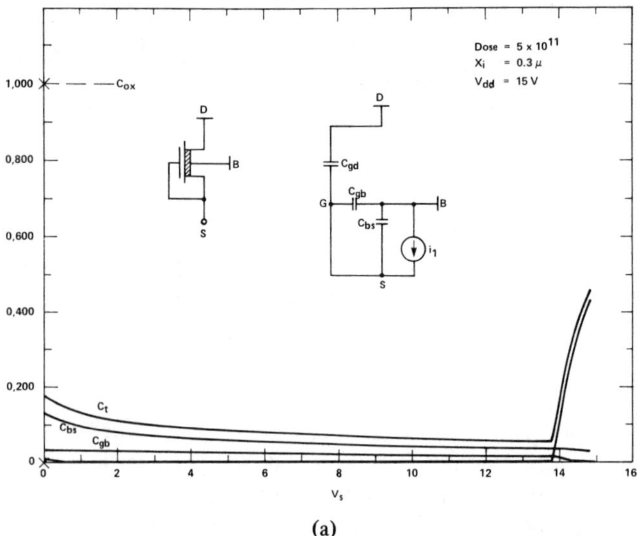

(a)

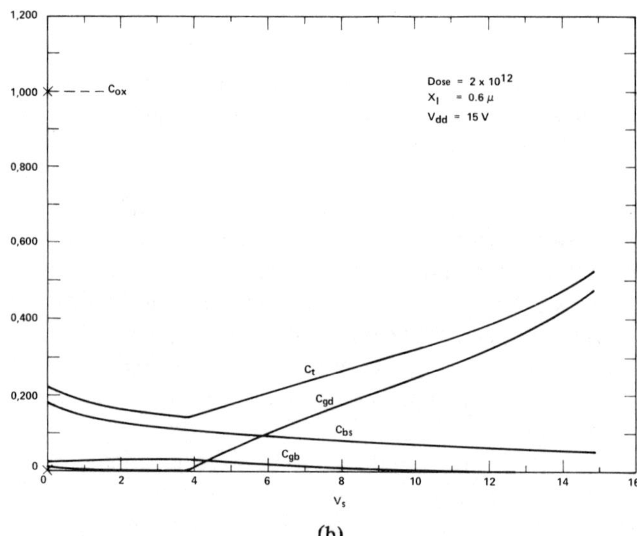

(b)

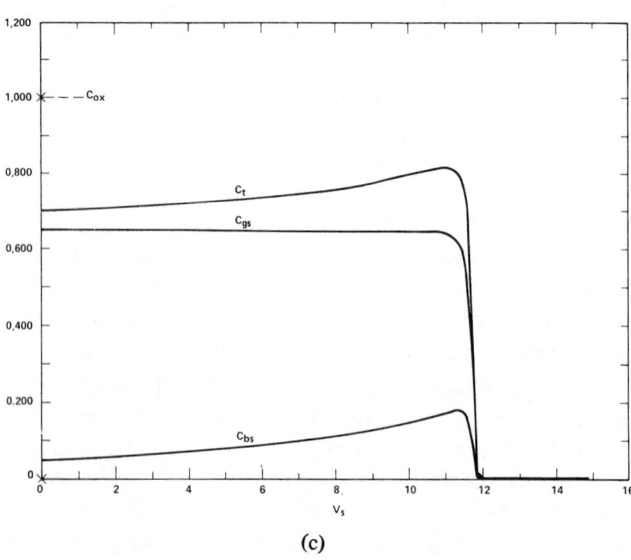

(c)

Fig. 10. A plot of capacitance components contributed by load device at the output node of an inverter as a function of the voltage at that node (a) for a lightly implanted device, (b) for a heavily implanted device, and (c) for an enhancement device.

The conductances are written as

$$g_d = \frac{\mu W}{L} [Q_i - (K_E + K_N) V_{md}^{1/2}] \tag{A7}$$

$$g_m = 0 \tag{A8}$$

$$g_s = -\frac{\mu W}{L} [Q_i - (K_E + K_N) V_{ms}^{1/2}] \tag{A9}$$

$$g_b = \frac{\mu W}{L} (K_E + K_N) (V_{md}^{1/2} - V_{ms}^{1/2}). \tag{A10}$$

The derivatives of the charge functions are

$$F_{GS} = -C_0 V_{mg} g_s \Big/ \left(\frac{\mu W}{L}\right) \tag{A11}$$

$$F_{GD} = -C_0 V_{mg} g_d \Big/ \left(\frac{\mu W}{L}\right) \tag{A12}$$

$$F_{GB} = (C_0 I_d - C_0 V_{mg} g_b) \Big/ \left(\frac{\mu W}{L}\right) \tag{A13}$$

and

$$F_{BS} = (K_N + K_E) V_{ms}^{1/2} g_s \Big/ \left(\frac{\mu W}{L}\right) - F_{GS} \tag{A14}$$

$$F_{BD} = (K_N + K_E) V_{ms}^{1/2} g_d \Big/ \left(\frac{\mu W}{L}\right) - F_{GD} \tag{A15}$$

$$F_{BG} = -F_G / V_{mg}. \tag{A16}$$

The six capacitance components can then be constructed using (16) and the relevant expressions for each capacitance component.

Acknowledgment

The author wishes to acknowledge the many stimulating discussions with his colleagues at BNR. Special thanks are due to A. R. Boothroyd for his contributions to this work and for constructive criticism of the manuscript. The comments made by the reviewers of the paper improved the clarity of the presentation for which the author is grateful.

References

[1] L. Forbes, "n-channel ion-implanted enhancement/depletion FET circuit and fabrication technology," *IEEE J. Solid-State Circuits*, vol. SC-8, pp. 226–230, June 1973.

[2] F. F. Fang and H. S. Rupprecht, "High performance MOS integrated circuits using ion-implantation technique," *IEEE J. Solid-State Circuits*, vol. SC-10, pp. 205–211, Aug. 1975.

[3] B. J. Hosticka *et al.*, "MOS sampled data recursive filters using switched capacitor integrators," *IEEE J. Solid-State Circuits*, vol. SC-12, pp. 600–608, Dec. 1977.

[4] See, for example, *1978 IEEE ISSC Dig. Tech. Papers:*
a) E. M. Blaser and D. A. Conrad, "FET logic configuration," pp. 14–15.
b) R. W. Knepper, "Dynamic depletion mode: An E/D MOSFET circuit method," pp. 16–17.
c) R. A. Blouschild *et al.*, "An NMOS voltage reference," pp. 50–51.

[5] J. R. Edwards and G. Marr, "Depletion-mode IGFET made by deep ion-implantation," *IEEE Trans. Electron Devices*, vol. ED-20, pp. 283–289, Mar. 1973.

[6] J. S. Huang and G. W. Taylor, "Modeling of an ion-implanted silicon-gate depletion-mode IGFET," *IEEE Trans. Electron Devices*, vol. ED-22, pp. 995–1000, Nov. 1975.

[7] C. G. Verbracken *et al.*, "Impurity profile determination and DC modeling of the JIGFET," *IEEE Trans. Electron Devices*, vol. ED-24, pp. 723–730, June 1977.

[8] R. A. Haken, "Analysis of the deep depletion MOSFET and the use of the DC characteristics for determining bulk-channel charge-coupled device parameters," *Solid-State Electron.*, vol. 21, pp. 753–761, 1978.

[9] A. M. Mohsen and F. J. Morris, "Measurements on depletion-mode field-effect transistors and buried channel MOS capacitors for the characterization of bulk transfer charge-coupled devices," *Solid-State Electron.*, vol. 18, pp. 407–416, 1975.

[10] G. Lubberts and B. C. Burkey, "Capacitance and doping profiles of ion-implanted buried-channel MOSFETs," *Solid-State Electron.*, vol. 22, pp. 47–54, 1979.

[11] J. A. Robinson, Y. A. El-Mansy, and A. R. Boothroyd, "A general four-terminal charging-current model for the insulated-gate field-effect transistor," *Solid-State Electron.*, vol. 22, 1979.

Section 1.3
Circuit Techniques

Eliminating Threshold Losses in MOS Circuits by Bootstrapping Using Varactor Coupling

REUBEN E. JOYNSON, JOSEPH L. MUNDY, MEMBER, IEEE, JAMES F. BURGESS, AND CONSTANTINE NEUGEBAUER, MEMBER, IEEE

***Abstract*—Threshold losses reduce speed and increase power consumption of MOS digital circuits. A method to eliminate these losses is described. This is accomplished by the application of bootstrapping, in which a temporarily isolated circuit node is capacitatively coupled to the input voltage. The advantages of a MOS varactor element and its use for the coupling capacitor are described.**

Notation

α	$= 1 - r$.
C_b	Coupling capacitance.
C_d	Depletion layer capacitance per unit area.
C_L	Output load capacitance.
C_0	Gate oxide capacitance per unit area.
C_S	Parasitic capacitance of node S.
ΔV_S	Change in voltage on node S during bootstrapping.
d_{ox}	Gate oxide thickness.
K_1	Backgate bias coefficient.
L	Length of varactor gate.
l	Overlap between varactor gate and drain.
μ_0	Hole mobility.
r	Bootstrap ratio.
$t_{\frac{1}{2}}$	Time required for the output voltage to rise to $\frac{1}{2}$ of its final value.
V_{BS}	Source to substrate potential difference.
V_d	Voltage on drain of transistor T_2.
V_d (max)	Voltage to which drain of transistor T_2 must be raised for maximum voltage on node S.
V_{in}	Input voltage.
V_{out}	Output voltage.
V_{prech}	Precharge voltage.
V_S	Voltage on node S.
V_S (max)	maximum voltage to which node S can be raised by varactor bootstrapping.
V_{S0}	Initial voltage on node S.
V_T	Threshold voltage.
V_{T0}	Threshold voltage without back-gating correction.
W	Width of varactor gate.

Introduction

IT IS A characteristic of the MOS transistor that the source voltage cannot rise higher than within one threshold voltage of the gate voltage. If the source rises higher (higher negative voltage for p-channel devices), then the surface under the gate is no longer inverted, but is depleted. Since charge carriers are therefore no longer available, the current is cut off and the source potential cannot rise further.

Manuscript received April 5, 1971; revised July 26, 1971.

The authors are with the General Electric Corporate Research and Development Center, Schenectady, N. Y.

TABLE I
OUTPUT VOLTAGES FOR MOS DIODES IN SERIES AS A FUNCTION OF INPUT VOLTAGE

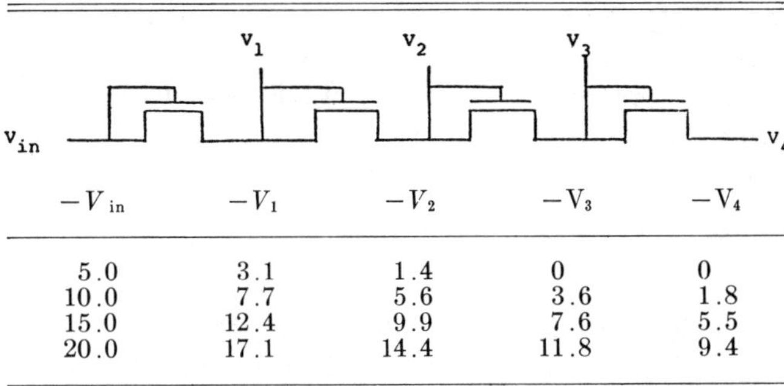

$-V_{in}$	$-V_1$	$-V_2$	$-V_3$	$-V_4$
5.0	3.1	1.4	0	0
10.0	7.7	5.6	3.6	1.8
15.0	12.4	9.9	7.6	5.5
20.0	17.1	14.4	11.8	9.4

Diodes are p channel; substrate resistivity—5 Ωcm; d_{ox}—1000 A, $V_{T0} = -1.0$ V, $V_{BS} = +3.0$ V.

In integrated circuits, where the source is generally not at the substrate potential, the channel becomes reverse biased with respect to the substrate and the threshold voltage varies with the voltage difference between source and substrate V_{BS} according to [1]

$$V_T = V_{T0} - K_1(\sqrt{2\phi_F + V_{BS}} - \sqrt{2\phi_F}) \quad (1)$$

where

V_{T0}	threshold voltage if source and substrate are at equal potentials,
K_1	$= d_{0x}/\epsilon_{0x} \sqrt{2q\epsilon_s N}$,
d_{ox}	gate oxide thickness,
ϵ_{ox}	gate oxide permittivity,
q	electronic charge,
ϵ_s	silicon permittivity,
N	substrate doping density,
ϕ_F	amount Fermi level is displaced from the midgap position.

Therefore, the source voltage can rise to only

$$V_{(source)} = V_{(gate)} - V_{T0} + K_1(\sqrt{2\phi_F + V_{BS}} - \sqrt{2\phi_F}). \quad (2)$$

According to (2), the source voltage can be considerably below the gate voltage, depending on the gate oxide thickness, substrate doping, and substrate bias. Table I

Reprinted from *IEEE J. Solid-State Circuits*, vol. SC-7, pp. 217–224, June 1972.

illustrates this by listing the voltage at the output nodes of four MOS diodes connected in series as a function of various input voltages. The output voltages can be seen to be considerably lower than the input voltages. To compensate for this voltage loss, high input voltages are required, considerably higher than T^2L levels, for instance. This requirement is a major disadvantage of MOS circuitry.

In this paper, a method is described that reduces or completely eliminates this voltage loss in dynamic MOS circuits by bootstrapping with the use of a voltage-variable capacitor (varactor). While bootstrapping is well known in circuits, the use of varactors for this effect is new.

Storage Nodes and Capacitative Coupling in Dynamic MOS Circuits

A unique feature of the MOS transistor is its almost infinite input resistance. Dynamic logic circuits utilize this high input resistance in the form of charge stored on a capacitor. The basic feature of dynamic MOS circuits is the storage node S, which can be raised to various voltage levels through transitor T_1, as illustrated in Fig. 1. Thus, by storing a logic "0" (below V_T) on S, transistor T_2 can be cut off; while by storing a logic "1", T_2 is conducting.

Two facts should be noted about the circuit in Fig. 1. First, V_{out} cannot rise to a voltage higher than two threshold voltages below V_{g1}. By referring to Table I, for example, it is found that for a value of $V_{g1} = -15$ V, V_{out} becomes -9.9 V. Second, with the gate of transistor T_1 off (below threshold), storage node S is isolated from the rest of the circuit, except for small leakage currents through the reverse-biased junction. The voltage on node S can now be changed by capacitively coupling to it. In particular, if S is considered to be one plate of a capacitor, then its voltage will change with the voltage on the other plate according to

$$\Delta V_s = \frac{\Delta V_b \cdot C_b}{C_s + C_b}$$

where

- ΔV_s change of voltage on node S,
- ΔV_b voltage change of the other plate of the coupling capacitance,
- C_b coupling capacitance,
- C_s parasitic capacitance between S and ground or other parts of the circuit.

Bootstrapping

Capacitative coupling can be used effectively to reduce or eliminate entirely the voltage loss due to gate thresholds. This is accomplished by using pulsed input voltages and inserting a coupling capacitance C_b between it and node S, as shown in Fig. 2.

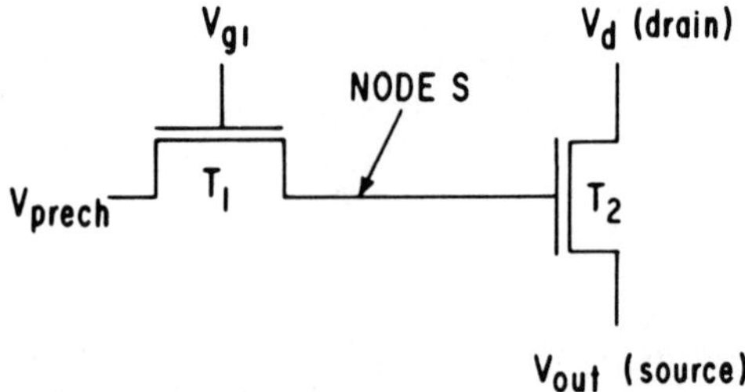

Fig. 1. Storage node S in dynamic MOS circuit.

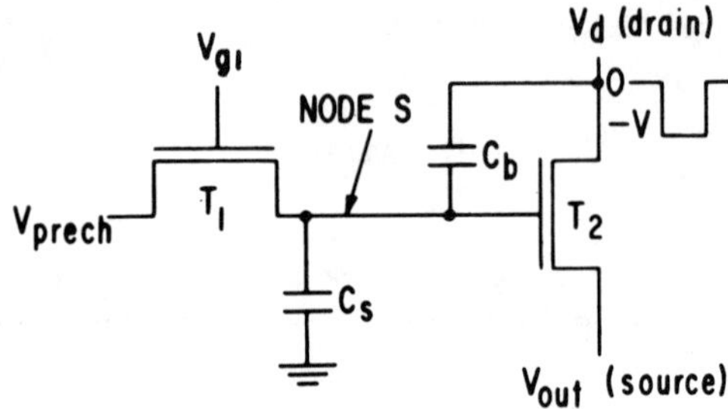

Fig. 2. Circuit incorporating bootstrap capacitor C_b.

When input voltage V_d turns on, node S will be bootstrapped to a higher voltage according to (3). In particular, if the ratio:

$$r = \frac{C_b}{C_s + C_b} \tag{4}$$

(called hereafter the bootstrap ratio) is large enough, the voltage on node S may rise sufficiently high that the full voltage of pulse V_d will appear at V_{out}. It should be noted that this requires that node S achieve a voltage at least V_T higher than V_d.

Bootstrapping by MOS Varactors

An interesting case of bootstrapping is encountered if the coupling capacitor in Fig. 2 is not of the ordinary voltage invariant kind, but changes its capacitance with the voltage across it (varactor). Varactors are easy to fabricate by MOS techniques as shown in Fig. 3(a).

The significance of using a varactor for bootstrapping in Fig. 2 is as follows. When the silicon surface is not inverted, the capacitance from gate to drain is only due to overlap. If inversion takes place, the channel forms a parallel-plate capacitor with the gate. Since current can flow from the channel to the drain, this relatively high capacitance appears effectively between the gate and drain.

Fig. 3(b) shows the capacitance between the gate and drain contact as a function of gate voltage. Below threshold the capacitance is small, given by

$$C = C_0 Wl, \qquad V_g < V_T. \tag{5}$$

Above threshold the surface under the gate is inverted and the whole gate area contributes to the capacitance:

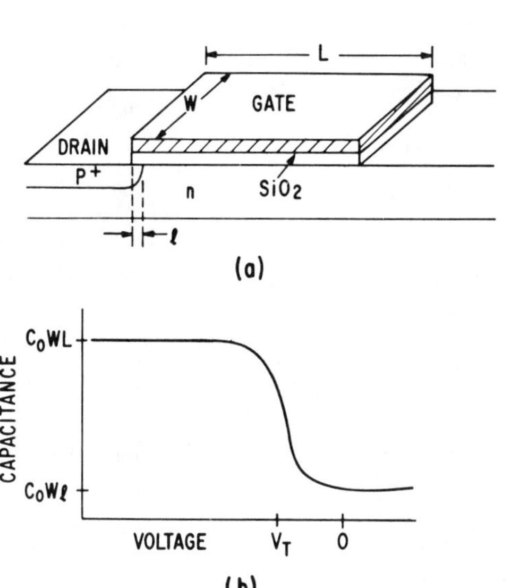

Fig. 3. (a) Schematic of MOS varactor. (b) Capacitance as function of voltage for MOS varactor.

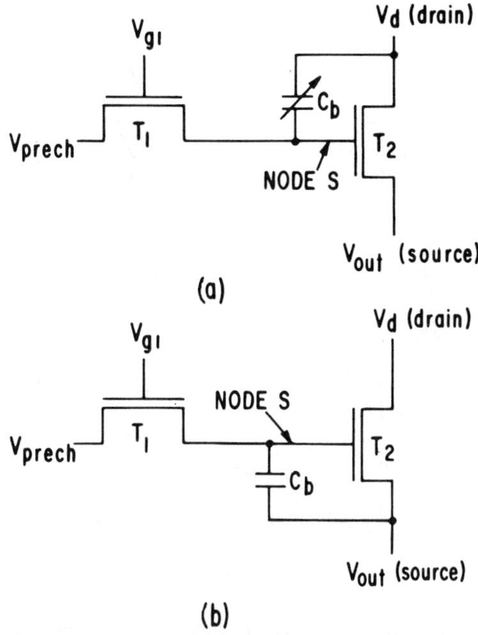

Fig. 4. Varactor bootstrapping of node S. (a) From drain of transistor T_2. (b) From source of transistor T_2.

$$C = C_0WL, \qquad V_g > V_T. \tag{6}$$

The transition is sharp and occurs within a few tenths of a volt. In Fig. 2 if node S is made the gate of a varactor, the drain of which is at potential V_d, it will couple only weakly to V_d if it is below the threshold voltage of V_d. In fact, below the threshold, C_b will add an amount somewhat less than $WC_0(L - l)$ to the parasitic capacitance C_s. Only if node S is above the threshold of T_2 will there be appreciable capacitative coupling between S and V_d.

Analysis of Bootstrapping by MOS Varactors

The basic elements for bootstrapping node S are shown in Fig. 4. The maximum voltage $V_s(\max)$ to which node S can be raised by varactor bootstrapping and the rise time of V_{out} will now be calculated.

Bootstrapping from Drain of T_2

If C_b had a fixed capacitance, the final voltage on node S would be given by

$$V_s = V_{S0} + rV_d \tag{7}$$

where V_s is the voltage on node S, V_{S0}, the initial voltage on node S, given by V_{prech} and V_{g1}, and V_d, the height of the pulse at the drain of T_2. However, if C_b is a varactor of the type shown in Fig. 3, its capacitance will decrease drastically when $V_s - V_d < V_T$. Therefore, maximum bootstrapping has taken place if V_d has risen to within one threshold voltage of V_S, i.e., if

$$V_s(\max) = V_d(\max) + V_{T0} + K_1(\sqrt{V_d + 2\phi_F} - \sqrt{2\phi_F}) \tag{8}$$

and if ϕ_F is neglected, one can solve (8) for V_d (max):

$$V_d(\max) = \frac{(2\alpha\gamma + K_1^2)}{2\alpha^2}\left[1 - \sqrt{1 - \frac{4\gamma^2\alpha^2}{(2\alpha\gamma + K_1^2)^2}}\right] \tag{9}$$

where

$$\alpha = 1 - r$$

$$\gamma = V_{S0} - V_{T0}.$$

$V_s(\max)$ then is obtained by substituting this result in (7). Values of $V_s(\max)$ are shown in Fig. 5 for 5-Ωcm material and for $K_1 = 0.5$ as a function of various ratios r and V_{S0}. Since V_{T0} is variable due to impurities and substrate bias, it is left as a parameter. It is clear that bootstrapping becomes more effective at higher values of r and the initial voltage on node S.

Not only does the enhanced voltage on node S increase the output voltage at the source of T_2, but the rise time of V_{out} is also decreased. Applying a step voltage to V_d, the rise time of the source follower configuration in Fig. 4(a) is given by

$$t_{1/2} = \frac{2C_L}{\beta V_{out}(\max)} \tag{10}$$

where $t_{1/2}$ is the time for the output to rise to $\frac{1}{2}$ its final value β, the gain of T_2,C_L, the load capacitance at the source output, and $V_{out}(\max)$, the final value of the output voltage. For example, consider the case $r = 0.9$ and $(V_{S0} - V_{T0}) = 4$. From Fig. 5 one gets $V_s(\max) - V_{T0} \approx V_{out} = 20$ V. The rise time is decreased and the value of the output voltage is increased by a factor of 5 due to varactor bootstrapping.

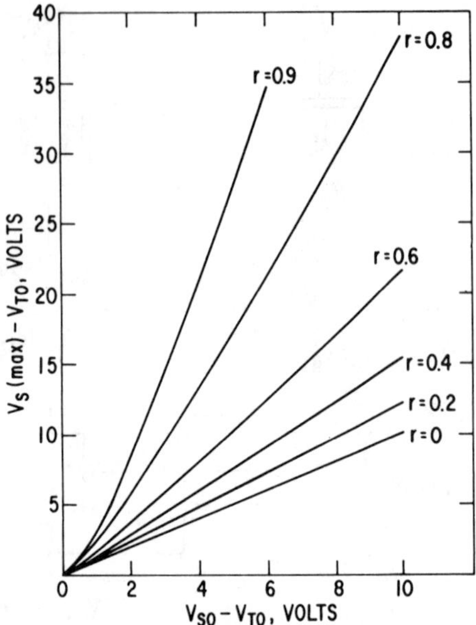

Fig. 5. Maximum voltages to which node S can be raised by varactor bootstrapping as a function of the initial voltage for various bootstrap ratios.

Bootstrapping from the Source of T_2

The sharp switching characteristic of the varactor is necessary to prevent an appreciable increase in the voltage of node S if it is not selected, i.e., if it is initially below threshold. An alternative approach, which has been indicated earlier by Lund *et al.* [2], also results in an enhanced gate voltage but does not require a nonlinear capacitor. This approach is shown in Fig. 4(b).

Here a capacitor is placed between the source and gate of T_2. If the initial voltage on node S is above the threshold, the source will rise, and thus, through capacitative coupling, node S will rise also. If, on the other hand, the initial voltage is below the threshold, the source will not rise and no coupling to node S through the bootstrap capacitor will occur. The maximum voltage $V_S(\max)$ to which node S can be raised by this method is identical to that described above for the case of bootstrapping from the drain side of T_2 and is shown in Fig. 5. However, in this case, the maximum voltage on node S is reached when the source of T_2 (V_{out}) has risen to within V_T of node S, i.e., (8) now becomes

$$V_S\ (\max) = V_{\text{out}} + V_{TO} + K_1\sqrt{V_{\text{out}}} \tag{11a}$$

(neglecting ϕ_F) and (7) becomes

$$V_S = V_{SO} + rV_{\text{out}}. \tag{11b}$$

This is in contrast to $V_s(\max)$ being determined when V_s is previously within a threshold of V_d. Therefore, for bootstrapping from the source of T_2, a varactor is not needed and can be replaced by an ordinary metal plate capacitor.

While $V_s(\max)$ and therefore also $V_{\text{out}}(\max)$ will be the same for both cases, the rise times will be much longer for the case of bootstrapping from the source side of T_2. To calculate the rise time of V_{out} after applying a step voltage to the drain of transistor T_2, we write the instantaneous current through T_2 (assuming T_2 operating in the pinched-off region) as

$$C_L\frac{dV_{\text{out}}(t)}{dt} = \frac{\beta}{2}[V_s - V_T - V_{\text{out}}(t)]^2 \tag{12}$$

where C_L is the output load capacitance, including the bootstrap capacitor. Substituting (11b) and letting $K_1 = 0$ for simplicity gives

$$C_L\frac{dV_{\text{out}}(t)}{dt} = \frac{\beta}{2}[(V_{SO} - V_{TO}) - \alpha V_{\text{out}}(t)]^2. \tag{13}$$

Integrating and solving for the time needed to reach $\frac{1}{2}$ the ultimate value $V_{\text{out}}(\max)$:

$$t_{1/2} = \frac{2C_L}{\alpha^2\beta V_{\text{out}}(\max)}. \tag{14}$$

Equation (14) is similar to (10), except for the presence of α^2. For the example previously considered, namely $r = 0.9$ and $V_{SO} - V_{TO}) = 4$, the rise time of V_{out} would be 100 times longer.

"Intrinsic" Bootstrapping by Transistor T_2 Alone

For the purpose of the above calculations, it was assumed that the entire coupling capacitance between the drain of T_2 and node S resided entirely in capacitor C_b. However, this assumption is justified only if the area of the gate of transistor T_2 is negligible compared to the area of the gate capacitor C_b, or if C_b and V_d are pulsed from different power supplies. If the gate of T_2 is not small, significant bootstrapping of node S will take place through coupling between the gate and channel capacitance. For practical purposes, $\frac{1}{2}$ of this capacitance couples to the drain side of T_2 and $\frac{1}{2}$ to the source side. Thus, the rise time of V_{out} for "intrinsic" bootstrapping of node S is somewhere between the rise times given by (10) and (14).

Dynamics of Channel Charge Redistribution in MOS Varactor

After the drain of the varactor has been subjected to a step voltage V_d, the excess positive charge in the channel will need some nonzero time to flow into the drain. The application of V_d causes a potential well to form at the drain and the holes in the vicinity of this well will flow into it by field-assisted diffusion. The situation becomes quite comparable to that involving surface change transport in silicon described by Engeler *et al.* [3], who give for the time dependence of the charge density in the channel

$$\frac{\partial f}{\partial t} = \frac{\partial}{x}\left(\frac{\mu_0 C_0(V_{SO} - V_T)}{C_0 + C_d} f \frac{\partial f}{\partial x}\right) \tag{15}$$

TABLE II

Time (ns) Required for ΔV_s to Reach 90 Percent of Its Final Value, as a Function of Precharge Voltage V_{S0} and Varactor Gate Lengths L (in mils) According to (16).

$V_{S0} - V_T$	$L = 0.3$	$L = 0.5$	$L = 1.0$	$L = 5.0$
1	36	104	390	10 400
2	18	52	190	5200
3	12	35	130	3500
4	9.2	26	98	2600
5	7.3	21	78	2100
6	6.1	18	66	1800
10	3.6	10	39	1000

where

- f channel charge density function $= \rho_x/\rho_L$,
- x distance of charge from the drain,
- ρ_x channel charge density at a distance x from the drain,
- ρ_L channel charge density at a distance L from the drain,
- μ_0 hole mobility,
- C_d depletion-layer capacitance.

An approximate solution for 90 percent change transfer, which for this application corresponds to the time required for the voltage increase ΔV_S of the gate being bootstrapped to reach 90 percent of its final value after the application of a step voltage V_d, is

$$t_{90\text{ percent}} = 6.2 \frac{C_0 + C_d}{C_0\mu_0} \frac{L^2}{(V_{S0} - V_T)} \text{ s.} \qquad (16)$$

Approximate values are given in Table II for some values of V_{S0} and L. Gate lengths should in general be kept below 1 mil, particularly if V_{S0} is small.

For a more exact evaluation, (15) is plotted in Fig. 6(a) and (b). In Fig. 6(a) the channel charge density function ρ_x/ρ_L is plotted as a function of the distance from the drain X/L, for various values of the time t/T after application of a step voltage V_d to the drain. Here T is defined as $T = 4L^2/D_0$; D_0 is the hole diffusivity, given by $D_0 = [\mu_0 C_0(V_{S0} - V_T)]/(C_0 + C_d)$. Fig. 6(b) shows the total channel charge under the gate of the varactor Q/Q_0 as a function of time t/T. In constructing these curves, the value of $C_0/(C_0 + C_d)$ was taken to be 0.5.

If varactor gate lengths smaller than 0.5 mil are used, the time required for channel charge redistribution will, in general, be negligible compared to the rise times of V_{out} calculated above. However, if these times become comparable, they should be added together for a worst case estimate.

Comparison With Experiment

Circuits incorporating three different bootstrap ratios were constructed and tested. Two circuits will be discussed. The first is the precharged node circuit shown in Fig. 4(a), in which the isolated node is the output of a

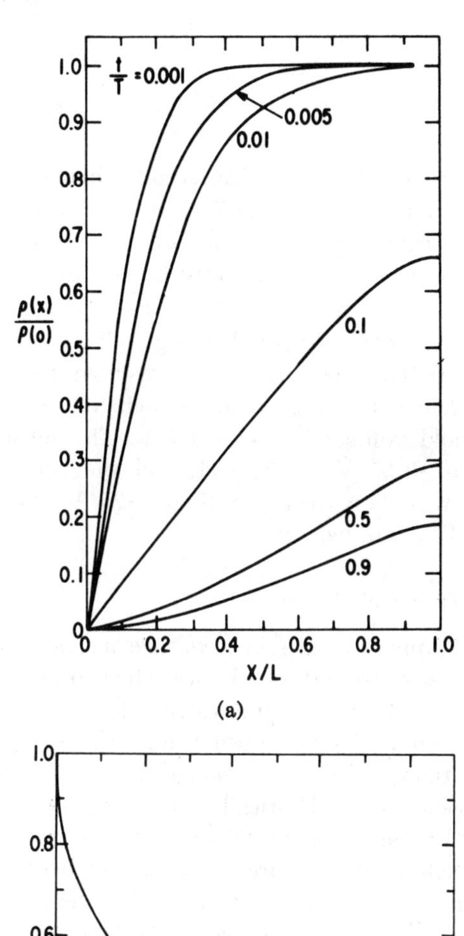

(a)

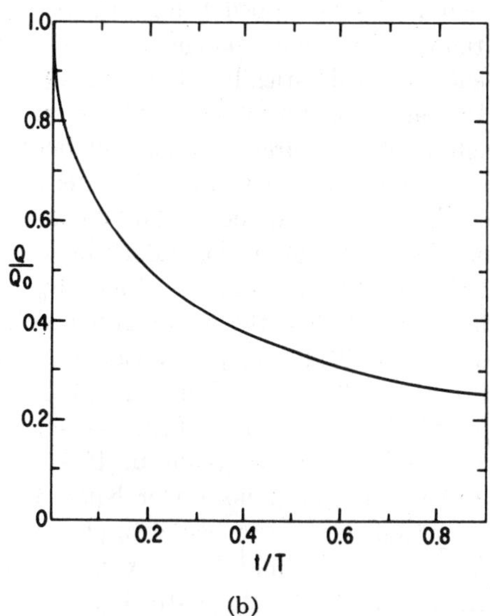

(b)

Fig. 6. (a) Channel charge density under gate of MOS varactor as a function of distance from the drain, for various times elapsed after the application of a step voltage to the drain. (b) Total channel under gate of MOS varactor as a function of time after application of a step voltage to the drain.

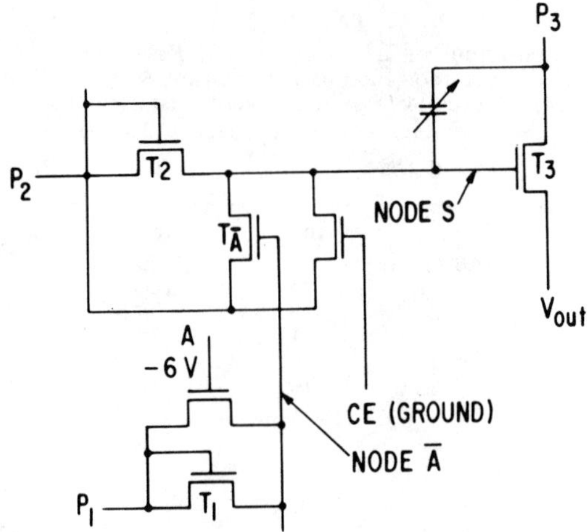

Fig. 7. NOR gate decoder circuit.

diode precharged with dc. The second circuit is the NOR gate decoder shown in Fig. 7. Output voltages are compared to calculated values according to the equations above, for various bootstrap ratios and precharge voltages.

Circuits were fabricated using self-registering gate techniques. The (100) orientation was used in conjunction with 5-Ωcm resistivity, to make p-channel circuits with a threshold voltage $V_{TO} = -1.0$ V. The substrate was biased at +2.5 V during test, and the field threshold voltage was more negative than −25 V. All voltages (except V_{BS}) are negative.

A. *Precharged Node Circuit*

Bootstrapping results in a voltage increase of node S when V_{in} goes from 0 to $-V$, according to (3). Of particular interest is the maximum value of the voltage to which node S can be bootstrapped before $V_s - V_T$ becomes smaller than a threshold voltage and the coupling capacitance decreases drastically. Therefore, a pertinent test for MOS varactor bootstrapping is to measure V_s (max) as a function of precharge voltage and bootstrap ratio and compare the results with the calculated values given in Fig. 5. Since V_s cannot be measured directly without disturbing the bootstrap ratio, values of V_s (max) are obtained in the following manner. First, V_{prech} is set to a particular value. Then the pulsed input voltage V_{in} is increased in amplitude; V_{out} is measured and plotted against V_{in}. V_{out} will equal V_{in} up to a voltage V_{out} (max). At this point the capacitance of the varactor decreases and bootstrapping is much reduced. If V_{in} is now increased further, V_{out} will no longer equal V_{in}, but will increase much slower, since bootstrapping is limited to the overlap capacitance only. V_s (max) is then determined by adding a threshold voltage to V_{out} (max). This is illustrated in Fig. 8 for the case of $V_{prech} = 10$ V.

Values of V_s (max) determined in this manner are plotted against V_{prech} in Fig. 9 for bootstrap ratios of 0.12, 0.42, and 0.52. The points represent the experimental

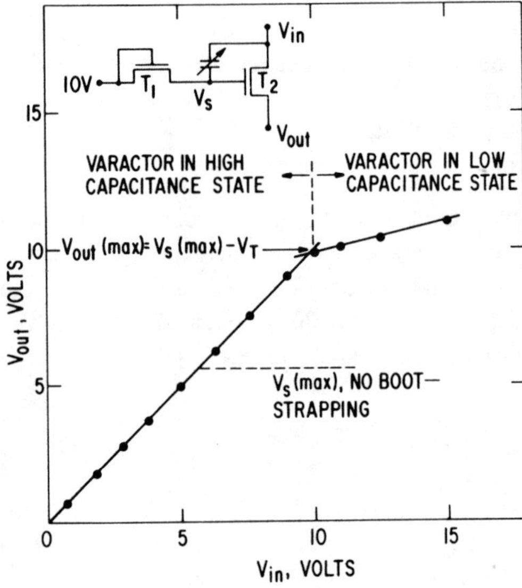

Fig. 8. V_{out} as a function of V_{in} for precharged node circuit, demonstrating method to obtain V_S(max).

values, while the lines are calculated from the geometry of the circuit and materials and process parameters. Calculated curves for $r = 0$, 0.9, and 1.0 are also given for reference.

An important practical parameter is the precharge voltage above which the voltage amplitude of V_{out} (max) is no longer limited by V_{prech}. Above the dotted line in Fig. 9 V_{out} (max) > V_{prech} and below it V_{out} (max) < V_{prech}. For instance, for a value of $r = 0.9$, a precharge voltage of more than 4 V must be reached if a value of $V_{out} > 4$ V is desired.

B. *NOR Gate Decoder (Fig. 7)*

Circuit operation is as follows. Phase P_1 precharges node $\bar{A}$ of transistor T_1. Since gate A is above threshold, however, $\bar{A}$ will discharge again when P_1 returns to ground. Phase P_2 precharges node S. Since transistor $T_{\bar{A}}$ is cut off before P_2 returns to ground, node S will remain

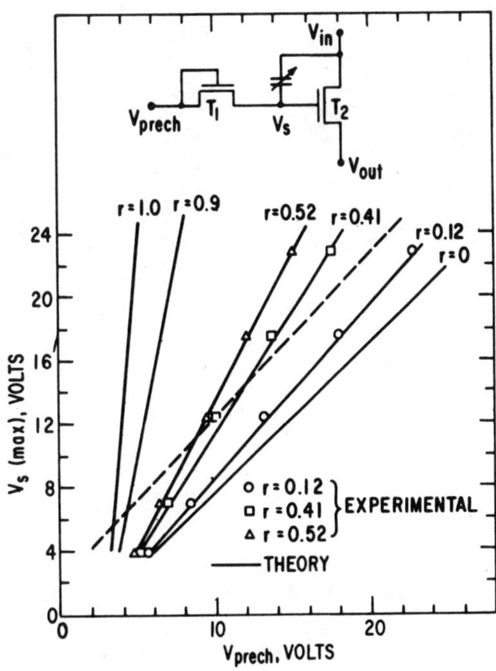

Fig. 9. V_S(max) as a function of V_{prech} for precharged node circuit. Above the dotted line V_{out}(max) > V_{prech}.

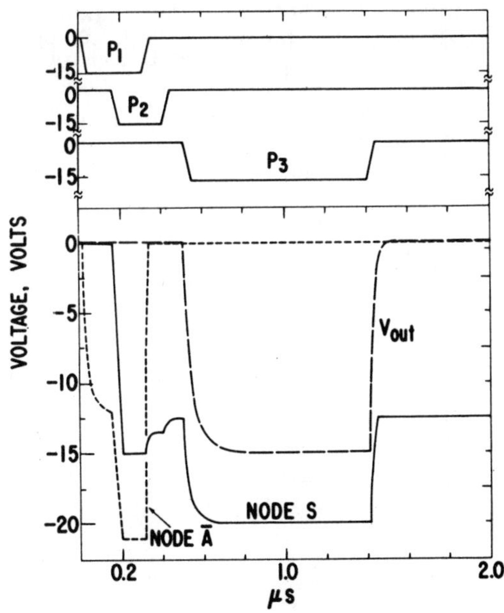

Fig. 10. Transient voltages on node $\bar{A}$, node S, and V_{out} calculated for the NOR gate decoder circuit in Fig. 7. Output load capacitance—2pF. Input voltage—15 V.

precharged. Phase P_3 will now bootstrap gate S through both, bootstrap capacitor C_b and the gate to channel capacitance of T_3. The final value of the output voltage then indicates how much bootstrapping of gate S actually occurred.

In addition to node S, node $\bar{A}$ is also isolated and can be subjected to bootstrapping. This is indeed the case if pulse P_2 follows but overlaps pulse P_1. Under these conditions, pulse P_2 turns on when node $\bar{A}$ is still above the threshold voltage of transistor $T_{\bar{A}}$, giving rise to "intrinsic" bootstrapping. In particular, if node $\bar{A}$ rises to a voltage that is a threshold above the phase voltage, node S can be precharged to a voltage equal to the height of pulse P_2.

Fig. 10 shows the voltage on node $\bar{A}$, node S, and V_{out} during circuit operation for $P_1 = P_2 = P_3 = 15$ V, and

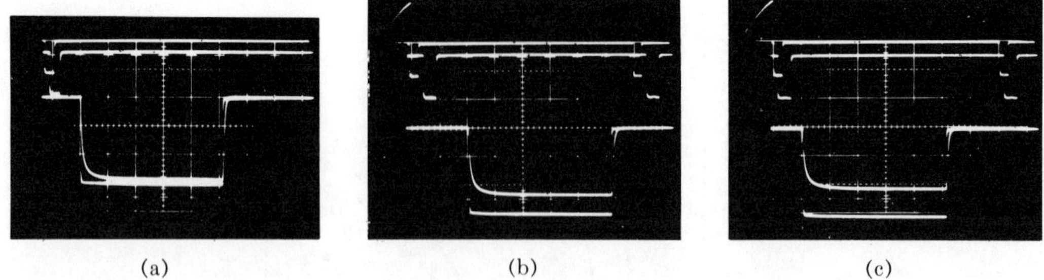

(a) (b) (c)

Fig. 11. Experimental values of V_{out} for the NOR gate decoder circuit shown in Fig. 7 for input voltages $P_1 = 12$ V, $P_2 = 15$ V, $P_3 = 15$ V, and output load capacitance = 15 pF. Horizontal scale: 5 μs/div. Vertical scale: Upper two traces P_1 and P_2, 10 V/div; lower two traces P_3 and V_{out}, 5 V/div. (a) $r = 0.41$, P_1 and P_2 overlap. (b) $r = 0.12$, P_1 and P_2 overlap. (c) $r = 0.41$, P_1 and P_2 do not overlap.

$r = 0.41$. The curves were obtained from calculations using geometric, material, and process parameters only and assuming an output load capacitance of 2 pF. It is seen that voltages in excess of 20 V are obtained on these nodes, although input voltages do not exceed 15 V. When P_1 and P_2 return to ground, capacitative coupling results in some voltage decreases on node S. This is due to the presence of some stray coupling capacitance between P_1 and P_2 and S.

Scope traces of the input and output pulses from actual circuit tests are shown in Fig. 11(a)–(c). The output voltage charged a 15-pF load capacitance. The input pulses are $P_1 = 12$ V; $P_2 = 15$ V; $P_3 = 15$ V. Fig. 11(a) gives the traces for the circuit ($r = 0.41$), for which the calculated behavior is shown in Fig. 10. The output voltage equals P_3, which is in agreement with prediction. The traces in Fig. 11(b) show the input and output voltage for the same circuit, except that here $r = 0.12$. The output voltage is now 3.5 V lower due to the smaller bootstrap ratio. Fig. 11(c), on the other hand, is again for a ratio of 0.41, but phases P_1 and P_2 do not overlap, as they do in Fig. 11(a). This eliminates varactor bootstrapping to node $\bar{A}$ and reduces the voltage to which node S is precharged, thus leading to a lowered V_{out}.

References

[1] R. Crawford, *Mosfet in Circuit Design.* New York: McGraw-Hill, 1967, pp. 37–45.

[2] D. Lund, C. A. Allen, S. R. Andersen, and G. K. Tu, *1970 Fall Joint Computer Conf., AFIPS Conf. Proc.*, vol. 37, 1970, p. 53.

[3] W. E. Engeler, J. J. Tiemann, and R. D. Baertsch, "Surface charge transport in silicon," *Appl. Phys. Lett.*, vol. 17, p. 469, 1970.

A MOST Inverter With Improved Switching Speed

JAN KOOMEN AND JOOP VAN DEN AKKER

Abstract—**A modified MOST inverter circuit consisting of a driver, load, and bias MOST is proposed. The gate voltage of the load MOST is supplied by the bias MOST. This leads to an improvement of both the output pulse height and the switching speed if the circuit is applied in dynamic logic.**

The switching transients are studied by considering first the dynamic loadlines of the driver and the load MOST, and second an analytical function has been developed predicting the 10–90 percent turnoff time of the circuit. The theoretical turn-off times are found to be in agreement with measurements on a breadboard circuit and from this a maximum gain in 10–90 percent turn-off time of the modified inverter of about a factor of 3, as compared with a conventional MOST inverter, appears to be attainable.

The modified inverter circuit may also be used in static logic with conservation of its full advantages, provided that the minimum switching period is about 50 ns.

I. Introduction

Usually a MOST inverter consists of an active driver and a passive load MOST in series [1], both of the p-channel type (Fig. 1). A disadvantage of this type of circuit is that the output pulse is characterized by a relatively large turn-off time.

A modified MOST inverter consisting of three p-channel MOST's is presented. In this inverter the active load MOST remains in the conductive state during the switching transients due to a capacitive feedback to its gate, which leads to an improved output-pulse shape and a decreased turn-off time.

Section II deals with the operation of the modified inverter circuit on the basis of the dynamic loadlines of the driver and the load MOST. Furthermore the 10–90 percent turn-off time will be expressed in an analytical form. The principle of the modified inverter will be demonstrated with measurements on a breadboard circuit in Section III and compared with measurements on a conventional MOST inverter in Section IV.

Manuscript received March 8, 1971; revised September 1, 1971.

The authors are with the Department of Electronics, Twente University of Technology, Enschede, the Netherlands.

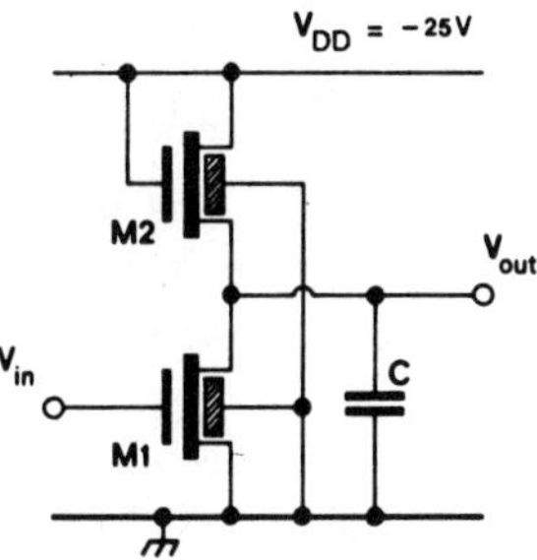

Fig. 1. Conventional MOST inverter circuit.

It is to be emphasized that all voltages are defined with respect to the bulk.

II. Modified MOST Inverter Circuit With Improved Switching Speed

This MOST inverter consists of three p-channel MOST's and the circuit together with a load capacitor C as shown in Fig. 2. The gate of the load MOST $M2$ has been connected to V_{DD} by a bias MOST $M3$ instead of being directly connected to V_{DD}.

A. Static Off and On States

In the static off and on states of the modified inverter, there is a small current flowing across the reverse-biased $p^+ - n$ junction formed by the $M3$ source-bulk junction.

Reprinted from *IEEE J. Solid-State Circuits*, vol. SC–7, pp. 231–237, June 1972.

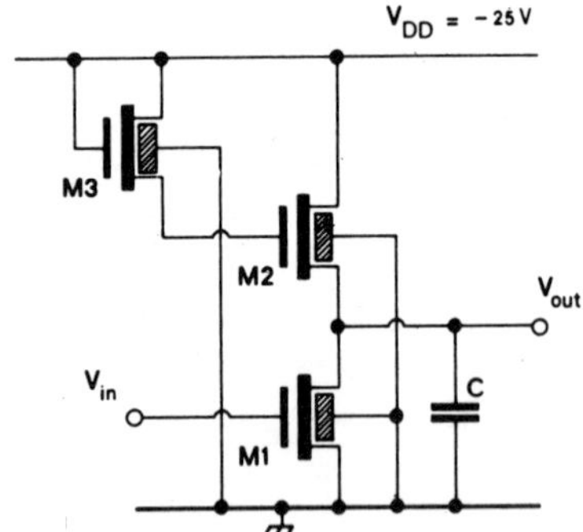

Fig. 2. Modified MOST inverter circuit.

This very small current must be supplied by channel conduction of $M3$, which is therefore operating on the verge of turn-on. Hence, the $M3$ source and the $M2$ gate are at the pinch-off potential V'_p corresponding to the gate voltage V_{DD}. This voltage V'_p can be found from the V_g versus V_p plot in Fig. 3 with $V_g = V_{DD}$.[1]

When the driver MOST $M1$ is turned off, $M2$ also operates on the verge of conduction because a similar reverse current is flowing across the source-bulk junction of $M2$. The potential V''_p of the source of $M2$ can now be found by the substitution of $V_g = V'_p$ in the V_g versus V_p graph of Fig. 3.

When $M1$ is turned on, V_{in} is large and negative and V_{out} assumes its maximum value V'_{max}, and $|V'_{max}|$ should be so small that an eventual subsequent inverter stage is turned off.

The $M1$ and $M2$ static-current characteristics of the modified inverter I_1 and I_3 are drawn in Fig. 4 together with the static characteristic I_2 of a conventional inverter with identical driver and load MOST.

B. Switching Transients

It is assumed that the internal response of $M1$ and $M2$ upon gate input signal has negligible delay [1, pp. 71–73] and that the charging and discharging of the load capacitance C in Fig. 2 limits the switching speed of V_{out}. This implies that during the switching transients the $M1$ driver and $M2$ load current-voltage characteristics remain quasi-static.

1) Turnoff Time: The advantage of incorporating the bias MOST $M3$ lies in the dynamic behavior of the circuit of Fig. 2. If the driver MOST $M1$ is on and suddenly switched off, the output voltage V_{out} falls towards a more negative value due to charging of the load capacitor C via $M2$. By action of the gate–source capacitance of $M2$, this decrease in V_{out} is transferred to the gate of $M2$ and the source of $M3$, and for simplicity this signal transfer is assumed to be complete. As described previously the source voltage of $M3$ was already equal to V'_p, the pinch-off voltage of the $M3$ source region corresponding to $V_g = V_{DD}$. A further decrease of the $M3$ source voltage will turn $M3$ completely out of conduction. This is obvious from the V_g versus V_p plot in Fig. 3. Both the $M3$ source- and drain-diffused regions now have a more negative potential than the pinch-off voltage V'_p, corresponding to the gate voltage $V_g = V_{DD}$. The $M3$ source and $M2$ gate are now isolated from the surroundings and follow the change of V_{out}. This means that during the decrease of V_{out} of the inverter, $M2$ keeps a constant gate–source voltage $V'_p - V'_{max}$, allowing V_{out} to make a full excursion to the battery voltage V_{DD}. The dynamic $M2$ load line I_4 during turnoff is illustrated in Fig. 4. $M2$ is in saturated operation in the first stage AB of its trajectory ABC during turnoff, the $M2$ pinch-off potential near its drain region follows the $M2$ gate voltage (in accordance to Fig. 3) until it reaches the value V_{DD}. At this moment $M2$ enters unsaturated operation (point B in Fig. 4). The corresponding $M2$ gate voltage V_{gB} can be obtained from Fig. 3 by the substitution $V_p = V_{DD}$ and, hence, it follows that the output voltage at state B is equal to $V_{gB} - (V'_p - V'_{max})$. When the output voltage approaches the battery voltage V_{DD}, the drain–source voltage of $M2$ approaches zero, so the current supplied by $M2$ will become zero and the gate voltage of $M2$ assumes a value $V_{DD} + (V'_p - V'_{max})$.

2) Analytical Description of the Turnoff Time: If it is supposed that the threshold voltage $V_{DD} - V_p$ is constant for all V_p values between V_{max} and V_{DD} (which appears to be justified by the measurement in Fig. 3); that

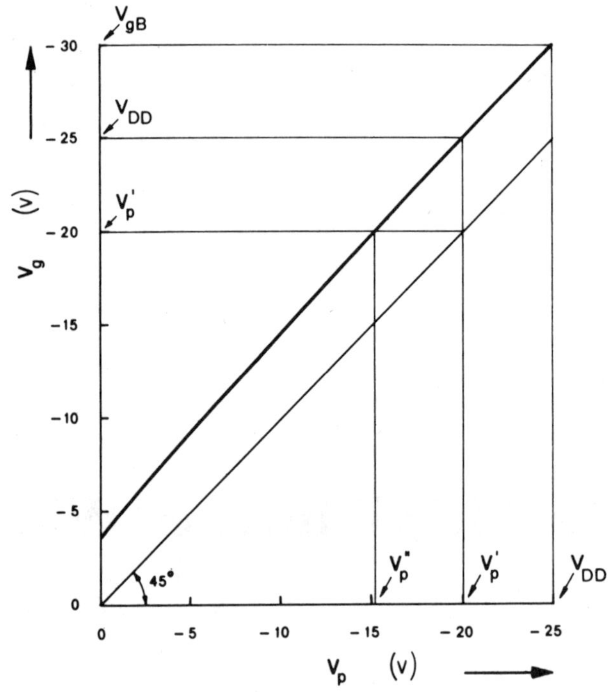

Fig. 3. V_g versus V_p plot.

[1] V_g versus V_p plots can be determined on MOS transistors by a measurement method described by Wallinga [2] and they are characteristic of a given MOS structure and independent of MOST geometry.

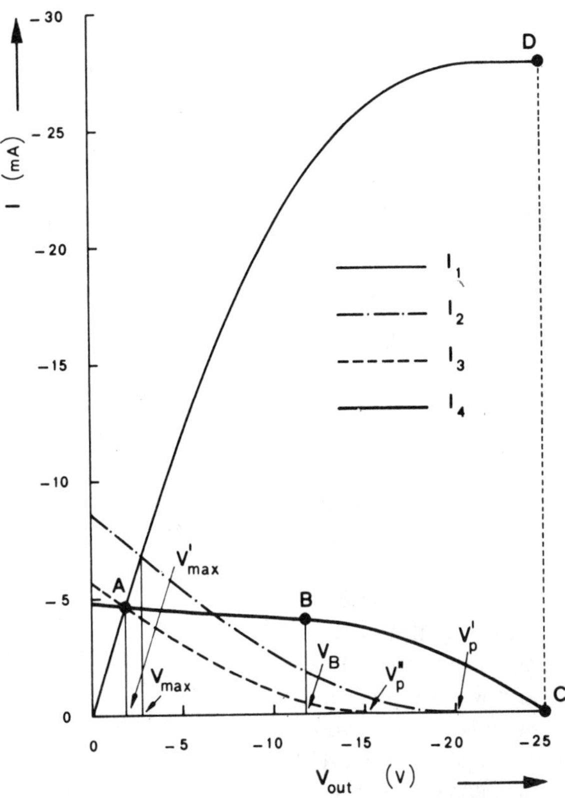

Fig. 4. $M1$ driver MOST current I_1 together with the static $M2$ load MOST currents I_2 and I_3 of the conventional and the modified inverters, respectively. The dynamic $M2$ loadline I_4 of the modified inverter is represented by the heavy solid line.

the $M1$ and $M2$ current characteristics are described by the MOST equations of van Nielen et al. [3], [4]; and that the signal transfer to the $M2$ gate of the modified inverter is complete, then the 10–90 percent turnoff time can be fixed in the following analytical form, as derived in the Appendix [5]

$$t_{off} = \frac{C}{\beta_{M2}a}\left\{2\left(\frac{0.9b - a}{a}\right) + \ln\left(\frac{2a - 0.1b}{0.1b}\right)\right\} \tag{1}$$

where

β_{M2} $= \mu A_{M2}C_0$,
μ mobility of the holes in the channel,
A_{M2} $M2$ aspect ratio,
C_0 gate oxide capacitance per unit area,
a $= |V''_p - V'_{max}|$,
b $= |V_{DD} - V'_{max}|$.

3) Turn-On Time: When the gate of the driver MOST $M1$ is switched to a negative voltage, we assume that the gate voltage of $M2$ is still equal to $V_{DD} + (V'_p - V'_{max})$. This will be true if the inverter is used dynamically, so that the switching periods will be short with respect to the leakage time constant of the $M3$ source-bulk junction. Now the state of operation of $M1$ is moved from state C to D in a negligible time (see Fig. 4). The output voltage V_{out} rises due to the discharge of C via $M1$. The load MOST $M2$ with isolated gate still tends to keep its gate–source voltage $V'_p - V'_{max}$. The path of operation of $M1$ and $M2$ is given in Fig. 4 by the trajectories CDA and CBA, respectively, and the load capacitor C will be discharged by the current $I_1 - I_4$.

The turn-on will be slightly longer than the turn-on time of the conventional inverter, because on the average the $M2$ load current I_4 is larger and the discharge current $I_1 - I_4$ is smaller.

The modified inverter is most suitable for dynamic use where the maximum switching period is limited. The behavior of the modified inverter, if used statically, will be treated in the discussion.

III. Measurements

The effect of a bias MOST was investigated on a breadboarded inverter circuit. The characteristics of the driver, load, and bias MOST are given in Table I. This inverter circuit is compared with a conventional inverter composed of the same driver and load MOST, $P16$ and $P17$ of Table I, respectively. The bias MOST $M3$ in the modified inverter circuit is of the type $P16$ of Table I. The V_g versus V_p plot of the MOST was measured by the method described by Wallinga [2] and is shown in Fig. 3. The measured driver and load characteristics of the two inverters are presented in Fig. 4. The dynamic

TABLE I

CHARACTERISTICS OF THE CIRCULAR SYMMETRIC MOS TRANSISTORS USED FOR THE MEASUREMENT

Sample number[a]	*P* 16	*P* 17	Dimensions
Oxide thickness	1300	1300	Å
Channel length	12	52	μm
Aspect ratio	44	12.2	
Type of silicon	n	n	
Bulk donor concentration	5×10^{14}	5×10^{14}	cm^{-3}
Mobility	130	130	$cm^2\ V^{-1}\ s^{-1}$
Source area	4.6×10^{-4}	4.8×10^{-4}	cm^{-2}
Gate area	3.1×10^{-5}	3.4×10^{-4}	cm^{-2}
Drain area	1.2×10^{-4}	1.2×10^{-4}	cm^{-2}

[a] Samples prepared in our laboratory.

load line of the modified inverter was measured as the $M2$ drain–source current as a function of its source voltage, while the drain and gate–source voltages were kept constant at $V_{DD} = -25$ V and $V'_p - V'_{\max} = -18.3$ V (see Section II-B1) and Fig. 4). The input pulse on the gate of the driver MOST, which had a repetition frequency of 10 Hz, is shown in Fig. 5 and was supplied by a Philips PM5729 pulse generator. The pulse shapes were measured with a Tektronix 547 oscilloscope with a 1*A*1 dual-trace input unit coupled with a P6045 measuring probe. The output pulses of the conventional and modified inverter are given in Figs. 6 and 7 for a battery voltage V_{DD} of -25 V. The total output load capacitance of both inverters, probe included, was 20 pF. Furthermore, the output of the modified inverter circuit with the gate and drain of bias MOST $M3$ connected to a separate voltage supply $V'_{DD} = -30$ V, while the drain of load MOST $M2$ is connected to a voltage supply $V_{DD} = -25$ V is shown in Fig. 8.

Important for the operation of the modified inverter is a complete signal transfer from the output to the gate of the load MOST $M2$ during the switching transients. The $M3$ source-bulk and the parasitic $M2$ gate-bulk capacitances, however, cause an attenuated capacitive signal transfer. In order to obtain a minimum attenuation and an adequate transfer, the gate of $M2$ should extend over its source-diffused region. This was simulated in the breadboarded circuit by an external capacitor of 22 pF connected between the $M2$ source and gate.

IV. DISCUSSION

In the first two rows of Table II the 10–90 percent turnoff times, as measured from Figs. 6 and 7, are given. The theoretical value for the conventional inverter is obtained from the following expression that has been derived by Crawford [1, pp. 78–80]:

$$t_{\text{off}} = \frac{18C}{\beta_{M2} V'_p} \tag{2}$$

for the following values: $\beta_{M2} = 3.9 \times 10^{-5}$ A/V^2; $C = 20$

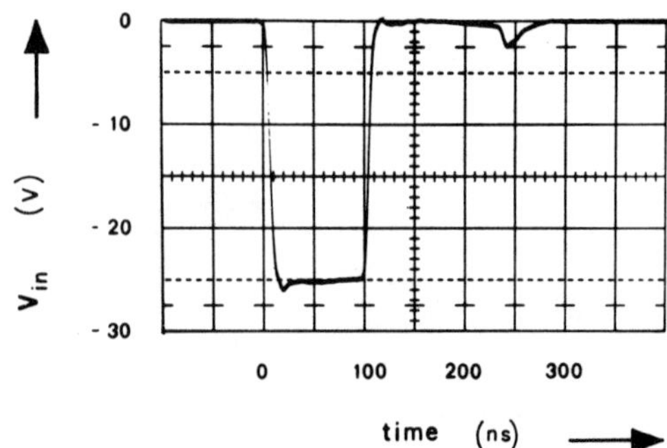

Fig. 5. Input pulse on the gate of the driver MOST $M1$.

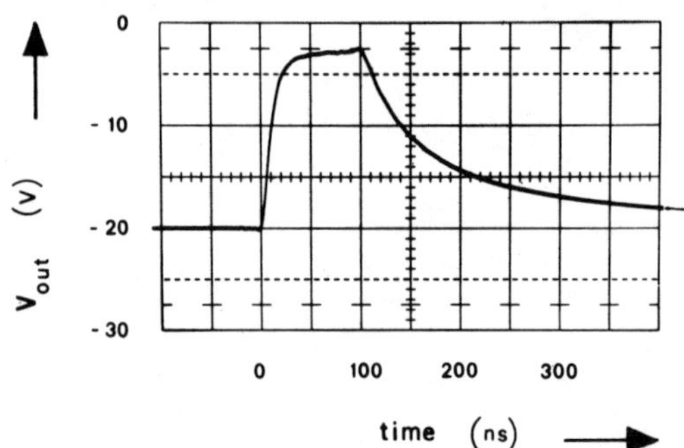

Fig. 6. Output pulse of the conventional inverter.

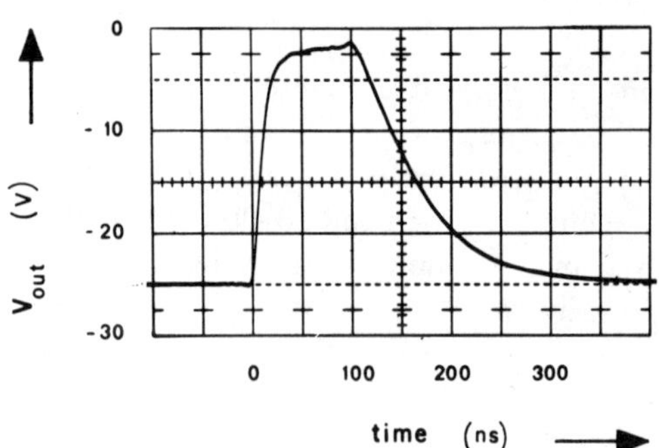

Fig. 7. Output pulse of the modified inverter.

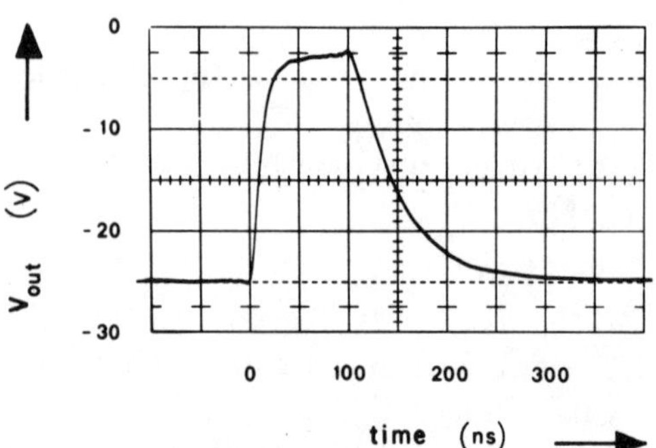

Fig. 8. Output pulse of the modified inverter if the drain of $M2$ is connected to -25 V and both the gate and drain of $M3$ to -30 V.

TABLE II
MEASURED AND THEORETICAL 10–90 PERCENT TURNOFF TIMES OF THE MODIFIED AND CONVENTIONAL INVERTERS

Inverter	10–90 Percent Turnoff Time Measured (ns)	Theoretical (ns)	Energy Dissipation (mW)
1 conventional	380	460	165
2 modified	135	120	121
3 modified	100	95	165

The energy dissipation in the static ON state is calculated from Fig. 4.

pF; and $V'_p = -20$ V as obtained from Figs. 3 and 4. The theoretical 10–90 percent turnoff time for the modified inverter circuit has been obtained from (1) for the values: $\beta_{M2} = 3.9 \times 10^{-5}$ A/V^2; $C = 20$pF; $V''_p = -15$ V; $V_{DD} = -25$ V; and $V'_{\max} = -1.7$ V, also obtained from Figs. 3 and 4. From this it can be concluded that the turnoff time can be predicted well by (1) derived from the first-order MOST equations [3]. Furthermore, a gain in turnoff time of about a factor of 3, as compared with the conventional inverter, appears to be possible.

If equal power dissipation in the static ON state for both types of inverters should be a criterion of comparison instead of equal MOST geometries, a larger aspect ratio A for the modified inverter load MOST could be allowed, causing an additional reduction in turnoff time. If the first-order MOST equations are used again it will be clear that in the condition of equal power dissipation in the static ON state, the ratio of aspect ratios should be:

$$\frac{A_{M2}(\text{mod})}{A_{M2}(\text{conv})} = \left(\frac{V'_p - V_{\max}}{V''_p - V'_{\max}}\right)^2 \tag{3}$$

Equal power dissipation as mentioned before can also be achieved by decreasing and adjusting the $M3$ gate and drain voltage as has been performed in the measurement of Fig. 8. For the condition of this last measurement the turnoff time has been computed by inserting V'_p and $V_{\max}$ for V''_p and $V'_{\max}$, respectively, into (1) and is included in the third row of Table II together with the measured value. The measurement of Fig. 8 gives a satisfactory impression of the maximum gain in turnoff times attainable, roughly a factor of 5; however, in practice it is advisable to optimize the turnoff time of the modified inverter by adjustment of the ratio of aspect ratios.

The application of the modified inverter in static logic is restricted and will be discussed briefly by considering its behavior in the sequence: static OFF state, turn-on, and turnoff. If the modified inverter is in the static OFF state and switched ON, the output voltage V_{out} increases from V''_p to near zero due to discharging of the output load capacitor C. By the $M2$ gate–source capacitance this increase is transferred to the gate of $M2$ and the source of $M3$. This means that during the turn-on transient the small near pinch-off current of $M2$ does not alter significantly, as the $M2$ gate–source bias remains unaltered at $V'_p - V''_p$.

When $M1$ is directly turned off after turn-on, the charging of the load capacitor C will require an excessive amount of time as $M2$ is badly conducting due to its unfavorable near-threshold gate–source bias $V'_p - V''_p$.

If on the other hand $M1$ is kept in conduction for a longer time, the gate of $M2$ will recover to the stationary voltage V'_p by the current flowing via $M3$ into the $M3$ source-bulk load capacitance. This charging of the $M2$ gate is analogous to the charging of the output load capacitor of a conventional inverter during the turnoff transient. Therefore, the recovery time can be estimated by [1, pp. 78–80]:

$$\tau = \frac{18C_s}{\beta_{M3}V'_p} \tag{4}$$

where C_s is the M3 source-bulk load capacitance. Hence, when $M1$ is turned off after a longer period than τ, the $M2$ gate voltage has sufficiently decreased to allow a shorter turnoff time.

The influence of the $M2$ gate recovery on the modified inverter turnoff transient is demonstrated in Fig. 9, where V_{out} of the breadboarded modified inverter is shown as a function of time in the sequence: static OFF state, turn on, and turnoff for two different periods of conduction of $M1$; 50, and 100 ns, respectively. By the substitutions $C_S = 28$ pF and $\beta_{M3}\, V'_p = 2.8 \times 10^{-3}$ mho into (4), the $M2$ gate recovery time for this inverter appeared to be 180 ns. In an integrated modified inverter circuit recovery times of 25 ns are feasible, because C_S can be made very small $\simeq 0.4$ pF. This allows operation in static logic for pulse lengths of 50 ns or more with the same favorable turnoff time as described in Section II-B1).

V. CONCLUSION

Under dynamic operation the modified inverter circuit offers a reduction in turnoff time by a factor of about 3, as compared with a conventional inverter of the same MOST geometries, provided the signal transfer to the gate of the load MOST is complete. If the energy dissipation in the static ON state for both types of inverters is equal, then the maximum gain in turnoff time might be 4. There is the added advantage that the output voltage makes the full excursion to the battery voltage V_{DD}.

If the circuit is to be operated statically, the same improvement in switching time can be obtained under the restriction that the minimum switching period is longer than the charging time of the capacitance, associated with the gate of the load MOST, towards negative voltages. The minimum charging time is estimated to be 25 ns for integrated modified MOST inverters.

ACKNOWLEDGMENT

The authors are indebted to O. W. Memelink for helpful suggestions and to the members of the technology group of their laboratory for providing the MOST devices.

VI. APPENDIX

ANALYTICAL DESCRIPTION OF THE 10–90 PERCENT TURNOFF TIME OF THE MODIFIED INVERTER

For reasons of convenience, it is assumed in this Appendix that all voltages occurring in the modified p channel inverter have positive signs.

Assume at time $t = 0$, that $M1$ is turned off and $V_{out} = V'_{max}$. Directly after the $M1$ turnoff the output capacitance C will be charged by $M2$, being in the saturated state, while its gate–source voltage keeps to be constant at $V'_p - V'_{max}$, because the signal transfer to the $M2$ gate is supposed to be complete. The charging of C is governed by the current equation:

$$C\frac{dV_{out}}{dt} = \tfrac{1}{2}\beta_{M2}a^2 \tag{5}$$

where

$$a = |V''_p - V'_{max}|.$$

Integrating this expression, taking into account the boundary condition $t = 0$ and $V_{out} = V'_{max}$ yields:

$$t = \frac{2C}{\beta_{M2}}\cdot\frac{V_{out} - V'_{max}}{a^2}. \tag{6}$$

It is worthwhile to emphasize that V_{out} decreases linearly with time with a slope s equal to:

$$s = \frac{\beta_{M2}a^2}{2C}. \tag{7}$$

For $C = 20$ pF; $\beta_{M2} = 3.9 \times 10^{-5}$ A/V² and $a = 14.3$ V, s calculates to be 2×10^8 V/s, which is in agreement with the corresponding slope in the measurement of Fig. 7: 2.2×10^8 V/s. $M2$ enters unsaturated operation if V_{out} has reached the value:

$$V_{out} = V_B = V_{gB} - V'_p + V'_{max} \tag{8}$$

[see Section II-B1)]. Because $V_{DD} - V_p$ is assumed to be constant for $V_{DD} < V_p < V'_{max}$ [see Section II-B2) and Fig. 3], $V_{gB} - V'_p$ in (8) can be replaced by $V_{DD} - V''_p$ (see Fig. 3), resulting in:

$$V_B = V_{DD} - V''_p + V'_{max}. \tag{9}$$

Inserting 9 into 6 gives:

$$t_B = \frac{2C}{\beta_{M2}}\cdot\frac{V_{DD} - V''_p}{a^2}. \tag{10}$$

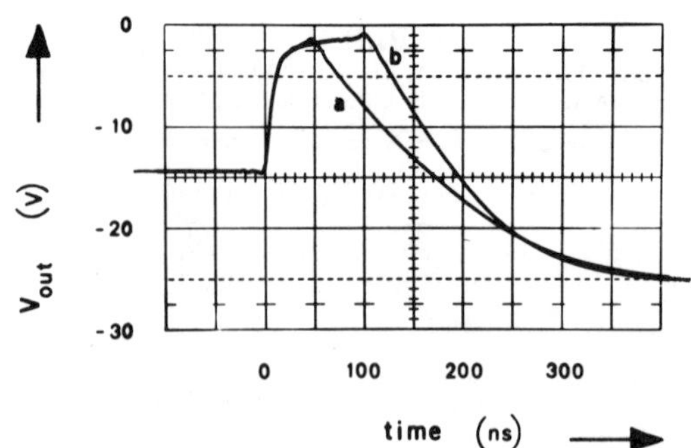

Fig. 9. Output voltage of the modified inverter circuit in the sequence: static OFF state, turn-on, and turnoff, for two different periods of conduction of $M1$; 50 and 100 ns for the curves a and b, respectively.

Substitution of $V_{out} = 0.1\ (V_{DD} - V'_{max}) + V'_{max}$, the 10 percent value of the output amplitude, into (6) delivers:

$$t_1 = \frac{2C}{\beta_{M2}}\cdot\frac{0.1(V_{DD} - V'_{max})}{a^2}. \tag{11}$$

If $M2$ is in unsaturated operation the charging of C obeys the following current equation:

$$C\frac{dV_{out}}{dt} = \beta_{M2}(a(V_{DD} - V_{out}) - \tfrac{1}{2}(V_{DD} - V_{out})^2). \tag{12}$$

Changing of the parameter $V_{DD} - V_{out}$ in V_m yields:

$$-C\frac{dV_m}{dt} = \beta_{M2}(-\tfrac{1}{2}V_m + a)V_m. \tag{13}$$

Integration of this equation and use of the initial conditions $t = 0$, $V_m = a$, gives [6]:

$$\frac{a\beta_{M2}}{C}\cdot t = \ln\left(\frac{-V_m + 2a}{V_m}\right). \tag{14}$$

Inserting $V_m = 0.1\ (V_{DD} - V'_{max})$, the 90 percent value of the output voltage amplitude, into (14) delivers:

$$t_2 = \frac{C}{\beta_{M2}a}\ln\left(\frac{-0.1b + 2a}{0.1b}\right) \tag{15}$$

where

$$b = |V_{DD} - V'_{max}|.$$

Finally the 10–90 percent turnoff time is equal to

$$t_B - t_1 + t_2$$

$$= \frac{C}{\beta_{M2}a}\left\{2.\frac{0.9b - a}{a} + \ln\left(\frac{-0.1b + 2a}{0.1b}\right)\right\}. \tag{16}$$

REFERENCES

[1] R. H. Crawford, *MOSFET in Circuit Design.* New York: McGraw-Hill, 1967, chs. 3 and 4, pp. 71–73, and pp. 78–80.
[2] H. Wallinga, "A method for the measurement of the turn-on

condition in MOS transistors," *Solid-State Electron.*, to be published.

[3] J. A. van Nielen and O. W. Memelink, "The influence of the substrate upon the DC characteristics of silicon MOS transistors," Philips Res. Rep., vol. 22, pp. 55–71, Feb. 1967.

[4] S. R. Hofstein and F. P. Heiman, "The silicon insulated-gate field-effect transistor," *Proc. IEEE*, vol. 51, pp. 1190–1202, 1963.

[5] J. van den Akker, "An integrated square wave oscillator in MOST with voltage controlled frequency," Dep. Elec. Eng., Twente Univ. Technol., Int. Rep., Enschede, the Netherlands, June 1971.

[6] E. Kamke, *Differentialgleichungen, Lösungsmethoden und Lösungen*, vol. 1. Leipzig: Akademische Verlagsgesellschaft Geest & Portig K.—G., 1961, p. 297, eq. I.26.

FET Logic Configuration

Eugene M. Blaser and Donald A. Conrad

IBM Corp.

Hopewell Junction, NY

BECAUSE CONVENTIONAL FET circuits use logic signal swings equal to the supply voltage, a great deal of power is dissipated to charge and discharge nodal capacitances. As is well known, reducing the logic signal swing can substantially improve the power-performance figure of merit, provided that noise margins and transconductance remain adequate. A circuit with this capability is shown in Figure 1, along with a conventional FET circuit.

In the circuit to be described, the input device is a depletion-mode FET with its gate tied to ground. The load device is a conventional depletion-mode pullup device. The outputs are taken from the drains of multiple enhancement-mode devices.

In logic format, the circuit is very similar to I^2L; that is, it has a single input and multiple outputs. When the input is at ground, device T1 is on and keeps node A close to ground; this keeps devices T3 and T4 off. When the input is at a threshold above ground (+2V for VTD = −2V), device T1 turns off. Device T2 can then charge up node A to +5V and turn on devices T3 and T4. Performance improvement is obtained due to the nodes seeing the bulk of the wiring and fan-in and fan-out capacitance swing only between +2V and ground. Logic would be implemented with this circuit, just as with I^2L, by dotting the outputs.

Figure 2, a plot of nominal average delay versus loading capacitance for the circuit with fan-in and fan-out equal to three, shows that this circuit can obtain, with one-fourth the power, the same performance as a conventional circuit. With equal power, moreover, this circuit performs twice as fast and is less sensitive to capacitance. This lower sensitivity can be a key feature in the design of large LSI chips for which wiring capacitance is a dominant factor.

Reducing the logic signal swing reduces the internal noise margins. To verify the reliability of the circuit under these conditions, a statistical noise analysis was made. The results are shown in Figure 3; a two-stage open-loop transfer function is plotted with statistical limits representing the 3σ points of a 1000-case Monte Carlo analysis. The noise margins are 175mV for the down level, and 275mV for the up level. These numbers are consistent with the general design criteria that the noise margin be about 10% of the logic signal swing.

The layout of a cell for this circuit for a conventional metal gate process is shown in Figure 4. The circuit in this cell has a fan-out of four. The total area of the cell, including power bussing, is slightly less than 4.5 mil^2. By using conventional process enhancements, one can reduce the cell area further and also improve the power-performance figure of merit.

Acknowledgments

The authors would like to thank K. Mathews for his continuing support and encouragement, and P. Cook for his helpful suggestions and additional analysis.

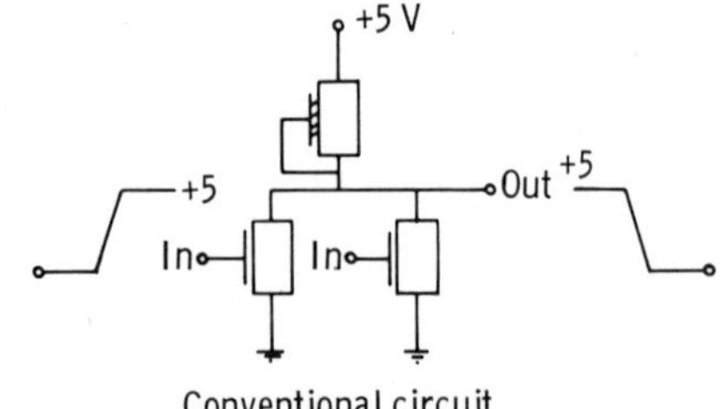

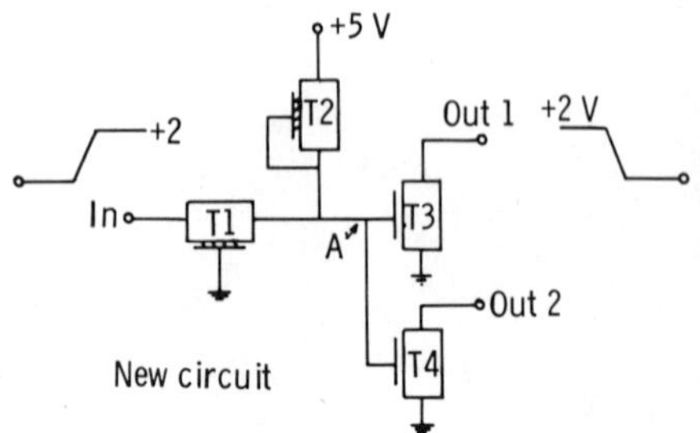

FIGURE 1—Comparisons of conventional and new circuits.

Reprinted from *IEEE Int. Solid State Circuits Conf.*, pp. 14–15, 1978.

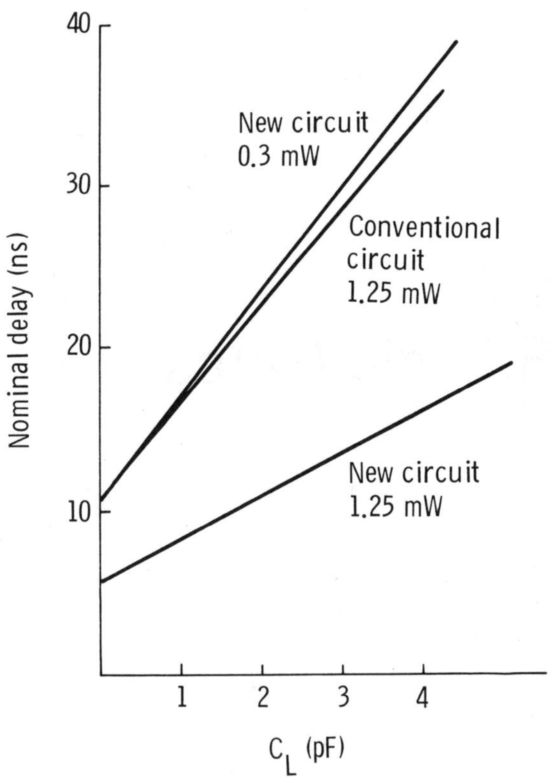

FIGURE 2—Nominal delay versus loading capacitance.

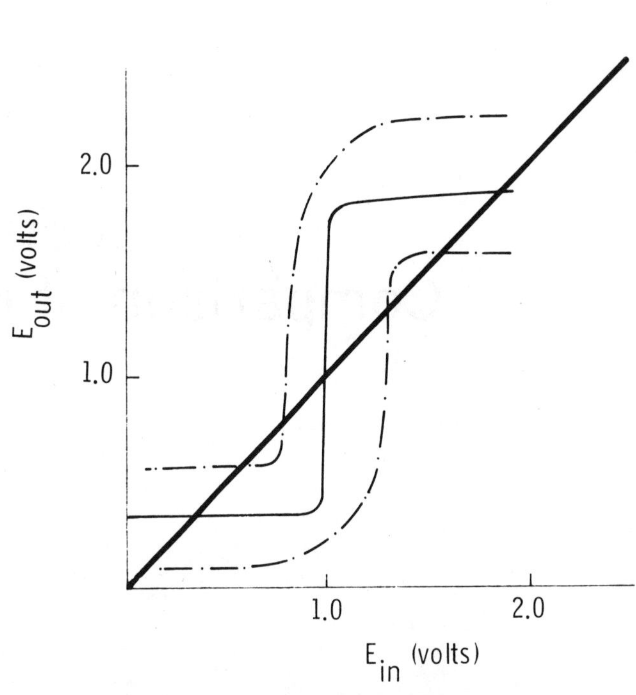

FIGURE 3—Noise analysis, illustrating noise margins for down level (175mV,) and up level (275mV).

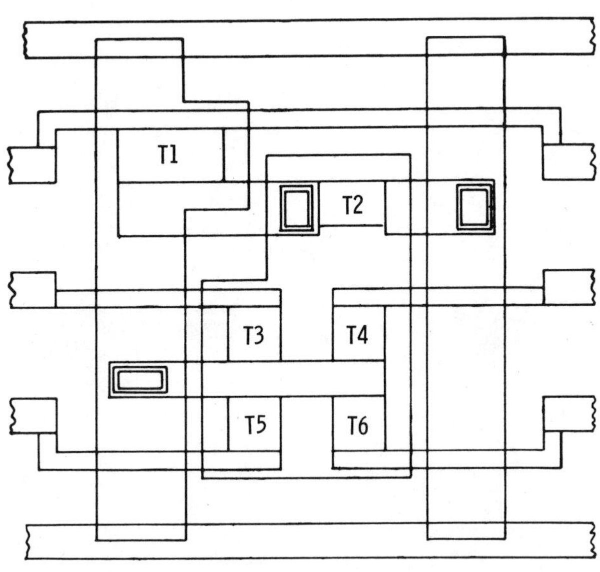

FIGURE 4—Cell layout.

Section 1.4
Comparison of MOS Logic Gates

Comparison of MOSFET Logic Circuits

PETER W. COOK, DALE L. CRITCHLOW, AND LEWIS M. TERMAN

Abstract—**Linear load, depletion-mode load, four-phase dynamic, and complementary MOSFET logic circuits are compared on the basis of power, delay, and density for two specific master slice layouts. The circuits were designed in a common technology base, and normalized power and delay characteristics were calculated by simulation. Chips of 1280 circuits were designed in images having one and two layers of metal, and power versus delay curves were calculated. The effect of an insulating substrate was also considered.**

I. Introduction

SINCE its advent over a decade ago, the MOSFET device has found wide usage in logic and memory circuits. As a result of unique device characteristics and flexibility, a variety of logic circuits have been developed, each with its own characteristics and proponents. Comparison of these circuits is of great interest; however, the literature offers no real basis for fundamental quantitative comparison of power and delay, since the various results reported have been done with differing technology levels, design approaches, capacitive environments, power dissipation needs, and for different applications. The MOSFET device is highly nonlinear, and variations in device parameter values and spreads, supply voltages, capacitive loading, etc., can radically affect the performance of a given circuit.

The purpose of the study reported here was to compare several MOSFET logic circuit types directly. The approach was to design the circuits in a common technology base, and to determine their intrinsic power and delay characteristics by simulation. Then, a 1280 circuit random logic chip was designed using each circuit type. From this, circuit and wiring area and capacitive loading were determined, and power versus delay curves calculated.

Manuscript received May 9, 1973; revised June 21, 1973.

The authors are with the IBM Thomas J. Watson Research Center, Yorktown Heights, N. Y. 10598.

Reprinted from *IEEE J. Solid-State Circuits*, vol. SC-8, pp. 348–355, Oct. 1973.

II. Approach

A. Circuits and Technology

The four basic circuit types chosen for the comparison are shown in Fig. 1. They are static linear load FET (LLFET) [1], static depletion-mode load FET (DLFET) [2], dynamic four phase nonoverlapping clock FET (DYNFET) [3], and complementary MOS (CMOS) [4]. Only positive logic NOR (actually negative logic NOR or positive logic NAND for CMOS) circuits were considered in detail. Details of the circuits are well known, and can be found in the references or elsewhere in the literature. Static saturated load NOR logic was not included because it was felt to have no significant advantages except for the single power supply over LLFET and adequate comparisons have already been published [5], [6]. There are numerous dynamic logic circuits; the four-phase nonoverlapping clock version has found wide usage, and was felt to be representative.

For the device technology a hypothetical self-aligned gate technology was assumed, typical of present day manufacturing capabilities. Typical device parameter values and spreads are given in Table I. Devices were N-channel except where indicated in the CMOS circuit. The photolithography capability assumed was basically 3.75-μ at the oxide opening level, with 7.5-μ metal line-width and 5.6-μ spacing between lines.

B. Normalized Delay and Power Constants

If all capacitances in a MOSFET circuit are increased by some factor, the waveforms will be slowed down by the same factor. Similarly, if all device W/L ratios (WLR's) are increased by some factor (without changing the capacitances), the waveforms are speeded up by the same factor. In both cases the changes in the waveforms occur only as a slowing or speeding, not in a change of their shapes, i.e., if the time axis is normalized in units of C/WLR, the waveforms will be identical. Thus, delay can be expressed as

$$T_d = K_d\ (C_{\text{node}}/\text{WLR}) \qquad (1)$$

where C_{node} is the total capacitance on the output node of the circuit, and WLR is arbitrarily taken to be the WLR ratio of an active or switching device (e.g., a parallel input device in a NOR block).[1] K_d is a constant for a given circuit design, i.e., ratio of active and load device WLR's, power supply voltages, device parameter values and tolerances, noise margin, etc.

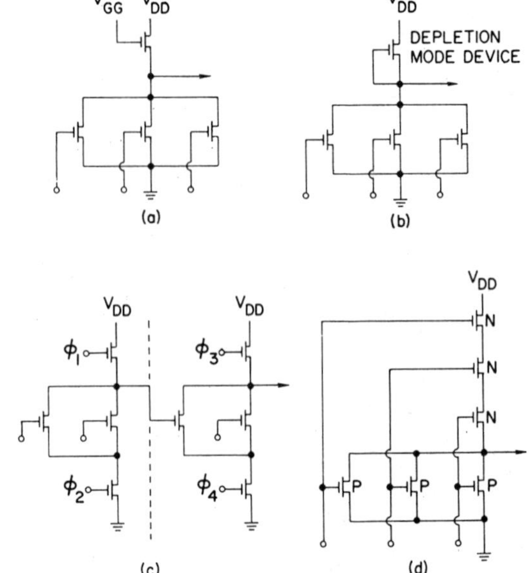

Fig. 1. Logic circuits used in comparison. (a) LLFET. (b) DLFET. (c) DYNFET. (d) CMOS.

TABLE I

	Noncomplementary N-channel	Complementary N-channel	Complementary P-channel
$\mu(\epsilon_{ox})/(T_{ox})$ (μ℧/V)	14 ± 20 percent	14 ± 20 percent	6 ± 20 percent
V_t (enh)	2.0 ± 0.6	2.7 ± 0.6	−2.25 ± 0.45
(dep)	−4.4 ± 0.6		
Supply tolerence	± 10 percent		± 10 percent

Assumed technology parameters. Device tolerances shown are 3 sigma variations. Gate insulator thickness is 1000 Å.

Similarly, the current through a MOSFET is proportional to its WLR, and an analogous equation for power may be written

$$P = K_p\ (\text{WLR})\ (SF) \qquad (2)$$

where, again, K_p is a constant for a given design, but is a function of device and design parameters, and the switching factor SF depends upon circuit operations.[2] For LLFET and DLFET, it is the probability that a NOR circuit is in the ON condition. Similarly, for DYNFET the switching factor is the probability that a NOR circuit is ON when clocked. CMOS circuits dissipate power only during a change of logic state, and the switching factor is defined by

[1] Any change in WLR will also change some circuit capacitances. For all circuits except DYNFET, this fact may be accommodated by deriving an equivalent nodal capacitance. In the case of DYNFET, changes in coupling between the clock lines and the output node that occur as WLR is varied result in a K_d that is a function of WLR. Subsequent curves include this effect.

[2] For CMOS, which dissipates only dynamic power, $P = CV^2f/2$, and it is possible to relate K_p and K_d, Taking f_T, the transition frequency, to be the product of the reciprocal of delay and the switching factor, and using equations (1) and (2), K_p may be expressed as $K_p = V^2/2K_d$. A similar argument may be made for the case of DYNFET; however, the V^2 term must be replaced with the product of the supply voltage and the logic swing.

$$SF\ (\text{CMOS}) = T_d \cdot f_T \quad (3)$$

where f_T is the average frequency of transitions, and is a function of the logic being performed and the system clock rate.

For the noncomplementary circuits, a switching factor of 2/3 was used. For CMOS, there is essentially no data available on the average switching frequencies of logic circuits, so results were calculated for a range of switching factors from 0.01 to 0.25.

Calculations of K_p and K_d were made for LLFET, DLFET, and CMOS using computer simulation. A string of six identical circuits were simulated, approximating an infinite chain, and pair delay was measured between the third and fifth stages. A second simulation run was made with the node capacitances incremented by a small amount, and the new delay measured. Then

$$\Delta T_d = \frac{\Delta T_{d(3\rightarrow 5)}}{2}$$

and

$$K_d = \frac{\Delta T_d}{\Delta C_{\text{node}}}(\text{WLR}).$$

For DYNFET, the minimum clock width for proper circuit operation was determined as a function of the WLR's of the pull-up and discharge devices for a given capacitive loading. The delay time was taken as a single clock width.[3]

Power was calculated from the ON current and supply voltage for LLFET and DLFET, and from the capacitive power for the DYNFET and CMOS.

III. Results

A. K_p and K_d: Values and Tolerances

The circuits were initially designed for equal logic swings. A 7.5-V V_{dd} supply was used for the LLFET, DLFET, and CMOS circuits. The V_{gg} supply for LLFET was 12.75 V. The DYNFET circuit used 12.75-V V_{dd} and clock supplies.[4] It was found that the limiting performance of 7.5-V CMOS was about a factor of 2 slower than the LLFET and DLFET circuits; the 12.75-V CMOS design has essentially the same limiting performance as the other circuits. (It should be noted that this results in higher fields on the chip, which may affect reliability.) The LLFET design had a ratio of load WLR to active device WLR of 1:16, while that for DLFET was 1:4. For CMOS, the ratio of N-channel to P-channel WLR was chosen to give equal rise and fall times.

TABLE II

	Supply Voltage	K_d (ns/pF)	K_p (mW)	$T_{\min}$ (ns)
CMOS	(12.75)	50.1	1.64	4.3
	(7.5)	118	0.236	10.5
LLFET	(7.5/12.75)	113	0.265	4.3
DLFET	(7.5)	102	0.226	3.7
DYNFET	(12.75/12.75)	67	0.223	5.1

K_d and K_p values. Values for DYNFET are a function of WLR, because of capacitance between clock line and output node. Values shown are for WLR = 2, and are typical of values for moderate WLR. $T_{\min}$ is the limiting delay for very large active WLR for average fan-out and fan-in (see text). For LLFET and DLFET, there is a slight dependence of $T_{\min}$ on the chip image employed.

Nominal values of K_p and K_d obtained from simulation are given in Table II. Simulation runs were also made to determine the effects on K_p and K_d of device parameter and power supply tolerances. The resulting variations of K_p and K_d with parameter and supply variations, normalized to nominal values, are given in Fig. 2. The individual data points for these curves were obtained by a worst case analysis with all parameters perturbed from nominal by the amounts indicated on the abcissa.

For K_p, CMOS (assumed running at a fixed system clock speed) shows the least sensitivity; it is due only to a square law dependence on power supply voltage. DYNFET is almost as good. Its variation is due to the supply variation and the effect on precharge level of threshold voltage. DLFET and LLFET are the most sensitive; DLFET has a square law dependence on threshold voltage and a linear dependence on supply voltage, and LLFET has a cubic dependence upon the supply voltage and a small dependence upon threshold voltage.

With regard to K_d, the 7.5-V CMOS design is the most sensitive, because of higher thresholds and the stacked N-channel devices, while the 7.5-V DLFET design is the least sensitive, because the current available to charge capacitive loads is independent of supply voltage. The other circuits are essentially equivalent.

B. Chip Layouts

It is possible to gain some insight into circuit comparisons from the K_p and K_d data presented so far, but such insights are indeed limited. Normalized delay, power, and power-delay products are all implicit in K_p and K_d. However, the normalization factor is the capacitive load on a given circuit output node, and there is no reason to expect that this loading will be the same in the several circuits. (Specifically, with two devices per input, one might reasonably expect that the CMOS loading would be higher than the others.) Therefore it is necessary to size the environment for each different circuit type in order to arrive at comparisons that accu-

[3] This implies overlapping decision time; i.e., some logic circuits are driven by clocks 1 and 2, others by 2 and 3, etc. Thus, a given clock may be used for both precharging and discharging. This results in restricted intercircuit interconnections, since the valid output time for some circuits will not overlap the required input valid time for others. In practice this appears to be a minimal problem.

[4] In DYNFET, use of a separate 7.5-V V_{dd} supply gives close to the same performance and reduces power dissipation by the ratio of 7.5 to 12.75.

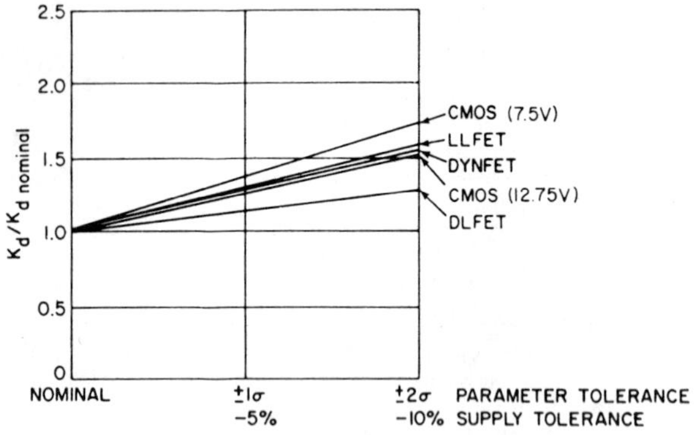

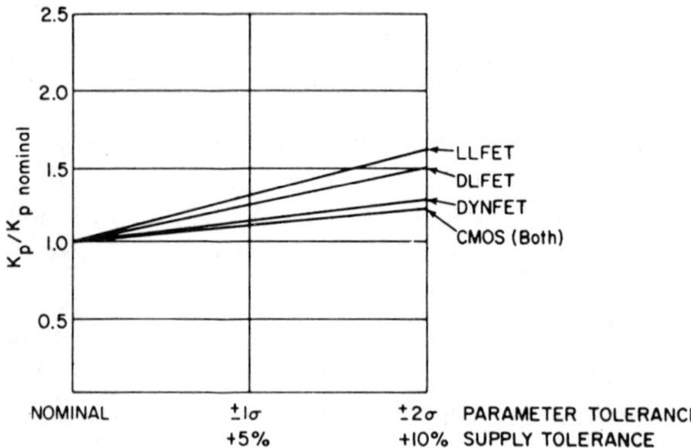

Fig. 2. Sensitivity of K_p and K_d to device parameter tolerances and supply variations with worst case analysis.

rately reflect integrated circuit performance. This involves placing the various circuits into appropriate chip images, and calculating the expected nodal capacitance in each image, for each circuit family. Capacitances were calculated using the familiar parallel plate formula.

Two different images were employed. Both are of the master slice type, and both used the same technology and photolithography rules. One uses two layers of metal, the other requires only a single layer. The first, sketched in Fig. 3, is what may be termed a square array. The chip is assumed to accommodate up to 1600 individual circuit sites, arranged in a 40 × 40 grid. Of these sites, only 1280 were expected to be used. In this chip image, wiring is accomplished by two levels of metallurgy, with a total of 16 tracks placed over the circuit area[5], and circuits are essentially buried under the wiring tracks, except for some first-level metal space required by device gates. LLFET, DLFET, and CMOS fit into this image; DYNFET does not fit with ease and was not considered. The circuits look identical in this image; the wiring requirements dominate the area. This is true until parallel device WLR's are increased over about ten to one; then, an area penalty is paid to place circuits in this image. This is particularly true of CMOS.

The second image, using only one level of metal, is a

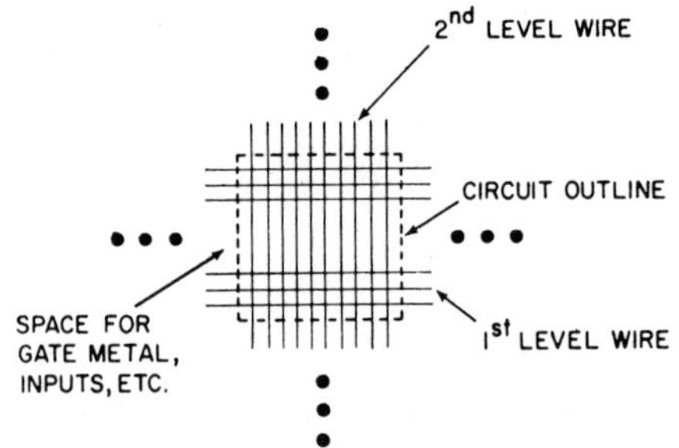

Fig. 3. Single circuit of square array chip image.

modification of what has been termed the "Weinberger arrangement" [8]. The arrangement is modified to divide the entire 1600 circuit chip into 16 "clusters" of 100 circuits each. The 100 circuit clusters are laid out in a Weinberger arrangement of two columns of 50 circuits each. An overall view of the entire chip appears in Fig. 4. The image provides 44 wiring tracks in each direction between clusters. Diffusions are used to cross under aluminum wiring where necessary. The chip is subdivided into clusters because a Weinberger arrangement of 1600 circuit sites would require far too many wiring tracks; 100 circuit clusters are about optimum from an area standpoint.

Some details of the individual circuits in the clusters appear in Fig. 5. The overall arrangement of source and drain "rails" with active devices spaced arbitrarily along the rails is that given in [8]. Two variations are employed. For LLFET and DLFET, a shared source diffusion is employed that is connected to a ground bus. In the case of DYNFET, a separate source diffusion is provided for each circuit, since the source is connected to a ground bus through an FET driven by one of the clock lines; source sharing here would imply that adjacent pairs of circuits have the same timing, a constraint that was felt to be rather undesirable, and certainly not worth the relatively small density penalty paid.

For the modified Weinberger image, provision must be made not only for intercluster wiring, but also for intracluster wiring. For this, enough space for 27 wiring tracks was allocated. In addition to the wiring track space, space was allocated for 4 input devices. The width of the columns was increased as the WLR's of individual active devices increased. In this way, as WLR is varied the number of wiring tracks is not affected. As has been pointed out earlier, this same independence of WLR is also achieved in the square array. CMOS does not fit this image well, and was not considered.

While comparisons of circuits on a density basis was not one of the main purposes of this study, it is significant to note that no major differences in density were noted among the images or circuit types. When a "circuit" is understood to include not merely device area but also all wiring area, all circuits required approximately 0.028 square mm (45 square mils) area. This does not include added area due to pads, kerf, off-chip drivers, etc.

[5] All wiring track estimates were made from wiring studies [7]. In the various different chip images, it was estimated that equal wireability was achieved.

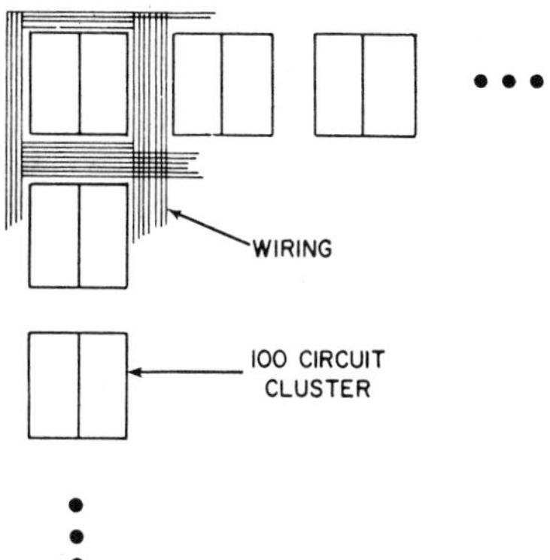

Fig. 4. Modified Weinberger chip image using 100 circuit "clusters."

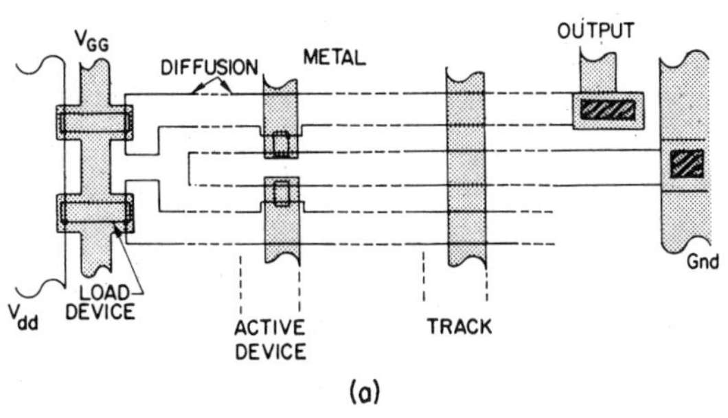

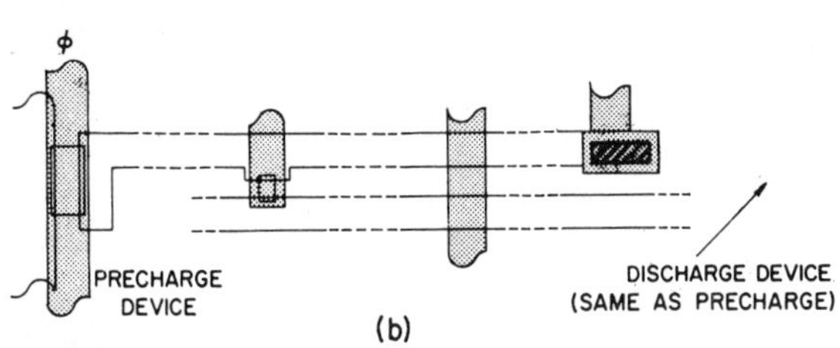

Fig. 5. Details of circuit layout in modified Weinberger image.

In all of the chip images, fan-in and fan-out were taken to be an average value. Fan-in was taken to be 2.7, and fan-out was taken to be 2.2. These numbers were obtained by examining several large-scale intergration (LSI) chips typical of a small machine implementation in MOSFET circuits. For all circuits except CMOS, designs were based on these average numbers. For CMOS, the stacked devices have a WLR which depends upon the fan-in, and it was not reasonable to treat the circuits as having a uniform fan-in of 4, with some inputs unused; such an approach results in a high performance or power penalty. Instead, circuits of varying fan-in (2–4) were designed and were assumed to exist in the chip with the same distribution observed on the LSI chips from which the average fan-in was measured.

Several practical differences among the various images and circuits should be pointed out. First, the square array image requires more complex processing because of the second level of metal. Second, the CMOS circuitry requires further process complication to implement the complementary devices.

C. Power-Delay Curves

With chip images defined, it is possible to calculate nodal capacitance for an average circuit. This capacitance is comprised of several parts: wiring capacitance, the capacitance of driven gates (including Miller effect, with an assumed average gain of 2), and the self capacitance of the circuit. In the square array case, a total average wire length of 0.94 mm (37 mils) was used. In the case of the modified Weinberger image, two separate lengths were calculated. Average intercluster wiring length was 3.75 mm (150 mils); average intracluster wiring length was about 0.26 mm (10.5 mils) [7]. When such capacitance calculations are done, application of the K_p and K_d factors will give a comparison of the circuits. Before actually presenting such results, it is useful to consider the sort of tradeoffs available to the FET circuit designer.

Once power supply voltages, ratio of active device WLR to load device WLR and noise margins have been fixed, the basic parameter the designer is free to vary is the WLR of devices. Generally, increasing WLR will give more current drive capability, and will increase both speed and power. However, there are limits to the speed that can be obtained; as WLR is increased, the capacitance of each circuit input is increased; when WLR is high enough that this capacitance dominates the circuit load, no further delay improvements can be achieved [5], [6].

Varying the circuit WLR's, calculating the corresponding node capacitances, and using the values of K_p and K_d, the curves of Fig. 6 are obtained. Shown in the figure are plots of power as a function of delay for the several circuit families in the different chip images. Increasing WLR is from lower right to upper left; along the curves specific points marked show WLR of 1, 2, 4, 8, and 16. If lower power is desired, the curves may be extrapolated with a -1 slope from the WLR $= 1$ point. For CMOS and DYNFET, this is accomplished by slowing the system clock, while for LLFET and DLFET, the active device WLR is fixed at 1 while the load device WLR is made smaller.

Several comments are in order on the data in Fig. 6(a). First, for all circuits a switching factor of 1 is assumed. This is why the CMOS curves appear much higher in power than the other circuits. Second, the limiting delay for all circuits is approximately the same; it is expected that limitations on DYNFET speed will be imposed by the clocks. Third, the differences between the two chip images are evident in the cases of LLFET or DLFET. The modified Weinberger image, where wiring is confined to diffusion and a single metal layer, has a higher wiring capacitance than the square array. As WLR increases, the significance of this is lost in the WLR-dependent capacitances, and the same circuit in either image approaches the same limiting speed.

The curves for DYNFET exhibit a deterioration of performance from what might be expected from comparisons of K_p and K_d; again, this results from sig-

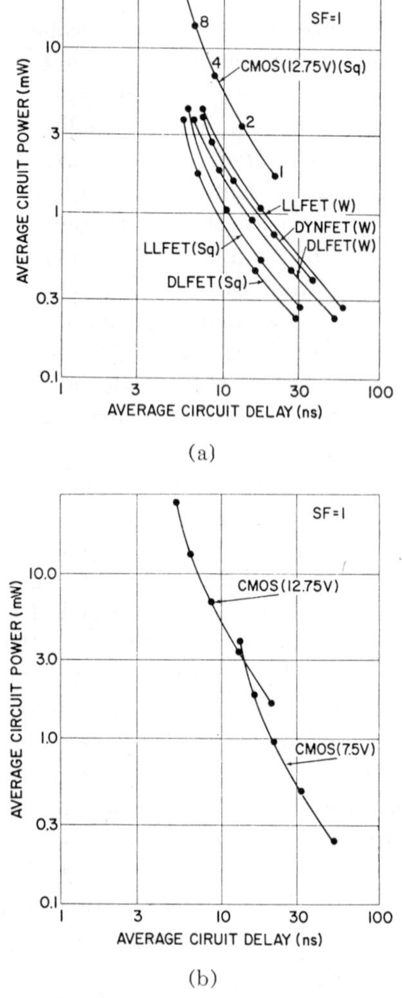

Fig. 6. Average circuit power versus delay curves for 1280 circuit chip at unity switching factor. *Sq* = square array; *W* = Weinberger layout; *SF* = switching factor. Both power and delay are nominal.

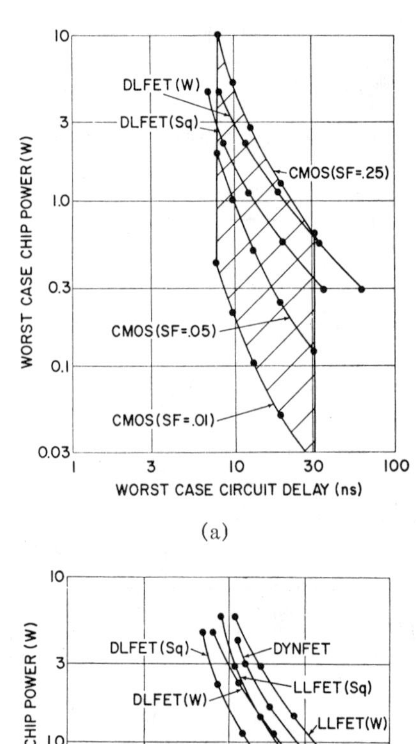

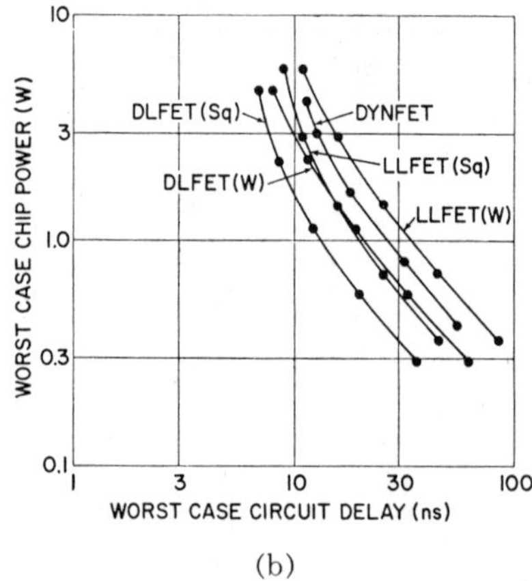

Fig. 7. Curves of worst case chip power versus worst case delay for 1280 circuit chips. $SF = \frac{2}{3}$ for LLFET, DLFET, and DYNFET; *SF* is varied over the indicated range for CMOS. Off-chip driver power is not included.

nificant changes in the capacitive environment. The DYNFET circuit must charge and discharge the capacitance of both source and drain rails in the Weinberger arrangement; the discharge is done through two stacked devices (clock device and active device), and the performance reflects these effects. If a 7.5-V V_{dd} supply is used, power dissipation is reduced by about 40 percent; performance is essentially unchanged.

Fig. 6(b) shows the power-delay curve of a 7.5-V CMOS chip and the power delay curve of an 12.75-V CMOS chip. The approximately 2:1 decrease in limiting speed for the 7.5-V design is evident.

Fig. 7 shows the power-delay curves for the several circuits and images when realistic switching factors and worst case power and delay constants are employed.

Several conclusions can be drawn from the data of Figs. 6 and 7. First, within a given image, the differences between non-CMOS circuit families are small. Second, except in the case of limiting performance, the square array offers a lower power for any given delay than the Weinberger arrangement; this is due to the capacitive differences noted previously.

The switching factor for CMOS is quite critical. If the switching factor is less than about 10 percent, CMOS gives the best power delay product. If the switching factor is substantially greater than 10 percent, other circuits offer superior performance. CMOS performance is limited by three factors: relatively low mobility of the P channel devices, the necessity to "stack" the N devices, and the higher capacitance presented by a single input (two devices).

D. Silicon on Insulating Substrate Technology

The use of sapphire or other insulating substrate material can substantially reduce the capacitance driven by a logic circuit [9]. Devices are fabricated by a thin (perhaps 1 μ) layer of silicon epitaxially grown on the insulating material, and unused silicon between devices is removed by a moat etch, thus largely eliminating the ground plane represented by the bulk silicon. Capacitance is reduced, but K_p and K_d values remain unchanged for the same design.

In calculating the capacitance of the silicon on insulating substrate (SOIS) circuits, diffusion sidewall capaci-

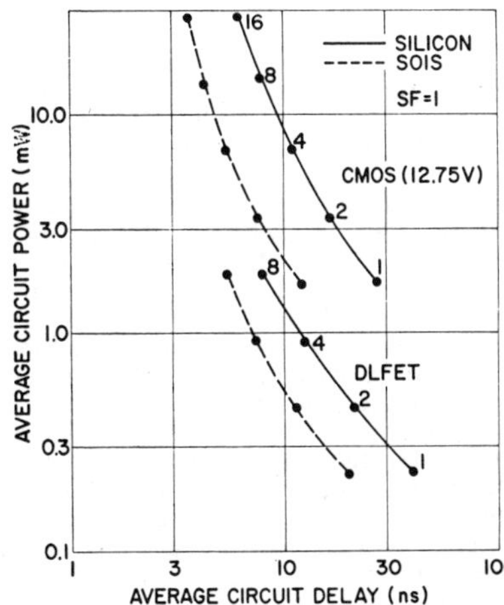

Fig. 8. Average circuit power versus delay curves for 1280 circuit chip in SOIS technology. Effects of fringing fields included.

TABLE III

Variable	Scale Factor
Current (I)	V^2/T_{ox}
Capacitance (C)	L^2/T_{ox}
Circuit density (D)	$1/L^2$
Delay (T)	L^2/V
Power (P)	V^3/T_{ox}
Power $\times$ delay ($P \times T$)	L^2V^2/T_{ox}
Power/area ($P \times D$)	$V^3/(L^3T_{ox})$
Delay constant (K_d)	T_{ox}/V
Power constant (K_p)	V^3/T_{ox}

First order scaling equations. L is all lateral dimensions, T_{ox} is all oxide thicknesses, V is all voltages, including thresholds. Junction capacitance is assumed to scale with the same factor as oxide capacitance. This implies a change in doping levels.

tance was ignored where the moat etch removed the adjoining silicon, as was the diffusion bottom wall capacitance. Capacitance of the interconnection lines over the insulating substrate was calculated by a computer program, which includes the effects of fringing fields [10], rather than just the parallel-plate value used before. The effect of fringing fields on capacitance is minor on a silicon substrate, but is important on an insulating substrate. It was assumed, on the basis of wiring studies [7], that a given line had one of its two adjacent wiring channels occupied.

The resulting power-delay curves for the 1280 circuit chip in SOIS technology are shown in Fig. 8. Only the square array chip image was considered, since it was low capacitance to begin with, and the Weinberger arrangement is only minimally improved by an insulating substrate. The solid curves are for a silicon substrate, but here include the effects of fringing fields on capacitance. Comparison with Fig. 6 shows the effect is small. The SOIS curves are better by a factor of about 2 in delay at constant power. At constant delay, a power improvement somewhat over 2:1 is observed. It should be pointed out that in SOIS, higher cross-coupling capacitance exists; first-order sizings of the resulting increased noise indicate that this is not an intolerable problem.

IV. Conclusions and Discussions

If the switching factor is low, CMOS is superior in power, and DLFET is superior in delay at the same supply voltage. The CMOS circuit can very effectively tradeoff the power for better performance by using a higher supply voltage. The limit of this tradeoff is determined by maximum allowable on-chip fields. With the supply voltages indicated, the crossover with other circuits occurs at about a 10–25 percent switching factor for CMOS. The other circuits are relatively close together. The asymptotic performance of all circuits is about the same (except for the 7.5-V CMOS design, which is slower). For intermediate performance (greater than about 30 ns), the power dissipation of LLFET and DLFET, while higher than CMOS, would still be low enough to permit convection cooling, and would be acceptable except where power is a constraint. At the low performance/low power end, both CMOS and DYNFET can be scaled to lower power by simply slowing the system clock; LLFET and DLFET may be scaled to lower power by decreasing load device WLR, but this eventually has an affect on circuit density, especially for LLFET. For designs of around 75 ns and faster, there are minimal differences in density for the several circuits in either of the chip images.

The results presented here were obtained for a specific set of dimensions, voltages, etc. It is possible, however, to scale results to other assumptions. The factors in Table III are the appropriate scale factors as lateral dimensions L, voltages (including thresholds) V, and oxide thicknesses T_{ox}, are changed. Junction capacitance is assumed to scale by the same factor as oxide capacitance. This is true if the substrate doping is changed with oxide thickness and voltage in order to maintain the same substrate characteristics. A more rigorous discussion of MOSFET device scaling has been given in [11].

The results presented here are for logic circuits in very regular chip images with NOR/NAND circuit implementation. This is the simplest implementation, and is most amenable to layout and design, particularly at high levels of integration. Improvement in circuit area and performance can generally be obtained by going to free form layouts where circuits may be placed arbitrarily, and by employing complex logic where a more involved function than a single NOR (e.g., an AND-OR-INVERT) may be implemented in a single circuit. Very limited experience indicates that free form layout may improve density by a factor of 2 or so for random logic chips; in special cases the improvement may be greater. Performance and/or power can also be improved similarly. Likewise, limited experience in complex logic indicates a density improvement of less than a factor of 2 at the chip level and a power reduction of around 2 for a constant function performance. Dynamic circuits seem most amenable to complex logic, although the design considerations become rather involved, as does layout. LLFET and DLFET can do a limited level of complex logic but suffer from the problem at a given noise margin of sinking the ON current through series devices. CMOS seems to become somewhat cumbersome in complex logic.

Acknowledgment

The authors wish to thank J. W. Allen, A. R. Desroches, W. D. Devine, R. Y. Hung, A. E. Ruehli, and Y. L. Yao for their contributions to the work reported in this paper.

References

[1] M. Axelrod, "Integrated IGFET logic circuit with linear resistive load," U. S. Patent 3 406 298, Oct. 15, 1968.
[2] R. Crawford, "Implanted depletion load boosts MOS array performance," *Electronics,* pp. 85–90, Apr. 24, 1972.
[3] L. Cohen, R. Rubenstein, and F. Wanlass, "MTOS four phase clock systems," in *NEREM Rec.,* 1967, pp. 170–171.
[4] F. M. Wanlass and C. T. Sah, "Nanowatt logic using field effect metal-oxide semiconductor triodes," in *ISSCC Dig. Tech. Papers,* Feb. 1963, pp. 32–33.
[5] D. L. Critchlow, R. H. Dennard, and S. E. Schuster, "Design of large-scale integrated logic using MOS devices," presented at the 1967 Microelectron. Symp., St. Louis, Mo.
[6] D. L. Critchlow and S. E. Schuster, "Computer aided design of large scale integrated MOS logic circuits," presented at the 1968 Microelectron. Symp., St. Louis, Mo.
[7] W. E. Donath, private communication.
[8] A. Weinberger, "Large scale integration of MOS complex logic, a layout method," *IEEE J. Solid-State Circuits,* vol. SC-2, pp. 182–190, Dec. 1967.
[9] J. P. Allison, F. P. Heiman, and J. P. Burns, "Silicon-on-sapphire complementary MOS memory cells," *IEEE J. Solid-State Circuits,* vol. SC-2, pp. 208–212, Dec. 1967.
[10] A. E. Reuhli and P. A. Brennan, "Accurate metallization capacitances for integrated circuits and packages," *IEEE J. Solid-State Circuits,* to be published.
[11] R. H. Dennard, F. M. Gaesslen, L. Kuhn, and H. Yu, "Design of micron MOS switching devices," presented at the 1972 Int. Electron Devices Meeting, Paper 24.3.

Part II
Digital VLSI

The 1980s will be the years of very large scale integration (VLSI). More specifically, they will be the years of digital MOS VLSI, the topic of this Part.

Section 2.1 deals with scaling MOSFET devices in terms of a scaling theory and the device physical limitations. The topic of modeling these scaled-down devices is quite involved because two dimensional [1–2] as well as three dimensional [3–4] effects should be considered. Moreover, the analysis of such effects as the subthreshold region of operation [5–6] becomes important. The reader is referred to references [1–15] and to Section 2 of the bibliography for further readings on recent contributions to MOS device modeling.

The classic paper by Dennard *et al*. introduces the reader to the topic of MOSFET device scaling. The scaling approach discussed is the direct (or the constant-electric field) scaling approach where voltages and both horizontal and vertical dimensions are scaled down by the same scaling factor. Some of the challenging problems related to MOS device scaling are also discussed. The second paper by Dennard *et al.* reports on the continued effort to design and characterize scaled down MOS devices. A new aspect to the improvement of MOS performance, which is discussed in this paper, is operation at liquid nitrogen temperature. The following five papers discuss the physical and the practical limitations of minimum size MOS devices. The paper by Toyabe and Asai offers analytical models for the threshold voltage and the breakdown voltage of short-channel MOS devices from a two-dimensional analysis. The paper by Masuda *et al.* offers a simple emperical expression for the threshold voltage. It also concludes that the smallest feasible device should have a channel length of $0.52\mu m$ and a gate oxide thickness, of 9.4nm when the supply voltage is 1.5V. The paper by Brews *et al*. offers an empirical relation for the minimum channel length for which long channel subthreshold behavior will be observed. It relates the device dimensions, voltages, junction depths, oxide thickness, and substrate doping. The paper by Ratnakumar *et al.* discusses the fundamental limits for enhancement/depletion VLSI, concluding that this limit is for $L = 0.3\mu m$, $V_{DD} = 0.5V$ and $Pt_d = 0.5fJ$. The final paper by El-Mansy discusses the effect of parasitic resistances on the performance of scaled-down MOSFETs.

In Section 2.2, the first paper by Lyman discusses VLSI processing techniques in, for example, lithography, etching, and interconnections. A review of the state-of-the-art and future projections are given. This is followed by papers on state-of-the-art MOS processing technologies. Finally, the paper by Yu *et al.* provides an overview of the challenging problems related to MOS VLSI in terms of processing technology, physics, and engineering approaches.

Section 2.3 deals with another approach to VLSI, namely circuit structures which rely on *merging or vertically stacking* MOS devices. The merging technique is widely used in bipolar circuits, in the multiemitter transistors of T^2L [16], in multicollector transistors and in the merged npn-pnp structures in I^2L [17–19]. Scaling these MOS structures offers even further advantages for VLSI.

The first paper discusses the merging of two MOS devices in the same device well, resulting in SDW (single device well) MOSFETs. The second paper discusses QSA (quadruply self-aligned) MOS which overcomes some of the performance limits of conventional scaled down MOS in terms of interconnection RC time constants and short channel effects. The third paper applies the merging technique, resulting in B^2L (buried load logic) where the load device of a NMOS driver (which is fabricated in a CMOS process) is a vertical JFET buried under the driver MOSFET. The final paper uses the principle of stacking with new processing steps resulting in JMOS (joint-MOS). It uses a laser recrystallized polysilicon layer to stack a PMOS device on top of a NMOS device, resulting in a CMOS inverter with a joint gate.

Section 2.3 deals with the circuit and subsystem aspects of VLSI. VLSI had a tremendous impact on such areas as digital system architecture [20–26], computer-aided-design (CAD) tools for logic [27–28], timing [29–30], circuit [31–36], and processing simulations [37–38], as well as automated layout [39–40]. Because of the limited space, these areas are not discussed in this section and the reader is referred to references [20–47] for further readings on the subject.

The paper by Keyes offers an interesting treatment of the recent evolution of digital electronics towards VLSI and offers even more interesting conclusions. The paper by Mead and Rem deals with optimal subsystem design for VLSI using cost functions. General guidelines for the organization of large integrated systems are offered. The paper by Foster and Kung discusses some of the important issues related to the system design of digital VLSI chips. Examples of layout using "stick" diagrams are given. The paper by Cook *et al.* discusses logic design methodology for VLSI. Design examples are given which includes both static and dynamic PLAs. The final paper by Mohsen and Mead discusses optimizing delay times in a VLSI chip environment, giving simple analytical tools to be used in VLSI chip design and analysis.

One important aspect of VLSI, not covered in this Part is reliability. The reader is referred to [48] and Section 10 of the bibliography for further sources. Moreover, Sections 3 and 4 of the bibliography contain references on MOSFET processing technologies and VLSI related topics respectively.

References

[1] M. S. Mock, "A Two-Dimensional Mathematical Model of IGFET," *Solid-State Electronics*, Vol. 16, 1973, pp. 601–609.

[2] J. J. Barnes, K. Shimohigashi, and R. W. Dutton, "Short-Channel MOSFETs in the Punchthrough Current Mode," *IEEE JSSC*, , Vol. SC-14, April 1979, pp. 368–375.

[3] P. P. Wang, "Device Characteristics of Short Channel and Narrow Width MOSFETs," *IEEE Trans. on ED*, Vol. ED-25, July 1978, pp. 779–786.

[4] A. Husain and S. G. Chamberlain, "Three Dimensional Simulation of VLSI MOSFETs," *The Digest of the 1980 Custom Integrated Circuits Conference*, May 1980, pp. 12–14.

[5] G. W. Taylor, "Subthreshold Conduction in MOSFETs," *IEEE Trans. on ED*, Vol. ED-25, March 1978, pp. 337–350.

[6] D. B. Scott and S. G. Chamberlain, "A Calibrated Model for the Subthreshold Operation of a Short Channel MOSFET Including Surface States," *IEEE JSSC*, Vol. SC-14, June 1979, pp. 633–644.

[7] Y. A. El-Mansy and A. R. Boothroyd, "A New Approach to the Theory and Modeling of Insulated-Gate Field-Effect Transistors," *IEEE Trans. on ED*, Vol. ED-24, March 1977, pp. 241–253.

[8] Y. A. El-Mansy and A. R. Boothroyd, "A Simple Two-Dimensional Model for IGFET Operation in the Saturation Region," *IEEE Trans. on ED*, Vol. ED-24, March 1977, pp. 254–262.

[9] Y. A. El-Mansy and D. M. Caughey, "Characterization of Silicon-on-Sapphire IGFET Transistors," *IEEE Trans. on ED*, Vol. ED-24, September 1977, pp. 1148–1153.

[10] Y. A. El-Mansy, "Analysis and Characterization of the Depletion-Mode IGFET," *IEEE JSSC*, Vol. SC-15, June 1980, pp. 331–340.

[11] R. R. Trautman, "Ion-Implanted Threshold Tailoring for Insulated Gate Field-Effect Transistors," *IEEE Trans. on ED*, Vol. ED-24, March 1977, pp. 182–192.

[12] R. R. Trautman and A. G. Fortino, "Simple Model for Threshold Voltage in a Short-Channel IGFET," *IEEE Trans. on ED*, Vol. ED-24, October 1977, pp. 1266–1268.

[13] L. Mo Dang, "A Simple Current Model for Short-Channel IGFET and its Application to Circuit Simulation," *IEEE JSSC*, Vol. SC-14, April 1979, pp. 358–367.

[14] *IEEE Trans. on ED*, Special Issue on SOS Technology and Non-Volatile Memory Technology, August 1978.

[15] *IEEE Trans. on ED*, Special Issue on Very-Large-Scale Integration, April 1979.

[16] C. S. Meyer, D. K. Lynn, and D. J. Hamilton, "Analysis and Design of Integrated Circuits," McGraw-Hill, 1968.

[17] K. Hart and A. Slob, "Integrated Injection Logic—A New Approach to LSI," *IEEE JSSC*, Vol. SC-7, October 1972, pp. 346–351.

[18] H. H. Berger and S. K. Wiedmann, "Merged Transistor Logic (MTL)—Low Cost Bipolar Concept," *IEEE JSSC*, Vol. SC-7, October 1972, pp. 340–346.

[19] N. C. DeTroye, "Integrated Injection Logic—Present and Future," *IEEE JSSC*, October 1974, pp. 206–211.

[20] C. Mead and L. Conway, "Introduction to VLSI Systems," Addison-Wesley, 1980.

[21] R. Rice, "Tutorial: VLSI," IEEE Computer Society Publication, Catalog No. EHO 158-6, 1980.

[22] D. A. Patterson and C. H. Sequin, "Design Considerations for Single-Chip Computers of the Future," *IEEE JSSC*, Vol. SC-15, February 1980, pp. 44–52.

[23] R. A. Cliff, "Acceptable Testing of VLSI Components which Contain Error Correctors," *IEEE JSSC*, SC-15, February 1980, pp. 61–70.

[24] J. A. Arulpragasam et al., "Modular Minicomputers Using Microprocessors," *IEEE JSSC*, SC-15, February 1980, pp. 85–96.

[25] J. J. Lenahan and F. K. Fung, "Performance of Cooperative Loosely Coupled Microprocessor Architecture in an Interactive Data Base Task," *IEEE JSSC*, SC-15, February 1980, pp. 97–116.

[26] D. Tabak and G. J. Lipovski, "MOVE Architecture in Digital Controllers," *IEEE JSSC*, SC-15, February 1980, pp. 116–126.

[27] Y. S. Chen and R. M. Jacobs, "A Systematic Approach to VLSI Design," The Digest of the 1980 Custom Integrated Circuits Conference, May 1980, pp. 63–66.

[28] K. Hirabayashi and M. Kawamura, "MACLOS-Mask Checking Logic Simulator," *IEEE JSSC*, Vol. SC-15, June 1980, pp. 368–370.

[29] B. R. Chawla et al., "MOTIS—An MOS Timing Simulator," *IEEE Trans. Circuits Systm.*, Vol. CAS-22, December 1975, pp. 901–910.

[30] Y. Puri, "On the Logic Delay in MOS LSI Static NOR Designs," *IEEE JSSC*, Vol. SC-14, August 1979, pp. 715–723.

[31] E. Seewann, "Switching Speeds of MOS Inverters," *IEEE JSSC*, Vol. SC-15, April 1980, pp. 246–352.

[32] L. W. Nagel, "SPICE 2—A Computer Program to Simulate Semiconductor Circuits," Univ. of Calif. Berkeley, ERL Memo ERL-M520.

[33] I. Hajj, K. Singal, J. Vlach, and P. R. Bryant, "WATAND—A Program for the Analysis and Design of Linear and Piecewise-linear Networks," *Midwest Symp. Circuit Theory*, Waterloo, Ont., Canada, April 1973.

[34] T. K. Young and R. W. Dutton, "Mini-MSINC—A Minicomputer Simulator for MOS Circuits with Modular Built-in Model," *IEEE JSSC*, Vol. SC-11, October 1976, pp. 730–732.

[35] R. C. Foss, "A Fresh Look at MOS Circuit Simulation," *The Digest of 1980 Custom Integrated Circuits Conference*, May 1980, pp. 38–41.

[36] M. I. Elmasry, "Adaptive MOS Macromodeling," *The Digest of 1980 Custom Integrated Circuits Conference*, May 1980, pp. 112–116.

[37] D. A. Antoniadis and R. W. Dutton, "Models for Computer Simulation of Complete IC Fabrication Process," *IEEE JSSC*, ED-26, April 1979, pp. 412–422.

[38] J. Compreers, H. J. DeMan, and W. M. C. Sansen, "A Process and Layout Oriented Short-Channel MOST Model for Circuit-Analysis Programs," *IEEE Trans. on ED*, Vol. ED-24, June 1977, pp. 739–746.

[39] D. G. Schweikert, "Automatic Layout of Custom MOS/LSI Integrated Circuits," *The Digest of the 1980 Custom Integrated Circuits Conference*, May 1980, pp. 99–100.

[40] R. M. Jennings, "ICDS: A Symbolic Layout and Mask Verification System for VLSI," *The Digest of the 1980 Custom Integrated Circuits Conference*, May 1980, pp. 101–102.

[41] G. Persky et al., "LTX—A System for the Directed Automatic Design of LSI Circuits," *Proc. 13th. Design Automation Conf.*, San Francisco, 1976, pp. 399–416.

[42] M. J. DeMan, "Computer-Aided Design for Integrated Circuits: Trying to Bridge the Gap," *IEEE JSSC*, Vol. SC-14, June 1979, pp. 613–621.

[43] B. Konemann, J. Mucha, and G. Zwiehoff, "Built-in Test for Complex Digital Integrated Circuits," *IEEE JSSC,* Vol. 15, June 1980, pp. 315–319.

[44] *IEEE Trans. on ED*, Special Issue on Non-Volatile Semiconductor Memory, Vol. ED-24, May 1977.

[45] *IEEE JSSC*, Special Issue on Semiconductor Materials, Processing, Process Modeling for IC Technology, August 1978.

[46] *IEEE Trans. on ED*, Special Issue on Very-Large-Scale Integration, April 1979.

[47] *IEEE JSSC*, Special Issue on Very-Large-Scale Integration, April 1979.

[48] *IEEE Trans. on ED*, Special Issue on Device Reliability, Vol. ED-26, January 1979.

Section 2.1
Scaling-Down MOSFETs

Design of Ion-Implanted MOSFET's with Very Small Physical Dimensions

ROBERT H. DENNARD, MEMBER, IEEE, FRITZ H. GAENSSLEN, HWA-NIEN YU, MEMBER, IEEE, V. LEO RIDEOUT, MEMBER, IEEE, ERNEST BASSOUS, AND ANDRE R. LeBLANC, MEMBER, IEEE

Abstract—**This paper considers the design, fabrication, and characterization of very small MOSFET switching devices suitable for digital integrated circuits using dimensions of the order of 1 μ. Scaling relationships are presented which show how a conventional MOSFET can be reduced in size. An improved small device structure is presented that uses ion implantation to provide shallow source and drain regions and a nonuniform substrate doping profile. One-dimensional models are used to predict the substrate doping profile and the corresponding threshold voltage versus source voltage characteristic. A two-dimensional current transport model is used to predict the relative degree of short-channel effects for different device parameter combinations. Polysilicon-gate MOSFET's with channel lengths as short as 0.5 μ were fabricated, and the device characteristics measured and compared with predicted values. The performance improvement expected from using these very small devices in highly miniaturized integrated circuits is projected.**

Manuscript received May 20, 1974; revised July 3, 1974.
The authors are with the IBM T. J. Watson Research Center, Yorktown Heights, N.Y. 10598.

List of Symbols

α	Inverse semilogarithmic slope of subthreshold characteristic.
D	Width of idealized step function profile for channel implant.
ΔW_f	Work function difference between gate and substrate.
ϵ_{Si}, ϵ_{ox}	Dielectric constants for silicon and silicon dioxide.
I_d	Drain current.
k	Boltzmann's constant.
κ	Unitless scaling constant.
L	MOSFET channel length.
μ_{eff}	Effective surface mobility.
n_i	Intrinsic carrier concentration.
N_a	Substrate acceptor concentration.
Ψ_s	Band bending in silicon at the onset of strong inversion for zero substrate voltage.

Reprinted from *IEEE J. Solid-State Circuits*, vol. SC–9, pp. 256–268, Oct. 1974.

Ψ_b	Built-in junction potential.
q	Charge on the electron.
Q_{eff}	Effective oxide charge.
t_{ox}	Gate oxide thickness.
T	Absolute temperature.
V_d, V_s, V_g, V_{sub}	Drain, source, gate and substrate voltages.
V_{ds}	Drain voltage relative to source.
V_{s-sub}	Source voltage relative to substrate.
V_t	Gate threshold voltage.
w_s, w_d	Source and drain depletion layer widths.
W	MOSFET channel width.

Introduction

NEW HIGH resolution lithographic techniques for forming semiconductor integrated circuit patterns offer a decrease in linewidth of five to ten times over the optical contact masking approach which is commonly used in the semiconductor industry today. Of the new techniques, electron beam pattern writing has been widely used for experimental device fabrication [1]–[4] while X-ray lithography [5] and optical projection printing [6] have also exhibited high-resolution capability. Full realization of the benefits of these new high-resolution lithographic techniques requires the development of new device designs, technologies, and structures which can be optimized for very small dimensions.

This paper concerns the design, fabrication, and characterization of very small MOSFET switching devices suitable for digital integrated circuits using dimensions of the order of 1 μ. It is known that reducing the source-to-drain spacing (i.e., the channel length) of an FET leads to undesirable changes in the device characteristics. These changes become significant when the depletion regions surrounding the source and drain extend over a large portion of the region in the silicon substrate under the gate electrode. For switching applications, the most undesirable "short-channel" effect is a reduction in the gate threshold voltage at which the device turns on, which is aggravated by high drain voltages. It has been shown that these short-channel effects can be avoided by scaling down the vertical dimensions (e.g., gate insulator thickness, junction depth, etc.) along with the horizontal dimensions, while also proportionately decreasing the applied voltages and increasing the substrate doping concentration [7], [8]. Applying this scaling approach to a properly designed conventional-size MOSFET shows that a 200-Å gate insulator is required if the channel length is to be reduced to 1 μ.

A major consideration of this paper is to show how the use of ion implantation leads to an improved design for very small scaled-down MOSFET's. First, the ability of ion implantation to accurately introduce a low concentration of doping atoms allows the substrate doping profile in the channel region under the gate to be increased in a controlled manner. When combined with a relatively lightly doped starting substrate, this channel implant reduces the sensitivity of the threshold voltage to changes in the source-to-substrate ("backgate") bias. This reduced "substrate sensitivity" can then be traded off for a thicker gate insulator of 350-Å thickness which tends to be easier to fabricate reproducibly and reliably. Second, ion implantation allows the formation of very shallow source and drain regions which are more favorable with respect to short-channel effects, while maintaining an acceptable sheet resistance. The combination of these features in an all-implanted design gives a switching device which can be fabricated with a thicker gate insulator if desired, which has well-controlled threshold characteristics, and which has significantly reduced interelectrode capacitances (e.g., drain-to-gate or drain-to-substrate capacitances).

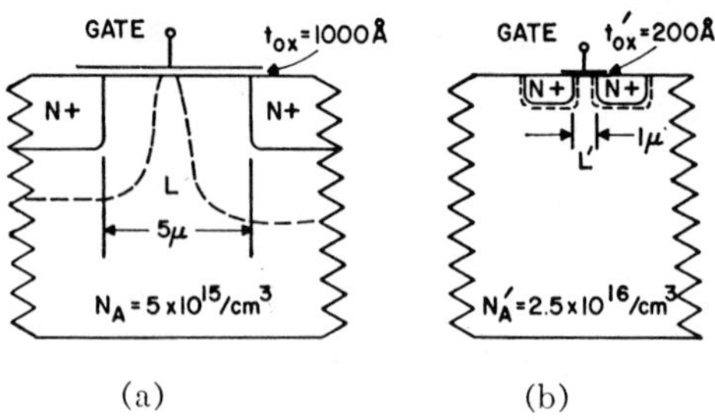

Fig. 1. Illustration of device scaling principles with $\kappa = 5$. (a) Conventional commercially available device structure. (b) Scaled-down device structure.

This paper begins by describing the scaling principles which are applied to a conventional MOSFET to obtain a very small device structure capable of improved performance. Experimental verification of the scaling approach is then presented. Next, the fabrication process for an improved scaled-down device structure using ion implantation is described. Design considerations for this all-implanted structure are based on two analytical tools: a simple one-dimensional model that predicts the substrate sensitivity for long channel-length devices, and a two-dimensional current-transport model that predicts the device turn-on characteristics as a function of channel length. The predicted results from both analyses are compared with experimental data. Using the two-dimensional simulation, the sensitivity of the design to various parameters is shown. Then, detailed attention is given to an alternate design, intended for zero substrate bias, which offers some advantages with respect to threshold control. Finally, the paper concludes with a discussion of the performance improvements to be expected from integrated circuits that use these very small FET's.

Device Scaling

The principles of device scaling [7], [8] show in a concise manner the general design trends to be followed in decreasing the size and increasing the performance of MOSFET switching devices. Fig. 1 compares a state-of-the-art n-channel MOSFET [9] with a scaled-down device designed following the device scaling principles to be described later. The larger structure shown in Fig. 1(a) is reasonably typical of commercially available devices fabricated by using conventional diffusion techniques. It uses a 1000-Å gate insulator thickness with a substrate doping and substrate bias chosen to give a gate threshold voltage V_t of approximately 2 V relative to the source potential. A substrate doping of 5×10^{15} cm^{-3} is low enough to give an acceptable value of substrate sensitivity. The substrate sensitivity is an important criterion in digital switching circuits employing source followers because the design becomes difficult if the threshold voltage increases by more than a factor of two over the full range of variation of the source voltage. For the device illustrated in Fig. 1(a), the design parameters limit the channel length L to about 5 μ. This restriction arises primarily from the penetration of the depletion region surrounding the drain into the area normally controlled by the gate electrode. For a maximum drain voltage of approximately 12–15 V this penetration will modify the surface potential and significantly lower the threshold voltage.

In order to design a new device suitable for smaller values of L, the device is scaled by a transformation in three variables: dimension, voltage, and doping. First, all linear dimensions are reduced by a unitless scaling factor κ, e.g., $t_{ox}' = t_{ox}/\kappa$, where the primed parameters refer to the new scaled-down device. This reduction includes vertical dimensions such as gate insulator thickness, junction depth, etc., as well as the horizontal dimensions of channel length and width. Second, the voltages applied to the device are reduced by the same factor (e.g., $V_{ds}' = V_{ds}/\kappa$). Third, the substrate doping concentration is increased, again using the same scaling factor (i.e., $N_a' = \kappa N_a$). The design shown in Fig. 1(b) was obtained using $\kappa = 5$ which corresponds to the desired reduction in channel length to 1 μ.

The scaling relationships were developed by observing that the depletion layer widths in the scaled-down device are reduced in proportion to the device dimensions due to the reduced potentials and the increased doping. For example,

$$w_s' = \{[2\epsilon_{Si}(\psi_b' + V_{s-sub}/\kappa)]/q\kappa N_a\}^{1/2} \simeq w_s/\kappa. \quad (1)$$

The threshold voltage at turn-on [9] is also decreased in direct proportion to the reduced device voltages so that the device will function properly in a circuit with reduced voltage levels. This is shown by the threshold voltage equation for the scaled-down device.

$$V_t' = (t_{ox}/\kappa\epsilon_{ox})\{-Q_{eff} + [2\epsilon_{Si}q\kappa N_a(\psi_s' + V_{s-sub}/\kappa)]^{1/2}\} + (\Delta W_f + \psi_s') \simeq V_t/\kappa. \quad (2)$$

In (2) the reduction in V_t is primarily due to the decreased insulator thickness, t_{ox}/κ, while the changes in the voltage and doping terms tend to cancel out. In most cases of interest (i.e., polysilicon gates of doping type opposite to that of the substrate or aluminum gates on p-type substrates) the work function difference ΔW_f is of opposite sign, and approximately cancels out ψ_s'. ψ_s' is the band bending in the silicon (i.e., the surface potential) at the onset of strong inversion for zero substrate bias. It would appear that the ψ' terms appearing in (1) and (2) prevent exact scaling since they remain approximately constant, actually increasing slightly due to the increased doping since $\psi_b' \simeq \psi_s' = (2kT/q)\ \ln\ (N_a'/n_i)$. However, the fixed substrate bias supply normally used with n-channel devices can be adjusted so that $(\psi_s' + V_{sub}') = (\psi_s + V_{sub})/\kappa$. Thus, by scaling down the applied substrate bias more than the other applied voltages, the potential drop across the source or drain junctions, or across the depletion region under the gate, can be reduced by κ.

All of the equations that describe the MOSFET device characteristics may be scaled as demonstrated above. For example, the MOSFET current equation [9] given by

$$I_d' = \frac{\mu_{eff}\epsilon_{ox}}{t_{ox}/\kappa}\left(\frac{W/\kappa}{L/\kappa}\right)\left(\frac{V_g - V_t - V_d/2}{\kappa}\right)(V_d/\kappa) = I_d/\kappa \quad (3)$$

is seen to be reduced by a factor of κ, for any given set of applied voltages, assuming no change in mobility. Actually, the mobility is reduced slightly due to increased impurity scattering in the heavier doped substrate.

It is possible to generalize the scaling approach to include electric field patterns and current density. The electric field distribution is maintained in the scaled-down device except for a change in scale for the spatial coordinates. Furthermore, the electric field strength at any corresponding point is unchanged because $V/x = V'/x'$. Thus, the carrier velocity at any point is also unchanged due to scaling and, hence, any saturation velocity effects will be similar in both devices, neglecting microscopic differences due to the fixed crystal lattice dimensions. From (3), since the device current is reduced by κ, the channel current per unit of channel width W is unchanged by scaling. This is consistent with the same sheet density of carriers (i.e., electrons per unit gate area) moving at the same velocity. In the vicinity of the drain, the carriers will move away from the surface to a lesser extent in the new device, due to the shallower diffusions. Thus, the density of mobile carriers per unit volume will be higher in the space-charge region around the drain, complementing the higher density of immobile charge due to the heavier doped substrate. Other scaling relationships for power density, delay time, etc., are given in Table I and will be discussed in a subsequent section on circuit performance.

In order to verify the scaling relationships, two sets of experimental devices were fabricated with gate insulators of 1000 and 200 Å (i.e., $\kappa = 5$). The measured drain voltage characteristics of these devices, normalized to $W/L = 1$, are shown in Fig. 2. The two sets of characteristics are quite similar when plotted with voltage and current scales of the smaller device reduced by a factor of five, which confirms the scaling predictions. In Fig. 2, the exact

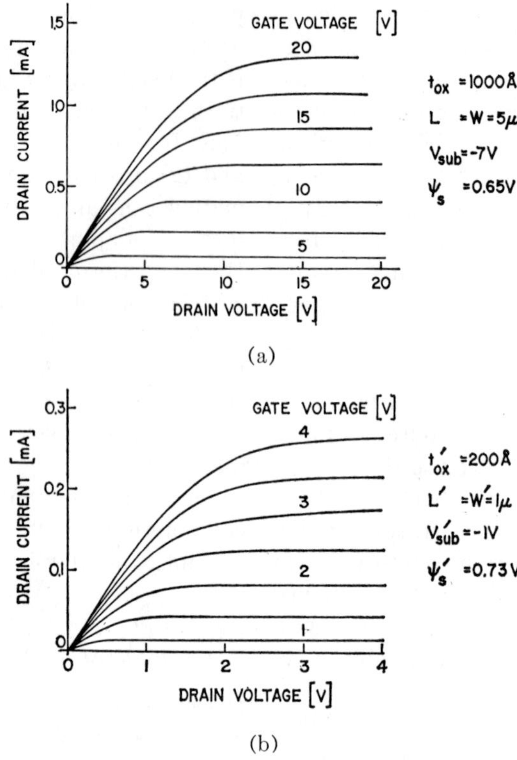

Fig. 2. Experimental drain voltage characteristics for (a) conventional, and (b) scaled-down structures shown in Fig. 1 normalized to $W/L = 1$.

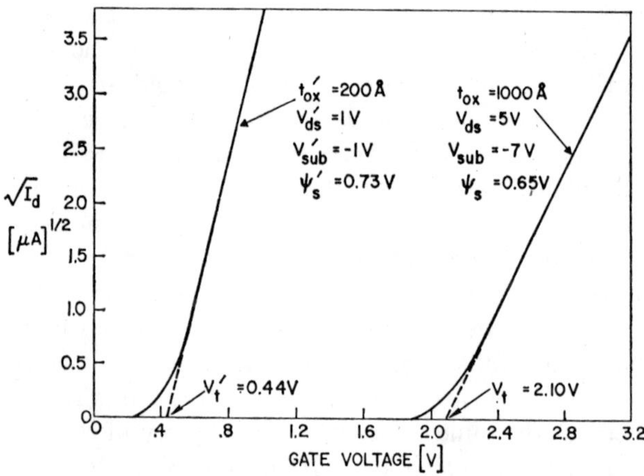

Fig. 3. Experimental turn-on characteristics for conventional and scaled-down devices shown in Fig. 1 normalized to $W/L = 1$.

match on the current scale is thought to be fortuitous since there is some experimental uncertainty in the magnitude of the channel length used to normalize the characteristics (see Appendix). More accurate data from devices with larger width and length dimensions on the same chip shows an approximate reduction of ten percent in mobility for devices with the heavier doped substrate. That the threshold voltage also scales correctly by a factor of five is verified in Fig. 3, which shows the experimental $\sqrt{I_d}$ versus V_g turn-on characteristics for the original and the scaled-down devices. For the cases shown, the drain voltage is large enough to cause pinchoff and the characteristics exhibit the expected linear relationship. When projected to intercept the gate voltage axis this linear relationship defines a threshold voltage useful for most logic circuit design purposes.

One area in which the device characteristics fail to scale is in the subthreshold or weak inversion region of the turn-on characteristic. Below threshold, I_d is exponentially dependent on V_g with an inverse semilogarithmic slope, α, [10], [11] which for the scaled-down device is given by

$$\alpha'\left(\frac{\text{volts}}{\text{decade}}\right) = \frac{dV_g'}{d\log_{10} I_d'}$$

$$= (kT/q \log_{10} e)\left(1 + \frac{\epsilon_{\text{Si}} t_{\text{ox}}/\kappa}{\epsilon_{\text{ox}} w_d/\kappa}\right), \quad (4)$$

which is the same as for the original larger device. The parameter α is important to dynamic memory circuits because it determines the gate voltage excursion required to go from the low current "off" state to the high current "on" state [11]. In an attempt to also extend the linear scaling relationships to α one could reduce the operating temperature in (4) (i.e., $T' = T/\kappa$), but this would cause a significant increase in the effective surface mobility [12] and thereby invalidate the current scaling relationship of (3). In order to design devices for operation at room temperature and above, one must accept the fact that the subthreshold behavior does not scale as desired. This nonscaling property of the subthreshold characteristic is of particular concern to miniature dynamic mem-

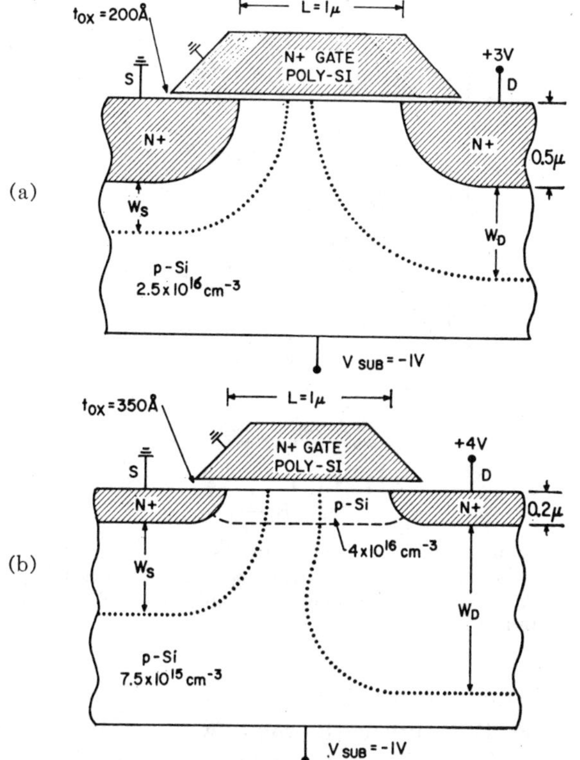

Fig. 4. Detailed cross sections for (a) scaled-down device structure, and (b) corresponding ion-implanted device structure.

ory circuits which require low source-to-drain leakage currents.

Ion-Implanted Device Design

The scaling considerations just presented lead to the device structure with a 1-μ channel length shown in Fig. 4(a). In contrast, the corresponding improved design utilizing the capability afforded by ion implantation is shown in Fig. 4(b). The ion-implanted device uses an initial substrate doping that is lower by about a factor of four, and an implanted boron surface layer having a concentration somewhat greater than the concentration used throughout the unimplanted structure of Fig. 4(a). The concentration and the depth of the implanted surface layer are chosen so that this heavier doped region will be completely within the surface depletion layer when the device is turned on with the source grounded. Thus, when the source is biased above ground potential, the depletion layer will extend deeper into the lighter doped substrate, and the additional exposed "bulk" charge will be reasonably small and will cause only a modest increase in the gate-to-source voltage required to turn on the device. With this improvement in substrate sensitivity the gate insulator thickness can be increased to as much as 350 Å and still maintain a reasonable gate threshold voltage as will be shown later.

Another aspect of the design philosophy is to use shallow implanted n^+ regions of depth comparable to the implanted p-type surface layer. The depletion regions under the gate electrode at the edges of the source and drain are then inhibited by the heavier doped surface layer, roughly pictured in Fig. 4(b), for the case of a turned-off device. The depletion regions under the source and drain extend much further into the lighter doped substrate. With deeper junctions these depletion regions would tend to merge in the lighter doped material which would cause a loss of threshold control or, in the extreme, punchthrough at high drain voltages. However, the shallower junctions give a more favorable electric field pattern which avoids these effects when the substrate doping concentration is properly chosen (i.e., when it is not too light).

The device capacitances are reduced with the ion-implanted structure due to the increased depletion layer width separating the source and drain from the substrate [cf. Figs. 4(a) and 4(b)], and due to the natural self-alignment afforded by the ion implantation process which reduces the overlap of the polysilicon gate over the source and drain regions. The thicker gate insulator also gives reduced gate capacitance, but the performance benefit in this respect is offset by the decreased gate field. To compensate for the thicker gate oxide and the expected threshold increase, a design objective for maximum drain voltage was set at 4 V for the ion-implanted design in Fig. 4(b), compared to 3 V for the scaled-down device of Fig. 4(a).

Fabrication of Ion-Implanted MOSFET's

The fabrication process for the ion-implanted MOSFET's used in this study will now be described. A four-mask process was used to fabricate polysilicon-gate, n-channel MOSFET's on a test chip which contains devices with channel lengths ranging from 0.5 to 10 μ. Though the eventual aim is to use electron-beam pattern exposure, it was more convenient to use contact masking with high quality master masks for process development. For this purpose high resolution is required only for the gate pattern which uses lines as small as 1.5 μ which are reduced in the subsequent processing. The starting substrate resistivity was 2 Ω·cm (i.e., about 7.5×10^{15} cm^{-3}). The method of fabrication for the thick oxide isolation between adjacent FET's is not described as it is not essential to the work presented here, and because several suitable techniques are available. Following dry thermal growth of the gate oxide, low energy (40 keV), low dose (6.7×10^{11} atoms/cm^2) B^{11} ions were implanted into the wafers, raising the boron doping near the silicon surface. All implantations were performed after gate oxide growth in order to restrict diffusion of the implanted regions.

After the channel implantation, a 3500-Å thick polysilicon layer was deposited, doped n^+, and the gate regions delineated. Next, n^+ source and drain regions 2000-Å deep were formed by a high energy (100 keV), high dose (4×10^{15} atoms/cm^2) As^{75} implantation through the same 350-Å oxide layer. During this step, however, the

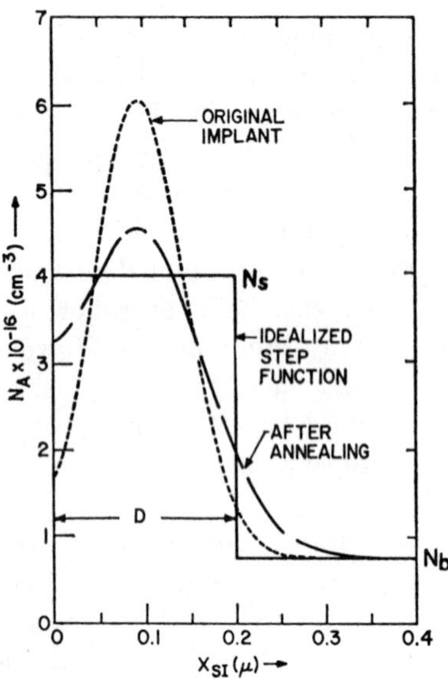

Fig. 5. Predicted substrate doping profile for basic ion-implanted device design for 40 keV B^{11} ions implanted through the 350-Å gate insulator.

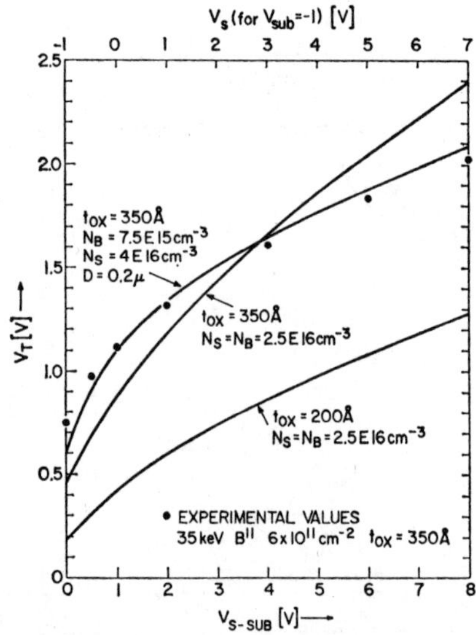

Fig. 6. Calculated and experimental substrate sensitivity characteristics for non-implanted devices with 200- and 350-Å gate insulators, and for corresponding ion-implanted device with 350-Å gate insulator.

polysilicon gate masks the channel region from the implant, absorbing all of the As^{75} dose incident there. The etching process used to delineate the gates results in a sloping sidewall which allows a slight penetration of As^{75} ions underneath the edges of the gates. The gate-to-drain (or source) overlap is estimated to be of the order of 0.2 μ. The high temperature processing steps that follow the implantations include 20 min at 900°C, and 11 min at 1000°C, which is more than adequate to anneal out the implantation damage without greatly spreading out the implanted doses. Typical sheet resistances were 50 Ω/□ for the source and drain regions, and 40 Ω/□ for the polysilicon areas. Following the As^{75} implant, a final insulating oxide layer 2000-Å thick was deposited using low-temperature chemical-vapor deposition. Then, the contact holes to the n^+ and polysilicon regions were defined, and the metalization was applied and delineated. Electrical contact directly to the shallow implanted source and drain regions was accomplished by a suitably chosen metallurgy to avoid junction penetration due to alloying during the final annealing step. After metalization an annealing step of 400 °C for 20 min in forming gas was performed to decrease the fast-state density.

One-Dimensional (Long Channel) Analysis

The substrate doping profile for the 40 keV, 6.7×10^{11} atoms/cm^2 channel implant incident on the 350-Å gate oxide, is shown in Fig. 5. Since the oxide absorbs 3 percent of the incident dose, the active dose in the silicon is 6.5×10^{11} atoms/cm^2. The concentration at the time of the implantation is given by the lightly dashed Gaussian function added to the background doping level, N_b. For 40 keV B^{11} ions, the projected range and standard deviation were taken as 1300 Å and 500 Å, respectively [13]. After the heat treatments of the subsequent processing, the boron is redistributed as shown by the heavier dashed line. These predicted profiles were obtained using a computer program developed by F. F. Morehead of our laboratories. The program assumes that boron atoms diffusing in the silicon reflect from the silicon-oxide interface and thereby raise the surface concentration. For modeling purposes it is convenient to use a simple, idealized, step-function representation of the doping profile, as shown by the solid line in Fig. 5. The step profile approximates the final predicted profile rather well and offers the advantage that it can be described by a few simple parameters. The three profiles shown in Fig. 5 all have the same active dose.

Using the step profile, a model for determining threshold voltage has been developed from piecewise solutions of Poisson's equation with appropriate boundary conditions [11]. The one-dimensional model considers only the vertical dimension and cannot account for horizontal short-channel effects. Results of the model are shown in Fig. 6 which plots the threshold voltage versus source-to-substrate bias for the ion-implanted step profile shown in Fig. 5. For comparison, Fig. 6 also shows the substrate sensitivity characteristics for the nonimplanted device with a 200-Å gate insulator and a constant background doping, and for a hypothetical device having a 350-Å gate insulator like the implanted structure and a constant background doping like the nonimplanted structure. The nonimplanted 200-Å case exhibits a low substrate sensitivity, but the magnitude of the threshold voltage is also low. On the other hand, the nonimplanted 350-Å case shows a higher threshold, but with an undesirably high substrate sensitivity. The ion-implanted case offers both a sufficiently high threshold voltage and a reasonably low substrate sensitivity, particularly for $V_{s\text{-sub}} \geq$ 1 V. For $V_{s\text{-sub}} < 1$ V, a steep slope occurs because the surface inversion layer in the channel is obtained while the depletion region in the silicon under the gate does not exceed D, the step width of the heavier doped implanted region. For $V_{s\text{-sub}} \geq 1$ V, at inversion the depletion region now extends into the lighter doped substrate and the threshold voltage then increases relatively slowly with $V_{s\text{-sub}}$ [11]. Thus, with a fixed substrate bias of -1 V, the substrate sensitivity over the operating range of the source voltage (e.g., ground potential to 4 V) is reasonably low and very similar to the slope of the nonimplanted 200-Å design. However, the threshold voltage is significantly higher for the implanted design which allows adequate design margin so that, under worst case conditions (e.g., short-channel effects which reduce the threshold considerably), the threshold will still be high enough so that the device can be turned off to a negligible conduction level as required for dynamic memory applications.

Experimental results are also given in Fig. 6 from measurements made on relatively long devices (i.e., $L = 10\ \mu$) which have no short-channel effects. These data agree reasonably well with the calculated curve. A 35 keV, 6×10^{11} atoms/cm^2 implant was used to achieve this result, rather than the slightly higher design value of 40 keV and 6.7×10^{11} atoms/cm^2.

Two-Dimensional (Short Channel) Analysis

For devices with sufficiently short-channel lengths, the one-dimensional model is inadequate to account for the threshold voltage lowering due to penetration of the drain field into the channel region normally controlled by the gate. While some models have been developed which account for this behavior [14], the problem is complicated for the ion-implanted structure by the nonuniform doping profile which leads to an electric field pattern that is difficult to approximate. For the ion-implanted case, the two-dimensional numerical current transport model of Kennedy and Mock [15], [16] was utilized. The computer program was modified by W. Chang and P. Hwang [17] to handle the abrupt substrate doping profiles considered for these devices.

The numerical current transport model was used to calculate the turn-on behavior of the ion-implanted device by a point-by-point computation of the device current for increasing values of gate voltage. Calculated results are shown in Fig. 7 for two values of channel length in the range of 1 μ, as well as for a relatively long-channel device with $L = 10\ \mu$. All cases were normalized to a width-to-length ratio of unity, and a drain voltage of 4 V was used in all cases. As the channel length is reduced to the order of 1 μ, the turn-on characteristic shifts to a lower gate voltage due to a lowering of the threshold voltage. The threshold voltage occurs at about 10^{-7} A where the turn-on characteristics make a transition from the exponential subthreshold behavior (a linear response on this semilogarithmic plot) to the $I_d \propto V_g^2$ square-law behavior. This current level can also be

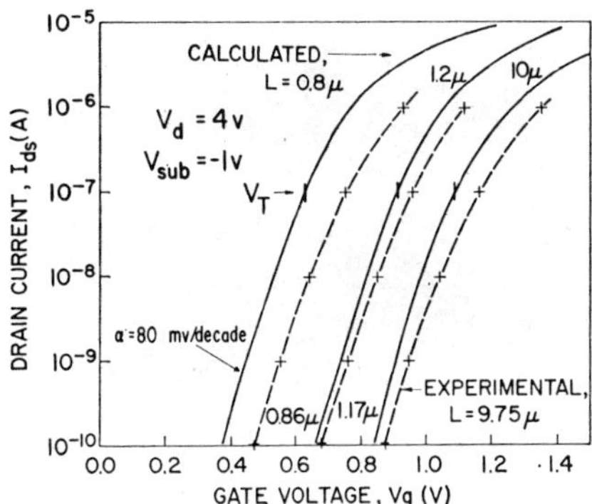

Fig. 7. Caluculated and experimental subthreshold turn-on characteristic for basic ion-implanted design for various channel lengths with $V_{sub} = -1$ V, $V_d = 4$ V.

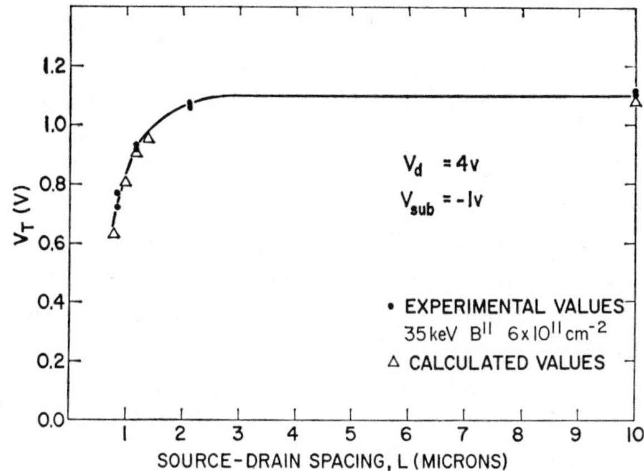

Fig. 8. Experimental and calculated dependence of threshold voltage on channel length for basic ion-implanted design with $V_{sub} = -1$ V, $V_d = 4$ V.

identified from Fig. 3 as the actual current at the projected threshold voltage, V_t. When the computed characteristics were plotted in the manner of Fig. 3 they gave 4×10^{-8} A at threshold for all device lengths. The band bending, ψ_s, at this threshold condition is approximately 0.75 V. Some of the other device designs considered with heavier substrate concentrations gave a higher current at threshold, so, for simplicity, the value of 10^{-7} A was used in all cases with a resultant small error in V_t.

MOSFET's with various channel lengths were measured to test the predictions of the two-dimensional model. The technique for experimentally determining the channel length for very short devices is described in the Appendix. The experimental results are plotted in Fig. 7 and show good agreement with the calculated curves, especially considering the somewhat different values of L. Another form of presentation of this data is shown in Fig. 8 where the threshold voltage is plotted as a function of channel length. The threshold voltage is essentially constant for $L > 2\ \mu$, and falls by a reasonably small amount as L is decreased from 2 to 1 μ, and then decreases more rapidly with further reductions in L. For

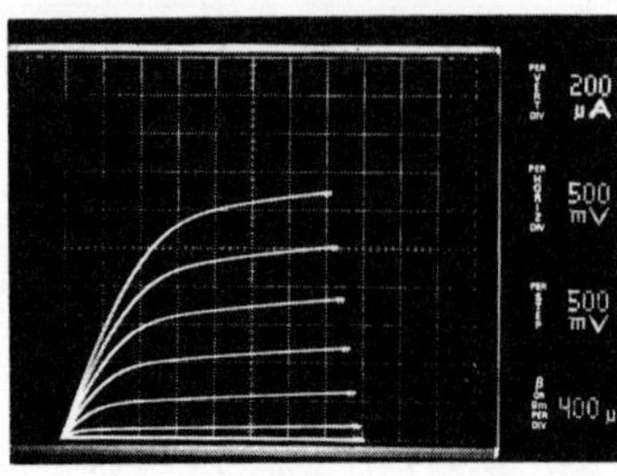

Fig. 9. Experimental drain voltage characteristics for basic ion-implanted design with $V_{sub} = -1$ V, $L = 1.1\ \mu$, and $W = 12.2\ \mu$. Curve tracer parameters; load resistance 30 Ω, drain voltage 4 V, gate voltage 0–4 V in 8 steps each 0.5 V apart.

circuit applications the nominal value of L could be set somewhat greater than 1 μ so that, over an expected range of deviation of L, the threshold voltage is reasonably well controlled. For example, $L = 1.3 \pm 0.3\ \mu$ would give $V_t = 1.0 \pm 0.1$ V from chip to chip due to this short-channel effect alone. This would be tolerable for many circuit applications because of the tracking of different devices on a given chip, if indeed this degree of control of L can be achieved. The experimental drain characteristics for an ion-implanted MOSFET with a 1.1-μ channel length are shown in Fig. 9 for the grounded source condition. The general shape of the characteristics is the same as those observed for much larger devices. No extraneous short-channel effects were observed for drain voltages as large as 4 V. The experimental data in Figs. 6–9 were taken from devices using a B^{11} channel implantation energy and dose of 35 keV and 6.0×10^{11} atoms/cm^2, respectively.

The two-dimensional simulations were also used to test the sensitivity of the design to various parameters. The results are given in Fig. 10 which tabulates values of threshold voltage as a function of channel length for the indicated voltages. Fig. 10(a) is an idealized representation for the basic design that has been discussed thus far. The first perturbation to the basic design was an increase in junction depth to 0.4 μ. This was found to give an appreciable reduction in threshold voltage for the shorter devices in Fig. 10(b). Viewed another way, the minimum device length would have to be increased by 20 percent (from 1.0 to 1.2 μ) to obtain a threshold comparable to the basic design. This puts the value of the shallower junctions in perspective. Another perturbation from the basic design which was considered was the use of a substrate doping lighter by a factor of 2, with a slightly higher concentration in the surface layer to give the same threshold for a long-channel device [Fig. 10(c)]. The results for smaller devices proved to be similar to the case of deeper junctions. The next possible departure from the basic design is the use of a shallower boron implantation in the channel region, only half as deep, with a heavier concentration to give the same long-channel threshold [Fig. 10(d)]. With the shallower profile, and

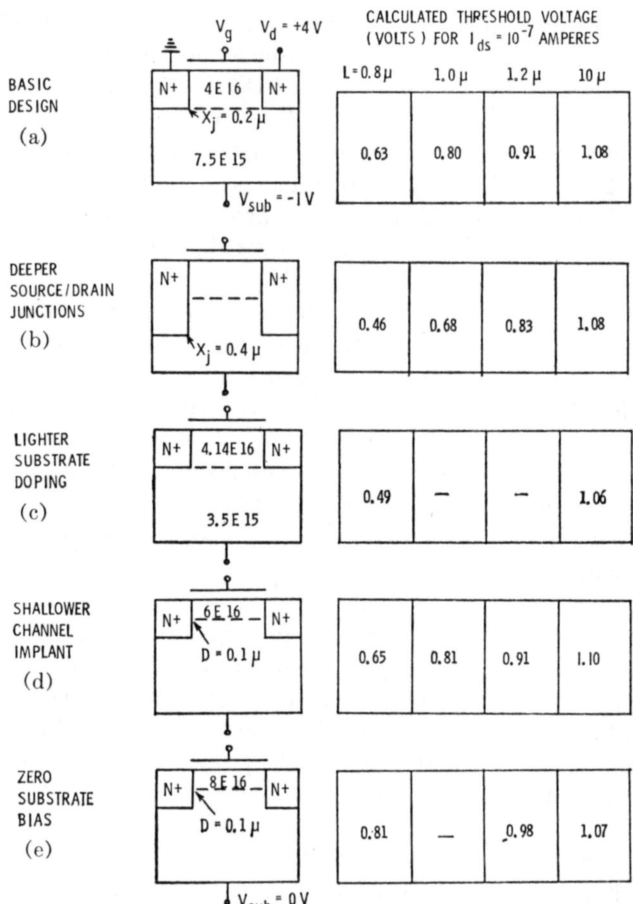

Fig. 10. Threshold voltage calculated using two-dimensional current transport model for various parameter conditions. A flat-band voltage of −1.1 V is assumed.

considering that the boron dose implanted in the silicon is about 20 percent less in this case, it was expected that more short-channel effects would occur. However, the calculated values show almost identical thresholds compared to the basic design. With the shallower implantation it is possible to use zero substrate bias and still have good substrate sensitivity since the heavier doped region is completely depleted at turn-on with a grounded source. The last design perturbation considers such a case, again with a heavier concentration to give the same long-channel threshold [Fig. 10 (e)]. The calculations for this case show appreciably less short-channel effect. In fact, the threshold for this case for a device with $L = 0.8\ \mu$ is about the same as for an $L = 1.0\ \mu$ device of the basic design. This important improvement is apparently due to the reduced depletion layer widths around the source and drain with the lower voltage drop across those junctions. Also, with these bias and doping conditions, the depletion layer depth in the silicon under the gate is much less at threshold, particularly near the source where only the band bending, ψ_s, appears across this depletion region, which may help prevent the penetration of field lines from the drain into this region where the device turn-on is controlled.

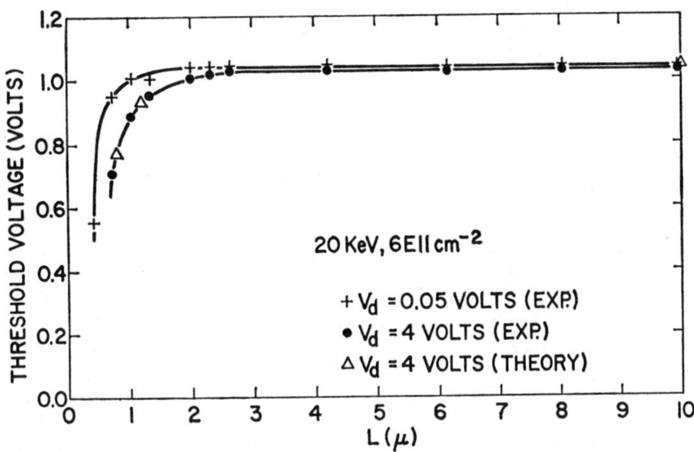

Fig. 11. Experimental and calculated dependence of threshold voltage on channel length for ion-implanted zero substrate bias design.

Characteristics of the Zero Substrate Bias Design

Since the last design shown in Fig. 10(e) appears to be better behaved in terms of short-channel effects, it is worthwhile to review its properties more fully. Experimental devices corresponding to this design were built and tested with various channel lengths. In this case a 20 keV, 6.0×10^{11} atoms/cm^2 B^{11} implant was used to obtain a shallower implanted layer of approximately 1000-Å depth [11]. Data on threshold voltage for these devices with 4 V applied to the drain is presented in Fig. 11 and corresponds very well to the calculated values. Data for a small drain voltage is also given in this figure, showing much less variation of threshold with channel length, as expected. The dependence of threshold voltage on source-to-substrate bias is shown in Fig. 12 for different values of L. The drain-to-source voltage was held at a constant low value for this measurement. The results show that the substrate sensitivity is indeed about the same for this design with zero substrate bias as for the original design with $V_{sub} = -1$ V. Note that the smaller devices show a somewhat flatter substrate sensitivity characteristic with relatively lower thresholds at high values of source (and drain) voltage.

The turn-on characteristics for the zero substrate bias design, both experimental and calculated, are shown in Fig. 13 for different values of L. The relatively small shift in threshold for the short-channel devices is evident; however, the turn-on rate is considerably slower for this case than for the $V_{sub} = -1$ V case shown in Fig. 7. This is due to the fact that the depletion region in the silicon under the gate is very shallow for this zero substrate bias case so that a large portion of a given gate voltage change is dropped across the gate insulator capacitance rather than across the silicon depletion layer capacitance. This is discussed in some detail for these devices in another paper [11]. The consequence for dynamic memory applications is that, even though the zero substrate bias

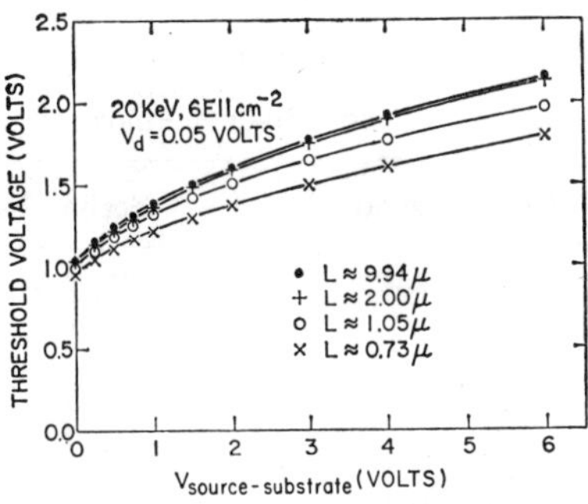

Fig. 12. Substrate sensitivity characteristics for ion-implanted zero substrate bias design with channel length as parameter.

design offers improved threshold control for strong inversion, this advantage is offset by the flatter subthreshold turn-on characteristic. For such applications the noise margin with the turn-on characteristic of Fig. 13 is barely suitable if the device is turned off by bringing its gate to ground. Furthermore, elevated temperature aggravates the situation [18]. Thus, for dynamic memory, the basic design with $V_{sub} = -1$ V presented earlier is preferred.

Circuit Performance with Scaled-Down Devices

The performance improvement expected from using very small MOSFET's in integrated circuits of comparably small dimensions is discussed in this section. First, the performance changes due to size reduction alone are obtained from the scaling considerations given earlier. The influence on the circuit performance due to the structural changes of the ion-implanted design is then discussed.

Table I lists the changes in integrated circuit performance which follow from scaling the circuit dimensions, voltages, and substrate doping in the same manner as the device changes described with respect to Fig. 1. These changes are indicated in terms of the dimensionless scal-

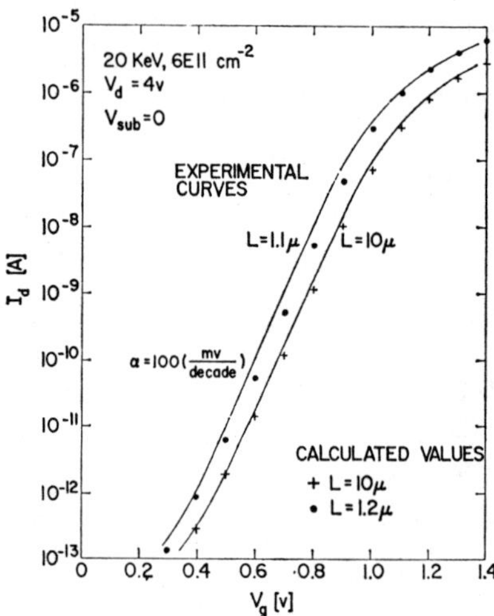

Fig. 13. Calculated and experimental subthreshold turn-on characteristics for ion-implanted zero substrate bias design.

TABLE I

SCALING RESULTS FOR CIRCUIT PERFORMANCE

Device or Circuit Parameter	Scaling Factor
Device dimension t_{ox}, L, W	$1/\kappa$
Doping concentration N_a	κ
Voltage V	$1/\kappa$
Current I	$1/\kappa$
Capacitance $\epsilon A/t$	$1/\kappa$
Delay time/circuit VC/I	$1/\kappa$
Power dissipation/circuit VI	$1/\kappa^2$
Power density VI/A	1

ing factor κ. Justifying these results here in great detail would be tedious, so only a simplified treatment is given. It is argued that all nodal voltages are reduced in the miniaturized circuits in proportion to the reduced supply voltages. This follows because the quiescent voltage levels in digital MOSFET circuits are either the supply levels or some intermediate level given by a voltage divider consisting of two or more devices, and because the resistance V/I of each device is unchanged by scaling. An assumption is made that parasitic resistance elements are either negligible or unchanged by scaling, which will be examined subsequently. The circuits operate properly at lower voltages because the device threshold voltage V_t scales as shown in (2), and furthermore because the tolerance spreads on V_t should be proportionately reduced as well if each parameter in (2) is controlled to the same percentage accuracy. Noise margins are reduced, but at the same time internally generated noise coupling voltages are reduced by the lower signal voltage swings.

Due to the reduction in dimensions, all circuit elements (i.e., interconnection lines as well as devices) will have their capacitances reduced by a factor of κ. This occurs because of the reduction by κ^2 in the area of these components, which is partially cancelled by the decrease in the electrode spacing by κ due to thinner insulating films

TABLE II

SCALING RESULTS FOR INTERCONNECTION LINES

Parameter	Scaling Factor
Line resistance, $R_L = \rho L/Wt$	κ
Normalized voltage drop IR_L/V	κ
Line response time R_LC	1
Line current density I/A	κ

and reduced depletion layer widths. These reduced capacitances are driven by the unchanged device resistances V/I giving decreased transition times with a resultant reduction in the delay time of each circuit by a factor of κ. The power dissipation of each circuit is reduced by κ^2 due to the reduced voltage and current levels, so the power-delay product is improved by κ^3. Since the area of a given device or circuit is also reduced by κ^2, the power density remains constant. Thus, even if many more circuits are placed on a given integrated circuit chip, the cooling problem is essentially unchanged.

As indicated in Table II, a number of problems arise from the fact that the cross-sectional area of conductors is decreased by κ^2 while the length is decreased only by κ. It is assumed here that the thicknesses of the conductors are necessarily reduced along with the widths because of the more stringent resolution requirements (e.g., on etching, etc.). The conductivity is considered to remain constant which is reasonable for metal films down to very small dimensions (until the mean free path becomes comparable to the thickness), and is also reasonable for degenerately doped semiconducting lines where solid solubility and impurity scattering considerations limit any increase in conductivity. Under these assumptions the resistance of a given line increases directly with the scaling factor κ. The IR drop in such a line is therefore constant (with the decreased current levels), but is κ times greater in comparison to the lower operating voltages. The response time of an unterminated transmission line is characteristically limited by its time constant R_LC, which is unchanged by scaling; however, this makes it difficult to take advantage of the higher switching speeds inherent in the scaled-down devices when signal propagation over long lines is involved. Also, the current density in a scaled-down conductor is increased by κ, which causes a reliability concern. In conventional MOSFET circuits, these conductivity problems are relatively minor, but they become significant for linewidths of micron dimensions. The problems may be circumvented in high performance circuits by widening the power buses and by avoiding the use of n^+ doped lines for signal propagation.

Use of the ion-implanted devices considered in this paper will give similar performance improvement to that of the scaled-down device with $\kappa = 5$ given in Table I. For the implanted devices with the higher operating voltages (4 V instead of 3 V) and higher threshold voltages (0.9 V instead of 0.4 V), the current level will be reduced in proportion to $(V_g - V_t)^2/t_{ox}$ to about 80 percent of the current in the scaled-down device. The power dissipation per circuit is thus about the same in both cases. All device capacitances are about a factor of two less in the implanted devices, and n^+ interconnection lines will show the same improvement due to the lighter substrate doping and decreased junction depth. Some capacitance elements such as metal interconnection lines would be essentially unchanged so that the overall capacitance improvement in a typical circuit would be somewhat less than a factor of two. The delay time per circuit which is proportional to VC/I thus appears to be about the same for the implanted and for the directly scaled-down micron devices shown in Fig. 4.

Summary

This paper has considered the design, fabrication, and characterization of very small MOSFET switching devices. These considerations are applicable to highly miniaturized integrated circuits fabricated by high-resolution lithographic techniques such as electron-beam pattern writing. A consistent set of scaling relationships were presented that show how a conventional device can be reduced in size; however, this direct scaling approach leads to some challenging technological requirements such as very thin gate insulators. It was then shown how an all ion-implanted structure can be used to overcome these difficulties without sacrificing device area or performance. A two-dimensional current transport model modified for use with ion-implanted structures proved particularly valuable in predicting the relative degree of short-channel effects arising from different device parameter combinations. The general objective of the study was to design an n-channel polysilicon-gate MOSFET with a 1-μ channel length for high-density source-follower circuits such as those used in dynamic memories. The most satisfactory combination of subthreshold turn-on range, threshold control, and substrate sensitivity was achieved by an experimental MOSFET that used a 35 keV, 6.0×10^{11} atoms/cm^2 B^{11} channel implant, a 100 keV, 4×10^{15} atoms/cm^2 As^{75} source/drain implant, a 350-Å gate insulator, and an applied substrate bias of -1 V. Also presented was an ion-implanted design intended for zero substrate bias that is more attractive from the point of view of threshold control but suffers from an increased subthreshold turn-on range. Finally the sizable performance improvement expected from using very small MOSFET's in integrated circuits of comparably small dimensions was projected.

Appendix

Experimental Determination of Channel Length

A technique for determining the effective electrical channel length L for very small MOSFET's from experimental data is described here. The technique is based on the observation that

$$WR_{chan} = L\rho_{chan} \tag{A1}$$

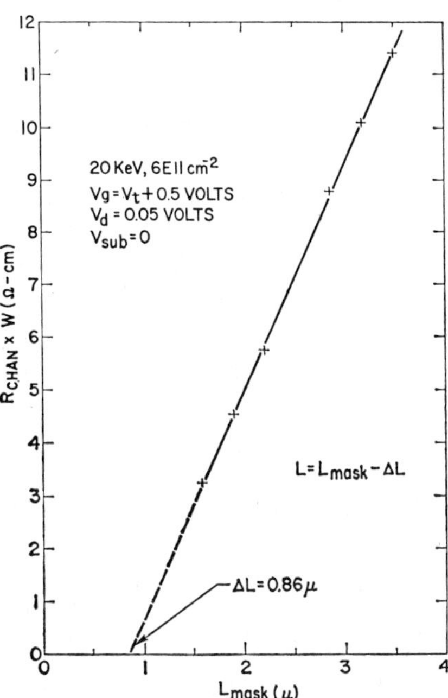

Fig. 14. Illustration of experimental technique used to determine channel length, L.

where R_{chan} is the channel resistance, and ρ_{chan} the sheet resistance of the channel. For a fixed value of $V_g - V_t > 0$, and with the device turned on in the below-pinchoff region, the channel sheet resistance is relatively independent of L. Then, a plot of WR_{chan} versus L_{mask} will intercept the L_{mask} axis at ΔL because $\Delta L = L_{mask} - L$, where ΔL is the processing reduction in the mask dimension due to exposure and etching. An example of this technique is illustrated in Fig. 14.

The experimental values of W and R_{chan} used in Fig. 14 were obtained as follows. First, the sheet resistance of the ion-implanted n^+ region was determined using a relatively large four-point probe structure. Knowing the n^+ sheet resistance allows us to compute the source and drain resistance R_s and R_d, and to deduce W from the resistance of a long, slender, n^+ line. The channel resistance can be calculated from

$$R_{chan} = V_{chan}/I_d = (V_d - I_d(R_s + R_d + 2R_c + R_{load}))/I_d, \tag{A2}$$

where R_c is the contact resistance of the source or drain, and R_{load} is the load resistance of the measurement circuit. I_d was determined at $V_g = V_t + 0.5$ V with a small applied drain voltage of 50 or 100 mV. The procedure is more simple and accurate if one uses a set of MOSFET's having different values of L_{mask} but all with the same value of W_{mask}. Then one needs only to plot R_{chan} versus L_{mask} in order to determine ΔL.

Acknowledgment

We wish to acknowledge the valuable contributions of B. L. Crowder and F. F. Morehead who provided the ion implantations and related design information. Also important were the contributions of P. Hwang and W. Chang to two-dimensional device computations. J. J. Walker and V. DiLonardo assisted with the mask preparation and testing activities. The devices were fabricated by the staff of the silicon technology facility at the T. J. Watson Research Center.

References

[1] F. Fang, M. Hatzakis, and C. H. Ting, "Electron-beam fabrication of ion implanted high-performance FET circuits," *J. Vac. Sci. Technol.*, vol. 10, p. 1082, 1973.

[2] J. M. Pankrantz, H. T. Yuan, and L. T. Creagh, "A high-gain, low-noise transistor fabricated with electron beam lithography," in *Tech. Dig. Int. Electron Devices Meeting,* Dec. 1973, pp. 44–46.

[3] H. N. Yu, R. H. Dennard, T. H. P. Chang, and M. Hatzakis, "An experimental high-density memory array fabricated with electron beam," in *ISSCC Dig. Tech. Papers,* Feb. 1973, pp. 98–99.

[4] R. C. Henderson, R. F. W. Pease, A. M. Voshchenkow, P. Mallery, and R. L. Wadsack, "A high speed p-channel random access 1024-bit memory made with electron lithography," in *Tech. Dig. Int. Electron Devices Meeting,* Dec. 1973, pp. 138–140.

[5] D. L. Spears and H. I. Smith, "X-Ray lithography—a new high resolution replication process," *Solid State Technol.,* vol. 15, p. 21, 1972.

[6] S. Middlehoek, "Projection masking, thin photoresist layers and interference effects," *IBM J. Res. Develop.,* vol. 14, p. 117, 1970.

[7] R. H. Dennard, F. H. Gaensslen, L. Kuhn, and H. N. Yu, "Design of micron MOS switching devices," presented at the IEEE Int. Electron Devices Meeting, Washington, D.C., Dec. 1972.

[8] A. N. Broers and R. H. Dennard, "Impact of electron beam technology on silicon device fabrication," *Semicond. Silicon* (Electrochem. Soc. Publication), H. R. Huff and R. R. Burgess, eds., pp. 830–841, 1973.

[9] D. L. Critchlow, R. H. Dennard, and S. E. Schuster, "Design characteristics of n-channel insulated-gate field-effect transistors," *IBM J. Res. Develop.,* vol. 17, p. 430, 1973.

[10] R. M. Swanson and J. D. Meindl, "Ion-implanted complementary MOS transistors in low-voltage circuits," *IEEE J. Solid-State Circuits,* vol. SC-7, pp. 146–153, April 1972.

[11] V. L. Rideout, F. H. Gaensslen, and A. LeBlanc, "Device design considerations for ion implanted n-channel MOSFET's," *IBM J. Res. Develop.,* to be published.

[12] F. F. Fang and A. B. Fowler, "Transport properties of electrons in inverted Si surfaces," *Phys. Rev.* vol. 169, p. 619, 1968.

[13] W. S. Johnson, IBM System Products Division, E. Fishkill, N. Y., private communication.

[14] H. S. Lee, "An analysis of the threshold voltage for short channel IGFET's," *Solid-State Electron.,* vol. 16, p. 1407, 1973.

[15] D. P. Kennedy and P. C. Murley, "Steady state mathematical theory for the insulated gate field effect transistor," *IBM J. Res. Develop.,* vol. 17, p. 1, 1973.

[16] M. S. Mock, "A two-dimensional mathematical model of the insulated-gate field-effect transistor," *Solid-State Electron.,* vol. 16, p. 601, 1973.

[17] W. Chang and P. Hwang, IBM System Products Division, Essex Junction, Vt., private communication.

[18] R. R. Troutman, "Subthreshold design considerations for insulated gate field-effect transistors," *IEEE J. Solid-State Circuits,* vol. SC-9, p. 55, April 1974.

1 μm MOSFET VLSI Technology: Part II—Device Designs and Characteristics for High-Performance Logic Applications

ROBERT H. DENNARD, MEMBER, IEEE, FRITZ H. GAENSSLEN, EDWARD J. WALKER, MEMBER, IEEE, AND PETER W. COOK, MEMBER, IEEE

Abstract—**Micrometer-dimension n-channel silicon-gate MOSFET's optimized for high-performance logic applications have been designed and characterized for both room-temperature and liquid-nitrogen-temperature operation. Appropriate choices of design parameters are shown to give proper device thresholds which are reasonably independent of channel length and width. Depletion-type devices are characterized at room temperature for load device use. Logic performance capability is demonstrated by test results on NOR circuits for representative fan-out and loading conditions. Unloaded ring oscillators achieved switching delays down to 240 ps at room temperature and down to 100 ps at liquid nitrogen temperature.**

I. INTRODUCTION

CONSIDERABLE WORK has been done up to this time on experimental micrometer-dimension MOSFET devices, and a good understanding of design principles has been achieved [1]-[5]. The work described in this paper is part of a comprehensive effort to develop and demonstrate a MOSFET technology for very large scale integration using direct electron-beam pattern exposure with 1 μm minimum linewidth and with typical layout dimensions of 1.25 to 1.5 μm. The choice of device design parameters (doping profiles, insulator thickness, etc.) was made to satisfy specific requirements for high-performance logic circuits while being compatible with fabrication processes.

One aim of the work is to show the performance level obtainable at micrometer dimensions with optimized silicon-gate FET's. The scaling principles show that the circuit delay should decrease directly with linewidth due to the reduction of device and circuit capacitances, while power dissipation decreases in proportion to the square of the linewidth due to reduced circuit voltages and currents [4]. Use of 1 μm minimum linewidth in comparison to typical present-day FET products with 3-4 μm minimum linewidth promises an order of magnitude density improvement with 3-4 times higher speed, while maintaining the same power density. Some of this improvement can be realized, of course, with refinements in optical photolithography currently being pursued in many places. Another aim is to demonstrate the performance enhancement gained from operation at liquid nitrogen temperature. It has been shown that low-temperature FET operation produces increased transconductance, a sharper turn-on characteristic, greatly improved interconnection line conductivity, better thermal conductivity, and potentially better reliability [6]. The increased transconductance, which is about 2-3 times greater at liquid nitrogen temperature depending on the applied lateral field, gives a proportionate increase in circuit speed.

Manuscript received December 4, 1978.

The authors are with the IBM Thomas J. Watson Research Center, Yorktown Heights, NY 10598.

The first section of this paper discusses the choice of FET design parameters such as doping profiles and insulator thickness. Following this, a comprehensive set of characteristics is presented based on measurements on fabricated devices and compared in some cases to the results of two-dimensional simulations which were used to establish the design. The room-temperature data includes the variation of threshold voltage as a function of channel length and width for both enhancement- and depletion-type devices. Design changes and characteristics are given for liquid-nitrogen-temperature operation of enhancement-type FET's. Finally, various types of ring oscillator test circuits for NOR circuit performance are described, and experimental results are given for both room- and liquid-nitrogen-temperature cases. Thus far, the depletion device has been used only for room-temperature circuit experiments because of the excessive change of threshold at low temperature caused by freezeout of the implanted donor impurities [7]. Enhancement devices with a positive gate bias have been used instead for low-temperature circuit experiments.

II. DEVICE DESIGN AND CHARACTERIZATION

A. Device Structure and Choice of Parameters

A cross section of the device structures which have been designed and tested in this study is shown in Fig. 1. These enhancement- and depletion-type devices were implemented in an ion-implanted silicon-gate technology with semirecessed oxide isolation. General design conditions for small MOS devices based on scaling were given in a previous paper along with detailed criteria for optimizing ion-implanted devices with lightly doped substrates [4]. Specific designs were given for memory applications which require careful consideration of subthreshold leakage. The structures of Fig. 1 follow the same general design criteria with somewhat different choices of the various parameters appropriate for the logic applications considered in this study.

The channel length of the enhancement device is nominally 1.3 μm with an anticipated tolerance of ±0.3 μm. These values

Reprinted from *IEEE J. Solid-State Circuits*, vol. SC-14, pp. 247-255, Apr. 1979.

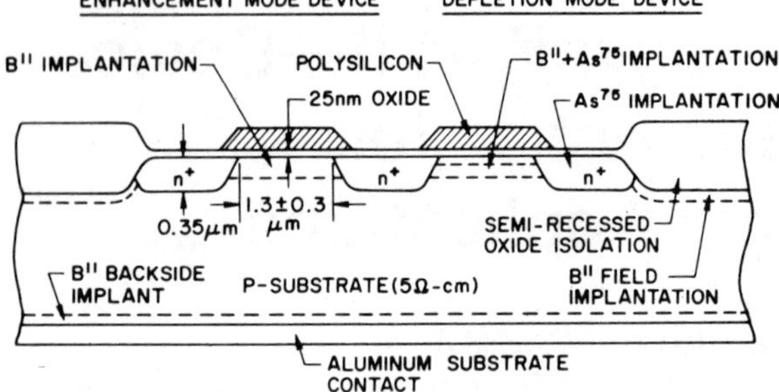

Fig. 1. Cross section of experimental device structure.

were based on an estimate of processing biases and dimensional control made at the beginning of the study when experience with the particular processes was limited. Confirming or possibly tightening this specification was one of the goals of the study. Test devices with smaller as well as larger channel lengths were included in a basic set of test structures made in all process runs. The depletion device was designed with a somewhat longer channel length (1.8 µm) on most test circuits to provide greater immunity to geometry variations, particularly since the threshold value changes appreciably with length at shorter channel lengths, as will be shown.

A gate insulator thickness of 25 nm was used in this study in comparison to 35 nm in [4]. The thinner insulator was used to achieve better threshold control and larger transconductance in a given device area. In principle, threshold spreads due to oxide charge variations are less with thinner oxides, and the substrate sensitivity (change of threshold with source-substrate bias) is also smaller.

The depth of the n$^+$ junction, which is a function of ion-implantation energy and dose and subsequent drive-in temperatures, is an important design choice. Shallower junctions are desirable to minimize lateral diffusion under the edge of the gate and under the field oxide, which would tend to give increased gate-to-source and gate-to-drain capacitance and larger layout dimensions. Shallow junctions also tend to minimize short-channel effects by giving a more favorable field pattern. On the other hand, deeper junctions are desirable to obtain good conductivity for n$^+$ interconnection paths, to minimize hot-electron injection into the gate insulator near the drain, and to be less susceptible to junction penetration from metal contacts. For arsenic implant doses of the order of 10^{16} cm^{-2} and greater, sheet resistivity varies approximately inversely with junction depth and is fairly independent of dose and temperature cycles for a given depth. Based on these considerations, a junction depth of 0.35 µm was chosen. This allows a sheet resistance as low as 20–25 Ω/sq which is important for circuit wiring.

The dose of the shallow implanted boron layer under the gate was chosen to give a threshold voltage of about 0.6 V for the enhancement-mode device. This threshold voltage is consistent with logic designs using a power supply voltage of about 2.5 V. Higher supply voltages are used for some dynamic logic circuits in array applications. For liquid nitrogen operation, the implanted boron dose was decreased somewhat to compensate for the threshold increase at low temperature [6]. The depletion device has a shallow phosphorous or arsenic implant to shift the threshold negative and to provide a normally conducting device for use as a load resistor.

One of the major advantages of an ion-implanted FET technology is that the substrate doping can be made very light, since the thresholds in the device and field regions can be readily adjusted and more tightly controlled by implanting additional impurities near the surface. For the design shown in Fig. 1, the substrate doping concentration is nominally $2.5 \times 10^{15}/\text{cm}^3$ (5-Ω · cm resistivity). This was chosen to be as light as possible to minimize substrate sensitivity which is particularly important with depletion load devices in order to maintain a fairly constant pinch-off current. The light substrate doping also minimizes junction capacitance. On the other hand, this doping level is heavy enough to prevent punch-through and obtain reasonable immunity from short- and narrow-channel effects. The one-dimensional depletion width is a little more than 1 µm at the maximum junction bias. Two-dimensional simulations have been used to optimize the channel doping profile in conjunction with the background level to achieve satisfactory short-channel behavior for a minimum channel length of 1 µm. Results are shown in the next section.

The field oxide, which is grown thermally prior to the silicon-gate deposition, is scaled down in thickness to control "bird's beak" growth to an amount reasonable for dense layout groundrules. A CVD layer, not shown in Fig. 1, is added prior to the deposition of aluminum contacts and interconnections. Proper choice of field implant conditions gives satisfactory device isolation. A low-resistance substrate connection is provided by aluminum on the back of the wafer, using an enhanced boron surface doping to assure ohmic contact at low temperatures.

III. Room-Temperature Device Characteristics

A large number of test devices of various dimensions have been fabricated and tested during the course of this study. The characteristics shown in this section are from typical devices on test wafers which are thought to be representative of the technology. They are reproducible within reasonable bounds and match the original goals and design predictions fairly well.

The turn-on characteristics, current versus gate voltage measured with a small drain voltage, are shown in Fig. 2 for enhancement and depletion devices with the same physical dimensions. A threshold value V_T of gate voltage at turn-on is defined by matching the experimental curve to a straight-line segment corresponding to a simple device model which is valid for low gate voltages. The straight-line model is matched to the experimental curve at the region of maximum slope and projected to zero current, intersecting the axis at $V_T + V_{DS}/2$ from which V_T is determined. When the gate voltage is below $V_T + V_{DS}$, the device is in pinch-off, and the current varies as $(V_{GS} - V_T)^2$ according to a well-known simple theory. The depletion device behaves somewhat differently in this region and has a definite (but small) current level at $V_{GS} = V_T$ which is presumably due to subsurface conduction in the implanted n-type layer. The straight-line segment matches the depletion-device current very well at $V_{GS} = 0$ which is the usual bias condition for a depletion-type load device in standard logic circuits, so this threshold definition is meaningful for model-

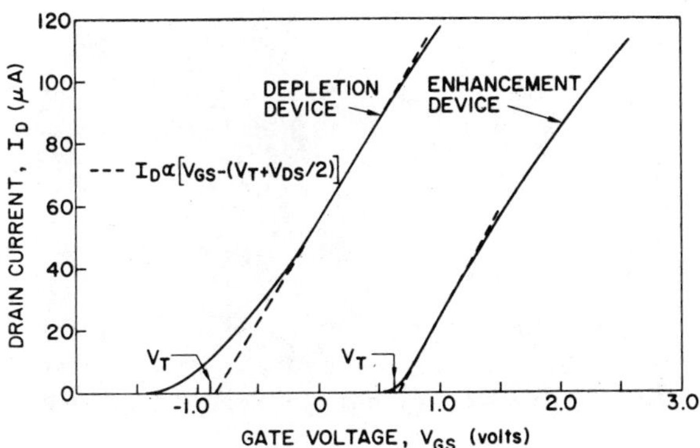

Fig. 2. Turn-on characteristics of experimental devices, showing threshold definition. $V_{DS} = 0.1$ V.

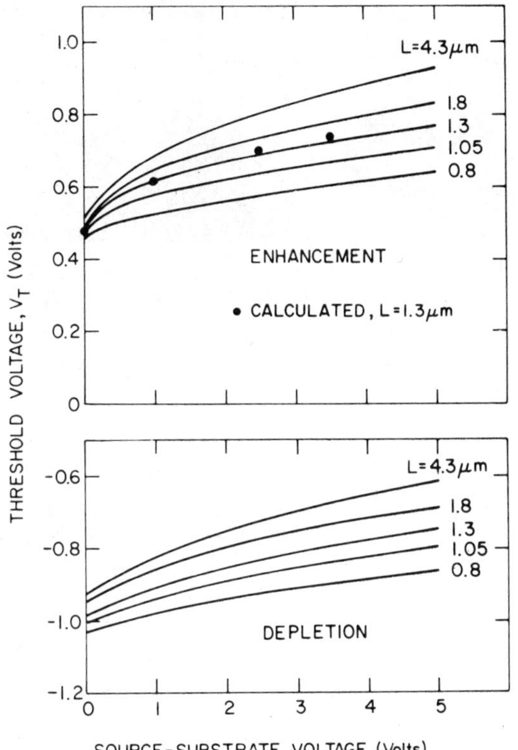

Fig. 3. Substrate sensitivity curves for various values of channel length L. $V_{DS} = 0.1$ V, $W = 15.3$ μm.

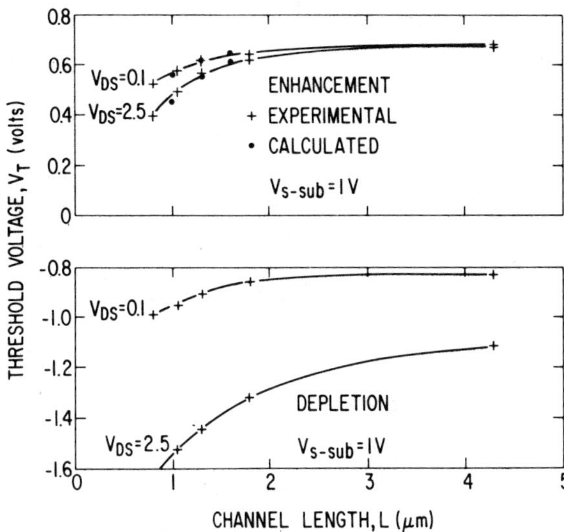

Fig. 4. Threshold voltage as a function of channel lengths for indicated drain–source voltages. $V_{S\text{-}SUB} = 1$ V.

ing of such circuits. The slopes of the straight-line segments are similar for the enhancement and depletion devices. Careful measurements accounting for external resistances, etc., indicate a mobility of about 550 $cm^2/V \cdot s$ for the enhancement device.

Measurements of the threshold voltage as a function of source–substrate voltage are shown in Fig. 3 for various values of channel length L. The channel length is defined as the separation between the n^+p junctions for the enhancement device and is determined experimentally from conductance measurements on devices of various gate dimensions (as shown in [4, Appendix]). Design values for the nominal 1.3 μm channel length are also shown in Fig. 3 and are matched well by the measured results. The design values are based on two-dimensional simulations [8] using a doping profile in the silicon determined with the SUPREM simulation program which accounts for redistribution of the implanted boron during the gate oxidation and other thermal cycles [9]. The simulated boron profile is roughly Gaussian with a concentration which peaks at about 4×10^{16} cm^{-3} near the surface and falls to half-value at a depth of nearly 0.2 μm. An adjustment of the total boron dose in the silicon was necessary to match calculated and experimental curves at one point since the diffusion rate and the segregation coefficient during oxidation are not accurately known for the process which was used. The room temperature design is intended for a substrate bias of −1 V which allows operating over a fairly flat portion of the curve of Fig. 3 for circuit cases where the source varies between ground and the positive power supply level. Use of a fairly low substrate bias helps minimize short-channel effects (changes of threshold with L) for a grounded source device.

These same threshold data are plotted as a function of channel length in Fig. 4 for a fixed 1-V source-substrate bias. Data for a relatively large drain voltage of 2.5 V are also given. For the high drain voltage, the device is in pinch-off for a wide range of gate voltages, and the threshold is determined by matching experimental turn-on data to an idealized square-law model. In the case of the enhancement device, the lowering of the threshold voltage with the higher drain voltage is fairly well controlled down to channel lengths of less than 1 μm. The experimental data confirms simulation results and shows that short-channel effects have indeed been minimized by the choice of design parameters for this device. For the depletion device, on the other hand, the change of threshold with drain voltage is substantial at short channel lengths. Even at long channel lengths there is a threshold shift for high drain voltage, probably due to increased subsurface current which adds to the surface current to cause an apparent lowering of the threshold value. The depletion-type device is relatively susceptible to short-channel effects because the depletion region created by the applied source–substrate bias extends farther below the silicon surface at the threshold condition. This removes the substrate "ground plane" farther from the region controlled by the gate and allows the drain electrode to play a more active role in establishing the potential in that region. The depletion device

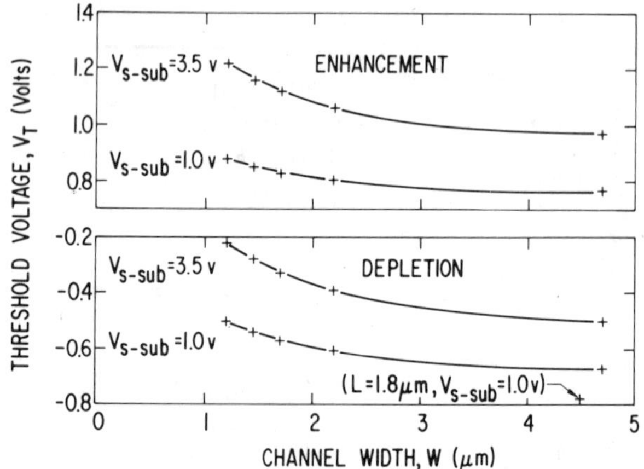

Fig. 5. Dependence of threshold on channel width and source–substrate voltage. $L = 15$ μm, $V_{DS} = 0.1$ V.

apparently requires a more elaborate representation for accurate circuit modeling than the enhancement device. This is thought to be true in general and not necessarily related to the small dimensions used in these particular devices.

The effect of channel width on threshold voltage is shown in Fig. 5. The threshold rises as channel width is decreased due to fringing of the electric field lines from the gate to the substrate at the edges of the device [10]. The effect becomes significant when the depletion depth under the gate is comparable to the channel width. As shown in Fig. 5, the threshold increases more when the source-substrate bias is larger. In other words, narrow devices have greater substrate sensitivity due to the greater depletion depth under the gate at large values of substrate bias. For the same reason, these characteristics are sensitive to substrate doping and would be degraded if a lighter doping concentration were used. The data of Fig. 5 are for a constant channel length of 15 μm. Similar results are obtained with shorter channel lengths except for a general lowering of threshold levels due to the short-channel effect. One data point for a shorter depletion device is shown for a particular geometry used extensively in the ring oscillator tests.

The source-drain current-voltage characteristics for an enhancement device having the nominal 1.3 μm channel length are given in Fig. 6. The conduction characteristics are well controlled over the intended operating voltage range and beyond. Avalanche multiplication and breakdown effects are seen to occur at reasonable voltage levels. The breakdown voltage is lower for shorter channels, but even at $L = 1$ μm the lowest drain-source voltage which will sustain high breakdown currents is about 7 V.

The corresponding drain characteristics of a depletion device are not greatly different than those of an enhancement device except for an offset in gate voltage. The load device characteristics are of particular interest for logic applications. These are shown in Fig. 7 for various values of channel length, normalized by dividing the current by the width-to-length ratio W/L. The desired characteristic is to have a constant current over a wide range, and this can be achieved approximately by having the current pinch off when the drain-source voltage is greater than $|V_T|$. However, the load current in pinch-off is not constant even for long channel lengths due to the change of threshold

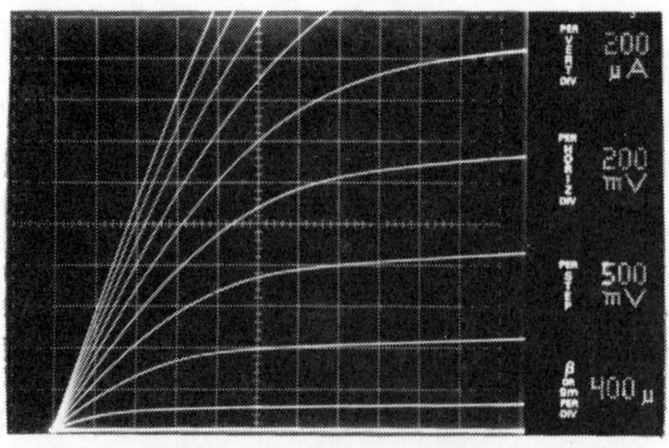

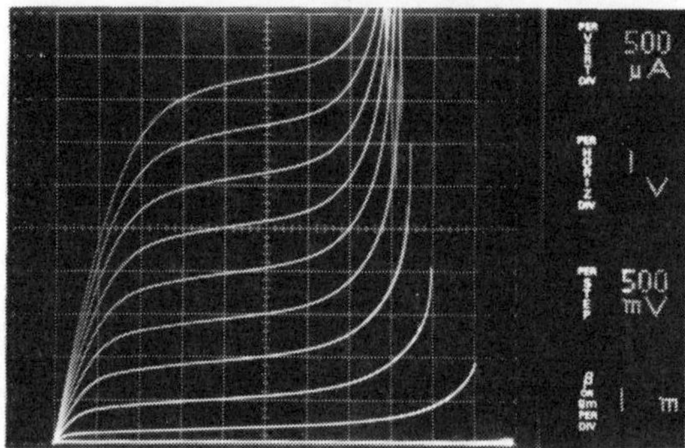

Fig. 6. Drain characteristics for enhancement device. $L = 1.3$ μm, $W = 15.3$ μm. Ten gate steps. $V_{S\text{-}SUB} = 1$ V.

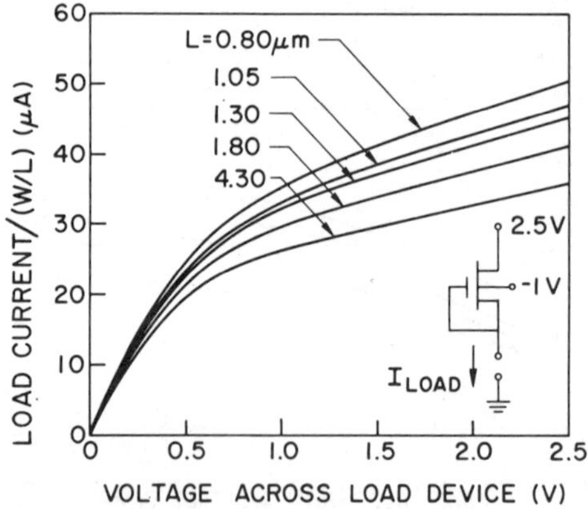

Fig. 7. Load current as a function of source voltage for different channel lengths, normalized to $W/L = 1$. Actual $W = 15.3$ μm.

voltage with both source-substrate voltage and drain-source voltage. The change of threshold with the drain voltage is greater for shorter channel lengths, as shown in Fig. 4, giving a greater change in the pinch-off current level. A nominal channel length of 1.8 μm has been used in the circuit experiments in most cases, and 1.3 μm has been used for unloaded ring oscillators. The load device characteristics are fairly attractive in both cases. The larger channel length gives a somewhat better characteristic and is more tolerant to dimensional variations; however, it takes more area and has a higher capacitance for a given current level, which is significant for lightly loaded inverter circuits with low fan-out.

IV. Low-Temperature Characteristics

The enhancement device design for liquid-nitrogen-temperature operation has a boron channel implant dose about 2/3 as

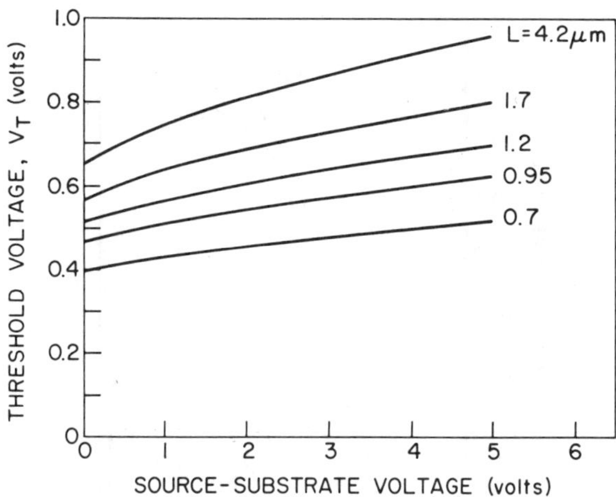

Fig. 8. Substrate sensitivity curves for liquid-nitrogen-temperature case. $V_{DS} = 0.1$ V.

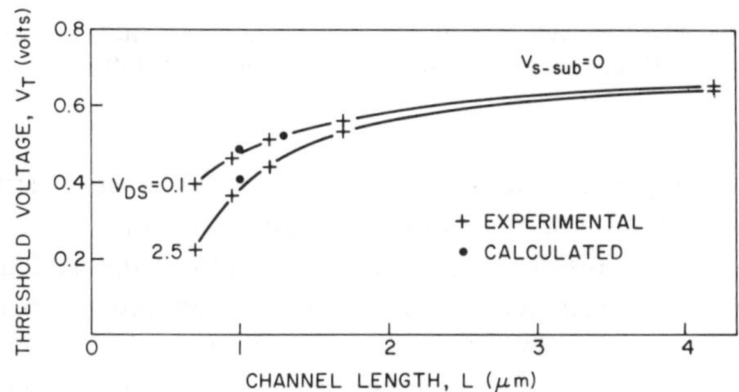

Fig. 9. Short-channel characteristics for liquid-nitrogen-temperature case. $V_{S\text{-}SUB} = 0$.

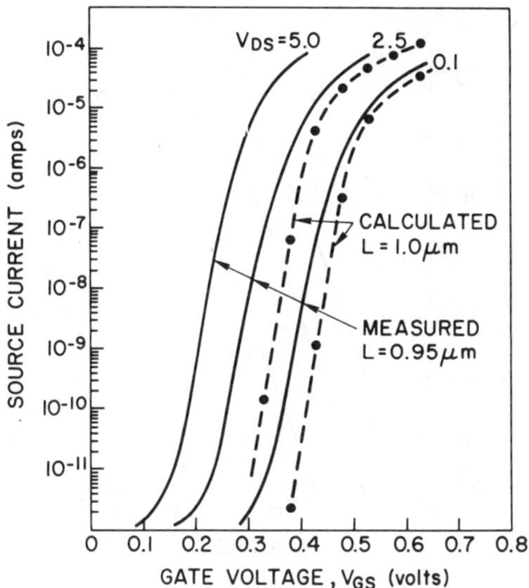

Fig. 10. Log plot of turn-on characteristic at liquid nitrogen temperature with drain voltage as a parameter for experimental device with $L = 0.95$ μm. Simulation for $L = 1.0$ μm, $W = 15.3$ μm, $V_{S\text{-}SUB} = 0$.

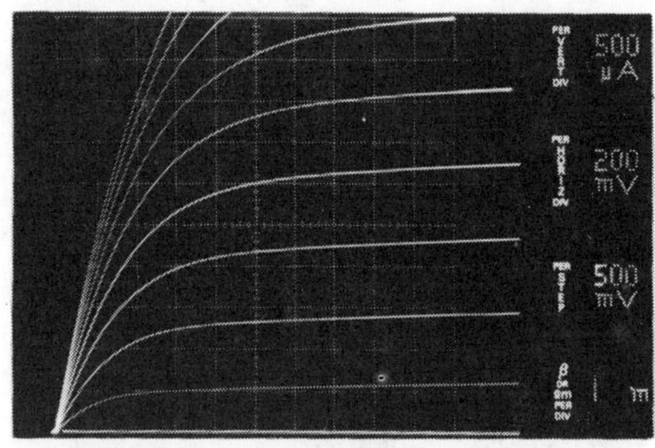

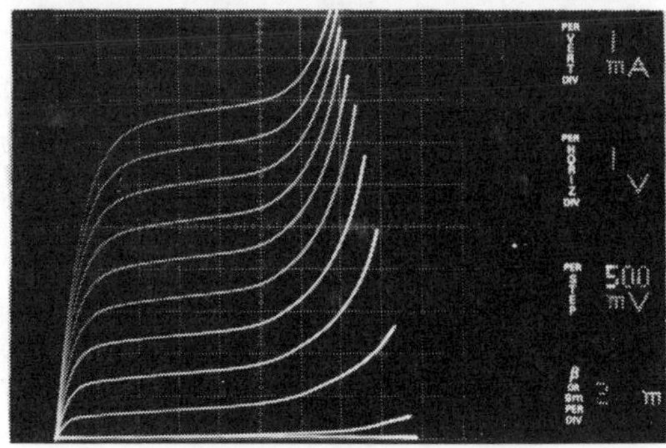

Fig. 11. Drain characteristics for liquid-nitrogen-temperature case. $L = 1.2$ μm, $W = 15.3$ μm, $V_{S\text{-}SUB} = 0$.

large as the room-temperature case. This compensates for the increase in threshold voltage at low temperature due to the increased voltage drop across the depletion region in the silicon under the gate (increased band bending) [6]. Threshold characteristics are shown in Figs. 8 and 9. The aim here was also to achieve a nominal 0.6-V threshold for a 1.3 μm long device but at zero source-substrate bias for the low-temperature design. The experimental value came out somewhat lower due to variations of oxide thickness and implant dose, and the simulated characteristics were adjusted to match at that point. The substrate sensitivity characteristic of Fig. 8 is flatter than the room-temperature result (Fig. 3) at low source-substrate voltage due to the lower channel doping and due to the increased band bending in the silicon at threshold, which acts like an increased source-substrate bias. The depletion depth with zero substrate bias is about the same as for the room-temperature case with -1 V substrate bias. Changes of threshold with channel length and drain voltage are seen to be similar to the room-temperature results.

Measurements of the turn-on behavior at liquid nitrogen temperature are shown in Fig. 10 for various values of drain voltage for a channel length of just less than 1 μm. On these curves, threshold corresponds to a current level of about 10^{-6} A. For lower (or subthreshold) current levels, these curves demonstrate the improvement in the turn-on rate which has been previously described [6]. Simulation results for a 1 μm device are also shown. The shift along the gate-voltage scale with increasing drain voltage reflects the change of threshold plotted in Fig. 9. The data shows that this short-channel device cuts off properly and does not punch through with up to 5 V on the drain.

The drain characteristics of the low-temperature device are shown in Fig. 11. The increase in transconductance at liquid nitrogen temperature reflects a mobility increase by more than a factor of three at low drain voltage, taking into account the shorter channel length on this sample. Most of this mobility increase is due to reduced phonon scattering, and a small part (~5 percent) is due to less impurity scattering with the smaller channel implant doping concentration. At higher drain voltages

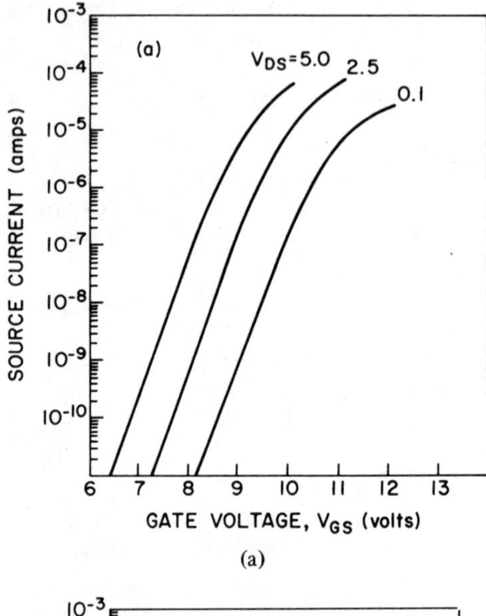

(a)

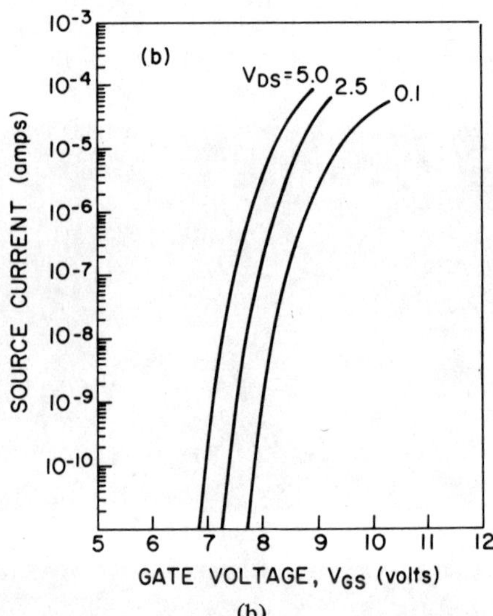

(b)

Fig. 12. Turn-on behavior of aluminum-gated parasitic thick-oxide device with layout spacing of 1.5 μm. $W = 43\ \mu$m. (a) Room temperature, $V_{S\text{-}SUB} = 1$ V. (b) Liquid nitrogen temperature, $V_{S\text{-}SUB} = 0$.

the increase in transconductance is smaller because the electrons are approaching saturation velocity, which is only about 25 percent greater at liquid nitrogen temperature than at room temperature [11].

V. Characteristics of Parasitic Isolation Devices

Test structures were fabricated to test the isolation region between two n$^+$ implanted lines separated by a minimum layout dimension. Fig. 12 shows the current flow between those n$^+$ lines as a function of the voltage applied to an aluminum conductor crossing the thick-oxide (~0.5 μm) isolation region. Turn-on curves for these parasitic thick-oxide FET's are shown as a function of drain-source voltage for both room- and liquid-nitrogen-temperature operating conditions. The peak doping concentration of the implanted boron layer under the field oxide is slightly less than for the room-temperature enhancement device, but it extends considerably deeper due to diffusion during the thermal growth of the semirecessed field oxide.

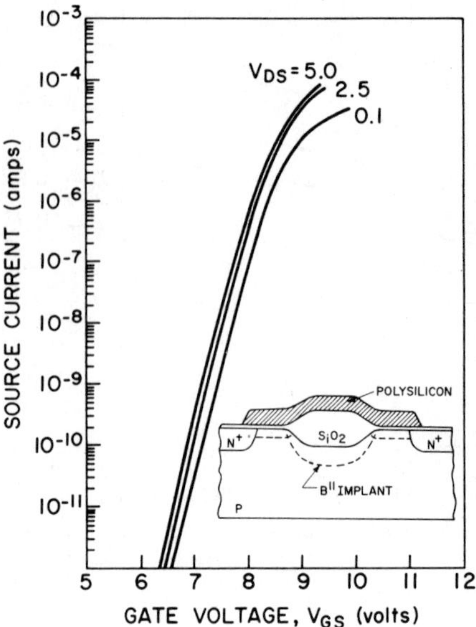

Fig. 13. Turn-on behavior of polysilicon-gated parasitic thick-oxide device with layout spacing of 1.5 μm. Room temperature, $V_{S\text{-}SUB} = 1$ V.

The doping under the field oxide is not reduced for the structures used for low-temperature operation; however, reducing the substrate bias to zero reduces the depth of the depletion region and hence reduces the amount of ionized impurities within the depletion region which contribute to the threshold. The net result is that the threshold of the thick-oxide device is lower for the liquid-nitrogen-temperature case than for the room-temperature case. However, the turn-off rate below threshold is much faster at low temperature, and the shift of threshold at high drain voltages is less due to the reduced depletion depth discussed above. Therefore, there is little difference in the net effectiveness of the isolation regions. Both room-temperature and low-temperature cases have a considerable margin in comparison to the applied voltages used in the circuit experiments.

Another important isolation region is the separation between two thin-oxide devices connected by a common silicon gate passing over the semirecessed field oxide. Fig. 13 shows characteristics for a test structure of this type for the minimum spacing allowed by the ground rules for this study. This gives the same width of the thickest portion of the recessed oxide as for the aluminum-gated device discussed above, but without the n$^+$ source/drain regions extending partially under and below the bird's beak portion of that recessed oxide. This device thus behaves like it has a longer channel and is less sensitive to drain voltage. The oxide thickness of the semirecessed field oxide under the silicon conductor is about 0.35 μm which tends to lower the threshold compared to the aluminum-gated thick-oxide device, but this is largely offset by reduced short-channel effects.

VI. Ring Oscillator Performance

Several types of ring oscillator circuits having various fan-out and wiring-capacitance conditions were included on all test wafers fabricated in this study. The simplest type is a 21-stage "unloaded" ring oscillator with a fan-in and fan-out of 1 made

Fig. 14. Fabricated 19-stage ring oscillator test circuit with a fan in and fan-out of 3, with dummy loading on output nodes.

TABLE I
RING OSCILLATOR RESULTS; AVERAGE DELAY AND POWER PER STAGE

	UNLOADED F.I., F.O.=1	LOADED F.I., F.O.=3 with C_{wire}=50fF
Room Temperature, Depl. Load		
L=1.3 μm, V_d=2.5 V	0.35 ns	1.9 ns
	0.48 mw	0.13 mw
L=1.05 μm, V_d=2.5 V	0.23 ns	1.1 ns
	0.63 mw	0.17 mw
Liquid Nitrogen Temp., Enh. Load		
L=1.05 μm, V_d=2.0 V	0.10 ns	0.46 ns
	1.3 mw	0.37 mw

with relatively wide switching devices (26 μm) to minimize the effect of wiring capacitance. This gives the fastest switching speed which is possible with this technology and is a good upper bound on performance. Another type of ring oscillator uses 19 stages of NOR logical gates with a fan-in and fan-out of 3 (two grounded inputs and two output connections to dummy switching circuits). This case includes a lumped capacitance load representing additional wiring capacitance connected to each NOR output. The total wiring capacitance per stage is about 50 fF which is thought to be representative of custom logic layouts in VLSI circuits using this technology. The switching devices were made smaller in this case (6.5 μm wide) to give a denser layout and an acceptable level of power dissipation. Even smaller devices could be used without drastically affecting the performance. Fig. 14 shows a photomicrograph of this test circuit implemented with the minimum dimension ground rules described in Part V of this paper.

Test results on these two types of ring oscillator circuits are shown in Table I for devices with two different channel lengths. The switching delay per stage and the average power dissipation (including the duty cycle) are given for both room- and liquid-nitrogen-temperature cases. The measured electrical device channel length is given for the data quoted. There are small spreads in other parameters which affect the results but should not greatly affect the power-delay product. The low-temperature results are considerably faster because of the higher device transconductance referred to previously. The power is also correspondingly greater due to the higher current, since the switching device size is kept constant. An enhancement-mode load device with a separate gate bias was used at liquid nitrogen temperature to avoid freezeout effects which make it difficult to achieve a sufficiently negative threshold voltage in depletion devices to give the desired load current in a reasonable size load device [7]. The size of the enhancement-mode load device was adjusted to give at room temperature about the same current as the depletion load device; this current more than doubles at liquid nitrogen temperature. The general experience with enhancement-mode load devices at room temperature is that they give about 20 percent greater average switching delay at a given load current and power level compared to depletion load devices. Also, the noise margins are not as wide, and the output impedance of the circuit in the high-voltage state is not as low. These problems are somewhat less in a liquid nitrogen environment because the output level in the low-voltage state is improved by the larger mobility in the switching device for this condition of low drain-source voltage. Also, the operating temperature range is smaller which gives less parameter variation. Saturation-velocity effects are beneficial in the load device for high drain-source voltage, limiting the load current and providing a more favorable load device characteristic. However, this can be utilized fully only in relatively high power circuits where the width-to-length ratio is unity or greater for the load device, so that a minimum channel length can be used.

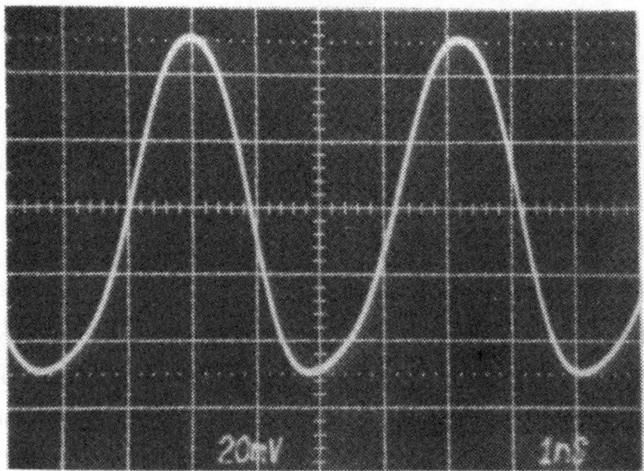

Fig. 15. Output waveform of 21-stage ring oscillator at liquid nitrogen temperature. Signal attenuated by source-follower output circuit driving 50-Ω termination.

The output waveform of the unloaded ring oscillator at low temperature is shown in Fig. 15. The high-frequency components are filtered out by the circuits used for the measurement. The period of the oscillation is 4.2 ns. Dividing by the number of stages (21) and by two switching transitions per cycle gives the average switching time of 100 ps per stage.

VII. CONCLUSIONS

Design parameters have been presented for MOS devices optimized for use in high-performance VLSI circuits. Characteristics of experimental devices match the design objectives and show acceptable control of threshold voltage as a function of channel length and width over the intended range of applied voltages. Depletion-type devices are shown to be more sensitive to threshold change as a function of channel length at high drain voltage, but attractive and fairly reproducible load-device characteristics are possible with proper choice of dimensions.

Design changes for operation of the enhancement-type device at liquid nitrogen temperature are shown to give similar threshold characteristics to those observed at room temperature. A substantial improvement in transconductance and a sharper turn-on rate in the subthreshold region are in line with previously published liquid-nitrogen-temperature data. This shows that the oxide charge and fast surface state density, which affect those characteristics, have been kept within reasonable bounds.

Characterization of isolation regions with narrow separation between components shows that good isolation is achieved. Both surface inversion and punch-through are avoided with normal expected operating voltages for both room- and low-temperature cases.

Test logic circuits fabricated with ground rules using 1 μm minimum dimensions have nominal switching delays of 1.9 ns for depletion-load NOR elements with a fan-in and fan-out of three and a 50-fF wiring capacitance at an average power level of 0.12 mW. Circuits with a smaller channel length, reduced from 1.3 to 1.05 μm, demonstrated a 1.1-ns delay for the typical circuit described. From the electrical characteristics and experience gained in the course of the study, it appears that even smaller channel lengths can be fabricated with the same process steps with adequate control. Unloaded ring oscillators exhibit much faster switching speeds, as expected. Operation at liquid nitrogen temperature gives substantially improved performance with some increase in power level. A switching delay of 0.46 ns was achieved for the typical NOR circuit described above, using an enhancement-type load device for a channel length of 1.05 μm. Unloaded ring oscillators demonstrated 100-ps switching delays for the same channel length at liquid nitrogen temperatures.

Acknowledgment

The authors gratefully acknowledge the support of the Silicon Fabrication Technology group, the Exploratory Silicon Materials group, and the Electron Beam Lithography Applications group at IBM Research in developing the processes and fabricating the devices and circuits. We are thankful to V. DiLonardo and J. J. Walker for laying out and digitizing the patterns for the test structures and to R. P. Havreluk, J. T. Parrish, and M. B. Wordeman for performing the electrical tests.

References

[1] F. F. Fang and B. L. Crowder, "Ion-implanted microwave MOSFET's," presented at the IEEE Int. Electron Dev. Meeting, Washington, DC, Nov. 1970.

[2] B. Hoeneisen and C. A. Mead, "Fundamental limitations in microelectronics–I. MOS technology," *Solid-State Electron.*, vol. 15, pp. 819–829, 1972.

[3] F. F. Fang and M. Hatzakis, "Electron-beam fabrication of ion implanted high performance FET circuits," *J. Vac. Sci. Technol.*, vol. 10, no. 6, pp. 1082–1085, Nov./Dec. 1973.

[4] R. H. Dennard, F. H. Gaensslen, H. N. Yu, V. L. Rideout, E. Bassous, and A. R. LeBlanc, "Design of ion-implanted MOSFET's with very small physical dimensions," *IEEE J. Solid-State Circuits*, vol. SC-9, pp. 256–268, Oct. 1974.

[5] H. N. Yu, R. H. Dennard, T. H. P. Chang, C. M. Osburn, V. DiLonardo, and H. E. Luhn, "Fabrication of a miniature 8K-bit memory chip using electron beam exposure," *J. Vac. Sci. Technol.*, vol. 12, no. 6, pp. 1297–1300, Nov./Dec. 1975.

[6] F. H. Gaensslen, V. L. Rideout, E. J. Walker, and J. J. Walker, "Very small MOSFET's for low-temperature operation," *IEEE Trans. Electron Devices*, vol. ED-24, pp. 218–229, Mar. 1977.

[7] F. H. Gaensslen, R. C. Jaeger, and J. J. Walker, "Low temperature threshold behavior of depletion mode devices–Characterization and simulation," in *IEDM Tech. Dig.*, Dec. 1977, pp. 520–524; also, F. H. Gaensslen and R. C. Jaeger, "Temperature dependent threshold behavior of depletion mode MOSFET's–Characterization and simulation," *Solid-State Electron.*, vol. 22, pp. 423–430, Apr. 1979.

[8] M. S. Mock, "A two-dimensional mathematical model of the insulated-gate field-effect transistor," *Solid-State Electron.*, vol. 16, pp. 601–609, 1973.

[9] D. A. Antoniadis, S. E. Hansen, R. W. Dutton, and A. G. Gonzalez, "SUPREM 1–A program for IC process modeling and simulation," Stanford Electron. Lab, Stanford, CA, Tech. Rep. 5019-1, May 1977.

[10] K. E. Kroell and G. H. Ackermann, "Threshold voltage of narrow channel field effect transistors," *Solid-State Electron.*, vol. 19, no. 1, pp. 77–81, Jan. 1976.

[11] F. F. Fang and A. B. Fowler, "Hot electron effects and saturation velocities in silicon inversion layers," *J. Appl. Phys.*, vol. 44, pp. 1825–1831, 1970.

Analytical Models of Threshold Voltage and Breakdown Voltage of Short-Channel MOSFET's Derived from Two-Dimensional Analysis

TORU TOYABE, MEMBER, IEEE, AND SHOJIRO ASAI, MEMBER, IEEE

Abstract—Analytical models of threshold voltage and breakdown voltage of short-channel MOSFET's are derived from the combination of analytical consideration and two-dimensional numerical analysis. An approximate analytical solution for the surface potential is used to derive the threshold voltage, in contrast with the charge conservation approach which has been usually taken. It is shown that the surface potential depends exponentially on the distance from the drain, and this causes the threshold voltage to decrease exponentially with decreasing channel length. The analytical dependence of threshold voltage on device dimensions, doping, and operating conditions is verified by accurate two-dimensional calculations, and the accuracy of the model is attained by slight modification.

The breakdown voltage of a short-channel n-MOSFET is lowered by a positive feedback effect of excess substrate current. From two-dimensional analysis of this mechanism, a simple expression of the breakdown voltage is derived.

Using this model, the scaling down of MOSFET's is discussed. The simple models of threshold and breakdown voltage of short-channel MOSFET's are helpful both for circuit-oriented analysis and process diagnosis where statistical use of the model is often needed.

I. Introduction

DEMAND for larger scale integration of MOS circuits has urged miniaturization of MOSFET's with the support of the progress of the lithographic technique. When the channel length of MOSFET's is of the order of 1 μm, the threshold voltage decreases with the decrease in channel length [1], and breakdown voltage also decreases in the case of an n-channel device [2]. These short-channel effects pose many problems in the device design in the development of modern MOS LSI.

The threshold voltage of a short-channel MOSFET has been analyzed by Lee [3] and Yau [4], using a charge-conservation condition including a drain and source depletion layer charge. They used simple geometrical division of the depletion layer in the substrate to derive the expressions of threshold voltage.

On the other hand, two-dimensional numerical analysis has been used to calculate threshold voltage of short-channel MOSFET's [1], [5], [6] and breakdown voltage [2]. This approach gives accurate prediction of these quantities.

However, two-dimensional analysis is not quite adequate for the application to circuit analysis or statistical modeling in process diagnosis because it is complex and takes much computation time. In this paper, threshold and breakdown voltage models are proposed in an analytically closed form as a function of structural parameters and operating conditions. Two-dimensional analysis is fully utilized to derive the models. Implications of the present models are discussed in relation to the scaling down of MOSFET's.

II. Threshold Voltage Model

A. Automatic Threshold Voltage Calculation Method in Two-Dimensional Analysis

When the channel length of MOSFET's becomes smaller, the threshold voltage V_T begins to decrease due to the two-

Manuscript received August 11, 1978; revised October 14, 1978.

The authors are with the Central Research Laboratory, Hitachi, Ltd., Kokubunji, Tokyo 185, Japan.

Reprinted from *IEEE J. Solid-State Circuits*, vol. SC–14, pp. 375–383, Apr. 1979.

dimensional field effect of the drain junction. This behavior cannot be explained by a one-dimensional model. Therefore, a computer program for numerical analysis is developed to analyze short-channel effect in MOSFET's. This program, called CADDET,[1] solves Poisson's equation and the current continuity equation for electrons (an n-channel device is considered) as a set of difference equations. Poisson's equation linearized by Gummel's algorithm [7] is solved using Stone's method. The current continuity equation is solved introducing the stream function [5] and using the line iteration method.

A practical definition of the threshold voltage V_T is employed here. The threshold voltage is defined as the gate voltage for which the drain current is equal to a specified value, I_{th}. In this paper, I_{th} is chosen to be 10^{-8} A. The channel width is 13.5 μm for all the devices in this paper.

Then the Newton-Raphson method is applied to determine V_T by the following iterative approximation:

$$V_T^{(j)} = V_T^{(j-1)} + \ln \frac{I_{th}}{I_D^{(j-1)}} \left(\frac{\Delta \ln (I_D/I_{th})}{\Delta V_G} \right)^{-1} \tag{1}$$

where $V_T^{(j)}$ is the jth approximation of V_T and $I_D^{(j-1)}$ is the drain current for $V_G = V_T^{(j-1)}$. The derivative in (1) is obtained from two-dimensional numerical solutions for $V_G = V_T^{(j-1)}$ and $V_T^{(j-1)} + \Delta V$, where ΔV is $\pm$ 50 mV. The well-known expression which is valid for long-channel MOSFET's is taken as the initial value, $V_T^{(0)}$. The Newton-Raphson iteration is made until the precision of V_T is less than 1 mV. It has turned out that the number of iterations is usually around two. This function of automatic V_T calculation is very useful in the practical use of the two-dimensional analysis and is used extensively to obtain the results in the following section.

B. Analytical Model of Threshold Voltage Supported by Two-Dimensional Analysis

Threshold voltage is a gate voltage which can induce enough carriers to support the current. An approach to obtaining threshold voltage is to use the charge-conservation condition [3], [4]. Since the inversion charge is related to surface potential, there is another possible approach, which we use here, dealing directly with the potential distribution.

A cross section of a MOSFET is shown in Fig. 1. Two-dimensional analysis made for the device shows that at the threshold the surface potential ψ_s has a minimum $\psi_{\min}$ around the middle point of the channel. The surface potential distribution is shown in Fig. 2. It is seen that $\psi_s - \psi_{\min}$ is an exponential function of x, which is different from a quadratic function in the case of planar junction.

The potential distribution in y-direction is plotted in Fig. 3. The potential distribution is a concave curve similar to the depletion layer potential distribution in the middle of the channel [curve (a)], while it is convex near the drain [curve (b)] when the drain voltage V_D is larger than the gate voltage V_G. Based on this observation, but using solely analytical

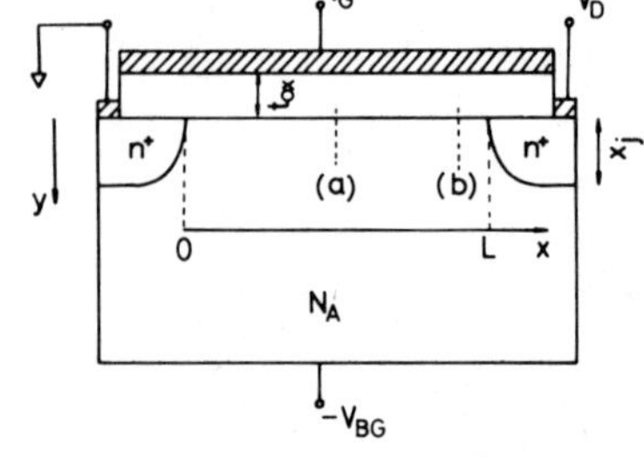

Fig. 1. Cross section of a MOSFET.

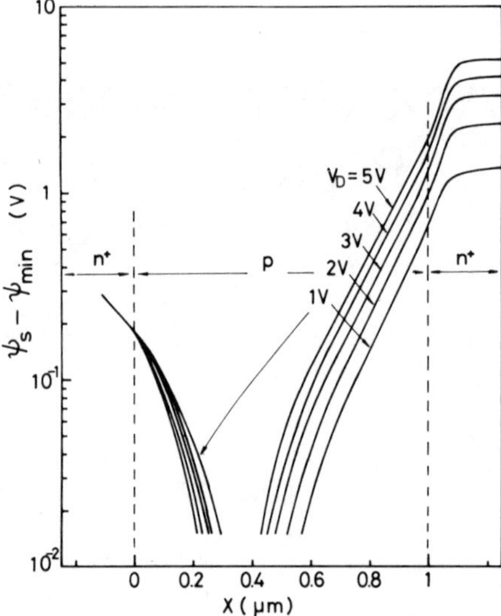

Fig. 2. Surface potential distribution for varied drain voltage. L = 1 μm, $N_A = 1 \times 10^{16}$ cm^{-3}, t_{ox} = 25 nm, x_j = 0.25 μm, V_{BG} = 2 V.

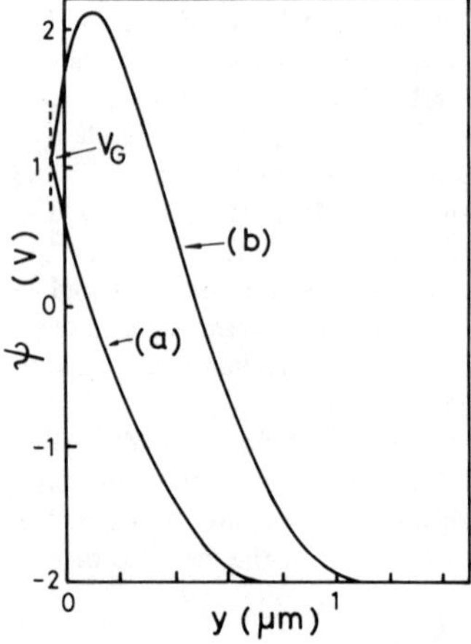

Fig. 3. Potential distribution in the direction from surface to substrate. Curves (a) and (b) are potential distributions on the lines (a) and (b) in Fig. 1, respectively.

methods, an analytical expression for threshold voltage is derived, the procedure of which is given in the Appendix.

It is given as

$$V_T = V_{FB} + \psi_{\min} + \frac{t_{ox}}{\epsilon_{ox}} \sqrt{2\epsilon_s q N_A (\psi_{\min} + V_{BG})} \, (1 - \eta) \tag{2}$$

[1]CADDET is an acronym for computer-aided device design in two dimensions.

where η is a factor representing the short-channel effect and is given as

$$\eta = \eta_0 \exp(-L/l_0). \tag{3}$$

In (3), η_0 is given as

$$\eta_0 = \frac{\epsilon_{ox}}{\epsilon_s} \frac{\sqrt{(V_D + V_{bi} - \psi_{min})(V_{bi} - \psi_{min})}}{\psi_{min} + V_{BG}} \cdot \left(\frac{1}{t_{ox}}\sqrt{\frac{2\epsilon_s(\psi_{min} + V_{BG})}{qN_A}} + \frac{3}{2}\frac{\epsilon_s}{\epsilon_{ox}}\right) \tag{4}$$

and l_0 is a characteristic length given as

$$l_0 = \sqrt{\frac{2\epsilon_s(\psi_{min} + V_{BG})}{qN_A}} \cdot \left(\frac{3}{2} + \frac{\epsilon_{ox}}{\epsilon_s}\frac{1}{t_{ox}}\sqrt{\frac{2\epsilon_s(\psi_{min} + V_{BG})}{qN_A}}\right)^{-1/2}. \tag{5}$$

It should be noticed that (2) reduces to the classical formula in the limit $L \gg l_0$. The exponential dependence of η on L is the direct consequence of the important finding in the present work; that is, the surface potential varies exponentially with distance. This fact is seen in the results of numerical analysis (Fig. 2) as well as in the analytical treatment (see Appendix).

The expression (2) is derived under some assumptions made in the Appendix, and therefore its accuracy is still to be scrutinized. In the following, two-dimensional analysis is used to prove the validity of the functional form of (2)-(5). By modifying the numerical coefficients in the above equations, a quantitative model is obtained.

Representative values of the device parameters and bias voltages are chosen as follows:

$$N_A = 10^{16}\ \text{cm}^{-3} \quad V_{BG} = 2\ \text{V} \quad t_{ox} = 25\ \text{nm}$$
$$V_D = 5\ \text{V} \quad x_j = 0.25\ \mu\text{m}. \tag{6}$$

A number of V_T - L curves are generated from the two-dimensional analysis varying each parameter around the above values.

The minimum of the surface potential ψ_{min} at the threshold is obtained at the same time. Here, the Brown factor [3], [8] B is defined as

$$B = \psi_{min}/\phi_F \tag{7}$$

where ϕ_F is the hole Fermi potential given as

$$\phi_F = \frac{kT}{q}\ln\frac{N_A}{n_i}. \tag{8}$$

The two-dimensional analysis shows that the Brown factor B depends exponentially on the channel length L and weakly on the back-gate voltage V_{BG}. Representing B in the long-channel limit by B_0, B_0 is well approximated by an expression as

$$B_0 = 1.9 + \frac{kT}{2q\phi_F}\ln\frac{2\phi_F + V_{BG}}{2\phi_F}. \tag{9}$$

The deviation of B from B_0 is plotted in Fig. 4 as a function of L for nine cases of two-dimensional calculations varying N_A, t_{ox}, V_{BG}, and V_D. Thus, an empirical equation of B is determined as

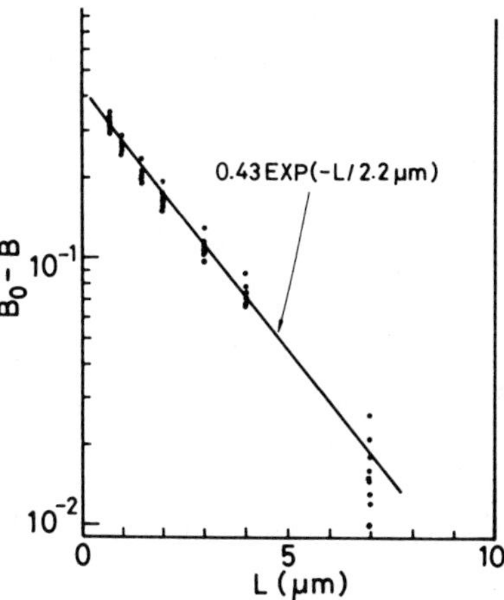

Fig. 4. Deviation of the Brown factor B from a constant B_0 versus channel length L for nine cases with varied N_A, t_{ox}, V_{BG}, and V_D.

$$B = B_0 - 0.43 \exp(-L/2.2\ \mu\text{m}). \tag{10}$$

The short-channel factor η is obtained by substituting V_T and ψ_{min} obtained from two-dimensional analysis into (2). Relations between η and L with varying N_A and t_{ox} are shown in Fig. 5(a) and (b), respectively. All these curves show exponential dependence on L and, therefore, (3) is verified by the two-dimensional analysis.

The values of η_0 and l_0 can be obtained from such curves for η as shown in Fig. 5. Using η_0 thus obtained, its analytical dependence on V_{BG} and V_D which has been predicted in (4) can be examined. The vertical and horizontal axes in Fig. 6 are chosen so that a straight line is obtained if the prediction of (4) is correct. Actually, the following equation,

$$\eta_0 = \frac{\epsilon_{ox}}{\epsilon_s} \frac{\sqrt{(V_D + V_{bi} - B\phi_F)(V_{bi} - B\phi_F)}}{B\phi_F + V_{BG}} \cdot (7.4\sqrt{B\phi_F + V_{BG}} + 2.2), \tag{11}$$

which is very close to (4), approximates the behavior shown in Fig. 6. However, the numerically calculated η_0 does not change with varying N_A and t_{ox}, and does not show a dependence on them such as predicted in (4). Although the reason for the discrepancy is not clear at present, (11) is adopted here as a quantitatively accurate model.

It is shown that the numerically calculated l_0 does not depend on V_D, which is consistent with (5). It is possible to rewrite (5) as

$$\frac{W_0^2}{l_0^2} = \frac{3}{2} + \frac{\epsilon_{ox}}{\epsilon_s}\frac{W_0}{t_{ox}} \tag{12}$$

where W_0 is given by

$$W_0 = \sqrt{\frac{2\epsilon_s(B\phi_F + V_{BG})}{qN_A}}. \tag{13}$$

Thus, W_0^2/l_0^2 is plotted against W_0/t_{ox} in Fig. 7. The results of two-dimensional analysis are not on a single straight line.

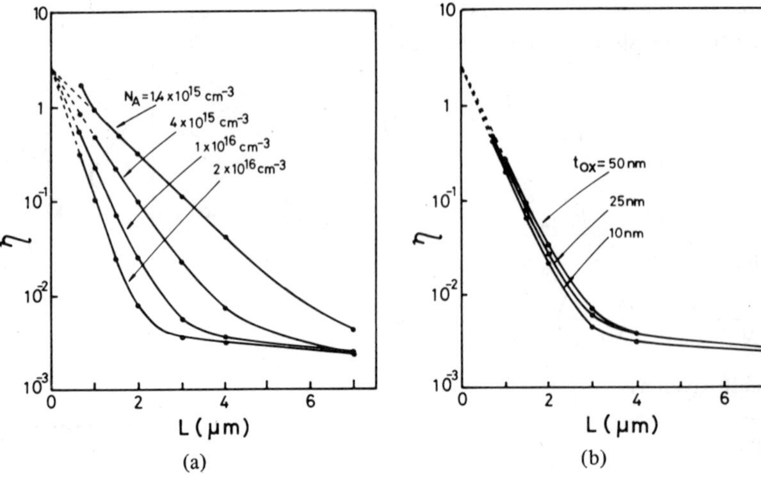

Fig. 5. Short-channel factor η versus channel length L with varying N_A in (a) and with varying t_{ox} in (b). $V_{BG} = 2$ V, $V_D = 5$ V, $x_j = 0.25$ μm.

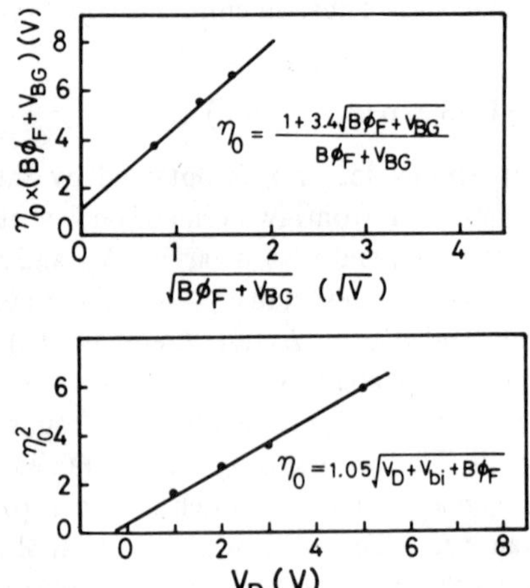

Fig. 6. Relations of pre-exponential factor η_0 with V_{BG} and V_D.

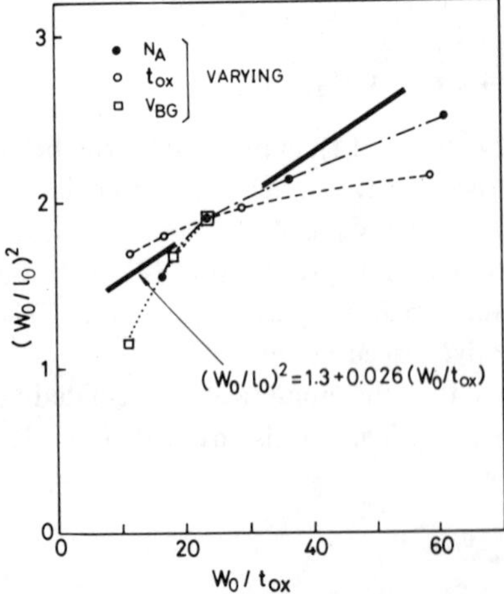

Fig. 7. Plot for examining a relation between $(W_0/l_0)^2$ and W_0/t_{ox}.

However, an approximate expression in the figure, which gives the values of l_0 within the error of ±15 percent is found to be

$$l_0 = W_0 \left(1.3 + 0.078 \frac{\epsilon_{ox} W_0}{\epsilon_s t_{ox}}\right)^{-1/2}. \tag{14}$$

TABLE I
THE PRESENT MODEL OF THRESHOLD VOLTAGE

Device parameters	Expression
Threshold voltage	$V_T = V_{FB} + B\phi_F + \frac{t_{ox}}{\epsilon_{ox}} \sqrt{2\epsilon_S q N_A (B\phi_F + V_{BG})}\ \times$ $\times\ (1 - \eta_0 \exp(-L/l_0))$
Brown factor	$B = c_1 + \frac{kT}{2q\phi_F} \ln\left(\frac{2\phi_F + V_{BG}}{2\phi_F}\right) -$ $- c_2 \exp(-L/c_3)$
Characteristic length	$l_0 = W_0 \left(c_4 + c_5 \frac{\epsilon_{ox}}{\epsilon_S} \frac{W_0}{t_{ox}}\right)^{-\frac{1}{2}}$
Pre-exponential factor of short channel factor	$\eta_0 = \frac{\epsilon_{ox}}{\epsilon_S} \frac{\sqrt{(V_D + V_{bi} - B\phi_F)(V_{bi} - B\phi_F)}}{B\phi_F + V_{BG}}\ \times$ $\times\ (c_6\sqrt{B\phi_F + V_{BG}} + c_7)$
Depletion layer width	$W_0 = \sqrt{2\epsilon_S (B\phi_F + V_{BG})/(qN_A)}$
Constants	$c_1 = 1.9$, $c_2 = 0.43$ $c_3 = 2.2$ μm, $c_4 = 1.3$ $c_5 = 0.078$, $c_6 = 7.4$ $c_7 = 2.2$,

The threshold voltage model obtained in the above is summarized in Table I. This model is initially derived analytically and corrected afterwards by two-dimensional analysis to attain improved accuracy.

In order to see how well the analytic model approximates accurate solution, these are compared in Figs. 8-11. The agreement is very good. Comparison between this model and the experimental results is shown in Fig. 12 and the agreement between them is very satisfactory.

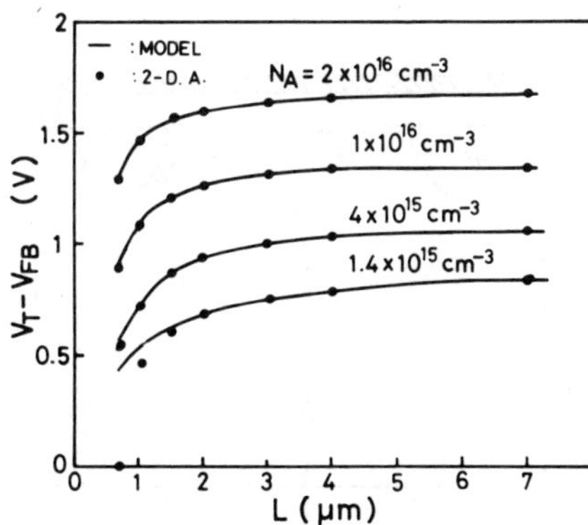

Fig. 8. $V_T - L$ characteristics with varying N_A. t_{ox} = 25 nm, x_j = 0.25 μm, V_{BG} = 2 V, V_D = 5 V.

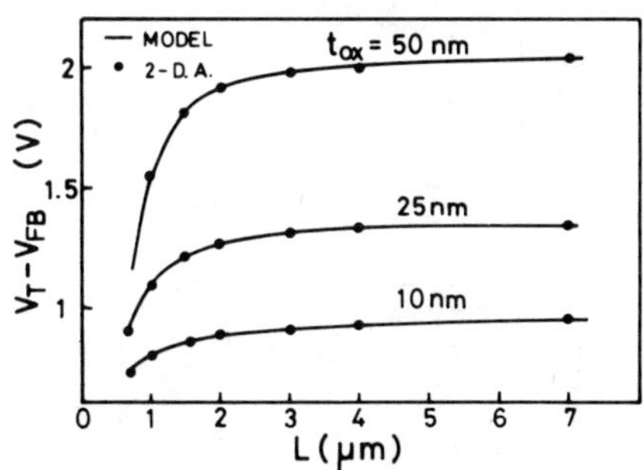

Fig. 9. $V_T - L$ characteristics with varying t_{ox}. $N_A = 1 \times 10^{16}$ cm^{-3}, x_j = 0.25 μm, V_{BG} = 2 V, V_D = 5 V.

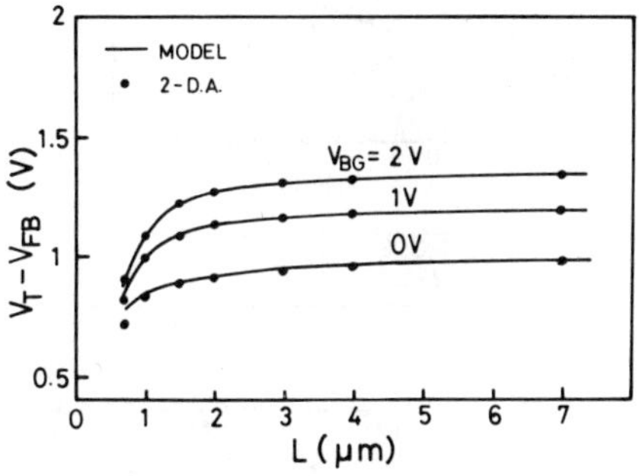

Fig. 10. $V_T - L$ characteristics with varying V_{BG}. $N_A = 1 \times 10^{16}$ cm^{-3}, t_{ox} = 25 nm, x_j = 0.25 μm, V_D = 5 V.

The effect of the junction depth x_j is not explicitly included in this model since two-dimensional analysis does not show any strong influence of x_j. As a result, this model is valid in the range of

$$4 \times 10^{15}\ \mathrm{cm^{-3}} < N_A < 2 \times 10^{16}\ \mathrm{cm^{-3}}$$

$$10\ \mathrm{nm} < t_{ox} < 50\ \mathrm{nm}$$

$$0.15\ \mu\mathrm{m} < x_j < 0.35\ \mu\mathrm{m}$$

$$0\ \mathrm{V} < V_{BG} < 2\ \mathrm{V}$$

$$1\ \mathrm{V} < V_D < 5\ \mathrm{V}.$$

By suitably chosen numerical coefficients, the model can be applied to a different domain of device parameters and operating conditions.

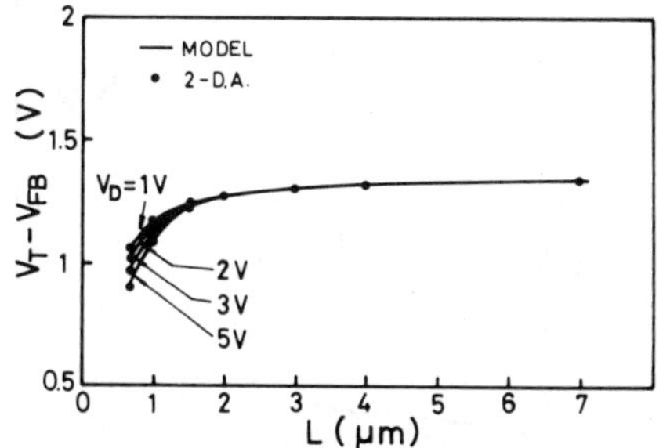

Fig. 11. $V_T - L$ characteristics with varying V_D. $N_A = 1 \times 10^{16}$ cm^{-3}, t_{ox} = 25 nm, x_j = 0.25 μm, V_{BG} = 2 V.

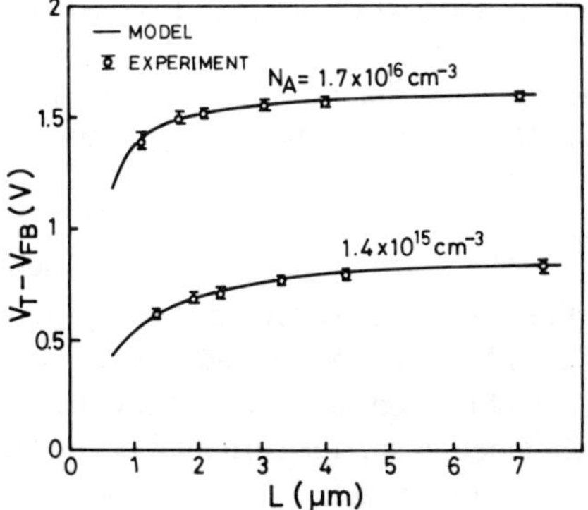

Fig. 12. Comparison between this model and the experimental results. t_{ox} = 25 nm, x_j = 0.25 μm, V_{BG} = 2 V, V_D = 5 V.

III. Breakdown Voltage Model

A. *Breakdown Voltage Calculation Method in Two-Dimensional Analysis*

Drain-source breakdown in short-channel n-MOSFET's is somewhat different from in long-channel MOSFET's or p-MOSFET's [2]. A negative resistance is often observed in short-channel n-MOSFET's. Also, the breakdown voltage BV_{DS} is much smaller than the conventional breakdown voltage BV_{DSO} which is expected from the experience with long-channel MOSFET's as shown in Fig. 13. This reduced breakdown voltage is brought about by a feedback effect of the excess substrate current [2].

Excess substrate current generated from channel current I_S by impact ionization causes a significant voltage drop across the substrate resistance R_{sub} as shown in Fig. 14. This voltage forward-biases the source-substrate junction and increases channel current. The increase in channel current increases the excess substrate current back again. Therefore, a positive feedback loop is formed, and this results in a decrease in the breakdown voltage and can even lead to negative resistance characteristics.

The important relation which determines the state of the device having an avalanche breakdown is given as

$$(M^* - 1)\, I_S = (V_{BG} - V_{BGi})/R_{sub} \tag{15}$$

where M^* is the multiplication factor for the channel current I_S; V_{BGi} is the internal back-gate voltage; and R_{sub} is the substrate resistance. The left-hand side of (15) is the excess substrate current by the multiplication of I_S and is naturally

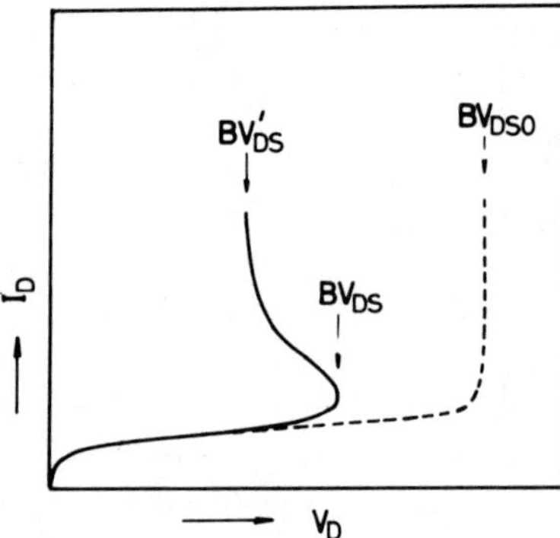

Fig. 13. $I_D - V_D$ characteristics with breakdown of a short-channel n-MOSFET (solid line). A curve is shown by a broken line, which would result without feedback effect of the excess substrate current.

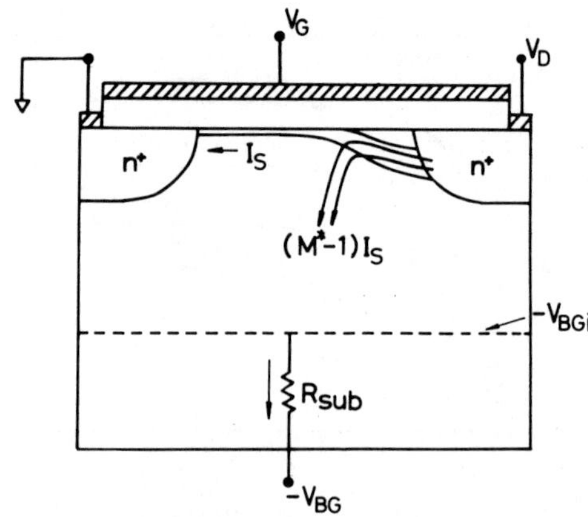

Fig. 14. Cross section of a MOSFET having the excess substrate current.

equal to the voltage difference divided by R_{sub}. The multiplication factor M^* is obtained from the ionization integral I^*_{ion} as

$$M^* = 1/(1 - I^*_{\text{ion}}). \tag{16}$$

The integration to obtain I^*_{ion} is made along the current path shown in Fig. 14. Therefore, two-dimensional analysis must be utilized to obtain an accurate electric field distribution near the drain junction and the current flow for the determination of the integration path.

It is shown [2] that the breakdown of BV_{DS} occurs when $-V_{BGi}$ reaches the cut-in voltage V_c of the forward source-substrate junction; that is, $V_{BGi} = -V_c = -0.65$ V. Thus, the breakdown condition is given as

$$I^*_{\text{ion}} I_S = (V_{BG} + V_c)/R_{\text{sub}}. \tag{17}$$

The quantities I^*_{ion} and I_S are obtained by two-dimensional analysis as functions of V_D, and consequently, BV_{DS} is obtained as V_D, which satisfies (17).

B. Empirical Expression of Breakdown Voltage Deduced from the Two-Dimensional Analysis

Two-dimensional analysis was carried out for the device shown in Fig. 1. The device parameters were varied within the range:

$0.5\ \mu\text{m} < L < 5\ \mu\text{m}$

$3 \times 10^{14}\ \text{cm}^{-3} < N_A < 10^{17}\ \text{cm}^{-3}$

$20\ \text{nm} < t_{ox} < 200\ \text{nm}$

$0.1\ \mu\text{m} < x_j < 2\ \mu\text{m}.$

For simplicity, V_G and V_{BGi} were chosen to be $V_T + 1$ V and 0 V, respectively.

The calculated I^*_{ion} shows cubic dependence on V_D in the range of $10^{-2} \lesssim I^*_{\text{ion}} \lesssim 10^{-1}$ where the breakdown usually occurs. Here, an empirical expression is used for I^*_{ion}:

$$I^*_{\text{ion}} \propto \frac{N_A V_D^3}{x_j t_{ox}^{1/2}}. \tag{18}$$

Gradual channel theory shows that the channel current I_S is inversely proportional to $L\, t_{ox}$. However, the drain current at a breakdown voltage (around 10 V) behaves differently from the simple theory due to the finite drain conductance. Rough approximation of I_S which is obtained by two-dimensional analysis is given as

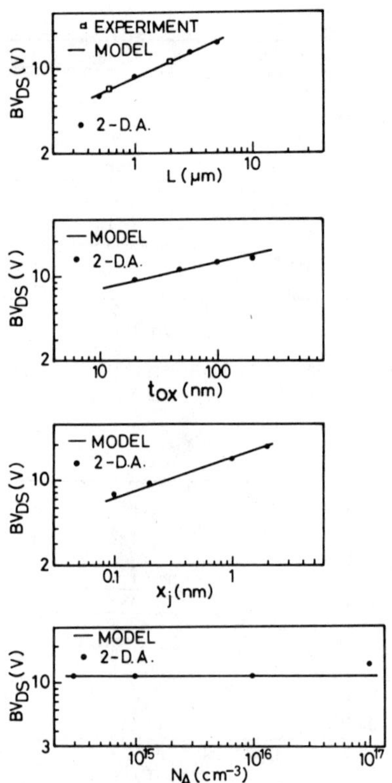

Fig. 15. Relations between breakdown voltage BV_{DS} and each device parameter.

$$I_S \propto \frac{1}{t_{ox} L} \left(\frac{t_{ox}}{N_A L} \right)^{1/3} (1 + \xi(N_A, t_{ox})\, V_c) \tag{19}$$

where the last factor represents the increase of I_S due to the forward substrate bias effect (ξ is related to the substrate bias constant and therefore to N_A and t_{ox}).

The substrate resistance R_{sub} is inversely proportional to the impurity concentration of deep substrate N'_A. Then the breakdown voltage is obtained from (17), (18), and (19) as

$$BV_{DS} \propto x_j^{1/3} L^{4/9} t_{ox}^{7/18} N_A^{-2/9} N_A'^{1/3} (1 + \xi V_c)^{-1/3} \cdot (V_{BG} + V_c)^{1/3}. \tag{20}$$

The breakdown voltage BV_{DS} is obtained directly from two-dimensional analysis [2] and it is shown that the dependence of BV_{DS} on L and x_j agrees well with the curves representing (20). The dependence on t_{ox} and N_A can be determined from the results of two-dimensional analysis. Thus, an empirical formula of BV_{DS} based on the two-dimensional analysis is obtained as

$$BV_{DS} = c_b(V_{BG} + V_c)^{1/3} x_j^{1/3} L^{4/9} t_{ox}^{2/9} N_A^{-1/3} N_A'^{1/3} \quad (21)$$

where $c_b = 2.6 \times 10^5$ $V^{2/3}$/cm. Comparison between the model and two-dimensional analysis as well as experimental results are shown in Fig. 15.

IV. Discussion and Conclusion

Advantage of the present model is analytical transparency and it is utilized in the following discussion of guidelines in designing a miniaturized MOSFET in the micron and submicron region.

Dennard *et al.* [1] proposed a simple scale-down approach, in which the lengths L, t_{ox}, and x_j are made κ times smaller, N_A are made κ times higher, and voltages V_G, V_{BG}, V_D are made κ times lower than the standard device. In this manner, depletion layer width as well as the threshold voltage also scale down approximately since the electric field is maintained approximately constant. The above approach results in a κ times smaller electric current, and power dissipation per unit area remains unchanged. The time required to charge or discharge the load capacitance, which is the measure of the delay per gate, becomes κ times shorter, fulfilling the high-speed requirements. Breakdown voltages BV_{DS} and BV_G also scales, since the electric field strength is maintained. Therefore, the above approach of simple scale down provides a general guideline toward miniaturization of MOS devices.

However, the electric field is kept constant only approximately when the externally applied voltages are scaled down. This is because of the presence of the junction built-in voltages. We can utilize the analytical expressions derived in the previous sections to examine the guidelines in the scaling down of MOSFET's.

When the simple scale-down approach is taken, the sensitivity of V_T to the channel length L, $\partial V_T/\partial L$ should remain unchanged. Using the model in Table I, the effect of scaling is calculated as

$$\frac{\left.\dfrac{\partial V_T}{\partial L}\right|_\kappa}{\dfrac{\partial V_T}{\partial L}} = 1, \quad \text{when } V_{BG} >> kB\phi_F \quad (22a)$$

$$= \frac{1}{\sqrt{\kappa}} \exp \frac{L}{W_{00}}\left(1 - \frac{1}{\sqrt{\kappa}}\right) \quad \text{when } V_{BG} \ll \kappa B\phi_F \quad (22b)$$

where

$$W_{00} = \sqrt{\frac{2\epsilon_s B\phi_F}{qN_A}}. \quad (23)$$

The above equation implies that the scaling can be harmful to the threshold voltage control unless the back-gate voltage is kept higher than $B\phi_F \approx 0.6$ V.

Although the simple scaling provides an idealistic guiding principle, a device engineer often encounters the situation in which he is requested to realize a device with higher speed without altering the supply voltage. Miniaturization is again a straightforward solution. Analytic expressions for the device characteristics give a guideline.

Instead of the simple scaling [1], the following nonlinear scaling is taken:

$$\begin{aligned} &\text{lengths } L, t_{ox}, x_j \rightarrow L/\kappa, t_{ox}/\kappa, x_j/\kappa \\ &N_A \rightarrow \kappa^2 N_A \quad (24) \\ &\text{voltages } V_{BG}, V_D \rightarrow \text{unchanged.} \end{aligned}$$

It is easy to see from (2) or the model in Table I that V_T remains unchanged by this scaling, and that threshold voltage controllability is maintained.

This nonlinear scaling results in a power dissipation density κ^3 times higher, but gate delay κ^2 times shorter. Therefore, the above approach can be attractive in a dynamic circuit technology such as CMOS, where power dissipation is not critical.

Closed-form expressions of electrical characteristics of MOSFET's are useful also in the analysis and diagnosis of the device fabrication process. Statistical analysis, in which the effects of fluctuation in processing parameters on device characteristics are analyzed, provides a powerful tool. Such an analysis is possible only if the following conditions are satisfied. The relation between the processing conditions and the structural parameters of device such as geometrical dimensions and impurity profiles have to be established. In addition, it is necessary to know the electrical characteristics of the device, which specifies the design-objectives, as functions of the structural parameters. The above relationship must be expressed in a rather simple form to give results within reasonable amount of time. The expressions derived in this paper are to constitute a subset of relations to be used in such analysis for the purpose of establishing a processing schedule of MOSFET's near the 1-μm range.

Appendix
Analytical Expression of the Threshold Voltage in Short-Channel MOSFET's

The electrostatic potential ψ in the substrate depletion layer is described by Poisson's equation

$$\frac{\partial^2 \psi}{\partial x^2} + \frac{\partial^2 \psi}{\partial y^2} = \frac{q}{\epsilon_s} N_A \quad (A.1)$$

where carrier density is ignored and impurity concentration is assumed to be constant. To derive an equation for the surface potential ψ_s, y-dependence of ψ is approximated by a simple form as described in the following. As shown in Fig. 3, it cannot be approximated by a quadratic function of y near the drain, and therefore, the cubic function of y,

$$\psi = a_0 + a_1 y + a_2 y^2 + a_3 y^3 \quad (A.2)$$

is used here. Boundary conditions for ψ are given as

$$\psi = \psi_s, \qquad \frac{\partial \psi}{\partial y} = \frac{\epsilon_{ox}}{\epsilon_s} \frac{\psi_s - V_G}{t_{ox}}, \qquad \text{for } y = 0 \tag{A.3}$$

$$\psi = -V_{BG}, \qquad \frac{\partial \psi}{\partial y} = 0, \qquad \text{for } y = W \tag{A.4}$$

where (A.3) is obtained from the continuity of the normal component of electric displacement, W is the depletion layer width, and the flat-band voltage V_{FB} is assumed to be zero for simplicity.

The coefficients, a_i $(i = 0 \sim 3)$, are determined from (A.2), (A.3), and (A.4). Then, the value of $\partial^2 \psi / \partial y^2$ at the surface is easily obtained, and from (A.1), an equation for ψ_s is obtained as

$$\frac{d^2 \psi_s}{dx^2} - A \psi_s = D \tag{A.5}$$

where

$$A = 4 \frac{\epsilon_{ox}}{\epsilon_s} \frac{1}{t_{ox} W} + \frac{6}{W^2}, \tag{A.6}$$

$$D = \frac{q}{\epsilon_s} N_A - 4 \frac{\epsilon_{ox}}{\epsilon_s} \frac{V_G}{t_{ox} W} + \frac{6 V_{BG}}{W^2}. \tag{A.7}$$

The boundary condition for ψ_s is given as

$$\psi_s = V_{bi} \qquad \text{for } x = 0 \quad \text{(at source junction)},$$

$$\psi_s = V_D + V_{bi} \qquad \text{for } x = L \quad \text{(at drain junction)}$$

where V_{bi} is the built-in voltage. The depletion layer width W is assumed to be constant. Then, (A.5) can be solved as

$$\psi_s = -D/A + (V_D + V_{bi} + D/A) \exp(\sqrt{A}(x - L)) + (V_{bi} + D/A) \exp(-\sqrt{A}\, x). \tag{A.8}$$

The exponential dependence of ψ_s on x which is shown in Fig. 2 is derived in (A.8). The surface potential ψ_s has a minimum $\overline{\psi}_{min}$, which is given as

$$\overline{\psi}_{min} = -\frac{D}{A} + 2 \sqrt{\left(V_D + V_{bi} + \frac{D}{A}\right)\left(V_{bi} + \frac{D}{A}\right)} \cdot \exp - \frac{\sqrt{A}}{2} L. \tag{A.9}$$

A relation between V_G and $\overline{\psi}_{min}$ is obtained by substituting (A.6) and (A.7) in (A.9) as

$$V_G = \overline{\psi}_{min} + \frac{t_{ox}}{\epsilon_{ox}} \sqrt{2 \epsilon_s q N_A (\overline{\psi}_{min} + V_{BG})} - 2\left(1 + \frac{3 \epsilon_s t_{ox}}{2 \epsilon_{ox} W}\right) V_e \exp - \frac{\sqrt{A}}{2} L \tag{A.10}$$

where the depletion layer width is replaced by the typical value

$$W = \sqrt{\frac{2 \epsilon_s (\overline{\psi}_{min} + V_{BG})}{q N_A}} \tag{A.11}$$

and V_e is given as

$$V_e = \sqrt{\left(V_D + V_{bi} + \frac{D}{A}\right)\left(V_{bi} + \frac{D}{A}\right)}. \tag{A.12}$$

The term D/A in (A.12) is approximately equal to $-\overline{\psi}_{min}$.

Supposing that $V_G = V_T$ and $\overline{\psi}_{min} = \psi_{min}$ at the threshold which is defined by $I_D = I_{th}$, an analytical expression of V_T is derived from (A.10) as

$$V_T = V_{FB} + \psi_{min} + \frac{t_{ox}}{\epsilon_{ox}} \sqrt{2 \epsilon_s q N_A (\psi_{min} + V_{BG})} (1 - \eta), \tag{A.13}$$

$$\eta = \eta_0 \exp -L/l_0, \tag{A.14}$$

$$\eta_0 = \frac{\epsilon_{ox}}{\epsilon_s} \frac{\sqrt{(V_D + V_{bi} - \psi_{min})(V_{bi} - \psi_{min})}}{\psi_{min} + V_{BG}} \cdot \left(\frac{1}{t_{ox}} \sqrt{\frac{2 \epsilon_s (\psi_{min} + V_{BG})}{q N_A}} + \frac{3}{2} \frac{\epsilon_s}{\epsilon_{ox}}\right) \tag{A.15}$$

$$l_0 = \sqrt{\frac{2 \epsilon_s (\psi_{min} + V_{BG})}{q N_A}} \cdot \left(\frac{3}{2} + \frac{\epsilon_{ox}}{\epsilon_s} \frac{1}{t_{ox}} \sqrt{\frac{2 \epsilon_s (\psi_{min} + V_{BG})}{q N_A}}\right)^{-1/2}. \tag{A.16}$$

The flat-band voltage V_{FB} contributes to V_T additively and is included in (A.13). The quantity ψ_{min} lies between ϕ_F and $2\phi_F$ [3].

Acknowledgment

The authors wish to thank Dr. M. S. Mock of Rutgers University for his contributions to the construction of the CADDET program, especially with the perturbation method described in Section II-A. Thanks are also due to Dr. T. Masuhara, Dr. H. Masuda, K. Yamaguchi, and Dr. M. Kubo for helpful discussions and to Y. Wada for providing experimental results. We are also indebted to Dr. H. Kodera and Dr. M. Nagata for their encouragement and guidance throughout this study.

References

[1] R. H. Dennard, F. H. Gaensslen, H. N. Yu, V. L. Rideout, E. Bassous, and A. LeBlanc, "Design of ion-implanted MOSFET's with very small physical dimensions," *IEEE J. Solid-State Circuits*, vol. SC-9, pp. 256–268, Oct. 1974.

[2] T. Toyabe, K. Yamaguchi, S. Asai, and M. S. Mock, "A numerical model of avalanche breakdown in MOSFET's," *IEEE Trans. Electron Devices*, vol. ED-25, pp. 825–832, July 1978.

[3] H. S. Lee, "An analysis of the threshold voltage for short-channel IGFET's," *Solid-State Electron.*, vol. 16, pp. 1407–1417, 1973.

[4] L. D. Yau, "A simple theory to predict the threshold voltage of short-channel IGFET's," *Solid-State Electron.*, vol. 17, pp. 1059–1063, 1974.

[5] M. S. Mock, "A two-dimensional mathematical model of the insulated-gate field-effect transistor," *Solid-State Electron.*, vol. 16, pp. 601–609, 1973.

[6] H. Masuda, M. Nakai, R. Hori and M. Kubo, "Device design of short channel MOS-FET's based on two dimensional numerical analysis program," *Trans. IECE Japan*, vol. 60-C, pp. 205–212, 1977.

[7] H. K. Gummel, "A self-consistent iterative scheme for one-dimensional steady state transistor calculations," *IEEE Trans. Electron Devices*, vol. ED-11, pp. 455–465, 1964.

[8] W. L. Brown, "n-type surface conductivity on p-type germanium," *Phys. Rev.*, vol. 91, pp. 518–527, Aug. 1953.

Characteristics and Limitation of Scaled-Down MOSFET's Due to Two-Dimensional Field Effect

HIROO MASUDA, MEMBER, IEEE, MASAAKI NAKAI, MEMBER, IEEE, AND MASAHARU KUBO, MEMBER, IEEE

Abstract—**Practical limitations of minimum-size MOS-LSI devices are investigated through measurement of experimental devices. It is assumed that scaled-down MOSFET's are limited by three physical phenomena. These are 1) poor threshold control which is caused by drain electric field, 2) reduced drain breakdown voltage due to lateral bipolar effects, and 3) hot-electron injection into the gate oxide film which yields performance variations during device operation. Experimental models of these phenomena are proposed and the smallest possible MOSFET structure, for a given supply voltage, is considered. It is concluded that the smallest feasible device has a channel length of 0.52 μm and a gate oxide thickness of 9.4 nm when the supply voltage is 1.5 V. Reliable threshold control is most difficult to realize in an MOS-LSI with the smallest devices.**

I. Introduction

IN THE PAST FEW YEARS, integration density has doubled every year in MOS-LSI's. This advancement has been supported by several technological developments such as accurate process control, fine-pattern photolithography, improved short-channel MOSFET structure, and low-power circuit. One approach to realize higher performance MOS-LSI's was proposed by Dennard [1], which is called the scaled-down approach because the significant device dimensions are reduced according to a scaling principle. However, this approach is limited by physical and practical problems for the minimization of MOS-LSI's.

The physical limitations on minimizing MOS-LSI's have been studied recently by Hoeneisen and Mead [2] and Keyes [3]. Hoeneisen and Mead pointed out that the fundamental limitation of the short-channel MOSFET is gate oxide breakdown. However, throughout present efforts to develop a small-size device, it has been clarified that several limiting factors occur before oxide breakdown voltage is reached. These are poor controlability of threshold voltage and reduced drain breakdown voltage due to lateral bipolar effects which factors are related to the power supply voltage.

Manuscript received March 23, 1978; revised May 31, 1978.

The authors are with the Central Research Laboratory, Hitachi Ltd., 1-280 Higashikoigakubo, Kokubunji-shi, Tokyo, Japan.

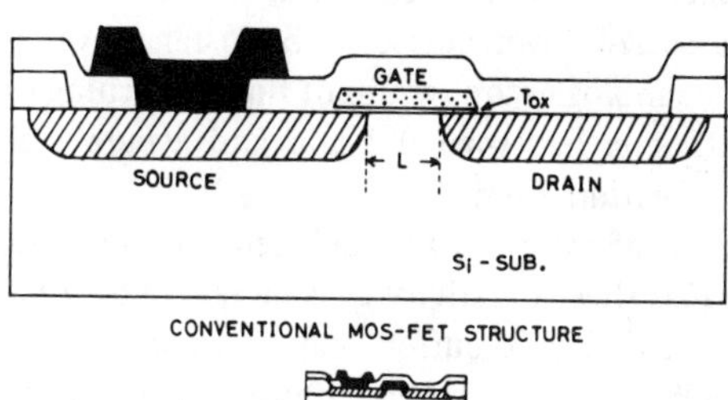

Fig. 1. Scaled-down concepts in MOSFET structure.

In this paper, the practical limitations for minimizing MOS devices are studied through experimental investigations.

II. Scaling-Down Concept

A scaling down of MOS devices means a proportional minimization of device dimensions, patterned geometries, and the power supply voltage. This is one of the ways to realize an MOS-LSI with high integration and performance. A MOSFET structure with a $\frac{1}{5}$ scaled-down model (scaling factor $K = 5$), which can, in principle, bring about 25 times higher integration density and performance, is shown in Fig. 1. The advantages of the scaled-down structure on device and circuit performance are very large as shown in Table I, where performance is illustrated as a scaling factor. It is noticed that the scaling concept yields high circuit performance, that is, a power-delay product of $P_W \cdot \tau_L = 1/K^2$. However, the following points must be taken into account for high-speed MOS-LSI performance:

Reprinted from *IEEE Trans. Electron Devices*, vol. ED–26, pp. 980–986, June 1979.

TABLE I
ADVANTAGES OF SCALING DOWN ON DEVICE AND CIRCUIT PERFORMANCE

Circuit or device parameters	Symbol	Scaling factor	Scaling
Power supply voltage	V_{DD}	$1/K$	
Drain current	I_D	$1/K$	$I_D(K)=\frac{\varepsilon_{ox}}{T_{ox}/K}\left(\frac{W/K}{L/K}\right)\left(\frac{V_G-V_{TH}-V_D/2}{K}\right)(V_D/K)=I_D/K$
Capacitance	C_L	$1/K$	$C_L(K)=\frac{\varepsilon_{ox}}{T_{ox}/K}(W/K)(L/K)=C_L/K$
Conductance	g_m	1	$g_m(K)=\frac{\varepsilon_{ox}}{T_{ox}/K}\left(\frac{W/K}{L/K}\right)\frac{V_G-V_{TH}}{K}=g_m$
Sub-threshold const.	α	1	$\alpha(K)=kT/q\cdot\ln 10\left(1+\frac{\varepsilon_s T_{ox}/K}{\varepsilon_{ox} W_d/K}\right)=\alpha$
Drain breakdown volt.	BV_j	$(K)^{-0.5}$	$BV_j(K)=\mathrm{const.}\times(2\varepsilon_s/qKN_A)^{0.5}=BV_j/(K)^{0.5}$
Sheet resistivity	ρ_s	K	$\rho_s(K)=\rho_B(T/K)=K\rho_s$
Voltage drop across the signal lines	δV	K	$\delta V(K)=I(K)\rho_s(K)/V(K)=K\delta V$
Line delay	τ_L	1	$\tau_L(K)=\rho_s(K)C_L(K)=\tau_L$
Power	P_W	$1/K^2$	$P_W(K)=I(K)V(K)=P_W/K^2$
Power and delay products	$P_W\cdot\tau$	$1/K^2$	$P_W(K)\cdot\tau(K)=P_W.\tau_L/K^2$

1) In general, advanced technologies should be developed to fabricate a scaled-down device. For instance, in Fig. 1, the following technologies are required: fine patterning of 1-2 μm, shallow diffusion less than 0.2 μm, and accurate photomask alignment of within 1 μm.

2) The line delay τ_L is not reduced by the simple scaling down, because sheet resistivity ρ_s is increased by a factor of K.

3) Subthreshold leak current causes poor switching operation in MOS circuits, thereby limiting the lowest possible supply voltage in dynamic-type MOS circuits.

4) An increased voltage drop across high-resistive signal lines lowers a noise margin of digital circuits.

Therefore, some modifications of the simple scaled-down approach must be considered for high-speed oriented MOS-LSI design. One is a technical effort to fabricate signal lines with lower resistance and another is to employ supply voltages higher than those dictated by the scaled-down principle.

III. LIMITING FACTORS OF SHORT-CHANNEL MOSFET [4]

As previously described, the scaled-down approach creates several difficulties in the attempt to achieve high-speed MOS-LSI's. In this section, physical phenomena that limit the scale down of MOSFET's are studied.

A. Threshold-Voltage Control

In a short-channel MOSFET, the channel current is affected not only by the gate field but by the drain field as shown in Fig. 2. The results of this analysis clearly indicate that electrons are swept out into the bulk near the drain edge, which results in a shortening of the effective channel. The computed quasi-Fermi potential distribution, furthermore, reveals that the drain field affects the channel as far as 1 μm from the drain junction. Such a drain field leads to poor cutoff characteristics of the device that are observed as the threshold voltage (V_{TH}) changes with the drain voltage (V_D).

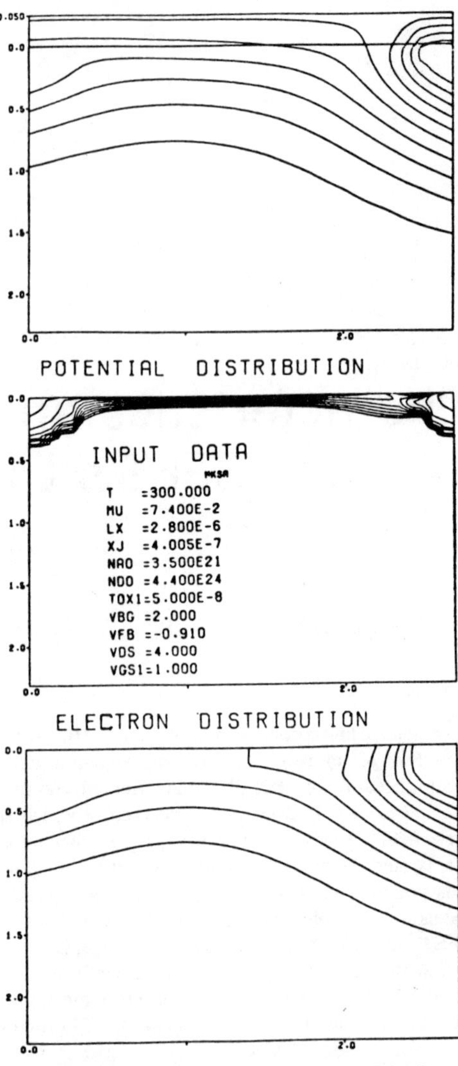

Fig. 2. Two-dimensional numerical analysis of 2-μm channel MOSFET. Potential lines: 0.346-6.579 (V); electron concentration lines: 4.8 × 10^{16}-7.1 × 10^{25} (m^{-3}); quasi-Fermi potential lines: 0.62-6.02 (V).

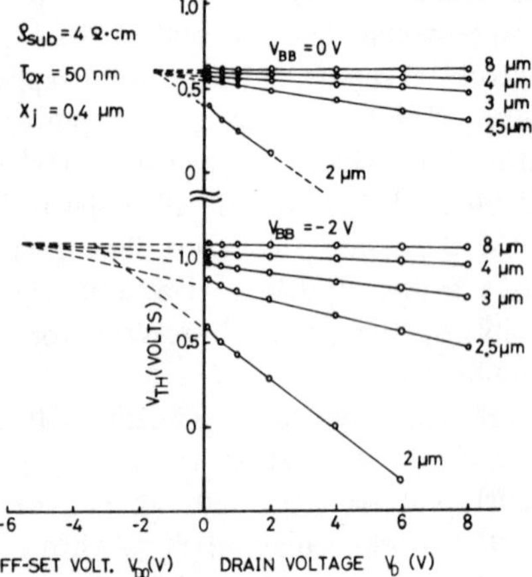

Fig. 3. Experimental V_{TH}-V_D characteristics of devices with various channel lengths.

Typical V_{TH}-V_D characteristics of the fabricated devices with various channel lengths are shown in Fig. 3. The following expression of the threshold voltage model has been derived from the experimental results shown in Fig. 3:

$$V_{TH} = V_{FB} + 2\phi_F + \frac{1}{C_0}\sqrt{2\epsilon_S q N_B(|V_{BB}| + 2\phi_F)} - \eta/C_0 \cdot (V_D + V_{D0}) \quad (1)$$

$$V_{D0} = 2(|V_{BB}| + V_{Bi}) \quad (2)$$

where η is the drain coefficient, V_{FB} the flat-band voltage, ϕ_F the Fermi potential, C_0 the gate capacitance per unit area, ϵ_S the dielectric constant of silicon, N_B the impurity concentration of the silicon substrate, V_{BB} the back gate bias voltage, and V_{Bi} the built-in voltage. The newly introduced drain coefficient has a strong dependence on channel length which is given as

$$\eta = \eta_0(x_j, N_B)\, L^{-n}. \quad (3)$$

Here, η_0 and n have the following values for MOSFET's with 10^{15} cm^{-3} $\leqslant N_B \leqslant 10^{16}$ cm^{-3}, 0.15 μm $\leqslant x_j \leqslant 0.41$ μm, and a gate oxide thickness of 50 nm:

$$\eta_0/C_0 = 4.1 \times 10^{-2}\text{-}8.8 \times 10^{-2} \quad (4)$$

$$n = 2.6\text{-}3.2. \quad (5)$$

The strong channel-length dependence of the drain coefficient reflects the well-known V_{TH} variation in short-channel structures.

The empirical equation showing the V_{TH} variation is indicated by following equation:

$$|\delta V_{TH}/\delta L| = n(\eta_0/C_0)\,(V_D + V_{D0})\, L^{-(n+1)}. \quad (6)$$

The dependence of the factor, η/C_0, on channel length L with the junction depth as a parameter is shown in Fig. 4. It is seen that η_0 is smaller for shallow n$^+$ junctions whereas n is unchanged. The η_0/C_0 and n obtained for fabricated MOSFET's are listed in Table II. In addition, it was found that punchthrough-like I_D-V_D curves can be interpreted by taking this model into account. A comparison of the experimental value and a gradual-channel MOSFET model with V_{TH} given by the empirical relationship of (1) is given in Fig. 5. These are in a very good agreement, when considering the carrier mobility reduction due to the gate field. The above results indicate that the punchthrough-like drain current in the short-channel MOSFET is not actually punchthrough current itself but the modulated drain current induced by threshold lowering by the drain voltage.

This threshold change due to the drain voltage and the channel length fluctuation of fabricated devices lead poor threshold control and punchthrough-like drain characteristics which limit the scale down of MOSFET's.

B. Drain Breakdown Voltage

The drain breakdown voltage of a MOSFET is determined by the following phenomena:

1) The avalanche breakdown of the p-n drain junction caused by the high electric field between the gate and drain.

2) I_D-V_D characteristics with a negative resistance (switchback) originating from lateral bipolar action, which is induced by weak avalanche hole current [5].

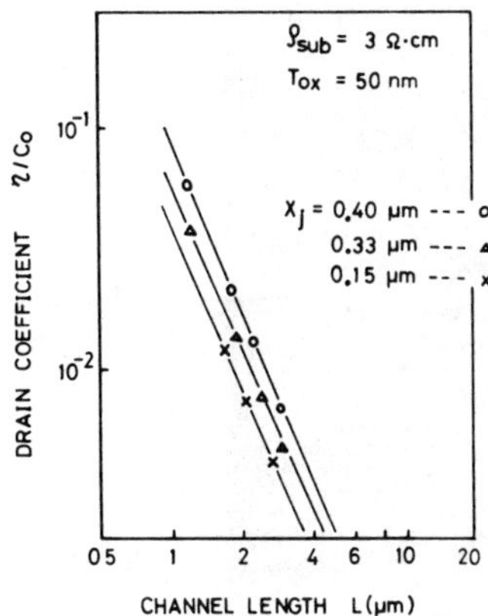

Fig. 4. Relationship between drain coefficient and channel length of the fabricated devices with junction depths of 0.40, 0.33, and 0.15 μm.

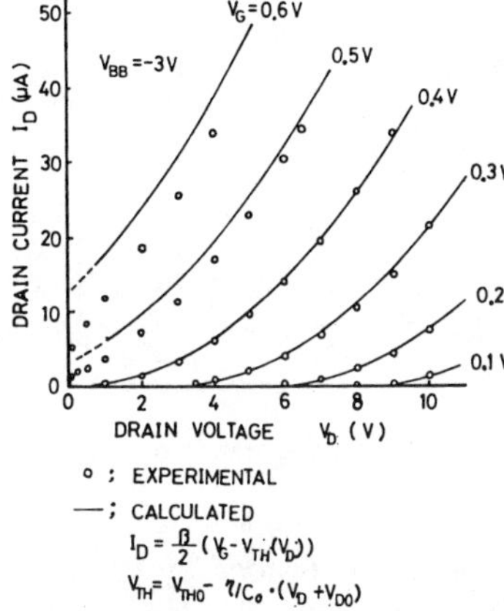

Fig. 5. Comparison of experimental punchthrough-like I_D-V_D curves with the proposed gradual-channel model with drain voltage-dependent threshold voltage.

TABLE II
MEASURED DRAIN COEFFICIENT PARAMETERS η_0 AND n OF FABRICATED MOSFET's

$\eta/C_0 = \eta_0/C_0 \cdot L^{-n}$

ρ_{sub} Ω·cm	x_j μm	T_{ox} nm	n	η_0/C_0
10	0.4	50	2.6	8.4×10^{-2}
3	0.4	50	3.0	7.8 〃
1	0.4	50	3.2	4.1 〃
3	0.40	50	3.2	8.8 〃
3	0.33	50	3.2	6.7 〃
3	0.15	50	3.2	4.1 〃

Typical drain breakdown characteristics and a MOSFET structure are shown in Fig. 6. The effective channel length and channel width of the experimental device are 2 and 13 μm, respectively. The characteristic features of the drain breakdown are described below. When the gate is biased in a cutoff condition ($V_G = 0$ V), the drain breakdown voltage (BV_{DS0}) is about 18 V. The drain breakdown voltage drops abruptly when applying a small positive with an increased gate voltage. The BV_{DS} has a minimum value (BV_{DS}(min)) of 12 V, when the gate is biased at 5 V. Further increases in gate voltage above 5 V result in a proportional rise in the breakdown voltage.

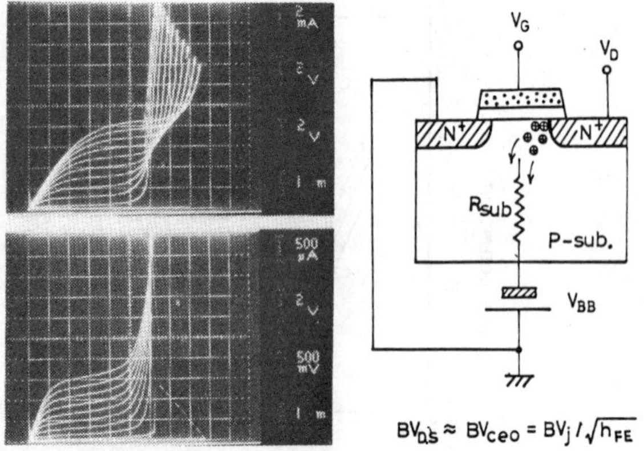

Fig. 6. Drain characteristics of a 2-μm channel MOSFET and physical structure of the MOSFET.

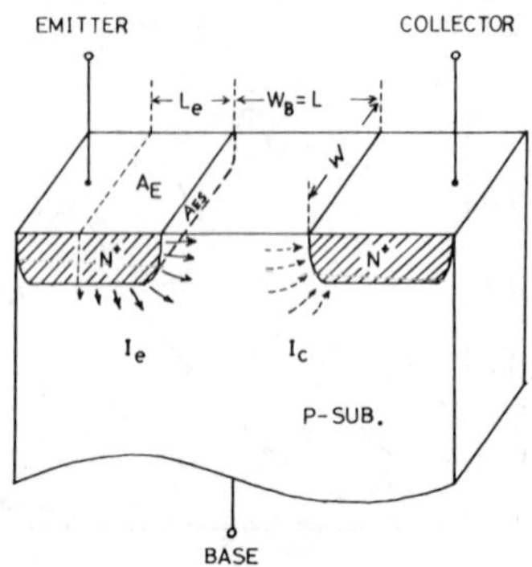

Fig. 7. Parasitic lateral bipolar transistor structure in a MOSFET.

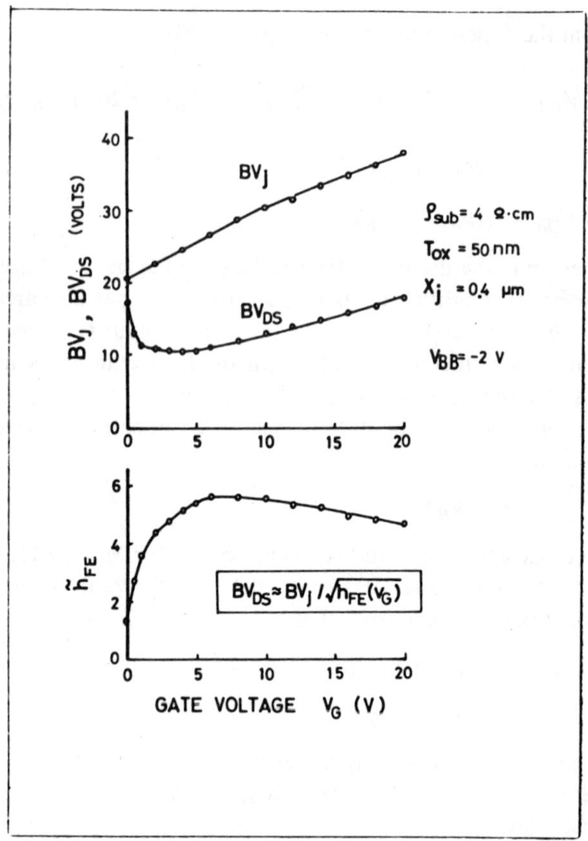

Fig. 8. Gate bias dependence of drain–substrate and drain–source breakdown voltages.

These results can be understood by taking a parasitic lateral bipolar effect into account. The hole current generated by weak avalanche multiplication is injected into the substrate (base), eventually forward biasing the source (emitter)–substrate junction. This means a direct electron current flows between the source and the drain (collector) if the current gain of the device is larger than unity.

From this point of view, the following bipolar equations can be used to explain the switching phenomena (Fig. 7):

$$I_e = A_E\,(\text{eff})\,\frac{qD_n n_p}{L_n}\,(e^{-U_{BE}} - 1) + A_{ES}\,\frac{qD_n n_p}{W_B}\,(e^{-U_{BE}} - 1) \quad (7)$$

$$I_c = A_{ES}\,\frac{qD_n n_p}{W_B}\,(e^{-U_{BE}} - 1) \quad (8)$$

$$\alpha = I_c/I_E \quad (9)$$

$$= \frac{A_{ES}/W_B}{A_E(\text{eff})/L_n + A_{ES}/W_B} \quad (10)$$

$$= \frac{x_j/L}{L_e/L_n + x_j/L} \quad (11)$$

$$h_{FE} = \alpha/(1 - \alpha) \quad (12)$$

$$= \frac{L_n}{L_e}\left(\frac{x_j}{L}\right). \quad (13)$$

Here, A_E(eff) and L_e are the effective emitter area and length, respectively, D_n the diffusion coefficient of electron, n_p the minority carrier density in the bulk silicon, L_n the electron diffusion length, U_{BE} the potential difference normalized with thermal voltage between the base and the emitter, A_{ES} the side area of the emitter, and W_B the base width (= L).

The breakdown voltage between the collector and the emitter, which corresponds to the drain breakdown voltage, is described by a well-known equation in the open-base condition [6]

$$BV_{CEo} = BV_j/\sqrt{h_{FE}} \quad (14)$$

$$= BV_j \Bigg/ \sqrt{\frac{L_n}{L_e}\left(\frac{x_j}{L}\right)} \quad (15)$$

$$BV_{DS} = BV_{CEo}. \quad (16)$$

The drain breakdown voltage (BV_{DS}) is approximated by BV_{CEo} because the holes generated at the drain junction flow easily to the nearby source in an ordinary MOSFET structure with a substrate resistance of several kilohms.

Experimental dependence of the drain–substrate breakdown voltage (BV_j) and drain–source breakdown voltage (BV_{DS}) on the gate voltage are shown in Fig. 8. In the figure, the proportional gate voltage dependence on the drain–substrate breakdown voltage comes from a high electric field effect caused by the gate and drain voltage difference. The estimated h_{FE} (= BV_j^2/BV_{DS}^2) of the lateral bipolar transistor was derived from the above results using (14), and is shown in the

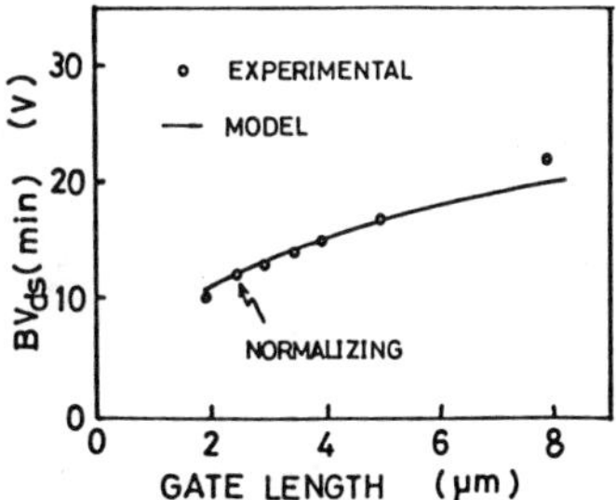

Fig. 9. Comparison between experimental and calculated BV_{DS}(min)-L characteristics.

lower half of Fig. 8. The h_{FE} estimated from the device dimensions ($L_e = 4$ μm) agrees well with the calculated h_{FE} of 6. The h_{FE} reduction near threshold voltage can be interpreted in terms of surface recombination of the injected hole current. The validity of the drain breakdown model is also verified by an examination of the BV_{DS}-L relationship, as shown in Fig. 9.

A MOSFET with a shorter channel obviously has a higher h_{FE}. Therefore, the reduction in the drain breakdown voltage becomes more remarkable.

C. Hot-Electron Injection into Gate Oxide

When a dc stress voltage is applied to the gate and drain electrodes, the device threshold increases during operation [7], [8]. Experimental results of the short-time stress tests using MOSFET's with $x_j = 0.4$ μm, $T_{ox} = 50$ nm, and $N_B = 3.5 \times 10^{15}$ cm^{-3} are shown in Figs. 10 and 11. Most notable results obtained from these experiments are the reduction of channel conductance at the drain edge introduced by hot-electron injection and the threshold change of all devices with various channel lengths, that arose when the drain current density per 1-μm channel width is 0.42 mA, as well as a well-known threshold shift. The conductance reduction results in lower g_m drain characteristics of the device when the drain and source are reversely connected as shown in Fig. 10. The latter provides the maximum current density available for device operation. In other words, the following inequality is predicted for these devices as the practical limitation of channel length reduction:

$$L \geqslant \frac{\beta_0(V_G)\,(BV_{dc} - V_{TH})^2}{2 \times 0.42 \times 10^{-3}\ (\mathrm{A})} \tag{17}$$

where $\beta_0(V_G)$ is the effective channel conductance of a MOSFET with an aspect ratio of one and BV_{dc} the maximum stress voltage. The maximum current density measured by using devices with $X_j = 1$ μm, $T_{ox} = 75$ nm, and $N_B = 10^{15}$ cm^{-3} shows about the same value of this experiment. Therefore, it seems that junction temperature at the drain edge affects the energy distribution of the hot electron, resulting in the threshold shift in the case of a short-time stress test.

D. Subthreshold Leak Current

The lowest power supply voltage for a digital MOS-LSI can be predicted by the subthreshold cutoff characteristics of the MOSFET, as shown in (A3) of the Appendix

$$V_{DD} \geqslant 5\ V_{TH} \tag{18}$$

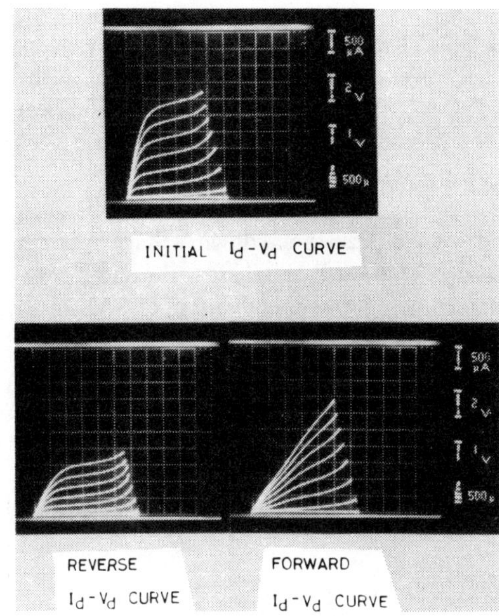

Fig. 10. Typical experimental results obtained from short-time stress test. The voltage (9 V) was applied to the gate and drain electrodes for 10 s.

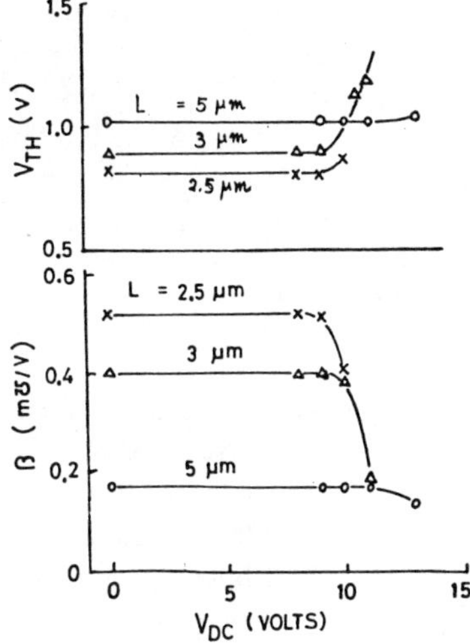

Fig. 11. Experimental variations of threshold and channel conductance due to the stress voltage.

$$V_{DD} = 5 \times (5 \cdot \alpha\,(\min)) \tag{19}$$

where α is the gate bias change needed for a drain current change of one decade with the gate voltage below threshold. As shown in Table I, α will not be decreased by the scaled-down structure and, furthermore, it has a minimum value at room temperature of $\alpha(\min) = \ln(10)\,kT/q = 57$ mV. Therefore, the power supply voltage must be higher than 1.43 V in MOSFET circuits for room-temperature operation.

IV. Practical Limitations of a Scaled-Down MOSFET

The experimental studies of short-channel MOSFET's clarify the practical limiting factors of scaled-down devices. At this point, the smallest MOSFET structure for MOS-LSI devices is examined, assuming the miniaturization of a 5-μm device structure with $x_j = 1$ μm, $T_{ox} = 100$ nm, and $N_B = 10^{15}$ cm^{-3}.

A. Channel Length

The available channel length for MOS-LSI devices as a function of the power supply voltage is bounded by the hatched region in Fig. 12. Here, the controlability of fabrication technology (δL) is assumed to improve with channel length by a factor of $\delta L/L = 0.23$.

An important result is that the minimum channel length is dominated by the drain breakdown voltage when the power supply voltage is above 8 V, whereas threshold controlability prevails below the power supply voltage of 8 V. In addition to this consideration, it should be noted that carrier velocity saturation by the drain field, in a channel shorter than 0.5 μm, reduces the improvements obtained by the scale down. The predicted value of the minimum channel length in this work is about two times larger than that estimated by Hoeneisen and Mead [2] based on the physical limitations approach shown in the figure.

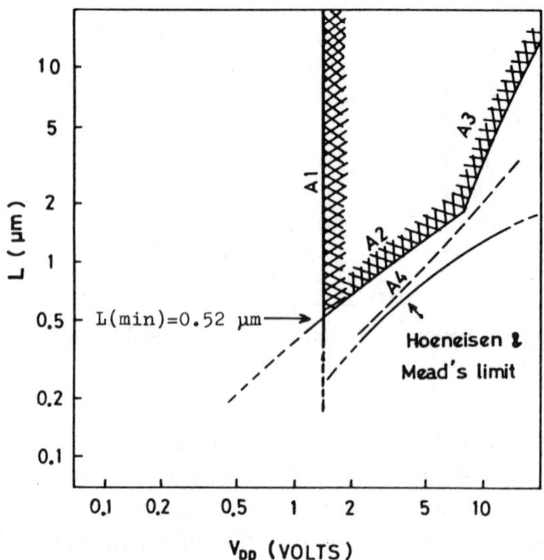

A1 ; $V_{DD} \geq 5V_{TH} = 5\times 5kT/q \cdot \ln(10)$

A2 ; $|\delta V_{TH}| = n(\eta_0/C_0)(V_{DD}+V_{DO})L^{-(n+1)}\delta L \leq 0.25V_{TH}$

A3 ; $BV_{DS}(\min) = BV_j/(L_n x_j/W_e L)^{0.5} \geq 1.5V_{DD}$

A4 ; $BV_{DC} = (2xI_D(\max)L/\beta(V_G))^{0.5} \geq 1.5V_{DD}$

Fig. 12. Limitations of channel shortening in scaled-down MOSFET's.

B. Gate Oxide Thickness

Obviously, the gate oxide breakdown is one important limiting factor for a thinner gate oxide film. Before breakdown is reached, the Fowler-Nordheim tunnel current flows when a high electric field is applied across the oxide film [9]. The experimental I-V characteristics of the gate oxide film show the F-N current with an exponential rise to the gate voltage and the maximum electric field of $\epsilon_m = 7.5 \times 10^6$ V/cm which causes oxide breakdown. Therefore, the limiting inequality of thinner gate oxide films is derived as follows taking into account the effect of F-N tunnel current (see Appendix):

$$T_{ox} \geqslant BV_G/2 \cdot (\epsilon_m + 2\alpha_G)^{-1} \tag{20}$$

$$= V_{DD} \cdot (\epsilon_m + 2\alpha_G)^{-1} \tag{21}$$

where BV_G is the gate oxide breakdown voltage and α_G the electric field change for F-N current change of one decade.

The junction breakdown is assumed for another limiting phenomenon of the gate oxide reduction. Threshold voltage control of the device with a thinner gate oxide requires a high impurity doping at the Si surface, which results in a reduced drain junction breakdown voltage.

The possible gate oxide thickness limited by these two phenomena is depicted in Fig. 13. As shown in the figure, the gate oxide breakdown, taking F-N current into account, limits the gate oxide thickness before the junction breakdown is reached.

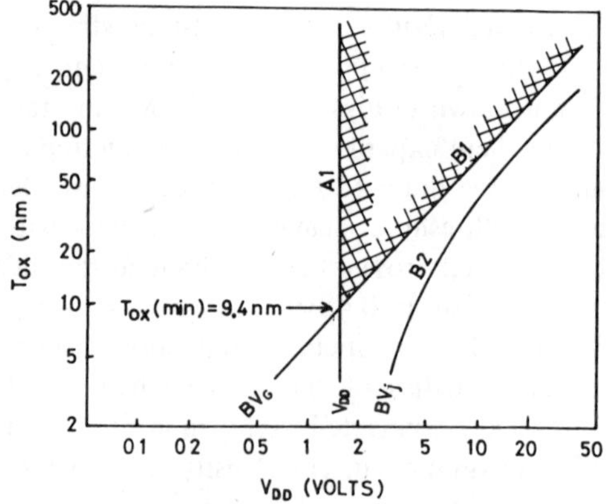

A1 : $V_{DD} \geq 5V_{TH} = 5\times 5kT/q \cdot \ln(10)$

B1 : $T_{ox} \geq V_{DD}/(\epsilon_m + 2\alpha_G)$

B2 : $BV_j\,(V_{TH} = 0.3V, N_B) \geq 2V_{DD}$

Fig. 13. Limitations of thinning gate oxide film in scaled-down MOSFET's.

C. The Smallest MOSFET

The minimum size of a MOSFET, for a given power supply voltage, can be determined from Figs. 12 and 13. The smallest possible MOSFET is shown in Fig. 14, when the power supply voltage is 1.5 V. The minimum channel length will be 0.52 μm and threshold voltage control below 0.08 V should be the most difficult problem to overcome to utilize this device in an MOS-LSI.

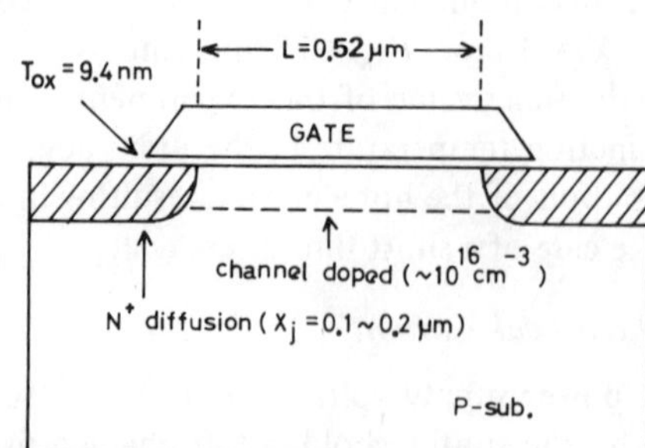

Fig. 14. Predicted smallest MOSFET structure when power supply voltage is 1.5 V.

V. Conclusion

Practical limitations in the minimization of MOS-LSI devices have been considered through measurement of small experimental devices. Experimental models for threshold and drain-source breakdown voltage in short-channel MOSFET's were proposed and the validity of the models examined. The threshold model introducing drain field effects agrees well with the experiments and it is clarified that the punchthrough-like I-V current is caused by threshold lowering due to drain voltage. The drain-source breakdown model based on a lateral bipolar effect satisfactorily explains the switch-back I_D-V_D characteristics of short-channel MOSFET's which reduce breakdown voltage to one half of the drain-junction breakdown voltage.

The practical limitations of the minimum scaled-down MOSFET were investigated using these models and experiments of hot-electron injection phenomena into the gate oxide, that yields a change in device performance during operation. As a result, it appears that the minimum channel length is determined by drain breakdown phenomena when the supply voltage is above 8 V, whereas it is limited by difficulties related to threshold control below the supply voltage of 8 V. It can, therefore, be concluded that the minimum MOSFET structure for a power supply voltage of 1.5 V has a channel length of 0.52 μm and a gate oxide thickness of 9.4 nm.

Appendix I
Limitation of Power-Supply Voltage

In circuit design of single-channel MOS-LSI's, the minimum power supply voltage is determined by input-output voltage transfer characteristics as shown in Fig. 15. Here, V'_{TH} is the threshold voltage including a threshold fluctuation (δV_{TH})

$$V'_{TH} = V_{TH} + \delta V_{TH}. \quad \text{(A1)}$$

Therefore, if the threshold fluctuation is controled under $0.25 V_{TH}$, the minimum power supply voltage of MOS circuits can be predicted by the following equations:

$$V_{DD} \geqslant 4 V'_{TH} \quad \text{(A2)}$$

$$V_{DD} \geqslant 5 V_{TH}. \quad \text{(A3)}$$

The threshold voltage in (A3) should be designed from considerations of MOSFET subthreshold leak current when the gate is biased at zero volt. Suppose the leak current is lower than the junction leak current of 1 pA/(100 μm^2). If the threshold voltage is defined as the gate bias voltage at a unit MOSFET ($W/L = 1$) drain current of 0.1 μA, it is required that the subthreshold leak current at $V_G = 0$ V be 10^{-5} times smaller than the drain current in the case of $V_G = V_{TH}$.

Appendix II
Limitation of Gate Oxide Thickness

Gate oxide breakdown is one of the most important factors in an MOS circuit for its unreversible characteristics. Therefore, the gate oxide thickness should be determined carefully through the experimental and theoretical considerations.

Experimental data of gate breakdown measured by Osburn and Ormond [10] showed a wide distribution of typical final oxide breakdown field. These experiments imply that the maximum gate field applied across the oxide should be designed below one half of the final oxide breakdown field of 7.5×10^6 V/cm. On the other hand, F-N tunnel current which flows before the oxide breakdown limits the power supply voltage for a leak current problem. There is the need to design the F-N current 10^{-2} smaller than the gate current at the oxide field of 7.5×10^6 V/cm (= 10^{-6} A/cm^2) for the purpose of lowering the gate current below the junction leak level of some 10^{-8} A/cm^2.

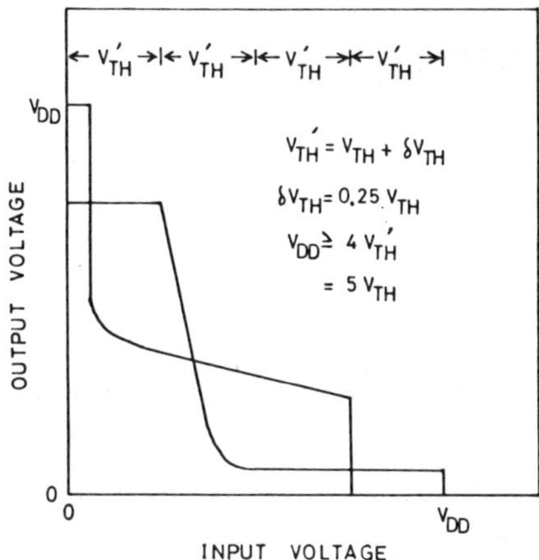

Fig. 15. Schematic input-output transfer curve of single-channel MOS circuit.

Acknowledgment

The authors wish to thank K. Sato for his continued encouragement and device fabrication and T. Toyabe for his cooperation during two-dimensional device analysis.

References

[1] R. H. Dennard *et al.*, "Design of ion-implanted MOSFET's with very small physical dimensions," *IEEE J. Solid-State Circuits*, vol. SC-9, p. 256, 1974.

[2] B. Hoeneisen and C. A. Mead, "Fundamental limitation in microelectronics–I. MOS technology," *Solid-State Electron.*, vol. 15, p. 819, 1972.

[3] R. W. Keyes, "Physical limits in digital electronics," *Proc. IEEE*, vol. 63, p. 740, 1975.

[4] H. Masuda *et al.*, *Tech. Paper of Electronic. Commun. Eng. Japan*, vol. SSD76-34, 1976.

[5] D. P. Kennedy *et al.*, "Source-drain breakdown in a insulated gate field effect transistor," in *IEEE IEDM Tech. Dig.*, p. 160, 1973.

[6] A. B. Phillips, *Transistor Engineering.* New York: McGraw-Hill, 1962.

[7] A. Shakir *et al.*, "N-channel IGFET design limitations due to hot electron trapping," in *IEEE IEDM Tech. Dig.*, p. 35, 1973.

[8] A. Phillips *et al.*, "IGFET hot electron model," in *IEEE IEDM Tech. Dig.*, p. 39, 1973.

[9] M. Lenzlinger and E. H. Snow, "Fowler-Nordheim tunneling into thermally grown SiO_2," *J. Appl. Phys.*, vol. 40, p. 278, 1969.

[10] C. M. Osburn and D. W. Ormond, "Dielectric breakdown in SiO_2 film on Si I: Measurement and interpritation," IBM Research, Tech. Rep. RC3470, July 23, 1971.

Generalized Guide for MOSFET Miniaturization

J. R. BREWS, W. FICHTNER, MEMBER, IEEE, E.H. NICOLLIAN, SENIOR MEMBER, IEEE, S. M. SZE, FELLOW, IEEE

Abstract — **As MOSFET dimensions are reduced, lower voltages, shallower junctions, thinner oxides, and heavier doping help to maintain long-channel behavior. A simple, empirical relation has been found between these parameters and the minimum channel length for which long-channel subthreshold behavior will be observed. This approximate relation provides an estimate for MOSFET parameters not requiring reduction of all dimensions by the same scale factor.**

INTRODUCTION

The proposed empirical relation is:

$$L_{min} = A.[x_j t_{ox} (w_s + w_d)^2]^{1/3} \quad (1)$$

where L_{min} is the minimum channel length for which long-channel subthreshold behavior will be observed, A is a proportionality factor, x_j is junction depth, t_{ox} is oxide thickness, and $w_s + w_d$ is the sum of source and drain depletion depths in a one dimensional abrupt junction formulation. That is,

$$w_d = \sqrt{2}L_B\,[\beta(V_{DS}+V_{bi}+V_{BS})]^{1/2} \quad (2)$$

where the bulk Debye length, L_B, is given by:

$$L_B = [\epsilon_s/(\beta q N_A)]^{1/2} \quad (3)$$

and $\beta = (kT/q)^{-1}$, V_{DS} is drain-to-source voltage, V_{bi} is the built-in voltage of the junctions, and V_{BS} is body-to source reverse bias. For $V_{DS} = 0$, $w_d = w_s$.

Equation (1) has been compared with computer results and with experiment. Eq. (1) fits observation with an accuracy of about 20% in the worst cases, and usually is more accurate. No simple model leading to Eq. (1) is known, and other expressions are not precluded. Nonetheless, Eq. (1) is a useful summary of our results.

EXPERIMENTAL STUDY

Experimentally, the boundary between a long-channel and a short-channel device was based upon two criteria. The first criterion was agreement of the dependence of the drain current on channel length with the long-channel dependence: $I_D \propto 1/L$. A ten percent departure from linear dependence upon (1/L) was taken to indicate short-channel behavior. The second criterion was related to the dependence of the subthreshold drain current on drain voltage [1], [2]. For long-channel devices I_D is independent of V_{DS} in the subthreshold region when $V_{DS} > 3kT/q$. Short-channel devices display a drain bias dependence for all values of V_{DS}.

The reciprocal slope of the subthreshold $\ln I_D$ *versus* gate bias curves was much less sensitive to short channel effects than the above two criteria. That is, a shift in these curves is the primary short channel effect, rather than a change of slope.

In Fig. 1, a comparison of the experimental L_{min} with the prediction of Eq. (1) is made. The two agree within experimental error. To make a more stringent test, comparisons with computer calculations also were made.

COMPUTER CALCULATIONS

To determine L_{min} from two-dimensional computer calculations, the channel length was reduced until the drain current measured ten percent above the Pao-Sah long-channel prediction for the same device [2], [3]. Parameters were varied individually with fixed bias conditions. The computer calculations used a finite difference solution of the coupled Poisson and transport equations [4].

The proportionality constant A in Eq. (1) was fixed by fitting Eq. (1) to one data point. We arbitrarily fitted the point $L_{min} = 7.2\mu m$, $N_A = 10^{14} cm^{-3}$, $t_{ox} = 250$ Å, $x_j = 0.33\mu m$, $V_{DS} = 1$ volt, $V_{BS} = 0$. For this point, we found A = $0.41(\text{Å})^{1/3}$. If this A-value is used in Eq. (1) with t_{ox} in angstroms, x_j in microns and with $w_s + w_d$ in microns, then L_{min} will be in microns. With A given, there are no further adjustable parameters.

Figure 2 shows the dependence of L_{min} upon doping level with oxide thickness as parameter. For thin oxides, Eq. (1) exaggerates L_{min} at all dopings. This point is brought out in Figure 3.

Figure 3 shows the oxide thickness dependence of L_{min} with doping density as parameter. The t_{ox} dependence of Fig. 3 may be a surprise, because a strong dependence of the electrostatic potential upon t_{ox} is not anticipated unless t_{ox} is comparable to L_{min}. The origin of the t_{ox} dependence of Fig. 3 is the *criterion* for L_{min}: as t_{ox} is reduced, a larger short-channel deviation in device behavior is necessary before the current level is altered by ten percent.

The dependence of L_{min} on drain-to-source bias, V_{DS}, and body-to-source reverse bias, V_{BS} also were studied. This dependence is so weak that the fit of Eq. (1) to these results is not a severe test.

Finally, Fig. 4 is a comparison of all the computed values with Eq. (1), analogous to Fig. 1 for experiment.

Manuscript received October 15, 1979; revised November 7, 1979. The authors are with Bell Laboratories, Murray Hill, New Jersey 07974

Reprinted from *IEEE Electron Device Letters*, vol. EDL–1, pp. 2–4, Jan. 1980.

Conclusions

A simple formula for the minimum channel length compatible with long-channel subthreshold behavior has been tested over a limited range of oxide thickness (100 - 1000 Å), doping level (10^{14}-10^{17}cm^{-3}), junction depth (.3 - 1.5μm), and bias (0-5 volts). Equation (1) allows a more flexible miniaturization than scaling of all device parameters by the same factor [5]. This flexibility should allow the choice of other than strictly scaled geometries, *e.g.* new geometries which are easier to make or which optimize other aspects of MOSFET operation.

Acknowledgments

We wish to thank G.E. Smith for criticism, E.N. Fuls and his group for fabrication, C.C. Chen, E.E. Labate, and S. Pang for device measurements, T.T. Sheng for TEM measurements, and S.E. Haszko and W.E. Willenbrock for SEM measurements.

References

[1] M.B. Barron, "Low-level currents in IGFETs", Solid-State Electron. *15* 293 (1972).

[2] J.R. Brews, "A charge-sheet model of the MOSFET," Solid-State Electron. *21* 345 (1978).

[3] H.C. Pao and C.T. Sah, "Effects of diffusion current on characteristics of MOS transistors", Solid-State Electron. *9,* 927 (1966).

[4] W. Fichtner, "Two-dimensional modelling of SOS transistors", IEE J. Solid-State and Electron Dev. *2,* 47 (1978).

[5] R.H. Dennard, F.H. Gaensslen, H.N. Yu, V.L. Rideout, E. Bassous and A. Le Blanc, "Design of ion-implanted Mosfet's with very small physical dimensions", IEEE J. Solid-State Circuits, SC-9, 256 (1974).

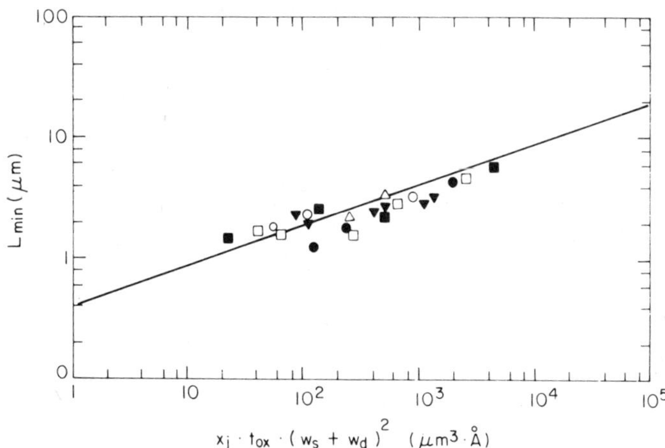

Fig. 1. Variation of L_{min} with $[x_j t_{ox} (w_s + w_d)^2]$ of Eq. (1). Points are experimental values. The straight line of slope (1/3) is the predicted value using Eq. (1) with A = 0.41 (Å)$^{1/3}$. Three junction depths are illustrated: ○ = .33μm, □ = .7μm, △ = 1.46μm. Open symbols denote V_{DS} = 1 V, V_{BS} = 0 V. Filled symbols denote V_{DS} = 5V, $V_{BS} \doteq$ 0 V. ▽ denotes $V_{BS} \neq 0$ with open symbols x_j = 0.33μ and filled symbol x_j = 0.7μ. Other device parameters were 10^{14} cm^{-3} ≤ N_A ≤ 10^{16} cm^{-3} and 130Å ≤ t_{ox} ≤ 1000Å.

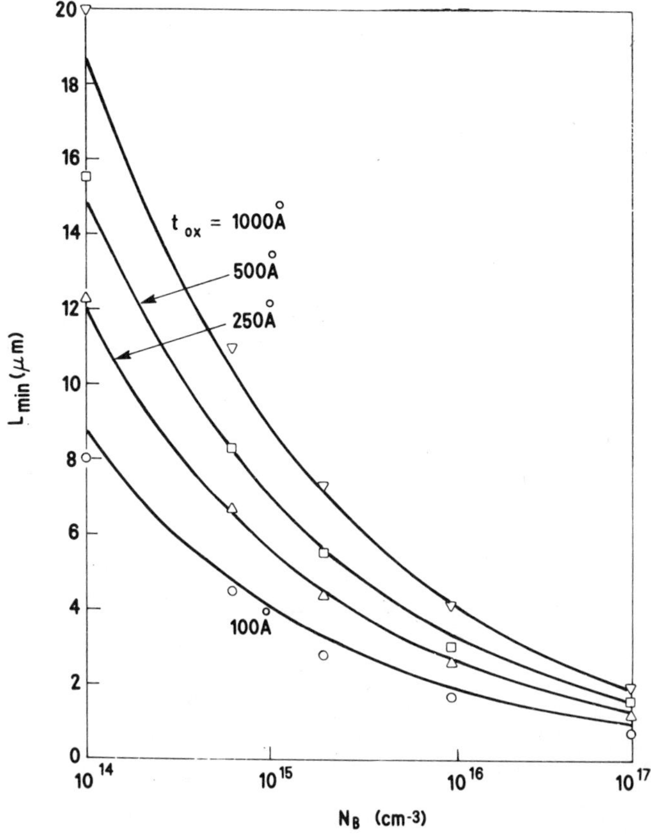

Fig. 2. L_{min} vs. doping level, N_A (cm^{-3}) with t_{ox} as parameter. Points are two-dimensional computer calculation, solid lines are Eq. (1). Junction depth is x_j = 1.46μ. Oxide thickness decreases from the upper to the lower curve, with t_{ox} = 1000 Å, 5000 Å, 250 Å and 100 Å respectively.

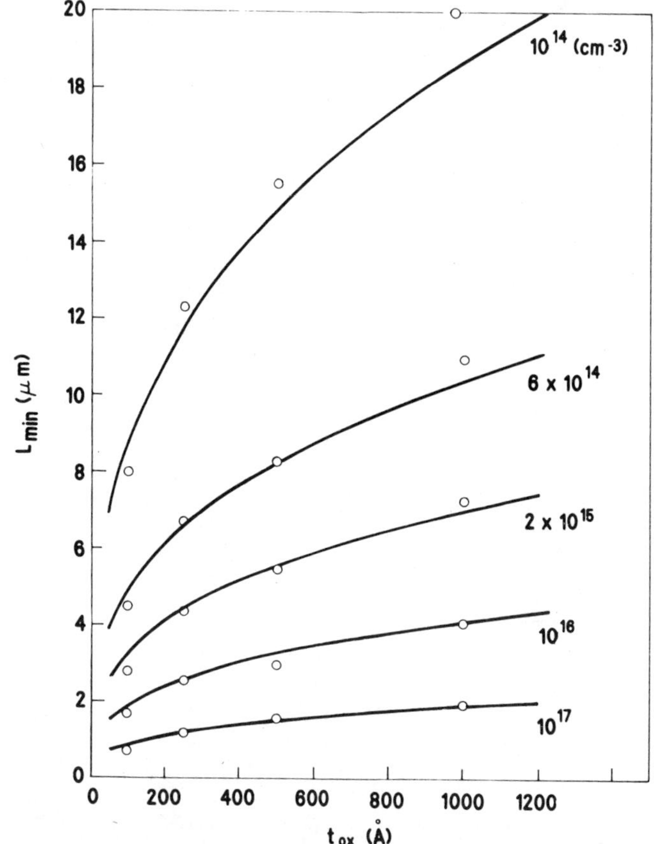

Fig. 3. L_{min} vs. t_{ox} with doping as parameter. Points are computer results; the solid lines are Eq. (1). Again x_j = 1.46μ.

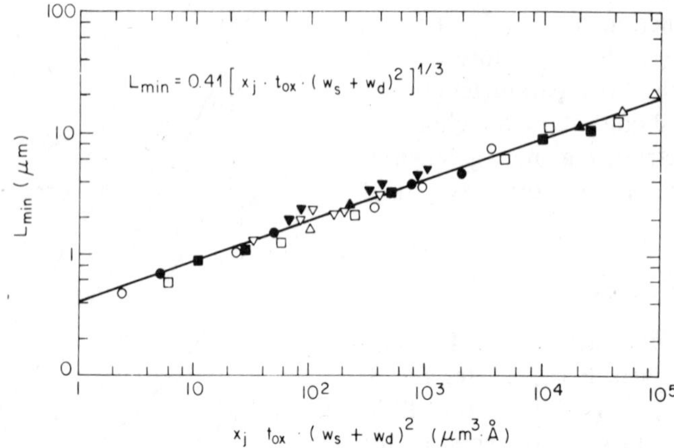

Fig. 4. L_{min} vs. $[x_j\, t_{ox}\, (w_s + w_d)^2]$ of Eq. (1). Points are values using two-dimensional computer solution. The straight line of slope (1/3) is the predicted value using Eq. (1). Symbols as in Fig. 1.

Performance Limits of E/D NMOS VLSI

K. Nirmal Ratnakumar and James D. Meindl

Stanford University

Stanford, CA

Dirk J. Bartelink

Xero Research Center

Palo Alto, CA

AN ANALYTIC MOST model including both weak inversion and short-channel effects describing accurately measured MOST characteristics for channel-lengths down to 1.0μm will be offered. Rigorous predictions based upon this model indicate that fundamental limits on an optimal E/D inverter for VLSI are:

$$L=0.3\mu m, V_{DD}=0.5V \text{ and } Pt_d=0.5fJ.$$

The optimized inverter structure is shown in Figure 1. The channel-length L_e of the enhancement device and the width W_d of the depletion device are set equal to the minimum feature size L. The geometric ratio β is chosen as, $\beta^{1/2} = W_e/L_e = L_d/W_d$ to minimize the inverter active area. The enhancement implant is done with the depletion channel regions masked, so that the substrate bias sensitivity of the load is small. Since the implanted regions are shallow (~1000Å) and are separated from the channel-stop P^+ regions by the P^- substrate the threshold-voltage sensitivity to the channelwidth can be neglected.

Assuming symmetrical noise margins and idealized device characteristics, the minimum power-delay product Pt_d is given by equation (*1*), (the numbered equations are listed in Table 1) where V_{Te} and V_{Td} are the enhancement and depletion threshold magnitudes respectively. For long-channel devices, the lower limit for V_{DD} is set by subthreshold currents[1,2] and using equation (*2*) it can be shown that the minimum V_{DD} for noise margins $\geqslant kT/q$ is $8kT/q$.

For short-channel devices, it will be shown that, contrary to an earlier scaling theory[3], V_{DD} must be increased. Equation (*3*)[4] represents the variation of threshold voltage V_{TS} of a short-channel MOST, where ΔV_T and η are functions of the device structure discussed hereafter.

For the output voltage to be close to V_{DD} in the logic *one* state, equation (*2*) predicts that $V_{TS} \geqslant 4kT/q$ and $V_{DD_{min}}$, the supply voltage corresponding to $(Pt_d)_{min}$ is given by equation (*4*).

Since ΔV_T and η increase as L decreases, $V_{DD_{min}}$ must increase. Hence, at some value $L=L_{min}$, the Pt_d product will be a minimum. Also, from equation (*1*), for this value of V_{DD}, the long-channel thresholds correspond to $(Pt_d)_{min}$.

Experimentally verified analytical expressions for ΔV_T and η are derived from a simple quasi-two-dimensional model illustrated in Figure 2. First ΔV_T at zero drain-bias is evaluated. The model assumes that, due to the rapid variation of the surface potential near the junctions, the surface is strongly inverted. Hence, it can be approximated that, up to a distance d from the junctions, all the gate fields terminate on the inversion charge, and that the entire channel depletion charge of qN_a is bound by junction fields. By a comparison of the inversion charge with the depletion charge, d is found to be approximately equal to half the depletion-depth W. The fringing junction fields beyond d terminate a charge corresponding to δN_a; Figure 2*c*. The potential distributions $V_1(y)$ at the source, and $V_2(y)$ at $x = L/2$ are assumed to be due to the junction and gate potentials respectively. By solving the resulting one-dimensional Poisson's equation ΔV_T is given by equation (*5*). Figure 3 shows the excellent fit between the measured threshold data of devices with values of L down to 1.0μm and the predictions of the above model compared with those of a *trapezoidal* charge-sharing model described in 1974[5].

With a drain-bias V_D, if N_a is not too small, the threshold-reduction is due mainly to the shift ΔL_s towards the source of the location of the surface potential minimum from $x = L/2$ and is calculated to be equation (*6*). Noting that $\eta = d\Delta V_T/dV_D$, equation (*6*) predicts a L^{-3} dependence for η which agrees with experimental data[6]. Figure 4 shows the agreement between the measured and predicted V_T versus V_D for the same set of devices as in Figure 3.

Substituting $E_{max} \simeq 6 \times 10^6$ V/cm and $V_{fb} \simeq -1V$ in equation (*7*), t_{ox}, the oxide thickness is calculated to be 50Å and using equations (*1* to *6*), it can be shown that $(Pt_d)_{min}=0.5$ fJ, $t_d=30$ ps, $V_{DD}=0.5V$, $L=0.3\mu m$, and $N_a=1.5 \times 10^{17}$ cm^{-3}. The drain break-down voltage is set by the avalanche breakdown of the parasitic NPN bipolar transistor[6]. Hence, it is concluded that the avalanche breakdown voltage V_{av} of the drain should satisfy

---

[1] Swanson, R.M. and Meindl, J.D., "Ion-implanted Complementary MOS Transistors in Low Voltage Circuits", *IEEE J. Solid-State Circuits,* SC-7, p. 146-153; 1972.

[2] Henderickson, T.E., "A Simplified Model for Subpinchoff Conduction in Depletion-mode IGFETs", *IEEE Trans. Elec. Dev.,* ED-25, p. 435-441; 1978.

[3] Dennard, R.H., Gaensslen, F.H., Yu, H.N., Rideout, V.L., Bassous, E. and LeBlanc, A.R., "Design of Ion-implanted MOSFET's with Very Small Physical Dimensions", *IEEE J. Solid-State Circuits,* SC-9, p. 256-268; 1974.

[4] Troutman, R.R. and Fortino, A.G., "Simple Model for Threshold Voltage in a Short-Channel IGFET", *IEEE Trans. Elec. Dev.,* ED-24, p. 1266-1268; 1977.

[5] Yau, L.D., "A Simple Theory to Predict the Threshold Voltage of Short-Channel IGFET's", *Solid-State Electron.,* 17, p. 1059-1063; 1974.

[6] Masuda, H., Nakai, M. and Kubo, M., "Characteristics and Limitation of Scaled-Down MOSFET's Due to Two-Dimensional Field Effect", *IEEE Trans. Elec. Dev.,* ED-26, p. 980-996; 1979.

[7] Jaeger, R.C. and Gaensslen, F.H., "Simple Analytical Models for Temperature-Dependent Behaviour of Depletion-Mode Devices", *IEEE Trans. Elec. Dev.,* ED-26, p. 501-508; 1979.

[8] Cottrell, P.E., Troutman, R.R. and Ning, T.H., "Hot-Electron Emission in N-channel IGFET's", *IEEE Trans. Elec. Dev.,* ED-26, p. 520-533; 1979.

Reprinted from *IEEE Int. Solid State Circuits Conf.*, pp. 72–73 and p. 260, 1980.

the condition, $V_{av} \geqslant 2(V_{DD} + V_{bi})$ where V_{bi} is the built-in junction potential. From an analysis of cylindrical junctions, the minimum source-drain junction-radius is found to be 800Å corresponding to a junction-depth of 1000Å. To minimize body-effect on the depletion load, N_{sub}, the substrate doping is kept small being just sufficient to prevent punch-through current. For the assumed voltages and junction radius, it is found that $N_{sub} = 8 \times 10^{15}$ cm^{-3}. The depletion implant dose is calculated to be 2×10^{11} cm^{-2}. In order that this implanted layer be pinched off, the depth of this channel should be <1000Å[7].

The transfer characteristics of the inverter corresponding to L=0.2, 0.3μm, respectively, are shown in Figure 5. Since, increased subthreshold currents at shorter channel-lengths, is the main cause for the poorer transfer characteristics, a CMOS inverter with the same magnitudes of N and P channel doping will perform better. Hence, as shown in Figure 5, for the same V_{DD}, the channel-lengths of CMOS inverters can be smaller by 50% or more. Since, the drain and substrate biases are low, the channel and substrate hot electron currents are negligible[8]. For the same reason, the electric fields are not sufficient to cause velocity saturation. However, to increase the storage time in dynamic gates, larger supply voltages may be required[6] and these effects, would then have to be considered.

Acknowledgment

This project was supported by DARPA contract no. MDA903-79-C-0680.

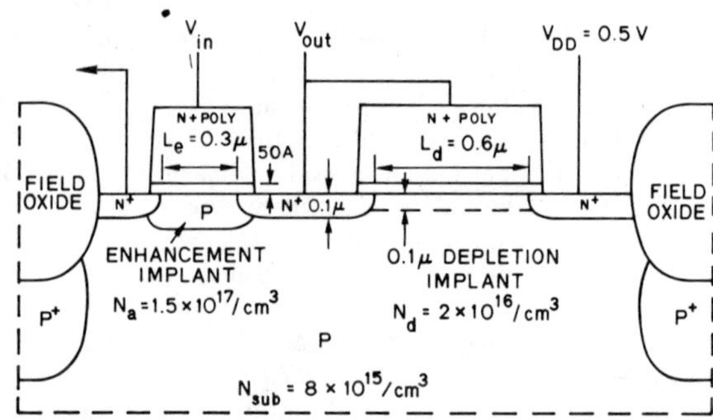

FIGURE 1—E/D inverter structure for minimum power-delay product.

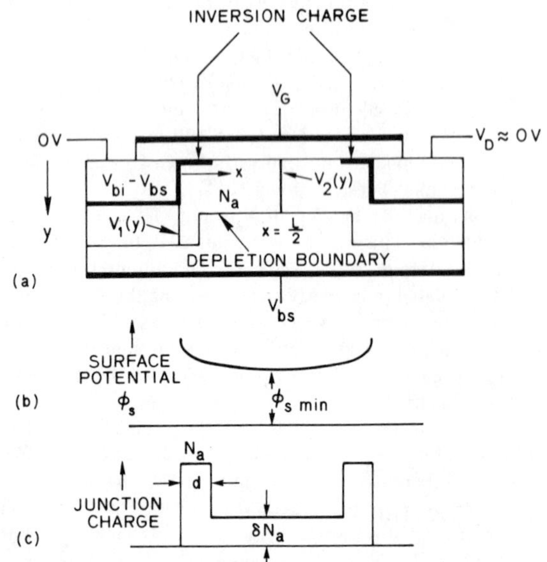

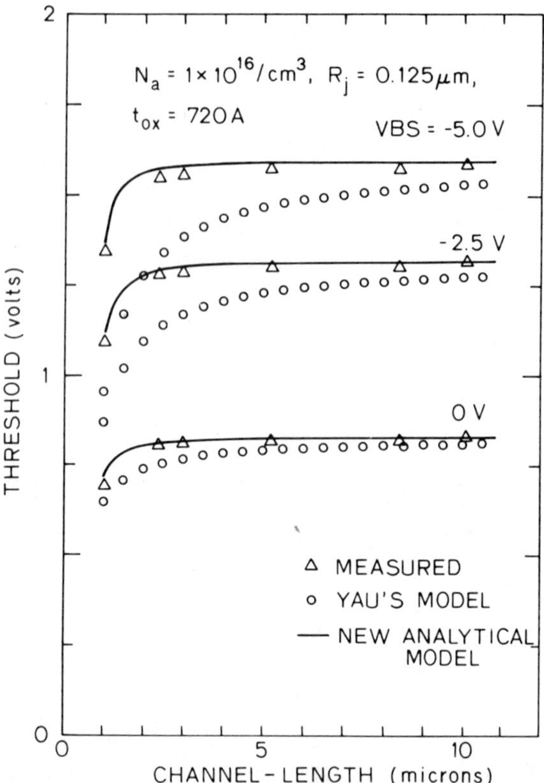

FIGURE 3—Analytical and experimental threshold-voltage versus channel length characteristics.

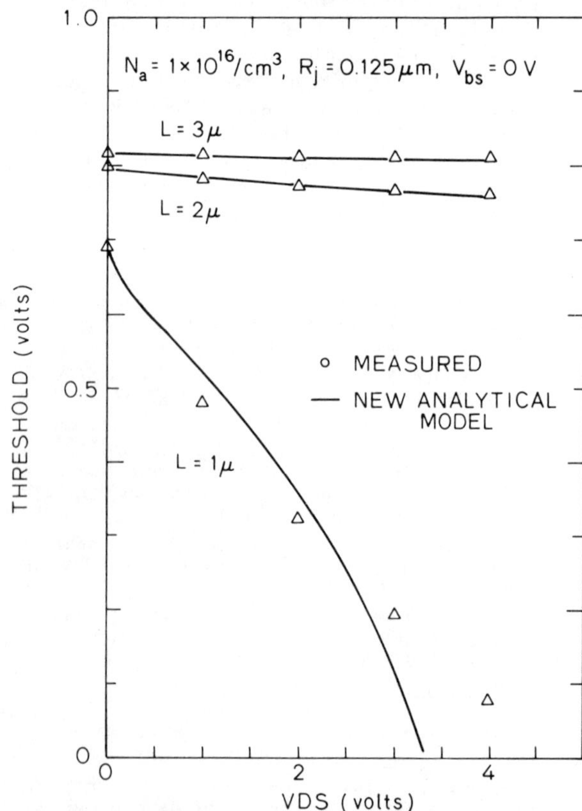

FIGURE 4—Analytical and experimental drain voltage dependence of short-channel threshold voltage.

[Left]

FIGURE 2—Illustration of the simple two-dimensional model for predicting short-channel threshold voltage.

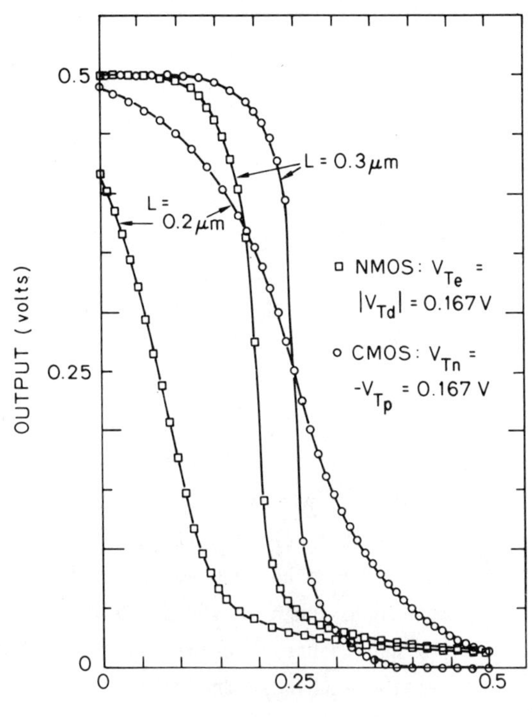

FIGURE 5—Comparison of predicted transfer characteristics of NMOS E/D and CMOS inverters for channel-lengths of 0.2 and 0.3μm.

$$(P t_d)_{min} = 2 C_o L^2 V_{DD}^2 \quad ; V_{Te} = V_{Td} = \frac{V_{DD}}{3} \; ; \quad \beta = 4 \tag{1}$$

$$I_D = \mu C_o \frac{W}{L} \, n \left(\frac{kT}{q}\right)^2 [\exp\{\frac{q(V_G - V_T)}{nkT}\}][1 - \exp(-\frac{qV_D}{kT})] \tag{2}$$

$$V_G - V_T \leq n \frac{kT}{q}$$

$$V_{TS} = V_{Te} - \Delta V_T - \eta V_D \tag{3}$$

$$V_{DD_{min}} = 3\left(\frac{4\frac{kT}{q} + \Delta V_T}{1 - 3\eta}\right) \tag{4}$$

$$\Delta V_T = \frac{1}{3} \frac{q N_a W^3}{C_o \{(\frac{L}{2})^2 - d^2\}} \tag{5}$$

$$\Delta V_T(V_D) = \frac{1}{3} \frac{q N_a W^3}{C_o \{(\frac{L}{2} - \Delta L_s)^2 - d^2\}} \; ; \Delta L_s = \frac{1}{2} \left\{\frac{2 \epsilon V_D}{q N_a}\right\}^{1/2} \tag{6}$$

$$t_{ox} = \frac{V_{DD} - V_{FB}}{E_{max}} \tag{7}$$

TABLE 1—List of equations.

On Scaling MOS Devices for VLSI

Yousset A. El-Mansy

Intel Corporation
Aloha, Oregon

ABSTRACT

Scaling down MOS device lateral and vertical dimensions is done systematically to achieve high density high performance technologies. It is shown that device gains however peak for a channel length of around 1μm below which it starts dropping again. Factors causing this effect, including the non scalability of voltage supplies, are discussed.

I. INTRODUCTION

MOS device scaling theory as presented in 1974[1] offered a methodology of designing devices and processes for high density high performance circuits. The procedure involved scaling down device lateral and vertical dimensions and supply voltage while increasing the substrate doping, all by the same scaling factor (S). Scaled devices would have higher currents, less capacitance and a power delay product that is reduced by the factor S^3. In practice, however, voltage supplies were not scaled down for various reasons such as TTL compatibility and operating margins. The power delay product could only be reduced by a factor in the range S to S^2. Nonscalability of voltages combined with shrinking of device lateral dimensions resulted in a number of effects on device characteristics that are caused by high fields. Some of these effects are related to material physical properties such as carrier velocity saturation while others could be reduced by proper process techniques such as threshold voltage geometry dependence. Shrinking the vertical dimensions enhanced the role of parasitic resistance and capacitance in affecting device currents. It also made the thickness of the inversion channel an important parameter for thin gate oxide devices.

For scaled devices, three physical factors have a major role in defining the terminal behaviour of the device. These are:

1) Velocity saturation of mobile channel charge.
2) Source and drain ohmic and contact resistances.
3) Finite Inversion channel thickness screening.

What makes these effects significant is that the first and third are dependent on material physical properties and as such, innovations in processing techniques would have little impact on them, while the second emphasizes the need for advanced source, drain and contacting technologies. An effect that is also important for small devices is the threshold voltage dependence on geometry. However, it has been the subject of numerous publications[2] and will not be treated here.

Reprinted from *IEEE Int. Conf. on Circuits and Computers*, vol. 1, pp. 457–460, 1980.

We start by looking at the drain current of a long channel device. Various effects are then introduced, one at a time. Finally, some results are presented and conclusions are drawn as to future scaling of MOS devices. For proper comparisons of various stages of scaled devices, a square device is considered throughout the analysis.

II. DRAIN CURRENT OF SCALED MOS DEVICES

II.1 Long Channel Device Current

The basic long channel device model assumes that the channel charge lies at the semiconductor surface and that the substrate fixed depletion charge is lumped into a threshold term. Referring to the terminology in Fig. 1 the drain current in the linear region for a square device (width = length) is written as

$$I_D = \mu C_O \cdot F(V_G, V_D, V_S) \qquad (1)$$

where

$$F(V_G, V_D, V_S) = \left(V_G - \frac{V_D + V_S}{2}\right)(V_D - V_S)$$

$$V_G = V_{GG} - V_T$$

V_D, V_S and V_{GG} are the applied voltages to the drain, source and gate terminals respectively.

V_T is the threshold voltage.

μ is the low field mobility

and C_O is the oxide capacitance per unit area.

As the drain voltage is increased, a point is reached where $\partial I_D/\partial V_D = 0$ and the current saturates at a drain voltage $V_{DSAT} = V_G$. The current in this region is obtained by substituting V_{DSAT} for V_D in equation (1).

II.2 Carrier Velocity Saturation

As the channel length L_E is reduced, the electric field along the channel increases and the carrier velocity deviates from the linear dependence on field and finally saturates at a scatter limited value. A simple way to express such behaviour is

$$\mu_e = \frac{1}{1 + \frac{\mu}{\nu_O} \cdot E}$$

where ν_O is the scatter limited value and E is the electric field. The drain current in equation (1) is modified to

$$ID = \mu C_O \cdot F_\nu \cdot F(V_G, V_D, V_S) \qquad (2)$$

where

$$F_\nu = \left(1 + \frac{\nu_{av}}{\nu_O}\right)^{-1}$$

and

$$V_{av} = \frac{\mu(V_D - V_S)}{L_E}$$

The saturation voltage V_{DSAT} now becomes

$$V_{DSAT} = V_S + \frac{\nu_O L_E}{\mu}\left\{\sqrt{1 + \frac{2\mu(V_G - V_S)}{\nu_O L_E}} - 1\right\}$$

As can be seen from equation (2), the effect of carrier velocity saturation is that the

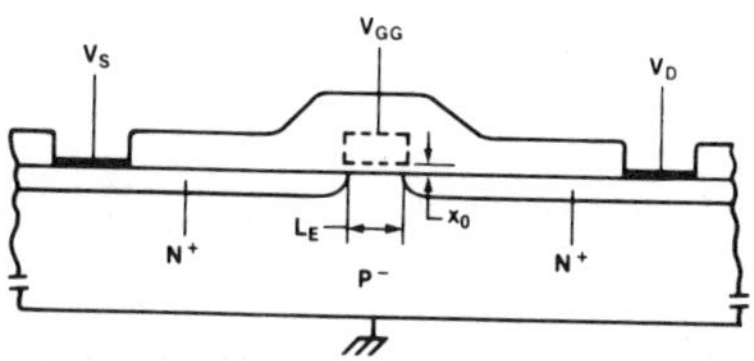

Fig. 1. Cross-Section of Scaled MOS Device

current in a square device reduces as the channel length is decreased ($F_\nu < 1$). The current also saturates at a lower drain voltage.

II.3 Source and Drain Resistance

As devices are scaled down, junctions get shallower and contact openings to these junctions become smaller. Both lead to an increased parasitic resistance in series with the device. The effect of such resistance is enhanced by the fact that the intrinsic device resistance becomes smaller for scaled devices. The resistance of each of the source and drain regions can be written as

$$R_S = R_\square \frac{L_D}{L_E} + R_C = R'_\square \cdot \frac{L_D}{L_E}$$

where $R_\square$ and R_C are the diffusion (per square) and contact resistances respectively. It is assumed that the ratio L_D/L_E is constant[3] as it is determined by lithographic alignment and resolution capabilities which normally track each other. For very small dimensions ($\lesssim$ 1μm) R_C will be a dominant factor. The effect of the parasitic resistance can be incorporated in equation (2) to give (refer to Fig. 2)

$$I_D = \mu C_o \cdot F_{\nu R} \cdot F(V_G, V_D, V_S) \qquad (3)$$

where $F_{\nu R} = (1 + \frac{\nu av}{\nu_o} + \frac{2R_S}{R_{CH}})^{-1}$

$$R_{CH} = \left\{\mu C_o (V_G - \frac{V_D + V_S}{2})\right\}^{-1}$$

The increased value of R_S reduces the current of square device as the junctions and contacts are scaled down.

II.4 Finite Inversion Layer Thickness

Recent experimental results,[4,5] on thin insulator devices have shown a degradation of device currents and transconductances. In those devices, the gate insulator thickness is of the same order as the inversion layer thickness. This causes the potential drop across the inversion layer to be a large portion of the applied gate to source voltage.[6] A simple model to describe that effect is illustrated in Fig. 3, where it shows that, in strong inversion, the effective gate capacitance is less than C_o and is the series combination of C_o and C_{CH}. This can be incorporated in the drain current expression by modifying the capacitance C_o by a factor F_{CH} to give

$$I_D = \mu C_o \cdot F_{\nu R} \cdot F_{CH} \cdot F(V_G, V_D, V_S) \qquad (4)$$

where $F_{CH} = (1 + \frac{C_o}{C_{CH}})^{-1}$

and the final gain constant of the device is

$$K = \mu C_o \cdot F_{\nu R} \cdot F_{CH} \qquad (5)$$

For a device with a gate capacitance of the order of the channel capacitance (70Å nitride or 35Å oxide) this effect causes the measured current to be half of the expected value (of an equivalent device with zero inversion layer thickness).

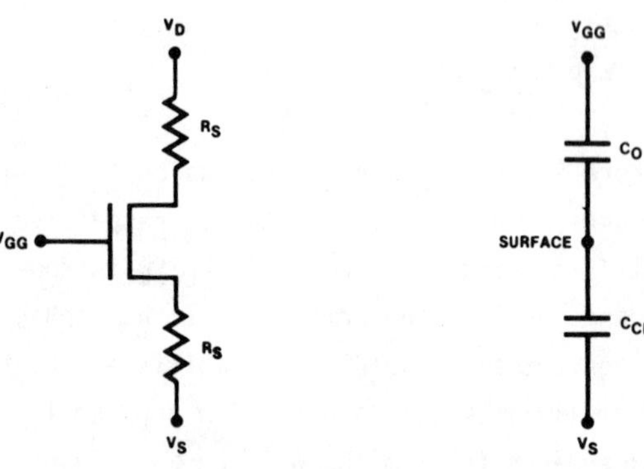

Fig. 2. Series Resistance

Fig. 3. Channel Capacitance

III. RESULTS AND DISCUSSION

Using an NMOS 1975 process as a reference (scaling factor S of 1) and using the relationships derived here, the data in Table I & Fig. 4 was generated. Scaling factors of 0.7 and 0.4, applied to channel lengths, oxide thickness and junction depth, produce scaled technologies that have existed in 1977 and 1979 respectively. As can be seen from the data, the physical mechanism with most effect on those technologies has been velocity saturation while other mech-

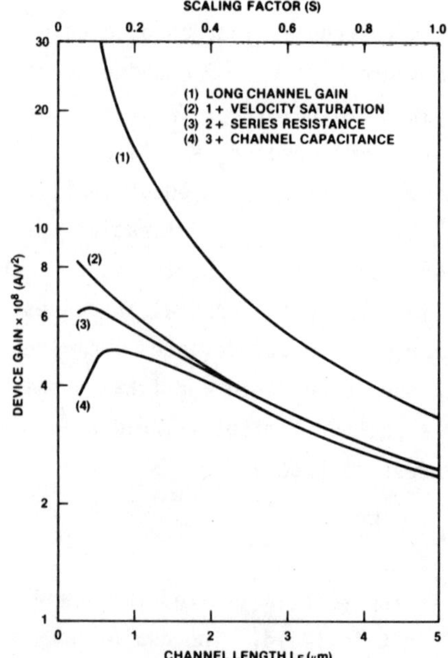

Fig. 4. Effect of Various Parameters on Device Gain Factor

TABLE I. THE CONTRIBUTION OF THE DIFFERENT FACTORS TO CURRENT REDUCTION IN SCALED DEVICES

SCALING FACTOR S	PROCESS PARAMETERS			VELOCITY SATURATION & RESISTANCE PARS			CHANNEL CAPAC.	LONG CHANNEL GAIN	SHORT CHANNEL GAIN
	x_o (Å)	L_E (μm)	$R'_{\square}$ (Ω)	$\frac{\nu_{av}}{\nu_o}$	$\frac{2R_S}{R_{CH}}$	$F_{\nu R}$	F_{CH}	$\mu C_o x10^8$	$K \times 10^8$
1	1000	5	20	0.35	0.007	0.74	0.97	3.3	2.35
0.7	700	3.5	28.5	0.5	0.015	0.66	0.95	4.7	2.96
0.4	400	2	50	0.83	0.044	0.53	0.92	8.25	4.06
0.3	300	1.5	66.7	1.17	0.078	0.44	0.9	11	4.35
0.2	200	1	100	1.75	0.175	0.34	0.86	16.5	4.8
0.1	100	0.5	200	3.5	0.7	0.19	0.75	33	4.73
0.05	50	0.25	400	7	2.8	0.09	0.6	66	3.67

anisms discussed here were nonsignificant. Results on technologies with scaling factors in the range 0.3 to 0.05 are also shown. The ratio of the oxide thickness to channel length has been kept constant while the equivalent parasitic resistance has been increased by the inverse of the scaling factor. As contact windows become smaller, contact resistance contribution becomes significant[7] and this is (as opposed to making the junctions shallower) the major factor in increasing $R'_{\square}$. As devices are scaled down, the current gain peaks for a device with a scaling factor of 0.2 (1μm channel length and 200Å gate oxide). For that device, the finite inversion layer thickness and series resistance reduce the gain by about 14% and 7% respectively. Matters get worse for smaller scaling factors. Considering that the peak in current gain represents devices that will likely be in next generation products, scaling of MOS devices is reaching a dead end. This is even more so since the factors resulting in such limitations are related to material physical properties and high electric fields. By lowering the operating voltages, the turn around point will move to smaller channel lengths and some gain advantage can be obtained going to 0.5μm devices.

IV. CONCLUSIONS

Scaling basic device parameters (channel length, oxide thickness and series resistance) by the same factor, we have shown that device gain has a peak at a channel length of 1μm beyond which the gain starts dropping. The mechanisms responsible for that are velocity saturation, finite inversion layer thickness and parasitic series resistance combined with the nonscaling of voltage supplies. Reducing voltage supplies, could extend the scaling trend one more generation provided that loading effecting associated with interconnects are reduced by processing techniques.

V. ACKNOWLEDGEMENTS

The author wishes to express his thanks to R. Burghard, R. Chwang and Bill Siu for stimulating discussions and their critical comments of the manuscript.

REFERENCES

(1) R. H. Dennard et al, J. Solid State Circuits, vol. SC-9, p. 256, Oct. 1974

(2) F. Klaassen, Solid State Electronics, vol. 23, p. 237, 1980

(3) P. Chatterjee, Solid-State Technology Workshop, New York, 1980

(4) T. Ito et al, ISSCC-1980, p. 74

(5) C. G. Sodini et al, Device Research Conference, 1980

(6) Y. El-Mansy and A. R. Boothroyd, IEEE Trans. Electron Devices, March 1977

(7) H. Nozawa et al, IEDM 1979, p. 366

Section 2.2
Processing Technologies

Scaling the barriers to VLSI's fine lines

The limits of IC technology are being forced outward by new and improved lithography and etching, beam processing, and silicides

by Jerry Lyman

☐ The integrated circuit industry is in the first surge of a great wave of change that will carry it into a new era of very large-scale integrated circuits with low-micrometer to submicrometer features—denser, faster, and more complex devices. To produce these fine-line chips, new processes, equipment, and materials will gradually replace much of today's IC processing equipment.

Among the most important new IC processing techniques are:

- Major new lithography (optical and nonoptical) methods capable of low-micrometer and submicrometer exposures.
- Replacement of wet etching by three dry methods—plasma etching, reactive ion etching (RIE), and ion-beam milling—to bypass the deficiencies of wet etching.
- The use of low-resistivity silicides and refractory metals as replacements for high-resistivity polysilicon interconnections.
- Multiple-resists to compensate for wafer surface variations that thwart accurate fine-line lithography.
- Laser and electron-beam processing to purify and reduce defects in IC materials.
- Nonoptical methods of inspecting line widths and layer-to-layer registration to replace optical methods incapable of measuring these parameters at low-micrometer levels.

The main driving force for VLSI has always been the two undeniable advantages of scaling device dimensions down—reduced cost and increased performance.

Scaling down boosts circuit density by the square of

Reprinted with permission from *Electronics*, vol. 53, pp. 115–126, June 19, 1980.
Copyright © 1980 by McGraw-Hill, Inc. All rights reserved.

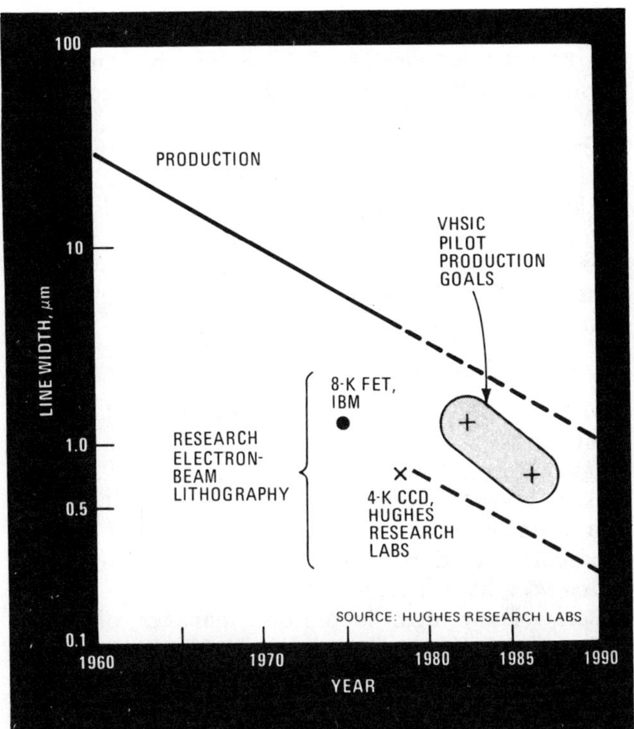

1. Shrinking lines. Current minimum production line widths for ICs are about 3 μm and are expected to drop to 1 μm by 1990. Pilot production-line goals set by the VHSIC program are 1.25 μm by 1982 and 0.7 μm by 1985, widths already achieved in the lab.

the scale factor. The scale factor is defined as the ratio of the original dimension to the reduced dimension. The result, of course, is more gates per chip area and more devices per wafer, the latter cutting the cost of manufacture—the bottom line in any business.

Scaling down also cuts a circuit's operating power, capacitance, and delay. An example of what happens to circuit factors when a typical MOS device is scaled from 4- to 1-micrometer line widths is shown in Table 1. Note that line resistance goes up and line response time is constant (the RC time constant is unchanged).

With these advantages it is no surprise that the IC industry has gradually been shrinking line widths. At present, the minimum production line width is 3 to 3.5 μm in high-performance MOS circuits. However, since 1978 an additional stimulus to VLSI has appeared: a $210 million U. S. Department of Defense triservice program to develop very high-speed integrated circuits (VHSIC) with up to 250,000 gates and with device dimensions as small as 0.5 μm.

The program is now in Phase 0 [*Electronics*, March 27, 1980, p. 41]. Nine teams have been awarded study contracts to define approaches to system and chip architecture, circuit processing technologies, and testing. Between four and six of the competitors of Phase 0 will be chosen to compete in Phase 1A in 1981, during which pilot lines producing circuits with 1.25-μm features are to be set up. Later phases (1982–1983) are expected to push submicrometer ICs into pilot-line production.

The VHSIC program is providing an extra stimulus to the appearance of low-micrometer and submicrometer semiconductor devices. Since such IC firms as Texas

TABLE 1: DEVICE AND CIRCUIT SCALING

Parameter	Change with linear scaling, factor of 4*
Circuit density	16
Operating voltage	1/4
Device current	1/4
Power per circuit	1/16
Circuit capacitance	1/4
Delay per circuit	1/4
Line resistance	4
Line response time	1

*Line width scaled from 4 μm to 1 μm; oxide thickness scaled from 100 nm to 25 nm

Instruments, Motorola, Signetics, National Semiconductor, Fairchild Semiconductor, and TRW are all members of teams working on VHSIC Phase 0, these companies will gain valuable know-how in VLSI processing that will surely be applied to in-house programs for commercial devices. It should be kept in mind that VHSIC is a research and development program and that the next production chips using newer forms of lithography will probably have about 2-μm details.

A new ballgame

As lithography limits were pushed back in the middle 1970s—typically 7 μm for production devices and close to 1 μm for research devices—IC processing engineers quickly discovered that the methods of the 1970s were not going to work. Wafer properties, resists, etching, alignment of mask levels, inspection, and cleanliness problems all became magnified. This led to the development of the methods listed above.

From about 1 μm down, the mechanical, physical, chemical, and electrical properties of the wafer become critical. For instance, poor wafer surface flatness (the potato-chip effect), which is relatively unimportant in the neighborhood of 10-μm features, can virtually prevent workable lithography at low-micrometer levels.

Resistivity of the silicon wafer, again not critical in the 10-μm process, now affects circuit speed in the new chips, since as line width goes down, interconnection resistance and RC delays go up.

In order to put down fine details, the thicknesses of both resist and oxide must be cut down. These thin coatings are easy to damage and often fill the hills and valleys of an etched surface unevenly.

Photoresist layers create still another problem at the 1-μm level and below. Consider the case of a 1-μm image exposed in a 0.5-μm resist layer spun onto a silicon wafer. If standard wet etching were used, the resist image would be undercut by the isotropic (equal in all directions) action of the wet etch. Thus this type of etching does not faithfully reproduce the dimensions of a photomask and cannot be used for low-micrometer work. Some other type of etching is required to reproduce completely vertical side walls.

Still another problem that becomes critical near or below 1 μm is level-to-level registration. Aligning 4-μm details on alternate mask levels is no problem with optical 1:1 and direct-step-on-wafer optical projection systems. But holding a 1-μm detail to 0.1 μm is currently impossible in production with optical lithography. That sort of accuracy can only be achieved with a scanning–electron-beam lithography system, which is low in throughput and extremely high in cost.

Assuming the low-micrometer devices can be fabricated, a further problem exists in inspecting them. Optical instruments fall off in accuracy in this range and scanning electron microscopes are simply too expensive to be production instruments. In addition, the cleanliness problem is compounded at this level. Particulates 1-μm in size (which could be ignored at 10 μm) now become a serious problem.

Making fine-line VLSI devices is quite complicated. The costs of implementing the 10 to 20 mask levels and 130 to 150 steps of the late 1980s will be staggering. But it will be done under industry and VHSIC pressure.

Improving images

IC lithography has always been the driving force behind each step forward in the IC industry. From 1976 to 1980, great strides were made in lithography [*Electronics*, April 12, 1979, p. 105] with the emergence of improved 1:1 optical projection, electron-beam, direct-step-on-wafer (DSW), and X-ray systems in commercial and in-house versions (Fig. 1).

At the present time, it appears that the transition to ICs with 0.5- to 0.8-μm details will take place in two stages at firms involved in the VHSIC competition. The rest of the IC world will be trying to push the geometries of production chips from 3 to about 2 μm and will proceed more cautiously.

The VHSIC participants will most likely use DSW, direct electron-beam writing, and a simple flood-beam X ray to expose 1.25-μm features. There is also a possibility that Perkin-Elmer Corp.'s 1:1 optical projection system, fitted with a deep-ultraviolet source and optics, may be used for this purpose, since it will have a resolution limit of about 1.2 μm.

In the second stage, which will be for chips with 0.5- to 0.8-μm line widths, direct electron-beam writing and X-ray lithography may dominate, though there is a good possibility that optical lithography (DSW in particular) will be extended down to 0.75 or 0.8 μm. An outside possibility for these submicrometer VLSI chips could be a DSW with either an X-ray or ion-beam source.

On the production side of the industry, the major producers will use DSW for only the most critical masking levels and 1:1 projection for the other levels of their next-generation 2-μm VLSI. This lithography mix will achieve a reasonably high throughput, since most operations will be on fast (60 levels per hour) projection aligners instead of the slower wafer steppers.

The Federal effort

VHSIC competitors are a mix of research and development firms plus independent IC production houses. Hughes Research Laboratories, Malibu, Calif., will do its initial VHSIC work on in-house direct-writing electron-beam systems. A long range possibility for Hughes' later chips could be an ion-beam lithography system [*Electronics*, March 27, 1980, p. 142].

Barry Dunbridge, laboratory manager of TRW's Defense and Space System group, Redondo Beach, Calif., and leader of a VHSIC team, notes that his group has been developing 1-μm chips since 1976 using a Canon FPA DSW machine equipped with a 4:1 reduction lens. That same system is targeted for the early VHSIC 1.25-μm chips. Dunbridge's group has been fabricating bipolar VLSI using a triple-diffused method which is presently being employed at the TRW LSI Products division to produce a commercial 8-bit high-speed analog-to-digital converter with 2-μm details.

Rockwell International's Electronics Research Center, Anaheim, Calif., is another prime contractor on VHSIC. Its lithography effort is based on two Cambridge Scientific Instruments scanning electron-beam systems used exclusively for direct writing of IC patterns onto resist-covered wafers. The most advanced machine is a Rockwell modification of Cambridge's latest unit, the EBMF-2. The modification allows design iterations to be done interactively on a terminal adjacent to the lithography system. In the fall of 1977, Rockwell fabricated an

2. Plasma-etched polysilicon. Polysilicon, heavily doped with phosphorus, was etched by an LFE planar plasma-etching machine to produce the 1μm-wide lines shown in this scanning electron micrograph. The pattern was exposed in AZ1370 photoresist using a step-and-repeat system.

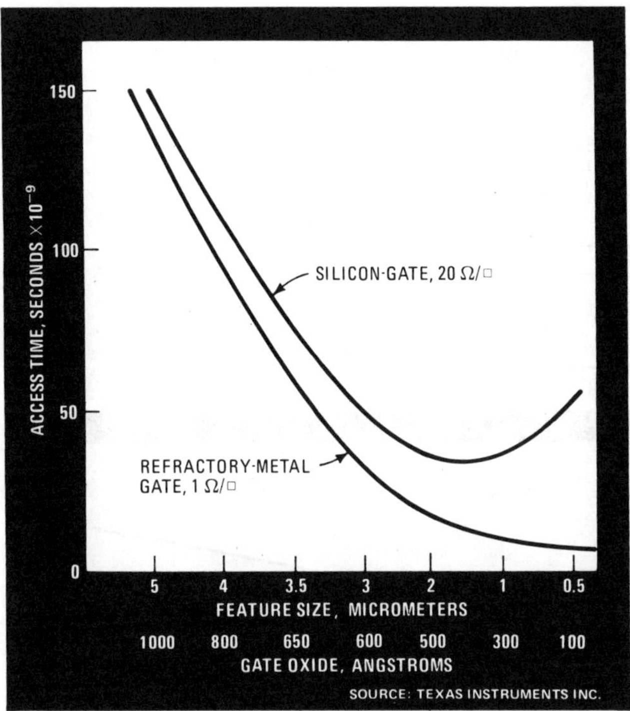

3. Faster metal. Given sheet resistivities of 20 and 1 ohm per square, silicon and refractory-metal gate materials in a 4-K static RAM have the plotted effect on access time with decreasing feature size. Silicon gates cause access times to rise below 1 μm.

n-channel-MOS ring oscillator boasting 0.25-μm channel lengths with direct electron-beam writing and dry processing. Rockwell also has an X-ray lithography program, but this is in the research stage. For producing small-geometry units, Rockwell has received or ordered DSW machines from both the Burlington, Mass., division of GCA Corp. and Electromask Inc.

Jim Dey, manager of image technology at National Semiconductor, is in charge of his company's lithography effort for VHSIC. According to Dey, "the early generation of VHSIC chips will be done on wafer steppers." National will try both the GCA and the Optimetrix 8010 in its VHSIC effort. For the submicrometer phase of the VHSIC program, National plans direct writing on wafers with an electron-beam system.

Two of the electronic giants in the VHSIC competiton—Texas Instruments Inc., Dallas, and International Business Machines Corp.—will base their efforts on scanning electron-beam systems developed in house for direct wafer writing. Both firms are leaders in the development of electron-beam technology.

What is surprising is that another electronics giant, Bell Laboratories—whose EBES electron-beam machine [*Electronics*, May 12, 1977, p. 95] led to commercial electron-beam mask-making machines from the Extrion division of Varian Inc., Gloucester, Mass., and Etec Corp., Hayward, Calif.—is putting X-ray lithography onto a production line. Martin Lepselter, director of Bell's advanced LSI development lab, Murray Hill, N. J., says that by 1981, the company will set up X-ray lithography systems at Western Electric for production of 1-μm n-MOS integrated circuits. The machines will be improved versions of Bell's X-ray II systems [*Electronics*, April 12, 1979, p. 115] using an improved X-ray source. With new faster X-ray resists, Lepselter feels a goal of 1,000 wafers per hour could be achieved with a relatively low $1.5 million investment in these new machines.

Intel, the third largest independent IC manufacturer in the U. S., is not a VHSIC competitor and is currently at the 3-μm level with its standard high-performance HMOS chips, which are imaged with Perkin-Elmer 1:1 projection systems. Intel is already purchasing and considering lithography equipment for its next chips, but will not reveal what line widths it is shooting for. Contenders for Intel's next chips are Perkin-Elmer's deep-ultraviolet 1:1 system and wafer steppers from GCA, Optimetrix or Censor. Gerry Parker, director of technology development for Intel, emphasizes that there is now a two-year wait for GCA and Perkin-Elmer equipment.

Across the water

In Europe and Japan, investigations are already under way to select lithography for resolving 1 μm and below. Both NV Philips Gloeilampenfabrieken of the Netherlands and Intermetall GmbH, the headquarters company of the ITT Semiconductor Group, favor direct electron-beam writing for submicrometer VLSI.

Joseph Borel, vice president for research and development at EFCIS, the Grenoble-based company that is

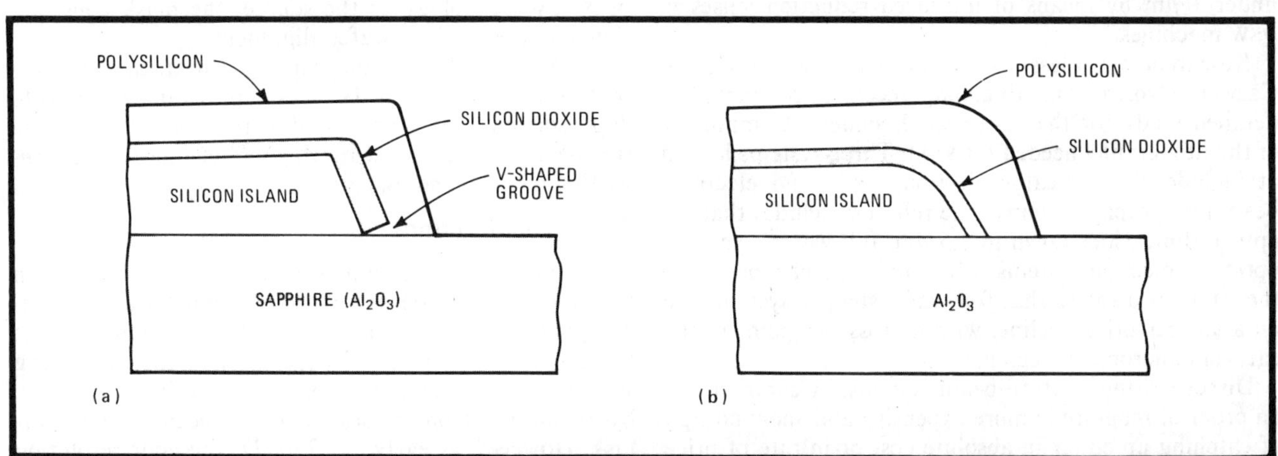

4. Laser smoothed. An unwanted V-shaped groove in the oxide covering a silicon island (a) is common in C-MOS-on-sapphire work. Energy from a laser rounds off the edge and eliminates the groove (b), preventing electrical breakdown and increasing channel mobility.

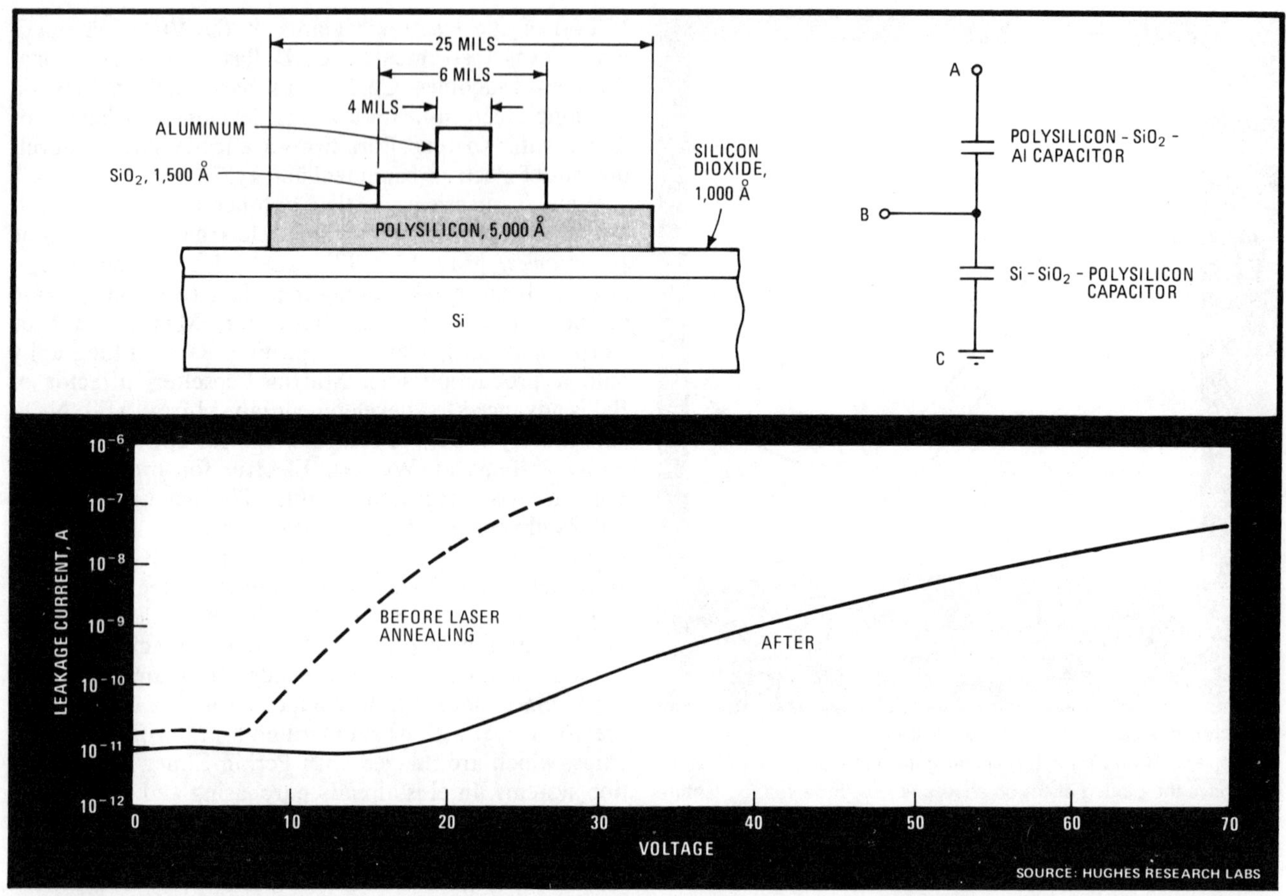

5. Annealed stack. Stacked capacitors with a polysilicon layer that has been exposed to pulses from a ruby laser show a dramatic improvement in electrical properties over unannealed devices. Breakdown voltage goes up and leakage current is cut by a factor of 1,000.

jointly run by Thomson-CSF and the French Atomic Energy agency, says, "Capital costs will become an overriding factor in determining which technologies will prevail for submicron circuits." He points out that the shift from direct exposure of wafers with 1:1 masks to reduction exposure using reticles and step-and-repeat machines has tripled fabrication machine costs. He figures the increase will be even higher when equipment like direct-writing electron-beam machines and X-ray equipment arrives at the mass production stage. Borel, like many others, thinks it will be possible to get a little under 1 μm by means of improved reduction lenses in DSW machines.

Researchers at Plessey's Allen Clark Research Centre Caswell, Northants., England, recently completed a detailed study for the European Economic Community of the lithography needed for VLSI. Three systems looked at include 1:1 optical projection, DSW, and electron-beam lithography systems. The report concludes that for optical dimensions down to 1.5 μm, full-wafer–exposure optical projection systems will remain the cheapest. But the study also shows that full-wafer stepper systems are on a steeper price decline, with a crossover point in the early submicrometer region.

Direct-writing electron-beam systems, by contrast, are an order of magnitude more expensive and show no sign of catching up either in absolute cost or in rate of price decline. So the report concludes that these systems will be used for mask making and for specialized applications like discretionary wiring, but will have no major production role until optical techniques finally run out of steam, as they will below 0.75 μm, or until there is a technological breakthrough in high-speed resists.

In Japan, as in the rest of the VLSI world, direct electron-beam writing is seen as the first route to submicrometer dimensions. Shojiro Asai, senior researcher at Hitachi's central research lab, says that "E-beam will remain the only means to get 1-μm or lower circuits for several years, until X-ray lithography's problems are solved." Asai lists the major problems to be worked out in X-ray technology as the source, the mask construction, and the mask-to-wafer alignment.

To Asai, ion-beam lithography is an attractive possibility for the long haul. He sees it providing a means to dope isolated regions addressed by the beam. In addition, the beam is free of scattering effects in its pattern-writing mode, he notes.

Etch considerations

Etching is second in importance only to lithography in the processing of fine-line chips. Micrometer and submicrometer lines on resists are worthless unless their images can be transferred accurately to the underlying substrate. Traditionally, wet etches using sulphuric, hydrochloric, or phosphoric acid have been assigned this task. However, as early as 1976–77, the poor resolution and undercutting of wet etching on the 5-to-7-μm chips being produced at the time allowed a form of dry plasma

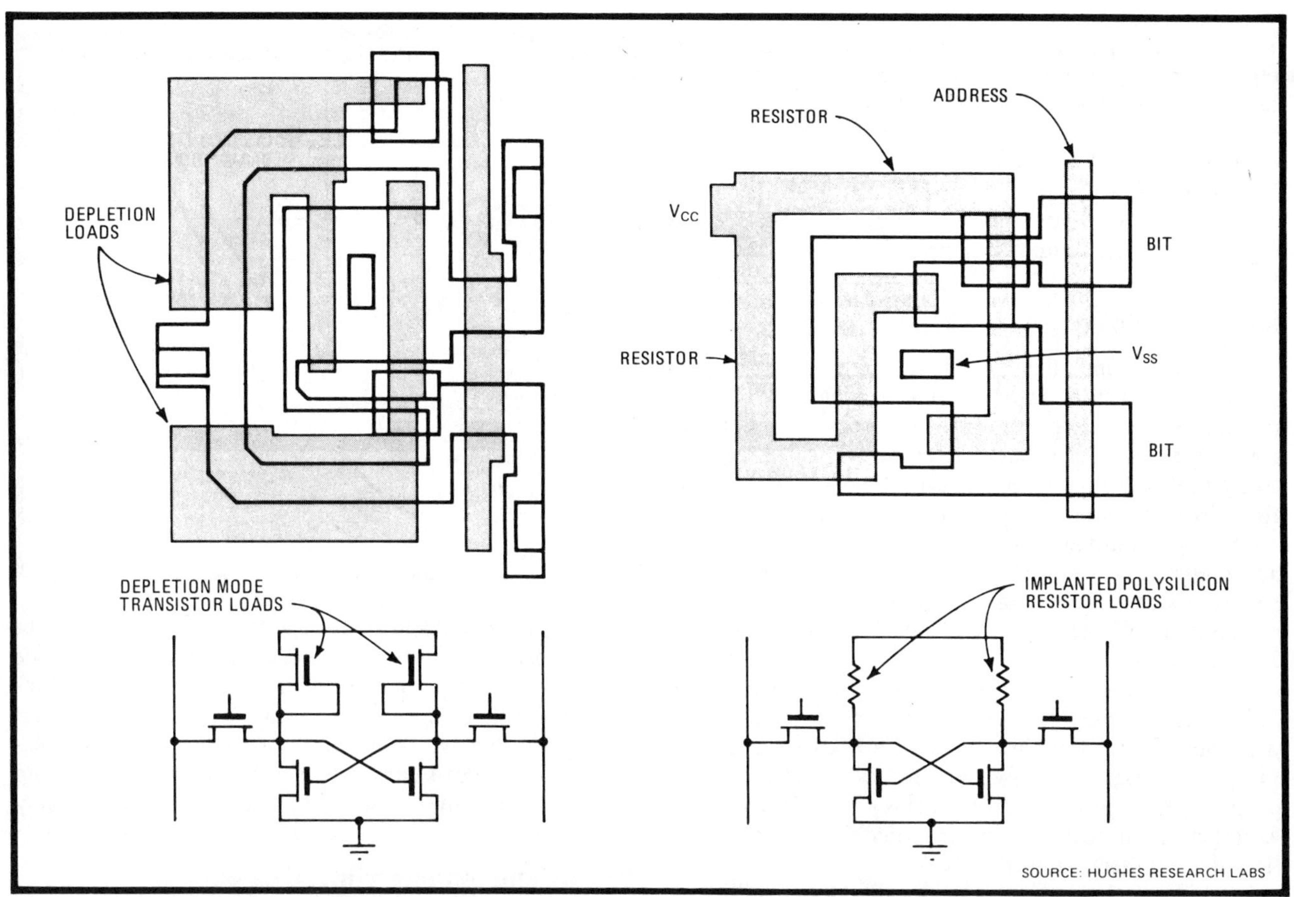

6. Polysilicon resistors. The relatively high resistivity of polysilicon is very useful in the design of static random-access memories. When the depletion-mode transistor loads in the cell at left are replaced by implanted polysilicon resistor loads, the cell size can be cut by 40% (right).

etching to get its foot in the door.

Since that time, plasma etching has been considerably refined and is in place on most IC fabrication lines, particularly the new H-MOS types (2.5 to 3.0 μm). So it is natural that both the future commercial producers of fine-line chips and the VHSIC teams will initially use plasma etching in the 1-to-2-μm range. But it appears that two other dry etching techniques—reactive ion etching (RIE) and reactive ion milling—will be applied to VLSI in the submicrometer range. Both techniques etch a wide range of materials anisotropically—a vital factor for submicrometer VLSI fabrication.

A plasma is a volume of ionized gas atoms capable of supporting a current. The plasma contains a substantial group of free radicals—electrically neutral atoms that can form chemical bonds. The free radicals react with photoresists and substrate coatings to etch them.

Early commercial plasma reactors, called barrel reactors, were built around a chamber with external electrodes. Wafers were stored vertically in a suitable carrier inside the chamber. Although such units had high throughput, they could not be used for anisotropic etching, for etching aluminum, or for selective etching of silicon dioxide over silicon at practical rates. Still, many hundreds of these systems are in use for dry etching in the 3-to-5-μm range. Below 3 μm, the planar plasma reactor takes over.

The planar plasma or parallel-plate reactor has two internal flat electrodes. Normally the top electrode is driven by a radio-frequency voltage while the lower one holds the wafer. The parallel-plate reactor can perform high-resolution (1-to-2-μm) anisotropic etching in silicon, polysilicon, silicon nitride, silicon dioxide, and aluminum. An example of plasma-etched 1-μm lines in doped polysilicon on a planar plasma reactor from LFE Corp. is shown in Fig. 2.

A new type of dry etching was reported at IBM in 1976. It was called reactive ion etching and it combined chemical (plasma) etching and plasma sputtering with chemically reactive ions bombarding the surface of the substrate. Reactive ion etching takes place in a plasma-filled planar reactor run at a higher voltage and a lower pressure than a comparable plasma reactor. For RIE, the electrode bearing the wafer is driven by rf and the other electrode is grounded (the opposite of a planar plasma reactor). The new method results in improved image-size control, anisotropic etching capability, higher etching rates, and better selectivity than straight plasma etching [*Electronics*, Aug. 31, 1978, p. 117], making it ideal for the narrow lines of VLSI and the submicrometer circuitry of the VHSIC program.

IBM has been using RIE and its IC processing on a production basis since 1976. In fact, IBM developed its own dry-etching system that does RIE, plasma, or a combination of both processes. Bell Labs and Hitachi both have considerable experience in RIE and have applied it both in production and prototype IC devices.

Manufacturers of plasma etchers have been quick to

recognize the potential new market for RIE by coming out with new machines that can operate either as plasma or RIE systems. Examples are LFE's model 501P, Plasma-Therm Inc.'s model PK-2440PE/RIE and the model 4440 from the Ultek division of Perkin-Elmer Corp., Mountain View, Calif. The latter is Perkin-Elmer's first entry into this field and it undoubtedly heralds the entrance of large equipment firms into the plasma and RIE business.

Ion-beam milling

The third contender for the etching process of the 1980s is ion-beam milling. In this technique a collimated beam of argon ions is focused onto a resist-covered wafer in a vacuum chamber. The beam selectively mills out unmasked material by displacing ions of the substrate under bombardment.

Ion-beam milling has many advantages. It can etch any material (plasma and RIE cannot claim this); it can generate anisotropic or tapered walls up to 45° and has no undercut. Its ability to mill fine lines is only limited by lithography.

However, straight ion-beam milling has several major disadvantages. For one, the ion beam is not selective and will continue to mill through the desired material into the underlying layer. Plasma and RIE systems have chemical etch stops that prevent this effect. Other disadvantages of ion-beam milling are trenching and redeposition of the milled material.

In spite of these disadvantages, ion-beam milling is being used extensively in magnetic-bubble work, in milling gallium arsenide (GaAs) ICs, and for making ultra-thin masks for X-ray lithography.

A modified form of ion-beam milling has been developed, however, that eliminates its lack of selectivity. This method, called reactive ion-beam milling, substitutes a reactive gas mixture (typically argon mixed with hexafluoroethane, C_2F_6) for the normal pure argon. This makes possible etching of silicon dioxide over silicon or aluminum with a selectivity of up to 8:1. In addition, typical etching rates are increased as much as two to three times—1,000 angstroms per minute for silicon dioxide. Reactive ion-beam milling is already available in machines from Extrion, Veeco Instruments Inc., Plainview, N. Y., and Technics Inc., Springfield, Va.

Of the three dry-etching techniques, plasma etching represents the greatest body of experience; it is still being refined. However, for the submicrometer chips of the future, most industry experts agree that either RIE or reactive ion-beam milling is necessary. It is worth noting that any dry-etching method for the 1981–85 period will have to etch a wide range of new materials—silicides, refractory metals, and polyimides.

Actually the three methods may coexist. At Rockwell International's Electronics Research Center, Thousand Oaks, Calif., planar GaAs LSI integrated circuits are fabricated in a process flow using all three dry-etching techniques. In an early step, a silicon nitride "cap" is etched shallowly with plasma. Later, RIE is used to etch via windows in a layer of silicon nitride separating two levels of interconnections. Finally, second-level titanium-gold metalization is ion-milled to desired widths.

TABLE 2: RESISTIVITY OF REFRACTORY-METAL FILMS

Metal, deposition method	Bulk resistivity at 20°C, μΩ-cm	Film thickness	Ohms/square	
			As deposited	After annealing
Molybdenum,	4.8			
• Electron-beam evaporation		3,048	0.95	0.27
• Radio-frequency sputtering		3,302	1.7	0.43
• Magnetron (S-gun) sputtering		3,000	0.72	0.35
Tungsten,	5.5			
• Electron-beam evaporation		3,302	2.6	0.4
• Rf sputtering		3,810	5.0	0.87
• S-gun sputtering		3,000	0.98	0.69
Tantalum	50	5,524	24.0	14.0
Titianium-tungsten	–	3,125	6.32	3.87
Polysilicon, diffusion or implantation	–	4,500	–	20-30
Aluminum, electron-beam evaporation	2.26	5,334	0.054	–

Conventional MOS silicon-gate devices cannot be scaled down indefinitely. One reason is the performance limitation presented by the rising resistance of the thinning polysilicon interconnections, which stretch out propagation delays. Two solutions to lower interconnection resistance are currently being evaluated: replacing the polysilicon interconnections with a silicide (an alloy of metal and silicon) or depositing metal over them.

Silicide and refractory-metal gates

The resulting sheet resistivity of either approach is orders of magnitude lower than that of polysilicon, which measures about 20 to 30 ohms per square. Often referred to as refractory—high-temperature—metals, those most often used in either application are molybdenum, tungsten, tantalum, titanium, and mixtures thereof.

Most companies favor the silicide approach, since it is more easily inserted into an existing process line. The pure refractory metal, however, has the lower sheet resistivity of the two. Silicides can be formed on polysilicon by several methods: sputtering or evaporation of a metal, co-sputtering metal and silicon, or co-evaporating metal and silicon.

Shyam Murarka, a member of the technical staff at Bell Lab's Murray Hill, N. J., facility has done extensive research on finding optimum materials and methods for the fabrication of silicides. His results show that sheet resistivities of 1 and 2 Ω/sq can be obtained by using 1,000-Å titanium and tantalum films, respectively, on polysilicon.

Murarka notes that tantalum silicide (TaSi) is mechanically strong and can resist the conditions and temperatures of MOS processing. Thus a retrofit in existing processing is possible. The potentially more valuable titanium silicide films, although mechanically strong, react violently with acids used in wet etching.

Dry etching of tantalum or titanium silicides has proven successful. Bell has used plasma etching to etch both the silicide and its underlying polysilicon and to stop at the gate oxide. Etching was carried out in a radial-flow (planar) or standard barrel reactor. Bell Labs has successfully made and tested MOS ICs with

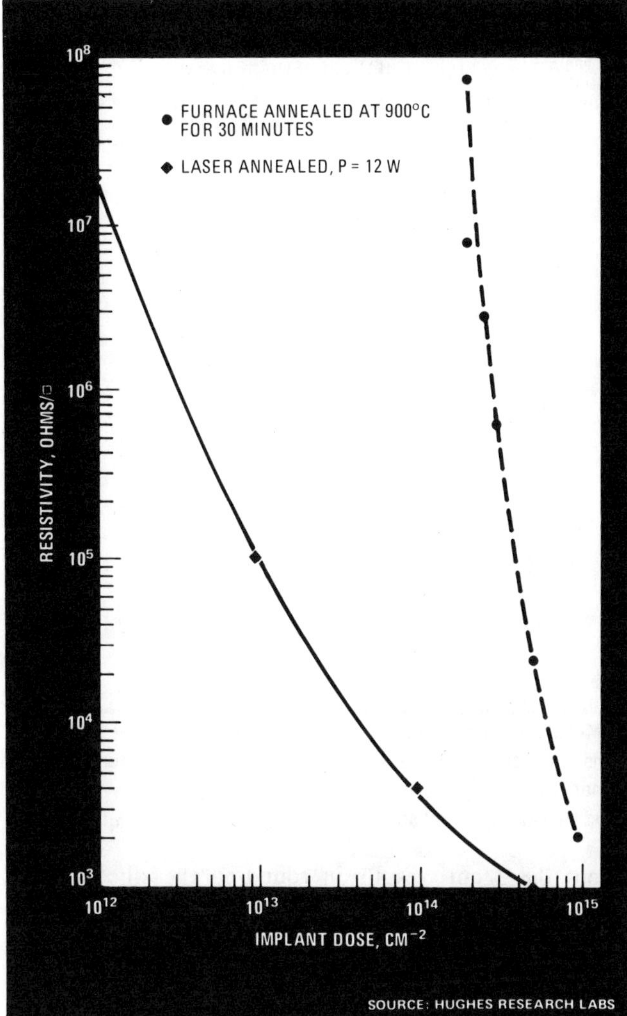

7. Implantation sensitivity. A 10% variation in implantation dose changes the resistivity of furnace-annealed polysilicon by a factor of 10. The resistivity of laser-annealed polysilicon resistors, given the same 10% variation in dose, changes by only a factor of 2.

tantalum silicides. The lower-resistance titanium silicide is still in an evaluation stage.

Other silicide experiments are going on at Texas Instruments, IBM, and in Japan. Texas Instruments has built test devices using molybdenum silicide with a sheet resistance of 5 Ω/sq. IBM is fabricating VLSI MOS devices with tungsten silicide gates. A dual–electron-beam evaporator co-evaporates tungsten and silicon onto polysilicon. Arnold Reisman, manager of exploratory semiconductor technology at IBM's Thomas J. Watson Research Center, Yorktown Heights, N. Y., notes, "Silicides are not a panacea; they will help you in places where polysilicon is used, but will not solve the problem of scaling aluminum, for instance."

In Japan, Nippon Electric Co. (NEC) and Hitachi Ltd. are both involved in silicide research. NEC is already using silicides, specifically platinum silicide, in bipolar products. For MOS, it is studying molybdenum gates, which can be used at 1-to-1.5-μm levels. The molybdenum silicide's resistivity of 0.3 Ω/sq substantially betters platinum silicide's 3 Ω/sq.

At Hitachi, Shojiro Asai says, "We won't be able to get rid of silicide in VLSI." Hitachi is devoting considerable efforts to such silicide problems as deposition, interfacing with oxides, and oxidation of surfaces. Molybdenum and tungsten are attracting the most attention at Hitachi, but platinum is also of some interest for interconnecting metals and heavily doped regions.

Refractory metals used for gates and interconnections were first investigated in the early years of MOS circuitry. However, the advantage of their low resistivity was more than offset by the process simplicity and passivation capability of silicon-gate technology. In 1977, the fundamental limitation of polysilicon interconnections in VLSI became apparent and metal gates reemerged.

Pradeep Shah, manager of MOS device technology at Texas Instruments, comments, "Interconnection technology is one of the neglected aspects of IC technology. This led us to look into both refractory metal gates and silicides."

Texas Instruments has run an extensive investigation of refractory-metal gate processes for VLSI end use. Molybdenum, tungsten, titanium-tungsten, and tantalum were chosen as likely refractory-gate candidates. Table 2 lists TI's figures for the resistivity of the sampled refractory metals deposited by different methods, before and after annealing at 1,000° and 450°C. Electron-beam–evaporated tungsten and molybdenum had the lowest sheet-resistance. Tantalum and titanium-tungsten films had comparatively higher sheet resistivities and so were eliminated as contenders.

In TI's refractory-metal work, molybdenum and tungsten films 3,500 Å thick were patterned at 1-to-2-μm geometries using electron-beam techniques and photoresists coupled with conventional plasma etching, ion milling, and wet etching. The sheet resistances of 0.25 and 0.4 Ω/sq for molybdenum and tungsten are 50 to 100 times lower than conventional polysilicon.

MOS test devices were fabricated with 1-to-2-μm gates and molybdenum-aluminum-silicon double-level metal structures. These units demonstrated significantly better performance than silicon-gate chips with the same geometries.

Figure 3 is a simulation of a 4-K static random-access memory's performance with both silicon and refractory-gate structures. Notice that the silicon-gate RAM's address time reverses its downward trend at about the 1.5-μm level, whereas the refractory-gate device's address time decreases with geometry.

Refractory-metal gates and silicide gates will both improve VLSI circuit performance. Refractory-metal gates offer a hundredfold reduction in sheet resistance over polysilicon, but silicides are only an order of magnitude better. However, pure refractory metals cannot be easily passivated by oxidation as polysilicon can be; this leads to additional processing steps. Silicides, on the other hand, are self-passivating, which results in higher device stability and makes self-aligned and two-level structures possible.

With the advent of VLSI, the classic material problems of IC processing such as ion-implantation damage, interconnection resistance, impurities in the substrate, and leakage current and dielectric breakdown at interfaces become magnified. Laser and charged-particle beams can potentially provide the localized processing technology to solve these problems.

At the present time, laser processing is more advanced than electron-beam processing, due to the ready availability of all types of laser hardware. Laser processing has the following advantages:

- Localized heating.
- High temperature for short time periods.
- Improved device performance (compared with conventional processing).
- Increased packing density, yield, and reliability.
- The ability to produce new material properties.

The possible applications of laser processing include ion-implantation annealing without dopant redistribution, large-grain polysilicon crystal regrowth on dielectric material, reflow of island structures, ohmic contact formation, gettering, and replanarization.

Annealing refers to the repair of lattice damage and dopant activation following ion implantation. A pulsed laser anneals by melting the surface of the wafer to a depth significantly beyond ion-implantation damage. As the melted area refreezes, the single-crystal structure is reestablished by liquid-phase epitaxy. The implanted dopant is distributed very evenly throughout the melted area.

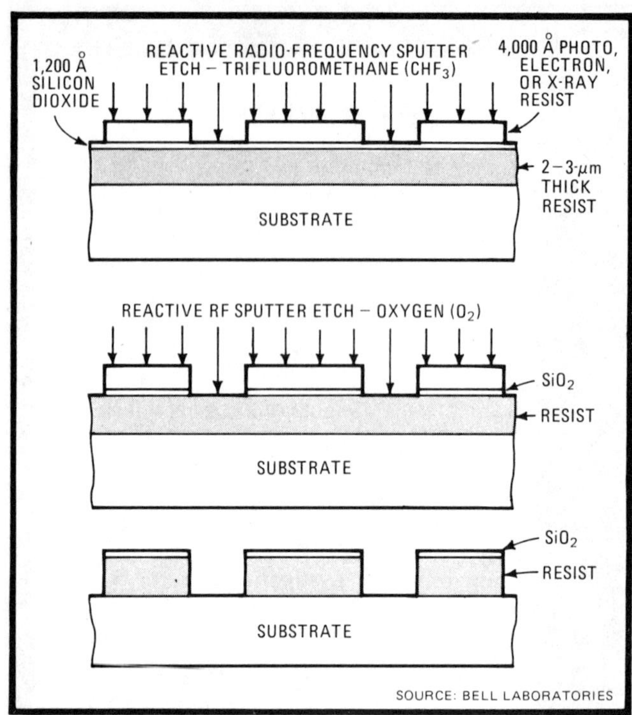

8. Multilayer. To prepare a wafer for X-ray imaging, Bell Labs first spins on a thick layer of organic resist, making the surface more planar. Layers of SiO_2 and X-ray resist are added. The results are good line-width control and step coverage and high resolution.

Removing damage

Annealing ion-implantation damage by continuous-wave laser heating involves a process known as solid-state epitaxy. This technique has the advantage that it does not redistribute the implanted dopant atoms.

Laser annealing, since it only heats the top of the wafer, eliminates the potato-chip effect of furnace annealing. This factor (wafer flatness) is vital to accurate lithography at levels near and below 1 μm. In addition laser annealing achieves a greater degree of dopant activation than furnace annealing.

Although the annealing of ion-implantation damage is basic to IC processing, uses of the laser in semiconductor processing that go beyond annealing are already on the horizon. In a paper given at the conference on laser and electro-optical systems and inertial confinement fusion (CLEOS/ICF) held during February 1980 in San Diego, Calif., Laverne Hess, head of the laser chemistry section of Hughes Research Laboratories, Malibu, Calif., discussed the results of work conducted by scientists at three Hughes facilities. Their research shows how lasers can improve step coverage in silicon-on-sapphire circuitry by eliminating the V-shaped groove common in such technology; how lasers can improve polysilicon stacked-structure oxide by annealing prior to oxidation; and how lasers can make polysilicon resistors less sensitive to implantation dose.

In Hughes' complementary-MOS-on-sapphire process, silicon islands are first defined photolithographically on the sapphire wafers and then etched. The islands are exposed to radiation from an excimer laser operating at a 2,490-Å wavelength with an energy density in the range of 0.5 to 1 joule per square centimeter. The islands are ion-implanted with gate oxidation; polysilicon deposition, contact, and metalization steps then follow.

It was found that exposure at an energy density of about 0.8 J/cm^2 results in rounding the silicon island edges, thus eliminating a grooved profile of the gate oxide and improving aluminum step coverage. The electrical characteristics of MOS transistors fabricated over laser-annealed islands showed a 30% increase in channel mobility. The gate oxide contour for an unannealed island is illustrated in Fig. 4a. In Fig. 4b, laser annealing has smoothed and rounded the island's edges, eliminating the oxide groove.

Stacking oxides

Polycrystalline silicon is a material of great importance in solid-state electronics. Devices like floating-gate memory systems, charge-coupled devices, and static and dynamic RAMs depend on the electrical characteristics of polysilicon and on oxides grown over polysilicon.

A major problem with these ICs, which rely on alternating layers of silicon and oxide, is that asperities on the surface of polysilicon lead to electric-field enhancement and consequent breakdown problems. One solution to the problem is to expose the polysilicon film to an intense laser beam prior to oxidation so as to melt down and smooth the surface asperities without creating unwanted heating in underlying material.

In order to test this theory, Hughes workers built up the stacked structure shown in Fig. 5. Radiation from a ruby laser was used to smooth the surface of a 5,000-Å polysilicon film. The resulting structure, consisting of two capacitors, was dramatically improved by exposure to the laser process (Fig. 5). Leakage current was reduced by 10^3 and breakdown voltage increased.

Another application of polysilicon is in load resistors replacing active load elements. This can save 40% in the

Fine lines demand defect-free wafers

Ultrapure, defect-free silicon will be vital to high-yield fabrication of submicrometer very large-scale integrated circuits. That is why all large U. S. silicon suppliers, such as Siltec Corp., Menlo Park, Calif., Monsanto Electronics division, Palo Alto, Calif., and Wacker Siltronic Corp., Portland, Ore., are currently engaged in research to stay ahead of the IC industry's tightening silicon specifications.

And that is why the subject of defects in silicon and gallium arsenide rates an entire session at the June 24–25, 1980, Electronics Materials Conference (EMC) at Cornell University, Ithaca, N. Y. Two of the papers point out the effects on silicon wafer defects of trace impurities such as carbon and thermal and oxidation process steps.

Robert Lorenzini, president of Siltec, states, "One of the things becoming increasingly evident is that the quality of the raw silicon wafers starting into a fabriction line becomes critical as we head into the VLSI era. All small wafer defects become a problem at narrow line widths."

Siltec engineers are finding that the yields of certain high-speed devices are enhanced by combining a higher oxygen content in wafers with a proprietary form of gettering. In addition, Siltec is engaged in research involving the ultrasonic measurement of microcracks (mechanical defects) in silicon ingots.

basic cell size of memories (Fig. 6), for example—an important consideration in VLSI design. Normally, implanted polysilicon resistors are furnace-annealed; but laser annealing produces a superior resistor, as Fig. 7 illustrates. The reason is that a 10% variation in ion-implant dose results in a change in resistance of furnace-annealed resistor of a factor of 10. Laser-annealed resistors, on the other hand, change by only a factor of 2 over the same dosage variation.

Bob Kaplan, manager of engineering for Quantronix Corp., Smithtown, N. Y., which makes the only commercial laser cold-processing (LCP) system—the Epitherm Model 610 [*Electronics*, February 28, 1980, p. 137]—sees gettering as the first significant application of LCP, followed by diffusion and annealing. Quantronix has sold machines to both Motorola and Western Electric.

Better gettering

Gettering is an important part of most semiconductor processes. The term refers to the reduction of mobile defects and certain impurities in the crystalline structure of wafers at their active or critical portions of the circuits built on them by physically damaging or chemically treating the back side of the wafer.

Gettering is more important in leakage-sensitive devices such as dynamic RAMs and C-MOS circuits. As junctions get shallower (as in VLSI) and narrower, defects are more of a problem and gettering becomes a necessity.

Two of the most heavily used chemical gettering methods involve diffusion of phosphorus at a high doping level into the back side of the wafer and ion-implanting the back side of the wafer with argon. Both have drawbacks. The first method often results in contamination of the front side of the wafer; in the second, the argon ions may often be annealed out in a later process step.

A more satisfactory method is to use a pulsed laser to getter the back side of the wafer. There is no problem of contamination or doping of the front side with laser gettering. The individual pockets of damage created seem to resist annealing longer than the damage created by the other two methods. In addition, lasers cost less than ion implanters.

In the laser diffusion method, a doped silicate is spun on the wafer and then radiated with a laser. The silicate becomes transparent and the laser energy goes into the silicon, melting the dopant. Laser diffusion puts a larger concentration of dopant into the material, resulting in lower resistivity.

Another form of beam processing being considered for VLSI wafers in the not-so-distant future is done with pulsed electron beams. Instead of heating a spot, as in laser processing, this system heats the entire surface of a wafer to a high temperature with a single submicrosecond pulse of a 7- to 10-cm beam. This method was developed by Spire Corp., Bedford, Mass., in 1974. Like laser processing, pulsed electron beams have applications in annealing ion-implantation damage in silicon and gallium arsenide, in epitaxial regrowth and in the formation of silicides.

In Japan and Europe, laser and electron-beam processing is being investigated extensively. At Plessey Co. in Ilford, Essex, England, laser annealing is still at the research stage and, according to a Plessey spokesman, "probably a good three years away from being a production process." Plessey is looking at both the continuous and pulsed laser techniques of annealing. Plessey engineers make the significant point that there is now evidence that the perfection of the crystal lattice of laser-annealed silicon is higher than that of thermally annealed silicon.

Hitachi last year published a paper on its research in laser-beam annealing with arsenic-ion implantation to make source and drain regions for MOS devices. Hitachi favors electron-beam annealing for building three-dimensional (stacked) VLSI by constructing single-crystal regions on insulating substrates. This, however, is a long way off. The Japanese firm is also looking into both laser epitaxy and electron-beam annealing each for different applications but of the two it is keenest on laser epitaxy.

Multiple resists

As the microelectronic evolution has proceeded from 10 to 3 to 1 μm and below, another complication occurs. Finer features require thinner resist coatings, which are fragile, causing a serious lithography problem. If a thin resist film is spun over a nonplanar surface, the resist will be distributed unevenly over the wafer. This results in a distorted exposure image.

Bell Labs and IBM have addressed this problem with

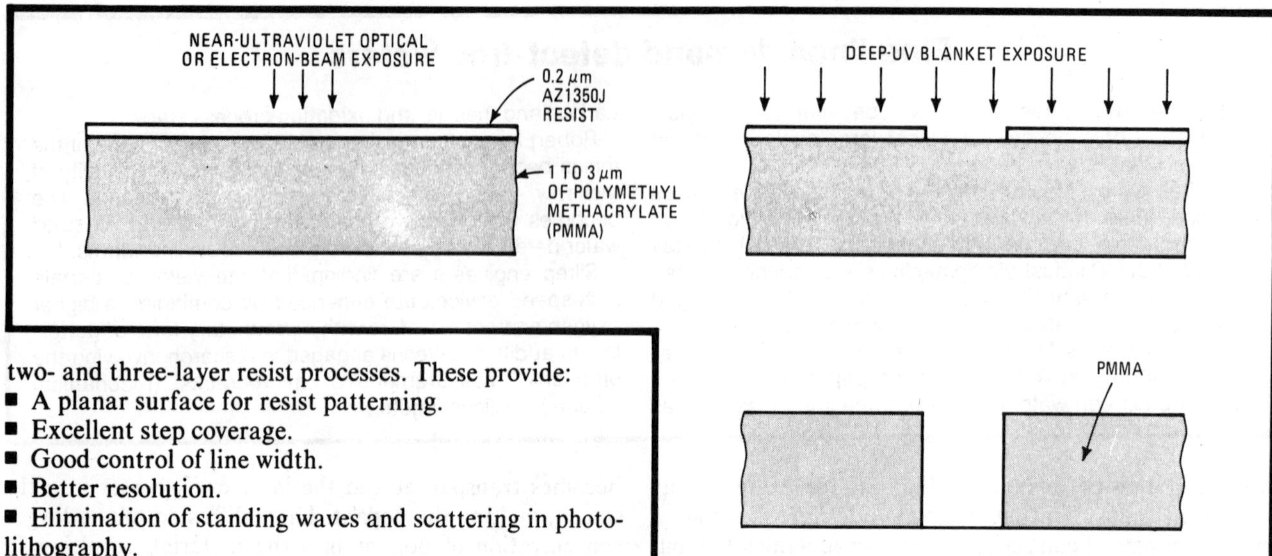

9. Portable comfortable mask. IBM puts a thin resist layer (sensitive to light or an electron beam) atop a layer of deep-ultraviolet resist. The top layer, once patterned, serves as a portable mask that can be carried with the wafer to a deep-UV blanket-exposure station.

two- and three-layer resist processes. These provide:

- A planar surface for resist patterning.
- Excellent step coverage.
- Good control of line width.
- Better resolution.
- Elimination of standing waves and scattering in photolithography.
- Reduced proximity effects in electron-beam imaging.
- Minimum resist erosion during substrate etch by plasma or ions.

In the Bell approach (Fig. 8), a 2- to 3-μm layer of polymer is first placed over the surface of the wafer, making it more planar. This is then covered with 1,200-Å photo, electron-beam, or X-ray resist. The thin photoresist is now highly planar and is capable of high-resolution lithography. After exposure and development of the top layer, the silicon dioxide is etched by trifluoromethane (CHF_3) reactive ion etching. The thick layer is etched by oxygen-ion reactive etching. Bell Labs has demonstrated 1-μm line and spaces using this technique.

IBM uses two multiple-resist methods. In its earliest system, developed specifically for electron-beam lithography, a two-layer resist has been developed. A thin (typically 400-nanometer) top layer of an IBM copolymer resist is the imaging layer, and a much thicker bottom layer of polymethyl methacrylate (PMMA) is used to provide an undercut profile suitable for metal lift-off patterning. The thickness of the bottom level is usually in the 700-to-1,300-nm range.

Again, the image is developed in the thin top resist, allowing better size and image control. After complete development of the top layer, the developer is changed and the PMMA main layer is developed in a solvent that does not attack the top layer. Thus, the thick bottom resist serves to make the thin top resist more planar.

IBM's other multiple-resist system employs two types of exposure. Called the portable conformable masking technique, it combines either electron-beam or near-ultraviolet (370-nm) lithography with a deep-UV (240-nm) blanket exposure.

Electron-beam lithography can write low- and submicrometer features into resist-covered surfaces. However, backscattered electrons from the substrate limit the resist images exposed by an electron beam to a relatively low height-to-width aspect ratio. On the other hand, deep-UV conformable printing has demonstrated a nearly 4:1 aspect ratio for 0.5- to 5-μm features.

In this method a thin resist is directly applied to a deep-UV resist as shown in Fig. 9. IBM used a 0.2-to-0.4-μm layer of AZ1350J (a standard positive photoresist from Shipley Co., Newton, Mass.) as the electron-beam or near-UV resist and a 1-to-3-μm layer of PMMA as the deep-UV resist.

In the process, the image is directly written by an electron beam or patterned by UV light into the top layer. The underlying PMMA layer is not sensitive to the electron-beam or near-UV exposure. After development, the AZ1350J layer serves as the deep-UV mask for the PMMA resist. The wafer is then moved to a blanket deep-UV station where it is exposed with deep-UV light and then developed. Lines 0.6 μm wide with 2-μm pitch on a 2.2-μm-thick PMMA resist have been demonstrated with this method. The AZ1350J cap of the portable conformable masks was removed during PMMA development.

If process or resist requirements call for it, a 50- to 200-nm layer of aluminum can be inserted between resists. An example of this would be to expose the top resist with X rays and then the second resist, unaffected because of the shielding aluminum, with deep-UV light.

Most IC companies are in the process of evaluating the use of multiple resists. However, many feel they can reach the 1-to-1.25-μm area with single resists. Multiple resists add several process steps and therefore raise cost and complexity. But when IC processing reaches the 0.5-to-0.8-μm level, this processing step will be almost impossible to avoid.

Measuring the unmeasurable

Anyone fabricating VLSI devices must routinely measure 1-μm line widths and narrower and check layer-to-layer registration to within ±0.1 μm. At these levels, the optical microscope can no longer be used to make absolute measurements; it can be used only for comparative measurements. A manufacturer must either go to special chip-test patterns or use a scanning electron

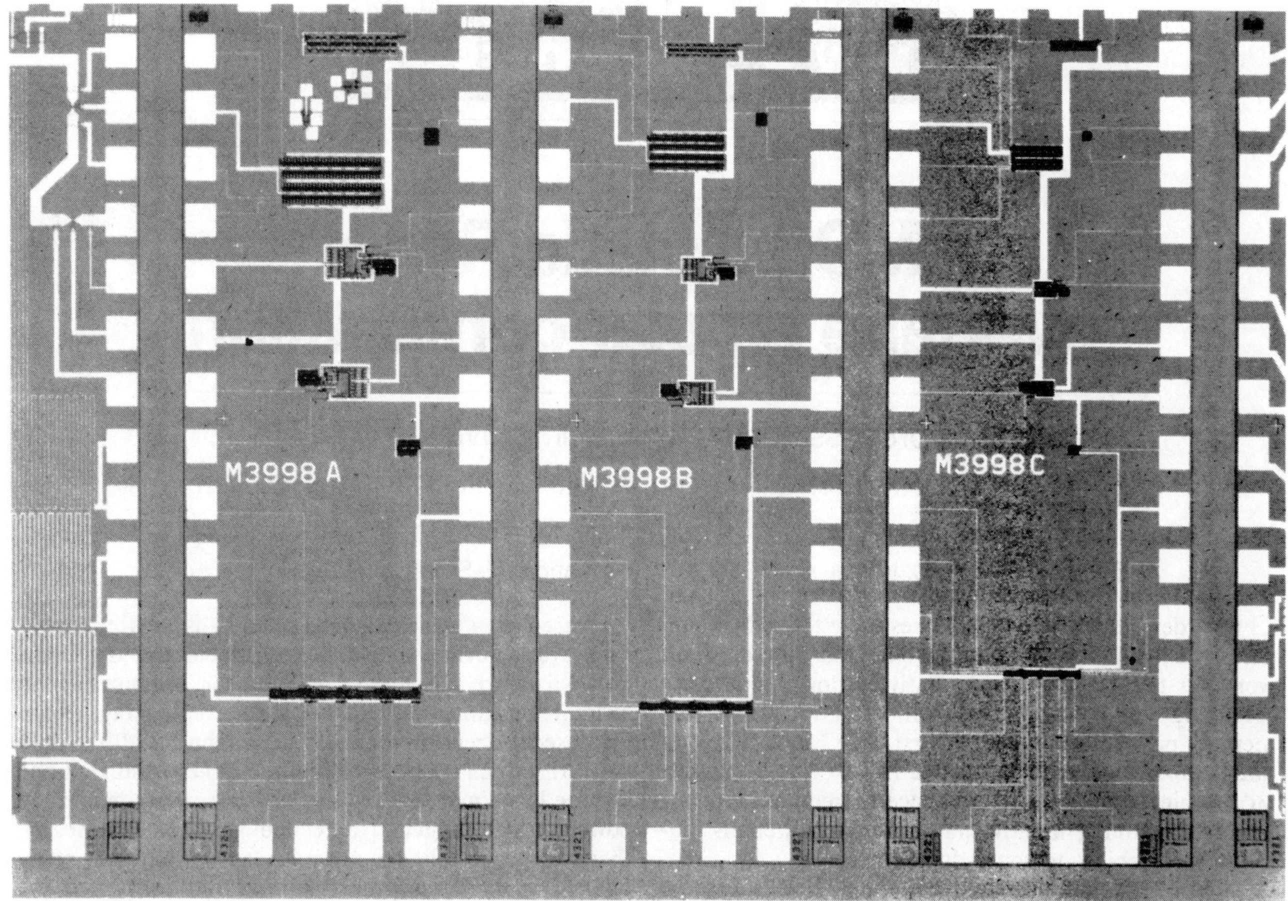

10. Monitors. This section of a Bell Labs wafer is devoted to testing. At left are resistive patterns that allow electrical measurement of line width, resistivity, and layer-to-layer alignment. Active devices shown are for measuring circuit speed at 2-, 1.5-, and 1-μm line widths.

microscope (SEM).

Bell Labs and Rockwell International's Electronics Research Center are already using so-called process monitors to electrically check parameters such as line width, sheet resistance, oxide thickness, and device performance. In Japan, Hitachi is also using these structures but is considering a special type of SEM. In general, most IC manufacturers opt for the SEM.

Electrical methods are based on voltage measurements made across a resistor, voltage divider, or resistance bridge. These measurements can be converted to resolution, layer alignment, and sheet resistivity. Oxide thickness can be checked by capacitance measurements. The National Bureau of Standards pioneered the resistive-pattern measurement of optical parameters.

Bell Labs has an extensive program for putting test structures on VLSI chips. An example is shown in Fig. 10: a process monitor comprising three resistive patterns for measuring line width, resistivity, and layer-to-layer alignment shares a wafer with 2-, 1½, and 1-μm versions of a test circuit for confirming speed predictions for each line width. Harry Boll, supervisor of the VLSI group at Bell Labs, Murray Hill, N. J., points out that test structures for process development can be used to monitor a process in full production as well as in a prototype stage. This method generates continuous data for each wafer at a relatively low cost.

At Rockwell's Thousand Oaks facility, a process-monitor chip takes up about 11% of a GaAs digital LSI wafer. This chip tests the capacitance-voltage (CV) profile of the implant, alignment of layers, overcrossings, via integrity, active test circuits, and resistivities of all implants and metalization.

The SEM, on the other hand, can check only wafer line resolution and layer-to-layer alignment—and it is a slow and expensive instrument. The industry would like to see in-line cassette-to-cassette versions of the SEM so that it could be integrated into a production line.

Hitachi has done some exploratory work on an advanced SEM specifically aimed at submicrometer measurements. This unit would have laser-positioned stages for greater positioning accuracy.

A beaming future

Past 1985 some radical changes may take place in IC processing. For instance, a futuristic piece of apparatus has already been constructed at Hughes Malibu, consisting of an electron-beam evaporator and an ion implanter in a vacuum chamber. A window allows the entrance of a laser beam. This is a piece of research and development equipment, but as more experience is gained on laser and electron-beam processing and ion beams, more IC processing steps will involve some form of beam. Possibly by this time, one or more ion beams in a single chamber will deposit, remove, and etch materials in addition to being able to expose a pattern in a resist. □

HMOS II static RAMs overtake bipolar competition

Shrinking process comes up with improved access times, new production remains compatible with HMOS fabrication

by R. M. Jecmen, C. H. Hui, A. V. Ebel, V. Kynett, and R. J. Smith, *Intel Corp., Santa Clara, Calif.*

☐ MOS devices have pushed aggressively towards higher performance and density during the past decade. This work has taken MOS from a relatively slow, low-density technology to a leadership position in random-access memory performance. For the first time, with the introduction of static RAMs fabricated in HMOS II, n-channel MOS achieved a superiority in access time over bipolar, while maintaining its advantages of low power dissipation and the ability to power down.

A number of different technological improvements have contributed to the MOS cause over the years (see "The evolution of MOS," p. 127). But the main differences between this second generation of the Intel HMOS process (the H is for high performance) and its immediate ancestors have to do with device scaling. To understand its key features requires an understanding of basic scaling theory.

Scaling

Figure 1 illustrates several of the device dimensions critical to scaling theory. Generally, to maintain the characteristics while shrinking an MOS device, all of the physical dimensions—channel length (L), gate-oxide thickness (T_{OX}), junction depth (X_J), and lateral diffusion of the source and drains under the gate (L_D)—must be reduced by the scaling factor 1/K. At the same time, threshold and punchthrough voltage levels are maintained by increasing the substrate doping concentration by a factor of K and reducing the power-supply voltage by a factor of 1/K.

HMOS II does not follow scaling theory exactly, however. Since industry compatibility demands that the supply voltage not be scaled down from the standard 5 volts, deviations from first-order scaling theory were necessary. To be sure, the impact of maintaining a 5-V supply is significant. All of HMOS II's deviations from scaling theory (Table 1) originate from three effects intrinsic to maintaining the 5-V supply voltage.

First, reduced dimensions result in more intense electric fields, so channel doping concentrations must be increased by a factor of αK (where α is greater than 1) to prevent device punchthrough. Secondly, the scaled MOS structure has higher gain, which produces higher currents per unit width. HMOS II takes advantage of this increased current drive by scaling channel width (W) by αK rather than simply by K. Finally, the constant supply voltage has a major impact on the power dissipation and power-delay product of a technology. Whereas scaling theory predicts that the power-delay product and power dissipation would drop by $1/K^3$ and $1/K^2$ respectively, a constant 5-V supply allows a less dramatic reduction of $1/\alpha K$ for the power-delay product—and no change in power dissipation.

New lows

By scaling the active transistors down to gate lengths of 2 micrometers and oxide thicknesses of 400 angstroms, HMOS II achieves a minimum gate delay of 400 picoseconds and a power-delay product of 0.5 picojoule. As shown in Fig. 2, the figures represent a scaling factor of 3 compared to 1976 industry-standard MOS

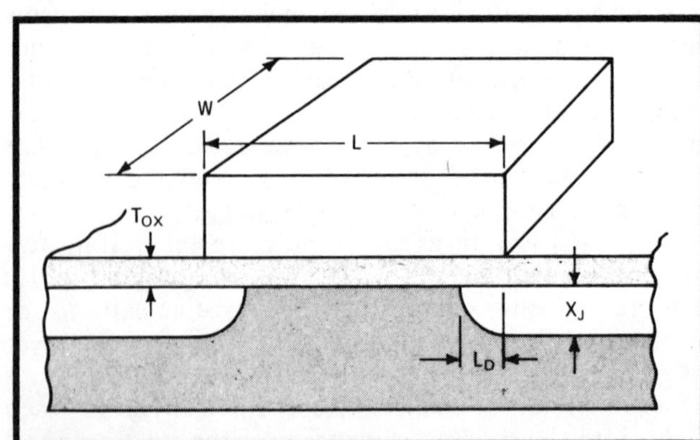

1. MOS scaling. The basic operating characteristics of MOS devices can be maintained if all dimensions—channel length (L) and width (W), oxide thickness (T_{OX}), junction depth (X_J), and lateral underdiffusion (L_D)—are reduced in the same proportions, while the substrate doping concentration is increased by that proportion.

Reprinted with permission from *Electronics*, vol. 52, pp. 124–128, Sept. 13, 1979.
Copyright © 1979 by McGraw-Hill, Inc. All rights reserved.

technologies. The performance improvement, however, is nearly tenfold.

Much of the HMOS II development centered on optimizing the scaling parameters. The emphasis was on boosting speed instead of density, but rapid development of a commercial product was deemed equally important. Therefore, HMOS II was designed to use most of the same process steps as HMOS; only those process blocks critical to switching speed were modified. Limiting engineering development to the scaled MOS transistor resulted in a very short turnaround time for the new process, with minimum impact on manufacturing.

The performance improvement did not add significantly to process complexity or expense. Since HMOS techniques are used for all major process blocks of HMOS II except the active transistor definition (Table 2), the compatibility of HMOS II with existing HMOS manufacturing lines is excellent. Even the finer transistor definition does not require any major modification to the existing production process or equipment. The 2-μm gate lengths are generated with standard optical photolithography and etching techniques. Moreover, the first HMOS II parts use the same single-level polysilicon depletion-mode transistors for loads as the HMOS parts. These keep process defect levels low and avoid the manufacturability and potential reliability problems of polysilicon-load approaches.

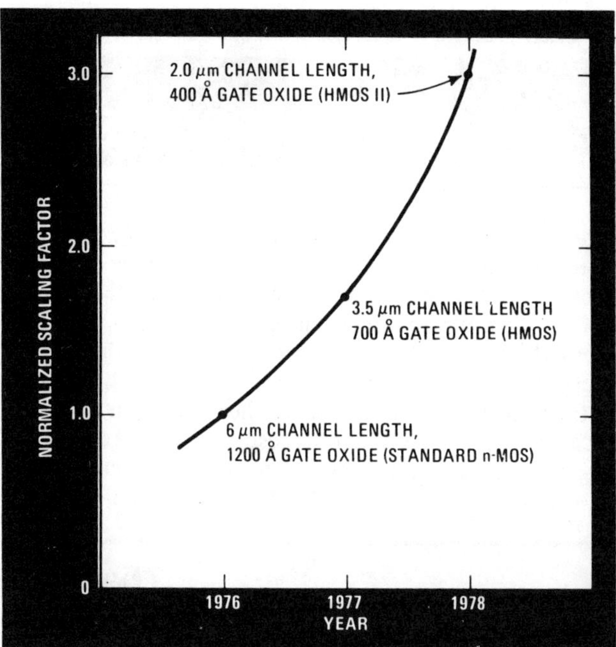

2. Progress. Recent improvements in processing have enabled the scaling to 2-μm channel lengths and 400-angstrom oxide thicknesses in HMOS II. The scaling factor of 3 relative to 1976 standards represents an eightfold drop in power-delay product.

Soft errors pose a potential reliability problem for static RAMs that use polysilicon loads, which have been shown to be sensitive to alpha radiation. Alpha-induced errors are inversely proportional to cell capacitance and load current, and polysilicon resistors significantly reduce both compared to depletion-load approaches. Great care must therefore be taken in cell design and processing of polysilicon-load technologies. HMOS II static RAMs have depletion loads, and accelerated testing using high-dose sources of alpha radiation have shown a zero failure rate per 1,000 hours.

Short channels revisited

The short lengths and high electric fields associated with HMOS II do have an impact on MOS device characteristics that goes beyond the first-order scaling theory. Besides the increased gain of the scaled MOS device, a number of short-channel effects occur that must be characterized in detail to optimize any design for HMOS II. Two of the effects are also apparent in HMOS.

Both threshold voltage and source-to-drain punchthrough voltage are inversely proportional to channel length for devices with the shortest channels. As with HMOS, those effects are a result of the drain voltage affecting the turn-on characteristics of the channel. Falling threshold voltage with rising drain voltage or decreasing channel length is a result of the electric field region around the drain depleting part of the channel charge. Thus a lower gate voltage is necessary to form the channel inversion region. Punchthrough voltage characteristics for HMOS II show the same second-gate effect seen with HMOS [*Electronics*, Aug. 18, 1977, p. 94]. In this case, the drain field inverts the channel from the terminated field lines at the oxide-silicon interface. HMOS II prevents each of these short channel effects from becoming catastrophic by scaling down the gate-oxide thickness (thereby reducing the impact of the second gate) and by increasing the channel doping concentration to a greater extent than the scaling factor.

Add velocity saturation

Another short-channel effect that only begins to show at those fields and channel lengths used in HMOS II is one

TABLE 1: DEVICE SCALING APPROACHES

Device parameter	Scaling factor	
	Theoretical	HMOS II approach
Device dimension T_{OX}, L, W	1/K	1/K ($K_W = \alpha K$), $\alpha > 1$
Doping concentration	K	αK
Voltage	1/K	1
Current	1/K	~1
Capacitance	1/K	1/αK
Propagation delay	1/K	1/αK
Power dissipation	$1/K^2$	1
Power-delay product	$1/K^3$	1/αK

TABLE 2: COMPARISON OF HMOS AND HMOS II TECHNOLOGIES

Characteristic	HMOS	HMOS II
Gate thickness	700 Å	400 Å
Gate length	3.5 μm	2.0 μm
Isolation definition		unchanged
Contact definition		unchanged
Metal definition		unchanged
Layout density		120% of HMOS
Gate delay	1 ns	0.4 ns
Power-delay product	1 pJ	0.5 pJ

that reduces the drain-to-source current. Called velocity saturation, it occurs when the electric fields become high enough to excite electrons moving from the source toward the drain to higher energies than the equilibrium thermal energy of the silicon lattice. At these high energies, electrons interact with the optical phonons instead of with the acoustic phonons as is normal; because of this, the electrons lose energy more rapidly. The net result is a saturating of average electron drift velocity at high electric fields, with the consequence that increasing channel fields actually reduces mobility.

When the MOS transistor operates in the saturation region, its channel is pinched off and the potential drop becomes a function of $V_{GS} - V_T$, where V_{GS} is the gate-to-source voltage and V_T is the threshold voltage. Velocity saturation will limit the rise in drain current with increasing gate voltage to a linear function instead of the normal square function. This result is illustrated in Fig. 3, which shows the current-voltage characteristics of a normal MOS device and one in velocity saturation. The compression of the current-voltage curves at high gate voltages is direct evidence of the reduction in mobility occurring as a result of electron-phonon interaction.

The impact of velocity saturation is the reduction in current gain of an HMOS II transistor. This works against the original intent of device scaling, since larger devices

The evolution of MOS

No fewer than four major changes in MOS technology have occurred over the past 10 years that have fostered its rapid improvement in performance without changing the basic nature of its operation.

In 1969, the standard MOS technology was an aluminum-gate p-channel process that exhibited low density and speed relative to today's standards. The first major advance in MOS performance came when silicon-gate processing replaced the original metal-gate approach. The silicon gate offered the great advantage of self-alignment: the usual overlap design required to accommodate misregistration of the gate with respect to source and drain regions was no longer necessary. With parasitic overlap capacitance greatly diminished, the pathway to greater speeds was cleared.

In 1972, the arrival of n-channel MOS meant an immediate boost in device speed, since the mobility of electrons is superior to that of the holes in p-channel MOS. At the time, Intel introduced the 2102 1-K static random-access memory, which was built only with enhancement-mode transistors using 6-micrometer channel lengths. Its typical address-access time was 500 nanoseconds.

Two years later, faster circuit speeds were made possible by the introduction of producible depletion-mode devices used as active loads. Using them, the 2102A dropped its typical access time down to 150 ns.

Since then, advances in MOS circuit speed have been attributable to device scaling. First, the 2115 1-K static RAM used 4.5-μm channels and 1,000-angstrom oxides for its typical access time of 55 ns.

In 1977 a comprehensive approach to scaling was applied in Intel's HMOS process. The result was the 2115A, built with 3.5-μm gate lengths and 700-Å oxides, to reach down to a typical access time of 35 ns. Through selective scaling of many critical physical and electrical parameters of the MOS devices, the trend toward higher speeds was maintained. At the same time, power requirements were reduced, thus significantly improving the power-delay product of MOS technology.

HMOS II goes a step farther. A direct descendant of HMOS, it employs device-scaling principles to improve performance beyond any MOS technology currently in production. The 15-ns typical address-access time (at room temperature) of the 2125H, made with HMOS II, is twice the speed of the 2115A, and an incredible 33-fold improvement over the 2102, which was introduced only seven years ago.

HMOS II is not the end of the road by any means. With the introduction of improved lithographic equipment such as direct-wafer-stepping exposure systems, resolution well below 1 μm will soon be possible. Yet even though the technology to produce the submicrometer devices of the 1980s might be well within reach, the introduction of such devices in a commercial process could be delayed by another factor—the adherence of industry to today's standard 5-volt power supply. Although HMOS II and possibly the next generation of scaled devices are achievable without reducing the supply voltage, there is no question that industry acceptance of a new voltage standard—say, a 2- or 3-V level—is inevitable. But that hurdle could turn out to be more difficult to get over than the technology development itself.

EVOLUTION OF MOS TECHNOLOGY

Device/circuit parameter	Al-gate p-MOS 1969	Si-gate p-MOS 1970	Si-gate n-MOS 1972	Depletion mode n-MOS 1974	HMOS 1977	HMOS II 1979
Gate length L (micrometers)	20	10–12	6	6	3.5	2
Lateral diffusion L_D (μm)	5	2	1.4	1.4	0.6	<0.6
Junction depth X_J (μm)	2.5	2.5	2.0	2.0	0.8	<0.8
Gate oxide thickness T_{OX} (angstroms)	1500	1200	1200	1200	700	400
Power supply voltage V_{CC} (volts)	12	12	12	5	5	5
Minimum gate delay T (nanoseconds)	80–100	40–50	12–15	4	1	0.4
Power delay product (picojoules)	60–80	30–40	18	4	1	0.5

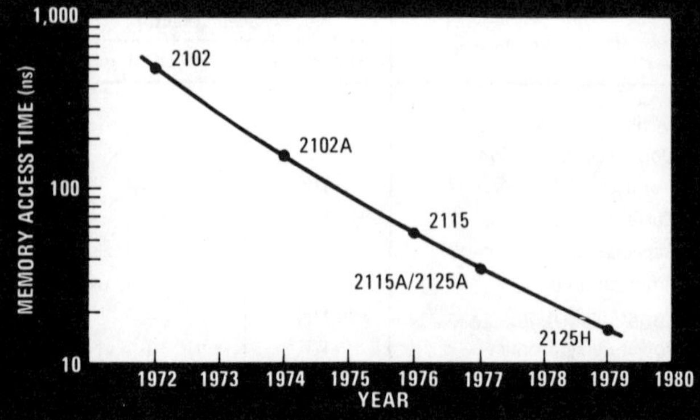

will be necessary to provide the same current drive as a device not in velocity saturation. Again, the unscaled power-supply voltage takes a performance toll.

Reliability key

One critical question that arose during the course of HMOS II development was the long-term reliability of short-channel, thin-oxide technology. With the supply fixed at 5 V, substantially higher electric fields occur both laterally and vertically within the scaled-down MOS structure. One possible effect of these high fields that impacts long-term reliability is the generation of hot electrons. Electrons become hot when accelerated to such a high energy that their temperature is greater than the equilibrium temperature of the lattice.

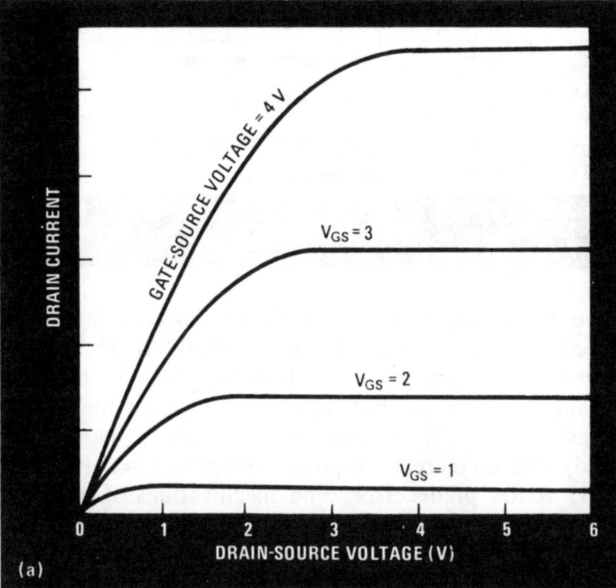

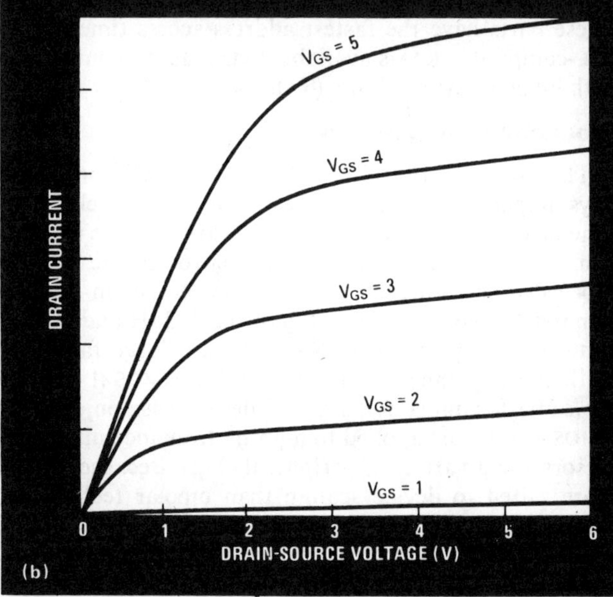

3. Saturation. Scaling can produce velocity saturation, which occurs when increased electric fields cause electrons to interact with lattice phonons. The effect on the current-voltage characteristics of a normal (unscaled) MOS device (a) is compression of the I-V curves at high gate voltage (b) due to a reduction in current gain.

The danger is that hot electrons can overcome the potential barrier at the oxide-silicon interface; once injected into the oxide they may become trapped. Electrons trapped in the oxide cause a positive shift in a device's threshold voltage that increases with the concentration of trapped charge. Thus, cumulative hot-electron trapping can cause a time-dependent threshold-voltage shift with a corresponding degradation in circuit performance over time.

Fortunately, charge-trapping effects have been successfully modeled. Theory predicts that the trapping rate increases with lateral and vertical electric fields (thus the concern for HMOS II) as well as with reduced temperatures. These relationships work to the advantage of reliability testing by allowing accelerated evaluation of threshold-voltage and circuit-performance implications. Stressing at high voltages (8 V) and low temperatures (−70°C) for 1,000 hours can simulate the hot-electron trapping effects of 50 years of standard operation. This accelerated stress-testing procedure was performed on both 4-K memories and discrete transistors fabricated with the HMOS II process. The results: address-access time of the 4-K memory increased less than 1 nanosecond, and the discrete transistors displayed no observable threshold shift. HMOS II simply does not have a hot-electron trapping problem.

IBM concurs

That conclusion is supported by a recent study by IBM Corp. Researchers at IBM who fabricated devices with even smaller geometries than those used in HMOS II showed that the current injected into the oxide of devices at normal voltages can only be observed at extremely low temperatures—for instance, −196°C. The temperature and channel-length dependence of the injected current indicates that HMOS II is still in an operating range where hot-electron effects will be unmeasurable.

A second reliability issue intrinsic to HMOS II is the integrity of the 400-Å gate oxide. Improved oxidation techniques have made HMOS II oxide integrity equivalent to the 700-Å oxide of HMOS despite the higher fields associated with the new technology. The breakdown voltage for the 400-Å oxide is typically well above 20 V with acceptably low defect densities. Moreover, the final testing procedure stresses the thin oxides at 10.5 V to guarantee product reliability. Since oxide breakdown is a time-dependent effect that increases exponentially with electric field, the short stress test eliminates all of the infant failure population.

A detailed product-reliability program has been completed for two static RAMs built with HMOS II: the 1-K 2125H and the 4-K 2147H. The reliability qualification includes 125°C dynamic burn-in with test intervals of 48 to 1,000 hours. The program also includes low-temperature testing, static-temperature cycling and a 250°C bake for 500 hours. Failure rates on HMOS II indicate long-term reliability should be at least as good as for HMOS. After 3.6 million device-hours of testing at 125°C, the HMOS II failure rate was 0.016% per 1,000 hours at 70°C and 0.010% per 1,000 hours at 55°C.

The 2125H, a 1,024-by-1-bit static RAM, became the yield and development vehicle for HMOS II. A previous

HMOS product, the 2125A, provided the basic layout. Some of its internal circuits were modified to optimize their design for the new technology; but since the basic layout remained intact, the 2125H has the same die size and organization as its HMOS counterpart.

Although the improved circuit density of HMOS II was not capitalized upon in the 2125H, the part provides information about the technology's potential circuit performance. A twofold improvement in performance or density is generally necessary to justify a major technology development; HMOS II is no exception. Typically the 2125H exhibits an address-access time of 15 ns with a power dissipation of 370 milliwatts. The 15-ns access time (at room temperature) is better than twice as fast as the typical 35-ns time of the 2125A.

Fully optimized

The first complete design to be fully optimized for HMOS II is the 2147H 4-K-by-1-bit static RAM. Since it is an entirely new design, the chip layout takes advantage of the 20% density improvement over HMOS offered by HMOS II. The die size of the 2147H is 120 by 177 mils, or 21,240-mil², compared to the 25,000-mil² 2147.

The 2147H is organized similarly to the 2147, with two memory planes separated by a common row decoder. This type of a layout conserves space for the decoder while minimizing the slowdown of access time due to word line resistance-capacitance delays that bits far from the row decoder suffer.

The peripheral circuitry is located mainly at one end of the chip. The 2147H has its substrate-bias generator, column decoders, output buffer, and all of the control circuitry at one side; only half the address buffers are found at the other side of the chip.

The main feature of the 2147H is not its die size or layout, however, but its performance specifications. The speed offered by the shrunken HMOS II technology together with some design improvements in the row decoders, chip-select buffer, and output allow the 2147H to achieve a typical access time of 22 ns (35 ns guaranteed) with no increase in power dissipation over its 55-ns 2147 HMOS predecessor. The specifications of both the 2125H and the 2147H are summarized in Table 3. The typical access times noted above for both products have allowed the announcement of a 20-ns 2125H and 35-ns 2147H over the full commercial temperature range. These parts have the fastest address-access time of any TTL-compatible RAMs available today, as the comparison with bipolar devices shows (Table 4).

TABLE 3: TYPICAL CHARACTERISTICS OF HMOS II RANDOM-ACCESS MEMORIES

Parameter	2125H	2147H
Physical characteristics		
Die size	10,816 mil²	21,240 mil²
Organization	1,024 x 1	4,096 x 1
Dc characteristics (typical)		
Supply voltage	5 V	5 V
Active power dissipation	330 mW	500 mW
Standby power dissipation	–	45 mW
Input/output levels	TTL	TTL
Output sink current (V_0 = 0.45 V)	26 mA	31 mA
Output source current (V_0 = 2.4 V)	31 mA	33 mA
Ac characteristics (typical)		
Address-access time	15 ns	22 ns
Chip-select access time	6 ns	22 ns
Power-down time	–	10 ns
Read-cycle time	15 ns	22 ns
Write-cycle time	15 ns	22 ns

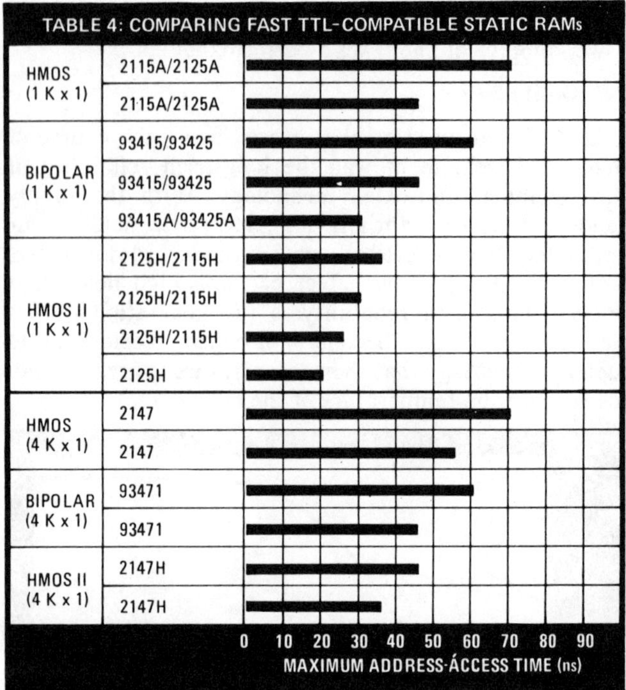

TABLE 4: COMPARING FAST TTL-COMPATIBLE STATIC RAMs

Production compatibility

The fact that HMOS II is based so heavily on HMOS pays important dividends. Not only was development time held to a minimum, but the always-delicate transfer from engineering to production control of the process proceeded smoothly. As a result, HMOS II is in production today, and the availability of the 2125H and 2147H static RAMs is excellent. Not only is a large family of static RAMs planned for the future, but HMOS II exhibits the same flexibility for a broad design base enjoyed by HMOS—it will be applied to high-performance microprocessors and a variety of peripheral chips. Because MOS is more suited to device scaling than bipolar technology, recent advances in photolithography and scaled wafer processing indicate a bright future for MOS performance.

The fast rate of its improvement in the 1970s should continue in the 1980s with the incorporation of direct wafer-stepping equipment and advanced dry-etching techniques. The performance improvement record for MOS over the past decade will be difficult to match; however, the tools and techniques are available today to make it happen. □

C-MOS LSI: comparing second-generation approaches

Using either isolated or ubiquitous p wells, new C-MOS processes get set for high-performance memories and analog circuits

by Donald L. Wollesen, *American Microsystems Inc., Santa Clara, Calif.*

☐ As complementary-MOS circuits grew in density and silicon-gate technology emerged in the early 1970s, the first generation of large-scale integrated C-MOS was born. C-MOS LSI was initially used for watch and calculator chips, and to this day the battle in those applications between the simpler metal-gate process and the denser though more expensive silicon-gate technology yields no clear winner.

But today's memories and microprocessors demand far greater speed than watches and calculators, and for these uses silicon-gate C-MOS is clearly the victor. Products at the density level of 4-K static random-access memories, which also demand high speed, mandate an entirely new approach in process technology and device structures. Moreover, the burgeoning analog-digital LSI that mixes linear circuits with logic makes new demands in terms of performance and density.

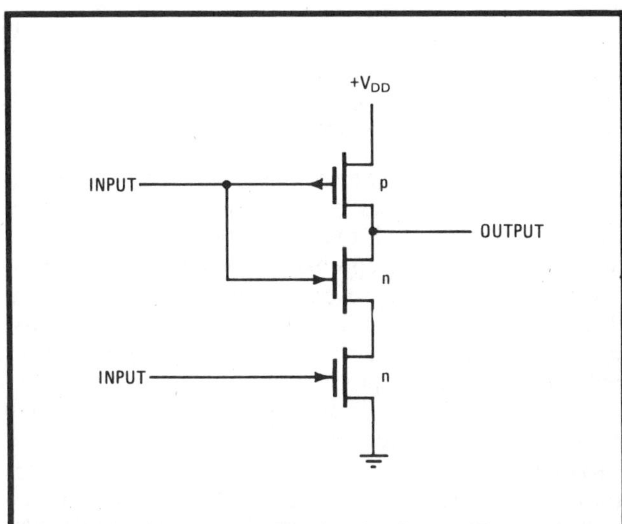

1. Gate portion. This simple portion of a gate will serve to compare C-MOS layouts. Two series n-channel transistors mark a key difference between the approaches, which either put all n-channel devices in a single p well or give each device its own well.

Those demands have been answered by a second generation of C-MOS LSI. The C-MOS circuits of fast converters, microprocessors, and memories are catching up with n-channel MOS in speed while retaining the advantage of low power dissipation. Three somewhat similar approaches to this new generation have evolved, each with its own advantages.

Several reasons make it important to understand the operation of each type. One reason is that a potential second-sourcing manufacturer may be unable to build a particular process if his tooling is not compatible. Another is that anyone who contemplates a custom circuit should be fully aware of the differences, because his layout may be suitable to one technology and not to the other two. The good news, though, is that a single layout can be done to accommodate all three.

The second generation

Looking at a portion of a C-MOS gate (Fig. 1) will be helpful in comparing the three C-MOS approaches. Simple plan-view and section drawings illustrate the differences; for all examples, the line width and spacing rules are consistent, so that a comparison in gate layout area may be made.

The first implementation of the gate portion is a process that uses both n^+ and p^+ polysilicon. The basic structure is a first-generation approach to which a selective field-oxidation process has been added. (At American Microsystems Inc., the selective field-oxidation process is used only to shrink existing designs down to 5-micrometer rules; it is not applied to new designs.)

Figure 2 shows the plan and section views of the three-device gate portion. Because the p well in the top view spans both n-channel devices, it is referred to as ubiquitous, and the process is called ubiquitous p well.

In this planar process, p^+ guard rings are used to reduce surface leakage. Polysilicon cannot cross the rings, however, so that bridges must be built. Note the use of n^+ polysilicon in the p-channel areas. The plan view shows the construction of the bridges linking p^+ to

Reprinted with permission from *Electronics*, vol. 52, pp. 116–123, Sept. 13, 1979.
Copyright © 1979 by McGraw-Hill, Inc. All rights reserved.

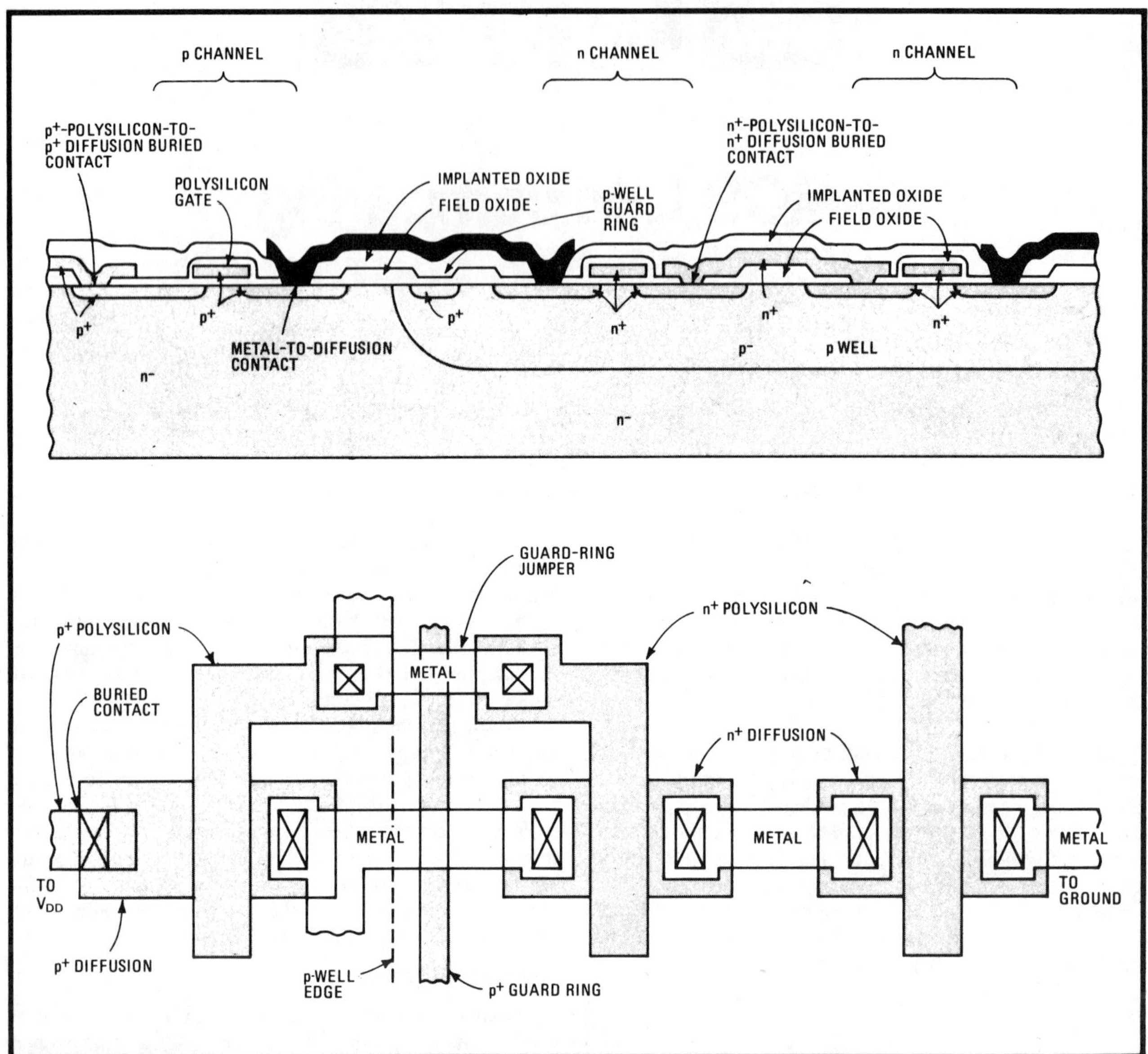

2. Two-polysilicon approach. The first high-performance complementary-MOS process upgraded earlier designs for 5-μm geometry. Its drawbacks: two types of polysilicon are used, and the unavailability of field implant doping ties field threshold to device thresholds.

metal to n^+. (Were the process to be used for a low-voltage, first-generation application like a watch circuit, the guard rings would not be necessary and polysilicon could directly connect n-channel and p-channel devices; however, to ensure good ohmic contact from one type of polysilicon to another, polysilicon-diode contacts must be capped with metal.)

This process provides a buried contact (n^+ polysilicon to n^+ diffusion) that can yield a circuit-density advantage. However, neither of the other two second-generation approaches provides buried contacts. Therefore, if a layout in this process is to be compatible with the others, the buried contact must be eliminated. Though there will be a penalty in real estate, the gain for custom applications is a great increase in the number of available C-MOS vendors.

The planar process of n^+p^+ ubiquitous p well is a disadvantage in that it precludes field-implant doping. The result is that the field threshold voltages are unavoidably linked to device thresholds. For example, if the gate-oxide thickness is 1,200 angstroms for a device with a 1-volt threshold, then a 12,000-Å field oxide fixes the field threshold at approximately 10 V. That dependency constrains the process designer, since low device thresholds will force low field thresholds—field oxide cannot be made much thicker than 15,000 Å without ensuing step-coverage problems.

Nor does the process lend itself to small-geometry devices. The gate oxide cannot be made too thin lest a phenomenon called boron penetration occur. Thin oxides allow boron from the p^+ doped polysilicon in the p-channel device to diffuse through the gate oxide to the channel region, causing thresholds to be changed so radically that sometimes the enhancement-mode transistor actually turns into a depletion-mode device—highly undesirable for complementary-MOS.

The second-generation C-MOS approach that offers the most advantages uses a selective field-oxidation process

and requires only n⁺ polysilicon. The selective field-oxidation process (referred to as Isoplanar or Planox by certain manufacturers) is preferable, since it not only eases metalization step coverage, but also allows for field implantation, so that field thresholds are not tied to device thresholds.

The n^+-only approach

Both of the second-generation C-MOS processes that follow are variants of the n^+-only, selective-field-oxide approach. One closely resembles the p^+n^+ ubiquitous-p-well process, since it, too, has a ubiquitous p well that is implanted before the field oxidation and thus runs under the field oxide. The other, called isolated p well, has separate wells for each n-channel device that are implanted after field oxidation.

Figure 3 shows the section and plan views of the n^+-only ubiquitous-p-well approach used to build the partial gate of Fig. 1. This is the 5-μm process recommended by AMI and others for new, high-performance C-MOS designs. The layout is simpler than with the two-polysilicon ubiquitous-well approach (there are no buried contacts and no polysilicon-diode contacts), and it occupies less area for the same line widths. Also, since the process permits implanting in the field region, no guard rings are required. Polysilicon can thus cross directly from p- to n-channel device areas without the need for bridges or polysilicon-dioxide contacts.

Note that all polysilicon is n^+, even in p-channel devices. Because of that, however, a buried contact between n^+ polysilicon and p^+ diffused areas is impossible. Moreover, even though a buried contact between n^+ polysilicon and n^+ diffused silicon is possible, the benefit rarely outweighs the cost of the extra mask step, and therefore the contact is usually unavailable in this type of process.

The problem of boron penetration is eliminated because all polysilicon is doped with phosphorus. Consequently, the process makes possible thinner gate oxides than the two-polysilicon approach, and that means tran-

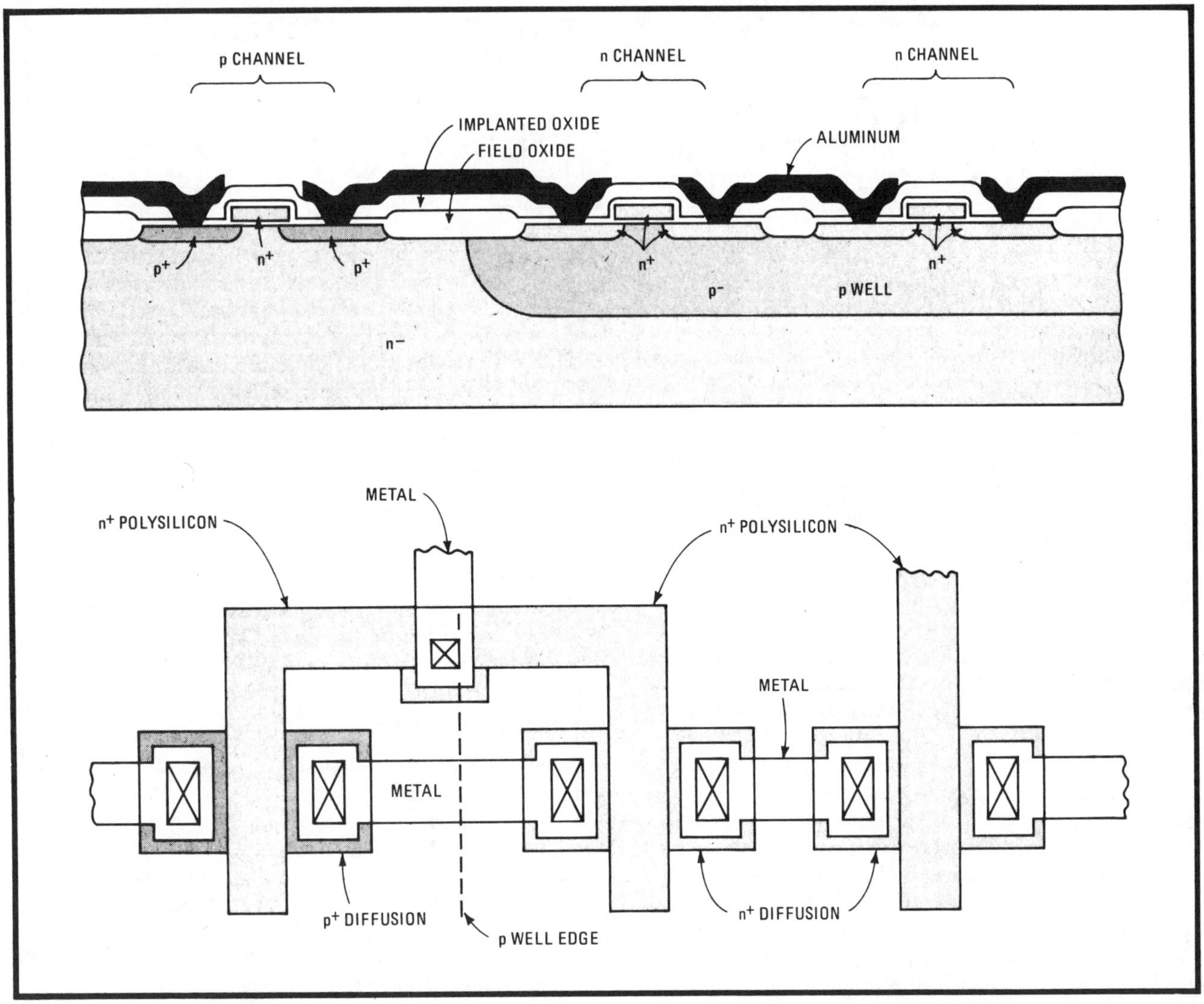

3. One-polysilicon approach. All new high-performance C-MOS circuits will use one type of polysilicon. This version has a ubiquitous p well; that is, series n-channel devices sit in a common p well, which, implanted before field oxidation, runs under the field oxide.

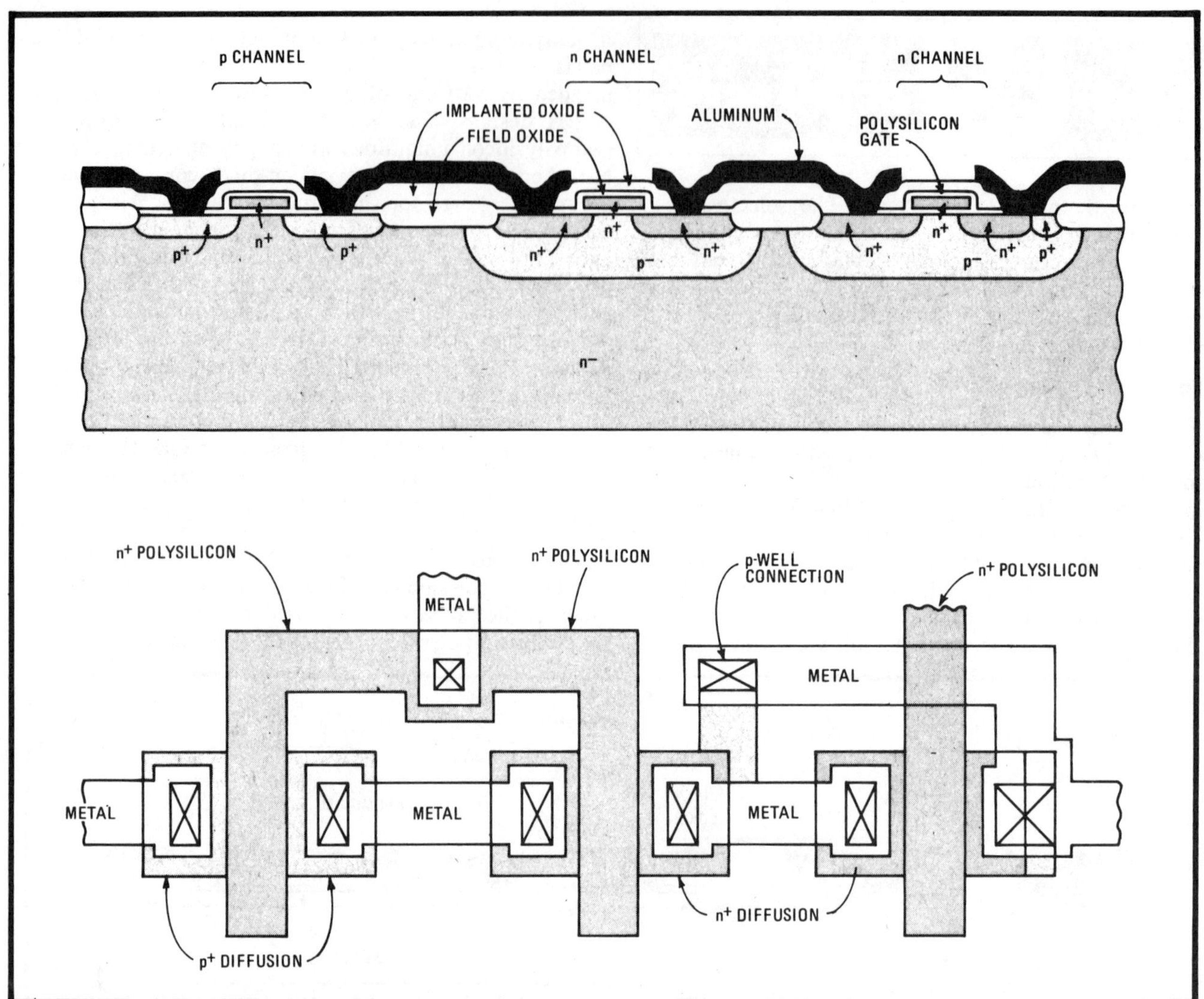

4. Isolated wells. The third C-MOS approach isolates all n-channel devices in separate p wells. Since the isolated wells must be doped much more heavily than those of the ubiquitous-well approach, n^+-to-p-well capacitance is greater and switching speeds lower.

sistors can have higher gain and lower threshold voltages with no adverse affect on field thresholds. On the other hand, thanks to field implants, field threshold voltages can be made higher with no direct effect on transistor thresholds. Since the field oxide is selectively grown, fairly thick field-oxide regions can be obtained without paying the penalty of the precipitous oxide steps found in planar approaches.

A variant of the all-n^+ polysilicon process just discussed uses basically the selective field-oxide approach except that the p wells are not continuous under the field-oxide areas; they are instead bounded by field-oxide edges. Since the p wells are naturally isolated from one another, the process is called n^+ isolated p well. The isolated wells must all be connected to ground; if they are left floating, circuit malfunctions are bound to occur. The grounding is done either with p^+ diffusions or with top-side metalization that covers a p^+-to-p-well contact diffusion.

In the isolated-well process, the p wells must be doped much more heavily than in the ubiquitous-well process. One result is a higher junction capacitance between the n^+ areas and the wells that both slows switching speeds and raises the power dissipation of a device. Even though the speed loss could be compensated for by slightly shorter channel lengths, the operating power still remains high.

Although currently available from AMI and other manufacturers, the isolated-well process is in fact not recommended for new designs by AMI. Its layout takes up more area than does one using the ubiquitous-well approach, even though its p-well-to-p^+-area spacing is slightly less.

Compatibility is key

A layout with the isolated-well approach appears to almost guarantee process compatibility with the ubiquitous-well approach. However, there are two hitches: first, the ubiquitous-well approach needs about 5 μm more space between n-channel and p-channel transistors; second, p wells in the isolated-well approach will often be purposely separated using only the field mask, thereby linking the wells to one another if the mask set is used with the ubiquitous p-well process.

Though the former presents no serious layout-compatibility problems, the latter could in practice prove troublesome. Consider, for example, a circuit requiring that the isolated wells not both be tied to ground but instead be operated at different potentials. That could be accomplished only if both the p-well and field-oxide masks are used. Figure 5 shows such a situation and how it can be handled. The rule is that if the p-well mask is merged (that is, the wells are not separated) in the isolated-well process and isolation accomplished only with the field mask, the process will not be compatible with the ubiquitous-well process.

Table 1 summarizes the major layout concerns for process compatibility. The most versatile layout would:

- Eliminate buried contacts.
- Include polysilicon-diode contacts.
- Use layout rules of the ubiquitous-well process.
- Assume the isolated-well process.
- Make contact to all isolated p wells.

The circuit takes up more area using the versatile layout approach, but it may be a small price to pay for compatibility.

Comparing the density of different processes is more a sport than a science; a manufacturer who wants to prove his process is better can present his design rules in the best light but is unlikely to do the same for his competitors' approaches. Here, though, the simple cells shown all have the same 5-μm line widths and spacings, as was noted earlier.

In all fairness, it must be pointed out that the gate portion of Fig. 1, from which the data in Table 2 was derived, was chosen to illustrate a compatibility risk between processes. In practice, a designer would not use series n-channel devices in the isolated-well process because such an arrangement occupies more area than other circuits and because in this process the body effect, which slows circuit speed, is particularly pronounced in n-channel devices. Also, the n^+ regions between the two n-channel devices would be merged, instead of using a metal or polysilicon jumper. In general, therefore, it is fair to regard the densities of both n^+-only processes as roughly equal.

It should also be pointed out that certain types of circuits tend to favor different layout schemes. For example, in the classic six-transistor static random-access memory cell, the buried contact that is available in the two-polysilicon process actually reduces cell area by about 5%. Fabrication costs, however, are higher because of the extra mask step required by buried contacts, and that offsets the area advantage.

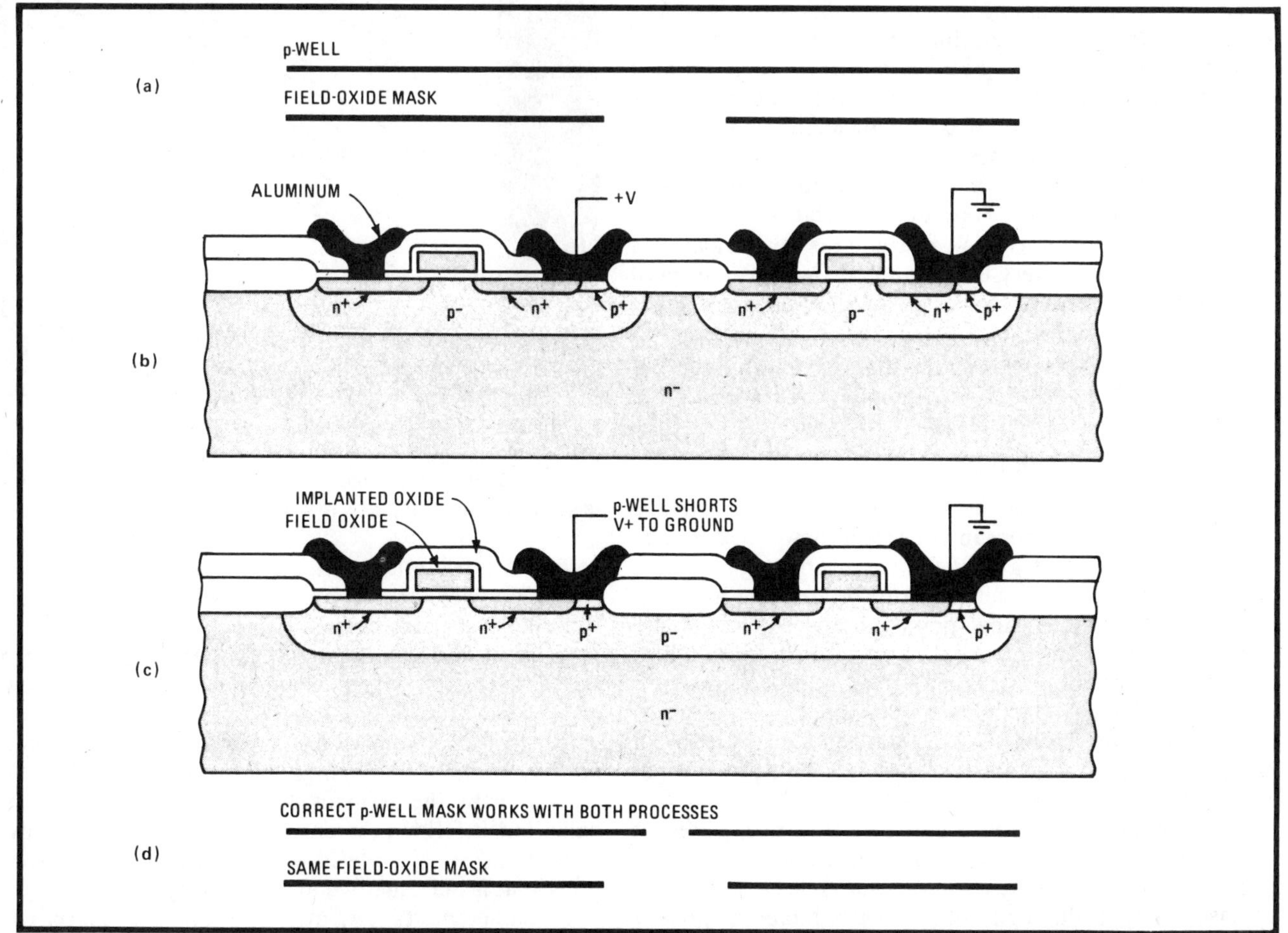

5. Compatibility. If p wells are isolated only with the field-oxide mask (a), the isolated-well (b) and ubiquitous-well (c) processes are compatible—but the power supply could short to ground if the wells are at different potentials. Solution: use the p-well mask, too (d).

TABLE 1: LAYOUT COMPATIBILITY CONCERNS FOR C-MOS PROCESSES			
Layout feature	**n^+/p^+ polysilicon ubiquitous p well**	**n^+-only polysilicon ubiquitous p well**	**n^+-only polysilicon isolated p well**
Buried contact	X	no	no
Polysilicon diode contact	yes	X	X
p well isolation with diffusion mask	no	no	yes
Tight p-well-to-p^+ spacing	no	no	yes
Layout care required for p-well electrical contacts	no	no	yes

X = does not matter

TABLE 2: COMPARING AREAS FOR C-MOS PROCESSES			
Process	**Area (mil^2)**	**Area (percentage)**	**Number of masks**
n^+/p^+ polysilicon ubiquitous p well (Fig. 2)	4.1	114	9–11
n^+-only polysilicon ubiquitous p well (Fig. 4)	3.6	100	8–9
n^+-only polysilicon isolated p well (Fig. 5)	4.0	111	8–10

Note: All processes done with 5-μm lines and spaces

TABLE 3: COMPARING PERFORMANCE OF SINGLE C-MOS INVERTERS			
Process	**Rise time (ns)**	**Gate power-supply current (μA)**	**Speed-power product (pJ)**
n^+/p^+ polysilicon ubiquitous p well	2.4	900	10.8
n^+-only polysilicon ubiquitous p well	1.4	900	6.3
n^+-only polysilicon isolated p well	1.4	1,300	9.1

Notes: All processes use 5-μm lines and spaces. Data is based 13-stage ring counters.

The n^+-only ubiquitous-well process uses the fewest number of masks, is the simplest to lay out, and takes up the least area in most cases. It is therefore the most cost-effective C-MOS process available today.

Whereas the first generation of C-MOS LSI was applied to products that demanded low power consumption—watches, calculators, and military gear—the second generation is beginning to change that situation. The new C-MOS LSI will certainly make inroads into places where C-MOS has not been used before, such as large memories of all types. Moreover, it will build microprocessors of the same complexity and capability as existing n-channel parts and—besides being much lower in power consumption—will be faster. Performance figures of 5-μm C-MOS approaches are shown in Table 3.

Critics of C-MOS technology argue that although it can be fast and draws very little standby power, at top speed it draws considerable power. Actually, that dependence can be used to advantage: higher speed does incur power costs, but since C-MOS automatically reduces its power as the switching speed goes down—it is the only technology to do so—the choice is left to the user.

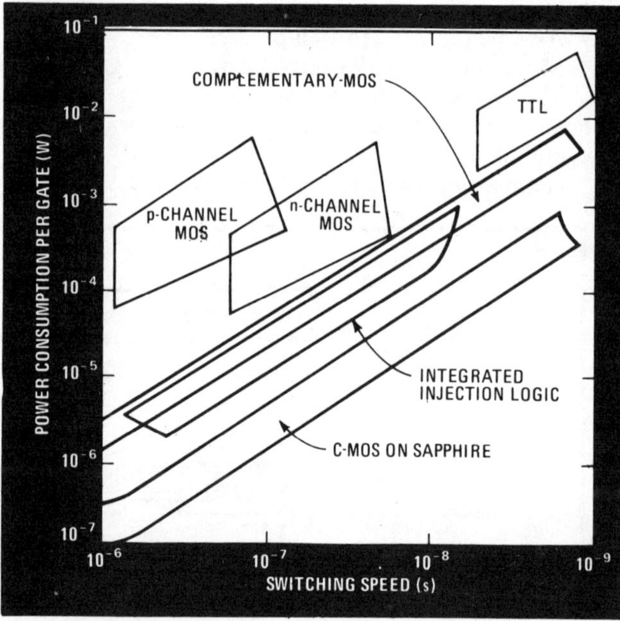

6. Energies. This comparison of switching energies (based on performance of a single 5-μm gate) shows bulk C-MOS equal in speed to C-MOS on sapphire. The former's junction capacitance is offset by the latter's losses in majority-carrier mobility.

Comparative judgments

Figure 6 compares several technologies in switching speed versus power consumption. It is, however, based on the performance of a single-input inverting gate; every gate in the system would have to be toggling at maximum rate for an extrapolation of gate-level performance to system-level performance. But it at least gives an idea of relative performance. C-MOS does tend to slow down as a function of the number of gate inputs—for a single-gate switching speed of 2.5 nanoseconds, a four-input gate would switch in about 10 ns—but with only a slight penalty in power dissipation.

The data is based on 5-μm technologies operated at 5 V. It is worth noting that, from the standpoint of speed, 5-μm bulk silicon matches 5-μm C-MOS on sapphire. The reason is that although bulk C-MOS exhibits far greater junction capacitance, C-MOS on sapphire is limited in its majority-carrier mobility, which holds it to a lower gain constant for a given device. Still, C-MOS on sapphire retains a substantial advantage in gate power. However, it may not yield any advantage at a system level because its standby leakage current is much higher. Also, it is a very expensive technology. Still, C-MOS and C-MOS on sapphire are the only technologies that dissipate power only on logic transitions.

Integrated injection logic is a constant loss-load technology, unlike C-MOS—high speed is traded off against low power by the designer. I^2L has a broad speed-power band, but it follows the entire speed-power curve only if its bias current is changed from standby to active, something that is not usually done in small systems.

The inherent standby attribute of static C-MOS technology is one of its greatest strengths from a system standpoint. Consider an 8-bit microprocessor with 16-K bytes of RAM. Because the microprocessor can perform only one address operation at a time, 16,383 bytes of memory do nothing but remember while 1 byte is being accessed. Moreover, in most cases any peripheral interfacing circuits will also be having to wait while memory is being accessed.

Current comparison

Table 4 compares the currents required for C-MOS, n-channel (2114 type), and n-channel power-down memories, based on the assumption that the 16-K bytes of memory are made up of 32 4-K-by-1-bit static RAMs. At any given time, 8 chips are active and 24 are inactive. The memory system's total current, which is the sum of the standby and active currents, is 30 times greater with n-channel than with C-MOS RAMs. Even power-down n-channel RAMs, which are not often used in microprocessor systems because the cost or the increased system complexity is rarely worth the trouble, draw almost nine times as much current as C-MOS.

C-MOS is the only logic form that operates in an automatic power-down mode. Even if I^2L static RAMs were available commercially, they would at best compete with edge-triggered n-channel RAMs and would probably have similar operating currents; only the standby currents would be less than with n-MOS.

Although the world of linear integrated circuits is currently dominated by bipolar technology, C-MOS has invaded such LSI devices as digital-to-analog and analog-to-digital converters, coder-decoders (codecs), and most dramatically, fixed filters using switched-capacitor designs.

There are two main reasons why MOS technology in general has been unable to compete with bipolar circuits in the field of linear ICs: offset voltage and noise. For a matched dual-input transistor pair, bipolar transistors have about 0.5 millivolt of offset voltage, whereas MOS devices often match so poorly that their offset is 10 mV or more. Similarly, 1/f noise at 100 hertz is about 20 $nV/Hz^{1/2}$ as against 500 $nV/Hz^{1/2}$ for the MOS device pair.

However, certain circuit techniques have made possible the development of competitive linear circuits, despite those noise and offset handicaps. As an example, the 5-μm n^+-only ubiquitous-p-well process has been used to build an operational amplifier competitive in performance with the general-purpose bipolar types. Table 5 compares the internally compensated C-MOS op amp with its bipolar counterpart, the popular 741. Figure 7 is a photograph of an oscilloscope showing the C-MOS op amp's large-signal unity-gain output response. Note that, unlike the case with a 741, the positive and negative slew ramps are nearly equal and are well behaved.

Converting

Other circuit design tricks have allowed C-MOS to work around the shortcomings of its linear-circuit performance. The best example is in a-d conversion. There, analog signals are quantized, and as long as the exact value of the signal is known at the end of the quantizing period—the most accurate quantization

The complexity of C-MOS

Historically, complementary-MOS has been the most complex MOS technology; since p-channel and n-channel MOS technologies each use only one device type, they would naturally build lower-cost circuits. Over time, the drive for increased performance has de-emphasized p-MOS. But the combined demand for higher density and a lower power-delay product has jacked up the process complexity of n-MOS.

The techniques used by circuit designers to reduce the power-delay product have, in fact, raised the complexity of n-MOS processes to the level of C-MOS technology (see the table). One way is by boosting speed with circuits that combine devices of several different thresholds—a few enhancement types, a few depletion types, and even devices with 0-volt thresholds—which require extra mask and implant steps.

Another, the use of clocked, or dynamic, circuit design, is aimed at reducing power consumption. Clocked logic definitely reduces power dissipation, but it also increases circuit complexity. What's more, because the attendant clock lines must run throughout the chip, clocked logic sacrifices density. Clocked n-channel logic is not as fast as and dissipates more power than C-MOS of equivalent line width. Thus, compared with past circuits, the area and cost penalties for going to C-MOS in today's high-performance world are continually growing smaller.

Another advantage of C-MOS coming to light is that for gate lengths of 5 micrometers or less, device modeling is more accurate than in n-MOS and therefore circuit simulations fit actual circuit performance better. The result is not only lower cost for circuit development, but greater ease in predicting development time and adhering to a schedule—simply because the C-MOS circuit is more likely to work the day it is supposed to without redesign or process adjustments.

Of course, more closely controlled development time is especially important to custom-circuit scheduling. Indeed, computer-aided simulation techniques will become increasingly important as circuits graduate in density to the very large-scale integration level.

COMPARING THE COMPLEXITY OF C-MOS PROCESSES

	Line width (μm)	Number of masks		
		Silicon-gate p-channel MOS	Silicon-gate n-channel MOS	Silicon-gate complementary MOS
1973	7.5	5–7	5–7	8–9
1975	6	6–8	6–8	8–9
1977	5	–	7–9	8–10
1979	3–4	–	8–10	8–10

TABLE 4: CURRENT REQUIREMENTS OF 16-K BYTES OF RANDOM-ACCESS MEMORY (mA)					
Technology	Standby		Active		Total
	Each chip	24 chips	Each chip	8 chips	
C-MOS	0.005	0.12	5	40	40
N-channel	35	840	45	360	1,200
N-channel (with power-down)	3	72	35	280	350

Note: All memory elements are 4-K-by-1-bit static RAMs.

TABLE 5: COMPARING C-MOS AND BIPOLAR OPERATIONAL AMPLIFIERS		
Parameter	C-MOS op amp	Bipolar (741 type)
Offset voltage (typical, mV)	6.3	1.0
Offset current (typical, nA)	≪1	20
Bias current (typical, nA)	≪1	80
Power-supply voltage (V)	±5	±15
Power-supply current (mA)	0.5	1.4
Output voltage swing (V)	±4.5	±13
Open-loop gain (dB)	96	106
Common-mode rejection ratio (dB)	66	70
Slew rate (V/μs)	10	0.5
Cell area (mil^2)	172	1,100

occurs at the exact end of the sample period—what goes on between the beginning and the end of the period is immaterial. C-MOS can make good use of that time between samples.

An example of what can be performed during the sample period is reset stabilization of an op amp. By measuring the offset voltage of the op amp, storing that voltage value on a capacitor, and then algebraically subtracting the potential on the capacitor from the offset error of the op amp during the quantizing period, an op amp with extremely low offset voltage, regardless of temperature, can be built.

The technique is a viable one that has already been used in codecs. There, a 3.3-kilohertz voice bandwidth is used, and the sampling frequency is 8 kHz. Thus the analog signal is quantized every 125 microseconds, and there is enough time between quantizing periods to perform the reset stabilization.

That technique is extremely important in telephony, because it allows the offset voltage to be lowered to less than 1 microvolt over the entire temperature range, and it reduces 1/f noise at 100 Hz. Since the principal contribution to 100-Hz 1/f noise is in the region where the 1/f corner frequency falls for MOS devices—around 8 kHz—sampling at that rate neatly sidesteps the inherent noise problem of MOS transistors.

C-MOS or n-MOS

As for whether n-channel alone or C-MOS builds better linear circuits, there is a good historical comparison in the history of bipolar linear devices. The 709 op amp was built using only npn transistors. Compared with the 741 and the 101A, which use both npn and pnp transistors, the 709 is vastly inferior.

Likewise, an n-MOS op amp will simply not perform as well as an op amp that uses both n-channel and p-channel devices. One good reason is that p-channel

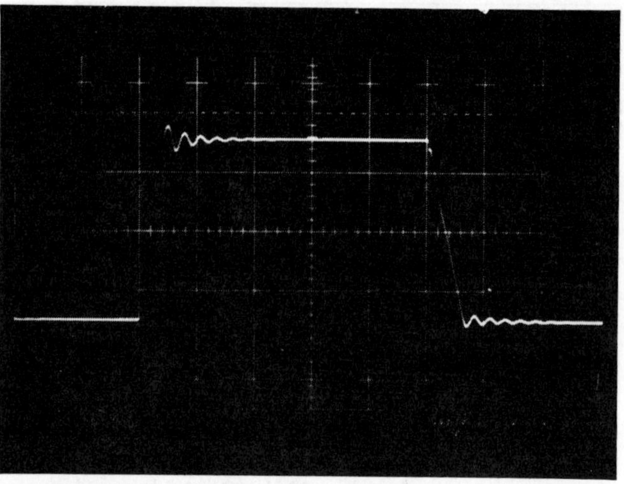

7. C-MOS linear. C-MOS is proving itself in linear circuits as well as digital. Here, the large-signal unity-gain output response of a C-MOS operational amplifier shows equal, well-behaved positive and negative slewing ramps—unlike those in the bipolar 741.

transistors are required for building current mirrors referred to the positive voltage supply. The lack of a good current mirror is a serious handicap for the n-MOS circuit designer.

Switched-capacitor and charge-coupled-device filter techniques are available in both n-MOS and C-MOS for building high-pass, low-pass, and bandpass filters from audio to video frequencies, a feat that bipolar technology will have difficulty matching. Interestingly, the area penalty that C-MOS pays versus n-MOS in digital designs is actually reversed in these applications. Despite smaller actual transistors in n-MOS, because fewer circuit elements are available and so many more devices are required, n-channel linear circuits take up more real estate than C-MOS.

Other pluses

Other elements, too, are available in the C-MOS process—for one, zener diodes, which can regulate power-supply voltages on chip. That is a boon for digital applications in which power-supply regulation is poor, as in automotive circuits. Zeners can also protect a chip from voltage surges, and they serve in linear circuits as voltage references. The zener reference diodes in AMI's C-MOS processes have been designed with an avalanche of just under 6 V.

Also inherent in the C-MOS process is a bipolar device. The p well serves as a base region, an n^+ diffusion as an emitter, and the substrate as the collector. Because the collector is tied to the substrate, the transistor is limited to an emitter-follower configuration, but it is a handy device nonetheless. The npn transistor has a breakdown voltage of over 50 V and, depending on the geometry used, a gain (h_{fe}) of 50 to 300.

One use for the built-in npn device is an output-stage pull-up transistor. Since it supplies more current for a given topological area than a p-MOS transistor, it takes up less die area for a given drive capability. A pair of transistors can even be used as a bandgap voltage reference, offering the designer the choice of zener or bandgap techniques in the same process. □

TWIN-TUB CMOS - A TECHNOLOGY FOR VLSI CIRCUITS

L. C. Parrillo, R. S. Payne, R. E. Davis*
G. W. Reutlinger and R. L. Field

Bell Laboratories
Murray Hill, New Jersey 07974

ABSTRACT

CMOS technology has been developed through several generations of design rules with an n-type substrate (where p-channel transistors were formed) and with a p-tub implanted and diffused region (where n-channel transistors were formed). In order to enable a separate optimization of both transistors and to utilize the dopant control available with implanted layers, a two-tub approach was adopted. Utilizing lightly doped epi on an n^+ substrate (for latch-up protection), nitride-masked self-aligned tubs, $10^{16}cm^{-3}$ surface doping and 600Å gate oxides, an 8-mask CMOS process (named "Twin-Tub") was formulated. The combination of n on n^+ epi and careful I/O layout renders the circuits latch-up free. Novel aspects of the process, the devices it produces and finally the resultant circuit performance are herein described.

I. INTRODUCTION

CMOS provides an inherently low power static circuit technology which has the capability of providing lower power-delay product than a comparable design-rule NMOS technology. In the VLSI era, large random logic devices (like microprocessors) are often power limited, i.e., the total power dissipation can limit the gate count of a chip and hence limit its scale of integration and ultimate performance.

The n-channel transistor in the classic bulk CMOS process was formed in a p-tub which is diffused into a moderately doped ($2-4 \times 10^{15}$ cm^{-3}) n-substrate where the p-channel transistor was formed. For control purposes, the p-tub had to be doped approximately an order of magnitude greater ($\sim 2 \times 10^{16}cm^{-3}$) than the n-substrate. In scaling to finer design rules, the doping in the n-substrate has to increase to support voltage in the shorter channel length p-channel transistors. Correspondingly, the p-tub doping has to be raised proportionately, and the n-channel transistor will suffer from excessive source/drain to p-tub capacitance. In order to avoid these scaling problems, a new Twin-Tub CMOS process was designed to provide separately optimized tubs and hence a lower capacitance n-channel transistor than could be obtained with the conventional process. With n^+ polysilicon doped with a separate phosphorus diffusion the parasitic thresholds of the field regions were designed to be 12V (without extra channel stoppers) with the n-channel active transistor thresholds at 0.6V and the p-channel active transistor thresholds at -1.9V. A p-channel threshold adjustment implant was added to reduce the threshold to -0.6V and enable circuits to be designed with operation down to 2V. In an effort to save masking steps, all the sources and drains are implanted nonselectively with boron and n^+ sources and drains are selectively implanted with a higher dose of phosphorus. Both implants are done through the gate oxide obviating the need to expose and possibly contaminate the gate edges. The structure is completed with a flowed p-glass, aluminum metallization and plasma deposited SiN cap layer.

* Present Address: Analog Devices, Wilmington, Mass. 01887

The resultant technology has 1 μm junction depths for the source and drain regions, 2 μm electrical channel lengths, $\sim 10^{16}cm^{-3}$ surface concentration with $\pm 0.6V$ active device thresholds, 12 and -20V parasitic n- and p-channel device thresholds, and the ability to shrink in an evolutionary way as patterning technology improves. The remainder of this paper will describe the process, the device properties and examples of circuit performance demonstrated in the Twin-Tub technology.

II. THE PROCESS

Figures 1a-e show the the wafer in cross section as the process develops. Key features of the process are the tub formation, thinox etching, source and drain implantations, window definition in the p-glass, and metallization.

1. Tub Formation

The tubs are formed in a self-aligned manner by first defining an oxide-nitride sandwich (MASK 1). The n-tub is implanted (Fig. 1a) and selectively oxidized. The remaining nitride is removed and the p-tub is implanted self-aligned to the oxide masked n-tub (Fig. 1b). Both tubs are driven to a depth of 5-6 μm. The field oxide is then grown to a thickness of ~1 μm.

2. Thinox Definition

The 1 μm thick field oxide is nonselectively implanted with argon at a low energy(1). This generates a fast etching surface layer which in turn generates a 40° taper of the field oxide during BHF etching (MASK 2) of the areas where gate oxide will be grown (Fig. 2). The definition of the 1 μm oxide with sloped walls requires a 2 μm compensation of the masks. Hence, it is envisioned that this is probably the last generation of design rules where a tapered field oxide will be used. Anisotropic, steep-wall definition or a selective oxidation process for the formation of the gate regions along with steep-wall-tolerant lithography will be required in future technologies.

3. Polysilicon Processing

The gate oxide of 600Å is grown and the resultant structure has a surface doping of $\sim 10^{16}cm^{-3}$ in each tub. The fact that the two tubs have comparable surface concentration is made possible by the Twin-Tub approach. Since n^+ polysilicon is used, the unadjusted thresholds would be 0.6V for the n-channel and -1.9V for the p-channel. The desired p-channel threshold is -0.6V and hence boron (MASK 3) is selectively implanted to reduce the threshold to the desired value. The sensitivity of the threshold to the implant doses is shown in Fig. 3. The polysilicon is then deposited and doped with phosphorus. The polysilicon is defined and etched (MASK 4) with an anisotropic plasma technique(2).

4. Source and Drain Formation

In order to save another mask, the source and drain formation has been done by first implanting boron into *all* sources and drains (Fig. 1c) and then masking (MASK 5) everything but the n^+ (n-channel) sources, drains and contacts. Phosphorus is implanted at

Reprinted from *IEEE Int. Electron Devices Meeting*, pp. 752–755, 1980.

4X the boron dose, overcompensating the existing boron and forming the n^+ sources and drains (Fig. 1d). Subsequent glass flow processing will drive the junctions to ~1 μm deep.

5. Intermediate Oxide

Phosphorus doped glass is deposited (low pressure CVD), flowed, gettered (front of glass and back of wafer) with a phosphorus diffusion and patterned (MASK 6) with plasma etching(3). The windows are reflowed, cleaned and aluminum is then deposited.

6. Aluminum

The aluminum is patterned (MASK 7) with plasma etching, sintered and capped with plasma deposited SiN (4). Finally, vias are opened in the SiN for bonding (MASK 8). The completed device cross-section is shown in Fig. 1e.

III. RESULTANT DEVICE PROPERTIES

1. Active Transistor Properties

The polysilicon gates for both types of transistors are defined in the same step and are designed to have the same nominal polysilicon gate length. Since the n^+ and p^+ source/drain junctions are diffused to the same junction depth (1.0-1.2 μm), the channel lengths are approximately equal. This physical symmetry aids in the control of the ratio of current drive per unit gate length for the two types of transistors. Small variations in etching or thermal drive have proportional effects on both types of transistors and hence cause little variation in their beta ratio. It is notable that while the transistor betas of both types of transistors vary ±35% about nominal, the beta ratio varies less than ±15% for minimum length transistors.

The active channel length for each type of device is nominally 2.0 μm, and is consistent with a 7V maximum supply voltage. For higher voltage operation, the avalanche current in the n-channel transistor becomes significant and longer channel lengths must be employed.

To first order, the threshold voltages of the n- and p-channel transistors are independent. The tubs are independent of the epi doping and determined to first order by the separate tub implants. Second order effects like dopant contamination during tub oxidations and drive-ins can effect one, the other or both of the tub surface concentrations. Furthermore, the p-channel devices have their thresholds reduced by more than 1V with a threshold adjust implant. Only gate oxide thickness and Q_{SS} affect both devices in a correlated way.

2. Parasitic Transistor Properties

The two tubs, outside of the active transistor regions, are covered by ~1 μm of field oxide. The n^+ polysilicon runners over the tubs define parasitic transistors with 13V thresholds over the p-tub and -19V thresholds over the n-tub. The most critical region of the devices is the border of the tubs. Inter-diffusion of the two tubs makes a region of almost 10 μm wide where the surface concentration of both tubs is well below its value far from the edge. The lightly doped region can be inverted at low voltage and hence an adjacent drain must be well removed from the edge. A 7 μm design rule for n^+ diffusion to p-tub edge has been established to account for the out-diffusion of the p dopant at the edge of the tub. Both two-dimensional calculations (Fig. 4) and experimental measurements (Fig. 5) have justified the need for this much space.

IV. CIRCUIT PERFORMANCE AND SIMULATIONS

The circuit performance of the technology has been initially characterized by measuring the propagation delay through, and simulating, ten strings of circuits of various types. The ability to match the simulations of these simple strings of devices with measured propagation delays has been utilized to provide confidence in the computer simulations of complex circuits which proceeded in parallel with the process development. A procedure was established whereby simulation parameters were automatically extracted from test chips on specific wafers. The circuit operation was then simulated using these extracted model parameters. The simulated results were then compared with the actual circuit performance measured on the specific wafers from which the model parameters had been extracted. This procedure was carried out on a large number of wafers(5). The agreement between simulations and measurements was typically 10%, with the simulation being faster.

Distributions of values for model parameters in this technology have been established from routine parameter extraction on many lots. From these distributions, a worst case, nominal, and best case set of technology simulation files was created to predict the circuit performance variations which reflect processing variations. An example of the distribution of circuit performance displayed against the technology simulation files is shown in Fig. 6 for a simple inverter with fan-out of two. Figure 7 illustrates the results for a 3 input NAND gate with fan-out of 6. In each figure, the arrows represent the simulated performance using the worst case, nominal, and best case simulation files.

SUMMARY

A new 8-mask Twin-Tub CMOS technology has been developed which allows separate optimization of each type of transistor. The initial applications are in the field of microprocessors, microcomputers and custom logic. The device properties are well controlled and designed to be scaled smoothly into the improved lithography of the future.

ACKNOWLEDGMENT

The development of a new generation of IC technology requires a large team effort. From the first debates on performance needs to the final transfer to manufacture, many individuals have contributed to the Twin-Tub CMOS technology development. To these colleagues we extend our thanks.

References

(1) R. A. Moline, et al., *IEEE Trans.* **ED-20**, No. 9, p. 840 (September 1973).

(2) T. M. Mayer, J. H. McConville, "Linewidth Control in Anisotropic Plasma Etching of Polycrystalline Silicon," *IEDM*, Paper 3.2, December 1979.

(3) R. A. Porter, W. R. Harshbarger, J. T. Clemens and J. D. Cuthbert, "Plasma Etching of Phosphosilicate Glass," *Electrochem. Soc. Mtg.*, Extended Abst. No. **193**, October 1978.

(4) A. K. Sinha, H. J. Levinstein, T. E. Smith, G. Quintana, S. E. Haszko, *J. Electrochem. Soc.*, **125**, p. 601 (April 1978).

(5) H. H. Lehner (to be published).

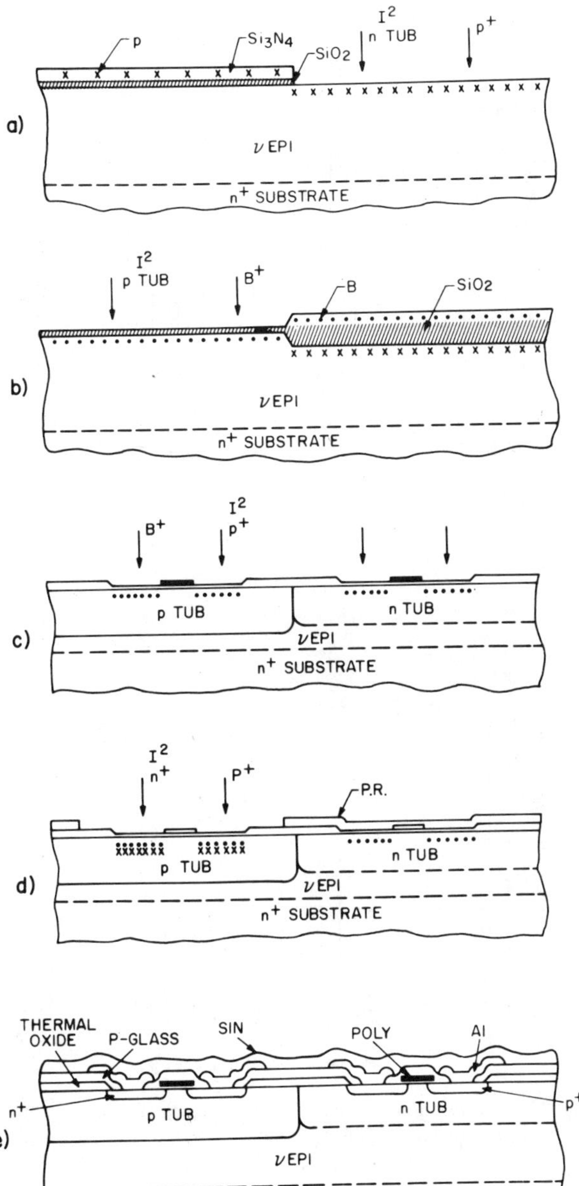

Fig. 1 Cross sections of Twin-Tub devices at several stages of the process.

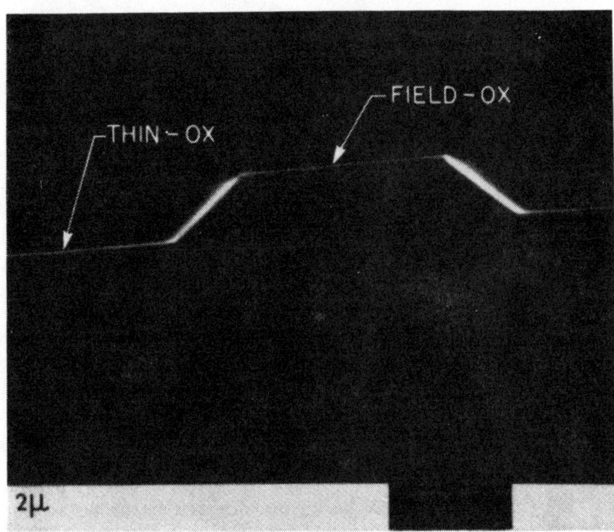

Fig. 2 SEM cross section of a device after the etching of the thinox regions.

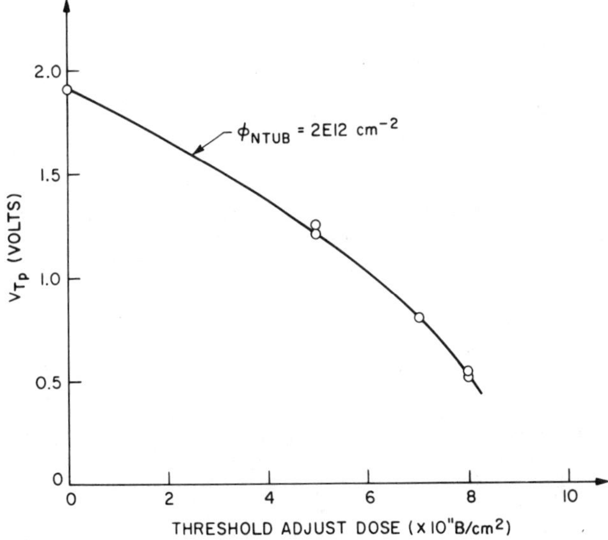

Fig. 3 Sensitivity of the p-channel transistor threshold to n-tub dose and threshold adjust dose.

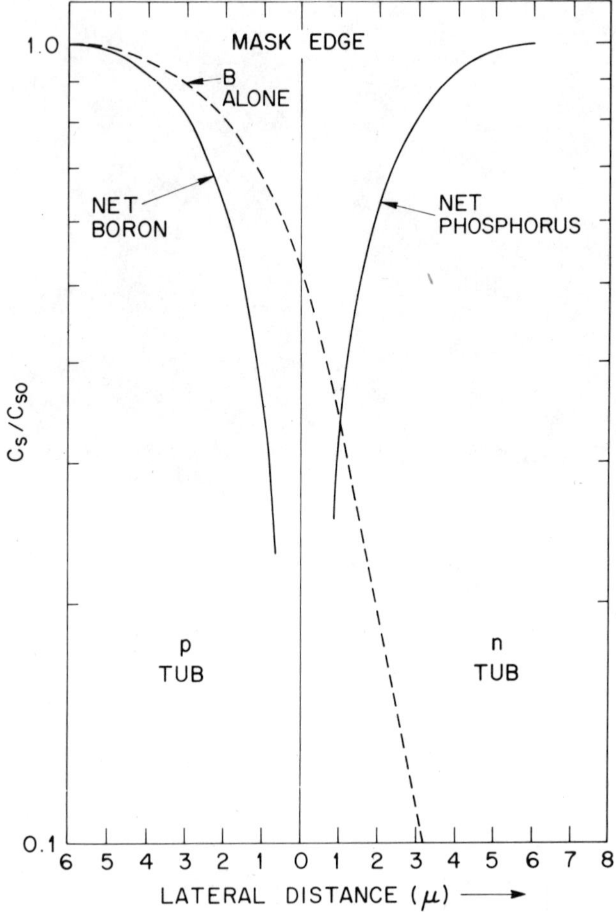

Fig. 4 Two dimensional diffusion profiles of boron and phosphorus at the border of the two tubs.

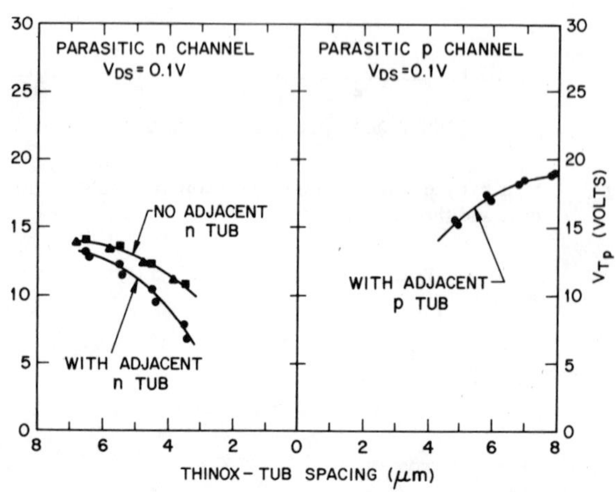

Fig. 5 Threshold voltage of the parasitic n- and p-channel transistors as a function of thinox to tub-edge spacing.

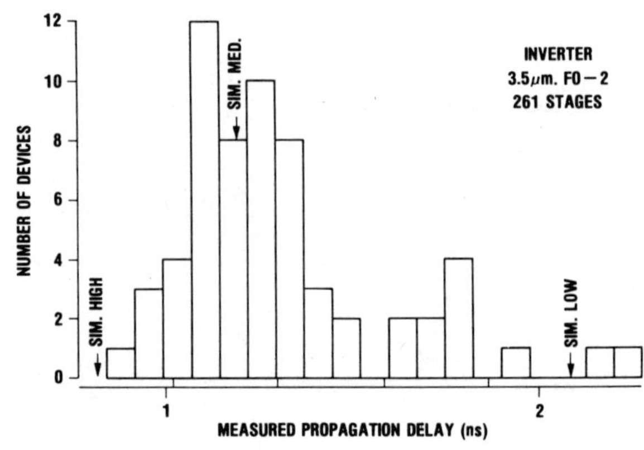

Fig. 6 Distribution of circuit performance displayed against the simulation file limits, inverter with fan-out of 2.

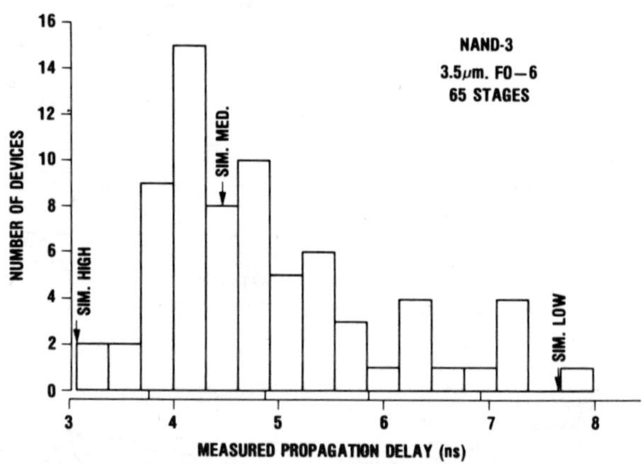

Fig. 7 Distribution of circuit performance displayed against simulation file limits, 3 input NAND with fan-out of 6.

Silicon-Gate n-Well CMOS Process by Full Ion-Implantation Technology

TAKASHI OHZONE, HIDEKICHI SHIMURA, KAZUHIKO TSUJI, AND TAKASHI HIRAO

Abstract—A silicon-gate n-well CMOS process for an application of digital circuits operated by TTL compatible supply voltage was developed. Full ion-implantation technology, a new photolithography technique, n^+-doped polysilicon gate which contain no boron impurities, and thin gate oxide of 65 nm can realize CMOS circuits of 2-μm gate length.

Average impurity concentrations measured from substrate bias effect of MOSFET's and junction depth are in good agreement with those expected from impurity profiles calculated by a simple diffusion theory. So, the process design for CMOS circuits operated by any supply voltage is possible by adjusting threshold voltages.

The process can easily be extended to n-MOS/CMOS process (E/D MOS and CMOS on the same chip), if a photomask to fabricate depletion-type n-MOSFET's is provided.

Manuscript received July 29, 1979; revised December 22, 1979.

The authors are with Semiconductor Research Laboratory, Matsushita Electric Industrial Company, Ltd., 3-15, Yagumo-nakamachi, Moriguchi, Osaka 570, Japan.

I. Introduction

IN STANDARD CMOS processes, n-MOSFET's are placed inside a p well. Recently, a new CMOS process with aluminum gate has been developed to realize analog and analog-digital LSI circuits operated by a supply voltage of 10-30 V, which uses an n well fabricated in a p substrate for the fabrication of p-MOSFET's [1]-[3]. n-well silicon-gate n-MOS/CMOS LSI circuits with a gate length of 4 μm also have been developed [4]. The process technologies combining high packing density n-MOS and low-power CMOS have become important for applications of high-performance digital MOS LSI circuits operated at TTL compatible supply voltage [4]-[5]. n-well CMOS circuits are superior to a p-well CMOS, because substrate bias effect of threshold voltages and parasitic capacitances of source/drain in both n- and p-MOSFET's become lower, resulting from low impurity concentrations in

Reprinted from *IEEE Trans. Electron Devices*, vol. ED-27, pp. 1789–1795, Sept. 1980.

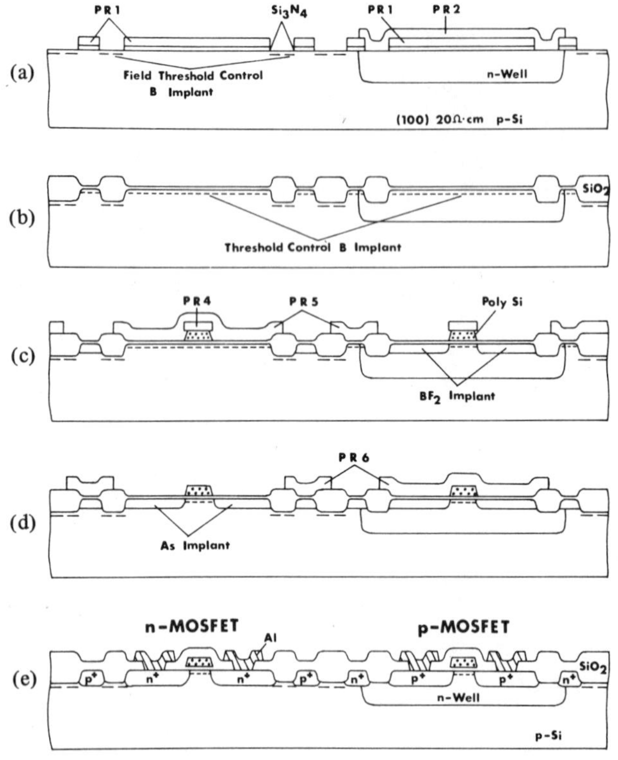

Fig. 1. Process sequence of n^+ polysilicon-gate n-well CMOS.

both p substrate and n well [3]. For improvements in density, performance, and power at lower cost, the size of MOSFET's has been scaled down by refining process technologies and photolithography techniques.

In this paper, a silicon-gate n-well CMOS process technology and a process design technique to realize gate length of 2 μm in both n- and p-MOSFET's are described.

II. Fabrication Process

The process sequence mainly differs from that of a standard silicon-gate CMOS by using an n well for p-MOSFET's in a p substrate and n^+ polysilicon gate in both n- and p-MOSFET's.

According to the scaling theory of MOSFET's [6], the physical parameters, such as gate oxide thickness and diffusion depth of source/drain, must be scaled down to avoid short-channel effects. But it has been known that the threshold voltage of p-MOSFET's with heavily boron-doped polysilicon gate is shifted under some heat treatments, even in thick oxide thickness such as 100-150 nm [7]. To prevent the instability in p-MOSFET's, n^+ polysilicon gates which contain no boron impurities in both n- and p-MOSFET's are introduced and n^+ polysilicon interconnections with low sheet resistance are also realized.

The n^+ silicon-gate n-well CMOS process presented is accomplished with six photomasks and eight photolithography steps, as shown in Fig. 1. In this process, both positive and negative photoresists are used to mask complementary regions by a single photomask. Five ion-implantation steps are employed, for n-well formation, field threshold-voltage adjustment in p substrate, threshold-voltage control of both n- and p-MOSFET's, and source/drain formations of n- and p-MOSFET's. The process conditions are summarized in Table I. A brief description of major process steps is given as follows.

1) The silicon wafer used is p-type (100) orientation having a resistivity of 20 Ω · cm. Phosphorus ions are implanted into Si substrate at 100 keV with doses in the range 0.8-2.0 × 10^{12} cm^{-2} to form an n-well region. A drive-in of the implanted phosphorus is performed at 1158°C for 16 h in an N_2 atmosphere. SiO_2 is completely etched off, SiO_2 of 50 nm is thermally grown all over the substrate, and then Si_3N_4 of 120 nm is deposited by the CVD method. Si_3N_4 is selectively removed by using photoengraving technology while photoresist remains on the Si_3N_4. In the next step, n-well regions are selectively covered by photoresist. The process step described previously is called a two-step photolithography technique, hereafter. Finally, boron ions are implanted into the field regions outside the n well at 60 keV with a dose of 1.0 × 10^{13} cm^{-2}.

2) After the photoresist is removed, a field oxide of 550 nm is formed by LOCOS technology [8]. Si_3N_4 is selectively removed and boron ions are implanted through the SiO_2 of 50 nm at 50 keV with doses of 0-8 × 10^{11} cm^{-2} to control threshold voltages of n- and p-MOSFET's simultaneously [1]. After the SiO_2 of 50 nm is removed, the gate oxide is newly formed by wet oxidation at 900°C to a thickness of 65 nm to avoid gate-oxide contaminations during implantation steps [9].

3) n^+ doped polysilicon of about 350 nm is deposited and selectively etched off to form silicon gates of n- and p-MOSFET's and interconnections. All regions except p^+ diffusion regions such as source/drain of p-MOSFET's and contact areas to p substrate are selectively covered by photoresist while the photoresist on the polysilicon is retained (two-step photolithography technique). BF_2 ions are implanted at 150 keV with a dose of 3 × 10^{15} cm^{-2}. Implantation of boron ions into polysilicon gates of p-MOSFET's is prevented by the photoresist on the polysilicon.

4) After photoresists are removed, n^+ diffusion regions such as source/drain of n-MOSFET's and contact areas to the n well are selectively defined by employing the same photomask used to define p^+ diffusion regions, while an opposite type of photoresist is used. Arsenic ions are implanted at 180 keV with a dose of 4 × 10^{15} cm^{-2}. An n^+ doped polysilicon in the n-MOSFET's regions is doped by additional arsenic implantation, resulting in lower sheet resistance than that in the p-MOSFET's regions.

5) After the photoresist is removed, CVD SiO_2 of 600 nm is deposited and the thermal treatment at 1000°C for 30 min in N_2 atmosphere is performed for the annealing of implanted layers and the densification of CVD SiO_2. Contact windows are opened and aluminum of about 1-μm thickness is evaporated. Finally, aluminum is selectively etched and the sintering step is performed.

The oxide thickness and final junction depth are also

TABLE I
PROCESS STEPS OF n^+ POLYSILICON-GATE n-WELL CMOS.

Process Step	Thickness (nm)	Energy (keV)	Dose (cm^{-2})	Final Junction Depth (µm)
1. Initial Oxide	900			
2. P Implant (n-Well)		100	$(0.8-2)x10^{12}$	3.2-4.8
3. n-Well Drive-In				
4. Si_3N_4 Deposition	120			
5. B Implant (Field of n-MOSFET's)		60	$1x10^{13}$	
6. Field Oxide	550			
7. B Implant (threshold Voltage Control of n- and p-MOSFET's)		50	$(4-8)x10^{11}$	
8. Gate Oxide	65			
9. n^+ Polysilicon	350			
10. BF_2 Implant (p^+ Diffusion)		150	$3x10^{15}$	0.55
11. As Implant (n^+ Diffusion)		180	$4x10^{15}$	0.40
12. CVD SiO_2	600			
13. Annealing				
14. Contact Window				
15. Al Metallization	1000			

shown in Table I. Sheet resistances of polysilicon in n- and p-MOSFET's regions are 45 and 55 Ω/□, respectively. Sheet resistances of n^+ and p^+ diffusion regions are 55 and 60 Ω/□, respectively.

III. ELECTRICAL CHARACTERISTICS OF MOSFET'S

The n-well CMOS process has been applied for the development of digital circuits operated by a TTL compatible supply voltage: 5 ± 0.5 V. Field inversion voltages V_{TFn} and V_{TFp} of n- and p-MOSFET's must satisfy a condition of $V_{TFn} = -V_{TFp} \geqslant 6$ V for both polysilicon and aluminum gates. Fig. 2 shows V_{TFn} and V_{TFp} as a function of an n-well phosphorus dose. A boron dose of 1×10^{13} cm^{-2} for field regions of n-MOSFET's and a phosphorus dose for an n-well higher than 1.0×10^{12} cm^{-2} can satisfy the condition for V_{TFn} and V_{TFp}. A boron implant for threshold-voltage control has little influence on both V_{TFn} and V_{TFp}, because the field oxide of 550 nm prevents boron ions from penetrating into the substrate.

Fig. 3 shows threshold voltages V_{Tn} and V_{Tp} of n- and p-MOSFET's as a function of boron dose for threshold-voltage control. V_{Tn} increases with the increase of boron dose, as is the case in the usual threshold-voltage control of n-MOSFET's. V_{Tp}, in a case when boron implantation is not carried out, increases with the increase of n-well phosphorus dose, and V_{Tp} decreases with the increase of boron dose. Symmetrical

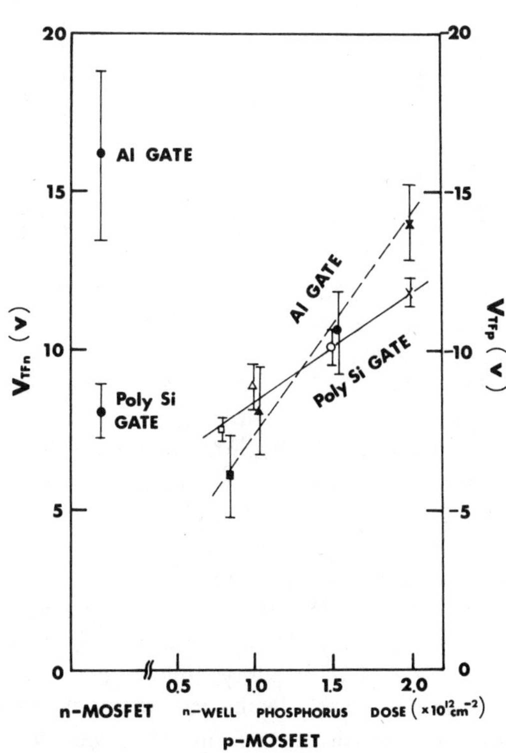

Fig. 2. Field-inversion voltages V_{TFn} and V_{TFp} of n- and p-MOSFET's as a function of implantation dose.

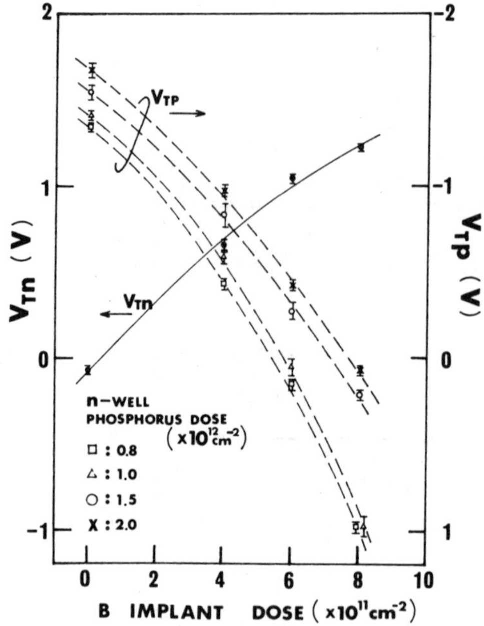

Fig. 3. Threshold voltages V_{Tn} and V_{Tp} of n- and p-MOSFET's as a function of boron dose for threshold-voltage control.

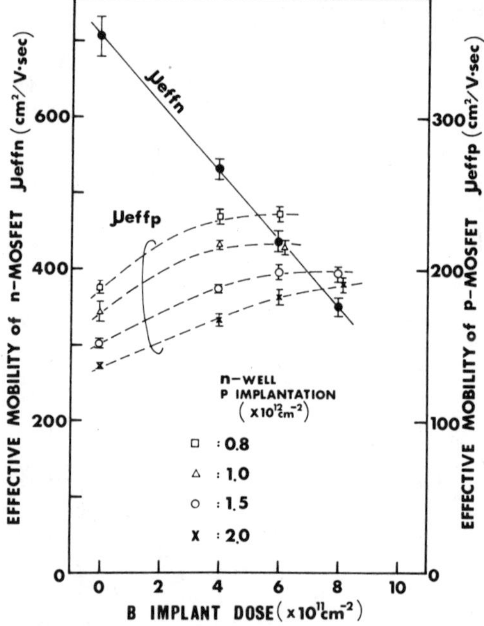

Fig. 4. Effective surface mobilities μ_{effn} and μ_{effp} of n- and p-MOSFET's as a function of boron dose for threshold voltage control.

threshold voltages $V_{Tn} = -V_{Tp} = 0.5\text{–}1.0$ V are favorable for 5-V operation CMOS circuits. For example, doses of 1.5×10^{12} cm^{-2} phosphorus and 4.0×10^{11} cm^{-2} boron result in $V_{Tn} = -V_{Tp} = 0.7$ V.

Fig. 4 shows effective surface mobilities $\mu_{eff\,n}$ and $\mu_{eff\,p}$ in n- and p-MOSFET's. The value of μ_{effn} decreases with the increase of boron dose. The decrease in μ_{effn} is caused by an increase of surface impurity concentration due to the additional boron doping. In the case of p-MOSFET's, μ_{effp} increases with the increase of the boron dose because of counterdoping, which results in lower surface impurity concentration, and consequently higher mobility [3]. For MOSFET's

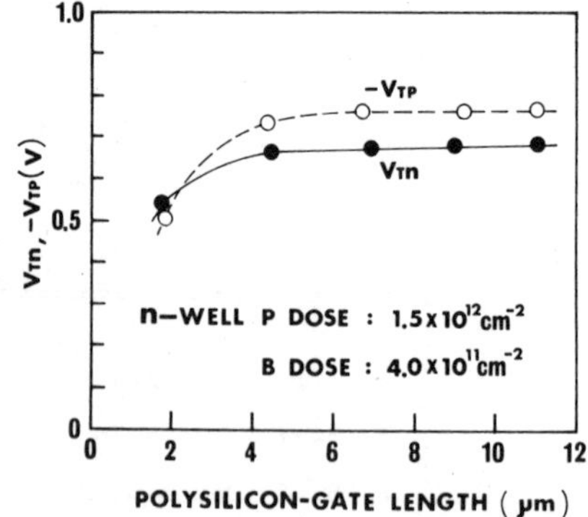

Fig. 5. Threshold voltages V_{Tn} and V_{Tp} as a function of polysilicon-gate length. Phosphorus dose for n-well formation and boron dose for threshold-voltage control are 1.5×10^{12} and 4.0×10^{11} cm^{-2}, respectively.

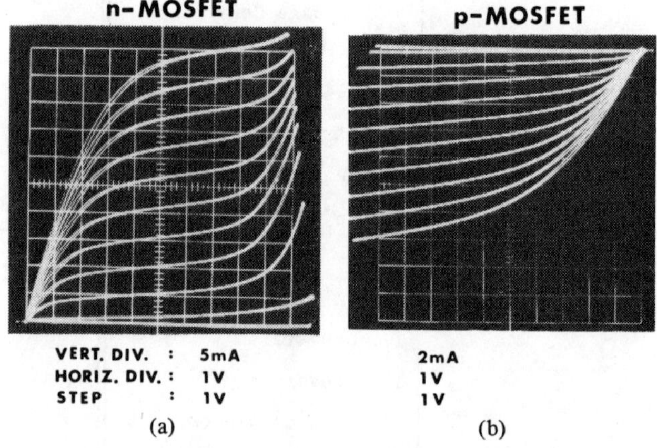

Fig. 6. V-I characteristics of (a) an n-MOSFET and (b) a p-MOSFET of about 1.8-μm polysilicon-gate length with channel width of 160 and 80-μm, respectively. Thickness of gate oxide is 65 nm.

with $V_{Tn} = -V_{Tp} = 0.7$ V, μ_{effn} and μ_{effp} are 550 and 190 $cm^2/V \cdot s$, respectively.

Changes in V_{Tn} and V_{Tp}, depending on polysilicon-gate length, are shown in Fig. 5 for the case of $V_{Tn} = -V_{Tp} = 0.7$ V. A decrease in threshold voltages by 0.15 and 0.25 V is observed in n- and p-MOSFET's of about 2-μm gate length, respectively. Characteristics of decrease in other MOSFET's of different threshold voltages are nearly the same as that shown in Fig. 5. A decrease of V_{Tn} and V_{Tp} in 2-μm gate length MOSFET's calculated by Poon's equation [10] is 0.11 and 0.16 V, respectively. The larger discrepancy in V_{Tp} may be caused by shorter effective channel length than that measured by means of the stain-etching technique, and a gradual change of impurity profile in p^+ diffusion region in contrast to a steep change in n^+ diffusion region.

Fig. 6 shows V-I characteristics of n- and p-MOSFET's of about 2-μm polysilicon-gate length with a channel width of 160 and 80 μm, respectively. The thickness of gate oxide is 65 nm. Breakdown voltages of p-n junctions at gate voltage $V_G = 0$ V are 12 and 22 V for n- and p-MOSFET's, respectively. The breakdown voltage of 12 V is determined by the voltage of the p-n junction between the n^+ diffusion and the channel stop regions under field oxide. Device characteristics shown in Fig. 6 allow fabrication of n-well CMOS circuits

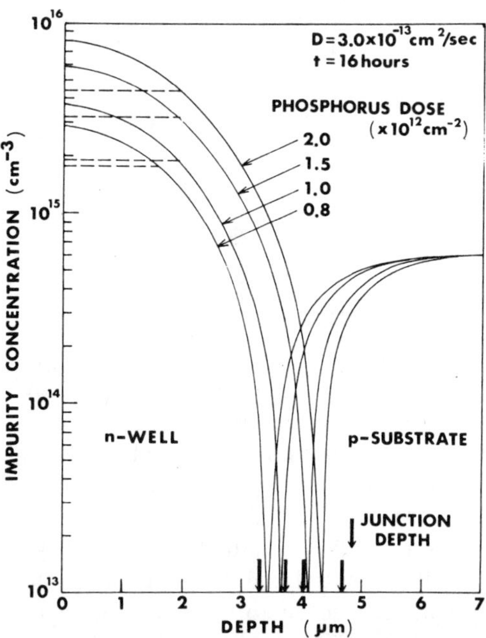

Fig. 7. Comparison between calculated n-well profiles and measured junction depth and effective surface impurity concentration (shown by dotted lines) derived from substrate bias effect without boron dose for threshold-voltage control.

operated by a supply voltage of 5 V to a polysilicon-gate length as short as 2 μm.

IV. Discussion of Impurity Profiles

The process modeling and experimental verification are presented for the impurity profiles of the n well to enable the development of other CMOS processes of different characteristics, such as threshold voltages.

Impurity profiles for different n-well implantation doses without boron implantation for threshold-voltage control are calculated. Calculations are performed as a case of "diffusion from a limited source" [11], assuming all the implanted phosphorus ions are diffused into a p-type substrate of uniform impurity concentration N_{sub}. The impurity profile of an n well N_{well} is given by the following equation:

$$N_{well} = \{(S/\sqrt{\pi D t})\exp(-x^2/4Dt)\} - N_{sub} \quad (1)$$

where S, D, t, and x are the implanted phosphorus dose, diffusion constant of phosphrous, diffusion time, and depth from a surface of p-type substrate, respectively. Fig. 7 shows the calculated profiles for $D = 3.0 \times 10^{-13}$ cm^2/s [12], $t = 5.8 \times 10^4$ s, and $N_{sub} = 0.6 \times 10^{15}$ cm^{-3} (20-$\Omega \cdot$cm, p-type silicon).

Fig. 8 shows the substrate bias effect of p-MOSFET's without boron implantation for threshold-voltage control. When the substrate bias voltage increases, breakdown, at which leakage current through the n well increases abruptly, is observed. It can occur because the n well under the drain is completely depleted. The breakdown voltage becomes lower with lower phosphorus doses. The breakdown voltages are calculated by the model shown in Fig. 9. Spreading of the depletion layer into n well at zero bias voltage between p-type substrate and n well is calculated by a linear graded-junction approximation [13]. In this case, spreading of the depletion layer into n well is about 1.0 μm. The average impurity concentration N_{av} is then calculated by integrating the n-well profile from the edge of the p$^+$ diffusion region to the edge of the depletion spreading in n well. Breakdown voltages are obtained by calculating the voltages at which n well of N_{av} is completely depleted. The calculated breakdown voltages are also shown in Fig. 8 in comparison with the measured breakdown voltages. Fairly good agreement between measured and calculated breakdown voltages is obtained.

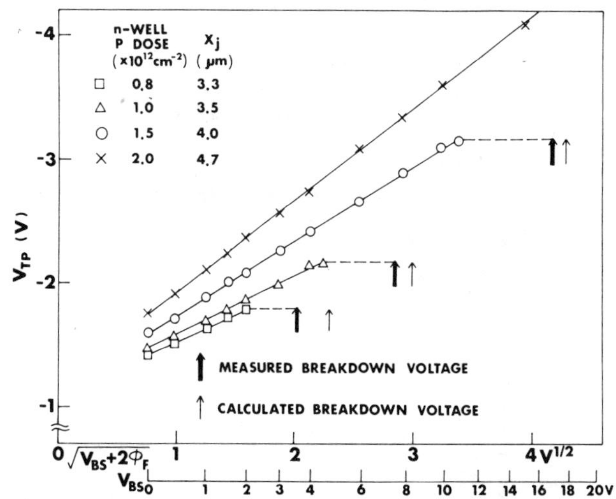

Fig. 8. Substrate bias effect of p-MOSFET's without boron dose for threshold-voltage control in case of a shallow n well.

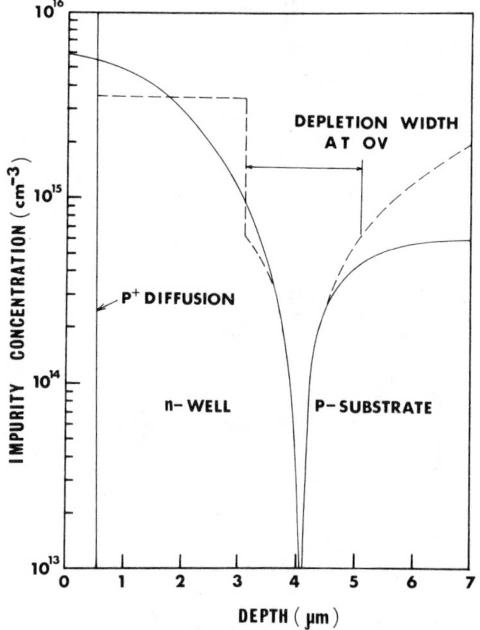

Fig. 9. A model for calculation of depletion-layer spreading in a shallow n well.

The average impurity concentration near the surface of n well $\overline{N_{well}}$ can also be derived from a change in V_{Tp}, depending on substrate bias voltage from the following equation [14]:

$$\Delta V_{Tp} = (\sqrt{2q\epsilon_{Si}\overline{N_{well}}}/C_{OX})\sqrt{V_{BS} + 2\phi_F} \quad (2)$$

where ΔV_{Tp}, q, ϵ_{Si}, C_{OX}, V_{BS}, and ϕ_F are a change of V_{Tp}

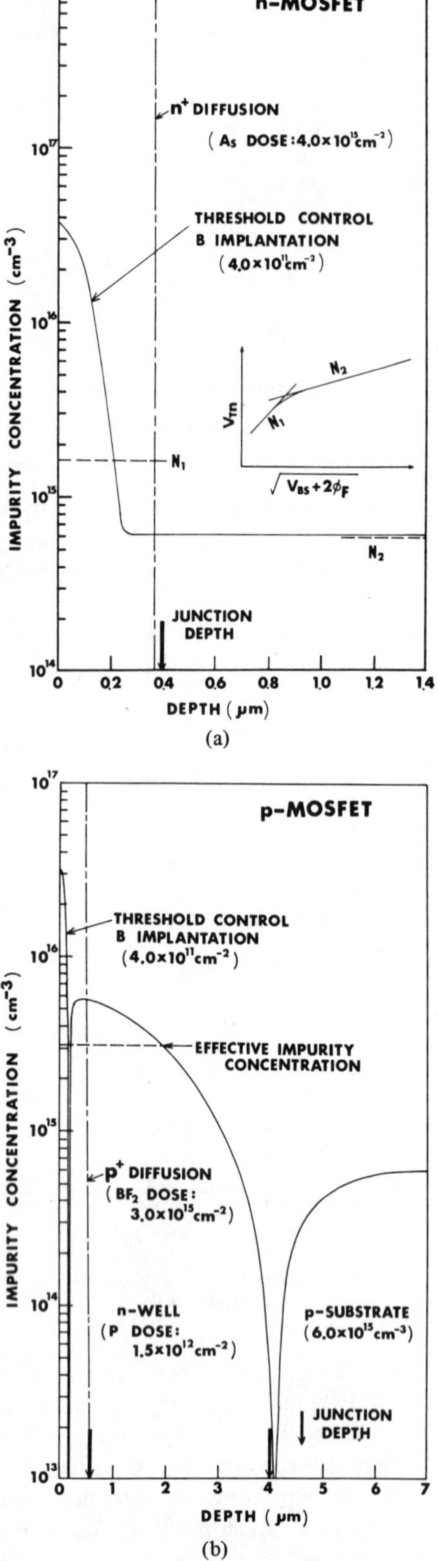

Fig. 10. Calculated impurity profiles of (a) an n-MOSFET and (b) a p-MOSFET with a symmetrical threshold voltages: $V_{Tn} = -V_{Tp} = 0.7$ V. Phosphorus dose for n-well formation and boron dose for threshold-voltage control are 1.5×10^{12} and 4.0×10^{11} cm^{-2}, respectively.

caused by substrate bias, electronic charge, permittivity of silicon, gate capacitance, substrate bias voltage, and Fermi potential, respectively. $\overline{N_{well}}$ obtained from (2) is shown by the dotted lines in Fig. 7. The measured $\overline{N_{well}}$ agrees with $\overline{N_{av}}$,

TABLE II

Comparison Between Effective Surface Impurity Concentration $\overline{N_{well}}$ Measured by Means of Substrate Bias Effect of p-MOSFET's and Average Impurity Concentration N_{av} of n Well Calculated from the Impurity Profiles Shown in Fig. 7

n-Well Phosphorus Implant Dose ($\times10^{12}$cm^{-2})	$\overline{N_{well}}$ ($\times10^{15}$cm^{-3})	N_{av} ($\times10^{15}$cm^{-3})
0.8	1.8	2.1
1.0	1.9	2.6
1.5	3.0	3.8
2.0	4.3	5.0

which is the average impurity concentration of n well as shown in Table II. Junction depths of n well, obtained by means of a stain-etching technique, are also shown in Fig. 7.

Finally, impurity profiles of MOSFET's with $V_{Tn} = -V_{Tp} = 0.7$ V can be estimated. Fig. 10 shows calculated profiles in the cases of (a) an n-MOSFET and (b) a p-MOSFET, respectively. Boron profiles resulting from the implantation of threshold-voltage control and p^+ diffusion profiles are calculated by equations similar to (1). Arsenic impurity profiles are calculated by equations presented in [15]. Measured impurity concentrations (N_1 and N_2) derived from substrate bias effect and junction depths are also shown in Fig. 10. N_1 and N_2 give the impurity concentrations at minimum depletion depth [3] and at the substrate, respectively. The value of the minimum depletion depth is obtained to be about 0.22 μm by assuming that implanted boron impurities of 4×10^{11} cm^{-2} are uniformly distributed to a thickness of 0.22 μm. The calculated impurity concentration of about 2×10^{15} cm^{-3} at the depth of 0.22 μm is in relatively good agreement with that of the measured value of $N_1 = 1.7 \times 10^{15}$ cm^{-3}. Junction depths of n well, and n^+ and p^+ diffusion regions are also in good agreement with those calculated.

V. Conclusion

A silicon-gate n-well CMOS process technology for digital circuits operating at TTL compatible supply voltage is presented. A full ion-implantation process is utilized to develop short-channel MOS LSI devices as short as 2-μm gate length.

The process parameters, such as impurity concentration of n well and junction depths of n well and n^+ and p^+ diffusions, were correlated with the impurity profiles calculated by using simple diffusion theories. It was found that agreement between experiment and theory is excellent.

For example, symmetrical threshold voltages of +0.7 and -0.7 V with effective surface mobilities of 550 and 190 cm^2/V · s for n- and p-MOSFET's are obtained, respectively.

Acknowledgment

The authors wish to thank T. Kondo, Dr. S. Horiuchi, and T. Ishihara for their encouragement, H. Esaki and H. Kawakami for their useful discussions, and I. Kitahiro, T. Komeda, and H. Kuroda for the device fabrication.

References

[1] W. C. Black, Jr., R. H. McCharles, and D. A. Hodges, "CMOS process for high-performance analog LSI," in *IEDM Tech. Dig.*, pp. 331-334, Dec. 1976.

[2] R. Dawson, J. Preisig, J. Carnes, and J. Pridgen, "A CMOS/buried-

n-channel CCD compatible process for analog signal processing applications," *RCA Rev.*, vol. 38, no. 3, pp. 406-435, Sept. 1977.

[3] J. Schneider, G. Zimmer, and B. Hoefflinger, "A compatible NMOS, CMOS metal gate process," *IEEE Trans. Electron Devices*, vol. ED-25, no. 7, pp. 832-836, July 1978.

[4] M. Suzuki, K. Matsumoto, E. Sugimoto, K. Takemae, and H. Yamamoto, "A high-speed NMOS/CMOS single-chip 16-bit microprocessor," in *ISSCC Dig. Tech. Papers*, pp. 206-207, Feb. 1978.

[5] T. Masuhara, O. Minato, T. Sasaki, Y. Sakai, M. Kubo, and T. Yasui, "A high-speed, low-power hi-CMOS 4K static RAM," in *ISSCC Dig. Tech. Papers*, pp. 110-111, Feb. 1978.

[6] R. H. Dennard, F. H. Gaensslen, H. N. Yu, V. L. Rideout, E. Bassous, and A. R. LeBlanc, "Design of ion-implanted MOSFET's with very small physical dimensions," *IEEE J. Solid-State Circuits*, vol. SC-9, pp. 256-268, Oct. 1974.

[7] J. T. Clemens and E. F. Labuda, "Impurity diffusion in SiO_2 layers and related effects on the MOS properties of the Si-gate technology," in *Proc. Electrochem. Soc. Meet.*, pp. 125-127, 1974.

[8] J. A. Appels, E. Kooi, M. M. Paffen, J. J. H. Schatorgé, and W. H. C. G. Verkuylen, "Local oxidation of silicon and its application in semiconductor-device technology," *Philips Res. Rep.*, vol. 25, no. 2, pp. 118-132, Apr. 1970.

[9] T. Ohzone, T. Hirao, K. Tsuji, S. Horiuchi, and S. Takayanagi, "A 2K × 8-bit static RAM," in *IEDM Tech. Dig.*, pp. 360-363, Dec. 1978.

[10] H. C. Poon, L. D. Yau, and R. L. Johnston, "DC model for short-channel IGFET's," in *IEDM Tech. Dig.*, pp. 156-159, Dec. 1973.

[11] A. S. Grove, *Physics and Technology of Semiconductor Devices*. New York: Wiley, 1967, pp. 49-52.

[12] T. Hirao, K. Inoue, S. Takayanagi, and Y. Yaegashi, "Annealing behaviors of phosphorus implanted in silicon," *Ion Implantation in Semiconductors*, F. Chernow, J. A. Borders, and D. K. Brice, Eds. New York: Plenum, 1976, pp. 1-9.

[13] A. S. Grove, *Physics and Technology of Semiconductor Devices*. New York: Wiley, 1967, pp. 163-166.

[14] R. H. Crawford, *MOSFET in Circuit Design*. New York: McGraw-Hill, 1967, pp. 40-46.

[15] K. Inoue, T. Hirao, G. Fuse, and S. Takayanagi, "A practical method for predicting the implanted-diffused arsenic profiles," to be published in *Japan J. Appl. Phys*.

COMPARISON OF BULK SILICON AND SOS FOR VLSI CMOS

A. Aitken

Mitel Semiconductor
Bromont, Quebec, Canada

ABSTRACT

Results will be discussed which indicate that both 2um bulk silicon and SOS/CMOS technologies have potential for nanosecond gate delays. The potential reduction in performance of SOS devices due to the floating substrate will be discussed. The analogue capability of present generation CMOS will be described as it can be very efficiently interfaced on-chip with high speed digital circuitry for combined analogue-digital applications.

INTRODUCTION

CMOS technology is now recognized as a leading contender for future VLSI designs. This paper will consider bulk silicon and SOS/CMOS devices from the following viewpoints.

1) Fabrication and Design of Bulk Silicon and SOS/CMOSFETS
2) Device Characteristics
3) Gate Density
4) Analogue Applications
5) Performance of VLSI Digital Circuits

Due to the dielectric isolation available with SOS/CMOS devices, this technology has been predicted to offer the highest CMOS operating frequencies. Results to date, however, have not indicated any clear advantage of SOS over bulk silicon. Studies of the SOS floating substrate have shown that the potential taken by the substrate during switching can strongly influence the gate propagation delay.

SOS/CMOS requires less processing effort than bulk silicon partly offsetting the high material cost of SOS wafers, however, it will be demonstrated that the number of critical stages are the same and also comparable to that of the high performance H-MOS technologies. To overcome the relatively large area required for CMOS memory, a number of CMOS designs use polysilicon load, n-MOS static memory combined with CMOS peripheral logic. In this case, the low power and high density is maintained without sacrificing speed.

An important development has been the introduction of high performance CMOS operational amplifiers and integration of analogue and digital functions in complex designs. The CMOS analogue designs can be optimized for high gain, low noise or any other parameter required by the application and still maintain high density and speed while drawing low power.

Fabrication and Design of Bulk Silicon and SOS/CMOSFETS

There is no single process flow which is being used to fabricate high performance CMOS devices, however, there is enough similarity between processes to draw conclusions on the relative complexities of the above technologies. The scaling of bulk silicon devices is similar to that discussed for H-MOS, however, in bulk silicon CMOSFETS, the device designer does not have the same freedom to modify substrate concentrations to minimize capacitance and the SOS devices must contend with a minimum feasible thickness of silicon (Fig. 1).

Summarized process flows are shown in Table I.

There are four critical masking stages:

1) Device Well
2) Gate
3) Contacts
4) Aluminium

These are the same critical stages which one requires for H-MOS technology. Other process stages may be added as required, e.g. buried contacts, second layer polysilicon, etc. SOS/CMOS has always used low temperature processing.

Reprinted from *IEEE Int. Electron Devices Meeting*, pp. 244–247, 1980.

The shallower junctions and thinner gate oxides now used for scaled CMOS means that virtually the same low temperature processing (except for P^-Well drive) is now used for bulk silicon. In both technologies, extra implants are required to prevent source-drain punch-through at voltages close to the operating voltage. For SOS, these implants also serve to reduce backside leakage.

Minimizing the parasitic capacitances is fundamental to improving performance. Table II shows the typical capacitances for bulk silicon and SOS/CMOS. With a fan-out of greater than 2, the dominant capacitances are related to gate oxide thickness. The use of over-lapping contacts in bulk silicon minimizes junction areas reducing the contribution of the junction capacitances.

Device Characteristics

Proper design of the channel region using ion implantation minimizes short channel effects and can result in sub-threshold voltage characteristics similar to those of longer channel devices. For bulk silicon, the expected transient characteristics of the MOSFETS are obtained provided there is a firm V_{DD} and V_{SS} close to the P-Channel and N-Channel devices respectively.

A more complicated picture emerges when one studies SOS and the effect of the floating substrate (1). Eaton (2) has shown that there is a gate delay component which depends on the switching period. Kim (3) has studied the transient response of the channel region when a gate potential is applied. The potential of the substrate rises with repetitive switching of the gates reducing the device drive capability. Fig. 2 demonstrates the effect of skewing high and low periods of the input pulse. The output is offset after a number of cycles due to charging of the substrate during the long pulse period and insufficient discharging time during the short pulse period. This phenomena will also give rise to increased gate delays when a node is repetitively switched.

Gate Density

Similar layout design rules can be used for SOS and bulk silicon. The extra constraint which exists with bulk silicon is the sideways diffusion of the P^-Well and the spacing between the P-Well and P^+ diffusion. With the layout usually used, this does not prove to be a major problem in most circuit elements as the area between the P and N-Channel devices is usually used for interconnect. Scaling of bulk silicon CMOS, however, does include scaling of the P^-Well to a depth of 3-4um (4) to improve circuit packing density.

The density advantage of SOS/CMOS lies mainly in cross-coupled flip-flop structures where the P and N-Channel devices can be butted together provided the junction depths are deep enough to prevent any leakage between the N and P substrate regions (Fig. 1). This is not difficult for channel lengths greater than 4um. However, when shorter channel lengths are used, SOS material problems may restrict comparable scaling of the silicon substrate thickness due to defect density and mobility reduction.

Because of the less critical demands on ratioing of CMOS devices c.f. H-MOS, similar logic gate density can be achieved even although the former requires more transistors. The static nature of CMOS logic implies any on-chip memory will also be static. In a number of applications, CMOS memory has been replaced by static N-MOS memory using polysilicon load (5) (Table III). While there is some increase of quiesscient power dissipation, the functional density on complex processor chips is significantly increased without sacrificing the maximum operating frequency.

Analogue Applications

In many VLSI applications, it is necessary to look at integrating analogue and digital functions on the same chip. CMOS is in an excellent position to take advantage of this combination as low power, high performance operational amplifiers can be designed. Dingwall (5) has demonstrated a $20MH_z$ SOS/CMOS A/D converter which dissipates only 50mw at V_{DD} = 5V and $15MH_z$. Because of the large voltage swings required for a number of analogue applications, shorter channel lengths will not always be feasible.

Fig. 3 shows the performance characteristics of an operational amplifier optimized for low noise and fabricated in Mitel's ISO^2CMOS technology. Effective channel lengths of 4um were used to allow operation between 3 volts and 18 volts. CMOS operational amplifiers have the advantage of high input impedance and are comparable in many features to bipolar designs. Higher gain and lower noise can be expected from bulk silicon operational amplifiers c.f. SOS/CMOS designs, however, the latter benefits from the complete electrical isolation which is achievable between circuit elements.

Performance of VLSI Digital Circuits

A number of performance comparisons of bulk silicon vs SOS/CMOS have been published (6) (7) which provide conflicting evidence on the relative merits of the two technologies.

Fig. 4 shows the results for Mitel's high performance CMOS and published SOS results. This is not a precise comparison but clearly both technologies have the capability to achieve nanosecond gate delays.

A more meaningful result is obtained by looking at the output of a ÷ 2 dynamic divider designed and characterized by Cadwallader and Sims (8) and fabricated with effective channel lengths of 1.5um on Mitel's technology. Fig. 5 shows the $250MH_z$ output signal obtained with a $500MH_z$ input signal.

Using the above results, the performance of CMOS (assuming bulk silicon and SOS to be similar) vs high speed bipolar technologies is shown in Fig. 6. At 5um geometries, the performance is comparable to low power Schottky while at 2um geometries ECL gate delays are being approached.

The CMOS power-speed product for nanosecond gate delays is less than 1 picojoule so thousands of gates can be integrated on a chip while still maintaining power dissipation within levels which are acceptable for standard packaging techniques.

SUMMARY

The high performance of bulk silicon and SOS/CMOS technology has been demonstrated. SOS/CMOS will maintain a theoretical advantage over bulk silicon but this is not substantiated to-date by experimental results. The successful development of CMOS analogue techniques has opened a wide array of applications for low power analogue-digital circuits.

ACKNOWLEDGEMENTS

I would like to thank my colleagues at Mitel Semiconductor for their contributions to this paper, in particular J. Morris and C. Groves for the results on the performance of the bulk silicon CMOS technology and T. Foxall and M. Foster for their results on the operational amplifiers. I would also like to thank R.W. Cadwallader and J.R. Sims of G.T.E. Sylvania for permission to use their results on the CMOS 2um technology and Dr. C.S. Kim of Digital Equipment Corporation for permission to use his results on the effect of the SOS floating substrate.

REFERENCES

(1) Y.A.El-Mansy,D.M.Caughey,"Characterization of Silicon-on-Sapphire IGFET Transistors," IEEE Trans.Electron Devices, Vol.ED-24,no. 9, pp.1148-1153:Sept. 1977.

(2) S.S.Eaton,B.Lalevic,"The Effect of a Floating Substrate on the Operation of Silicon-on-Sapphire Transistors," IEEE Trans.Electron Devices, Vol.ED-25,no. 8, pp.907-912:Aug. 1978.

(3) C.S.Kim, Private Communication.

(4) Y.Sakai,T.Masuhara,O.Minato,N.Hashimoto,"High Packing Density High Speed CMOS (Hi-CMOS) Device Technology," Japanese Jnl. of Appl. Physics, Vol.18,supplement 18-1,pp.73-78: 1979.

(5) O.Minato,T.Masuhara,T.Sasaki,Y.Sakai,M.Kubo, K.Uchibori,T.Yasui,"A High Speed Low-Power Hi-CMOS 4K Static Ram," IEEE Trans.Electron Devices, Vol.ED-26,no. 6, pp.882-885.

(6) A.G.F.Dingwall,"Monolithic Expandable 6 Bit $20MH_z$ CMOS/SOS A/D Converter," IEEE Jnl. of Solid-State Circuits, Vol.SC-14, no. 6, pp.926-932:Dec. 1979.

(7) A.Aitken,A.T.P.MacArthur,R.Abbott,J.D.Morris, "The Relative Performance and Merits of CMOS Technologies," I.E.D.M. Digest,pp.327-340:1976.

(8) S.Laguchi,H.Tango,K.Maeguchi,L.M.Dang, "Performance of Downward Scaled CMOS/SOS," I.E.D.M. Digest, pp.589-593:1979.

(9) R.W.Cadwallader,J.R.Sims, Private Communication.

Table I
2um Technology Process Flow

SOS/CMOS

1) Initial Oxidation (1000°C)
2) Mask and Define Active Regions
3) Mask and Boron Implant (P^-islands)
4) Gate Oxide (900°C)
5) Mask and Phos. Implant for P-MOS V_{DS}
6) Boron Implant for P-MOS V_T
7) Mask and Deep Boron Implant for N-MOS V_{DS} and Backside Leakage Control

Bulk Silicon/CMOS

1) Initial Oxidation (1000°C)
2) Mask and Boron Implants (P^-Well)
3) P^-Well Drive-In (1100°C)
4) SiO_2 + Si_3N_4 Deposition
5) Mask and Define Active Regions
6) N^-Field Implant
7) Mask and Boron Implant P^-Field Region
8) Field Oxidation (1000°C)
9) Gate Oxidation (900°C)
10) Mask and Phos. Implant for P-MOS V_{DS}
11) Boron Implant for P-MOS V_T
12) Mask and Boron Implant for N-MOS V_{DS} and V_T Control

Bulk Silicon and SOS/CMOS

13) Polysilicon Deposition
14) Mask and Define Gates
15) Mask and Phosphorus or Arsenic Implant (N+)
16) Mask and Boron Implant (P+)
17) Diffusion (900°C)
18) Phos. Glass Deposition Plus Anneal
19) Mask and Etch Contacts
20) Al. Deposition
21) Mask and Etch Al.
22) Alloy

Table II

	Bulk Silicon (Si)/SOS	Node cap.(Pf)
Node	cap(Pf)/u^2	
Gate	$6.7x10^{-4}$	$2x10^{-2}$
$P^+ - N^-$	$1.4x10^{-4}$(Si)	$.9x10^{-2}$(Si)
$N^+ - P^-$	$2.0x10^{-4}$(Si)	$.9x10^{-2}$(Si)
Al Interconnect	$2.0x10^{-5}$(Si)	$3.5x10^{-2}$(Si)
Al-Poly (Diff.)	$6.0x10^{-5}$	$.7x10^{-2}$
Gate/Source-Drain	$1.1x10^{-4}$Pf/u	$.16x10^{-2}$

Table III

Cell Design	Area(u^2)
Bulk Silicon CMOS 6T cell	2400
SOS/CMOS 5T cell	1140
N-MOS Poly. Si. Load	600

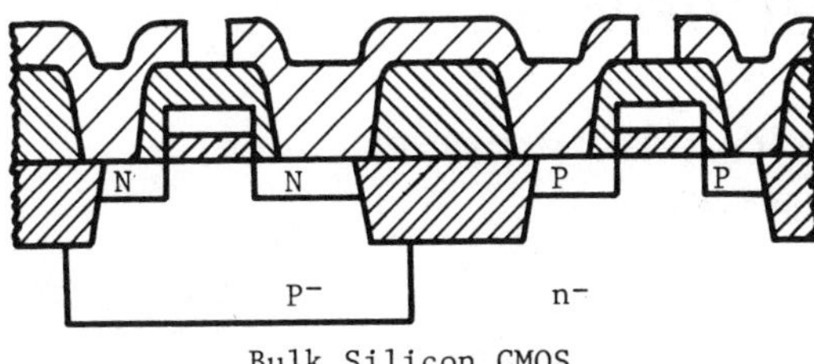

Bulk Silicon CMOS

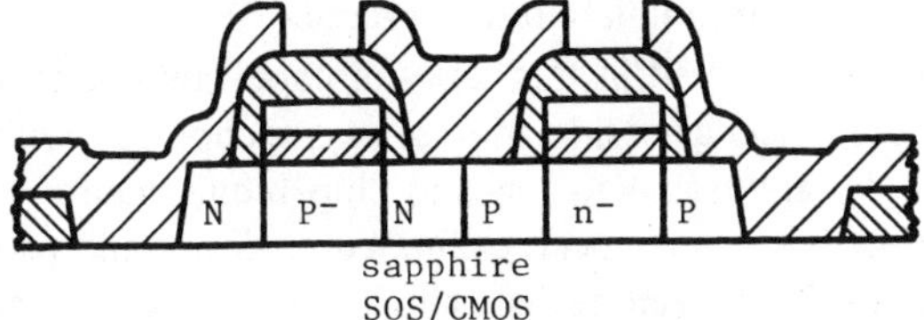

sapphire
SOS/CMOS

Fig. 1 X-section of Bulk Silicon and SOS/CMOSFETS

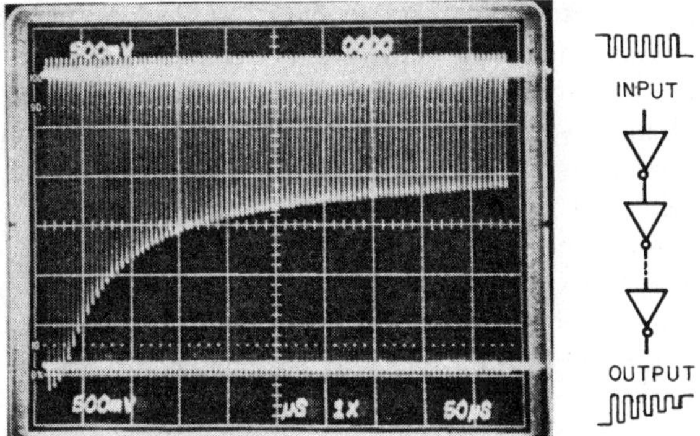

Fig. 2 Output of SOS/CMOS Inverter Chain

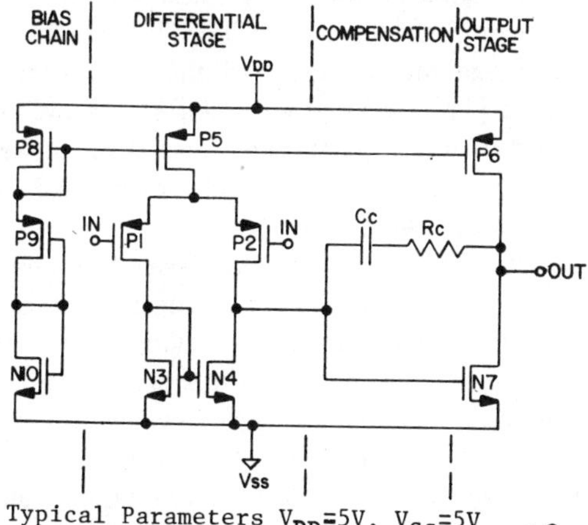

Typical Parameters V_{DD}=5V, V_{SS}=5V	
Input Impedance	$10^{10}\Omega$
Offset Voltage	5mV
Open Loop Gain	75db
Unity Gain Bandwidth	1.5MH_z
Common-Mode Input Range	±4.0V
Common-Mode Rejection Ratio	75db
Slew Rate	2V/μs
Equivalent Input Noise Voltage	75nv/$\sqrt{H_z}$
Power Dissipation	1mw
Layout Area	100 sq.mils

Fig. 3 Performance characteristics of ISO^2-CMOS™ Operational Amplifier

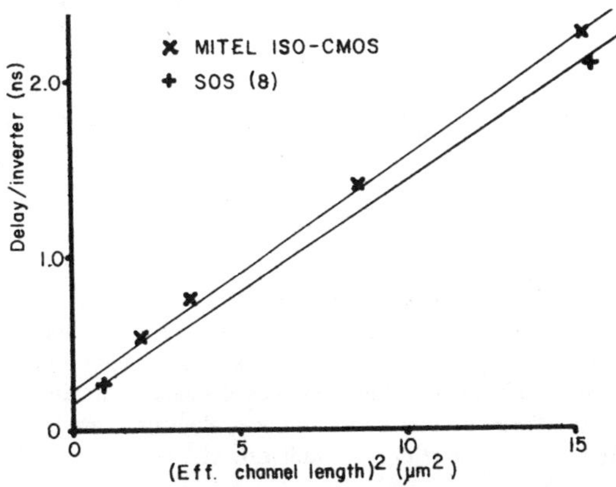

FIG. 4 COMPARISON OF BULK SILICON AND SOS/CMOS PERFORMANCE

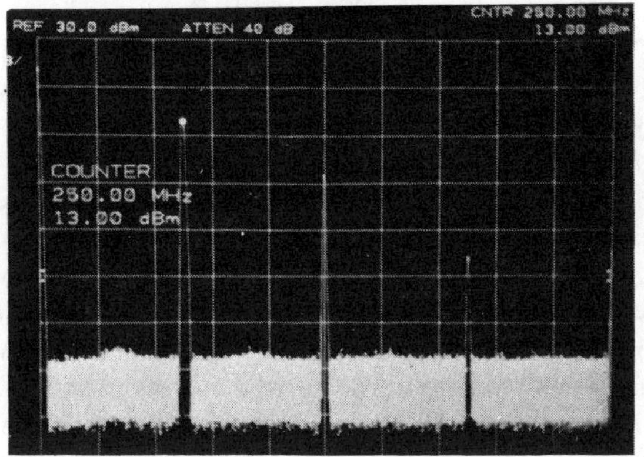

Fig. 5 Output of CMOS ÷ 2 divider

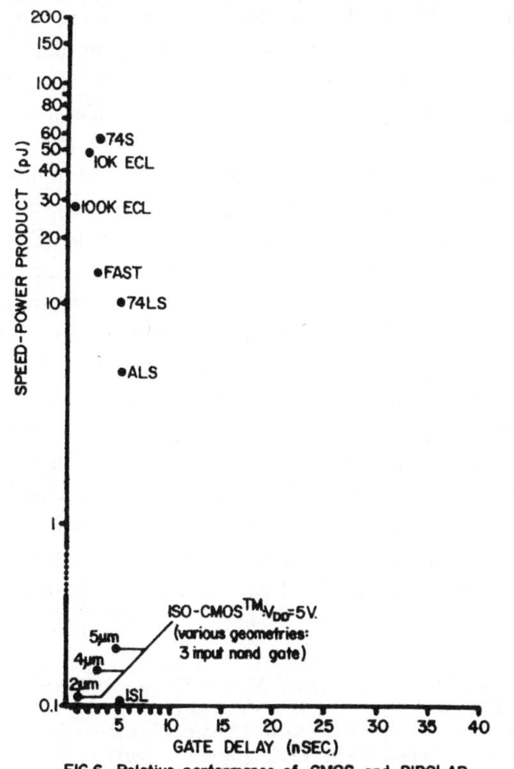

FIG.6 Relative performance of CMOS and BIPOLAR logic families

1 μm MOSFET VLSI Technology: Part I—An Overview

HWA-NIEN YU, MEMBER, IEEE, ARNOLD REISMAN, CARLTON M. OSBURN, AND DALE L. CRITCHLOW, MEMBER, IEEE

Abstract—**This paper attempts to provide a technical perspective for a 1 μm MOSFET VLSI technology described in the technical papers that follow. Highlights of various aspects of the technology development are discussed briefly. These include device design, circuit design, hot-electron effects, processing technology, electron-beam lithography, metal silicide interconnections and radiation effects.**

I. Introduction

THE EXTENSION of any semiconductor technology to small dimensions brings with it a host of new technology, physics, and engineering challenges. The potential rewards in logic and memory applications are performance and cost improvements which in addition to the normal desire to overcome technological problems have been the driving force from the beginning. The series of papers [1] - [7] following this overview describe the development of a 1 μm MOSFET technology in a project called the logic and array test vehicle (LATV) containing two comprehensive test chips, a device test chip, and a circuit test chip. It is a feasibility study to determine what the problems are and how they can be overcome. The study was aimed primarily at demonstrating the extendibility of silicon-gate MOSFET technology to 1 μm dimensions for VLSI applications. It also serves as a vehicle to consolidate and firm up device and circuit designs, processing technologies, reliability issues, and electron-beam exposure ground rules and to expose reliability issues. Logic circuit performance is examined using NOR circuit ring oscillators at both room and liquid nitrogen temperatures. Array logic performance is demonstrated by measuring cycle times of programmed logic array (PLA) microprocessor cross sections implemented in dynamic and static configurations. Package-induced delays and inductance-related noise problems due to fast rise times pose peripheral problems of equal magnitude which are important but have not been addressed here. Related to the packaging issues, heat dissipation concerns must also be taken into serious consideration.

At the 1 μm or sub-μm lithography level, direct electron-beam writing appears to be the most suitable method for patterning complex VLSI chips at the present time. Although optical lithographic techniques including deep UV [8] and X-ray lithography [9] are under intensive investigation, the use of the direct writing electron beam is still not being seriously challenged in laboratory practice.

The work discussed in this series of papers represents the result of a total engineering address of a technology which appears to be applicable to realistic chip requirements. Major technology issues have been examined critically and engineering designs have been realistically implemented. Analytical and experimental work has been aimed at demonstrating the basic feasibility of a 1 μm MOSFET technology within the dimensional control and tolerance limits defined in the overall study. It is anticipated that once the process technology base has been more thoroughly exercised to obtain more information on tolerances, specific designs of MOSFET chips or systems at 1 μm minimum lithography can be implemented even more aggressively than has been attempted here, in terms of density and performance. For example, based on the results to be described it appears reasonable that the 1.3 ± 0.3 μm channel length design studied here can be enhanced to 0.8 ± 0.2 μm with significant performance and possible density advantages resulting.

II. Device Design

Device design dictates some of the primary requirements of a high-performance high-density MOSFET technology. The basic device design method involved the application of the scaling principle [10] modified by potential improved designs due to the use of ion implantation. Part II of this series of papers discusses in detail these device designs and presents experimental verification of them.

Fig. 1 is a photomicrograph of the device test chip image. Both enhancement- and depletion-mode device test sites with a range of channel lengths and channel widths, such as the one shown in Fig. 2, are incorporated in this image to provide an assessment of the ability to fabricate hardware having required dimensional tolerances and electrical parameters. Additional test sites are present to provide information on flat-band voltage, leakage current, sheet resistivity, hot-electron effects, and contact resistance.

It was recognized in the course of developing the scaling theory [10] that we cannot geometrically scale the weak inversion region of the turnon characteristic (the temperature-dependent subthreshold conduction) of a MOSFET as operating voltages are scaled along with the other structural and electrical parameters. A point is reached at which we can no longer implement a practical design for certain types of dynamic circuits such as dynamic RAM's which require low

Manuscript received December 4, 1978.

H.-N. Yu, A. Reisman, and C. M. Osburn are with the IBM Thomas J. Watson Research Center, Yorktown Heights, NY 10598.

D. L. Critchlow was with the IBM Thomas J. Watson Research Center, Yorktown Heights, NY 10598. He is now with IBM, Data Systems Division, Hopewell Junction, NY 12533.

Reprinted from *IEEE J. Solid-State Circuits*, vol. SC–14, pp. 240–246, Apr. 1979.

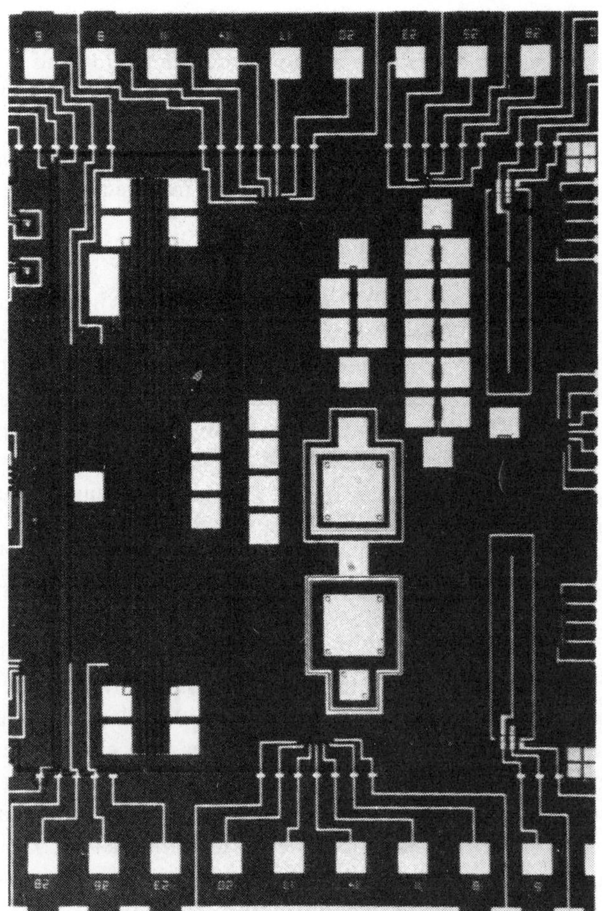

Fig. 1. Photomicrograph of the LATV device test chip.

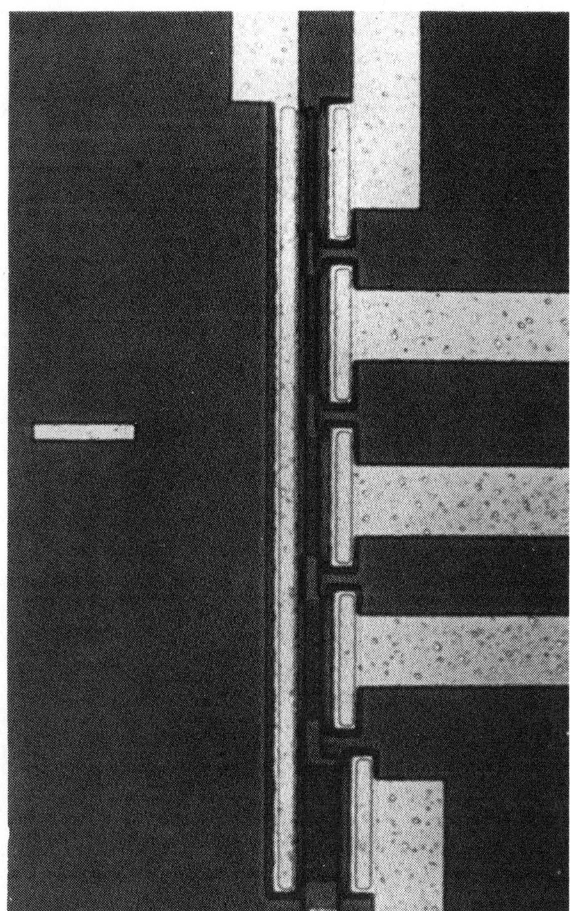

Fig. 2. Photomicrograph of a typical device test site.

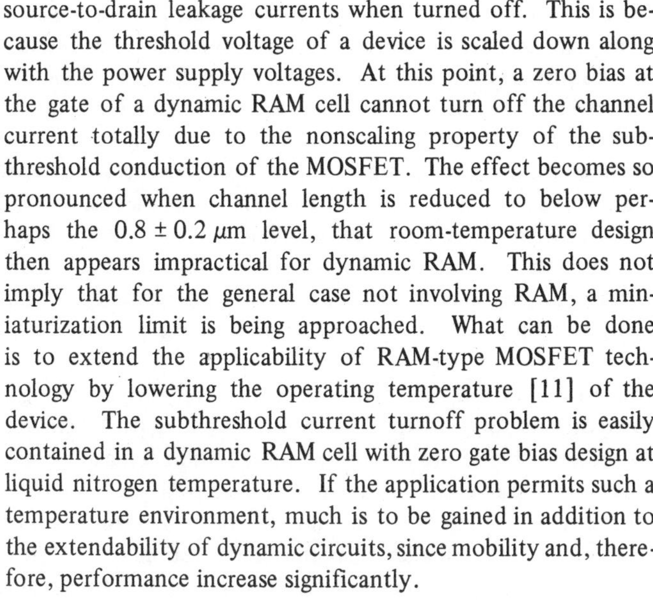

source-to-drain leakage currents when turned off. This is because the threshold voltage of a device is scaled down along with the power supply voltages. At this point, a zero bias at the gate of a dynamic RAM cell cannot turn off the channel current totally due to the nonscaling property of the subthreshold conduction of the MOSFET. The effect becomes so pronounced when channel length is reduced to below perhaps the $0.8 \pm 0.2\ \mu m$ level, that room-temperature design then appears impractical for dynamic RAM. This does not imply that for the general case not involving RAM, a miniaturization limit is being approached. What can be done is to extend the applicability of RAM-type MOSFET technology by lowering the operating temperature [11] of the device. The subthreshold current turnoff problem is easily contained in a dynamic RAM cell with zero gate bias design at liquid nitrogen temperature. If the application permits such a temperature environment, much is to be gained in addition to the extendability of dynamic circuits, since mobility and, therefore, performance increase significantly.

III. Reliability

Gate-oxide breakdown and contact metallurgy are two of the major reliability concerns in devices with reduced dimensions. Gate-oxide reliability or wear-out phenomena [12], [13], in terms of time to failure t, can be expressed as

$$t = t_{\max} \exp\left[A(E_{BD} - E_i)\right]$$

where $t_{\max}$ is the wear-out time for an intrinsic oxide, E_{BD} is the experimentally observed breakdown field of the oxide, E_i is the intrinsic oxide breakdown field, and A is a constant. For given $t_{\max}$, it has been determined experimentally that the time to failure t is about 1 decade for each MV/cm difference between intrinsic and experimentally observed breakdown field. When the thickness of the oxide is decreased, the breakdown field increases [14]. As a result, the time to failure of a thin oxide increases, favoring thin-oxide devices for a given field.

However, the wear-out phenomenon is also electrode dependent. Fig. 3 is a replot of data published previously in the literature [12], [13]. It gives a comparison of maximum time to failure of Al and Si electrodes on MOS capacitor structures. The results of such wear-out studies on simple capacitor structures can only provide relative data on the reliability behavior of different material systems. With this understanding, it is clear from the results of the cited study that for a given applied field on the MOS structures, those with silicon electrodes resist wear-out about 3 orders of magnitude in time better than do aluminum electrodes over a 25 nm oxide layer. Thus, in addition to the well-known advantages of self-aligned silicon-gate MOSFET technology for achieving greater density and superior performance, the enhanced resistance to wear-out of an oxide layer further strengthens the case for employing a silicon-gate approach in scaled-down devices. One of the technological

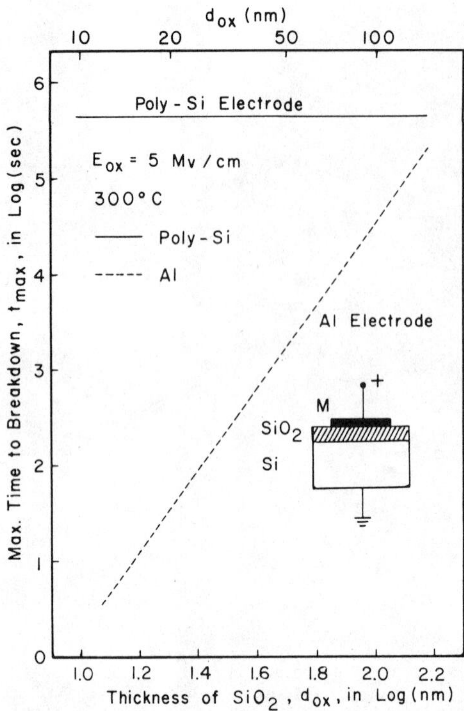

Fig. 3. Maximum time to breakdown verus thickness of SiO_2 with Al and Si electrodes in MOS capacitor structures.

problems associated with scaled-down structures is the making of contacts which can withstand the necessary postfabrication annealing procedures. The specific concern with Al contact metallurgy to shallow junctions is the penetration of the metal through the junction due to interdiffusion of Al and Si during heat treatment at around 400°C (and perhaps higher temperatures) while trying to eliminate process-induced trapping centers and interface states. Alternate solutions to this problem include the use of deeper junction depths in the contact region, buried polysilicon contact layers, Al-Si metallurgy, and a barrier metallurgy interposed between Al and the contact region. While discussions continue over the pros and cons of each approach, the choice of a Pd_2Si barrier metallurgy layer [15] stems basically from its process simplicity and good contact resistance characteristics. Although the use of a Pd_2Si barrier metallurgy does not prevent the dissolution of Si in Al, the reaction is sufficiently slow and uniform so as not to cause junction degradation during short-term heat treatments. For future extensions certainly, and even to improve the present status, an even better refractory contact metallurgy would be desirable. This will become more apparent in the discussion on annealing necessary to minimize radiation effects.

Contact resistance is fast becoming of considerable importance because it may represent a fundamental limit or at least a major obstacle that must be contended with as device dimensions continue to shrink [16]. The resistance of a 1 μm contact to silicon could range between 1000 and 10 Ω if contact interfacial resistivity falls into the 10^{-5} to the 10^{-7} $\Omega \cdot cm^2$ range, respectively. A 0.25 μm^2 contact could exhibit values ranging from 4000 to 40 Ω. For the 1 μm MOSFET technology, the smallest contact holes gave contact resistances of 10-20 Ω which are small compared to circuit impedances. However, the design problem for MOSFET's could be serious if additional problems such as process contamination and interfacial imperfections were to come into the picture. Thus, like temperature, contact resistance is a potential limit to be considered, and work is needed to understand the limits imposed by surfaces and the manner in which surfaces are processed.

IV. Threshold Stability

Threshold voltage shifts caused by hot-electron injection and trapping have been discussed extensively in the literature. These phenomena are addressed further in Part IV of this series of papers. In general, the stability of device threshold voltage is related to applied gate, source, and drain voltages, the current and leakage levels in the device, the emission probability of electrons across the Si-SiO_2 interface, and the field-dependent trap cross sections and trap densities present in the insulator. Given a good quality of insulator, i.e., one with a reasonably reproducible number of traps, proper circuit design can control the amount of threshold voltage shift experienced by scaled devices so as to provide adequate electrical stability over a required chip lifetime with an assumed duty cycle to contend with. In addition to "normal" hot-electron effects, the most advanced processing techniques, e.g., electron-beam exposure, plasma based etching and deposition, etc., pose some new hot-electron-related problems, because ionizing radiation can generate significant levels of additional traps, both charged and neutral, in the gate insulator. The positively charged traps are readily discernible by flat-band measurements on completed devices, but the neutral traps only become evident under long-term electrical stress as they are filled by electrons injected into the gate insulator. Fortunately, process-induced radiation damage up to the metal level is annealed during normal processing, and it is only the damage introduced at the metal(s) level that need concern us. This level cannot, at present, be subjected to high enough annealing temperatures to remove all of the electron-beam exposure damage introduced at the last patterning stage. This topic has been discussed earlier [17] and is the focus of Part VIII of this series.

Because of the importance of radiation effects, it is valuable at this point to place the problem in proper perspective and point out methods of attacking it. The probability of trapping is to the first order proportional to the product of the density of a trap (N) and its cross section (σ), $N\sigma$. The potential threshold shift associated with such trapping however, is, proportional only to the density of a given trap. When trapping experiments are conducted on radiation-damaged insulators, it is observed that positively charged traps are annihilated first. This implies that since the neutral trap cross section is some 100 times smaller than the cross section of a positive trap, the density of neutral traps is less than 100 times more than the density of positive traps. In fact, from trap filling experiments, the densities are found to be comparable. Fig. 4 attempts to show these combined effects. From Fig. 4 it is seen that in order to obtain an equivalent threshold shift of 0.1 V, it is necessary to inject electrons (at a constant injection rate) 100 times longer to annihilate the same number of neutral as positive traps. Thus, the major concern with process-

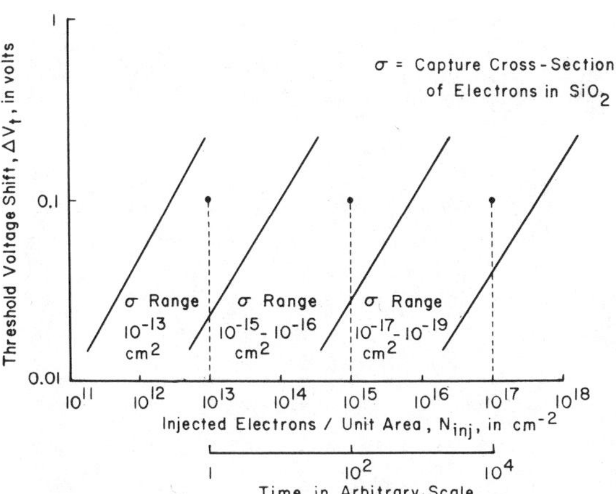

Fig. 4. Trapping dependence of threshold voltage shift as a function of electrons injected or time.

induced radiation damage is positive traps. Fortunately, while neutral traps require annealing temperatures in excess of 550°C, a large fraction of the radiation-induced positive traps are annealable at 400°C. The net is that for present very advanced technology applications, such as LATV, electron-beam-induced radiation-damage effects can be contained by design and process accommodations. Nonetheless, it is the case that such effects do cause a possible decrease in either useable chip lifetime and/or performance. For example, lowering operating voltages to reduce the electron injection rate into the insulator results in a performance degradation. There are, for the future, a number of ways the problem can be greatly minimized or eliminated completely. These involve application of one or more of the combination of the following to chip design and processing: a) employing electron-beam resists with greater sensitivity, e.g., 10^{-6} C/cm^2 exposure flux, b) developing barrier and/or interconnect and contact metallurgies which enable higher temperature postprocess annealing, and c) designing devices with smaller field gradients. All of these methods are being currently pursued along with others discussed in Part VIII.

V. Dimensional Control

One of the assumptions inherent in the scaling principle is that dimensional variations or tolerances can be scaled proportionately in fabricating smaller devices. Therefore, it is extremely important to keep dimensions under good control during patterning and etching. Table I lists the critical minimum mask dimensions to be patterned at various mask levels. Even though the patterning of 1 μm linewidths and spacing can be achieved, they were not employed at mask levels other than the contact hole level. Essential steps of the fabrication process follow generally those described previously in the fabrication of an 8 kbit memory chip [18]. Refined processes are discussed in Part V of this series. In addition, electron-beam patterning of resist using automatic proximity correction has been employed to minimize dimenional distortions due to electron scattering, as described in Part VI of this series.

Reactive ion etching (RIE) [19] appears to be the most suitable way for accurately delineating or etching small device structures without undercutting problems. At present, RIE does not provide the etch-rate selectivity between silicon and

TABLE I
Minimum Linewidth Used at Various Mask Levels of the LATV Technology

Minimum n^+-region linewidth:	1.75 μm
Minimum polysilicon linewidth:	1.5 μm
Minimum contact hole linewidth:	1.0 μm
Minimum metal linewidth:	1.25 μm
(Device channel length L:	1.3 ± 0.3 μm)

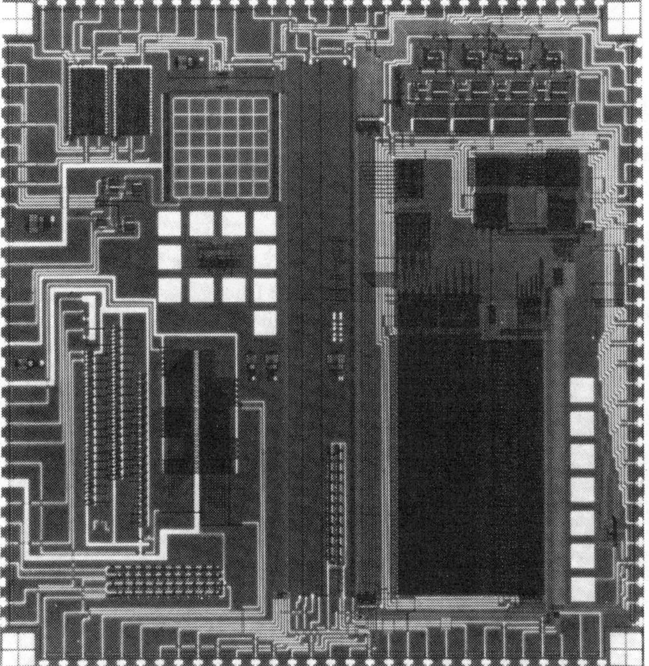

Fig. 5. Photomicrograph of the LATV circuit test chip.

SiO_2 that is possible with chemical etching. Recent advances in the RIE technique with the addition of H_2 to CF_4 [20], however, do provide an etch-rate ratio of SiO_2 to silicon of 35 to 1 or more. This new technique is now being employed to etch contact holes with good results.

VI. Circuit Design and Performance

Extensive effort has been devoted to the design and implementation of VLSI circuits in a logic system-like environment with the 1 μm MOSFET technology. Part III of this series gives a comprehensive treatment of the logic circuit design methodology in terms of random and array logic. The random logic chip design is simulated by using a particular "Weinberger" type of layout [21] in a ring oscillator in order to examine NOR circuit performance in an 8000-circuit chip. In order to maximize the performance capability of the 1 μm MOSFET in a Weinberger logic layout, it is shown that performance can be greatly improved by partitioning these 8000 circuits into clusters of interconnected circuit islands similar to a number of small circuit chips or "macros."

As the number of circuits per chip increases in future VLSI designs, logic circuit chip design becomes increasingly complex. Array logic design provides an alternative route to random logic design and may be implemented with PLA's. Both dynamic and the more advanced static PLA implementations of a micro-

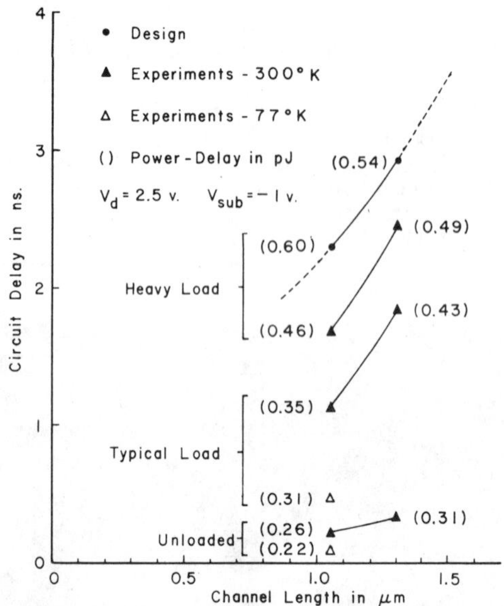

Fig. 6. Performance range of MOSFET in NOR circuits with 1 μm lithography.

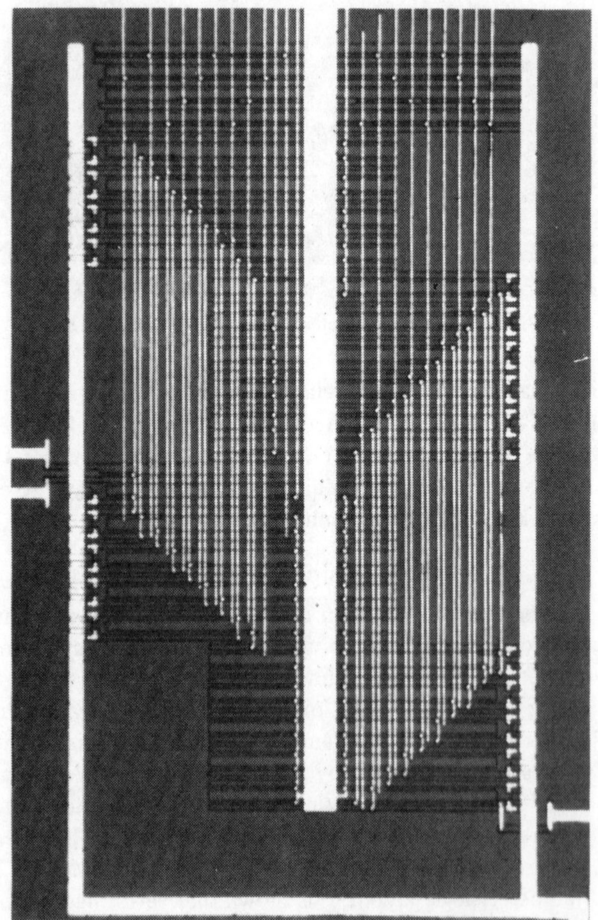

Fig. 7. Photomicrograph of a ring oscillator with heavy wiring load (Weinberger layout, fan in = fan out =3).

processor cross section have been designed and implemented in the LATV exercise. Studies of both types of PLA implementations are discussed in Part III. Experimental confirmation of NOR circuit performance in random and custom logic designs was obtained with ring oscillators having realistic loading conditions.

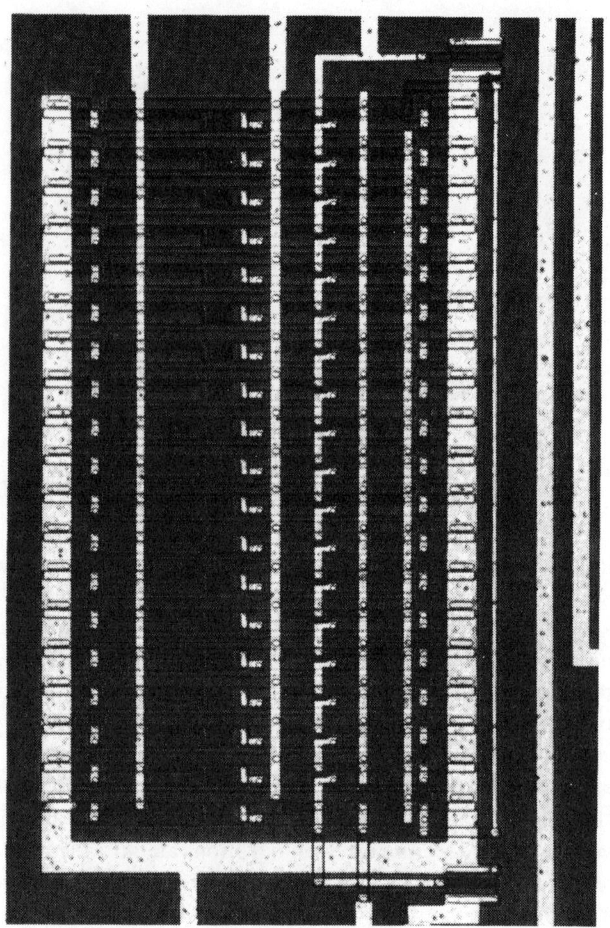

Fig. 8. Photomicrograph of a ring oscillator with typical wiring load (fan in = fan out =3).

Fig. 5 is photomicrograph of one implementation of the LATV circuit test chip image. The left side of the chip is devoted to circuit experiments for confirming NOR circuit performance in random logic while the right side of the chip is devoted to the microprocessor cross section experiment using PLA's. Two such total images have been fabricated, one containing dynamic PLA, the other containing static PLA circuitry.

With the device channel length design accommodating variations of from 1.0 to 1.6 μm (1.3 ± 0.3 μm), performance of NOR circuits, in terms of delay per circuit, can vary considerably. Fig. 6 gives the range of performance of the nominally 1 μm MOSFET technology in a NOR circuit. Experimental data were taken from chips whose device channel lengths tracked at 1.05 and 1.3 μm. The measured delay of a NOR circuit with heavy load (Weinberger layout) at a fan in and fan out of 3 for a 1.05 μm channel length device is about 1.7 ns with a power-delay product of 0.46 pJ. For a typical load condition (custom design), the corresponding delay is 1.12 ns at 0.35 pJ. The unloaded NOR circuit (fan in = fan out = 1) with larger devices (W/L=20) gave a delay of 230 ps at room temperature and 100 ps at liquid nitrogen temperature. Figs. 7-9 are photomicrographs of ring oscillators used for

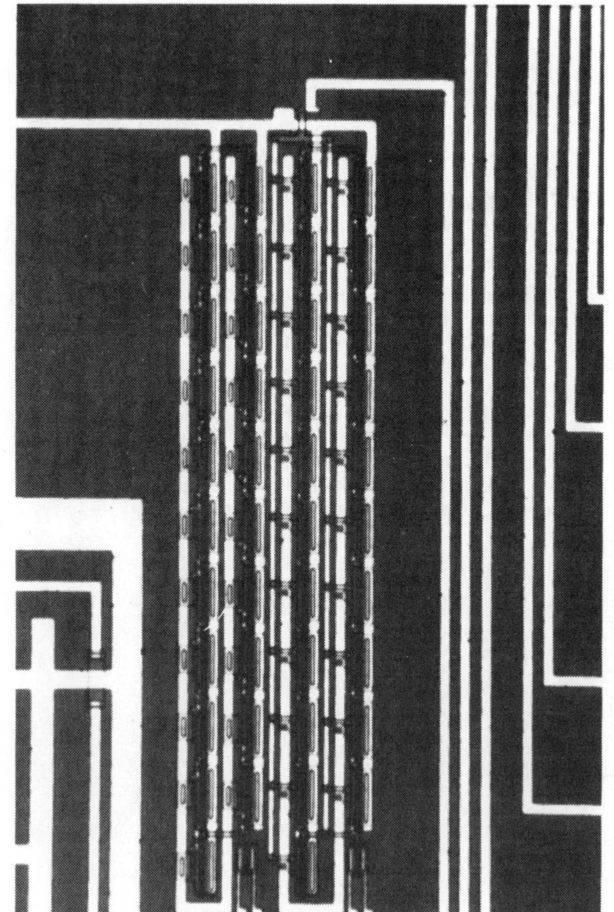

Fig. 9. Photomicrograph of a high-speed ring oscillator (fan in = fan out = 1).

measuring NOR circuit delays. As mentioned earlier with the same 1 μm lithography, more aggressive design of devices with channel lengths of 0.8 ± 0.2 μm should provide loaded NOR circuit delays in the subnanosecond region.

VII. Interconnection Technology

Logic circuit or memory array performance can be improved significantly if the time constant of polysilicon conductors can be reduced. Part VII of this series discusses the prospects for the use of refractory metal silicides such as WSi_2 on top of the polysilicon, "polycide" line [22] in order to reduce the resistance of a polysilicon line by perhaps 20 times. Polycide technology appears to be fully compatible with silicon-gate processing technology. Future extensions of LSI to VLSI technology will be further enhanced by the polycide technology.

VIII. Conclusions

An overview of the development of a 1 μm MOSFET VLSI technology has been presented. The following series of seven technical papers discuss the details of various aspects of the technology and attempts to indicate its feasibility for VLSI applications. While our effort continues in the direction of further reducing dimensions of MOSFET's for future VLSI applications, the following conclusions can be drawn at this time.

1) 1 μm MOSFET technology using electron-beam lithography has been demonstrated experimentally for VLSI applications in logic and array configurations and appears readily extendible to memory systems. The feasibility of such a technology is supported by separate studies of device design, reliability, stability, density, and performance. With more aggressive ground rules at the 1 μm level, performance numbers appear extendable by some 50 percent, and there may be some density enhancement in addition. LATV technology is capable, at the present ground rules, of yielding a 256 kbit memory chip or a 10K logic circuit chip using Weinberger-type layouts.

2) The loaded circuit performance range of a VLSI logic chip using LATV technology ranges between 1.1 and 2.5 ns per stage depending upon the channel length and exhibits a power-delay product ranging from 0.35 to 0.49 pJ at room temperature. At liquid nitrogen temperature, the delay of a typically loaded NOR circuit (1.1 ns at 300 K) was measured to be 0.46 ns. Unloaded NOR circuits exhibit a delay of 100 ps at liquid nitrogen temperature with a power-delay product of 0.22 pJ.

3) Based on the results of the 1 μm MOSFET technology, submicron MOSFET technology should be feasible, resulting in further improvements in density, power, and performance in future VLSI systems.

Acknowledgment

The authors wish to thank the entire staff of the Exploratory Semiconductor Technology area and the Electron-Beam Technology group for their efforts and dedication to the success of this project.

References

[1] R. H. Dennard, F. H. Gaensslen, E. J. Walker, and P. W. Cook, "1 μm MOSFET VLSI technology: Part II–Device designs and characteristics for high-performance logic applications," this issue, pp. 247-255.

[2] P. W. Cook, S. E. Schuster, J. T. Parrish, V. DiLonardo, and D. R. Freedman, "1 μm MOSFET VLSI technology: Part III–Logic circuit design methodology and applications," this issue, pp. 255-268.

[3] T. H. Ning, P. W. Cook, R. H. Dennard, C. M. Osburn, S. E. Schuster, and H.-N. Yu, "1 μm MOSFET VLSI technology: Part IV–Hot-electron design constraints," this issue, pp. 268-275.

[4] W. R. Hunter, L. Ephrath, W. D. Grobman, C. M. Osburn, B. L. Crowder, A. Cramer, and H. E. Luhn, "1 μm MOSFET VLSI technology: Part V–A single-level polysilicon technology using electron-beam lithography," this issue, pp. 275-281.

[5] W. D. Grobman, H. E. Luhn, T. P. Donahue, A. J. Speth, A. D. Wilson, M. Hatzakis, and T. H. P. Chang, "1 μm MOSFET VLSI technology: Part VI–Electron-beam lithography," this issue, pp. 282-290.

[6] B. L. Crowder and S. Zirinsky, "1 μm MOSFET VLSI technology: Part VII–Metal silicide interconnection technology–A future perspective," this issue, pp. 291-293.

[7] J. M. Aitken, "1 μm MOSFET VLSI technology: Part VIII–Radiation effects," this issue, pp. 294-301.

[8] B. J. Lin, "Deep UV lithography," *J. Vac. Sci. Technol.*, vol. 12, no. 5, pp. 1317-1320, Nov./Dec. 1975.

[9] S. E. Bernacki and H. I. Smith, "X-ray lithography applied to silicon device fabrication," in *Proc. 6th Int. Conf. Electron, Ion Beam Sci. Technol.*, Princeton, Electrochem. Soc., 1974, pp. 34-46.

[10] R. H. Dennard, F. H. Gaensslen, H. N. Yu, V. L. Rideout, E. Bassous, and A. R. LeBlanc, "Design of ion-implanted MOSFET's with very small physical dimensions," *IEEE J. Solid-State Circuits*, vol. SC-9, pp. 256-268, Oct., 1974.

[11] F. H. Gaensslen, V. L. Rideout, E. J. Walker, and J. J. Walker,

"Very small MOSFET's for low temperature operation," *IEEE Trans. Electron Devices*, vol. ED-24, pp. 218–229, Mar. 1977.

[12] C. M. Osburn and N. J. Chou, "Accelerated dielectric breakdown of silicon diode film," *J. Electrochem. Soc.*, vol. 120, no. 10, pp. 1377–1384, Oct. 1973.

[13] C. M. Osburn and E. Bassous, "Improved dielectric reliability of SiO_2 films with polycrystalline silicon electrodes," *J. Electrochem. Soc.*, vol. 122, no. 1, pp. 89–92, Jan. 1975.

[14] C. M. Osburn and D. W. Ormond, "Dielectric breakdown in silicon dioxide film on silicon," *J. Electrochem. Soc.*, vol. 119, no. 5, pp. 597–603, May 1972.

[15] C. K. Kircher, "Contact metallurgy for shallow junction Si devices," *J. Appl. Phys.*, vol 47, no. 12, pp. 5394–5399, Dec. 1976.

[16] H. M. Naguib and L. H. Hobbs, " Al/Si and Al/Poly-Si contact resistance in integrated circuits," *J. Electrochem. Soc.*, vol. 124, no. 4, pp. 573–577, Apr. 1977.

[17] J. M. Aitken, D. R. Young, and K. Pan, "Electron trapping in electron beam irradiated SiO_2" *J. Appl. Phys.*, vol. 49, pp. 3386–3391, 1978.

[18] H. N. Yu, R. H. Dennard, T. H. P. Chang, C. M. Osburn, V. DiLonardo, and H. E. Luhn, "Fabrication of a miniature 8K-bit memory chip using electron-beam exposure," *J. Vac. Sci. Technol.*, vol. 12, no. 6, pp. 1297–1300, Nov./Dec. 1975.

[19] L. M. Ephrath, "The effect of cathode materials on Reactive ion etching of silicon and silicon dioxide in CF_4 plasma," *J. Electron. Mater.*, vol. 7, no. 3, pp. 415–428, 1978.

[20] —, "Selective etching of silicon dioxide using reactive ion etching with CF_4–H_2," to be published.

[21] A. Weinberger, "Large scale integration of MOS complex logic: A layout method," *IEEE J. Solid-State Circuits*, vol. SC-2, pp. 182–190, 1967.

[22] B. L. Crowder, S. Zirinsky and L. M. Ephrath, *Recent Newspaper*, no. 464, Electrochem. Soc. Fall Meeting, Atlanta, GA, 1977.

Section 2.3
Novel Circuit Structures for VLSI

Single-Device-Well MOSFET's

ESMAT Z. HAMDY, STUDENT MEMBER, IEEE, MOHAMED I. ELMASRY, SENIOR MEMBER, IEEE, AND YOUSSEF A. EL-MANSY, MEMBER, IEEE

Abstract—**A novel MOSFET structure based on merging a surface enhancement-type device and a buried depletion-type device in a Single Device Well (SDW) is described. The SDW MOSFET structure utilizes the inherent two-dimensional geometry of a MOSFET device well to obtain two devices perpendicular to each other, having the same gate, thereby utilizing the hitherto nonutilized volume of the well. The two perpendicular currents of the devices in the merged structure are analyzed. An analytical model is developed and circuit CAD simulations are performed. A test chip is fabricated and the structure performance is evaluated. Some circuit examples are given.**

List of Symbols

C_{ox}	Oxide capacitance per unit area.
K_S	Relative permittivity of silicon.
k'	$\mu_p C_{ox}$.
kT/q	Thermal voltage, = 0.026 V at room temperature.
L	Length of MOSFET channel.
n_i	Intrinsic impurity concentration.
N_W	Well impurity concentration.
N_{sub}	Substrate concentration.
q	Electron charge.
Q_D	Charge in the depletion region.
Q_s	Accumulation charge in the semiconductor.
V_B	Substrate to source potential.
V_{bi}	Built-in barrier potential.
V_{DN}	Drain to source potential of n-channel device.
V_{DP}	Drain to source potential of p-channel device.
V_{FB}	Flat-band potential.
V_{GN}	Gate to source potential of n-channel device.
V_{GP}	Gate to source potential of p-channel device.
V_{T0}	Threshold voltage without substrate bias effect.
W	Width of MOSFET channel.
X_W	Depth of the SDW well.
ϕ_F	Equilibrium Fermi potential.
μ_n	Effective electron mobility.
μ_p	Effective hole mobility.
ϵ_0	Permittivity of free space.

Manuscript received May 27, 1980; revised November 29, 1980. This work was supported in part by NSERCC Grant A9334 and PRAI 7705.

E. Z. Hamdy was with the Department of Electrical Engineering, University of Waterloo, Waterloo, Ontario, Canada N2L 3G1. He is now with Intel, Aloha, OR 97006.

M. I. Elmasry is with the Micro-components Organization, Burroughs Corporation, San Diego, CA 92127, on leave from the Department of Electrical Engineering, University of Waterloo, Waterloo, Ontario, Canada N2L 361.

Y. A. El-Mansy was with Bell-Northern Research, Ottawa, Ontario, Canada. He is now with Intel, Aloha, OR 97006.

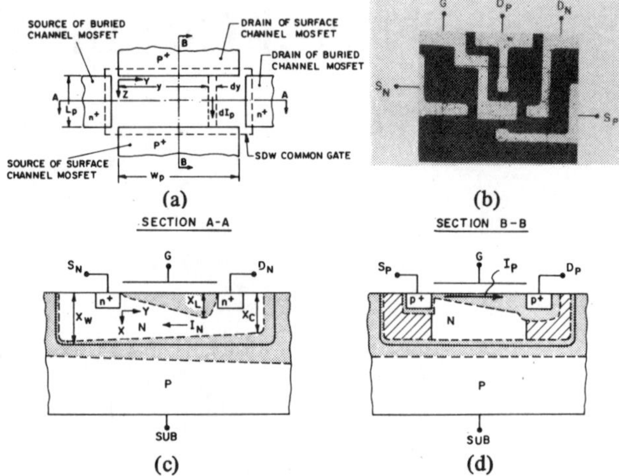

Fig. 1. (a) Top view of SDW MOSFET. (b) Photomicrograph of SDW. (c) Cross section *AA* in the n-channel buried device. (d) Cross section *BB* in the p-channel surface device.

I. Introduction

Recent advances in integrated circuit technology towards Very-Large-Scale Integrations (VLSI) have narrowed the performance and the complexity gaps between bipolar and MOSFET; performance in terms of speed and power dissipation, complexity in terms of number of devices and number of masks. Based on these facts, one type of circuit can (and should) benefit from techniques used in the other. Circuit techniques normally used in MOSFET shift registers has been applied to bipolar structures and the results have been reported [1]. In this work device merging, similar to that used in bipolar I^2L, is applied to MOSFET's resulting in the development of the Single-Device-Well (SDW) MOSFET [2]. The SDW is based on merging two devices; a surface-channel enhancement device with a buried channel depletion device sharing the same well and the same gate.

II. The Structure

The SDW structure utilizes the inherent two-dimensional geometry of a MOSFET device well to obtain two devices perpendicular to each other, having the same gate. The source and drain of the surface device are of opposite doping type relative to the well material while the source and drain of the buried device are of the same doping type. Fig. 1(a) shows a diagramatic layout of the SDW and Fig. 1(b) shows a photomicrograph.

SDW's can be fabricated in different technologies: In MOSBI

Reprinted from *IEEE Trans. Electron Devices*, vol. ED-28, pp. 322–327, Mar. 1981.

[1] (a technology which accommodates MOSFET devices in a bipolar environment) the isolated n-epitaxial layer acts as a well accommodating a p-channel surface device and a n-channel buried device. In CMOS, the isolated N (or P) well accommodates a p- (or n-) channel surface device and a n- (or p-) channel device. In CMOS/SOS technology, the isolated N (or P) island accommodates a p- (or n-) channel surface device and a n- (or p-) channel buried device.

Fig. 1(c) and (d) shows two perpendicular crossections. A surface channel current I_P flows in the p-channel device. A buried channel current I_N of the n-channel device flows perpendicular to I_P in the neutral region bounded by the surface depletion region and the depletion region associated with the well-substrate p-n junction. Hence, I_N and I_P are isolated from each other by depletion regions. The currents of adjacent buried channel devices fabricated on the same chip are isolated by a dielectric or p-n junctions.

III. Theory of Operation

The two channel currents of the surface enhancement device and the buried depletion device are separated by a depletion region. They do not interact directly, but each is affecting the operation of the other through the sustained boundary conditions.

A. The Surface Current

The current in the p-channel enhancement surface device can be modeled by the usual drain current equations [3]. However, the potential distribution across the n-channel buried device is in effect a substrate bias on the p-channel surface device. Hence, the threshold voltage along the *width* of the p-channel surface device varies and the threshold voltage of the p-channel surface device at a point y is given by

$$V_T(y) = V_{T0} + \frac{Q_D}{C_{ox}} \left\{1 - \sqrt{1 - \frac{V(y)}{2\phi_F}}\right\} \tag{1}$$

where

$$2\phi_F = -2\left(\frac{kT}{q}\right) \ln\left(\frac{N_W}{n_i}\right)$$

where V_{T0} is the threshold voltage of the surface p-channel enhancement device with no applied voltage across the n-channel buried device and $V(y)$ is the potential along the buried channel.

Integrating the incremental channel current $dI_p(y)$ in a strip of width dy at position y (see Fig. 1(a)) from the source to the drain, and assuming a linear distribution for the substrate potential, we obtain in the nonsaturated region

$$I_P = k'\left(\frac{W}{L}\right)_p [(V_{GP} - V_{T\,\mathrm{eff}})\, V_{DP} - V_{DP}^2/2] \tag{2a}$$

and in the saturation region

$$I_P = \frac{k'}{2}\left(\frac{W}{L}\right)_p [V_{GP} - V_{T\,\mathrm{eff}}]^2 - I_{\mathrm{eff}} \tag{2b}$$

where

$$V_{T\,\mathrm{eff}} = V_{T0} + \frac{2}{3}\frac{Q_D}{C_{ox}}\left(\frac{2\phi_F}{V_{DN}}\right) \cdot \left[\left\{\left(1 - \frac{V_{DN}}{2\phi_F}\right)^{3/2} - 1\right\} + \frac{3}{2}\left(\frac{V_{DN}}{2\phi_F}\right)\right] \tag{3a}$$

and

$$I_{\mathrm{eff}} = \frac{k'}{2}\left(\frac{W}{L}\right)_p \frac{2}{3}\left(\frac{Q_D}{C_{ox}}\right)^2 \left(\frac{2\phi_F}{V_{DN}}\right)^2 \cdot \left[\left\{\left(1 - \frac{V_{DN}}{2\phi_F}\right)^{3/2} - 1\right\}^2 - \left(\frac{3}{2}\frac{V_{DN}}{2\phi_F}\right)^2 - \frac{9}{8}\left(\frac{V_{DN}}{2\phi_F}\right)^3\right]. \tag{3b}$$

It is clear from (2) that the p-channel surface device can be modeled with the usual current equations with an effective threshold voltage $V_{T\,\mathrm{eff}}$ and an effective current I_{eff} component. An increase in the threshold voltage of the surface device is predicted by (3a) due to the substrate bias effect of the buried device. This agrees with our experimental results.

B. The Buried Current

In case of the n-channel buried device [4], [5] the current equations are modeled as follows. Two modes of operation are possible, depending upon if the gate potential is less than or greater than the magnitude of the flat band voltage V_{FB}; namely mode A, and mode B respectively.

1) Mode A: With reference to Fig. 1(c), with the application of a gate voltage less than the flat-band voltage, we obtain a depletion region across the channel extending from the $Si\text{-}SiO_2$ interface down to X_L. The depth of the surface depletion region X_L depends upon the magnitude of the applied negative gate voltage. Hence, the gate voltage modulates the resistance (R) between X_L and X_C, where X_C is the depth of the boundary of the depletion region associated with the substrate-epitaxial (substrate-well in CMOS) p-n junction. This resistance is given by

$$R = \frac{L}{q\mu_n N_W W(X_C - X_L)}. \tag{4}$$

Using the depletion approximation we obtain

$$X_C = X_W - BD\sqrt{V_{bi} + V_B + V(y)} \tag{5}$$

$$X_L = B\sqrt{V(y) - \phi_s(y)} \tag{6}$$

where

$$\phi_s(y) = V_{GN} - V_{FB} - \frac{A}{2} + A^{1/2}\sqrt{V(y) - V_{GN} + V_{FB} + \frac{A}{4}} \tag{7}$$

and

$$A = \frac{2\epsilon_0 K_S q N_W}{C_{ox}^2}, \quad B = \sqrt{\frac{2\epsilon_0 K_S}{qN_W}}, \quad D = 1/\sqrt{1 + N_W/N_{sub}}.$$

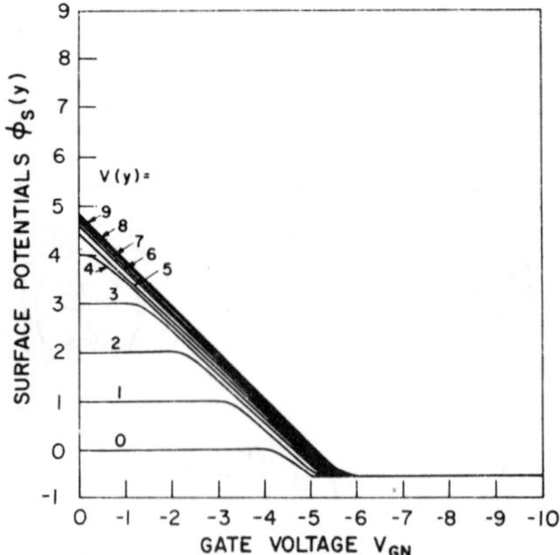

Fig. 2. Variation of surface potential in the buried device.

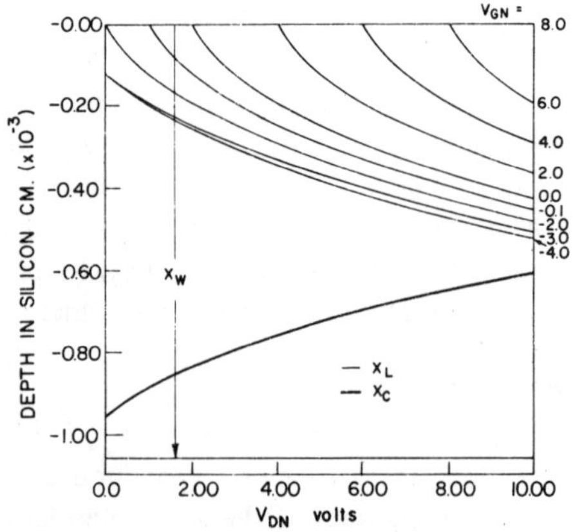

Fig. 3. Computer plot of the depletion boundaries in the buried device.

Fig. 2 shows the surface potential $\phi_s(y)$ as a function of the gate potential V_{GN} and the potential along the buried channel $V(y)$. Fig. 3 is a computer plot of the variation of the two depletion boundaries X_C, X_L as a function of the gate potential. It should be noted that at large negative gate potential the surface is completely inverted and no more control on the buried resistor R is possible. At this point $\phi_s(y) = 2\phi_F$, and the surface depletion region depth is given by

$$X_L' = B\sqrt{(V(y) - 2\phi_F)}. \tag{8}$$

Due to the variation of $V(y)$ across the buried channel, part of the surface depletion region is inverted from the source S_N where $V(y) = 0$ to a point where $V(y) = V_{IN}$ which is given by

$$V_{IN} = \frac{(-V_{GN} + V_{FB} + 2\phi_F)^2}{A} + 2\phi_F. \tag{9}$$

Hence, the drain current is given by

$$I_N = \int_0^{V_{IN}} (1/R')\, dV + \int_{V_{IN}}^{V_{DN}} (1/R)\, dV \tag{10}$$

where R' is the value of the channel resistance given by (4) when the surface inverts (i.e., $X_L = X_L'$).

Case (i): The gate voltage is less than the flat-band voltage V_{FB} but not sufficient to invert any part of the channel. Hence, $V_{IN} = 0$, and the corresponding gate voltage is given by

$$V_{GN1} = -\sqrt{A(-2\phi_F)} + 2\phi_F + V_{FB}. \tag{11}$$

Integrating (10) we obtain

$$I_{N1} = I_1 + I_{21} + I_{31} + I_5 \tag{12}$$

where

$$\left.\begin{aligned}
I_1 &= G_0(1 + F)\, V_{DN}\\
I_{21} &= G_0 H V_{DN}\\
I_{31} &= -G_1\left[\left(\frac{A}{4} - V_{GN} + V_{FB} + V_{DN}\right)^{3/2} - \left(\frac{A}{4} - V_{GN} + V_{FB}\right)^{3/2}\right]\\
I_5 &= -G_2\left[(V_{bi} + V_B + V_{DN})^{3/2} - (V_{bi} + V_B)^{3/2}\right]\\
G_0 &= q\mu_n N_W \left(\frac{W}{L}\right)_n X_W\\
G_1 &= G_0\left(\frac{2}{3}\right)\left(\frac{B}{X_W}\right) \qquad G_2 = G_1 D \qquad H = \frac{B\sqrt{A}}{2X_W}
\end{aligned}\right\}. \tag{13}$$

The current component I_1 includes a subcomponent ($G_0 F \cdot V_{DN}$) which is not modulated by the gate. This current flows perpendicular to the cross section (Fig. 1(d)) in the hatched region. The factor F is a function of the geometrical layout of the SDW structure. In our experimental structures, F was found to be 0.2.

Case (ii): The gate voltage is less than V_{GN1}. Hence, part of the channel is inverted from the source up to a point where $V(y) = V_{IN}$. Integrating (10) we obtain

$$I_{N2} = I_1 + I_2 + I_3 + I_4 + I_5 \tag{14}$$

where I_1 and I_5 are given by (13) and

$$I_2 = G_0 H\left[V_{DN} - 2\phi_F - \frac{1}{A}(-V_{GN} + V_{FB} + 2\phi_F)^2\right]$$

$$I_3 = -G_1\left[\left(\frac{A}{4} - V_{GN} + V_{DN} + V_{FB}\right)^{3/2} - \frac{1}{A\sqrt{A}}\left(\frac{A}{2} - V_{GN} + 2\phi_F + V_{FB}\right)^3\right]$$

$$I_4 = -G_1\left[\frac{1}{A\sqrt{A}}(-V_{GN} + 2\phi_F + V_{FB})^3 - (-2\phi_F)^{3/2}\right].$$

Case (iii): Large negative gate potential is applied such that all the channel is inverted. Hence, $V_{IN} = V_{DN}$, and no more gate control is possible, the corresponding gate voltage at which this occurs is given by

$$V_{GN2} = -\sqrt{A}\,(V_{DN} - 2\phi_F)^{1/2} + 2\phi_F + V_{FB}. \tag{15}$$

The drain current is obtained by substituting $V_{GN} = V_{GN2}$ in (14)

$$I_{N3} = I_{N2}\big|_{V_{GN} = V_{GN2}}. \tag{16}$$

2) Mode B: With the application of a gate potential larger than the flat-band voltage, the enhancement surface device will be in the cut off region, while accumulation will start to occur at the surface of the buried device extending from the source to V_{AN} where

$$V_{AN} = V_{GN} - V_{FB}. \tag{17}$$

Hence, for $V_{DN} > V_{AN}$ part of the surface is accumulated. For $V_{DN} \leqslant V_{AN}$, all the surface will be accumulated and the corresponding gate voltage is given by

$$V_{GN3} = V_{FB} + V_{DN}. \tag{18}$$

In the accumulation region, in addition to the current due to the accumulated charge Q_s [6], we have an additional current component due to bulk resistance of the channel. The resultant drain current is given by

$$I_N = \left(\frac{W}{L}\right)_n \mu_n \int_0^{V_{AN}} (-Q_s)\, dV + \int_0^{V_{AN}} (1/R'')\, dV + \int_{V_{AN}}^{V_{DN}} (1/R)\, dV \tag{19}$$

where R'' is the value of the channel resistance given by (4) when the surface depletion width is zero (i.e., $X_L = 0$).

Case (i): In this case $V_{GN3} > V_{GN} \geqslant V_{FB}$, and the surface is partly accumulated from the source to $V(y) = V_{AN}$, the drain current from (19) is given by

$$I_{N4} = I_A + I_B + I_{DEP} \tag{20}$$

where

$$I_A = \mu_n C_{ox} \left(\frac{W}{L}\right)_n \left(\frac{1}{1 + 2\sqrt{\left(\frac{kT}{q}\right)\Big/A}}\right) \cdot \left[(V_{GN} - V_{FB})\, V_{AN} - \frac{V_{AN}^2}{2}\right]$$

$$I_B = G_0(1 + F + H)\, V_{AN} - G_2\left[(V_{AN} + V_{bi} + V_B)^{3/2} - (V_{bi} + V_B)^{3/2}\right]$$

$$I_{DEP} = G_0(1 + F + H)(V_{DN} - V_{AN}) - G_1\left[\left(V_{DN} + V_{FB} - V_{GN} + \frac{A}{4}\right)^{3/2} - \left(V_{AN} + V_{FB} - V_{GN} + \frac{A}{4}\right)^{3/2}\right]$$

$$- G_2\left[(V_{DN} + V_{bi} + V_B)^{3/2} - (V_{AN} + V_{bi} + V_B)^{3/2}\right].$$

Case (ii): For gate voltages $V_{GN} \geqslant V_{GN3}$, the surface is totally accumulated and the drain current is obtained by substituting $V_{AN} = V_{DN}$ in (20)

$$I_{N5} = I_{N4}\big|_{V_{AN} = V_{DN}}. \tag{21}$$

The above current relations ((12) to (21)) are summarized in Table I.

TABLE I
REFERENCE TO THE BURIED CURRENT EQUATIONS

CASE	GATE VOLTAGE RANGE	DRAIN CURRENT	EQUATION USED
A-(i)	$V_{GN1} < V_{GN} < V_{FB}$	$I_N = I_{N1}$	12
A-(ii)	$V_{GN2} < V_{GN} \leqslant V_{GN1}$	$I_N = I_{N2}$	14
A-(iii)	$V_{GN} \leqslant V_{GN2}$	$I_N = I_{N3}$	16
B-(i)	$V_{GN3} > V_{GN} \geqslant V_{FB}$	$I_N = I_{N4}$	20
B-(ii)	$V_{GN} \geqslant V_{GN3}$	$I_N = I_{N5}$	21

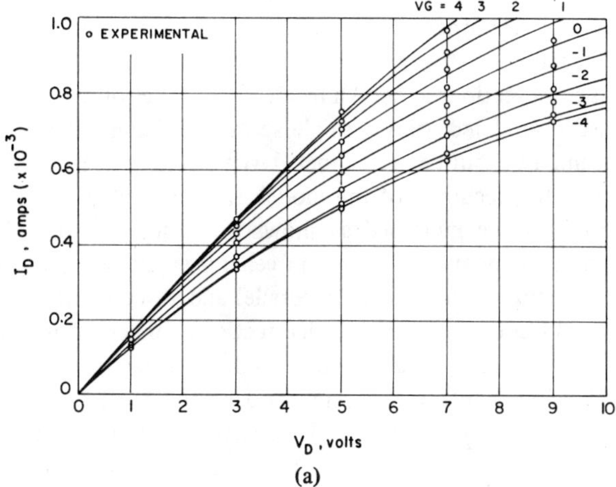

(a)

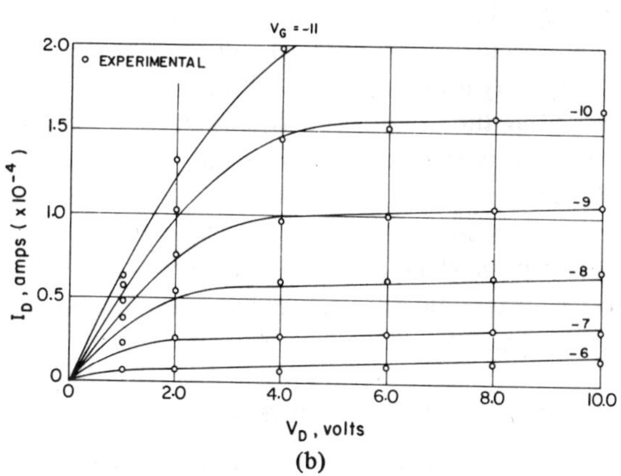

(b)

Fig. 4. Computed and experimental *I-V* characteristics of (a) n-channel buried device. (b) p-channel surface device.

A computer model was developed based on these relations, and was implemented in WATAND [7] to simulate SDW circuit performance. The *I-V* characteristics of the SDW surface and buried devices are shown in Fig. 4.

IV. Functional Modeling

The SDW can be represented by a lumped model as shown in Fig. 5(a). It consists of two transistors, a surface channel enhancement and a buried channel depletion MOSFET's, having

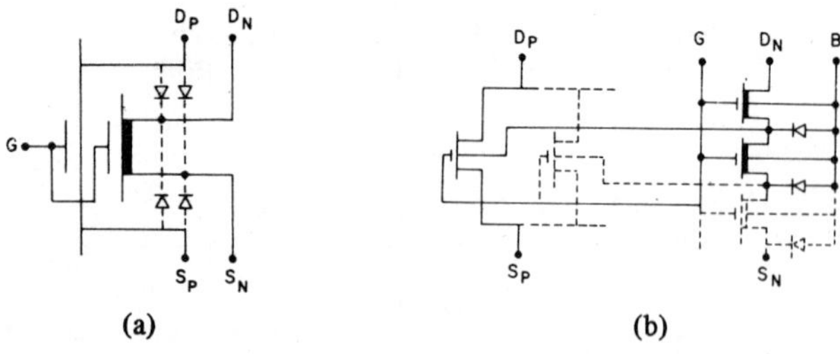

Fig. 5. (a) SDW lumped component model. (b) SDW distributed model.

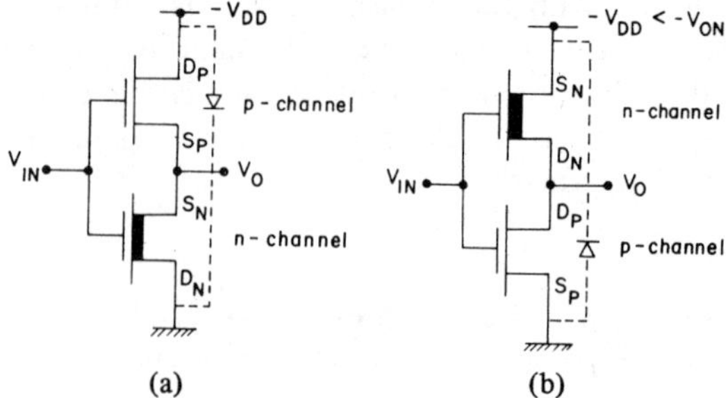

Fig. 6. SDW Noninverting mode of operation (a), and inverting mode of operation (b).

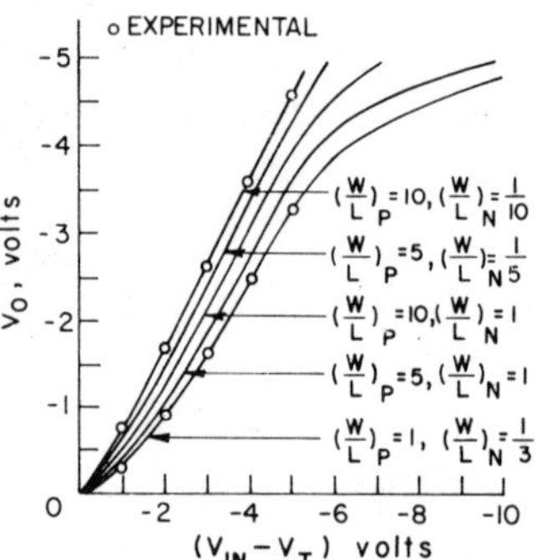

Fig. 7. Transfer characteristic of SDW source follower.

the same gate. Four parasitic diodes also exists between the different source and drain regions.

The effect of the buried device on the surface device was modeled in Section III-A using an effective threshold voltage $V_{T\,\mathrm{eff}}$ and an effective current I_{eff}. Another method to emphasize the variation of the threshold voltage along the buried channel, is by functionally modeling the distributed nature of the structure. This is done by partitioning the SDW into a number of sections as shown in Fig. 5(b). The solid lines show the SDW modeled using a single surface p-channel device section and two buried n-channel device sections. In order to increase the accuracy of the model, the number of the device sections can be increased as shown doted in Fig. 5(b). Here the model consists of two (or in general m) surface p-channel device sections connected in parallel and three (or in general $(m + 1)$) buried n-channel device sections connected in series. The aspect ratio of the surface p-channel device sections is $[(W/L)_p/m]$ while the aspect ratio of the buried n-channel device is $[(W/L)_n\ (m + 1)]$. This partitioning allows the substrate terminal of each surface p-channel section to be biased at an average voltage level which is function of the two adjacent buried n-channel sections.

In modeling the surface channel sections a model similar to that given in [8] is used. While the buried channel sections are modeled using the dc-current relations given in Section III-B. Because the gate is common to all sections, the capacitive effects are only included in the surface channel models. SDW parasitic diodes which are shown in Fig. 5(a) are included in the surface channel model, while the parasitic diodes of the epitaxial-substrate junctions are added in the functional model as shown in Fig. 5(b).

V. Experimental Results and Applications

SDW's can be integrated in both Si-gate and metal-gate MOSBI technologies. Also they can be integrated in a CMOS technology having well-substrate junction isolation or dielectric isolation and in CMOS/SOS having complete channel dielectric isolation. An experimental test chip was fabricated in a MOSBI technology with a metal gate and an oxide thickness of 800 Å. A 10.6-μm n-type epitaxial layer of 9.43-Ω · cm resistivity and a p-type substrate of 10-Ω · cm resistivity were used. The experimental I–V characteristics of both devices are shown in Fig. 4, which agrees with the computed aided I–V model developed in Section IV. The I–V characteristics of the p-channel surface device is similar to the well-known behavior of that device (see Fig. 4(a)); while the n-channel buried device shows a characteristic of a modulated resistor (see Fig. 4(b)). At gate voltages less than −4 V, the surface inverts and no more control on the buried channel current is possible.

SDW's can be used in any circuit where an n-channel, and a p-channel MOSFET's having the same gate are utilized. The only constraint is that the parasitic diodes shown in Fig. 5(a) should not be turned on. Two circuit modes of operation results. If the diodes are reverse biased a noninverting building block is obtained as shown in Fig. 6(a). If the diodes are allowed to be forward biased with a voltage less than the turn-on voltage V_{ON}, then an inverting building block results as shown in Fig. 6(b). This inverting mode puts constraints on the technology used because the maximum supply voltage should be in the order of 500 mV, and this requires a few hundred millivolts for the threshold voltage of the devices.

In the noninverting mode, the p-channel enhancement device is used as a driving transistor and the n-channel depletion device is used as a load transistor, in a source follower configuration as shown in Fig. 6(a). Based on the functional model presented in Section IV, it has been found that a model with $m = 1$ or 2 is sufficient to model SDW's in almost all circuits of interest. Using $m = 1$, the dc-transfer characteristics of the source follower is obtained, and it agrees with the experimental results as shown in Fig. 7.

Computer simulation of the small signal gain of the source follower was also obtained for different values of $(W/L)_p$ and $(W/L)_n$, as shown in Fig. 8. These results predict that for a gain approaching unity we require a larger value for $(W/L)_p$ and smaller values for $(W/L)_n$. This can be easily obtained due to the *inherent* geometric layout of the SDW; increasing $(W/L)_p$ reduces $(W/L)_n$.

Fig. 10 shows a simulated transient response of the source followers circuits shown in Fig. 9. The output voltage swing and the load capacitor C_0 are taken the same. The turn-on

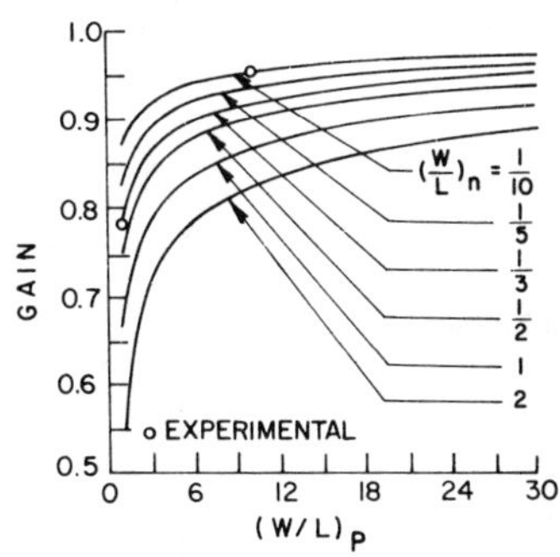

Fig. 8. Small signal gain of SDW source follower.

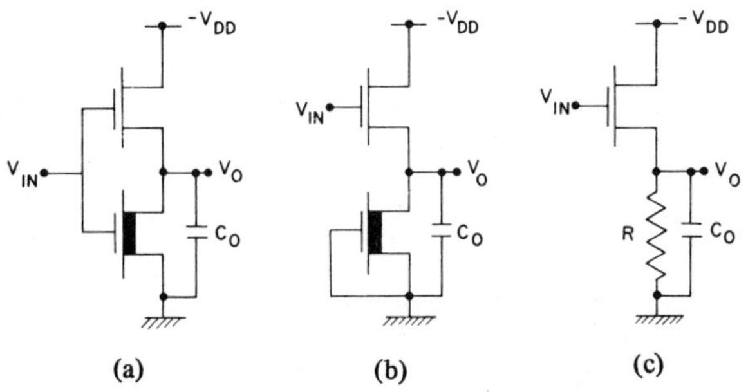

Fig. 9. (a) SDW source follower. (b) PMOS source follower with depletion load. (c) PMOS source follower with resistive load.

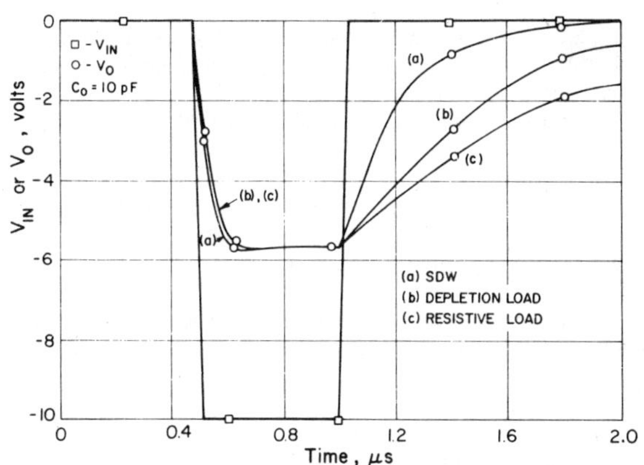

Fig. 10. Computed transient waveforms of source followers shown in Fig. 9.

times are almost the same for the three cases, since this time depends mainly upon the PMOS driver. For the turn-off times, the depletion load is better than the resistive load, as was expected [9]. However, the SDW source follower with the PMOS as the driver and the buried n-channel as a load has a smaller turn-off time. This has been confirmed experimentally and can be explained as follows. As the input gate swings from the supply potential towards ground the buried n-channel device tends to be in a higher conducting state, hence causing the load capacitor C_0 to discharge faster.

VI. Conclusions and Comments

SDW's can be implemented in MOSFET technologies, e.g., NMOS, PMOS, CMOS, SOS, and MOSBI with some modifications in the processing steps. SDW's can be used in analog and digital circuit design with a potential reduction in silicion area [10]. A major impact of SDW's is in the design of a compact static memory cell [11]. Most important of all, we feel that SDW MOSFET's is introducing a new concept in the design of VLSI integrated structures by making use of the volume in the silicon bulk.

Acknowledgment

The authors wish to thank R. Grant and M. Vlach of the University of Waterloo for their valuable assistance.

References

[1] E. Z. Hamdy and M. I. Elmasry, "Bipolar structures for BIMOS technologies," *IEEE J. Solid-State Circuits*, vol. SC-15, pp. 229–236, Apr. 1980.

[2] E. Z. Hamdy, M. I. Elmasry, and Y. A. El-Mansy, "A novel single-device-well MOSFET gate," in *IEDM Tech. Dig.*, Dec. 1979, pp. 576–580.

[3] A. S. Grove, *Physics and Technology of Semiconductor Devices*. New York: Wiley, 1967.

[4] S. R. Hofstein, "An analysis of deep depletion thin-film MOS transistor," *IEEE Trans. Electron Devices*, vol. ED-13, pp. 846–855, Dec. 1966.

[5] Y. A. El-Mansy, "Analysis and characterization of the depletion mode IGFET," *IEEE J. Solid-State Circuits*, vol. SC-15, pp. 331–340, June 1980.

[6] S. M. Sze, *Physics of Semiconductor Devices.* New York: Wiley, 1969.

[7] I. Hajj, K. Singhal, J. Vlach, and P. R. Bryant, "WATAND–A program for the analysis and design of linear and piecewise-linear networks," presented at Midwest Symp. Circuit Theory, Waterloo, Ont., Canada, Apr. 1973.

[8] N. A. Zakhary, M. Vlach, and M. I. Elmasry, "An adaptive MOS macromodel for VLSI," presented at 22nd Midwest Symp. on Circuits and Systems, Philadelphia, PA, June 1979.

[9] R. H. Crawford, *MOSFET in Circuit Design.* New York: McGraw-Hill, 1967.

[10] E. Z. Hamdy and M. I. Elmasry, "SDW MOSFETs in LSI analog circuit design," submitted for publication to *IEEE J. Solid-State Circuits.*

[11] M. I. Elmasry and E. Z. Hamdy, "SDW MOSFET static memory cell," to be published in *IEEE J. Solid-State Circuits.*

A QUADRUPLY SELF-ALIGNED MOS (QSA MOS) A NEW SHORT CHANNEL HIGH SPEED HIGH DENSITY MOSFET FOR VLSI

Kuniichi Ohta, Kunio Yamada, Kyozo Shimizu and Yasuo Tarui

Cooperative Laboratories,
VLSI Technology Research Association
4-1-1, Miyazaki, Takatsuku, Kawasaki, 213, Japan

ABSTRACT

A new device named Quadruply Self-Aligned (QSA) MOS is proposed to overcome speed and density limit of conventional scaled down MOS VLSI circuits.

This device includes four mutually self-aligned areas: poly Si gate area, shallow source drain area to eliminate short channel effect, deep junction area with high conductance and specific contact area to afford efficient metallic interconnection, thus achieving high speed and high density.

Fabrication processes involve undercutting of poly Si gate, anisotropic ion etching of SiO_2 and source drain ion implantation.

Experimental results of the device and feasibility of MOS RAM with a density of 1 Mbit/6 x 4 mm^2 storage area are described.

INTRODUCTION

Despite the inherent high speed nature of scaled down MOS devices (1), scaled down MOS VLSI circuits show speed limits due to RC time constant (Fig. 1). This is the major source of using metals and deep junction interconnect lines (1) and also the need for the effective self-aligned contact means (2) – (5). Elimination of short channel effects is also one of the main problems of device design. A new short channel MOS device is proposed to meet these requirements.

BASIC CONCEPT AND DEVICE STRUCTURE

Basic fabrication processes are described. (Fig. 2) After usual Si gate processes, the subsequent Si_3N_4 deposition, undercutting of SiO_2 and gate poly Si, and poly Si side wall oxidation lead to the structure shown in Fig. 2. (a). Oxide film in active region is etched off by anisotropic reactive ion etching (6) (7) except the area shadowed by Si_3N_4 film (Fig. 2 (b)). Removing the remaining Si_3N_4 and subsequent sources drain ion implantation give rise to shallow and deep implanted regions (Fig. 2 (c)). Then, source drain contact formation by selective oxidation with Si_3N_4 masking (Fig. 2 (d)), opening of contact hole to poly Si and metal interconnection process lead to the final structure shown in Fig. 2 (e).

This device has four mutually self-aligned areas: namely, poly Si gate area, shallow source drain area, deep junction area and contact area. The edges of these four areas (① ~ ④ in Fig. 3) are formed in a self aligned manner by successive processing steps from the initial gate pattern edge ⓐ, and thus the name Quadruply Self-Aligned MOS (QSA MOS) emerges.

The main features of this device are summarised as follows.

(1) Use of undercutting allows channel length shorter than minimum feature size, resulting in a smaller intrinsic delay of the device.
(2) Short channel effect can be eliminated by shallow source drain junctions.
(3) Overlap capacitance between source drain and gate electrode can be reduced.
(4) Extensive use of high conductance interconnections is permitted by deep N^+ junctions and metallic interconnections readily available from self-aligned contact means.
(5) This device has a highly self-aligned structure.

Thus, design of high speed high density VLSI circuits will be feasible by this QSA technique.

A modification of QSA MOS is shown in Fig. 2 (f). This device called SCA (Self Aligned Contact by Anisotropic Etching) MOS can be obtained by eliminating shallow source drain area. It can be made by a slightly simpler process and has all the features of QSA MOS except (2).

EXPERIMENTAL

A Device Design –– Basic Equations

Basic equations are derived in reference to Fig. 3.

The gain factor β of the MOSFET is given by

$$\beta = \frac{\mu_o \epsilon_{ox}}{t_{ox}} \frac{W}{L_{SD}} \frac{1}{1 + \theta (V_G - V_T)} \quad (1)$$

where t_{ox} and ϵ_{ox} are the thickness and dielectric constant of gate oxide, W is channel width, V_G is gate voltage, V_T is threshold voltage, μ_o is surface mobility and θ is a constant.

Source drain distance L_{SD} and gate drain overlapping L_{ovl} are given by

$$L_{SD} = L_{mask} - 2L_u - 1.6x_j + \ell_{ox} \quad (2)$$

$$L_{ovl} = 0.8x_j - (\ell_{ox} + 0.5\ell'_{ox}) \quad (3)$$

The notations of these device parameters are shown in Fig. 3. Equation (2) shows that L_{SD} is controlled by gate patterning, undercutting, side wall oxidation and source drain formation processes.

Equation (3) shows that the gate drain overlapping capacitance is smaller than that of conventional MOSFET.

When

$$L_u = \frac{1}{2} \ell_{ox} \quad (4)$$

then, eq (2) reduces to

$$L_{SD} = L_{mask} - 1.6x_j \quad (5)$$

Eqs. (4) and (5) are the basic equations of SCA MOS. Thus, QSA MOS includes SCA MOS as a special case.

B Fabrication Process

The key fabrication steps are outlined here.

Undercutting is controlled by prescribed time schedule, yielding the splitting of duplicated lines as shown in Fig. 4 (a).

The basic assumption of QSA MOS process is selectivity and anisotropy in reactive ion etching: namely, the masking Si_3N_4 film and the oxide film shadowed by it must remain unetched when RIE of SiO_2 in the unshadowed region is completed. This can be accomplished by the proper choice of etch rate ratio (6) (7) and thicknesses of films as shown in Table I and Fig. 2. Fig. 4 (b) shows this is the case.

Breakdown voltage V_B of poly Si gate side wall oxide were measured by an overlapping electrode, obtaining V_B above 20V. This electrical test result gives another verification of the anisotropy in RIE.

C Device Characteristics

Fig. 5 shows the drain current I_D vs. drain voltage V_{DD} of the QSA MOS. This result verifies the proper operation of the device.

Reprinted from *IEEE Int. Electron Devices Meeting*, pp. 581–584, 1979.

SOME VLSI DESIGN ASPECTS

Figs. 6 and 7 show the minimum area one transistor RAM cell with area $6F^2$ in comparison with the cell of present day dynamic MOS RAMs. Here, F is the minimum feature size. This minimum area cell can be realized by the self-algined structure of the QSA MOS on the assumption that the ratio of the storage capacitance to bit line capacitance is large enough for sensing.

This cell area means 1 Mbit MOS RAM with storage area of 6 x 4 mm^2 and 3 x 2 mm^2 with 2 μm and 1 μm design rule, respectively.

Fig. 8 shows a layout of the gated flip-flop type of the sense amplifier widely used in the present day dynamic MOS RAM. Minimum bit line pitch of 4F is realized by QSA MOS. The self-aligned contact and deep N^+ source drain interconnect lines are effectively used.

CONCLUSION

A new type of high speed, high density MOS was proposed and its proper operation was experimentally verified. The significance of the device in VLSI design was discussed.

REFERENCES

(1) H. Y. Yu, A. Reisman, C. M. Osborn and D. L. Critchrow, "1 μm MOSFET VLSI Technology: Part I-An Overview", IEEE J. Solid-State Circuits, Vol. SC-14, pp240–246, April 1979, and references cited therein.

(2) Y. Tanigaki, S. Iwamatsu and K. Hirobe, "A New Self-Aligned Contact Technology", J. Electrochem. Soc., Vol. 125 (3), pp471–472, 1978.

(3) H. Sunami, M. Koyanagi, "Selective Oxide Coating of Si Gate (SELOCS)", Proc. 10th Conf. on Solid State Devices, Tokyo, 1978: Japan J. Appl. Phys., Vol.18 (1979) Suppl. 18-1, pp255–260.

(4) S. Muramoto, T. Hosoya and S. Matsuo, : A New Self-Aligning Contact Process for MOS LSI", IEEE IEDM 1978, pp185–188.

(5) V. L. Rideout, and V. J. Silvestri, "MOSFETs with Polysilicon Gates Self-Aligned to the Field Isolation and the Source/Drain Resistors", IEEE IEDM 1976, pp593–596.

(6) H. W. Lehman and R. Widmer, "Profile Control by Reactive Sputter Etching", J. Vac. Sci. Tech., Vol 15, pp319–326, 1978.

(7) H. Komiya, H. Toyoda and H. Itakura, "Etching Characteristics of SiO_2 in CHF_3 gas plasma", to be published in J. Electronic Material, Vol 8, Dec., 1979.

TABLE I

The rate of reactive ion etching in cathode coupled CF_4 + H_2 system: CF_4 flow rate 30 cc/min, H_2 flow rate 20 cc/min, power density 0.25 W/cm^2, total pressure 0.03 Ton.

	Rate	Ratio
SiO_2	400 Å/min	1
Si_3N_4	360 Å/min	~0.9
Si	40 Å/min	0.1
lateral etching rate of SiO_2	~0	~0

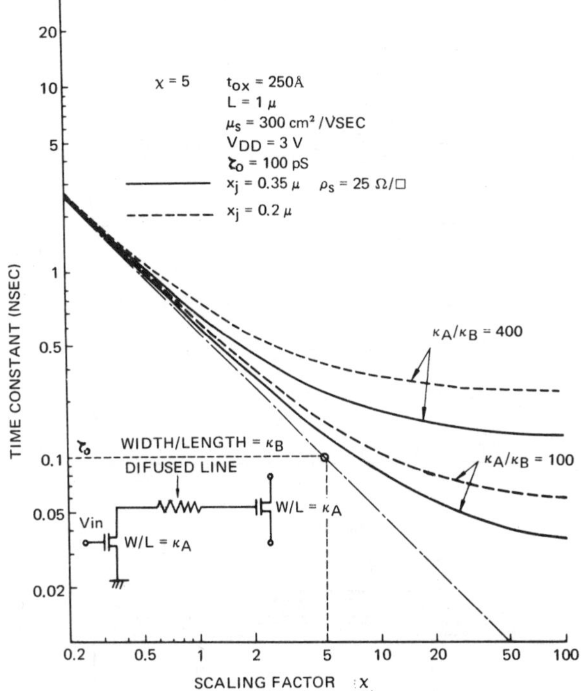

Fig. 1 The circuit time constant vs. scaling factor κ. The curves are extended from the point χ = 5.

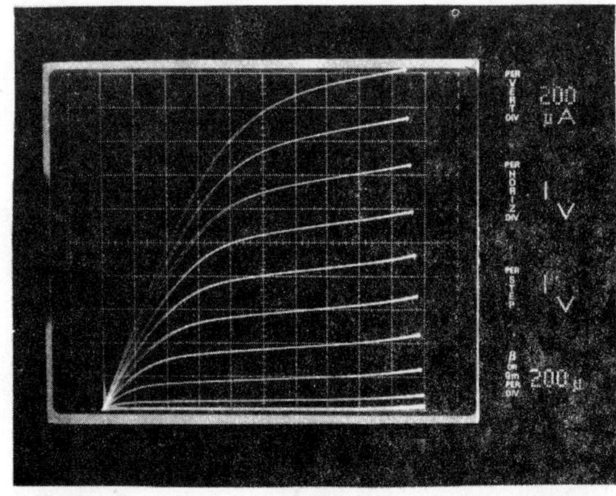

Fig. 5 Drain current ... ..ain voltage characteristics as a function of gate voltage. L_{SD} = 1 μ and W = 5 μ. t_{ox} = 400A.

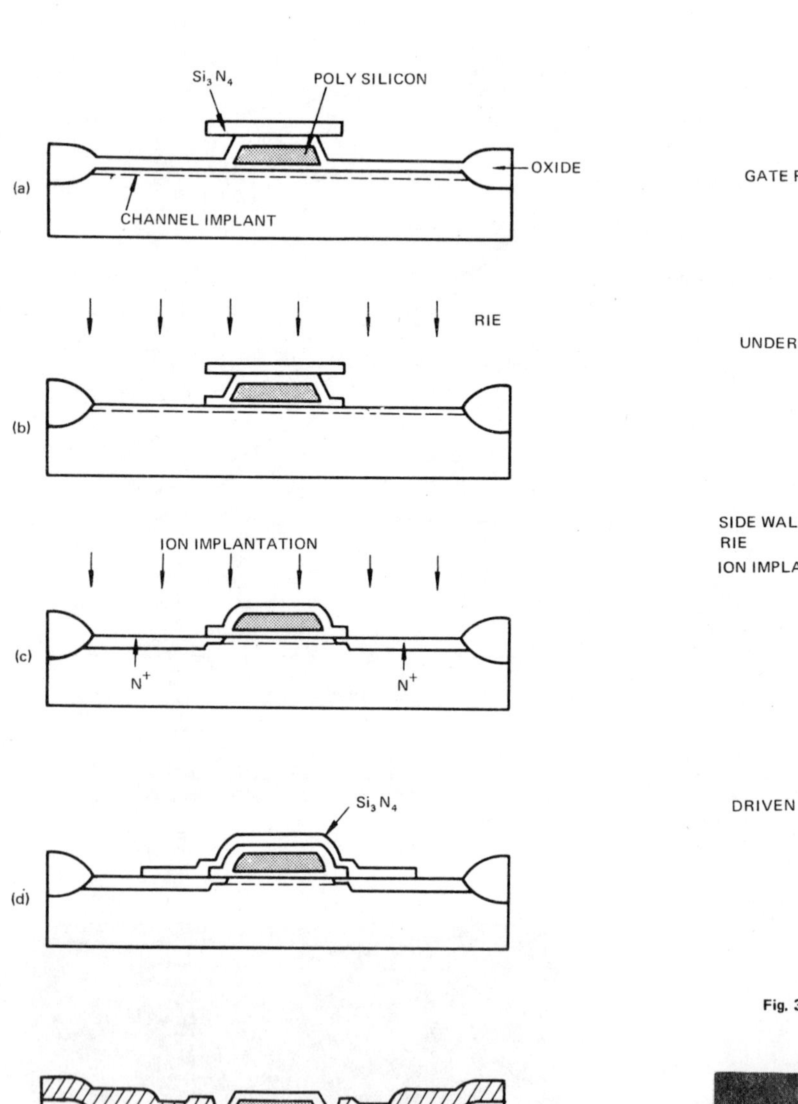

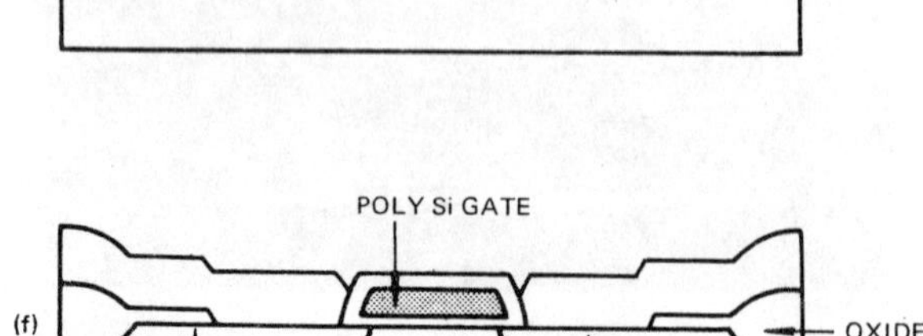

Fig. 2 Device structure and processing steps. Typical film thicknesses: gate oxide 400 Å, poly Si gate 0.3 μ, interlayer oxide 0.3 μ, masking Si_3N_4 for RIE 0.22 μ, poly Si side wall oxide 0.15 μ, oxide in the active region after side wall oxidation 0.1 μ.

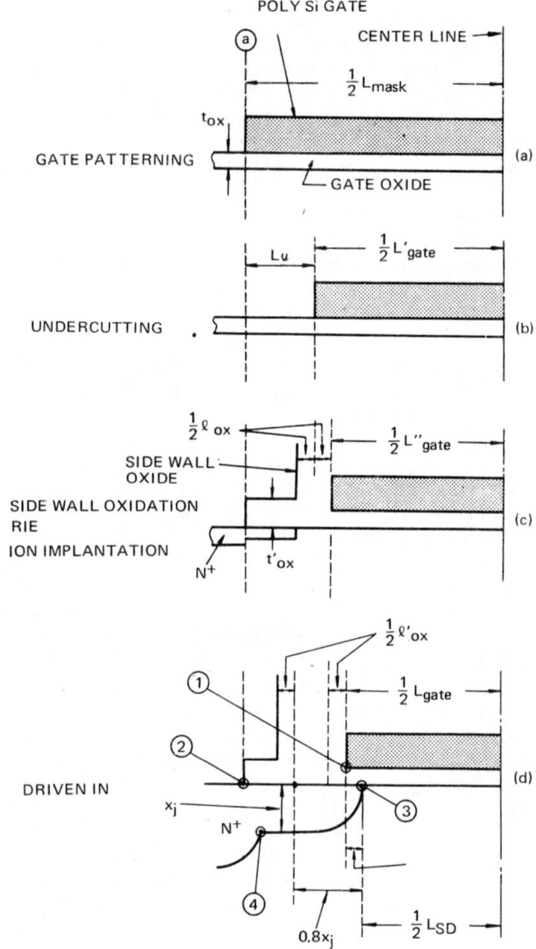

Fig. 3 The details of Quadruple Self-Aligning processes.

Fig. 4 (a) The plan view of the device after the undercutting of poly Si gate.

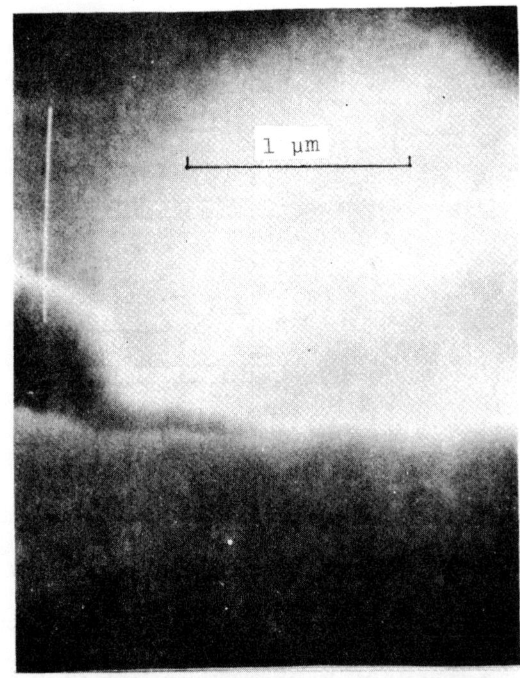

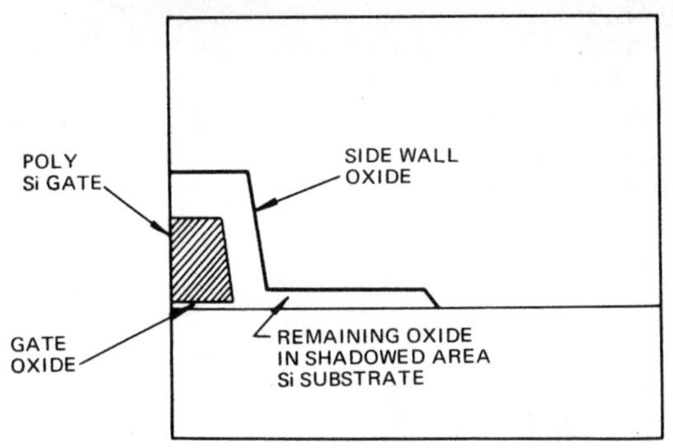

Fig. 4 (b) The cross sectional view of the device after the reactive ion etching of SiO_2 and the removal of Si_3N_4 are made.

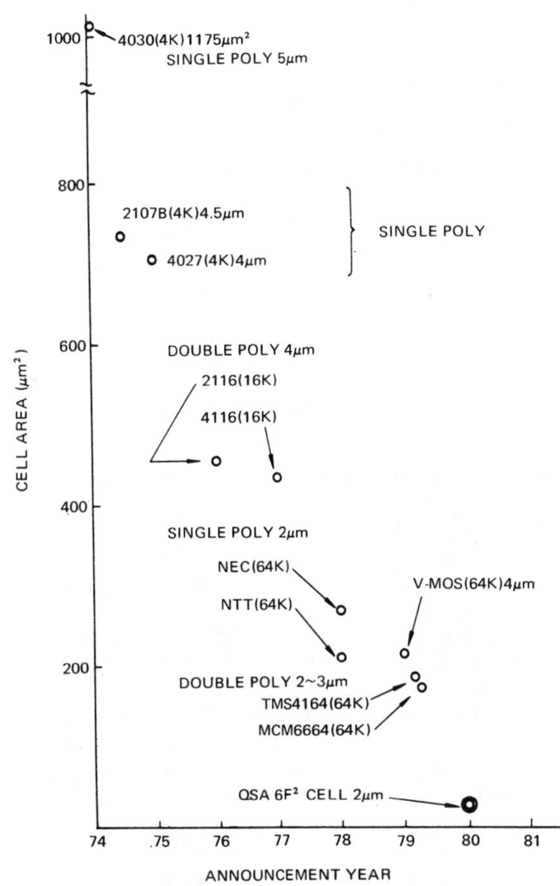

Fig. 7 Comparison of the cell area between dynamic random access memories.

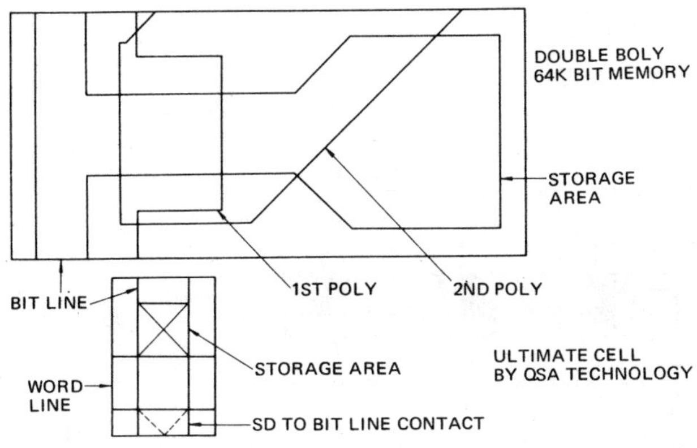

Fig. 6 The layout of dynamic random access memory cell.

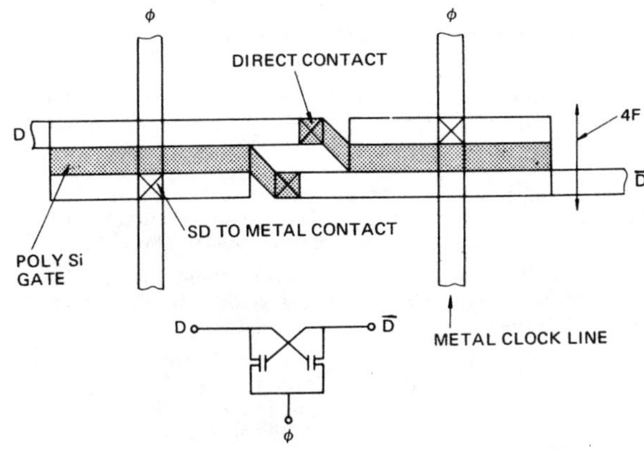

Fig. 8 A layout of 4 F pitch sense amplifier in dynamic MOS random access memory.

MOS Buried Load Logic

Yoshio Sakai, Toshiaki Masuhara, Osamu Minato and Norikazu Hashimoto

Hitachi Central Research Laboratory

Tokyo, Japan

RECENTLY, HIGH PERFORMANCE MOS devices have been developed using scaling technologies[1] and three-dimensional device structures such as VMOS[2]. However, complex processing is required. This paper will describe a three-dimensional device structure which utilizes a buried JFET load fabricated with simple processing.

The device and circuit – MOS *b*uried *l*oad *l*ogic (BLL or BL^2) – are shown in Figure 1. Driver MOSTs are located in the low concentration P-wells formed by the CMOS process[3]. The load device is a vertical JFET (or SIT)[4] buried under the driver MOST. The P-well windows under the driver MOST drains are the channel regions of the load devices. The N type substrate is the common drain for the load devices. The MOST drains are the sources of the buried JFETs. Therefore, the BL^2 is a merged device which achieves high packing density. A photomicrograph of the BL^2 inverters is shown in Figure 2 with E/D and CMOS inverters: the BL^2 has the smallest inverter area. The load device has triode-like I-V characteristics, as shown in Figure 3. These characteristics result from the low impurity concentration of the channel regions. The load current is determined mainly by three device parameters: size of the P-well window (channel thickness), P-well depth (channel length) and impurity concentration of the channel region. The latter two parameters are determined by the CMOS process[3]. Therefore, the first is the main design parameter of the load device. The depleted channel regions of the load devices reduce the drain junction capacitance of the driver MOSTs. Therefore, the parasitic load capacitance consists mainly of the gate capacitance of the driver MOST; this provides high speed, low power logic. The BL^2 is completely CMOS compatible. Therefore, one can design VLSIs using both BL^2 for high speed logic and CMOS for low power logic.

The transfer characteristic curves of BL^2 inverters are shown in Figure 4. The BL^2 inverter provides the maximum output voltage level corresponding to the V_{cc} supply value. In BL^2 inverters, large inverter gains can be obtained with small load device areas. Eighty-eight stage inverter chains were fabricated using 3μm gate length MOSTs. Figure 5 shows the propagation delay time versus power dissipation of BL^2 inverters. High performance of the BL^2 was confirmed by a minimum gate delay of 0.34ns and a minimum power delay product of 0.17pJ using a 5V supply. The performance is better than that of E/D NMOS logic.

A four-stage BL^2 binary counter was fabricated; its photomicrograph and circuit are shown in Figure 6. The BL^2 counter size is 3.52×10^{-2} mm^2, which is much smaller than conventional TTL counters. The maximum toggle frequency and the power dissipation were measured and are presented in Table 1. The BL^2 maximum toggle frequency of 72.5MHz is comparable to that of a high-speed Schottky counter. BL^2 power dissipation has been reduced to 4.1mW at the maximum toggle frequency, which is thirty times smaller than for a high-speed Schottky counter.

The BL^2 is most suitable for the Weinberger arrangement[5] because the load device permits a large degree of freedom in layout. Furthermore, in the BL^2 layout, power supply lines are not necessary because of the buried loads, and the output nodes are P-well windows in the diffusion N^+ layers. A BL^2 full adder was designed with the area of 1.04×10^4 μm^2, which is more than twice as dense as the same VMOS layout[2].

Acknowledgments

The authors wish to thank M. Kubo and T. Funabashi for their helpful discussions.

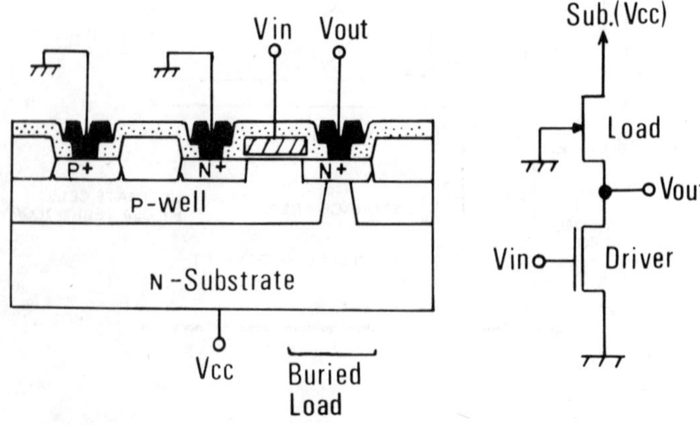

FIGURE 1–Device structure and circuit diagram of the BL^2.

---

[1] Jecmen, R.M., Ebel, A.A., Smith, R.J., Kynett, V., Hui, C.H. and Pashley, R.D., "A 25ns 4K Static RAM", *ISSCC DIGEST OF TECHNICAL PAPERS*, p. 100-101; Feb., 1979.

[2] Rogers, T.J., Meindl, J.D., "VMOS: High-Speed TTL Compatible MOS Logic", *IEEE Journal of Solid-State Circuits*, SC-9, p. 239-250; 1974.

[3] Sakai, Y., Masuhara, T., Minato, O., Hashimoto, N., "High Packing Density, High Speed CMOS (Hi-CMOS) Device Technology", *Proceeding of the 10th Conf. on Solid-State Devices*, Tokyo; 1978: *Japanese Journal of Appl. Physics*, 18, Supplement 18-1, p. 73-78; 1979.

[4] Nishizawa, J., Terasaki, T., Shibata, J., "Field Effect Transistor Versus Analog Transistor (Static Induction Transistor)", *IEEE Trans. Electron Devices*, ED-22, p. 185-197; 1975.

[5] Weinberger, A., "Large Scale Integration of MOS Complex Logic: A Layout Method", *IEEE Journal of Solid-State Circuit*, SC-2, p. 182-190; 1967.

Reprinted from *IEEE Int. Solid State Circuits Conf.*, pp. 56–57, 1980.

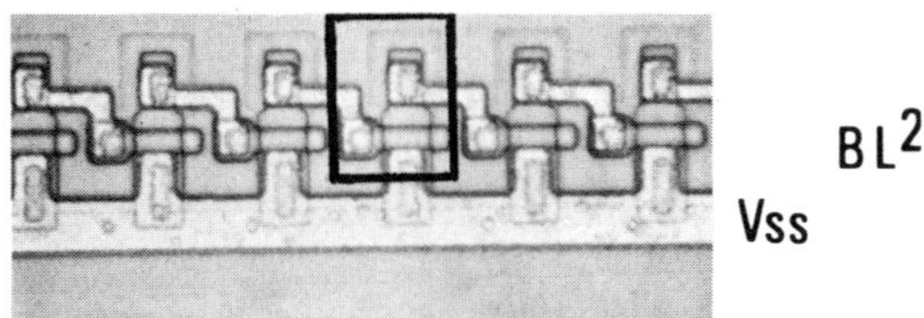

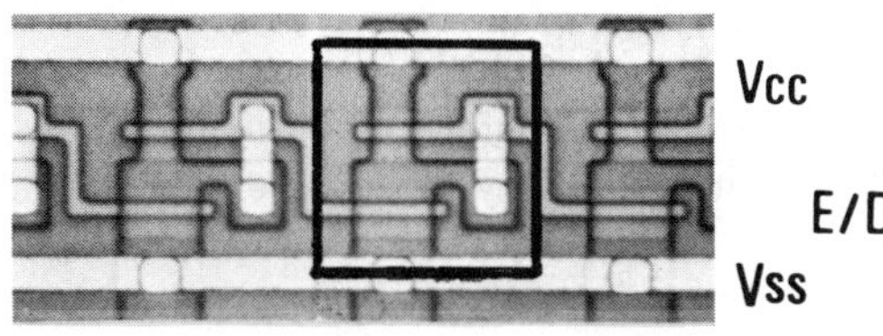

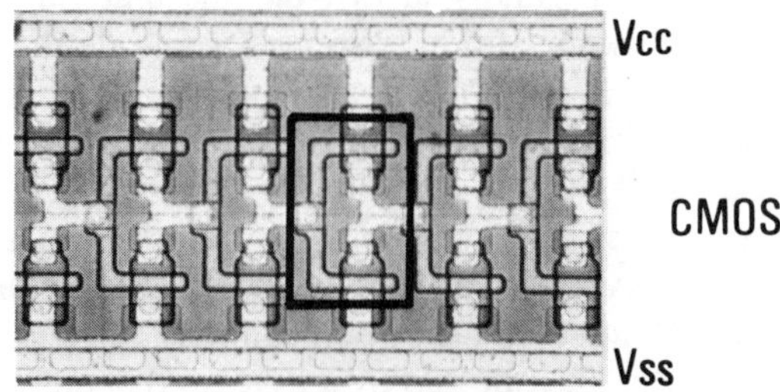

FIGURE 2—Photomicrograph of BL^2, E/D and CMOS inverters.

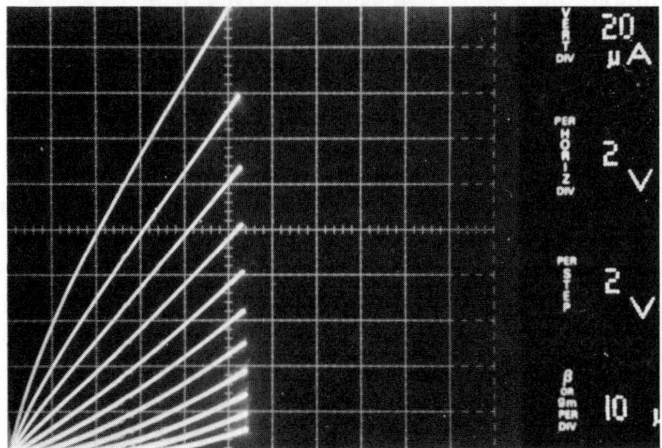

FIGURE 3—Current-voltage characteristics of buried load device.

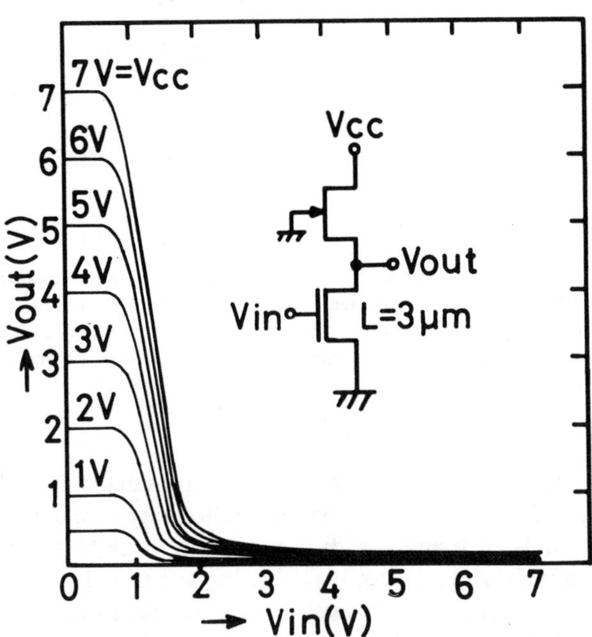

FIGURE 4—Transfer characteristic curves of BL^2 inverter.

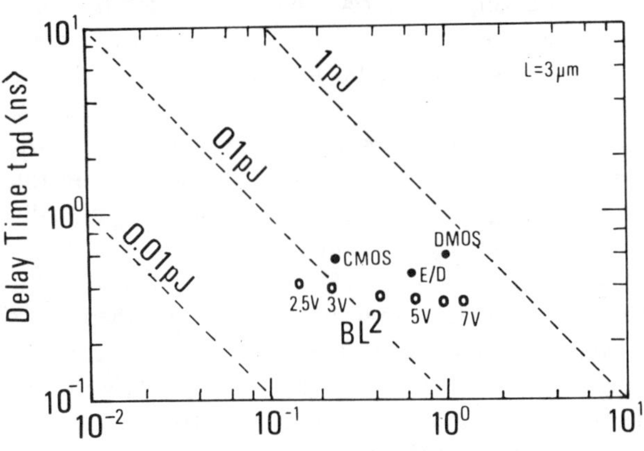

FIGURE 5—Propagation delay time versus power dissipation/gate of BL^2 inverters.

[Right]

FIGURE 6—Four-stage BL^2 binary counter with circuit diagram.

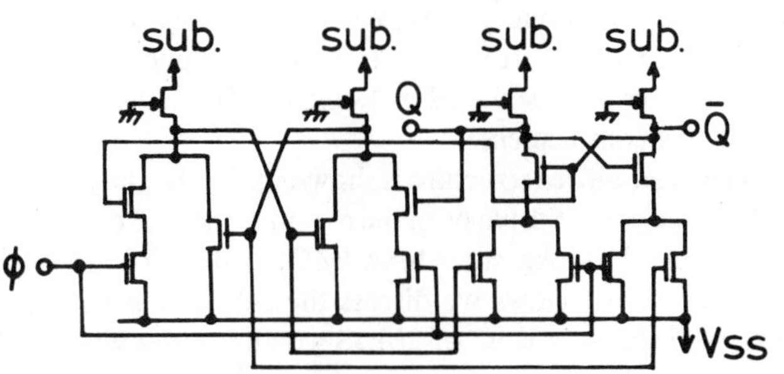

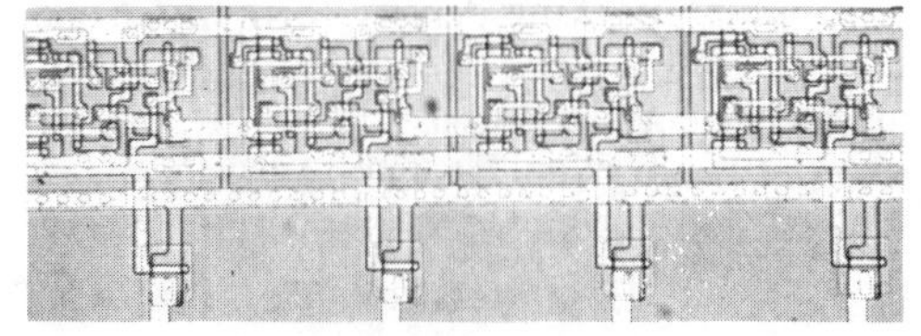

Device	Max. Freq. (MHz)	Power (mW)
High Speed Schottky	101	124
Low Power TTL	12	7.9
BL^2	72.5	4.1

Table I

One-Gate-Wide CMOS Inverter on Laser-Recrystallized Polysilicon

J.F. GIBBONS, FELLOW, IEEE, AND K.F. LEE

Abstract—**A CMOS inverter having a single gate for both n and p channel devices has been fabricated using bulk silicon for the p channel device and a laser-recrystallized silicon film for the n channel device. The fabrication details and dc electrical performance of this device are described.**

INTRODUCTION

Several recent publications have shown that 0.5 μm thick CVD Si films can be recrystallized by a scanning cw argon laser beam to produce material in which MOS devices can be fabricated directly [1]-[4]. In particular, Lee et al. [1] showed that both enhancement and depletion mode devices could be made on the *top* surface of such films using conventional techniques for fabrication of source and drain wells, gate oxidation, and so on. The channel mobilities deduced from the drain characteristics of these devices gave values that were found to be 60-70% of the values obtained on single crystal substrates. Q_{SS} values at the oxide/recrystallized polysilicon interface were found to be $10^{11}/cm^2$, which is device-worthy even though it is somewhat more than an order of magnitude higher than Q_{SS} for a high-quality oxide/single crystal silicon interface.

In a more recent paper, Kamins et al. [5] measured the interface properties that are obtained when a single crystal/SiO_2/polysilicon sandwich is exposed to laser radiation under conditions that recrystallize the polysilicon layer. They found that under appropriate processing conditions, Q_{SS} values at both the crystalline silicon/SiO_2 interface and the SiO_2/laser recrystallized polysilicon interface could be kept at or below the mid-$10^{10}/cm^2$ level. These results together with the previous results of Lee et al. led us to attempt to make a one-gate-wide CMOS inverter in which the bulk silicon is used for the p-channel device and the *bottom* of the laser recrystallized polysilicon film is used for its n-channel complement.

The basic device structure is shown in Fig. 1. The *j*oint use of a single gate to drive both the n- and p-channel devices led Kleitman [6] to suggest the term JMOS to describe this structure. In what follows we discuss the fabrication and basic electrical characteristics of JMOS structures that were made to explore the central idea. The electrical characteristics obtained appear to warrant further investigation of the JMOS structure as a high packing density form of CMOS.

Manuscript received April 21, 1980.

The authors are with Stanford Electronics Laboratories, Stanford, CA 94305

EXPERIMENTAL

To obtain the highest surface mobility for the particle with the lower bulk mobility, it is preferable to build the p-channel device in the single crystal substrate. Accordingly, fabrication is performed on an n-type <100> single crystal of Si of resistivity 1-4 Ω-cm. A layer of 5000 Å of field oxide was thermally grown on this material, after which source and drain regions were defined by photolithographic patterning and chemical etching. A boron predeposition was then done at 950°C for 30 min., followed by a 900°C, 15 min. dry O_2 oxidation. The field oxide was removed at the gate region by another patterning step, and 1000 Å gate oxide was grown at 1000°C in dry O_2. A layer of 1 μm of CVD polysilicon was then deposited as the gate material, followed by a $POCl_3$ predeposition at 975°C for 30 min. to dope the gate. 2000 Å of CVD SiO_2 was then deposited and the gate was defined by a photolithographic patterning step plus chemical etching of the CVD SiO_2 and polysilicon. The gate dimensions utilized in these experiments were $100\mu/50\mu$ (W/L). After fabrication of the gate, the CVD SiO_2 was removed by chemical etching, and 1000 Å SiO_2 was grown on the gate polysilicon at 1100°C in dry O_2. A layer of 0.5 μm of CVD polysilicon was then deposited, followed by a B^+ implant of $1 \times 10^{12}/cm^2$ at 100 keV. This layer of CVD polysilicon acted as device material for the n-channel device on the top level. A thermal anneal at 1100°C in N_2 for 1 hour was carried out to improve the surface structure during subsequent laser recrystallization [3]. A scanning cw argon laser was used, with a laser power of 10W, a spot size of 40μm, a scan speed of 12 cm/sec, a step size of 15μm, and a substrate temperature of 350°C. The top level device region was defined by deposition of 2000 Å of CVD SiO_2, a patterning step, and chemical etching of the CVD SiO_2 and laser recrystallized polysilicon. The CVD SiO_2 was then removed. 5000 Å of CVD SiO_2 was deposited to cover up the structure and densified at 900°C. Source and drain regions to the top level devices were defined and formed by a $POCl_3$ predeposition at 975°C for 30 min. Contact holes were then defined. Al was evaporated, patterned and alloyed at 450°C in N_2 for 30 min. to complete the structure.

DEVICE CHARACTERISTICS

The drain characteristics of devices obtained from the

Reprinted from *IEEE Electron Device Letters*, vol. EDL-1, pp. 117-118, June 1980.

fabrication schedule outlined above are shown in Fig. 2(a) and 2(b). In part (a) we show the drain characteristics for the p-channel device, which was made on the single crystal silicon. From analysis of these drain characteristics we find a threshold voltage of −2.2 volts and a surface mobility for holes of 180 cm^2/V-sec. These values are consistent with a Q_{SS} value of approximately 1.6×10^{11}; threshold shifting could be performed using conventional implantation techniques and thermal annealing prior to fabrication of the gate as outlined above.

The drain characteristics for the n-channel device are shown in Fig. 2(b), and lead to a threshold voltage of 2.1 volts and a surface mobility for electrons in the laser recrystallized film of 160 cm^2/V-sec. These values are somewhat lower than those obtained in previous experiments [4] but nonetheless sufficient to indicate that well-machined CMOS devices can be made in the two-level ("high-rise") configuration envisaged as JMOS.

Acknowledgements

The authors would like to acknowledge their indebtedness to ARPA (Contract MDA903-78-C-0128) for support and Dr. R. Reynolds for his continuing interest in this work. They would also like to acknowledge Nancy Latta and Zora Norris for expert technical assistance.

References

[1] K.F. Lee, J.F. Gibbons, K.C. Saraswat, and T.I. Kamins, Appl. Phys. Lett. *35*, 173 (15 Jul 1979).

[2] T.I. Kamins, K.F. Lee, J.F. Gibbons, and K.C. Saraswat, IEEE Trans. Electron Devices *ED-27*, 290 (Jan 1980).

[3] A.F. Tasch, Jr., T.C. Holloway, K.F. Lee and J.F. Gibbons, Electronics Letters *15*, 14, 435 (5 Jul 1979).

[4] K.F. Lee, J.F. Gibbons, K.C. Saraswat, T.I. Kamins, H.W. Lam, A.F. Tasch, and T.C. Holloway, *AIP Conference Proceedings*, No. 50, Materials Research Society, Boston, 1978.

[5] T.I. Kamins, K.F. Lee, and J.F. Gibbons, IEEE Electron Device Lett. *EDL-1*, 5 (Jan 1980).

[6] D. Kleitman, private communication.

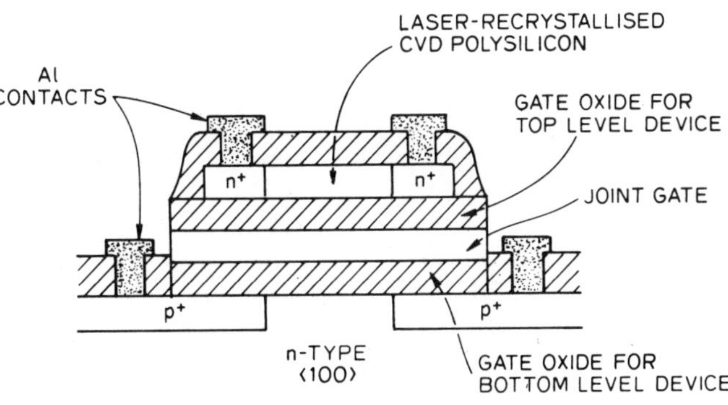

Fig. 1. Schematic of a JMOS structure.

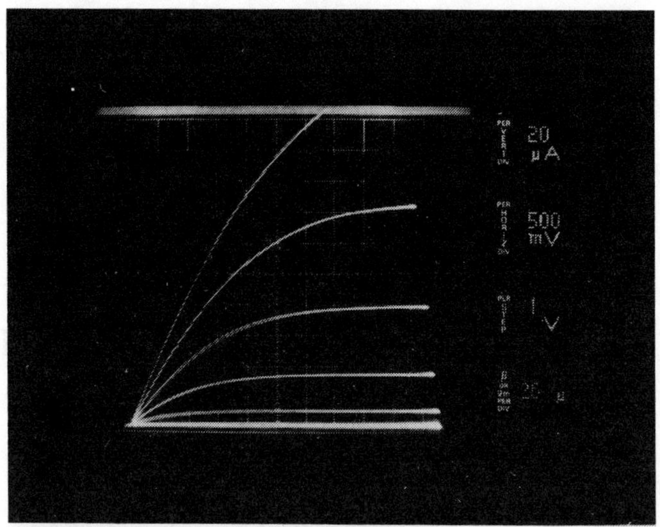

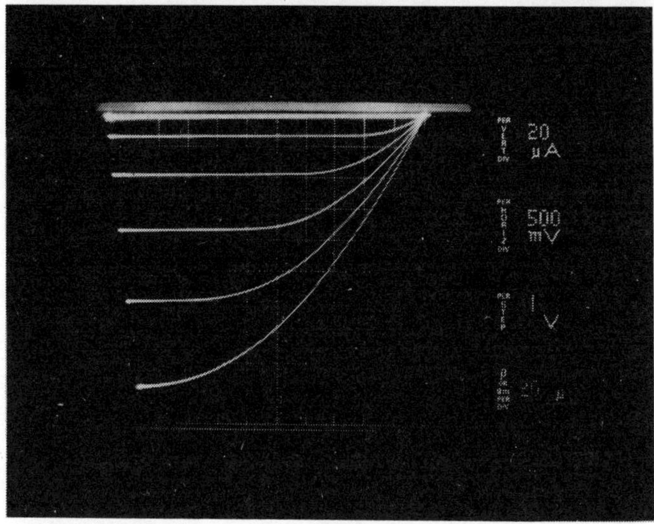

Fig. 2. (a) I-V characteristics of upper-level n-channel enhancement mode device fabricated in laser-recrystallized polysilicon, V_G = 7 V to 0 V.
(b) I-V characteristics of lower level p-channel enhancement mode device fabricated in single crystal, V_G = -7 V to 0 V.

Section 2.4
Circuit and System Design for VLSI

The Evolution of Digital Electronics Towards VLSI

ROBERT W. KEYES

Abstract—Technological trends are extrapolated to the end of this century. Problems of utilizing high levels of integration are noted, and the capabilities of technology are viewed in the perspective of the problems to provide a forecast of the levels of integration that will be found in large computing systems. A physical model and some more speculative system assumptions are used to estimate the performance of the systems. The physical characteristics forecast for the system are summarized.

I. Introduction

PROGRESS in microelectronics has been extremely rapid. All aspects of electronic data processing have benefited from the great improvements that have taken place in the cost, reliability, and performance of electronic components. It is possible to extrapolate the history of integrated-circuit technology into the future and foresee a long continuation of this rapid progress [1]-[5]. However, the extrapolation implies certain changes in the intensive parameters of a system, such as increasing impurity concentrations and electric fields in semiconductor components and increasing density of power dissipation in large systems containing many components. One is thus forced to ask how far extrapolation can be carried before the changing intensive parameters lead to fundamental alterations in the phenomena which are basic to the operation of semiconductor devices. In other words, one must consider the extrapolation of semiconductor technology to ever-smaller dimensions in the light of known semiconductor phenomena and the laws of physics.

The purpose of this paper is to extrapolate the basic properties of increasingly powerful integrated-circuit chips through the remainder of this century. Models will then be used to derive performance, as measured by time per operation, from the physical description of the chip. Such performance projections will also require assumptions about the packaging of the chips. Certain parameters of the model have been derived by fitting to existing systems. Somewhat more speculative system assumptions will be introduced to provide a forecast of the evolution of large computers through the time period considered. Most of the quantitative description of the models is relegated to the Appendixes.

The relation of computer performance to technology requires a physical model of a complete computing system. The physical implementation of a system, however, offers a great many opportunities for choice, so that a wide variety of physical designs are actually encountered. In addition, physical implementations are extremely complex in detail. Thus any model that aims to be generally applicable must be greatly simplified and can only hope to represent a limited number of important features in a semiquantitative way. In most cases neither theory nor experience suffices to provide accurate and unique relationships between the properties of chips and the characteristics of system components built from the chips. Such relationships must be regarded as deterministic in modeling, and are described by simple mathematical formulas fitted to the qualitative and semiquantitative information that is available.

The application of projections of the capability of technology to the highest performance systems will be considered. It will be assumed that the development of large computers will occur by evolution, i.e., that no drastic revolutions will change the basic character of such machines. Thus the subject is "what might happen" rather than "what will necessarily happen." The scenario could be drastically changed by, for example, the development of techniques for using many millions of slow components to process information at the same rate as hundreds of thousands of fast components, or the development of a superconducting computer operating at cryogenic temperatures.

II. Extrapolation to VLSI

Extrapolations are broadly based on the assumptions that present levels of development effort will continue and produce results comparable to those achieved in the past. They also assume that such results will be economically desirable, that they will enable a user to exercise data-processing functions at reduced cost. Extrapolation through the earlier part of the period covered has been substantially guided by available projections of others [1]-[5]. It is influenced by judgements as to where the physical limits will be found in the latter part of the period. Fig. 1 shows an extrapolation of the basic capabilities of semiconductor technology as measured by chip size and minimum dimension produced by the lithographic process. The dates used in plotting the extrapolations of this section are intended to mean the dates of delivery of systems incorporating the technologies in question. There is no fundamental physical barrier to the achievement of the progress shown [6].

Fig. 2 shows how a chip may be regarded as composed of a large number of squares, each with side equal to the minimum lithographic dimension shown in Fig. 1. The character of each small square can be controlled independently of the other squares. Thus the number of such small squares on the chip is the number of independently controllable or resolvable ele-

Manuscript received August 1, 1978; revised November 10, 1978.

The author is with the IBM Thomas J. Watson Research Center, Yorktown Heights, NY 10598.

Reprinted from *IEEE J. Solid-State Circuits*, vol. SC-14, pp. 193–201, Apr. 1979.

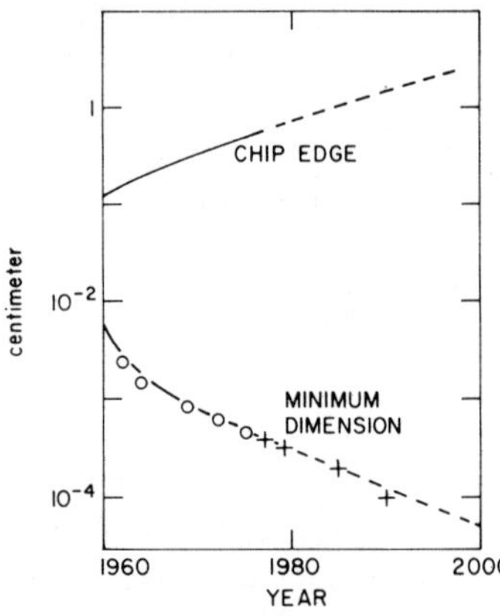

Fig. 1. History and projection of the minimum lithographic dimension and the maximum technologically feasible chip size. The points used to extrapolate minimum dimension are taken from [1] (O) and [3] (+).

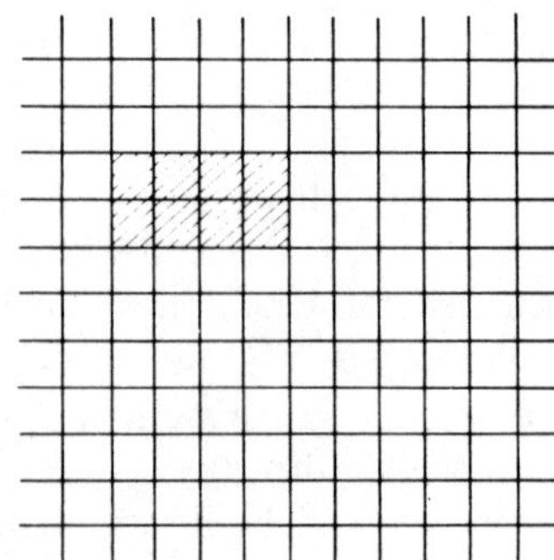

Fig. 2. Illustrating the concept of a resolvable element, a square with side equal to the minimum lithographic dimension. For example, the shaded area may be used to make an ohmic contact of sufficiently low resistance.

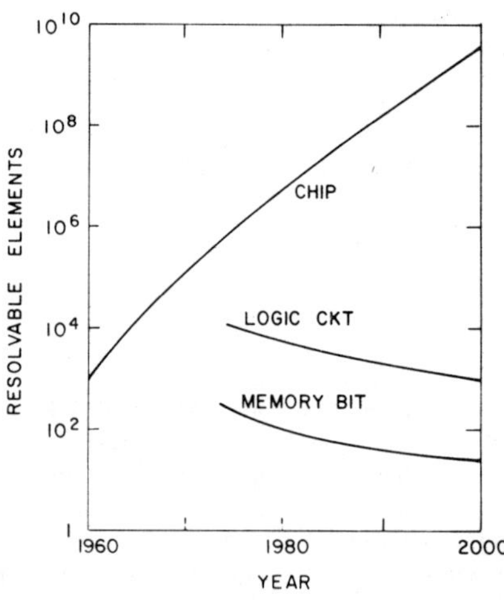

Fig. 3. The number of resolvable elements on a chip of maximum dimension, calculated from Fig. 1, and estimates of the number of such elements needed to construct a logic circuit and a memory bit plus the other elements, such as wires, decoders, and drivers that accompany them on the chip.

ELECTROMIGRATION
HOT ELECTRONS AND BREAKDOWN
WIRING COMPLEXITY
OHMIC RESISTANCE
INTERCONNECTIONS
POWER DISSIPATION

Fig. 4. The phenomena that will limit the advance of integrated digital electronics.

ments. Quite a few such resolvable elements are needed to fabricate, for example, the source, drain, and gate electrodes of a transistor and the insulating regions between circuits.

The number of resolvable elements per chip as derived from the extrapolated technological capabilities of Fig. 1 is shown in Fig. 3. Fig. 3 also shows an extrapolation of the number of elements needed to construct a logic gate or a memory bit together with its associated wiring and off-chip communication devices. Ingenuity has reduced the complexity of circuits in the past, at least as measured by resolvable elements in the surface plane of the chip, and the continuation of the exercise of this kind of ingenuity is anticipated [7], [8]. Increasing chip size, decreasing minimum dimension (miniaturization), and circuit inventiveness all contribute to the progress of integration [1].

Achievement of the extrapolated capabilities shown in Figs. 1 and 3 will require continuous process-development programs and substantial investments in tooling. Thus the projected advances will not take place unless they can be economically utilized to construct functional devices. Some of the phenomena that apparently are likely to limit the functioning of miniaturized, highly integrated semiconductor devices are listed in Fig. 4. It is clear that the degree to which these factors can be analyzed quantitatively varies widely. Consider them in order.

The first, electromigration, the motion of atoms induced by current in metallic wires, we believe will be fully contained by the development of better alloys.

Circuits based on lithography with minimum dimensions down to 1 μm promise to have superior performance that can be advantageously utilized. Beyond this point, high electric fields in devices will produce hot electrons and dielectric breakdown phenomena that will slow progress [9]-[12]. For example, exploiting the ultimate capacity of lithography may necessitate the development of devices in a material other than silicon. Nevertheless, economics favors progress towards the reduction of dimensions, since process costs tend to depend on the area processed rather than the number of devices. It is assumed, as shown in Fig. 1, that the hot-electron phenomenon will not prevent the development of devices with 0.5-μm dimensions in the year 2000.

On the other hand, several factors constitute more immediate limits to progress to larger substrates. In logic the complexity of the design of chips containing many circuits impedes progress. The resistance of interconnecting wires increases as dimensions are reduced. The increasing length of interconnections on a chip (measured in units of the average circuit-to-circuit distance) with increasing number of circuits exacerbates this problem [13], [14]. A guide to the dependence of the length on circuit count is shown in Fig. 5. The total line length on the chip, in the same units, is also shown in Fig. 5. Increasing the number of circuits on a chip increases the number of connections that must be made between the chip and its substrate, and the provision of the

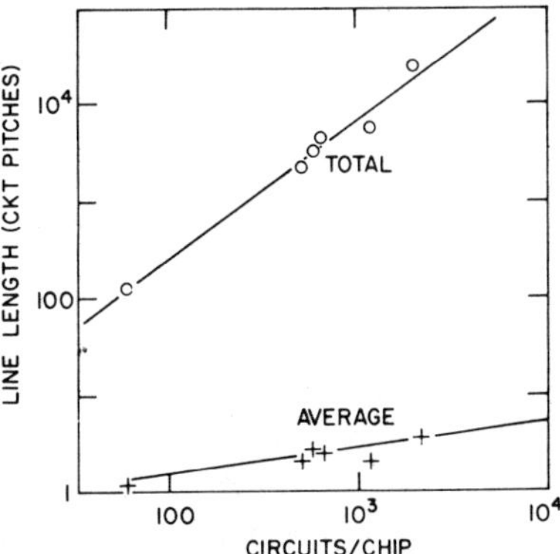

Fig. 5. The average interconnection length and the total wire length on a logic chip as a function of the level of integration, after the work of Donath [13] and Heller *et al.* [14]. The lengths are measured in circuit "pitches." The circuits are assumed to be placed on a square lattice, and the "pitch" is the circuit-to-circuit distance, which is the square root of the area per circuit.

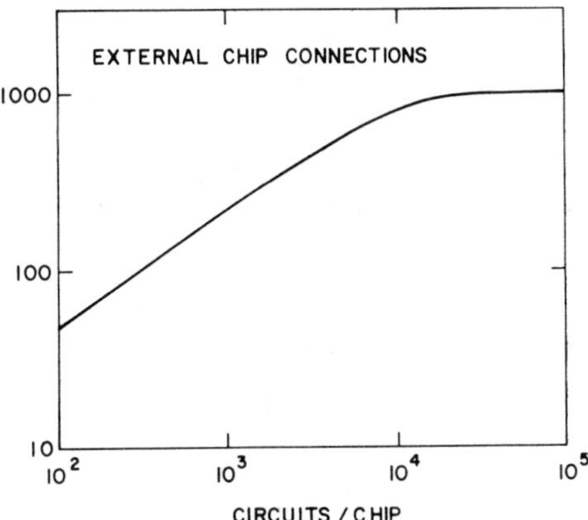

Fig. 6. The number of signal-carrying connections that must be made to a logic chip as a function of the level of integration [15]. The number of connections is proportional to the two-thirds power of the number of circuits at low levels of integration, but is not extrapolated beyond 1000 connections.

hundred or so connections now required is already difficult. An estimate of the dependence of the number of connections required in random logic on the number of circuits on a chip is shown in Fig. 6 [15]. Further, it is not clear that system speed is increased by striving for the highest possible number of circuits on a single substrate. The technical difficulties of utilizing very large random logic chips will prevent levels of integration from achieving the high values that could be attained by straightforward development of material science and lithographic processing.

Fig. 6 is an extrapolation of the results of Landman and Russo [15] at low circuit counts, but it is assumed that the number of connections to the chip will not exceed 1000. If a chip contains a reasonably complete functional entity or subsystem, the number of external connections may be even smaller.

Memory is more directly responsive to the cost per function, rather than to performance as measured by speed of operation, than is logic. Since the achievement of high logic speeds is one of the forces driving miniaturization of logic devices, memory devices will not demand such aggressive exploitation

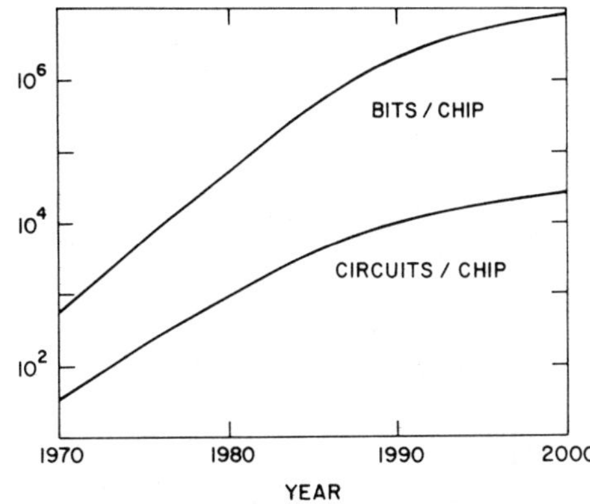

Fig. 7. An extrapolation of the levels of integration of main memory and logic chips, tempering the capabilities presented in Fig. 1 with the difficulties listed in Fig. 4.

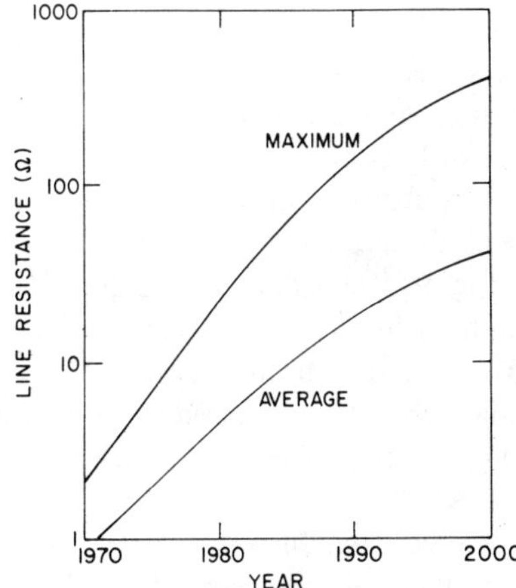

Fig. 8. The resistance of aluminum interconnecting lines, on logic chips, as calculated from the dimensions of Fig. 1, the average line lengths of Fig. 5, and maximum line lengths taken to be half of the chip edge.

of advanced lithographic capability. However, advances will eventually be slowed by the hot-electron effects that will inevitably become more serious as device dimensions fall towards 1 μm or less.

Thus our guess at the rate of growth of bits/chip and logic circuits per chip, Fig. 7, shows a slower growth for logic than for memory and a declining rate of growth after 1990 as the limits are more firmly felt. These projections do not strain the ability of technology to provide larger chip sizes, and it is assumed that chip size grows at a rate that will accommodate the component growth shown in Fig. 7. For comparison with Fig. 1, the logic-chip edge is 0.25 cm and the memory-chip edge is 1.6 cm in the year 2000. The projections imply that miniaturization of off-chip connections will be achieved; the chip area per connection decreases to a value less than 10^{-4} cm^2.

One of the consequences of the assumption about the size of logic chips presented in Fig. 7 is shown in Fig. 8: The increase in interconnection resistance on the chip. The resistance of the average interconnection increases both because of the decrease in the dimensions of a wire and because of the increase in length shown in Fig. 5. The resistance of the maximum length wire, taken to have a length one-half the chip

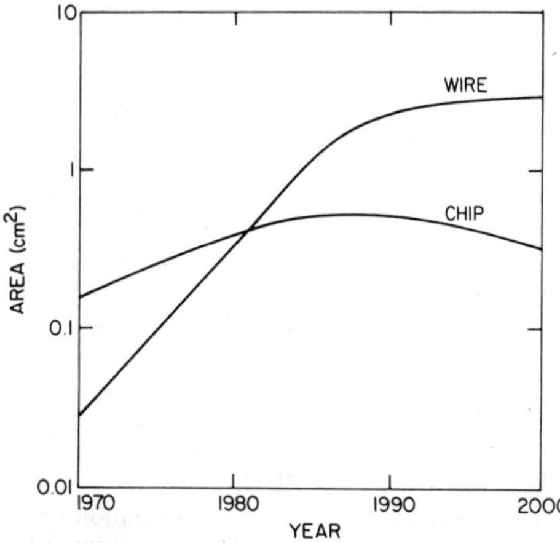

Fig. 9. The area of logic chip wiring, as calculated from the dimensions of Fig. 1 and the total line lengths of Fig. 5, compared with the area of a chip.

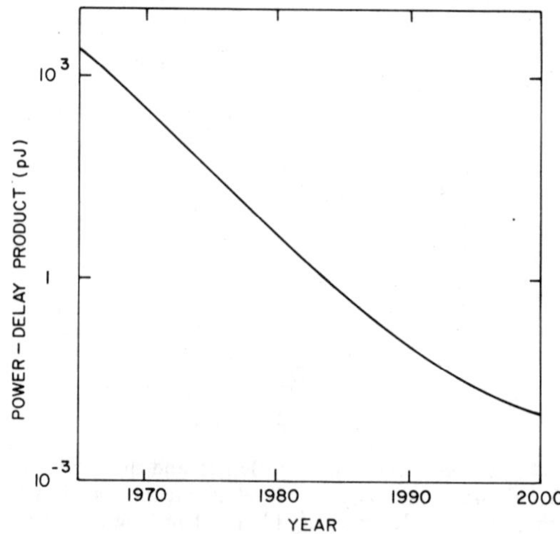

Fig. 10. The power-delay product of logic, including early vacuum tube as well as transistorized computers. The extrapolation is drawn to approach a limit of 0.01 pJ.

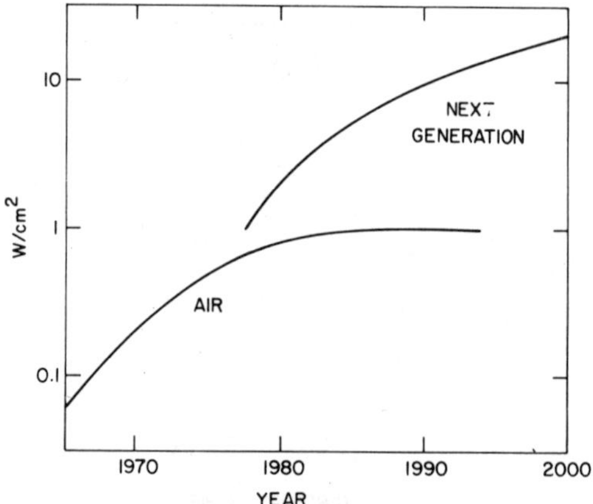

Fig. 11. A projection of cooling capabilities for logic chip packages. Forced-air cooling is probably limited to about 1 W/cm². New cooling technologies, in which heat is transferred to a liquid without the intermediary of air, are emerging [17], [18], and it has been assumed that they will extend cooling capability to 20 W/cm².

edge, becomes quite large, and is intolerable with present methods. Wiring designs and circuit layouts must find ways to avoid these longest wires.

Another consequence of the assumed level of integration of logic chips and the growth of line length shown in Fig. 5 is presented in Fig. 9. Here the area required for the wiring, assuming that the wire width and the spacing between wires are equal to the minimum dimension and that 25 percent of the wiring channels can be utilized, is plotted and compared with the area of the chip. The more rapid growth of area needed for wiring implies that a substantial increase in the number of wiring layers will be required.

The progress in miniaturization can be expected to yield improvements in performance; that is, in speed of logic circuits. Part of the improved performance is a direct result of shorter distances that signals must travel between circuits. Miniaturization also plays a large role in the steady decrease of the energy utilized per switching operation since the introduction of transistors into computers. The trend of this parameter, the product of power per circuit and logic delay (*pt*) is shown in Fig. 10 [16]. The energy dissipated has decreased by about four orders of magnitude since 1957. The sources of this decrease may be very roughly assigned as follows. One order of magnitude to decrease in voltage; we have suggested that the voltage is approaching a lower limit and cannot be decreased much further [6]. Two orders of magnitude to miniaturization. One order of magnitude to improved designs, such as replacing p-n junction area with semiconductor/insulator interface. Historically, the power-delay product of integrated logic chips has decreased nearly in proportion to the area per circuit. Thus it can be expected that circuits will be operated with less power. Nevertheless, because of the projected rapid increase in the number of circuits per chip, it is desirable to increase the density of power dissipation. Difficulties in removing heat directly degrade circuit speed because of the power/speed tradeoff.

There is room for optimism concerning the power-dissipation limit, at least in the near future. The decrease in the *pt* product of high-speed logical operations that has characterized the last 30 years will continue through several more orders of magnitude, as forecast in Fig. 10. The value shown for *pt* in the year 2000 is only about 10^6 times the thermal energy of an electron or molecule at ordinary temperatures.

Advances in cooling technology also seem imminent. Circuits are conventionally cooled by transfer of heat from a semiconductor or semiconductor module to air. However, air cooling is limited to a power density of about 1 W/cm², as shown in Fig. 11. Emerging technologies, in which heat is transferred directly to a liquid without the intermediary of air [17], [18], break through the 1-W/cm² limit and are probably limited to something like the maximum rate of heat transfer to boiling Freon, about 20 W/cm², as also illustrated in Fig. 11.

As mentioned, there are many choices to be made in the physical design of a system, and many factors other than performance to be considered. Optimization is not done on a day-to-day basis, so that the technological parameters change in a series of steps rather than as a continuous curve. Thus the projections shown in Figs. 6-11 are trends and can only be expected to represent the state of technology semiquantitatively at any given time.

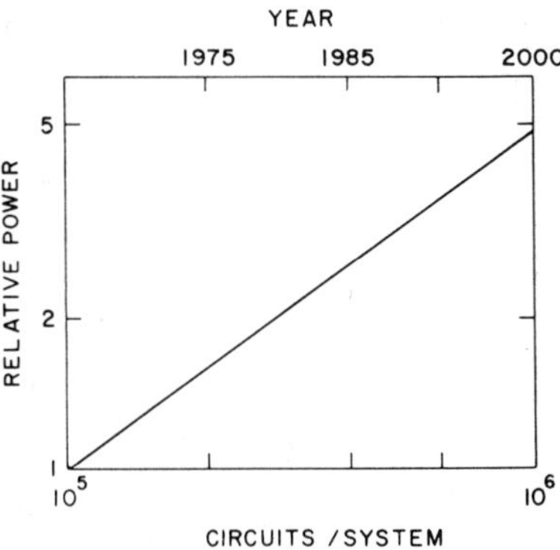

Fig. 12. An assumption that research in the "computer sciences" will make it possible to use increasing amounts of hardware to process information faster. The information processing power of a computer is assumed to increase as the 0.7 power of the number of circuits. As used in the present model, this means that 60 packaged delay times (see Appendix A) are used to process an instruction in a system of 2×10^5 circuits, and that the number decreases to 20 for a system of 10^6 circuits. The projected rate of system learning, only a very rough guess, is also indicated.

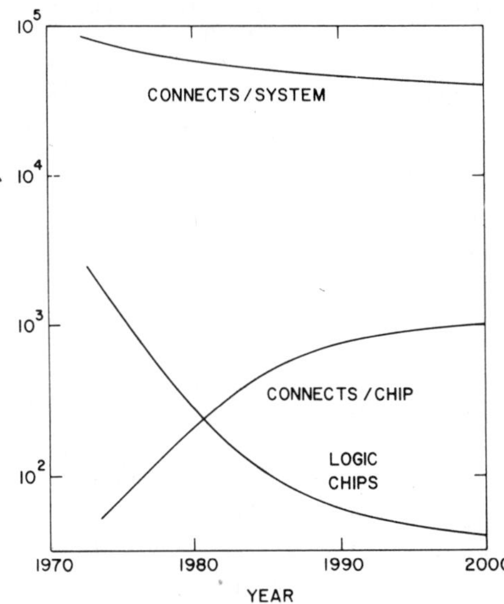

Fig. 13. The provision of chip-to-package connections is regarded as a costly element of computer system manufacture. Thus, one of the objectives of the projection of the level of integration of logic chips shown in Fig. 7 was to decrease the total number of off-chip connections used in the light of the growth of system size shown in Fig. 12. The results, calculated from Figs. 6, 7, and 12, are shown.

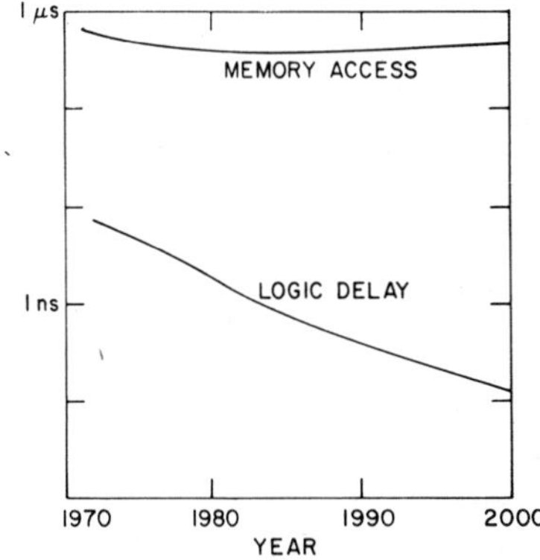

Fig. 14. Packaged logic delays and main-memory access times calculated from the models presented in Appendixes A and B, and the extrapolations of technology.

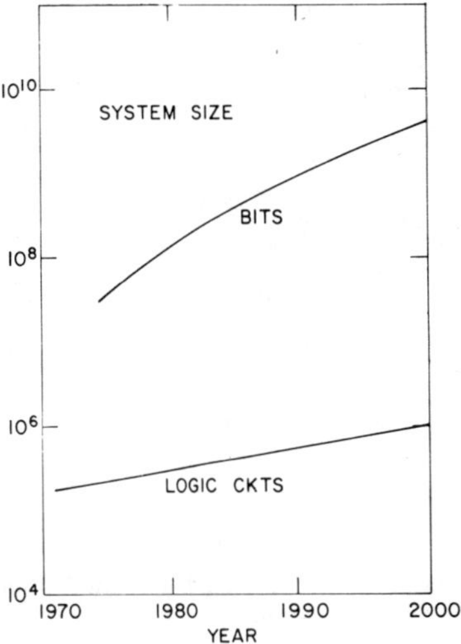

Fig. 15. The rapid growth of memory utilization resulting from the assumption that the number of bits grows in proportion to MIP's.

III. Modeling System Performance

It is anticipated that system learning will occur, and that it will be possible to utilize ever-increasing numbers of circuits in a single system to speed the instruction stream. The relative power of a system is assumed to grow slightly slower than proportionately to the system circuit count, as shown in Fig. 12, and the circuit count is allowed to grow from 2×10^5 in 1975 to 10^6 in the year 2000. The meaning of this in the model of performance is that the time per instruction is assumed to decrease from 60 packaged logic delays to 20 packaged logic delays during the period.

The implications of this system assumption for the chip-connection problem are shown in Fig. 13. The number of logic chips decreases because of the rapid increase in the level of integration. The number of chip connections also decreases somewhat. The prevention of a substantial growth in total number of chip connections is regarded as an objective of design in these projections, and implies that a much lower level of integration of the logic chips would be unacceptable.

The forecasts of integration level, *pt* product, and cooling capability (Figs. 7, 10, and 11) can be used in a physical theory to predict the progress of packaged logic delay. The limiting delay is regarded as the sum of two parts, the circuit delay, which is obtained by dividing the *pt* product by power, and the chip-to-chip transit time [19]. The latter, however, increases with power; since the power density is limited to values shown in Fig. 11, the more power expended per chip, the further apart the chips must be placed. The power per circuit can be chosen to minimize the total delay, as described in more detail in Appendix A.

The resulting logic delay is shown in Fig. 14. The calculation predicts that it will decrease through more than another order of magnitude through the remaining part of the century.

For comparison, the main memory access time, estimated in Appendix B, is also shown in Fig. 14. This does not decrease much through the time period in question because of the rapid growth in memory size. It has been assumed that the main

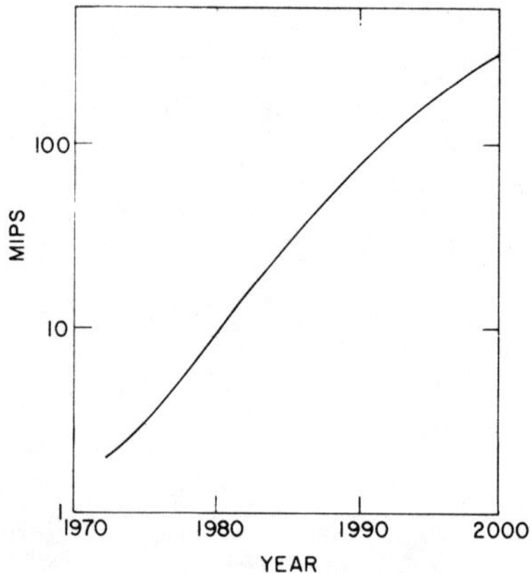

Fig. 16. The projected growth of processing power as measured by millions of instructions performed per second.

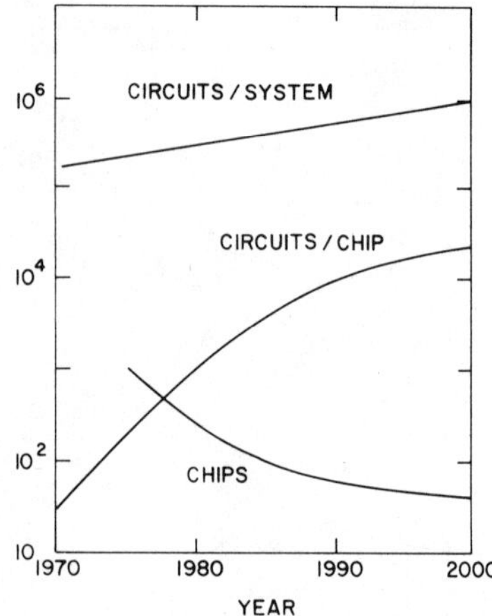

Fig. 17. A summary of the projected evolution of numbers of logic components.

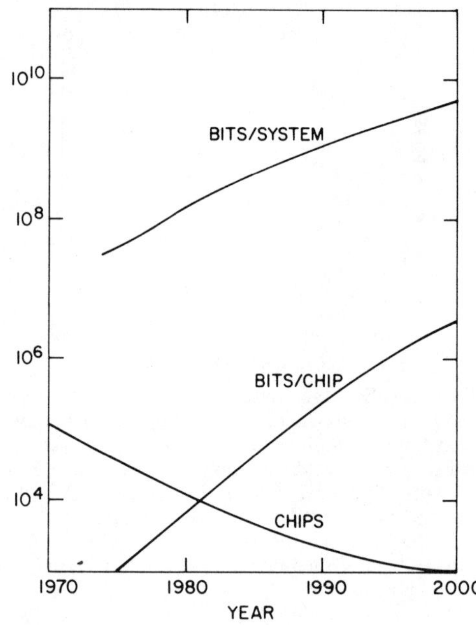

Fig. 18. A summary of the projected future numbers of memory components.

memory will continue its historical trend to grow in proportion to computer power, resulting in the number of bits per system shown in Fig. 15.

The increasing gap between logic speed and memory access will have to be taken up by increasing attention to buffers and cache memory, and, perhaps, by innovations in memory hierarchy. The model used to determine the effect of memory access time and the interposition of a cache memory on system performance is described in Appendix B. Assuming that this can be successfully done, the growth of large system power, as measured by millions of instructions per second, shown in Fig. 16, can be forecast.

IV. Physical Characteristics of the VLSI System

A few additional results follow from the calculations presented.

The system parameters—that is, total component count, components per chip, and number of chips—are summarized in Figs. 17 and 18 for logic and memory.

The assumptions about lithography and the level of integration lead to values for the chip area. The projections relating to area are summarized in Fig. 19. The memory chip grows steadily in area through the period. The rapid growth of total memory compensates the advantages gained from lithography

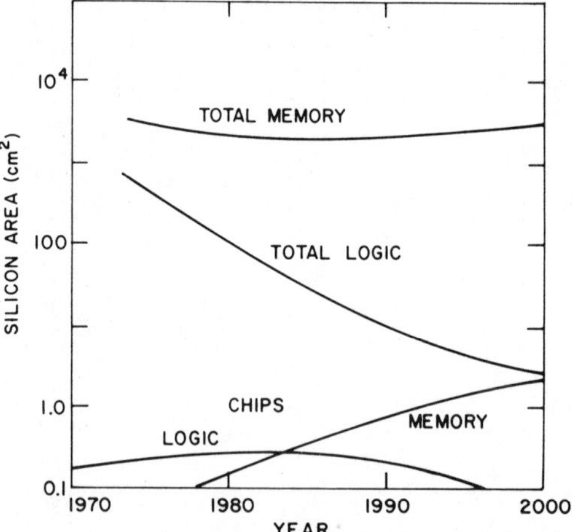

Fig. 19. The projected utilization of silicon area.

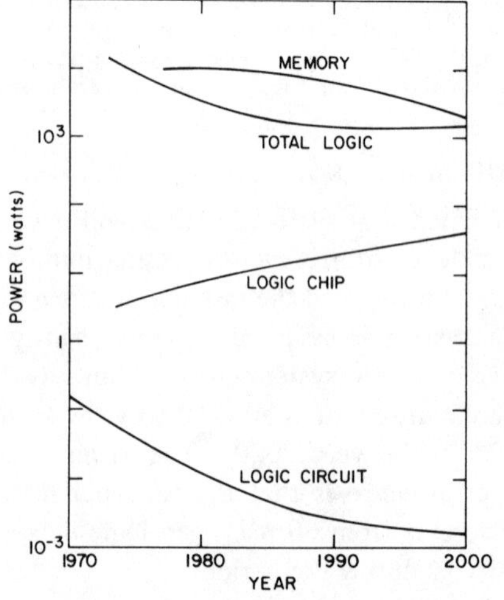

Fig. 20. The power demands predicted by the model.

and ingenuity to keep the total silicon area in the memory nearly constant. On the other hand, the limitation of the size of logic chips to 25 000 circuits implies a decreasing chip size, and the slow growth of circuit count in the system leads to a decrease in the silicon area required for logic. Thus over 100 times more silicon area will be devoted to memory than to logic by the end of the period.

Power utilization by the electronic components is summarized in Fig. 20. Power consumption is increasingly dominated by memory during the period.

V. Conclusions

Utilization of the advanced capabilities for the fabrication of integrated circuits that will become available for random logic chips will require solution of several difficult problems: Design and construction of the increasingly complex chip wiring, provision of many more external electrical connections to increasingly small chips, and devising circuits that can tolerate large interconnection resistances. Assuming that some progress can be made in these areas, the evolutionary development of large machines should lead to single processors capable of handling 300 million instructions per second by the end of the century. Such large machines will be physically dominated by memory; for example, the silicon area in the memory will be three orders of magnitude greater than the area in logic.

Appendix A
Model of Packaged Delay

The removal of the heat generated in the semiconductor devices is a performance-limiting aspect of packaging. It is possible to quantify this limit as follows. The characteristic heat-transfer parameter of a planar packaging technology is the maximum rate per unit area at which heat can be removed from the package. A widely used measure of the performance of semiconductor circuits is their power-delay product. Assume that device-design changes within a given technology can be used to trade speed with power while maintaining a fixed power-delay product, i.e., if p is the power per circuit and t_c is the delay per circuit, then the semiconductor technology only requires that

$$pt_c = U. \tag{A1}$$

The energy dissipated per switching operation, the pt product, is an important parameter of switching circuits. The progress of the pt product in simple circuits, is shown as a function of time in Fig. 10. In complex logic circuits, it depends on circuit fan-out and wire loading. Energy must be supplied to change the capacitance of several other devices and of the wiring that interconnects devices in actual logic circuits. A term proportional to the average wire length is added to the pt product of Fig. 10 to take account of the effect of the wiring. The term proportional to length has the form $C'V^2l$, where C' is the capacitance per unit length, V is a voltage, and l is the total wire length driven by the circuit, taken to be three times the average wire length given by Fig. 5. $C'V^2$ is about 2 pJ/cm in advanced modern chips; a value 1 pJ/cm is used here to allow room for improvement in wire geometry and reduction of voltage. Summing up, the energy per operation used in the model is

$$U = (pt) + 3 \times (1 \text{ pJ/cm}) \times l_{av}. \tag{A2}$$

Here (pt) must be understood to mean the pt product given by Fig. 10.

An analytic representation of l_{av} is used in the calculations. From Fig. 5

$$l_{av} = 0.3N^g \tag{A3}$$

where N is the number of circuits on a chip and g has the value 0.325.

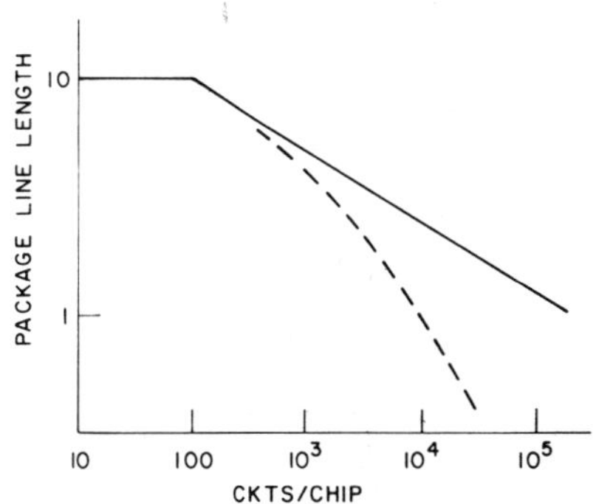

Fig. 21. The weighting factor m for off-chip delays in the minimization of average packaged delays. The solid line is an interpolation between values $m = 10$ for low levels of integration and $m = 1$ for integration approaching the total systems on a single chip. The dotted line shows the additional reduction in m that results from the reduced incidence of off-chip connections as the level of integration increases. The latter factor is based on the assumption that off-chip delays are only encountered with probability (1/12) if the number of circuits per chip exceeds 50 000.

Delays encountered by signals in passing from chip to chip also constitute an appreciable part of the average logic delay. The contribution of the off-chip delays to the average depends on the frequency with which signals leave a chip and the length of the off-chip wiring on the package. Little accurate information that sheds light on either of these quantities is available.

Almost every logic stage sends its output off-chip in systems with low levels of integration, and it appears that the off-chip delays amount to the time needed for a signal to traverse about ten chip pitches. "Chip pitch" is the center-to-center distance between chips on a planar package. This component of delay might be expected to decrease with increasing levels of integration. More lengthy sequences of operations can be completed on a chip if it contains many logic gates, and a signal leaving a chip would seem to have a greater probability of having a receptor at a shorter distance if the level of integration is high. These results are obvious in the limit in which a system can be constructed from only one or a very few chips. Thus the weighting of off-chip delays used here is essentially an interpolation between the simple views of the very low and very high levels of integration just described. The form of the assumed relationships is plotted in Fig. 21. Here the average number of chip pitches included in the logic delay per stage is plotted as a function of the number of logic circuits per chip. These numbers are the values of the quantity m in the theory of packaged delay given below.

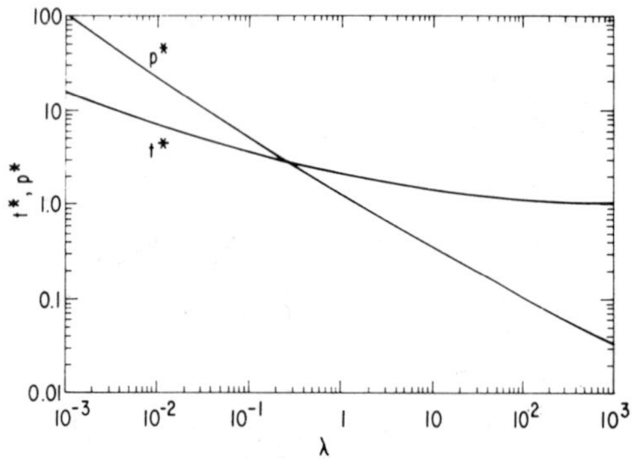

Fig. 22. The values of p^* and t^* which provide the solution of (A6)–(A9).

Let semiconductor chips, each containing N logic gates with the property described by (1) be packaged on a planar substrate from which heat can be removed at a maximum density Q per unit area, with each chip occupying an area L^2. Assume, further, that an amount of power P_D is dissipated in the high-current circuits that drive the transmission lines that connect one chip to another. Then heat removal requires

$$P_D + Np \leqslant QL^2. \tag{A4}$$

The time taken for a signal to propagate from one chip to another is mL/c_1, where c_1 is the velocity of electromagnetic waves on the interconnections and m is the length of interconnections measured in units of the distance between chips L. It is also required that L be larger than the chip edge a. The total packaged delay t_p is the sum of the circuit delay t_c and the chip-to-chip propagation time. All of these effects are taken into account by expressing t_p as a function of the power as

$$t_p = (U/p) + (m/c_1)\left((Np + P_D)/Q)^{1/2} + a\right) \tag{A5}$$

where m is the factor that weights the chip-to-chip delays shown in Fig. 21. There is a value of p that minimizes t_p, given by the equation

$$(1 + Np/P_D)^{1/2} = mNp^2/2c_1UQ^{1/2}P_D^{1/2}. \tag{A6}$$

Equation (4) can be solved with the aid of Fig. 22, in which $p^* \equiv Np/P_D$ is plotted as a function of a parameter λ, defined by

$$\lambda \equiv (m/2c_1NU)\,(P_D^3/Q)^{1/2}. \tag{A7}$$

The propagation time τ_p then is given by

$$\tau_p = (ma/v) + (mP_D^{1/2}/c_1Q^{1/2})\,\tau^*. \tag{A8}$$

The quantity τ^* here is also plotted in Fig. 22 and is related to λ and p^* by

$$\tau^* = (\tfrac{1}{2}\lambda p^*) + (1 + p^*)^{1/2}. \tag{A9}$$

The results given by (A6)–(A9) are used to determine the packaged delays.

Appendix B
Memory Access and Cache

As is the case with most of the quantitative relationships that are needed for a model of system performance, no simple, unique relation between memory access time and memory size, power dissipation, and chip characteristics can be found. Qualitatively, it is seen that memory access time decreases with an increase in chip power, with miniaturization, and with decreasing memory-system size. Memory access time does not directly enter into the model of system performance. Thus, a relatively simple view of memory access time was adopted. The expression used for memory access time is

$$T_M = K_M C_M^{\alpha} p^{-1} A^{1/2}. \tag{B1}$$

Here K_M is a constant, C_M is the number of chips in the memory, p is the power per chip, and A is the chip area, α is a parameter, estimated to have the value 0.2.

Since the memory-chip size grows steadily in the model, memory access times do not decrease significantly according to (B1). It is assumed that the increasing gap between processing time and memory access time is taken up by a fast buffer or cache memory, built essentially with the technology used for the logic chips.

Assume that a small buffer memory or cache with fast access time holds the information that is currently needed by the processor. The cache is small enough that occasionally the desired information is not found there, and it must be obtained by transfer from the main memory. In such a case, a main memory access time must be added to the cycle time of the processor. The size of the cache is determined in practice by economic considerations. The cache is very expensive, and the minimum amount that will optimize system performance per unit cost is used. Performance is measured by the reciprocal of t_I, the instruction time, and costs are measured roughly by the number of chips in the model used here. Thus the quantity to be optimized is

$$F = t_I(hn_L + n_C) \tag{B2}$$

where n_C is the number of cache chips, n_L is the number of logic chips, and h is a factor that accounts for the added cost per logic chip attributable to the more complex physical design of logic. The instruction time consists of the time calculated without references to the main memory plus the product of the "miss ratio" r and the main memory access time T_M

$$t_I = k_L t_p + k_M r T_M. \tag{B3}$$

Here k_L is the number of logic delays per instruction, t_p is the logic delay calculated in Appendix A, and k_M is the number of memory references per instruction. The miss ratio r is approximately related to the size of the cache by [20], [21]

$$r = K_C/n_C N \tag{B4}$$

where N is the number of bits on a cache chip. When (B3) and (B4) are substituted into (B2) and the resulting expression for F is minimized with respect to n_C, it is found that

$$n_C = (hk_M K_C n_L T_M/Nk_L t_p)^{1/2}. \tag{B5}$$

The following values were used in the application of this model: $h = 5$ and $K_C = 2000$; n_L is obtained by dividing the circuits per system by the circuits per chip; N is taken to be two times the number of logic circuits per chip; t_M is obtained from (B1); and k_L and k_M are both assumed to vary inversely as the "relative power" factor given in Fig. 12 and have the ratio $k_M/k_L = 1/12$.

References

[1] G. E. Moore, "Progress in digital integrated electronics," in *Tech. Digest 1975 Int. Electron Devices Meet.* (IEEE, New York, 1975), pp. 11-13.

[2] R. N. Noyce, "Large scale integration: What is yet to come?", *Science*, vol. 195, pp. 1102-1107, Mar. 18, 1977.

[3] G. Marr, "Perspectives on MOS directions," in *Fall COMPCON 77 Digest* (IEEE Catalog No. 77CH1258-3C), pp. 242-244.

[4] "Semiconductors face the '80s," *IEEE Spectrum*, vol. 14, pp. 42-48, Oct. 1977.

[5] E. Bloch and D. Galage, "Component progress: Its effect on high-speed computer architecture and machine organization," *Computer*, vol. 11, pp. 64-76, Apr. 1978.

[6] R. W. Keyes, "Physical limits in semiconductor electronics," *Science*, vol. 195, pp. 1230-1235, Mar. 18, 1977.

[7] J. M. Oliphant, "Technological impact on semiconductor memories," in *1976 Fall COMPCON Digest* (IEEE, New York, 1976), pp. 174-177.

[8] P. R. Schroeder, "Prospects for the 64K RAM," in *1977 Fall COMPCON Digest* (IEEE, New York, 1977), pp. 114-115.

[9] T. H. Ning, C. M. Osburn, and H. N. Yu, "Effect of electron trapping on IGFT characteristics," *J. Electron. Mat.*, vol. 6, pp. 65-76, Feb. 1977.

[10] B. Hoeneisen and C. A. Mead, "Fundamental limitations in microelectroncs–I. MOS technology," *Solid-State Electron.*, vol. 15, pp. 819-829, Aug. 1972.
—, "Fundamental limitations in microelectronics–II. Bipolar technology," *ibid.*, vol. 15, pp. 981-987, Sept. 1972.

[11] S. A. Abbas and R. C. Dockerty, "Hot carrier instability in IGFET's," *Appl. Phys. Lett.*, vol. 27, pp. 147-148, Aug. 1, 1975.

[12] D. R. Collins, "Excess current generation due to reverse bias p-n junction stress," *Appl. Phys. Lett.*, vol. 13, pp. 264-266, Oct. 15, 1968.

[13] W. E. Donath, "Placement and average interconnection lengths of computer logic," IBM Res. Rep. RC4610 (submitted to *IEEE J. Solid-State Circuits*).

[14] W. R. Heller, W. F. Mikhail, and W. E. Donath, "Prediction of wiring space requirements for LSI," in *Proc. 14th Design Automation Conf.*, (New Orleans, LA), June 20-22, 1977, pp. 32-42.

[15] B. S. Landman and R. L. Russo, "On a pin versus block relationship for partitions of logic graphs," *IEEE Trans. Comput.*, vol. C-20, pp. 1469-1479, 1971.

[16] K.-U. Stein, "Technologischer Stand in der Mikroelektronik," *Electrotech. Maschinenbau*, vol. 93, pp. 240-248, 1976.

[17] E. A. Wilson, "True liquid cooling of computers," in *1977 National Computer Conf. Proc.* (Montvale, NJ.: AFIPS Press, 1977), pp. 341-348.

[18] R. M. Russell, "The CRAY-1 computer system." *Commun. Ass. Comput. Mach.*, vol. 21, pp. 63-72, Jan. 1978.

[19] R. W. Keyes, "A figure of merit for IC packaging," *IEEE J. Solid-State Circuits*, vol. SC-13, pp. 265-266, Apr. 1978.

[20] S. I. Rege, "Cost, performance, and size tradeoffs for different levels in a memory hierarchy," *Computer*, vol. 9, pp. 43-51, Apr. 1976.

[21] T. Makino and N. Ohno, "Characteristics of not found probability in memory hierarchy system," *NEC Res. Develop.*, vol. 20, pp. 51-58, Oct. 1976.

Cost and Performance of VLSI Computing Structures

CARVER A. MEAD AND MARTIN REM

Abstract—**Using VLSI technology, it will soon be possible to implement entire computing systems on one monolithic silicon chip. Conducting paths are required for communicating information throughout any integrated system. The length and organization of these communication paths place a lower bound on the area and time required for system operations. Optimal designs can be achieved in only a few of the many alternative structures. Two illustrative systems are analyzed in detail: a RAM-based system and an associative system. It is shown that in each case an optimum design is possible using the area-time product as a cost function.**

I. Introduction

THE SILICON integrated-circuit technology is evolving continuously toward smaller elementary devices and denser, more complex functions on each single silicon chip. It appears that new processing and lithographic techniques will make possible the fabrication of chips containing 10^7 or 10^8 individual transistors. One such chip will contain more function than today's largest computers. A large amount of effort has been put into fabrication questions, and much more effort will be required to reach the practical limits of device compactness. However, there is at present essentially no theoretical basis for optimizing the overall organization of systems implemented in this technology.

The conventional complexity theory is inadequate because its measure of cost is the number of steps of a sequential machine. No account is taken of the size of the machine (and hence the time required for each step). Possible concurrency is ignored, thereby ruling out the most important potential contribution of the silicon technology. The traditional switching theory is also inadequate. While it provides a beautiful formalism for describing elementary logic functions, its optimization methods concern themselves with logical operations rather than communication requirements. Even in current integrated circuits, the wires required for communicating information across the chip account for most of the area, and driving these wires accounts for most of the time delay. In very large scale integrated systems, the situation becomes even more extreme. In this paper, we describe a method by which the conceptual organization of a large chip can be analyzed, and a lower bound placed on its size and cycle time before a detailed design is undertaken. The results of this analysis suggest rather general guidelines for the organization of large integrated systems.

II. Metrics of Space and Time

A. Physical Properties

Devices used to construct monolithic silicon integrated circuits are universally of the charge-controlled type. A charge Q placed on the control electrode (gate, base, etc.) results in

Manuscript received September 18, 1978; revised January 10, 1979. This work was supported in part by BMD under Contract DASG60-77-C-0097, and the Office of Naval Research under Contract N00014-16-C-0367. (California Institute of Technology, Computer Science Department Contribution 1584.)

C. A. Mead is with the Department of Computer Science, California Institute of Technology, Pasadena, CA 91125.

M. Rem is with the Department of Computer Science, California Institute of Technology, Pasadena, CA 91125, on leave from the Department of Mathematics, Eindhoven University of Technology, Eindhoven, The Netherlands.

Reprinted from *IEEE J. Solid-State Circuits*, vol. SC–14, pp. 455–462, Apr. 1979.

a current $I = Q/\tau$ flowing through the device. The transit time τ is the time required for charge carriers to move through the active region of the device.

All times in an integrated system can be formulated as simple multiples of τ. For one transistor to drive another identical to it, a charge Q must flow through its active region, requiring time τ. If the capacitance C_L of the load being driven is K times the gate capacitance C_g of the driving transistor, a time $K\tau = (C_L/C_g)\tau$ is required.

B. Linear Versus Hierarchical Structures

In large integrated systems it is necessary to communicate information throughout the entire system. As an example, a bit of information stored on the gate of a minimum size transistor in a random-access memory must be communicated to the memory bus of a CPU. Since there are many words of data in the memory, there are many possible sources for each wire in the memory bus. Fig. 1 illustrates two possible approaches to organizing such a bus. In the first approach, a transistor associated with each bit drives the bus wire directly. If the bus wire has a capacitance C_w, the time required to drive the bus wire is $t = \tau(C_w/C_g)$. In a typical computer memory, C_w is many orders of magnitude larger than C_g, and the delay introduced by such a scheme is very long. Since C_w is proportional to the length of the wire, it is also proportional to S, the number of driver transistors connected to the wire.

$$t = \tau S. \tag{1}$$

A second scheme is shown in Fig. 1(b). Here each transistor drives a wire only long enough to reach its neighbor. Each such wire is connected to the gate of a transistor twice as large as the transistor driving it. The arrangement is repeated upward until the top level where all sources have a path to the bus. In this scheme the delay in driving the lowest level wire is 2τ (assuming the primary capacitance is due to the gate of the larger transistor). The delay introduced by the wires at each level is the same, since each driver transistor is twice as large as those driving it. Hence the delay in driving the bus line is $2\tau N$ where N is the number of levels in the structure. Since there are $S = 2^N$ transistors at the lowest level, the delay may be written

$$t = 2\tau \log_2 S \tag{2}$$

Comparing (2) and (1), we see that for large S the delay has been made much shorter by using a hierarchical structure.

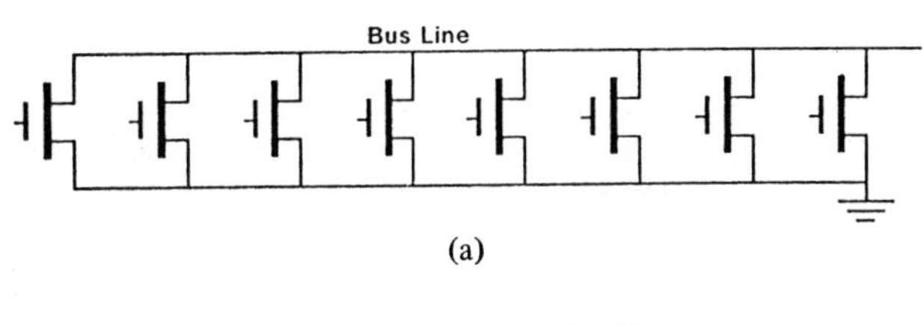

(a)

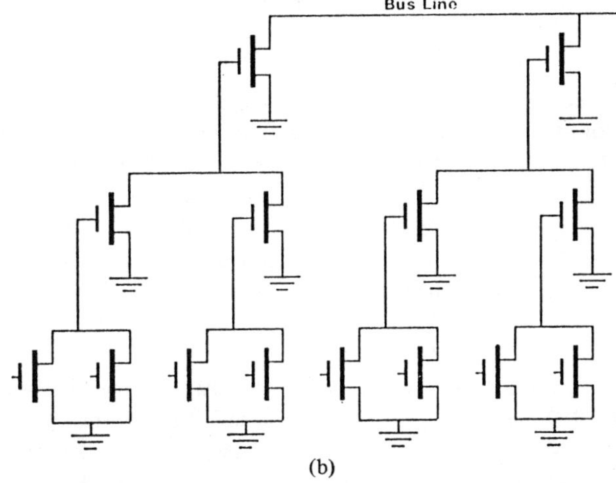

(b)

Fig. 1. (a) A bus driven directly by memory cells. (b) A bus driver tree.

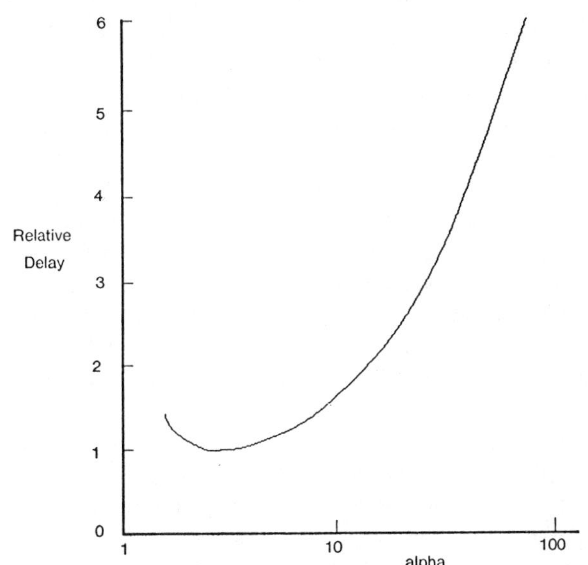

Fig. 2. Delay of a hierarchical structure as a function of α.

C. A Cost Criterion

A hierarchy such as that shown in Fig. 1(b) may be built using any integral number α of transistors driving each wire. The driver transistors will in general be α times the size of those driving them. The delay for such a structure is $t = \alpha\tau \log_\alpha S = \tau(\alpha/\log \alpha) \log S$. All system delays are thus proportional to $\tau \log S$, with a penalty factor $\alpha/\log \alpha$ dependent upon the branching ratio of the hierarchy. This delay is plotted in Fig. 2, normalized to its minimum value which is attained at $\alpha = e$.

While dramatic improvements in the performance of integrated structures can be achieved by a hierarchical organization, a penalty is always paid in the area required for wires. In the simple case shown, a bus requiring one wire when driven directly requires $\log_\alpha S$ wires when organized as a hierarchy. For this reason it is not possible to optimize a design without a cost function involving both area and time. In this paper we will use the area-time product as our basic cost function. For the above simple example, the cost function is area · time = $\tau(\log S)^2\ \alpha/(\log \alpha)^2$. The cost is minimized for $\alpha = e^2 \approx 7.4$.

D. Hierarchical Computing Systems

The analysis given above suggests a very general structure for computing systems. Lowest level cells are grouped together into modules in such a way that α cells drive their outputs onto an output wire. Each output wire is connected to a driver transistor which is α times as large as those driving the wire. Modules are grouped in such a way that α of those modules drivers are connected to an intermodule communication wire. This wire in turn is connected to a driver transistor α^2 times as large as the lowest level transistors. This process is continued until the appropriate size system has been realized.

III. Random-Access Memory

In this section we discuss the cost and performance of a random-access memory (RAM) of S words of $\log S$ bits each. As the unit of length we employ the minimum distance of two conducting paths. For the unit of time we choose the time it takes a basic element to charge a wire of unit length plus another transistor like itself. One unit of time is thus slightly larger than the transit time of a transistor.

A. Organization of the RAM

We organize the RAM in a hierarchical fashion. The elements of level 0 are the bits themselves, each bit consisting of two crossing wires: a select wire and a data wire. When the select wire is signaled it puts its contents on the data wire. We group α^2 bits into an $\alpha \times \alpha$ square to form a module of level 1. If the width of an element (a bit) is b_0, the elements have to drive wires of length αb_0. A module on level 1 consists of an array of crossing select and data wires, constituting the α^2 bits of level 0, and some additional logic and wires at the side. We group again α^2 of these modules into a square to form a module of level 2, etc. Fig. 3 shows three levels of the hierarchy for $\alpha = 4$.

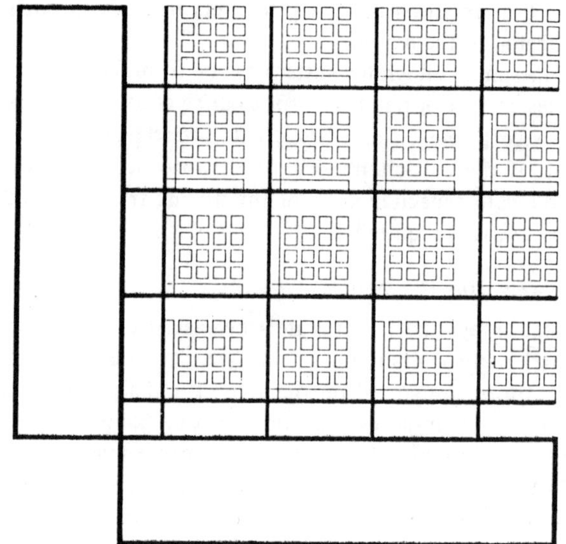

Fig. 3. Three levels of a memory hierarchy for $\alpha = 4$.

To study the memory in more detail we look at a module of level i (Fig. 4). We describe how one extracts one of its α^{2i} bits. In order to select 1 bit of storage, $2i \log \alpha$ address wires are required. We run $i \log \alpha$ of them, called the row address wires, vertically along the side of the module and the other $i \log \alpha$; the column address wires, horizontally. Its α^2 submodules are organized into α rows of α submodules each. When the select wire of the module is asserted $\log \alpha$ of the row address wires are used by the decoder to select one of the α rows of submodules; the select wire running through that row is asserted. The other $(i - 1) \log \alpha$ row address wires are run horizontally into each of the α rows of submodules, where they serve as column address wires for the submodules. Of the $i \log \alpha$ column address wires $(i - 1) \log \alpha$ are run vertically into each of the α columns of submodules, where they serve as row addresses. The other $\log \alpha$ address wires are used by the multiplexor to select one of the α data wires coming out of the columns of submodules. The signal on the selected data wire is driven onto the data wire of the module itself.

If we wish to have a memory of S words with $N + 1$ levels (level 0 through N) we choose $N = \log S/2 \log \alpha$ or $S = \alpha^{2N}$. This gives a hierarchical structure with S bits from which we can extract 1 bit at a time. If we want the word length to be $\log S$ we employ $\log S$ of these structures in parallel. To select one word we select 1 bit in each of the $\log S$ hierarchies.

B. Area of the RAM

Fig. 4 allows us to compute the size of a RAM. Let L_i denote the width of a module of level i; then we have the following recurrence relation:

$$L_0 = b_0$$

$$L_i = i \log \alpha + 1 + \log \alpha + \alpha \cdot L_{i-1}.$$

The solution to the above relation is

$$L_i = \alpha^i b_0 + \frac{\alpha^i - 1}{\alpha - 1} + \left(\frac{2\alpha^{i+1} - \alpha^i - \alpha}{(\alpha - 1)^2} - \frac{i + 1}{\alpha - 1} \right) \log \alpha.$$

Rather than the width itself we are interested in the width per bit. In one direction, horizontal or vertical, module i has α^i bits; therefore, we compute L_i/α^i.

$$\frac{L_i}{\alpha^i} = b_0 + \frac{1}{\alpha - 1} + \frac{2\alpha - 1}{(\alpha - 1)^2} \log \alpha - \frac{1}{(\alpha - 1)\alpha^i} \left[\left(\frac{\alpha}{\alpha - 1} + 1 + i \right) \log \alpha + 1 \right]. \tag{3}$$

An interesting property of the width per bit, as expressed by (3), is that its limit for $i \to \infty$ is finite.

$$\lim_{i \to \infty} \frac{L_i}{\alpha^i} = b_0 + \frac{1}{\alpha - 1} + \frac{2\alpha - 1}{(\alpha - 1)^2} \log \alpha. \tag{4}$$

This means that the width per bit L_i/α^i is bounded from above by (4) independent of the number of levels of a RAM. Expression (3) converges in an exponential fashion towards its limit. For small values of i, (3) is already very close to (4). Therefore, we use (4) as the width per bit for a RAM; its square is then the area per bit. By dividing the area per bit by the bit area b_0^2 we obtain the total area per bit area for a RAM. Fig. 5 shows this quotient as a function of α for four different values of b_0. It gives the overhead factor in the area that is due to the wires. For a memory of 64K bits with $N = 2$, α should be 16. Expression (4) is then equal to $b_0 + 0.6$. This shows that in 2-level 64K dynamic MOS memories, for which b_0 lies between 1 and 2, roughly half of the area will be occupied by wires.

One may wonder why we have not discussed the area that is

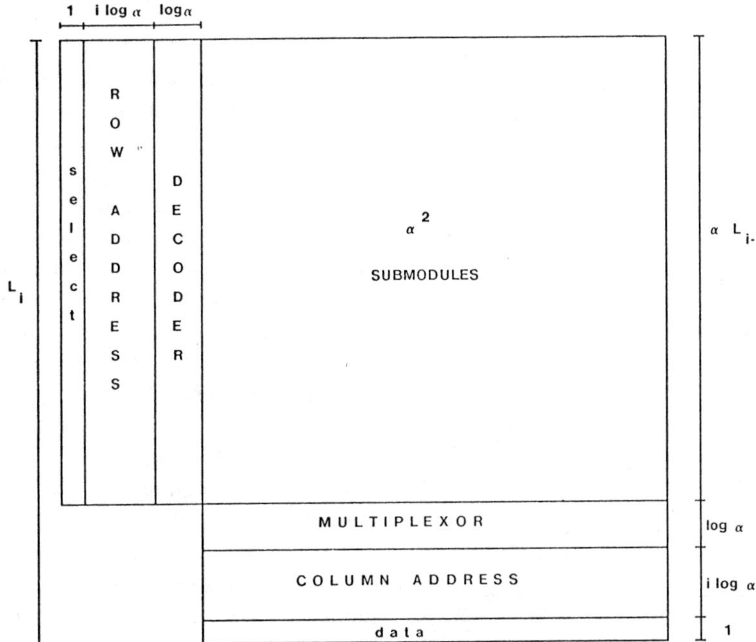

Fig. 4. A RAM module of level i ($i > 0$).

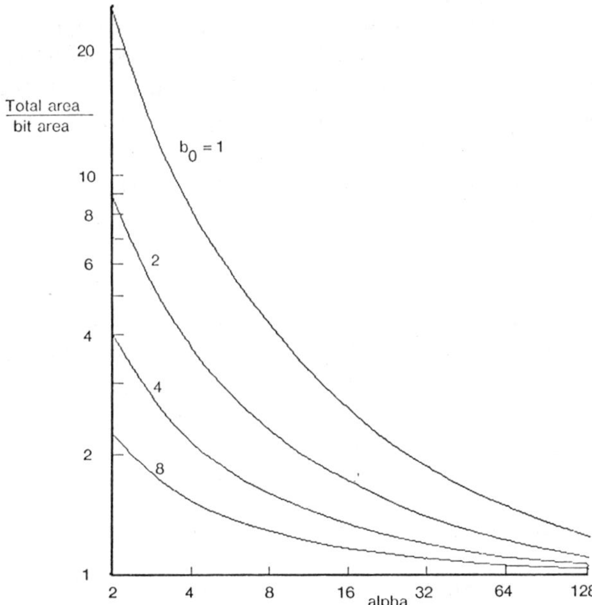

Fig. 5. Total area per bit of a RAM as a function of α.

consumed by the wires for power and ground. The reason for this is that these wires can be thought of as increasing only the width b_0 of each bit; they do this by an amount that is roughly independent of α, as is shown in the following analysis.

For simplicity we assume that the wires for power and ground run in opposite directions, say parallel to the data and select wires. We compute how much one of them contributes to the width of a module i. The width of a power or ground wire is proportional to the number of bits served by it. Let the width at the highest level be u; given S and the design of the lowest level memory cell, this parameter is easy to compute. The width of the wire in a module on level i is proportional to the current it must supply and is hence $u(\alpha^{2i}/\alpha^{2N})$. In one direction, horizontal or vertical, there are (α^N/α^i) such modules. The total contribution of all modules on level i is thus $u(\alpha^i/\alpha^N)$. Taking the sum of this expression for $i = 0, 1, \cdots, N$ yields

$$\frac{u}{\alpha^N}\,\frac{\alpha^{N+1}-1}{\alpha-1} \approx u\,\frac{\alpha}{\alpha-1}.$$

There are $\sqrt{S}$ bits in one direction; the increase of the bit width, due to power and ground, therefore, is

$$\frac{u}{\sqrt{S}}\,\frac{\alpha}{\alpha-1}$$

which is roughly equal to $u/\sqrt{S}$.

We are interested in the optimal choice of α, but to make that choice we will have to look at the access time, which also depends on α as well.

C. Access Time of the RAM

Each element of level 0 drives a wire of length αb_0 to reach the periphery of its module on level 1; this takes time αb_0. Each module on level 1 drives in the same amount of time as a wire that is α times longer to reach the periphery of its module on level 2, etc. With N being the level of the highest module, the time required to extract 1 bit of storage adds up to $\alpha b_0 N$. We use this figure as the access time. For a RAM of S words, the access time is then $\alpha b_0(\log S/2 \log \alpha)$.

D. The Cost of the RAM

We take the product of the area and the access time as the cost function of the RAM. A RAM of S words of $\log S$ bits each has the following area–time product.

$$\left(b_0 + \frac{1}{\alpha-1} + \frac{2\alpha-1}{(\alpha-1)^2}\log\alpha\right)^2 \frac{\alpha b_0}{2\log\alpha}\; S\log^2 S. \qquad (5)$$

Fig. 6 shows (5), normalized with respect to $S \log^2 S$, as a function of α for different values of b_0. One notices that for increasing bit sizes the branching ratio of the hierarchy should decrease. Static memories, therefore, should have a smaller α

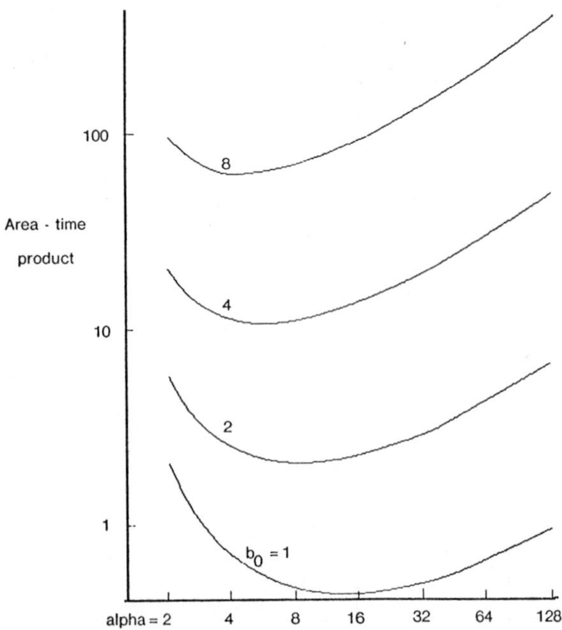

Fig. 6. Area-time product of a RAM as a function of α.

than dynamic ones. For dynamic MOS memories the optimal choice for α lies between 8 and 16, for static MOS memories ($b_0 \approx 4$) between 4 and 8. One may speculate that "smart memories," structures in which part of the processing task is distributed over the memory cells, will have small branching ratios and hence relatively deep hierarchies.

IV. Content Addressable Memory

The basic elements of the RAM were bits. The content addressable memory (CAM) is an example of a word organized memory. We consider a "pure" CAM. It consists of words of w bits each. We access a word by applying w bits of data to the system. We assume that there is only one word in the memory with that contents, and the address of that word is produced by the memory.

A. Organization of the CAM

The basic elements are the bits, each of width b_1. The bits do not constitute the modules of level 0. The modules on level 0 of the hierarchy consist of αw words of w bits each. [See Fig. 7(b)] The w data bits are run via parallel wires vertically through the module. Out of each word comes one horizontal match wire going to the right. A word asserts its match wire if each data bit received is equal to the corresponding bit stored. There are αw words in a module of level 0; the address of the matching word leaves the module via the $\log \alpha w$ address wires.

The above organization of a module of level 0 has one defect. It would require the individual bits of storage to drive wires of length wb_1, which may be greater than the desired αb_1, to reach the address wires. In Section II, we discussed that this type of communication should be achieved by a hierarchy. We, therefore, organize the driving of the match wire by the w bits in a word in the same manner as shown in Section II.

Each word is chopped up into (w/α) subwords of α bits each [Fig. 7(a)]. Each of the (w/α) subwords sends a signal to a "match tree" which has a branching ratio of α and delivers, via $\log_\alpha w$ levels, the logical product of its inputs. The top node of the match tree can drive a wire of length $b_1 \alpha^{\log_\alpha w} = b_1 w$, the length of a word in the memory. Therefore, the word itself can drive a wire of length $b_1 \alpha w$, and we may group together αw words into module 0 [Fig. 7(b)]. Notice that the module's length is roughly equal to α times its width. This will be true for modules on higher levels as well.

We now describe a module of level i (Fig. 8). It contains $w\alpha^{4i+1}$ words and consists of α^4 submodules of level $i - 1$, grouped into α^2 rows of α^2 submodules each. Each such row contains, besides the α^2 submodules, w data wires to transport the data to each of the submodules and $\log w\alpha^{4i-1}$ outcoming address wires to transport to the right the address of the matching word. Each submodule has $w\alpha^{4i-3}$ words, and, hence, one row contains $w\alpha^{4i-1}$ words which explains the number of address wires. A module on level i has α^2 of these rows and thus requires $\log w\alpha^{4i+1}$ outcoming address wires; they are placed to the right of the rows.

In the CAM we have α^4 submodules per module, in the RAM only α^2. This is only a seeming difference. In the CAM, for simplicity, we have combined two steps in the hierarchy; we have maintained, however, our multiplication factor α for the wire lengths. L_{i-1}, the length of a module of level $i - 1$, is roughly equal to α times W_{i-1}, the width of a module of level $i - 1$. Therefore, module $i - 1$ can already drive wires of length αW_{i-1}. As a consequence, we can put α^2 submodules into one row as this would only require the driving of wires of length $\alpha^2 W_{i-1}$ in each row. But then we can, and this is the second step, combine α^2 rows as this would require the driving of wires of a length about $\alpha^2 L_{i-1}$, which is roughly equal to $\alpha^3 W_{i-1}$.

B. Area of the CAM

We compute the length and the width separately. For the length L_i of a module on level i, we have the relation [cf. Figs. 7(b) and 8]

$$L_0 = \alpha w \left(b_1 + \frac{\log w}{\log \alpha}\right)$$

$$L_i = \alpha^2 (w + L_{i-1} + \log w\alpha^{4i-1}).$$

The solution to this recurrence relation is

$$L_i = \alpha^{2i+1} w \left(b_1 + \frac{\log w}{\log \alpha}\right) + (w + \log w) \frac{\alpha^{2i+2} - \alpha^2}{\alpha^2 - 1} + \left(\frac{4\alpha^{2i+2} - 4\alpha^2}{(\alpha^2 - 1)^2} + \frac{3\alpha^{2i+2} - 4i\alpha^2 - 3\alpha^2}{\alpha^2 - 1}\right) \log \alpha.$$

A module on level i has $w\alpha^{2i+1}$ bits in the vertical direction. The length per bit, therefore, is $L_i/w\alpha^{2i+1}$. This has the following limit for $i \to \infty$:

$$b_1 + \frac{\log w}{\log \alpha} + \frac{\alpha(w + \log w + 3 \log \alpha)}{w(\alpha^2 - 1)} + \frac{4\alpha \log \alpha}{w(\alpha^2 - 1)^2}. \tag{6}$$

As in the case of the RAM, $L_i/w\alpha^{2i+1}$ is already very close to the limit for small values of i; the rate of convergence is again exponential. We use (6) as the length per bit of a CAM.

We find for the width W_i of a module on level i the following

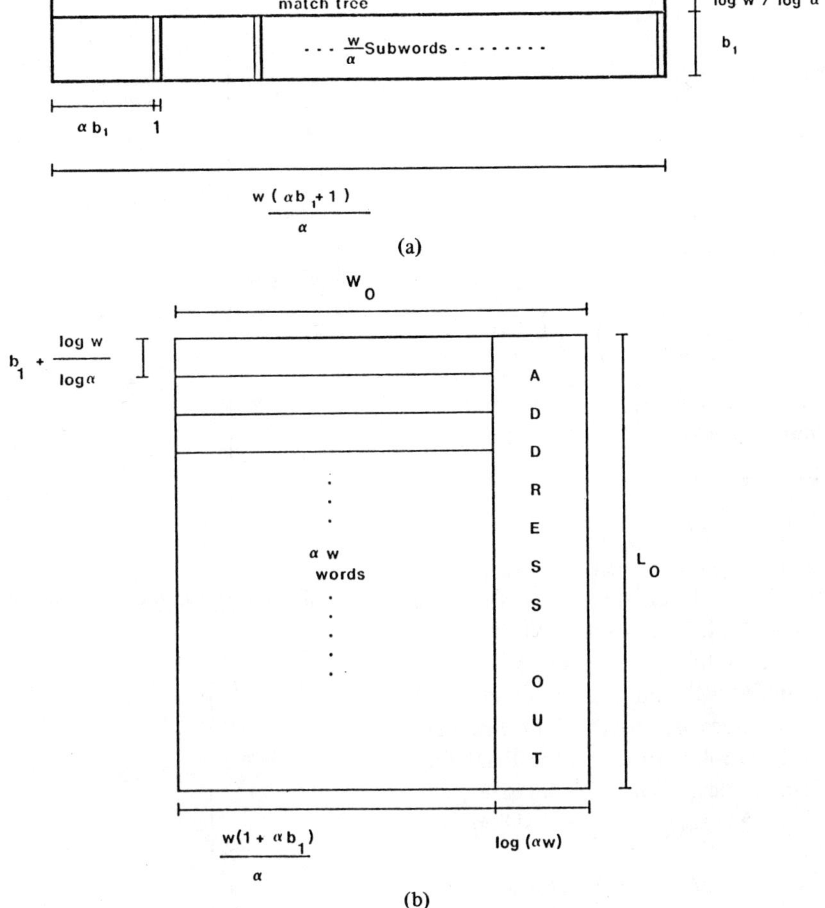

Fig. 7. (a) One word of storage in the CAM. (b) A CAM module of level zero.

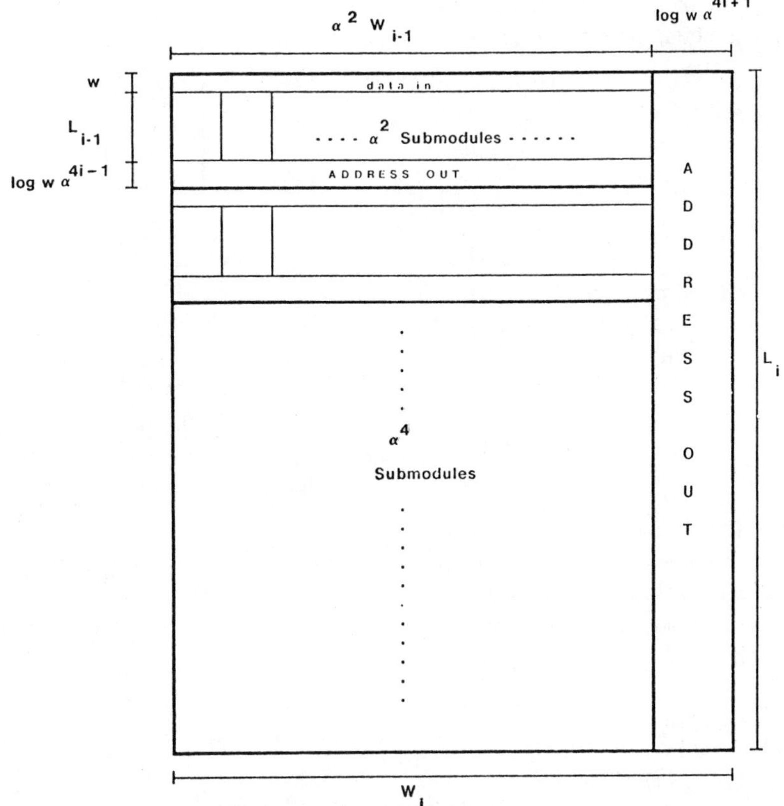

Fig. 8. A CAM module of level i ($i > 0$).

recurrence relation [cf. Figs. 7(b) and 8]:

$$W_0 = \frac{w}{\alpha}(\alpha b_1 + 1) + \log \alpha w$$

$$W_i = \alpha^2 W_{i-1} + \log w\alpha^{4i+1}.$$

Its solution is

$$W_i = \alpha^{2i} w \left(b_1 + \frac{1}{\alpha}\right) + \frac{\alpha^{2i+2} - 1}{\alpha^2 - 1} \log w + \left(\frac{4\alpha^{2i+2} - 4\alpha^2}{(\alpha^2 - 1)^2} + \frac{\alpha^{2i+2} - 4i - 1}{\alpha^2 - 1}\right) \log \alpha.$$

In the horizontal direction there are $w\alpha^{2i}$ bits. The width per bit $W_i/w\alpha^{2i}$ has as its limit for $i \to \infty$

$$b_1 + \frac{1}{\alpha} + \frac{\alpha^2 \log \alpha w}{w(\alpha^2 - 1)} + \frac{4\alpha^2 \log \alpha}{w(\alpha^2 - 1)^2}. \tag{7}$$

We take the product of (6) and (7) as the area per bit.

By dividing the area per bit by the bit area b_1^2 we obtain the total area per bit area for a CAM. Fig. 9 shows this quotient for $w = 32$ as a function of α for different values of b_0.

If we compare Figs. 5 and 9, we notice that for small values of α the wires in the CAM cause less overhead in area than those in the RAM. For large values of α it is the RAM that enjoys a smaller overhead in area. For equal bit sizes, i.e., with $b_0 = b_1$, the area overhead factor for the RAM and the CAM are about equal at $\alpha = 8$.

As in the RAM we can compute by how much we should increase the bit width b_1 if we wish to take power and ground into account. Both power and ground give an increase of $u(\alpha^2/\alpha^2 - 1)$ to the length and the width of the CAM. This is even closer to u than in the case of the RAM. If we wish to ammortize this amount over the bits, the bit width b_1 should be incremented by

$$\frac{2u}{\sqrt{S w}} \frac{\alpha^2}{\alpha^2 - 1}$$

for a CAM of S words of w bits each.

C. Access Time of the CAM

For the access time we take the time required to extract the address of the matching word of data from a memory of S words. With the highest level being level N, we have $S = w\alpha^{4N+1}$ or

$$N = \frac{\log S - \log w}{4 \log \alpha} - \frac{1}{4}.$$

A word of storage has a response time of $(\log w/\log \alpha)\alpha b_1$; for a module of level 0 this becomes $[(\log w/\log \alpha) + 1]\,\alpha b_1$. Each new level of the hierarchy multiplies the wire lengths by a factor α^2 and hence requires an additional time of $2\alpha b_1$. For N levels we find, hence,

$$\text{access time} = \left(2N + \frac{\log w}{\log \alpha} + 1\right)\alpha b_1$$

$$= \left(\frac{\log S + \log w}{2 \log \alpha} + \frac{1}{2}\right)\alpha b_1. \tag{8}$$

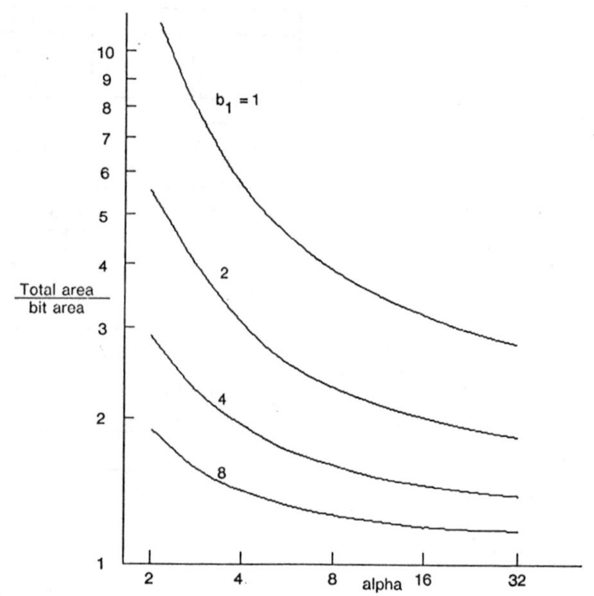

Fig. 9. Total area per bit as a function of α for a CAM with word length 32.

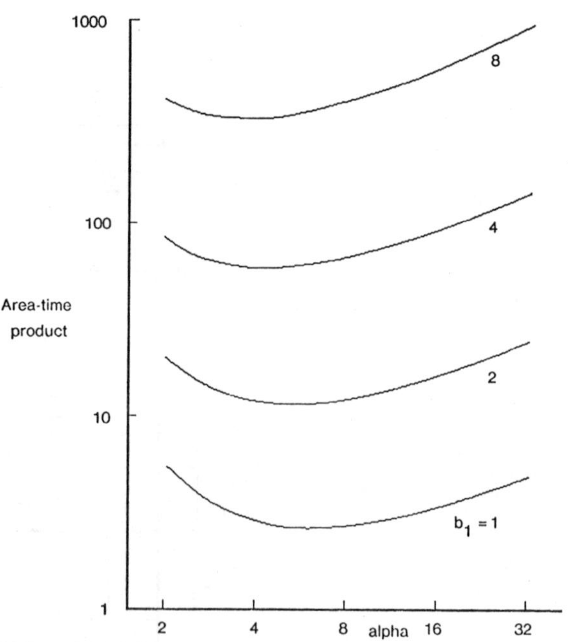

Fig. 10. Area–time product for a CAM of 65K 32-bit words.

D. The Cost of the CAM

We again take the product of the area and the access time as the cost function. For a CAM of S words of w bits each, formulae (6), (7), and (8) yield the cost function

$$\left(b_1 + \frac{\log w}{\log \alpha} + \frac{\alpha(w + \log w + 3 \log \alpha)}{w(\alpha^2 - 1)} + \frac{4\alpha \log \alpha}{w(\alpha^2 - 1)^2}\right) \cdot \left(b_1 + \frac{1}{\alpha} + \frac{\alpha^2 \log \alpha w}{w(\alpha^2 - 1)} + \frac{4\alpha^2 \log \alpha}{w(\alpha^2 - 1)^2}\right) \cdot \left(\frac{\log S + \log w}{2 \log \alpha} + \frac{1}{2}\right)\alpha b_1 w S.$$

Fig. 10 shows the cost function as a function of α for a CAM of 65K words of 32 bits each. The curves are fairly independent of the choice of w provided we choose w great enough, say $w \geqslant 16$. A change in S will basically move the curves only up and down; it will not affect the positions of their minima.

We notice again that increasing the bit size will decrease the optimal choice of α. Comparing Figs. 6 and 10 we see that content addressable memories should have smaller branching ratios than random-access memories. For $b_1 = 4$, which seems a reasonable figure, the optimal choice of α is 4.

V. Conclusion

We have presented a general method for analyzing the cost and performance of recursively defined VLSI structures. Parameters of any such structure may be optimized with respect to time, area, or some combination of the two. While we have chosen the area-time product, it is clear that some other choice may be appropriate for any given application.

The results of this study indicate that as more processing is available in each module at level zero, the optimal value of α will decrease. A system with $\alpha = 4$ would seem to be appropriate for memories in which substantial processing is comingled with storage.

Very general arguments were used to generate the basic recursive structure. For that reason it appears that a very large fraction of VLSI computing structures will be designed in this way. We have discussed two examples, one in which the basic elements were bits of storage, and one with words of storage at the lowest level. They gave rise to rather different recursive structures. The way in which their area and time measures were established should make it clear how to apply these techniques to other recursively defined computing structures.

Structured VLSI design proceeds from algorithm to logic cell to cell array to special-purpose chip, yielding cheap, powerful, and modular hardware that will permanently alter the systems landscape of the 80's.

The Design of Special-Purpose VLSI Chips

M. J. Foster
H. T. Kung
Carnegie-Mellon University

We have now entered a technological domain in which many of the problems previously encountered in building special-purpose hardware are much less severe. LSI technology allows tens of thousands of devices to fit on a single chip, and the advance to VLSI should increase this number. Devices once requiring many components can now be built with just a few chips, reducing the difficulties in reliability, performance, and heat dissipation that arise from combining many standard SSI or MSI components. In addition, the development of simplified techniques[1] and implementation guides [2] for structuring IC system design—an area often regarded as difficult—allows relatively naive designers to achieve success.

Special-purpose VLSI chips can function as peripheral devices attached to a conventional host computer. If many types of chips are attached, the resulting system can be considered an efficient general-purpose computer. Figure 1 illustrates how special-purpose chips such as a pattern matcher, FFT device, and sorter might form part of such a general-purpose system.

Construction of complex special-purpose VLSI chips will be feasible only if we hold down design cost (i.e., design time). We will argue that chip design time can be reduced significantly if the underlying algorithm is "good"—i.e., designed carefully in the first place. We will characterize such algorithms below and will examine a concrete example of one—the design of a pattern matching chip. (We completed this design in the spring of 1979 and have had prototype chips fabricated, with testing now under way. Preliminary results show that the chip can achieve a data rate of one character every 250 nanoseconds, which is higher than the memory bandwidth of most conventional computers. This high performance is achieved in spite of little effort given to circuit and layout design. We attribute this performance mainly to the careful design of the underlying algorithm.)

We will also identify the major steps in special-purpose VLSI chip design according to the good algorithm philosophy, and will offer a methodology for transforming a good algorithm into a final layout in a more or less mechanical way. With this approach, designing a special-purpose chip should not be more difficult than designing a high-level algorithm for the same job.

Design philosophy

Algorithms that perform well on conventional random access computers are not always the best for VLSI implementation. As Sutherland and Mead[3] point out, good algorithms for VLSI implementation are not necessarily those requiring minimal computation. Computation is cheap in VLSI; *communication* determines performance. Thus, in this new era of computation, we need to reconsider the algorithms for many tasks.

A "good" algorithm in this context should possess one or more of the following properties:

- The algorithm can be implemented by only a *few* different types of *simple* cells.
- The algorithm's data and control flow is *simple* and *regular,* so that cells can be connected by a network with local and regular interconnections. Long distance or irregular communication is thus minimized.

Reprinted from *IEEE Computers*, vol. 13, pp. 26–40, Jan. 1980.

- The algorithm uses extensive *pipelining* and *multiprocessing*. Typically, several data streams move at constant velocity over fixed paths in the network, interacting at cells where they meet. In this way a large number of cells are active at one time so that the computation speed can keep up with the data rate.

Algorithms with these properties have been named *systolic algorithms** by Kung and Leiserson.[4] Many have been designed recently and are surveyed by Kung.[5]

Since most special-purpose chips will be made in relatively small quantities, the design cost must be kept low. Systolic algorithms have several advantages which help reduce this cost:

- One can design and test only a few different, simple cells, since most of the cells on the chip are copies of a few basic ones.
- Regular interconnection implies that the design can be made modular and extensible, so one can design a large chip by combining the designs of small chips.
- By pipelining and multiprocessing, one can meet the performance requirement of a special-purpose chip simply by including many identical cells on the chip.

*The word "systole" was borrowed from physiologists, who use it to refer to the rhythmically recurrent contractions of the heart, which pulse blood through the body. For a systolic algorithm, the function of a cell is analogous to that of the heart. Each cell regularly pumps data in and out (performing some short computation before each "contraction"), so that a regular flow of data is kept up in the network.

All these imply that if a good algorithm is used, the design time, and therefore the design cost, can be substantially reduced.

In VLSI special-purpose chip design, then, the most crucial decision is the choice of the underlying algorithm, since the suitability of the algorithm largely determines the design cost and performance. Given the importance of algorithm design, it should receive the largest part of the design effort. Low-level optimizations at the circuit or layout design level are probably not worthwhile, as these will lead only to minor improvements in the overall performance while increasing design time.

The design of a pattern matching chip

A specific VLSI chip—one that performs on-line pattern matching of strings with wild card characters—illustrates our design philosophy and methodology. The design of the underlying algorithm demonstrates that it can be mapped to circuit and layout designs in a straightforward way.

The string pattern matching problem. Our chip accepts two streams of characters from the host machine, and produces a stream of bits as shown in Figure 2. One of the input streams, the text string, is an endless string of characters over some alphabet Σ. The other input stream, the pattern, contains a fixed-length vector of characters over the alphabet $\Sigma \cup \{X\}$, where X is the wild card character. The output is a stream of bits, each of which corresponds to one of the characters in the text string. The data streams move at a steady rate between the host computer and the

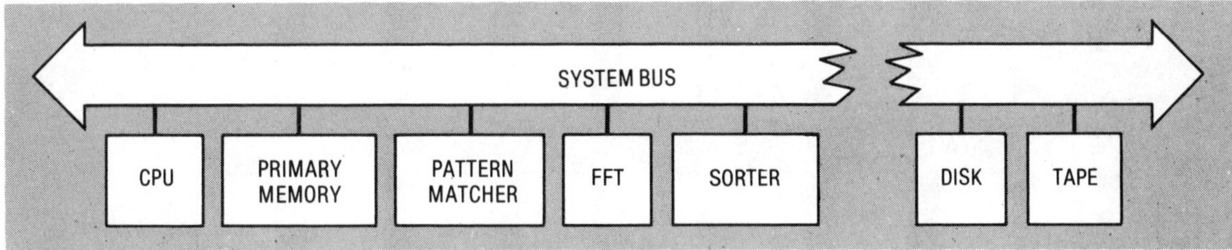

Figure 1. Special-purpose chips attached to a general-purpose computer.

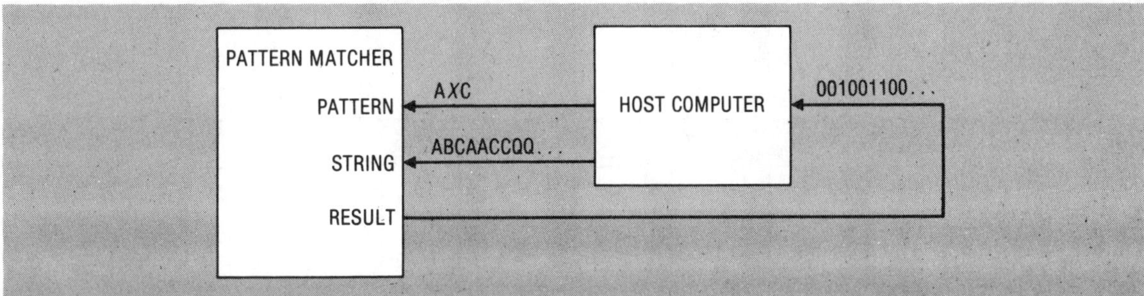

Figure 2. Data to and from the pattern matcher.

pattern matcher, with a constant time between data items.

Let us denote the input text stream as $s_0s_1s_2 \ldots$. The finite pattern stream will be denoted as $p_0p_1 \ldots p_k$ and the output result stream as $r_0r_1r_2 \ldots$. Characters in the two input streams may be tested for equality, with the wild card character X deemed to match any character in Σ. The output bit r_i is to be set to 1 if the substring $s_{i-k}s_{i+1-k} \ldots s_i$ matches the pattern, and 0 otherwise, i.e.,

$$r_i \leftarrow (s_{i-k} = p_0) \wedge (s_{i+1-k} = p_1) \wedge \ldots \wedge (s_i = p_k).$$

In Figure 2, for example, the pattern AXC matches the substrings $s_0s_1s_2$, $s_3s_4s_5$, and $s_4s_5s_6$ (ABC, AAC, and ACC). Result bits r_2r_5, and r_6 are thus set to 1, and all other result bits are 0.

This problem is important in many applications. String pattern matching is a basic operation in SNOBOL-like languages[6] and in data base query languages. String matching hardware has been proposed for use in office automation systems.[7] Many artificial intelligence systems make heavy use of pattern matching as a search method. Furthermore, string pattern matching is similar to many stressing numerical computations such as convolutions and correlations. All of the linear product problems discussed by Fischer and Paterson[8] are also similar to string matching.

Several fast algorithms are known for solving the string matching problem without wild card characters on a normal random access machine.[9, 10] These methods use information about partial matches of the pattern with itself to avoid redundant comparisons, skipping over parts of the string where partial match results may be inferred from previous comparisons. When wild card characters exist in the pattern these methods break down, since the "matches" relation is no longer transitive. The strings AC and XB both match AX, for example, but do not match each other. Information about matchings of the pattern with itself is therefore irrelevant if wild card characters are present. The fastest algorithm known for string matching with wild card characters is based on multiplication of large integers[8] and requires more than linear time. The pattern matching chip solves the problem in linear time by performing comparisons in parallel.

The chip design. We designed our chip according to the methodology discussed earlier, beginning with the careful design of a systolic algorithm and proceeding to its hardware implementation.

Algorithm design—data flow. The pattern and the text string arrive alternately over the bus one character at a time. We will call the interval during which one character arrives from either stream a beat. During each pair of consecutive beats the chip must input

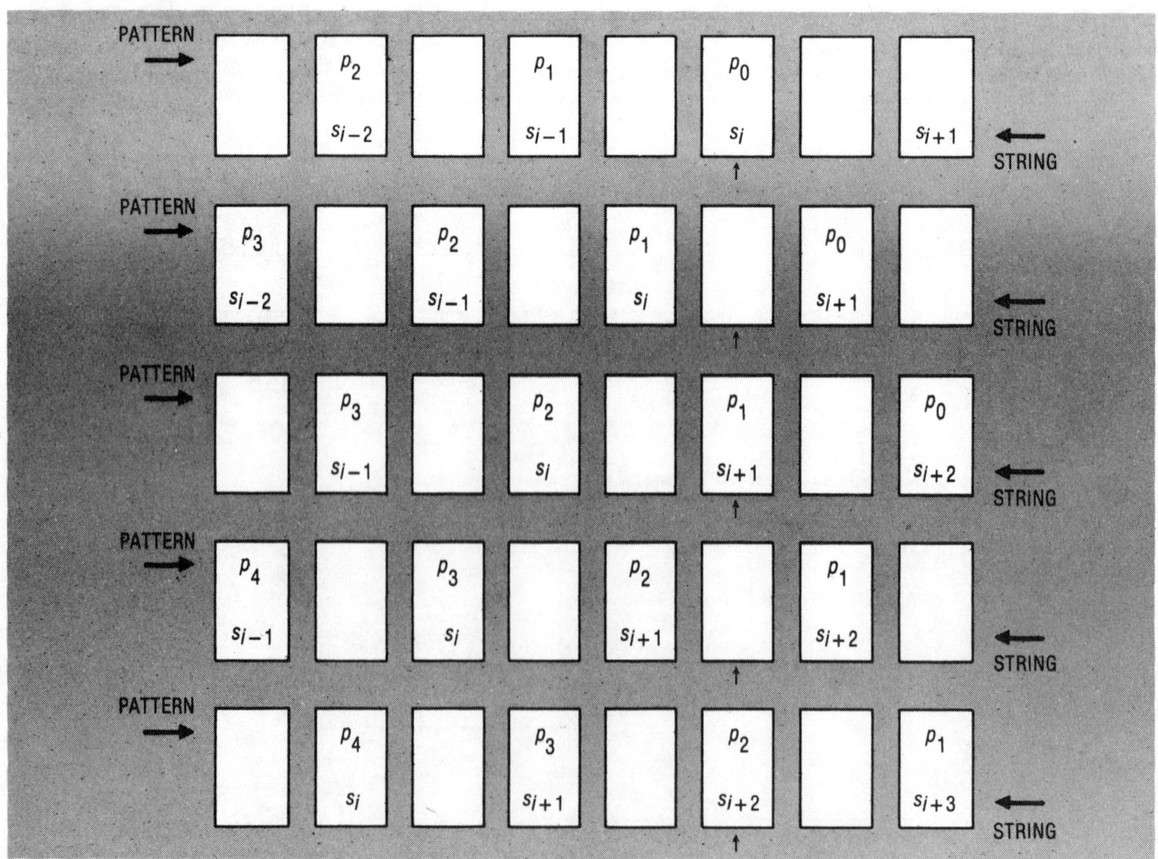

Figure 3. The flow of characters through a linear array of cells.

two characters and output one result. All characters on the chip move during each beat.

The chip is divided into character cells, each of which can compare two characters and accumulate a temporary result. The pattern and string follow a preset path of cells from the time they enter the chip until the time they leave it. On each beat every character moves to a new cell. We use a linear array of cells, with the pattern and string moving in opposite directions, to make each character of the string move past all characters of the pattern. To make each pair of characters meet rather than just pass, we must separate them by one cell so that alternate cells are idle. Each cell is then active on alternate beats. Figure 3 traces the flow of characters for several beats.

Following the pointer in Figure 3 illustrates the history of the character cell, starting when the first character of the pattern, p_0, is present. Suppose the string character s_i is present during this beat. During the next beat the cell is idle, but during the beat after that it contains p_1 and s_{i+1}. Two beats later, p_2 and s_{i+2} are together, then p_3 and s_{i+3}, and so on. By the time the last pattern character p_k leaves the cell, the substring $s_i s_{i+1} \ldots s_{i+k}$ will have met the whole pattern. We can therefore keep the partial match results in this cell, update it whenever a new pair of characters enters the cell, and output the results after the last character of the pattern goes past. To output results we shift them along with the string, so that each match result leaves the array with the last character of its substring. If we recirculate the pattern so that the first character follows two beats after the last one, we can output the completed result and initialize a new partial result on the same beat. The number of character cells required is therefore no more than the number of characters in the pattern.

Each character cell performs two separate functions—it compares characters of the pattern and string, and it updates and outputs match results. We can divide these functions between two modules, so that there are two linear arrays with connections between corresponding cells as shown in Figure 4. The cells on the top are the comparators; the pattern flows through them from left to right, the string from right to left. The bottom cells, or accumulators, receive the results of the comparison from above. They maintain partial results and shift completed results right to left. Two bits associated with the pattern flow through the accumulators from left to right. One of these bits, called λ, marks the end of the pattern. It is one for the last character of the pattern and zero for the others. The other bit is x, the "don't care" bit, which marks wild card characters. A one in this bit tells the accumulator to ignore the result from the comparator, since this pattern character matches anything.

We can further divide the comparators. Rather than using one large circuit to compare whole characters, we can divide each comparator into modules that can compare single bits. Two characters are equal if corresponding bits are equal. By staggering the bits so the high-order bits enter the array before the low-order ones, we can make a pipeline comparator. Each single-bit comparator shifts its result down to meet the bits coming into the next lower comparator. The active and idle comparators alternate vertically as well as horizontally, so that on each beat the active comparators form a checkerboard pattern as shown in Figure 5.

Algorithm design—cell algorithms. Two kinds of cells must be designed to build a pattern matching chip exhibiting the data flow described above:

- The *one-bit comparator* has one bit of the pattern flowing from left to right, one bit of the string flowing from right to left, and the comparison result for the pair of characters flowing from top to bottom. The cell uses this algorithm to update the comparison result:

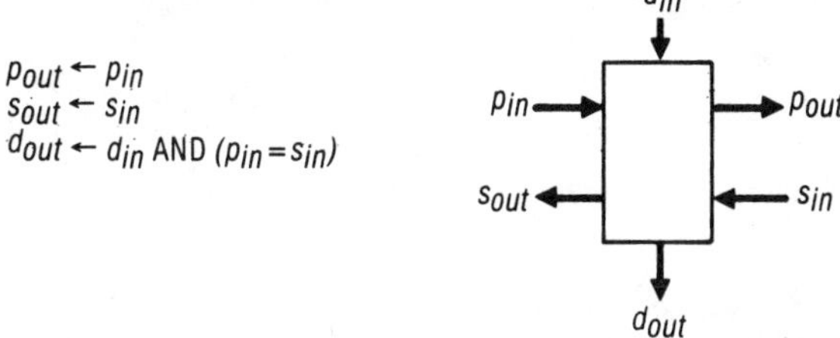

- The *accumulator* receives d_{in} (the result from the comparator above), λ_{in} (the end-of-pattern indicator), and x_{in} (the don't care bit). It maintains a temporary result t, and at the end of the pattern uses t to replace the result r that flows from right to left:

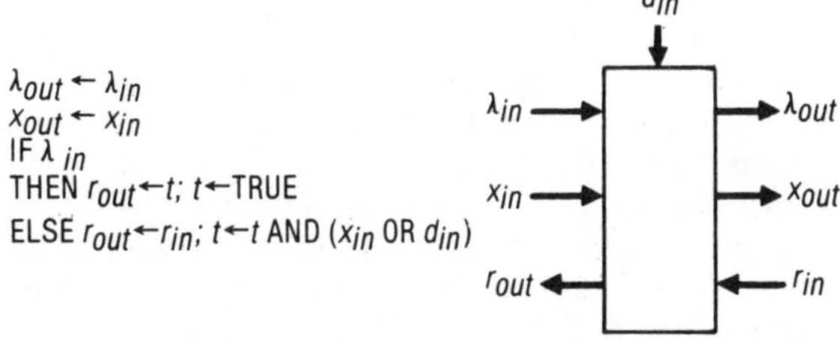

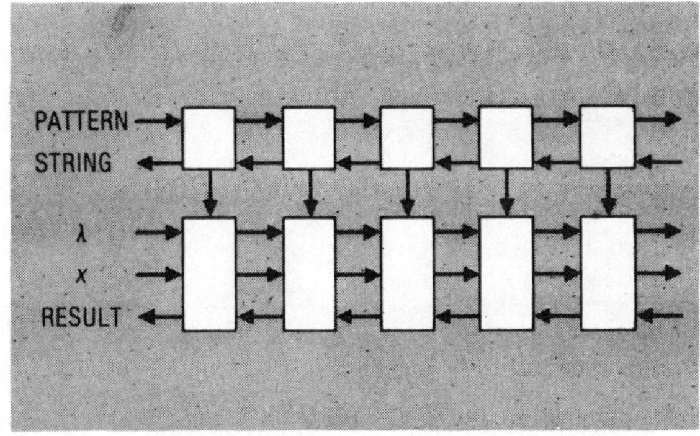

Figure 4. Pattern matching achieved in two modules, each consisting of a linear array of identical cells. Comparators are on the top and accumulators on the bottom.

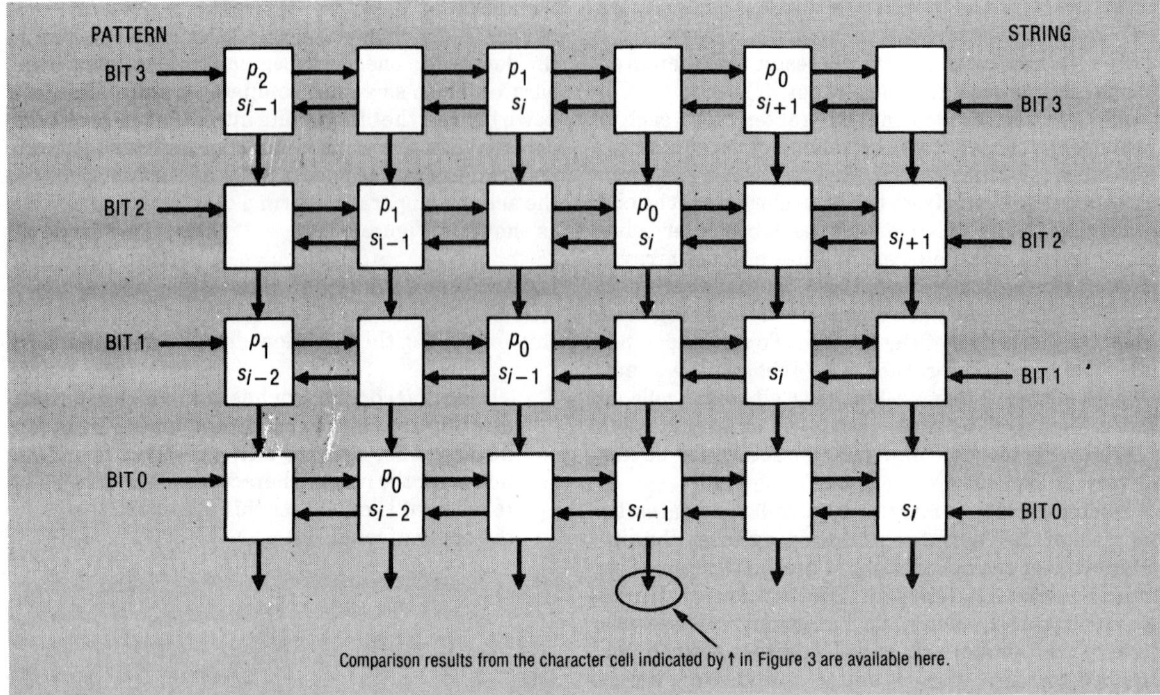

Figure 5. Comparators for single bits.

Circuit and layout design—data flow circuit. Each pipeline used by the algorithm for data flow is implemented as a unidirectional shift register shifting on each beat. Every other cell of the shift register contains valid data. In the NMOS technology used for this chip, a shift register is a chain of inverters separated by pass transistors as shown in Figure 6. When the voltage on the gate of a transistor is near the supply voltage V_{dd}, its channel conducts current, while if the voltage is near ground it does not. The inputs to the inverters can store charges, so data is stored within the inverters; the pass transistors control the inverter inputs. A clock with two non-overlapping phases controls the pass transistors. Because adjacent transistors are turned on by opposite phases of the clock, there is never a closed path between inverters that are separated by two transistors. Alternate inverters can therefore store independent data bits.

The dynamic alternation of active and idle inverters in the NMOS shift register mirrors the alternation of active and idle cells in the algorithm (compare with Figure 5). Each cell can thus contain one gated inverter from each of the shift registers that passes through it. The clock controlling the shift register stages in a cell can activate the cell. The shift register components are then fully utilized—all idle inverters are in idle stages.

Circuit and layout design—cell circuit. Since each cell inverts its inputs before sending them to its neighbors, two versions of each cell must be constructed. One version operates on positive inputs to produce inverted outputs, while the other computes positive outputs from inverted inputs. Transforming a cell algorithm to its inverted twin is straightforward, so the existence of two versions presents no problem. Using the cell algorithms, we can design circuits for the twin versions of each cell. From the circuit designs, we can lay out the masks for fabricating the chip. The positive version of the comparator cell illustrates the process. It takes positive inputs and

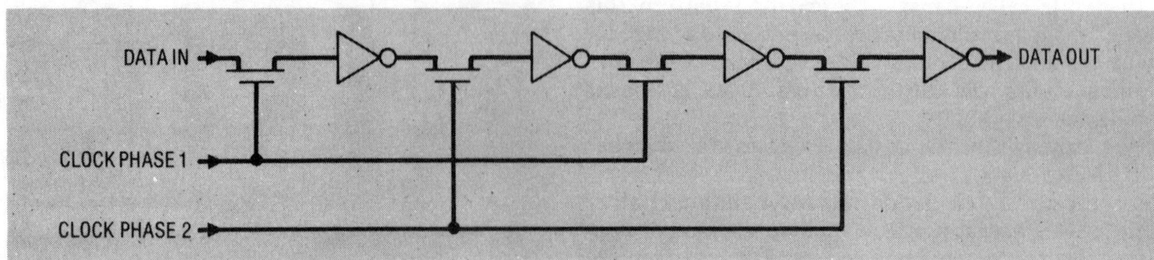

Figure 6. A shift register in NMOS.

produces inverted outputs, so the outputs in the comparator algorithm must be inverted:

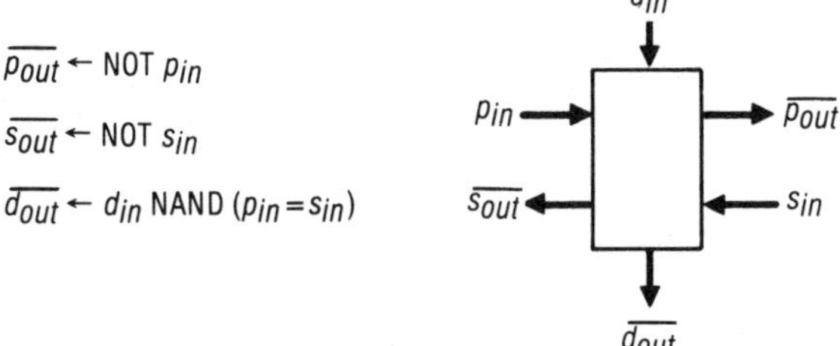

$\overline{p_{out}} \leftarrow$ NOT p_{in}
$\overline{s_{out}} \leftarrow$ NOT s_{in}
$\overline{d_{out}} \leftarrow d_{in}$ NAND $(p_{in} = s_{in})$
d_{in}
p_{in}
$\overline{p_{out}}$
$\overline{s_{out}}$
s_{in}
$\overline{d_{out}}$

In NMOS, data storage can take place on the input to any logic gate, as long as a pass transistor can isolate that input. The *p* and *s* shift registers can be implemented with inverters as planned, but a NAND gate can be used as the stage for the *d* shift register. Figure 7 is the circuit for the positive comparator. When the clock input goes from ground to V_{dd}, the power supply voltage, all three pass transistors turn on. The pattern and string inputs are then stored on the inverters, and the *d* input is stored on one input to the NAND gate. The exclusive NOR gate outputs TRUE if the two inputs are equal, and FALSE otherwise. The output of this equality test goes to the other input of the NAND gate, which computes d_{out}. After the inputs have stabilized, the clock goes to ground. The outputs of this cell then provide stable inputs to neighboring cells until the clock goes high again.

Circuit and layout design—cell sticks. The next step after completing the circuit diagram is the design of the cell's topological layout, or stick diagram, which shows the relative positions of all signal paths, power connections, and components but hides their absolute sizes and positions. Most of the circuit's components can be implemented in several ways, and a choice among these must be made at this stage of the design. Figure 8 is an example of a stick diagram.

Silicon-gate NMOS technology uses three conduction layers (differentiated by color in Figure 8). Following Mead and Conway's [1] convention, blue lines represent metal conduction paths, red lines polycrystalline silicon (polysilicon), and green lines diffusion into the substrate. The three layers are insulated from each other except at contact cuts, represented by round black dots. The yellow squares are areas of ion implantation, used to create depletion mode transistors. These serve as pull-up resistors in the gates and inverters.

NMOS field-effect transistors are created by crossing a diffusion path (green) with a polysilicon area (red). The green path is the channel, and the red area is the gate. If no ion implantation is present, the channel conducts current only when the gate is at V_{dd}.

The positive comparator cell uses pass transistors and inverters to implement the shift registers; it also uses a NAND gate and an equality, or NXOR, gate. These basic components are combined as shown in Figure 8 to produce the stick diagram for the positive comparator cell. Power and ground run horizontally across the cell on metal (blue) paths. The clock is in polysilicon (red) at the top and right edges, and dips below the upper power wire near the middle of the cell to allow the cell above to connect to the power wire. Data paths for *p* and *s* run horizontally along the top, while *d* runs downward in diffusion (green).

Let us trace the *p* data path through the cell. It enters at the left in diffusion and passes through the channel of a transistor that is gated by the clock. Contact is made to a polysilicon path that goes to the input of the *p* inverter. The inverter output, in metal, crosses the *d* data path with no interaction and provides an input to the equality gate. It then passes over the *s* inverter and leaves the cell at the right.

Circuit and layout design—final layout and masking. When stick diagrams have been designed for all of the cells, actual layouts can be produced. These follow the topology of the stick diagrams, but also include the absolute sizes and positions of all components. Designing a layout involves choosing electrical parameters for all transistors as well as following minimum spacing rules for the intended fabrication process. Care must be taken to line up power connections and data paths that cross several

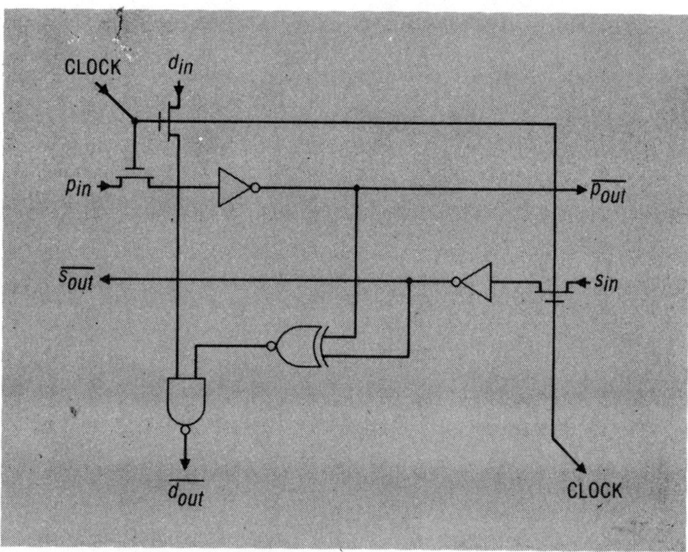

Figure 7. Positive comparator circuit.

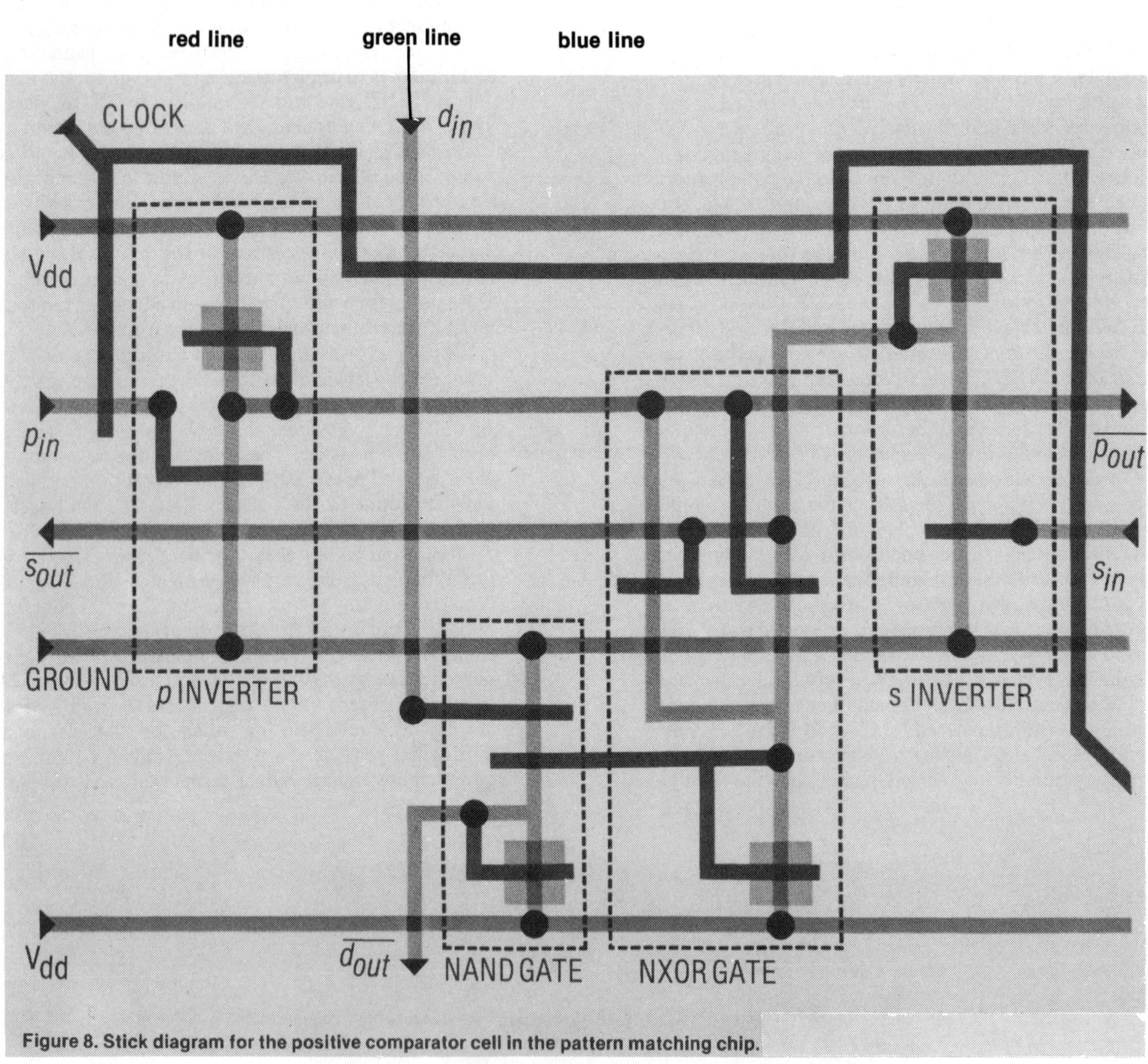

Figure 8. Stick diagram for the positive comparator cell in the pattern matching chip.

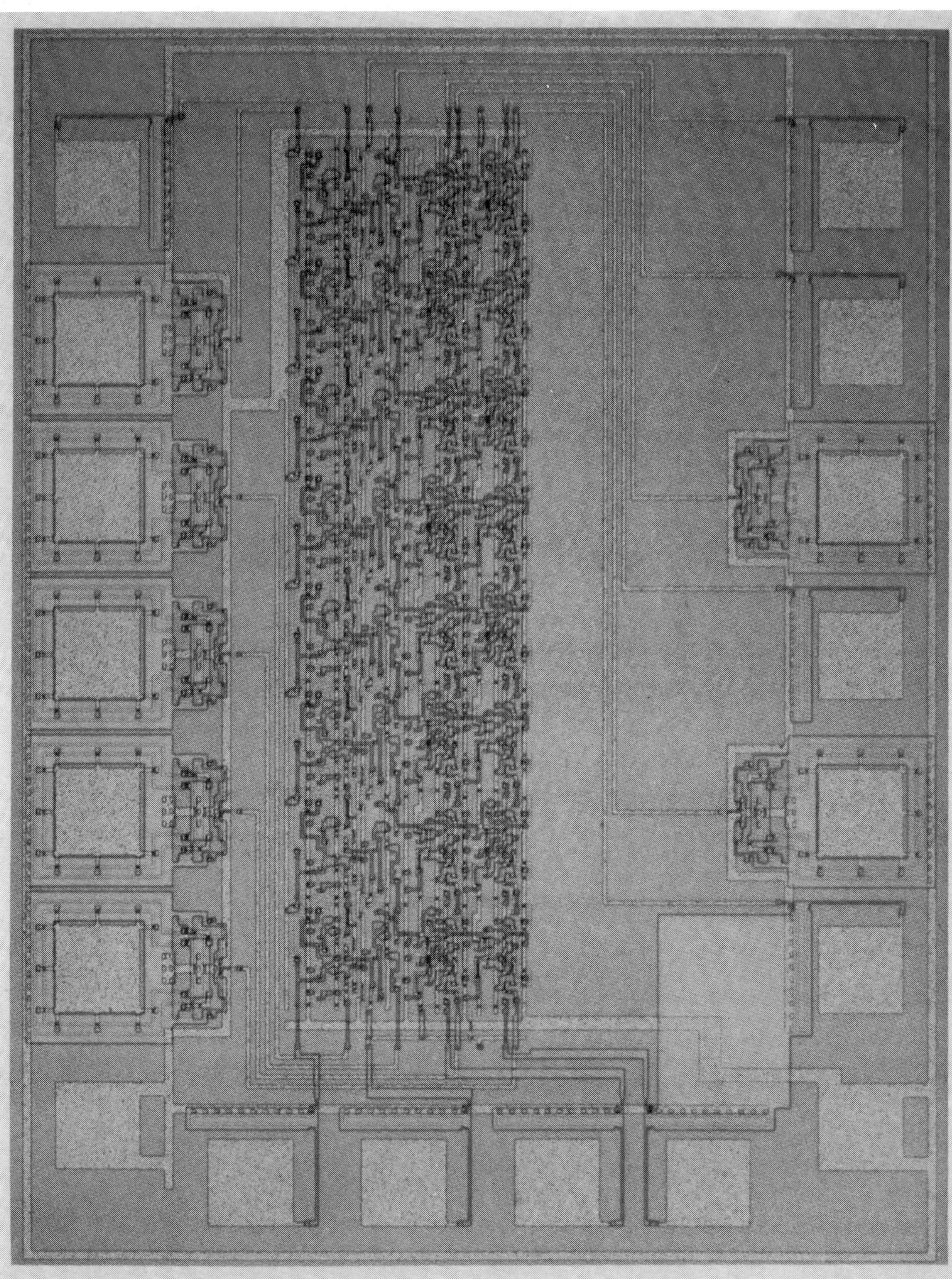

Figure 9. The CMU pattern matching chip prototype. The pattern matching array at left center measures 472 by 1528 microns and is connected to bonding pads on a rectangle measuring 1536 by 1884 microns.

cells. In principle, the layout can be designed mechanically from the circuit and stick diagrams.

When the layouts for all cells are complete, they can be assembled into a working array with the inputs and outputs hooked to contact pads. The layouts can be described using a graphics language (such as the Caltech Intermediate Form[1]) that can be interpreted to make the masks. These masks can then be used to fabricate the chips.

Figure 9 is a photograph of the prototype pattern matcher we constructed according to the methodology outlined above. It can handle patterns containing up to eight two-bit characters.

Design alternatives. In designing the chip we often reached points where we had to choose among several alternatives. There were three major decision-making areas—choice of an algorithm, choice of a data flow implementation, and choice of a method for cell implementation.

Alternative algorithms. A bewildering variety of algorithms could form the basis for a pattern matching chip. The desire for simple and regular data flow rules out the fast sequential algorithms described by Boyer and Moore[9] and Knuth et al.[10] Since these algorithms require dynamically changing communication, their hardware implementation will be too complex to be modular.

Mukhopadhyay[11] has proposed several machines which store a character of the pattern in each cell and which broadcast the text string character by character to all cells. This broadcasting is the major disadvantage of this algorithm. Each cell requires a connection to the broadcast channel, increasing the power requirements of the system as a whole or decreasing its speed. Our algorithm requires no broadcasting of data.

A chip designed by Mead et al.[12] uses another algorithm in which pattern characters are stored in the cells. The text string passes through all of the cells, and the results of character matches are combined using a common wired-NOR bus. We wished to avoid unbounded fan-in of this type, since it may degrade performance when a design is extended to VLSI.

Another algorithm—similar to ours—uses a linear array of cells with data flowing in only one direction. The pattern is permanently stored in the array of cells, and the text string moves past it. Partial results move at half the speed of the text so that they accumulate results from an entire substring match. We rejected this algorithm because of the static storage of the pattern—loading the cells in preparation for a pattern match would require extra time and circuitry.

Our algorithm is well suited to VLSI implementation. All communication is local, since each character cell communicates only with its left and right neighbors. This enhances modularity and extensibility, as well as avoiding the large drivers needed for long-range transmission. Only a few types of cells are used, with many copies of each type. By replicating the basic cells, pattern matching chips of any size can be formed. Finally, control of the chip is simplified since our algorithm requires no separate operation to set up the system for a new pattern.

Alternative data flow implementations. Although the global flow of data is determined by the choice of algorithm, several methods of implementing the data flow may be possible. Serial or parallel data transmission between cells may be selected, for example. Communication may be coordinated in several ways. The data flow can even be transformed to combine several cells into one circuit. We will discuss two of the choices that arose in implementing the data flow of the pattern matching chip.

The existence of idle cells can be avoided by combining pairs of neighboring cells when implementing the data flow. Because each cell pair contains one active and one idle cell at each beat, the two cells can share circuitry. In the pattern matching chip, for example, neighboring comparators could have shared the equality gate, and the d data path could have been multiplexed.

If the amount of sharable circuitry is large enough, it may be advantageous to combine two or more cells in this way. Some additional circuitry will of course be needed to coordinate the sharing and may wipe out the savings. The increased interdependence of the circuit components may also offset the savings, since design changes may become more difficult and errors may be made. The pattern matcher cells are too small to profit from this data flow transformation.

Another choice in data flow implementation is between self-timed and clocked (synchronous) data paths. In a clocked data flow implementation, all data movement is under centralized control. The data flow controller sends signals to each cell to enable data transfers. The pattern matching chip uses this method. In fact, the data flow control signals are the same clock signals needed for data refreshing, although this need not be true in general.

In a self-timed implementation, data flow control is distributed among the cells so that each cell controls its own data transfers. Neighboring cells must obey a signaling convention to coordinate their communication. Self-timed data flow has advantages in modularity and extensibility, since no common clock is needed. Each of the cells may run at its own pace, synchronizing with its neighbors only when communication is needed. Self-timing's disadvantage lies in the extra circuitry needed to implement the signaling conventions. For systems small enough to use a common clock—like the pattern matching chip—clocked data flow is best. For larger systems, of course, self-timed communication may be the better choice.[13]

Alternative cell implementations. Two major choices affected the design of the cells. We rejected static shift registers, which can hold data for long periods without shifting it, in favor of dynamic shift registers, which can not. Also, we chose a random logic implementation of the cell circuitry rather than a more structured approach using standard PLA—programmed logic array—and register layouts.

The dynamic shift registers we used can not hold data for more than about 1 millisecond without shifting. Data is refreshed only by shifting. Static shift registers, the alternative choice, have regeneration circuitry in every stage so that data can be held indefinitely without shifting. In addition to the two clock phases, static registers need a third signal for the shift command.

Static shift registers are probably the better choice for most systems. They do not invert data between stages, as do dynamic shift registers, and they simplify testing. For our chip, however, dynamic shift registers have advantages. The alternation of active and idle cells allows just one inverter from each shift register to be placed in each cell. This permits the two-phase clock to do double duty as a data flow control signal. The cells and the global layout are thus greatly simplified.

The simplicity of the cell functions dictated the use of random logic. If cells contain more than a few gates, the state-machine design approach should be taken. The state of the cell can be held in a register, and the combinational logic used for changing states can be implemented with a PLA. Standard layouts for registers and PLA cells are available, simplifying design and layout tasks and shortening design change and error correction time. However, the small size of our pattern matcher cells, each containing only four gates, made the use of random logic possible. Design and layout of such simple circuits is easy.

Uses and extensions of the pattern matching chip. A pattern matching chip with n character cells can directly match patterns of length only up to n. Longer patterns require the existence of more than n partial results at each beat. Since any chip must be of finite size, it is important that the chip be extensible. It should be possible to combine several chips to form a larger pattern matcher.

In order to make the chip extensible, an input for the result stream and outputs for the pattern and text streams must be provided. Several pattern matching chips can then be cascaded (Figure 10). The inputs to each chip in the figure are taken from the outputs of its neighbors, so that the cells on all of the chips form a single linear array. The pattern is fed to the inputs of the leftmost chip, and the text string is input to the rightmost chip. The result output is taken from the leftmost chip. A cascade of k chips with n cells each can thus match patterns of up to kn characters.

If the pattern to be matched is longer than the capacity of the available pattern matching system, the pattern can be run through the system several times to match it against the entire string. If the system contains a total of n character cells, each run will match the complete pattern against n substrings. To cover all substrings, all we need do is delay the string by n characters on succeeding runs.

Modifying the design of the pattern matcher can provide special-purpose hardware for problems similar to string matching. For example, we might wish to count how many characters in a substring match corresponding characters in a pattern. This problem can be solved by replacing the result bit stream with a stream of integers, and replacing the accumulator cell with a counting cell:

$\lambda_{out} \leftarrow \lambda_{in}$
$x_{out} \leftarrow x_{in}$
IF λ_{in}
THEN $r_{out} \leftarrow t$; $t \leftarrow 0$
ELSE IF x_{in} OR d_{in}
THEN $t \leftarrow t+1$; $r_{out} \leftarrow r_{in}$
ELSE $r_{out} \leftarrow r_{in}$

d_{in}
λ_{in} → → λ_{out}
x_{in} → → x_{out}
r_{out} ← ← r_{in}

A problem of more practical interest is the computation of correlations. Here, the pattern, string, and result are all numbers. The result r_i of a correlation is defined as

$$r_i=(s_{i-k}-p_0)^2 + (s_{i+1-k}-p_1)^2 + \ldots + (s_i-p_k)^2.$$

A good match of substring to pattern results in a high correlation.

Correlations can be computed by a machine with a data flow identical to the string matching chip, except that all streams contain numbers. The comparator is replaced by a difference cell that computes

$$d_{out} \leftarrow s_{in}-p_{in}.$$

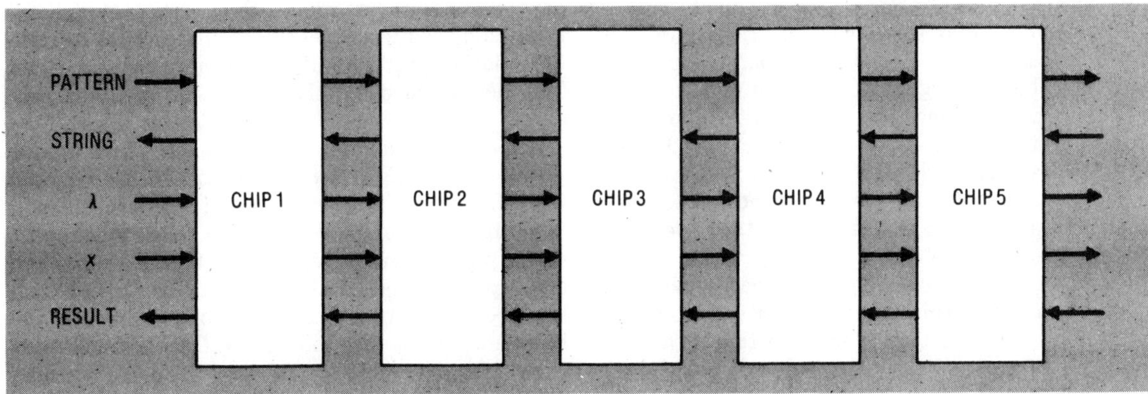

Figure 10. A five-chip pattern matcher—cascading of chips permits the direct matching of longer strings.

Like the character comparison, this difference computation may be pipelined bit by bit. An adder cell replaces the accumulator. The algorithm for the adder cell is

$$\begin{array}{l} \text{IF } \lambda_{in} \\ \text{THEN } r_{out} \leftarrow t;\ t \leftarrow 0 \\ \text{ELSE } r_{out} \leftarrow r_{in};\ t \leftarrow t + d_{in}^2. \end{array}$$

Other problems such as convolutions and FIR filtering have algorithms using the same data flow.[4,5] It should be clear that special-purpose hardware similar to the pattern matching chip can be built for any of these problems.

Design methodology

A systematic approach is essential when designing a complex system of any kind. The design task must be broken into manageable subtasks, with a well-defined flow of information between them. Each subtask can then be performed separately with no need to consider more than one subtask at a time. This allows division of labor and, more importantly, prevents mistakes and eases design changes.

Because of the diversity of tasks and concerns in VLSI design, a systematic method is especially important in designing a special-purpose chip. It is impossible, for example, to take global data flow, circuit design, and transistor characteristics into account all at once. We must find small subtasks, with boundaries between them that hide the implementation details of one from another. Of course, any set of subtasks is unlikely to be completely independent, since problems that crop up in performing one may require redoing another—difficulties in layout, for example, may mandate a circuit redesign. However, these design iterations will be easier if the interactions between subtasks are few.

VLSI system structure suggests several natural information boundaries. One advantage of geometrically regular algorithms is the spatial separation that they impose between subsystems. The interior of one cell can be designed in ignorance of the interior details of another (although exterior details such as size and data path positions must be known). If cells are complex, the separation of circuit functions within each cell may provide an additional information boundary. The design of each functional block of a cell can then be largely independent of the others. The existence of a hierarchy of abstract chip models, from algorithm to gate to layout level, is a further aid to VLSI design. Each level of the hierarchy deals with an independent set of design issues and serves as an implementation of the next level up and as a specification for the next level down.

Chip design can thus be decomposed geometrically, functionally, and hierarchically. These decompositions must be consistent to be used to best advantage. Tasks separated geometrically should also be separated functionally and hierarchically. It would be unfortunate, for example, if all cell circuits had to be considered at once in order to construct a stick diagram for a chip. Careful construction of a *task dependency graph,* before beginning the design, avoids this problem. This graph should contain all of the subtasks to be performed and include the information needed for each and the precedence relations among them. Of course, backtrack paths resulting in several iterations of one task because of difficulties in another need not be shown. The chip design task is not yet understood well enough to predict such backtracking.

The task dependency graph ensures that no more than a small amount of knowledge is required for any subtask. Each of the subtasks in the graph should deal with the design of one geometric area at one level of abstraction. The circuit design of the entire chip all at once is too large a task because it covers too much chip area. Generating a layout from a cell's function is too large a task, since it spans too many levels of the hierarchy. Designing a single cell circuit from a cell's function is probably a task of the proper size, although if the cell performs several different functions the task should be further subdivided.

Figure 11 is a task dependency graph for the design of a pattern matching chip like ours. Our own project in fact brought out the need for the task dependency graph and suggested its structure. It should be suitable for designing other chips of about the same scale. Each subtask deals with only one geometric region, one circuit function, and one level of the VLSI chip model hierarchy. The arrows indicate the flow of information between the subtasks, each of which we briefly describe below.

Data flow and cell type function. The chip design must begin with an algorithm design conceptually specifying the overall chip structure. Several algorithms will exist for any problem, and the best one should be found at this stage. The algorithm is a level of abstraction at which to think about important properties such as regularity and modularity, without worrying about low-level issues. It should integrate two distinct bodies of information. One is the data flow pattern, including the number of cells, their geometric placements, and the choreography of data. The types of cells should be distinguished and the beats on which each is active should be identified. The other body of information is the function of each cell type, comprising not just the circuit function but also the relative positions of signal inputs and outputs and the sequence of activity on each beat.

Cell combinations and placements. Cells in the implementation might not correspond one to one with the cells in the algorithm. Several cells may be combined to share components or rarely used communication paths in the algorithm may be multiplexed onto one physical data path. The first task in implementing the algorithm is to choose among these combinations and to position cells and cell combinations on the chip.

This subtask requires information about the pattern of active and idle cells on each beat and the use of each communication path, which the data flow and geometry subtask provides. It also requires information about the sharable subfunctions and complexity of each cell type, which the cell function subtask provides. The output of this subtask is a skeleton layout for the chip, with each cell group assigned a location and a set of contained cells.

Data flow control circuit. Data flow control circuitry ensures the orderly movement of data on the correct beats. To perform this subtask we must learn the correct sequence of beats from the algorithm data flow and which elements are active on each beat. From the cell combination subtask we learn which cell groups and physical data paths contain the active elements.

Based on the size and intended use of the chip we can decide whether the data flow should be clocked or self-timed. If we choose to clock we must decide whether to generate the signal externally or on the chip. We can then design the shift registers for data movement and route any clock wires or synchronization signals among the cell groups on the skeleton layout.

Cell logic circuits. We now have the three pieces of information needed to design circuits for the cells—the cell functions (from the cell type function step), the group of cells to be implemented by each circuit (from the cell combination step), and the shift register stages that must be included in each cell (from the data flow control). If the cell functions are simple enough, ad hoc circuit design techniques may be adequate. If the functions are complex, the cells may be split into subsystems to be designed independently. In this way, full advantage may be taken of the functional decomposition of each cell. In addition, the circuit for each cell type can be designed without reference to the others, since all communication needs have been considered in the data flow control. In designing the circuits, however, consideration must also be given to how the chip will be tested after fabrication.

Cell timing signals. A cell function may comprise several distinct sequential steps performed on each beat. In the pattern matching accumulator, for example, the assignments

$$r_{out} \leftarrow t;\ t \leftarrow \mathrm{TRUE}$$

must take place in the correct order. The cell circuit, especially in a clocked system, may require signals to

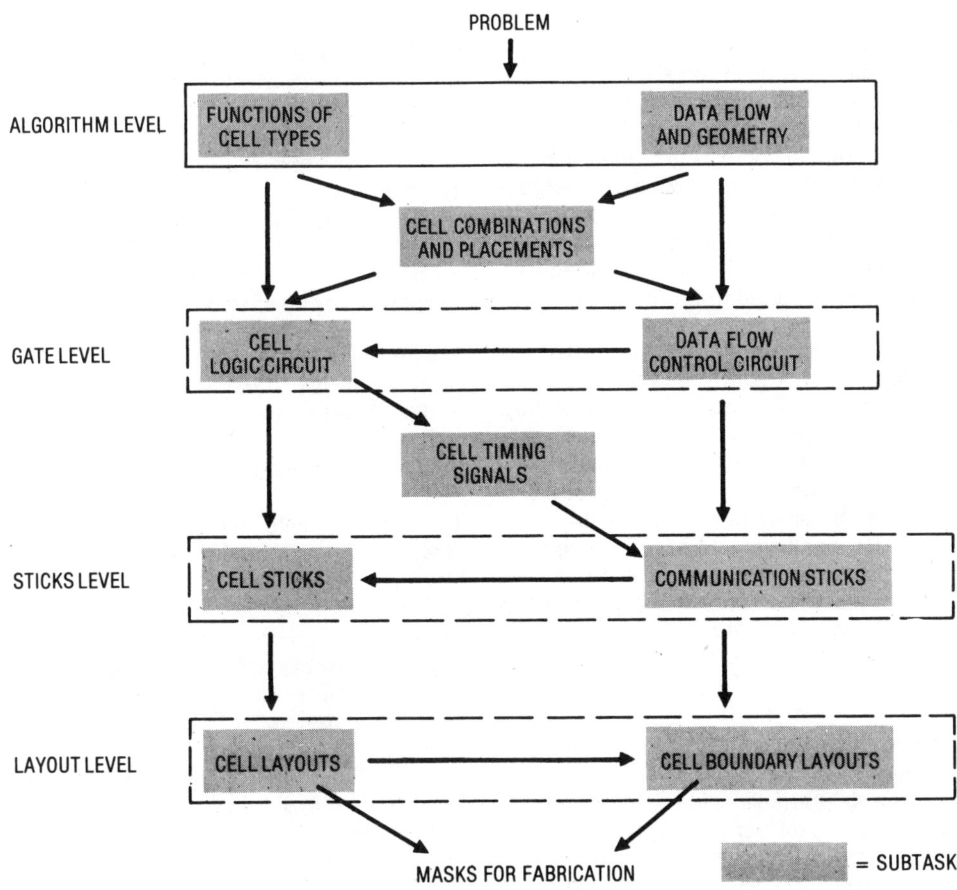

Figure 11. A task dependency graph can guide the designer of a special-purpose VLSI chip. This graph—for a pattern matching chip—shows how the design effort can be decomposed into simpler tasks.

control such sequences, in addition to the signals needed for cell activation. These should be supplied by the data flow control. Such signals should be identified as soon as the cell circuits are complete, and circuits to generate them added to the data flow control.

Communication sticks. When the data flow control circuitry is complete we can draw its stick diagram. For geometrically regular chips this will consist of an open communication path network, control circuitry, and blank spaces for the cells. If the chip has centralized clock circuitry, its topology can be designed. The distribution network for power and ground should also be designed at this stage.

Cell sticks. The topological layouts of the individual cells can now be designed. The relative locations of power, ground, and all inputs and outputs are known from the communication sticks. We must now choose implementations for the circuit elements and decide on the relative positions of internal data paths.

Cell layouts. Once the topological layouts of the cells are complete, the detailed layout of each cell is possible. Following the design rules for the intended fabrication process, actual dimensions for each electrical component and distances between circuit elements must be chosen. This subtask's output is a scale drawing of the cell.

Cell boundary layouts. With cell sizes known, the cell boundaries can be laid out. The communication path and data flow control topology is known from the communication sticks. Wire lengths and spacings can be chosen, as can distances between cells. Inputs and outputs can be connected to contact pads. The cell and cell boundary layouts form a complete description of the chip; once they are complete, masks can be made and the chip fabricated.

Summary of the design methodology. With the help of the task dependency graph, the seemingly complicated process of designing a special-purpose chip can be carried out systematically, one subtask at a time. The graph presented here, although based on limited design experience, seems to be a good starting point. The design tasks below the algorithm level are relatively routine and may at least in principle be helped a great deal by various (future) computer-aided design systems. Eventually only the algorithm design level will require substantial effort and experience.

Over the past few years efforts in several fields of computer science have converged to make possible the design of special-purpose chips as described in this article. The study of parallel algorithms, particularly those for mesh-connected computers, has provided techniques for VLSI algorithm design.[14] The work of Mead and Conway[1] in developing structured NMOS design techniques has eased the design of reliable circuits and layouts. Improvements in computer-aided design and graphics systems have reduced the drudgery of mask design. Finally, the development of suitable intermediate languages makes the design and fabrication processes relatively independent and allows several users to share designs.

These developments allow the relatively inexperienced designer to develop chips quickly and confidently for his own application. By concentrating on algorithms, he can construct—with minimal design time—chips of good performance and fairly small area. The design of the pattern matching chip described here took only about two man-months.

Further developments can make the designer's task even easier. It is possible, for example, to build libraries of standard cells similar to subroutine libraries. If a designer needs, say, an inner product step cell, he can select it from a library rather than construct it himself. Libraries of data flow implementations are also possible, although their forms are less obvious.

Advances in fabrication technology may increase the scale of projects that can be attempted. Aside from reductions in feature size, techniques such as wafer-scale integration will increase the size and power of special-purpose devices. The modularity inherent in our philosophy is especially appropriate to wafer-scale integration, where a wafer's chips are interconnected rather than cut apart for individual packaging. Since some of the wafer's chips may be defective, the fabricator must be able to reroute the interconnections to replace a faulty chip with a functioning one. He can do this easily if the chips have regular interconnections and if they include only a few types.

The philosophy and methodology described here will make practical the design of special-purpose VLSI chips by their users. Connected to a general-purpose computer, these devices will provide rapid solutions to a variety of computations. Given the ease of the design process and the availability of new design tools, VLSI modularity will become a common architectural strategy in the 80's. ■

Acknowledgments

We received help from many people during our research. Using a preliminary version of Mead and Conway's *Introduction to VLSI Systems,* Bob Sproull taught us basic NMOS design techniques in his VLSI design course at CMU. Our pattern matching chip prototypes are included in the XEROX PARC multiproject chips for spring 1979 and have been fabricated at XEROX facilities. Larry Stewart checked our layouts for violations of design rules. Bob Hon provided much needed help, including building the layout design system we used, converting our designs into ICARUS format, and mounting chips for testing. Philip Lehman and Siang Song offered suggestions in the early stages of the algorithm design. Lynn Conway, Bob Hon, Dick Lyon, Siang Song, and Bob Sproull reviewed this paper. To these people, and to the others who helped us directly or indirectly, we express our thanks.

This research was supported in part by the Defense Advanced Research Projects Agency under Contract F33615-78-C-1551 (monitored by the Air Force Office of Scientific Research), the National Science Foundation under Grant MCS 78-236-76, the Office of Naval Research under Contract N00014-76-C-0370, and an NSF Fellowship.

References

1. C. A. Mead and L. A. Conway, *Introduction to VLSI Systems,* Addison-Wesley, Reading, Mass., 1980.
2. R. Hon and C. Sequin, "A Guide to LSI Implementation," 2nd ed., XEROX Palo Alto Research Center Technical Report, 1979.
3. I. E. Sutherland and C. A. Mead, "Microelectronics and Computer Science," *Scientific American,* Vol. 237, No. 3, Sept. 1977, pp. 210-228.
4. H. T. Kung and C. E. Leiserson, "Systolic Arrays (for VLSI)," in I. S. Duff and G. W. Stewart, eds., *Sparse Matrix Proc. 1978,* Society for Industrial and Applied Mathematics, Philadelphia, Pa., 1979, pp. 256-282. A slightly different version appears in C. A. Mead and L. A. Conway, *Introduction to VLSI Systems,* Addison-Wesley, Reading, Mass., 1980, sec. 8.3.
5. H. T. Kung, "Let's Design Algorithms for VLSI Systems," *Proc. Caltech Conf. Very Large Scale Integration,* California Institute of Technology, Pasadena, Calif., Jan. 1979., pp. 65-90. Also available as a Carnegie-Mellon University Computer Science Department Technical Report, 1979.
6. R. E. Griswold, J. F. Poage, and I. P. Polansky, *The SNOBOL4 Programming Language,* Prentice-Hall, Englewood Cliffs, N. J., 1968.
7. P. J. Warter and D. W. Mules, "A Proposal for an Electronic File Cabinet," *MICRO-DELCON,* IEEE Computer Society, Long Beach, Calif., Mar. 1979, pp. 56-63.
8. M. J. Fischer and M. S. Paterson, "String Matching and Other Products," Massachussetts Institute of Technology, Project MAC, Technical Report 41, 1974.
9. R. S. Boyer and J. S. Moore, "A Fast String Searching Algorithm," *Comm. ACM,* Vol. 20, No. 10, Oct. 1977, p. 762.
10. D. E. Knuth, J. H. Morris, and V. R. Pratt, "Fast Pattern Matching in Strings," *SIAM J. Computing,* Vol. 6, No. 2, June 1977, pp. 323-350.
11. A. Mukhopadhyay, "Hardware Algorithms for Nonnumeric Computation," *IEEE Trans. Computers,* Vol. C-28, No. 6, June 1979, pp. 384-394.
12. C. A. Mead, R. D. Pashley, L. D. Britton, Y. T. Daimon, and S. F. Sando, "128-Bit Multicomparator," *IEEE J. Solid State Circuits,* Vol. SC-11, No. 5, Oct. 1976, pp. 692-695.
13. C. L. Seitz, "Self-Timed VLSI Systems," *Proc. Caltech Conf. Very Large Scale Integration,* California Institute of Technology, Pasadena, Calif., Jan. 1979, pp. 345-355.
14. H. T. Kung, "The Structure of Parallel Algorithms," in M. C. Yovits, ed., *Advances in Computers, Volume 19,* Academic Press, N.Y., 1980.

1 μm MOSFET VLSI Technology: Part III—Logic Circuit Design Methodology and Applications

PETER W. COOK, MEMBER, IEEE, STANLEY E. SCHUSTER, MEMBER, IEEE, JAMES T. PARRISH, VICTOR DILONARDO, AND DARRYL R. FREEDMAN, MEMBER, IEEE

Abstract—Logic circuits were designed and fabricated in a 1 μm silicon-gate MOSFET technology. First, conventional random logic chip images using the largely one-dimensional "Weinberger" layout are examined. The image is able to provide chips with an average circuit delay of 3 ns at the 8000 circuit level of integration. Second, two forms of PLA and PLA-based macros are discussed. A dynamic PLA, used in a microprocessor cross section and including 105 product terms, which achieves a 56 ns cycle time is described. A static PLA, designed for 21-ns delay and achieving measured delays from 13 to 21 ns, is also described. Extensions, particularly into low-temperature operation, are discussed.

I. INTRODUCTION

IMPROVING lithographic capabilities to achieve smaller dimensions remains one of the most attractive means to enhance MOSFET circuit performance. The so-called "constant field" scaling [1], [2] shows that for a k-fold reduction in linewidth, the circuit performance increases by k while the power decreases by k^2, and the density increases by k^2. The present 1 μm silicon-gate MOSFET project [3]-[7] has been directed towards the comprehensive development of a silicon-gate MOSFET technology with minimum lithographic dimensions of 1 μm and typical device channel lengths of 1.3 μm. It is further directed towards the development of advanced circuits and chip images that will take full advantage of the performance potential of 1 μm MOSFET's.

The performance improvement predicted by constant field scaling is dramatic but may not be achieved at high levels of integration if chip images are not carefully thought out. The simple extension of chip sizes from, e.g., 1000 to 8000 circuits, leads to increased wiring lengths on typical NOR circuits and rapidly increasing design problems. Section II of this paper will describe in detail the analysis of chip images of 8000 circuits per chip and will show specific designs capable of maintaining the performance expected for a 1 μm technology. If random NORs are retained as basic building blocks, these problems can be partially alleviated by the use of an "island" approach in which the total chip is built-up of islands of relatively small size and high density. Each island may look like a present-day chip, with interisland wiring accommodating what is presently done at the card level. This island approach is one form of the macro method of chip design and is motivated by the desire to maintain the performance implied by scaling while impacting design methods as little as possible. A more radical approach to macro design is found in the use of a set of blocks completely different from the NOR. The goal in this approach is to simplify the design process by working with single blocks that are equivalent to many NOR's while still maintaining good power and performance in the final design. The particular approach presented involves a set of parts including PLA's (for combinatoric logic), registers (for data and state storage), and buses (for interconnection). Clock generators are included as support circuits. The third section of this paper will describe in detail circuits worked out for use in this design approach using both dynamic and static building blocks.

Manuscript received December 4, 1978.

P. W. Cook, S. E. Schuster, J. T. Parrish, and V. DiLonardo are with the IBM Thomas J. Watson Research Center, Yorktown Heights, NY 10598.

D. R. Freedman is with the IBM Systems Communications Division, Kingston, NY.

II. NOR CIRCUITS AT HIGH LEVELS OF INTEGRATION

The potential for a technology is closely allied to the design approach. When the Weinberger chip image [8] is utilized for high chip circuit counts, there is a significant performance

Reprinted from *IEEE J. Solid-State Circuits*, vol. SC-14, pp. 255-268, Apr. 1979.

degradation due to reduced power or increased wiring capacitance (or both). In the 1 μm technology, a standard Weinberger design with 8000 circuits will have an average delay of 10-12 ns. An analysis of the image led to improvements, notably a second level of metal for wiring and a chip image made up of an array of Weinberger islands or macros. These changes bring the performance of the 8000 circuit chip to the 3-4 ns range.

A. *Weinberger Image*

Variations of the Weinberger image have been used at IBM to design random logic MOSFET chips from the time of the original paper [8] to the present. Over that period, chip circuit counts have increased from about 55 in the 1965 time frame to current counts of around 2000. There is a large amount of data relating to performance, chip size, logic power, etc. available within IBM for Weinberger designs, and newer approaches are usually compared to Weinberger designs for evaluation.

The Weinberger array (Figs. 1-3) evolved in the context of metal-gate MOSFET technologies. It is characterized by circuits (typically NOR's) arranged in columns. Within a column, circuits are built between source and drain diffusion "rails" which extend from one edge of the column to the other. As needed, MOSFET active devices are made between these rails to provide NOR inputs. Outputs from a circuit are taken from the circuit's drain rail. The circuit column is bounded on one side by a metal V_{DD} line and, on the other, by a metal ground line. A load device is wired between the metal V_{DD} line and the drain rail of a circuit, and the source rail is tied to the ground line. Usually two circuits share a single source rail, as shown for the typical (metal-gate) circuit pair of Fig. 1. Power distribution in a simple Weinberger image is by column buses and "horizontal" intercolumn power buses, ultimately tied to chip I/O pins. A typical power distribution scheme appears in Fig. 2. Off-chip drivers (OCD's) for the Weinberger image are usually placed at the periphery near the pads they drive to minimize power distribution and wiring problems associated with these circuits.

An extension to the simple Weinberger image is found in the "coupled" Weinberger image. This image, which appears in skeletal form in Fig. 3, is really two separate Weinberger images "coupled" through common power supplies and a central intercolumn wiring area.

Wiring within a column is provided by metal wires orthogonal to the diffused source and drain rails. The position of active devices and outputs along a rail are chosen to facilitate this largely one-dimensional wiring problem. While in principal it is possible for inputs and outputs to be placed anywhere along a rail, it is more common to divide the rail into "wire channels." Inputs and outputs are then placed in wire channels. Most of the width of a column is taken up by intracolumn wiring rather than by active devices. The wireability of a column will depend on the number of circuits in the column and the number of wire channels in the column. Intercolumn wiring is on the n^+ level, and, although it is minimized in placement and wiring programs, it may take up to 25-30 percent of the column height.

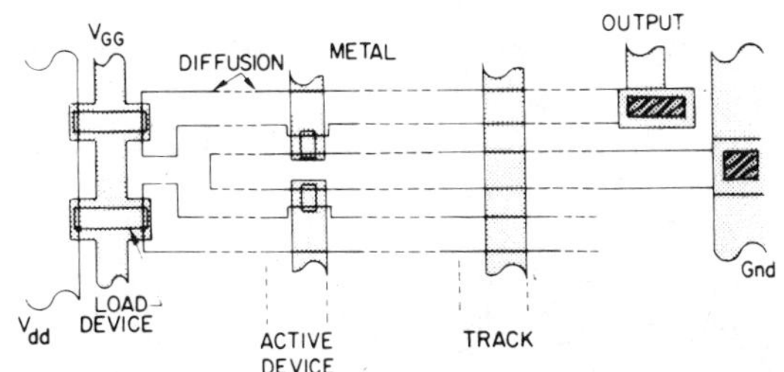

Fig. 1. A pair of circuits from a Weinberger image using a metal-gate MOSFET process.

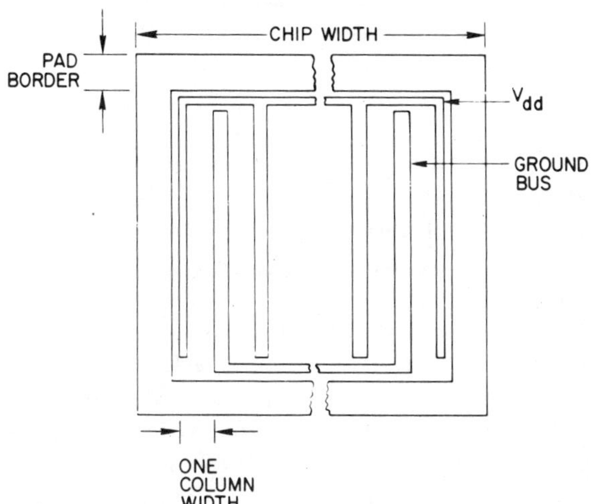

Fig. 2. Weinberger image: power distribution.

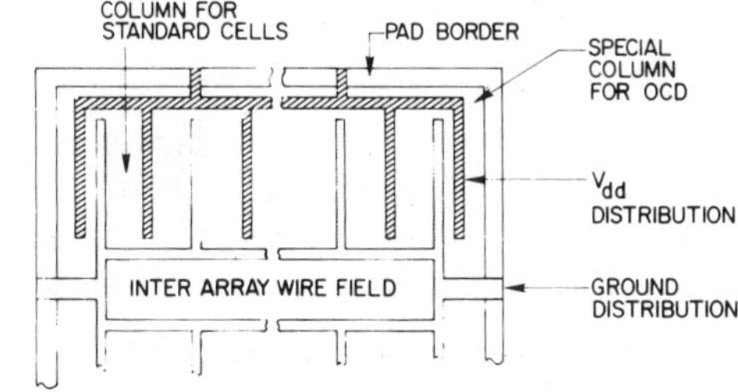

Fig. 3. "Coupled" Weinberger image: power distribution.

The most used circuit is the NOR. Within any particular chip, circuits may have various values of fan-in, fan-out, power, and different capacitive loading. The columns often have different widths to accomodate special circuits. Off-chip drivers designed to handle the very large capacitive load encountered by nets that leave the chip are usually placed around the periphery of the chip to be near the I/O pads and to minimize their interference with the intrachip wiring.

B. *DC Design*

The dc design of a static NOR is given by the width-to-length ratio (W/L) of both active and load devices. These W/L values are typically related by the "ratio of ratios" which is determined by circuit down level requirements, so that a given circuit is normally characterized by only a single parameter, the W/L ratio of the active device. This W/L ratio cannot be chosen with complete freedom because of IR drops in getting power to a circuit; any design must be carried out in the context of an "*IR* budget," defined as the sum of voltage drops from the V_{DD} input of the chip to the ground pin of the chip, exclusive of the drops across devices. This *IR* budget is set by such factors as noise margin, parameter spreads, and tradeoffs in the chip, module, and power supply. In a scaled design, the *IR* budget must be porportional to V_{DD}; this produces a difficult design problem, since with constant field scaling, *IR* drops do not scale with decreasing device dimensions. For the designs presented in this paper, circuit dc designs (as specified by the *IR* budget and ratio of ratios) are kept constant as the chip size and circuit power are varied; the image is adjusted by modifying the power bus or rail width to maintain these dc design characteristics.

C. Delay

For a given MOSFET circuit, the delay depends on the power of the circuit, the total capacitive load on the circuit, and the details of the input waveform. In assessing a technology, this last dependence may be eliminated by treating a long chain of identical circuits, each with "average" loading and power. The delay through two stages of such a chain is readily determined and is twice the average delay of a single stage. Normally, signal propagation delays are not significant in MOSFET circuits. However, in the Weinberger image, intercolumn wiring is done on n^+ lines. Such lines are distributed *RC* transmission lines and may have significant delay. For the 1 μm technology, such lines have a time constant of 10^{-14} s/μm^2. While this is not a problem for short runs, long lines of 1 mm will have limiting delays of ~10 ns.

D. Wiring Analysis of the Weinberger Image

General theories applicable to the wiring demands of the Weinberger image have been developed by Rent, Donath, and others [9]-[13]. These theories incorporate empirically derived constants to match them to observed data. Most of the equations describing the wiring demand of Weinberger and "coupled" Weinberger images are based on extrapolations of a relationship widely known as Rent's rule. Stated simply, if one assembles N blocks of logic, with each block having W wires connected to it, the number of nets F entering or leaving the assemblage is given by

$$F = WN^P$$

where P is a constant referred to as the Rent exponent and is from ~0.5 to ~0.7, depending upon the logical organization of the chip.

The number of wire channels needed for intracolumn wiring is given by the mean wire length (expressed in units of "cell height") multiplied by the number of wires per cell. An expression for the mean wire length is derived by Donath [11]. A curve showing results from this expression is given in Fig. 4.

A clean analytical expression for the number of horizontal intercolumn wires is harder to arrive at. The computed number varies widely with the assumptions made regarding how to include primary I/O in the computation. Satisfactory agreement with a limited number of experiments was obtained with a simple formula that has the same asymptotic behavior as does the expression used in the intracolumn wiring. The horizontal intercolumn wiring demand is taken to be proportional to the total number of circuits on the chip raised to P, the Rent exponent.

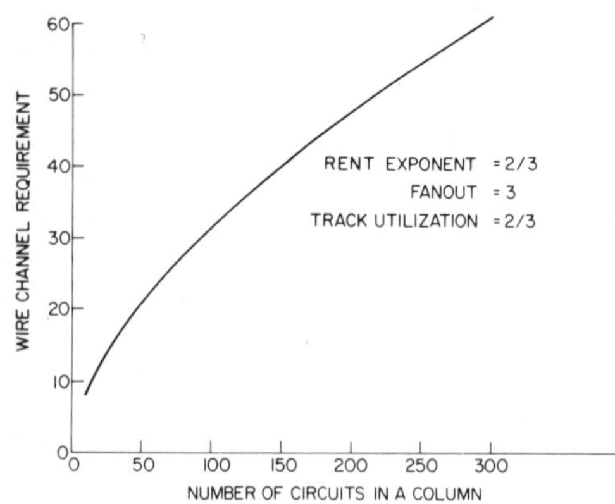

Fig. 4. Wire channel requirements in a Weinberger column as a function of the number of circuits in the column.

E. Analysis Method

It is difficult to analyze a specific Weinberger image chip. Such an analysis is equivalent to a complete chip design. Therefore, to provide information on typical performance, a hypothetical average chip has been analyzed. In this chip, all circuits are equal in fan-in, fan-out, wiring capacitance, and power. Fan-in and fan-out were set at 3, a typical number for Weinberger chips. The Rent exponent was 2/3. Significant layout parameters (column widths, length of wire on an average circuit, etc.) are taken from the appropriate analytical work described above. The power-line width is set to provide the required *IR* budget. This type of analysis is performed for a variety of chip images produced by varying the number of circuits in a column and the best results taken as an appropriate characterization of the technology and image at a given level of integration.

The 1 μm Weinberger performance is shown in Fig. 5(a). Note that performance varies from ~3 ns for 2000 circuit chips to ~10 ns for 8000 circuit chips.

F. The Weinberger Macro Image

Because the chips presented in Fig. 5(a) have constant power, the observed degradation in performance is to be expected. However, it is possible to improve performance significantly. The circuits of the 2000 circuit chip have a total load capacitance that is slightly dominated by the wiring capacitance; by the time power is reduced for the 8000 circuit chips, wiring capacitance is strongly dominant. Thus these dense Weinberger layouts are not optimum; they can be improved by reducing wiring capacitance. Also, functional groups of circuits with high local connectivity will appear at circuit counts less than 8000. Thus an improvement in overall performance can be expected if the Weinberger image is restricted to relatively small islands in a chip. The resulting image is analogous to a card populated with several small Weinberger chips.

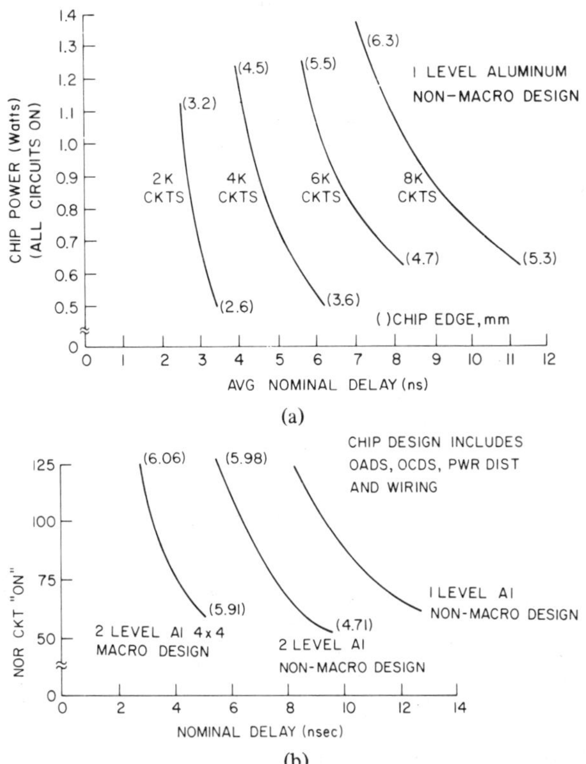

Fig. 5.(a) Power versus delay for the 1 μm technology for several chip sizes. A single "coupled" Weinberger image is assumed. To estimate wiring track requirements, the partitioning exponent is 2/3. The number of OCD's is taken as the square root of the number of circuits, with OCD power being 5 times normal circuit power. Chip power is total, under the assumption that all circuits are on; this is essentially equivalent to worst case power under the assumption that 2/3 of the circuits are on at any one time. (b) Circuit power versus delay for 8000 circuit chips. The cases shown are for a chip designed as a single image with a single level of aluminum, the same single image design with two levels of aluminum, and a 4 X 4 array of 500 circuit islands, also using two levels of aluminum.

Such an image was analyzed using the same approach taken for the original Weinberger image. To facilitate interconnection of islands, a second metal wiring layer was assumed. With this added metal, intermacro wiring was done exclusively on metal, and horizontal intramacro wires formerly on n^+ diffusions were done on the second level of metal. OCD's of the Weinberger chip were replaced with off-island drivers matched to interarray capacitances. Normal off-chip drivers were assumed at the periphery. The results are given in Fig. 5(b) for a 4 X 4 array of macros of 500 circuits. A delay of ~3 ns can be achieved.

G. Summary

Random logic Weinberger islands can deliver average NOR delays of ~3 ns in chips of 8000 circuits using the 1 μm silicon-gate MOSFET technology with two levels of metal wiring. This represents a significant advance over what can be achieved with a conventional single-level metal Weinberger image.

III. Dynamic PLA Circuits

A. Introduction

Section II of this paper has shown how random logic can be used in an island chip image to maintain the high performance promised by scaling to 1 μm dimensions. The islands are still relatively complex, and the impact on chip design methodology is not trivial. Therefore, there has been interest in examining higher level blocks for use in implementing chip designs. Ideally, these higher level blocks would be quite flexible, so that they could be used in a broad range of applications while remaining easy to design. The retention of the power and performance characteristics seen in random logic is also desirable.

In 1974, a study was initiated to evaluate the possible capabilities of a set of PLA-based macros in implementing small processors. In that study [14] an 8 bit microprocessor was redesigned using a set of blocks including PLA's, registers (of several types), and buses. Those blocks were designed in the same metal-gate MOSFET technology used in implementing the original microprocessor, so that differences between the original and PLA-based designs would be the result of the design approach and not technology changes. That study took the position that the merits of PLA-based design were to be measured by the performance, density, and power of the entire processor rather than by the number of bits equivalent to a NOR circuit [15]. The result for the particular microprocessor was a PLA design that offered equivalent performance and density at one-third the power of the original Weinberger NOR design. This power reduction was largely due to the exclusive use of dynamic circuits in the PLA macros.

The parts of this early microprocessor study were never implemented in the metal-gate process. However, as a part of the present study of the potential of 1 μm silicon-gate MOSFET's, a cross section of the PLA version of the microprocessor was implemented and has been previously reported on briefly [16]. Details on circuit designs and results follow.

B. Description of the Microprocessor Cross Section

The microprocessor is shown in Fig. 6; the cross section actually fabricated is encircled. Fig. 7 is a photograph of the microprocessor cross section. Included are two type-*D* registers and two PLA's (an ALU and a control PLA) interconnected by buses. The control PLA provides a simple means of generating complex clock waveforms to test the remaining parts on the chip. Typical operations implemented by the control PLA include "load register" and "form sum in ALU and load register."

The larger PLA in the cross section is an arithmetic and logic unit (ALU) PLA adapted from the ALU of the microprocessor study. It performs addition and bit-by-bit AND, OR, and EXCLUSIVE OR on a pair of single-byte arguments including, for addition, input carry. Results are typically 8 bits wide with an added output carry generated on addition. The PLA has 105 product terms, 20 inputs (40 actual AND array inputs), and 9 outputs; it is typical of a moderately large PLA.

Like the parts of the original microprocessor study, the parts in the cross section use dynamic circuitry almost exclusively. The clocks which are embodied in four nonoverlapping phases and used as follows:

Φ1) turns on register load device, writes data into registers and precharges the AND arrays of PLA's;

Φ2) drives output of 2 bit decoder into AND arrays and precharges the OR arrays of PLA's;

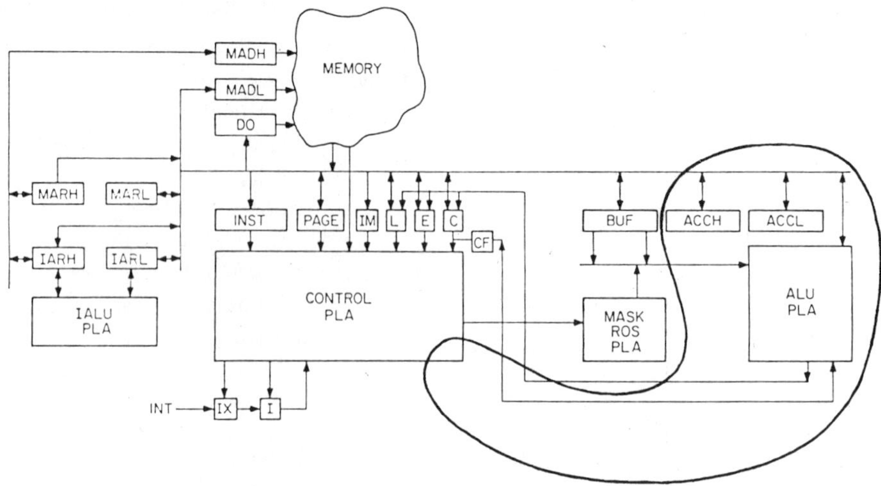

Fig. 6. Microprocessor cross section. The entire microprocessor is shown; the cross section is encircled.

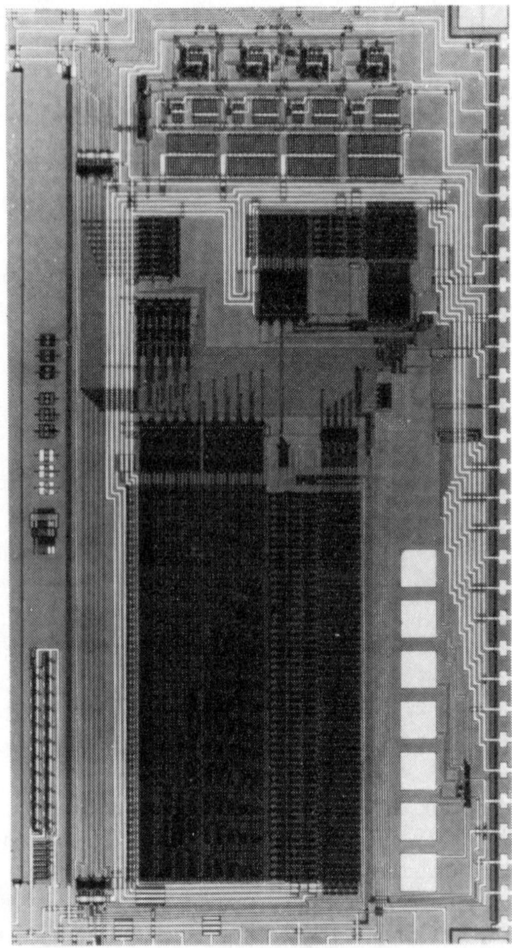

Fig. 7. Photograph of microprocessor cross section. The large PLA which dominates the test site is the ALU; the clock generator circuitry dominates the top of the site.

Φ3) drives output of interarray driver into OR array and precharges buses;

Φ4) drives output of OR array or register onto data buses and clears registers.

Several features are to be noted in this timing information. Firstly, some operations are conditional. These operations include writing data into registers (Φ1), driving the output of the OR array or register onto data buses (Φ4), and clearing registers (Φ4). Such actions are the result of control pulses produced by control logic; when such pulses occur, they are essentially in synchronism with the indicated phase pulse (being, in fact, derived from such phase pulses). Other than the four operations indicated above, actions initiated by phase pulses take place unconditionally.

Secondly, control pulses are only needed in two distinct phase times: Φ4- and Φ1-time. Because the output of the PLA OR array becomes valid during Φ3 (and remains valid during the following Φ4- and Φ1-times), a PLA can be used to generate control pulses by provision of an appropriate driver at the output of the PLA OR array. This feature was used in the original microprocessor study and in the cross section where PLA's are used as controls.

Finally, the parts have been so timed as to allow a PLA to communicate with itself on a data bus. Thus, the same bus that provides input to a PLA may also receive data from the output of the same PLA. The circuitry used at the PLA input and output ensures that there is no race of data through the PLA, as each stage of the PLA acts approximately like a sample and hold circuit.

The original microprocessor simulation study [14] resulted in PLA's with ~800 ns cycle times. The "on" time of a single phase was thus 100 ns. Such clocks were readily generated at off-chip sources and were brought into the chip with little difficulty. However, PLA cycles of 56 ns can be achieved with the 1 μm technology, which implies phase times of 7 ns with rise and fall times of the order of 1 ns. As clock lines on the cross section are loaded with approximately 20 pF, it is possible to bring the clocks in from external sources and maintain fast rise and fall times. Larger chips, however, will begin to face problems with this off-chip clock generation approach. Therefore, on-chip clock sources have been designed for the cross section. Driven by a single lightly loaded "timing" waveform, the on-chip circuitry derives the four phases and drives on-chip clock lines from a dc source.

Three different voltage levels are used in the cross section. V_{DD1} is the drain supply used for all logic levels, and V_{DD2}

supplies the on-chip clock generators and also sets the up level of "control pulses" produced by the control PLA. The final voltage (V_{CLOCK}) is the peak voltage of the timing waveform brought into the on-chip clock generators. For the microprocessor cross section, $V_{DD1} = 2.5$, $V_{DD2} = 3.5$, and $V_{CLOCK} = 5$. One supply may be eliminated by setting V_{DD1} to 3.5 V; this would increase the power.

Two different logic levels are used in the cross section. For all data buses, a logical 1 is defined as a ground or near-ground level. Thus when buses are precharged, they are precharged to logical 0. Since data are driven to buses during Φ4 when the bus precharge path is off, a single bus may be simultaneously driven by several sources. In this case, the bus acts to perform the "dot-OR" of data from the several sources.

For control pulses, a logical 1 is defined as a high level, with logical zero being defined as ground or near ground. The specific drivers which convert the PLA OR array output into control pulses are open-circuited when producing a zero output. Thus a control pulse line may receive control pulses from several simultaneously active sources (or even from sources "active" in different phase times). Like the data buses, such control pulse lines will perform a "dot-OR" of pulses from their several sources. While this feature has not been used in the cross section, it was used in the original microprocessor study to allow a large and complex control function to be shared among several compact PLA's.

C. PLA Design

The overall arrangement of a PLA is shown in Fig. 8. Shown are the arrays, 2 bit decoders, and interarray drivers used to drive and retime signals between the two arrays.

As circuits, the PLA arrays are trivial. In the AND array, each "product term" (or word) is implemented with a single pull-up device, whose gate is connected to Φ1. Thus, during Φ1, all product terms are precharged to V_{DD1}. Also connected to the product term are a multiplicity of input (or "bit") devices, whose drains are connected to the product term, whose sources are grounded, and whose gates are connected to 2-bit decoders in a pattern dictated by the "personality" of the PLA. Since the 2 bit decoder outputs are at ground except during Φ2, the product terms unconditionally precharge to V_{DD1} during Φ1 and assume proper logical values during Φ2; product terms will remain at these values until Φ1 of the next cycle. The OR terms in a PLA are similar, except that they are precharged during Φ2 and become valid during Φ3. On the surface, the design of such circuits would seem to require merely the provision of a large enough device to ensure either precharge or discharge in a single-phase time. In fact, it is somewhat more complex.

The array sections of a PLA can, in a polysilicon-gate technology, exist in two forms, as illustrated in Figs. 9 and 10. In Fig. 9 the input to the array is distributed on a metal level. The second basic arrangement shown in Fig. 10 distributes the input to the array on polysilicon. Choice of the cell arrangement is dictated by the effects of the distributed RC line associated with each cell. For the ALU PLA in the cross section, the first cell was used in the AND array, and the second was used in the OR array. Other PLA's performing other functions may have different optimum organizations.

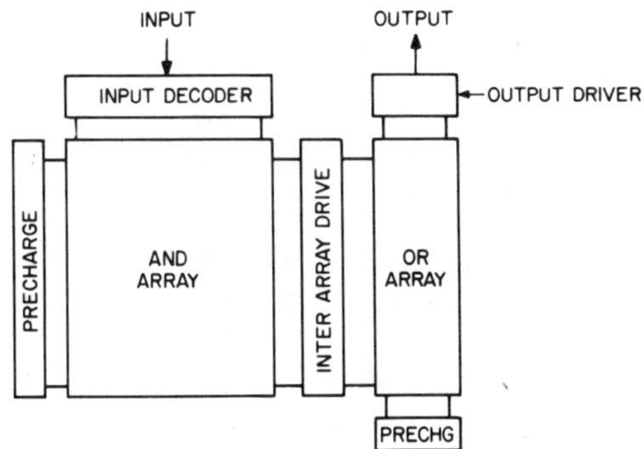

Fig. 8. General PLA showing basic parts.

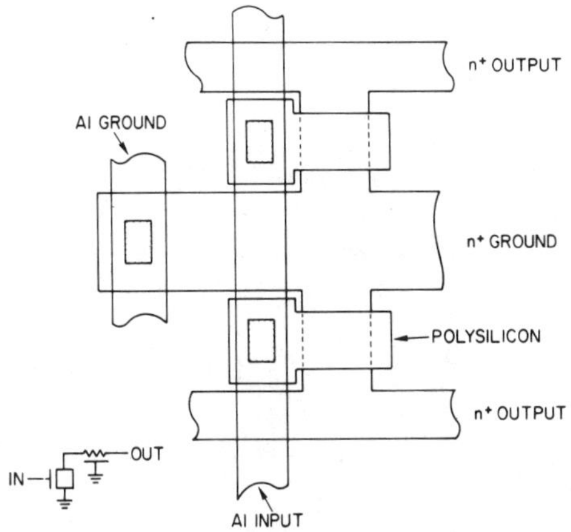

Fig. 9. Metal input array cell layout.

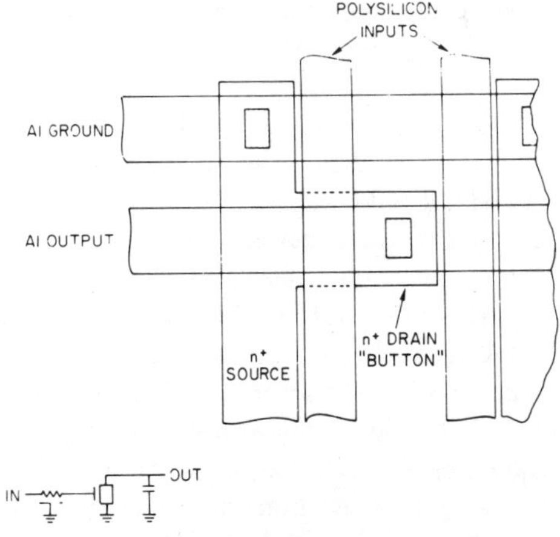

Fig. 10. Polysilicon input array cell layout.

The support circuits for the PLA (including 2 bit decoders, interarray drivers, and array output drivers) are all variations of a single basic circuit which finds its most complex embodiment in the 2 bit decoder. That decoder appears in Fig. 11. The schematic, shown in Fig. 11(b), shows a single path consisting of an inverter and a NAND to generate the $L + \overline{R}$ signal. The output of the inverter actually has a fan out of 2, because it also drives the $\overline{L} + \overline{R}$ NAND circuit. (For purposes of notation, "L" and "R" designate the "left" and "right" inputs to a 2 bit decoder.)

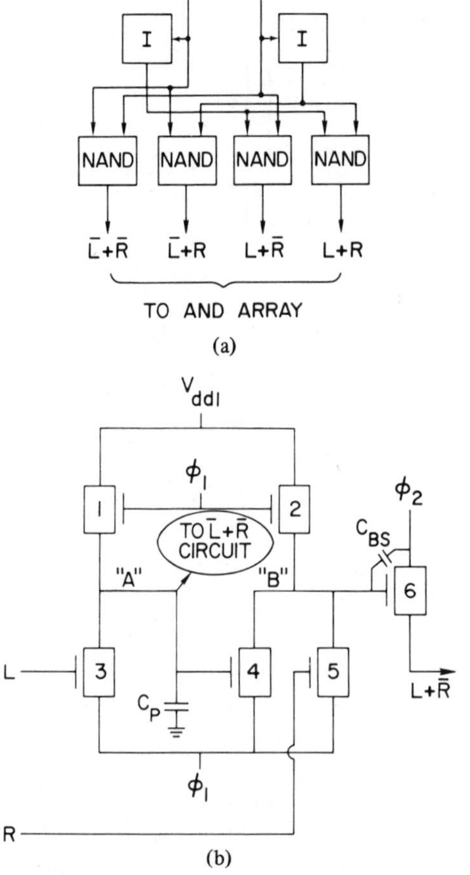

Fig. 11. (a) 2 bit decoder: logic function. (b) 2 bit decoder: partial schematic diagram.

The operation of the circuit is divided into two parts: Φ1 high and Φ1 low after high. The operation with Φ1 high is simple; both nodes *A* and *B* precharge to V_{DD1} through devices 1 and 2 (and possibly other devices). When Φ1 falls after this precharge, the operation depends upon the values of *L* and *R*. If *L* is low, then node *A* will remain high, and, independently of the level at *R*, node *B* will be discharged through device 4 as Φ1 falls. Likewise, node *B* discharges if *R* is high, regardless of the state of *L*, with the discharge now taking place through device 5. Operation is most complex when *L* is high and *R* is low. In this case, the logic function of the circuit demands that *A* discharge to ground while *B* remains high. However, when Φ1 begins to fall, both *A* and *B* are high; thus device 4 may be turned on, causing a malfunction of the circuit. It is seen that the circuit operation includes a built-in race when *R* is low and *L* is high, and device sizes must be chosen so that under these conditions node *A* falls to ground rapidly enough to keep node *B* essentially at the V_{DD1} level. Because C_{BS} is moderately large, this is not difficult. At the same time, sufficient "pad" capacitance (C_P) must be provided so that when *L* is low and node *A* is to remain high, the effects of parasitic coupling from the Φ1 line and node *A* are minimized.

In Fig. 11, device 6 is a bootstrap driver. The bootstrap capacitance C_{BS} is dominated by a gate-to-inversion layer capacitance to provide a maximum bootstrap effect when an output pulse in required and a minimum of drain-to-gate coupling when no output is desired. Ideally, C_{BS} would be zero under the no-output condition (*B* low). In fact, this cannot be achieved, and it is desireable to keep either device 3 or 4 on (if on during Φ1) until the end of Φ2. The 2 bit decoder is normally used at the input of a PLA; that input typically comes from a clocked bus. Thus, as implied by the timing given earlier, *L* and *R* will be logically valid from the end of Φ4 to the beginning of the next Φ3 (when both *L* and *R* unconditionally become high). Since *L* and *R* are stable during Φ2, *A* and *B* are also stable during that time, and, when *B* is pulled low, it is also clamped low through either device 4 or 5, and coupling from Φ2 to *B* is absorbed by the clamp.

Performance of the PLA arrays was sized after the layouts were completed. In the AND array, one 2 bit decoder circuit required a 25 μm width; this space may be occupied by up to 3 AND array input devices and allows a *W*/*L* ratio of 2.23:1 for the AND array device. The entire AND array "rail" is ~300 μm long, with a capacitance of 0.2 pF and a resistance of 5.2 kΩ. Under nominal conditions, the rail can be discharged from V_{DD1} to 0.25 V in 3.7 ns; under "worst case" conditions, the rail is discharged in 6.4 ns. The OR array has a pitch limited by the interarray driver (7.5 μm) and allows a device *W*/*L* ratio of 3.2:1. Rail capacitance in the OR array is ~0.3 pF; because the OR array output is distributed on aluminum, and because each polysilicon input wire to the OR array is short, there are negligible *RC* line effects in the OR array. Again, under "worst case" conditions, the OR array discharges in 5.7 ns.

In addition to the 2-bit decoder, the PLA parts require three other drivers. The interarray driver retimes and drives the AND array output into the OR array; the control pulse driver allows a logic level from an OR array output to be converted into a pulse on Φ4 or Φ1 (thereby allowing a PLA to be used as control logic), and the data bus driver allows OR array outputs to be driven onto a data bus. All of these circuits are derived from the 2-bit decoder and are similar in design and layout. Specifically, the interarray driver is identical to the 2-bit decoder except that it is precharged during Φ2 and produces an output pulse during Φ3; also, it has no *R* input or device 5, and the output of a product term replaces the *L* input. The control pulse driver is identical to the interarray driver except that its input comes from an OR output, and it is precharged during Φ3 and driven during either Φ4 or Φ1. (Since the OR output remains valid from the end of Φ3 to the beginning of Φ2, the clamping of the driver discussed above is maintained for the control-pulse driver.)

D. Registers

The basic *D*-type latch of the register macro is shown in Fig. 12(a). The latch is designed so information can be read from the bus into the latch during Φ1 and written from the latch onto the bus during Φ4 by means of the control pulse Φ4*W*. Reading data into the latch requires two control pulses: a Φ4*R* pulse to clear the latch and a Φ1*R* pulse to enter new data. Both pulses may come from control logic; alternatively, optional circuitry for locally generating the second control pulse appears in Fig. 12(b). The latch is actually a static cir-

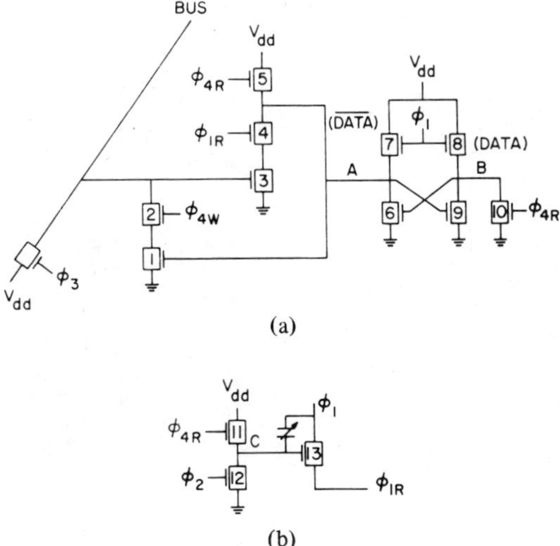
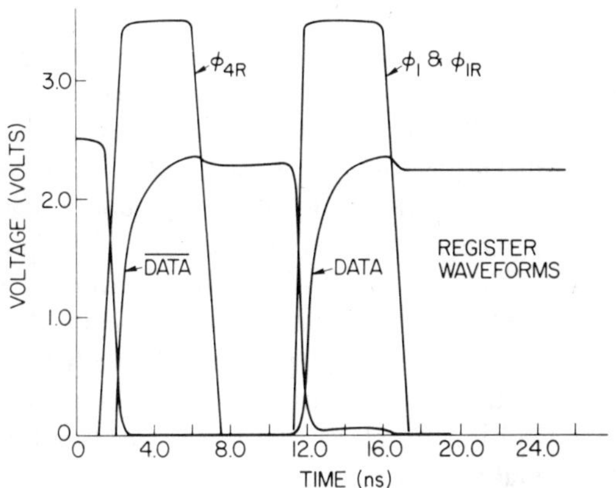

Fig. 12. Basic D-type latch and locally generated second control pulse.

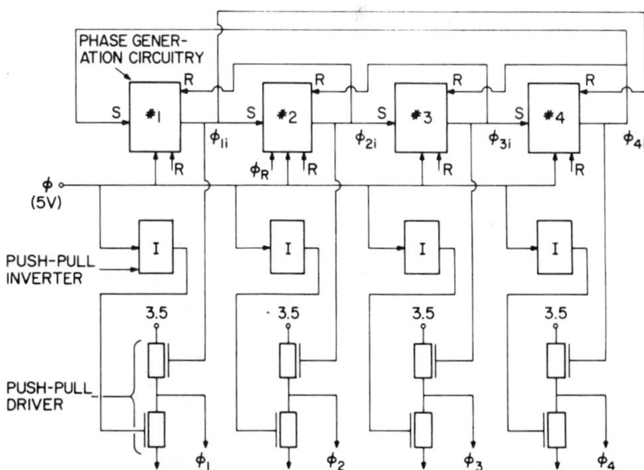

Fig. 14. Overall clock generator.

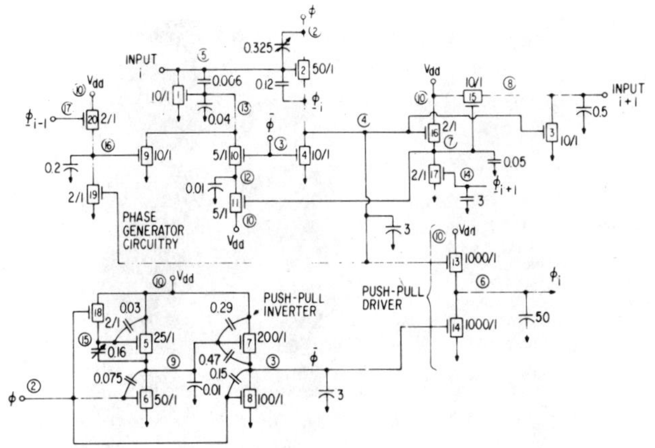

Fig. 15. Single clock phase generator.

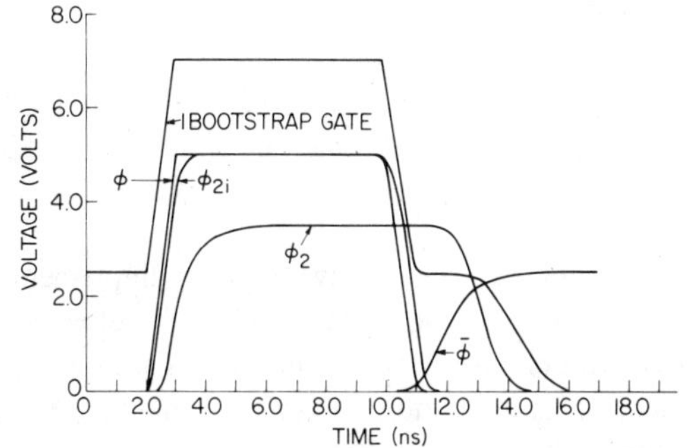

Fig. 16. Clock waveforms (simulated).

Fig. 13. Simulated waveforms for D latch in 1 μm logic technology.

cuit, but since load devices are pulsed during $\Phi 1$, power is kept low.

The latch shown is arranged to interface to a single bus. More than a single bus can be interfaced by replication of devices 1-4. Simulated waveforms for the latch under nominal conditions appear in Fig. 13.

E. On-Chip Clock Generation

An overall block diagram of the clock generator is given in Fig. 14. The clock generator consists of three basic building blocks: 1) the phase generation circuitry, 2) a push-pull inverter, and 3) a high-capacitance push-pull driver. A single off-chip clock is supplied to the phase generators and inverters; this off-chip clock must have slightly shorter rise and fall times than the desired on-chip phases. However, the capacitance driven by this clock is relatively small. The clock generator circuitry, shown in detail in Fig. 15, operates very much like a shift register, with a single "1" propagating from stage to stage and activating push-pull drivers which provide the on-chip clocks. Reset circuitry to provide proper initialization of the phase generator and inverters to generate a complementary clock are also provided on chip. Simulated waveforms at key nodes in the circuit under nominal conditions are shown in Fig. 16. The driver is capable of delivering pulses with ~1 ns rise and fall times into loads of ~50 pF.

The 5-V timing waveform, bootstrap drivers of the phase generator, and hot-electron limits of the MOSFET devices combine to form a difficult design problem. It is necessary to keep voltage limits on each device within the limits required to avoid hot-electron effects. The general approach [6] is to clamp device gates to ground when device drain-to-source voltage is high and to make bootstrap driver devices large enough to ensure safe drain-to-source voltage when the device is actually conducting. A plot showing the maximum voltages seen by the key devices of the clock generation circuitry and the hot-electron boundary is shown in Fig. 17. (The various

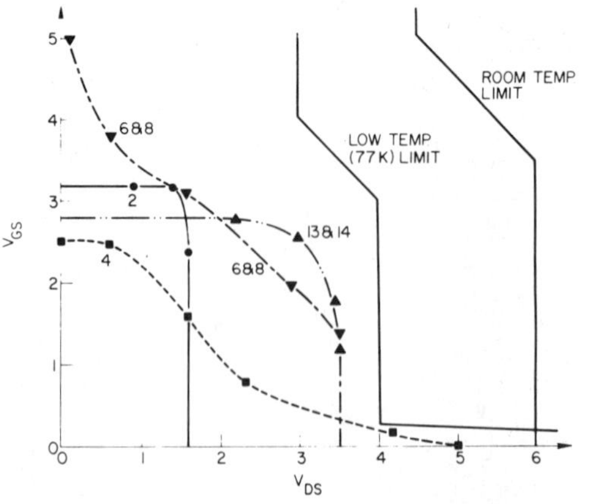

Fig. 17. Single clock phase generator: Device voltages and hot-electron limits.

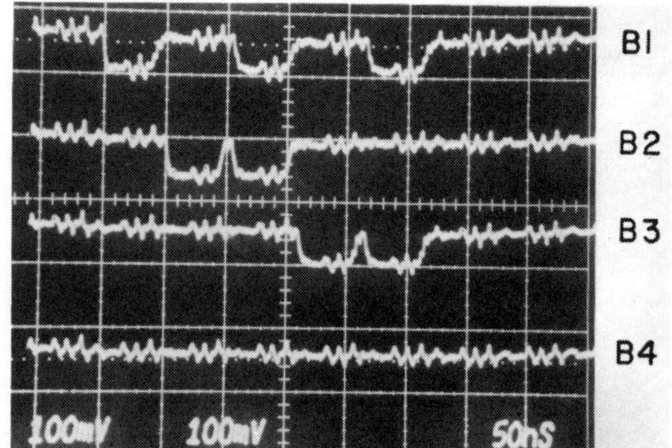

Fig. 18. ALU PLA operation at high frequency. For this test, bus data are incremented by one on each PLA cycle. Operation shown has a cycle time of 56 ns.

devices correspond to those of Fig. 15.) The plot shows that hot-electron requirements have been satisfied.

F. Results

The cross section described above has been implemented as a part of the 1 μm silicon-gate MOSFET technology development. Test wafers have been fabricated. A number of chips have been diced and bonded to facilitate high-speed testing. Fig. 18 shows the operation of an ALU PLA with a 56 ns clock period. For this test, all clocks and control lines were brought in from off chip. Clock generators have also been run successfully at high speed. Shown in Fig. 19 are waveforms from a clock generator running with a four-phase period of ~45 ns. The clock generator is isolated from the scope load by source followers but is loaded on chip with ~20 pF.

However, there are definite limitations that can be seen to the extension of the use of dynamic parts. As levels of integration rise, the loading on clock lines will tend to increase. As far as on-chip drivers are concerned, this can be accomodated by an increase in the driver W/L ratio; eventually, however, a point is reached where performance is limited by package inductances (particularly on the V_{DD1} and V_{DD2} lines). As an example, consider the fact that one phase of the clocks swings through 3.5 V in ~1 ns; with a clock load of 20 pF, average

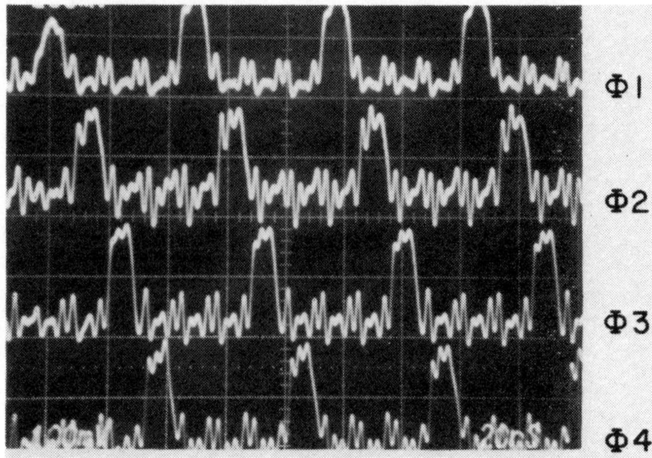

Fig. 19. Clock generator operation with 45-ns period for all four phases. On-chip load is approximately 20 pF; displayed signals are monitored through source followers.

current during the clock rise must be 70 mA. A simple triangular current pulse with this average value will have a current rise rate (di/dt) of 0.28×10^9 A/s. Lead inductance must be kept very small indeed to tolerate this current spike. An increase in performance by a factor of 2.5 (as could be achieved ideally by operating the chips at liquid nitrogen temperature) will increase the average current to 175 mA and gives $di/dt = 1.75 \times 10^9$ A/s. Thus the dynamic PLA parts appear most useful for performance levels requiring PLA cycle times no faster than ~50 ns or in applications where power is at a premium. In such applications, the parts described represent a powerful but simple to use set of high-level building blocks for digital machines.

IV. Static PLA's

In Section III of this paper, dynamic circuits were chosen for the PLA's because of the peculiar nature of PLA's; while conventional NOR's have restricted fan-in and fan-out, PLA's do not. A PLA used in the ALU of the machine above contained some circuits with fan-out > 100 and other circuits with fan-in > 20 and maximum allowed fan-in ~ 100. Such a circuit "environment" leads to limited performance and high power if conventional NOR's are used; the 2-bit decoders (fan-out ~ 100) are limited by loads external to the decoders and can be made to operate at high speed but only at substantial power. The array circuits (maximum allowed fan-in ~ 100) are limited by the "internal" loads associated with a structure capable of accomodating high maximum fan-in and thus do not offer a substantial power-delay tradeoff. On the other hand, dynamic circuits, especially using bootstrap drivers, do allow high performance at low power. The superiority of the dynamic approach is clearly seen in Fig. 20, where power versus delay curves are shown for a PLA with about 100 product terms which has been simulated using both dynamic circuits and conventional NOR's.

But if dynamic circuits offer advantages within a PLA, they offer several disadvantages at the system level. First, they require clocks and, unless rather complex multiclock systems are to be built, will tie all PLA's to the slowest PLA: small

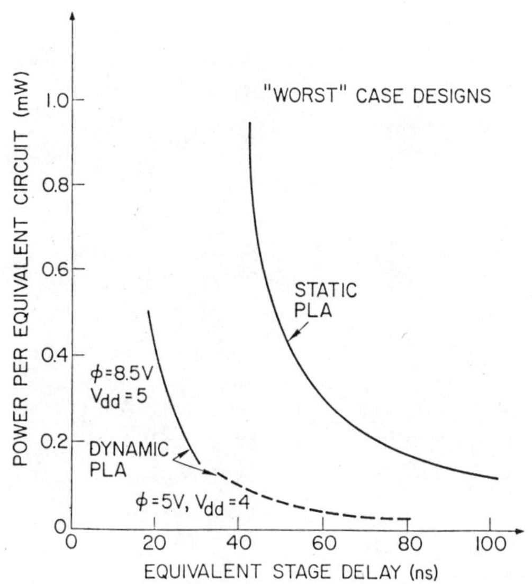

Fig. 20. Power-delay tradeoff comparison between static PLA's (with conventional NOR circuits) and dynamic PLA's.

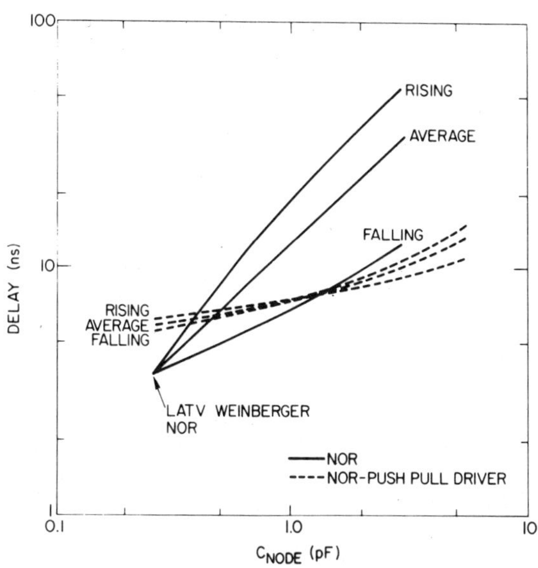

Fig. 22. NOR and NOR push-pull driver: delay versus C_{NODE}.

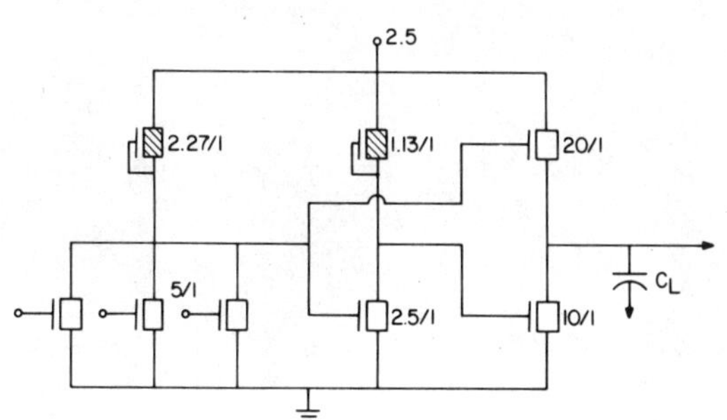

Fig. 21. Schematic diagram of NOR push-pull driver.

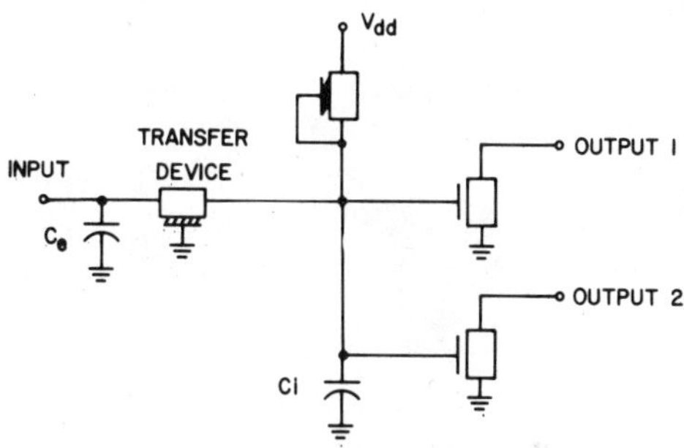

Fig. 23. Schematic of F^2L logic circuit.

PLA's, which can theoretically offer greater performance, will not. In addition, dynamic PLA's at high performance exhibit the severe current transients described earlier. While these problems are not severe in low-performance technologies, they become increasingly difficult as technologies and performance levels advance.

Fortunately, the development of static circuits has not stopped at the conventional NOR. Recent improvements in static circuits have allowed the design of static PLA's that offer the speed of their dynamic counterparts while providing nearly the same power level. In addition, the system problems mentioned above are largely solved by the static design. Finally, the static circuits offer greater flexibility, as size can be traded for performance without severe impacts to major clock cycles. The two circuits that have allowed high-performance static PLA's are a NOR push-pull circuit used in instances with a high fan-out and the F^2L circuit described by Blaser and Conrad [17] and used in instances of high fan-in.

The NOR push-pull circuit provides improved delay at high fan-out. The circuit schematic, shown in Fig. 21, consists of a standard NOR followed by an inverter and a push-pull stage. The input capacitance is the same as a standard NOR stage. It achieves high drive capability by a true push-pull output stage. The output stage dissipates no dc power because of the use of enhancement-mode devices in both pull-down and pull-up positions; because of this, the output high level is reduced. To compensate for this reduced up level from the push-pull stage (which is a threshold below that of a normal stage), the active device of the receiving stage is made slightly larger than normal to give, at its output, the same down level as a normal stage. (Alternatively, a higher V_{DD} supply could be provided for the NOR push-pull driver.) Delay as a function of total output node capacitance for both a conventional NOR and the NOR push-pull driver are given in Fig. 22. The NOR push-pull driver exhibits a much flatter delay versus capacitance characteristic than the conventional NOR but also exhibits higher unloaded delay due to its internal structure. Thus, at low capacitances, the NOR is faster, while at high capacitance, the NOR push-pull is faster. Therefore, the circuit is useful in those instances where the driver capacitance is high.

The F^2L circuit provides improved delay for high fan-in. The circuit schematic shown in Fig. 23 is similar to I^2L in that it has a single input and multiple outputs. The key feature of the F^2L circuit is that while the internal circuit node swings the full power-supply voltage level, the voltage swing of the external node, which is separated from the load device by a transfer device, is reduced. The voltage level is determined by the threshold voltage of the transfer device. The circuit achieves a reduction in delay since part of the total node capacitance has to charge and discharge only part way. Simulations of the

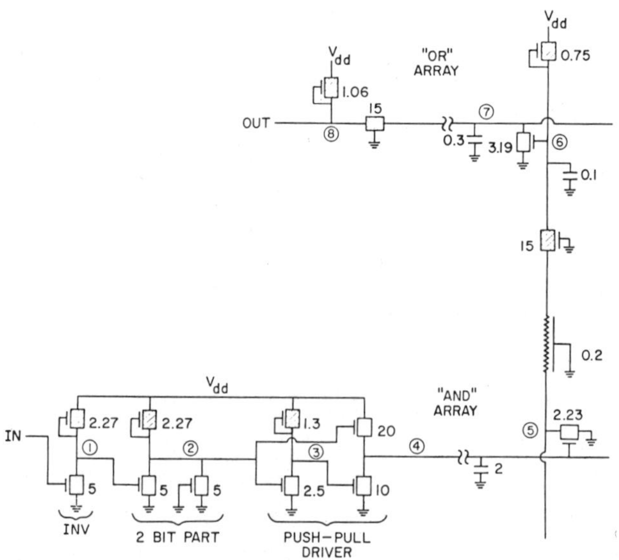

Fig. 24. Static PLA: detailed schematic diagram. Numbers by FET's are device width-to-length ratios; capacitor values are in picofarads.

TABLE I
PERFORMANCE OF STATIC PLA

Node	Delay (ns)		Voltage	
	Rising	Falling	On	Off
1	1.15	0.95	0.12	2.5
2	2.05	0.9	0.12	2.5
3	1.4	1.15	0.14	2.5
4	5.0	2.05	0.0	1.8
5	-	-	0.14	0.94
6	11.55	5.8	0.24	2.5
7	-	-	0.09	0.94
8	7.75	1.9	0.13	2.5

Delay (rising input) = 21.55 ns
Delay (falling input) = 18.95 ns
Delay (average) = 20.25 ns

Fig. 25. Photomicrograph of static PLA test site.

circuit with parameters suitable to the 1 μm MOSFET technology show that the sensitivity of circuit delay to capacitance on the external node is substantially less than the sensitivity of circuit delay to the capacitance on the internal node. For those cases where the external node capacitance is larger than the internal node capacitance, the reduction in delay is significant. Since there is a voltage drop across the transfer device which results in a higher ON voltage for the F^2L circuit, care must be taken in the design to insure that an adequate noise margin exists.

The combination of the NOR push-pull driver and the F^2L circuit results in a high-performance static PLA circuit shown in Fig. 24. The NOR push-pull driver is used in the 2 bit partitioning circuits and the F^2L circuit in the arrays. This arrangement utilizes the improved delay of the NOR push-pull driver for the high fan-out of the partitioning circuit and the improved delay of the F^2L circuit for the high fan-in of the PLA "AND" and "OR" arrays. Simulation for the static PLA which implements the 8 bit ALU in the 1 μm technology have been performed for both rising and falling waveforms. Results under nominal conditions for the most heavily loaded paths are given in Table I. This delay is for the 8 bit ALU PLA from the dynamic cross section of Section IV, suitably modified to use the static circuitry. Actual measurements made on chips from several wafers given typical delays of 13–21 ns at power levels of 15–24 mW. A photomicrograph of the static PLA is shown in Fig. 25.

The circuit for the test site appears in Fig. 26; waveforms showing typical data are shown in Fig. 27. The static PLA experiment consisted of connecting the static PLA to a "bus switch" so that with proper control-line values, the output of the static PLA would be fed back into the input of the static PLA, with a "rotate" of bits one position to the left. When this is traced out in detail, the entire circuit acts like a ring oscillator, each "stage" of which is comprised of a PLA delay and a bus switch delay. Whether such a "ring" actually oscillates depends upon the function to be performed by each PLA stage. For the experiments reported here, the PLA was set to do the EXCLUSIVE OR function; one set of bits was input to the PLA from external pads; the other was provided by the feedback arrangement described above. By setting an odd number of external inputs to logical 1, the whole circuit acts like a ring oscillator with an odd number of inverters (PLA stages with external input = 1) and an even number of identity elements (PLA stages with external inputs = 0). Alternatively, this arrangement allows performance testing even in the absence of fully working PLA's by supplying one of the external inputs to the PLA from a pulse generator.

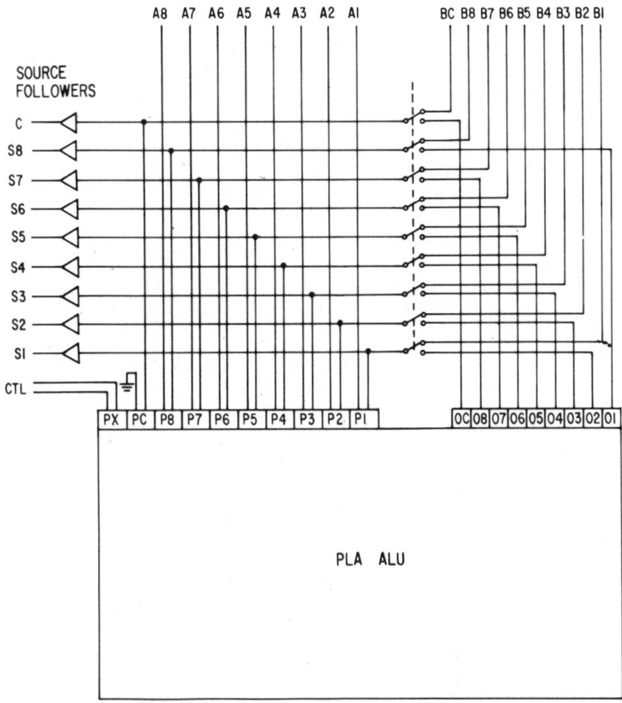

Fig. 26. Schematic of static PLA test site.

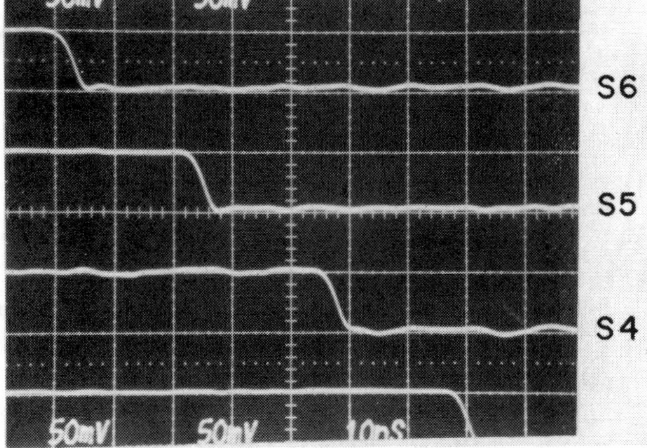

Fig. 27. Waveforms on a typical static PLA test site.

V. Conclusion

Section II of this paper has concerned itself with random logic circuits in a 1 μm silicon-gate MOSFET technology. The analysis there presented shows that while extrapolations from simple chips suggests 3 ns performance should be attainable, "brute force" extension of the chip size to 8000 circuits produces problems that severely degrade this performance. The analyses also develop a hierarchical chip image using an array of Weinberger arrays and a second level of metallurgy to reduce average wiring capacitance and achieve ~3 ns performance.

Section III of this paper has described a set of PLA-based macros useful in digital hardware design. Designed around a four-phase clock, which can be generated on chip, the parts constitute a set of flexible building blocks for digital system design. Analyses and experimental results based on an 8 bit ALU leads to PLA's with cycle times of ~56 ns. Because of problems associated with lead inductance, such a performance level is probably near a limit for all dynamic PLA's.

Finally, Section IV of this paper has described a high-performance static PLA intended to extend the utility of the PLA macro concept of design by reducing the current transient problems implicit in the all-dynamic approach. Measured PLA delay (13-21 ns) and power (15-24 mW) are in good agreement with results predicted from simulations. The static PLA retains the flexibility of any PLA while eliminating many of the limitations inherent in a dynamic approach at high performance. Thus the static PLA approach is extremely attractive for high levels of integration and applications which are performance driven.

Within appropriate performance limits, all of these approaches appear viable and give to the digital designer a variety of ways of dealing with the complexity of VLSI while retaining the potentials of a VLSI technology.

VI. Extensions

In all of the above discussions, designs have centered about the room-temperature operation of MOSFET circuits. It is well known [18] that low-temperature operation of MOSFET's can lead to a performance improvement by about a factor of 2.5, with a corresponding power increase. It would be desirable to achieve similar performance improvements in the circuits described in this paper by low-temperature operation. This is possible but requires some modifications.

For random logic, the design problems outlined in Section III of this paper are aggravated by the significantly higher current levels in circuits. This leads to very wide diffused rails where such rails are used to conduct dc current; because of this, Weinberger layouts, even in small islands, are probably not well suited to low-temperature operation. Square arrays of circuits, with dc supply paths placed on one of two levels of metal, are more suited to low-temperature operation.

For the PLA circuits, two cases must be considered. The dynamic PLA, from a circuit point of view, can run very fast at low temperatures. However, such operation aggravates the lead inductance problem described above; evidently the ~56 ns cycle time of the parts on the cross section described in Section IV of this paper is nearing the limit imposed by the packaging. The static PLA, conversely, has no significant current spike problems and can achieve very high performance with suitable modifications to the technology.

The key problem that arises with low-temperature operation of static PLA's concerns voltage drops along the diffused rails of the AND array. This drop is large but tolerable for room-temperature environments. However, in liquid-nitrogen-temperature environments, the current nearly triples, while the line resistance remains essentially unchanged. This leads to intolerable *IR* drops along the AND rail and forces, from dc design considerations, the use of the polysilicon input cell (Fig. 10) in the AND array of the PLA. With a conventional polysilicon-gate technology, the resistance of this line is relatively high. In addition, on high fan-out lines from the 2 bit decoders, the capacitance distributed along the line is also very high; the combination leads to a distributed *RC* line with

TABLE II
STATIC PLA'S IN VARIOUS DESIGNS AND ENVIRONMENTS

Case	<------Cell Type------>		Delay	On level v		Resistivity	
	AND Array	OR Array	ns.	AND	OR	n+	Poly
1	Metal Gate	Metal Gate	22.48	.242	.413	20	--
2	Poly Input	Poly Input	40.4	.175	.127	20	40
3	Al Input	Poly Input	22.5	.242	.127	20	40
4	Poly Input	Poly Input	23.3	.175	.127	20	2
5	Al Input	Poly Input	9.23	.342	.127	20	40
6	Poly Input	Poly Input	9.9	.175	.127	20	2

Resistivity is measured in ohms per square. Cases 1–4 are for operation at room temperature; cases 5–6 are for operation at low temperature. Cases 4 and 6 include low-resistivity polysilicon (2 Ω/sq, rather than 40 Ω/sq). Cases 1 and 5 are of questionable use because of the high level at an array output. Case 3 is approximately the room-temperature design described in this paper.

a relatively long time constant. Thus, without technology modifications, low-temperature operation of PLA's of the size being considered here would offer no real advantages in performance.

Current work on interconnections [19] indicates that it is possible to develop polysilicon layers that exhibit very low sheet resistivity. Such polysilicon layers may be applied to the low-temperature PLA's to overcome the RC time constant problem described above. Simulation of static PLA circuits in a variety of layouts and technologies leads to the data of Table II; it is evident that use of low-resistivity polysilicon can provide low-temperature PLA's that should operate at nominal delays of 9.9 ns. These PLA's have not been fabricated at this time.

ACKNOWLEDGMENT

The work described in this paper required the close cooperation of many people. The authors would like to acknowledge specifically the contributions of C. M. Osburn and the staff of the Silicon Processing Facility and W. D. Grobman and the staff of the Electron Beam Lithography area, without whose work the experiments described in this paper would not have been possible. We would also like to acknowledge the continued support of H.-N. Yu and A. Reisman during the entire project.

REFERENCES

[1] R. H. Dennard *et al.*, "Design of ion implanted MOSFETs with very short channel lengths," in *Int. Electron Devices Meeting Dig. Tech. Papers*, 1973.

[2] R. H. Dennard, F. H. Gaensslen, H. N. Yu, V. L. Rideout, E. Bassous, and A. LeBlanc, "Design of ion implanted MOSFET's with very small physical dimensions," *IEEE J. Solid-State Circuits*, vol. SC-9, pp. 256–268, Oct. 1974.

[3] H. N. Yu *et al.*, "The evolution of FET technology for VLSI applications," in *Int. Electron Devices Meeting Dig. Tech. Papers*, 1978.

[4] W. R. Hunter *et al.*, "One micron electron beam lithography FET technology," in *Int. Electron Devices Meeting Dig. Tech. Papers*, 1978.

[5] W. D. Grobman *et al.*, "Electron beam lithography for 1-μm FET logic circuit fabrication," in *Int. Electron Devices Meeting Dig. Tech. Papers*, 1978.

[6] T. H. Ning *et al.*, "Hot electron design constraints for one micron IGFET's," in *Int. Electron Devices Meeting Dig. Tech. Papers*, 1978.

[7] R. H. Dennard *et al.*, "MOSFET designs and characteristics for high performance logic at micron dimensions," in *Int. Electron Devices Meeting Dig. Tech. Papers*, 1978.

[8] A. Weinberger, "Large scale integration of MOS complex logic: A layout method," *IEEE J. Solid-State Circuits*, vol. SC-2, pp. 182–190, Feb. 1967.

[9] B. S. Landman and R. L. Russo, "On a pin vs block relationship for partitions of logic graphs," *IEEE Trans. Comput.*, vol. C-20, pp. 1469–1479, 1971.

[10] W. E. Donath, "Stochastic model of the computer logic design process," IBM T. J. Watson Research Center, Yorktown Heights, NY, unpublished.

[11] —, "Placement and average interconnection lengths of computer logic," IBM T. J. Watson Research Center, Yorktown Heights, NY, unpublished.

[12] W. E. Donath, W. R. Heller and W. F. Mikhail, "Prediction of wiring space requirements for LSI," unpublished.

[13] W. E. Donath and D. R. Freedman, "Random logic modelling applied to 1-μm FET technology," unpublished.

[14] P. W. Cook, C. Ho, S. E. Schuster, "A study in the use of PLA-based macros," unpublished.

[15] W. E. Donath, "Equivalence of memory to random logic," *IBM J. Res. Dev.*, vol. 18, pp. 401–407, 1974.

[16] P. W. Cook, S. E. Schuster, D. R. Freedman, J. T. Parrish and V. Dilonardo, "One micron MOSFET PLA's," in *Int. Solid-State Circuits Conf. Dig. Tech. Papers*, 1979.

[17] E. M. Blaser and D. A. Conrad, "FET logic configuration," in *Int. Solid-State Circuits Conf. Dig. Tech. Papers*, pp. 14–15, 1978.

[18] F. H. Gaensslen, V. L. Rideout, E. J. Walker, and J. J. Walker, "Very small MOSFETs for low-temperature operation," *IEEE Trans. Electron Devices*, vol. ED-24, pp. 218–229, Mar. 1977.

[19] B. L. Crowder and S. Zirinsky, "1 μm MOSFET VLSI technology: Part VII—Metal silicide interconnection technology—A future perspective," this issue, pp. 291–293.

Delay-Time Optimization for Driving and Sensing of Signals on High-Capacitance Paths of VLSI Systems

AMR M. MOHSEN, MEMBER, IEEE, AND CARVER A. MEAD

Abstract—Transmission of signals on large capacitance paths in a VLSI system may result in substantial degradation of the overall system performance. In this paper minimization of the delay times associated with driving and sensing signals from large capacitance paths by optimizing the fan-out factor of the driver stages, the gain of the input sensing stages, and the path voltage swing are examined. Examples of driving signals on a high capacitance path with two driving schemes are: a push-pull depletion-load driver chain and a fixed driver; and of sensing signals with two sensing schemes: a single-ended depletion-load inverter input stage and a balanced regenerative strobed latch are presented. We conclude that minimum delay time is achieved when the delay times of the successive stages of the driver chain, the high capacitance path, and the input sensing stage are comparable. In general, transmission time of signals in a system is minimized when the delay times of the different stages of the system are comparable.

A. M. Mohsen is with Intel Corporation, Santa Clara, CA, and the California Institute of Technology, Pasadena, CA 91125.

C. A. Mead is with the Department of Computer Science, California Institute of Technology, Pasadena, CA 91125.

I. Introduction

THE OVERALL PERFORMANCE of VLSI systems may be seriously degraded if signals need to be transmitted from one part to other parts in the system across large capacitance paths [1]. This large fan-out situation often occurs in the case of control drivers that are required to drive a large number of inputs to memory cells or logic-function blocks across a chip, or in the case of sensing stored information from small cells of large memory arrays. A similar and even more serious problem is driving wires which go off the silicon chip to other chips or input and output devices. In such cases, the

Reprinted from *IEEE J. Solid-State Circuits*, vol. SC–14, pp. 462–470, Apr. 1979.

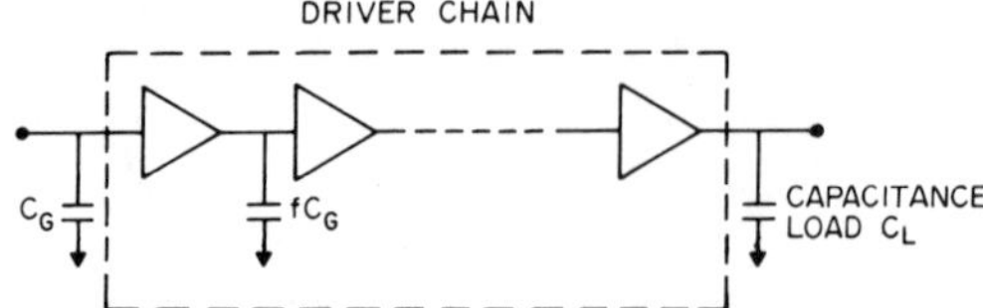

Fig. 1. Driver chain driving a high capacitance load C_L.

ratio of the capacitance that must be driven to the inherent capacitance of a gate circuit on the chip is often many orders of magnitude, causing a serious delay and degradation of system performance.

In this paper we examine, in general terms, optimum means of minimizing the delay time associated with transmitting information on large capacitance paths. In Section II, we analyze the driving of capacitive loads in the minimum possible time. In Section III, we examine the driving and sensing circuits with minimum possible delay times. In Section IV, we consider the sensing of signals on large capacitance lines driven by fixed sources. The general guidelines for designing the driver and sensing circuits of signals on high capacitance paths for minimum delay time are summarized in Section IV.

II. Driving Large Capacitive Loads

Consider how we may drive a capacitive load C_L in the minimum possible time. Let us assume we are starting with a signal V_i at the input of an elementary driver of input capacitance C_G. The elementary driver can be a simple static inverter or a dynamic clocked driver. Define the ratio of the load capacitance to the input capacitance C_L/C_G as Y. It seems intuitively clear that the optimum way to drive a large capacitance is to use the elementary driver to drive a larger driver and that larger driver to drive a still larger driver until at some point the larger driver is able to drive the load capacitance directly, as shown in Fig. 1. Let the delay time associated with the elementary driver driving a similar driver be τ_{Dr}. Thus the delay associated with the elementary driver driving a larger driver by a factor f is $f\tau_{Dr}$. If N such stages are used, each larger than the previous by a factor f, then the total delay of the driver chain τ_{ch} is given by

$$\tau_{ch} = Nf\tau_{Dr}. \tag{1}$$

Also, the capacitance ratio Y is related to N and f by

$$Y = f^N, \quad \ln Y = N \ln f. \tag{2}$$

Substituting (2) into (1)

$$\tau_{ch} = \ln Y \cdot \left[\frac{f}{\ln f}\right] \tau_{Dr}. \tag{3}$$

Thus the total delay is always proportional to ln Y as a result of the exponential growth in successive stages of the driver. The multiplicative factor $f/\ln(f)$ is plotted as a function of f in Fig. 2 normalized to its minimum value e. Total delay time is minimized when each stage is larger than the previous one by a factor of e, the base of natural logarithms. Minimum total delay $\tau_{ch/min}$ is given by

$$\tau_{ch/min} = \tau_{Dr} e \ln \left(\frac{C_L}{C_G}\right). \tag{4}$$

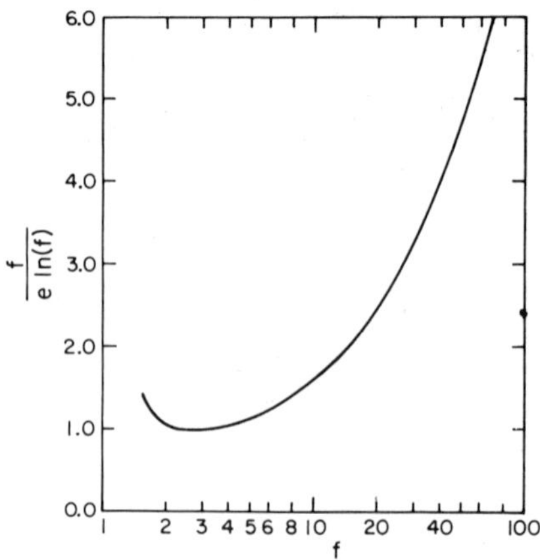

Fig. 2. Relative time penalty ($f/e \ln f$) versus fan-out factor f.

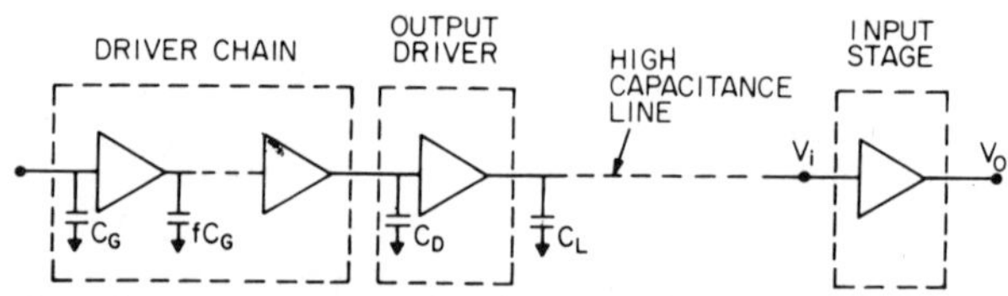

Fig. 3. Driver chain and output driver drives a high capacitance line C_L. Input stage receives input signal V_i to generate output voltage V_o.

The minimum of the driver-chain delay in Fig. 2 is rather broad with a relatively small delay-time penalty for fan-out factor f above e.

III. Driving and Sensing Signals on Large Capacitance Lines

Consider how we may minimize the time to transfer a signal through a high capacitance line by optimizing the driver circuit at one end of the line and the input sensing circuit at the other end of the line. It has been shown previously that a driver chain can be optimized to minimize the delay time required to drive the line capacitance C_L. We will consider below the implications of optimizing the input sensing circuit with the driver circuit by examining the effect of the gain of the input stage and the line voltage swing on the total delay time of signal transmission on the high capacitance path.

In Fig. 3 the driver is made of a driver chain as described in Section II, where the voltage swing is equal to the supply voltage, and an output driver that drives the large capacitance line with a voltage swing equal to V_i. The input stage senses the signal at the other end of the line and generates an output voltage V_o equal to the supply voltage. The input stage can be a single-ended circuit or a differential regenerative or non-regenerative circuit. The gain of the input stage G is defined as

$$G = \frac{V_o}{V_i}. \tag{5}$$

The delay associated with the input stage sensing τ_i is a function of the input voltage swing V_i required to generate V_o at the output, i.e., it is a function of the input-stage gain

$$\text{Input-Stage Delay} = \tau_i(V_i). \tag{6}$$

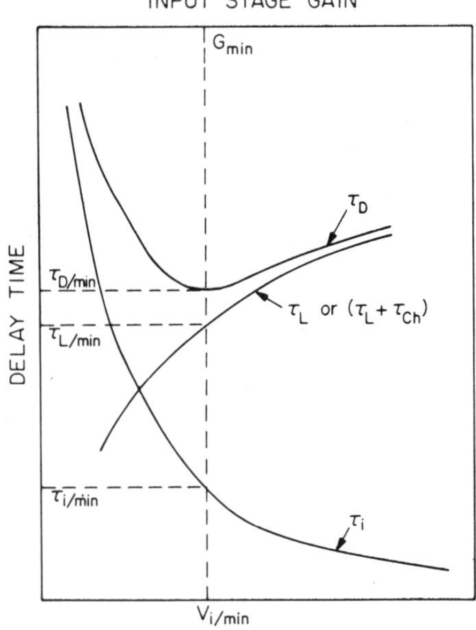

Fig. 4. Delay time of driver stages τ_{ch}, output driver τ_L, and input stage τ_i versus input-stage gain and input voltage swing.

For smaller V_i, the input stage sensing delay τ_i is larger as shown in Fig. 4. The functional relationship can be written as

$$\tau_i(V_i) = \tau_0 f(V_i) \tag{7}$$

where τ_0 is the characteristic transit time of the technology (transit time across the channel in the MOS technology or across the base in the bipolar technology).

The time required for the output driver to charge and discharge the large capacitance line by a voltage V_i is given by

$$\tau_L = \frac{C_L}{I_o} V_i \tag{8}$$

$$\tau_L = \frac{C_L}{I_o} \frac{1}{G} V_o = C_L R_o \frac{1}{G} = \frac{T_0}{G} \tag{9}$$

where

$$R_o = \frac{V_o}{I_o} \quad \text{and} \quad T_0 = C_L R_o. \tag{10}$$

I_o represents the current driving capability of the output driver and is given [1] by

$$I_o = C_D \frac{V_o}{\tau_{Dr}} \tag{11}$$

where C_D is the input capacitance of the output driver. The minimum possible driver-chain delay, as shown in Section II, is given by

$$\tau_{ch} = \tau_{Dr} e \ln \frac{C_D}{C_G}. \tag{12}$$

If the input-stage circuit configuration is such that the input voltage V_i is sampled and it is then clocked to amplify V_i to V_o, the total delay time τ_D is approximately equal to the driver-chain delay τ_{ch} plus the delay associated with driving the large capacitance line τ_L plus the input stage sensing delay τ_i

$$\tau_D = \tau_{ch} + \tau_L + \tau_i. \tag{13}$$

As shown in Appendix A, the above sum previously given still represents approximately τ_D for other input circuit configurations if $\tau_L \gtrsim \tau_i$. Substituting in (13), we get

$$\tau_D = \tau_{Dr} e \ln \frac{C_D}{C_G} + \frac{C_L}{C_D} \tau_{Dr} \frac{V_i}{V_o} + \tau_i(V_i). \tag{14}$$

An optimum value of C_D results by putting the partial derivative $(\partial \tau_D / \partial C_D) = 0$, and is given by

$$C_{D/opt} = \frac{C_L}{e} \frac{V_i}{V_o} = \frac{C_L}{e} \cdot \frac{1}{G}. \tag{15}$$

Substituting in (13),

$$\tau_D = \tau_{Dr} e \ln \frac{C_L}{C_G} \frac{V_i}{V_o} + \tau_i(V_i). \tag{16}$$

The first term in (16) represents the delay in the driver chain τ_{ch} and the output driver τ_L and is less than the delay τ_{ch} in (4), as the signal swing on the output lines is reduced by the gain V_o/V_i. Thus, the optimum output driver delay is equal to the delay per stage of the driver chain. The delay times are plotted in Fig. 4 versus V_i. By equating the partial derivative $(\partial \tau_D / \partial V_i) = 0$, we get the optimum swing $V_{i|min}$ of the line for minimum delay time τ_D

$$\tau_{Dr} e \frac{1}{V_{i|min}} + \frac{\partial \tau_i}{\partial V_i} (V_{i|min}) = 0 \tag{17}$$

which defines $V_{i|min}$ and by substituting in (16) results in the minimum possible delay $\tau_{D|min}$ for transferring a signal on such a high capacitance path.

The input-stage delay τ_i in (6) can be written as a monotonic function of the gain G defined in (5)

$$\tau_i = \tau_0 f\left(\frac{V_o}{G}\right) = \tau_0 g(G). \tag{18}$$

The total delay time in (17) can also be written as a function of the gain G

$$\tau_D = \tau_{Dr} e \ln \frac{C_L}{C_G} \frac{1}{G} + \tau_0 g(G). \tag{19}$$

The dependence of τ_i, $(\tau_{ch} + \tau_L)$ and τ_D on the gain G is illustrated in Fig. 4.

If the input-stage circuit configuration is such that

$$\tau_i = \tau_0 \alpha G^n, \quad n \geqslant 1 \tag{20}$$

then (19) reduces to

$$\tau_D = \tau_{Dr} e \ln \frac{C_L}{C_G} \frac{1}{G} + \tau_0 \alpha G^n. \tag{21}$$

Since the frequency bandwidth (BW) of the input sensing stage is proportional to $1/\tau_i$, (20) can be rewritten as

$$G \cdot \text{BW} = \frac{1}{\tau_0 \alpha G^{n-1}}. \tag{22}$$

Thus the input-stage sensing delay τ_i dependence on the gain G is a reformulation of the gain-bandwidth product of the input

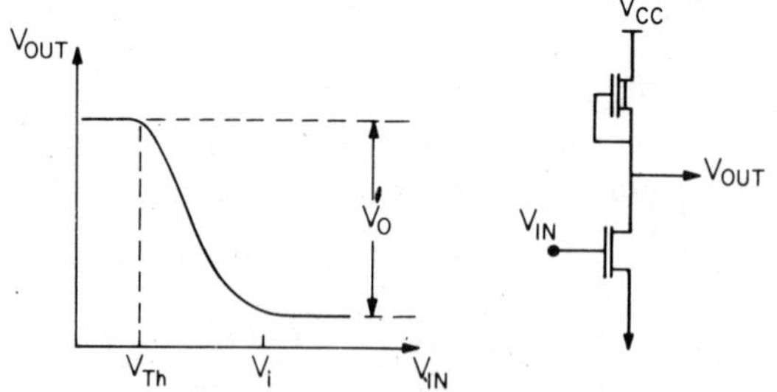

Fig. 5. Depletion-load-inverter input stage.

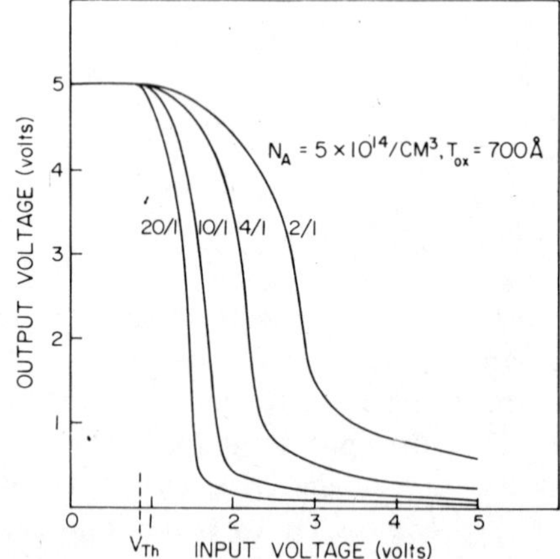

Fig. 6. Input–output voltage characteristics of a depletion-load-inverter input stage for different aspect ratios of the pull-down to pull-up transistors.

stage, which is limited by the characteristic transit time of the technology τ_0. The minimum delay time occurs at

$$G_{|\min} = \left(\frac{\tau_{\mathrm{Dr}} e}{n\alpha\tau_0}\right)^{1/n} \qquad V_{i|\min} = V_o\left(\frac{n\alpha\tau_0}{e\tau_{\mathrm{Dr}}}\right)^{1/n}$$

$$\tau_{i|\min} = \frac{e\tau_{\mathrm{Dr}}}{n} \tag{23}$$

where $\tau_{i|\min}$ is independent of the ratio of load capacitance to gate capacitance (C_L/C_G). The minimum possible delay $\tau_{D|\min}$ for transferring the signal through the high capacitance path is given by

$$\tau_{D|\min} = \tau_{\mathrm{Dr}} e\left[\frac{1}{n} + \ln\frac{C_L}{C_G}\left(\frac{n\alpha\tau_0}{\tau_{\mathrm{Dr}} e}\right)^{1/n}\right]. \tag{24}$$

We consider below two numerical examples of a single-ended depletion-load-inverter input stage and a differential regenerative strobed-latched input stage.

A. Depletion-Load-Inverter Input Stage

For the depletion-load MOS inverter input stage in Fig. 5, the input-output characteristics for different aspect ratios are shown in Fig. 6. The gain of the stage is given [2] by

$$\frac{V_o}{V_i - V_{\mathrm{th}}} = K\sqrt{r} \tag{25}$$

where r is the aspect ratios of the load and pull-down transistors and K is a constant given by

$$K = \frac{2}{\alpha f}\sqrt{V_Q + V_{BB}}$$

where α is the body factor $= \sqrt{(2eN_A\epsilon_s/C_{ox})}$; V_{BB} is the substate bias; V_Q is the quiescent output voltage $\cong (V_{cc}/2)$; and f is a constant. The input-stage delay is dominated by the rise time of the stage and is given [1] by

$$\tau_i = 4(O+p)\tau_0(r+1) \simeq 4(O+p)\tau_0 r \tag{26}$$

where

- O inverter output fan-out;
- p parasitic to intrinsic gate capacitance;
- τ_0 transit time across gate of pull-down transistor, and is given by

$$\tau_0 = \frac{L}{V_d} \simeq \frac{L^2}{\mu_{\mathrm{eff}}(V_G - V_{\mathrm{th}})} \tag{27}$$

where

- L gate length of the pull-down transistor;
- V_d carrier drift velocity under the gate;
- μ_{eff} effective carrier mobility;
- $(V_G - V_{\mathrm{th}})$ voltage drop across inversion layer in saturation.

Thus the relationship in (6) reduces to

$$\tau_i = \tau_0 \frac{EV_o^2}{(V_i - V_{\mathrm{th}})^2} \tag{28}$$

where E is a dimensionless constant equal to $[4(O+p)/K^2]$.

Assuming the voltage swing on the high capacitance path is between V_{th} and V_i, the delay times for the depletion-load-inverter input stage reduce to

$$\tau_{\mathrm{ch}} + \tau_L = e\tau_{\mathrm{Dr}} \ln \frac{C_L}{C_G}\frac{(V_i - V_{\mathrm{th}})}{V_o}$$

$$\tau_i = \tau_0 E \frac{V_o^2}{(V_i - V_{\mathrm{th}})^2}$$

$$\tau_D = e\tau_{\mathrm{Dr}} \ln \frac{C_L}{C_G}\left(\frac{V_i - V_{\mathrm{th}}}{V_o}\right) + \tau_0 E\left(\frac{V_o}{V_i - V_{\mathrm{th}}}\right)^2. \tag{29}$$

In Fig. 7 τ_i, $(\tau_{\mathrm{ch}} + \tau_L)$ and τ_D are plotted for a depletion-load-inverter input stage with the following parameters: $L = 4\ \mu$m; $\mu_{\mathrm{eff}} \cong 500$ cm^2/V · s; $(V_G - V_{\mathrm{th}}) \cong 4$ V; $\tau_0 = 1/20$ ns; $O + p = 5$; $k = 3$; and $E = 2.2$. The driver chain consists of depletion-load push-pull buffers with the following parameters: $P = 5$, $\tau_0 = 1/20$ ns; $r = 4$; $\tau_{\mathrm{Dr}} = 20$; $\tau_0 = 1$ ns; $C_G = 0.1$ pF; $C_L = 50$ pF; $C_L/C_G = 500$. τ_D has a minimum at

$$(V_i - V_{\mathrm{th}})_{\min} = W_o\sqrt{\frac{2\tau_0 E}{e\tau_{\mathrm{Dr}}}} \tag{30}$$

where the values of τ_i, $(\tau_{\mathrm{ch}} + \tau_L)$, τ_0 and G are given by

$$\tau_{i|\min} = 0.5\,\tau_{\mathrm{Dr}} e$$

$$\tau_{\mathrm{ch}} + \tau_{L|\min} = e\tau_{\mathrm{Dr}} \ln \frac{C_L}{C_G}\sqrt{\frac{2\tau_0 E}{e\tau_{\mathrm{Dr}}}}$$

$$\tau_{D|\min} = \tau_{\mathrm{Dr}} e\left[0.5 + \ln\frac{C_L}{C_G}\sqrt{\frac{2\tau_0 E}{e\tau_{\mathrm{Dr}}}}\right]$$

$$G_{|\min} = \sqrt{\frac{e\tau_{\mathrm{Dr}}}{2\tau_0 E}}. \tag{31}$$

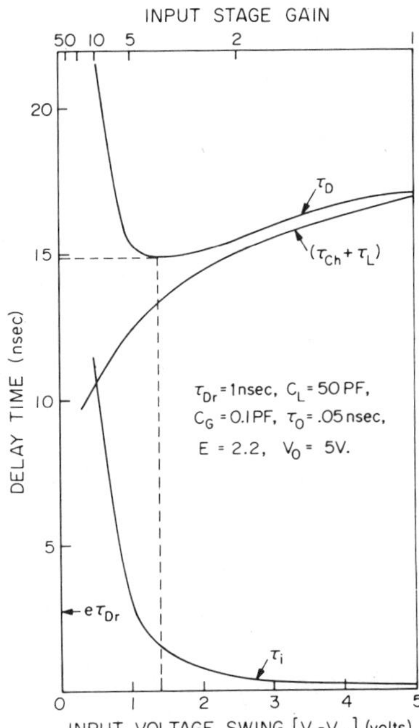

Fig. 7. Delay time versus line voltage swing V_i and input-stage gain G for a depletion-load push-pull driver chain driving 50-pF load and a depletion-load-inverter input stage.

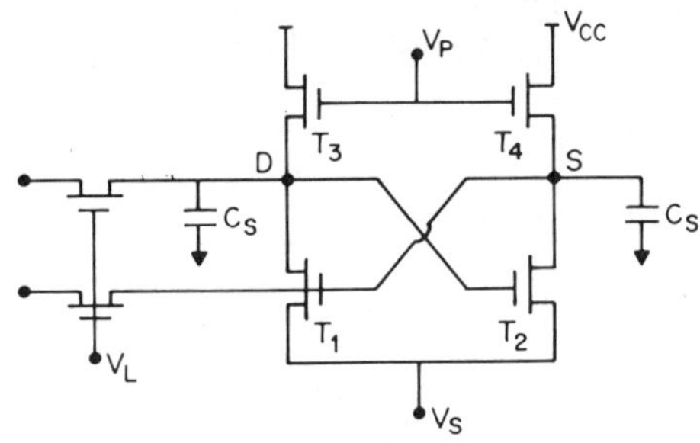

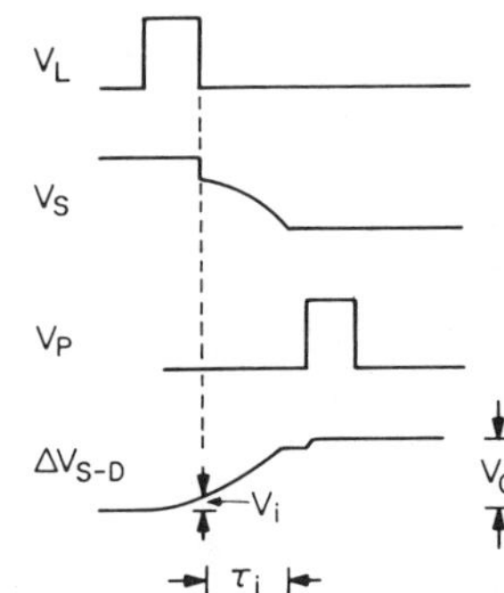

Fig. 8. Regenerative balanced strobed-latch input stage.

In Fig. 7 the delay of the driver chain is the dominant component of the total delay time for input voltage swing $V_1 >$ 0.8 V and input-stage gain $G < 8$. The total delay time increases logarithmically with the line voltage swing for line voltage swings above the optimum value. The increase in τ_D by increasing the voltage swing on the high capacitance line from 1.4 to 5 V is only 15 percent. Therefore, in such cases full supply-voltage swing on the high capacitance line provides better immunity against interfering signals with a relatively small delay-time penalty. However, increasing the input-stage gain by a factor of 3 from the optimum value increases the total delay time τ_D by about 50 percent. Irrespective of the line-to-gate capacitance C_L/C_G, the minimum transmission delay time τ_D on the large capacitance line is achieved with a driver-chain fan-out f equal to e and an input stage of sensing delay τ_i, half the delay per stage of the driver chain ($e\tau_{\mathrm{Dr}}$).

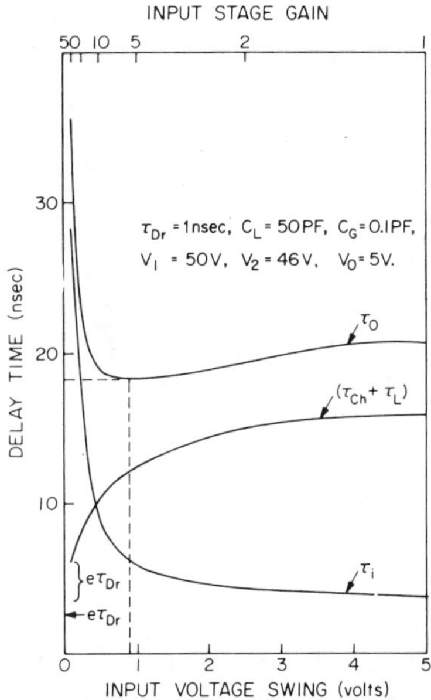

Fig. 9. Delay time versus line voltage swing V_i and input-stage gain G for a depletion-load push-pull driver chain driving 50-pF load and a regenerative balanced strobed-latch input stage.

B. Strobed-Latch Input Stage

For the strobed-latch input stage in Fig. 8 the latching delay time τ_i is inversely proportional to V_i with an optimum latching waveform and no off-side conduction [3] (as shown in Appendix B). The delay times associated with transmission on the high capacitance path with such an input stage are given by

$$\tau_i = \tau_0 \left(\frac{V_1}{V_i} + \frac{V_2}{V_{\mathrm{th}}} \right)$$

$$(\tau_{\mathrm{ch}} + \tau_L) = e\tau_{\mathrm{Dr}} \ln \frac{C_L}{C_G} \frac{V_i}{V_o}$$

$$\tau_D = e\tau_{\mathrm{Dr}} \ln \frac{C_L}{C_G} \frac{V_i}{V_o} + \tau_0 \left(\frac{V_1}{V_i} + \frac{V_2}{V_{\mathrm{th}}} \right). \tag{32}$$

The delay times are plotted in Fig. 9 for a strobed input latch with the following parameters:

$$C_S = 0.1 \text{ pF} \quad C_g = 0.03 \text{ pF} \quad \frac{W}{L} = \frac{15}{5} \quad \frac{W_{el}}{L_{el}} = \frac{12}{3.8}$$

$$f = 0.77 \quad t_{ox} = 700 \text{ Å} \quad p = 12.6 \times 10^{-6} \text{ A/V}^2$$

$$\tau_0 = 0.05 \text{ ns} \quad V_1 = 50 \text{ V} \quad V_{\mathrm{th}} = 0.7 \text{ V} \quad V_2 = 46 \text{ V}$$

$$V_o = 5 \text{ V} \quad \tau_{\mathrm{Dr}} = 1 \text{ ns} \quad C_L = 50 \text{ pF} \quad C_G = 0.1 \text{ pF}.$$

The total delay time has a minimum at

$$V_{i/\min} = \frac{\tau_0}{e\tau_{\mathrm{Dr}}} V_1, \tag{33}$$

where the delay times are given by

$$\tau_{i|\min} = e\tau_{\mathrm{Dr}} + \tau_0 \frac{V_2}{V_{\mathrm{th}}}$$

$$(\tau_{\mathrm{ch}} + \tau_L)_{\min} = e\tau_{\mathrm{Dr}} \ln \frac{C_L}{C_G} \frac{\tau_0}{e\tau_{\mathrm{Dr}}} \cdot \frac{V_1}{V_o}$$

$$\tau_{D|\min} = e\tau_{\mathrm{Dr}} \left[1 + \ln \left(\frac{C_L}{C_G} \frac{\tau_0}{e\tau_{\mathrm{Dr}}} \frac{V_1}{V_o} \right) + \frac{\tau_0}{e\tau_{\mathrm{Dr}}} \frac{V_2}{V_{\mathrm{th}}} \right]$$

$$G_{|\min} = \frac{V_o}{V_i} = \frac{V_o}{V_1} \frac{e\tau_{\mathrm{Dr}}}{\tau_0} \tag{34}$$

Similarly, in this case the increase in the total delay time τ_D for a voltage swing on the high capacitance path larger than the optimum value is rather small. Also, minimum transmission delay τ_D across the high capacitance path is achieved with a sensing delay τ_i of the input stage comparable to the delay per stage of the driver chain $e\tau_{\mathrm{Dr}}$.

IV. Sensing Signals on Large Capacitance Lines

In many cases, the driver circuit at one end of the line is limited by constraints that limit the driver optimization previously discussed. Such cases are often encountered in sensing signals from small cells of large memory arrays. We consider below how we may minimize the total delay time of signal transmission on a high capacitance path with a fixed drive source at one end by optimizing the gain of the input stage and the line voltage swing.

In Fig. 10, the output driver is represented by a fixed current source I_o which drives the large capacitance line C_L with a voltage swing equal to V_i. The input stage senses the input signal at the other end of the line and generates an output voltage V_o equal to the supply voltage. The total transmission delay time τ_D in this case is equal to the sum of the sensing delay time τ_i of the input stage and the line delay time τ_L associated with the charging and discharging of the line capacitance C_L. Using (7) and (9), the delay time τ_D is given by

$$\tau_D = \tau_0 f(V_i) + T_o \frac{V_i}{V_o}. \tag{35}$$

If the input-stage delay τ_i is given by (20), the minimum delay time occurs at

$$G_{|\min} = \left[\frac{T_o}{n\alpha\tau_0} \right]^{1/(n+1)}$$

$$V_{i|\min} = V_o \left[\frac{n\alpha\tau_0}{T_o} \right]^{1/(n+1)}$$

$$\tau_{i|\min} = \frac{\tau_{L|\min}}{n}. \tag{36}$$

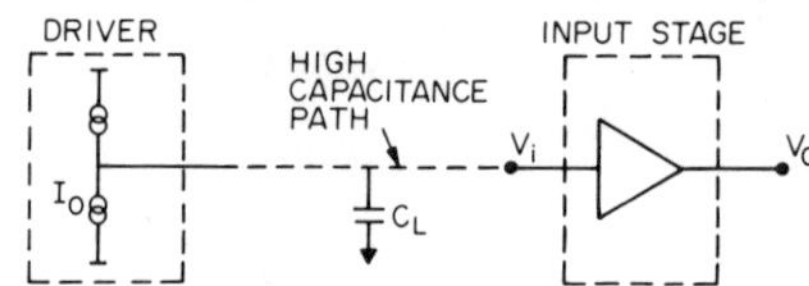

Fig. 10. Fixed driver drives a high capacitance load C_L. Input stage receives input signal V_i to generate output voltage V_o.

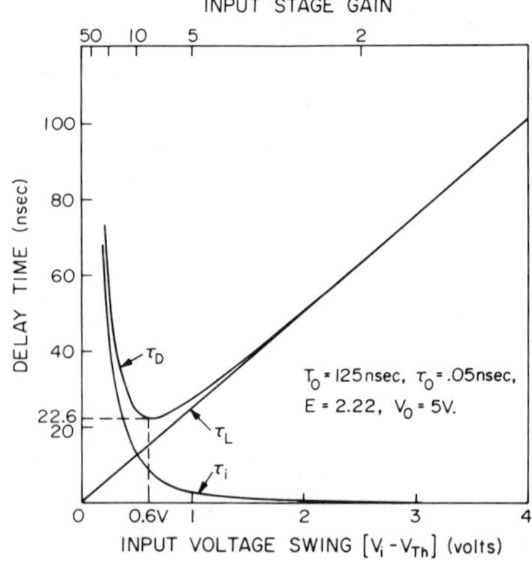

Fig. 11. Delay times versus line voltage swing V_i and input-stage gain G for a fixed driver driving a large capacitance load with a drive-time constant T_0 = 125 ns, and a depletion-load-inverter input stage.

The minimum delay time $\tau_{D|\min}$ for transferring the signal across the high capacity path is given by

$$\tau_{D|\min} = \left[1 + \frac{1}{n} \right] \tau_{L|\min} = \left[1 + \frac{1}{n} \right] T_0 \left[\frac{\tau_0 \alpha n}{T_0} \right]^{1/(n+1)}$$

We consider below two numerical examples for a single-ended depletion-load-inverter input stage and a differential regenerative strobed-latch input stage.

A. Depletion-Load-Inverter-Input Stage

For the depletion-load-inverter input stage in Fig. 6, the input delay time is given by

$$\tau_i = \tau_0 E \frac{V_o^2}{(V_i - V_{\mathrm{th}})^2}. \tag{37}$$

Assuming the voltage swing on the high capacitance line C_L is between V_i and V_{th}, the total delay time τ_D reduces to

$$\tau_D = \tau_0 E \frac{V_o^2}{(V_i - V_{\mathrm{th}})^2} + T_o \frac{(V_i - V_{\mathrm{th}})}{V_o}. \tag{38}$$

In Fig. 11, τ_i, τ_L, and τ_D are plotted for the following parameters:

$L = 4\ \mu\mathrm{m}$ $\mu_{\mathrm{eff}} = 500\ \mathrm{cm}^2/\mathrm{V}\cdot\mathrm{s}$ $(V_o - V_{\mathrm{th}}) = 4$ V

$\tau_0 = 1/20$ ns $E = 2.2$ $C_L = 1$ pF $I_o = 40\ \mu\mathrm{A}$

$T_o = 125$ ns.

τ_D has a minimum at

$$(V_i - V_{\text{th}}) = \left[\frac{2\tau_0 E}{T_o}\right]^{1/3} V_o$$

where the values of τ_i, τ_L, τ_D, and G are given by

$$\tau_{i|\min} = \tau_0 \left[\left(\frac{T_o}{2\tau_0}\right)^2 E\right]^{1/3}$$

$$\tau_{L|\min} = 2\tau_{i|\min}$$

$$\tau_{D|\min} = 3\tau_{i|\min}$$

$$G_{|\min} = \left[\frac{T_o}{2\tau_0 E}\right]^{1/3} \tag{39}$$

In Fig. 11, a minimum of τ_D at 22 ns exists at an input voltage swing of 0.6 V, which is about a factor of 5 less than the delay time τ_D with full supply voltage swing. The minimum delay time is achieved with the input-stage delay time τ_i equal to half the line delay time τ_L.

B. Strobed-Latch Input Stage

For the strobed-latch input stage with an optimum latching waveform and no off-side conduction, the total delay time is given by

$$\tau_D = \tau_0\left(\frac{V_1}{V_i} + \frac{V_i}{V_{\text{th}}}\right) + T_o \frac{V_i}{V_o}. \tag{40}$$

The delay times are plotted in Fig. 12 for a strobed input latch with the following parameters:

$C_S = 0.1$ pF $\quad C_g = 0.03$ pF $\quad \frac{W}{L} = \frac{15}{5} \quad \frac{W_{el}}{L_{el}} = \frac{12}{3.8}$

$f = 0.77 \quad t_{ox} = 700$ Å $\quad \tau_0 = 0.05$ ns $\quad V_1 = 50$ V

$V_{\text{th}} = 0.7$ V, $\quad V_2 = 46$ V $\quad V_o = 5$ V $\quad C_L = 1$ pF

$I_o = 40\ \mu$A $\quad T_o = 125$ ns.

τ_D has a minimum at

$$V_{i|\min} = \sqrt{\frac{\tau_0}{T_0}}\, V_o V_1$$

where the values of τ_i, τ_L, τ_D, and G are given by

$$\tau_{i|\min} = \tau_0\left[\sqrt{\frac{T_0}{\tau_0}\frac{V_1}{V_o}} + \frac{V_{\text{th}}}{V_2}\right]$$

$$\tau_{L|\min} = \tau_0 \sqrt{\frac{T_0}{\tau_0}\frac{V_1}{V_o}}$$

$$\tau_{D|\min} = \tau_0\left[2\sqrt{\frac{T_0}{\tau_0}\frac{V_1}{V_o}} + \frac{V_{\text{th}}}{V_2}\right]$$

$$G_{|\min} = \sqrt{\frac{\tau_0}{T_0}\frac{V_1}{V_o}}. \tag{41}$$

In Fig 12 the minimum delay time τ_D is 18.5 ns for $V_i = 0.3$ V. Similarly, in this case the minimum total delay time to transmit the signal across the large capacitance line is achieved with a line voltage swing and input-stage gain such that the sensing delay τ_i of the input stage is comparable to the line delay time τ_L.

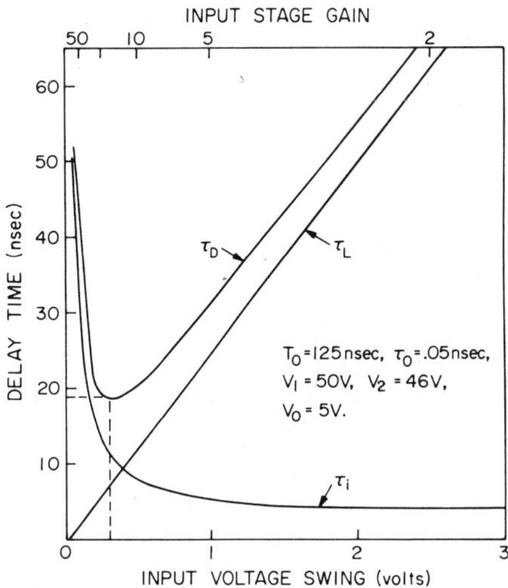

Fig. 12. Delay time versus line voltage swing V_i and input-stage gain G for a fixed driver driving a large capacitance load with a drive-time constant T_0 = 125 ns and a regenerative balanced strobed-latch input stage.

V. Conclusions

We have examined how to minimize the delay time associated with the transmission of signals across large capacitance paths by optimizing the driving and sensing circuits. In our analysis we have considered the design of the driver and sensing circuits in general terms by optimizing the fan-out of the driver-stages chain, the gain of the input sensing circuit, and the path voltage swing.

For driving large capacitive loads, we have found that the drive delay time of a chain of successive drivers has a broad minimum at a fan-out factor f around e, the base of the natural logarithms. The delay times of each stage of the driver chain are equal to $e\tau_{\text{Dr}}$, where τ_{Dr} is the delay time of a driver driving a similar driver. This is a result of the exponential growth of the drive capabilities of the successive stages of the driver chain. At this minimum, the number of stages in the driver chain is equal to the natural logarithm of the load capacitance to the gate capacitance C_L/C_G. The minimum driver-chain delay time τ_{ch} is equal to the delay per stage of the driver chain $e\tau_{\text{Dr}}$ times the number of stages $\ln(C_L/C_G)$. For fan-out factor f larger than e, the relative delay time penalty is relatively small.

Minimization of the total transmission time on a large capacitance path, in cases where the fan-out factor of the driver chain, the gain of the input sensing stage, and the path voltage swing can be optimized, have been examined. Minimum total delay is achieved with a driver chain of fan-out f equal to e and an input stage with an input sensing delay related to the delay per stage of the driver chain according to the delay-time gain characteristic of the input stage. Irrespective of the ratio of the path-to-gate capacitance, the total delay time has a broad minimum for line voltage swings above the optimum swing, but a rather sharp minimum for input-stage gain above the optimum gain. For line voltage swings above the optimum value, the driver chain and line delay times are dominant and the total delay times increase logarithmically with the line voltage swing. Therefore, in such cases full supply voltage swing on the high capacitance line provides better noise immunity against interferring signals with a relatively small time penalty. Delay times for push-pull depletion-load-driver stages with a single-ended depletion-load-inverter input stage and with a balanced regenerative strobed latch have been analyzed. For a single-ended depletion-load-inverter input stage (delay time $\tau_i \alpha^{al}$ 1/(gain)^2), the minimum total delay is achieved with an input-stage delay τ_i equal to one-half the delay per stage of the driver chain $e\tau_{\mathrm{Dr}}$. For a regenerative balanced strobed-latch input stage (delay time $\tau_i \alpha^{al}$ 1/(gain)), minimum delay time occurs when the input-stage delay τ_i is comparable to the delay per stage of the driver chain.

Minimization of the total transmission time on a large capacitance path in cases where the driver is fixed and the line voltage swing and the gain of the input stage can be optimized, have been presented. Cases of fixed drivers of large capacitance lines are encountered in sensing stored information from memory cells of large arrays. Minimum total delay is achieved with a line voltage swing and an input stage such that the line delay time is related to the input sensing delay according to the delay-time gain characteristics of the input stage. For a single-ended depletion-load-inverter input stage (delay time $\tau_i \alpha^{al}$ 1/(gain)^2), the minimum total delay is achieved at a line voltage swing and input-stage gain such that the input-stage delay time τ_i is half the line delay time τ_L. For a differential regenerative balanced strobed-latch input stage (delay time $\tau_i \alpha^{al}$ 1/(gain)), the minimum total delay occurs when the input-stage delay τ_i is comparable to the line delay time τ_L. Deviations of the gain and line voltage swing by a factor of 2 from the minimum may increase the total delay time by as much as 75 percent for the examples considered in this paper.

In general, we may conclude that a minimum transmission time of signals in a system consisting of several stages is achieved when the delay times of the different stages are comparable. For the case of driving and sensing signals from large capacitance paths, minimum delay time is achieved when the delay times of the successive stages of the driver chain, the high capacitance path, and the input sensing stage are comparable.

Appendix A

The output of the input-stage circuit can be represented by a source voltage V_s that corresponds to the amplified undelayed input voltage V_i to the stage and a delay τ_i provided by a simple RC circuit as shown in Fig. 13(a). We show below that if the input-stage delay τ_i is less than the line delay τ_L, the total delay τ_D is approximately equal to the sum of the input stage delay τ_i and the line delay τ_L.

In Fig. 13(b) the responses of the input-stage equivalent circuit to a step, a ramp, and a sinusoidal input are shown. For a step input

$$t > 0 \quad V_S = V_0 \quad V_{\mathrm{out}} = V_0 [1 - \exp(-t/\tau_i)]. \tag{A-1}$$

For a ramp input

$$t > 0 \quad V_S = \frac{t}{\tau_L} V_0 \quad V_{\mathrm{out}} = \frac{(t - \tau_i)}{\tau_L} + \frac{V_0}{\tau_L} \exp(-t/\tau_i). \tag{A-2}$$

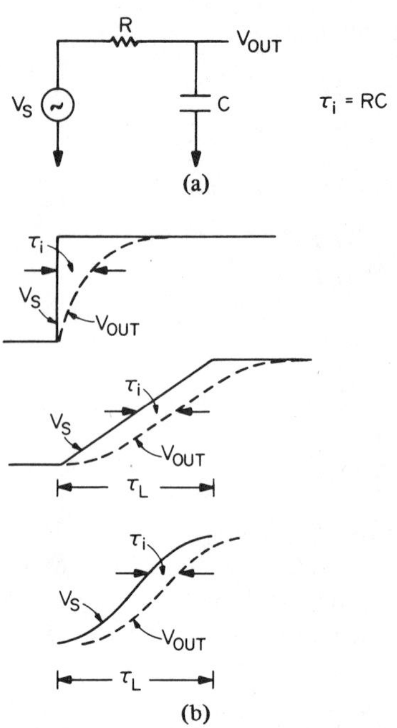

Fig. 13. (a) Equivalent circuit of the input sensing stage. (b) The output responses of the input stage to a step, a ramp, and a sinusoidal input.

If $\tau_L > \tau_i$, then

$$V_{\mathrm{out}} \simeq \frac{(t - \tau_i) V_0}{\tau_i}. \tag{A-3}$$

For a sinusoidal input

$$t > 0 \quad V_S = \frac{V_0}{2}\left[1 - \cos\frac{\pi t}{\tau_L}\right] \quad V_{\mathrm{out}} = \frac{V_0}{2} \cdot \left[1 - \cos\frac{\pi(t - \theta)}{\tau_2}\right] \quad \theta = \frac{\tau_L}{\pi}\tan^{-1}\frac{\pi\tau_i}{\tau_L}. \tag{A-4}$$

If $\tau_L > \tau_i$, then

$$V_{\mathrm{out}} \simeq \frac{V_0}{2}\left[1 - \cos\frac{\pi(t - \tau_i)}{\tau_L}\right]. \tag{A-5}$$

From (A-3) and (A-4), it is apparent that for $\tau_L > \tau_i$ the output voltage V_{out} is delayed from the amplified undelayed input voltage V_s by the input stage delay τ_i. Thus, in general, if $\tau_i < \tau_L$, the total delay τ_D is the sum of the line delay τ_L and the input-stage delay τ_i

$$\tau_D \simeq \tau_L + \tau_i. \tag{A-6}$$

Appendix B

Dynamic MOS regenerative latch sensors, as in Fig. 8, can amplify a small initial imbalance V_i between the two internal nodes D and G to a voltage difference comparable to the initial power-supply voltage V_0. For smaller initial voltage imbalance the latch-up time is, in general, larger. For any given initial imbalance V_i, there is an ideal latching waveform that minimizes the latch time [3]. The initial imbalance represents the sum of the real voltage imbalance and any threshold imbalance of the MOS crosscoupled transistor pair. The general shape of the optimum latching waveform is shown in Fig. 8. It consists of an initial step followed by a ramp of gradually increasing slope to the final voltage value.

The internal latch nodes D and G are precharged to V_0. The input voltage introduces an imbalance V_i on nodes D and G. To minimize threshold imbalances and reduce power dissipation, the flip-flop load devices are turned off during latchup. The latch-up waveform $V_s(t)$ can be selected such that no current flows through the off-side during latchup to maximize the final latched imbalance. However, coupling capacitances to the off-side lower its final voltage and lowers the conduction of the on transistor, thus increasing the latching time. The optimum latching waveform [3] consists of two portions given by

$$V_s(t) = V_0 - V_{th} - \frac{V_i - t/\tau}{1 - t/\tau} \quad \text{for} \quad t < t_{sat} \tag{B-1}$$

and

$$V_s(t) = V_0 + V_{in} - V_{th} - \frac{V_{th}}{2f}\{3 + \exp[(t - t_{sat})/\tau_1]\} \quad \text{for} \quad t > t_{sat} \tag{B-2}$$

where

$$f = \frac{C_s}{(C_s + C_g)}$$

$$\tau = \frac{2C_s}{\beta f^2 V_i}$$

$$\tau_1 = \frac{C_s}{\beta f V_{th}}$$

$$t_{sat} = \frac{2C_s(V_{th} - fV_i)}{\beta f^2 V_{th} V_i} \tag{B-3}$$

where C_g, β, and V_{th} are the gate capacitance, current factors, and threshold voltages of T_1 and T_2; and C_s is the capacitance of latch nodes D and G. The latch time τ_i is given by

$$\tau_i = \tau_0\left(\frac{V_1}{V_i} + \frac{V_2}{V_{th}}\right) \tag{B-4}$$

where τ_0 is the transit time across gate and is given by

$$\tau_0 = \frac{C_g}{\beta(V_G - V_{th})} = \frac{L^2}{\mu(V_G - V_{th})}$$

$$V_1 = \frac{2C_s}{C_g}\frac{(V_{th} - fV_i)}{V_{th}}\frac{V_0}{f^2}$$

$$V_2 = \frac{C_s}{C_g}\frac{V_0}{f}\ln\left[\frac{f(V_0 \pm V_i - V_{th}) - V_{th}/2}{V_{th}/2}\right]. \tag{B-5}$$

Thus the total latch τ_i is approximately inversely proportional to the initial unbalance V_i.

References

[1] C. A. Mead and L. A. Conway, *Introduction to VLSI Systems*, Limited Printing, 1978.

[2] D. Senderowicz, D. A. Hodges, and P. Gray, "High-performance NMOS operational amplifier," *IEEE J. Solid-State Circuits*, vol. SC-13, pp. 760–766, Dec. 1978.

[3] W. T. Lynch and H. J. Boll, "Optimization of the patching pulse for dynamic flip-flop sensors," *IEEE J. Solid-State Circuits*, vol. SC-9, pp. 49–55, Apr. 1974.

Part III
MOS Memory Cells and Circuits

MOS memory cells and circuits is an area which has received a great deal of attention from semiconductor as well as system houses and has enjoyed the talent of many circuit, device, and process designers in order to compete with nonsemiconductor memories in a high volume market.

In Section 3.1 the classic paper by Terman provides the reader with basic circuit design concepts for the design of static and dynamic MOS memories. It is followed by two review papers on dynamic RAM memory cells. The following two papers are examples of new static memory cell designs. The paper by Ohzone *et al.* discusses the use of polysilicon resistors as loads in the design of 16Kb static RAMs. The paper by Iizuka *et al.* also discusses the use of polysilicon to construct the load structures in a CMOS technology. However, the polysilicon load is an active transistor rather than a passive resistor. The last two papers in this section discuss memory cells for PROMs. The paper by Salsbury *et al.* discusses the commonly used stacked gate cell which is electrically programmed by means of hot electrons injection and erased by exposure to ultraviolet light. A new memory PROM cell is presented in the paper by Tanimote *et al.* and uses an irreversible resistivity transition phenomenon in polysilicon resistors.

In Section 3.2 the first two papers by Foss and by Foss and Harland discuss basic design circuit techniques and peripheral circuits which are used in RAM memory chip design. The following three papers, starting with the classic paper by Stein *et al.*, discusses different techniques in the design of sense amplifiers.

Section 3.1
Memory Circuits and Cells

MOSFET Memory Circuits

LEWIS M. TERMAN, MEMBER, IEEE

Invited Paper

Abstract—Metal-oxide-semiconductor first effect transistors (MOSFETs) are currently being used in a variety of memory applications. The requirements of memory usage and the characteristics of MOSFET devices and technology have led to a number of unique circuits for these applications. Organization and design considerations of memory systems using MOSFET devices are reviewed, and examples of specific circuits are presented and analyzed. These include random access cells, shift registers, read only storage, and on-chip support circuits; both complementary and noncomplementary circuits are discussed.

I. MOSFET Memory Considerations

THE POSSIBILITY of using semiconductor circuitry for a large fraction of the memory requirements in computing and other digital systems has received increasing attention over the past several years [1]–[5]. Cost is a very important consideration in memory, and the advent of large scale integration holds the promise of drastically reducing the cost of an individual semiconductor circuit; appreciable reductions in digital circuit costs have already occurred. In addition, the use of circuitry as a storage technology offers a degree of flexibility unavailable with other memory technologies. Consider the block diagram of a memory system shown in Fig. 1. The basic elements of a memory are the array, in which the information is stored, and the supporting circuit blocks, which carry out the functions of selection, driving the array, and amplification and detection of sense signals. In a conventional magnetic memory system different technologies are used for the array and the support circuits and, as a result, there is a pronounced interface between them. This interface is both electrical and physical. Relatively complex circuitry is required to provide signals to drive the array, as well as to amplify and detect the sense signals coming out of the array, and different packaging is necessary for the circuits and the array. The use of circuitry in the storage array greatly reduces the interface. Clearly, the packaging can be done in the same technology, but more important, since the use of circuitry permits placing gain in the system anywhere it is desirable, the electrical interface can also be reduced. Conceptually, the entire memory system could be operated at logic levels, eliminating any need for special driver, sense amplifier, and detector circuits. In practice, this is not done because it is more efficient to simplify the storage circuits at the expense of support circuit complexity because of the far greater number of the former, but there exists considerable freedom in tradeoffs between the various circuit functions to achieve an optimum system, and, in fact, storage, decode, drive, and sense circuits may be intermixed as desired for this end.

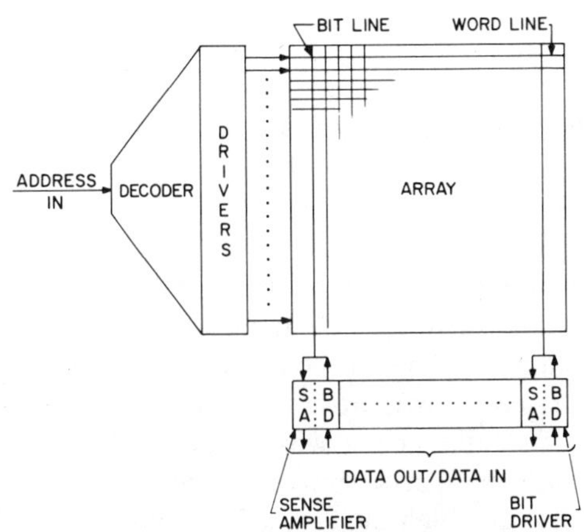

Fig. 1. Memory system block diagram.

There are additional advantages in a semiconductor memory system. Nondestructive reading is easily achieved, as is a dc base sense signal, and it is easier to obtain high performance because of the reduction of the array-support circuit interface, and the characteristics of the technology. On the other hand, there are also disadvantages. These include the power dissipation necessary to retain information, the volatility of storage which this implies if input power is lost, the reliability of a system having a great many chips and interconnections, and the question of whether or not sufficient circuit cost reduction can be achieved through large scale integration to allow semiconductor memory systems to be cost competitive with other memory technologies, especially ferrites, over a wide range of applications.

One important result of easing the interface between the array and support circuits is flexibility in choosing array size without affecting per bit cost. In magnetic systems, the support circuitry is comparatively expensive, while the cost of the individual storage bit is relatively low; thus, as the array is made larger, the support circuitry is spread over a larger number of bits, and the cost per bit declines. In contrast with a semiconductor memory the major cost is in the bit storage circuitry, and the cost per bit will remain essentially constant as the array size increases or decreases. These trends are sketched in Fig. 2. The ability to fabricate smaller systems at relatively low cost has given semicon-

Manuscript received September 21, 1970; revised January 20, 1971. *This invited paper is one of a series planned on topics of general interest—The Editor.*

The author is with the IBM Thomas J. Watson Research Center, Yorktown Heights, N. Y. 10598.

Reprinted from *Proc. IEEE*, vol. 59, pp. 1044–1058, July 1971.

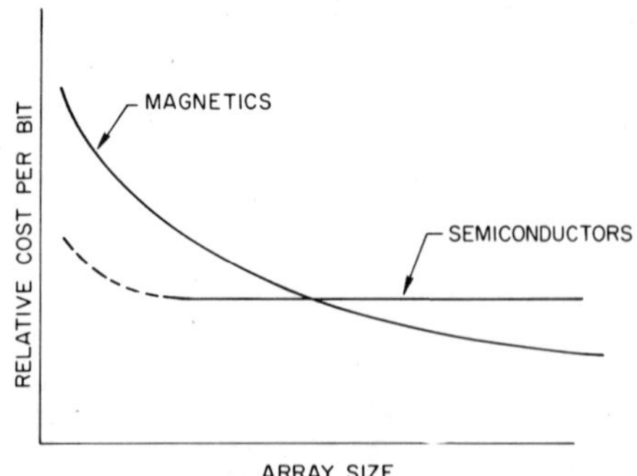

Fig. 2. Trends of cost per bit as a function of array size for magnetic and semiconductor memories.

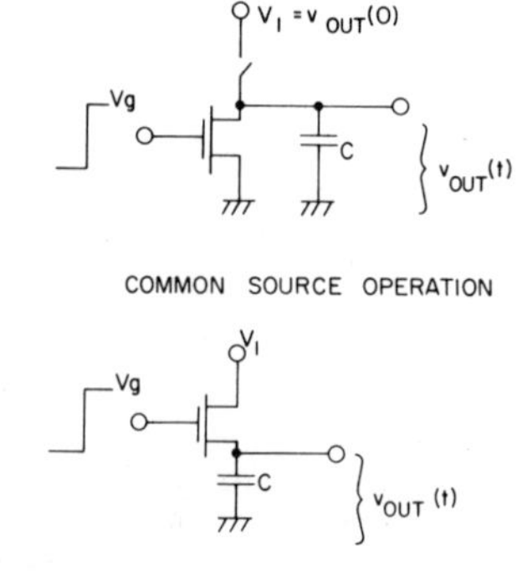

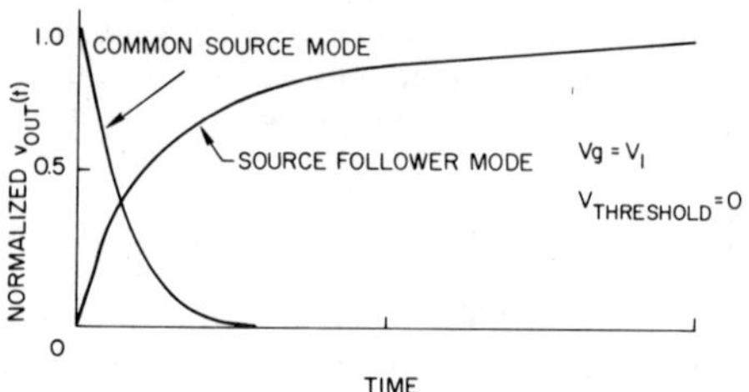

Fig. 3. Comparison of MOSFET switching transients. The effect of substrate voltage on threshold voltage has been ignored.

ductor technology a toehold in the memory market, and, as larger systems become economically competitive, will result in the possibly advantageous flexibility that the memory does not have to be made in a single large system to keep the cost down, but rather can be segmented into a number of smaller units, which can be placed as desired through the system in order to optimize it.

The point at which the crossover occurs in Fig. 2 is very important, as it indicates the relative areas of application of the technologies (it is, of course, dependent upon the performance range being considered). Since with time the magnetic system curve will go to lower and lower costs, the semiconductor system cost must drop even faster in order to expand its area of application. Cost, therefore, is very important.

The circuit used to store information, the memory cell, is a prime element in determining semiconductor memory cost. Desirable characteristics are small area, allowing high bit storage density, light loading to the drive and sense circuitry, and the ability to be written and read with a reasonable delay. It also should be able to retain information with low power dissipation.

Metal-oxide-semiconductor field effect (MOSFET) devices are attractive for memory because the technology offers the potential of low cost and of fulfilling the previously mentioned requirements. The processing itself is simple, requiring four masking steps and only a single diffusion, which should result in higher yields and/or capability for larger chips. High circuit density can be obtained because the devices themselves are small, self-isolated, amenable to efficient layouts, and can be combined in simple dc coupled circuits without requiring additional resistors or capacitors. In addition, the devices themselves have a number of characteristics that are useful in designing the circuits. These include an absence of minority carrier storage effects, bidirection conduction between the source and drain of the device, the absence of any appreciable dc loading imposed by the gate circuit, low capacitive loading per device, and the high impedance level of the device. The last permits the fabrication of high values of resistance in relatively small areas which is helpful in reducing power dissipation, and allows the use of relatively long diffused lines without having their impedance affect the circuit performance, which can be advantageous in chip layouts.

Performance has been considered a major drawback of MOSFET devices, and it is true that the best present MOSFET logic circuits operate at the low performance end. However, in the context of a memory system, the combination of MOSFET device characteristics and the requirements of memory usage permit operation of a memory system with sufficient performance to encompass a much wider range of applications. The access or cycle times of most core or film memories are much longer than the delay of the associated logic circuitry in the remainder of the system (a computer main frame memory is an example). Although a MOSFET system may have a long transient which limits performance, the system can still operate in conjunction with much higher speed processor logic.

The longest delays in MOSFET circuits occurs in driving off-chip, where the high impedance level of the devices is relatively slow in driving large interconnections and stray capacitances. With proper system organization the MOSFET transients can be kept on-chip, eliminating the need for off-chip FET drivers, and avoiding the resultant long transients.

The speed of a MOSFET switching transient depends upon the mode in which the device is operated. As shown in Fig. 3, the common source transient is much faster than the source follower transient; it also avoids the voltage attenuation of the latter.[1] Transient speed depends upon

[1] An exposition on MOSFET switching transients is given in [6]. The source–follower curves given therein are calculated for the substrate connected to the device source, which is impractical in an integrated circuit, and which eliminates the augmentation of the device threshold with increasing source to substrate voltage. A satisfactory qualitative correction can be made.

the voltages applied to the devices. Judicious use of clocking pulses to sequentially turn devices on and off, such as in multiphase logic schemes, [7]–[10], can eliminate dc paths and gain ratio requirements in switching circuits, permitting further improvement in performance. In addition, the MOSFET device exhibits essentially no delay in the source–drain current in response to a voltage pulse, applied either to the gate to turn the device on, or on the drain when the device is already on [11]. Neither of these modes of operation is applicable to logic circuits, since a current output is obtained for a voltage input, but either may be used to sense the state of a storage element without delay. This permits high speed reading of the state of a memory circuit.

For many applications, the optimum system is obtained by interfacing the MOSFET array chips with bipolar support circuit chips [12], [13]. This permits interconnection lines which have large capacitive loads to be driven by low impedance bipolar circuits, resulting in much faster transitions than if MOSFET circuits were used to drive the lines. Similarly, in sensing, transition time delay can be minimized by the use of a low impedance sense amplifier, which essentially senses current. The low impedance sense amplifier keeps the sense line time constant short, and, as outlined previously, current sensing results in minimum cell delay. The result is a hybrid system, the goal of which is to combine MOSFET cost advantages with bipolar performance capabilities. MOSFET chips are used in the array, which has the great majority of total circuits, and thus determines system cost. Bipolar chips are used for support circuits, which basically determine the performance, and are much more adept at driving larger capacitive loads. As a result, the best characteristics of both technologies are obtained simultaneously, and the approach is widely used where performance is a requirement.

The best performance in a hybrid system is obtained if the array chips contain no decoding. This permits the bipolar support circuits to have direct access to the on-chip word and bit lines, and in system operation the only delay involving MOSFET circuitry occurs in the cell itself. In reading, the delay can be essentially zero; in writing, there is a delay due to the transient of the cell as it switches, but since within the cell the device or devices causing the switching are comparatively lightly loaded with an inherent fan-out of 1, the delay can be made small compared to the system cycle time. The performance is largely determined by the bipolar support circuits.

The price paid for this organization is the number of connections to the chip required. Consider Table I, where the number of the chip address and information connections required for various organizations of hypothetical 256 and 1024 bit memory chips is given.[2] It is clear that the chip with full binary decoding has many fewer chip connections, which in turn should be advantageous from the standpoint of reliability and packaging yield, and the bit organization of a binary decoded chip has advantages of ease and flexibility in assembling a complete system. The decoded array chip is still interfaced with bipolar support circuit chips to obtain the best performance.

TABLE I

	256	1024	Bits per Chip
Undecoded chip:	16 × 16	32 × 32	organization
	16	32	word line connections
	32	64	bit line connections
	—	—	
	48	96	total connections
X–Y selected chip:	256 × 1	1024 × 1	organization
	16	32	*X* connections
	16	32	*Y* connections
	2	2	bit line connections
	—	—	
	34	66	total connections
Full binary decoded chip:	256 × 1	1024 × 1	organization
	8	10	binary address lines
	2	2	bit lines
	—	—	
	10	12	total connections

There are also a number of drawbacks to a decoded chip. The decode circuits require chip area and increase power dissipation on the chip. There is also more total capacitance in the system which must be driven. There is a significant effect on performance. On-chip decoding requires MOSFET logic circuits, and at least some decoding at MOSFET rather than bipolar speeds. Although the circuits do not have to drive off-chip (thus avoiding interconnection capacitances), they must drive large fan-outs and the associated capacitive loading, such as occur on the word line or the outputs of the address inverters.[3] The result is longer chip transients and a lengthening of the chip access and cycle times. This is quite apparent in present-day commercially available chips, as is discussed in subsequent sections.

There is still appreciable controversy over decoded versus undecoded chips, and currently there are examples of chips and systems using both approaches [15]–[18]. The key to the undecoded chip is the interconnection technology, which must have sufficient reliability and density. As the number and density of bits on a chip increase, there will be increasing requirements on the interconnection technology. Historically, improvements in chip size and density have occurred faster than corresponding interconnection capabilities, and it seems likely that the ability to put bits on a chip will outstrip the interconnection technology eventually, if this has not already occurred. Further, evolutionary im-

[2] A memory cell with 1 word line and 2 bit lines has been assumed in Table I.

[3] Actually, the address inverters can be eliminated, at a cost of increased address connections, by presenting double rail address information to the chip, or by the use of combinatorial logic [14]. Neither approach has seen appreciable use.

provements in MOSFET devices should result in improved device performance, and reduce the performance difference between decoded and undecoded chips.

II. Random Access read/write p- or n-Channel Memory Cells

The first [19] and still most common MOSFET memory cell is the six-device circuit shown in Fig. 4.[4] Devices T_1–T_4 form a conventional bistable cross-coupled flip-flop circuit. T_1 and T_2 are the cross-coupled or "active" devices, T_3 and T_4 are the load devices. The interior nodes of the flip-flop are connected to the bit lines through two gating devices, T_5 and T_6, which can be switched on by the word line. Coincident selection versions of the cell have been shown in the literature [20]–[21]. The basic cell operation is similar.

In the quiescent state, the word line is at ground and T_5 and T_6 are off, isolating the flip-flop from the bit lines. Information is retained in one of the two stable states of the flip-flop circuit. The cell dissipates power due to current flowing through the load device in the on side of the flip-flop. The off-node load device conducts only the very small amount of current necessary to supply leakage current to the substrate from the off node, and essentially dissipates no power.

For the purposes of illustration, assume node 1 is high, and node 2 is low. Then T_2 is on and T_1 is off. To read the cell the word line is pulsed turning on gating devices T_5 and T_6. Both bit lines are kept at a supply potential. Current flows between the one bit line and ground through the on flip-flop device T_2 and the gating device T_6. No current flows in the zero bit line because T_1 is off.[5] The state of the cell is determined by detecting on which bit line the sense current occurs. There is essentially no cell delay in reading. The sense current will flow in the gating device in direct response to the word line voltage pulse (once the threshold voltage has been exceeded) as previously discussed. The drain of the gating device is connected to the bit line supply, and its source is connected to ground through the on flip-flop device, which is a comparatively low impedance. To the first order, the sense current does not charge or discharge capacitance, and it can flow to the sense circuitry without delay.

To write the cell, the word line is pulsed and one of the bit lines is grounded. In the illustrative state, if the one bit line is grounded, the cell is already in the state to which it was to be written, and no change occurs. If the zero bit line is grounded, node 1 is pulled down towards ground through the gating device T_5. As the level of node 1 drops below the threshold voltage of T_2, the device turns off, and node 2 is pulled up through T_6 and T_4. The writing process thus consists of two transients: discharging the initially high node through a gating device operating in common source mode, and charging the initially low node through the other gating device and a load device in source follower operation. The transients overlap somewhat, but it is the charging transient which largely determines cell writing delay in practice.

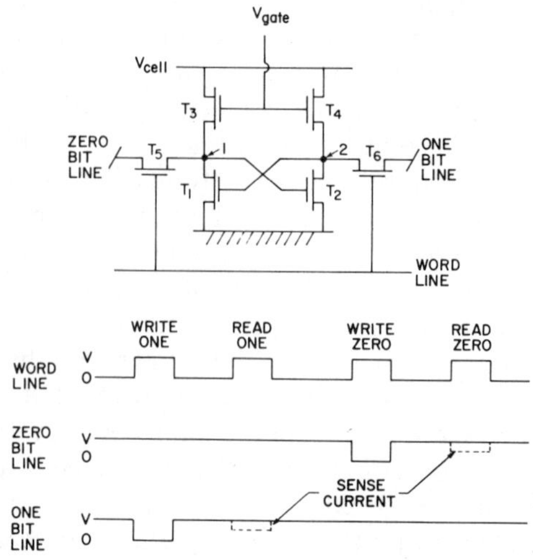

Fig. 4. Six-device memory cell.

There are two limiting cases for the writing operation. In the "low voltage" mode, the word line is kept on only until the cell node voltages have sufficient offset that threshold voltage variations and other circuit asymetries cannot cause the cell to lapse back to the initial state. At this point the word pulse is terminated, and the remainder of the pull-up of the high node occurs through the associated load device. In the "high voltage" mode, the pull-up transient occurs through the gating device, and the word pulse remains on until the final level of the high node is obtained. In the limiting case the contribution to the pull-up transient by the load device is negligible. Clearly, a spectrum of intermediate combination modes also exist.

The low voltage mode permits the use of a lower word line voltage pulse, but is unattractive because of poor performance. Low cell standby power requires a high impedance load device, while a fast writing pull-up transient requires a high gain (low impedance) device. These are conflicting requirements, and result in the performance and standby power of the cell being interrelated. To achieve a reasonable cell standby power, poor write performance must be accepted.

In the high voltage writing mode, the pull-up transient occurs through a gating device, which is turned off in the quiescent condition and which does not affect cell standby

[4] Most of the circuits shown (with the exception of the complementary circuits) will operate in the same general manner whether made in p-channel or n-channel technology, assuming the appropriate voltage supply polarity. Because of this, the device technology type and supply polarity are not explicitly shown on the circuit diagrams, although descriptive terminology as "high" or "low" level, "charge" or "discharge," etc., will be used as if n-channel devices and positive supplies were used. Enhancement mode devices have been assumed throughout except where contra-indicated in the text.

[5] Actually, there can be a current in the off side bit line through the gating device and the load device if the cell supply is larger than the bit line supply. This current will be in the opposite direction to the "1" sense current.

power. As a result, the performance and the standby power are independent, and may be designed for separately. Arbitrarily low standby power can be achieved by raising the load device impedance, since the only requirement on a load device is that it deliver enough current to the flip-flop off side node to compensate the node leakage current, which is quite small. In practice, a lower limit on cell power arises because higher impedance load devices take increasing area, and the cell becomes too large to be economically attractive.

Write delay is primarily determined by charging a node capacitance through the associated gating device. Since this capacitance consists mainly of the gate capacitance of the active cross-coupled device and some additional stray capacitance, write performance may be improved by increasing the gain of the gating device. However, there is an upper limit on the gain of the gating device. During reading, the cell can be disturbed if the current through the on-side active device is sufficient to raise the drain on the on-side active device above the threshold of the off-side active device to where the positive feedback of the circuit, and possible asymetries in device characteristics, can cause the cell to change state. This places an upper limit on the gain of the gating devices (or more precisely upon the ratio of gating device gain to active device gain).

Thus write delay and sense current are interrelated;[6] however, worst case write delay is associated with minimum sense current conditions, and the disturb condition occurs generally at or near the maximum sense current conditions. Thus tolerances on device characteristics and supply levels also affect the write performance. The looser the tolerances, the smaller the gating device must be made to avoid possibly disturbing the cell, and the worst case write delay is correspondingly increased. A limit on the minimum gating device size is imposed by the minimum sense current requirement and the necessity, during writing, of discharging the initially high node, which occurs through voltage division between the load and gating devices. An alternative, increasing the active device gain, generally increases cell area, which is undesirable.

A significant reduction in standby power dissipation of the cell may be achieved by pulsing the load devices off through the load device gate line, and occasionally pulsing them on. While the load devices are off, standby power is virtually eliminated. The read operation is unchanged and the write operation must be in the high voltage mode but is otherwise unaffected. This is termed "stored charge" operation, in that information is retained dynamically as charged stored on the capacitance of the off node of the flip-flop. There is effectively no leakage through the gate structure of the active device; however, since the nodes of the flip-flop are partially diffusion areas, the back biased p-n junction leakage currents potentially cause eventual loss of information. To overcome this, the load devices must be periodically pulsed on to "restore" or "refresh" the original charge condition. While the load devices are on, the cell does dissipate power. In practice, the interval between restore pulses is on the order of milliseconds, while the restore pulsewidth is in the microsecond range or less, and the duty cycle on the load devices is on the order of 10^{-2} to 10^{-3}. Average power dissipation is reduced by the same factor.

[6] One way to break the interrelation is to use a bilevel word pulse, with reading done at the lower voltage, and writing done at the higher. This requires additional complexity in the word driver circuits, and has not been used in practice.

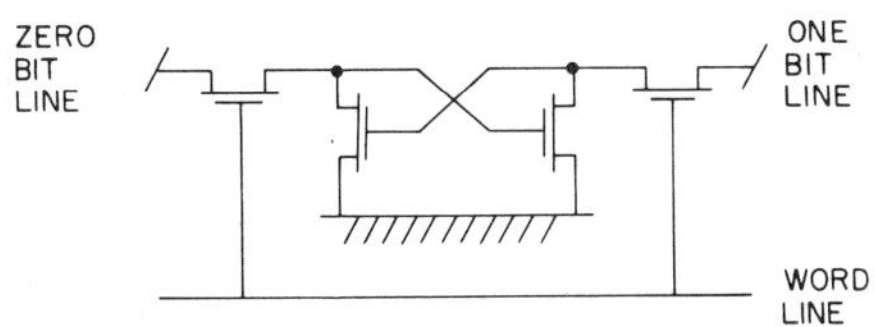

Fig. 5. Four-device stored charge cell.

Reading and writing operations can be unaffected by stored charge operation, and can continue through the restore cycle. The cell design must take into account the droop in the off-node level due to leakage, and also due to the capacitive coupling to the trailing edge of the restore pulse, but otherwise the design criteria are essentially the same as for the conventional six-device cell. The possibility of the load devices being on during a read or write operation due to a simultaneous restore cycle must be included.

The load devices are not necessary for the read or write operations and, in fact, are also unnecessary for the restore cycle, and thus may be eliminated, resulting in the four-device cell [4], [22] shown in Fig. 5. Restoring the cell is accomplished by a read cycle (although no actual detecting of the cell state need take place). When the word line is pulsed, the gating devices turn on and act as load devices to the active devices, forming a cross-coupled flip-flop and the off-side node is restored by charge flowing from the associated bit line. Basic cell operation and design are similar to that of the six-device stored charge cell, except that the load devices are absent. The basic advantage this cell has over the six-device stored charge cell is in circuit area. The elimination of two load devices and two power supply lines result in a cell area about two-thirds to a half that of the six-device cell.

A flip-flop in stored charge operation is actually unnecessarily redundant, and information may be stored on the gate of a single device. Elimination of one cross-coupling device in the four-device cell leads to the three-device cell shown in Fig. 6 [17]. Information is stored on the capacitance of node 1. This is one of a class of memory cells in which information is stored on a node capacitance associated with the gate of a device, and which do not use a cross-coupled flip-flop circuit.

The cell is written by turning on the gating device T_1 with the word line, which establishes the condition of the write bit line on node 1. In reading the cell, the word line is turned on. Devices T_2 and T_3 form an AND gate. T_3 will be on or off, depending upon the charge condition of node 1,

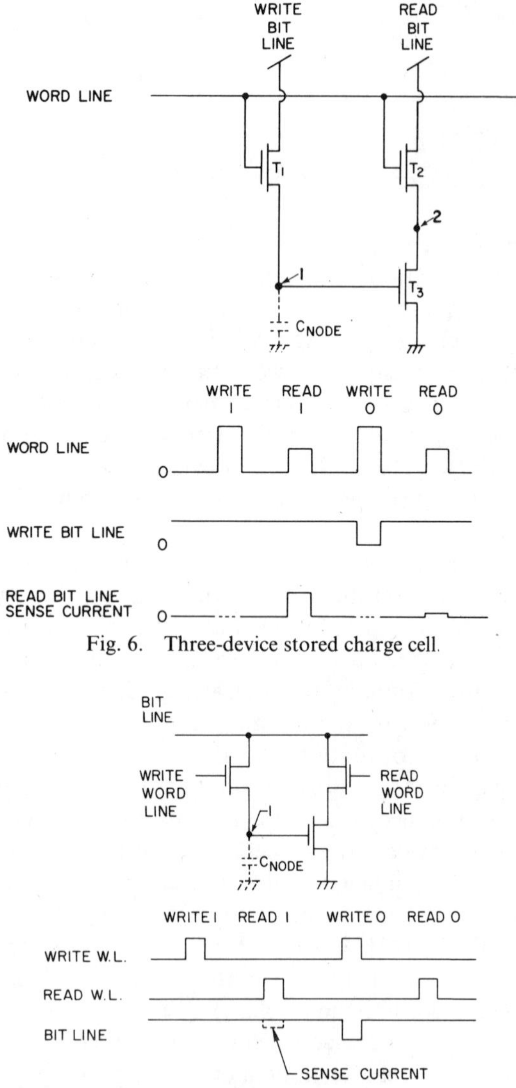

Fig. 6. Three-device stored charge cell.

Fig. 7. Alternate three-device cell.

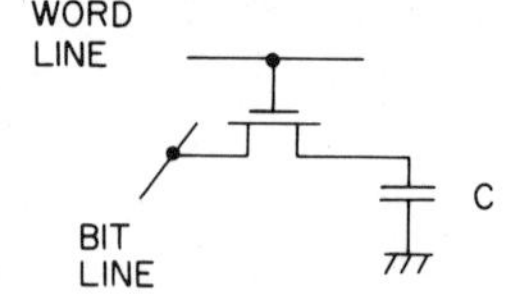

Fig. 8. Capacitor stored charge cell.

and the presence or absence of current in the read bit line can be detected to determine the state of the cell. A lower word line voltage is used in read to prevent inadvertent writing of the cell. This is aided by the fact that the word line must be at least two threshold drops above ground in order to turn on T_3, while it need be only one threshold drop above ground to turn on T_2 if T_3 is already on. An alternate version of the three-device cell which eliminates this possibility by having two word lines is shown in Fig. 7 [23].

The design of these cells is significantly different than that of the cross-coupled circuits. The absence of the cross-coupling device and the associated positive feedback paths results in the elimination of device gain ratio requirements. The cells cannot be disturbed by excessive sense current. As a result, the devices may be laid out for minimum cell area rather than being restricted to certain size ratios due to circuit requirements.

The write transient of the three-device cell can be inherently faster than that of the cross-coupled cells due to the absence of a gain ratio requirement. In both circuits, the worst case write transient is a source–follower pull-up of an information node through a gating device. In cross-coupled circuits, the capacitance of the information node is largely determined by the flip-flop active device which must be larger than the gating device by some ratio. This results in a slower transient than for the three-device cells, where no such adverse ratio of device sizes is necessary. The three-device cell also has the advantage that only a single transient is required for writing, rather than the discharge transient, followed by an overlapping but still somewhat sequential pull-up transient that occurs in the cross-coupled circuits.

Read may be slightly slower in the three-device cells because (at the beginning of the read cycle) some sense current may be lost in charging node 2, or because a false sense current spike may charge node 2 even if T_3 is off. Such delays are generally minor from a system standpoint.

The three-device cells occupy much smaller circuit area than the six-device cell, not only because of fewer devices used, but also because they are ratioless circuits, and can be laid out for minimum area. In practice, an area advantage of perhaps a factor of four is obtained for the circuit of Fig. 6; that of Fig. 7 is somewhat less.

Perhaps the simplest stored charge random access cell is that using the circuit of Fig. 8 [24]. It consists of a capacitor, upon which information is stored, and a single gating device. The cell is written by establishing the bit line level on the capacitor through the gating device; reading occurs by connecting the capacitor to the bit line through the gating device, and sensing the charge on the capacitor, either as an ac base current pulse, or as a quasi-dc base voltage on the bit line capacitance. The cell has a number of drawbacks—the readout is destructive, the stored charge redistributes between the cell and bit line capacitances, and the writing speed is limited by the information storage capacitor which must be made large enough to yield a reasonable sense charge. On the other hand, the cell is simple, and the word and bit line loading can be about the minimum possible for any cell.

Each of the various stored charge cells must be refreshed periodically, but the procedure varies for different cells. The six-device cell in stored charge operation is refreshed through the load device gate lead, independent of read or write operations, and a chip, a block of the memory, or the whole memory system may be refreshed simultaneously at any time. The four-device cell is refreshed by pulsing the word line, similar to a conventional read operation, and consequently read and write operations must be inhibited during the refresh cycle. Block refreshing can be done by turning on all the word lines on a chip simultaneously, although there may be a problem with chip power dissipation and the difficulty of delivering sense current to all cells simultaneously.

Cells which are not cross-coupled, such as the three-device cells, will not automatically refresh themselves into the proper state when driven. The information to be refreshed must be read out first, and then be rewritten. This results in a longer refresh cycle, and also means that only one word line on a chip (or in any block of memory which shares the same sense amplifiers and bit drivers) can be refreshed at a time. A fully decoded bit organized chip will require an on-chip sense amplifier for each chip bit line, since writing one bit along a word line results in all bits along the word line being written into whatever state the respective bit lines are in, and in a bit organized chip, only one bit line is connected off chip at a time. The on-chip sensing can basically be a logic circuit, and can be relatively simple (as in Section VI), but additional chip circuitry is required. There will also be additional delay involved, and if the on-chip sensing is used in the read operation, the chip read access delay will be longer compared to using bipolar off-chip sensing.

The present state of the art, as reported in the literature, is 256 bits per chip using the six-device cell, and 1024 bits per chip using the three-device cell, indicating the density advantage of the latter. Chip and system performance depend upon chip organization. Using chips without decoding, cycle times of 150 ns or better for the full memory system have been reported using bipolar support circuits [1], [15]. Systems using fully decoded bit organized chips generally have cycle times in the 500-ns to 1-μs range [17], [18].

III. p- or n-Channel Shift Register Circuits

An alternative to the random access systems of the previous section is serial access systems using shift registers. The shift register is essentially an electronic delay line. As shown in Fig. 9, memory circuits are connected serially, so that the output of one feeds the input of the next. Under the control of clock pulses, all information bits are simultaneously shifted from one stage or cell to the next throughout the shift register. The output of the shift register may be fed back into the input to form a closed loop, around which information can be circulated.

Once a bit enters a shift register, it must be shifted through all stages before it becomes available at the output.[7] To access a particular bit of information it may be necessary to shift it through every stage in the shift register, which results in a long delay, and for this reason shift registers are not attractive for random access applications. On the other hand, there are numerous applications where data are generated, manipulated, or transmitted serially. Also, if a sequential block of information is to be accessed, the long delay in obtaining the first bit of information may be outweighted by a high bit rate for transferring the rest of the information in the block. In this case a possible system organization is sketched in Fig. 10. Each shift register contains 1 bit of N words. To access a word, one shift register for each bit in the word are shifted synchronously so that all bits of the same word arrive at the shift register outputs simultaneously. The next word is obtained after the next shift. Worst case access time depends upon the length of the shift register; a shorter length results in faster access, but requires more decoding to select between the larger number of shift registers required in a system of a given size.

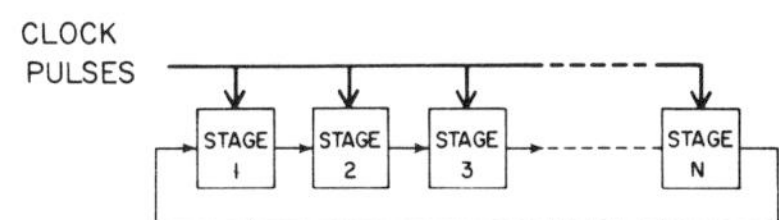

Fig. 9. Shift register block diagram.

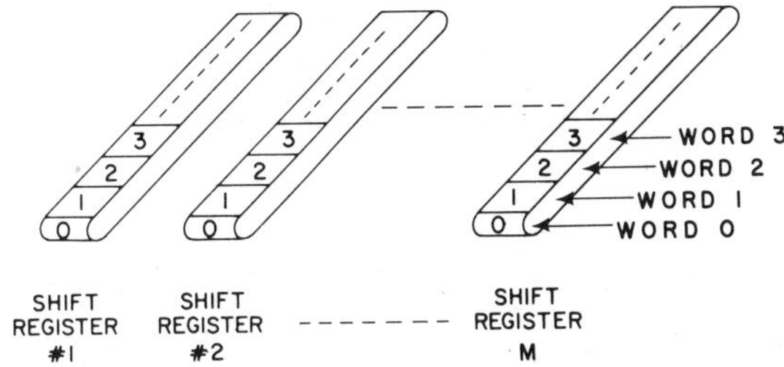

Fig. 10. Possible shift register memory system organization.

A shift register chip may require no decoding since any number of bits may be handled by a single set of input and output connections, and the number of connections to the chip needed is correspondingly low. The area of a single stage can be made quite small, and reasonable shifting rates can be obtained. A shift register stage is essentially a logic circuit which must drive another similar circuit with a fan out of 1; there is no large lumped capacitance which the cell must drive, such as the word or bit line of a random access chip. The shifting rate will be limited by the slowest cell in the shift register, and care must be taken to avoid having performance unduly limited by a single stage with an unusually large load, such as might occur at the output stage or as a result of nonuniform cell layout on the chip, because the shift register circuit must physically turn a corner or loop back. Interfacing the shift register chips with bipolar support circuits results in advantages similar to those obtained for random access systems; in particular, the clock pulse drivers must drive every cell on the chip, and thus see an appreciable capacitive load. Bipolar devices result in faster transition times on the clock pulses, particularly if a number of chips are to be driven in parallel.

The serial nature of the shift register has implications in reliability. If one cell in a shift register fails, the cell information passing through the shift register subsequently is lost, as all bits must pass through the bad cell. On the other hand, the low number of chip interconnections required per bit is favorable from a reliability standpoint; the net effect depends upon which failure mode predominates.

A shift register stage must be able to transfer an information bit to the next stage, while simultaneously receiving an information bit from the previous stage; subsequently, the received bit must be transferred within the stage, preparatory to the next stage-to-stage transfer. Thus a complete

[7] It is possible to have intermediate tap-off points.

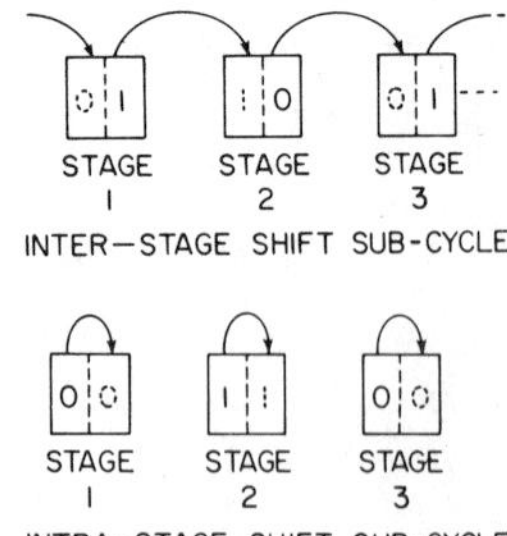

Fig. 11. Shift register subcycles.

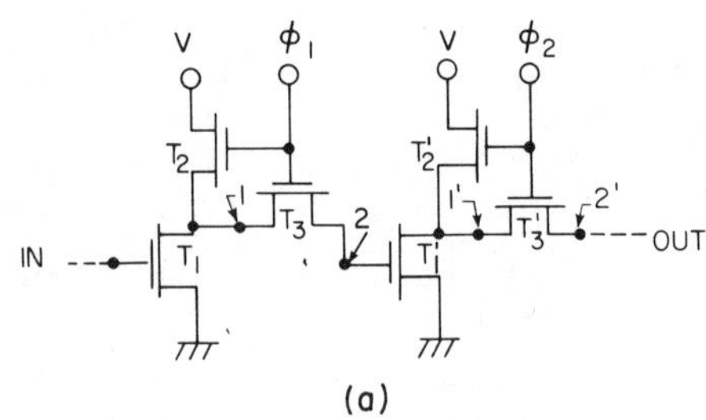

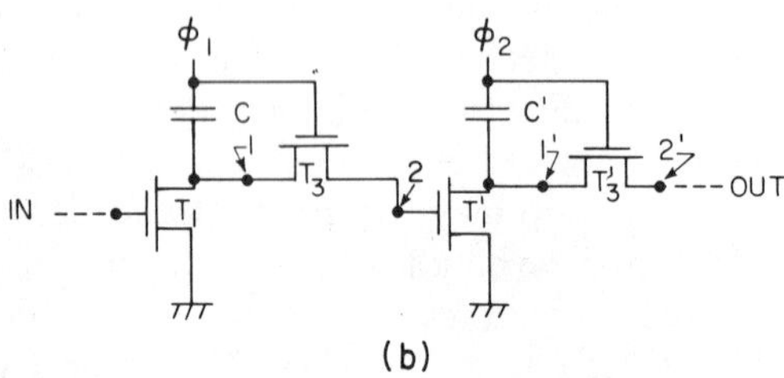

Fig. 12. Two phase shift register circuits.

shifting cycle actually requires two shifts, as shown in Fig. 11, and the stage is made up of two substages, which are usually identical. In a dynamic shift register, an information bit is generally stored on the gate capacitance of a device in an inverter and is transferred by pulsing the subsequent inverter properly, or through a series connected device used as a transmission gate which is pulsed on at the appropriate time. An inverter circuit provides gain, while the transmission gate may operate in the source–follower mode, resulting in voltage attenuation.

A two-phase shift register circuit is shown in Fig. 12(a) [25]. There are two identical substages; in each, T_1 and T_2 form an inverter, and T_3 acts as a series transmission gate connecting it to the inverter to the next substage. Prior to the application of phase (clock) pulse ϕ_1, information is retained as charge stored on the capacitance of the input node, as in the stored charge random access memory cells discussed previously. When ϕ_1 is applied, the inverter action establishes node 1 at the inverse of the input level, and node 2 follows through device T_3. When ϕ_1 terminates, device T_3 turns off, locking in the charge condition of node 2, and the information has been transferred in inverted form, from the input to node 2. In a similar manner, ϕ_2 transfers the information to the output node 2′ where, because it has undergone a second inversion, it has the same "sense" that it had at the input to the stage. To prevent interaction of successive bits of information, the phase pulses are kept from overlapping.

Performance is limited by the necessity of an impedance ratio between load and active devices in the inverters. Conventional dc inverter operation dictates this be around 1:10, which results in a comparatively low gain to capacitance ratio for the pull-up transient, where the load device charges the capacitances of nodes 1 and 2, the latter being primarily determined by the gate capacitance of the active device in the next inverter. The pull-down transient, occurring through T_1 and T_3 in the common source mode is much faster. The necessity of a gain ratio also results in a larger cell area. The transmission gate device has no dc requirement for a gain ratio with the load or active devices, but cannot be made too small or it will cause appreciable further slowing of the pull-up transient, and cannot be made too large because of the gate to source capacitive coupling on the trailing edge of the associated phase pulse. This coupling will reduce the amplitude of a high level (or "1") stored on node 2, and may cause the substrate diode to become forward biased if a low level (or "0") is stored there. In practice the gain of the transmission gate device is in the middle between those of the load and active devices.

The stage dissipates dc power while the phase pulses are on, since during that time there is then a possible path between the phase lines and ground. A modification of the two-phase circuit which eliminates this problem is shown in Fig. 12(b) [26], where the load device is replaced by a capacitor C. Operation is similar to the previous circuit. Node 2 is charged through C and T_3 if the input is low (T_1 is off), and is discharged as in the previous circuit if the input is high (T_1 in on). The capacitor eliminates the dc current path from the phase pulse. The charging transient of node 2 is faster than before because of the elimination of the load devices and dc gain ratio requirements. The discharge transient is longer than before, since the load capacitor C must be charged. This capacitor is made several times larger than the sum of the capacitances of nodes 1 and 2 to reduce loss in the phase line level coupled into node 2,[8] and a longer discharge transition results. An additional performance limitation arises from the possible injection of carriers into the substrate from the source of T_3, due to the coupling to the trailing edge of the phase pulse forward biasing the substrate diode. Overall, however, the performance is somewhat better with the capacitor load. Cell area is roughly the same, since the capacitor occupies appreciable area.

Both circuits in Fig. 12 are dynamic; i.e., similar to the stored charge random access cells, and the information is stored as the presence or absence of charge on a node capacitance. Leakage necessitates periodic refreshing of the information, which is accomplished when information is shifted to the next inverter. Thus the information is continually circulating in the shift register, with the leakages determining the minimum shift rate.

A widely used four-phase dynamic shift register stage with improved performance is shown in Fig. 13(a) [9]. The

[8] Reducing the value of load capacitor C can be compensated for by raising the phase pulse level, but this aggravates the problem of capacitive coupling to node 2 from the trailing edge of the phase pulse.

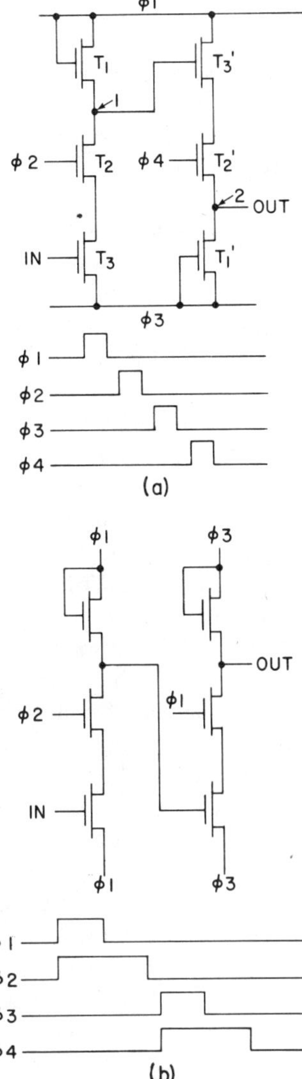

Fig. 13. Four-phase shift register circuits. (a) Nonoverlapping clock pulse circuit. (b) Overlapping clock pulse circuit.

stage consists of two identical pulsed inverters with the second drawn upside down to simplify the circuit schematic. Clock pulse ϕ_1 unconditionally charges node 1 through device T_1, irrespective of the conditions of the input line, since ϕ_2 is off. When ϕ_2 goes on, node 1 is conditionally discharged through the two-device AND gate formed by T_2 and T_3. At the end of ϕ_2, the input information has been shifted, in inverted form, to node 1. ϕ_3 and ϕ_4 perform the corresponding operations on the second inverter, and shift the information (now reinverted to true form) to the output node 2.

The clock pulses are kept from overlapping to avoid interference of adjacent information bits, and to prevent any dc current paths during shifting. This eliminates any requirements of a gain ratio between devices and allows a stage to be laid out for minimum area. The four-phase stage has a particularly efficient layout, and is similar in area to that of the three-device random access cell, despite having twice as many devices.

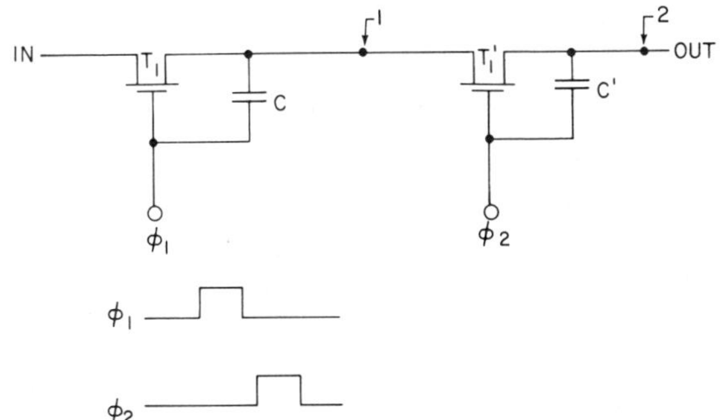

Fig. 14. Bucket brigade shift register circuit.

The elimination of any gain ratio requirements also results in improved performance because the possibility of a small device having to charge or discharge the gate capacitance of a much larger device is avoided and large capacitances, such as the load capacitance of the circuit of Fig. 12(b), are not present. The shift register performance can be improved by raising the amplitude of the clock pulses. This places extra strain on the supporting drive circuits and increases the power dissipation of a stage. Only dynamic power is dissipated in a stage, arising from the charge and discharge of the various capacitances. It is normally small but can become appreciable for high clock pulse amplitudes and shifting rates.

This four-phase shift register is widely used because of good performance and small layout area. One of the ultimate limitations to high speed shift register operation is the necessity of generating four separate nonoverlapping clocks. A four-phase shift register with somewhat simple clocking is shown in Fig. 13(b).[9] Operation is similar to the previous four-phase circuit, but the phase clocks can overlap without allowing a dc current path. Design considerations are similar to the nonoverlapping clock circuit, performance is slightly better, especially at low clock pulse amplitude, but the layout area is perhaps 25 to 50 percent larger.

The shift register stages shown so far have gain in each stage. This, in fact, is not necessary. Fig. 14 shows a shift register stage using the so-called "bucket brigade" technique [27]. It is a simple circuit requiring comparatively small layout area. A simplified explanation of the operation follows, assuming enhancement mode devices with a zero volt threshold. Initially, node 1 is charged to e_0 V and the phase lines are at ground. When ϕ_1 is pulsed to e_0 V node 1 is raised to 2 e_0 by capacitive coupling through C. Device T_1 now operates as a source follower in the saturation mode. Assume the input node is uncharged (i.e., at zero volts). Charge flows from node 1 to the input node until it charges up to e_0 V, at which point device T_1 turns itself off through normal source–follower action. At this point, node 1 is also at e_0 V. When ϕ_1 returns to ground, e_0 is coupled out of node 1, which ends up at ground potential. If the input node had been at e_0 V initially, no charge would have flowed through T_1, and node 1 would have ended up at e_0 V after

[9] The circuit is related to logic circuits shown in [9] and [51].

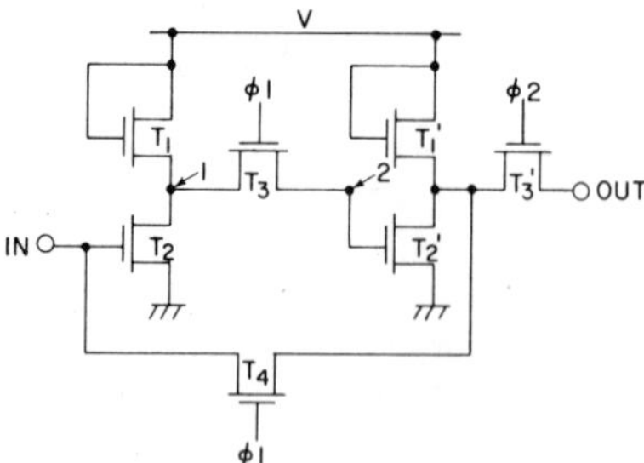

Fig. 15. Static shift register circuit.

ϕ_1 terminated. In this manner, the state of the input node is transferred to node 1 by ϕ_1. Clock pulse ϕ_2 performs a similar transfer of the information to the output node.

Since the devices operate in the source–follower mode, there is voltage attenuation at each transfer, and gain must be placed in the shift register periodically to reestablish the "1" and "0" levels. In order to avoid requiring gain too frequently, as little voltage attenuation as possible in each transfer is desired, which implies limited performance due to long source–follower transients. Capacitance C must be large in order to couple the phase pulse to the internal node, further limiting performance.

Information is stored dynamically on node capacitances, and must be periodically refreshed. The effect of leakage is cumulative between amplifying stages, and the low frequency clock rate must be adjusted accordingly.

A shift register can be made dc stable by incorporating a flip-flop circuit in each stage. An example is shown in Fig. 15 [28]. The stage consists of a pair of inverters and a pair of series transmission gates. Information is shifted by alternately pulsing ϕ_1 and ϕ_2 very much as in the two-phase shift register stage previously discussed. When ϕ_1 is on, a cross-coupled flip-flop circuit is formed, which statically retains the information. A potential race condition occurs in setting the flip-flop where ϕ_1 is turned on; it is overcome by designing the response time of the forward path through T_3 to be faster than that of the reverse path through T_4. The use of dc inverters result in gain ratio requirements with attendent power dissipation and performance limitations. The stage may be made bidirectional by adding a device between node 1 of each stage and node 2 of the previous stage [29], and altering the phase pulse pattern. Alternately pulsing the forward path series gates shifts information to the right; alternately pulsing the reverse connected gates shifts it to the left.

Static shift registers have found use because they do not require continual shifting of the stored information. However, in comparison to dynamic shift registers, they have generally lower performance, require more power, and occupy larger layout area.

For currently available shift registers, shifting rates run typically 1 to 5 MHz for p-channel devices, and up to 15 MHz has been reported using n-channel devices [4]. Chips are available with from several hundred bits of storage to as much as a thousand bits, operating in the megacycle range.

IV. Complementary Circuits

In complementary MOSFET circuits both n- and p-channel devices are used [30]–[33]. Such circuits have some unique characteristics and advantages. Consider the simple complementary inverter circuit in Fig. 16(a). When the input is low, the n-channel device is off and the p-channel device is on. The output node is high. If the input is high, the n-channel device is on and the p-channel device is off. The output node is low. The circuit acts as an inverter, but has the very desirable characteristic that in either quiescent condition, one of the two devices in the circuit is off. No dc current flows (other than leakages), and standby power dissipation is essentially eliminated.

When the input goes from a low to a high level, the output node is pulled down through the n-channel device in the common source mode of operation. Similarly, the upward output node transient occurs through the p-channel device, also in common source operation. Thus the source–follower transient is eliminated. This not only gives a faster mode of operation for the transients, but also eliminates the voltage loss between gate and source which occurs with enhancement mode devices in source–follower operation.[10] A further reason for improved transient performance is that the load device is turned off and is not pulling against the active device in the inverter. This also eliminates any requirement for gain ratios between the devices, which, as before, leads to better transient response. Complementary circuits are advantageous from the standpoints of having a firmer on state and better noise immunity.

The complementary circuit analog of a series transmission gate device is shown in Fig. 16(b) [34]. The polarity of the pulses on the clock lines are chosen so that both devices are either on or off. When the gate is on, there is always one device in the pair operating in the common source mode, and although the other device operates as a source follower, the limitations of source–follower operation are avoided.

Two complementary inverters can be cross-coupled to form a bistable memory element with essentially zero standby power. Addition of two gating devices leads to the memory cell of Fig. 17 [35], which is the complementary analog of the cell shown in Fig. 4. Operation is qualitatively similar. In writing, the complementary load device can be used to help the pull-up transient; however, initiating the writing cycle is more difficult because the initial pull-down transient of the high node must be accomplished against a common source load device that is turned on hard. If the load device is made low gain, the writing becomes easier to initiate, but the speed advantage gained in the upward transient is sacrificed.

Historically, complementary memory cells have been designed for high performance, and have been relatively complex and have required large layout areas to achieve that

[10] Augmentation of the device threshold as the magnitude of the source to substrate voltage increases due to the source–follower transient is also avoided.

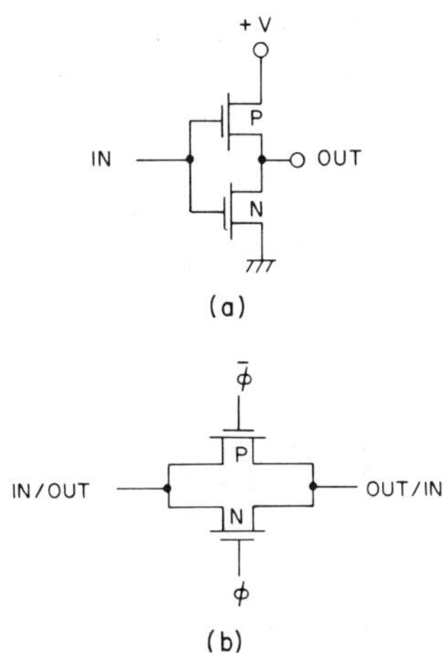

Fig. 16. (a) Complementary MOSFET inverter. (b) Complementary series transmission gate.

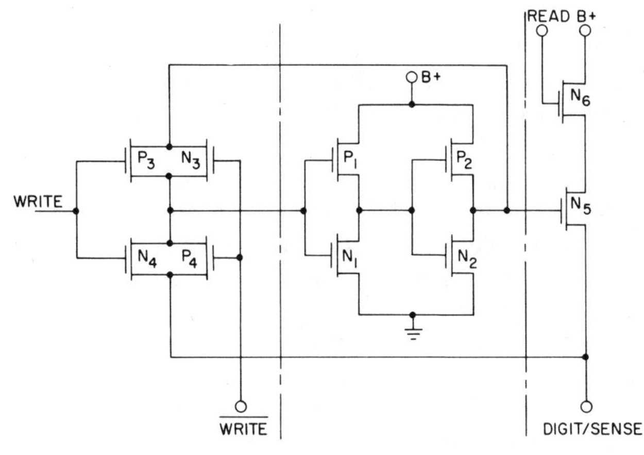

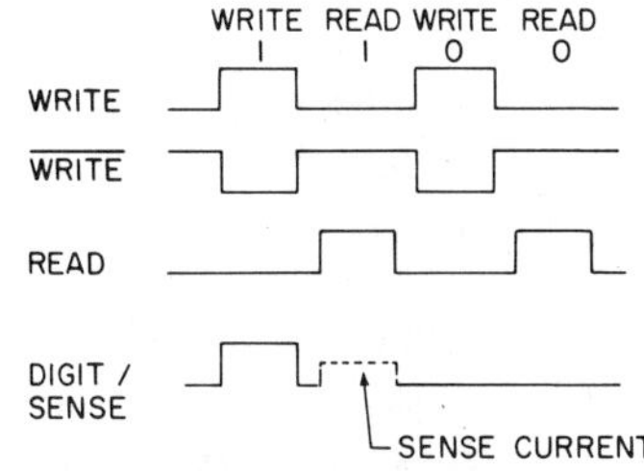

Fig. 18. High performance complementary cell.

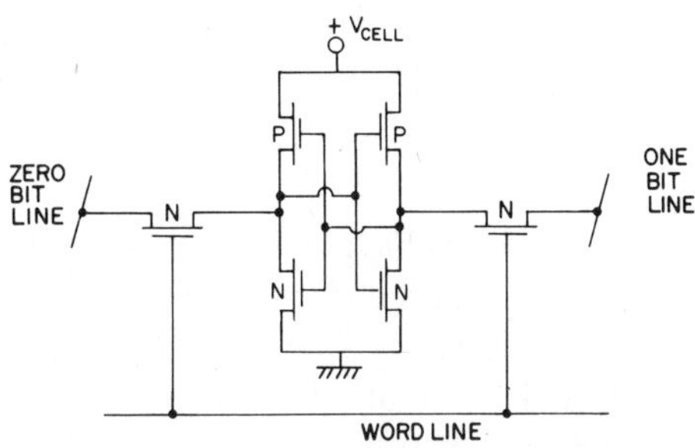

Fig. 17. Complementary six-device cell.

end. An example is shown in Fig. 18 [36]. In the quiescent condition, the transmission gate formed by P_3 and N_3 cross-coupled the inverters formed by P_1/N_1 and P_2/N_2, while the P_4/N_4 transmission gate is off. To read, sense current conditionally flows through the AND gate formed by N_5 and N_6, depending upon the state of the cross-coupled flip-flop circuit. To write, the polarity of the WRITE and $\overline{\text{WRITE}}$ lines are reversed. This turns off the transmission gate formed by P_3 and N_3, and breaks the feedback path in the cross-coupled circuit. At the same time, the transmission gate formed by P_4 and N_4 is turned on, forcing the information on the digit/sense line onto the gate of the P_1/N_1 inverter, from where it propagates through to the output node of the P_2/N_2 inverters in one pair delay. The WRITE and $\overline{\text{WRITE}}$ lines are then returned to their original polarity, reestablishing the cross-coupling of the cell. The fast write speed of the cell is obtained through the operation of the complementary circuits and the breaking of the feedback loop. The performance is obtained on the cost of circuit complexity, which is clearly greater than with the previous cells. A variety of complementary memory cells are shown in [31].

Quiescent standby power of both noncomplementary stored charge and complementary memory cells is determined by leakage currents. The stored charge cells require a periodic refresh cycle, during which power is dissipated. In practice, complementary systems dissipate only nanowatts per cell in standby, while a stored charge system will be two or three orders of magnitude higher. In both cases, power is low enough that volatility of stored information can be overcome by a battery back-up power supply.[11]

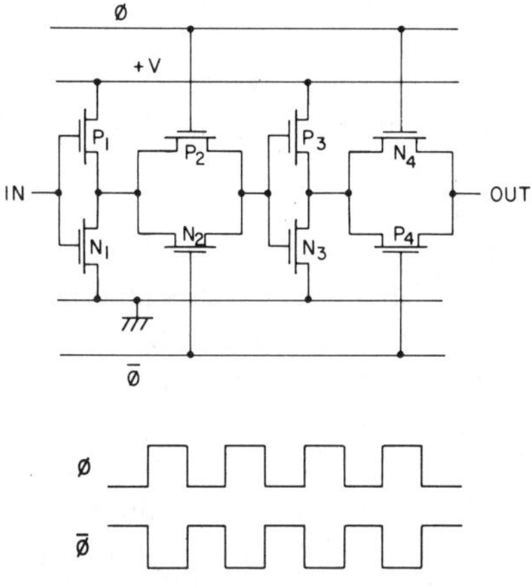

Fig. 19. Complementary shift register.

A high speed complementary shift register circuit is shown in Fig. 19 [37]. A stage consists of alternating two inverters and two transmission gates. Pulsing the clock lines to turn on the P_2/N_2 transmission gate allows the information at the input to propagate to the gates of the P_3/N_3 inverter in inverted form. Reversing the polarity of the clock lines locks the information in on the gates of the P_3/N_3 inverter, and allows it to propagate forward into the next stage through the P_4/N_4 transmission gate.

The performance of this shift register is better than that of noncomplementary circuits for a number of reasons. The

[11] A battery back-up is possible for dc cells where the system standby dissipation is not too high.

complementary inverter and transmission gate operation, which eliminates source–follower limitations and gain ratio requirements, is important. In addition, 1) the capacitive coupling from the clock lines to the information nodes is balanced and cancels; 2) information transfer requires only a single transient per shift, rather than an unconditional charge followed by a conditional discharge, as is done in the four-phase and similar circuits; and 3) the phase clock pulsing is much simpler.

At present, only a limited amount of complementary circuit hardware is available. Almost all of this has been aimed for the high performance end. Shifting rates of 75 to 100 MHz have been reported for the shift register circuit shown [37], and random access chips of 64 to 256 bits with cycle times in the 10–20-ns range have been reported for both undecoded and fully decoded bit organized chips [36], [39], [40]. These performance figures are significantly better than that reported for available p-channel counterparts.

The performance difference with n-channel circuits would be much less. Pulsed logic circuits are clocked to avoid dc current paths and gain ratio requirements, thus achieving low standby power operation and device geometry requirements similar to complementary logic, and the use of a p-channel common-source load device in complementary circuits is not inherently significantly faster than the n-channel source–follower transient of an n-channel load device, due to the higher mobility of electrons (approximately a factor of three [38]) and the greater capacitive loading of complementary circuits, where two gates must be driven per unit of fan-out. Also, electron mobilities reported in complementary integrated circuits tend to be lower than that obtainable in n-channel circuits. Thus it is not clear that complementary circuit transients are inherently faster than those of n-channel pulsed circuits. On the other hand, pulsed n-channel logic will suffer from the voltage attenuation of source–follower operation; the necessity of serial transients to do logic, which may be at least partially overcome by overlapping transients, and the generation, timing, and distribution of the clock pulses, which can add significantly to the complexity of a system. As devices improve, the clocking could become a major inhibitant to utilization of improvements in inherent device performance.

The eventual importance of complementary devices is still not definite. In the past, they have suffered from a more complex technology and larger circuit areas, which has resulted in higher costs and tended to restrict applications to areas where the very low standby power characteristics are of prime importance. Some recent efforts have been made towards achieving competitive cell density, and achievement of similar comparable density between the six device noncomplementary and complementary cells has been reported [39]. Complementary circuitry does not improve the density of high density storage arrays, such as those using the three-device cells, and noncomplementary circuits have an edge for low cost applications.

With effort now being directed towards a wider range of applications, predictions have been made that complementary circuits will approach noncomplementary circuits in cost, although perhaps lagging behind some time in development [41]. It remains to be seen whether design claims and laboratory hardware can be carried through to a wide range of product applications, or if they will continue to be used in special applications only.

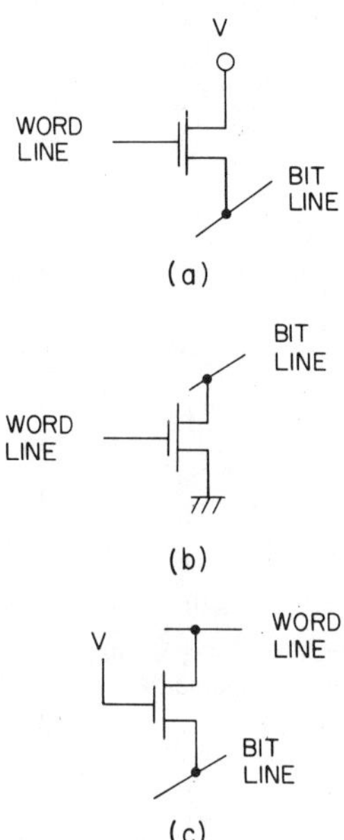

Fig. 20. Read only memory array circuits.

V. Read Only Memory and the MNOS Device

A frequent area of application for MOSFET devices is read only memories (or ROMs). In such a memory, the information is written in permanently during the fabrication process. In operation, the memory is read to retrieve the stored information, but the contents cannot be altered and there is no write cycle. There are many uses for a ROM; among them are control memories, code conversion, table look-up character generation, etc. [42].

Because of the elimination of the write requirement, only a single device is needed per bit. Circuits for the storage array are shown in Fig. 20. The information storage mechanism is the thickness of the gate oxide, which is determined during fabrication in the gate oxide mask step. If the device has a normal thin gate oxide, its threshold voltage will be low; if the gate oxide is thick, the threshold voltage is high. In response to a pulse on the word line, the low threshold device will conduct, while the high threshold device will not, and the presence of a bit line current or voltage swing can be detected for a "1" or "0". In Fig. 20(a) and (b), the word line voltage must overcome the device threshold to turn it on, but there is no dc load on the word line, and the noise immunity is good. The circuit shown in Fig. 20(c) can operate with lower word line voltage because of the absence of a threshold between word and bit lines, but accordingly has no noise immunity and is susceptible to sneak paths as a result of the bidirectional source–drain coupling through on devices.

Since only a single device is required per bit of information and very efficient array layouts are possible, the density of bits on ROM chips is much higher than with read/write chips. 2K bit chips are routinely available, and at least two sources sell 4K bit chips. Because of the high bit densities possible, on-chip binary decoding is used. This is reflected in the chip performance; cycle times run 500 ns to about 1 μs.

The density of a ROM array can be approached in a read/write array with the MNOS device [43]–[49], a MOSFET structure in which the threshold may be set by tunneling of charge in or out of the gate insulator by a high voltage pulse applied to the gate. The threshold may be interrogated subsequently by a low voltage pulse, as in a ROM. Only a single device per bit is needed. The MNOS device is still in the laboratory stage of development at present.

VI. On-Chip Support Circuits

On-chip support circuits are used to decode the input address and select the corresponding information bit or bits. On-chip sense signal amplification can be provided; this is necessary where the MOSFET chip is designed to be completely compatible with a bipolar logic family, such as TTL. There are numerous methods of obtaining the necessary functions. The circuits shown in this section are examples of what can be done. ROM arrays have been shown for simplicity; the extension to read/write cells is straightforward.

A cross section of a decoded chip using simple dc coupled logic is shown in Fig. 21 [50]. Address inputs are inverted on chip. The output of a NOR block will be low if any input is high, and will be high only if all inputs are low. The selected word line drives the gates of all devices along it. One bit line is selected by the corresponding bit NOR block turning on the series transmission gate which connects the bit line to the dot–OR bus. The dot–OR bus is conditionally discharged to ground, depending upon the threshold voltage of the array device. The remainder of the output circuitry provides off-chip drive capability. It should be noted that the basic information storage array is word organized, and that selection is done at the periphery of the array similar to the 2½ dimension organization used in magnetic film memories. This keeps the array simple and minimizes the decode circuitry.

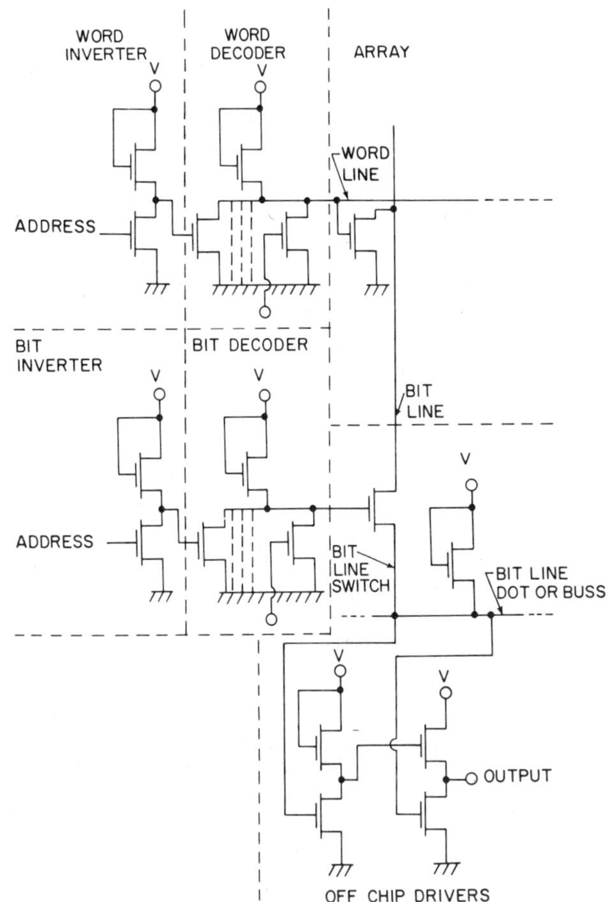

Fig. 21. Cross section of a fully decoded chip using dc logic.

The dc coupled circuitry has a number of drawbacks. It is slow because of gain ratio requirements between load and active devices, and the worst case path involves several load device source follower transients. Power dissipation is high because dc current flows in all unselected NOR blocks, and can flow in the inverters, the array, and the output drive circuits as well.

An example[12] of a decoded chip using pulsed support circuitry is shown in Fig. 22. The pulsed logic circuits are similar to the four phase nonoverlapping clock shift register circuits described previously. The sequence of operation is as follows: the word inverter and NOR block output nodes are precharged on ϕ_4 and ϕ_1, respectively. The inverter nodes are conditionally discharged on ϕ_1 and the NOR block nodes are conditionally discharged on ϕ_2. The bit inverter operation is similar to the word inverter, and uses ϕ_1 and ϕ_2. Thus as the end of ϕ_2, only one word line remains charged, and only one bit NOR block has all its inputs low. Also during ϕ_2 the bit line is unconditionally charged. On ϕ_3 all bit lines are conditionally discharged. All unselected bit lines have a discharge path through their respective bit NOR blocks; the selected bit line can be discharged only if the array device at the intersection of the selected bit and word lines has a thin gate oxide. Thus, at the end of ϕ_3, only the selected bit line can remain charged, and then only if the selected array device has a high threshold. ϕ_3 also serves to precharge the bit NOR block node. On ϕ_4 the bit NOR block output node is conditionally discharged. All unselected bit line inputs are low; therefore, the NOR block output is the inverse of the state of the selected bit line. The output may be sampled during either or both of the ϕ_1 and ϕ_2 periods.

No dc current flows during the operation of the chip, greatly reducing power dissipation. Dynamic power is dissipated due to the charging and discharging of the various information node capacitances on the chip, but this tends to

[12] The circuits described here are similar to, but not identical with, the approach used in [51].

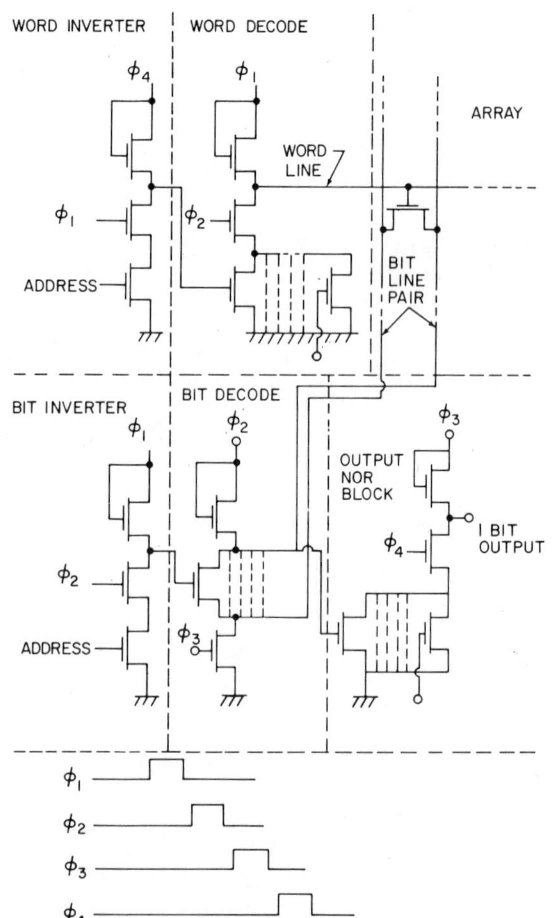

Fig. 22. Cross section of a fully decoded chip using pulsed logic.

be small in absolute value, using 2.5 mW at 1 MHz/100 pF for a 5 V swing. The pulsed logic eliminates gain ratio requirements with the attendant advantages. The result is a system which is faster and lower power than the dc coupled system, but which requires generation and timing of the clock pulses. On-chip generation of some clock pulses from others can reduce timing problems between pulses.

The circuits given above illustrate approaches to on-chip support circuits. There are, in fact, innumerable variations which are possible, each with particular advantages and disadvantages [22], [23], [51], [52].

A source–follower transient can be markedly sped up by use of the so-called "super one" technique [53], [22]. The circuit is shown in Fig. 23(a). Initially as the result of conventional pulsed logic operation, a voltage level V_g is stored on the gate of T_1. As long as ϕ_1 is low, the output remains low, and the feedback capacitance C_F has a voltage V_g across it. When ϕ_1 is pulsed, the load capacitance is charged through T_1. As the output rises, the voltage on the gate of T_1 is higher than the output voltage by the voltage across the feedback capacitor, and to the extent that C_F is much greater than the stray capacitance of the gate node, that voltage will remain close to the initial value of V_g V. Thus it is possible at the end of the transient to achieve a voltage on the gate of T_1 higher than any supply voltage

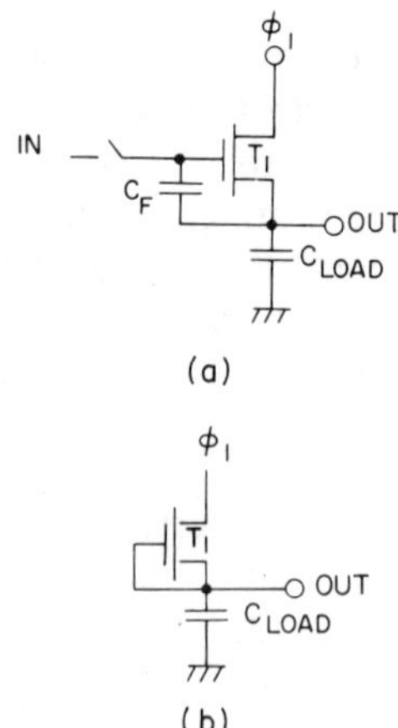

Fig. 23. (a) "Super one" circuit. (b) Depletion mode load device connection with similar operation.

present. In this manner the self-turning off action of the source–follower mode can be overcome, and in the limiting case then the voltage across the feedback capacitance does not change, the pull-up transient becomes identical with the common source transient.

Similar operation can be obtained using a depletion mode device connected as shown in Fig. 23(b) [54]. The built-in potential of the depletion mode threshold acts similarly to the feedback capacitor voltage of the "super one" circuit, except that the gate–source voltage is not reduced by charging the stray capacitance, and the gate node is not loaded by the feedback capacitance C_F.

VII. Epilogue

At present, the MOSFET device has applications in a wide variety of memory applications, due to unique characteristics of the devices and the technology. As overall semiconductors technology improves, MOSFET technology will share in the advances; in fact, MOSFET technology is newer and will probably undergo more rapid development. In addition, there are technology advances specifically applicable to MOSFET devices. These include n-channel technology, insulating substrates, thinner gate oxides, self-aligned and zero overlap gate structures, ion implantation, lower thresholds, charge free oxides, etc.; the result can be significant additional improvement in MOSFET devices, and it is not unreasonable that the performance gap with bipolars will narrow, and perhaps eventually vanish. Further, memory phenomena (as opposed to memory circuits) in MOSFET structures such as the MNOS and charge coupled devices [55], [56] have the potential of further reducing the area and complexity required to store an information bit.

References

[1] D. A. Hodges, "Large-capacity semiconductor memory," *Proc. IEEE*, vol. 56, July 1968, pp. 1148–1162.

[2] W. B. Sander, "Semiconductor memory circuits and technology," *AFIPS Fall Joint Computer Conf., Proc.*, Dec. 1968, pp. 1205–1211.

[3] "Semiconductor memory," *1970 Digest INTERMAG Conf.* (session 11), Apr. 1970, pp. 11.1–11.6, also *IEEE Trans. Magn.*, vol. MAG-6, Sept. 1970, pp. 584–589.

[4] J. W. Bremer, "A survey of mainframe computer memories," *Computer Design*, May 1970, pp. 63–71.

[5] R. Graham and M. Hoff, "Why semiconductor memories?" *Electron. Prod.*, Jan. 1970, pp. 28–34.

[6] R. H. Crawford, *MOSFET in Circuit Design*. N. Y.: McGraw-Hill, 1967, ch. 4, pp. 71–86.

[7] J. Karp and E. De Atley, "Use four-phase MOS IC logic," *Electron. Des.*, Apr. 1, 1967, pp. 62–66.

[8] B. G. Watkins, "A low-power multiphase circuit technique," *IEEE J. Solid-State Circuits*, vol. SC-2, Dec. 1967, pp. 213–220.

[9] L. Cohen, R. Rubenstin, and F. Wanlass, "MTOS four phase clock systems," *NEREM Rec.*, 1967, pp. 170–171.

[10] L. L. Boysel and J. P. Murphy, "Four phase LSI logic offers new approach to computer design," *Comput. Des.*, Apr. 1970, pp. 141–146.

[11] K. Goser, "Channel formation in an IGFET and its equivalent circuit for CAD," *Internat. Solid State Circuits Conf., Digest of Tech. Papers*, Feb. 1970, pp. 98–99.

[12] P. Pleshko and L. M. Terman, "An investigation of the potential of MOS transistor memories," *IEEE Trans. Electron. Comput.*, vol. EC-15, Aug. 1966, pp. 423–427.

[13] R. Igarashi, T. Kurosawa, and T. Yaito, "A 150 ns associative memory using integrated MOS transistors," *Internat. Solid State Circuits Conf., Digest of Tech. Papers*, Feb. 1966, pp. 104–105.

[14] F. S. Greene and W. B. Sander, "Address selection by combinatorial decoding of semiconductor memory arrays," *IEEE J. Solid-State Circuits* (Corresp.), vol. SC-4, Oct. 1969, pp. 295–296.

[15] T. W. Hartz, D. W. Hillis, J. Marley, R. C. Lutz, and C. R. Hoffman, "A main frame semiconductor memory for fourth generation computers," *AFIPS Fall Joint Computer Conf., Proc.*, Nov. 1969, pp. 479–488.

[16] Y. Tarui, Y. Hayashi, T. Koyanagi, H. Yamamoto, M. Shiraishi, and T. Kurosawa, "A 40 ns 144 bit n-channel MOS-LSI memory," *IEEE J. Solid-State Circuits*, vol. SC-4, Oct. 1969, pp. 271–279.

[17] W. M. Regitz and J. Karp, "A three transistor cell, 1024 bit, 500 ns MOS RAM," *Internat. Solid State Circuits Conf., Digest of Tech. Papers.*, Feb. 1970, pp. 42–43.

[18] L. L. Vadasz, A. S. Grove, T. A. Rowe, and G. E. Moore, "Silicon-gate technology," *IEEE Spectrum*, vol. 6, Oct. 1969, pp. 28–35.

[19] J. D. Schmidt, "Integrated MOS random-access memory," *Solid-State Design*, Jan. 1965, pp. 21–25.

[20] D. E. Brewer, S. Nissim, and E. V. Podraza, "Low power computer memory system," *AFIPS Fall Joint Computer Conf., Proc.*, Nov. 1967, pp. 381–393.

[21] J. H. Friedrich, "A coincident-select MOS storage array," *Internat. Solid State Circuits Conf., Digest of Tech. Papers*, Feb. 1968, pp. 104–105.

[22] D. Lund, C. Allen, S. Anderson, and G. Tu, "Design of a megabit semiconductor memory system," *AFIPS Fall Joint Computer Conf., Proc.*, Dec. 1970, pp. 53–62.

[23] L. Boysel, W. Chan, and J. Faith, "Random access MOS memory packs more bits to the chip," *Electronics*, Feb. 16, 1970, pp. 109–115.

[24] R. H. Dennard, "Field-effect transistor memory," U.S. Patent 3 387 286, June 4, 1968.

[25] H. Z. Bogert, "Metal Oxide Silicon Integrated Circuits," *SCP Solid-State Technol.*, Mar. 1966, pp. 30–35.

[26] R. H. Crawford and B. Bazin, "Theory and design of MOS capacitor pull-up circuits," *IEEE J. Solid-State Circuits*, vol. SC-4, June 1969, pp. 145–158.

[27] F. L. J. Sangster, "Integrated MOS and bipolar analog delay lines using bucket-brigade capacitor store," *Internat. Solid State Circuits Conf., Digest of Tech. Papers*, Feb. 1970, pp. 74–75.

[28] General Instrument Corp. Tech. Spec., MEM 501, May 1965.

[29] M. N. Shen, "Two-way four phase MOSFET dynamic shift register," *IBM Tech. Disclosure Bull.*, vol. 12, no. 12, May 1970, p. 2149.

[30] F. M. Wanlass and C. T. Sah, "Nanowatt logic using field effect metal-oxide semiconductor triodes," *Internat. Solid State Circuits Conf., Digest of Tech. Papers*, Feb. 1963, pp. 32–33.

[31] J. R. Burns, "Switching response of complementary-symmetry MOS transistor logic circuits," *RCA Rev.*, Dec. 1964, pp. 627–661.

[32] E. J. Boleky, "The performance of complementary MOS transistors on insulating substrates," *RCA Rev.*, vol. 31, no. 2, June 1970, pp. 372–395.

[33] T. Klein, "Technology and performance of integrated complementary MOS circuits," *IEEE J. Solid-State Circuits*, vol. SC-4, June 1969, pp. 122–130.

[34] J. R. Burns and J. J. Gibson, "Complementary field effect transistor transmission gate," U.S. Patent 3 457 435, July 22, 1969.

[35] G. B. Herzog *et al.*, "Large scale integrated circuit arrays," RCA Interim Tech. Rep. 5, May 1967, pp. 46–47.

[36] J. F. Allison, F. P. Heiman, and J. R. Burns, "Silicon-on-sapphire complementary MOS memory cells," *IEEE J. Solid-State Circuits*, vol. SC-2, Dec. 1967, pp. 208–212.

[37] J. E. Meyer, J. R. Burns, and J. M. Scott, "High speed silicon-on-sapphire 50 stage shift register," *Internat. Solid State Circuits Conf., Digest of Tech. Papers*, Feb. 1970, pp. 200–201.

[38] G. Cheroff, D. L. Critchlow, R. H. Dennard, and L. M. Terman, "IGFET circuit performance, n-channel versus p-channel," *IEEE J. Solid-State Circuits*, vol. SC-4, Oct. 1969, pp. 267–271.

[39] J. R. Burns, NASA contract work, to be published.

[40] J. R. Burns and J. H. Scott, "Silicon-on-sapphire complementary MOS circuits for high speed associative memory," *AFIPS Fall Joint Computer Conf., Proc.*, Nov. 1969, pp. 469–477.

[41] J. A. Rajchman, "Computer memories and the impact of semiconductor technology," presented at Internat. Electron Devices Meeting, Oct. 1969.

[42] J. Wunner and R. Colino, "Applying the versatile MOS ROM," *Electron. Prod.*, Jan. 1970, pp. 35–40.

[43] H. A. R. Wegener, A. J. Lincoln, H. C. Pao, M. R. O'Connell, and R. E. Oleksiak, "The variable threshold transistor, a new electronically alterable, non-destructive read only storage device," presented at Internat. Electron Devices Meeting, Oct. 1967.

[44] J. T. Wallmark and J. H. Scott, "Switching and storage characteristics of MIS memory transistors," *RCA Rev.*, vol. 30, no. 2, June 1969, pp. 335–365.

[45] E. C. Ross and J. T. Wallmark, "Theory and switching behavior of MIS memory transistors," *RCA Rev.*, vol. 30, no. 2, June 1969, pp. 366–381.

[46] H. A. R. Wegener and F. A. Sewell, "Metal-insulator-semiconductor transistor for use as a nonvolatile digital storage element," Sperry Rand Tech. Rep. AFAL-TR-69-187, July 1969.

[47] D. Frohman-Bentchkowsky, "An integrated metal-nitride-oxide silicon (MNOS) memory," *Proc. IEEE* (Lett.), vol. 57, June 1969, pp. 1190–1192.

[48] ——, "The metal-nitride-oxide-silicon (MNOS) transistor—characteristics and applications," *Proc. IEEE*, vol. 58, Aug. 1970, pp. 1207–1219.

[49] F. W. Flad, C. J. Varker, and H. C. Lin, "The application of MNOS transistors in a preset counter with nonvolatile memory," *Internat. Solid State Circuits Conf., Digest of Tech. Papers*, Feb. 1969, pp. 46–47.

[50] L. Boysel, "Memory on a chip: a step toward large-scale integration," *Electronics*, Feb. 6, 1967, pp. 93–97.

[51] A. Varadi and R. Rubinstein, "2048 bit MTOS read only memory," *1968 Computer Group Conf. Digest*, June 1968.

[52] L. Boysel and J. Murphy, "Multiphase clocking achieves 100 ns MOS memory," *EDN*, June 10, 1968, pp. 50–55.

[53] A. K. Rapp, presented at the Internat. Solid State Circuits Conf., Session THE 7, Feb. 1969.

[54] J. MacDougall and K. Manchester, "Ion implantation offers a bagful of benefits for MOS," *Electronics*, June 22, 1970, pp. 86–90.

[55] W. Boyle and G. Smith, "Charge coupled semiconductor devices," *Bell Syst. Tech. J.*, vol. 49, no. 4, Apr. 1970, pp. 587–593.

[56] G. Amelio, M. Tompsett, and G. Smith, "Experimental verification of the charge coupled device concept," *Bell Syst. Tech. J.*, vol. 49, no. 4, Apr. 1970, pp. 593–600.

A Survey of High-Density Dynamic RAM Cell Concepts

PALLAB K. CHATTERJEE, MEMBER, IEEE, GEOFFREY W. TAYLOR, MEMBER, IEEE, ROBERT L. EASLEY, HORNG-SEN FU, MEMBER IEEE, AND AL F. TASCH, JR., MEMBER, IEEE

Abstract—**The performance capabilities of a variety of dynamic RAM cell concepts proposed in recent years are compared to the industry standard one-transistor cell. The new concepts are divided into three categories. The lateral charge sensing cells such as the Charge-Coupled cell, Hi-*C* cell, Merged-Charge cell, and Stacked-Capacitor cell. Vertical cells such as VMOS, the Punchthrough Isolated, and the Buried-Bit-Line cell which make use of the third dimension to achieve higher density. The Stratified-Charge cell and Taper-Isolated cell use current sensing of a dynamic change in the threshold voltage of a buried-channel transistor. The various cells were fabricated and compared on the basis of signal size, leakage rates, packing density, and fabrication and operational complexity. An overall figure of merit for a dRAM cell is suggested which combines all three considerations. Based on the cell concepts reported to date and this figure of merit, the Stacked-Capacitor, VMOS, and Punchthrough-Isolated cells are the most promising charge storage cells. The Taper-Isolated cell, however, is shown to have significant overall advantage compared to the charge storage cells.**

I. Introduction

THE TREND toward lower cost per bit, and higher performance memories has driven various integrated circuit technologies to very high density. Dynamic Random Access Memories (dRAM's) have evolved in the past few years to densities of 16K bit per chip in routine production today; and, 65K bit dRAM's are being developed by various semiconductor houses. The evolution of the dynamic RAM has been largely due to two main factors. Firstly, the lithography techniques have been refined continuously so that today we may optically print 3-4-μm geometries with ± 1-μm level-to-level registration routinely over 3-in diameter silicon wafers. Secondly, clever memory cell structures have simplified the cell design thereby increasing the packing density.

In this paper the performance of various new cell design concepts are compared with the industry-standard one-transistor-one-capacitor (1T) cell [1] used in dRAM's today. The basic principle of operation of such a cell is the storage of a charge packet on an MOS capacitor. An MOS transistor serves as a switch to charge and discharge the storage capacitor. The cross section of a conventional NMOS dRAM cell is shown in Fig. 1. A charge storage cell of this kind operates with a non-

Manuscript received November 7, 1978; revised February 8, 1979.

P. K. Chatterjee, G. W. Taylor, R. L. Easley, and A. F. Tasch, Jr., are with Texas Instruments Incorporated, Central Research Laboratory, Dallas, TX 75265.

H-S. Fu was with Texas Instruments Incorporated, Central Research Laboratory, Dallas, TX 75265. He is now with the Integrated Circuit Laboratory, Hewlett-Packard Company, Palo Alto, CA.

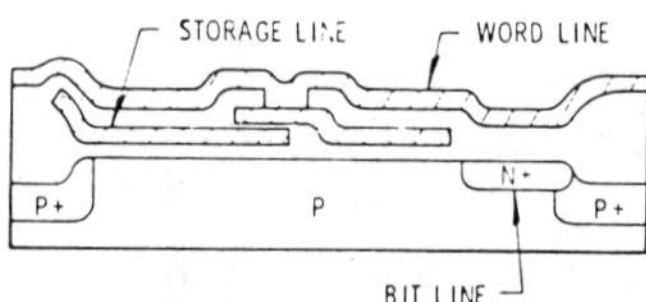

Fig. 1. Cross section of a one-transistor two-level polysilicon dynamic RAM cell.

equilibrium condition under the storage gate. Minority carriers generated in or near the vicinity of the depletion region under the storage electrode are collected as leakage charge in the storage well. Data in the storage well must, therefore, be periodically refreshed in order to avoid errors. The size of the charge packet and the leakage rate are thus two major performance factors. In large memory applications, the fabrication complexity of the cell has a significant impact on the choice of a cell structure. In addition, the logic and clock circuits required to address the array are built into the memory chip. Thus the complexity of clocks that need to be generated dictate the size of the entire memory. New memory cells must be evaluated on the basis of all these considerations.

Many novel dRAM cell structures have been reported in recent years which laterally rearrange the elements of the 1T cell [2]-[5]. In addition, cell structures utilizing the third dimension have been reported [6]-[8]. All of these concepts are based on capacitive charge storage. In contrast, novel dRAM concepts based on a dynamic change in threshold have been disclosed [9], [10]. This concept is radically different from all other concepts and merits careful consideration because of its high-performance potential. We categorize these various dRAM concepts as lateral charge storage cells, vertical charge storage cells, and dynamic threshold cells.

Two novel lateral charge storage cell structures have been reported which merge two of the three major elements of the 1T cell: The Charge-Coupled (CC) cell [2] and the Merged-Charge Memory (MCM) [4] cells. These two cells afford important advantages in structural simplicity. The Hi-*C* cell [3] which uses ion-implantation techniques to improve storage capacity, has the important advantage of improving the signal size at a given density. The Stacked-Capacitor (STC) cell [5] uses a high dielectric constant insulator to increase storage capacity.

Vertical charge storage concepts were introduced with the VMOS cell [6], [7]. It is shown in this paper that the process complexity introduced by the use of V grooves is not neces-

Reprinted from *IEEE Trans. Electron Devices*, vol. ED-26, pp. 827-839, June 1979.

sary and punchthrough conduction may be used in the vertical cell configuration. Two versions of these vertical concepts are discussed. In the first, the storage and transfer elements are stacked and the bit line is laterally placed [8]. In the second all three are vertically stacked.

Two versions of the dynamic threshold concept have been reported. The Stratified-Charge Memory (SCM) cell uses a buried channel and a series-enhancement device for the cell which is used to perform the select function. The Taper-Isolated Dynamic-Gain (TIDG) cell eliminates the series enhancement device and uses a bipolar-like selection scheme.

It is our purpose in this paper to propose a scheme to rate dRAM cells, rather than to uniquely and unambiguously select the cell of the future. To this end, all the above cells are compared on the basis of signal size, leakage rates, packing density, and fabricational and operational complexity. An overall figure of merit for a dRAM cell is suggested which combines all these considerations.

The Punchthrough cell concepts are demonstrated using structures fabricated by conventional lithography. All these cell structures were fabricated and characterized except the VMOS and STC cell where data from [5]-[7] were used.

Electron-beam lithography provides the attractive capability of small geometry patterning and accurate level-to-level registration (±1500 Å) and has been used to fabricate the ~65-μm^2 (0.1-mil^2) lateral charge storage cells using 2.0-μm minimum features. The results demonstrate that advanced dynamic MOS devices using multilevel silicon gates and metallization can be fabricated in an electron-beam compatible process. Since dynamic MOS devices are very sensitive to the damage created by electron-beam radiation, proper anneal sequences have been introduced in the process. The excellent leakage characteristics of our dynamic RAM's (~0.4 nA/cm^2 at 23°C) and the characteristics of NMOS devices fabricated simultaneously, clearly indicate that the use of electron-beam lithography will not degrade the performance of these devices.

II. Dynamic RAM Cell Concepts

The series of cell structures described in the previous section were aimed at achieving higher density compared to the basic 1T cell. In this section, we shall briefly review these structures for the benefit of readers who may not be totally familiar with all the concepts. The particularly attractive aspects of each cell structure from a conceptual point of view will be emphasized. In the later sections we shall compare the performance of these cells on the basis of experimental data.

A. The Charge-Coupled RAM Cell (CC)

The storage and transfer functions are combined into a single gate in the Charge-Coupled (CC) cell to obtain an increased lateral packing density (see Fig. 2). In the storage region, p-type ions are implanted into the silicon at a depth of several thousand angstroms. This implant results in a ϕ_s versus V_G characteristic in which ϕ_s varies slowly with V_G compared to the stronger dependence of ϕ_s on V_G in the unimplanted transfer region. The p-type implant is then followed by a

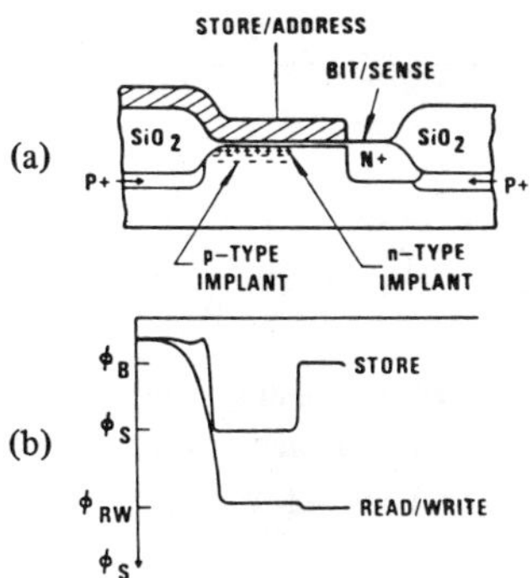

Fig. 2. (a) Cross section of the charge-coupled RAM cell. (b) Surface potential configuration for READ, WRITE, and STORE modes.

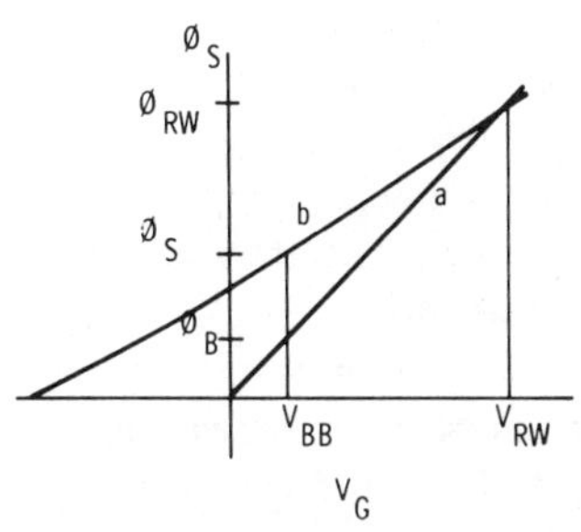

Fig. 3. Surface potential versus gate voltage. Curve *a* is for low-doped p-type material. Curve *b* is for the same material with combined n- and p-type implants near the surface.

shallow n-type implant, which shifts the ϕ_s versus V_G characteristic for the storage region which is shown by curve *b* in Fig. 3. Also shown is the ϕ_s versus V_G curve (curve *a*) for the transfer region.

The operation of the CC cell is identical (voltages and timing) to the operation of the conventional one-transistor cell. With the word line turned off (STORE mode), a potential well exists for storing charge in the storage region. When the word-line gate voltage is turned on, the surface potential in the transfer region is more positive than that of the storage region so that charge can flow between the bit line and the storage region. Any charge present in the storage cell may be dumped onto the bit line and sensed.

The CC cell may be fabricated using a standard n-channel self-aligned gate process (n-SAG) with the addition of the storage region implants, which have to be critically registered to avoid potential barriers between transfer and storage region. That is, the p-type implant must lie (laterally) within the n-type implant.

B. The Hi-C RAM Cell

The implantation technique used in the CC concept may also be applied to a 1T cell to increase the effective charge capacity of the cell. This is established in the Hi-*C* cell [3]. In dynamic operation, the MOS storage capacitor stores charge at the Si/SiO_2 interface. The charge is thus stored on the depletion layer capacitance C_D in addition to the oxide capacitance C_O. For substrate dopings normally used, $C_D \ll C_O$ and C_D is usually neglected. The Hi-*C* RAM concept demon-

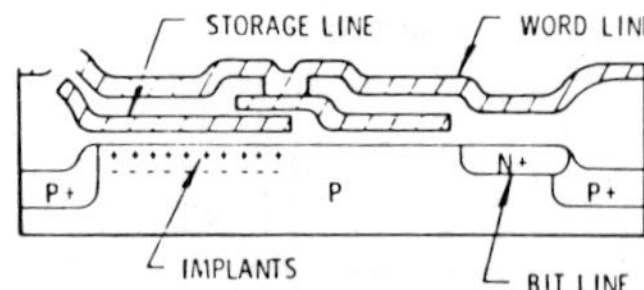

Fig. 4. Cross section of the Hi-C RAM cell structure.

strates an effective way of increasing the depletion-layer capacitance without reducing the surface potential so that the charge capacity (which is the product of capacitance and storage potential) is increased.

The Hi-C RAM cell concept is shown in Fig. 4. As mentioned earlier, for a given applied gate voltage, the maximum surface potential (empty well) decreases when the substrate doping is increased, say, by a p-type implant. However, this decrease can be cancelled by shifting the flat-band voltage to a more negative value using a shallow n-type implant. This is similar to the n-type implant employed for depletion-mode NMOS transistors. As a result, the surface potential difference $\Delta\phi_s$ does not decrease when the total capacitance increases, and there is a net increase in charge capacity. Following the analysis in [3] it can be easily shown that the charge capacity per unit area $Q_{\text{Hi-}C}$ of the Hi-C cell can be written as

$$Q_{\text{Hi-}C} = Q_{1\text{T}} + Q_{\text{CC}} \tag{1}$$

where $Q_{1\text{T}}$ and Q_{CC} are the capacities of the one-transistor and charge-coupled RAM cells, respectively. That is, the Hi-C cell structure combines the charge-coupled and the one-transistor cells, and the resulting charge capacity is exactly the sum of the capacities of these two cells.

The fabrication and operation are identical to that of a 1T cell with the two additional storage region implants which must be critically aligned as for the CC cell.

C. Merged-Charge Memory Cell (MCM)

The merged-charge memory (MCM) cell [4] combines the bit storage and sense (BSS) functions on a single-gate electrode as shown in Fig. 5. Parallel to every n of these BSS lines is a diffusion stripe which serves as a fill-and-spill charge injector. This provides a better storage to cell area ratio and a simple and very dense structure.

In the MCM array, the information charge is stored in a potential well under the cross point of the word line and the polysilicon BSS line, as shown in Fig. 5. The charge storage potential wells on a particular BSS line are defined by regions of thin oxide; they are separated from the adjacent storage potential wells along the BSS line by intervening areas of thick oxide.

During a write operation, the BSS line is kept at the high voltage V_H to create a deep potential well (1). The BSS line is kept at the high voltage V_H for storage and is allowed to float during the read operation. The diffusion stripes function as "fill-and-spill" charge injectors to all the storage potential wells under a selected word line. The charge injected from the n^+ diffusion stripes is gated and metered by the potential well under the word line ($V_{WI} = V_H/2$) into a succes-

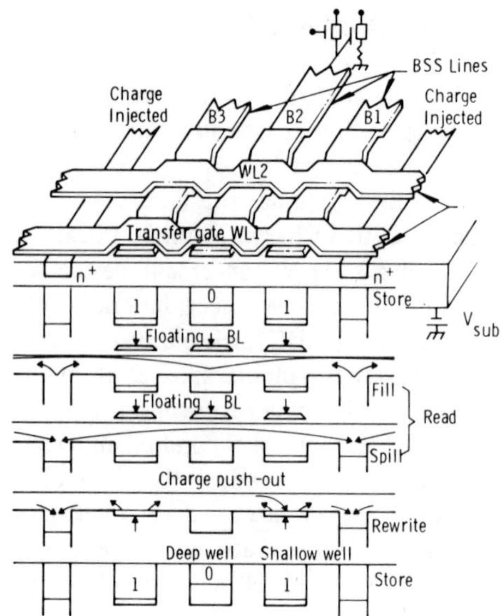

Fig. 5. Cross section and operation principle of the merged-charge memory cell. (After Lee [4].)

sion of pulsed storage capacitors of deep and shallow potential wells. This results in an array of charge packets as shown in Fig. 5.

A 1 or 0 signal is stored as a near empty or half filled level, respectively, in the potential well at the storage node. Information in a particular word is read by first floating the BSS lines and pulsing the diffusion stripes to ground. The word line is then pulsed on from a negative offset voltage to $V_H/2$. Because of the substrate bias, the diffusion stripes are still reverse biased so that charge can flow only under the selected word line. As the injected charge from the diffusion stripes successively fills up the potential wells, output signals proportional to the net charge flowing into each of the potential wells are induced in the corresponding BSS lines. Those potential wells only slightly filled initially receive more electrons than those wells already half filled and, thereby, cause a greater drop in the corresponding BSS line voltages. Thus the difference between the 1 and 0 signal is proportional to the difference in the initial stored charge levels or the associated surface potential difference. After flooding all the potential wells, the diffusion stripes are then strongly reverse biased so that excess charge flows out from the entire channel until the surface potentials underneath the BSS lines approach those under the word line. During the "read spill" time the floating voltages on the BSS lines increase; however, the difference of 1 and 0 signal is maintained.

Reading is destructive because following a read operation, the potential wells are all half filled (0) and therefore indistinguishable. The rewrite operation is essentially a "selective spill" process. A word is written by clamping each BSS line to the high voltage V_H for a deep potential well (0) or pulsed down to $V_H/2$ for a shallow potential well (1) while the word line remains on. Selected shallow potential wells now push out charges (see Fig. 5) and these charges are drained off by the strongly reverse-biased diffusions at the ends. The word

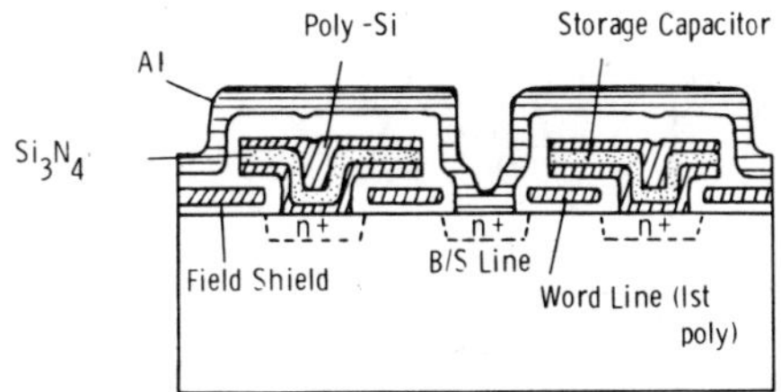

Fig. 6. Cross section of the stacked-capacitor cell. (After Koyangi *et al.* [5].)

line is then turned off, which isolates the potential wells. Next, the potential wells are pulsed back to the V_H store condition. Thus information is stored as a half filled well because of half select considerations. This results in a smaller charge packet per unit area.

D. Stacked-Capacitor Cell (STC)

The cell area of a 1T cell is generally limited by the storage capacitor area required to provide a detectable signal. The Hi-*C* cell is an example of an attempt to increase the storage capacitance per unit area by utilizing the depletion capacitance in the semiconductor. Another way to increase the storage capacity [5] is to increase the effective dielectric constant of the insulator used to form the capacitor. In the Stacked-Capacitor cell (STC) the storage capacitor is stacked above the address transistor (Fig. 6). The STC cell has a triple-level polysilicon structure. The address transistor gate electrode is composed of a first polysilicon layer and each stacked capacitor is composed of a second polysilicon layer, Si_3N_4 film (~2 × dielectric constant compared to SiO_2) and a third polysilicon layer. Aluminum bit lines may be used to effectively reduce bit-line capacitance. The operation of the cell is, of course, identical to the 1T cell.

The cell area may be reduced significantly in the STC cell at the cost of very complex processing. The use of Si_3N_4 as a dielectric also raises questions on reliability and reproducibility of deposited Si_3N_4 dielectrics compared to thermally grown SiO_2.

E. VMOS Cell

The VMOS technology allows the fabrication of an RAM cell in which the charge transfer and storage are accomplished almost vertically with respect to the bit line [6], [7]. A cross section of the cell is illustrated in Fig. 7. The storage region is the isolated n^+ area located at the bottom of the V groove and the word (transfer) line is the VMOS transistor connecting the storage region to the surface.

The fabrication sequence of the cell is similar to the VMOS process sequence. The n^+ storage region is implanted or diffused initially into a p^+ substrate, similar to the DUF (diffusion under field) step in bipolar technology. The high-resistivity p layer (π) is then grown and the grooves are defined and etched to terminate in the n^+ region. The remaining steps follow the normal VMOS process sequence [6]. The bit line in this case is a diffused n^+ line.

The operation of the cell is identical to the 1T cell discussed above.

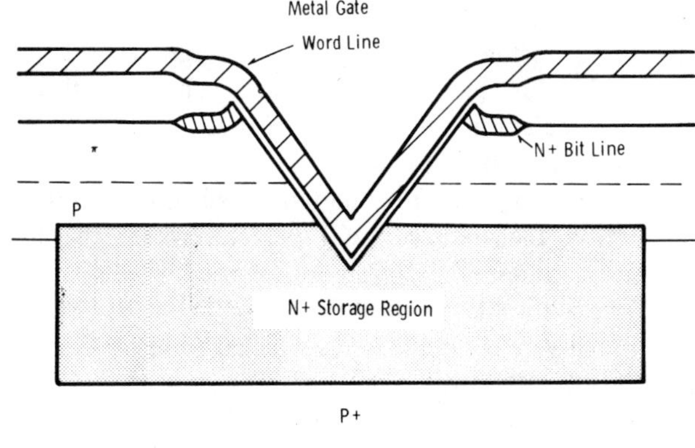

Fig. 7. Cross section of the buried-storage VMOS dynamic RAM cell [6].

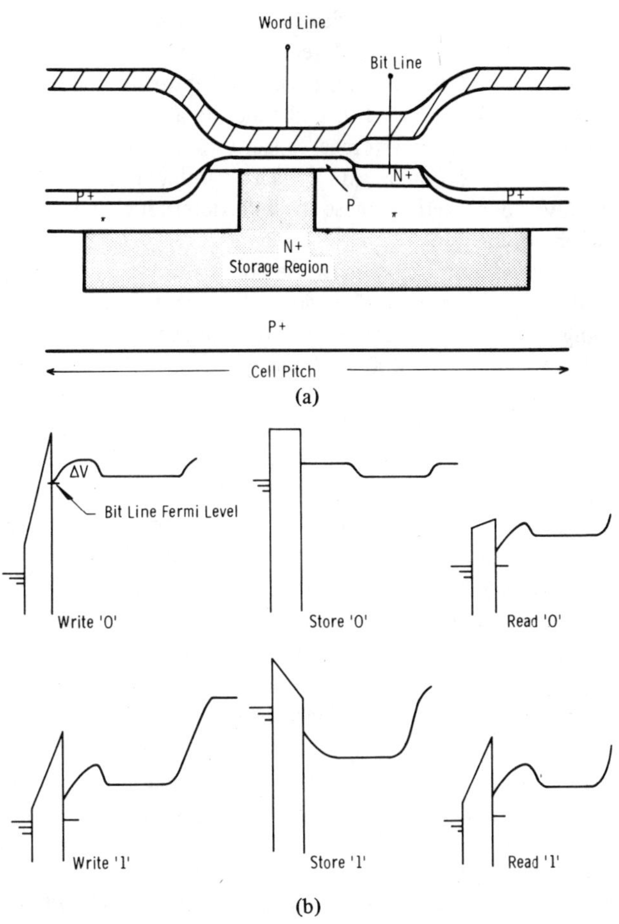

Fig. 8. (a) Cross section of the punchthrough isolated cell showing the version fabricated using epi and implants. (b) Energy diagram describing the operation.

F. Punchthrough RAM Cells

The use of punchthrough conduction in the design of a memory cell may offer advantages as described by the following two configurations.

1) Punchthrough Isolated Cell (PTI): A cross section of the cell is shown in Fig. 8(a). The cell is a planar structure in which the transfer line and storage line have been combined into the gate of one transistor to form the word line. The source of the transistor is buried below the surface and acts as the storage region for the cell. The storage region is junction isolated and is accessed from the surface by punchthrough of the gate depletion region [8]. The drain of the transistor also forms the diffused bit line.

The punchthrough cell may be fabricated by a modified n-channel self-aligned-gate (n-SAG) process, where the main modification addresses the formation of the buried n^+ storage region. The allowable depth of this region below the transfer/punchthrough gate is determined by leakage and subthreshold considerations. This buried n^+ storage region may either be fabricated as a DUF or by a set of ion implants.

Following the first alternative, the n^+ region is defined on a p^+ substrate by a long diffusion on which an epitaxial π region is then grown over the surface of the wafer. The standard n-SAG process is then used to fabricate the gate and bit line along with the peripheral devices. The advantages of using this method are that the n^+ region may be made as deep as possible, so that the sidewalls will contribute to the storage capacitance. The n^+ DUF is embedded in a p^+ substrate, thus further enhancing the storage capacity, and reducing leakage due to carrier diffusion [11]. The epi-thickness has to be critically controlled because it will determine the punchthrough voltage.

The second alternative is to use compensating ion implants to fabricate the buried n^+ region. Excellent dimension and doping control can be achieved. Using phosphorus and boron ion implants of 300–400 keV, we may achieve a deep n^+ region with an adjustable p-type doping for both the deep and shallow dimension (Fig. 9). The deep p implant increases the storage capacity. It also extends beyond the n^+ buried storage region in the lateral dimension because of the larger lateral straggle of the boron implant. The shallow boron (p) implant may also be used to control the punchthrough voltage. In this fabrication scheme, buried n^+ regions of ~0.5-μm depth may easily be achieved. This scheme will be even more useful for VLSI memories where device dimensions are scaled.

It is, of course, possible to combine both approaches to achieve the large buried storage region area with the epi and the controlled depth using the ion implants. The combined scheme should be very powerful since it has the advantage of exploiting the third dimension and tight process control available from ion implantation. This scheme is shown in the cross section of Fig. 8(a).

The operation of the cell is similar to that of the 1T cell. A 0 is written with the bit line at ground potential. With the word line high, the gate depletion region connects to the storage region via punchthrough and the storage region remains at ground (Fig. 8(b)). The signal is stored with ground potential on the word line, so that the storage region is isolated from the surface. For the read operation, the bit line and word line are high and the signal charge flows from the storage region to the bit line via punchthrough conduction until the storage region potential is equal to the bit-line potential minus a threshold voltage. For the 1 state, the potentials are similar to the 0 state except that the bit line is held high during the write sequence.

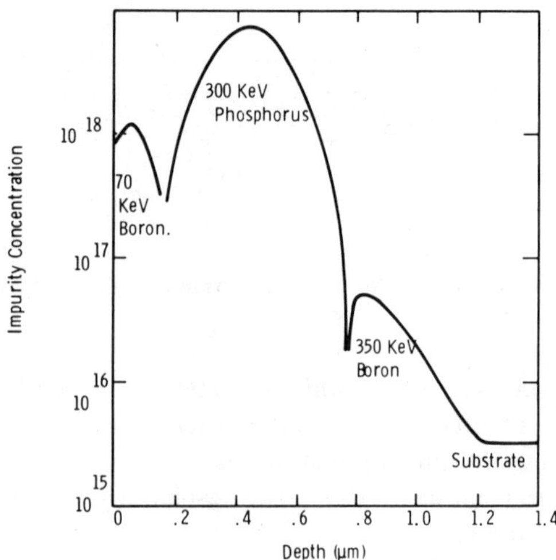

Fig. 9. Ion-implant profile used to generate a punchthrough cell without epitaxy.

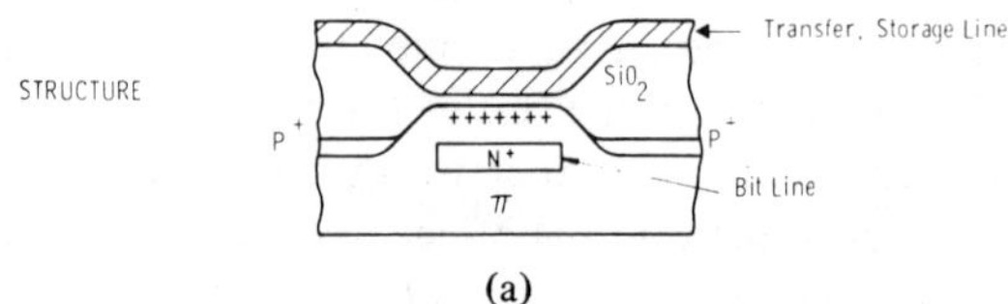

(a)

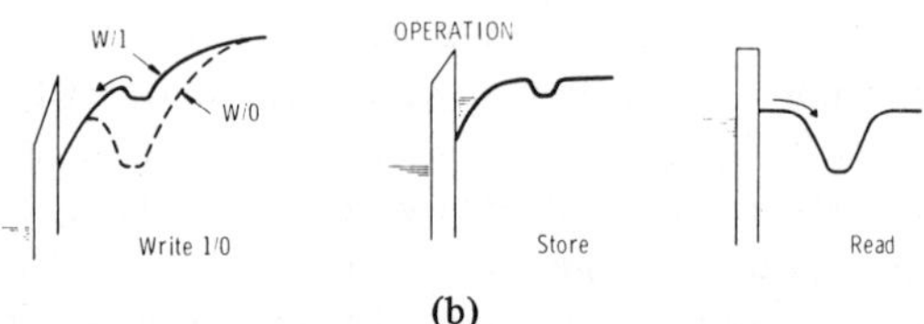

(b)

Fig. 10. (a) Cross section of the buried-bit-line RAM. (b) Energy diagram describing the operation of this cell.

2) Buried-Bit-Line Cell (BBL): A cross section of the cell is shown in Fig. 10. The cell is a planar structure in which the bit line is located below the surface, parallel to the *X* direction, and the word/storage line (transfer and storage functions have been combined into one electrode) is formed by a polysilicon or metal line running in the *Y* direction on the surface. The charge storage region is the surface depletion region of the MOS capacitor and the charge is transferred to the surface from the bit line by punchthrough of the gate depletion region.

The fabrication of this cell is similar to the punchthrough isolated cell described previously. The buried n^+ bit line may be fabricated as a DUF using a diffusion followed by the growth of an epitaxial layer or through the use of a set of ion implants. The epitaxial-layer technique is probably preferable in this case to achieve the lowest possible bit-line resistance. After the epitaxial layer has been grown, standard n-SAG processing is used except for the one step of making contact to the buried line. Wherever a contact is required, an orientation-dependent silicon etch may be used to make a groove extending from the surface to the buried line. This step will ensure reliable contacts without the use of a prolonged high-temperature cycle to allow penetration of a surface diffusion to the buried line.

In order to achieve charge storage with zero volts on the word/storage line, an additional set of boron and phosphorus ion implants may be used after polysilicon deposition to create a potential well at the surface in the low-voltage condition in a fashion similar to the Hi-*C* cell described earlier. With all of these processing options, the control on the punch-through or write voltage will be determined by the epi thickness and resistivity.

The operation of the cell is based upon the flow of charge between the surface and the buried electrode which serves as the bit/sense line. The operations of writing, storing, and reading a 0 and a 1 are shown by the energy diagrams normal to the surface in Fig. 10. The bit line has a high- and a low-value potential which correspond to the operation of writing a 1 and 0, respectively. The word line can be at a high, a low, and an intermediate potential which correspond to the write, read, and store modes, respectively. To write a 0, the word line is pulsed to the high level with the bit line at the high potential. The channel/buried diode junction is reverse biased and no signal charge is collected at the surface (deep-depletion condition). The storage condition is maintained with the word line at the intermediate level and the bit line at the high potential. In this condition the bit line serves the function of inhibiting the flow of leakage charge from the bulk to the surface.

Writing of a 1 is accomplished with the bit line at the low potential and the word line at the high level. As shown in Fig. 10(b) (write 1/0) the surface potential never attains the value it did in the case of the 0 because the junction becomes forward biased and inverts the surface. When the word line is reduced to the intermediate level, the inversion charge remains at the surface in the steady-state condition.

The read function is accomplished with the word line at the low and the bit line at the high potential. In the resulting flat-band condition any surface charge flows immediately to the bit line and the resulting voltage change is detected by the sense amplifier.

G. Stratified-Charge Memory (SCM)

The stratified-charge memory [9] concept has recently been proposed as a means of circumventing the problems presently encountered in the design of RAM's for VLSI. The cells described above provide a finite charge packet which must charge the bit-line capacitance to provide the signal. This capacitive voltage division causes the voltage swing on the bit line to be small and increases access time. The SCM cell differs from the conventional RAM structures because the signal current is determined by the threshold voltage of a buried-channel transistor rather than the charge on a capacitor. The threshold voltage is determined by the storage of minority carriers (holes) at the oxide-silicon interface. The structure of the cell is shown in cross section in Fig. 11(a).

The cell consists of two orthogonal electrodes for row and column address as well as source and drain busses that run parallel to the column electrode. The column electrode has a deep n-type implant under it, much like a buried-channel

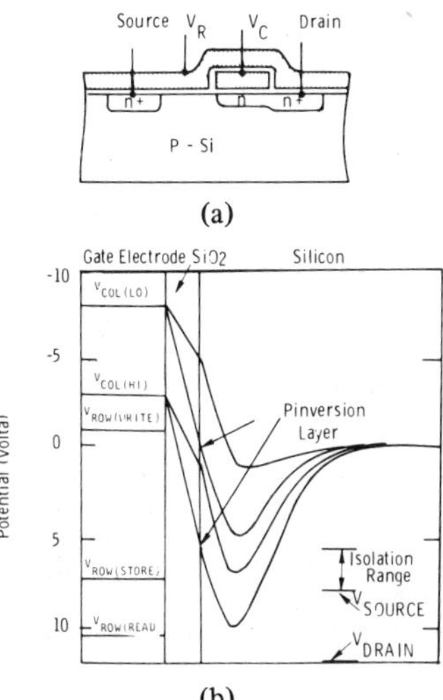

Fig. 11. (a) Cross section of a stratified-charge memory cell. (b) Potential configurations for the various modes.

CCD. The information is stored as a packet of holes at the Si/SiO_2 interface under this column electrode. The hole packet is derived from the substrate by biasing the row electrode into accumulation and selecting the gate bias on the column electrode such that the surface potential in the buried channel region attracts holes (1) or rejects holes (0) (Fig. 11(b)). If the holes are attracted, a hole inversion layer is formed which clamps the surface potential and changes the effective gain of the column transistor for a given gate potential. The holes are dynamically held at the interface by the n^+ drain on one side, surface potential on the row electrode on the other, and the n-buried channel at the bottom. However, the two edges of this column electrode which adjoin the channel stop region will, in a normal process, allow the holes to escape into the substrate. To avoid this, the channel/channel stop transition region must be carefully designed. This is the most critical consideration in the ability to realize the SCM cell.

The fabrication of this cell is straightforward since it is identical to a conventional double-polysilicon n-SAG process with the additions of a buried-channel implant.

H. Taper-Isolated Dynamic Gain Cell (TIDG)

Very recently [10] a one-transistor *only* ROM-like dRAM cell has been introduced. Its operation depends on the modulation of the threshold of a buried-channel device by a hole packet derived from the substrate and channel stop region.

The cross section of this memory cell is shown in Fig. 12. It consists of a source, drain, and gate fabricated essentially in a standard n-channel process. The channel region contains a deep n-type implant (much like a depletion MOSFET) and a shallow p-type implant. The surface potential across the width direction of this transistor is shown in Fig. 12(b). The energy of the n-type implant may be adjusted so that a significant fraction of the implanted ions penetrate the normally occurring taper region between the gate oxide and the channel stop. The shallow p-type implant is, of course, stopped in the oxide in this region. Consequently, the surface potential in the taper region will be more positive than that under the thin gate

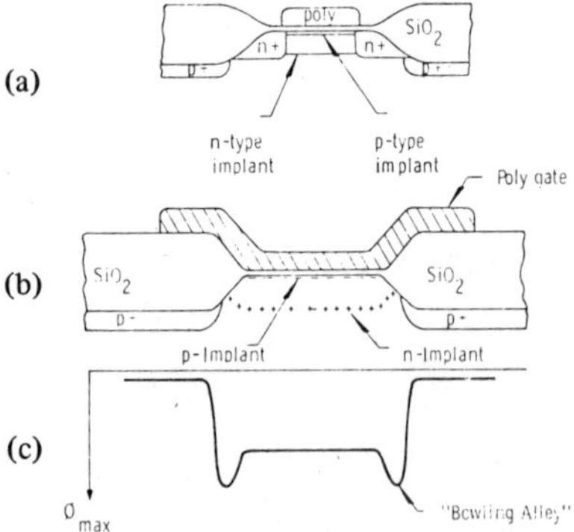

Fig. 12. (a) Cross section of the taper-isolated dynamic-gain RAM cell along the channel direction. (b) Cross section of the TIDG cell across the channel direction. (c) Potential distribution across the width of the taper region.

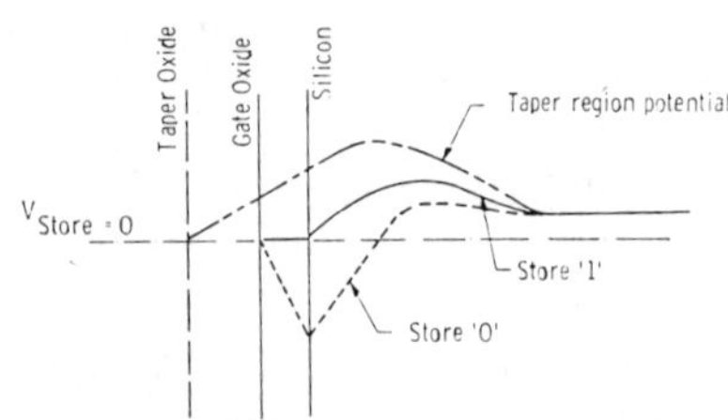

Fig. 13. Potential distribution into the depth of the silicon at the thin gate region for the STORE condition.

region, as shown in Fig. 12(c). The potential distribution across the channel is thus analogous to a "bowling alley." The surface potential in the field region is essentially at the substrate potential, if the Q_{ss} at the field oxide-silicon interface is small as is usually the case. Thus the "bowling alley" provides a potential barrier for the lateral flow of *holes* into the channel region.

The potential distribution into the depth of the silicon substrate is shown in Fig. 13, for the channel (gate oxide) and taper oxide regions. With the gate electrode held at or near zero, the taper region surface potential is *positive* with respect to both the channel and the substrate. This provides a potential barrier for *holes*. If the shallow p-type implant in the channel region is sufficiently heavy, then the surface potential under the channel region may be negative in the absence of holes at the surface (deep depletion for holes), and the potential distribution in the channel region is as shown by the label STORE 0 in Fig. 13. If, however, a packet of holes could be introduced in the channel region, then they would be trapped by the "bowling alley" on the edges of the channel and the n^+ source-drain at each end of the transistor. This sheet of holes (positive charge) would then cause a more negative V_T on the transistor such that the potential distribution under the channel region would be as labeled by STORE 1 in Fig. 13.

A selective WRITE scheme is shown in Fig. 14. The key to the understanding of the select function is the fact that the drain/source potential may be lowered to fill the channel with electrons thus eliminating the hole barrier to the substrate and channel stop region. To WRITE a 0 state, the gate is held high to obtain a surface potential ϕ_s. The drain potential is then lowered to $V_{DD} < \phi_s$ when all trapped holes flow into

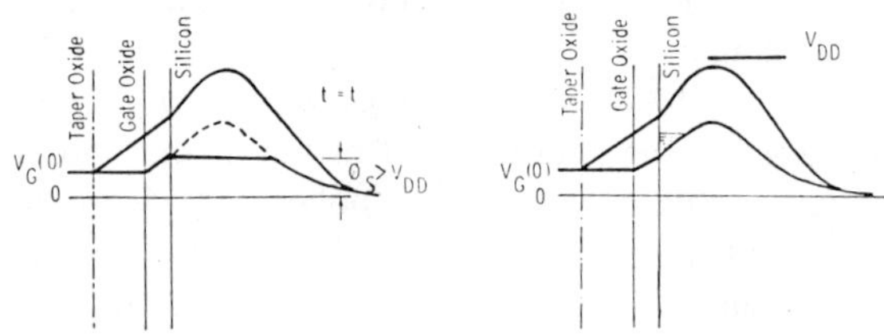

Fig. 14. Selective writing of the 0 state may be accomplished by using the drain to provide for electrons to lower the hole potential barrier and pulsing the gate on.

the substrate and channel stop. The drain potential is then raised and the gate potential lowered to obtain the 0 state. The inhibit function is performed by holding the drain high while the gate is pulsed. Similarly the WRITE 1 is performed by pulsing the gate low to where the surface potential in the bowling alley is still positive; the drain potential is then lowered to WRITE, and held high to inhibit. The p-type surface implant may be adjusted such that all the operating voltages are positive.

III. Signal Size

The primary figure of merit of a dynamic RAM cell is the effective signal it can produce to distinguish between the two binary states. In the case of the charge storage cells, it is the charge in the storage area times bit line capacitance that effectively determines the signal voltage. For the dynamic threshold cells a constant source-to-drain current rather than a constant charge is used to charge the bit-line capacitance. The differences in bit-line capacitance of the various cells need to be compensated by the charge packet size and will be considered further in Section V. In this section we shall compare the drive capabilities of different cells in terms of the charge per unit storage area for charge-storage cells and the change in current for the dynamic-threshold cells.

The comparison of the lateral-charge-storage cells was performed on devices simultaneously fabricated using electron-beam lithography, since these cells are process compatible. A nine mask, two-level polysilicon n-SAG process was used in this fabrication. Since the 1T, CC, and Hi-*C* cells are identical in operation they were fabricated to share the same bit-line and read/write circuitry. Cells with a minimum area of 65 μm^2 (0.1 mil^2) were fabricated corresponding to a packing density of ~1.5 million bits/cm^2, using 2-μm minimum features. A scaled n-SAG process with 500-Å gate oxide, 0.4-μm junctions, and ion implants to adjust threshold and punch-through voltages was used.

These cells were operated with the substrate grounded and $V_{DD} = 5$ V. The reduced voltages were required to ensure that the electric field in the oxide region was not excessive for the gate oxide thicknesses used (500 Å). In Table I we have listed the charge capacity and leakage rates per unit area of storage for 195 μm^2 and 71 μm^2 1T, CC, Hi-*C*, and 98-μm^2 MCM RAM cells. The charge capacity of the 1T, CC, and Hi-*C* cells are determined by measuring the current in the precharge node to calibrate a source follower output. The charge capacity of the MCM cell is experimentally difficult to determine since the detection involves a displacement cur-

TABLE I
COMPARISON OF THE PERFORMANCE OF dRAM CELLS

Type of Cell	Area $\mu m^2 (mil^2)$	DRIVE CAPABILITY: Charge Capacity e/cm^2	DRIVE CAPABILITY: Threshold Change Volts	LEAKAGE RATE: nA/cm^2 at 23°C	LEAKAGE RATE: $\mu A/cm^2$ at 90°C	Susceptibility to Alpha Particles
1-T	195 (.3)	1.28×10^{12}	-	1.1	1	Yes
	71 (.11)	1.2×10^{12}	-	1.3	1.1	Yes
CC	182 (.28)	1.04×10^{12}	-	.45	.22	Yes
	65 (.1)	$.99 \times 10^{12}$	-	.4	.2	Yes
Hi-C	195 (.3	2.1×10^{12}	-	.95	.98	Yes
	11 (71)	1.95×10^{12}	-	.89	.92	Yes
MCM	98 (.15)	5.4×10^{11}		8	.3	Yes
STC*	65 (.1)	2.4×10^{12}		.4	.3	Yes
VMOS**	218 (.33)	3.2×10^{12}		.8	.2	Yes
PTI	195 (.3)	3.1×10^{12}		.5	.4	Yes
BBL	195 (.3)	1.3×10^{12}		.8	.9	No
SCM***	98 (.15)	-	2.0	.3	.2	No
TIDG	80 (.125)	-	2.5	.25	.1	No

*Reference 5
**Reference 6, 7
***Reference 9

rent rather than a particle current at the output. The numbers quoted in Table I are based on capacitance ratio estimates, which may involve ±20-percent error, and is thus reflected in the output voltage swing. The CC cell shows that ~80 percent of the charge capacity of the 1T cells, whereas the charge capacity of the Hi-*C* cell is about 80 percent greater than 1T. These results bear out the high density predictions made in [2] and [3]. It is seen that the charge capacity per unit area of the 195-μm^2 cells is slightly larger than the 0.1-mil^2 cells under identical structure and operating conditions. This strongly suggests that the storage well size is really dependent on the periphery to area ratio. For the 71-μm^2 cell size, the tapered region between the gate and field oxide has a significant dimension even with scaling, this is not very surprising. This result points out a need to move away from the self-aligned thick-oxide (or LOCOS) process as higher densities are approached! The MCM cell has been operated as described in [4], but with voltage levels similar to the 1T cell. The charge capacity of the MCM cell is seen to be much smaller than that of the 1T cell.

Some of the aspects of the operation of these cells at these dimensions and voltages need to be noted. All double-level cells were fabricated assuming adequate fringing effects may be relied upon to control the interelectrode surface potential. However, in two-level polysilicon gate structures, significant interelectrode potential barriers may be introduced due to a combination of gate-oxide nonuniformity and impurity segregation effects in the interelectrode region especially in cases where implants are used for controlling the surface potentials. These interelectrode barriers are especially significant at lower operating voltages where overdrive margins are reduced, and they may cause a significant degradation of charge-storage capacity.

In order to perform the "read" operation for the MCM cell, the word line must be pulsed while the storage gate is floating which tends to mask the change in potential due to signal charge. The clock rise times are thus extremely critical to the operation of the cell. Further, the bit-line capacitance is pattern sensitive so that for the worst case where all the cells along the line are full of charge, the signal swing is small. Increasing the charge-storage capacity also increases the bit-line loading providing little advantage in signal voltage in the MCM cell. We shall discuss this further in Section V. It has been suggested that a pair of MCM cells may be used to store charge to avoid this problem. This would, of course, result in a smaller packing density.

The effective charge storage area of the VMOS cell is larger than that of a 1T cell since the entire surface of the buried-storage junction is available for charge storage. This area advantage is offset partially by the fact that the MOS capacitance per unit area can generally be made higher than the p-n junction reverse-bias capacitance per unit area. For our purposes, we shall use the projected area of the buried-storage region on the silicon surface to normalize the charge capacity in order to make a fair comparison with the lateral-charge-storage cells. The data on the VMOS cells (Table I) have been obtained from [6] and those on the PTI and BBL cells are obtained from devices fabricated by optical lithography using similar process parameters for the lateral cells, and for the n-SAG part of the process. It is instructive to note that the storage capacity per unit area on a VMOS cell is effectively 2.4 times that of the 1T cell. The PTI cell is very similar to the VMOS cell in its storage mechanism. Some tradeoffs are involved because a small fraction of the supply voltage is required to punch through to the cell; this is not a linear tradeoff because the storage capacitance decreases as the square root of the storage voltage. The BBL cell has a storage capacity that is similar to the 1T cell, for the same storage voltage.

In contrast to the charge-storage concepts where the charge packet representing the signal will shrink in direct proportion to cell area, the SCM cell may be designed to offer a signal almost invariant to scaling. This result follows from the fact that two states of threshold are being detected and the current in the high conduction state is proportional to g_m which may be adjusted by choosing an appropriate width-to-length ratio of the device to compensate for the reduction in the threshold window due to scaling. If the bit-line capacitance which the cell has to drive is reduced in scaled devices, the output signal per unit area can actually improve as the size of the memory chip is reduced. The actual signal size from this device has not been included in Table I since the mechanism is so different for this cell. However, if we consider a typical bit-line capacitance (C_b) for, say, a 64K dRAM memory and specify an access time (τ) and signal voltage swing ΔV to set a latch, the current drive Δi may be estimated from

$$\Delta i = \frac{\Delta V \cdot C_b}{\gamma \tau} \tag{2}$$

where γ represents the fraction of the access time that may be allotted to allow the bit line to be charged. The current differential between the 0 and 1 state, which may be written as

$$\Delta i = \frac{W}{L} \frac{\mu C_O'}{2} \left[V_G - (V_{T0} + V_{T1}) \right] \Delta V_T \tag{3}$$

is supplied by the device. In this expression C_O' is the effective capacitance of the buried-channel device. Thus for a given $V_G = V_{\text{STORE}}$, V_{T0} and V_{T1} one may compute the device size required to obtain the current. As an example, for

$$C_O' = 3.45 \times 10^{-8} \text{F/cm}^2, \quad V_{\text{STORE}} = 3 \text{ V}, \quad V_{T0} = -1 \text{ V},$$

$$V_{T1} = -3 \text{ V}, \quad \gamma\tau = 20 \text{ ns}$$

$\Delta V = 200$ mV, $C_b = 0.6$ pF [13], we calculate $W/L < 0.1$. This example shows how effective this cell concept is in terms of signal voltage for a given cell area. If $W/L = 1$ is used as minimum features, the access time will be significantly reduced.

IV. Leakage Considerations

Since all dynamic RAM's use a nonequilibrium condition to achieve one of the binary states, there will be a time-dependent decay process which results in this information ultimately being transformed to the other binary state. In all charge storage cells, this process occurs by the generation of minority carriers in or near the depletion region under the storage electrode which are collected in the storage well. Data in dynamic RAM cells must, therefore, be periodically refreshed in order to avoid errors. Because device geometries and charge packets are being reduced for VLSI dynamic memories, it is extremely important to understand the relative importance of various mechanisms that contribute to leakage current in dRAM cells. It has recently been shown [11], [12] that for the 1T dRAM cell, in addition to the space-charge current generated in the depletion region, and the surface-state emission under the storage electrode itself, peripheral effects are very significant for small geometries. Improved gettering techniques have now resulted in large bulk lifetimes (1-2 ms) in VLSI devices which reduce the source of leakage under the gate itself. Large bulk lifetimes, however, result in long diffusion lengths. Thus the contribution of diffusion to leakage becomes very important. This contribution has a higher activation energy than the first two and is, therefore, even more significant at high temperatures, since memory chips are typically required to operate over a wide temperature range. It is shown in [11] that the contribution to leakage from the peripheral region of an MOS storage capacitor fabricated using a local or self-aligned oxidation isolation technique may be up to 10 X higher than leakage generated under the storage itself. This is because the transition region between the gate and field oxide regions has a higher generation rate and because the periphery acts as a gated diode with the storage well as a virtual drain. Diffusion components of leakage from the bulk of the silicon substrate become dominant for processes which yield a very high bulk lifetime τ since diffusion current is proportional to $1/\sqrt{\tau}$ but the space-charge-generated current is proportional to $1/\tau$. Thus the leakage rate may be improved by using heavier doping p^+ in the substrate region, to reduce the effective minority-carrier concentration and hence the diffusion component.

With the preceeding discussion in mind, the leakage rates expected from the various cell structures may now be compared. The leakage rate is measured by emptying the storage well of the cell, stopping the clocks in a stroage mode for a known interval, and then reading the analog output of the cell due to the leakage charge. These rates as shown in Table I.

The CC cell can effectively cut off the contribution of peripheral component because the storage electrode is a ground potential during the store mode, whereas it is held at V_{DD} for the 1T and Hi-*C* cells. We have measured leakage rates in electron-beam fabricated CC cells which are as low as 0.4 nA/cm^2 at room temperature.

1T and Hi-*C* cells have a somewhat larger leakage rate at room temperature (Table I) because of added contribution from the periphery. This periphery component may be minimized if the storage region/surface potential is adjusted by the use of an ion implant allowing the cell to be operated with the storage electrode grounded. This leakage advantage in the grounded storage 1T cell has recently been demonstrated [11]. The VMOS and PTI cell structures have a strong advantage since the storage regions are isolated from the generation mechanism in the periphery. The buried region thus collects leakage charge only from the generation and diffusion components in the bulk, and not from the surface generation at the edge of the cell. The BBL cell, however, uses the MOS storage capacitor. In normal operation it would collect minority carriers from the periphery region like the 1T cell. The STC uses a double-poly capacitor for storage. Its leakage rate is proportional to that of the floating n^+ region connected to the second poly. Thus for a given cell structure, the leakage rate is expected to be higher if the storage mechanism uses an MOS capacitor with a high voltage on the gate electrode and if no provision is made for suppressing the peripheral contribution to leakage current. The vertical cells which have buried a storage region would be least affected by such peripheral effects.

The holes stored at the Si/SiO_2 interface provide the dynamic threshold shift for the SCM and TIDG cell. Only those holes which are thermally generated in the region between the Si/SiO_2 interface and the channel potential maximum contribute to leakage. Thus all leakage from field, periphery, and bulk is excluded and the cells have excellent leakage rates.

The temperature dependence of the leakage rate provides an estimate of the fractional contribution of the generation and diffusion components of leakage. The activation energy corresponding to a pure generation case is $E_g/2$ whereas that corresponding to a pure diffusion is E_g (where E_g is the silicon bandgap). The leakage rate of cells measured at 90°C is also listed in Table I. It is seen that the isolated CC cell has a lower activation of the leakage rate than the isolated 1T cell. This agrees with the data of [11] where the CC structure was shown to be capable of minimizing the field leakage component. The MCM cell shows a higher leakage rate at room temperature than the CC or 1T cell, probably because there are no bit lines in the vicinity of each cell which may attract leakage electrons, as is the case with 1T and CC cells. However, the activation energy corresponds largely to a space-charge generation condition. This may be because each cell is surrounded by accumulation gates on two edges and storage gates on the other two, so that very little peripheral contribution may be expected. The Hi-*C* cell has a leakage rate that tracks the 1T cell. The temperature dependence indicates that *all* the lateral cells have a significant diffusion contribution from the bulk and bare field region.

The leakage in the buried-storage vertical cell (VMOS and PTI) should be expected to be similar to that in a charge-coupled RAM cell for similar substrate doping. The data for the PTI cell shown in Table I agree with this prediction. The BBL cell leakage follow the 1T leakage on the basis of the periphery contribution to the storage region. However, the n^+ bit line collects the diffusion from the bulk, so that the activation energy should correspond to space-charge generation except for the bare-field component. Leakage rates reported for the VMOS cell built on p^+ substrate have a space-charge generation activation energy. The diffusion component of leakage in lateral cells may be reduced if they are constructed on a p-p^+ epitaxial substrate [11]. This allows the bulk minority carrier concentration to be reduced in the substrate, but leaves the device parameters unchanged. Thus from the leakage point of view, a CC or grounded-storage-gate cell built on such an epitaxial substrate would be comparable to a VMOS or PTI cell.

The SCM and TIDG cells have a pure space-charge generated activation so that they have ~10 X less leakage at 90°C.

Another leakage mechanism which becomes important at small geometries is the subthreshold component of current across the pass transistor in the charge-storage cells. Since the turn-off margin (V_{GS} - V_T) in the off-state and bit-line high voltage both exponentially determine this current, then a solution to this problem is to increase the channel doping concentration. However, this results in an increased threshold voltage and, therefore, in a decreased storage capacity for a given V_{DD}. The subthreshold current in a VMOS transistor accordingly is very dependent on the doping in the π region and may be significantly larger than the 1T if this doping is not increased. The PTI cell will avoid this problem since the punch-through voltage $V_P > V_T$. The SCM and TIDG cells do not have this limitation since they do not depend on charge storage.

At small geometry the generation of "soft errors" due to alpha particle tracks in the silicon [14] becomes important. Alphas are generated due to trace radioactivity in package materials and have energies of ~5 MeV. These particles generate electron-hole pairs as they come to rest in the silicon substrate. The electrons act as leakage spikes and may diffuse to the storage regions to cause soft errors. All lateral and vertical cells are prone to this error. However, BBL, SCM, and TIDG cells have a built-in mechansim which guards against soft errors, since electrons diffusing from the bulk are swept into the drain or bit line and do not disturb information. Measurements comparing 1T and TIDG cell have actually shown that the TIDG cell is ~200 X less sensitive to alpha particles than a 1T cell.

V. Packing Density

Comparison of the packing density available from the use of the various cell concepts is a major issue in the choice of the RAM cell which can be most effective for very high density memory. It is necessary, however, to select a basis on which such comparison is to be made. For the sake of objectivity we shall designate a fixed design rule as the fundamental basis. This would require the smallest patterned geometry to be 3 μm in dimension and with 3-μm spaces and ±0.5-μm alignment tolerance, based on the geometries of 64K dRAM's reported [13]. The other requirement is that the signal voltage available from the cell be equal in all cases. Thus for all charge storage cells, we require that the voltage sensed on the bit line be constant for 128 cells on a bit line. Bit-line capacitance/cell is shown in Table II. For the SCM and TIDG cells we compare the signal size following an analysis similar to that presented in Section III, where the bit-line capacitance is required to be charged to the same voltage as that obtained with the charge packet that would be available from the other cells.

Based on the above premises, cell layouts for each different concept have been generated with an effort to reduce the cell area to a minimum. The resulting cell areas for the various cells are shown in Table II. The 1T cell is based on a two-level polysilicon structure with a single contact shared between two cells [13]. As a benchmark for reference, the output voltage swing would be 200 mV as per our design rules. Thus the other cell layouts are generated so that they produce the same output voltage.

The CC cell has a slightly lower charge capacity per unit area (Table I) than the 1T but may be laid out with a similar bit-line capacitance so that it has a cell area slightly larger than that of the 1T cell. The Hi-*C* has a larger storage capacity per unit area so that it requires a smaller cell and hence has a smaller bit-line capacitance per cell.

The MCM cell is capable of high packing density conceptually. However, it has a low charge capacity, and the bit-line capacitance is pattern sensitive. Thus increasing cell area also in-

TABLE II
COMPARISON OF CELL AREAS FOR 3-μm DESIGN RULES AND EQUAL SIGNAL VOLTAGE

CELL	I-T	CC	HI-C	MCM*	STC	VMOS	PTI	BBL	SCM	TIDG
Area (μm^2)	190	216	126	120	70	190	128	220	81	55
Bit Line Capacitance/ Cell.(fF)	6	6	4.5	5-15	3.6	18	7.1	15	4.5	43.5

* Based on complementary storage on two cells to compensate for small signal and and bit pattern sensitivity as recorded for bit line capacitance.

creases bit-line capacitance and does not result in increased signal. The cell area in Table II is for complementary storage and readout which alleviates this problem partly. The signal size is still smaller (~50 percent) than the other cells.

The STC cell has an area advantage which results from the high dielectric capacitor stacked on the address gate, and a smaller pitch of the aluminum bit line which reduces the capacitance somewhat.

The VMOS cell layout is comparable to the 1T cell. As discussed in Section III the buried junction provides a larger surface area due to its three-dimensional nature, which increases the charge capacity. However, the bit line has to surround the V groove so that the bit-line capacitance is also substantially increased. Thus no real advantage in packing density is gained.

The PTI cell is very similar to the VMOS cell in its storage mechanism but has a bit line which almost resembles the 1T cell. Thus a real packing density advantage is obtained.

The vertical structure of the BBL cell loses its advantage because of the large bit-line capacitance. Since an MOS storage capacitor is used, the cell size is limited by storage area.

The SCM and TIDG cells were laid out with $W/L = 1$ for minimum geometry, although the available current was larger than that required to obtain the signal size of 200 mV in ~20 ns. The current drive in a minimum-geometry transistor is thus sufficient to provide a smaller access time.

VI. DISCUSSION AND CONCLUSIONS

We have thus far reviewed the various dRAM cell concepts and compared them on the basis of signal size, leakage current, and packing density. The signal size for the charge-storage cells was normalized to the area of storage so that a comparison of the drive capability available using various physical mechanisms could be made. It was shown that the SCM and TIDG cells could potentially provide a much larger signal for a given area. The leakage rates at room temperature and their activation energies were compared for all the cells. The packing density of the various cells was compared on the basis of a given design rule and equal signal voltage on the bit line. To complete the survey of the cells and establish an overall figure of merit, however, two other aspects must be considered. First is the relative fabrication complexity which relates directly to the yield that may be expected when the cell in question is incorporated in a memory chip. The second is the operation complexity which determines the peripheral circuitry required to exercise the memory arrays, and hence the chip size.

TABLE III
FABRICATION COMPLEXITY

Process Step	Complexity (10 Point Scale)
Epitaxy and Buried N^+	7
Thick Oxide Isolation	2
First Poly	3
Second Poly	6
Third Poly	6
Orientation Dependent Etch	5
Contact to Cell	5
Metal	3
Ion Implants (Pair)	4

Quantitative comparison of fabrication complexity is difficult since it requires an assessment of the relative yield loss probability due to various process steps. However, based on previous experience one may formulate such an assessment at least from a simplified standpoint, as shown in Table III. It is our purpose in designating these levels of process complexity, to generate a basis for arriving at an overall figure of merit for the cell structure. Each critical process step is rated on a ten point scale, based on its potential yield. Thus for example, the first level of polysilicon is rated at a complexity of 3 based on uniformity, geometry sizing, and sheet resistance consideration. In contrast, the second level of polysilicon has a complexity of 6 because of the probability of interlevel shorts. Other process complexity factors shown in Table III are generated on a similar basis.

The operational complexity is determined by the types of clock waveforms to be generated. A two-level-address clocking scheme is considered to be the simplest and is rated at 4 because it results in a peripheral circuit area which is approximately 40 percent of the memory chip area [13]. The

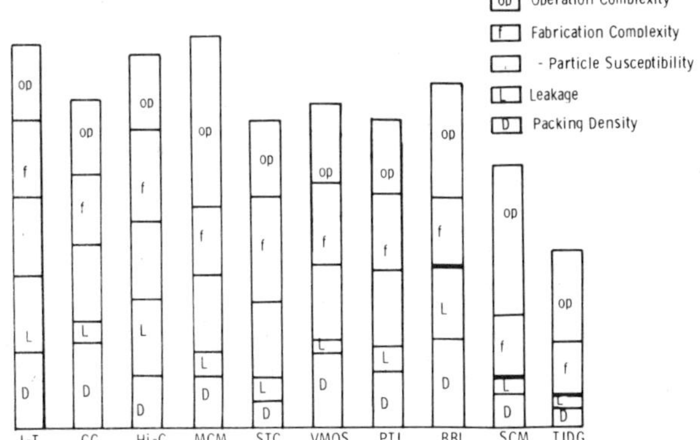

Fig. 15. Bar chart comparing the overall figure of merit of the various RAM cells. The bars are composed of cell area, fabrication complexity and operation complexity, leakage rate and alpha particle sensitivity.

TABLE IV
OPERATION COMPLEXITY

Operation	Complexity (10 Point Scale)
Two Level (Binary) Clocks	4
Three Level Clocks	6
Negative Clock Voltage	2
Critical Timing	2

increased peripheral area required for the clocking requirements of the other cells are estimated and scale factors are assigned in Table IV.

To arrive at the overall figure of merit of a dRAM cell, we combine the data of Tables I, II, III, and IV as follows. The 90°C leakage and alpha particle susceptibility data from Table I and packing density data of Table II are normalized to the 1T cell. Similarly, the process and operating complexity established for each cell by adding the assigned levels in Tables III and IV are normalized to the process and operating complexity evaluated for the 1T cell. Using these data we construct the bar chart of Fig. 15. To the extent that the cell layout used to generate this chart was on an equal signal-size basis, the bar size for each cell in Fig. 15 may be construed as its overall figure of merit. The cell with the minimum bar height will be considered the most suitable for high-density memories.

The CC cell has a slight fabrication advantage because a single polysilicon electrode process may be used. However, this is partly offset by the fact that the pair of ion implants necessary for its fabrication are to be critically registered (p implant must be contained, within the n implant laterally). The area advantage of the Hi-*C* cell is also offset by this requirement. The MCM cell can be fabricated in a very simple process and does not need a contact in the cell. However, complex three-level clocks are required with both negative and positive levels, and critical rise and fall times to operate the cell. In addition, the signal swing is pattern sensitive. The VMOS and PTI cells are functionally and structurally similar. The VMOS cell suffers from a large bit-line capacitance. In the latter, the V groove is replaced by a set of ion implants to generate an accurate punchthrough voltage. The operation of these cells is identical to the 1T cell. The density advantage of the STC cell is offset by its fabrication complexity. The BBL cell requires the V-groove etch to form the bias to the bit line. Its operation requires a three-level clocking scheme. The cell area and fabrication advantage of the SCM cell is also offset by the three-level positive/negative clock waveform.

The TIDG cell has more packing density than the SCM cell and may be operated with all positive voltages with binary clocks and an extra power supply.

The above discussion shows that based on this figure of merit the STC, VMOS, and PTI cells are the most promising charge-storage concepts. However, the TIDG cell is seen to have a very significant overall advantage over the charge-storage concepts.

The complexity factors attributed to various process and operation steps in this paper are based on our experience and are somewhat subjective. The reader may easily modify these factors to represent his own experience. It is our purpose to develop the concept of an overall figure of merit for dRAM cells which may be applied to evaluate innovative cell concepts in the future and should prove to be valuable to VLSI memory design.

ACKNOWLEDGMENT

The authors would like to thank H. G. Hurlbut, H. H. Chao, T. C. Holloway, T. G. Blocker, K. E. Bean, and A. H. Shah for their help in various stages of this work.

REFERENCES

[1] W. F. Kosonocky, "Charge coupled memory," U.S. Patent 3 720 933. W. E. Engeler, J. J. Tiemann, and R. D. Baertsch, "A surface charge random access memory system," *IEEE J. Solid-State Circuits*, vol. SC-7, p. 330, 1972.

[2] A. F. Tasch, Jr., R. C. Frye, and H-S. Fu, "The charge coupled RAM cell concept," *IEEE Trans. Electron Devices*, vol. ED-23, p. 126, 1976.

[3] A. F. Tasch, Jr., P. K. Chatterjee, H-S. Fu, and T. C. Holloway, "The Hi-C RAM cell concept," *IEEE Trans. Electron Devices*, vol. ED-25, p. 33, 1978.

[4] H. S. Lee, "Merged charge memory," *IBM J. Res. Develop.*, p. 402, Sept. 1977. Also, H. S. Lee and W. D. Pricer, in *IEEE IEDM Tech. Digest*, p. 15, 1976.

[5] M. Koyanaji, H. Surami, N. Hoshimoto, and M. Ashikawa, "Novel high density, stacked capacitor MOS RAM," in *IEEE IEDM Tech. Digest*, p. 348, 1978.

[6] J. J. Barnes, S. N. Shadbe, and F. B. Jenne, "The buried-source VMOS dynamic RAM device," in *IEEE IEDM Tech. Digest*, p. 272, 1978.

[7] D. V. Essl, R. Losehand, and B. Rehn, "A 64K bit VMOS RAM," in *ISSCC Tech. Digest*, Feb. 1979.

[8] G. W. Taylor, P. K. Chatterjee, H-S. Fu, and A. F. Tasch, Jr., "A punch-through isolated RAM cell," in *IEEE IEDM Tech. Digest*, p. 352, 1978.

[9] D. Erb, "Stratified charge memory," in *ISSCC Tech. Digest*, p. 24, 1978.

[10] P. K. Chatterjee, G. W. Taylor, and M. Malwah, "Taper isolated dynamic gain RAM cell," in *IEEE IEDM Tech. Digest* (Late News), 1978.

[11] P. K. Chatterjee, G. W. Taylor, A. F. Tasch, Jr., and H-S. Fu, "Leakage studies in high-density dynamic MOS memory devices," *IEEE Trans. Electron Devices*, vol. ED-26, pp. 564–576, Apr. 1979.

[12] R. C. Sun and J. T. Clemens, "Characterization of reverse-bias leakage currents and their effects on the holding time characteristics of MOS dynamic RAMs," in *IEEE IEDM Tech. Digest*, p. 254, Dec. 1977.

[13] G. R. M. Rao and J. Hewkins, "64-K dynamic RAM needs only one 5-volt supply to outstrip 16-K parts," *Electron.*, p. 109, Sept. 28, 1978.

[14] T. C. May and M. H. Woods, "Alpha-particle-induced soft errors in dynamic memories," *IEEE Trans. Electron Devices*, vol. ED-26, p. 2, Jan. 1979.

One-Device Cells for Dynamic Random-Access Memories: A Tutorial

V. LEO RIDEOUT, MEMBER, IEEE

Abstract—The evolutionary development of one-device cells for dynamic random-access memory (RAM) integrated circuits is described in this paper. From an examination of the areal layout (planar top view) and the cross section (vertical topography), various memory cells are compared in a systematic manner. Structural features such as contact via formation, bit-line and word-line pitch, metal step coverage, and cell placement along the bit line are also considered. Some new dynamic RAM cell concepts such as doubly doped storage capacitors, self-registering contacts, and VMOS FET's are discussed. From an examination of commercially available dynamic RAM chips, a basic lithographic groundrule was determined. It will be shown that, although this lithographic figure of merit has steadily decreased over the past four years, the number of lithographic squares per cell has remained constant for different cell types.

I. Introduction

THE COMBINATION of high packing density, moderate speed-power product, and low cost per bit of the one-device cell used in MOSFET dynamic random-access memories (RAM's) is unmatched by any other integrated-circuit memory product. For any given lithographic capability, the area of the memory cell layout is a crucial focal point for dynamic RAM design because cell density has a direct impact on chip performance and on production cost. In this paper, the evolutionary development of one-device cell design will be described. Then the structure of one-device memory cells will be compared in a systematic manner. By structure we mean the areal layout (planar top view) and the cross section (vertical topography). Other features such as metal step coverage, contact hole formation, cell placement along the bit line, and number of masking operations will be considered. In addition, some new dynamic RAM cell concepts such as doubly doped storage capacitors, self-registering contacts, and VMOS FET's will be discussed.

Manuscript received March 30, 1979.

The author is with IBM Thomas J. Watson Research Center, Yorktown Heights, NY 10598.

The structure of the memory cell results from the lithographic masking sequence and the thin-film (layer) processing steps which comprise the fabrication process. The number and sequence of processing steps and masking operations, the ease of electrically interconnecting various conductive regions of the MOSFET's, and the manner of isolating adjacent devices distinguishes one integrated-circuit process from another. Such comparisons constitute an important technical exercise, because the choice of a particular MOSFET structure and its associated fabrication process will determine the density and performance of the memory cell array and its peripheral support circuits, as well as the capability for fabricating other MOSFET products such as microprocessors, ROM's, or CCD's.

The dynamic memory cell layout is an excellent measure of a manufacturer's basic groundrule capability because in the cell the linewidth resolution, overlay capability, and edge bias tolerance are all brought into play. Often a less aggressive groundrule is used in sensing, addressing, and decoding circuits located peripherally to the array of cells. By the term groundrule, we mean the minimum exposable linewidth or linespacing of a photoresist image, a single-dimensional figure of merit which describes the lithographic capability. From an examination of commercially available dynamic RAM cells it will be shown that the basic lithographic groundrule used in production has steadily decreased from about 5 μm in 1974 to 4 μm in 1976, and to 3.5 μm in 1978. Furthermore, it will be shown that the number of lithographic squares per cell (i.e., a square with a side equal to the basic groundrule) depends on the cell type and is independent of the lithographic capability.

II. One-Device Cell Operation

A. Operation

The one-device memory cell and its read/write operation was invented by Dennard [1]. As shown in Fig. 1(a), a memory

Reprinted from *IEEE Trans. Electron Devices*, vol. ED–26, pp. 839–852, June 1979.

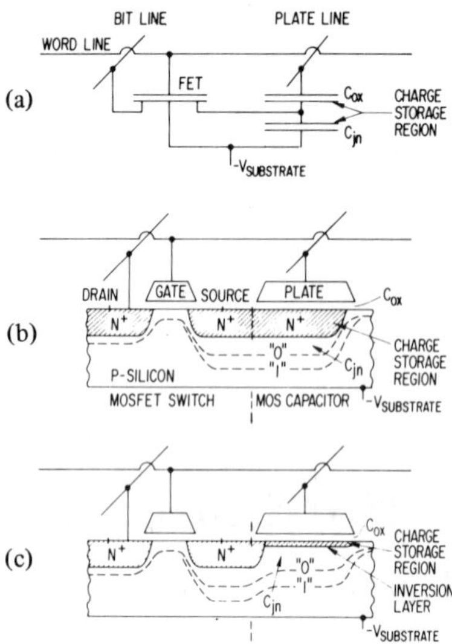

Fig. 1. One-device memory cell illustrating (a) circuit, (b) basic structure with diffusion storage, and (c) basic structure with inversion storage.

cell consists of a transistor (a MOSFET switch) and a charge storage capacitor. Because it contains a single active device, the cell is often referred to as a one-transistor or one-device cell. Typically, the storage capacitance consists of two components connected in parallel; an MOS capacitance and a junction capacitance. The bias-independent MOS capacitance is generally much larger (e.g., 5 to 10 times larger) than the voltage-dependent junction capacitance. The storage capacitor electrode that connects to the source region of the MOSFET can be an n-type diffused region as shown in Fig. 1(b), or an inversion layer of electrons as shown in Fig. 1(c). In this paper all examples will assume the n-channel or "NMOS" technology.

The MOSFET in the cell is used to electrically connect a selected capacitor storage element to an input/output line called the bit or column line. The control line that connects to the gate of the MOSFET switch is referred to as a word or row line. Typically, the charge storage capacitor is operated in two states, the neutral and the charged states which represent a binary "0" and "1," respectively. The stable or "0" state is established by the electrons normally present in an n-type doped region (Fig. 1(b)), or in a surface inversion layer under a biased plate electrode (Fig. 1(c)). The charged or metastable "1" state is established by removing some (e.g., 10^6 or more) of these electrons through the MOSFET switch. In the charged or "1" state, the charge storage region will gradually discharge to the "0" state due to leakage currents from the surface, the substrate, or the MOSFET switch, and hence the charged state must be periodically refreshed. For this reason, the cell is often referred to as a dynamic memory cell. Other names include charge switched or switched capacitor dynamic RAM cell.

As shown in Fig. 1, in its most general implementation, the one-device cell is connected to three array interconnection lines consisting of two address lines termed the MOSFET gate or word line and the MOSFET drain or bit line, and the upper capacitor electrode line referred to here as the plate line. The word and bit lines are orthogonal to each other and one of them must cross over and be insulated from the other. In addition, one of them must cross over or pass beside and be insulated from the plate line. The manner in which the three lines are electrically insulated from one another has a significant impact on the cell size and packing density. Another important density consideration is the manner in which the metal interconnection line pattern makes electrical connection to the drain region or to the gate region in the cell.

B. Figures of Merit

Two important figures of merit for a dynamic RAM cell are the number of lithographic squares per cell area, a density figure of merit, and the charge transfer ratio, a performance figure of merit [2]. The minimum exposable linewidth or linespacing in a photoresist pattern on the chip is termed the basic lithographic groundrule. Knowing the cell area and basic groundrule one can calculate the number of minimum lithographic squares per cell (i.e., a square whose side equals the basic groundrule). One-device cell areas typically range from 20 to 50 lithographic squares per cell.

The charge transfer ratio T is a measure of the voltage division that occurs when a charged storage capacitor is connected to a capacitive bit line, and is given by

$$T = \frac{C_s}{C_s + nC_{BL}} = \frac{1}{1 + nC_{BL}/C_s} \leqslant 1 \tag{1}$$

where C_s is the storage capacitance, C_{BL} the bit-line element capacitance in the cell, and n the number of cells on the bit line. Typical transfer ratios are of the order of 5 to 25 percent. The sense amplifier attached to the bit line has a gain-bandwidth product that partially determines the time to access a bit of information from a given cell location. Consquently, it is desirable to increase the transfer ratio by increasing C_s or by decreasing C_{BL}. The means for doing this and the resultant implications will be discussed later. In order to minimize the total number of sense amplifiers on the chip, n is maintained as large as possible. As illustrated in Fig. 2, in order to compare various dynamic RAM technologies it is useful to plot the transfer ratio versus the number of lithographic squares per cell for a fixed value of n and for a given lithographic groundrule.

Exercises comparing various RAM technologies must also consider other figures of merit relating to processing complexity (number of lithographic masking operations, etching steps, and high-temperature treatments), chip performance (access/cycle time, refresh period, and power dissipation), and cost (chip size, yield, and packaging). Thus making accurate comparisons of competing cell technologies is obviously a complicated procedure. In the polysilicon-gate MOSFET technology, however, a definite historical trend is evident; increased process complexity has been introduced to achieve higher cell packing density and smaller chips. As RAM chips progressed from 4 to 16 to now 64K bits, one can observe a transition from single polysilicon, to single polysilicon with buried contacts, to double polysilicon, then double polysilicon with buried contacts and depletion-mode loads, and recently even triple polysilicon. Circuit complexity

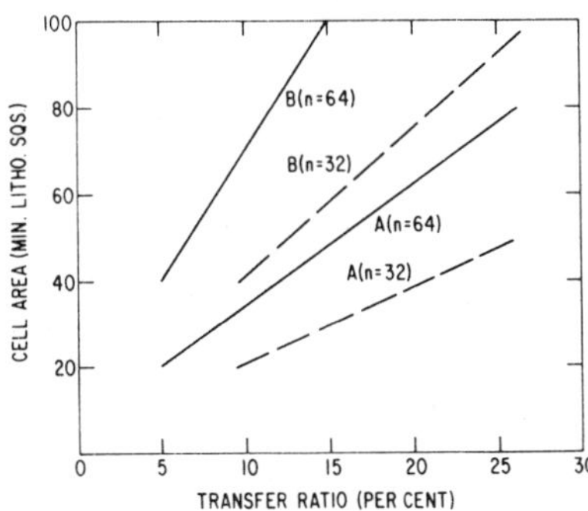

Fig. 2. Hypothetical transfer ratio versus cell area relationship for two cell types. Cell *A* exhibits the higher performance for a given cell area.

has also increased to help reduce chip power (e.g., dynamic circuitry) and the number of pin outputs (e.g., multiplexed inputs).

In the fabrication of one-device cell dynamic RAM's, several structural variations are feasible

- the MOSFET technology can be metal-gate, polysilicon-gate, or a hybrid of the two technologies;
- the cell capacitor can store charge in an inversion layer or in a diffused region of the semiconductor substrate;
- the isolation between cells can be conventional thick oxide, recessed thick oxide, or field shield;
- the word, bit, and plate lines can be fabricated from various combinations of metal, polysilicon, or diffused silicon wiring.

These structural features will now be discussed.

III. Cell Types

One-device cell RAM's emerged first as 2K-bit parts [3], but the first major commercial success was as 4K-bit NMOS parts. The initial acceptance of one-device cell RAM's was as minicomputer memories where cost is paramount, but more recently these RAM's (especially the 16K-bit parts) have also found acceptance as main memories for large computers where cost is important if the speed objective can be met. Although they offer low standby power consumption, dynamic RAM's are less attractive for microprocessor applications where the more costly static RAM's with their simpler operation are generally preferred. One means to overcoming this difficulty is exemplified by a recently announced 4K-bit RAM [4] in which each dynamic one-device cell has its own automatic refresh circuit so that, to the user, the chip operates as a static RAM.

Since the introduction of commercially successful, mass produced, 4K-bit, one-device cell dynamic RAM's in 1974, a confusing variety of cell types has emerged as the technology progressed from 4 to 16 and now 64K bits per chip. Later, we will develop a methodology for cataloging and comparing cell types based on the cell wiring, i.e., the arrangement of the bias and control lines to drain, gate, and plate. Initially, however, it is simpler to describe the evolution of one-device cell structures in terms of the development of various MOSFET technologies.

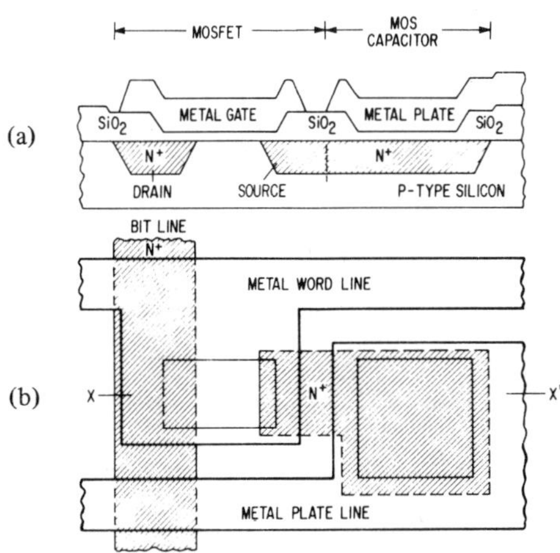

Fig. 3. Simple metal-gate cell. The cross section shown in (a) is taken along the line XX' of (b).

A. Metal-Gate Cell

In terms of processing simplicity, a major attraction of the one-device cell structure is that the technology used to form the MOSFET switch can also be used to form the MOS charge storage capacitor. This feature is illustrated in Fig. 3(a) which shows a cross section of the original cell disclosed by Dennard [1] using a simple four-mask metal-gate process [5] with conventional thick oxide isolation. The lower capacitor electrode is provided by extending the n^+ source diffusion under the metal (e.g., Al) capacitor plate. This is referred to as a junction or diffusion storage capacitor. Because they are made from the same material layer, the metal-gate word line and the metal capacitor plate line cannot pass over one another and still be electrically isolated. Consequently, as shown in Fig. 3(b), the two metal lines must pass alongside of each other and this consumes valuable chip area.

In order to reduce the cell area, the metal-gate word line should cross over and be insulated from the capacitor storage plate. Conceivably, to accomplish this, one could add a second layer of metal wiring to the cell of Fig. 3. One constraint to using a second level of metal wiring is cost because two masking operations must be added, one for the second metal layer pattern and one for the associated contact hole pattern.

A drawback of the non-self-aligned metal-gate structure of Fig. 3 is the larger parasitic overlap capacitance between the gate and the source or drain. Self-aligned metal-gate structures can be obtained by using a nonoxidizing silicon nitride layer in the gate region or by using a polysilicon gate, and the metal crossover can be facilitated by using a polysilicon plate as will now be discussed.

B. Metal-Gate/Polysilicon-Plate Hybrid Cell

In the hybrid approach, a polysilicon-gate technology is used to provide the plate and a metal-gate technology is used to provide the MOSFET's in the cells and in the peripheral circuits. A hybrid cell was used in one of the first commercial 4K-bit RAM's [6]. As shown in Fig. 4, the basic idea is to use an n-type polysilicon layer for the storage capacitor and thermally grow a thick SiO_2 insulation layer over it. Seven

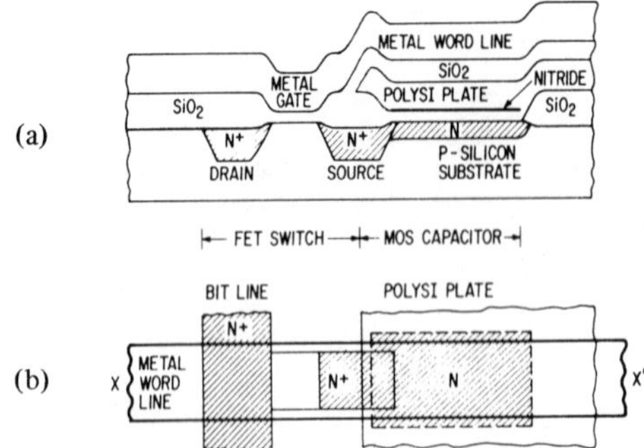

Fig. 4. Metal-gate/polysilicon-plate hybrid cell using recessed oxide isolation between cells. The cross section shown in (a) is taken along the line XX' of (b).

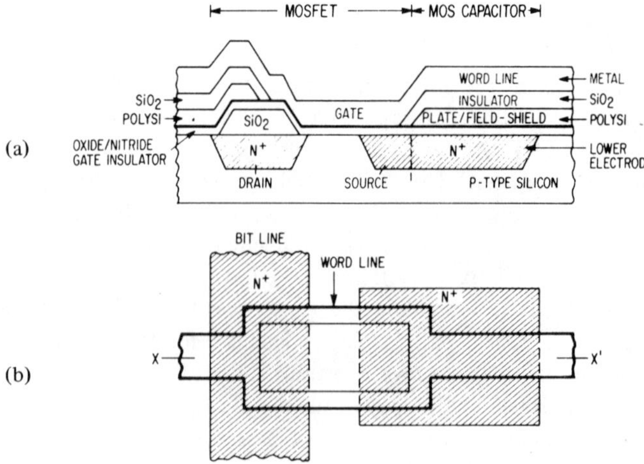

Fig. 5. Hybrid silicon and aluminum MOS cell with p-type polysilicon field shield. The cross section shown in (a) is taken along the line XX' of (b).

basic masking operations were required. Early in the process, a thin nitride layer prevented oxidation in the gate and capacitor regions. Later, the nitride in the gate area was removed and the gate oxide regrown.

The use of nitride layers to provide the gate or plate dielectric and a nonoxidizing layer presents several difficulties. For example, during high-temperature oxidation, the nitride layer may crack allowing local oxide islands to form. Also, oxide–nitride dual dielectrics are more susceptible to threshold shift problems due to hot-electron trapping at the oxide–nitride interface [7]. Nevertheless, these technical difficulties can be overcome.

Another form of hybrid cell [8] is shown in Fig. 5. Crossover capability is provided by a p-type polysilicon field-shield layer which serves as both the storage capacitor plate and the field isolation between cells. The p-type polysilicon field-shield material, however, generally is not available for use as an interconnection line material nor as a MOSFET gate electrode material due to its other functions. The field shield is maintained at substrate potential. The nitride layer serves as both a passivation layer and an oxidation barrier. This hybrid technology cell is relatively simple to fabricate and it offers diffusion storage and a compact cell layout with five basic masking operations. This cell is used by IBM in recently announced 18, 32, and 64K-bit dynamic RAM's [9].

The major attraction of a p-type field shield in the NMOS technology is that extremely low surface leakage can be obtained [10]. Attempts have been made to utilize n-type polysilicon-gate material as a field shield [11], but the built-in potential difference of about 1 V between n- and p-type polysilicon is critical to leakage control [10]. When a p-type field shield is maintained at substrate potential, pinholes in the plate oxide will lead to an inoperative cell, but no leakage current will flow from plate to substrate. This feature is attractive to on-chip redundancy in which faulty cells are switched out of operation but the storage plates for the bad cells are retained intact [9].

A major attraction of a metal-gate technology for dynamic RAM's is that a contact hole connecting the word line and the gate electrode is unnecessary as they are one and the same, while a major attraction of a polysilicon capacitor plate is that it may be easily insulated from a metal word line to facilitate the crossover. The hybrid metal-gate/polysilicon-plate cell of Fig. 5 combines these two features to obtain a relatively smaller cell than either a single-polysilicon-layer or single-metal-layer technology can provide. The smaller cell results from the very close spacing of gate and plate electrodes which removes the source region between them. Actually, the metal gate overlaps the polysilicon plate, a feature that can also be achieved and used to advantage with two layers of polysilicon, as will be discussed later in Section III-H.

Despite refinements of the metal-gate technology, the NMOS polysilicon-gate MOSFET technology is the most widely adopted integrated-circuit technology for dynamic RAM's by virtue of its dense cell structure, versatile low-capacitance interconnection wiring, and broad product commonality. Various polysilicon-gate cell types will now be considered.

C. Single-Polysilicon Cell with Diffused Bit Line

Fig. 6 shows a one-device cell [12] fabricated with a four-mask, single-polysilicon-layer process. The cell is characterized by a diffused bit line and a metal word line that connects to the polysilicon gate. The word-line connection is made using a contact hole or "via" etched through the oxide insulation layer over the polysilicon. The contact hole can be located at the side of the channel (as shown here) or over the channel [13] which offers a smaller cell area but requires a more stringent mask-to-mask alignment procedure. This type of cell has been successfully, used in a number of commercial 4K-bit dynamic RAM's [14].

Although the single-polysilicon cell is potentially not as small as a hybrid-technology cell because of the required separation between gate and plate (i.e., the source region in Fig. 6), the processing is simple (only four basic masks are required), the MOSFET gate is self-aligned to the source and drain, and no nitride layers are required. Because the polysilicon regions are covered with an insulating layer of silicon dioxide, the metal word line can cross over or connect to the

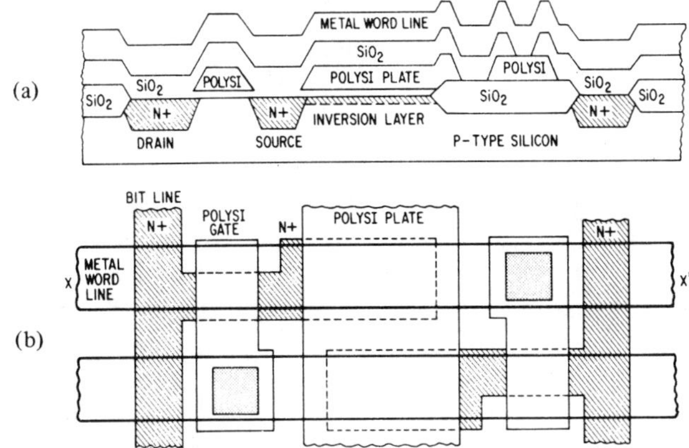

Fig. 6. Single-polysilicon cell with diffused bit line. The cross section shown in (a) is taken along the line XX' in (b).

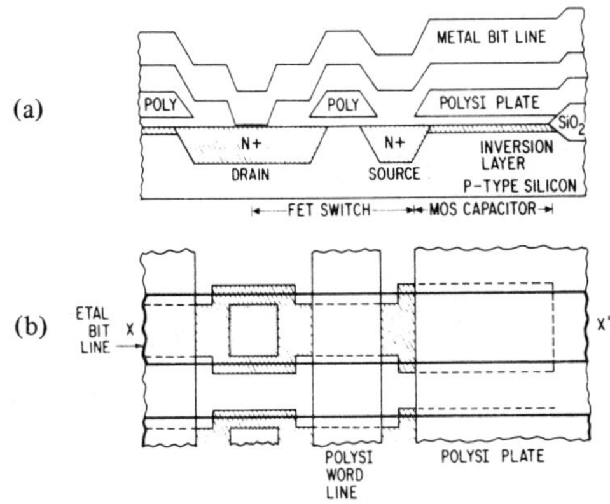

Fig. 7. Single-polysilicon cell with metal bit line. The cross section shown in (a) is taken along line XX' of (b).

polysilicon regions as desired. In addition to its functions as a MOSFET gate or MOS capacitor electrode, the polysilicon can also serve as an interconnection line, for example, for interconnecting adjacent plate electrodes in the cell array or gates in the decoder circuits. This extra wiring capability is particularly attractive for the support circuits located peripherally to the RAM cell array.

As shown in Fig. 6(a), the lower capacitor electrode is an inversion charge layer of electrons developed by biasing the plate with a large positive bias (e.g., 5 to 12 V) considerably in excess of the inversion threshold (e.g., 1 to 2 V). This is the neutral or stable "0" state. The charged metastable "1" state is established by removing some (e.g., 10^6 or more) of the electrons comprising the inversion charge. Inversion storage is commonly used in 4K-bit single-polysilicon and 16K-bit double-polysilicon dynamic RAM's. In contrast, metal-gate cells usually utilize diffusion storage (Figs. 3–5). Diffusion storage is generally considered preferable to inversion storage for several reasons and is utilized whenever it is feasible or required. One attraction of diffusion storage is that the capacitor plate need not be biased to the high positive bias required to form the inversion layer; on the contrary, the plate may be maintained at ground [6] or at negative substrate potential [9]. In one commercial polysilicon-gate 4K-bit RAM an additional masking step was used to deliberately provide an n-type implant in the capacitor region as in Fig. 4, thereby converting an otherwise inversion-storage capacitor to a depletion-storage capacitor. With inversion storage, the size of the charge packet is more likely to vary (skew) from cell to cell due to oxide charge problems, etc. Adding an n-type diffusion-storage region alleviates this problem.

In one-device cells, at least one of the control or bias lines is of metal, usually Al, due to the lower resistance. In metal-gate technology, the metal line to the cell is invariably the word line which also provides the metal gate of the MOSFET switch. An important structural feature that strongly influences the area of a polysilicon gate cell is the means for connecting the metal control line to the gate or the drain of the MOSFET in the cell. Incompletely etched contact holes are a potential reliability concern, and the contact holes generally utilize the minimum lithographic feature size in order to minimize cell area. The diffused bit-line cell of Fig. 6 uses a metal word line and requires one etched contact hole per cell.

D. Single-Polysilicon Cell with Metal Bit Line

A smaller cell may be fabricated with the four-mask single-polysilicon-layer process by using a metal bit line and polysilicon word line, as shown in Fig. 7. Here the contact hole connecting the metal bit line to the drain region is shared between two cells thereby halving the number of contact holes which leads to a density savings. This cell has been used in a number of commercial 4K-bit RAM's and in a 16K-bit [15] and a 64K-bit chip [16].

One difficulty with the polysilicon word-line cell of Fig. 7 relates to the relatively large *RC* time constant of the long polysilicon word line due to the inherently high sheet resistance of polysilicon (e.g., about 20 to 50 Ω/square). A metallized polysilicon line with much lower sheet resistance [17] would be advantageous here. Another difficulty with this cell is that the layout of the charge sense amplifiers cannot easily match the very small pitch of the bit lines. To compensate for this, buried contacts (i.e., direct polysilicon to diffusion contacts) are invariably used in the sense amplifiers and, in some cases [15], [16], the storage capacitor is rotated to increase the bit-line pitch.

E. Twin Cells

The use of a twin cell, i.e., two cells per binary bit [9], [18], [19], relieves the sense amplifier spacing problem of the metal bit-line cell of Fig. 7. As shown in Fig. 8, in a twin cell the two cells are placed side by side sharing a common word line and the two bit lines connect to a common sense amplifier. One cell stores a binary "1" and the other a "0," or *vice versa.* The most important attribute of the twin cell is very close tolerance tracking between the cell and its twin which alternately serve as the dummy comparison cell during sensing. Since the mask-to-mask misalignment in one cell tracks with the adjacent twin, excellent electrical balance is achieved naturally. In addition, the accessed cell and its twin are always

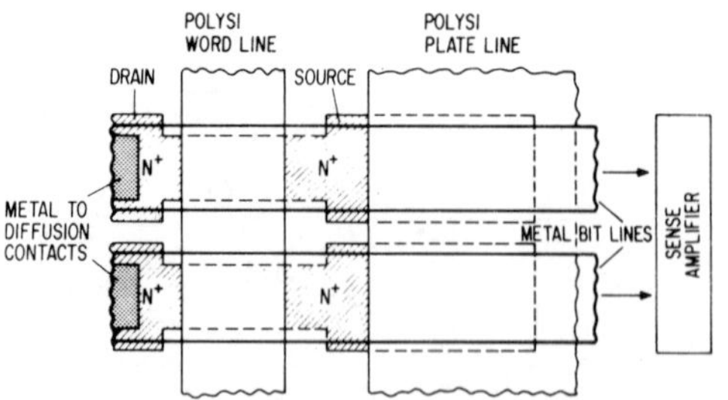

Fig. 8. Twin cells using single-polysilicon cells with metal bit lines and a common polysilicon word line.

equal bit-line distances away from the sense amplifier. This gives improved noise margins (i.e., due to common-mode rejection) over single cell arrays. Another attraction is that the sense amplifiers can be located at the side of the array and do not have to be located between two halves of the array. Because of its layout, the metal bit-line cell of Fig. 7 is ideally suited for use as a twin cell.

For a given number of bits on a chip, the twin cell offers potentially shorter cycle time at the expense of a larger array of cells [18]. Compared to the single-cell approach, the density penalty associated with the use of two cells per bit is somewhat diminished because the number and complexity of peripheral circuits are not necessarily increased when twin cells are used. In a dynamic RAM chip, only about 30 to 50 percent of the chip area is covered with cells, the rest being devoted to sense amplifiers, control and clocking circuits, protective devices, and bonding pads. Thus for example, doubling the array area may only cause an increase of about 25 percent in total chip area. This will be tolerable if the speed or yield improvements afforded by the twin cell are sufficiently attractive. The twin cell is used in several commercial 4K-bit RAM's [18] and in a recently announced 18K-bit RAM [9].

F. Extra Masking Operations

One of the most important attributes of MOSFET integrated-circuit technology is processing simplicity. The complexity and hence the cost of a process is directly proportional to the number of basic lithographic masking operations which is typically four to six for a MOSFET process. In comparison, bipolar processes often require eight or more masking operations. Notwithstanding the desire to keep MOSFET masking steps at a minimum, extra masking operations may be tolerated if the cell packing density or circuit performance improvement is large enough to offset the added processing cost and the potentially decreased fabrication yield. Examples of extra masking operations that may be added to a basic four-mask polysilicon-gate process include depletion-mode channel adjustment, direct ("buried") polysilicon-to-diffused region contacts, additional polysilicon layers, and self-registered metal-to-polysilicon contacts. For the highest density and highest performance RAM technology, such techniques offer important structural advantages, but at the expense of increased process complexity.

With the simple metal gate cell of Fig. 3, and with the hybrid field-shield cell of Fig. 5, the n$^+$ source and drain regions are formed prior to defining the metal-gate electrode pattern; consequently, the source diffusion can conveniently be extended under the capacitor plate to provide a diffused storage region. In the self-aligned polysilicon-gate technology, the polysilicon regions block the source and drain diffusion and the n$^+$ source region cannot be extended under the polysilicon plate without additional process steps. An extra masking operation can be used, however, to provide an implanted n-type diffused storage electrode as discussed earlier. The additional processing cost of a fifth masking operation may be compensated for by improved yield resulting from elimination of variations in the magnitude of the inversion storage charge. Similarly, if a lighter n-type depletion-mode implant is used in the peripheral circuits it might also be used in the diffused storage region [20].

An extra masking step can also be employed to provide a direct connection between n-type polysilicon and n-type diffused source and drain regions of the substrate [21]. Because the polysilicon is covered with an insulating silicon dioxide layer, and since a metal line may cross over it, the direct polysilicon-to-diffusion contact is often referred to as a "buried" contact. Wherever the polysilicon pattern crosses the contact area pattern, a contact is made. The buried contact improves the wiring capability of a polysilicon process and is frequently used in peripheral circuits of 4 and 16K-bit dynamic RAM's to improve circuit density and, additionally, to directly connect first-layer polysilicon to second-layer polysilicon. We will now discuss how the buried contact can also be used in the memory cell.

(a)

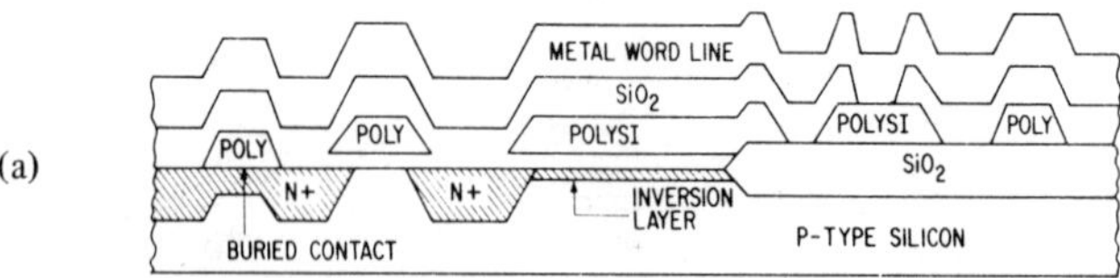

(b)

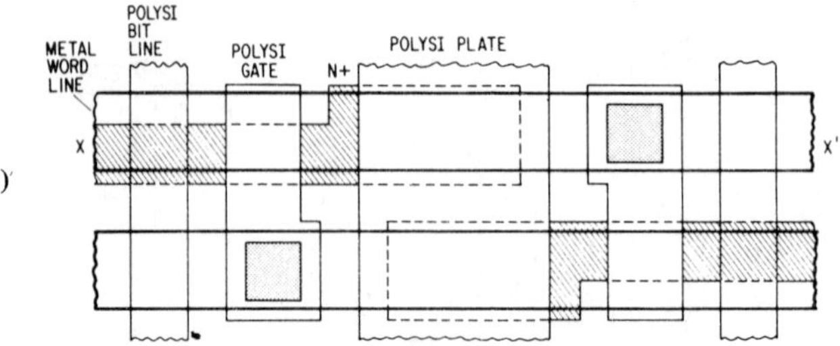

Fig. 9. Single-polysilicon cell with polysilicon bit line. The cross section shown in (a) is taken along line XX' of (b).

G. Single-Polysilicon Cell with Polysilicon Bit Line

The buried contact step can also be applied in the cell to provide a polysilicon bit-line cell as shown in Fig. 9. In the diffused bit-line cell of Fig. 6, the bit-line capacitance is largely due to the diffusion capacitance in the p-type silicon substrate. In contrast, with the polysilicon bit-line cell of Fig. 9, much of the bit-line area is separated from the substrate by the thick field isolation oxide which reduces the bit-line capacitance, thereby improving the transfer ratio (see (1)). An inherent difficulty with polysilicon bit-line cells relates to the misalignment between the bit line and the buried contact border which can create structural difficulties at the edge of the MOSFET channel.

An RAM chip using the single-polysilicon cell with a polysilicon bit line has not been commercially produced. A comparative study [16] of single-polysilicon-gate cells led to the conclusion that, for a given area cell, the metal bit-line cell of Fig. 7 had the highest transfer ratio, the diffused bit-line cell of Fig. 6 was less, and the polysilicon bit-line cell of Fig. 9 was the lowest. This is not unexpected because the polysilicon bit-line concept is not well suited to a single-polysilicon cell; the cell becomes elongated due to the two polysilicon spacings required per cell (see Fig. 9). However, the use of two overlapping layers of polysilicon with the buried contact step offers a number of interesting new cell layout possibilities that will be discussed in Section III-J.

H. Double-Polysilicon Cell with Diffused Bit Line

Early in the development of CCD shift-registor memory devices, it was discovered that two, or even three, overlapping layers of polysilicon improved the device performance and packing density. Subsequent to the CCD development, it was recognized that the use of a second layer of conductive polysilicon and a fifth masking operation offers two important structural advantages over a single-polysilicon process for one-device cells. Fig. 10 shows a double-polysilicon cell with a diffused bit line, a cell commonly used in commercial 16K-bit RAM's [22], [23] and in some 64K-bit chips. First, by overlapping the capacitor plate (first polysilicon layer) with the MOSFET gate (second polysilicon layer), the n^+ source region between the MOSFET switch and the storage capacitor is eliminated leading to a smaller cell (c.f., Figs. 6(a) and 10(a)). This area saving feature also occurs in the metal-gate/polysilicon hybrid cells (see Figs. 4(a) and 5(a)). The second favorable structural feature is that the second overlapping polysilicon layer allows two cells to share one polysilicon gate region and one contact via (c.f., Figs. 6(b) and 10 (b)). This results in a diffused bit-line cell with one contact hole per two cells. A reduction in cell area also results from this contact hole sharing because the hole is located, in effect, over the storage capacitors rather than over or at the side of the channel. The double-polysilicon RAM cell of Fig. 10 requires only about one-half to two-thirds the area of the single-polysilicon cell of Fig. 6 for the same lithographic feature size and transfer ratio. Another advantage of the double-polysilicon cell of Fig. 10 is the efficient cell placement on the bit line, a feature that will be discussed in Section IV-B.

The overlapping double-polysilicon RAM of Fig. 10 presents a number of technical difficulties related to the region of overlap. For example, one distinction between the single-polysilicon and the overlapping double-polysilicon RAM cells concerns the FET channel length definition in the cell. In the single-polysilicon cell, the channel length of the FET is determined by a single pattern masking operation (see Fig. 6(b)), while in the overlapping cell it is determined by the relative positions of the two polysilicon patterns (see Fig. 10(b)). Thus the mask-to-mask misregistration tolerance is an important consideration in determining the channel length

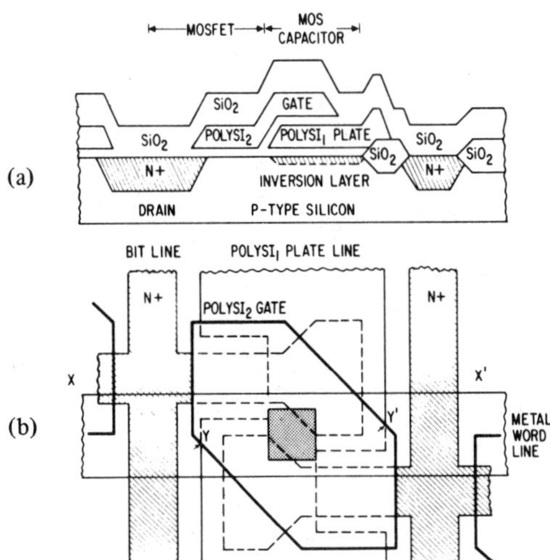

Fig. 10. Double-polysilicon cell with diffused bit line. The cross section shown in (a) is taken along line XX' of (b). Positions Y and Y' indicate a potential metal step coverage problem.

of the FET switch in the double-polysilicon cell and, hence, the overall length of the cell.

Another difficulty with double-polysilicon cells is related to the "thick" insulation oxide on the top and sides of the polysilicon plate which is formed by a thermal oxidation step which also provides the thin gate insulator. Even though the n^+ polysilicon plate oxidizes about twice as fast as the p-type silicon substrate, some compromise in insulation oxide thickness must be made. Yet another problem is the metal step coverage of the word line at a position where the borders of the two polysilicon layers coincide. This region is identified by positions Y and Y' in Fig. 10(b). Voids or breaks in the metal line can occur at the crossing point leading to a potential reliability concern [24]. One approach to relieving the step coverage is to cover the chip with a thick reflowed layer of phosphorus-rich glass prior to etching the contact holes and patterning the metal lines. Definition of small-area contacts in a phosphorous-rich glass layer is, however, a nontrivial problem.

The cell placement on the bit line can be changed to ease the coverage problem. For example, in one double-polysilicon 16K-bit RAM, the cells are placed head-to-head rather than interleaved as in Fig. 10(b). This insures that the edges of the two polysilicon layers never line up. The metal coverage problem can also be relieved by changing the cell layout from a diffused bit-line to a metal bit-line cell as discussed in the following section.

I. Double-Polysilicon Cell with Metal Bit Line

In double-polysilicon RAM cell development, the metal bit-line cell followed the diffused bit-line cell, as in the single-polysilicon development. Fig. 11 illustrates a double-polysilicon metal bit-line cell in which the gate and plate polysilicon layers do not overlap in the thin-oxide region of the cell. This results in improved metal step coverage but with some loss in density as the cell now contains an n^+ source region interposed between gate and plate. The gate length is well defined in the

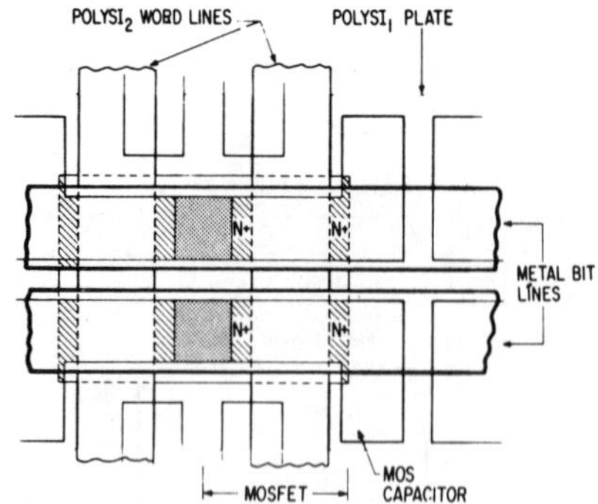

Fig. 11. Double-polysilicon cell with metal bit line.

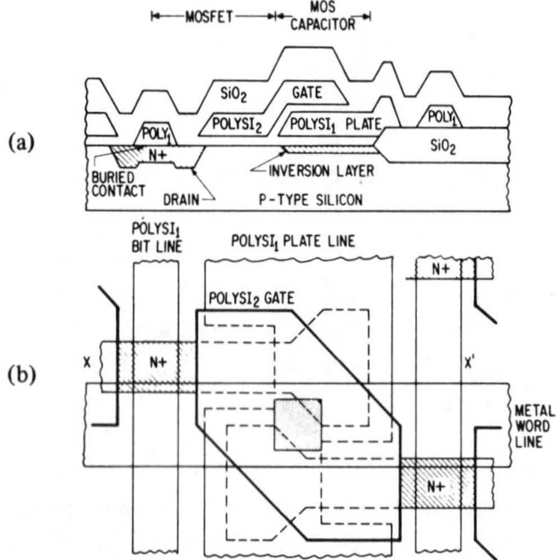

Fig. 12. Double-polysilicon cell with polysilicon bit line. The cross section shown in (a) is taken along line XX' of (b).

cell and, if desired, an n-type diffusion layer extending completely under the capacitor plate can be accommodated using the source region for misalignment tolerance. The inclusion of the n-type source region is, of course, optional and a denser cell can be achieved by eliminating it. In Fig. 11, two cells share one contact via which connects the metal bit line to a common n^+ diffused drain region. Other layout variations of the cell of Fig. 11 are possible; the two polysilicon layers may overlap in the thin-oxide region of the cell, the cell placement on the bit line may be staggered differently, or a third layer of polysilicon may be utilized [25].

J. Double-Polysilicon Cell with Polysilicon Bit Line

Analogous to the single-polysilicon cells, the third variant of the double-polysilicon cell is the polysilicon bit-line cell which is illustrated in Fig. 12. The buried contact can be made to either the first or second polysilicon layer. As illustrated in Fig. 12, the first polysilicon layer may be used to form the storage plate and the bit line with a buried contact [26]. The second polysilicon layer provides the gates in the cell array, but since the first polysilicon layer makes a buried contact, the first and second layers cannot be connected via the buried-contact step. If the buried contact is made to the second polysilicon layer, and if that layer is used to provide both the bit line and the MOSFET gates [27], the gate cannot overlap the bit line as they are made of the same polysilicon layer. However, the buried contact is then available to connect the two polysilicon layers together.

A major attraction of the polysilicon bit-line cell is reduced bit-line capacitance [27] which is the most effective way to increase the transfer ratio (see (1)). First-order calculations indicate that the bit-line capacitance of the polysilicon bit-line cell of Fig. 12 can be significantly less than that of the diffused bit-line cell of Fig. 10. Polysilicon bit-line cells are used in a recently announced 64K-bit RAM [27]. Other variants of the polysilicon bit-line cell are possible. For example, when two layers of polysilicon are available, both the bit line and the word line may be of polysilicon. In this case, no metal lines or metal-to-polysilicon contact vias are needed in the cell array.

K. Methodology of Categorization

A methodology for categorizing cell types can be established based on the choice of the material (metal, polysilicon, or diffused silicon) used to fabricate the three control elements of the cell; the drain (bit line), FET gate (word line), and capacitor plate. Table I illustrates various possibilities, some of which have not been discussed in this paper. For example, if the bit line is of diffused silicon, the FET gate may be of metal or polysilicon and the plate also may be of metal or polysilicon. This tabular approach has helped the author to discover a number of new cell layouts. VMOS dynamic RAM cells can be cataloged by the same table.

IV. Structural Features

A. Bit-Line and Word-Line Pitch

The width-to-length aspect ratio of the cell influences the bit-line and word-line spacings or "pitch." The popular single-polysilicon diffused bit-line cell of Fig. 6 gives a bit-line-to-word-line pitch ratio of about 3 : 1, while the double-polysilicon diffused bit-line cell of Fig. 10 gives a pitch ratio of about 2 : 1. Bit-line sense amplifiers and word-line decoders can be laid out to meet these dimensions. However, if the bit-line spacing becomes too small, as in VMOS cells (pitch ratio 1 : 1) or in the single-polysilicon metal bit-line cell of Fig. 7 (pitch ratio 1 : 2), it may be difficult to match the sense amplifier width-to-the-bit-line pitch. In such cases, several approaches are feasible; the bit-line pitch can be increased by rotating the storage capacitor [15], buried contacts can be employed to reduce the sense amplifier width, or sense amplifiers can be staggered rather than lined up.

B. Cell Placement

Cell placement on the bit line can have a significant effect on the bit-line capacitance, and on the position of the access lines from the bit-line decoders. Let us consider the diffused bit-line cells that use single polysilicon (Fig. 6) and double polysilicon (Fig. 10). Fig. 13(a) shows the alternating cell layout [2], [3] along the bit line of a single-polysilicon 4K-bit RAM. Alternation tends to balance out bit-line capacitance variations due to mask-to-mask misalignment. In comparison, the single-polysilicon 4K-bit RAM can use the same-side arrangement [14] shown in Fig. 13(b) which yields a relatively

TABLE I
CATEGORIZATION OF CELL TYPES

	FET GATE			
BIT LINE	METAL (SINGLE METAL)	METAL (HYBRID)	POLYSILICON (SINGLE POLYSI)	POLYSILICON (DOUBLE POLYSI)
DIFFUSED	METAL (FIG. 3) VMOS (FIG. 17)	POLYSI (FIGS.4,5)	POLYSI (FIGS. 6,14) VMOS	$POLYSI_1$ (FIG. 10) $POLYSI_2$
METAL	IMPOSSIBLE	IMPRACTICAL	POLYSI (FIG. 7)	$POLYSI_1$ (FIG. 11) $POLYSI_2$
POLYSILICON ($POLYSI_1$ or $POLYSI_2$)	METAL POLYSI	METAL POLYSI	POLYSI (FIG. 9)	$POLYSI_1$ (FIG. 12) $POLYSI_2$
	CAPACITOR PLATE			

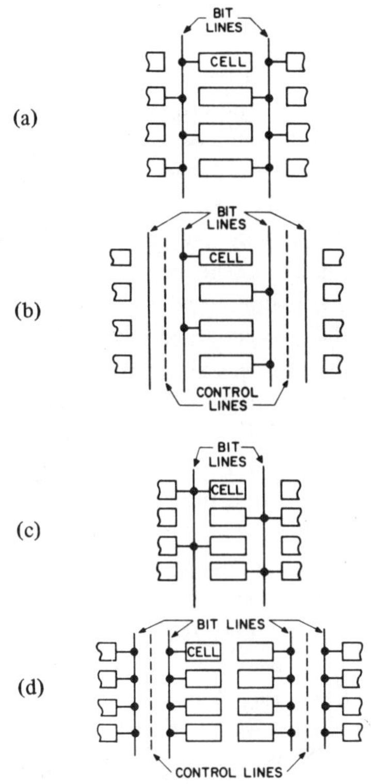

Fig. 13. Cell placement on bit line for (a) alternating single-polysilicon 4K-bit RAM, (b) same-side single-polysilicon 4K-bit RAM, (c) alternating double-polysilicon 16K-bit RAM, and (d) same-side double-polysilicon 16K-bit RAM.

larger bit-line diffusion capacitance per cell. However, this arrangement allows the sense amplifier control lines from the decoders to be placed between the bit lines so that the multiplexed decoder circuits can be placed outside of the cell array. With the alternating cell layout of Fig. 13(a), however, the decoders must be placed next to the sense amplifiers between two halves of the cell array.

Fig. 13(c) shows the alternating cell arrangement of a double-polysilicon 16K-bit RAM [22], [23]. As in Fig. 13(a), the cells of Fig. 13(c) alternate, but share a common contact point on the bit line (this illustrates why the polysilicon bit-line approach is more effective with double-polysilicon than with single-polysilicon cells). Furthermore, Fig. 13(a) and (c) exhibits essentially the same word-line spacing and bit-line capacitance per cell, but arrangement of Fig. 13(c) has significantly reduced bit-line pitch resulting from locating the word-line contact hole over the capacitor electrodes (c.f., Figs. 6(b) and 10(b)). Fig. 13(d) shows the head-to-head cell placement of a double-polysilicon 16K-bit RAM. This allows the decoder control lines to be routed between the bit lines as in the same-side single-polysilicon arrangement of Fig. 13(b).

C. First- or Second-Level Polysilicon Peripherals

When two layers of polysilicon are used, either may be chosen to fabricate the MOSFET's and bootstrap capacitors in the peripheral circuits. With the early double-polysilicon RAM chips [22], [23], the first polysilicon layer provided both the plate capacitors of the cells and the MOSFET gates of peripheral circuit devices. This is undesirable from several points of view. The first polysilicon layer experiences more high-temperature processing which may lead to reliability problems [28]. Also, the insulator should be as thin as possible under the plate to enhance the storage capacitance. Thus it is desirable to decouple the capacitor storage plate from the gates of the peripheral circuit MOSFET's. Also, if a buried contact is made to the second polysilicon layer, the two polysilicon layers may be connected via the buried contact step, an approach used in some recent 16K-bit RAM's. Recently, a transition to the use of second polysilicon in the peripherals and a buried contact made to the second polysilicon has become apparent in commercial 16K RAM's.

V. NEW CONCEPTS

This section will briefly consider a number of new dynamic RAM concepts, most of which are still in an exploratory stage. A detailed description of several novel cells has been given by Chatterjee *et al.* [29].

A. Self-Registering Contacts

The objective of the self-registering contact is to provide a smaller area contact by means of a misregistration-tolerant connection between a metal line and a polysilicon or diffused region. One such contact results in the so-called "GATE/PLATE" cell [30] which may be fabricated using either one [30] or two [31] layers of polysilicon. A single-polysilicon cell is shown in Fig. 14. An oxidation barrier layer of silicon nitride is used to define the MOSFET gate electrode pattern in the

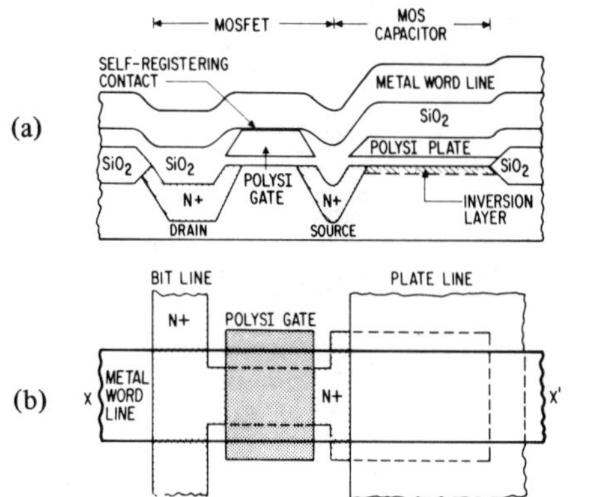

Fig. 14. Single-polysilicon GATE/PLATE cell. The cross section in (a) is taken along line XX' of (b).

cell array, while an oxidizable layer of silicon dioxide is used to define the polysilicon plate pattern. After the n^+ source and drain regions are formed by diffusion or ion implantation, a thick thermal oxide is grown everywhere except over the gate contact regions which are protected by the nitride layer. When the nitride regions are dissolved, polysilicon areas are revealed for contacting by metal interconnection lines. Exposed and oxide-protected polysilicon regions can be connected together by overlapping the nitride and oxide masking patterns for the polysilicon regions. In this manner, a dense peripheral wiring pattern can be built up [32].

The self-registering contact approach yields a small RAM cell because the gate contact area is relatively small, and because the masking patterns that determine the gate and plate patterns can be spaced closer together than one minimum lithographic spacing. In comparison with the double-overlapping-polysilicon cell of Fig. 10, the cell of Fig. 14 is about 25 percent larger for the same transfer ratio. Although the self-registering contact process also requires five basic masking operations, it requires only one layer of polysilicon and thus offers improved topography for metal coverage and requires somewhat fewer processing steps. Disadvantages are that each cell requires one metal contact, and that the metal-to-polysilicon contact is located over the thin gate insulator for the smallest cell layout.

Another version of the self-registering contact cell uses the so-called "recessed-gate" MOSFET as the switch in the cell [33]. With this device, the polysilicon gate electrode and the self-registering gate contact area correspond only to the channel region (i.e., the gate material does not overlap onto the field isolation). Although the gate polysilicon cannot be used for wiring, by using a second layer of polysilicon for the plate [33] the cell area can be made smaller than that of the double overlapping cell of Fig. 10.

The self-registering contact cell of Fig. 14 provides a single-polysilicon diffused bit-line cell like that of Fig. 6 but with a self-registering gate contact. A self-registering diffusion contact has also been described [34] that provides a cell analogous to the single-polysilicon/metal bit-line cell of Fig. 7. In this case, part of the nitride used initially to form the semirecessed oxide isolation regions is retained to later form the metal-to-diffusion contact areas.

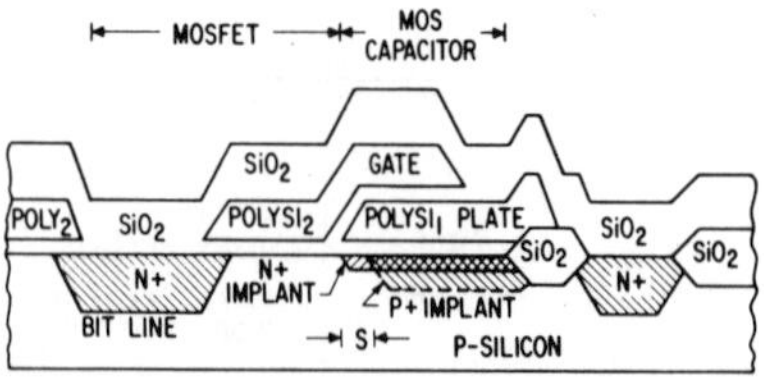

Fig. 15. Doubly doped storage capacitor cell using overlapping double polysilicon. The misalignment between n^+ and p^+ implanted regions is indicated by S.

B. Double-Doped Storage Capacitors

One way to increase the charge transfer ratio of the cell is to increase the junction capacitance component of the storage capacitor within the silicon substrate. Presently, most of the storage capacitance is made up of the MOS thin-oxide capacitor which is typically five to ten times larger than the substrate depletion layer capacitor in parallel with it. With the addition of an extra masking step one can increase the storage capacitance component in the silicon substrate by implanting a shallow n-type region and a deeper p-type region [35], [36] as shown in Fig. 15. The extra masking step is required to prevent the doubly doped layer from occuring under the MOSFET transfer gates in the cell and under the gates of MOSFET's in the peripheral circuits. In this so-called "Hi-*C*" RAM cell [36], the p-type doping is used to increase the depletion capacitance of the electron inversion layer, however, the presence of a highly doped p-type region also increases the threshold voltage for the capacitor plate, thereby requiring a much higher positive plate voltage to form the electron inversion layer. In order to counteract this, an n-type region is also provided to lower the threshold and facilitate formation of the inversion storage layer. If the n-type doping is high enough, a diffusion storage cell is achieved and the storage capacitor plate may be maintained at substrate potential.

Fabrication of the doubly doped storage capacitor region is facilitated by cell layouts which contain an n^+ "source" region located between the MOSFET and the MOS storage capacitor (Figs. 6-9, 11, 14). In these cases, alignment of the edge of the doubly doped storage region with respect to the edges of the polysilicon capacitor plate is relieved by the presence of the source region. In overlapping double-polysilicon cells (Figs. 10, 12) it is difficult to align the doubly diffused regions to each other and to the capacitor plate [37] (see Fig. 15). If the n-type boundary extends under the MOSFET, the MOSFET channel length is reduced which can lead to short-channel effects, while if the n-type underlaps the p-type region a potential barrier may occur preventing charge from leaving the capacitor. The doubly doped technique can increase the storage capacitor at most by about 50 percent, and the enhancement is quite alignment sensitive in overlapping polysilicon cells.

C. Contactless Cells

In the contactless or "charge-coupled" RAM cell [38] shown in Fig. 16 the polysilicon electrode serves as both the word line and the storage plate. This eliminates the need for in-

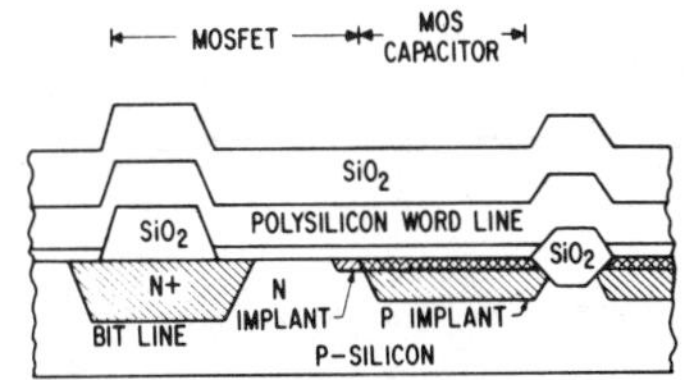

Fig. 16. Contactless single-polysilicon cell.

(a)

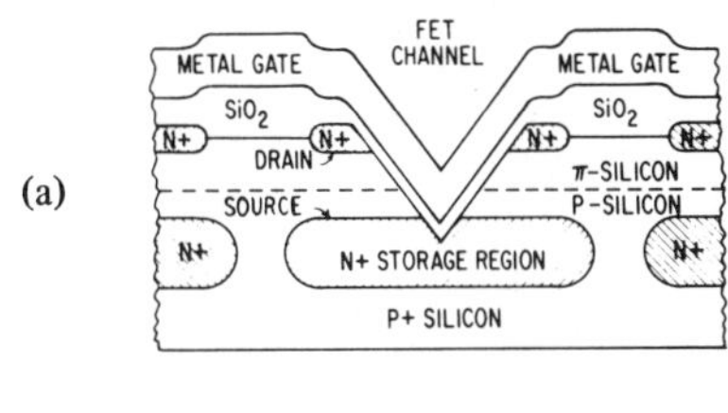

(b)

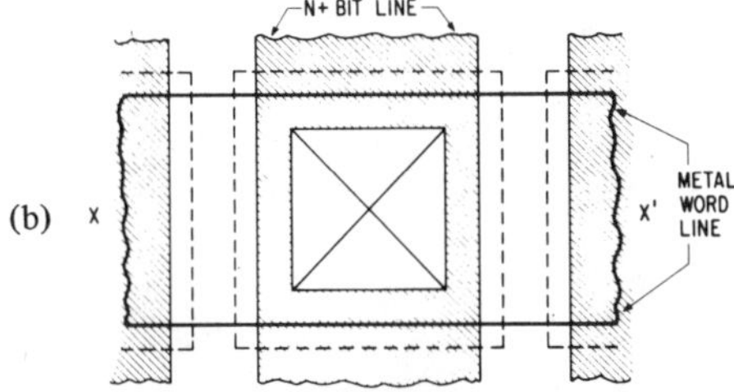

Fig. 17. VMOS cell with diffused bit line. The cross section in (a) is taken along line XX' of (b).

dependent gate and plate regions and for a connection between the metal word line and the polysilicon gate, leading to a smaller cell area without contacts. Difficulties with the contactless cell stem from accommodating the misalignment of the potential barrier edge which enlarges the cell, and the relative magnitude of the stored charge for a given cell area.

D. DMOS FET's

A MOSFET with a double-diffused source region called a DMOS FET offers higher transconductance and possibly better channel length control at the expense of an additional masking operation [39]. Such devices would appear to be more attractive for circuits with unidirectional current flow (e.g., an ROM array). The DMOS device has been applied to a dynamic RAM [40] which improved the sense amplifier performance, but required two-sided devices with poorer characteristics in the cells. In dynamic RAM's, the circuit speed improvement due to the DMOS FET probably is not attractive enough to warrent the extra masking step which may be better used to fabricate other advantageous structures such as buried contacts or depletion-mode loads.

E. VMOS Cells

Although the VMOS FET is a form of vertical DMOS device, the advantage exploited for dynamic RAM arrays is not transconductance enhancement, but rather small cell area because a junction storage capacitor can be located beneath the MOSFET [41], [42]. Fig. 17 shows a VMOS cell with a diffused bit line and metal word line and MOSFET gate which requires six masking operations. A polysilicon MOSFET and word line can be used, but this requires a seventh masking step. These cell types can be ascribed to various matrix positions in Table I. Locating the bit line, word line, and MOSFET switch over the storage capacitor results in the smallest possible one-device cell (about 15 to 20 lithographic squares), a cell area that can only be approached by contactless cells or by other vertical cells such as ones with a buried punchthrough region [29]. In addition, no contact vias are required in the array of VMOS cells.

The VMOS cell presents several problems such as outdiffusion of the buried n^+ regions and control of the p-type epitaxial layer thickness. Oxide charge problems from the four ⟨111⟩ surfaces and scaling of the anisotropically wet-etched V groove to smaller dimensions are also of concern. However, the primary problem is associated with the peripheral circuits which make up 50 to 70 percent of the chip area. The inherently large width-to-length ratio of the VMOS device and the difficulty in electrically contacting the buried-source region make the VMOS FET unattractive for exclusive use in the peripheral circuits unless an additional masking step is provided [43]. Consequently, a conventional lateral NMOS FET is usually fabricated on the chip using extra masking steps [41].

The innovative VMOS cell represents cell area reduction carried to the extreme, but if the cell technology cannot be used to fabricate the peripheral circuits, much of the array density advantage is lost to increased process complexity. In general, the dynamic RAM exemplifies not only the technological leading edge of MOSFET innovation, but also the economic cutting edge of mass production for MOSFET integrated circuits. In a mature and competitive market arena which has been characterized by evolutionary improvements to the initial four-mask single-polysilicon process, the VMOS dynamic RAM represents a radical technical departure which may not be commercially feasible unless the density advantage can offset the increased cost of a more complex process with potentially lower yield.

VI. Comparison of Commercial Cell Types

A. 16K-bit RAM's

Table II lists some information about various polysilicon-gate 16K-bit dynamic RAM's. A number of interesting observations can be made. For example, from the second column, we note that when a buried contact step is used with double overlapping polysilicon, the peripheral circuits and the buried contact are made using the second polysilicon layer. The chip utilization (fraction of chip area devoted to cells) ranges from 0.32 to 0.49. For double-polysilicon cells, the larger cells have the larger chip utilization, and *vice versa.*

B. Groundrule Comparison

Fig. 18 plots the number of minimum photolithographic squares/cell for a number of polysilicon-gate 4 and 16K-bit dynamic RAM's as a function of the year of introduction. These data were generated as follows. Chips were purchased and the cells photographed using the same microscope. Because of the required manufacturing tolerances associated with linewidths and spacings of the masking pattern, mask-to-

TABLE II
16K-bit One-Device Cell Dynamic RAM's
(NMOS Polysilicon-Gate Technology. 16 PIN DIP, +12 and ±5V)

Company (Part #)	Cell Type (B.C., Periph.Ckts)	Cell Area* (μ^2/mils^2)	Chip Area (mm^2/mils^2)	Chip Util.	Access/Cycle (nsec)
TI (4070)	Single-Fig. 7 (No, Poly 1)	640/.98 (619)$	32.26 50,000	.32	350 550
Intel (2116)	Double-Fig.10 (No, Poly 1)	455/.70 (-----)	21.98 34,075	.34	200 375
Intel (2117)	Double-Fig.10 (Yes, Poly 2)	510/.79 (483)$	18.97 29,500	.44	150 320
Mostek/TI (4116)	Double-Fig.10 (No, Poly 1)	510/.76 (449)$	17.89 27,600	.46	150 375
Motorola (6616)	Double-Fig.10 (No, Poly 1)	~450/.70 (410)$	18.20 28,200	.41	150 ---
Hitachi (4716)	Double-Fig.10 (Yes, Poly 2)	370/.58 (346)$	17.43 27,000	.35	150 ---
Fujitsu (8116)	Double-Fig.11 (Yes, Poly 2)	540/.84 (439)$	17.92 28,000	.49	150 375
NEC (416)	Double-Fig.13D (Yes, Poly 2)	~620/.96 (562)$	22.80 35,300	.45	150 ---

*Vendor Array Area/16384 $Author's Photograph at 675X

mask misalignments, and etching tolerances of fabricated patterns on the chip, fabricated features equal in size to the minimum lithographic groundrule are rarely encountered on the chip, particularly not in the complex RAM cell. Accordingly, if one sums the observed diffusion, polysilicon, and metal linewidths and spacings in the cell and divides by six, one can obtain an average fabricated image size (i.e., an average feature size) which can also serve as a dimensional figure of merit. These results are listed at the top of Fig. 18. One could include the contact hole width and divide by seven, but this had no effect on the results. Next, it was assumed that mask-masking equipment was graduated in 0.5-μm increments (i.e., approximately 20×10^{-6}-in increments). From personal experience, a rule of thumb had been established that the fabricated feature size is about 1.5 times the minimum lithographic image size. In ascribing 5 μm to 1974, 4 μm to 1975–1976, and 3.5 μm to 1978, the fabricated image size was found to be consistently larger than the lithographic image size by a factor of 1.3 to 1.6. This progress in the reduction of lithographic linewidths correlates well with other data [44].

The vertical scale of Fig. 18 was obtained by using the deduced value of the minimum groundrule. Of course, if one chooses to use the measured average feature size instead of the minimum groundrule, the number of squares per cell will be reduced by about 2.25 (i.e., 1.5^2) times. Misunderstanding about the use of average fabricated feature size versus minimum photoresist image size can lead to sizable discrepancies in the reported number of squares per cell.

The results of Fig. 18 indicate that the number of lithographic squares per cell remains essentially constant for a given cell type, and that by going to increasing cell cleverness (i.e., single polysilicon/one contact via per cell, single polysilicon/one contact via per two cells, double polysilicon/one contact via per two cells) the number of squares per cell decreases. Stated another way, this exercise illustrates that the reduction in photolithographic image size translates directly into a reduction of cell size, the number of squares per cell remaining constant for a given layout type. Consequently, in order to obtain additional improvements in RAM cell packing density and performance, one must also seek changes in cell structure or fabrication technique. Packing-density improvements usually result from reducing the number and area of contacts in the cell (often through improving self-registration within the cell), while performance improvements usually involve methods to increase storage capacitance and to decrease bit-line capacitance. In several of these areas, improvements have been carried about as far as commercial practicality will allow, and further progress will require additional masking operations and novel processing steps.

VII. Future Considerations

Although the dynamic one-device memory cell presently dominates the high-density/low-cost RAM market, it has been a mass manufactured product for only about five years. The processing techniques, structures, and masking sequences have already experienced several evolutionary improvements over the past few years leading to faster, denser, and more reliable memory chips. Undoubtedly, the ubiquitous one-device cell can still be improved in structure or extended in application.

In terms of improved cell structures for 64K-bit RAM's and beyond, cell designs that are less susceptable to alpha-particle radiation will be desirable. In this regard, sapphire substrates, polysilicon-to-polysilicon storage capacitors [26], or cells with larger signal voltages (e.g., twin cells) may be preferred. Development of a metallized or silicided polysilicon line with much lower sheet resistance of about 1 to 5 Ω/square would favor approaches that emphasize polysilicon wiring. A second level of metal wiring is often used in bipolar

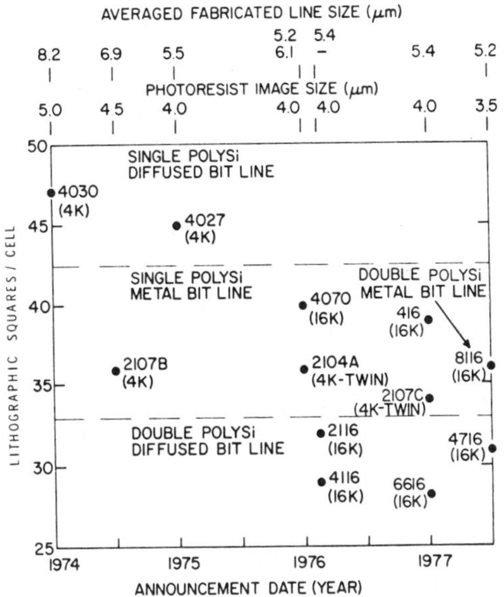

Fig. 18. Number of minimum photolithographic squares/cell for various commercial 4 and 16K-bit dynamic RAM's versus year of introduction.

processes and eventually may also prove to be technically attractive to the double-polysilicon process. Further development of on-chip redundancy techniques can also be anticipated. New cells with vertical structures will continue to receive attention [45], [46], but for the short term the emphasis has shifted to peripheral circuits (depletion-mode load, second polysilicon replacing first polysilicon, buried-contact wiring, etc.). Novel processing techniques such as metal liftoff, reactive-ion etching, all ion-implanted devices, and new field-isolation techniques will be needed to keep pace with consistently improving lithography.

In terms of applications, one may anticipate very large RAM arrays with rather slow access times that can compete with CCD or bubble shift-register arrays in terms of cost per bit. In comparison to shift-register array memories, dynamic RAM's may be better suited to redundancy wiring techniques which may become a prerequisite for very-large-scale integrated memory chips. Furthermore, like CCD's, dynamic RAM arrays can also be used for optical image sensing. Although it is difficult to imagine how nonvoltability could be introduced into today's dynamic RAM's, at low temperatures such as 77 K [47] the refresh time periods for dynamic MOSFET RAM arrays become so long (seconds to minutes) that a quasi-static mode of operation becomes feasible.

We conclude by noting that, although the one-device dynamic RAM cell has been maturing for almost a decade, it still holds the potential for a number of technical surprises.

Acknowledgment

Careful readings of the manuscript by colleagues B. A. Chappell, R. H. Dennard, L. M. Terman, and H. N. Yu at the T. J. Watson Research Center are gratefully acknowledged.

References

[1] R. H. Dennard, "Field-effect transistor memory," U.S. Patent 3 387 286, June 4, 1968.

[2] K. U. Stein and H. Friedrick, "A 1-mil^2 single-transistor memory cell in silicon-gate technology," *IEEE J. Solid-State Circuits*, vol. SC-8, pp. 319–323, Oct. 1973.

[3] L. Cohen, R. Green, R. Smith, and J. L. Seely, "Single-transistor cell makes room for more memory on an MOS chip," *Electron.*, pp. 69–75, Aug. 2, 1971.

[4] J. M. Caywood, J. C. Pathak, G. L. Van Buren, and S. W. Owen, "A self-refreshing 4K RAM with sub-mW standby power," in *IEEE Internat. Solid-State Circuits Conf. Dig.*, pp. 16–17 (Philadelphia, PA, Feb. 1979).

[5] *MOS Integrated Circuits*, W. M. Penney and L. Lau, Eds. New York: Van Nostrand Reinhold, 1972, p. 165.

[6] R. Proebsting and R. Green, "A TTL compatible 4096-bit n-channel RAM," in *IEEE Internat. Solid-State Circuits Conf. Dig.*, pp. 28–29 (Philadelphia, PA, Feb. 1973).

[7] T. H. Ning, "Hot electron emission currents in n-channel IGFET's," in *IEEE Internat. Electron Devices Meet. Tech. Dig.*, pp. 144–147 (Washington, DC, Dec. 1977).

[8] R. R. Garnache and W. M. Smith, "Integrated circuit fabrication process," U.S. Patent 3 841 926, Oct. 15, 1974.

[9] R. R. DeSimone, N. M. Donofrio, B. L. Flur, R. H. Kruggel, and H. H. Leung, "FET RAM's," in *IEEE Internat. Solid-State Circuits Conf. Tech. Dig.*, pp. 154–155 (Philadelphia, PA, Feb. 1979).

[10] S. A. Abbas, C. A. Barile, and R. C. Dockerty, "Low-leakage, n-channel silicon gate FET with a self-aligned field shield," in *IEEE Internat. Electron Devices Meet. Tech. Dig.*, pp. 371–373 (Washington, DC, Dec. 1973).

[11] M. Kayanagi, H. Sunami, N. Hoshimoto, and M. Ashikawa "Novel high density, stacked capacitor MOS RAM," in *IEEE Internat. Electron Devices Meet. Tech. Dig.*, pp. 348–351 (Washington DC, Dec. 1978).

[12] K. U. Stein, A. Sihling, and E. Doering, "Storage array and sense/refresh circuits for single-transistor memory cells," *IEEE J. Solid-State Circuits*, vol. SC-7, pp. 336–339, Oct. 1972.

[13] W. K. Hoffman and H. L. Kalter, "An 8K-bit RAM chip using the one-device FET cell," *IEEE J. Solid-State Circuits*, vol. SC-8, pp. 298–304, Oct. 1973.

[14] "An in-depth look at MOSTEK's high performance MK 4027," Application Note, Mostek Corp., Carrollton, TX.

[15] C. Kuo, U. Kitagawa, D. Ogden, and J. Hewkin, "16 K-RAM built with proven process may offer start-up reliability," *Electron.*, pp. 81–86, May 1976.

[16] T. Wada, O. Kudok, M. Sakamoto, H. Yamanaka, K. Nakamura, and M. Kamoshida, "A 64K × 1 bit dynamic ED-MOS RAM," *IEEE J. Solid-State Circuits*, vol. SC-13, pp. 600–606, Oct. 1978.

[17] S. Zirinsky and B. L. Crowder, "Refractory silicides for high temperature compatible I.C. conductor lines," presented at the Electrochem. Soc. Fall Meet., paper 463, Atlanta, GA, Oct. 1977.

[18] *Memory Design Handbook*. Santa Clara, CA: Intel Corp., 1977, sec. 3, p. 4.

[19] R. C. Foss and R. Harland, "Standards for dynamic MOS RAMS," *Electron. Des.*, p. 66, Aug. 16, 1977.

[20] V. L. Rideout, "Enhancement-mode FETs and depletion-mode FETs with two layers of polycrystalline silicon and fabrication of integrated circuits containing the FETs," U.S. Patent 4 085 498, Apr. 25, 1978.

[21] L. L. Vadasz, "Integrated circuit structure and method for making integrated circuit structure," U.S. Patent 3 699 646, Oct. 24, 1972.

[22] C. N. Ahlquist, J. R. Breivogel, J. T. Koo, J. L. McCollum, W. G. Oldham, and A. L. Renniger, "A 16,384-bit dynamic RAM," *IEEE J. Solid-State Circuits*, vol. SC-11, pp. 570–574, Oct. 1976.

[23] P. R. Schroeder and R. J. Proebsting, "A 16K × 1 bit dynamic RAM," in *IEEE Internat. Solid-State Circuits Conf. Dig.*, pp. 12–13 (Philadelphia, PA, Feb. 1977).

[24] V. J. Silvestri, V. L. Rideout, and V. Maniscalo, "Al coverage of surface steps at SiO_2 insulated polycrystalline Si boundaries: Al evaporation in vacuum and low pressure Ar," to be published in *J. Electrochem. Soc.*

[25] I. Lee, R. Yu, F. J. Smith, S. Wong, and M. P. Embrathiry. "A 64kb MOS dynamic RAM," in *IEEE Internat. Solid-State Circuits, Conf. Tech. Dig.*, pp. 146–147 (Philadelphia, PA, Feb. 1979).

[26] V. L. Rideout, "Double polysilicon dynamic memory cell with polysilicon bit line," *IBM Tech. Disc. Bull.*, vol., 21 pp. 3828–3831, Feb. 1979.

[27] R. P. Cenker, D. G. Clemons, W. R. Huber, J. B. Petrizzi, F. J. Procyk, and G. M. Trout, "A fault-tolerant 64K dynamic random-access memory," in *IEEE Internat. Solid-State Circuits Conf.*

Tech. Dig., pp. 150–151 (Philadelphia, PA, Feb. 1979). Also, this issue, pp. 853–860.

[28] C. R. Barret and R. C. Smith, "Failure modes and reliability of dynamic RAMs," in *IEEE Internat. Electron Devices Meet. Tech. Dig.*, pp. 319–322 (Washington, DC, Dec. 1976).

[29] P. K. Chatterjee, G. W. Taylor, R. L. Easley, H-S. Fu, and A. F. Tasch, Jr., "A survey of high density dynamic RAM cell concepts," this issue pp. 827–839.

[30] V. L. Rideout, J. J. Walker, and A. Cramer, "A one-device memory cell using a single layer of polysilicon and a self-registering metal-to-polysilicon contact," in *IEEE Internat. Electron Devices Meet. Tech. Dig.*, pp. 258–261 (Washington, DC, Dec. 1977).

[31] V. L. Rideout, "FET one-device memory cells fabricated with two layers of polycrystalline silicon and fabrication of integrated circuits containing arrays of the memory cells," U.S. Patent 4 075 045, Feb. 21, 1978.

[32] ——, "Self-registering metal-to-polysilicon contacting technique," *IBM Tech. Disc. Bull.*, vol. 21, pp. 3818–3821, Feb. 1979.

[33] V. L. Rideout and V. J. Silvestri, "MOSFET's with polysilicon gates self-aligned to the field isolation and to the source and drain regions," *IEEE Trans. Electron Devices*, vol. ED-26, July 1979.

[34] V. L. Rideout, "Polysilicon-gate field-effect transistors with self-registering metal contacts to both polysilicon and diffused silicon regions," *IBM Tech. Disc. Bull.*, vol. 21, pp. 3833–3835, Feb. 1979.

[35] C. G. Sodini and T. I. Kamins, "Enhanced capacitor for one-transistor memory cell," *IEEE Trans. Electron Devices*, vol. ED-23, p. 1187, Oct. 1976.

[36] A. F. Tasch, P. K. Chatterjee, H-S. Fu, and T. C. Holloway, "The Hi-*C* RAM cell concept," *IEEE Trans. Electron Devices*, vol. ED-25, pp. 33–41, Jan. 1978.

[37] V. L. Rideout, "Double polysilicon dynamic random-access memory cell with increased charge storage capacitance," *IBM Tech. Disc. Bull.*, vol., 21, pp. 3823–3825, Feb. 1979.

[38] A. F. Tasch, H-S. Fu, T. C. Holloway, and R. C. Frye, "Charge capacity analysis of the charge-coupled RAM cell," *IEEE J. Solid-State Circuits*, vol. SC-11, pp. 575–584, Oct. 1976.

[39] Y. Tarui *et al.*, "Diffusion self-aligned MOST–A new approach for high speed devices," in *Proc. 1st Conf. Solid-State Devices* (suppl. to *J. Japan. Soc. Appl. Phys.*, vol. 39, pp. 105–110, 1970).

[40] K. Shimatori, K. Anami, Y. Nagayama, I. Ohkura, M. Ohmori, and T. Nakano, "Fully ion implanted 4096-bit high speed DSA MOS RAM," in *IEEE Internat. Solid-State Circuits Conf. Dig.*, pp. 76–77 (Philadelphia, PA, Feb. 1977).

[41] T. J. Rodgers, W. R. Hiltpold, B. Frederick, J. J. Barnes, F. B. Jenné, and J. D. Trotter, "VMOS memory technology," *IEEE J. Solid-State Circuits*, vol. SC-12, pp. 515–523, Oct. 1977.

[42] K. Hoffman and R. Losehand, "VMOS technology applied to dynamic RAM's," *IEEE J. Solid-State Circuits*, vol. SC-13, pp. 617–622, Oct. 1978.

[43] D. V. Essl, R. Losehand, and B. Rehn, "A 64kb VMOS RAM," in *IEEE Internat. Solid-State Circuits Conf. Tech. Dig.*, pp. 148–149 (Philadelphia, PA, Feb. 1979).

[44] G. E. Moore, "Progress in digital integrated electronics," in *IEEE Internat. Electron Devices Meet. Tech. Dig.*, pp. 11–13 (Washington, DC, Dec. 1975).

[45] P. K. Chatterjee, G. W. Taylor, and M. Malweh, "Circuit optimization of the taper isolated dynamic gain RAM cell for VLSI memories," in *IEEE Internat. Solid-State Circuits Conf. Tech. Dig.*, pp. 22–23 (Philadelphia, PA, Feb. 1979).

[46] A. Mohsen, "Vertical charge-coupled devices," in *IEEE Internat. Solid-State Circuits Conf. Tech. Dig.*, pp. 152–153 (Philadelphia, PA, Feb. 1979).

[47] F. H. Gaensslen, V. L. Rideout, E. J. Walker, and J. J. Walter, "Very small MOSFET's for low temperature operation," *IEEE Trans. Electron Devices*, vol. ED-24, pp. 218–229, Mar. 1977.

A 2K × 8-Bit Static MOS RAM with a New Memory Cell Structure

TAKASHI OHZONE, TAKASHI HIRAO, KAZUHIKO TSUJI, SHIRO HORIUCHI, AND SHIGETOSHI TAKAYANAGI

Abstract—**A 2K × 8-bit static MOS RAM with a new memory cell structure has been developed. The memory cell consists of six devices including four MOSFET's and two memory load resistors. Two load resistors are fabricated in the second-level polysilicon films over the polysilicon gate MOSFET used as the driver. Thus the memory cell area is determined only by the area of four MOSFET's.**

By applying the new cell structure and photolithography technology of 3 μm dimensions, the cell area of 23 × 27 μm and the chip area of 3.75 × 4.19 mm have been realized.

The RAM is nonclocked and single 5 V operation. Access time of about 150 ns is obtained at a supply current of 120 mA.

Introduction

MEMORY size of the n-channel static MOS RAM has been increased by about two times in 2 years. It is important for the RAM of large memory size to realize smaller chip area as well as lower power dissipation. As the memory cell array occupies about 60-70 percent of the static RAM's chip area, a smaller memory cell area has been required to realize smaller chip size.

To realize smaller memory cell area and lower power dissipation in the memory cell, the ion-implanted polysilicon resistors [1] have been applied to the memory load resistors of the static MOS RAM's [2]-[6].

The ion-implanted polysilicon resistors are suitably applied to the memory cell resistors with desirable features as follows:

1) the resistors are superior with respect to process compatibility to MOS IC's, especially to polysilicon gate MOS IC's;

2) the resistance value can be controlled in extremely wide range by changing ion-implanted dosage. As the result, load current of the memory cell has been lowered to 1 μA-0.1 nA [3] in contrast to that of 1 μA in a conventional depletion-type MOSFET load memory cell [7];

3) the resistors have positive temperature coefficients, which can compensate the temperature dependence of subthreshold current in short channel MOSFET's and leakage current of source/drain junctions [2].

In this paper, the new double-polysilicon memory cell structure using the ion-implanted polysilicon load resistors, and then the fabrication process and electrical characteristics of the 16 kbit static RAM with new memory cells are described [5].

Manuscript received April 4, 1979; revised October 26, 1979.

The authors are with Semiconductor Research Laboratory, Matsushita Electric Industrial Company, Ltd., Moriguchi, Osaka, Japan.

Memory Cell Structure

A schematic of conventional polysilicon resistor load memory cell fabricated using a single-level polysilicon process is shown in Fig. 1(a). The load resistors occupy about 20-30 percent of the memory cell area as they are usually fabricated on the field oxide.

Fig. 1(b) shows the newly developed memory cell structure. The load resistors are successfully fabricated over the driver MOSFET by applying a double-level polysilicon process which has been commonly used in CCD's and dynamic MOS RAM's. As the result, the memory cell area can be determined by the area of four MOSFET's. The cell also uses the ion-implanted polysilicon resistors fabricated in the second-level polysilicon films. The resistance value of the memory load resistors is controlled to be above 50 MΩ to suppress the load current below 0.1 μA at a supply voltage of 5 V.

Fig. 2 shows the photomicrograph of the memory cell before aluminum metallization. Polysilicon gates of four MOSFET's (T_1-T_4) and voltage supply line V_{CC} are formed using the first-level polysilicon films. For the memory load resistors (R_1 and R_2) and interconnections between drain and the polysilicon gate of the driver MOSFET to form cross-coupling of the memory flip-flop, the second-level polysilicon films are used. As the memory load resistor can be fabricated over the driver MOSFET, the memory cell area is determined only by the area of the four MOSFET's.

Design rules of 3 μm are typically adopted in the RAM. The gate length of all the enhancement-type MOSFET's is below 3 μm. The minimum linewidth and separation of the first-level and the second-level polysilicon films are 3 μm. The minimum linewidth and separation of aluminum metallization are 3 and 4 μm, respectively. Minimum size of the contact area is 3 × 3 μm. The memory cell area of 23 × 27 μm can be realized by combining the new memory cell structure and the design rules of 3 μm dimensions. This small cell area is about half of that in conventional static MOS RAM's.

Fabrication Process

Gate length of all the enhancement-type MOSFET's is below 3 μm as mentioned in the preceding section. The lowering of threshold volatge and the increase of subthreshold current are observed in such short-channel MOSFET's [8]. The short-channel effects become more troublesome as the resistance value of the memory load resistors becomes higher, and nor-

Reprinted from *IEEE J. Solid-State Circuits*, vol. SC-15, pp. 201-205, Apr. 1980.

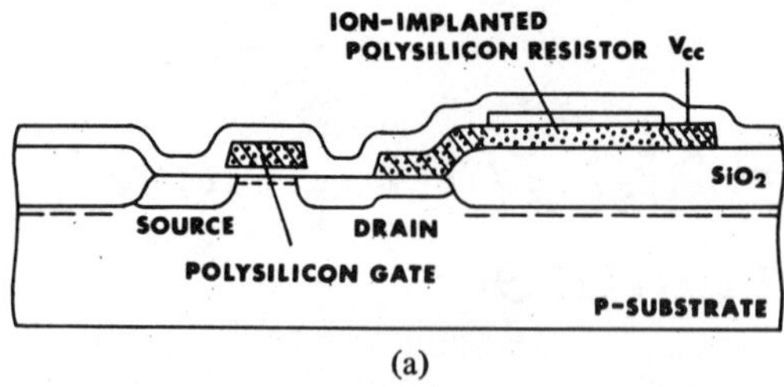

(a)

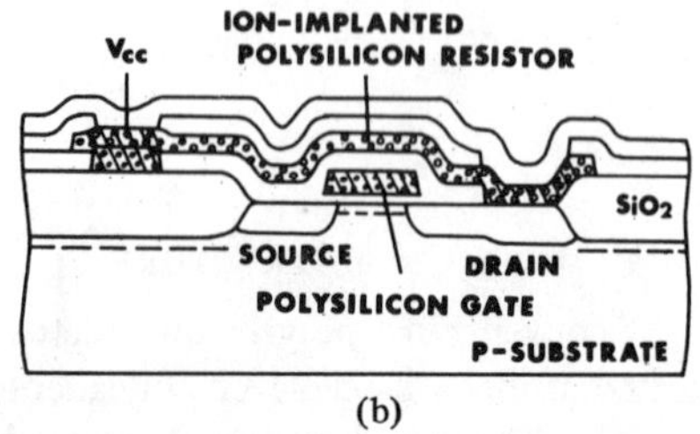

(b)

Fig. 1. Schematics of static MOS memory cell structures. (a) Conventional resistor load memory cell fabricated by single-level polysilicon process. (b) New resistor load memory cell structure fabricated by double-level polysilicon process.

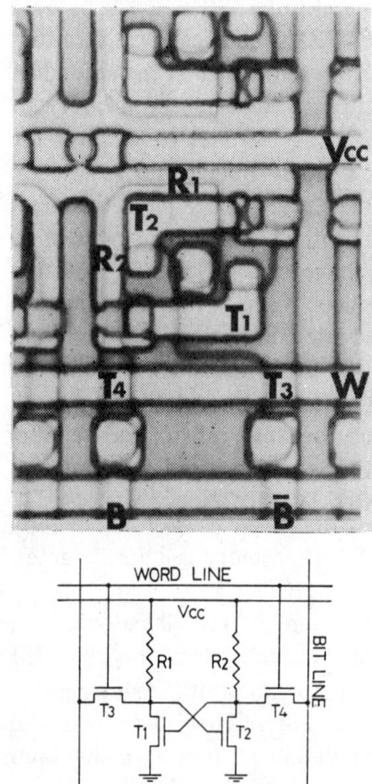

Fig. 2. Photomicrograph of the new memory cell before aluminum metallization.

mal flip-flop operations of the memory cells cannot be expected at last. To avoid the short-channel effects, the physical parameters of MOSFET's such as gate oxide thickness and diffusion depth of source/drain are scaled down based on the scaling theory [8].

Fig. 3 shows the process sequence of the RAM. The process is based on an n-channel E/D-type polysilicon gate MOS IC process combined with double-level polysilicon technology and LOCOS technology [9].

The features of the process sequence are described in the following.

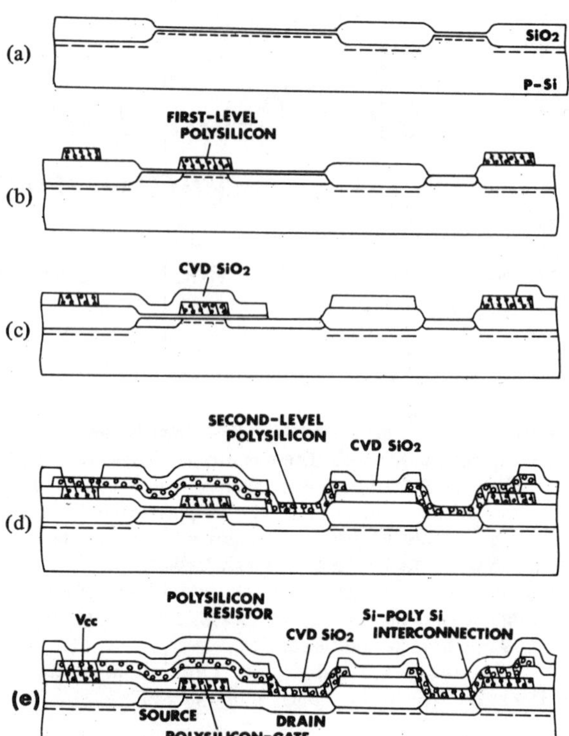

Fig. 3. Fabrication process sequence of the RAM.

1) Silicon substrate is p-type, (100) oriented wafer with a resistivity of 10-15 Ω · cm. The double layer film with a SiO_2 film of 50 nm and a Si_3N_4 film of 120 nm is formed all over the substrate, and then the Si_3N_4 film is selectively removed to define active areas. Boron ions are implanted into the substrate through the SiO_2 film to a dose of 10^{13} cm^{-2} at 60 keV in order to control the threshold voltage in the field regions to be above 7 V. Thick field oxide films of 600 nm are formed by thermal oxidation. After the Si_3N_4 films are selectively removed, boron and phosphorus ions are implanted through the SiO_2 film under the removed Si_3N_4 film to control the threshold voltage of enhancement-type and depletion-type MOSFET's, respectively. Three kinds of threshold voltage are used in the RAM as described in the next section: V_{TE} in enhancement-type MOSFET's and V_{TD1} and V_{TD2} in depletion-type MOSFET's. Boron ions are implanted at 50 keV to a dose of 6×10^{11} cm^{-2} for V_{TE} control. Phosophorus ions are implanted at 100 keV to doses of 9×10^{11} and 3×10^{11} cm^{-2} for V_{TD1} and V_{TD2} control, respectively.

2) After removing the SiO_2 film of 50 nm, gate oxide of 65 nm is formed. Immediately after the gate oxide formation, the first-level polysilicon film is deposited by thermal decomposition of SiH_4 to a thickness of ~350 nm. Phosphorus impurities are diffused in order to lower the sheet resistance value of the polysilicon films below 30 Ω/□. Then, the pattern definition of polysilicon gates and interconnections are performed. Arsenic ions are implanted into the substrate through oxide films of 65 nm at 180 keV to a dose of 4×10^{15} cm^{-2} to form source and drain regions by using the polysilicon gates as a mask to prevent arsenic implantation into the channel region. Both of the phosphorus and arsenic impurities are doped in the first-level polysilicon films. The sheet resistance

value and the junction depth of the arsenic ion-implanted region after process are ~40 Ω/□ and ~0.4 μm, respectively.

3) Nondoped CVD SiO_2 film of ~300 nm is deposited and densified at 1000°C for 15 min in an N_2 atmosphere. The first- and second-level polysilicon films are isolated by the CVD SiO_2 film. Then, contact holes to source/drain and the first-level polysilicon films are opened.

4) The second-level nondoped polysilicon film of ~300 nm is deposited. Arsenic ions are implanted at 100 keV to a dose of about $10^{14}cm^{-2}$ into the polysilicon film to control the sheet resistance value to be about 10 MΩ/□. Then, the second-level polysilicon film is formed to be memory load resistors, interconnections between source/drain regions and the first-level polysilicon films, and the protection films against aluminum spikes during aluminum–silicon sintering. CVD SiO_2 film of ~300 nm is deposited again. Contact holes are opened by the same photomask used in process 3), and then phosphorus impurities are diffused into the contact areas to lower the sheet resistance value of the second-level polysilicon films. The diffusion process also results in certifying the good contact between the second-level polysilicon film and the source/drain or the first-level polysilicon film. The junction depth of the contact area between the second-level polysilicon film and source/drain region becomes ~0.6 μm, because high concentration phosphorus impurities are diffused through the second-level polysilicon film.

5) CVD SiO_2 film of ~600 nm is deposited, and annealed at 1000°C for 15 min in an N_2 atmosphere. Then, contact holes to form aluminum interconnections are opened. Finally, aluminum metallization and aluminum–silicon sintering are performed.

Nine photomasks and ten photolithography steps are needed to fabricate the RAM. Three of the nine photomasks are used for the definition of ion-implanted areas to control threshold voltage.

Fig. 4 shows a cross-sectional SEM photomicrograph of a processed MOSFET. Fig. 5 shows *V-I* characteristics of MOSFET's with 3 μm gate lengths and experimentally fabricated 2 μm gate lengths. The breakdown voltage of the 3 μm-MOSFET is determined by junction breakdown voltage between the drain and boron implanted region under the field oxide. The punchthrough voltage above 10 V is obtained in case of the 2 μm-MOSFET.

Fig. 6 shows a photomicrograph of the processed 16 kbit RAM. About 101 100 elements are integrated on a chip of 3.75 × 4.19 mm. Memory cell array of 128 × 128 bits occupies about 65 percent of the chip area. It can be recognized that the new memory cell structure and fine photolithography technology contribute to the reduction of chip size.

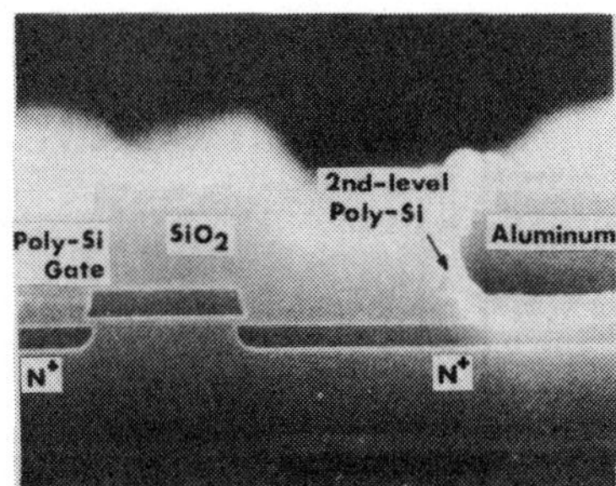

Fig. 4. A cross-sectional SEM photomicrograph of the processed MOSFET.

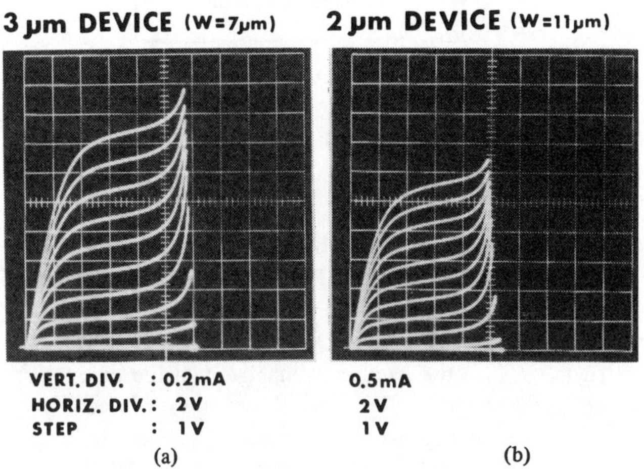

Fig. 5. *V-I* characteristics of MOSFET's with gate length of (a) 3 μm and (b) 2 μm, respectively.

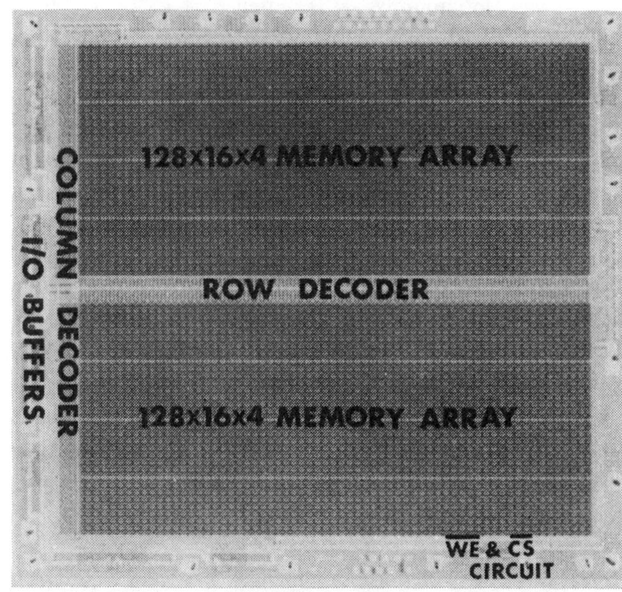

Fig. 6. Photomicrograph of the 2K × 8-bit static RAM. Chip size is 3.75 × 4.19 mm.

Circuit Diagram and Electrical Characteristics

The RAM is organized as 2K × 8 bits for the use of by-eight microprocessors. The RAM has socket compatibility to popular 16 kbit PROM's and ROM's in 24-pin packages. Fig. 7 shows the circuit block diagram of the RAM. The RAM uses a single 5 V supply and has nonclocked operation. The RAM has also powerdown-mode operation [7] which means that the dissipation current at $\overline{CS}$ = "1" (when the chip is deselected) is decreased about $\frac{1}{5}$ - $\frac{1}{10}$ of that at $\overline{CS}$ = "0" (when the chip is selected). Powerdown control signals (PDC's) generated in the control circuit block are supplied to the peripheral circuits such as row and column decoders and I/O circuits to realize effective powerdown-mode operation.

The peripheral circuits except for the memory cell array are E/D MOS circuits which are constructed by two kinds of inverters. Conventional inverters in which the gate and source of the depletion-type load MOSFET with V_{TD1} are connected are

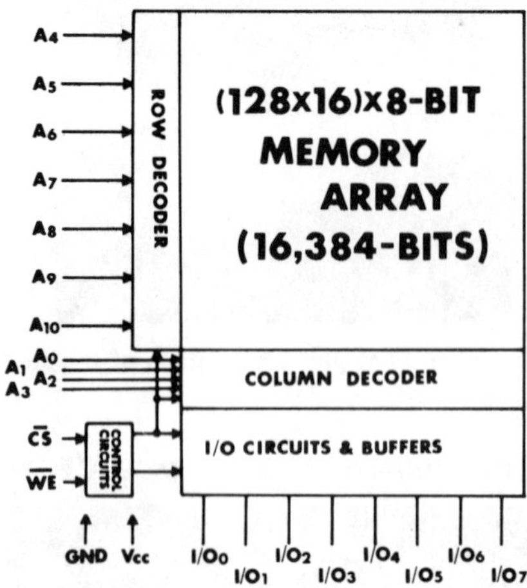

Fig. 7. Circuit block diagram of the RAM.

used only in part of the control circuit block. While the powerdown controlled inverter in which the PDC signal is supplied to the gate of the load MOSFET with V_{TD2}, as shown in Fig. 8(a), is used in almost all of the peripheral circuits. The latter inverter is active when the PDC signal is "1". When the PDC signal is "0," the inverter is inactive and the dissipation current is decreased. Fig. 8(b) shows a calculated V_{TD2} dependence of the powerdown ratio R_{PD}, which means the ratio of dissipation currents at PDC signal is "0" and "1." Fig. 8(b) also shows the maximum "1" level output voltage $V_{0\max}$ of the inverter. V_{TD2} is selected to be about -1 V, because minimum R_{PD} is obtained at $V_{0\max}$ = 5.0 V. Fig. 8(c) shows the measured dissipation current characteristics of the inverter as a parameter of PDC signal voltage V_{PDC}. R_{PD} of about 10 percent can be obtained at $V_{TD2} \simeq -0.8$ V.

To realize a more effective powerdown-mode operation, output voltages generated in row and column decoders are set to be "0" when chip is deselected. Consequently, the memory cell array is completely deselected, and the dissipation current which flows charging MOSFET's of each bit line decreases to zero.

Fig. 9 shows access time T_A versus supply voltage V_{CC} characteristics of the RAM. T_A of about 150 ns is obtained at a selected current of 117 mA and deselected current of 12 mA. T_A from 100-200 ns can be obtained by controlling the value of V_{TD2}. For example, T_A of 90 ns is measured at a selected current of 145 mA for $V_{TD2} \simeq -1.2$ V. The characteristics of the 16 kbit RAM are summarized in Table I.

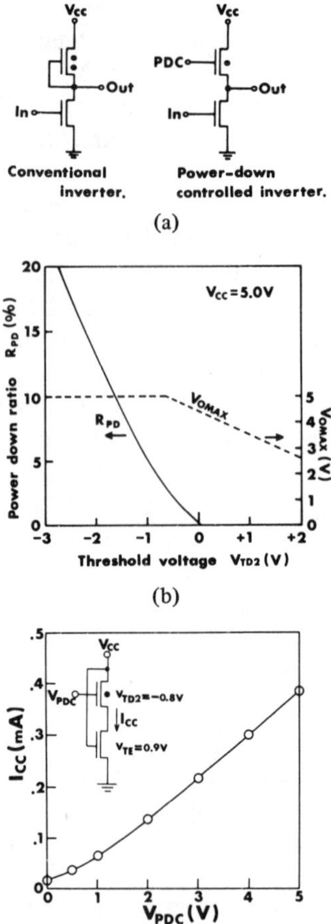

Fig. 8. Powerdown controlled E/D inverter. (a) E/D inverter circuit. (b) Powerdown ratio R_{PD} versus threshold voltage V_{TD2} characteristics. (c) Measured dissipation current characteristics of an E/D inverter.

SELECTED CURRENT : 117mA

DESELECTED CURRENT: 12mA

Fig. 9. Access time T_A versus supply voltage V_{CC} characteristics of a 16K RAM. Selected current and deselected current are 117 and 12 mA, respectively.

SUMMARY

Static memory cell area of 621 μm^2 has been successfully fabricated by combining a new memory cell structure and photolithography technology of 3 μm dimensions. The memory load resistors can be fabricated over the driver MOSFET by introducing double-level polysilicon process into the static RAM's fabrication process.

The new memory cell structure has been applied to a 16 kbit static RAM resulting in a chip size of 3.75 × 4.19 mm. The features of the RAM process are as follows:

1) higher packing density has been realized by fabricating the memory load resistors and interconnections in the second-level polysilicon films;

2) ion-implantations for threshold voltage control of MOSFET's are performed before gate oxidation. As the result, the first-level polysilicon film can be deposited immediately after gate oxidation to prevent oxide contamination and pinhole generation caused by photoetching steps;

3) there exists a low-resistance second-level polysilicon film in contact region between the aluminum film and the source/

TABLE I
CHARACTERISTICS OF THE 16K RAM

PARAMETERS	16K FULLY STATIC RAM
ORGANIZATION	2K×8
SUPPLY VOLTAGE	+5V
INTERFACE	TTL(THREE STATE I/O)
ACCESS TIME	150ns
CYCLE TIME	150ns
SELECTED CURRENT	120mA
DESELECTED CURRENT	15mA
CHIP SIZE	3.75×4.19mm
MEMORY CELL SIZE	23×27μm
PACKAGE	24 pin

drain region to prevent the formation of aluminum spikes during the sintering step. Leakage current in the source/drain regions through the substrate scarcely increase even at a sintering temperature of 490°C.

The memory cell area can be decreased to 270 and 70 μm^2 by applying lithography technology of 2 and 1 μm dimensions, respectively. The memory cell structure may be a promising one to realize larger memory size static RAM such as 64 kbits on a small chip.

ACKNOWLEDGMENT

The authors are most thankful to Dr. S. Kisaka and H. Hozumi for their encouragement. The authors would like to thank Mr. Esaki for his useful discussions, M. Noyori, S. Kondo, and T. Shiragasawa for their support of device measurements, Y. Nakagiri and K. Ichida for their support of circuit analysis, and I. Kitahiro, T. Komeda, and H. Kuroda for their device fabrication.

REFERENCES

[1] T. Ishihara, H. Hozumi, T. Hirao, and T. Ohzone, "Application of ion-implantation technology to resistor load MOS IC," (in Japanese) in *4th Symp. Ion-Implantation into Semiconductors*, Feb. 1973, pp. 227-238.

[2] T. R. O'Connell, J. M. Hartman, E. D. Errett, G. S. Leach, and W. C. Dunn, "A 4K static clocked and nonclocked RAM design," in *ISSCC Dig. Tech. Papers*, Feb. 1977, pp. 14-15.

[3] V. G. Mckenny, "A 5-V-only 4-K static RAM," in *ISSCC Dig. Tech. Papers*, Feb. 1977, pp. 16-17.

[4] G. S. Leach, J. M. Hartman, K. L. Clark, and T. R. O'Connell, "A 1K × 8-bit 5V-only static RAM," in *ISSCC Dig. Tech. Papers*, Feb. 1978, pp. 104-105.

[5] T. Ohzone, T. Hirao, K. Tsuji, S. Horiuchi, and S. Takayanagi, "A 2K × 8-bit static RAM," in *Tech. Dig. Int. Electron Devices Meeting*, Dec. 1978, pp. 360-363.

[6] R. D. Pashley, S. S. Liu, W. H. Owen, J. M. Owen, J. Shappir, R. J. Smith, and R. W. Jecmen, "A 16K × 1b static RAM," in *ISSCC Dig. Tech. Papers*, Feb. 1979, pp. 106-107, 287.

[7] R. D. Pashley, W. H. Owen, K. P. Kokkonen, R. M. Jecmen, C. N. Ahlquist, and P. Schoen, "A high performance 4K static RAM fabricated with an advanced MOS technology," in *ISSCC Dig. Tech. Papers*, Feb. 1977, pp. 22-23, 231.

[8] R. H. Dennard, F. H. Gaensslen, H. N. Yu, V. L. Rideout, E. Bassous, and A. R. Leblanc, "Design of ion-implanted MOSFET's with very small physical dimensions," *IEEE J. Solid-State Circuits*, vol. SC-9, pp. 256-268, Oct. 1974.

[9] J. A. Appels, E. Kooi, M. M. Paffen, J. J. H. Schatorjé, and W. H. C. G. Verkuylen, "Local oxidation of silicon and its application in semiconductor-device technology," *Philips Res. Rep.*, vol. 25, pp. 118-132, Apr. 1970.

VARIABLE RESISTANCE POLYSILICON FOR HIGH DENSITY CMOS RAM

T. Iizuka, H. Nozawa, Y. Mizutani, H. Kaneko and S. Kohyama

Semiconductor Device Engineering Laboratory
TOSHIBA Corporation, Kawasaki, Japan

ABSTRACT

A new and attractive structure of static RAM cell with a variable resistance polysilicon load, i.e. a polysilicon transistor load (PTL) has been developed. The resistance is controlled by "under gate" formed of underlying n^+-layer. Symmetric p- and n-MOSFET actions of the undoped polysilicon transistor are observed and theoretically analyzed. The PTL, operating as a p-MOSFET, enables data storage with a current as low as 10^{-10} ampere per bit. The PTL conductance in an "ON" state is high enough to overcome fabrication process fluctuations or radiation stimuli. Utilizing n^+-layer interconnections under the polysilicon, a small cell size of 899um^2, which is comparable to conventional polysilicon load four-transistor cells, is achieved with a 3um design rule. Test memory arrays have been fabricated and READ/WRITE operations are successfully verified.

INTRODUCTION

Polysilicon load cell is widely used in most of the existing high density static RAM's because of its small cell size capability (1). The passive load elements, however, have to consume rather high data-storage power in order to guarantee the noise immunity and stability. On the other hand, conventional six-transistor CMOS RAM cell has definite advantages of wide operational margin and extremely small data-retention power due to its active load elements. However, it is accompanied by several difficulties due to its large cell size and process complexity.

In this paper, a new structure of a static RAM cell using a polysilicon active load, i.e. polysilicon transistor load (PTL) is described. The polysilicon resistor is actually a polysilicon thin film transistor (TFT) (2), controlled by "under gate" which is the n^+-layer underlying beneath the polysilicon film and the thin gate oxide. Utilizing n^+-layer interconnections crossing under the polysilicon together, a small cell size, which is comparable to the conventional polysilicon load cell, can be achieved. Moreover, the cell with p-MOSFET mode PTL can store data with a low power consumption as in standard CMOS RAM cells.

FABRICATION

In principle, the RAM cell with the PTL can be fabricated with combination of polysilicon gate MOS process and high dose ion implantation technique. The cell structure is shown in Fig. 1.

Until the gate oxidation, the process is compatible with CMOS or NMOS processes. After the gate oxidation, about 700A in this study, the undergate of PTL is formed in p-type substrate or P-well by selective high dose Arsenic ion implantation, which is about 10^{15}atom/cm^2 or more. Then intrinsic polysilicon film of 4000A thickness is deposited on the gate oxide. For V_{TH} adjustment, Boron ions are implanted at the interface between the polysilicon film and the gate oxide through the polysilicon. After the polysilicon patterning, CVD SiO_2 is deposited and then selectively removed in order to keep the polysilicon transistor region to be undoped during an arsenic diffusion for source and drain. After the source and drain diffusion, the RAM process follows usual MOS process to the end. Therefore, the process requires only a minor modification of the conventional MOS processes.

POLYSILICON TRANSISTOR CHARACTERISTICS

Undoped polysilicon transistor with Ohmic source and drain junctions shows a symmetric I-V characteristics as shown in Fig. 2(a). Fig. 2(b) is an equi-current V_{DS}(drain voltage relative to source) vs. V_{GS}(gate voltage relative to source) curve at a drain current $I_D = 0.1\mu A$ obtained from Fig. 2(a).

Drain current I_C for a TFT with Ohmic source and drain junctions is given

by $$I_D=q(W/L)C_{OX}\int(\mu_n N_{nc} + \mu_p N_{pc})d\psi \quad (1)$$

Reprinted from *IEEE Int. Electron Devices Meeting*, pp. 370–373, 1979.

and $q(N^{+}_{pt} - N^{-}_{nt} + N_{pc} - N_{nc}) + Q_i$

$$= (\psi - V_{GS})C_{OX} \qquad (2)$$

where

- q : absolute value of electron charge,
- W, L : width and length of the TFT,
- C_{OX} : gate oxide capacitance per unit area,
- μ_p, μ_n : hole and electron mobility,
- N_{pc}, N_{nc} : mobile hole and electron density per unit area,
- N^{+}_{pt}, N^{-}_{nt} : occupied localized state-density for holes and electrons in the mobility gap,
- ψ : surface potential,
- Q_i : ionized impurity density in the polysilicon film.

From Eqs. (1)-(2), drain current in each regions shown in Fig. 2(c) is obtained

as $I_D = I_p + I_n$

where hole current I_p and electron current I_n are given by

$$I_p = \begin{cases} \pm(W/2L)\mu_p C_{ox}\left[V_{GS} - (V_{DS}, 0)_{max} - V_{tp}\right]^2 & \text{for PP(p-channel pentode)} \quad \pm : V_{DS} \text{ polarity} \\ -(W/L)\mu_p C_{ox}\left[(V_{GS} - V_{tp})V_{DS} - V_{DS}^2/2\right] & \text{for PT(p-channel triode)} \\ 0 & \text{for other regions} \end{cases}$$

$$I_n = \begin{cases} \pm(W/2L)\mu_n C_{ox}\left[V_{GS} - (V_{DS}, 0)_{min} - V_{tn}\right]^2 & \text{for NP(p-channel pentode)} \quad \pm : V_{DS} \text{ polarity} \\ (W/L)\mu_n C_{ox}\left[(V_{GS} - V_{tn})V_{DS} - V_{DS}^2/2\right] & \text{for NT(n-channel triode)} \\ 0 & \text{for other regions} \end{cases}$$

and threshold voltages for p-channel, V_{tp}, and for n-channel, V_{tn} are

$$V_{tp} = -(qN_{pt} + Q_i)/C_{ox}$$

$$V_{tn} = -(-qN_{nt} + Q_i)/C_{ox} .$$

The threshold voltage gap (V_{tn}-V_{tp}) is proportional to the sum of the total localyzed state-density N_{pt} and N_{nt} for holes and electrons in the mobility gap. In the case of polycrystalline silicon, the gap (V_{tn} -V_{tp}) is large enough to separate p- and n-MOSFET mode for low voltage power supply operations. As static RAM cell loads, the p-MOSFET mode polysilicon transistor is preferable. In order to obtain a lower threshold voltage for p-channel, B^+ ions with the dose of $5\times10^{12}cm^{-2}$ was implanted. The threshold was shifted down to -5V for p-channel, which is still not sufficiently low for standard 5V operations. However, it should be noted that the "OFF" state current was not increased by the implantation. The I_D vs. V_{DS} curve measured after the implantation is shown in Fig. 3.

TEST MEMORY CELL

A static RAM cell circuit using the PTL is shown in Fig. 4. The circuit operation is principally the same as that of six-transistor CMOS cell. Structures used in the cell is shown in Fig. 1. P-well in an n-substrate configuration is used to build CMOS peripheral circuits on the same chip. The left part of Fig. 1(b) is the p-MOSFET mode polysilicon transistor whose drain region is doped with arsenic impurities, when n^+-polysilicon gates and interconnections are formed. The n^+-layer under the n^+-polysilicon, as shown in Fig. 1(c), is also used as interconnections.

Photograph of the test memory cell array is shown in Fig. 5. The cell size of $899um^2$ is obtained using a 3µm-gate rule. READ/WRITE operations are tested on a 16 by 16 memory array test device. The data storage current was in the order of 10^{-10} ampere per bit. The minimum power supply voltage for data storage, however, was rather high as a consequence of high threshold voltage of the fabricated polysilicon transistors. This can be easily improved by optimizing the threshold voltage.

CONCLUSIONS

Undoped polysilicon film transistor with Ohmic source and drain junctions shows a good symmetric I-V characteristics. The threshold voltage gap (V_{tn} -V_{tp}) for the polysilicon transistor is wide enough to separate p- and n-MOSFET modes for the standard 5V-V_{CC} operation. As a cell load, threshold voltage can be shifted to a suitable value by ion implantation without any serious degradation of "OFF" state current.

A test memory cells with 899μm^2 area/bit, which is comparable to an advanced polysilicon load cell, has been fabricated and READ/WRITE operations has been successfully tested, with a data retention current as low as 10^{-10} ampere per bit.

REFERENCES

(1) T. Ohzone, T. Hirao, K. Tsuji, S. Horiuchi and S. Takayanagi, Tech. Dig. 1978 IEDM, Washington D.C., pp.360-363.

(2) G.W. Newdeck and A.K. Malhotra, Solid-State Electron. vol. 19, pp.721-729, 1976.

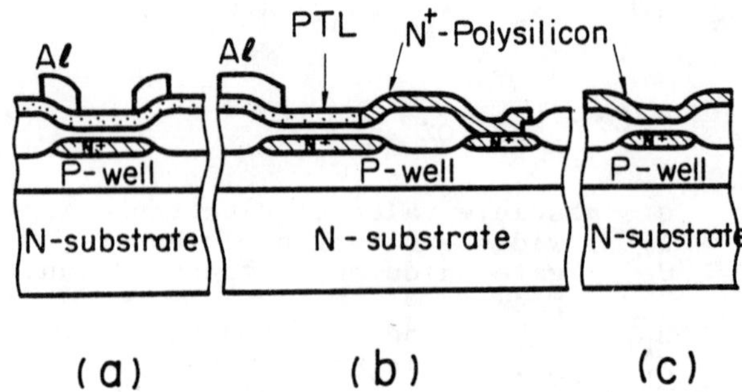

Fig.1. Cross sections of PTL cell structure.
(a) Polysilicon transistor with symmetric structure.
(b) PTL and polysilicon-to-n+-layer contact.
(c) Polysilicon-n+-layer crossover.

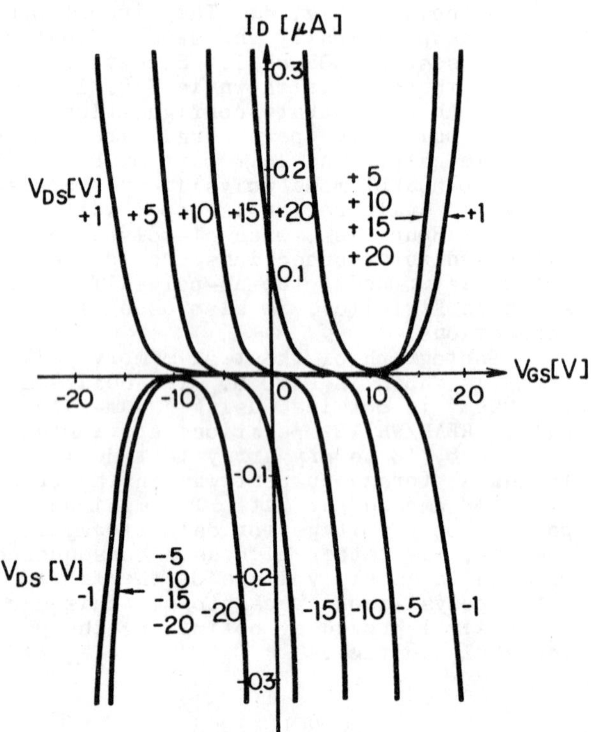

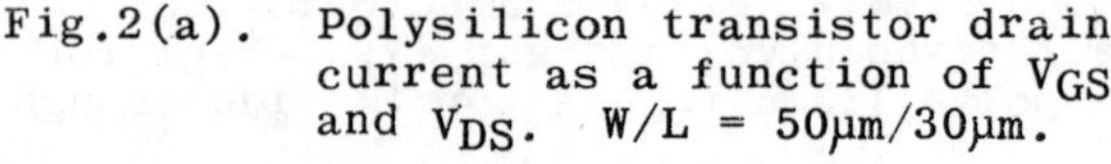

Fig.2(a). Polysilicon transistor drain current as a function of V_{GS} and V_{DS}. W/L = 50μm/30μm.

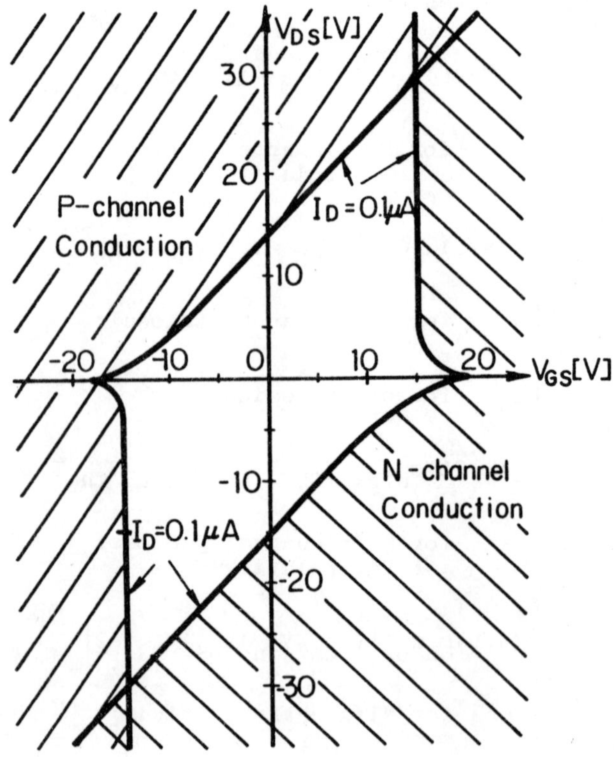

Fig.2(b). V_{DS} vs. V_{GS} curve at I_D =0.1uA derived from Fig.2(a).

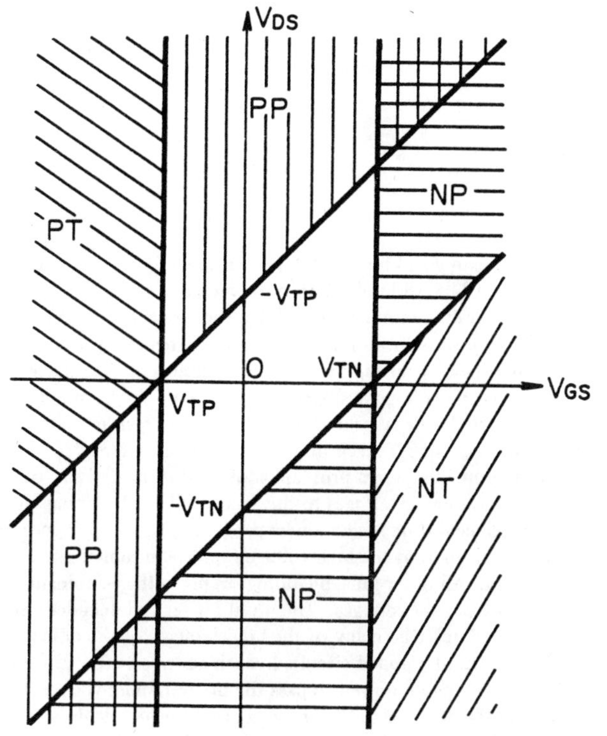

Fig.2(c). PTL operation mode map.
PP : p-channel pentode,
PT : p-channel triode,
NP : n-channel pentode,
NT : n-channel triode.

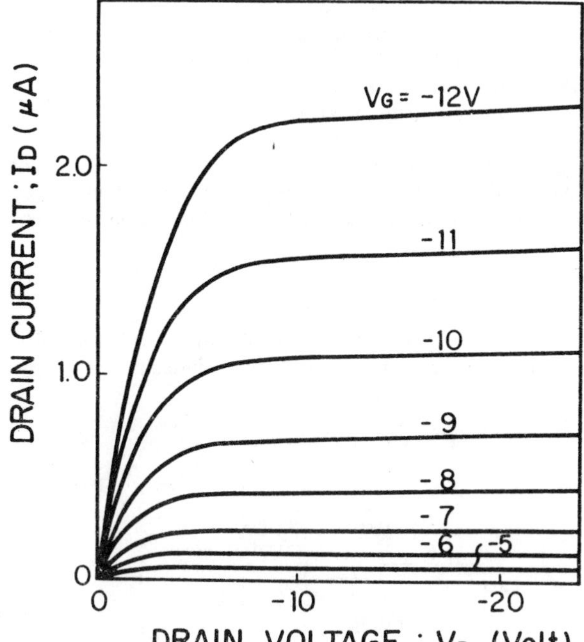

Fig.3. Drain characteristics of poly-silicon transistor.

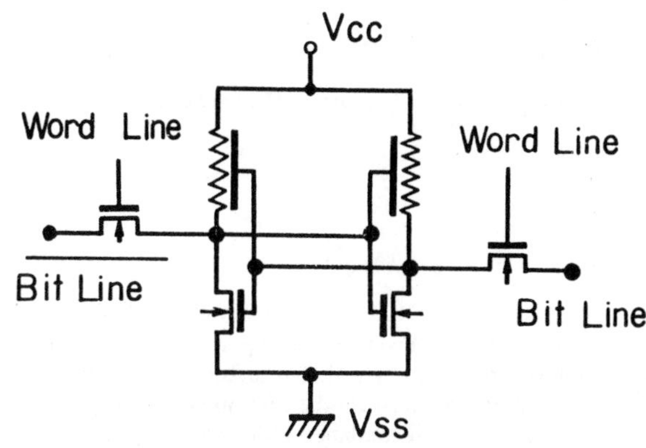

Fig.4. PTL cell circuit.

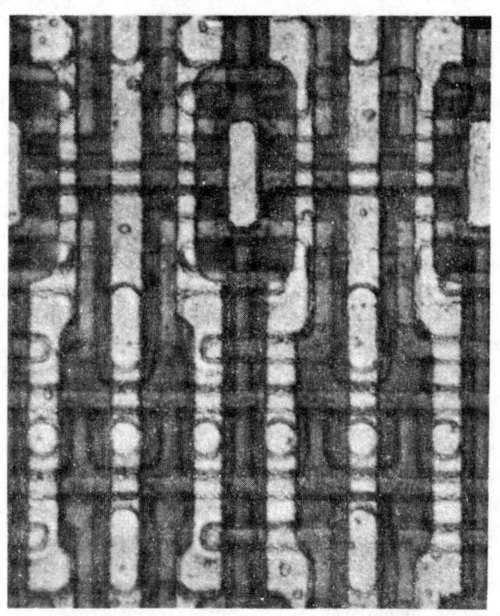

Fig.5. Photograph of the PTL cell array. The cell size is $899\mu m^2$.

High Performance MOS EPROMs using a Stacked-Gate Cell

Phillip J. Salsbury, William L. Morgan, George Perlegos and Richard T. Simko

Intel Corp.

Santa Clara, CA

A HIGH PERFORMANCE 8192-BIT Erasable PROM has been developed in response to the increasing requirements of second-generation microprocessors. The design goals of density and speed have been achieved through the development of an N-channel stacked-gate cell combined with novel peripheral circuits. The small cell size (1 mil^2) and fast memory access (450 ns max) extend EPROM performance beyond the levels established by the well known P-channel approach[1,2].

The stacked-gate device, implemented as a one-transistor cell, forms the heart of the memory. This cell, illustrated in Figure 1*(a)*, is fabricated via a dual-layer silicon-gate process and consists of a bottom floating gate and a top select gate. Both the first and second gate oxides are of standard production thickness; approx. 1000Å. The channel doping level is adjusted via ion implantation. A top view of the cell layout is shown in Figure 1*(b)*. The rows correspond to common polysilicon select gates, and the columns comprise common metal drain lines. The overlapped gate structure helps provide reproducible cell characteristics (e.g., programming margin and sense current) over a wide range of manufacturing tolerances. The 24x27-μ cell size is the smallest thus far achieved in a production MOS EPROM.

During the *read* mode, the stacked gate cell can be simulated using the capacitance-coupled circuit model of Figure 2. The *intrinsic* transistor (including C_{GS}' and C_{GD}') is readily modeled by conventional CAD techniques. The remaining *extrinsic* capacitance elements are calculated directly from layout geometry and oxide thicknesses, and are entered as normal network elements of the circuit simulation.

The cell is programmed by means of hot electrons injected through the oxide from the channel to the floating gate. This injected charge raises the effective threshold voltage measured from the top gate, as described by the programming characteristics of Figure 3. Once programmed, the charge retention characteristics are similar to the original FAMOS device. Reliability studies estimate 100 years as the time required for 5% failure of an 8K memory at 70°C[3]. Charge removal (erasure) is accomplished by exposure to ultraviolet light. Stability of the cell threshold window has been demonstrated through more than 10^3 program/erase cycles.

An 8192-bit EPROM based on the stacked gate cell is shown in Figure 4. The memory is organized 1024x8 bits, is fully decoded, and all address and data lines are TTL compatible. Chip size 134 x 189 mil. Within the memory array, the common-drain column lines perform the y-select function, and the *top-gate* lines source as x-select. Programming is accomplished by raising the selected column and the selected gate lines to a voltage of approximately 25V. Program inhibit of unselected cells is insured by column *pull-down* circuits plus careful design of *off* levels delivered by the decoders.

The principle design problem addressed is the delivery of high programming voltages to the array while maintaining high performance during *read*. A new programming circuit approach was chosen to limit the high voltage input requirements to a single pin. All other pins, including supply voltages, remain at their normal *read* voltages. The input buffer and decoder circuits of Figure 5 describe many of the key elements of the design solution. Bootstrapped circuits in each address buffer provide the voltage drive required to pass the programming voltage through the decoder to the array. Use of transfer devices for address buffer isolation, and a novel double-poly high voltage driver transistor avoid gate-controlled breakdown at key high voltage nodes. The series-parallel decoder was chosen for low power dissipation and solid *low* levels.

The column-sensing and column-programming circuitry is shown in Figure 6. Similar bootstrapped drivers deliver programming voltages to the array columns through a y-select network. The sense amplifier is a *cascode* circuit featuring a special column biasing network that is derived from the unprogrammed cell V_t. The column bias level is chosen to maximize performance while avoiding read disturb problems.

Performance figures for the 8K memory compare favorably with state-of-the-art N-channel mask programmable ROMs. The standard access time spec is 450ns, and a significant portion of the distribution falls below 325ns at 70°C. Programming speeds of 100ms/word are achieved using a 26-V programming waveform.

Acknowledgment

The authors gratefully acknowledge the contribution and guidance of D. Frohman-Bentchkowsky during the initial phase of this project.

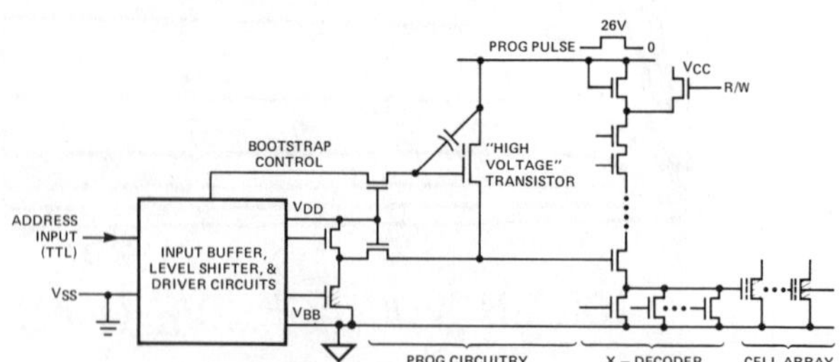

FIGURE 5 – Schematic of address buffer and row decoder circuits. Shaded transistors are ion-implanted.

---

[1] Frohman-Bentchkowsky, D., "A Fully Decoded 2048-Bit Electrically Programmable MOS ROM", *ISSCC Digest of Technical Papers*, p. 80-81; Feb., 1971.

[2] Frohman-Bentchkowsky, D., "FAMOS-A New Semiconductor Charge Storage Device", *Solid-State Electronics*, p. 517-529, Vol. 17; 1974.

[3] Gear, G., "FAMOS PROM Reliability Studies", *Proceedings of The International Reliability Physics Symposium*, p. 198-199; April, 1976.

Reprinted from *IEEE Int. Solid State Circuits Conf.*, pp. 186–187, 1977.

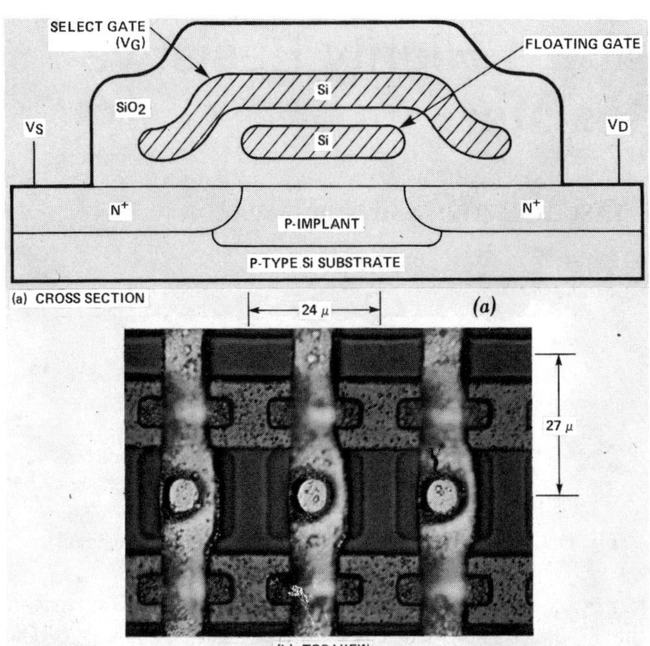

FIGURE 1 – Stacked gate memory cell: *(a)* cross-sectional view; *(b)* top view photo (cell area is $648\mu^2$).

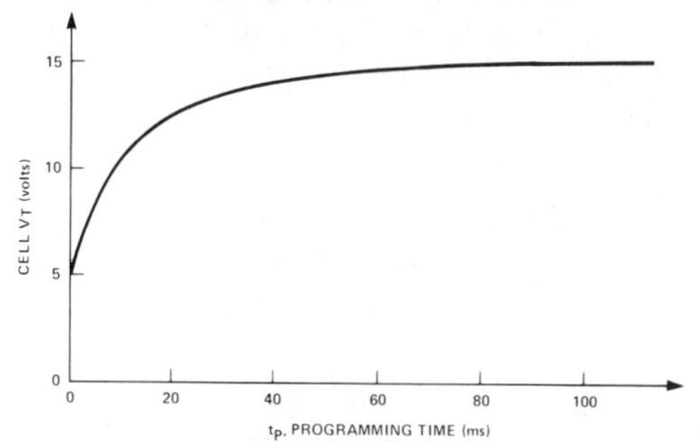

FIGURE 3 – Threshold voltage versus programming time for typical cell.

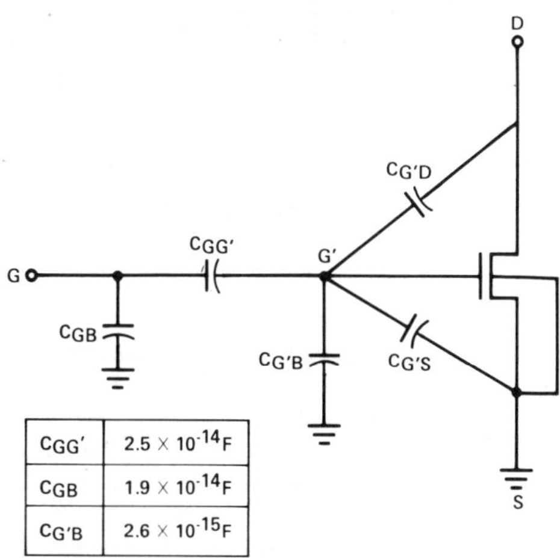

$C_{GG'}$	2.5×10^{-14}F
C_{GB}	1.9×10^{-14}F
$C_{G'B}$	2.6×10^{-15}F

FIGURE 2 – Circuit model of the cell.

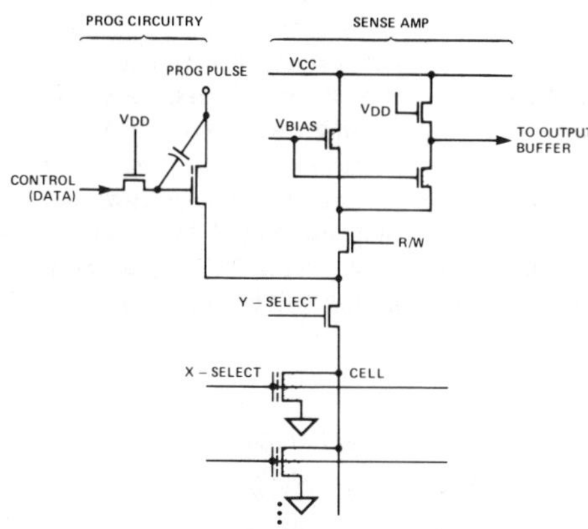

FIGURE 6 – Sense amplifier and column programming circuitry.

[Below]

FIGURE 4 – Photo of the 8K EPROM chip. Overall dimensions are 134 x 189 mils.

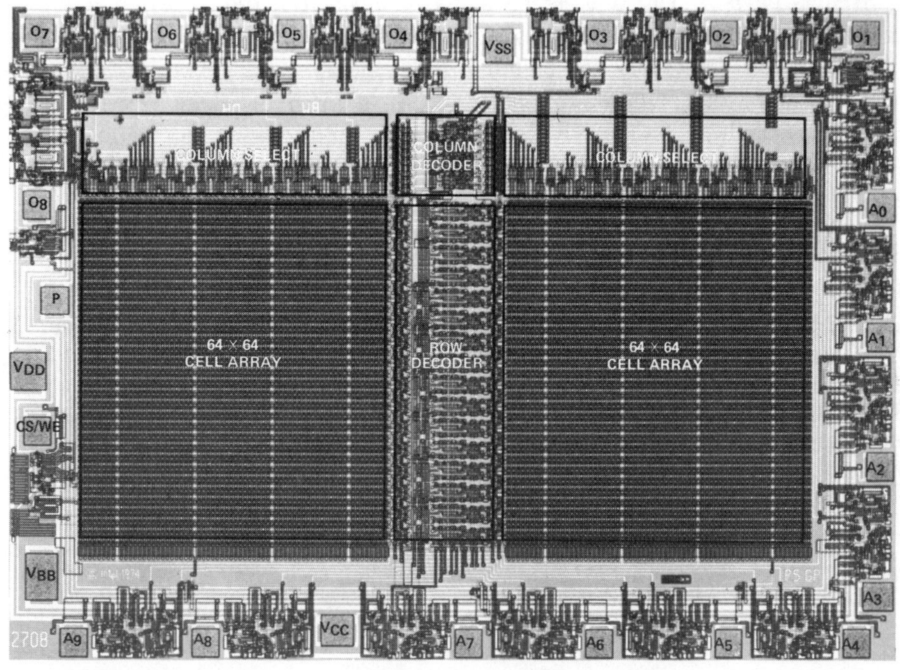

A Novel MOS PROM Using a Highly Resistive Poly-Si Resistor

MASAFUMI TANIMOTO, JUNICHI MUROTA, YASUO OHMORI, AND NOBUAKI IEDA

***Abstract*—A novel MOS electrically programmable read-only memory (PROM) using a highly resistive polycrystalline silicon (poly-Si) resistor as a memory element is proposed.**

In a highly resistive poly-Si, a new memory effect of an irreversible resistivity transition, from an initial highly resistive value to a low-resistive one, is observed. The dependencies of the transition voltage and current, which cause the transition, on the poly-Si deposition conditions, are studied, and the deposition conditions suitable for MOS PROM fabrication are obtained. The transition voltage V_t can be reduced down to 10 V by decreasing the poly-Si film thickness to 0.4 μm. The transition current is less than 10 mA.

A 36-bit MOS PROM, using the poly-Si resistor as a memory element, is fabricated. The programming voltage used in this work is 25 V and the programming time per bit is less than 10 μs. The read access time is less than 300 ns. The programming voltage, however, can be reduced down to 15 V by decreasing the poly-Si film thickness and the series resistance in the circuit. The novel PROM has another advantage in that the poly-Si resistor is compatible with a conventional silicon-gate process.

I. Introduction

A READ-ONLY MEMORY (ROM) is an important device for code conversion, character generation, and microprogramming. Various types of ROM's have been developed [1]-[7]. Among these ROM's, an electrically programmable ROM (PROM) is remarkably superior to a mask ROM in a small-volume memory system. Moreover, MOS PROM's have an advantage over bipolar PROM's in chip cost.

There are two types of MOS PROM's. One is an alterable PROM. Since alterable PROM's can be erased by applying voltage or by exposing to ultraviolet light, they can be programmed over and over again. They require, however, a high programming voltage, and some of them, such as MNOS, require a very thin gate oxide which is not used in MOS random-access memory. The other is a fusable-link PROM. The programmed state of the fusable-link PROM is stabler than that of the alterable PROM because the programming is carried out by blowing a fusable-link instead of storing charges into a floating gate or a trapping state. However, this PROM also requires a high programming voltage to flow a large programming current.

In this paper, a novel MOS PROM using a polycrystalline silicon (poly-Si) resistor as a memory element is proposed. A poly-Si resistor is composed of highly resistive poly-Si whose resistivity is above 10^3 Ω · cm. An irreversible resistivity

Manuscript received March 8, 1978; revised August 8, 1979.

The authors are with Musashino Electrical Communication Laboratory, Nippon Telegraph and Telephone Public Corporation, Musashino-shi, Tokyo, 180 Japan.

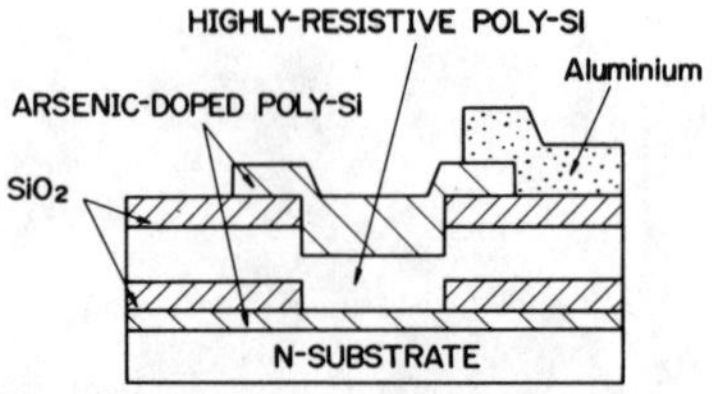

HIGHLY-RESISTIVE POLY-SI
Aluminium
ARSENIC-DOPED POLY-SI
SiO_2
N-SUBSTRATE

Fig. 1. Cross-sectional view of the highly resistive poly-Si resistor.

transition in highly resistive poly-Si is used for programming the PROM. This PROM is a kind of the fusable-link PROM. The voltage and current required for this transition can be reduced down to 10 V and less than 10 mA, respectively. Therefore, the programming voltage and current of the PROM are small, compared with those of other MOS PROM's. The fabrication process of the PROM requires no special technology because the poly-Si resistor is fabricated by a conventional silicon-gate process.

Section II describes some experimental results for the irreversible resistivity transition in poly-Si. The deposition condition of poly-Si, which is applicable to a memory element of MOS PROM, is also given. Section III covers the PROM fabrication and experimental results obtained from the PROM. Section IV summarizes the results of this work.

II. Memory Effect in Highly Resistive Poly-Si

A. Sample Preparation

The fabrication process of the poly-Si resistor, shown in Fig. 1, is as follows. First, a highly arsenic-doped poly-Si, whose resistivity is below 2×10^{-2} Ω · cm, is deposited on n-type, (100), 1.5-Ω · cm substrate as a lower electrode. Then, a highly resistive poly-Si, whose resistivity is higher than 1×10^3 Ω · cm, is deposited, by pyrolysis of SiH_4-H_2-AsH_3 system, in an RF-heated horizontal reactor at temperatures between 650 and 750°C. An upper electrode is composed of highly arsenic-doped poly-Si, whose resistivity is about 2×10^{-2} Ω · cm, and aluminum metallization on top of the poly-Si electrode. CVD SiO_2 is used to insulate the highly resistive poly-Si from each electrode, except for the active region, and the current path is constructed perpendicular to the substrate, as shown in Fig. 1.

B. Current-Voltage Characteristics

Typical current-voltage characteristics of the poly-Si resistor are shown in Fig. 2. In the initial highly resistive state, the current is proportional to the voltage in a low applied voltage region. Though the current becomes unproportional to the

Reprinted from *IEEE Trans. Electron Devices*, vol. ED-27, pp. 517-520, Mar. 1980.

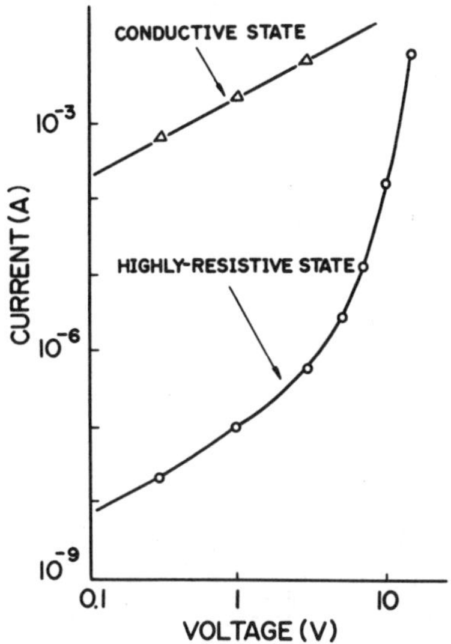

Fig. 2. Current-voltage characteristics of the poly-Si resistor.

voltage in a high applied voltage region, the current-voltage characteristic is reversible. When the applied voltage exceeds the transition voltage V_t, the highly resistive poly-Si resistor is changed irreversibly into a low-resistive one. In this low-resistive state, the current-voltage characteristic of the poly-Si resistor is linear over all the voltage region even when a reverse bias is applied.

The current path in this low-resistive poly-Si is observed by the following procedure. An aluminum metallization layer, an upper poly-Si electrode, and an upper SiO_2 film are removed by chemical etching. The highly resistive poly-Si film is Sirtl etched slightly. A selective etched area of about 1-μm diameter is observed. This means that the structure of poly-Si is changed locally. Therefore, it is suggested that 1) the current concentrates in a small area in the low-resistive poly-Si, and 2) the irreversible resistivity transition of the poly-Si resistor is caused by the structural change of highly resistive poly-Si.

A similar memory effect is obtained for a variety of sample structures. For example, it is obtained with a sample in which the lower and upper electrodes are made of an n^+-diffused layer and an aluminum (or molybdenum) metallization layer, respectively. It is also obtained with a sample in which the positions of the upper and lower electrodes are separated in parallel to the substrate, and the current path is constructed obliquely to the substrate.

In this work, arsenic-doped poly-Si is chosen as an upper electrode and the distance between the electrodes is controlled by the film thickness in order to obtain the uniformity of the transition voltage within a lot and for different lots. This memory element using the poly-Si resistor is expected to be compatible with a conventional MOS process.

C. Dependence of Transition Voltage V_t on Deposition Condition

To realize a memory device with the poly-Si resistor, it is indispensable to lower the transition voltage V_t. The relationships between the transition voltage and deposition conditions,

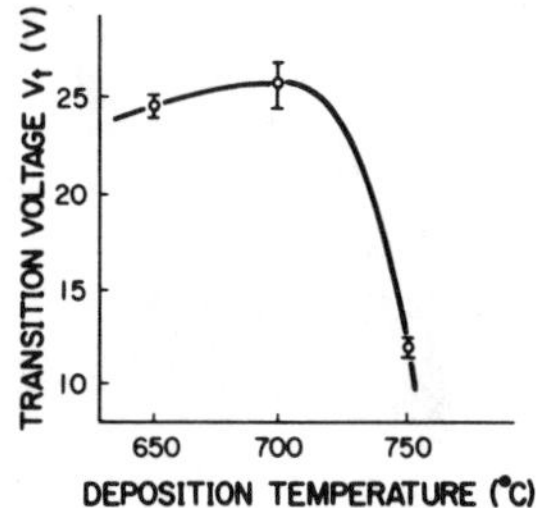

Fig. 3. Deposition temperature dependence of transition voltage V_t.

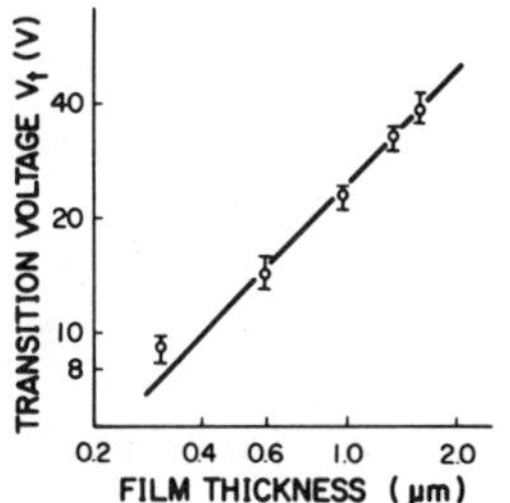

Fig. 4. Film thickness dependence of transition voltage V_t.

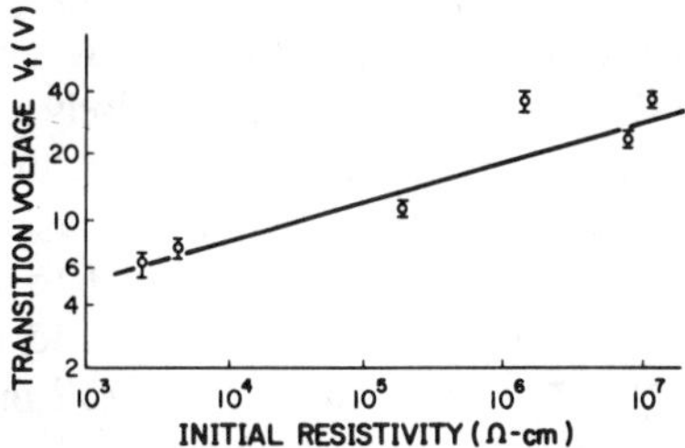

Fig. 5. Initial resistivity dependence of transition voltage V_t.

such as deposition temperature, film thickness, and partial pressure of AsH_3, are studied.

Fig. 3 shows the deposition temperature dependence of the transition voltage for an undoped poly-Si of 1.0-μm thickness. The transition voltage decreases abruptly above 700°C. The preferred orientation of the poly-Si film changes from the random orientation to the ⟨110⟩ orientation when the deposition temperature is above 700°C. It is considered that the transition voltage depends on the structure of the poly-Si film. To make the transition voltage variation small with the deposition temperature, the deposition temperature should be below 700°C.

Fig. 4 shows the film thickness dependence of the transition voltage for an undoped poly-Si deposited at 700°C. The transition voltage is proportional to the film thickness. The electric field in the film is approximately 2×10^5 V/cm. It is possible to obtain a transition voltage of less than 10 V by decreasing the film thickness down to 0.4 μm, as shown in Fig. 4.

Fig. 5 shows the initial resistivity dependence of the transition voltage for the highly resistive poly-Si with a 1.0-μm thickness, deposited at 700°C. The initial resistivity is varied from 1×10^3 to 1×10^7 Ω · cm by varying the AsH_3 partial pressure during deposition of the poly-Si. The transition voltage tends to increase with the initial resistivity. The transi-

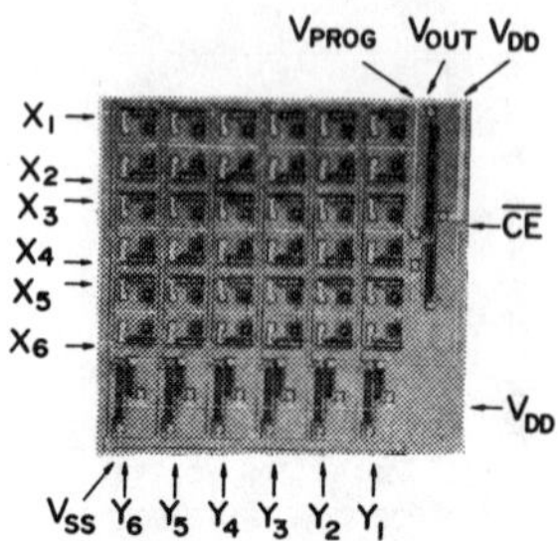

Fig. 6. Microphotograph of the MOS PROM. Effective area is 0.7 mm × 0.7 mm.

tion voltage can be made less than 10 V by lowering the initial resistivity down to $1 \times 10^4\ \Omega \cdot$cm, even for a 1.0-$\mu$m film thickness. Undoped poly-Si, however, is preferable because it is difficult to control the initial resistivity by varying the AsH_3 partial pressure.

D. Application to Memory Element in PROM

As described above, the poly-Si resistor has a memory effect and its transition voltage is low. The pulsewidth dependence of the transition voltage V_t is small; for example, V_t's at 0.1-μs pulsewidth and at 1.0 μs are larger than that under dc condition by only 15 and 5 percent, respectively. The current required for the irreversible transition (transition current I_t) depends on deposition conditions, electrode area, and film thickness. The transition current is from 1 to 10 mA, when the transition voltage is from 25 to 10 V and the electrode area is below 100 μm^2. The total deviations from the average value of the transition voltage V_t and current I_t for different lots are 10 percent for V_t and 30 percent for I_t.

The stability of the poly-Si resistor in low- and highly resistive state is tested at 100°C with an applied voltage of 10 V. The resistance of the poly-Si resistor does not change under these conditions.

The ratio of the resistance in a highly resistive state to that in a low-resistive state is larger than 10^4 in a low applied voltage region at temperatures below 70°C. The temperature dependence of the transition voltage V_t is small; for example, V_t at 70°C is only 10 percent smaller than V_t at room temperature.

From these results, it is confirmed that the poly-Si resistor will become an excellent memory element of an MOS PROM.

III. MOS PROM

A. Fabrication

A 36-bit MOS PROM using the poly-Si resistor is fabricated. Its microphotograph is shown in Fig. 6. The PROM is constructed with a 6 × 6 bit memory cell array, address selecting MOSFET's, and an output amplifier. Fig. 7(a) and (b) shows an equivalent circuit and a cross-sectional view of a memory cell, respectively. The cell consists of a poly-Si resistor and a selecting MOSFET, which are connected in series.

A conventional n-channel silicon-gate process is used to fabricate this device on a p-type, (100), 1.5-$\Omega \cdot$cm substrate. The MOSFET has a gate oxide thickness of 1000 Å and an

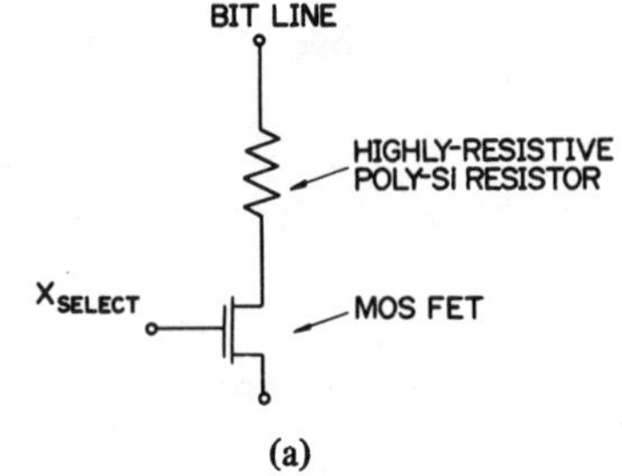

(a)

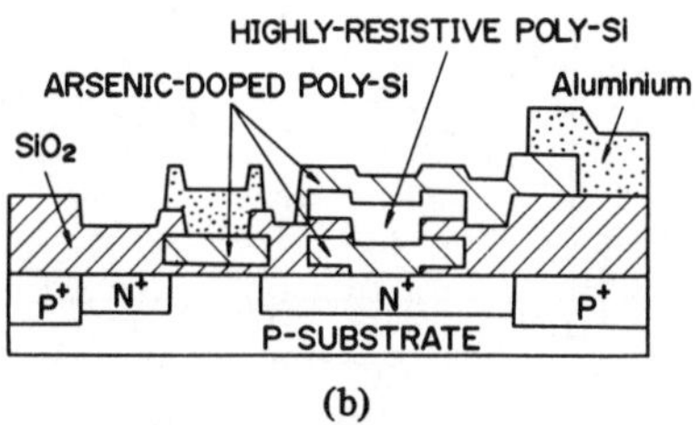

(b)

Fig. 7. Memory cell. (a) Circuit diagram. (b) Cross-sectional view.

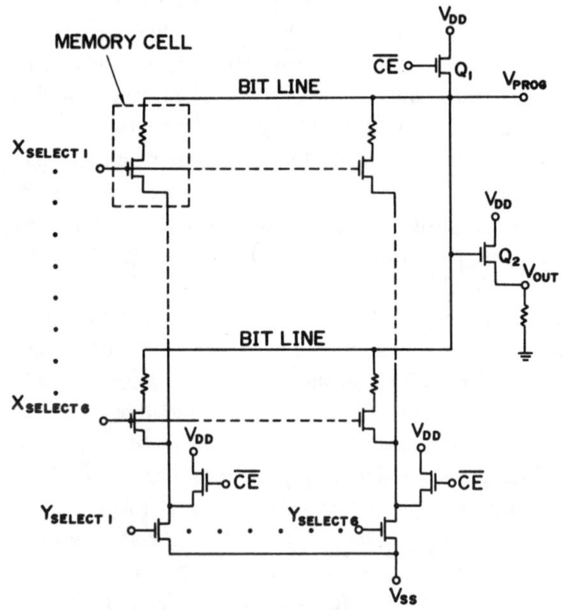

Fig. 8. Circuit diagram of the MOS PROM.

effective channel length of 5 μm. The threshold voltage of the MOSFET is 1.1 V when the substrate bias voltage is -2 V. The poly-Si resistor, as shown in Fig. 1, is constructed with undoped poly-Si on the n^+-diffused drain region of the FET. Undoped poly-Si is deposited at 700°C. The film thickness of poly-Si is selected as 0.6 μm because the transition voltage should be larger than the power supply voltage V_{DD} of the PROM. The transition voltage of this film is expected to be 15 V, while V_{DD} is 10 V.

B. Device Operation

A circuit diagram of the PROM is shown in Fig. 8. The programming operation can be performed as follows. A cell (X_i, Y_j) is selected by raising the $X_{\mathrm{SELECT}\,i}$ and $Y_{\mathrm{SELECT}\,j}$ line

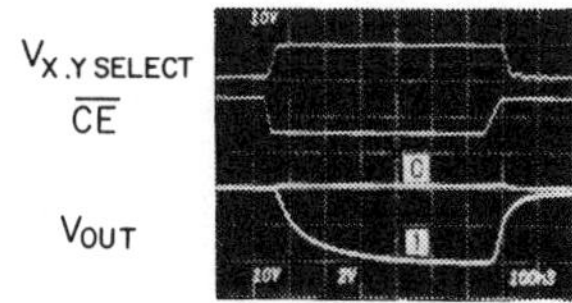

Fig. 9. Operation waveforms.

potentials and a voltage larger than the transition voltage is applied to the V_{PROG}. The resistance of a highly resistive poly-Si resistor is lowered and the programming operation is accomplished at this particular address location. Read operation can be performed in the following manner. The bit line is precharged through a transistor Q_1 by the $\overline{CE}$ signal. A cell (X_i, Y_j) is selected by raising the $X_{SELECT\,i}$ and $Y_{SELECT\,j}$ line potentials. As a result, the potential of the precharged bit line decreases. The time constant of this transient response is determined by the resistance of a highly resistive poly-Si resistor, g_m of the MOSFET, and parasitic capacitance. Since the ratio of the resistance for the poly-Si resistor in a highly resistive state to that in a low-resistive state is about 10^4, the time constant difference between "1" and "0" written in a cell is very large. Therefore, the information in a selected cell can be read by monitoring the bit-line voltage by the source-follower transistor Q_2.

The programming and read operations of the fabricated PROM are successfully verified. The programming voltage is 25 V and time required for programming is less than 10 μs per bit. Read access is less then 300 ns. Output waveforms of this PROM, when stored information "1" and "0" are read, are shown in Fig. 9. The resistor of 5 kΩ is connected to the V_{OUT}. The following voltages are used to operate this PROM:

PROGRAMMING: $V_{X,Y\,SELECT} = 20$ V $\quad V_{PROG} = 25$ V

READ: $V_{X,Y\,SELECT} = 10$ V $\quad \overline{CE} = 10$ V.

In the programming mode, $V_{X,Y\,SELECT}$ is chosen to be 20 V to provide the current required for the programming. On the other hand, $V_{X,Y\,SELECT}$ is chosen to be 10 V in the read mode. A dc bias voltage of 10 V is applied as V_{DD} and that of -2 V as the substrate bias V_{BB}.

In this fabricated PROM using 0.6-μm-thick poly-Si, the programming voltage is expected to be 20 V, taking into account the potential drops in the address selecting transistors. However, the programming voltage V_{PROG} used in this work is 25 V, because of potential drops in the upper poly-Si electrode and common line which is connected in series to the highly resistive poly-Si resistor. The resistance of an upper electrode is more than 500 Ω because it is composed of an arsenic-doped poly-Si whose resistivity is about 2×10^{-2} $\Omega \cdot$ cm as described in Section II-A. The common line, connecting memory cell and Y-select transistor, is composed of a diffused layer whose sheet resistance is about 15 $\Omega/\square$. The total resistance of the common line is, for example, about 1 kΩ for memory cell (X_1, Y_1). The potential drops in the upper poly-Si electrode and the common line can be reduced by optimizing cell structure and physical layout. Therefore, V_{PROG} can be lowered to 20 V. Moreover, V_{PROG} can be reduced down to 15 V since the transition voltage is expected to be 10 V by decreasing the poly-Si film thickness to 0.4 μm.

IV. Conclusions

A memory effect in a highly resistive poly-Si and a novel MOS PROM using this memory effect are described.

An irreversible transition from a highly resistive state to a low-resistive state is observed in a highly resistive poly-Si. The transition voltage V_t at which the highly resistive poly-Si resistor is changed to a low-resistive one can be reduced down to 10 V by increasing the deposition temperature and by decreasing the film thickness and the initial resistivity. The current necessary for this transition is less than 10 mA.

A 36-bit MOS PROM, using the poly-Si resistor as a memory element, is fabricated. This novel PROM has an advantage in that it can be programmed with a low voltage and a small current. In addition, its fabrication process requires no special technology, because the poly-Si resistor is fabricated by a conventional silicon-gate process.

Acknowledgment

The authors wish to thank Dr. H. Toyoda, Dr. H. Yoshimura, M. Kondo, and M. Hirai, for their support of this work, and Dr. T. Asaoka for his useful discussions and comments. They are also grateful to their colleagues at the Semiconductor Memory Technology Section, and Mask and Pattern Generation Section for the device fabrication.

References

[1] D. Kahng and S. M. Sze, "A floating gate and its application to memory devices," *Bell Syst. Tech. J.*, vol. 46, pp. 1288-1295, July-Aug. 1967.

[2] D. Frohmann-Bentchkowsky, "A fully-decoded 2048-bit electrically-programmable MOS ROM," in *ISSCC Dig. Tech. Papers*, pp. 80-81, Feb. 1971.

[3] J. T. Wallmark and J. H. Scott, "Switching and storage characteristics of MIS memory transistors," *RCA Rev.*, vol. 30, pp. 335-365, June 1969.

[4] Y. Uchida, N. Endo, S. Saito, M. Konaka, I. Nojima, Y. Nishi, and K. Tamaru, "A 1024-bit MNOS RAM using avalanche-tunnel injection," in *ISSCC Dig. Tech. Papers*, pp. 108-109, Feb. 1975.

[5] J. Scharbert and H. Murrmann, "A 1024-bit ECL-PROM with 15ns access," in *ISSCC Dig. Tech. Papers*, pp. 106-107, Feb. 1975.

[6] T. J. Rodgers, R. Hiltpold, J. W. Zimmer, G. Marr, and J. D. Trotter, "VMOS ROM," *IEEE J. Solid-State Circuits*, vol. SC-11, pp. 614-622, Oct. 1976.

[7] J. E. Schroder and R. L. Gosline, "A 1024-bit fused-link CMOS PROM," in *ISSCC Dig. Tech. Papers*, pp. 190-191, Feb. 1977.

Section 3.2
Peripheral Circuits

The Design of MOS Dynamic RAMs

Richard C. Foss

Mosaid, Inc.

Ottawa, Canada

AT ISSCC 72 a paper[1] representing the introduction of modern MOS dynamic RAM development was presented. A balanced flipflop sense amplifier and restore circuit with cells on either side of a divided bit line was described in that classic report. While the development milestones since then are seen externally as the move from 1K to 4K to 16K and now 64K bit densities, the key advances internally are rather subtle.

The original forms of sense amplifier[2] used simple clocked loads which created a speed power tradeoff between the active power consumed and the time taken to restore a one-level on the high-going bit line half. Two alternatives, both avoiding this tradeoff, have emerged as standard approaches. One is the *pre-charge high bit-line*[3] in which the cell one level is restored by connection to a bit line pre-charged to V_{DD} during the standby time. This also allows a dummy cell of about half the real cell area, pre-charged to ground, to give a *half charge* reference signal with which to compare stored one and zero levels.

The second approach is some form of *dynamic active restore* circuit in which one and zero levels are both restored in the active part of the cycle but current is shut off in the load on the low side; e.g., as shown in Figure 1. Such a sense amplifier is safer in its operation, but more complex and more difficult to fit in the bit line pitch.

When either kind of all-dynamic-sensing-and-restore circuit is used, it is also necessary to allow the Y access circuits to connect both sides of a selected bit line to a balanced data buss. This is needed to be able to execute read-modify-write cycles and is also a faster way of both reading and writing data. Two standard approaches have emerged for solving this problem. One is the so-called *folded bit-line*[4] shown in Figure 2. This makes balanced Y access particularly easy at the expense of some loss in cell layout efficiency. The alternative is to fit the Y decoder and access circuits into the center of the memory array alongside conventionally placed sense amplifers[3]; Figure 3.

Both forms of bit line architecture and both kinds of all-dynamic sense amplifier are now emerging in 64K RAM devices. Package well size limitations set typical cell dimensions of 22 x 8μ. Lower sensing margins make the extra safety of *active restore* desirable but a 22μ pitch makes such a design very difficult to lay out. The small signal margins also make it necessary to have the closest possible control over the reference. Two cells per bit[5] which allows comparison of a zero level with a one level and vice versa, would be ideal, but are hardly compatible with the area constraint in 64K parts. The derivation of a half-charge level from the pre-charged high bit line and half-area dummy cell found in most current designs is less well suited to the new generation of devices. If substrate bias is derived by an on-chip bias oscillator, it becomes difficult to pre-charge bit lines high without coupling a large positive transient into the $-V_{BB}$ supply. Also, accurate half-area cells are increasingly difficult to control as dimensions are reduced. Thus, a return to dummy cells identical in structure to real cells and the use of bit lines charge-shared at the end of the cycle to derive a half voltage level seems a promising alternative; Figure 4.

As the X and Y pitch of cells has progressively diminished, so the circuit and layout of decoders has grown more complex. Here, too, there is a conflict between the desirability of ensuring safe operation by actively holding low unselected decoder outputs[6]

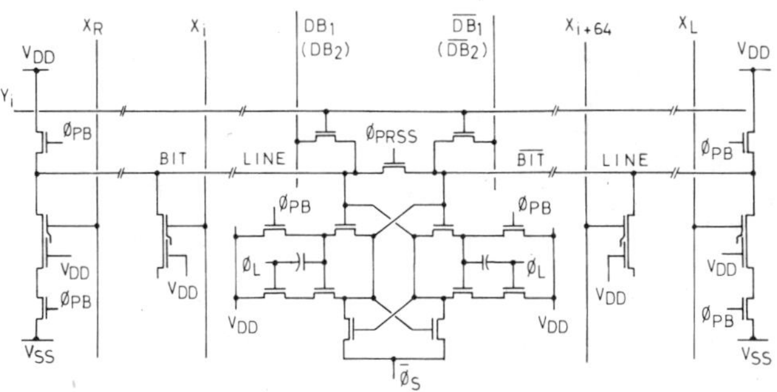

FIGURE 1—Dynamic-active-restore sense amplifier as used in NEC 16K RAM. ϕ_{PB} is high during the precharge time, ϕ_L goes high shortly after ϕ_S goes low to strobe the sense amplifier. Y access to both sides of the bit line is provided in this case by a Y decoder on one side of the array and an extra line into the centre.

[1] Stein, K.V., Sihling, and Doering, E., "Storage Array and Sense/Refresh Circuit for Single Transistor Memory Cells", *ISSCC DIGEST OF TECHNICAL PAPERS*, p. 56-57; Feb., 1972.

[2] Foss, R.C., and Harland, R., "Simplified Peripheral Circuits for a Marginally Testable 4K RAM", *ISSCC DIGEST OF TECHNICAL PAPERS*, p. 102-103; Feb., 1975.

[3] Schroeder, P.R., and Proebsting, R.J., "A 16K x 1 Bit Dynamic RAM", *ISSCC DIGEST OF TECHNICAL PAPERS*, p. 12-13; Feb., 1977.

[4] Harland, R., "MOS One-Transistor Cell RAM having Divided and Balanced Bit Lines Coupled by Regenerative Flipflop Sense Amplifiers and Balanced Access Circuitry"; U.S. Pat. 4,045,783.

[5] Foss, R.C., and Harland, R., "Standards for Dynamic MOS RAMs", *Electronic Design*, p. 66; Aug. 16, 1977.

[6] Hoffman, W.K., and Kalter, H.L., "An 8Kb Random Access Memory Chip Using the One-Device FET Cell", *J. SSCC*, vol. SC-8; Oct., 1973.

[7] Foss, R.C., and Brothers, J.S., "Total Design of High Speed Counters", *ISSCC DIGEST OF TECHNICAL PAPERS*, p. 44; Feb., 1968.

Reprinted from *IEEE Int. Solid State Circuits Conf.*, pp. 140–141, 1979.

and the growing problem of finding room for the extra circuit elements this feature requires. Smaller signal margins and the effects of substrate voltage movements make it especially desirable for 64K parts to have *active-hold-off* decoders, just as the space problem becomes most severe.

A major advance in dynamic RAM design came with the appearance of good address buffer designs in late generation 4K and 16K developments. It is now generally appreciated that a highly regenerative sense-amplifier type of buffer is essential. It becomes almost impossible to test a RAM if the decoders operate under conditions which are analog functions of the address input parameters.

The peripheral circuits of dynamic memory have greatly increased in complexity as a consequence of the search for performance. The technique of *balanced pipelining* is now universal. By strobing data and data signals using closely timed sequential clocks, high speeds are attainable, because relatively small differential signals are able to *steer* the succeeding regenerative stages. Thus MOS RAM designers are beginning to re-invent the principles long used in balanced ECL circuits[7]. As sub-micron geometries emerge, there will be even more incentive to use series-gating current-steering circuits for similar reasons to their use in bipolar work. With no base current and with easy V_T changes by ion implant such circuits will be simpler than their bipolar counterparts.

Acknowledgments

Any study into the *comparative anatomy* of dynamic RAM devices must acknowledge the contributions made by some outstanding circuit designers. The contributions of the author's colleague, R. Harland, are, in particular, gratefully acknowledged.

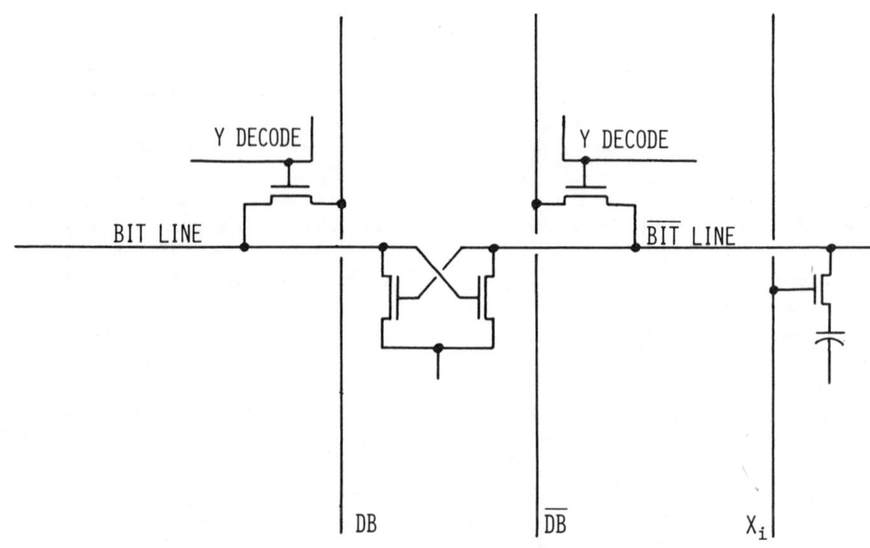

FIGURE 3—Central Y decoder arrangement, balanced Y access with conventional bit line placing requires Y decoder centrally located; or extra line as in Figure 1.

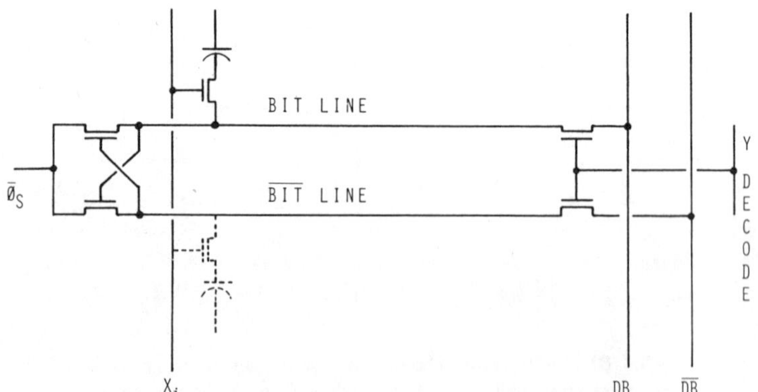

FIGURE 2—A folded bit line arrangement, where balanced Y access is obtained at either end of bit line halves at cost of some loss of cell efficiency. Two cells per bit avoiding need for any reference signal, dummy cells etc. are provided.

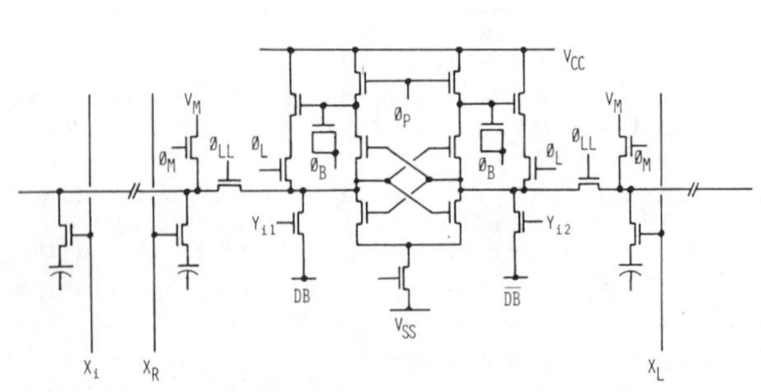

FIGURE 4—Mid-point reference for 64K RAM ϕ_M shorts all bit line halves together to produce a mid-point reference level during the precharge time. X_R and X_L are high to load this level into the dummy cells.

Peripheral Circuits for One-Transistor Cell MOS RAM's

RICHARD C. FOSS, SENIOR MEMBER, IEEE, AND ROBERT HARLAND

Abstract—The use of a single transistor and storage capacitor allows MOS dynamic memories to be built with cell areas of less than two square mils. The logic signals then available are unusually small and balanced sensing is commonly used. Such sense amplifiers and other on-chip circuits peripheral to the memory array are increasingly important in determining the total area and cost, the performance and testing difficulties.

This paper describes some of the key peripheral circuits used in a practical 4K random-access memory (RAM) design paying particular attention to these factors. A "margin test" facility is designed into the form of sense amplifier used and allows measurement of cell storage levels and sense amplifier offset to ensure that adequate signal margins exist in the memory.

Introduction

In a little over five years, MOS dynamic random access memories (RAM's) have developed from experimental 1024 (1K) bit chips, consisting of barely more than array plus decoders, to production-worthy 4K bit devices, with full on-chip buffering and timing. Processing technology has changed from p-channel silicon gate to n-channel coplanar with ion-implantation for field threshold control. Memory cell areas have shrunk from 6 square mils to 2 mil^2 or less while the cell structure has simplified to the limiting case of one access transistor and one storage capacitor. These trends have thrown more and more emphasis on the design limitations of the on-chip circuits peripheral to the memory array. As cell areas are reduced, the total area consumed by these functions becomes relatively more important: some memory designs use as little as 28 percent of total chip area for the memory array, tending to negate the potential advantages in chip size and cost reduction which should result from the one-transistor-cell approach. Also, as memory cell area is reduced the difficulty increases of achieving decoders, sense amplifiers, and access circuits which can be laid out to the same pitch as the X or Y spacings of the array. This trend runs counter to the need to increase the performance of these circuits as cell areas and the magnitude of the stored charge and the voltages representing logic signals is diminishing. The solutions to these problems cannot be bought at the price of speed: mainframe memory components are required to access data in 200 ns or less with TTL levels both in and out of the memory chip. Lastly, the user of the present kinds of MOS memory not only expects this TTL compatability, but also requires that all the timing of the internal sequence of operations be done on-chip. At most, one high-level clock is allowable and this must present a low capacitance load to the external clock driver.

Manuscript received April 14, 1975; revised June 9, 1975.

The authors were with Microsystems International Ltd., Ottawa, Ont., Canada. They are now with MOSAID, Inc., Ottawa, Ont., Canada.

Not surprisingly therefore, it is increasingly found that the circuit features peripheral to the memory array proper largely determine circuit cost, performance, power consumption, and any susceptibility to pattern sensitivity, i.e., failure modes dependent on bit pattern or accessing pattern of the memory. Furthermore, the trend to complete buffering and full on-chip timing of the internal workings makes it increasingly difficult to know what the internal operating margins are. This is not a new problem in a large-scale integration (LSI) context; the same is true in all but the simplest logic elements. What is new is when this situation is found in parts where logic signals are necessarily small because of the economics of cell area. Such signal levels may be literally only of the order of 10^6 electrons of stored charge or 160 mV of static potential difference. Such signal levels demand the use of regenerative amplifiers which by their nature do not "degrade gracefully," i.e., do not give any indication, short of failure to sense correctly, that internal margins are inadequate. In this manner peripheral circuits are also contributing to testing difficulties and potential reliability hazards.

Despite the factors outlined above, very little has been reported in the literature outside of the basic cells and some of the sense amplifier circuitry. This paper claims little originality in these areas but details an approach to the peripheral circuitry aimed at simplifying and reducing the area taken by such circuits in a 4K RAM. This results in a chip which is only 122 × 165 mils, of which 40 percent is cell array, built with a simple 4-mask (plus scratch protection) process. This is an area only 30 percent greater than the industry standard 1K p-channel part which also needs one extra masking step.

The circuits used also allow exploration of the internal margins of the part at the critical cell/sense-amplifier interface. This *margin test* capability is a new feature in such memory devices.

The Basic Cell

The basic cell used in a one-transistor (1T) cell memory can be readily built in silicon gate process technology using either of two approaches. In both cases, the single access transistor has its gate driven from a word (X) line and switches stored charge from a capacitor onto a bit (Y) line. The capacitor has as one plate a polysilicon electrode at V_{DD} (+12 V) supply potential overlying gate oxide dielectric. A depletion well forms under this dielectric and is contiguous with the source of the access transistor. Fig. 1 shows a widely used configuration [1] where the word line is metal and makes contact to

Reprinted from *IEEE J. Solid-State Circuits*, vol. SC–10, pp. 255–261, Oct. 1975.

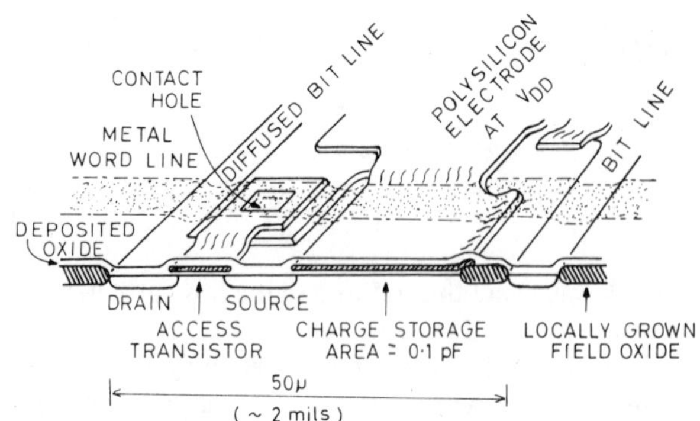

Fig. 1. Single transistor memory cell.

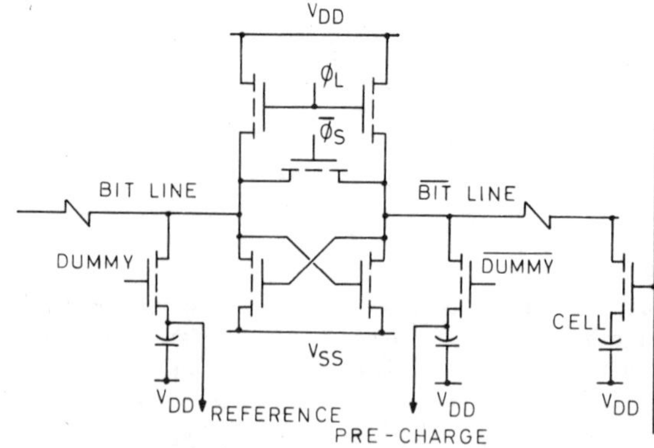

Fig. 2. Sense amplifier after Kuo *et al.* [3].

the polysilicon gate electrode. The bit line is diffused and contiguous with the drains of all the access transistors. The bias electrode for the cell capacitor runs parallel to the diffused bit line.

Note, however, that the layout shown differs from some published layouts in that contact to the gate polysilicon is made over the field oxide. In principal, this contact can overlie the active gate region, but this variant tends to increase the minimum gate lengths that can be used (i.e., to something longer than the minimum contact dimension plus two alignment tolerances) and represents a departure from conservative processing practice.

In the alternative approach, the word line is a polysilicon strip parallel to the capacitor bias electrode. The bit line is a metal run which can make contact to a drain diffusion common to two-cell access transistors.

The advantages and disadvantages of the two approaches are nicely balanced. Practical layouts of either show no significant differences in area utilization or in ratio of cell capacitance to bit line capacitance. The metal bit line avoids problems which can arise in writing due to the higher resistance of the bit line in diffused form. This resistance also forms a distributed *RC* structure which has a time constant which affects charge distribution as the sense-restore circuits are activated. The metal bit line avoids these problems and requires only half the number of contact openings. It however has a distributed *RC* delay along the word line and has an optimum layout with the smallest spacings normal to the bit line. This spacing is the pitch into which must be fitted the sense amplifiers and *Y* access circuits as well as the *Y* decoder. This is a much more difficult layout problem than the equivalent problem with a diffused bit line: in that case, the narrow spacing is normal to the word line and the problems are largely confined to the *X* decoder design. For these reasons, the realization using a diffused bit line with a total cell area of $50\ \mu \times 25\ \mu$ (just less than 2 mil^2) was adopted in the present design. This gives a storage node capacitance of about 0.12 pF using 1000 Å of gate oxide.

Sense-Restore Sense Flip-Flop

The readout of stored data from the storage capacitance onto the larger capacitance associated with the bit line represents a destructive readout of the stored data. With a capacitance ratio of, typically, 1:8, the resulting signal voltage is also necessarily small. The basic approach most commonly used to alleviate these problems is some variant of the divided bit line and balanced flip-flop sense amplifier proposed by Stein *et al.* [2]. The most widely used variant is that published by Kuo *et al.* [3]. This is shown in Fig. 2. In brief, this arrangement has the bit and $\overline{\text{bit}}$ lines shorted together floating at some potential less than +1 V_T above V_{SS} while the memory is quiescent. During this time a reference voltage level midway between those values representing one and zero levels is written into dummy cell structures on either side of the flip-flop. As the memory is activated, the two sides of the flip-flop are first unshorted. Data from a storage cell are then dumped onto one side or other as one word line is selected. At the same time the "reference" level is dumped from the dummy cell on the side of the flip-flop opposite to that of the selected cell. As a result, a voltage/charge differential is set up across the two nodes of the flip-flop. The load clock ϕ_L now turns on the two load transistors. Both nodes rise together until the higher side starts to turn on the opposite transistor. Regenerative action then results in amplification of the signal to full logic levels and the restoration of the zero or one level back into the cell.

Despite the practical success achieved by memories using this arrangement, it is not used in the present design. Although the bit and $\overline{\text{bit}}$ lines are shorted together during the quiescent time of the memory, this does not prevent their common mode potential from drifting down during this period. The degree to which this level falls below 1 V_T above V_{SS} depends on junction leakage of the bit line to substrate and the time since the memory was last active. When a new cycle is activated, the flip-flop loads must pull up both the bit and $\overline{\text{bit}}$ lines until the flip-flop reaches its active region. The time taken for this depends on the starting level of the lines and it is also critically important that the flip-flop load structures be well balanced so as not to give a differential rate of rise to the two sides. Again, depending on the initial common mode level, this could lead to an imbalance sufficient to overcome the initial signal differential between the two sides by the time the flip-flop reaches its active region.

To avoid any possible problems arising from the floating bit and $\overline{\text{bit}}$ lines, the alternative approach shown in Fig. 3 was adopted. In this arrangement, the bit and $\overline{\text{bit}}$ lines are clamped

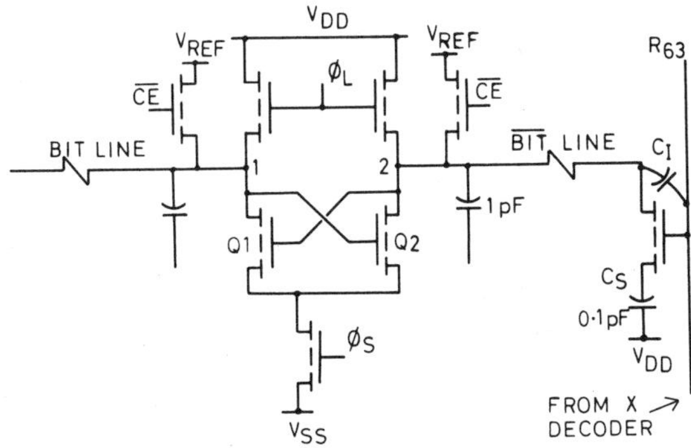

Fig. 3. New sense amplifier: clock sequence $CE \rightarrow \phi_X \rightarrow \phi_S \rightarrow \phi_L$.

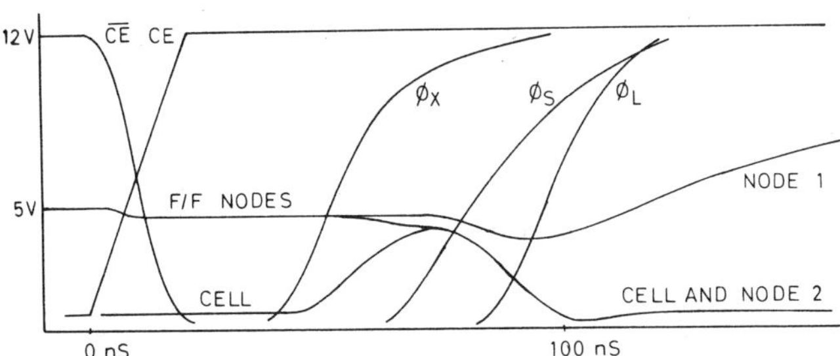

Fig. 4. Sensing and restoring logic 0 (cell on node 2 side).

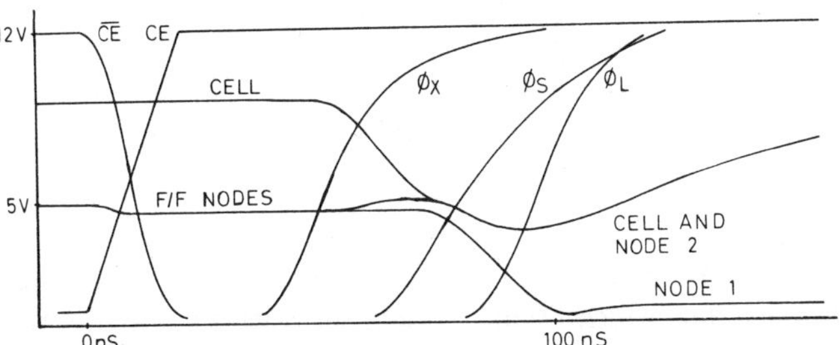

Fig. 5. Sensing and restoring logic 1 (cell on node 2 side).

to a reference potential by the internally generated inverse of the *CE* clock which activates the memory. During this time, the internally generated clocks ϕ_S (sense) and ϕ_L (load) are at a zero level and the flip-flop is inactive. The first-order description of the circuit operation is then as follows.

1) $\overline{CE}$ goes low unclamping bit and $\overline{\text{bit}}$ lines.

2) One of the 64 word lines is selected and goes high having been activated by the X address clock ϕ_X: suppose it is R_{63} on the right-hand side of the array.

3) If a stored one is present in the cell, the V_{ref} level on the $\overline{\text{bit}}$ line connected to node 2 of the flip-flop will be incremented: if a stored zero it will be decremented. Suppose a one is stored.

4) The sense clock ϕ_S now grounds the common sources of the flip-flop. As the source potential falls rapidly towards V_{SS}, node 2 being slightly higher ensures that Q_1 turns on slightly ahead of Q_2. Regenerative action ensues with the lower node going to V_{SS} and the higher one falling slightly before the transistor connected to it is fully turned off.

5) The load clock ϕ_L now turns on the load transistors. The low side rises to a level set by the ratio of the transistor geometries and the high side is pulled up relatively slowly to $V_{DD} - V_T$, assuming ϕ_L reaches a one level equal to V_{DD}.

The two cases where zero and one levels are stored are shown pictorially in the waveform diagrams (Figs. 4 and 5). In a circuit operating with such small signal levels, it is, of course, necessary to consider many second-order factors. Chief among these are the following.

1) The potential remaining on bit and $\overline{\text{bit}}$ lines is somewhat less than V_{ref} by virtue of the capacitative coupling through the clamp transistors. This coupling is relatively small because the lines are only left floating as $\overline{CE}$ falls below 1 V_T above V_{ref}. In a practical arrangement, a fall of about 0.25 V in the common mode potential is observed. Any imbalance between the clamp transistors will give a proportion of this shift as unwanted imbalance signal.

2) As the cell access transistor is turned on, significant charge coupling occurs through the gate to channel capacitance. This capacitance per unit area of the gate oxide is about 4.2×10^{-4} pF/μ^2.

Thus with an access transistor with gate dimensions $7 \times 7\ \mu$ and a gate voltage swing of $V_{DD} - V_T$, about 11 V, the charge coupled into the cell and bit line when a stored zero is present is

$$Q_C = 11 \times 0.0206 = 0.227 \text{ pC}.$$

To this term must be added the charge injected from the word line crossing the diffused bit line. With an area of $6 \times 8\ \mu$ and a capacitance per unit area of 0.44×10^{-4} pF/μ^2 this amounts to

$$Q_L = 11 \times 0.0021 = 0.0232 \text{ pC}.$$

Thus the total charge injected

$$Q_{I0} = Q_L + Q_C = 0.25 \text{ pC}.$$

When a stored one is present in the cell, the calculation is a little more complex since the gate-to-channel capacitance, other than the overlap term, is not effective until the gate voltage reaches 1 V_T above the bit line potential. This amounts to

$$Q_{I1} = 0.176 \text{ pC}.$$

These charge injections can be referred back to the cell as equivalent increments to the voltage levels representing logic zero and logic one. Thus the act of selecting a cell adds about 2 V to a stored zero and 1.5 V to a stored one.

It is, of course, possible to balance out most of this effect using "dummy cell" structures. The X decode circuitry can ensure that when a cell anywhere on, say, the right-hand side of the flip-flop is selected, a balancing amount of charge is injected by a dummy structure on the left-hand side, and vice versa. This involves additional complexity and adds extra terms into the tolerancing. On balance, it is rather simpler to adjust the level of V_{ref} to take into account the changed effective levels of the stored zero and stored one. Note too that a dummy cell cannot perfectly balance out the spurious injected charge because $Q_{I0} \neq Q_{I1}$. The other second-order factors which need to be considered are mainly connected with sense amplifier balance and the effects of bit line resistance.

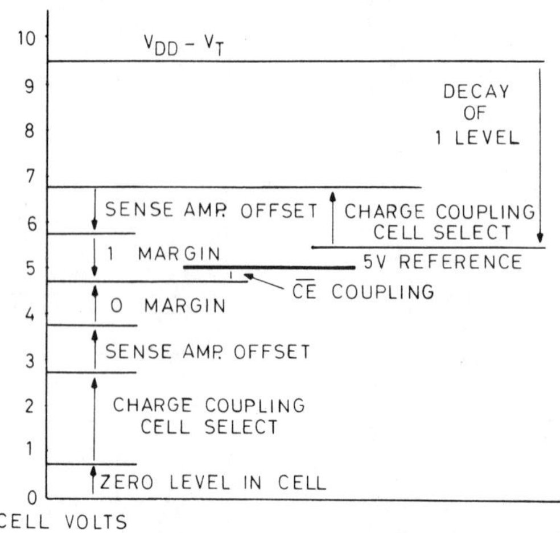

Fig. 6. Principal terms setting margins.

First, there is the simple effect of V_T imbalance in the flip-flop inverters which results in an offset voltage referred to the cell scaled by the ratio of bit line to cell capacitance. All the other factors are sufficiently complex as to require computer simulation. This is an essentially empirical approach and results depend greatly on the details of a practical layout. It is however useful to comment on the sense of the results and note some qualitative explanations.

A. Capacitance Balance

The sense amplifier may be thought of as sensing a voltage provided a perfect balance exists in the capacitance on either side. In practice this will not be the case and a difference in charge must be considered. It is found that an increase in capacitance is indeed equivalent to an increase in the voltage but not directly prorata as would be implied by a strict sensing of charge balance.

B. Spatial Balancing

Given a diffused bit line some 800 μ long and 6 μ wide end-to-end resistance of up to about 2 kΩ may exist. The distributed time constant this represents with about 1 pF of junction capacitance would appear to be negligible. However, it is found in circuit modeling and in practice that the effects of static capacitance remote from the sense amplifier are less than the same amount of capacitance nearby. The bit line resistance prevents the sense amplifier from "seeing" all the charge at the far end of the bit line at the critical instant of charge redistribution during sensing. It is thus desirable to preserve not only a balance of the static capacitance on either side of the sense amplifier but to ensure that the physical location of each item contributing to that capacitance is balanced. A slow rise time for ϕ_s minimizes this effect but slows memory access time.

C. Cell Location

As a consequence of the items 1) and 2) mentioned above, the position of the cell along the bit line is found to affect the level at which detection of one or zero becomes indeterminate. The capacitance of the cell itself added to that of the bit line ensures a bias towards a one state, but this diminishes as the cell increases in distance from the sense amplifier. In other words, an addition to the minimum "one" voltage level of about 0.5 to 0.75 V is needed in cells at the far end of the bit and $\overline{\text{bit}}$ lines. Note that a dummy cell cannot balance out this term since it is necessarily in a fixed location.

Complete tolerancing of what is perhaps the simplest variant yet published of this approach to a balanced sense amplifier is still not an easy task. Fig. 6 shows diagrammatically the principal factors which determine the actual minimum one and zero levels in the complete memory. As shown, allowing a total of 1 V referred back to the cell (i.e., about 120 mV at the sense amplifier) for all offset terms still results in design margins of ±1 V when a 5-V reference level is used. This is after allowing for the stored one level of 9.5 V decaying to about 5.6 V during the refresh time of the memory.

Possible Variations of Sense Amplifiers

The source-clocked sense amplifier as discussed in the preceding section seems close to an optimum way of sensing the necessarily small signals in a one-transistor cell memory. As a minor variant, it is possible for all of the sense amplifiers to share a common source-clocking transistor. This must carry the current flowing in every sense amplifier. It does however reduce the number of devices to be fitted into the pitch between adjacent bit lines. It is a variation which is thus more appropriate where this pitch is a significant problem.

A second variation is to use a common clock signal for ϕ_S and ϕ_L. As already noted, it is desirable to have the basic sensing action independent of the presence of the load devices. To achieve this, it is not essential to have ϕ_L as a separate clock. A single clock with finite rise time replacing ϕ_S and ϕ_L will automatically turn on the source-clocking transistor, with source at V_{SS} potential, before the load devices can be affected. What makes it advantageous to separate ϕ_S and ϕ_L is the desirability of having ϕ_L reach V_{DD} level quickly once it is activated, to speed up the rewriting of a one-level into the bit or $\overline{\text{bit}}$ line and cell. This is more easily achieved by a separate clock signal which is not loaded by the capacitance of the source-clocking transistors.

Finally, it may be noted that any sense amplifier which consists essentially of a static flip-flop creates a classic speed-power tradeoff between the power wasted in the flip-flop load current on the low side and the memory cycle time, as determined by the time taken for a load to pull the relatively large bit line capacitance back up to a good logic one level. As shown in the waveform diagram, Fig. 5, this is a relatively slow process with practical load geometries. Furthermore, geometry variations in production directly translate into cycle time tolerancing.

These factors strongly point to the desirability of replacing the simple clocked loads with dynamic circuitry which pulls only the off-side high. This does not appear practical without a major departure from the layout currently used. The complexity of the state-sensing load circuitry would be awkward to fit in the pitch between bit lines. More seriously, the use of "one-shot" loads would complicate the Y select circuitry in order to keep a read-modify-write (RMW) capability. If the state of the sense flip-flop is to be externally changed after the sense/read operation, within the same clock cycle, then *either* both clocked loads must be present to conduct current *or* access provided to both sides of the bit line to be able to write a one back into either side as needed. With the sense amplifier as shown in Fig. 3, access is needed to only one side of the split bit line for read, write, or RMW into a particular Y location.

Y Access Circuitry

With the bit line divided on either side of a centrally placed sense amplifier, as in Fig. 3, it is uneconomic of silicon area to provide access to more than one end of the bit line. This results in a number of design compromises that represent perhaps the chief shortfalls in this basic circuit/layout approach. The first such compromise is the choice between using a single transmission gate device for both reading out from the bit line and writing new data back in and the alternative of separate read and write structures. With the read and write functions separated, a transmission device is still needed for writing, but reading can be done using grounded source amplifying stages with gates connected to the bit lines. In the present design, the simplicity of a combined I/O device was chosen and the problems of output sensing thus created were solved in a manner closely similar to that used in each individual bit line sense amplifier.

The Y select and output sense circuit is shown in Fig. 7. As when sensing individual cells, the Y decoder selecting an individual bit line connects it to one side or other of a balanced flip-flop. Alternate bit lines go to opposite sides to balance the capacitance loading on this flip-flop. From the waveform diagrams, Figs. 4 and 5, it can be seen that the bit line voltage is either near zero or else at about 4.5 V depending on the logic state. The I/O bus lines are thus required to be precharged to about 2.5 V, i.e., about half the reference potential, V_{ref}, used on the bit lines. To achieve this, one I/O line is precharged to V_{ref} while $\overline{CE}$ is at a one level. The other is precharged to zero (V_{SS}). When CE goes to a one, the two lines are shorted together, averaging the charge and thus setting both lines to the desired level. The shorting transistor is turned off by the inverse of ϕ_S prior to the Y sensing function.

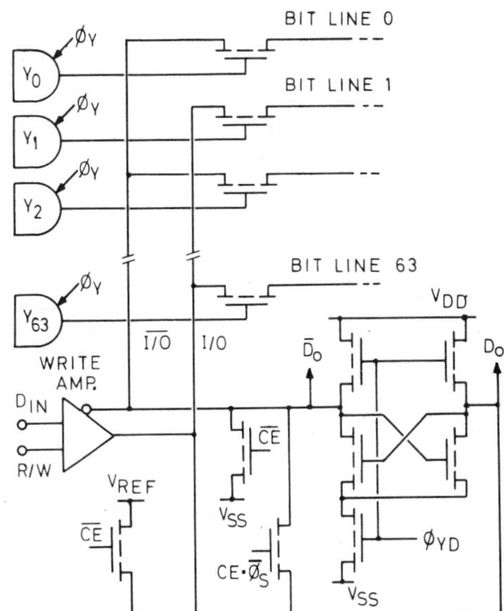

Fig. 7. Y select and output sense.

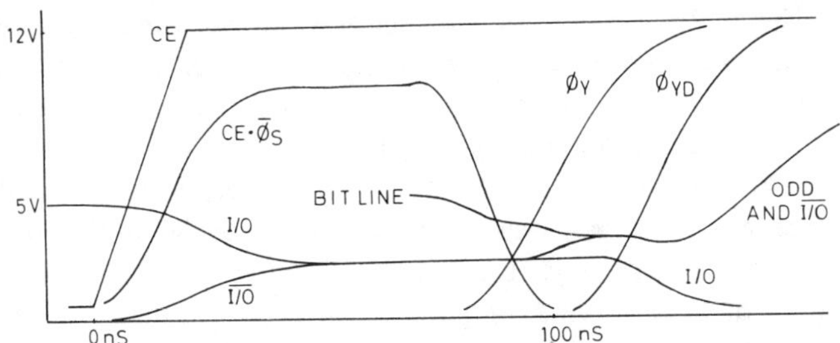

Fig. 8. Sensing 1 on odd numbered bit line.

After the Y enable clock ϕ_Y has strobed the Y access circuits, a bit line is connected to one side or other, incrementing or decrementing it, depending on the state existing on the bit line at that instant. Lastly, just as in the individual bit line sense amplifiers, the clock ϕ_{YD} activates the flip-flop. In this case, a common clock waveform is used for both the source transistor and the load devices. The waveforms illustrating this operation are shown in Fig. 8 for the case where a logic one level on an odd numbered bit line is being sensed. This use of balanced regenerative sensing gives the same kind of speed/sensitivity advantage to the Y axis as is achieved in the single bit sensing. The combination allows amplification of the minimal static charge in the cell up to complementary levels quite capable of driving the inverter and source follower of a TTL driving "totem-pole" output stage without passing through simple inverting amplifying stages at all. The signal path consists solely of transmission gates with all amplification by the rapid regenerative actions of the two cascaded sense amplifiers.

Block Diagram and Clock Sequencing

A complete memory block diagram is shown in Fig. 9. In addition to the circuitry already discussed, the functions of address buffering, X and Y decoding, write amplifier and clock

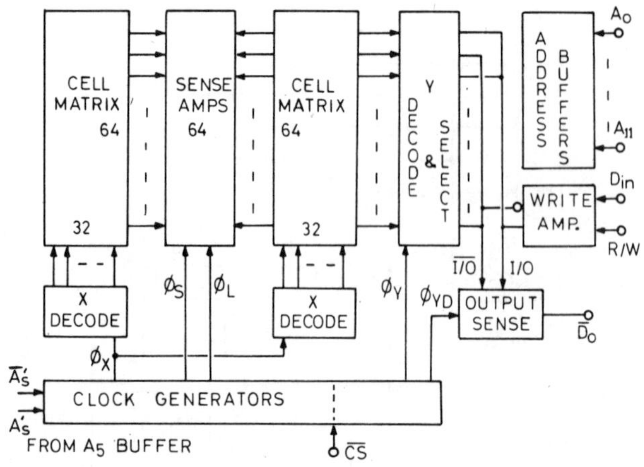

Fig. 9. Memory block diagram.

Fig. 10. Chip photo (Table I refers to this).

TABLE I
MEMORY CHIP AREA UTILIZATION

CELL ARRAY	512 x 10⁴μ²	39.4
SENSE AMPS	78	6.0
X DECODERS	94	7.2
Y DECODE & ACCESS	130	10.0
ADDRESS BUFFERS	67	5.2
OTHER CIRCUITRY	218	16.8
OTHER AREA (PADS ETC)	200	15.4
TOTALS	1299 x 10⁴μ² (20,000 SQ. MILS.)	100.0%

generation are required. Circuit techniques in these areas are relatively conventional using dynamic circuitry and "boot-strapped" inverters. Fig. 10 shows the chip photograph of the part and Table I indicates the area utilization. The term "other area" includes all those functions serving no electrical purpose such as the scribe channel, bonding pads, alignment marks, and identifiers.

The internal clock sequence governs all the timing of the part. This sequence of the principal clocks is illustrated in Fig. 11. Each major clock simply triggers the next in sequence with the exception that ϕ_S trips both the ϕ_Y clock enabling the Y decoders and the ϕ_L clock. This involves no race hazard since ϕ_L, as already shown, plays no part in the sensing but only serves to rewrite back the logic one level on one side or other of each bit sense amplifier. Provision was made on the initial layout for adjusting (by device size tailoring) the timing between clocks to set up an optimal timing interval. With one design iteration this achieved a high proportion of parts with 200 ns access with further scope for improvement as the process spreads became better known.

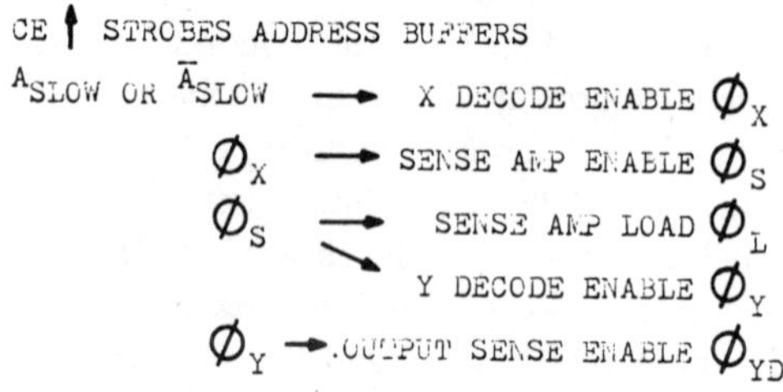

Fig. 11. Internal timing clocks.

In memory designs of this type it is usual to include not only the high-level *CE* clock but also a TTL level control input called chip select or *CS*. In this context *CE* and *CS* are thus not equivalent terms. A better term for the *CS* might be "refresh control." The *CE* clock activates the chip and one X line of 64 cells is read and restored by the bit sense amplifiers. 64 such cycles with the X address stepped in sequence are thus sufficient to refresh the entire memory. If however the *CS* control is not also in a valid low condition, then it is required that the memory, although active, shall neither read nor write, regardless of other control inputs.

In the present design, this is most easily achieved by allowing the generation of ϕ_Y and hence ϕ_{YD} to be dependent on valid *CS*. If ϕ_Y and ϕ_{YD} are inhibited, then no access is possible to any bit line and the output sense amplifier remains disabled and the output in a high-impedance state. An elementary three-transistor circuit thus achieves the desired *CS* function.

The sequence of clocks as described results in every write cycle being essentially an RMW cycle in that the ϕ_S clock activating the bit sense amplifier always precedes the ϕ_Y clock giving access to a bit line. A slight shortening of the write cycle is possible if the write condition is allowed to generate ϕ_Y earlier and so have the input data present on a given bit line, prior to the sensing function. In many large memory systems the RMW cycle is always used (as part of an error correction system) and so a slight speed-up of a standard write cycle is of little value. Furthermore the modification, although simple to design in, would separate the write and RMW testing conditions. The bit sense amplifier will readily take up a state preimpressed on one end of a bit line. It is not so simple to guarantee that a new state will reset the sense amplifier once it has been activated. If a one level exists on the half-bit line fed to the Y access circuits, it is easy to pull down and reset to a zero. Conversely however, a zero level held down by the "on" inverter transistor in the flip-flop can be difficult to pull up. The on resistance of the Y access transistor and the resistance of the diffused bit line can constitute a load for this inverter leaving the flip-flop holding down the zero level regardless of the new data impressed on the I/O bus lines.

Margin Test Facility

It is something of a common practice to design integrated circuits with little, if any, regard for the testability of the part. Memories are no exception and, as already noted, present special problems in that sensitive analog functions are performed with on-chip buffering, preventing access to such functions for test purposes. The testing technique designed into this memory is a "margin test" capability similar to that used in core memories and elsewhere. The line labeled V_{ref} in Fig. 3 is required to be halfway between the effective zero and worst case one levels, allowing for charge injection by the cell access transistor. As shown on the level diagram, Fig. 6, this is around the 5-V level. Since this is an external standard supply (V_{CC}) fed into the memory, the V_{CC} rail can be used as V_{ref}. Provided V_{CC} is not used elsewhere (except as the upper level for the TTL output buffer), then variation of this supply gives a direct indication of the internal operating margin at the critical cell interface. Increasing V_{CC} until memory failure occurs will measure internal one levels, and decreasing it measures zero levels. Differences noted on either side of the flip-flop measure sense amplifier offset. Such facility is invaluable as an engineering investigation tool and appears to have merit as an aid to production testing. Without it, final testing must ensure in some other way that failure will not occur at temperature and supply extremes.

There are disadvantages in using V_{CC} in this way. First, V_{CC} cannot be powered down or abolished, which would otherwise be possible. Second, the use of a separate V_{ref} supply reduces somewhat the dc operating range of V_{DD} since the reference level does not track with other internal levels. Finally, it is necessary to ensure that noise on the V_{CC} rail is not such as to impair the working margins.

The alternative source of V_{ref} is to derive it from V_{DD}. It is then still possible to arrange a probe test pad to allow an external override, so as to keep a margin test feature at the probe stage. The objections to the use of V_{CC} are thus removed but at some cost. Firstly, margin testing is of course not possible at the finished device level. There is also a small dc drain during the memory quiescent time, to operate the internal reference generator. Most serious however, is the much increased V_{DD} noise susceptibility. The reference level is effectively strobed into the bit lines as *CE* goes to zero. This is shortly after both internal circuits such as the address buffers and external clock drivers have placed heavy peak loads on V_{DD}. All memories of this type thus require careful decoupling of V_{DD} when V_{ref} is derived from it.

Conclusions

The rapid evolution of MOS dynamic memories has allowed little time for the standardization or stabilization of the circuit techniques. Many mistakes from earlier generations of memories are being replicated in new 4K memory designs. Careful consideration of the peripheral circuits used in a one-transistor cell design does allow a reasonably simple and tolerant part to be realized in no more than 20 000 square mils of chip area. This has a major effect on the attainable die yield and figures in excess of 20 good die per 2 in wafer were readily achieved in early production. Conversion of "good" die to finished parts depends most critically on the testability of the part. In this respect, margin testing was shown to give a substantial advantage over more conventional approaches to probe testing.

Acknowledgment

The coplanar version of the silicon gate process used was developed by a team lead by D. Gonsalves. Product engineering work was done by W. Woodley and the development of the memory described in this paper depended in large measure on these individuals' efforts. All circuit simulation work was done using the NANSIM program and MOS model developed by a group led by Dr. M. Caughey of Bell-Northern Research, Ottawa, Ont., Canada.

References

[1] W. K. Hoffman and H. L. Kalter, "An 8K b random access memory chip using the one-device FET cell," *IEEE J. Solid-State Circuits* (*Special Issue on Semiconductor Memory and Logic*), vol. SC-8, pp. 298–305, Oct. 1973.

[2] K. U. Stein, A. Sihling, and E. Doering, "Storage array and sense/refresh circuit for single transistor memory cells," *IEEE J. Solid-State Circuits* (*Special Issue on Semiconductor Memories and Digital Circuits*), vol. SC-7, pp. 336–340, Oct. 1972.

[3] C. Kuo, N. Kitagawa, E. Ward, and P. Drayer, "Sense amplifier design is key to one-transistor cell in 4096 bit RAM," *Electronics*, Sept. 1973.

Storage Array and Sense/Refresh Circuit for Single-Transistor Memory Cells

KARL U. STEIN, AARNE SIHLING, AND ELKO DOERING

Abstract—**The read signals of dynamic single-transistor MOS memory cells with destructive readout decrease with decreasing cell area. To achieve the required small cell area, a device with a high specific capacitance is needed for the storage capacitor and sensitive refresh amplifiers and noise compensating arrays are also required.**

For the cell layout in silicon-gate technology a storage capacitor is therefore proposed that uses a field-induced nonequilibrium inversion layer as an electrode.

As a sensitive refresh amplifier a gated flip-flop that can be used for one digit line at each of its two input nodes is presented. The symmetric array thus achieved is not only highly sensitive (undefined region of the input voltage difference about 0.3 of the transistor threshold voltage) and independent of the process parameters, but also permits noise compensation by the use of one dummy word line (with dummy cells) on each side of the flip-flop.

Different cells and refresh circuits have been realized in silicon-gate technologies. Cells with an area of 1600 μm^2 (2.6 mil^2) have been successfully operated with a READ/WRITE cycle time of 350 ns (storage capacitance 0.134 pF, digit line capacitance 0.32 pF for 64 cells per line or 128 cells per amplifier).

INTRODUCTION

THE GOAL of development over the last few years has been to reduce the cost per memory bit by putting more bits on a chip. This has primarily been achieved by reducing the area of the memory cells.

A quite successful way of reducing the cell area is to eliminate circuit elements of the storage cell. For example the progress from the dynamic four-transistor memory cell [1] [Fig. 1(b)], derived from the flip-flop cell [Fig. 1(a)], to the various three-transistor cells [2]–[5] was achieved by eliminating the feedback path (through T_2) in each individual flip-flop cell and sharing it among many cells.

In this development the next logical step was to eliminate the amplifying transistor T_3 and the read-selection transistor T_4 from the three-transistor memory cell and to share these devices also among many cells [Fig. 1(d)]. This led to the single-transistor memory cell [6]–[8].

A comparison of the most commonly used three-transistor cell [Fig. 2(a) [3] with the single-transistor cell [8] [Fig. 2(b)] makes clear the following advantages of the single-transistor cell:

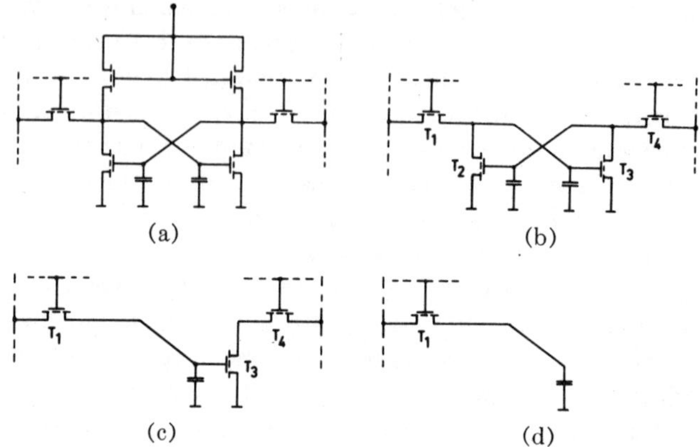

Fig. 1. Development of MOSFET memory cells. (a) Flip-flop cell (statically or dynamically operated). (b) Four-transistor cell. (c) Three-cell transistor cell. (d) Single-transistor cell.

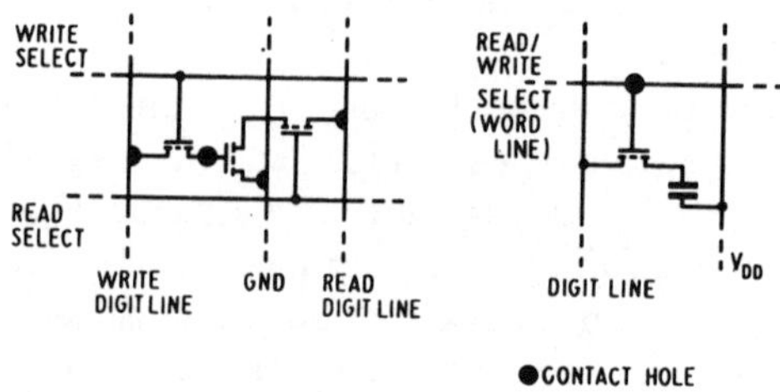

Fig. 2. Comparison of three-transistor and single-transistor memory cells. (●) Contact hole. (◗) Contact hole shared by neighboring cells.

1) fewer elements in the electrical circuit (one transistor and one capacitor instead of three transistors and one capacitor);
2) fewer lines (2 or 3 instead of 4 or 5); and
3) fewer contact holes (none or 1 instead of 2-½ or more, depending on the way in which the holes are shared by neighboring cells).

To summarize, the advantage of the single-transistor cell is that the number of elements in the layout is reduced by approximately one-half.

The disadvantages of the single-transistor cell, which arise from the elimination of the amplifying transistor, are the following:

1) a parasitic capacitor, such as is used in the three-transistor cell (the gate capacitance) cannot be used as a storage capacitor;
2) the readout of the cell is destructive (DRO); and
3) the output voltage of the cell is damped so that a sensitive refresh amplifier is needed.

Manuscript received April 18, 1972; revised June 5, 1972. This paper was presented at the ISSCC, February 16–18, 1972. This work was partially sponsored by the Bundesministerium für Bildung und Wissenschaft.

The authors are with Siemens AG, Forschungslaboratorien, Munich, Germany.

Reprinted from *IEEE J. Solid-State Circuits*, vol. SC–7, pp. 336–340, Oct. 1972.

The object of this paper is to offer solutions for these problems and thereby eliminate the disadvantages of single-transistor cells.

Cell Layout

The considerations regarding cell layout can be based on the simplified equivalent circuit of the single-transistor cell shown in Fig. 3. This shows the storage capacitor C_S, the selection transistor T, which is switched on for write in, in order to establish high or low potential across C_S and also for readout of the stored voltage. The capacitance C_D represents all parasitic capacitances of the digit line and the sense amplifier input. C_{W1} and C_{W2} are the parasitic capacitances of the selection transistor.

During readout, the voltage, e.g., V_H for a stored "1," at the storage capacitor is diminished by the distribution of the stored charge between the storage capacitor C_S and the digit line capacitance C_D. Neglecting the parasitic capacitances C_{W1} and C_{W2} of the selection transistor, the sensed quasi-dc voltage [1]V_s at the digit line is $V_s = V_H\ (1 + C_D/C_S)^{-1}$. For reliable detection the voltage V_s at the sense amplifier input must be outside the undefined region of voltage width V_{tr} within which (0) and (1) cannot be discriminated by the sense amplifier.

Taking account of this we get the following condition for the value of the storage capacitance: $C_S > C_D\ [V_H/V_{\mathrm{tr}} - 1]^{-1}$. To attain the required small cell area, which is determined primarily by C_S, a device for C_S with a high specific capacity, a digit line with low capacity C_D, and a sensitive amplifier (low V_{tr}/V_H) must be used.

The basic layout used for the cells realized in silicon-gate technology is shown in Fig. 4(b); a photomicrograph of actual cells is shown in Fig. 4(a). The digit lines are diffused areas, the selection transistor is a standard minimum size self-aligned silicon-gate transistor. The aluminum word lines lie on top of the cells.

Storage is effected by means of a silicon gate capacitor, which is also shown in the cross section of the memory cell in Fig. 5. In this device, the inversion layer under a silicon gate connected to the supply voltage is used as one electrode of the storage capacitor. As a result, two capacitors in parallel can be used: one from the inversion layer to the gate, the other from the inversion layer to the substrate.

Treating the situation from the point of view of semiconductor physics, the surface potential of a nonequilibrium semiconductor surface under inversion conditions is established via the selection transistor, its value being determined by the voltage of the digit line. The dependence of the surface potential and the total capacitance of the device on the charge of the inversion layer, which

[1] In the circuit discussed later, the digit lines are precharged to an intermediate voltage. For this case V_s is the voltage difference between the voltages of a stored "1" and a stored "0."

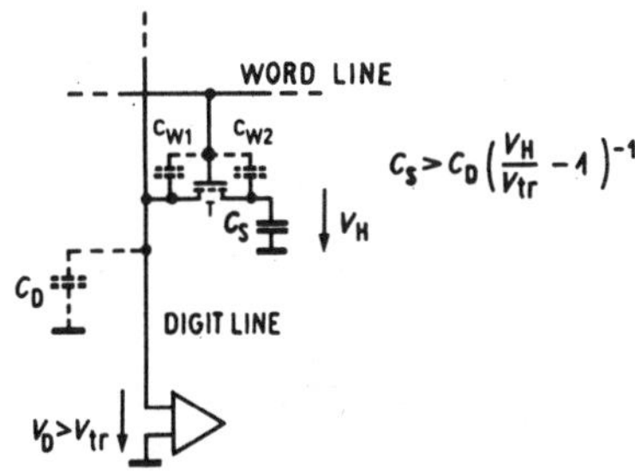

Fig. 3. Simplified equivalent circuit of the single-transistor cell with sense amplifier.

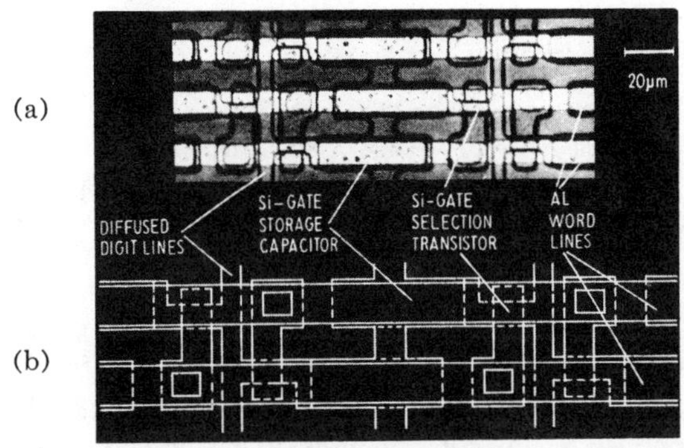

Fig. 4. Single-transistor silicon-gate memory cell with an area of 1600 μm^2. (a) Photomicrograph of realized cell. (b) Schematic layout.

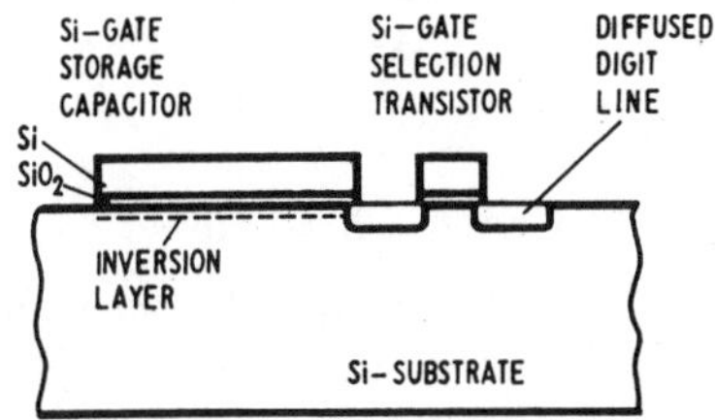

Fig. 5. Schematic cross section through memory cell shown in Fig. 4.

is similar to the behavior of the charge-coupled device [9], is shown in Fig. 6 for a device employing n-channel technology. As we see, the specific capacitance that can be used for the storage with the voltages 0 V for "0" and 10 V for "1" is about 0.31 pF/1000 μm^2, which is about 12 times the value of the junction capacitance alone ($C_J \approx 0.026$ pF/1000 μm^2). With this value the storage capacitance C_S of the memory cell of Fig. 4 is 0.134 pF, the parasitic digit line capacitance is $5 \cdot 10^{-3}$ pF per cell.

The leakage behavior of this storage capacitor is determined by the depletion layer around the inversion layer, as in the case of the charge-coupled device [9] and is closely related to the behavior of a p-n junction [10]. The leakage currents tend to build up the inversion layer and, therefore, decrease the surface potential, which is the voltage of the storage capacitor. This must be considered in evaluating the worst case voltages for readout.

Besides the small cell area, the layout of Fig. 5 also has the following characteristics: 1) digit-line length per cell as small as possible and 2) word-line length adapted to the width of the sense/refresh circuit.

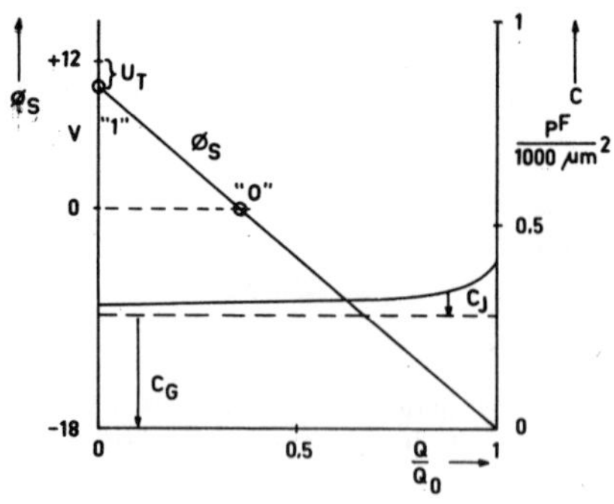

Gate voltage, V_G: +12 V.
Gate oxide thickness, X_0: 120 nm.
Threshold voltage, V_T: 2 V at U_{sub} = −18 V.
Substrate bias, U_{sub}: −18 V.
Substrate doping, N_A: $2 \cdot 10^{15}$ cm^{-3}.
Equilibrium charge density, Q_0: 8.3 pA/1000 μm².

Fig. 6. Dependence of the surface potential ϕ_s and the total capacitance C (gate capacitance C_G plus junction capacitance C_J) on the relative charge Q/Q_0 of a (nonequilibrium) inversion layer.

The following basic dimensions were used for the layout: 1) 10 μm for the aluminum linewidth and line separation, 2) 8 μm for the polysilicon linewidth and line separation, and 3) 6 × 8 μm for the contact holes.

Following these rules a digit-line length per cell of 20 μm was achieved using the minimum period for the aluminum lines. The word line length per cell adapted to the amplifier width is 80 μm. The area of the basic cell layout is therefore 1600 μm².

Gated Flip-Flop

For the sense/refresh circuit, a two-terminal amplifier is very suitable since no inversion of the polarity of the read signal on the digit line is required to refresh the stored charge. The circuit proposed for this purpose is a gated flip-flop (Fig. 7), which, if used as a symmetrical device, has the advantage as well as other symmetrical integrated circuits, of being insensitive to technological tolerances.

Further advantages of the gated flip-flops are the following.

1) Each of the two nodes can be used for a digit line, thus doubling the number of storage cells per amplifier.

2) A compensation for word-select noise effected by the parasitic capacitances C_{W1} and C_{W2} in Fig. 3 can easily be realized, as will be explained in the next section.

3) The stet V_{tr} of the undefined region of the sense/refresh amplifier depends only on small geometrical and turn-on voltage differences of neighboring identical transistors and is estimated to be of the order of 0.3 of the turn-on voltage.

4) A starting voltage for sensing near the switching point of the flip-flop can easily be achieved (precharging of digit lines).

The gating of the flip-flop (Fig. 7) is performed in two steps. The first step is activated by switching on the cross transistor T_C by means of clock ϕ_3 and thereby connecting both nodes of the flip-flop, establishing in the ideal case the voltage of the switching point. This voltage is used for precharging.

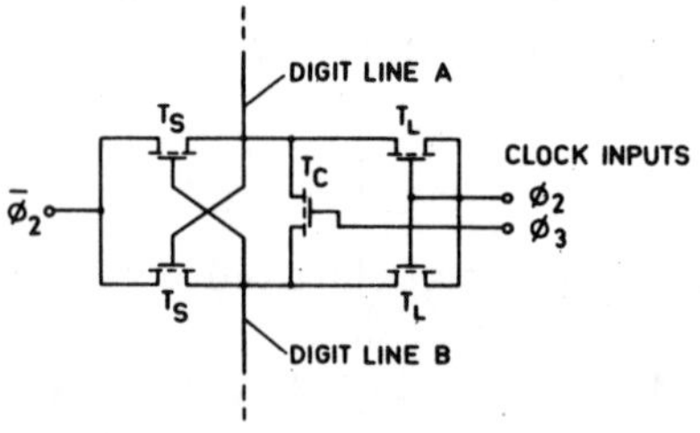

Fig. 7. Gated flip-flop with digit lines A and B and clock inputs for operating the load and switching transistors, T_S and T_L, respectively, and the cross transistor T_C.

In the second step, the supply voltage and ground voltage of the flip-flop are reversed by switching ϕ_2 and $\bar{\phi}_2$. Thereby, both the load transistors and the switching transistors T_L and T_S, respectively, are back biased, which leads to isolation of the nodes. This step is used for sensing the stored charge as a quasi-dc voltage difference between the nodes of the flip-flop. This voltage difference is amplified by switching on the flip-flop.

Storage Array and Sense/Refresh Operation

A storage array with two matrices A and B, each of n words with m bits, is shown in the block diagram in Fig. 8 (total storage capacity of the array, 2-nm bits). Next to each matrix there is a word line that is operated as a dummy word line to the opposite matrix. Ideally, the complete array is so designed as to be completely symmetrical with respect to the symmetry axis of the gated flip-flops used as sense/refresh circuits.

The selection of a single memory cell of one of the matrices for write in or readout is performed in the conventional manner by coincident selection of a word line and a digit line via the decoders.

A READ/REWRITE cycle will now be explained in the light of Figs. 9 and 10. A precharge of the whole circuit before sensing is initiated by switching on ϕ_3 [Fig. 10(a)]. This switches on the cross transistor T_c of the flip-flop and selects both dummy word lines. The conductance of T_c establishes the voltage of the switching point of the flip-flop on both digit lines and in the capacitors of both dummy cells. This is seen in the results of the computer-aided circuit analysis for standard n-channel silicon-gate technology shown in Fig. 10(b). Once a precharge voltage is established, the flip-flop is switched off by switching ϕ_2, $\bar{\phi}_2$, and ϕ_3.

Reading can now be performed by selecting the word line of the required storage cell in one of the storage matrices and, at the same time, the dummy word line associated with the other storage matrix. As we see in Fig. 10(b), the result is a voltage difference between the nodes of the flip-flop, which is determined only by the voltage of the storage capacitor. To amplify this voltage, the flip-flop is switched on by ϕ_2 and $\bar{\phi}_2$. In the example considered in our analysis about 200 ns are needed for

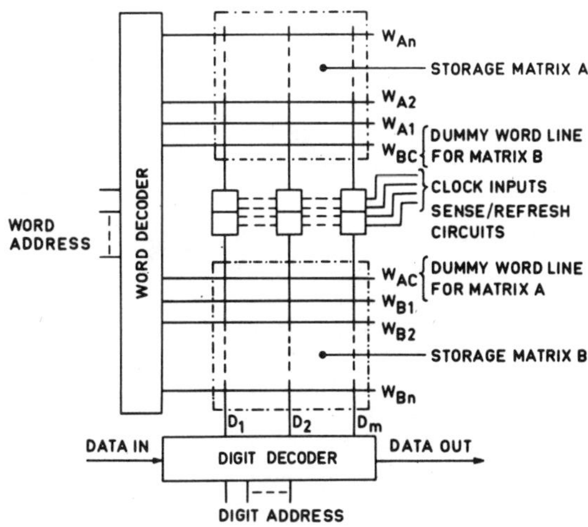

Fig. 8. Block diagram of a memory chip (total capacity 2-nm bit) with symmetrical storage matrices, dummy word lines, and sense/refresh circuits.

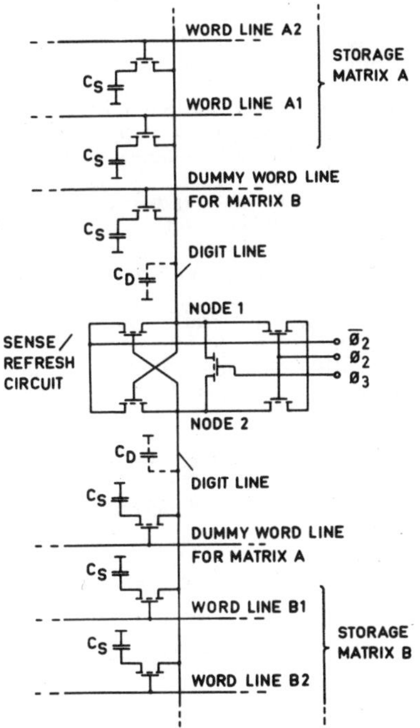

Fig. 9. Sense/refresh circuit with neighboring dummy and storage cells.

amplification if the digit lines are loaded with 64 words each.

If as shown in Fig. 10(a), the storage cell is selected during the amplification, rewriting is carried out simultaneously. The cycle is terminated by switching off the selected word line.

Experimental Results

Experimental circuits with sense/refresh amplifiers and memory cells with different capacitances (0.12–0.4 pF) have been realized in p- and n-channel silicon-gate technology. Both technologies produced good results with identical masks. Fig. 11 shows a micrograph of a sense/refresh circuit with the neighboring dummy and storage cells.

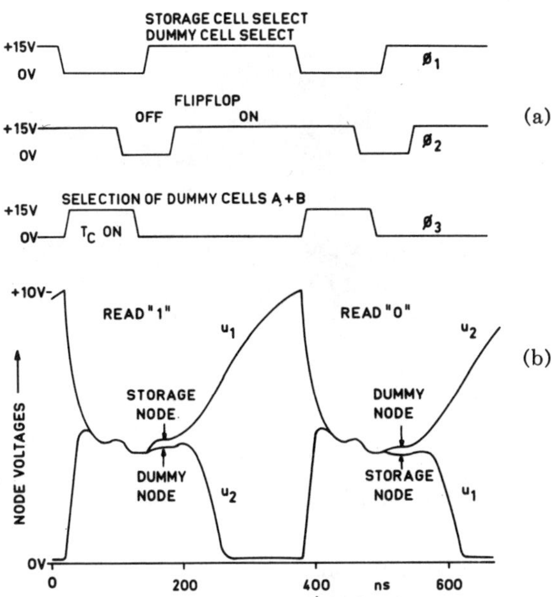

Fig. 10. (a) Timing diagram showing the signals for the sense/refresh amplifer [gated flip-flop (Fig. 9)] and cell select. (b) Computed node voltages u_1, u_2 of the flip-flop realized in a n-channel silicon-gate technology.

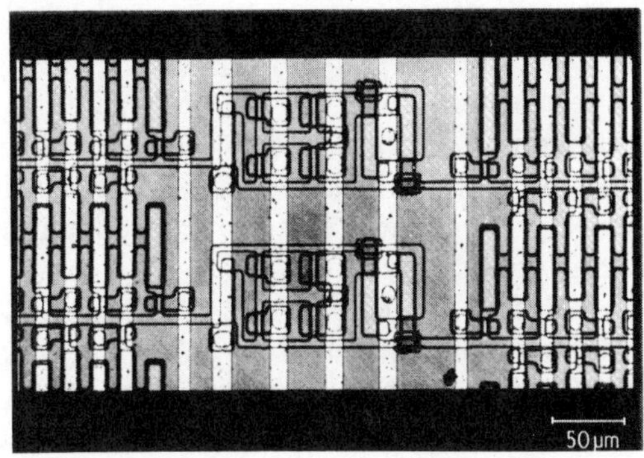

Fig. 11. Photomicrograph of a sense/refresh circuit with neighboring dummy and storage cells in silicon-gate technology.

The most significant representation of the experimental results is given by the waveforms of the node voltages of the flip-flop during a READ/REWRITE cycle (Fig. 12), these being similar to the computed results shown in Fig. 10(b).

The device under test was realized in n-channel silicon-gate technology. The threshold voltage U_T was +2 V at a substrate bias of −18 V. Each of the digit lines connected to the nodes of the flip-flop was loaded in this experimental circuit with eight realized memory cells plus a capacitance representing more than 64 cells. The waveforms observed are in good agreement with computed waveforms and can be compared with the curves of Fig. 10(b). This circuit can be operated at a READ/WRITE cycle time of about 350 ns.

The cell area of the device for which the results are shown in Fig. 12 was 1600 μm^2. Further experiments have shown that even the smallest realized cells with an

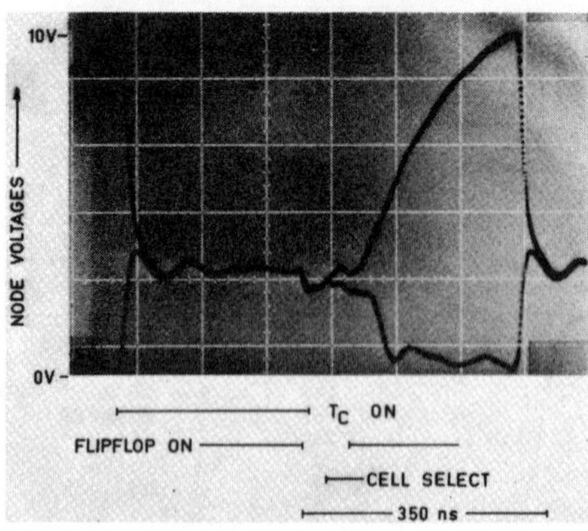

Fig. 12. Node voltages of a flip-flop realized in n-silicon-gate technology during a READ/REWRITE cycle [cf. Fig. 10(a)].

area of 1450 μm^2 could be operated in the same way. This confirms the value of the stet V_{tr} of the undefined region of the sense/refresh amplifier, estimated to be 0.6 V in this circuit. To get a more representative and reliable value of V_{tr}, yield and stability investigations need to be done.

Conclusion

It has been shown that the use of a gated flip-flop as a sense/refresh amplifier and memory cells with inversion-layer storage capacitors in standard silicon-gate technology eliminates the major disadvantages of single-transistor memory cells.

Realizing a 4096-bit chip with the present 1600-μm^2 cells would require a chip size of the order of 4×4.5 mm. For this chip an access time of about 250 ns and a cycle time of 350 ns are estimated. The cycle time includes the precharge of the digit lines and dummy cells, which is done simultaneously, as well as the sensing and rewriting.

Further development towards finer structures will yield smaller cell areas down to 625 μm^2 (1 mil^2) for structures characterized by 5-μm aluminum line width and line separation. With the storage density achieved thereby the 1-kbyte RAM chip seems feasible.

Acknowledgment

The authors would like to express their appreciation to M. Leitmeir and G. Lindert for their assistance in the design and the electrical measurements and to H. Friedrich for the n-silicon-gate processing.

References

[1] D. Lund, G. A. Allen, S. R. Andersen, and G. K. Tu, "Design of a megabit semiconductor memory system," *in Proc. AFIPS Fall Joint Computer Conf.*, pp. 53–62, Dec. 1970.
[2] W. M. Regitz and J. Karp, "A three-transistor cell, 1024-bit, 500 ns MOS RAM," *ISSCC Dig. Tech. Papers*, pp. 42–43, Feb. 1970.
[3] ——, "Fully decoded random-access 1024-bit dynamic memory 1103," Intel Corp., Mountain View, Calif., data sheet, Oct. 1970.
[4] J. A. Karp, W. M. Regitz, and S. Chou, "A 4096-bit dynamic MOS RAM," *ISSCC Dig. Tech. Papers*, pp. 10–11, Feb. 1972.
[5] L. M. Terman, "MOSFET memory circuits," *Proc. IEEE*, vol. 59, pp. 1044–1058, July 1971.
[6] R. H. Dennard, "Field-effect transistor memory," U. S. Patent 3 387 286, June 4, 1968.
[7] J. O. Paivinen, R. B. Rubinstein, L. Cohen, and L. T. Baker, "Read-write random-access memory system having single device memory cells," U. S. Ser. 809 223, Mar. 21, 1969.
[8] L. Cohen, R. Green, K. Smith, and J. L. Seely, "Single-transistor cell makes room for more memory on a MOS chip," *Electronics*, p. 69, Aug. 2, 1971.
[9] W. S. Boyle and G. E. Smith, "Charge-coupled semiconductor devices," *Bell Syst. Tech. J.* (Briefs), pp. 587–593, Apr. 1970.
[10] A. S. Grove and D. J. Fitzgerald, "Surface effects on p-n junction-characteristics of surface space-charge regions under nonequilibrium conditions," *Solid-State Electron.*, vol. 9, p. 783, Sept. 1966.

Optimization of the Latching Pulse for Dynamic Flip-Flop Sensors

WILLIAM T. LYNCH, MEMBER, IEEE, AND H. J. BOLL, MEMBER, IEEE

***Abstract*—Analysis of dynamic IGFET flip-flop charge sensors shows that the optimum latching waveform is an initial voltage step followed by a ramp of gradually increasing slope. Latchup time is approximately inversely proportional to the initial voltage imbalance. Capacitive coupling between the two sides of the flip-flop generates a voltage excursion of the off-side even when there is no off-side conduction. With a 10-V latching ramp, the off-side voltage excursion is typically about 2 V, and full latchup is attained in about 75 ns for an initial imbalance of 0.5 V. If a small off-side conduction is allowed, then latchup time can be reduced by a factor of two or more. The penalty is a few tenths of a volt added excursion of the off-side voltage. Computer circuit simulations were used to verify the analytic derivations.**

Manuscript received June 25, 1973.

The authors are with Bell Laboratories, Murray Hill, N. J. 07974.

I. INTRODUCTION

THE detection of small voltage signals has long been a serious difficulty in insulated-gate field-effect transistor (IGFET) circuit design. There are two basic causes: first, IGFET threshold voltage, V_T, is not accurately controlled; and second, transconductance increases only linearly with gate-source voltage above threshold.

In IGFET integrated circuits, adjacent devices are closely matched, so first-order threshold variations can be compensated for by using balanced detectors. Flip-flop detectors, besides being balanced, have the added advantage of regenerative action, so that a small initial imbalance grows during latchup until the imbalance,

Reprinted from *IEEE J. Solid-State Circuits*, vol. SC–9, pp. 49–55, Apr. 1974.

when fully latched, is comparable with the power supply voltage.

In a switched-capacitor memory [1], the high-speed detection of a small voltage is an essential part of the circuit function. Furthermore, to reduce unwanted power dissipation and current drain, the flip-flop load devices are turned off during latchup. In such a dynamic flip-flop, it is essential that there be almost no current flow through the *off*-side during latchup. Otherwise, the voltage of the *off*-side will be reduced along with the *on*-side, and the final (latched) imbalance will be reduced. Even in a flip-flop where the load devices remain on, a conduction in the *off*-side during latchup is undesirable because additional time may be required for the *off*-side load device to recharge its side.

In this paper we analyze the dynamics of flip-flop detectors, and show that the minimum time for latchup is approximately inversely proportional to the initial flip-flop imbalance, and that there is an ideal latching waveform that minimizes latch time for any given initial imbalance. By imbalance, we mean the sum of the real voltage imbalance and any threshold imbalance of the IGFET cross-coupled pair. The analysis, however, assumes only a real voltage imbalance. The waveform description would be more complicated if threshold variations were included, but the results would be essentially unchanged. A latch time of 75 ns can be achieved in the switched capacitor design of Boll and Lynch [1], with no *off*-side conduction, for an initial imbalance as small as 0.5 V. With a small *off*-side conduction that increases the *off*-side voltage excursion by ~25 percent, the latch time can be reduced to less than 40 ns.

II. Flip-Flop Latchup

A schematic of an IGFET flip-flop is shown in Fig. 1. n-channel devices are assumed in the discussion and derivation, but the final results are applicable to either n- or p-channel. In the initial state, both flip-flop devices *T*1 and *T*2 are off and are maintained off by the latch voltage V_S, which is held positive at V_0. A small initial voltage imbalance of v volts is indicated. The load devices *T*3 and *T*4 will be assumed to be gated off before the initial input imbalance and to remain off during the entire latchup. Their only function is to precharge the capacitances C_L of the input lines *D* and *G* to an initial voltage V_0. The positive imbalance of v volts is indicated as an input signal to node *G*, so that the initial conditions before latchup are $V_D = V_0$ and $V_G = V_0 + v$.

We wish to find an optimum latching voltage $V_S(t)$, which will minimize the latching times under the constraint that *T*2 may not conduct current. The optimum initial shape of the latch pulse V_S is a negative step from its initial positive level to a voltage value of $V_0 - V_T$, where V_T is the threshold voltage. This assures that *T*2 is marginally *off*, with a gate-to-source voltage of V_T, and *T*1 is *on*.

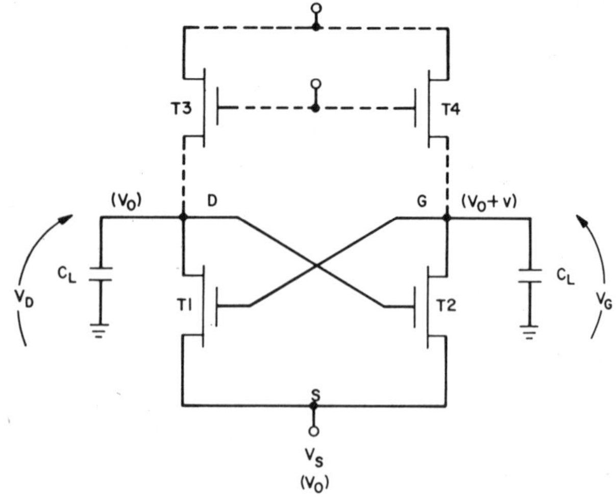

Fig. 1. IGFET flip-flop sensor. The initial voltage conditions are indicated in parentheses.

After this initial step, the current flow through *T*1 progressively increases the imbalance. The latch pulse V_S must be shaped so as to give the fastest possible waveform within the restriction that *T*2 must not turn on. V_G will then be reduced only by the capacitive coupling through C_G, the gate capacitance of *T*1.[1] Initially, the V_S ramp must be slow because the conductance level of *T*1 is initially low, and V_D must track V_S or else *T*2 will turn on. As V_S decreases, the conductance level of *T*1 increases (V_G remaining essentially constant), and the ramp speed may be progressively increased. Since V_D is decreasing as V_S decreases, *T*2 can be maintained in the *off* state throughout the latch sequence. Ideally, the V_S ramp should be chosen so that V_D always lags V_S by the threshold voltage V_T; that is, $V_D(t) = V_S(t) + V_T$. A faster ramp than this will partially turn on *T*2; a slower ramp will give a longer latch time.

III. Effects of *T*1 Gate Capacitance

If the gate capacitance, C_G, of *T*1 were zero, and if *T*2 was maintained *off*, the gate voltage V_G would remain at $V_0 + v$. However, since this is not the case, the negative going latch voltage V_S couples through *T*1 and reduces V_G. This in turn reduces the *on* conductance of *T*1 and increases the latchup time. Therefore, C_G has two undesirable effects which must be included in the latch derivation: it increases latchup time and reduces the *off*-side voltage.

The components of C_G are the gate-channel capacitance, C_{GC}, and the gate-source and gate-drain overlap capacitances, C_{GS} and C_{GD}. In the following analysis, the effects of C_{GS} and C_{GD} are neglected when the transistor is off. For a worst case analysis, the gate-drain capacitance of *T*2 should be added to C_G of *T*1 to ac-

[1] The latching condition which is being considered corresponds to the worst case read, i.e., reading and refreshing the node *G* side of the flip-flop when the cell being accessed on that side is initially uncharged.

count for the reduction in V_G due to the gate-drain overlap of $T2$.

When $T1$ is *on*, C_G takes from C_L (at node G) the charge

$$q = (V_G - V_S - V_T)C_G \tag{1}$$

where $V_G - V_S - V_T$ is the voltage above threshold of $T1$. This equation is valid for all four components of C_G, since it is being assumed that V_D is directly tracking V_S. The voltage reduction across C_L (at node G) is

$$\Delta V_G = -\frac{q}{C_L} = -(V_G - V_S - V_T)\frac{C_G}{C_L}. \tag{2}$$

In terms of the initial gate voltage, $V_0 + v$, the corrected gate voltage is

$$V_G = V_0 + v - (V_G - V_S - V_T)\frac{C_G}{C_L}. \tag{3}$$

By adding $- V_S - V_T$ to both sides of (3) and rearranging terms we obtain

$$V_G - V_S - V_T = (V_0 + v - V_S - V_T)f \tag{4}$$

where $f \equiv C_L/(C_L + C_G)$. $(1 - f)$ represents the voltage ratio of ΔV_G to ΔV_S as the result of coupling through C_G.

IV. Optimization of the Latch Pulse

As was discussed in Section II, the flip-flop node conditions, immediately after the negative step of V_S, are

$$V_D(0^+) = V_0 \tag{5a}$$

$$V_S(0^+) = V_0 - V_T \tag{5b}$$

$$V_G(0^+) = V_0 + vf \tag{5c}$$

where (5c) was obtained from (5b) through (4).

For $vf < V_T$, the current equation for the *on*-side of the flip-flop, $T1$, is

$$I = -C_L\frac{dV_D(t)}{dt} = -C_L\frac{dV_S(t)}{dt}$$

$$= \frac{\beta}{2}[V_G(t) - V_S(t) - V_T]^2. \tag{6a}$$

Again using (4), we obtain

$$-C_L\frac{dV_S}{dt} = \frac{\beta}{2}f^2[V_0 + v - V_T - V_S]^2. \tag{6b}$$

It is assumed that V_T is not a function of time, i.e., that the back gate-bias effects due to a changing V_S are negligible. Equation (6) can be readily solved for $V_S(t)$ as in the following:

$$V_S(t) - V_S(0^+) = -\frac{(\beta/2C_L)v^2f^2t}{1 - (\beta/2C_L)vf^2t}. \tag{7}$$

Equation (7) is valid as long as $T1$ is in saturation, i.e., as long as $V_G \le (V_D + V_T)$. At time $t = t_{\text{sat}}$, when $T1$ goes from saturation to triode operation, $V_G = V_D + V_T$. That is, the imbalance $V_G - V_D$ has grown from its initial value of v to the value V_T. Since $V_D = V_S + V_T$, we then have

$$V_G(t_{\text{sat}}) - V_S(t_{\text{sat}}) - V_T = V_T. \tag{8}$$

Again employing (4),

$$\frac{V_T}{f} = V_0 + v - V_S(t_{\text{sat}}) - V_T \tag{9}$$

and combining this with (5b),

$$V_S(t_{\text{sat}}) - V_S(0^+) = v - V_T/f. \tag{10}$$

The time t_{sat} is obtained by substituting (10) into (7), as in the following:

$$t_{\text{sat}} = 2C_L\frac{(V_T - fv)}{\beta f^2V_Tv} \qquad \text{for } V_T \ge fv. \tag{11}$$

Note that t_{sat} is zero if $fv \ge V_T$. In that case, there is no saturation regime, and we go immediately into the triode regime. It is readily verified that t_{sat} is minimized when β is chosen, so that $C_G = C_L$ (i.e. $f = .5$). Also for small v, i.e., $V_T \gg fv$, t_{sat} is inversely proportional to v.

The ideal shape for the latch pulse for the triode regime is also easily derived. The current equation now is

$$I = -C_L\frac{dV_S}{dt} = \beta[V_D - V_S]$$

$$\cdot\left[(V_G - V_S - V_T) - \left(\frac{V_D - V_S}{2}\right)\right] \tag{12}$$

where V_D, V_S, and V_G are time dependent. Using (4) and $V_D = V_S + V_T$, we obtain

$$-C_L\frac{dV_S}{dt} = \beta V_T\left[f(V_0 + v - V_T - V_S) - \frac{V_T}{2}\right]. \tag{13}$$

By inserting the boundary conditions at t_{sat} and at the end of the latch waveform, t_l,

$$V_S(t_{\text{sat}}) = V_0 - V_T + v - V_T/f$$

and

$$V_S(t_l) = 0. \tag{14}$$

Equation (13) can be solved for $(t - t_{\text{sat}})$ and $(t_l - t_{\text{sat}})$, as seen in the following:

$$(t - t_{\text{sat}}) = \frac{1}{f}\frac{C_L}{\beta}\frac{1}{V_T}\ln\left[\frac{V_S(t_{\text{sat}}) - V_S(t) - \dfrac{V_T}{2f}}{V_T/2f}\right] \tag{15}$$

$$(t_l - t_{\text{sat}}) = \frac{1}{f}\frac{C_L}{\beta}\frac{1}{V_T}\ln\left[\frac{f(V_0 + v - V_T) - V_T/2}{V_T/2}\right]. \tag{16}$$

When $t > t_l$, then $V_S = 0$. However, V_D is not yet 0 at $t = t_l$, but continues to decrease. For this discussion, the latchup is considered to be complete at $t = t_l$.

Table I lists t_{sat}, $(t_l - t_{\text{sat}})$, and t_l for $v = 0.5$ V and 1 V, and $V_T = 2$ V and 3 V. Parameters of $V_0 = 10$ V, $C_L = 0.7$ pF, $\beta = 52 \times 10^{-6}$ ℧/V, and $f = 0.833$ were

TABLE I

SUMMARY OF t_{sat}, $t_l - t_{sat}$, AND t_l FOR $\beta = 52 \times 10^{-6}$ ℧/V, $C_L = 0.7$ pF, AND $V_0 = 10$ V

	t_{sat} (ns)			
	$V_T = 2$ V		$V_T = 3$ V	
	$f = 1$	$f = 0.833$	$f = 1$	$f = 0.833$
$v = 0.5$ V	40	61	45	67
$v = 1.0$ V	13.5	23	18	28
	$t_l - t_{sat}$ (ns)			
$v = 0.5$ V	14	15	6	6
$v = 1.0$ V	14	15	7	7
	t_l (ns)			
$v = 0.5$ V	54	76	51	73
$v = 1.0$ V	27.5	38	25	35

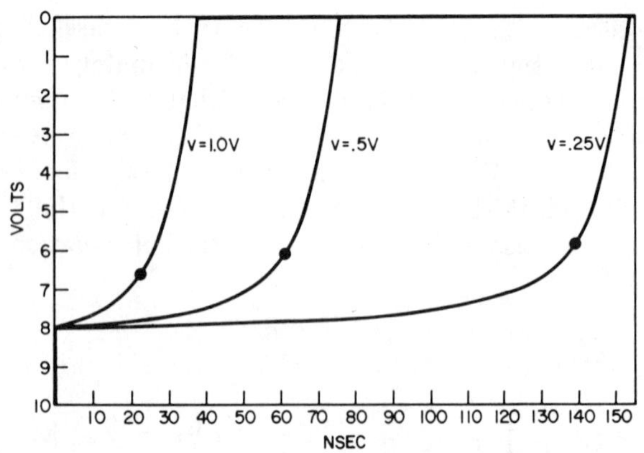

Fig. 2. Optimum latching waveforms for $V_T = 2$ V, $C_L = 0.7$ pF, $\beta = 52 \times 10^{-6}$ ℧/V, and $f = 0.833$, for initial voltage imbalances of $v = 0.25$, 0.5, and 1.0 V. The t_{sat} points are indicated as solid dots.

chosen to conform to the parameters of the flip-flop sensors in [1]. (The β value is a worst case value.) Latchup for $v = 0.5$ V and 1 V can be achieved in ~75 ns and 38 ns, respectively. It can also be seen that the time t_{sat} dominates for small v, since the latch ramp must be initially slow for small v. Fig. 2 shows the general shape of the latching waveforms. Note that the waveform for higher v can be fitted over the waveforms for lower v by positive displacements in both time and voltage. As an example, the t_{sat} points are indicated as solid dots. Additional equivalent points can be obtained by incrementing with the same voltage and time for each waveform. It is apparent that the only significant difference in the latch waveforms is the additional tail on the curves for low v. Once the imbalance has increased to the imbalance at $t = 0^+$ for the higher v curve, the waveshapes, as expected, are identical. It is also to be noted from Fig. 2 that to a high degree of accuracy, the latchup time for the three cases is inversely proportional to the initial imbalance. This effect is somewhat fortuitous because for the parameter values chosen, $t_l - t_{sat}$ from (16) very nearly compensates the $-fv$ term in the numerator of (11). However, because the logarithmic term in (16) varies slowly with its argument, the inverse relationship between latchup time and initial imbalance is approximately true over a wide range of parameter values.

In the above derivation, the off-side conduction was required to be zero. However, a considerable increase in speed, with only a minor reduction in V_G, can be achieved by allowing $T2$ to conduct weakly during the latchup. A particular case of interest is the case of constant conduction, i.e., with the $T2$ gate-to-source voltage maintained throughout the latching ramp at a small constant voltage v_c above threshold. This case is discussed in the Appendix, and the analytical solutions are derived. If, e.g., we use the parameters for Table I with $f = 0.833$, $V_T = 2$ V, $v = 0.5$ V, and $v_c = 0.5$ V, the required latching time is only ~36 ns, as compared to the latching time of ~76 ns for $v_c = 0$. That is, the latching time can be reduced by approximately a factor of two, if the latching ramp is modified so that the initial gate-to-source voltage of $T1$ is increased from $V_T + v$ to $V_T + v + v_c = V_T + 2v$, and the off-side is allowed to conduct throughout the latching ramp with a gate-to-source voltage of $V_T + v_c = V_T + v$. The only tradeoff for realizing this decrease in the latching time is a small increase in the voltage excursion, ΔV_G, of the *off*-side. At the time $t = t_l$, the ratio of ΔV_G, due to conduction by $T2$, to ΔV_G, due to coupling through C_G, is

$$\frac{\Delta V_G|_{T2\text{conduction}}}{\Delta V_G|_{C_G\text{coupling}}} = \frac{(\beta/2C_L)v_c^2 t_l}{(1-f)(V_0 - V_T)}. \tag{17}$$

For the example given in the Appendix ($v = v_c = 0.5$), this ratio is $\approx 0.33/1.34 \approx 0.25$. That is, the tradeoff for reducing the latch time by more than a factor of two is a 25 percent increase (0.33 V) in the voltage excursion of the unlatched side. Further reductions in latching time, with correspondingly larger increases in ΔV_G, can be realized by further increasing the value of v_c.

V. COMPUTER VERIFICATION

The circuit analysis program SERVICE [3] was used to analyze the flip-flop in Fig. 1. Throughout the analyses, the betas of $T1$ and $T2$ were set equal to 52 $\times 10^{-6}$ ℧/V, C_L was 0.7 pF, V_o was 10 V, and v was 0.5 V. Since the SERVICE program includes the back gate-bias effect on the threshold voltage V_T, the threshold was chosen so as to remain within ± 0.2 V of 2 V throughout the latch ramp. Three different latch ramps were employed, corresponding to the three curves of Fig. 2. One ramp is slower than necessary for the fixed initialization of $v = 0.5$ V, one is too fast, and the third is correct.

Although the SERVICE program does not require that f be specified since it automatically calculates the effects of capacitive coupling, the derivation of V_S (Section IV) requires a prior assumption for the value of f. An f value of 0.833 was chosen in deriving the V_S

TABLE II

SUMMARY OF ΔV_G EXCURSIONS FOR $v = 0.5$ V, $V_T = 2$ V, $\beta = 52 \times 10^{-6}$ ℧/V, $C_L = 0.7$ pF, AND $V_0 = 10$ V, FOR V_S WAVEFORMS OPTIMIZED FOR $f = 0.833$ AND $v = 0.25$, 0.5, AND 1.0 V, RESPECTIVELY

v for which V_S is optimized	ΔV_G	Comments
0.25 V	2.16 V	$T2$ remained off; $(V_D - V_S)$ decreased during the latchup
0.5 V	2.25 V	$T2$ conducted very slightly; $(V_D - V_S)$ remained essentially constant during the latchup
1.0 V	2.54 V	$T2$ conducted slightly; $(V_D - V_S)$ gradually increased during the latchup

waveforms of Fig. 2 with the assumption that the C_G capacitance consisted mainly of the gate-to-channel capacitance C_{GC} and was equal to approximately two-thirds of the total gate-oxide capacitance. This approximation is not a totally valid one since C_{GC} depends on both the device geometry and the conduction level of the IGFET; in particular, C_{GC} is more nearly equal to the total gate-oxide capacitance in the triode regime. Although the triode regime covers the largest voltage excursion of V_S, the saturation regime is more critical (Table I) in determining the total time for latchup. The choice of too small an f, i.e., a large C_{GC}, would unnecessarily lengthen the calculated latch time. A more accurate approach would be to use different f values for the saturation and triode regimes.

The computer results provide an excellent confirmation of the previous derivations. These results are summarized in Table II. For the latch ramp optimized for $v = 0.5$ V, the net excursion of V_G was 2.25 V (i.e., from 10.5 to 8.25 V). The chosen f value was in fact too large, particularly for the triode regime, since some minor conduction of $T2$ did occur in this regime. A more appropriate f value would have been $f \approx 0.77$. Voltage V_D lagged approximately one threshold voltage behind V_S throughout the saturation regime, but lagged further during the triode regime. For the ramp optimized for $v = 0.25$ V, ΔV_G was 2.16 V. The lower value for ΔV_G confirms the minor level of conduction in the prior computer run. Throughout the saturation regime, the value of $(V_D - V_S)$ was less than V_T and was monotonically decreasing; during the triode regime, $(V_D - V_S)$ was increasing. For the latch ramp optimized for $v =$ 1.0 V, ΔV_G was 2.54 V. Therefore, in reducing the ramp time to 38 ns, ΔV_G increased by only 18 percent. The increased latch speed resulted in a gradual increase in $(V_D - V_S)$ which only marginally turned on $T2$. The turn on of $T2$ is nearly equal to that predicted by the example for (17), but is not directly comparable. In the derivation of (17), not only was the ramp time reduced, but also, the initial V_S step was increased by 0.5 V to insure $T2$ turn on even at the beginning of the latch ramp. In addition, the effective f values are different for the two cases.

VI. CONCLUSIONS

The calculated derivation and the computer verifications show that there is an optimum latching waveform for IGFET flip-flops. This waveform is expressed in (7), (11), (15), and (16), and the general shape is shown in Fig. 2. The optimum waveform consists of an initial step followed by a ramp of gradually increasing slope to the final voltage value. The total latch time is approximately inversely proportional to the initial imbalance. Coupling capacitances to the *off*-side from either the latching node or the *on*-side, increase the latching time since they lower the *off*-side voltage and therefore lower the conduction of the *on* transistor. A latching speed off-side voltage-excursion tradeoff is possible by allowing the *off*-side to partially conduct during the latch. Analysis of the flip-flop sensors in [1] shows that, with ~25 percent increase in the voltage excursion of the *off*-side, a latching time of less than 40 ns can be achieved for an initial imbalance of 0.5 V. Moreover, since worst case beta values were used in the derivation, the quoted 40 ns value is typically 25 ns for a 0.5-V initial imbalance. For the expected imbalance of 1.5–2 V [1], the time for t_{sat} approaches 0 ns, and the value for t_l could be in the 10 ns range as experimentally confirmed by Waaben [3].

APPENDIX A

We wish to consider the case of weak conduction by the *off*-side ($T2$) during the latchup. In particular, we wish to consider the case of constant conduction, i.e., with the $T2$ gate-to-source voltage maintained throughout the latching ramp at a small constant voltage v_c above threshold. For a small v_c, $T2$ will remain in saturation with its current equal to $\beta/2 v_c^2$. V_G will now not only be reduced by capacitive coupling, but also by the conduction of $T2$. This additional reduction of V_G, as a function of time, is equal to

$$\Delta V_{G\ T2\text{conduction}} = -\frac{\beta}{2}\frac{v_c^2}{C_L}t \tag{A-1}$$

for $0 < t < t_l$. It is necessary to determine the effect of this additional V_G excursion on the conduction of $T1$ and, therefore, on the latchup time.

V_G of (3) is now modified to

$$V_G = V_0 + v - (V_G - V_S - V_T)\left(\frac{C_G}{C_L}\right) - \frac{\beta}{2}\frac{v_c^2}{C_L}t \quad \text{(A-2)}$$

where all terms have the same definitions as in the main body of the paper. By adding $-V_S - V_T + \beta v_c^2 t/2C_G$ to both sides of (A-2), and by rearranging terms, we obtain

$$V_G - V_S - V_T + \frac{\beta}{2}\frac{v_c^2}{C_G}t = f\left(V_0 + v - V_S - V_T + \frac{\beta}{2}\frac{v_c^2}{C_G}t\right) \quad \text{(A-3)}$$

where f is again defined as $C_L/(C_L + C_G)$.

In order to obtain an initial gate-to-source voltage of $v_c + V_T$ for $T2$, the initial conditions at $t = 0^+$ must be

$$V_S(0^+) = V_0 - V_T - v_c/f \quad \text{(A-4a)}$$

$$V_D(0^+) = V_0 - (v_c/f)(1-f) \quad \text{(A-4b)}$$

$$V_G(0^+) = V_0 + vf - (v_c/f)(1-f) \quad \text{(A-4c)}$$

$$(t - t_{sat}) = \frac{C_L}{\beta f(V_T + v_c)} \ln \left[\frac{V_S(t_{sat}) - V_S(t) - \frac{\beta}{2}\frac{v_c^2}{C_L}(t - t_{sat}) + \frac{V_T + v_c}{2f} - \frac{v_c^2}{2f(V_T + v_c)}}{\frac{V_T + v_c}{2f} - \frac{v_c^2}{2f(V_T + v_c)}} \right] \quad \text{(A-9)}$$

$$(t_l - t_{sat}) = \frac{C_L}{\beta f(V_T + v_c)} \ln \left[\frac{f(V_0 + v - V_T) - f\frac{\beta}{2}\frac{v_c^2}{C_L}t_l - \frac{v_c + V_T}{2} - \frac{v_c^2}{2(V_T + v_c)}}{\frac{V_T + v_c}{2} - \frac{v_c^2}{2(V_T + v_c)}} \right]. \quad \text{(A-10)}$$

where it is assumed that the coupling factor f is the same for both $T1$ and $T2$, since both transistors are now on.

Substitution of (A-3) into (6a), the current equation for the saturation region, gives, after some rearranging,

$$I = -C_L\frac{dV_S}{dt} = \frac{\beta}{2}f^2\left(V_0 + v - V_S - V_T - \frac{\beta}{2}\frac{v_c^2}{C_L}t\right)^2. \quad \text{(A-5)}$$

With the temporary substitution of $V_S' \equiv V_S + \beta v_c^2 t/2C_L$, this equation is easily solved. Substitution of the initial condition of (A-4a) gives as the final result, valid for $0 < t < t_{sat}$,

$$t = \frac{C_L}{\beta f v_c} \ln \left[\frac{V_S - V_S(0^+) + \frac{\beta}{2}\frac{v_c^2}{C_L}t - v}{V_S - V_S(0^+) + \frac{\beta}{2}\frac{v_c^2}{C_L}t - \frac{2v_c}{f} - v} \cdot \frac{\frac{2v_c}{f} + v}{v} \right]. \quad \text{(A-6)}$$

In the limit of $v_c \to 0$, (A-6) can be shown to reduce to (7).

In an identical way to the development of (10), it can be shown that

$$V_S(t_{sat}) - V_S(0^+) + \frac{\beta}{2}\frac{v_c^2}{C_L}t_{sat} = v - \frac{V_T}{f}. \quad \text{(A-7)}$$

Substitution of (A-7) into (A-6) gives

$$t_{sat} = \frac{C_L}{\beta f v_c} \ln \left[\frac{V_T}{V_T + 2v_c} \cdot \frac{fv + 2v_c}{fv} \right]. \quad \text{(A-8)}$$

If, e.g., we use the parameters for Table I with $V_T = 2$ V, $v = 0.5$ V, $v_c = 0.5$ V, and $f = 0.833$, then $t_{sat} \approx 26$ ns. This is only 3 ns longer than the results of Table I for $v = 1.0$ V. Even though the additional ΔV_G [see (A-1)] up to the time of $t = t_{sat}$ is equal to ~ -0.24 V, the effect on the conduction level of $T1$ is minor, and $T1$ acts very much as if the initial imbalance were $v + v_c = 1.0$ V. The additional ΔV_G is not significant, since the increase in ΔV_G at any point in time is small compared to the gate-to-source overvoltage, $V_G - V_S - V_T$, at that point in time. (For example, $V_G - V_S - V_T$ at t_{sat} is equal to $V_T + v_c$, which is equal to 2.5 V for the previous example.)

The solution for the triode region proceeds in an identical fashion to the solution in the main body of the paper. The results are (A-9) and (A-10) above.

In the limit of $v_c \to 0$, (A-9) and (A-10) reduce to (15) and (16), respectively. A good approximation to the implicit solution of (A-10) is to use (16) with V_T replaced by $(V_T + v_c)$.

If the parameters for the previous example are substituted into (A-10), the result for $(t_l - t_{sat})$ is 10 ns. The previously calculated time for t_{sat} was 26 ns. Therefore, when the *off*-side $T2$ is allowed to conduct with a gate-to-source voltage 0.5 V above threshold throughout the ramp, the net result is to reduce the required latching ramp time from $\sim$76 ns to $\sim$36 ns. The only penalty is an increase in the excursion of the *off*-side node voltage from ~ -1.34 V $(-(V_o - V_T)(1-f))$ to ~ -1.67 V $(-(V_o - V_T)(1-f) - \beta v_c^2 t_l/2C_L)$.

Acknowledgment

The authors wish to thank E. E. Labate for his assistance in executing the SERVICE computer runs.

References

[1] H. J. Boll and W. T. Lynch, "Design of a high performance 1024-b switched capacitor p-channel IGFET memory chip," *IEEE J. Solid-State Circuits*, vol. SC-8, pp. 310–318, Oct. 1973.

[2] J. D. Leggett and J. W. Shorter, private communication.

[3] S. Waaben, private communication.

Cross-Coupled Charge-Transfer Sense Amplifier

Lawrence G. Heller

IBM Corporation

Essex Junction, VT

FOR THE PAST SEVERAL YEARS, there has been considerable interest in the development of improved sensitivity/performance MOS sense amplifiers for one-device cell memory arrays[1,2,3]. The main impetus for this activity is the direct relationship between the array density of the one-device dynamic memory cell, consisting of a single gating transistor and a storage capacitor, and the sensitivity of the detection circuit[3].

A common approach to the sense amplifier for the one-device memory cell is a latch or flipflop[1,2]. More recently the application of charge-transfer concepts to MOS sense amplifiers has resulted in improved sensitivity[3].

This paper will describe an MOS sense amplifier that consists of a preamplifier and a latch. A circuit diagram of the preamplifier with timing waveforms is illustrated in Figure 1. High speed preamplification is achieved by the novel cross-coupling of devices T5 and T6 operated in a charge-transfer mode[4,5].

During $\phi 1$ time, the bit/sense lines are precharged to $(V_I - V_{th})$ by operating devices T5 and T6 in saturation and devices T1 and T2 in the linear region. Nodes N1 and N2 are charged to the power supply level V_I and devices T5 and T6 are precharged up to cutoff ($V_{gs} - V_{th} \approx 0$), effectively precharging out any offset due to V_{th} mismatch between T5 and T6[3]. Assume, for simplicity, that a stored "1" in the memory cell is a high voltage V_H and a stored "0" is ground, and that the precharged B/S line level $V_I - V_{th} \approx V_H/2$ is intermediate between the stored "1" and "0" levels.

After precharge a word line is accessed and depending on the stored information the sense signal will be positive or negative. Assume a negative signal (stored "0") is developed on the B/S line on the left of the amplifier. Application of the ramp voltage $\phi 2$ results in amplification of the imbalance between devices T5 and T6 due to cross-coupling action. During the $\phi 2$ ramp, amplification continues until device T5 comes out of saturation and at least one threshold voltage is developed across nodes N1 and N2. The preamplified signal is now fed to a second cross-coupled pair for further amplification.

The complete sense amplifier is indicated in Figure 2 along with the pulsing sequence. After preamplification, the B/S lines are charged to V_H by $\phi 3$. Then $\phi 5$ is ramped toward ground setting the second cross-coupled pair T11 and T12.

The left B/S line is discharged to ground through devices T5 and T11 and the word line is deactivated. The information has been written back into the cell. $\phi 4$ discharges the B/S lines to ground, completing the sensing cycle. The sensing of a positive signal, due to the reading of a "1", would flip the sense amplifier in the opposite direction and write a "1" back into the cell. In this case, device T6 turns on harder than device T5 during the $\phi 2$ ramp.

Cross-coupling of devices T5 and T6 results in rapid amplification due to positive feedback. In addition, amplification speed is enhanced because nodes N1 and N2 are isolated from the B/S line capacitance by devices T5 and T6, which are operated in saturation. An approximate linear analysis of the first cross-coupled pair T5 and T6 indicates that the preamplification switching time τ goes as

$$\tau \sim \frac{C_{B/S}}{g_m\left(\frac{C_{B/S}}{C_L} - 1\right)}$$

where $C_{B/S}$ is the B/S line capacitance and C_L is the total output capacitive load on nodes N1 and N2. For large open loop gain, $(C_{B/S}/C_L)^2$, the switching time associated with preamplification approaches that of a standard latch C_L/g_m with the same output load. However, the preamplifier is substantially more sensitive than a standard latch because any offset due to V_{th} mismatch is precharged out. A preamplified signal in the 0.4 – 1.0V range allows a rapid set time for the second cross-coupled pair T11 and T12.

Figure 3 is an experimental plot of the preamplifier sensitivity versus $\phi 2$ ramp time, indicating a sensitivity $\pm \Delta V$ in the low mV range. The test site used for this experiment has an open loop gain of approximately 16.

The cross-coupled charge-transfer sense amplifier concepts have been used in several one-device cell memory chip designs, including a 64K bit memory chip. Other applications include a previously described 1mV MOS comparator[6].

Dedication

The author would like to dedicate this paper to the late Dominic P. Spampinato, a colleague, a friend and an inspiration.

Acknowledgments

The author is indebted to K. S. Gray for proving the potential of the sense amplifier in product design, and to Y. S. Yee and M. B. Pettigrew of IBM, Yorktown Heights, N. Y., for providing the experimental curve of Figure 3. The support of B. Agusta is appreciated.

[1] Stein, K.-U., Sihling, A., and Doering, E., "Storage Array and Sense/Refresh Circuit for Single-Transistor Memory Cells", *IEEE J. Solid-State Circuits*, vol. SC-7, p. 336-340; Oct., 1972.

[2] Lynch, W.T., and Boll, H.J., "Optimization of the Latching Pulse for Dynamic Flipflop Sensors", *IEEE J. Solid-State Circuits*, vol. SC-9, p. 49-55; Apr., 1974.

[3] Heller, L.G., Spampinato, D.P., and Yao, Y.L., "High Sensitivity Charge-Transfer Sense Amplifier", *IEEE J. Solid-State Circuits*, vol. SC-11, p. 596-601; Oct., 1976.

[4] Kalter, H.L., "Parameter Independent FET Sense Amplifier", *U.S. Patent 3,993,917;* Nov. 23, 1976.

[5] Heller, L.G., and Spampinato, D.P., "Cross-Coupled Charge Transfer Sense Amplifier Circuits", *U.S. Patent 4,039,861;* Aug. 2, 1977.

[6] Yee, Y.S., Terman, L.M., and Heller, L.G., "A 1mV MOS Comparator", *IEEE J. Solid-State Circuits*, vol. SC-13, p. 294-297; June, 1978.

Reprinted from *IEEE J. Solid State Circuits Conf.*, pp. 20–21, 1979.

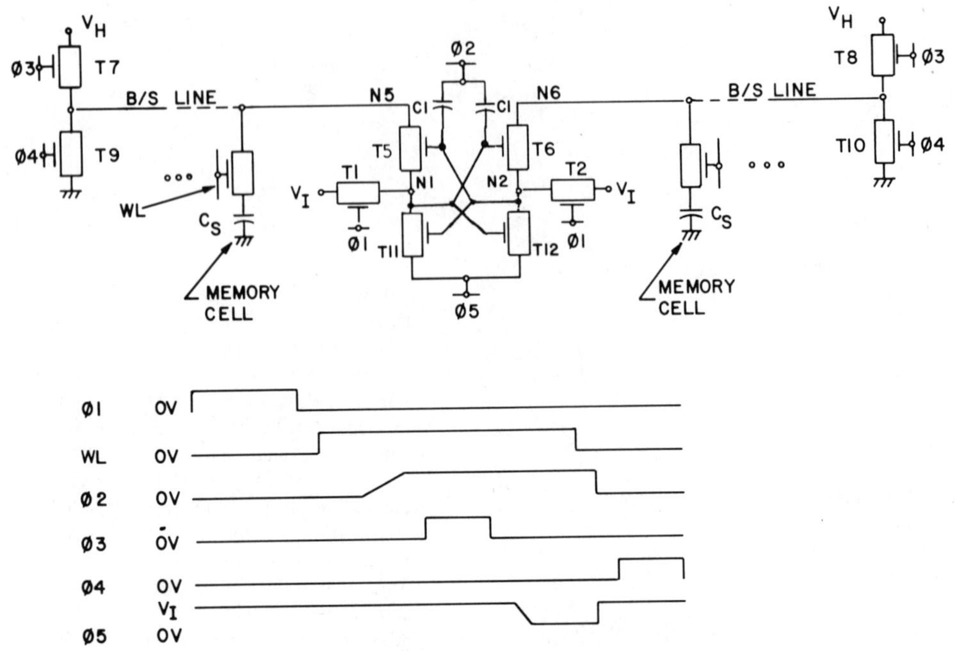

FIGURE 2—Charge-transfer sense/amplifier.

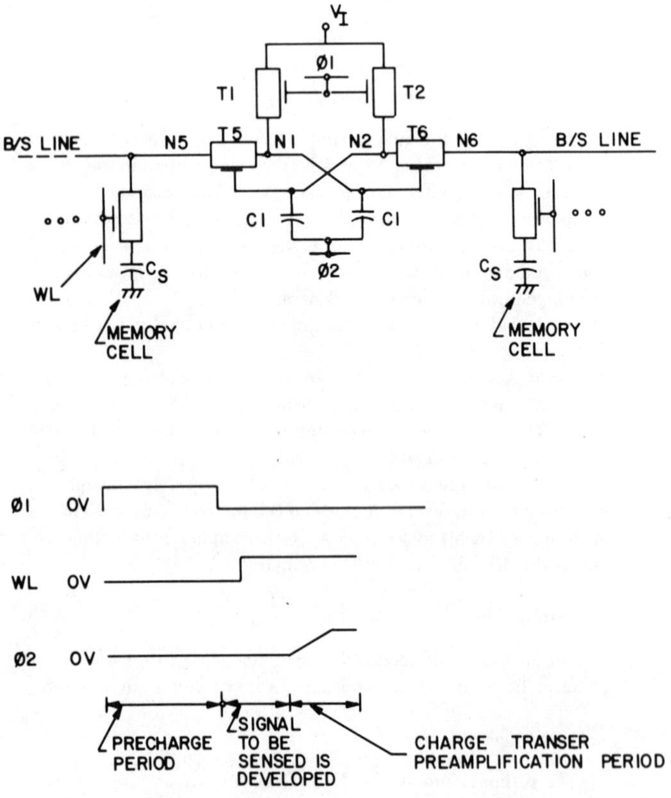

FIGURE 1—Cross-coupled charge-transfer preamplifier.

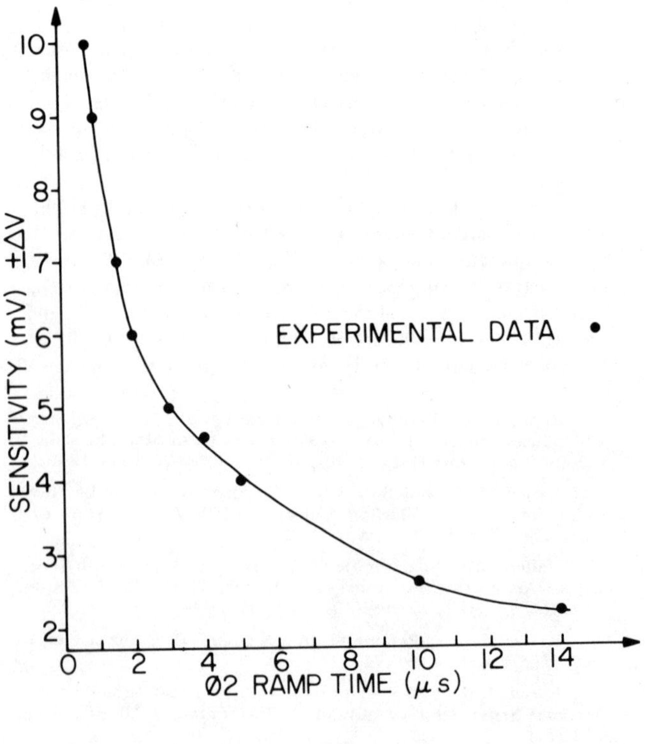

FIGURE 3—Sensitivity versus preamplification time.

Part IV
MOS Digital Circuit Applications

The continual evolution of digital MOS circuits towards higher degrees of integration has been associated with an increase in performance. This has offered the VLSI circuit designer a challenging opportunity to integrate digital subsystems or even complete systems on a single silicon chip. The application of VLSI in system/subsystem design can be generally grouped into the integration of:

1. large capacity memory chips [1–2],
2. data processing subsystems [3–4], and
3. signal processing subsystems [5–9].

The most recent impact of VLSI, both in terms of performance and silicon area, is in the area of signal processing. The demands of signal processing exceed that of data processing and memories. Signal processing requires realtime operations at high data rates. Moreover, data processing involves the integration of relatively small primitive operations (eg. add, subtract, mask, compare) while signal processing involves the integration of large primitives (eg. multipliers).

In data processing, VLSI impacts computer architecture especially at the microcomputer and microprocessor level [10–13]. For example, combining arithmetic and memory functions on a single chip eliminates the need to pass data off-chip to the memory. This reduction in data transfer requirement improves system performance and reduces the required I/O pins. Moreover, merging of arithmetic, logic, and memory functions in each cell of a data processing array would offer a modular array suitable for VLSI [14–28].

In memory, the advances of VLSI have offered higher density for both static (up to 64Kb from the early 256b) and dynamic (up to 256Kb from the early 1Kb) RAMs. The performance has also been enhanced in terms of 5V-only operation and access time. The area of ROMs, PROMs, and EPROMs has also taken advantage of advances in the technology as well as innovative circuit designs.

This Part deals with some applications of MOS digital circuits. Section 4.1 covers logic and circuit design using programmable logic arrays (PLAs). Section 4.2 deals with the integration of some basic building blocks used in digital signal processors. Section 4.3 addresses the impact of VLSI on microprocessors design and gives two typical design examples, the design of the 8086 and the 6800. Sections 4.5, 4.6, and 4.7 offer some key developments in MOS static and dynamic RAMs and ROMs, PROMs, and EPROMs respectively. The published work in the area of MOS memory alone in the last five years exceeds that reported on all other MOS digital applications combined. Thus, I have not attempted to present to the reader an accurate history of the developments in the area of MOS memory. Moreover, because of space limitations I had to be selective and excluded a number of papers which are considered important. However, most of these are used as references in the selected papers and the others are included in the bibliography.

Finally, the reader is referred to Sections 5–9 of the bibliography which contains references related to MOS digital applications in signal processing, microprocessors, static RAMs, dynamic RAMs and ROMs, PROMs, and EPROMs respectively.

References

[1] J. Eimbinger, "Semiconductor Memories," Wiley-Interscience, 1971.

[2] D. A. Hodges, "Semiconductor Memories," IEEE Press, 1972.

[3] G. K. Kostopoulos, "Digital Engineering," Wiley-Interscience, 1975.

[4] A. Barna and D. I. Porat, "Integrated Circuits in Digital Electronics," Wiley-Interscience, 1973.

[5] L. R. Rabiner and C. M. Rader, "Digital Signal Processing," IEEE Press, 1972.

[6] H. J. Blinchikoff and A. I. Zvereu, "Filtering in the Time and Frequency Domains," Wiley-Interscience, 1976

[7] R. E. Bogner and A. G. Constantinides, "Introduction to Digital Filtering," John Wiley, 1975.

[8] B. Gold and C. M. Rader, "Digital Processing of Signals," McGraw-Hill, 1969.

[9] A. Antonion, "Digital Filters Analysis and Design," McGraw-Hill, 1979.

[10] A. Barna and D. I. Porat, "Introduction to Microprocessors," Wiley-Interscience, 1976.

[11] B. Soncek, "Microprocessors and Microcomputers," Wiley-Interscience, 1976.

[12] D. R. McGlynn, "Microprocessors and Microcomputers," Wiley-Interscience, 1976.

[13] D. R. McGlynn, "Microprocessors: Technology, Architecture, and Applications," Wiley-Interscience, 1976.

[14] F. Faggin, "How VLSI Impacts Computer Architecture," *IEEE Spectrum*, May 1978, pp. 28-31.

[15] R. C. Minnick and R. A. Short, "Cellular Linear-Input Logic," Stanford Research Institute, SRI Project 4122, February 1964.

[16] R. C. Minnick et al., "Cellular Arrays for Logic and Storage," Stanford Research Institute, SRI Project 5087, April 1966.

[17] R. C. Minnick, "Cutpoint Cellular Logic," *IEEE Trans. Electronic Computers*, Vol. EC-13, December 1964, pp. 685-698.

[18] —, "Survey of Microcellular Research," *J. ACM*, Vol. 14, No. 2, April 1967, pp. 203–241.

[19] W. H. Kautz et al., "Cellular Interconnection Arrays," *IEEE Trans. Computers*, Vol. C-17, May 1968, pp. 443–445.

[20] A. Waksman, "A Permutation Network," *J. ACM*, Vol. 15, January 1968, pp. 159–163.

[21] W. H. Kautz, "A Cellular Threshold Array," *IEEE Trans. Electronic Computers*, Vol. EC-16, October 1967, pp. 680–682.

[22] H. S. Stone, "A Logic-in-Memory Computer," *IEEE Trans. on Computers*, January 1970, pp. 73–78.

[23] S. E. Wahlstrom, "Programmable Arrays and Networks," *Electronics*, December 11, 1967, pp. 91–95.

[24] W. H. Kautz, "Fault Testing and Diagnosis in Combinational Digital Circuits," *Proc. 1st Annual IEEE Computer Conf.*, Chicago, IL., September 1967.

[25] —, "Testing for Faults in Combinational Cellular Logic Arrays," *Proc. 8th Annual Symp. on Switching and Automata Theory*, Austin, Texas, October 1967, pp. 161–174.

[26] J. Goldberg et al., "Technique for the Realization of Ultra-Reliable Space-borne Computers," *Interim Scientific Report III*, SRI Project 5580, June 1968.

[27] W. H. Kautz, "Cellular Logic-in-Memory Arrays," *IEEE Trans. on Computers*, Vol. C-18, No. 3, August 1969, pp. 719–727.

[28] R. R. Seeber, "Associative Self-Sorting Memory," *Proc. 1960 Eastern Joint Computer Conf.*, Vol. 18, pp. 179–188.

Section 4.1
Programmable Logic Arrays

High-Speed Static Programmable Logic Array in LOCMOS

PETER MAY AND FRANS C. SCHIERECK

Abstract—A large static programmable logic array (PLA) with 20 inputs, 94 product terms, and 24 outputs has been designed and realized in LOCMOS, the complementary MOS technology with isolation by local oxidation of silicon. Layout and physical parameters of this technology resulted in a simple, dense, and low-capacity design. The dc and transient features of different realization possibilities have been simulated. Design automation tools have been developed to ensure error-free personalization of the PLA. A density of 160 gates per mm^2 has been achieved. Samples show average propagation delays of 100 ns, while dissipation is typically 120 mW.

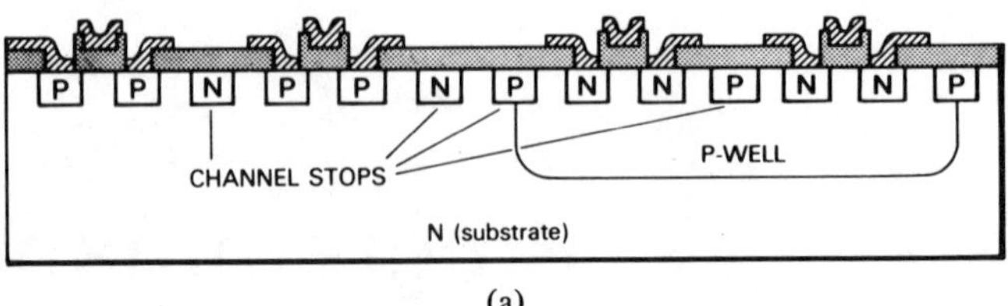

(a)

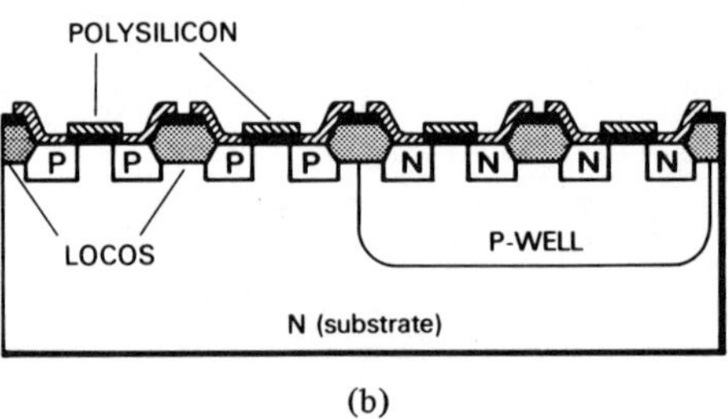

(b)

Fig. 1. (a) Conventional CMOS with aluminum gate. To prevent the possibility of parasitic transistors channel stops are necessary. (b) CMOS with local oxidation of silicon: LOCMOS. No channel stops are necessary and gate density is increased considerably.

INTRODUCTION

COMPLETELY new possibilities are offered to logic and electrical designers by the advent of large-scale integration (LSI). The computer on a chip is almost a reality. Bipolar and MOS technologies will improve the reliability and the performance and reduce production costs of computer systems. The differences between MOS and bipolar technologies with respect to gate density, speed, sensitivity for power supply, and temperature variations are well known. The main disadvantage of MOS was its rather low speed. This prevents its application in high-speed data processing equipment. New technologies, smaller parameter spreads in production, and improvements in electrical design enable some MOS techniques to enter the speed region of transistor–transistor logic (TTL).

Technologies like *silicon on sapphire* or *local oxidation of silicon* used for complementary MOS and n-channel depletion load MOS achieve delays of 10 ns per gate. One of these combinations, CMOS with isolation by local oxidation of silicon, LOCMOS [1]-[3], has been used for the design of large static programmable logic arrays (PLA's). A cross section of p- and n-channels transistors in LOCMOS in comparison with conventional CMOS is shown in Fig. 1. The performance of several technologies is listed in Fig. 2 [4].

Circuit type	*Nominal stage delay* [*ns*]
TTL medium speed	**8**
P MOS	**90 - 150**
N MOS silicon gate	**40 - 50**
CMOS silicon gate	**12 - 17**
LOCMOS	**7 - 11**
CMOS on sapphire	**6 - 10**

Fig. 2. Nominal stage delay of several available MOS technologies [4]. *Note:* Data are based upon 2-input NAND gate with fan-out of 3.

PLA–GENERAL

PLA's help in the more systematic implementation of decoding and similar logic networks [5]-[7] and can also provide a means to increase the packing density of random logic. There are PLA's on the market and they are well suited to manage combinational logic, to control sequential-state networks and to generate characters. However, for many applications these standard products are too small and input expansion nearly always gives uneconomic solutions. To overcome this restriction a large PLA in LOCMOS has been designed. Its block diagram is shown in Fig. 3; there are 20 inputs, 94 product terms, and 24 outputs; 4 outputs are used for sequential feedback.

This design is part of a custom LSI chip, which limits the area and dissipation of the PLA to 6 mm^2 and 300 mW, respectively. To fit in the machine cycle of the application the delay for the most complex Boolean function, of 15 product terms of 15 input variables each, has to be less than 250 ns at a supply voltage of 10 V.

The complementary structure of CMOS appears to be im-

Manuscript received November 14, 1975; revised February 6, 1976.
The authors are with the Philips Data Systems, Apeldoorn, The Netherlands.

Reprinted from *IEEE J. Solid-State Circuits*, vol. SC–11, pp. 365–369, June 1976.

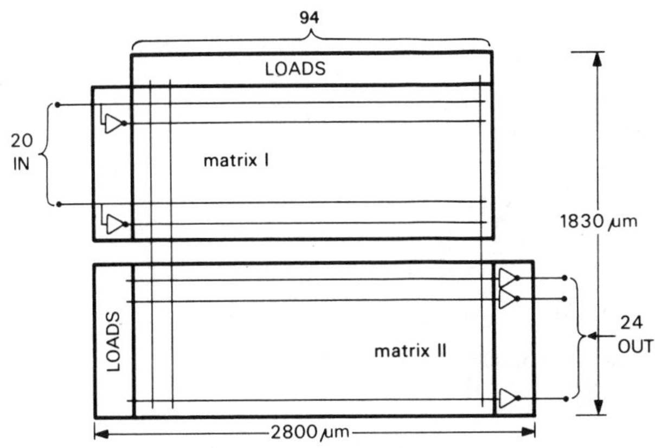

Fig. 3. Block diagram of the PLA.

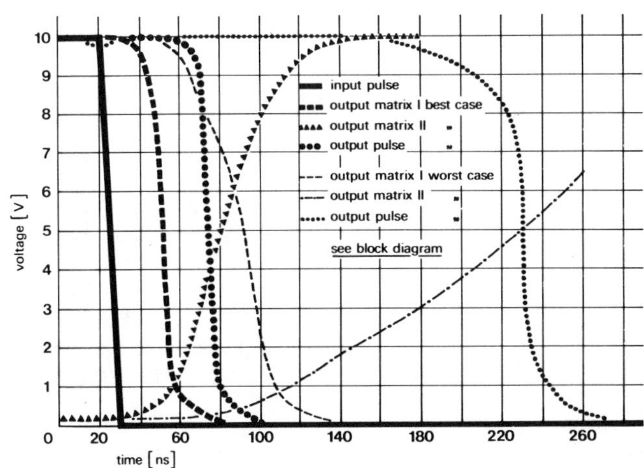

Fig. 5. Transient analysis of the propagation of a logical 0 (most complex Boolean expression and worst case load of the input) for best case and worst case physical parameters. W/L ratio of the load transistor is 1.4.

P-channel load matrix I W/L [μ/μ]	P-channel load matrix II W/L [μ/μ]	t_{pd} [ns]	logic level	physical parameters
18/6	18/6	110 160	'1' '0'	worst case
18/8	18/16	200 170	'1' '0'	"
18/15	18/15	200 240	'1' '0'	"
18/17	18/17	210 250	'1' '0'	"
18/17	18/17	50 80	'1' '0'	best case

Fig. 4. Propagation delay for different W/L ratio of the loads in matrix I and matrix II. In all calculations shown here the W/L ratio of the N drivers in both matrices was 18/6 [μm/μm]. The operating conditions are worst case. $VDD - VSS = 10$ V.

practical for the PLA itself, because of the tremendous increase in the number of transistors and their related wiring. Therefore, the complementary principle has not been used for the matrices of the PLA.

Circuit Design

The transistor matrices and their loads can be either p- or n-channels. For every logically and electrically consistent combination an equivalent circuit model for the PLA is developed. Together with best and worst case process parameters, the transient performance, the internal logic levels, and the dissipation of the PLA are calculated using Philpac, a simulation package for analysis of circuits. Besides the choice of p- and n-channels, the W/L ratio of loads and drivers and the complexity of the Boolean expression are also used as parameters in the analysis. The results for some combinations are shown in Fig. 4.

The result was a PLA, implemented with p-channel loads and n-channel drivers. Calculated transient response of internal and external nodes to input stimuli is shown in Fig. 5. The delay under worst case physical parameters and operating conditions is 250 ns. In both matrices the drivers are connected in parallel and form NOR functions.

Drivers in series, i.e., NAND functions, can be packed tighter, however this solution has been rejected due to the speed loss caused by the backgate effect. The bootstrap drivers in the product lines between the two matrices, which are in general required because of speed [8], [9], can be omitted due to the low parasitic capacitive load, specific for LOCMOS. At the outputs of the PLA these drivers appear to be useful to speed up the output edges.

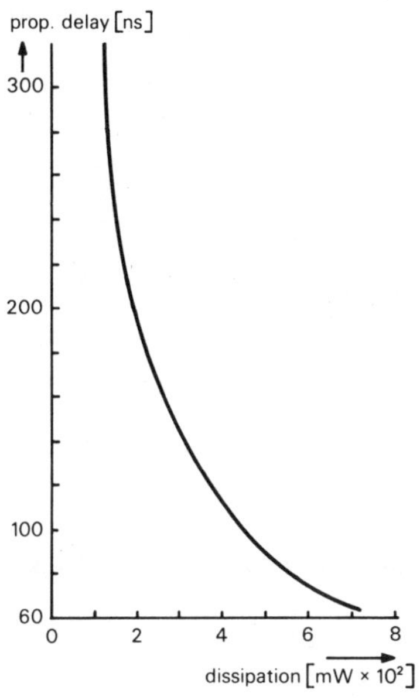

Fig. 6. Delay-dissipation curve for worst case electrical and physical conditions (see text). Values are calculated with different W/L ratios of the p-channel loads. W/L ratio of the drivers is constant. $VDD - VSS = 10$ V. Capacitive load: 0.6 pF.

Boolean functions like $\phi = (A \cdots X) + \cdots + (B \cdots Y)$ can be programmed in this array. Proposals for the logic content of this device show that most of the 94 product terms contribute to the dissipation. This is inherent to the NOR function. The calculated delay-dissipation curve for worst case conditions is shown in Fig. 6.

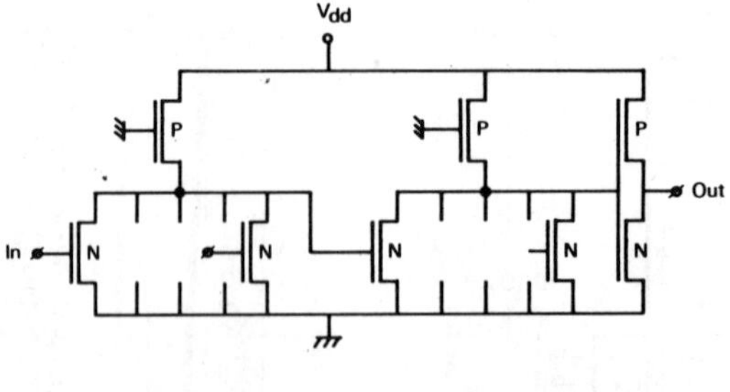

Fig. 7. Functional diagram of the PLA. NOR function with the inputs as parameters is in matrix I, the other in matrix II.

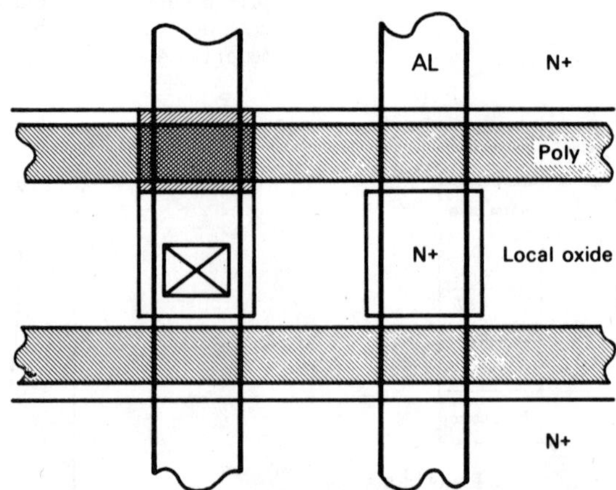

Fig. 8. PLA detail showing 2 storage cells. Each cell is the basis for 2 transistors.

If dissipation is a less important parameter or if the number of product terms is decreased, delays of less than 100 ns are possible.

A diagram on transistor level of a few cells of the PLA is shown in Fig. 7.

Layout Description

The 40 inputs of matrix I, the horizontal lines in Fig. 3, representing the true and inverted levels of the input signals, are realized in polysilicon. The product terms, the vertical lines, are aluminum in matrix I and polysilicon in matrix II. Aluminum is also used for the output lines of matrix II. In both matrices the polysilicon is the gate for the loads and the drivers. A part of the layout, two storage cells, is shown in Fig. 8. The polysilicon lines run over local oxide. n^+ lanes are above and below this oxide. These lanes are connected to ground and are the sources of the n-channel drivers. Within the local oxide the two n^+ regions, shown in the figure, are the drains. To personalize the PLA, a transistor is created by partly removing the local oxide defined by the appropriate mask under the polysilicon (shaded area).

Transistors used in this matrix have a real channel length of 3.9 μm and a real channel width of 16.6 μm. The vertical aluminum line is connected to the drain of the transistor. The area of this PLA cell is $26 \times 26\ \mu m^2$. At the cost of 40 percent speed reduction this area can be reduced by 30 percent. The fast version of the PLA has 6000 transistors. Chip area is 5.01 mm^2, loads, input inverters, and output bootstrap drivers included. Equivalent gate density in this array logic is about 160 gates per mm^2, which is twice as dense as with conventional gate logic in the LOCMOS process.

Experimental Results

Photographs of the PLA are shown in Figs. 9 and 10. With this realization the influence of the complexity of Boolean equations on the speed was measured. The most complex function implemented on this PLA, see Fig. 3, has the following characteristics:

1) the input is loaded with 40 gates of the upper matrix, i.e., matrix I;
2) the product term is a 15-input NØR;
3) this product term is loaded with 15 gates of the lower matrix, i.e., matrix II; and
4) the output is a 15-input NØR and drives 6 other LOCMOS gates outside the PLA.

Measured delays for this function are 140 ns for a rising edge

Fig. 9. Photograph of the PLA. Area is 5.01 mm^2.

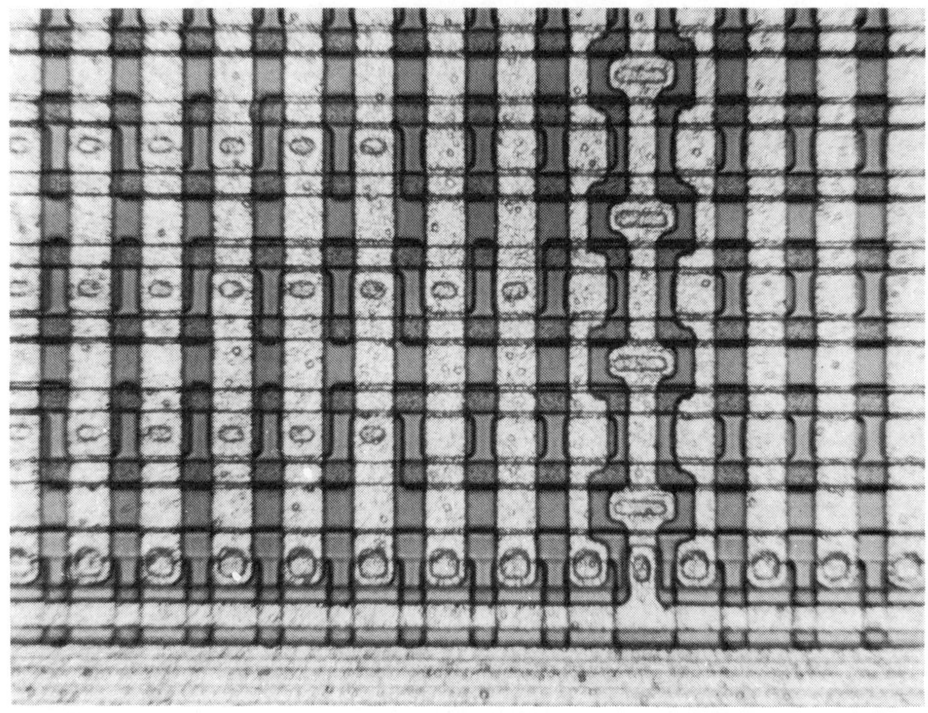

Fig. 10. Photograph of a part of the PLA. Personalization is clearly shown.

and 145 ns for a falling edge at a power supply of 10 V. Real channel width and length of the loads are 16.6 and 15.8 μm, respectively.

For a Boolean function, half as complex as the previous one in the upper matrix and with the same complexity in the lower matrix, the delays are 100 and 120 ns for the positive and negative edges, respectively. An oscillator implemented on this PLA shows a typical frequency of 11 MHz. The dissipation of the PLA is 120 mW. Power-supply variations of 10 percent result in a 10 percent deviation of these delay figures.

Simulation of the Logic Content

Design automation tools have been developed to provide fast and fault-free translation of the coding form to the layout. The contents, coded by the logic engineer, are fed into the program REPLAY, which generates four types of data:

1) the Boolean equations, as sum of product terms, realized by the coded content;
2) a simulation model to check the PLA in its logic environment on the LSI chip;
3) statistical data, like load of input lines, product terms, and output lines; and
4) mask-making control tapes.

Conclusion

It has been shown that PLA's realized in the LOCMOS technology can operate at speeds in the region of 100 ns. Densities of 160 gates per mm^2 have been achieved.

Acknowledgment

The authors wish to thank S. de Vree and L. de Groot for their technical assistance and B. Daniëlse for the design automation tools. The successful technological realization of the design is mainly due to the work of the groups of Dr. Van Iersel and I. Weyland.

References

[1] B. B. M. Brandt, W. Steinmaier, and A. J. Strachan, "LOCMOS, a new technology," *Philips Tech. Rev.*, no. 1, pp. 19-23, 1974.

[2] A. J. Strachan and K. Wagner, "Local oxidation of silicon/CMOS: Technology/design system for LSI in CMOS," in *ISSCC, Dig. Tech. Papers*, pp. 60-61, 1974.

[3] F. C. Schiereck, A. Drost, and P. May, "LOCMOS LSI circuitry, an example of its application in a minicomputer," in *Colloque Int. sur les Circuits Intégrés Complexes*, pp. 43-51, Paris, France, 1974.

[4] J. Jurison, D. A. Iser, and B. J. Russell, "Design considerations for aerospace digital computers," *Comput. Design*, pp. 113-123, Aug. 1974.

[5] W. N. Carr and J. P. Mize, *MOS LSI Designs and Applications.* New York: McGraw-Hill, 1972.

[6] H. Fleisher and L. J. Maissel, "An introduction to array logic," *IBM J. Res. Develop.*, pp. 98-109, Mar. 1975.

[7] P. May and F. C. Schiereck, "Design of a high speed, high density PLA in LOCMOS," in *1975 Proc. European Solid-State Circuits Conf.*, pp. 104-105, Canterbury, England, 1975.

[8] R. A. Wood, "High-speed dynamic programmable logic array chip," *IBM J. Res. Develop.*, pp. 379-383, July 1975.

[9] E. Hebenstreit and K. H. Horninger, "High speed programmable logic array in ESFI MOS technology," in *1975 Proc. European Solid-State Circuits Conf.*, pp. 107-108, Canterbury, England, 1975.

A Study in the Use of PLA-Based Macros

PETER W. COOK, MEMBER, IEEE, CHUNG W. HO, MEMBER, IEEE, AND STANLEY E. SCHUSTER, MEMBER, IEEE

Abstract—**This paper describes a study in which a PLA-based macro design of a small processer is carried out in the same technology as the original "random" logic design of the same processor. The objectives of the study were to determine gains or losses in "technology utilization" when a PLA-based approach is used to replace the more conventional "random" logic approach. The results in this case are a design of equal performance and density, with only one-third the power of the original design.**

Introduction

IN RECENT years, the PLA (programmable logic array) [1] has received considerable attention as a possible replacement for conventional random logic and/or ROS (read-only storage) in digital system design. This attention is largely due to growing difficulties in the areas of physical design, timing and logic verification, and testing, which lead to untenable design times and costs with conventional methods. Moreover, technological progress has reached the point where large arrays capable of implementing significant logical functions are physically realizable.

Comparisons of PLA's and conventional "random" logic implementations of systems that can pinpoint any advantages or disadvantages to the PLA approach are not common; at the time of this work, they were not existent. Such comparisons as existed [2] included not only a change in design methodology (the use of PLA's) but also included significant technological differences (LSI versus SSI), and the results attributable to PLA's alone were difficult to determine. The work of [2] also focused on what can be termed "fixed-image" PLA's: in such PLA's, the size of the array is fixed and the designer can only specify bit patterns in that fixed array image. This leads to the search for a universal image and, in specific designs, can lead to a forced use of the PLA.

In the context of LSI or VLSI, such a fixed-image approach seems unwarranted. As technology advances, it is unlikely that any logic chip will be simply one "thing" such as a PLA (present microprocessors that combine in a single chip logic, RAM and ROS are examples of this). An approach termed the "PLA-based macro" approach in which the chip designer has access to a limited number of flexible parts including PLA's, registers of several kinds and buses to provide the required combinatoric logic, storage, and communications functions has been chosen. All of these "parts" are flexible in their size, so that a register can be from one to many bits, and a PLA can range from several hundred bits to several thousand. This flexibility prevents any artificial forcing of functions into a fixed image of any kind.

Because there was no "common technology" comparison of PLA-based designs and more conventional "random logic" designs, the present study was begun. It objective was simple: to determine, in a common technology base, the possible advantages or disadvantages in using the PLA-based design approach. The method adopted was to design, in a known technology using the PLA parts described briefly above, a small low-end microprocessor. The final design was to be compared with a random logic design of the same processor in terms of power, speed, and density. The particular microprocessor (an 8-bit machine designed elsewhere in IBM as a 1200 circuit MOSFET chip) was chosen for this study because it was simple enough to be accommodated by a small group, already was designed in "random" logic, and was well enough defined to provide a fixed target. The design resulting from that study is the subject of this paper.

The basic approach taken in this study was to provide the designer with a set of three very flexible parts. The parts include PLA's for combinatoric and control functions, registers of several types, and appropriate means for interpart communication.

Conclusions

The results of this study show that the PLA-based macro approach to machine design can, with appropriate circuitry, result in a machine exhibiting equal or superior characteristics relative to the same machine designed in conventional random logic. The equality or superiority is measured in terms of power, performance, and density of a large function, such as an entire microprocessor, and is observed when both designs are implemented in an identical technology. The major area of superiority observed is in the power per function and is a result of the dynamic logic circuits employed essentially throughout. This form of dynamic logic is in turn made practical by the organization of the system into large macros, which simplifies clock distribution, and by the specific circuitry employed, which allows the use of simple drivers at the output of every logic stage.

This observed result is based upon a careful competitive design effort in a low-end machine; the extension of the result to higher performance environments may require further study.

Vehicle for Study

The microprocessor used in this study is a single-chip processor implemented in a MOSFET technology. The processor, considered equal to about 1200 circuits, fills a single 235 mil ×

Manuscript received March 1979; revised June 8, 1979.

The authors are with the IBM Thomas J. Watson Research Center, Yorktown Heights, NY 10598.

Reprinted from *IEEE J. Solid-State Circuits*, vol. SC–14, pp. 833–840, Oct. 1979.

235 mil chip. Worst case power is 400 mW. The basic measure of processor speed is taken as the instruction rate of the processor. The processor interfaces a 64K byte memory with a 3.2 μs cycle time. A single byte is read or written in a cycle. The instruction set of the machine consists of some 45 instructions, most of which employ single byte operands, though some are double byte operations. The (unweighted) average instruction time is 2.71 memory cycles, or 8.67 μs; this gives a processor speed of 115 000 instructions/s. The machine has general registers when viewed logically; the general registers are in fact implemented as the low address space of main memory, so that register accesses are actually memory accesses.

Macro Set

The set of macros used in this study has three members, all parameterized so as to achieve extensive use. Members of the set and their basic characteristics follow.

1) PLA: used for combinatoric elements, including next-state computation in sequential controls. As a macro, the PLA is parameterized in both size and function by its bit pattern. Additional parameters provide 2-bit partitioning options, output driver types, and electrical characteristics.

2) Registers: used for all on-chip storage, but not main memory. Parameters control latch type, data width, and electrical details.

3) Buses: used for all data transfers. The bus macro is also capable of dot-oring several inputs. Parameters include width and electrical parameters. The bus is an unusual macro in that it is not confined to a single area of a chip but rather is distributed; however, bus support circuits such as precharge paths, load devices, and clamp circuits are localized and parameterized.

With these macros in mind, a data flow for the PLA-based processor was created. A diagram of the data flow appears in Fig. 1. Several factors went into the partitioning of the machine as shown. First, most instructions are single byte operations. This, together with the complexity of a 16-bit ALU led to the use of an 8-bit ALU for all data path operations; 16-bit instructions were to be accommodated in two ALU passes. This was felt to represent no performance penalty since only a single byte path from memory was provided and fetching arguments for 16-bit operations would require two memory cycles in any case. On the other hand, all addressing in the processor is 16 bits. Address incrementing could have been done in the main ALU; however, it was believed to be more efficient to provide a separate 16-bit incrementing ALU (IALU) to provide the increment function. This function is, of course, much simpler than a general ALU, and so several other forms of address modification were subsequently incorporated into the IALU. Two major buses were provided in the system: the LOBUS and the HIBUS. The LOBUS is used for all operands and ALU operations; the HIBUS and LOBUS together are used for addressing paths. The shared use of the LOBUS together with the use of several registers that can communicate to both buses simplifies saving of instruction addresses during an interrupt or branch-and-link operation.

Key to the data flow is the ability of the clocked PLA to feed its output directly back into its own input, with no race problems. Details will be presented subsequently; basically, this results from the specific circuitry used in the PLA which

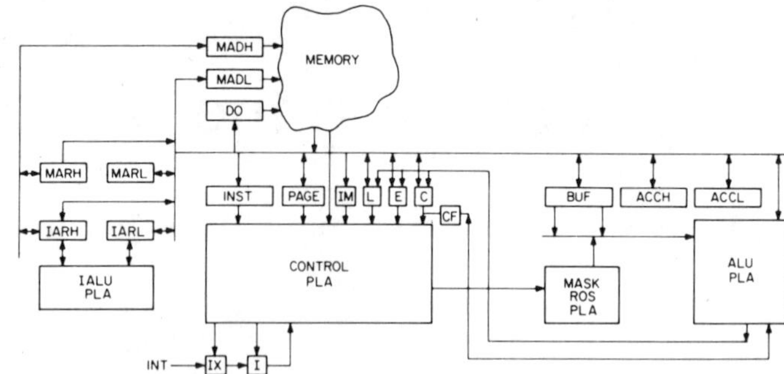

Fig. 1. PLA-based processor data flow. The PLA macros are designated in the diagram; the remaining blocks are registers of from 1 to 8 bits width, using several latch types.

behaves as if the input were provided with a sample-and-hold circuit. Thus, the single connection of the ALU PLA to the LOBUS serves as both input and output, the functions being separated in time. Likewise, most registers which tie to the LOBUS do so by a bidirectional path. In the data flow, a single PLA cycle can allow for data to be brought from a register to ALU, operated on, and returned to the same or another register.

At this point it became necessary to define in detail the various parts of the machine. This entailed the electrical design of the various macros and the verification of their operability under appropriate worst case circumstances. Second, it was necessary to define in rather careful detail the contents of the control PLA. In PLA's size not only implies silicon cost, it also implies delay. It was therefore desirable to implement the control function in as small a PLA as possible. While one can obtain rather general insights regarding the size of a PLA for certain combinatoric functions as might be found in ALU's, control functions are less structured, and detail was here considered important.

Circuit Family

The PLA-based macros used in this study were all based on dynamic circuits. This resulted from a need to drive some circuits under conditions of high (exceeding 100) fan-out, and the ability to provide low-power bootstrap drivers in simple dynamic circuits.

Dynamic logic, per se, is not new, and has been used in random logic arrangements, and the question naturally arises, why not use dynamic random logic. In an earlier study of various FET logic circuit alternatives [4], dynamic random logic was considered; it was found to offer no significant advantages over static random logic. This arises from problems associated with clock distribution, from the need to restrict the number of phases lying between two circuits that are connected to each other (a "phase 1" circuit cannot drive a "phase 1" circuit), and from the circuitry itself, with stacked devices, limited levels, and possibly higher node capacitance. The specific circuitry used in the PLA's in this study avoided these problems, and offered significant power reductions.

Timing

All circuitry in the PLA-based processor operated on a single four-phase clock. Each phase consisted of an on time followed by an identical interphase gap time. Thus, if T is the on time of a given phase pulse, the entire four-phase cycle will take $8T$. At the outset of the physical design process, the following timing assumptions were made.

Φ1: Loads register from bus; (precharge AND array in PLA).

Φ2: (Drive 2-bit partitioning outputs to AND array; precharge OR array.)

Φ3: (Precharge buses; refresh registers; drive AND array outputs into OR array.)

Φ4: Drive OR array output or register content to bus.

The actions described above are such as to have their effects remain in force until explicity altered. Thus, when a Φ4 signal drives a register content to a bus, the bus retains that register content until the subsequent Φ3 time, when buses are all unconditionally precharged.

In the list above, the items in parentheses are unconditional and ensure the proper operation of the macros themselves. Items not in parentheses are conditional, and must be controlled in such a way that the resulting machine performs the correct operations. Therefore, pulsed drivers, identical in structure to those used internally in the PLA's were designed as possible PLA output drivers. These are so arranged that when connected to a PLA output, they may provide conditional pulses at times Φ4 or Φ1. These are the times during which all conditional operations take place, and the drivers allow the use of an otherwise conventional PLA as a control for the machine.

The original processor was designed to interface a 3.2 μs memory. A preliminary examination of several of the instructions in the data flow of Fig. 1 indicated that four PLA cycles per memory cycle would ensure equivalent performance of the "random" and PLA-based processor machines. This translates to an 800 ns (worst case) PLA cycle, and a nominal 100 ns on-time for any phase.

Logic Levels

The PLA is normally thought of as an AND-OR device. In its simplest form it performs this function only if a ground level is taken as logical 1. While inverting drivers make such strict binding unnecessary, it was decided to adopt such a definition of logic levels for all data paths. This served to facilitate the construction of buses that could dot-or data from several sources.

For control pulses, the opposite approach was taken, with a high level taken as logical 1 for all control pulses. This is because it is far easier to initiate an action with such a signal than with a low level. Again, the choice proved useful when it became evident that simple bootstrap drivers used for such control pulses could also dot-or control pulses from several sources if such pulses were defined with a high logical 1.

Interface and Clocking

In the original processor, clocks control the interface to the memory: when the memory is busy, some processor clocks are stopped, thus placing the processor in a hold state. For the PLA-based processor, it was assumed that the basic four-phase clock was continuously running. A line (*DR*) was assumed available to the processor to signal when the memory had com-

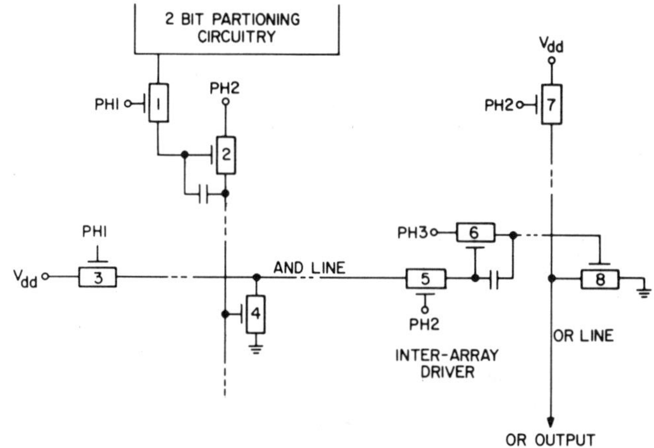

Fig. 2. Conceptual circuitry used in PLA's.

pleted the last action requested by the processor. This line is monitored by the control PLA of the PLA-based processor, which places that processor in a hold state whenever a requested memory action has not been serviced. The original processor did not directly drive the memory address bus, but drove that bus through an interface chip. In the PLA-based processor, it was assumed that memory address bus contention problems would be accommodated in that chip, just as the original processor accommodated such problems through the clock chip. In retrospect, it appears possible to accommodate the memory address contention problem in a manner more consistent with the original design by eliminating the *DR* signal, and providing a memory available (MA) signal. (This *DR* signal represents the only "architectural" difference between the original processor and the PLA-based design.)

Physical Design

The basic element in the design was the PLA itself, including peripherals for 2-bit partitioning and bus driving. This circuitry went through a number of modifications. Initially and conceptually, a simple circuit such as that of Fig. 2 was envisioned. Both AND and OR arrays are shown. The circuitry is similar to that in [5] in its extensive use of dynamic circuits and bootstrap drivers. Two-device bootstrap drivers (device 1,2 and 5,6) actually drive the two arrays. During Φ1, the 2-bit partitioning circuit is gated onto the bootstrap driver gate (device 2) while the AND array is precharged through device 3. When Φ1 falls and before Φ2 rises, the 2-bit partitioning circuitry operates in a manner to be described to provide the proper level at the gate of device 2. During Φ2, the driver operates and conditionally drives the output of the AND array circuits to their final value. This final value is gated into the interarray driver (device 6) and the OR array precharged during Φ2 also. During Φ3, the interarray driver operates and the OR array outputs assume their final values. At the same time, buses are unconditionally precharged. During Φ4, drivers similar to the interarray driver operate to place the OR array output on the bus. Alternatively, pulse drivers can deliver control pulses from the OR array during either Φ4 or Φ1 of the subsequent cycle.

The drivers of Fig. 2 may not operate properly in a technology with significant gate to drain overlap, where substantial gate-to-drain capacitance may cause a false turn-on of the

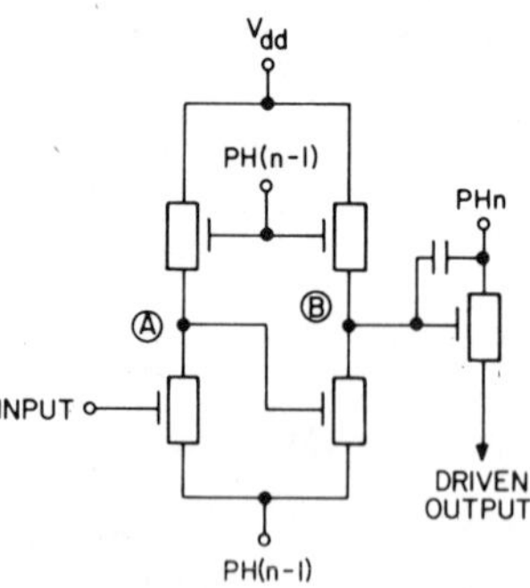

Fig. 3. Actual clamped bootstrap driver used throughout the design. The bootstrap capacitor is implemented by an MOS capacitor to minimize clamp requirements and yet provide high capacitance when a high output is to be driven.

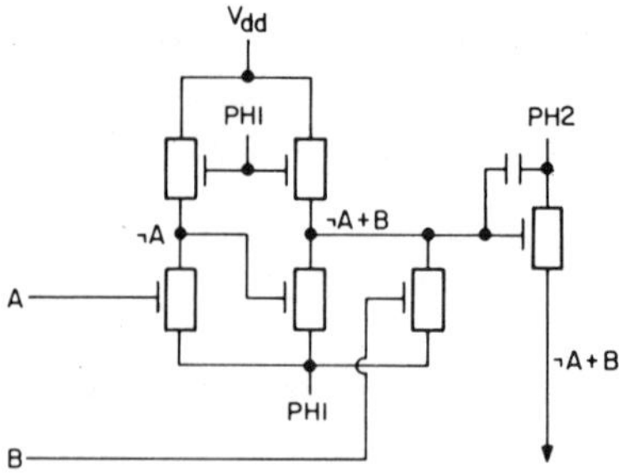

Fig. 4. Extension of basic driver into a 2-bit partitioning circuit for the PLA. Logic functions shown assume that a low (ground) level signifies logical 1, and are valid only at appropriate phase times (e.g., the driver output has the indicated value only during Φ2).

bootstrap device by coupling the phase pulse of the driver into the gate of the driver. To accommodate such a technology, the driver was redesigned, resulting in the circuit shown in Fig. 3. Here, two dynamic inverters precede the actual bootstrap driver device; the bootstrap capacitor of the driver is now connected from gate to drain, rather than from gate to source. Most of the bootstrap capacitance is formed between a metal electrode and an inversion layer under that electrode; the inversion layer is contiguous with the bootstrap device drain, and thus electrically connected to it. When the gate of the bootstrap device is at a high potential, the inversion layer is formed, and a high capacitance exists from gate to drain. The phase pulse on the drain of the bootstrap device couples into the gate and provides a very fast rising waveform at the driver output. Reasonable fall time is also achieved.

Conversely, when the gate of the bootstrap device is at a low potential, the inversion layer is not formed and coupling between gate and drain is much reduced. The double inverters provide added protection against this coupling. When the input to the first of the inverters is at a low level, both nodes A and B will precharge to a high level during $\Phi(n - 1)$, but node A will remain high after $\Phi(n - 1)$, while node B drops. Thus, the active device of the second inverter is on during Φ_n and serves to clamp the bootstrap device gate to ground. If the driver input is high, then as $\Phi(n - 1)$ falls both node A and node B begin to fall. Node B generally is the more heavily loaded node, and it falls more slowly than node A. Use of proper width-to-length ratios of the devices and occasional inclusion of a padding capacitor at node B will ensure a high level at node B. In this case, at Φ_n, the bootstrap device gate is high and unclamped, and a pulse will appear at the driver output. The only modification that this driver makes in basic timing concepts is that the driver input must remain valid until after the output pulse has been completed. This restriction does not alter the basic timing described earlier.

The driver is quite flexible and is the basic circuit in the PLA's. The clamp action of the second inverter stage works properly provided its input does not go high during the output time of the driver. Thus, the first inverter may be omitted and the driver used as an inverting driver at an array output. The basic driver circuit may also be expanded into a complete 2-bit partitioning circuit as shown in Fig. 4. The basic circuit shown is repeated four times (with appropriate modification) to provide the signals needed. The only timing requirement here is that inputs to the array become valid during Φ1 and remain valid to the end of Φ2. Since PLA inputs are usually on buses (which become valid during Φ4 and remain valid to the beginning of Φ3), this again is no modification to already assumed timing.

The array circuitry was laid out in the ground rules as the original "random" processor. The most complex part of the layout was the 2-bit partitioning circuitry just described. Once this was done, the AND array device sizes were set to match the input line pitch of the partitioning circuits. The interarray driver was laid out and the OR array device size set to similarly match pitches. The circuits were then simulated under 2-sigma worst case conditions including skews and level shifts on the nominally 100 ns clock pulses. Skews and level shifts were taken as consistent with low cost bipolar clock drivers. Device parameters available to the designer (width-to-length ratios and padding capacitors in some circuits) were adjusted to achieve a working worst case circuit for maximally loaded array paths. When this was done, the PLA was considered complete and attention turned to other elements in the design.

Register Macros

A register macro (or one of several) was used for all long term data storage within the PLA-based processor. The macros vary in complexity from a simple D-type latch with a single data path to a more complex T-type latch with multiple data paths. In order to reduce power, all latches employed "pulsed power" in which load devices were turned on only during a single phase of the clock. The register macros were also designed to have a single read control line and a single write control line, to minimize wiring and control space.

D-Type Latch

The most frequently used register macro consisted of the D-type latch shown in Fig. 5. The latch was designed so that information could be read from the bus into the latch during Φ1 and written from the latch onto the bus during Φ4. When no read or write operation was requested, the latch will store information indefinitely, dissipating power only during Φ3, when the information in the latch is "refreshed" to compensate for any decrease in levels caused by leakage. Nominally, load devices dissipate power for only 12.5 percent of a clock cycle.

Information is conditionally read from the bus into the latch

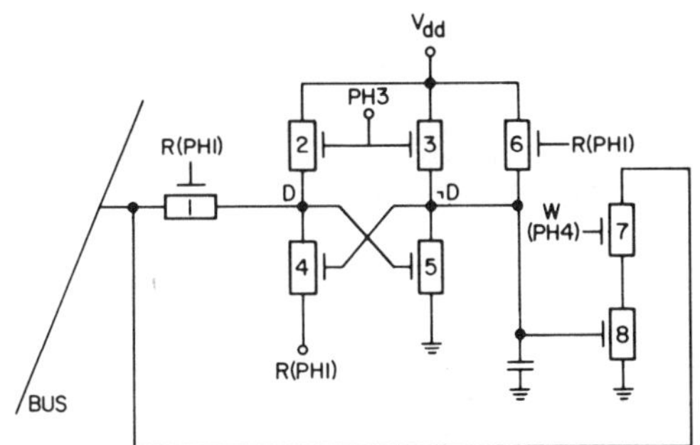

Fig. 5. Basic *D*-type latch used in PLA-based processor.

during Φ1. If a read control signal is generated, devices 1 and 6 will be turned on and the source of device 4 ($R\Phi 1$) which is normally low will also go high. Since Φ3 is low, devices 2 and 3 are turned off. Bringing the source of device 4 ($R\Phi 1$) high during a read operation makes it possible to transfer the information on the bus into the latch independently of the original state of the register. (One can see very quickly if this were not done and node $\neg D$ and the bus were both high during a read operation it is highly likely that the bus would be discharged through devices 1 and 4.) If the bus is high, node *D* will go high and node $\neg D$ will either remain low or be driven low through device 5. For the case where the bus is low, node *D* will go low (or remain low), since device 5 is now off node $\neg D$ will either remain high or charge to a high level through device 6. The WLR ratios of each of the devices have been carefully chosen under worst case conditions to meet these requirements. When the read control signal $R\Phi 1$ goes low the information which was previously on the bus is now stored in the dynamic latch, which is refreshed during Φ3 by pulsing load devices 2 and 3.

Information is conditionally written from the register onto the bus during Φ4. The write control line $W\Phi 4$ conditionally turns on device 7, causing the complement of $\neg D$ to be transferred to the bus which had been precharged during Φ3 through a device. Devices 7 and 8 have large WLR's since they are stacked and because of the possible high bus capacitance they must discharge.

A major driving force in the latch design was the minimization of the number of control wires. A much simpler latch design would be possible if two read control lines were used. This would allow the latch to be cleared during one phase and loaded during the next. The timing of the system overall appears to allow such operation, but it was not investigated in detail.

Toggle (and *JK*) Latch

The most complicated register macro consisted of the *T* type with multiple data paths shown in Fig. 6. The toggle register is used in connection with the IALU of the system, where incrementing is simplified by the toggle function. The toggle input to the register comes from the output of the IALU OR array. Information can also be loaded into the register from either of two buses.

The latch can be used either as a *T* or a *JK*. Truth tables for both modes of operation are given in Table I, where *D* and *Dn*

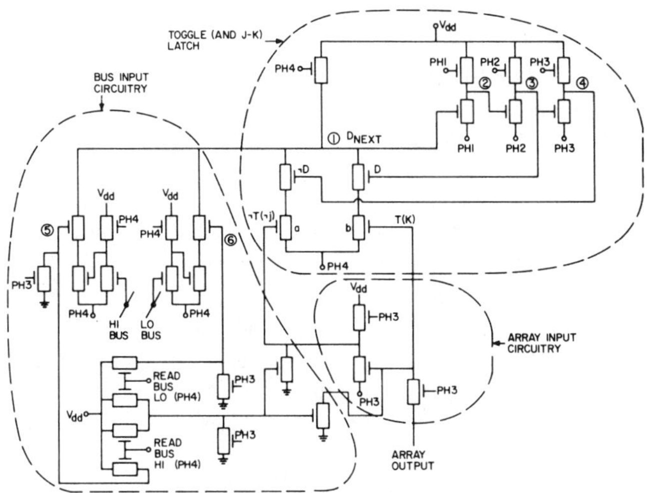

Fig. 6. *JK*/*T* latch with multiple input and output lines. This is the most complex single macro in the processor.

TABLE I
Latch Operation: *T* and *JK* Latches

¬T	T	D	¬D	Dn	¬Dn	
0	1	0	1	1	0	Toggle
0	1	1	0	0	1	Toggle
1	0	0	1	0	1	No change
1	0	1	0	1	0	No change

$$\neg Dn = \neg T \neg D + TD$$

(a) Toggle Latch (T)

¬J	K	D	¬D	Dn	¬Dn	
0	0	0	1	1	0	Set to 1
0	0	1	0	1	0	Set to 1
0	1	0	1	1	0	Toggle
0	1	1	0	0	1	Toggle
1	0	0	1	0	1	No change
1	0	1	0	1	0	No change
1	1	0	1	0	1	Set to 0
1	1	1	0	0	1	Set to 0

$$\neg Dn = \neg J \neg D + KD$$

(b) JK Latch Function

denote the datum stored in the register before and after the input is changed. The *T* register is really a subset of the *JK* as indicated in the table, so the latch operation will be described for the *JK* case. The table indicates that when no input is applied ($\neg J = 1, K = 0$) the state of the latch remains unchanged. When an input is applied to *J* only ($\neg J = 0, K = 0$) the latch either remains in the 1 state or switches to it. When an input is applied to *K* only ($\neg J = 1, K = 1$) the latch either remains in the 0 state or switches to it. When inputs are applied to both *J* and *K* ($\neg J = 0$, $K = 1$) the latch toggles to its complement state. At the end of Φ4 the new state of the latch is stored on node 1 of Fig. 6. By the end of the next Φ3 time this information has been transferred to node 3 and in complement form to node 4. Thus, it is available as shown to determine the next state of the latch during Φ4. During the time node 1 is changing, nodes 3 and 4 remain unchanged because of the isolation provided by the Φ1 "stage."

The array input circuitry as shown is used to generate the toggle signals (*T* and $\neg T$). If the latch were used as a *JK*, separate lines would be needed to generate $\neg J$ and *K* inputs to the latch.

The state of two buses (HIBUS and LOBUS) can be read into

the latch by means of the bus input circuitry. If READ.BUS.LO and READ.BUS.HI are not activated, nodes 5, 6, and 7 will be low during the up and down times of Φ4 and the input circuitry does not affect the state of the latch. However, if either READ.BUS.LO or READ.BUS.HI are activated the latch will take the state of the appropriate bus. For instance, if READ.BUS.LO goes high, nodes 6 and 7 will also go high. Input lines T and $\neg T$ will both go low turning off devices A and B. Since node 6 is high, device C is turned on and information on the LOBUS can be read into node 1 through the two-stage inverter circuit. This two-stage inverter is similar to the 2-bit partitioning circuitry previously described and has the same requirements for the discharge speeds of the stages.

Control Design

In a PLA, size implies delay. Therefore, the design of the control PLA emphasized a minimization of the number of words required to implement the control function. This was done manually by using two basic techniques. Where instructions could be made to have common sequences of steps this was done, and don't cares introduced as appropriate to allow one word of the control PLA to be shared among several instructions. Where, in addition, whole functions (such as I-Fetch) were used with sufficient frequency, the functions were coded as coroutines in the control PLA by adding a few input bits to the array to activate the coroutine, and by coding such coroutines to be invoked only by such added input bits, independently of the instruction being executed. In this way, it is possible to code such functions as I-Fetch only once in the control PLA, and yet to have the I-Fetch function run concurrently with other operations. These two methods, applied rather aggressively, led to a control PLA sufficiently small to meet the desired performance specifications.

In the end, two different control schemes were investigated. The first used a single control PLA as shown in the data flow, Fig. 1. Inputs to the control PLA came from the instruction register (INST), the ALU indicators (L, E, C), memory interface lines, and the interrupt interface. The rest of the inputs of the control are feedback lines from its own outputs which are used to implement a 2-bit counter (PLA cycles within a memory cycle), a microstep counter (sequencing of PLA cycles in an instruction), and a field of bits for activating the coroutines described earlier. The primary outputs of the control PLA consist of control wires for ALU, memory, IALU, buses, registers, etc.; most of these are pulsed output lines.

Each of the 45 instructions of the processor belongs to one of the several instruction groups such as byte instruction group, register instruction group, etc. Within a given group, portions of the microsteps are often the same for different instructions. To take advantage of the commonality, don't care bits can be introduced into the instruction field of the control so that one PLA word can be accessed by more than one instruction. Furthermore, certain actions are common among different instruction groups, such as ADD and SUBTRACT, which occur in both the register instruction group and the byte instruction group. In addition, the instruction fetch for the next instruction is common to all instructions and actually is performed while the

TABLE II

Comparison of Performance of Random and PLA-Based Microprocessor. Table Shows Time in Memory Cycles per Instruction. For the Case of Jump and Branch Instructions, Times Shown are Taken/Not Taken

OPERATION	INST	Original	PLA Based	
Add register	AR	3	3	
Subtract register	SR	3	3	
Load register	LR	3	3	
Store register	STR	3	3	
Load, decrement	LRD	5	5	
Load, increment	LRB	5	5	
Add byte	AB	3	3	
Subtract byte	SB	3	3	
Load byte	LB	3	3	
Store byte	STB	3	3	
Compare byte	CB	3	3	
And byte	NB	3	3	
Or byte	OB	3	3	
Xor byte	XB	3	3	
Add immediate	AI	2	3	+1
Subtract immediate	SI	2	3	+1
Load immediate	LI	2	2	
Compare immediate	CI	2	2	
And immediate	NI	2	2	
Or immediate	OI	2	2	
Xor immediate	XI	2	2	
Group immediate	GI	2	2	
Add 1	A1	2	2	
Subtract 1	S1	2	2	
Shift left	SHL	2	2	
Shift right	SHR	2	2	
Clear	CLA	1	1	
Transpose	TRA	1	2	+1
Input carry	IC	1	1	
Store indirect	STN	4	4	
Load indirect	LN	4	4	
Test and reset	TR	1	1	
Test and preserve	TP	1	1	
Input	IN	4	4	
Output	OUT	4	4	
Jump	J	3	2	-1
Jump on not =	JNE	3/1	2/1	-1/0
Jump on =	JE	3/1	2/1	-1/0
Branch	B	3	2	-1
Branch on not =	BNE	3/2	2	-1/0
Branch on =	BE	3/2	2	-1/0
Branch on high	BH	3/2	2	-1/0
Branch on low	BNL	3/2	2	-1/0
Branch and link	BAL	6	5	-1
Return	RTN	5	4	-1
Interrupt	INT	10	10	

last several steps of the instruction are performed. Hence, the concept of coroutine is adopted in which a group of PLA words are designated to accomplish a certain task such as ADD or I-FETCH and the coroutine field in the input is used to call or activate them. Note that the I-Fetch coroutine is called to run concurrently with the regular instruction tasks during the last memory cycle of a given instruction. This kind of parallelism certainly contributes to the fact that the PLA-based processor requires only two memory cycles for the BRANCH and JUMP macroinstructions, while three memory cycles are required in the original processor.

The memory cycles required for executing the instructions of the original and PLA-based processor are given in Table II on a per instruction basis. In general, the overall performance of the two processors is identical.

The PLA to implement the machine control was completely implemented, including all 45 instructions and interrupt processing, with 137 PLA words. Control inputs consisted of 14 primary inputs and 10 feedback inputs. The AND array of the control PLA is 48 bits (devices) wide. For the OR array, the 10 bits of feedback wires are also doubled (set and reset) to re-

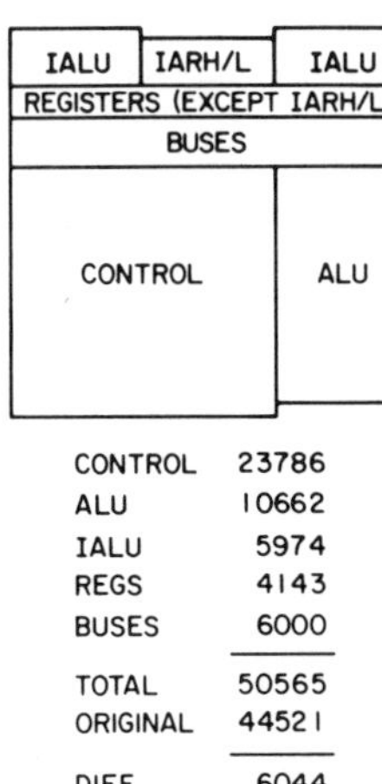

Fig. 7. Overall diagram of chip layout using a single control PLA. The subdivision of the control PLA into several smaller PLA's results in the reduction of total area at the expense of a somewhat more complex wiring problem.

quire 20 PLA outputs; in addition, there are 76 control lines used to activate various transfer paths in the rest of the system. The total control PLA is therefore 137 words × 144 bits, or 19 728 bits total.

Subsequent effort was made to divide up the single control PLA into several small PLA's to minimize the total bit count in the control, and hence save chip area. The single control PLA was divided into three sections and minimized using the programs of Hong *et al.* [3]. Three subdivided control PLA's were obtained which perform the identical function as the original single array. Sizes of these arrays (words × bits) are 59 × 77, 48 × 93, and 36 × 124, for a total of 13 471 bits. This subdivided control thus reduces the total control bit count by 32 percent.

Chip Layout

Fig. 7 shows the overall layout of the PLA-based processor chip using a single control PLA. The PLA and register areas in the layout have been calculated from detailed layouts of the register latches and PLA circuits. In this overall layout, the IALU PLA has been subdivided into two sections, each having half of the words of the original IALU. There is a small overhead penalty paid for this because of the necessity of duplicating some of the 2-bit partitioning circuits; the sectioning achieves a simpler overall layout.

Wiring space in the area between the registers and the major PLA's is estimated from the known number of data and control wires: it was assumed that a single wiring space could serve two control wires, as most control wires merely go to different registers. The subdivided control design was not completed in detail. An examination of the area saved (in control bits not required) and lost (again, the repetition of partitioning circuits) suggests that the overall chip area will be reduced by from 10 to 15 percent.

Power

Chip power for all dynamic circuits was calculated assuming full voltage swings on all active lines at a 1.25 MHz rate. The PLA's were all considered active whether they were serving a useful function or not. Thus, the ALU PLA is dissipating power even when its outputs are not gated to any bus; a modification of the drivers used to clock the PLA's can provide a mode of operation in which all unused PLA's are turned off. This type of circuitry will provide its greatest advantage in the design with the subdivided control PLA, where unused control functions may also be turned off.

TABLE III
Summary of Results

PARAMETER	Original	PLA based	Relative Utilization
Speed (us/cycle):	3.2	3.2	1.00
Power (mW):	400	131	3.05
Area (sq.mil):	44521	50565	0.88

Summary of Results

A summary of the results of this study appear in Table III. This table compares the power, speed, and density of the original processor with the PLA-based processor. The "relative utilization" compares the two designs, the original being used as a reference. Normalization is such that a large number indicates a better use of the appropriate aspect of the technology. The result is extremely exciting: the PLA-based processor exhibits nearly the same characteristics as the original design in all aspects except power, where it is significantly superior. The results are even more exciting when it is realized that they do not represent the limit of what can be done with PLA-based macros. Mention has been made already of the possibility of subdividing the control PLA to achieve higher density, and modifying circuits to turn off unused PLA's to reduce power. These techniques can also impact speed by reducing capacitance. They have not been explored in detail in this study.

It must be emphasized that these results are derived from a specific low-end test design. It is not clear how the results apply in a performance dominated environment. In the low end, however, it is evident that the PLA-based macro design concept can successfully compete with more conventional random logic approaches.

Acknowledgment

The authors wish to thank D. Lee, IBM Office Products Division, for his substantial help in mapping the ideas inherent in this study into the MOSFET technology of the original design. Without this "real world" base, the study would have remained purely academic. The leadership and encouragement of D. Critchlow is also acknowledged.

References

[1] H. Fleischer and L. I. Maissel, "An introduction to array logic," *IBM J. Res. Develop.*, vol. 19, p. 98, 1975.

[2] J. C. Logue *et al.*, "Hardware inplementation of a small system in programmable logic arrays," *IBM J. Res. Develop.*, vol. 19, p. 110, 1975.

[3] S. J. Hong, R. G. Cain, and D. L. Ostapko, "MINI: A heuristic approach for logic minimization," *IBM J. Res. Develop.*, vol. 18, p. 443, 1974.

Section 4.2
Digital Signal Processors

LSI's for Digital Signal Processing

NORIHIKO OHWADA, TADAKATSU KIMURA, AND MASANOBU DOKEN

Abstract—This paper describes high-performance CMOS LSI's for digital signal-processing (DSP) technology, such as digital filter, fast Fourier transform (FFT), discrete Fourier transform (DFT), and digital phase-locked loop (DPLL). First, DSP functions for communication use, functional blocks to compose DSP functions, and the types of arithmetic for LSI are discussed. It is explained that multiplier (MPL), variable-length shift register (VSR), and linear arithmetic processor (LAP) have been chosen as the most useful DSP LSI's. Device design for high-speed and low-power CMOS is described and its feasibility is shown as characteristics of propagation delay time at 430 ps and power delay product at 0.073 pJ. The 3-μm effective channel-length CMOS technology has been selected for the DSP LSI because of the high speed, 5 ns, in the case of two input NAND gates and high yield technology.

The multiplier architecture is pipeline and uses the Two's-complement representative, the variable-length shift register uses the binary-select method, and the linear arithmetic processor uses the method of changing the outside connections for realization of DSP functions. Maximum operating frequency of these LSI's is more than 23 MHz at the 5-V source voltage. Power dissipation of a VSR, which has been lossy, is less than 250 mW in the 8-MHz operation.

They have wider application to communication systems. High-speed CMOS technology is applied to the digital system equipment up to the second level of the PCM hierarchy.

I. Introduction

RECENT PROGRESS in LSI technology accelerates the applications [1], [2] of digital signal-processing (DSP) technology for communication use.

DSP technology, such as digital filter, fast Fourier transform (FFT), discrete Fourier transform (DFT), and digital phase-locked loop (DPLL), can cover many communication equipment functions. Therefore, by utilizing versatile, widely applicable LSI's, communication-system circuit design can be simplified and the performance, cost, maintainability, reliability, and equipment size of the system will be greatly improved. Some technical papers [3]-[6] on LSI's for DSP technology have been published and indicate advances in the reduction of multiplier delay time and power consumption, and integration of many functions.

In this paper, first, the DSP functions for communication use, the functional blocks to compose DSP functions, and the types of arithmetic for LSI are discussed. Then, the device design of the high-speed low-power CMOS, the circuit design and performances of the multiplier, the variable-length shift register, and the linear arithmetic processor, with high-speed and low power-consumption performances made by CMOS, are described. For an example of those LSI applications, a digital push-button receiver using a digital filter was also surveyed and the effects are demonstrated.

Manuscript received September 7, 1978; revised November 28, 1978.

The authors are with the Musashino Electrical Communication Laboratories, Nippon Telegraph and Telephone Public Corporation, Musashino-shi, Tokyo, Japan.

II. DSP Functions

As a first approach in designing LSI's, common fundamental functions have been extracted from communication equipment. The relation between the DSP functions and the communication equipment are shown in Fig. 1, in which the digital filter, fast Fourier transform, discrete Fourier transform, and digital phase-locked loop are the main DSP functions for use in communications. These functions can be realized with several fundamental circuit blocks, such as multipliers, adders, subtractors, and shift registers, as shown in Fig. 2. In preparing each of these components, it is easy to design DSP LSI's for their desired functions, or a single LSI chip which contains all of these components can be prepared. The desired function can be obtained by changing its internal connections by a final photomasking, its decoder on the chip, or the outside connections of its LSI terminals.

In the first step, a multiplier and a shift register have been designed because these are the most common components for a DSP and have a wide application area by themselves. Then follows a single-chip DSP LSI to cover the wide DSP functions, like the digital filter and FFT.

This paper describes three basic circuits, which have been designed and developed; that is, a multiplier LSI (MPL), a variable-length shift register LSI (VSR), and a linear arithmetic processor LSI (LAP).

III. Design Philosophy

A. Type of Arithmetic

The type of DSP system arithmetic is the most important choice because it is closely connected with the DSP LSI speed and function. Generally, the LSI is classified into parallel and serial. The latter is preferred because of its low input and output pin number. The serial-type multiplier comes in two types, the pipeline type and the serial-parallel type. If its coefficient word length is (m) and its data word length is (n), the pipeline-type operation speed is proportional to (n) only and independent of (m), while the operation speed of the serial-parallel type and the parallel-type increases in proportion to $(m + n)$. The number of gates of the pipeline and serial-parallel types are proportional only to (m), while the number for the parallel-type are proportional to $(m + n)$. Although the parallel type has several advantages in its applications, the pipeline type was chosen for multiplier arithmetic because of its smaller number of gates and pins, and its higher throughput. With these advantages, it is possible to realize a compact and low-power DSP LSI.

Reprinted from *IEEE J. Solid-State Circuits*, vol. SC-14, pp. 214–220, Apr. 1979.

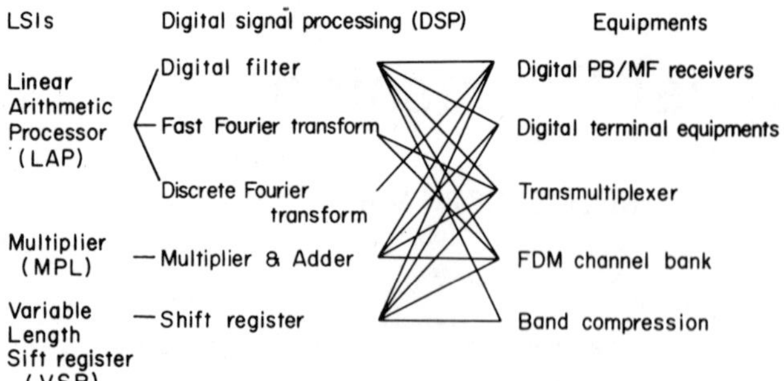

Fig. 1. Digital signal processing in communication equipment.

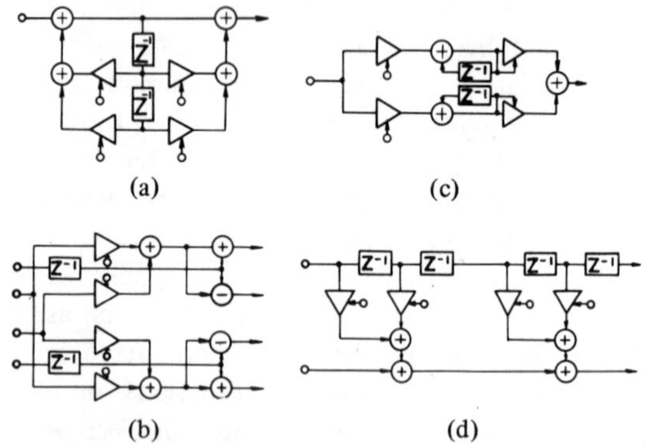

Fig. 2. Several kinds of digital signal processing. (a) Recursive second-order digital filter (DF). (b) Fast Fourier transform (FFT). (c) Discrete Fourier transform (DFT). (d) Nonrecursive digital filter (N-DF).

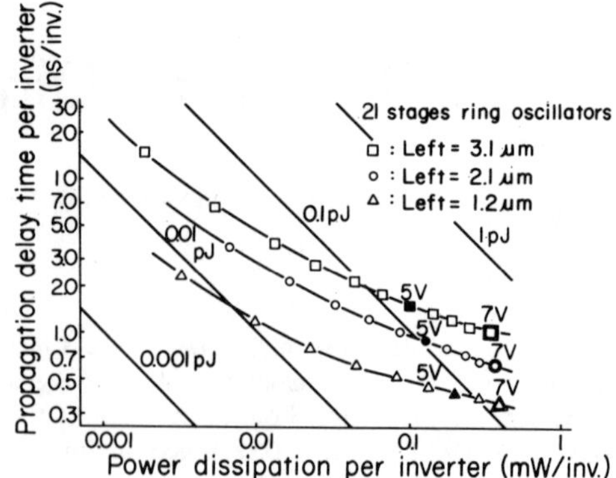

Fig. 3. CMOS power dissipation versus propagation delay time.

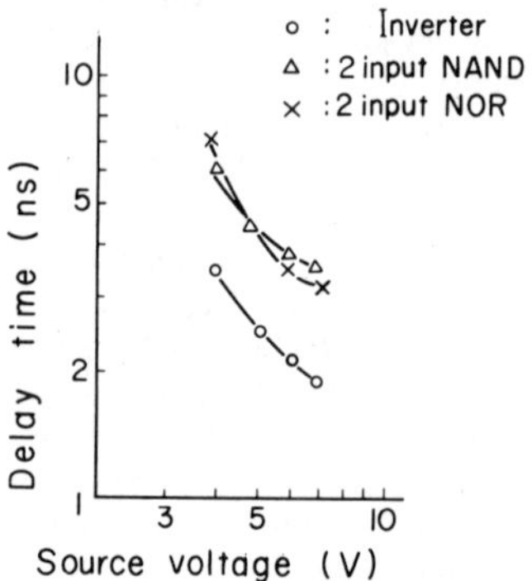

Fig. 4. 3-μm CMOS gates delay time versus source voltage.

The two's-complement representatives (2'C) and sign-magnitude representatives are generally used in the DSP. The former, 2'C, is convenient for treating the data in the addition and subtraction operations, and easily handles data overflow. For the number representative of the data and the coefficient, the 2'C are, therefore, used in DSP.

B. Device Technology

CMOS was preferred for its low power consumption and its wide operation range in source voltage and temperature, and its developmental work was focused on making its switching speed high enough for communication use. As a result, a CMOS with a short-channel length, isolation with insulator (SiO_2), and shallow source–drain junctions was fabricated. The p-well and source–drain junctions were formed by ion-implantation technology and had depths of 6.7 μm and 0.3 to 0.4 μm, respectively. The gate oxide thickness was 500 Å and the local oxide thickness for isolation was 2 μm. Channel doping was applied to the p-MOS to avoid punch-through and to adjust the threshold voltage as well.

Phosphorous-doped polysilicon was chosen to make the self-aligned gate electrodes for both p- and n-MOS. Interconnections through-holes for the gate electrodes have been reduced with this structure. In order to prevent shallow junction degradation due to the aluminum-to-silicon reaction, an Al/Si alloy (1-percent Si) was used for the interconnections.

Ring oscillators with 3.1-, 2.1-, and 1.2-μm effective channel lengths were fabricated and evaluated. From the oscillation frequency and the power of the 21-stage ring oscillator, the power P_d and the average circuit-switching delay per inverter stage T_{pd} were estimated. Results are shown in Fig. 3. The characteristics for an oscillator with a 1.2-μm effective channel length were T_{pd} of 430 ps, P_d of 170 μW, and power delay product $T_{pd} \cdot P_d$ of 73 fJ at 5-V applied source voltage, respectively. From these data, the delay time for the 2-input NAND gates is expected to be reduced to 1 or 2 ns.

These results have proved the feasibility of CMOS in high-speed DSP use and 3-μm effective channel length, with about 5-ns delay time, was considered appropriate to realize DSP LSI's having a maximum operation speed of 20 MHz. In the final design procedure, considering the LSI fabrication yield, the gate oxidation film thickness and the source–drain junction depth were chosen as 1000 Å and 1.5 μm, respectively, as a matter of course. Using these device parameters, an inverter, a 2-input NAND gate, and a 2-input NOR gate have been fabricated. As shown in Fig. 4, the delay time of the inverter, the 2-input NAND gate, and the 2-input NOR gate were 2.5 ns, 4.5 ns, and 5 ns, respectively, at a source voltage of 5 V and one fan-out. Moreover, the maximum operating frequency of a dynamic-type shift register was 33 MHz. Therefore, CMOS elements have been chosen for the DSP LSI.

IV. DSP LSI's

B. The Multiplier

The multiplier construction was of the pipeline type and the number representative was 2'C, as previously mentioned. A scaling circuit was introduced into this multiplier to avoid the degradation of precision in the case of an absolute-value imbalance between the data and the coefficient word length. To make it operate with higher precision, the rounding-off function

TABLE I
MULTIPLIER OPERATION ARCHITECTURE

Operation architecture		◦ Pipeline ◦ Fixed point ◦ Variable scaling
Representative numbers		Two's complement
Word length	Coefficient	16 bits (Multiplier) 12 bits (DF, FFT, DFT, etc)
	Data	Free
Input - Output form		Serial
Multiplex numbers		64 (Max)

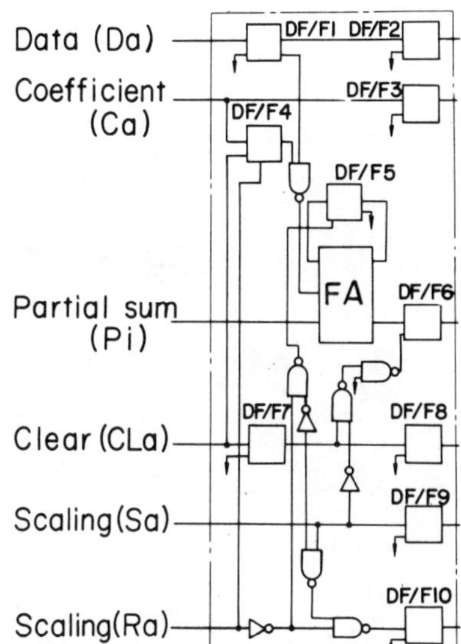

Fig. 5. Variable scaling multiplication circuit configuration.

was also added. With the terminal for this function, the multiplied data were made to raise fractions, to reduce fractions, or to count five and higher fractions as units. The coefficient word length was set at 16 bits because, backed by the introduction of the scaling circuit, most DSP functions can be satisfied by 16-bit operation. The multiplier operation architecture is shown in Table I. Because this multiplier algorithm was briefly explained by Lyon [7] and Baldwin *et al.* [4], the multiplier LSI configuration and the circuit design to implement high-speed operation are described below.

1) LSI Configuration: In Fig. 5, a fundamental 2'C multiplication circuit is shown. This circuit provides 1 bit of the coefficient words. D-type flip-flops (DF/F) 2, 3, 6, and 8 were used to make the pipeline type, and DF/F 4 was used to make the coefficient serial. The 2'C multiplication operation can be realized by subtraction of the most significant bit (MSB) and the expansion of the sign. The data length of the multiplication result is the sum of the data length plus the coefficient word length. To get maximum precision out of the multiplied data, a scaling function was added. In this device, scaling means to take out the data at an arbitrary position in the result. To scale the result, sign-bit expansion, lower bit clear, and reset of the carry, which exist among the data and the neighboring piece, are needed. Two control circuits (S_a and R_a) are added to the fundamental circuit. By the control circuit S_a, a lower bit and the neighboring data bits are cleared

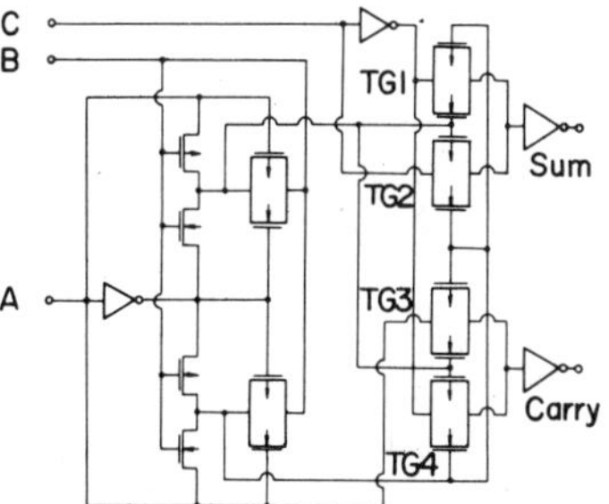

Fig. 6. Full-adder circuit configuration.

by reset signals from DF/F 4 and DF/F 5. Using control circuit R_a, the sign bits are expanded with the control of DF/F 6.

The multiplier is made up of a serial connection of this circuit, so this circuit has a simple pattern repeatability. The last circuit has a full subtractor instead of full adders in the other 15 circuits, according to the algorithm of 2'C multiplication.

2) Circuit Design: The most significant circuits in the multiplier are a serial full-adder, which determines this characteristic, and latch circuits, which occupy a large area. Therefore, to realize the high-speed multiplier with CMOS technology, the full adder and the D-type flip-flop were improved.

Full adders are usually composed of an exclusive-OR gate or a reduced majority function of their inputs. The exclusive-OR type has the drawback of a large delay time in the carry output, and the majority-function type has the drawback of a large delay time in the sum output. An exclusive-OR type adder has been designed with transfer gates (TG). This circuit, shown in Fig. 6, operates with two input signals, such as an exclusive-OR, and the exclusive-OR is in parallel to improve the speed. When $A \oplus B$ is at a low level, TG2 and TG4 are open and input C appears on the sum output, and input A or B appears on the carry output. When $A \oplus B$ is at a high level, TG1 and TG3 are open, $\overline{C}$ appears on the sum output, and C appears on the carry output. There is a total of 24 transistors, including inverters for polarity reversal, which is a smaller number than that used for the majority-function type full adder. The calculating speed of this adder is faster than either that of the exclusive-OR type or the majority-function type.

The pipeline multiplier uses many shift registers and latch circuits, which are basically composed of DF/F. Dynamic-type register cells were used for DF/F because of their advantages in circuit simplicity, high packing density, and high speed. For static operation needs, a chain-type register cell, shown in Fig. 7, was designed. In the design, feedback loops are settled like a long chain, and an inverter and a TG cell alternatively operate as a master or a slave at each time interval. With this chain-type register, the circuit area is widely reduced. Comparing the area of this type to a trickle inverter type, the former is about 30 percent smaller than the latter. As for speed, the chain-type resister is about 20 percent faster than the other types.

To operate a CMOS TG, two clocks that have antiphases with regard to each other are needed. Usually, antiphase is made with an inverter, but phase difference occurs due to inverter time delay. Then a TG is inserted in the in-phase clock line to compensate for the inverter delay time.

The simulations were performed by the worst case one. By

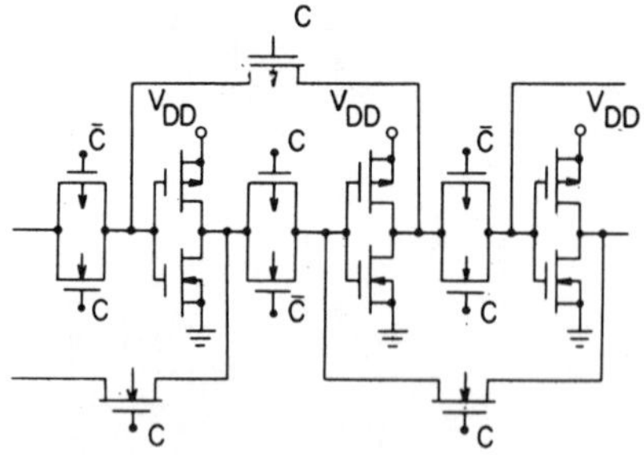

Fig. 7. Chain-type register cell.

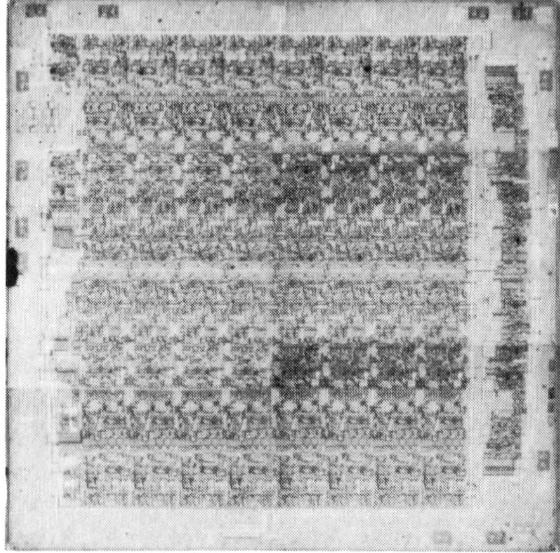

Fig. 8. 5-μm CMOS multiplier LSI.

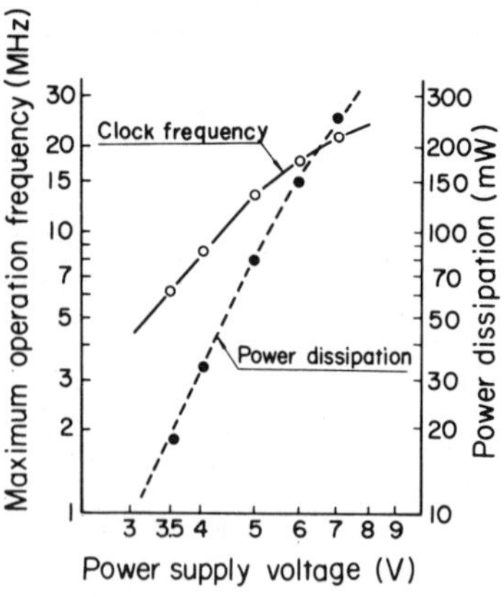

Fig. 9. 16-bit CMOS multiplier characteristics.

Fig. 10. 3-μm CMOS multiplier LSI.

applying the simulation values to the repetitive part of the multiplier, its critical paths were found to lie in the line from the partial sum to the sum output or the carry input, and the line from the carry output to the sum output or the carry input. The delay time of their critical paths was 70 ns, so this multiplier was expected to operate at 14-MHz clock frequency in the worst case, using 3-μm technology and 20 MHz in a typical condition. To prevent making the control path, such as the R_a or S_a lines, the critical path and to enclose the critical path in the full adder, a three-phase clock was used in the LSI. Clocks for the data line, the coefficient line, and the control line were set at a faster phase compared to that for the operation lines. By this means, 20 MHz of the operation speed was achieved, which was twice as high as in a single-clock operation.

3) Performance: The multipliers, which were made by the technology for the 5-μm effective channel-length CMOS static type and the 3-μm effective channel-length dynamic type, were evaluated. The 5-μm CMOS multiplier LSI is shown in Fig. 8. The total elements are 3814, and the total gates are 956, counting the 2-input NAND's as a gate. The multiplier occupied an area of about 90 percent, and the rest was for the full adder, full subtractor, and input-output circuits. The chip size was 4.25 × 4.64 mm. The operating frequency and the power consumption versus the power-supply voltage are shown in Fig. 9. The operation speed was in proportion to the square of the power-supply voltage, 14 and 21 MHz at V_{dd} of 5 and 7 V, respectively. These were almost the same values as the design values. The power consumption was proportional to the fourth power of the power-supply voltage, which was 80 and 280 mW at V_{dd} of 5 and 7 V, respectively.

At a 5-V ± 10-percent voltage range and an 8-MHz operation frequency, the phase margin was about 60 ns. The operating frequency varied by about 4 MHz with a 100°C temperature deviation. The speed-to-temperature coefficient was about 0.3 percent/°C, which was the same value as that for the ring oscillators. The phase margin varied by 20 ns at the 8-MHz operating frequency and 100°C temperature variation. Its temperature dependency was 0.1 percent/°C.

To achieve a high-performance DSP, a high-speed multiplier is indispensable. A dynamic multiplier was designed using 3-μm effective channel-length CMOS technology. This multiplier has the same LSI construction as the static one previously mentioned, but an overflow-detection circuit was added to the full adder. The total gate number is 800 and the chip size is 2.67 × 5.62 mm. The LSI is shown in Fig. 10. Its operation speed and power dissipation at a V_{dd} of 5 V were 25 MHz and 114 mW, respectively and the design value of the operation speed was 20 MHz. This value exceeded the design value by 5 MHz. It was clear that the performance of the high-speed multiplier was twice as good as that of the static one. Moreover, in spite of being a dynamic type, it was able

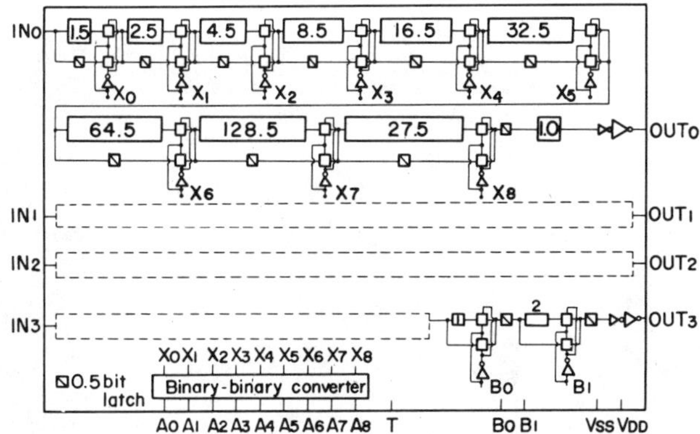

Fig. 11. Variable-length shift register block diagram.

to operate at a lower frequency, down to 1.2 MHz and the set-up time and the hold time were 32 and 35 ns, respectively. The output buffer was designed to drive a load capacitance of up to 35 pF. The delay time was 65 ns at 10 pF and 70 ns at 35 pF.

B. The Variable-Length Shift Register

Various word-length shift registers are needed for DSP, such as data latches or data stores for multiplex use. To satisfy these needs, a shift register, whose word length was able to be arbitrarily selected, was designed.

1) LSI Configuration: To realize this type of register, the decoder-select and binary-select methods are considered. The former needs a decoder circuit and the latter has a long critical path. The binary method, which puts a selector between two binary-length shift registers, was chosen. A 0.5-bit latch was introduced, which improves the critical path between the selectors. The selector is a wired OR circuit composed by a transfer gate. The configuration of this variable shift register is shown in Fig. 11. It consists of four blocks of 288-bit shift registers and a 3-bit variable shift register, which is able to change its bit length with one bit independently.

When all the blocks are serially connected, the word length is 1155 bits. By inserting the 3-bit register, 6 to 1155 bits can be arbitrarily selected. The bit shift signal of the binary representation does not correspond to a desirable bit length. The binary signal-conversion circuit is used in the following equation:

$$A_0'2^0 + A_1'2^1 + \cdots + A_8'2^8 = A_0 2^0 + A_1 2^1 + \cdots + A_8 2^8 - 6$$

provided that

$A_0'A_1', \cdots, A_8'$: desired binary signal

$A_0A_1, \cdots, A_8$: internal binary signal.

The 1-bit cell is an 8-element dynamic type composed of the usual master–slave flip-flop circuit. Maximum delay occurred in the path from the shift register passing the selector to the latch or the next shift register, or, similarly, from the latch passing the selector to the latch or the next shift register. These delay times were usually designed at 50 ns on both paths. Considering the convenience of its use, the clock driver was installed on the LSI, and the input capacitance of the clock input terminal was limited to below 10 pF.

Fig. 12. Variable-length shift register LSI.

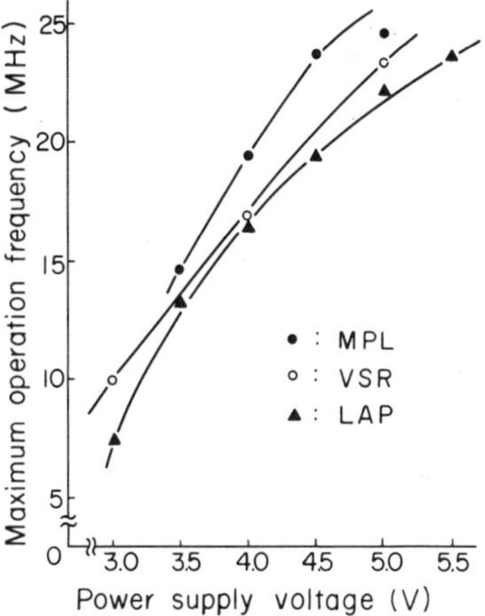

Fig. 13. Characteristics of DSP LSI's.

2) Performance: Fig. 12 shows an LSI with this variable-length shift register. Total transistors, chip size, and pin number are 12 000, 4.46 X 5.59 mm, and 22, respectively. The operating frequency and the power consumption versus the power-supply voltage are shown in Fig. 13. The maximum operating frequency, with a design value of 20 MHz, was 24 MHz at the applied source voltage of 5 V, and the power consumption was 680 mW for the worst pattern (10101010 · · ·), and is 390 mW for an all (1) or all (0) pattern at the same applied voltage. The clock driver occupied 63 percent of the total power consumption. Degrading the operation frequency from 24 to 8 MHz, the power consumption was reduced to 250 mW for the worst pattern.

The rise and fall times of the output buffer were about 20 ns with a 35-pF load capacitance. The output impedance was compatible to LSTTL, as is the case in the multipliers. The necessary minimum pulsewidth was 6 ns. Although the cells were the dynamic type, it was possible to operate at 1 Hz in an atmosphere of 130°C.

C. Linear Arithmetic Processor

The DSP function, such as recursive digital filter (RDF), nonrecursive digital filter (NDF), fast Fourier transform

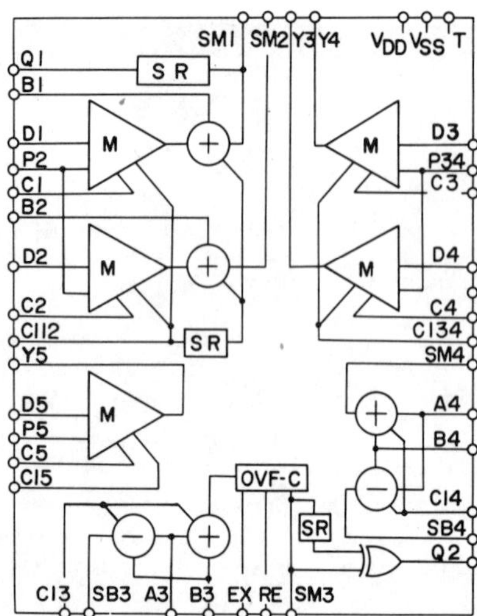

Fig. 14. Single-chip DSP LSI block diagram.

Fig. 15. Linear-arithmetic processor LSI.

(FFT), and discrete Fourier transform (DFT), can be realized with one chip DSP LSI having five multipliers, four full adders, and two subtractors in it.

The functions can be tailored by changing the outside or internal LSI connections. The outer-connection method has been chosen because of its flexibility and versatility. Because of the universal LSI usage, it was named a linear arithmetic processor (LSP).

1) LSI Configuration: A block diagram of the LSP LSI is shown in Fig. 14. The main five blocks are 1) a pair of multipliers and a full adder with a common control circuit; 2) a pair of multipliers; 3) a single multiplier; 4) a pair of full adders and full subtractor with a common control circuit; and 5) a full adder and a full subtractor with an overflow-detector circuit. The multiplier in this LSI abridged the two control circuits, S_a and R_a, used in the multiplier LSI to reduce the number of gates. Scaling was fixed at ±2. The coefficient bit of the multiplier was 12 under a decimal point.

The external LSI terminals were set so as to realize the DSP functions mentioned with the terminal connections. For example, a five-multiplication recursive digital filter will be realized by connecting the terminals as follows. Terminals *B*3 and *SM*4 are appropriated for input and ouput, and shift registers are externally added for the delay between terminal *Q*2 and terminals *D*1, *D*2 and between *D*1, *D*2 and terminals *D*3, *D*4, respectively. The other terminals have to be connected properly to make the five-multiplication recursive digital filter.

2) Performance: The LSI of this linear-arithmetic processor (LAP) is shown in Fig. 15. Its construction is dynamic and it has a total of 11 200 transistors. Made by 3-μm effective channel-length CMOS technology, with a chip size of 6.3 X 6.0 mm, the LSI is mounted in a 42-pin DIP package. The operating speed, with a design value of 20 MHz, was 23 MHz, and the power consumption was 250 mW at a 5-V source voltage, as shown in Fig. 13. The output-data delay time from external clock timing was less than 40 ns, with a 35-pF load capacitance. The output-waveform rise and fall times were less than 20 ns. With this performance, its operation up to

TABLE II
DSP LSI CHARACTERISTICS

LSI Family	Multiplier	Variable Shift Register	Linear Arithmetic Processor
Maximum operation frequency	25 MHz	23 MHz	23 MHz
Power consumption*	50 mW	250 mW	200 mW
PIN number	18	22	42
Circuit configuration	Coefficient bit length: 16	Maximum Word length: 1155 bits	Coefficient bit length : 12 (under a decimal point)
Note:* V_{dd} = 5 V , f_c = 8 MHz			

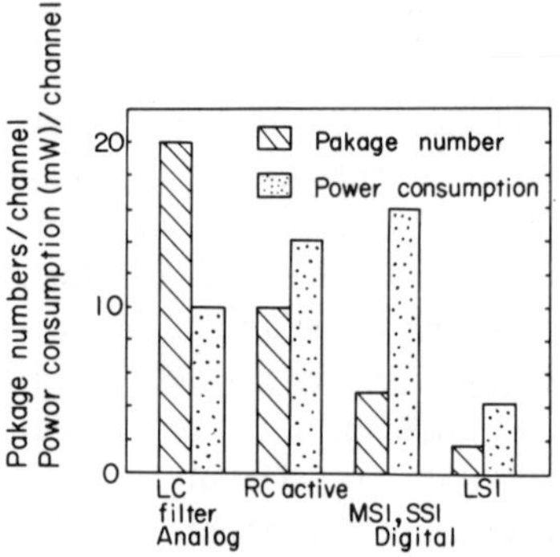

Fig. 16. DSP LSI's application for push-button receivers.

20 MHz was guaranteed, even when the DSP functions are realized by using external terminal connections.

V. APPLICATION

Table II shows the characteristics of the multiplier, variable-length shift register, and linear arithmetic processor. An example of these applications is the push-button receiver. The push-button receiver, now in commercial use, is composed either of a passive filter of the inductor and capacitor or *RC* active filters of hybrid IC technology. In Fig. 16, their packaging density per channel and power consumption are compared; DSP LSI's achieved one tenth the size and one half the power consumption.

Another example is the application as a transmultiplexer; that is, PCM/FDM conversion, which converts multiplexed

PCM signals into FDM signals, and vice versa. Five PCM T - 1 are nearly equal to two of the FDM SG group. Because a voice channel has to be represented as 24 bits in this case, a clock speed of 13.824 MHz is needed to form 72 multiplexed signals. Therefore, these LSI's can be used for this equipment, even in the worst conditions; i.e., a supply voltage of 4.75 V and an atmosphere of 70°C. Considering the input/output interface of these LSI's, the output is compatible with LSTTL and can drive four LSTTL's, but the input is not compatible and its threshold is $V_{DD}/2$.

VI. Conclusion

High-performance DSP LSI's, such as a multiplier, a variable-length shift register, and a linear arithmetic processor, have been realized by short-channel CMOS technology.

The multiplier LSI has an $AX + Y - Z$ function. It is mounted in an 18-pin DIP case. The variable-length shift register LSI has a total word length of 1155 bits. An arbitrary word length can be selected. It is mounted in a 22-pin DIP case. The linear arithmetic processor LSI has been designed to realize main DSP functions, such as digital phase-locked loops. It is mounted in a 42-pin DIP case.

The maximum operating frequency of these LSI's is up to 20 MHz. Their power consumption is below 250 mW at an 8-MHz operating frequency and 5-V power-supply voltage.

Besides their high performance of high speed and low power consumption, they have a wide operating range of temperatures and power-supply voltages. Because of their universal construction, low pin numbers, and TTL compatible output level, these DSP LSI's will lead to wider applications in communication systems.

Application to a transmultiplexer and push-button receiver improve equipment performance. Other high-performance DSP equipment would be realized with these LSI's. The high-speed CMOS technology used for these LSI's is to be applied to digital system equipment up to the second level PCM hierarchy.

Acknowledgment

The authors wish to thank M. Watanabe, Director of the Integrated Electronics Development Division, and H. Ariyoshi, Chief of the Electronic Circuit Section in the Musashino Electrical Laboratory, for direction and encouragement. They also wish to thank Y. Aoyama and F. Mano for their useful advice and discussions, and H. Yoshimura and R. Kasai for their technical assistance. Acknowledgment is also due H. Sasaki, Director, Dr. A. Morino, and M. Nakajima of the Nippon Electric Company for their cooperation in the LSI fabrication.

References

[1] S. L. Freeny, R. B. Kieburtz, K. V. Mina, and S. K. Tewksbury, "System analysis of a TDM-FDM translator/digital A-type channel bank," *IEEE Trans. Commun. Technol.*, vol. COM-19, pp. 1050–1059, Dec. 1971.

[2] M. G. Bellanger and J. L. Daguet, "TDM-FDM transmultiplexer: Digital polyphase and FFT," *IEEE Trans. Commun.*, vol. COM-22, pp. 1199–1205, Sept. 1974.

[3] J. D. Heightley, "Partitioning of digital filters for integrated-circuit realization," *IEEE Trans. Commun. Technol.*, vol. COM-19, pp. 1059–1063, Dec. 1971.

[4] G. L. Baldwin, B. L. Morris, D. B. Fraser, and A. R. Tretola, "A modular high-speed serial pipeline multiplier for digital signal processing," *IEEE J. Solid-State Circuits*, vol. SC-13, pp. 400–408, June 1978.

[5] S. L. Freeny, "Special-purpose hardware for digital filters," *Proc. IEEE*, vol. 63, pp. 633–648, Apr. 1975.

[6] D. Hampel, K. E. Mcguire and K. J. Prost, "CMOS/SOS serial-parallel multiplier," *IEEE J. Solid-State Circuits*, vol. SC-10, Oct. 1975.

[7] R. F. Lyon, "Two's complement pipeline multipliers," *IEEE Trans. Commun.*, Apr. 1976.

A Single-Chip Digital Signal Processor for Voiceband Applications

Yuichi Kawakami, Takao Nishitani, Eiji Sugimoto, Etsuro Yamauchi and Munekazu Suzuki

Nippon Electric Co., Ltd.

Kawasaki, Japan

A SINGLE-CHIP voiceband digital signal processor, organized as a high speed microprocessor containing a program ROM, a RAM, a data ROM, and a parallel multiplier on a chip, will be reported in this paper. The device has achieved high level digital signal processing capability, with all necessary functional blocks built on a single chip. Also, it can be tailored to various signal processing applications by only changing the ROM program.

A signal processor is required to perform complicated realtime data processing including a number of multiplications for every sampled data within a regular sampling period. For example, a voiceband signal processor composed of second-order digital filter sections has to perform four multiplies, four adds and two moves as many times as the number of filter stages within some 125μs of every sampling period. This heavy task has been impossible with the conventional microprocessors because of speed limitations.

These problems have been resolved by including a high speed parallel multiplier, sophisticated processor architecture with horizontal microprogramming and dual accumulator configuration, and high speed N-channel E/D MOS LSI with 3μ channel length.

Figure 1 shows the block diagram of the processor, designed to function either as a peripheral processor or a stand-alone single chip processor. Internally, all data are handled in two's complement for higher processing efficiency. This processor is controlled by 23-bit horizontal microinstructions stored in an on-chip program ROM. By this method, instruction decode time has been minimized and 250ns of instruction cycle time has been achieved. Figure 2 shows the instruction types of this processor, categorized into three types. Type A executes four operations simultaneously, including ALU operation, data move via main-bus, Data Pointer (DP) operation and O-register decrement. Type B executes branch operations including conditional branch and subroutine call. Type C loads immediate data into the register or the RAM location, as indexed by the destination field.

The multiplier is a high speed 16-bit parallel multiplier which uses Booth's algorithm[1,2] and 143 full adders. The multiplier and its input/output registers (K, L, M, N) occupy about 3mm^2 on the chip. With Booth's algorithm, the number of full adders and carry propagation time have been almost halved compared with the array multiplier; 16b multiply can be performed within 250ns. In addition, separate data paths are furnished from both DATA ROM and RAM to the multiplier registers, so that the multiplicator and the multiplicand can be transferred to the multiplier directly and simultaneously.

Internal Main-bus and Sub-bus can be disconnected by the Separator, and Sub-bus is connected to the ALU. By this, data transfer via Main-bus and the operation between accumulator and the data on Sub-bus can be performed simultaneously.

This processor has a dual accumulator configuration and dual flag register for the convenience of interrupt operation, double-precision real arithmetic operation and single-precision complex arithmetic operation. Two accumulators and two flag registers have duplicate functions, and instructions can directly designate which of the two should be used.

The DATA ROM can be used for various purposes, such as law conversion from nonlinear PCM to linear PCM codes or vice versa, coefficient storage for filtering, and so on.

For high efficiency of subroutine calls, DATA ROM and RAM addresses are pointed directly by the O-register and D.P. register, respectively.

As the fabrication process, 3μ N-channel E/D MOS technology has been adopted. The 3μ technology has improved the device speed by 40%, compared with the conventional NMOS technology. It has also contributed to the improvement of integration density. About 40,000 transistors are integrated in the area of 5.47 by 5.20mm die size. The device operates with an 8MHz main clock.

Table 1 summarizes hardware features and performance of this processor. The single chip processor can implement 55 second-order digital filter sections at 8kHz sampling of voiceband signals. This means four multiplies, four adds and four moves can be performed within 2.25μs for a second-order filter section. Figure 3 shows an example of digital signal processing system using this device as a peripheral preprocessor. Through various complicated calculations, realtime digital signal data are converted by the preprocessor and transferred to the host CPU in the form suited for its processing capability. Also, the processor is capable of multi-chip operation for very sophisticated applications.

The processor affords versatile digital signal processing applications such as digital filters, dual-tone multi-frequency receivers, data MODEMs, speech synthesizers and FET.

Acknowledgments

The authors wish to thank Y. Kato, A. Sawai and R. Maruta for their technical suggestions and assistance. They also wish to thank M. Sakai and M. Endo for their valuable contribution toward the realization of this project.

---

[1] Rubinfield, L.P., "A Proof of the Modified Booth's Algorithm for Multiplication", *IEEE Transaction on Computers*, Vol. C-24, No. 10, p. 1014-1015; Oct., 1975.

[2] Waster, S., et al, "Real Time Processing Gains Ground with Fast Digital Multiplier", *Electronics*, p. 93-99; Sept. 29, 1977.

Reprinted from *IEEE Int. Solid State Circuits Conf.*, pp. 40–41, 1980.

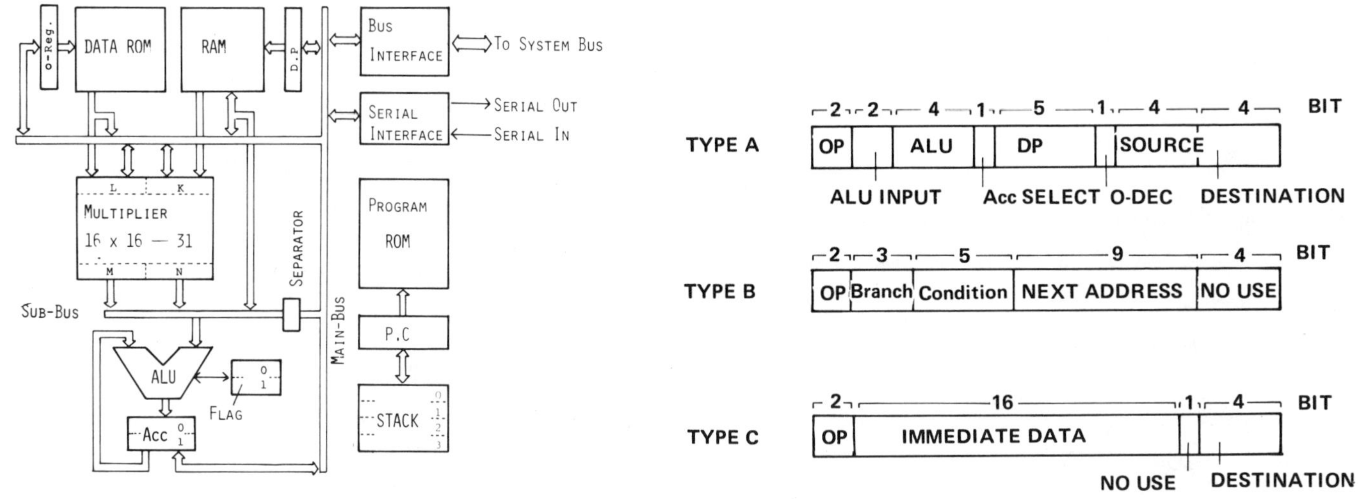

FIGURE 1—Block diagram of the signal processor.

FIGURE 2—Instruction types of the signal processor.

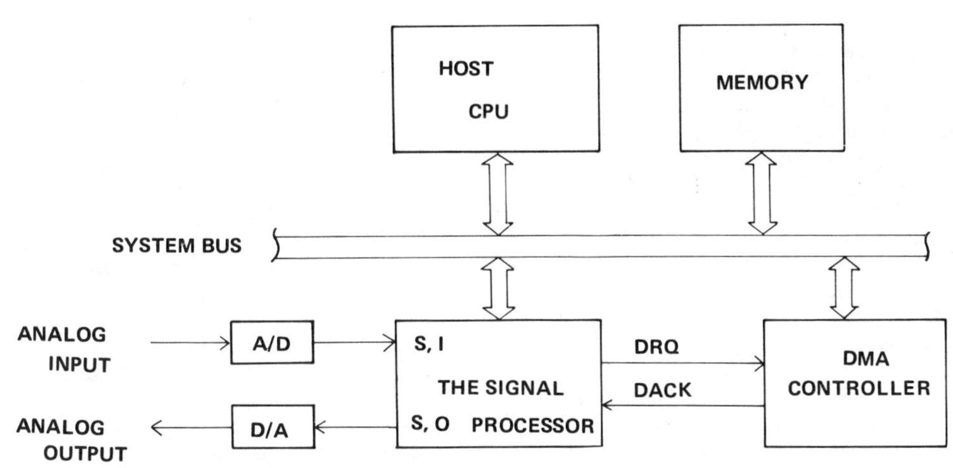

FIGURE 3—An example of digital signal processing system using this signal processor.

Instruction ROM Capacity	512 x 23 bits
Data ROM Capacity	512 x 13 bits
RAM Capacity	128 x 16 bits
Multiplier	16 x 16 to 31 bits (250 nano sec.)
Data Word Length	16 bits
I/O	8 bit Bus Interface and Serial In/Out Interface
Die Size	5.47 x 5.20 mm^2
Power Supply	+5v Single
Power Dissipation	900 mW (typ.)
Package	28 Pin Dip
Performance	
A Second-order Filter Section	2.25 μs (55 Filter sections within 125μs)
64-point Complex FFT	1.6 ms

TABLE 1—Summary of hardware features and performance.

A Digital Signal Processor for Telecommunications Applications

James R. Boddie, Gobind T. Daryanani, Ismail I. Eldumiati, Renato N. Gadenz, John S. Thompson and Stephen M. Walters

Bell Laboratories

Holmdel, NJ

Richard A. Pedersen

Bell Laboratories

Allentown, PA

A PROGRAMMABLE digital signal processor IC offering speed, precision, and flexibility for a variety of telecommunications applications will be discussed. Functionally, it is a special-purpose microcomputer whose instruction set and arithmetic and addressing capabilities are optimized for realtime signal processing functions including filtering, detection and modulation. The processor can decode an instruction, fetch data and perform a 16b by 20b multiplication and a full 36b product accumulation in one machine cycle of 800ns. Signal processing functions of such applications as dual tone multifrequency receivers or low-speed data modems with a single device are thus available. The arithmetic precision of the processor is sufficient for many voice-grade applications as well. The digital signal processor can function in a stand-alone fashion in many applications requiring only an external resonator or clock. However, it easily interfaces to microprocessors and additional devices to achieve a greater degree of signal processing capability. Highly flexible and separate serial input and output ports and the ability to convert between μ255 compressed PCM and two's complement binary code formats means that the processor needs few, if any, external interface circuits even when used in complex, multiprocessor applications.

Figure 1 shows a block diagram of the circuit including a 1024-word by 16b ROM for instruction and fixed coefficient storage, a 128 word by 20b RAM for variable data storage, an address arithmetic unit (AAU) with address registers for controlling memory access, an arithmetic unit (AU) with provision for multiplication, full product accumulation, rounding and overflow protection, an I/O unit to control serial data transmission in and out of the circuits and a control unit which provides instruction decoding and processor synchronization. Each of these units operate in parallel and, to a large extent, independently of each other. Communication between units is accomplished by an internal 20b data bus and a 10b address bus.

For program development and for some applications, external instruction and coefficient memory may be accessed over a 16b external data bus providing an alternate external address space of 1024 words. External memory access can be accomplished with no loss in processing capacity. Variable data transfers occur between the AU and either the data memory (RAM) or the I/O buffer registers. The AAU maintains an address register for the program counter and primary and auxiliary registers for coefficient read, variable read and variable write data addresses. Provision also exists for single-level subroutines and program looping. Once initial addresses are entered into the registers under program control, they are modified by the AAU as required.

The AU is responsible for the high speed arithmetic necessary for signal processing functions. It performs concurrently the primary operations of multiplication of a 16b coefficient by a 20b data word, the accumulation of a product to 40b and reduction of accumulations to 20b for data storage. The AU implements a number of variations upon its basic multiply/accumulate operation. It is possible, for example, to use the magnitude or sign of one operand in a multiplication rather than the operand itself or to shift or negate the contents of the accumulator before adding a product. Use of these special functions does not impose any execution time penalty over the conventional AU cycle. Multiplication and accumulation are performed concurrently, with the 36b product of one cycle being added, in the next cycle, to the accumulator. The contents of the accumulator are reduced to the 20b data storage size by either rounding or truncation.

Internal access to the separate input and output buffer registers by the AU can be made in place of data memory read and write operations. External access to these registers occurs asynchronously with respect to program execution. This buffering feature and special control logic simplify the problem of synchronizing a program of an arbitrary length with the data sample rate. The processor is designed to interface with a wide variety of serial data sources and sinks including other signal processors. Separate data transfer rates and synchronization modes are available for input and output as well as 8, 16 or 20b word sizes. To provide adequate flexibility for use as a system element, data can be transferred in and out of the processor by either internal or external clock and synchronization control. Program synchronization can occur either on data transfers or by application of a separate external signal. The processor can also provide separate synchronization control for other system elements when necessary.

One of the essential aspects of any efficient signal processor architecture is the ability to execute most of its basic functions in parallel. Thus memory access for instruction and coefficient fetch and data read and write occur concurrently with address modification, AU computations, and I/O operations. Effectively separate control of the AU and memory access is achieved through the design of the control fields of the processor instructions. Parallel activity is achieved with a minimum of communication paths between internal functional units through the use of a shared data bus and distributed instruction decoding. The control unit coordinates these operations and provides some special functions like condition checking and internal clock generation.

Figure 2 is a chip photomicrograph of the development version of the processor which does not include program and

Reprinted from *IEEE Int. Solid State Circuits Conf.*, pp. 44–45, 1980.

coefficient ROM. The processor is implemented with depletion load NMOS technology utilizing a single 5V power supply and is mounted in a 40-pin DIP. The chip ($68.5\ mm^2$) contains approximately 45,000 transistors (with program ROM) and has a maximum power dissipation of 1.5W. At the stated cycle time, based on a 5MHz clock rate, the processor can execute a four coefficient algorithm for a recursive filter section (two poles and two zeros) in 3.2μs or one tap of a nonrecursive filter in 0.8μs. This would, for example, be sufficient to realize nearly 39 second-order recursive filter sections at an 8kHz sample rate. This performance, with stored program flexibility, makes this circuit suitable as the basic signal processing element in many telecommunication systems.

Acknowledgments

The authors wish to acknowledge the efforts of F. E. Barber, T. J. Bartoli, R. L. Freyman, J. A. Grant, J. Kane, R. N. Kershaw, C. R. Miller, W. A. Stocker, E. F. Schweitzer and W. Witscher, Jr. in the implementation of this circuit, and the guidance of H. C. Kirsch and D. C. Stanzione throughout the project.

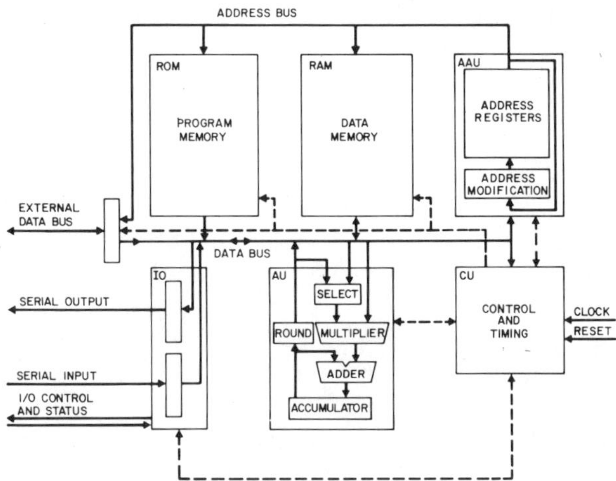

FIGURE 1–Block diagram of the programmable digital signal processor circuit.

FIGURE 2–Photomicrograph of the development version of the processor.

Section 4.3
Microprocessors

Projecting VLSI's impact on microprocessors

Single-chip microcomputers with 1 million bits of information, English-language programming, and canned software are seen ahead

One million devices on a single silicon chip by 1985? RAMs of 1024 kbits with prices as low as 0.002 cent per bit? Both developments will be possible in the next decade with a new generation of very-large-scale integrated circuits. Microprocessors and related components will be built on these ICs with new circuit-design techniques and advanced fabrication processes. Among the likely products are single-chip microcomputers with as much as 256 kbits of electrically erasable memory.

Contrast this progress with present silicon chip densities of less than 100 000 devices and prices at least an order of magnitude higher than 0.002 cent per chip.

Future ICs of high complexity will be intimately linked to the microprocessor. This is because this device, with its flexibility, opens up large-volume applications (and thus low costs per function). Until the microprocessor's advent, IC manufacturers were in a dilemma: they needed to increase IC densities to lower function costs, but in doing so, they started creating complex ICs that were limited in applications (and thus restricted in volume and costly).

Radical changes are ahead

Straight-line projections of IC complexities have been accurately forecast (see Fig. 1, based largely on a similar figure presented by H. W. Spence and R. W. Rozeboom at the 1977 International Conference on Microlithography). Recent trends in IC design and processing (Figs. 2, 3) suggest that these increases in complexity will continue. This gives rise to interesting speculations about the shape of future ICs.

For example, the present IC power dissipation of 1 to 2 W, imposed by conventional packaging, is bound to more than double to handle the higher densities. Thus radically new packaging ideas will evolve, which in turn will dictate new design standards.

One possibility is the gradual abandonment of the 5-V standard for TTL ICs. Since the demand for lower power dissipation and closer on-chip line spacing is tied to lower operating voltages, future high-density ICs are likely to operate at new standards of 3 or 1.5 V. Such voltages are compatible with those of batteries, which are likely to be used increasingly in future IC systems.

Microwatt power-dissipation levels will be necessary for each gate to achieve the high densities. In addition circuit designers will demand internal gate speeds below 1 ns.

But achieving million-component densities will require more than just lower operating voltages. With advances in fabrication and equipment, it is certain that the present barrier of 1-μm IC line widths and spacings will be overcome in production. Two-layer metal interconnections on the chip will become the rule rather than the exception.

In IC processing, plasmas are now replacing wet chemicals for deposition, oxidation, and other steps. This is making possible finer on-chip line geometries and lower processing costs. This trend will intensify.

NMOS technology indicated

NMOS technology can be the vehicle for future ICs. And CMOS is a likely supplement, more so than now. CMOS's major drawbacks of slower operating speeds and larger cell sizes, compared with NMOS, are being resolved.

Speeds from 20 to 40 MHz (depending on power-supply voltage) are possible if silicon-gate techniques, instead of metal-gate, are used. Up to 100-MHz operation has been achieved in the laboratory with isolated-substrate or dielectric-isolation designs. ICs with such speeds should become commercially available by the early 1980s. And CMOS cell sizes can be reduced by such design innovations as the use of a single MOS element in the output stage, instead of the classical complementary transistor pair.

The future architecture

Present IC complexities of 50 000 to 80 000 devices per chip can support, besides memory, a full range of very powerful, 16-bit peripheral chips. The peripheral chips of the 1980s could contain components for direct memory access, the bus arbitrator, memory segmentation, and the peripheral processor. The peripheral-processor components are likely to be programmed by the user for application in floppy-disk or CRT controllers, dedicated processors, memory sharing, and special communication protocols.

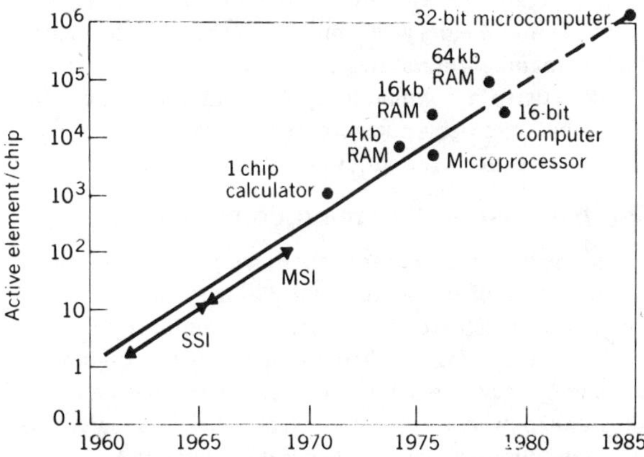

[1] By 1985, ICs with complexities of one million devices per chip will be possible. Microcomputers handling 32-bit operations are one manifestation.

Daniel Queyssac
Motorola Semiconductor Products

Reprinted from *IEEE Spectrum*, vol. 16, pp. 38–41, May 1979.

When we consider that the most powerful central processing unit available uses the equivalent of six million devices, the possibility of building single-chip CPUs of one million bits can be fully appreciated. More likely, future microcomputers will be apportioned as follows:

- 100 000 devices for the CPU.
- 400 000 devices for I/O adapters.
- 512 000 devices for an electrically erasable ROM (no RAM/ROM splitting).

Resident in memory will be powerful firmware in the form of a high-level-language compiler/interpreter and, probably, the most universal technical language: English. The CPU could have an 800-to-2000-word vocabulary, making it possible to instruct it directly in English. Recent speech-synthesizer ICs point the way.

The CPU will probably be 16 bits wide and feature a 20-ns cycle time. The I/O area will provide many direct inputs and outputs for interfacing to the outside world. With the type of organization projected, such a microcomputer system could have artificial intelligence.

How to reduce software costs

Producing more powerful computing machines does not, in itself, create a market for them, even if the cost does not increase in proportion with the increased capability. This is clearly indicated by sales of 16-bit microcomputers, which are only starting to be used by select customers for sophisticated applications. Less-powerful 8-bit microcomputer applications, on the other hand, have been growing significantly, and 4-bit microcomputer sales are literally exploding.

A major reason for such hesitant expansion of 16-bit microcomputers is the cost of software. As a rule of thumb, the generation of an average line of software costs approximately $10. One way to reduce software costs is to simplify programming.

From a hardware standpoint, the cost of computing power is dropping so drastically that by 1984 the capability of an IBM 1800 mainframe computer will be available for about $100 (Fig. 4). This creates an irresistible incentive for semiconductor manufacturers to plunge ahead with ever more sophisticated designs, so that new markets for microcomputers can open up. This is not an attempt to replace larger computers with 16-, 32-, and 64-bit microcomputers; rather it is a well-researched plan for taking advantage of the rapidly decreasing price/performance ratio of ICs to anticipate and stimulate the microcomputer market. It calls for using the increased device complexities to simplify the operation of powerful CPUs.

A few years ago the trend was to build more powerful CPUs every year, often in big mainframes. Then suddenly the microcomputer appeared with a downgraded CPU but many I/O and memory capabilities on the chip. Semiconductor manufacturers turned to this market, leaving 16-bit CPUs to a comparatively small market. The 4-bit and 8-bit microcomputer market began to take off because of easier use and lower costs.

The third-generation microcomputer

The next generation of microcomputers—the third generation—will be 8-, 16-, and 32-bit systems with architectures structured for programming simplicity instead of program length. Programmed with high-level languages, they will feature minicomputer-like architectures and powerful instruction sets. (Present single-chip microcomputers are second-generation systems.)

Two harbingers of third-generation microcomputers are the Motorola M6809, now available, and M68 000, which will be available shortly. The M6809 is an 8-bit microcomputer with 16-bit internal organization, and the M68 000 is a 16-bit microcomputer with 32-bit internal organization. The major features of both are architectures that support position-independent code and re-entrant programming. Such features will have a far-reaching impact on the way microcomputers are used.

The position-independent code allows written software to be executed in any location of the microcomputer's address map. The re-entrant feature permits interruption of a given program location in the address map, and the return to the proper address from a subroutine. Together these two design features lend themselves to modular programming, thus making possible "canned software."

With canned software, a large range of subprograms, 4 to 8 kbytes long, will become available from semiconductor manufacturers and other sources at very low prices. An applications program can then be developed by selection of the desired software. Program continuity can be provided with short, simple "patch" programs of high-level instructions. This technique can cut the cost of programming by an order of magnitude.

The availability of standard firmware in the form of fully debugged ROM-resident programs will enable users to build inexpensive software libraries and to split programming tasks into small, manageable modules. This, in turn, will reduce programming time and the knowledge needed for microcomputer applications. The microcomputer will then reach millions more of potential users.

To increase flexibility and expand throughput, third-

[2] Design innovations resulting in small IC cell sizes (A) and processing innovations for finer line-width and space control (B) are the tools of future high-density ICs.

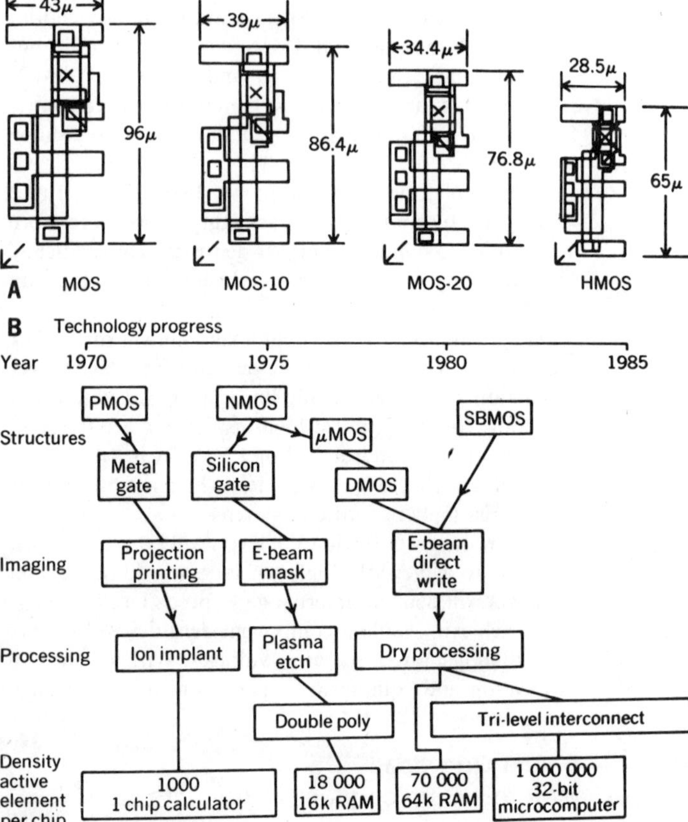

generation microcomputers will be supported by language-compatible software that permits movement from 8-bit operation to 16 bits and back again. Since the microcomputer will handle high-level languages efficienctly, the user's software library is not compromised by a move from an 8-bit to a 16-bit microcomputer, or even to a 32-bit system.

Will this compatibility apply across the board from 4 to 32 bits? Probably not. Low-end, 4-bit microcomputers, with mass use, will tend to be more hardware-sensitive. Since they will be used in applications where a single program will serve millions of parts, a small savings on hardware can quickly offset program development costs. At this point such microcomputers will sell below $1 in large quantities.

Improvements in processing needed

In view of the far-reaching nature of the microcomputer revolution, progress must be made in processing technology to reach the expected goals. Table I compares the progress in processing in the past few years with what will be needed to put a million devices on a chip by 1985. Similarly Table II shows IC electrical specifications and the improvements expected in emerging processing technologies.

The market inroads resulting from exploding microcomputer applications are listed in Table III. By 1983 the microcomputer market will be worth well over $2 billion in the United States and will represent nearly one-third of the domestic IC market. Microcomputers will account for over 20 percent of the world semiconductor market, compared with only 9 percent in 1978. A valid question is how will the semiconductor industry respond to this explosive demand? By spectacular increases in productivities. Let us illustrate:

In 1976 the number of good dies per 3-inch wafer (*GD/WF*) was around 200 for an average chip surface of 160 × 160 mils. Three basic considerations limit the possible good dies from what is obtained at the end of the production line:

1. Wafer yield (*Wy*).
2. Assembly yield (*Ay*).
3. Final test yield (*FTy*).

In 1976 the average values of microprocessor yields were: *Wy*, 40 percent; *Ay*, 80 percent; and *FTy*, 85 percent. By the formula

$$\text{Good finished products } (GFP) = (GF/WF)\,(Wy)\,(Ay)\,(FTy)$$

it is possible to calculate the approximate number of good finished products per wafer. Thus the 1976 overall yield per wafer was

$$(200)\,(0.4)\,(0.8)\,(0.85) = 54 \text{ units}$$

This means that with 10 000 wafer starts, it was possible to manufacture 540 000 microprocessors.

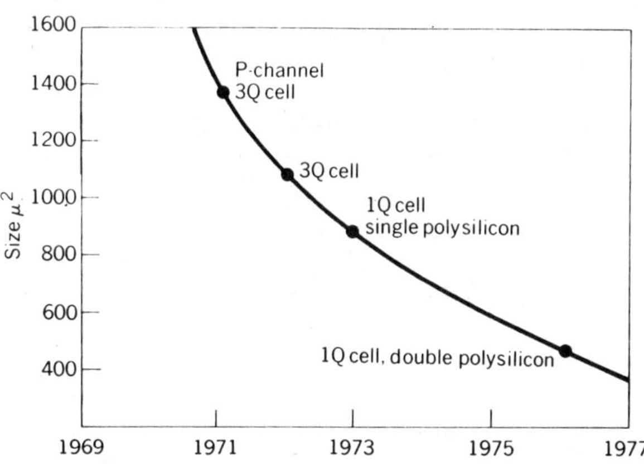

[3] The evolution of RAM cell sizes from 1400 μm² to 400 μm² in the last eight years is an example of how IC design innovations are bound to increase future chip densities.

[4] The cost of computing power (hardware) is dropping so drastically that by 1984 the capabilities of a much larger IBM 1800 computer will be available in a $100 IC chip.

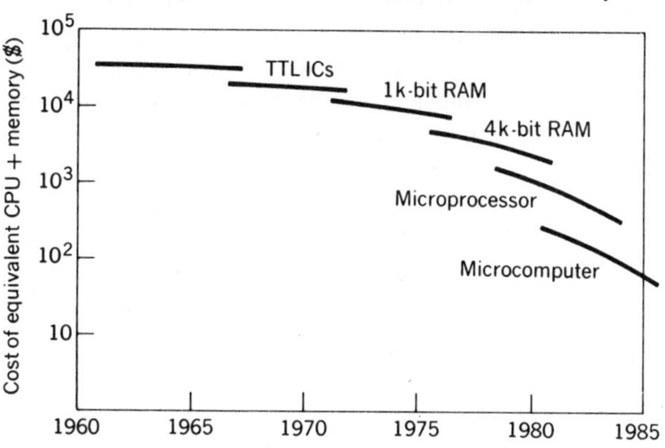

I. Comparative IC processing data

Parameter	1976	1979	1985
Die size (mil²)	160×160	250×250	450×450
(production level, mm²)	4.0×4.0	6.35×6.35	11.4×11.4
Resolution (μm) (production level)	6	3	1
Device per die (nonmemory)	10 000	80 000	>1 000 000
Wafer size (inches)	3	4	5 (ribbon technology)

II. Comparative IC performance data

Parameter	1976 (NMOS process)	1980 (HMOS II process)	1985 (SBMOS/ DIMOS processes) *
Speed, ns (internal gate)	6	2	1
Power dissipation, mW (per gate)	3	0.5	0.25
Speed-power product, pJ	18	1.0	0.25
Power dissipation per package, watts	1	1.5	5

* Schottky barrier MOS/dielectric-isolation MOS

III. The world market value for microcomputers

	1978	1979	1980	1981	1982	1983
Percentage of total semiconductor market	8.8	12.8	14.4	15.5	17	20.2
Percentage of IC market	14.9	20.6	22.5	23.1	24.4	28.5

Let's see what the situation will be in 1979 for the same type of product (160 × 160 mils). Manufacturing by then will be done on 4-inch wafers. Since the ratio of 4-inch to 3-inch wafers is approximately 1.8, the 200-chip maximum per wafer will increase to 360. At the same time we can expect the following yield values:

$$Wy = 50 \text{ percent}$$
$$Ay = 90 \text{ percent}$$
$$FTy = 90 \text{ percent}$$

This results in (360) (0.5) (0.9) (0.90) = 145 good finished products per wafer.

With the same wafer-start capability, it is now possible to manufacture 1 450 000 microprocessors, or nearly three times more than in 1976, without extra production capacity.

If we apply the above calculation to the 250 × 250-mil chip sizes expected for 1979 products, we find:

$$\text{Die surface ratio} = \frac{250 \times 250}{160 \times 160} = 2.44$$

$$\text{Wafer surface ratio} = \frac{4^2}{3^2} = 1.77 \text{ (from 3 to 4 inch)}$$

$$\text{Possible good dies per wafer} = \frac{200 \times 1.77}{2.44} = 145$$

Using 145 as the value of yield, we have:

$$GFP = (145)\,(0.5)\,(0.9)\,(0.90) = 58$$

Therefore even if we multiply the circuit complexity by 8 (an increase from 10 000 to 80 000 devices per chip), the same 10 000 wafer starts will yield 580 000 pieces—more than the 540 000 pieces available from today's less-complex 160 × 160 mil circuits.

This same progression should apply for the years beyond 1979, so that by 1985 it is reasonable to expect square 5-inch wafers with a new method of generating monocrystal silicon—ribbon technology. Here, once a laser remelts polycrystalline silicon after the silicon has been grown, the silicon is drawn out in ribbon form. At this point, with a small increase in yield, it is still possible to expect more than 100 good finished dies per wafer for systems of million devices-per-chip complexity, or 350 good finished dies for microprocessors of 1979 complexity.

Therefore productivity increases, coupled with straight-line production expansion, should provide the quantity of microcomputers needed by the market.

IV. Failure rates and mean time between failure (MTBF) for Motorola MC6800 microprocessor (ceramic package, 70°C ambient temperature)

Year	Failure rate (percent/1000 hours)	MTBF, hours (years)
1974	1.27	78 000 (9)
1975	0.5	200 000 (23)
1976	0.12	833 000 (95)
1977	0.08	1 700 000 (194)
1978	0.013	7 700 000 (877)
1979	0.006	16 666 666 (1901)

Reliability on the upswing

One final facet important to the expanding world of IC chip complexity is reliability. Just as power dissipation must be greatly reduced to accommodate one million devices on a single chip, so must reliability be improved by several orders of magnitude.

If one were to build a microprocessor of modern complexity using simple, plastic-packaged TTL gates, it would have a mean time between failure of only a few months. By contrast, the mean time between failure of a commercially available Motorola MC6800 CPU, a device with 3000-gate complexity and packaged in ceramic, was 877 years last year and is projected to reach 1900 this year. This clearly shows the reliability advantage of LSI.

As shown in Table IV, reliability is evolving asymptotically, with a failure rate of 10^{-9} as a trend. But even if we cannot realistically expect an improvement in this value for all new ICs, we can at least expect to see this value reached by new microprocessors of increased complexity. With a million devices per chip (300 000 equivalent gates, and a failure rate of 10^{-9}, the corresponding failure rate is 3×10^{-14} per gate.

Self-diagnostics for greater reliability

The impressiveness of these reliability figures is further magnified by the fact that the price will be low enough to allow the use of redundant systems equipped with self-diagnostics. Should a failure occur, it will be invisible.

Self-diagnostic features will become necessary for two major reasons: manufacturing costs and end-system reliability.

The increasing complexity of IC products makes their final testing very difficult. The necessarily large number of package leads will not allow convenient internal accessing, and this makes testing costly. One solution is to have internal circuitry, conveniently located on the chip, devoted solely to functional testing of all or part of the circuit. The testing of the product then becomes faster and more reliable.

The next logical step is to use this test function on the chip more than once in final testing and to make it available to the end user. At a given time interval, a test sequence of all microprocessors used in end equipment can be initiated and a go/no-go message transmitted to the user, who can immediately know if the equipment is fully operational. Another alternative is to design the system with redundancy of functions (a definite possibility in view of the evolution of the price/performance ratio of microprocessors). As soon as a defect is detected, another pathway will be used. ◆

The Intel 8086 Microprocessor: A 16-bit Evolution of the 8080

Stephen P. Morse
William B. Pohlman
Bruce W. Ravenel
Intel Corporation

The new Intel 8086 microprocessor was designed to be a compatible successor to the 8080, and yet it provides an order of magnitude increase in processing throughput over the older machine. The processor design was constrained to be assembly-language-level compatible with the 8080 so that existing 8080 software could be reassembled and correctly executed on the 8086. To allow this compatibility the 8080 register set and instruction set have to appear as logical subsets of the 8086 registers and instructions.

The goals of the 8086 architectural design were to provide symmetric extensions of existing 8080 features, as well as the following new processing capabilities not found in the 8080:

16-bit arithmetic, signed 8- and 16-bit arithmetic (including multiply and divide), efficient interruptible byte-string operations, improved bit-manipulation facilities, mechanisms to provide for re-entrant code, position-independent code, dynamically relocatable programs.

Another design goal was to be able to address directly more than 64K bytes and support multiprocessor configurations.[1]

The 8086 memory structure includes up to one megabyte of memory space and up to 64K bytes of input/output ports. The register structure includes three files of registers. Four 16-bit general registers can participate interchangeably in arithmetic and logic operations, two 16-bit pointer and two 16-bit index registers are used for address calculations, and four 16-bit segment registers allow extended addressing capabilities. Nine flags record the processor state and control its operation.

The instruction set supports a wide range of addressing modes and operations for data transfer, signed and unsigned 8- and 16-bit arithmetics, logicals, string manipulation, control transfer, and processor control. The external interface includes a reset sequence, interrupts, and a multiprocessor-synchronization and resource-sharing facility.

Intel 8086 Device Characteristics

ALU Width:		**16 bits**
Memory addressing capability:		**1,048,576 bytes**
Addressable I/O ports:		**64K**
Process:		**HMOS**
Gate propagation delay:		**≈ 2 ns**
Clock period:	**200 ns standard**	**125 ns selected**
Memory access:	**800 ns standard**	**500 ns selected**
Relative performance:		**7 to 12 times 8080A, depending on character of program**
Pins:		**40**
Power:		**+5V**

Memory structure

The 8086 memory structure consists of two components—the memory space and the input/

Reprinted from *IEEE Computer*, vol. 11, pp. 18–27, June 1978.

output space. All instruction code and operands reside in the memory space. Peripheral and I/O devices ordinarily reside in the I/O space, except in the case of memory-mapped devices.

Memory space. The 8086 memory is a sequence of up to 1 million 8-bit bytes, a considerable increase over the 64K bytes in the 8080. Any two consecutive bytes may be paired together to form a 16-bit word. Such words may be located at odd or even byte addresses (16-bit references to odd locations require two hardware memory cycles, while those to even locations require just one). The most significant 8 bits of word are located in the byte with the higher memory address.

Since the 8086 processor performs 16-bit arithmetic, the address objects it manipulates are 16 bits in length. Since a 16-bit quantity can address only 64K bytes, additional mechanisms are required to build addresses in a megabyte memory space. The 8086 memory may be conceived of as an arbitrary number of *segments*, each at most 64K bytes in size. Each segment begins at an address which is evenly divisible by 16 (i.e., the low-order 4 bits of a segment's address are zero). At any given moment the contents of four of these segments are immediately addressable. These four segments, called the *current code segment*, the *current data segment*, the *current stack segment*, and the *current extra segment*, need not be unique and may overlap. The high-order 16 bits of the address of each current segment are held in a dedicated 16-bit *segment register* and are called the *segment address*. In the degenerate case where all four segments start at the same address, namely address 0, we have an 8080 memory structure.

Bytes or words within a segment are addressed using 16-bit *offset addresses* within the 64K byte segment. A 20-bit physical address is constructed by adding the 16-bit offset address to the 16-bit segment address with 4 low-order zero bits appended, as illustrated in Figure 1.

Input/output space. In contrast to the 256 I/O ports in the 8080, the 8086 provides 64K addressable input or output ports. Unlike the memory, the I/O space is addressed as if it were a single segment, without the use of segment registers. Input/output physical addresses are in fact 20 bits in length, but the high-order 4 bits are always zero. Ports may be 8 or 16 bits in size, and 16-bit ports may be located at odd or even addresses.

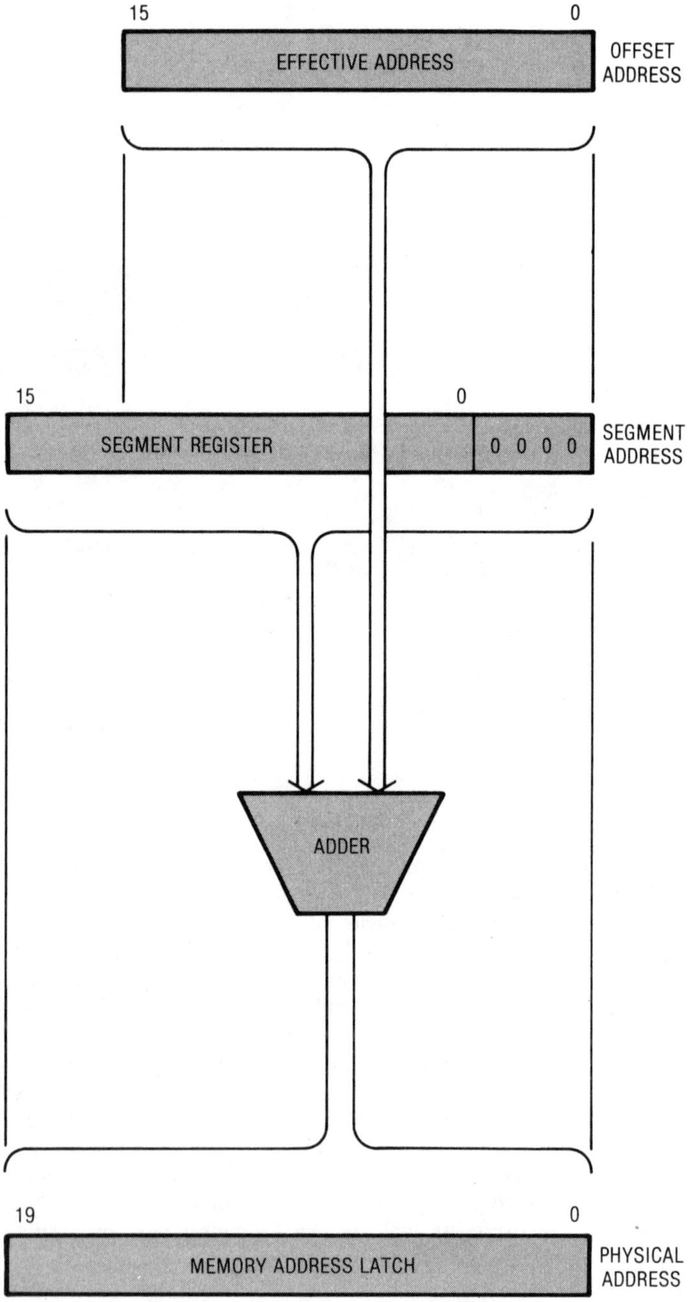

Figure 1. To address 1 million bytes requires a 20-bit memory address. This 20-bit address is constructed by offsetting the effective address 4 bits to the right of the segment address, filling in the 4 low-order bits of the segment address with zeros, and adding the two.

Register structure

The 8086 processor contains three files of four 16-bit registers and a file of nine 1-bit flags. The three files of registers are the general register file, the pointer and index register file, and the segment register file. There is a 16-bit instruction pointer which is not directly accessible to the programmer; rather, it is manipulated with control transfer instructions. The 8086 register set is a superset of the 8080 registers, as shown in Figures 2 and 3. Corresponding registers in the 8080 and 8086 do not necessarily have the same names, thereby permitting the 8086 to use a more meaningful set of names.

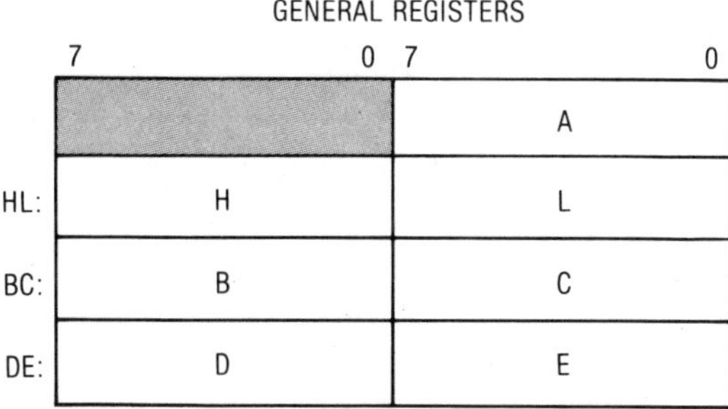

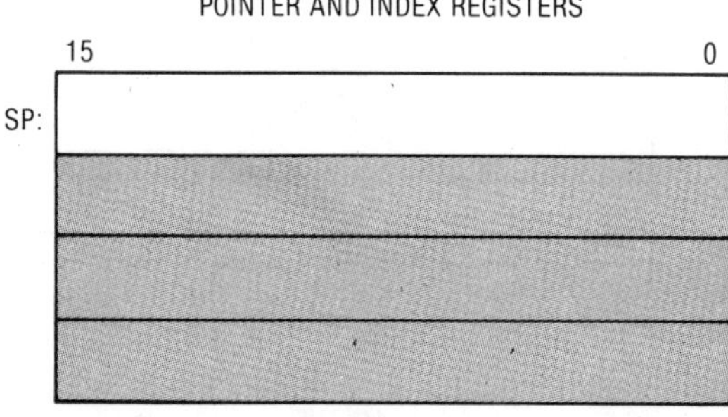

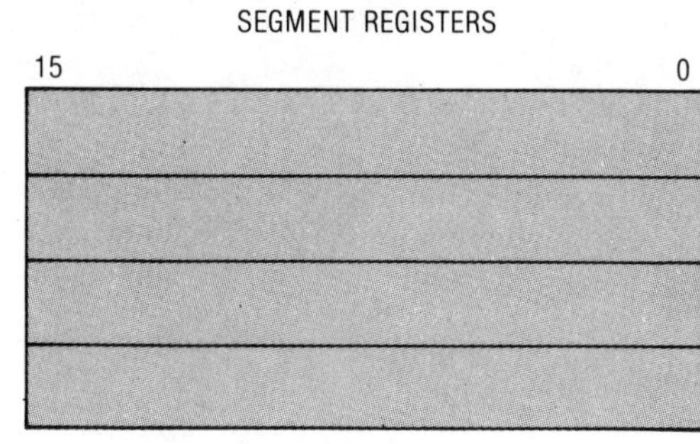

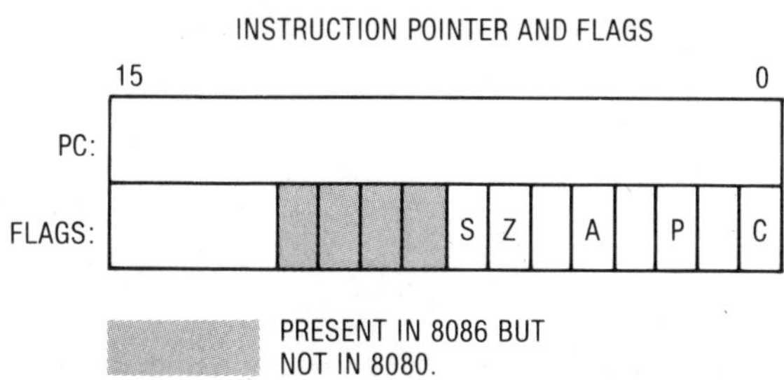

Figure 2. The 8080 register structure is a subset of the new 8086 register structure.

General register file. The AX-BX-CX-DX register set is called the general register file, or HL group (for reasons that will be apparent below). The general registers can participate interchangeably in the arithmetic and logical operations of the 8086. Some of the other 8086 operations (such as the string operations) dedicate certain of the general registers to specific uses. These uses are indicated by the mnemonic phrases in Figure 3. The general registers have a property that distinguishes them from the other registers—viz., that their upper and lower halves are separately addressable. Thus, the general registers can be thought of as two files of four 8-bit registers—the H file and the L file.

Pointer and index register file. The SP-BP-SI-DI register set is called the pointer and index register file, or the P and I groups. The registers in this file are similar in that they generally contain offset addresses used for addressing within a segment. Like the general registers, the pointer and index registers can participate interchangeably in the 16-bit arithmetic and logical operations of the 8086.

They are also similar in that they can enter into address computations. There are some differences, however, which result in dividing this file into two subfiles, the P or pointer group (SP, BP) and the I or index group (SI, DI). The difference is that the pointers are by default assumed to contain offset addresses within the current stack segment, and the indexes are by default generally assumed to contain offset addresses within the current data segment. There are also mnemonics associated with these registers' names, as shown in Figure 3.

Segment register file. The CS-DS-SS-ES register set is called the segment register file, or S group. The segment registers play an important role in the memory addressing mechanisms of the processor. These registers are similar in that they are used in all memory address computations (see description of memory structure). The segment registers' names have associated mnemonic phrases, as shown in Figure 3.

The contents of the CS register define the current *code* segment. All instruction fetches are taken to be relative to CS, using the instruction pointer (IP) as an offset. The contents of the DS register define the current *data* segment. Generally, all data references except those involving BP or SP are taken by default to be relative to DS. The contents of the SS register define the current *stack* segment. All data references which explicitly or implicitly involve SP or BP are taken by default to be relative to SS. This includes all push and pop operations, including those caused by call operations, interrupts, and return operations.

In general, the default segment register for the two types of data references (DS or SS) can be overridden. By preceding the instruction with a special 1-byte prefix the reference can be forced to be relative to one of the other three segment registers. The contents of the ES register define the current *extra* segment. The extra segment has no specific use, although it is usually treated as an additional data segment.

Programs which do not load or manipulate the segment registers are said to be *dynamically relocatable.* Such a program may be interrupted, moved in memory to a new location, and restarted with new segment register values.

Flag register file. The AF-CF-DF-IF-OF-PF-SF-TF-ZF register set is called the flag register file or F group. The flags in this group are all one bit in size, and are used to record processor status information and to control processor operation. The flag registers' names have the following associated mnemonic phrases:

AF: Auxiliary carry
CF: Carry
DF: Direction
IF: Interrupt enable
OF: Overflow
PF: Parity
SF: Sign
TF: Trap
ZF: Zero

The AF, CF, PF, SF, and ZF flags retain their familiar 8080 semantics, generally reflecting the status of the latest arithmetic or logical operation. The OF flag joins this group, reflecting the signed arithmetic *overflow* condition. The DF, IF, and TF flags are used to control certain aspects of the processor. The DF flag controls the *direction* of the string manipulation instructions (auto-incrementing or auto-decrementing). The IF flag enables or disables external *interrupts*. The TF flag puts the processor into a single-step mode for program debugging. More detail is given on each of these three flags later in the article.

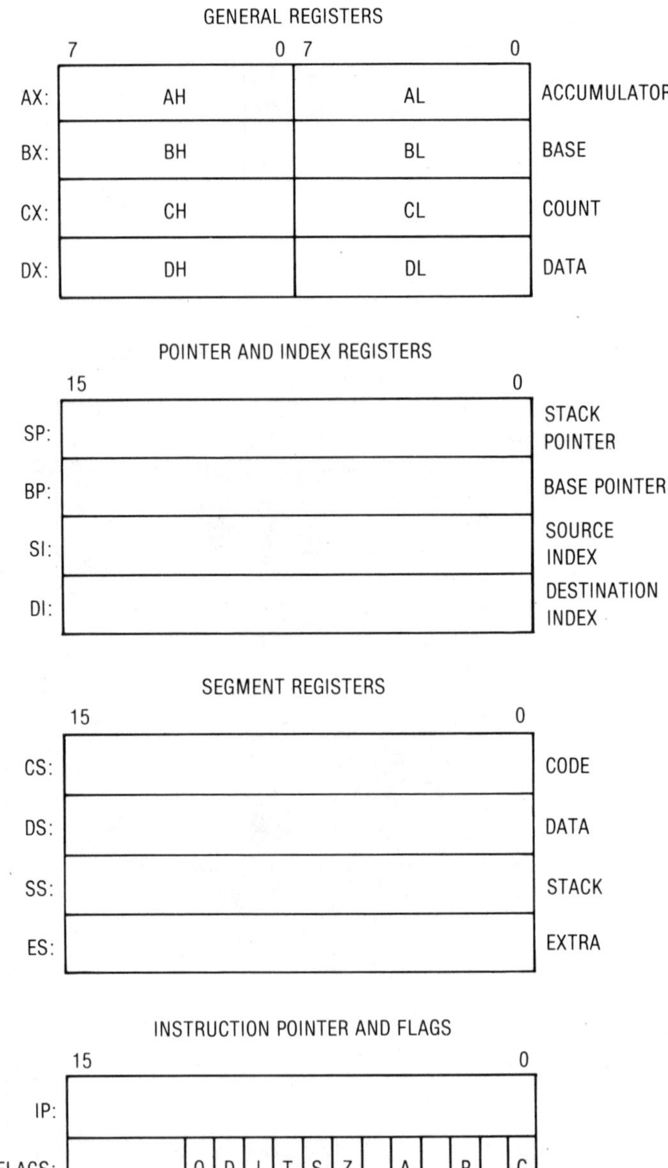

Figure 3. The powerful 8086 register structure has many more registers and four more flags than the 8080. The chief difference is that they can process 16-bit data. However, the general registers remain byte-addressable.

Instruction set

The 8086 instruction set—while including most of the 8080 set as a subset—has more ways to address operands and more power in every area. It is designed to implement block-structured languages efficiently. Nearly all instructions operate on either 8- or 16-bit operands. There are four classes of data transfer. All four arithmetic operations are available. An additional logic instruction, *test*, is included. Also new are byte and word string manipulation and inter-segment transfers.

Operand addressing. The 8086 instruction set provides many more ways to address operands than were provided by the 8080. Two-operand operations generally allow either a register or memory to serve as one operand, and either a register or a constant within the instruction to serve as the other operand. In general, operands in memory may be addressed *directly* with a 16-bit offset address, or *indirectly* with *base* (BX or BP) and/or *index* (SI or DI) registers added to an optional 8- or 16-bit *displacement constant*. The result of a two-operand operation may be directed to either of the source operands, with the exception, of course, of in-line immediate constants. Single-operand operations are applicable uniformly to any operand except immediate constants. Virtually all 8086 operations may specify 8- or 16-bit operands.

Memory operands. Operands residing in memory may be addressed in four ways:

direct 16-bit offset address;

indirect through a base register, optionally with an 8- or 16-bit displacement;

indirect through an index register, optionally with an 8- or 16-bit displacement;

indirect through the sum of a base register and an index register, optionally with an 8- or 16-bit displacement.

The general register, BX, and the pointer register, BP, may serve as base registers. When BX is the base, the operand by default resides in the current data segment. When BP is the base, the operand by default resides in the current stack segment. When both base and index registers are used, the operand by default resides in the segment determined by the base register. When an index register alone is used, the operand by default resides in the current data segment.

Register operands. The four 16-bit general registers and the four 16-bit pointer and index registers may serve interchangeably as operands in 16-bit operations. Three exceptions to note are multiply, divide, and the string operations, all of which use the AX register implicity. The eight 8-bit registers of the HL group may serve interchangeably in 8-bit operations. Again, multiply, divide, and the string operations use AL implicitly.

Immediate operands. All two-operand operations except multiply, divide, and the string operations allow one source operand to appear within the instruction as immediate data. Sixteen-bit immediate operands having a high-order byte which is the sign extension of the low-order byte may be abbreviated to 8 bits.

Virtually all 8086 operations may specify either 8- or 16-bit operands.

Addressing mode usage. The addressing modes permit registers BX and BP to serve as base registers and registers SI and DI as index registers. Possible use of this for language implementation is discussed below:

Simple variables and arrays: A simple variable is accessed with the direct address mode. An array element is accessed with the indirect access mode utilizing the sum of the registers SI (where SI contains the index into the array) and displacement (where displacement is the offset of the array in its segment).

Based variables: A based variable is located at a memory address pointed at by some other variable. If the contents of the pointer variable were placed in BX, the indirect addressing mode utilizing BX would access the based variable. If the based variable were an array and the index into the array were placed in SI, the indirect addressing mode utilizing the sum of the register BX and the register SI would access elements of the array.

Stack marker: Marking a stack permits efficient implementation of block-structured languages and provides an efficient address mechanism for reentrant procedures. Register BP can be used as a stack marker pointing to the beginning of an activation record in the stack. The indirect address mode utilizing the sums of the base register BP and a displacement (where displacement is the offset of a local variable in the activation record) will access the variable declared in the currently active block. The indirect address mode utilizing the sum of the base register BP, index register SI (where SI contains the index into an array), and displacement (where displacement is the offset of the array in the activation record) will access an element of the array. Register DI can be used in the same manner as SI so that two array elements can be accessed concurrently.

Example: An example of a procedure-calling sequence on the 8086 illustrates the interaction of the addressing modes and activation records.

```
;CALL MYPROC (ALPHA, BETA)
        PUSH  ALPHA             ;Pass parameters by
        PUSH  BETA              ;Pushing them on the stack
        CALL  MYPROC            ;Call the procedure
```

```
;PROCEDURE MYPROC (A, B)
MYPROC:                         ;Entry point
        PUSH  BP                ;Save previous BP value
        MOV   BP,SP             ;Make BP point at new record
        SUB   SP,LOCALS         ;Allocate local storage on stack
                                ;for reentrant procedures
;body of procedure

        MOV   SP,BP             ;Deallocate local storage
        POP   BP                ;Restore previous BP
        RET   4                 ;Return and discard 4 bytes
                                ;of parameters
```

Upon entry to the procedure MYPROC its parameters are addressable with positive offsets from BP (stack grows towards lower memory addresses). Since usually less than 128 bytes of parameters are passed, only an 8-bit signed displacement from BP is needed. Similarly, local variables to MYPROC are addressable with negative offsets from BP. Again, economy of instruction size is realized by using 8-bit signed displacements. A special return instruction discards the parameters pushed on the stack.

Data transfer. Four classes of data transfer operations may be distinguished: general-purpose, accumulator-specific, address-object transfers, and flag transfers.

The general-purpose data transfer operations are *move, push, pop,* and *exchange*. Generally, these operations are available for all types of operands.

The accumulator-specific transfers include *input* and *output*, and the *translate* operation. The first 256 ports can be addressed directly, just as they were addressed in the 8080. However, the 8086 also permits ports to be addressed indirectly through a register (DX). This latter facility allows 64K ports to be addressed. Furthermore, the 8086 ports may be 8 or 16 bits wide, whereas the 8080 only permitted 8-bit wide ports. The *translate* operation performs a table-lookup byte translation. We will see the usefulness of this operation below, when it is combined with string operations.

The address-object transfers—*load effective address* and *load pointer*—are an 8086 facility not present in the 8080. The *load effective address* operation provides access to the address of an operand, as opposed to the value of the operand itself. The *load pointer* operations provide a means of loading a segment register and a general or pointer register in a single operation. Such 32-bit pointers are used to gain access to the full megabyte of memory.

The flag transfers provide access to the collection of flags for such operations as *push, pop, load,* and *store*. A similar facility for pushing and popping flags was provided in the 8080; the load and store flags facility is new in the 8086.

Arithmetics. Whereas the 8080 provided for only 8-bit addition and subtraction of unsigned numbers, the 8086 provides all four basic mathematical functions. Both 8- and 16-bit operations and both signed and unsigned arithmetic are provided. Standard 2's-complement representation of signed values is used. Sufficient conditional transfers are provided to allow both signed and unsigned comparisons. The OF flag allows detection of the signed overflow condition. The 8080 provided a correction operation to allow addition to be performed directly on packed binary-coded representations of decimal digits. In the 8086, correction operations are provided to allow arithmetic to be performed directly on unpacked representations of decimal digits (e.g., ASCII) or on packed decimal representations.

Multiply and divide. Both signed and unsigned *multiply* and *divide* operations are provided. Multiply produces a double length product (16 bits for 8-bit *multiply*, 32 bits for 16-bit *multiply*), while *divide* returns a single-length quotient and a single-length remainder from a double-length dividend and single-length divisor. Sign extension operations allow one to construct the double-length dividend needed for signed division. A quotient overflow (e.g., divide by zero) will automatically interrupt the processor.

Decimal instructions. Packed BCD operations are provided in the form of an accumulator adjustment instruction. Two such instructions are provided—one for an adjustment following an addition and one following a subtraction. The addition adjustment is identical to the 8080 DAA instruction; the subtraction adjustment is similarly defined.

Unpacked BCD operations are also provided in the form of accumulator adjust instructions (ASCII is a special case of unpacked BCD). Four such instructions are provided, one each for adjustments involving addition, subtraction, multiplication, and division. The addition and subtraction adjustment are similar to the corresponding packed BCD adjustments except that the AH register is updated if an adjustment on AL is required. Unlike packed BCD, unpacked BCD byte multiplication does not generate cross terms, so multiplication and division adjustments are possible. The multiplication adjustment consists of converting the binary value in the AL register into BCD digits in AH and AL; the divide adjustment does the reverse. Note that adjustments for addition, subtraction, and multiplication are performed following the arithmetic operation; division adjustment is performed prior to a division operation.

The following examples show how these adjustments would be used.

ASCII addition: *a* + *b* — > *c*

```
0 — > (CARRY)
DO i = 1 to N
        (a[i] ) — >(AL)
        (AL) + (b[i] ) — >(AL)
            where "+" denotes add with carry
        add-adjust (AL) — >(AX)
        (AL) — >(c[i])
```

ASCII subtraction: *a* – *b* — > *c*

```
0 — > (CARRY)
DO i = 1 to N
        (a[i]) — > (AL)
        (AL) – (b[i]) — > (AL)
            where "–" denotes subtract with borrow
        subtract-adjust (AL) — > (AX)
        (AL) — > (c[i])
```

ASCII multiplication: *a* * *b* — > *c*

```
(b) AND 0FH — >(b)
0 — > (c[1])
DO i = 1 to N
        (a[i] AND 0FH — > (AL)
        (AL) * (b) — > (AX)
        multiply-adjust (AL) — > (AX)
        (AL) + (c[i]) — > (AL)
        add-adjust (AL) — > (AX)
        (AL) — > (c[i])
        (AH) — > (c[i + 1])
```

ASCII division: *a* / *b* — > *c*

```
(b) AND 0FH — >(b)
0 — > (AH)
DO i = N to 1
        (a[i]) AND 0FH — > (AL)
        divide-adjust (AX) — > (AL)
        (AL) / (b) — > (AL)
            with quotient going into (AH)
        (AL) — > (c[i])
```

Logicals. The standard logical operations AND, OR, XOR, and NOT are carry-overs from the 8080. Additionally, the 8086 provides a logical TEST for specific bits. This consists of a logical AND instruction which sets the flags but does not store the result, thereby not destroying either operand.

The four unit-rotate instructions in the 8080 are augmented with four unit-shift instructions in the 8086. Furthermore, the 8086 provides multibit shifts and rotates, including an arithmetic right shift.

String manipulation. The 8086 provides a group of 1-byte instructions which perform various primitive operations for the manipulation of byte and word strings (sequences of bytes or words). These primitive operations can be performed repeatedly in hardware by preceding the instruction with a special prefix. The single-operation forms may be combined to form complex string operations in tight software loops with repetition provided by special iteration operations. The 8080 did not provide any string-manipulation facilities.

Hardware operation control. All primitive string operations use the SI register to address the source operands, which are assumed to be in the current data segment. The DI register is used to address the destination operands, which reside in the current extra segment. The operand pointers are incremented or decremented (depending on the setting of the DF flag) after each operation, once for byte operations and twice for word operations.

Any of the primitive string operation instructions may be preceded with a 1-byte prefix indicating that the operation is to be repeated until the operation count in CX is satisfied. The test for completion is made prior to each repetition of the operation. Thus, an initial operation count of zero will cause zero executions of the primitive operation.

Primitive operations manipulating byte or word strings can be performed repeatedly in hardware, greatly increasing speed and efficiency.

The repeat prefix byte also designates a value to compare with the ZF flag. If the primitive operation is one which affects the ZF flag, and the ZF flag is unequal to the designated value after any execution of the primitive operation, the repetition is terminated. This permits the scan operation to serve as a scan-while or a scan-until.

During the execution of a repeated primitive operation the operand pointer registers (SI and DI) and the operation count register (CX) are updated after each repetition, whereas the instruction pointer will retain the offset address of the repeat prefix byte (assuming it immediately precedes the string operation instruction). Thus, an interrupted repeated operation will be correctly resumed when control returns from the interrupting task.

Primitive string operations. Five primitive string operations are provided:

- MOVB (or MOVW) moves a byte (or word) operand from the source operand to the destination operand. As a repeated operation this provides for *moving* a string from one location in memory to another.
- CMPB (or CMPW) subtracts the destination byte (or word) operand from the source operand and affects the flags but does not return the result. As a repeated operation this provides for comparing two strings. With the appropriate repeat prefix it is possible to *compare* two strings and determine after which string element the two strings become unequal, thereby establishing an ordering between the strings.
- SCAB (or SCAW) subtracts the destination byte (or word) operand from AL (or AX) and affects the flags but does not return the result. As a repeated operation this provides for *scanning* for the occurrence of, or departure from, a given value in the string.
- LODB (or LODW) *loads* a byte (or word) operand from the source operand to AL (or AX). This operation ordinarily would not be repeated.
- STOB (or STOW) *stores* a byte (or word) operand from AL (or AX) to the destination operand. As a repeated operation this provides for filling a string with a given value.

Software operation control. The repeat prefix provides for rapid iteration in a hardware-repeated string operation. Iteration-control operations provide this same control for implementing software loops to perform complex string operations. These iteration operations provide the same operation count update, operation completion test, and ZF flag tests that the repeat prefix provides.

The iteration-control transfer operations perform leading- and trailing-decision loop control. The destinations of iteration-control transfers must be within a 256-byte range centered about the instruction.

Four iteration-control transfer operations are provided:

- LOOP decrements the CX ("count") register by one and transfers if CX is not zero.
- LOOPZ (also called LOOPE) decrements the CX register by one and transfers if CX is not zero and the ZF flag is set (loop while zero or loop while equal).
- LOOPNZ (also called LOOPNE) decrements the CX register by one and transfers if CX is not zero and the ZF flag is cleared (loop while not zero or loop while not equal).
- JCXZ transfers if the CX register is zero. This is used for skipping over a loop when the initial count is zero.

By combining the primitive string operations and iteration-control operations with other operations, it is possible to build sophisticated yet efficient string manipulation routines. One instruction that is particularly useful in this context is the *translate* operation; it permits a byte fetched from one string to be translated before being stored in a second string, or before being operated upon in some other fashion. The translation is performed by using the value in the AL register to index into a table pointed at by the BX register. The translated value obtained from the table then replaces the value initially in the AL register.

As an example of use of the primitive string operations and iteration-control operations to implement a complex string operation, consider the following application: An input driver must transfer characters until one of several different EBCDIC control characters is encountered. The transferred ASCII string is to be terminated with an EOT character. To accomplish this, SI is initialized to point to the beginning of the EBCDIC buffer, DI is initialized to point to the beginning of the buffer to receive the ASCII characters, BX is made to point to an EBCDIC to ASCII translation table, and CX is initialized to contain the length of the EBCDIC buffer (possibly empty). The translation table contains the ASCII equivalent for each EBCDIC character, perhaps with ASCII NULs for illegal characters. The EOT code is placed into those entries in the table corresponding to the desired EBCDIC stop characters. The 8086 instruction sequence to implement this example is the following:

```
  JCXZ    Empty
Next:
  LODB    Ebcbuf ;fetch next EBCDIC character
  XLAT    Table  ;translate it to ASCII
  CMP     AL,EOT ;test for the EOT
  STOB    Ascbuf ;transfer ASCII character
  LOOPNE  Next   ;continue if not EOT
  .
  .
  .
Empty:
```

The body of this loop requires just seven bytes of code.

Transfers. Two basic varieties of calls, jumps, and returns are provided in the 8086: intra-segment transfers, which transfer control within the current code segment, and inter-segment transfers, which transfer control to an arbitrary code segment, which then becomes the current code segment. Furthermore, both direct and indirect transfers are supported; indirect transfers make use of the standard addressing modes, as described previously, to locate an operand which specifies the destination of the transfer. By contrast, the 8080 provides only direct intra-segment transfers.

Facilities for position-independent code and coding efficiency not found in the 8080 have been introduced in the 8086. Intra-segment direct calls and jumps specify a self-relative direct displacement, thus allowing position-independent code. A shortened jump instruction is available for transfers within a 256-byte range centered about the instruction, thus allowing for code compaction. Returns may optionally adjust the SP register so as to discard stacked parameters, thereby making parameters passing more efficient.

The 8080 provided conditional jumps useful for determining relations between unsigned numbers. The 8086 augments these with conditional jumps for determining relations between signed numbers. The seldom-used conditional calls and returns provided by the 8080 have not been incorporated into the 8086.

External interface. The 8086 processor provides both common and uncommon relationships to external equipment. The two varieties of interrupts, maskable and non-maskable, are not uncommon, nor is single-step diagnostic capability. More unusual is the ability to *escape* to an external processor to perform specialized operations. Also uncommon is the hardware mechanism to control access to shared resources in a multiple-processor configuration.

Interrupts. The interrupt mechanism of the 8086 is much more general than that of the 8080—and in fact bears no resemblance to it. The 8086 processor recognizes two varieties of external interrupt—the *non-maskable interrupt* and the *maskable interrupt.* A pin is provided for each variety.

Interrupts result in a transfer of control to a new location in a new code segment. A 256-element table (interrupt transfer vector) containing pointers to these interrupt service code locations resides at the beginning of memory. Each element is four bytes in size, containing an offset address and a segment address for the service code segment. Each element of this table corresponds to an *interrupt type*, these types being numbered 0 to 255. All interrupts perform a transfer by pushing the current flag settings onto the stack and then performing an indirect call (of the inter-segment variety) through the interrupt transfer vector.

The interrupt mechanism of the 8086 is much more general than that of the 8080—and in fact bears no resemblance to it.

Program execution control may be transferred by means of operations similar in effect to that of external interrupts. A generalized 2-byte instruction is provided that generates an interrupt of any type; the type is specified in the second byte. A special 1-byte instruction to generate an interrupt of one particular type is also provided. Such an instruction would be required by a software debugger so that breakpoints can be "planted" on 1-byte instructions without overwriting, even temporarily, the next instruction. And finally an interrupt return instruction is provided which pops and restores the saved flag settings in addition to performing the normal subroutine return function.

Single step. When the TF flag register is set, the processor generates an interrupt after the execution of each instruction. During interrupt transfer sequences caused by any type of interrupt, the TF flag is cleared after the push-flags step of the interrupt sequence. No instructions are provided for setting or clearing TF directly. Rather, the flag register file image saved on the stack by a previous interrupt operation must be modified so that the subsequent interrupt return operation restores TF set. This allows a diagnostic task to single-step through a task under test, while still executing normally itself.

External processor synchronization. Instructions are included that permit the 8086 to utilize an external processor to perform any specialized operations (e.g., exponentiation) not implemented on the 8086. Consideration was given to the ability to perform the specialized operations either via the external processor or through software routines, without having to recompile the code.

The external processor would have the ability to monitor the 8086 bus and constantly be aware of the current instruction being executed. In particular, the external processor could detect the special instruction ESCAPE, and then perform the necessary actions. In order for the external processor to know the 20-bit address of the operand for the instruction, the 8086 will react to the ESCAPE instruction by performing a read (but ignoring the result) from the operand address specified, thereby placing the address on the bus for the external processor to see. Before doing such a dummy read, the 8086 will have to wait for the external processor to be ready. The "test" pin on the 8086 processor is used to provide this synchronization. The 8086 instruction WAIT accomplishes the wait.

If the external processor is not available, the specialized operations could be performed by software subroutines. To invoke the subroutines, an interrupt-generating instruction would be executed. The subroutine needs to be passed the specific specialized-operation opcode and address of the operand. This information would be contained in an in-line data byte(s) following the interrupt-generating instruction.

The same number of bytes are required to issue a specialized operation instruction to the external processor or to invoke the software subroutines. Thus, the compiler could generate object code that could be used either way. The actual determination of which way the specialized operations were carried out could be made at load time and the object code modified by the loader accordingly.

Sharing resources with parallel processors. In multiple-processor systems with shared resources it is necessary to provide mechanisms to enforce controlled access to those resources. Such mechanisms, while generally provided through software operating systems, require hardware assistance. A sufficient mechanism for accomplishing this is a *locked exchange* (also known as test-and-set-lock).

The 8086 provides a special 1-byte prefix which may precede any instruction. This prefix causes the processor to assert its bus-lock signal for the duration of the operation caused by the instruction. It is assumed that external hardware, upon receipt of that signal, will prohibit bus access for other bus masters during the period of its assertion.

The instruction most useful in this context is an exchange register with memory. A simple software lock may be implemented with the following code sequences:

```
Check:
    MOV        AL,1      ;set AL to 1 (implies locked)
    LOCK XCHG  Sema,AL   ;test and set lock
    TEST       AL,AL     ;set flags based on AL
    JNZ        Check     ;retry if lock already set
    .
    .                    ;critical region
    .
    MOV        Sema,0    ;clear the lock when done
```

Conclusion

The Intel 8086 microprocessor architecture was designed to meet the requirements of a broad class of new microprocessor applications. Its symmetric operational organization will allow the efficient implementation of software systems, especially those written in higher-level languages. The arithmetic, logical, byte-string, and bit operations support the common computational needs of microprocessor applications. The ability to support reentrant code, position-independent code, and dynamically relocatable programs will allow reasonable operating system implementations in larger applications, while the large address space supports those applications' memory requirements. Other aspects of the architecture make feasible very efficient smaller applications, where the performance the 8086 offers is often crucial. As an evolution of the popular 8080 processor, the 8086 presents the most advanced microprocessor capabilities available today. ■

Acknowledgments

The 8086 could never have been realized without the work of a skilled device design team. The internal layout, logic design, and circuit were done by Jim McKevitt, John Bayliss, Kit Ng, and Peter Stoll. Much to their credit, functional 8086's were available within a month of the date predicted almost two years earlier.

The architecture design itself was greatly aided by the extensive analysis of Bruce MacLennan, and many hours of discussions with Bill Brown, Kevin Kahn, and Dean Schulz.

Reference

1. B. Jeffrey Katz, Stephen P. Morse, William B. Pohlman, and Bruce W. Ravenel, "8086 Microcomputer Bridges the Gap Between 8- and 16-Bit Designs," *Electronics*, February 16, 1978, pp. 99-104.

A Microprocessor Architecture for a Changing World: The Motorola 68000

Edward Stritter
Tom Gunter
Motorola Semiconductor

Microprocessor technology is entering a new and especially challenging era. While technology constraints have not completely disappeared, we are nearly to the point where the limiting factor in microprocessor design is not how much function can be included, but how imaginative and creative the designer can be.[1] As a result, several companies have introduced new-generation microprocessors. We describe how one of them, the Motorola 6800, responds to these unique conditions.

Motivations for a new microprocessor architecture

Previous generations of microprocessors were limited by the available technology. Brooks, in an overview article,[2] discusses how the technology constraints and the perceived microprocessor market motivated early microprocessor architecture. Microprocessors were limited in number of registers, data-path width, and instruction-set power primarily because technology could not support more features on a single chip. Other limitations of microprocessors, such as having too small an address space[3] and awkwardness of address computation,[4] may be attributed as much to prevailing perceptions of the potential market as to technology constraints.[5] Whatever the former sources of restraint, however, we are now in a period of technical innovation and spirited competition.

Technological advances. The basic microprocessor technology, MOS, has been steadily advanced in the last few years. The most noticeable improvement has been circuit density (Figure 1), which translates directly into the amount of capability that can be put on a single-chip microprocessor. Whereas earlier microprocessors contained from 5000 to 10,000 transistors per chip, current processors have from 25,000 to 70,000 transistors, which is less than an order of magnitude away from the number in many of the largest maxi-computers. Circuit density is not the only technology advance that has been made: corresponding improvements have been achieved in circuit speed and power dissipation.

Advances in technology have been more evolutionary than revolutionary. The major advance, increased circuit density, is the result of gradual improvements in processing techniques that permit smaller circuit dimensions. Density improvements are expected to continue, since they depend not on overcoming fundamental limitations but only on further evolutionary improvement of existing processes. New microprocessor architectures must be devised to take advantage of this future advancement.

Market demands. The demand for microprocessors in applications not foreseen just a few years ago is providing new opportunities for microprocessor manufacturers. Just as the original microprocessor designers could not predict the many uses that would be found for their devices, today's designers cannot hope to envision more than a few of the eventual applications of new microprocessors. The implication for the designer is that new designs must be flexible and general if they are to be useful in a large number of potential applications.

High software costs. The problem of software costs is even worse in microprocessor applications than it is with computers generally. Decreasing memory costs,

Reprinted from *IEEE Computer*, vol. 12, pp. 43–52, Feb. 1979.

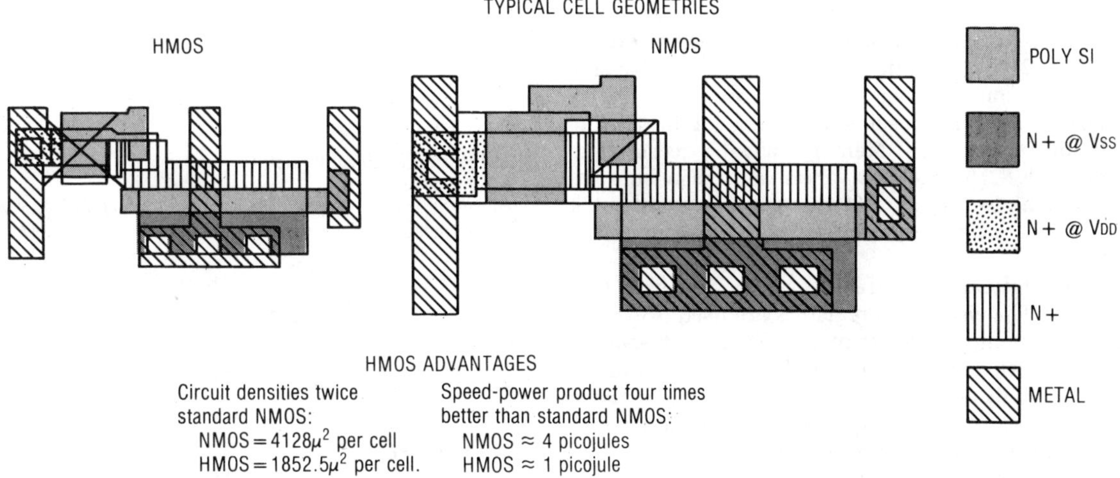
TYPICAL CELL GEOMETRIES
HMOS
NMOS
POLY SI
N + @ Vss
N + @ VDD
N +
METAL
HMOS ADVANTAGES
Circuit densities twice standard NMOS:
NMOS = 4128μ² per cell
HMOS = 1852.5μ² per cell.
Speed-power product four times better than standard NMOS:
NMOS ≈ 4 picojules
HMOS ≈ 1 picojule

Figure 1. Comparisons of HMOS and NMOS technologies. The HMOS technology used for the MC68000 results in significant improvements to circuit densities and speed-power products.

increasing processor functionality, and more complex applications are combining to increase the size and complexity of microprocessor programs. Software costs of $100,000 or more are clearly incompatible with hardware costs of hundreds of dollars. This cost disparity may be unimportant in large-volume applications, where software costs can be amortized over thousands of hardware units, but it often precludes the use of microprocessors in applications characterized by complex programs but low volume. To help reduce the high cost of software, microprocessor designers must make a strong commitment to supporting high-level languages and disciplined programming practices.

High design costs. The cost of designing and implementing a new device with tens of thousands of transistors is high. Computer design aids are indispensible, but they are also expensive. Designers must attack this design-cost problem in several ways. First, straightforward designs, using regular structures, are easier to implement, test, and correct, and are therefore less expensive than exotic designs. Second, each new architecture must be planned to last for as long as possible and must be easy to expand in the future. Manufacturers can no longer afford to produce new architectures every few years. Experience with trying to extend and improve the original 8-bit microprocessor architectures demonstrates the need for planned expansion. Designers must be careful to include as few limitations to future expansion as possible. The most common mistakes in the past have been limiting address size and not providing unused operation codes for future new instructions.

Design goals for the 68000. Motorola's 68000 microprocessor architecture has been designed to meet the requirements outlined above. (The MC68000's characteristics are summarized in Table 1.)

Architectural family. The 68000 design specifies a computer architecture of which a number of different versions or "implementations" will be produced.[6] The first version, the MC68000, implements only the subset of the complete 68000 architecture allowed by current technology constraints.

Flexibility and usefulness. The 68000 design ensures that the processor is easy to program. As much as possible, there are no unnatural limitations, artifacts, special cases, or other awkward features in the architecture.

Marketability. The 68000 is a general-purpose architecture, reflecting the increasing market acceptance of general-purpose microprocessors for diverse applications.

Expandability. The 68000 design specifies several features, such as floating-point and string operations, that are not implemented in the first version but have been specified now to guarantee future consistency. In addition, unused space has been left in the architecture to accommodate new features that future advances in technology will make possible.

Support of high-level languages. The 68000 architecture contains features for implementing high-level languages, and Morotola is commited to supplying software support for program development in well-known high-level languages.

Table 1.
Motorola MC68000 characteristics.

INTEGER SIZES	8, 16, and 32 bits
ADDRESSING CAPABILITY	16,777,216 bytes
INPUT/OUTPUT	memory-mapped
TECHNOLOGY	HMOS
INTERNAL CYCLE	250 nsec
MEMORY ACCESS	500 nsec
RELATIVE PERFORMANCE	10 to 25 times 6800
PINS	64
POWER	+5V

68000 internal architecture

Resources. The 68000 design provides an address space of 2^{32} bytes (limited to 2^{24} bytes in the initial implementation). Memory is byte addressable, with individual-bit addressing provided for bit-manipulation instructions. Memory may be accessed in units of 1, 8, 16, or 32 bits. CPU resources include sixteen 32-bit registers, a 32-bit program counter (24 bits in the initial implementation), and a 16-bit status register.

The registers (Figure 2) are divided into two classes. The eight data registers are used primarily for data manipulation; they may be operand sources or destinations for all operations but are used in addressing only as index registers. The eight remaining (address) registers are used primarily for addressing. The stack pointer is one of the address registers. The program counter and status word are separate registers.

Addressing. Memory is logically addressed in 8-bit bytes, 16-bit words, or 32-bit long words. The current implementation requires that word and long-word data be word aligned. Bits are individually addressable in the bit-manipulation instructions.

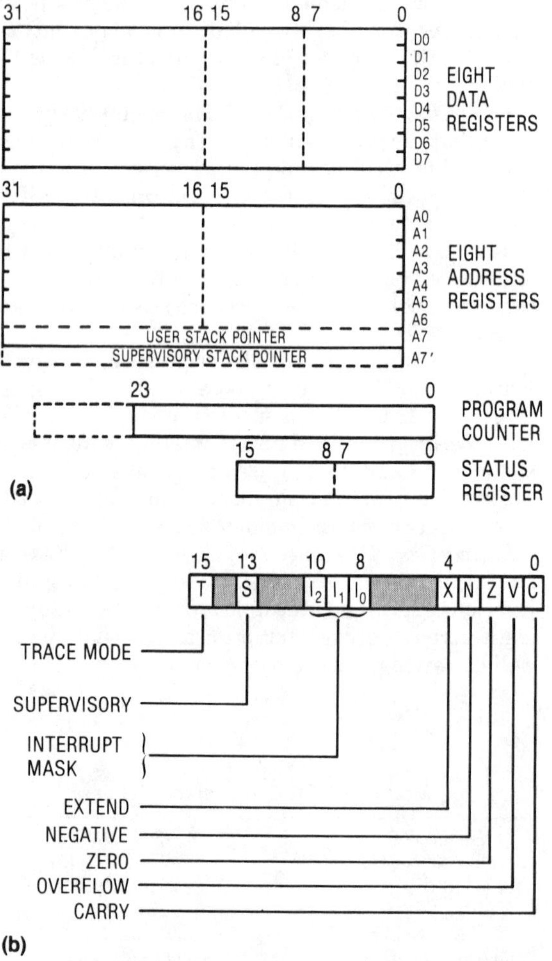

Figure 2. MC68000 programming model (a) and internal structure of status register (b).

Table 2. MC68000 addressing modes.

Mode	Specification
REGISTER DIRECT ADDRESSING:	
data register direct	EA = Dn
address register direct	EA = An
status register direct	EA = SR
REGISTER DEFERRED ADDRESSING:	
register deferred	EA = (An)
register deferred post-increment	EA = (An); An <– An + N
register deferred pre-decrement	An <– An – N; EA = (An)
base relative	EA = (An) + d16
indexed	EA = (An) + (Xn) + d8
PROGRAM COUNTER RELATIVE:	
relative with offset	EA = (PC) + d16
relative indexed	EA = (PC) + (Xn) + d8
short PC relative branch	EA = (PC) + d8
long PC relative branch	EA = (PC) + d16
ABSOLUTE ADDRESSING:	
absolute short	EA = (next instruction word)
absolute long	EA = (next two instruction words)
IMMEDIATE DATA ADDRESSING:	
immediate	DATA = next instruction word(s)
quick immediate	DATA = subfield of instruction (4 bits)

DEFINITIONS:

- EA = effective address
- An = address register
- Dn = data register
- Xn = address or data register used as index register
- SR = status register
- PC = program counter
- d8 = 8-bit displacement
- d16 = 16-bit displacement
- N = 1 for byte, 2 for word, and 4 for long word operands
- ( ) = contents of
- <– = replaces

The architecture specifies an optimal memory-management scheme that implements and enforces variable-length segmentation of the address space with access rights specifiable for individual segments. The processor can be used with or without memory management.

Address calculations (Table 2) are specified by 6-bit fields of the instruction. The addressing specification is orthogonal to the operation specification of the instruction; that is, any addressing mode can be used in any instruction that uses addressing.

Addresses are 32-bit quantities (24 bits in the current implementation). The architecture efficiently supports small systems (those with fewer than 2^{16} addressable bytes) by allowing 16-bit address quantities to be specified, moved, or calculated in almost every addressing situation. For example, an absolute address carried in an instruction can use 16 or 32 bits, or an index calculation can use 16 bits (sign extended to 24 bits) or 32 bits of a register as input. This feature allows the architecture to support very large addresses without penalizing the efficiency of programs that require only small addresses. The address size (16 or 32 bits) is individually specified for each use, so that large and small addresses can be intermixed arbitrarily in a program.

A variety of addressing modes are available:

Register direct. The data or address register contains the operand.

Address register deferred. The operand address is in the specified address register.

Address register deferred post-increment. The operand address is in the specified address register. After the operand is accessed, the address in the register is incremented by the operand size (1, 2, or 4).

Address register deferred pre-decrement. The operand address is in the specified address register. Before the operand is accessed, the address register is decremented by the operand size.

Base relative. The operand address is the contents of the specified address register plus a 16-bit signed displacement in the instruction.

Program counter relative. The operand address is the current program counter value plus a 16-bit signed displacement in the instruction.

Indexed. The operand address is the contents of the specified address register plus the contents of an additional (data or address) register specified plus an 8-bit signed displacement in the instruction.

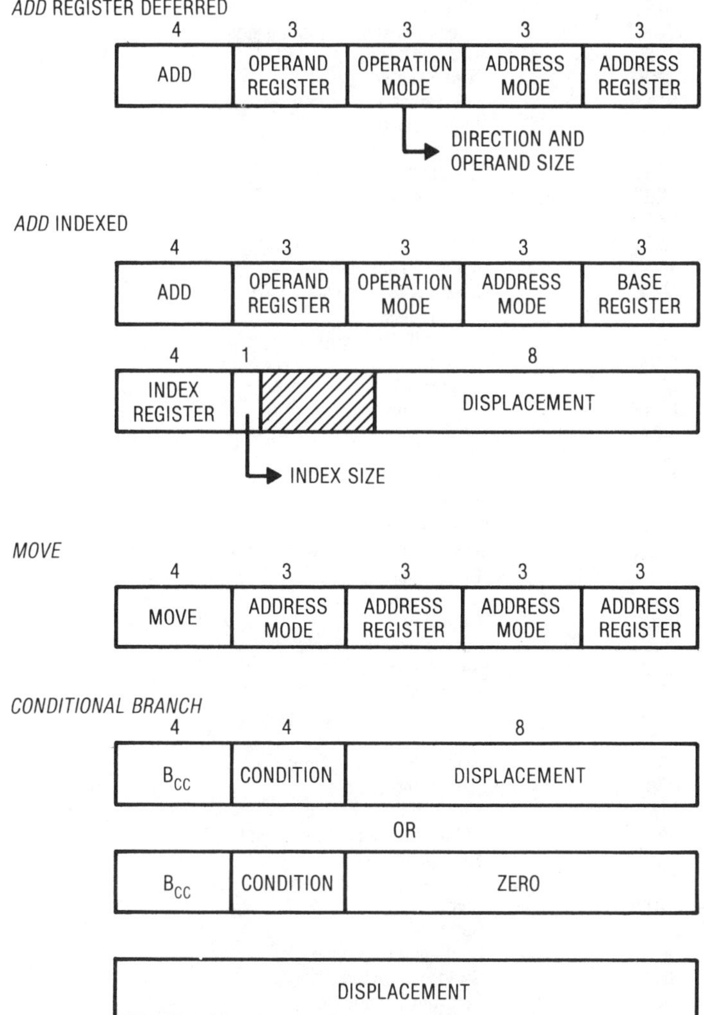

Figure 3. Typical MC68000 instruction formats.

Program counter indexed. The operand address is the current value of the program counter, plus the contents of the specified data or address register, plus an 8-bit signed displacement in the instruction.

Absolute. The operand address is in the instruction.

Immediate. The operand is in the instruction.

Bit addressing. A complete set of bit-manipulation instructions (SET, CLEAR, CHANGE, and TEST) is provided. For these instructions, an individual memory word is addressed using one of the above addressing modes. The individual bit to be manipulated is addressed by its bit number in that word. The bit specification is contained in the instruction or previously calculated in a data register. This mechanism allows bits to be addressed simply, without requiring the use of logical instructions and masks. For registers, all 32 bits are individually addressable.

In all cases, the addresses specified by the program can span the entire address space. No arbitrary segment sizes are imposed, and no separate segment numbers need be manipulated.

Address, like integer, is a fully supported data type. A complete set of address-manipulation operations (MOVE, COMPARE, INCREMENT, DECREMENT, ADD TO, SUBTRACT FROM) is implemented on the address registers. In addition, the LOAD EFFECTIVE ADDRESS instruction performs an arbitrary calculation and puts the result into a specified address register. This provides the programmer, in a single instruction, with the ability to precalculate addresses using any of the processor's addressing modes.

Because there are eight address registers, fewer memory accesses are required for loading and storing temporary address values, and addresses rarely need to be recalculated in different parts of the program. These features minimize the program time spent manipulating addresses, a common bottleneck in existing microprocessors. They also establish a degree of address-size independence;[7] the address-specification fields in instructions are most often only 6 bits, regardless of the fact that a large (32-bit) address is actually being specified.

Data manipulation. The 68000 supports a number of data types and supplies a complete set of operations for each type (Table 3 and Figure 3). In general, the addressing mode is independent of the data type. Also, in cases where it makes sense (integers, logicals, and addresses), the size of the operand may be specified independently of the operation. Operand sources may be either registers or addressed memory locations. The result may be stored either in the register or in the specified memory location. This class of "register-to-memory" operations reduces the number of register stores required to save results. Most operations can be specified to work memory-to-register, register-to-register, register-to-memory, immediate-to-register, or immediate-to-memory. The move instruction is more flexible, being a full two-address instruction. It can specify memory-to-memory move operations as well as the options listed above.

The 68000 data types and the operations that support them are:

Integer. The operations are ADD, SUBTRACT, MULTIPLY, DIVIDE, NEGATE, COMPARE, and ARITHMETIC SHIFT. Integers may be 1, 2, or 4 bytes. Shifts are multiple-bit shifts, either left or right, with shift count specified in the instruction or previously calculated in a data register, and indicate overflow as appropriate.

Multiprecision integer. ADD WITH EXTEND, SUBTRACT WITH EXTEND, NEGATE WITH EXTEND, UNSIGNED MULTIPLY, and UNSIGNED DIVIDE are the primitives supplied for easily implementing multiprecision integer arithmetic. Operands may be 1, 2, or 4 bytes, except for multiply and divide, which operate only on 2-byte quantities.

Logical. The operations are AND, OR, EXCLUSIVE OR, COMPLEMENT, COMPARE, SHIFT, and ROTATE (which allow multiple-position shifts and rotates, left or right, with or without extend bit). Logicals may be 1, 2, or 4 bytes.

Boolean. AND, OR, EXCLUSIVE OR, COMPLEMENT, IMPLICATION, and SET ACCORDING TO CONDITION CODES are provided. (SET ACCORDING TO CONDITION CODES is used to retrieve the logical value of any of the conditional tests that are available to the CONDITIONAL BRANCH instruction.) Boolean data are one-byte quantities.

Bit. The operations are SET, CLEAR, CHANGE, and TEST. Bits are individually addressable.

Decimal. ADD, SUBTRACT, NEGATE, and COMPARE are decimal operations. The decimal (BCD) instructions work on operands in memory (memory-to-memory) two digits (one byte) at a time. Combined with a looping instruction, the decimal instructions implement variable-length memory-to-memory decimal operations.

Character. Character instructions, MOVE and COMPARE, work on operands in memory (memory-to-memory).

Address. Address operations include INCREMENT (by 1, 2, or 4), DECREMENT (by 1, 2, or 4), ADD INTEGER, SUBTRACT INTEGER, COMPARE, and LOAD EFFECTIVE ADDRESS.

Real. Floating-point ADD, SUBTRACT, MULTIPLY, and DIVIDE are specified but not implemented in the first version.

String. STRING MOVE, STRING SEARCH, and TRANSLATE are specified but not implemented in the first version.

Program control. Program-control instructions include CONDITIONAL BRANCH (program counter relative), JUMP, JUMP TO SUBROUTINE, RETURN FROM SUBROUTINE, and RETURN FROM INTERRUPT, all of which are traditional instructions. Sixteen separate operating-system calls are specifiable with the TRAP instruction. Conditional traps, looping, and subroutine control are discussed below. The STOP instruction halts the processor, the RESET instruction reinitializes the system environment, and the MOVE instruction can manipulate the processor status word.

Privilege states. The 68000 processor can operate in user or supervisor state. In supervisor state, the entire instruction set is available. Indication of the current state is given to the external world so that, for instance, address translation can be inhibited when the processor is in supervisor state. In user state, certain instructions, such as STOP, RESET, and those that modify the status word, are not allowed; they cause a

Table 3.
MC6800 instruction set.

MNEMONIC	DESCRIPTION
ABCD	Add decimal with extend
ADD	Add
ADDX	Add with extend
AND	Logical and
ASL	Arithmetic shift left
ASR	Arithmetic shift right
BCC	Branch conditionally
BCHG	Bit test and change
BCLR	Bit test and clear
BRA	Branch always
BSET	Bit test and set
BSR	Branch to subroutine
BTST	Bit test
CHK	Check register against bounds
CLR	Clear operand
CMP	Arithmetic compare
DCNT	Decrement and branch non-zero
DIVS	Signed divide
DIVU	Unsigned divide
EOR	Exclusive or
EXG	Exchange registers
EXT	Signed extend
JMP	Jump
JSR	Jump to subroutine
LDM	Load multiple registers
LDQ	Load register quick
LEA	Load effective address
LINK	Link stack
LSL	Logical shift left
LSR	Logical shift right
MOVE	Move
MULS	Signed multiply
MULU	Unsigned multiply
NBCD	Negate decimal with extend
NEG	Two's complement
NEGX	Two's complement with extend
NOP	No operation
NOT	One's complement
OR	Logical or
PEA	Push effective address
RESET	Reset external devices
ROTL	Rotate left without extend
ROTR	Rotate right without extend
ROTXL	Rotate left with extend
ROTXR	Rotate right with extend
RTR	Return and restore
RTS	Return from subroutine
SBCD	Subtract decimal from extend
SCC	Set conditionally
STM	Store multiple registers
STOP	Stop
SUB	Subtract
SUBX	Subtract with extend
SWAP	Swap data register halves
TAS	Test and set operand
TRAP	Trap
TRAPV	Trap on overflow
TST	Test
UNLK	Unlink stack

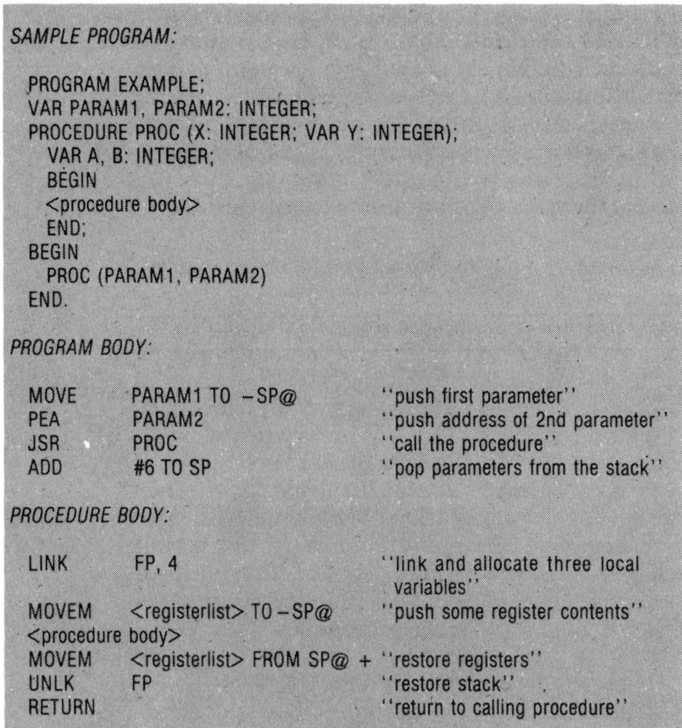

```
SAMPLE PROGRAM:

  PROGRAM EXAMPLE;
  VAR PARAM1, PARAM2: INTEGER;
  PROCEDURE PROC (X: INTEGER; VAR Y: INTEGER);
    VAR A, B: INTEGER;
    BEGIN
    <procedure body>
    END;
  BEGIN
    PROC (PARAM1, PARAM2)
  END.

PROGRAM BODY:

  MOVE      PARAM1 TO -SP@              ''push first parameter''
  PEA       PARAM2                      ''push address of 2nd parameter''
  JSR       PROC                        ''call the procedure''
  ADD       #6 TO SP                    ''pop parameters from the stack''

PROCEDURE BODY:

  LINK      FP, 4                       ''link and allocate three local
                                          variables''
  MOVEM     <registerlist> TO -SP@      ''push some register contents''
  <procedure body>
  MOVEM     <registerlist> FROM SP@ +   ''restore registers''
  UNLK      FP                          ''restore stack''
  RETURN                                ''return to calling procedure''
```

Figure 4. Sample Pascal program and equivalent 68000 code.

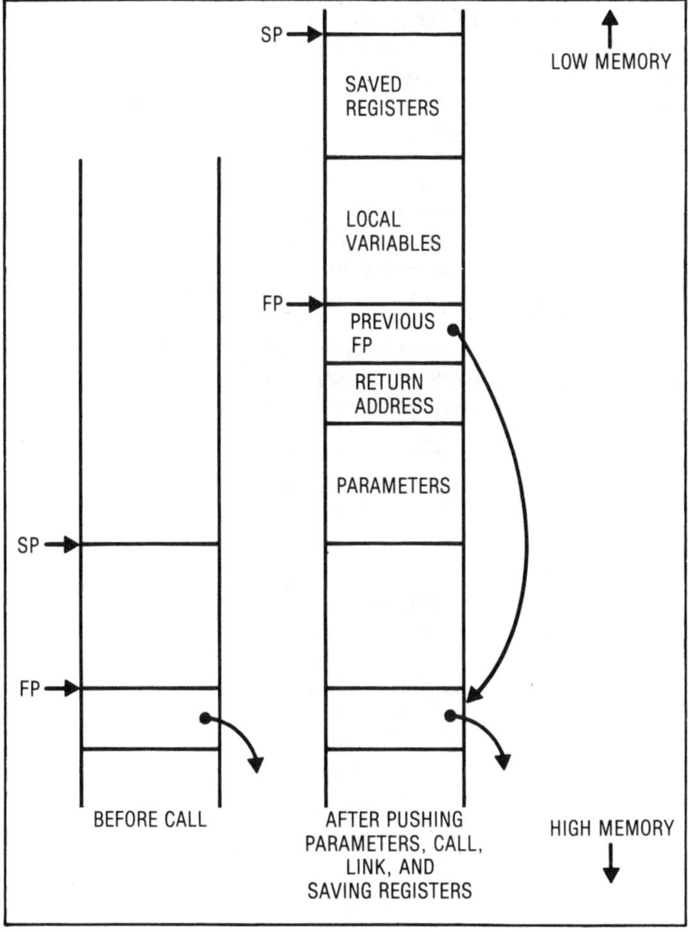

Figure 5. Stack activity on procedure call.

trap to supervisor state (by stacking the current program and status word and loading a new context from a pre-assigned trap vector). Illegal instructions, unimplemented instructions, interrupts, and traps (operating as system calls) all cause the processor to trap and switch to supervisor state. To ensure proper operation when returning to supervisor state, regardless of user-state activity, there are two stack-pointer registers—one active in user state, one in supervisor state. The user stack-pointer contents are available, by special instructions, to the supervisor-state program.

The 68000's user/system state distinction will allow a small operating-system kernel to provide fully protected virtual address spaces to any number of independent tasks or users.

Trapping on illegal and unimplemented instructions allows the operating system to provide a more functional virtual machine to user-state tasks. For instance, the operating system can transparently provide software implementation of any currently unimplemented instructions (such as floating-point or string manipulation) executed by a user-state task.

High-level-language support. A recent paper by Allison[8] suggests ways in which microprocessor architecture should be designed to support high-level languages. This method, followed by the 68000 designers, is to "examine . . . the runtime representation required for the class of languages to be implemented" and to "provide adequate instructions . . . to support the required runtime representation" and transformations on that representation "without extensive in-line computation."

The 68000 design supports high-level languages, at both compilation time and execution time, with a clean, consistent instruction set; with hardware implementation of commonly used functions (multiply, divide, and address calculation); and with a set of special-purpose instructions designed to manipulate the runtime environment of a high-level-language program. The language constructs aided by these special-purpose instructions include array accessing, limited-precision arithmetic, looping, Boolean-expression evaluation, and procedure calls.

Array accessing. The BOUNDS CHECK instruction compares a previously calculated array index (in a data register) against zero and a limit value addressed by the instruction. A trap occurs if the index is out of bounds for that array. This replaces a common sequence of instructions (at least four) with a single instruction.

Limited-precision arithmetic. The TRAP ON OVERFLOW instruction causes a trap if the preceding operation resulted in overflow. This allows efficient overflow testing to encourage proper checking of arithmetic results.

Looping. A restricted form of the FOR-loop construct is implemented in a single instruction that decrements a count and branches backward if the result is nonzero.

Boolean-expression evaluation. The CONDITIONAL SET instructions assign a true or false value to a Boolean variable on the same conditions that are used by the CONDITIONAL BRANCH instructions. These instructions help implement Boolean-expression evaluation by avoiding extra conditional branches, especially in the case (as with Pascal) where "short-circuited" evaluation may be undesirable because of possible side effects.

Procedure calls. The 68000 uses a stack—pointed to by one of the address registers, called the stack pointer—to build the nested environments of called procedures. Three instructions (plus an additional one for each parameter) implement a high-level-language procedure call (Figure 4). The entire call mechanism uses only the stack and is completely reentrant (Figure 5). These instructions are described in more detail below.

Push parameter values or addresses onto the stack. The MOVE instruction pushes a value onto the stack, and the PUSH EFFECTIVE ADDRESS (see LOAD EFFECTIVE ADDRESS explained earlier) pushes the result of an artitrary address calculation onto the stack for call by reference.

Call procedure. The JUMP TO SUBROUTINE instruction pushes the return address on the stack and jumps to the procedure entry point.

Establish new local environment. The LINK instruction does all of the following: saves the old contents of the frame pointer (an arbitrary address register) on the stack, points the frame pointer to the new top of stack, and subtracts the number of bytes of local storage required by the procedure from the stack pointer. This establishes local storage for the called procedure and a frame pointer (address register) for index addressing of local variables and parameters.

Save an arbitrary subset of the registers on the stack. The MOVE MULTIPLE REGISTERS instruction saves an arbitrary subset of the registers on the stack (or anywhere in memory) in a single instruction. The registers to be saved are indicated by setting the corresponding bits in a 16-bit field of the instruction.

A set of at most four instructions reverses the process for procedure return:

Reload saved registers. The MOVE MULTIPLE REGISTERS instruction is used here also.

Reestablish previous environment. The UNLINK instruction undoes the work of the LINK instruction.

Return from procedure. The RETURN instruction pops the return address from the stack and returns to the calling procedure.

Pop parameters from the stack. The ADD IMMEDIATE instruction used on the stack pointer pops any number of values off the stack.

The 68000 system architecture

A computer architecture specifies interactions between the processor and its environment by defining such things as interrupt structure, memory segmentation, bus interfaces, and input/output structure. The 68000 system architecture is designed to be as flexible as possible. For instance, I/O device registers are addressed as memory locations (memory-mapped I/O), as on other Motorola microprocessors. Memory-mapped I/O gives the programmer the flexibility and power of the entire instruction set for manipulating device-control and data registers. Since no additional instructions are required for I/O, the processor is simpler, and the instruction set is easier to remember. The I/O space is protected by the same memory-management facilities that are used to protect critical areas of memory.

The 68000 bus structure is also designed for simplicity, speed, and flexibilty. The address and data lines are separate; no multiplexing is needed. This avoids the need for any separate devices for demultiplexing, ensuring maximum performance for systems in which speed is important. The bus is asynchronous; transfers on the bus are controlled by accompanying handshake signals, so that no assumptions need be made about timing or system synchrony. The use of handshake signals allows devices and memories with large variations in response time to be used on the same processor bus. The processor waits an arbitrary amount of time until the accessed device or memory signals that the transfer is occurring.

A simple bus request/grant protocol is implemented on-chip so that processors and direct-memory-access devices can cooperatively share the system bus with no extra arbitration logic. Also, the chip has a bus-fault input pin that causes instruction execution to be terminated at any point and a trap to be taken if an illegal or faulty memory access is made. This facilitates memory protection.

The 68000 interrupt structure is like that of most minicomputers. Eight priority levels are implemented. Interrupts are vectored so that software has full control over the placement and execution of interrupt-handling routines. The current priority level of the processor is kept in its status word. Interrupts at or below the current priority are inhibited. Interrupts at higher levels may occur, so interrupt handling may be nested. When an enabled interrupt occurs, the processor sends an acknowledge signal. The interrupting device responds with a vector number. The vector number is used by the processor

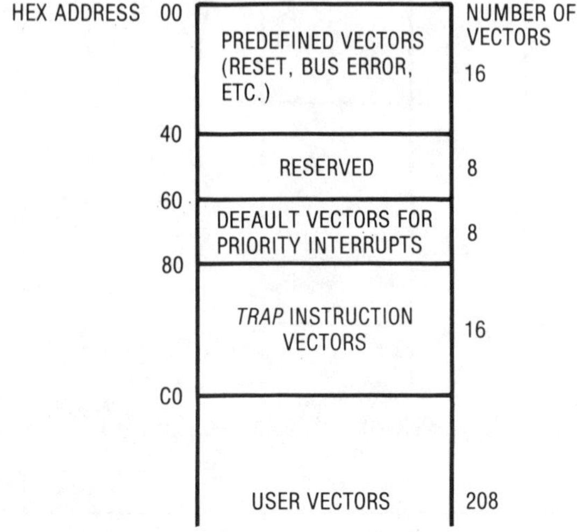

Figure 6. Trap and interrupt vector allocation.

to index into a table of interrupt vectors in low memory to find the appropriate entry point to the interrupt handler; there are 256 such vectors (Figure 6). Individual devices on the same priority level can be distinguished by different vector numbers, so no device polling is required. Software traps and exception conditions in the processor also transfer through the vector table; in these cases the vector numbers are assigned by the processor. The vector table is in main memory and therefore can be manipulated by the operating system as necessary. The processor implements a set of default vectors (one for each priority level) so that existing peripheral devices, not equipped to respond with vector numbers, can be used.

68000 systems can be configured with a processor directly connected to memory; the addresses generated by the program are then for the physical memory. This will suffice for many applications. More complex applications, especially those with multiple tasks or even multiple users, will require more sophisticated memory management. A separate single-chip device will be available to provide memory segmentation, address translation, and memory protection.

68000 design and implementation

The single-chip MC68000 microprocessor (Figure 7) is a partial implementation of the 68000 architecture. It implements as large a subset of the complete architecture as current technologies will allow. The relevant technological constraints are limitations on the number of pins and on circuit density. Addresses are limited to 24 bits by present-day packaging technology, which restricts the number of pins per package to 64. Similarly the data path to memory is only 16 bits wide. This is not an architectural limitation, but it does require that two memory accesses be made for each 32-bit datum.

Circuit density limits the number of instructions that can be implemented. One-eighth of the operation-code map is currently unimplemented. Some of this space is allocated in the architecture—for example, for floating-point and string operations. Some of the free space is currently unspecified and will be allocated for future architectural enhancement. All unimplemented instructions cause traps, so that software emulation is possible.

Future implementations of the architecture may expand upwards or shrink downwards in performance and functional capability. Technological advances will soon allow the full architecture to be implemented. As circuit densities improve further, new versions will be faster and smaller (and thus less expensive) and will consume less power. Increased circuit density will also allow the inclusion of on-chip memory and sophisticated speed-up techniques.

Today's state of the art in MOS LSI technology permits approximately one transistor per square mil

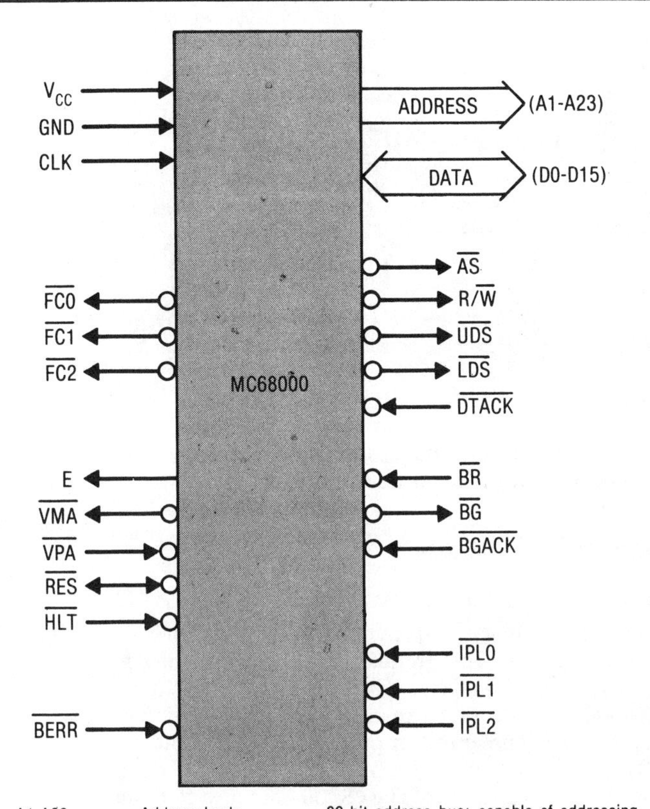

A1-A23	Address leads	23-bit address bus; capable of addressing 16,777,216 bytes in conjunction with UDS and LDS.
D0-D15	Data leads	16-bit data bus; transfers 8 or 16 bits of information.
AS	Address strobe	Indicates valid address and provides a bus lock for indivisible operations.
R/W	Read/write	Defines bus operation as read or write and controls external bus buffers.
UDS, LDS	Data strobes	Identifies the byte(s) to be operated on according to R/W and AS.
DTACK	Data transfer acknowledge	Allows the bus cycle to synchronize with slow devices or memories.
BR	Bus request	Input to the processor from a device requesting the bus.
BG	Bus grant	Output from the processor granting bus arbitration.
BGACK	Bus grant acknowledge	Confirmation signal from BG indicating a valid selection from the arbitration process.
IPL0, IPL1, IPL2	Interrupt priority level	Provides the priority level of the interrupting function to the processor.
FC0, FC1, FC2	Function code	Provides external devices with information about the current bus cycle and processor state.
CLK	Clock	Master TTL input clock to the processor.
RES	Reset	Provides reset (initialization) signal to the processor and peripheral devices.
HLT	Halt	Stops the processor and allows single stepping.
BERR	Bus error	Provides termination of a bus cycle if no response or an invalid response is received.
E	Enable	Enable clock for 6800 systems.
VPA	Valid peripheral address	Identifies addressed area as a 6800 compatible area.
VMA	Valid memory address	Indicates to 6800 family devices that a valid address is on the bus.
V_{CC}	+5 volt (2 pins)	—
GND	Ground (2 pins)	—

Figure 7. MC8000 pin identifications and definitions. The microprocessor is housed in a 64-pin package that allows the use of separate (non-multiplexed) address and data buses.

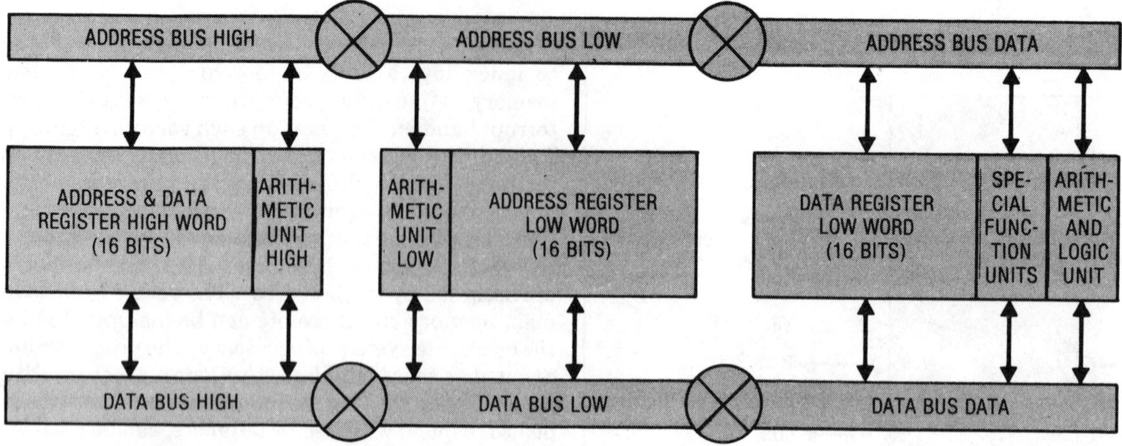

Figure 8. MC68000 execution unit configuration.

of circuit area and permits logic gates to be designed with a speed-to-power product of one picojoule. An advanced high-density *n*-channel silicon-gate MOS technology was selected for the design of the 68000. This technology supports three-micron device geometries and provides the designer with multiple MOS transistor threshold voltages. The technology allows the circuit designer to develop high-performance logic gates using minimum-size devices and to develop internal buffer circuits requiring little power.

The execution unit is a dual-bus structure that performs both address and data processing (Figure 8). The two buses are 16 bits wide, and each can be dynamically reconfigured into three independent sections as required by the microcode. Three independent arithmetic units are available to perform these calculations; also, special logic functions are provided to execute long shifts, priority encoding, and bit manipulation. Each of these units is connected to two internal buses and receives both input operands simultaneously from the registers. Each bus contains both the true and the complement logic values so that differential circuit design can be used for higher-speed operation. The execution unit directly interfaces to the external bus logic and buffers, but its operation is independent of the external timing requirements of the bus.

The control of the 68000 is implemented by microcode. The actual structure of the microprogrammed control structure is discussed in detail in another paper.[9] The microcontrol is implemented as a two-level structure. The first level contains sequences of microinstructions with short "vertical" format and complex branching capabilities. Microinstructions contain the addresses of nanoinstructions, wide "horizontal" control words, stored in the second level. The nanoinstructions directly control the execution unit. The use of microcode is motivated by the high design cost of new VLSI chips. The microcode's regularity of structure compared to combinatorial logic significantly decreases the design complexity. Microcode also permits some engineering decisions—for instance, details of specific instructions—to be delayed. In other words, once the micromachine architecture is determined, hardware implementation (circuit design) and firmware implementation (microprogramming) can be done in parallel.

Conclusion

The Motorola 68000 architecture combines advanced technology improvements with a better understanding of the architectural needs of microprocessor users and microprocessor applications. The 68000 is a step into an area previously occupied only by high-end minicomputers. It is a 32-bit architecture that supports many data types and data sizes. The advantages of the 68000 include a flexible addressing mechanism, a simple and effective instruction set that can be used to easily build complex operations, a multilevel vectored interrupt structure, and a fast, asynchronous, nonmultiplexed bus architecture. The 68000 architecture describes a family of microprocessors designed for the expanding high-end microcomputer market. ■

References

1. J. R. Rattner, "Microprocessor Architecture—Where Do We Go From Here," *COMPCON Spring 1977 Digest of Papers*, pp. 223-224.
2. F. P. Brooks, "An Overview of Microcomputer Architecture and Software," *Proc. EUROMICRO 1976*, North Holland, pp. 1-6.
3. C. G. Bell and W. D. Strecker, "Computer Structures: What Have We Learned From the PDP-11?," *Proc. 3rd Symposium on Computer Architecture*, 1976, pp. 1-14.
4. L. A. Levanthal and W. C. Walsh, "Addressing Considerations in Microprocessor Design," *COMPCON Spring 1977 Digest of Papers*, pp. 225-229.
5. B. L. Peuto and L. J. Shustek, "Current Issues in the Architecture of Microprocessors," *Computer*, Vol. 10, No. 2, Feb. 1977, pp. 20-25.
6. S. A. Ward, "Toward the Renaissance Computer Architecture," *MIDCON 1977 Preprints*, pp. 1-6.
7. P. E. Stanley, "Address Size Independence in a 16-bit Minicomputer," *Proc. 5th Symposium on Computer Architecture*, 1978, pp. 152-157.
8. D. R. Allison, "A Design Philosophy for Microcomputer Architectures," *Computer*, Vol. 10, No. 2, Feb. 1977, pp. 35-41.
9. E. P. Stritter and H. L. Tredennick, "Microprogrammed Implementation of a Single Chip Microprocessor," *Proc. 11th Annual Microprogramming Workshop*, Nov. 1978, pp. 8-16.

Section 4.4
Static RAMs

A High Performance Low Power 2048-Bit Memory Chip in MOSFET Technology and Its Application

ROLF REMSHARDT AND UTZ G. BAITINGER

Abstract—A 2048-bit read/write memory chip is described. It uses a modified 6-device memory cell in an n-channel MOSFET technology. To exploit the potential of the given MOSFET technology with respect to the cost/performance ratio and the power-delay product, special provisions are taken. The power is kept low by the gate driver concept as well as by clocked peripheral circuits. High performance is achieved with fast peripheral circuits, the delayed chip select concept, and a bipolar sense amplifier which also supplies the bit-line restore voltage.

Circuits are presented which successfully utilize the on-chip tracking to reduce the impact of device parameter tolerances on worst case power and performance.

It is shown how the memory chip is packaged on modules, cards, and boards to build up functional memory units.

I. Introduction

THE MODELS 115 and 125 of the IBM System/370, together with the memory extensions for the models 158 and 168, are the first IBM computers which use large monolithic memories in MOSFET technology for the main stores and for control stores. These memories have proven their feasibility and reliability in several thousand systems during the last three years.

The heart of these memories, which range from 64 kbytes (for the model 115) up to 8 Mbytes (for the model 168), is a 2048-bit array chip in MOSFET technology. Its nominal standby power dissipation is 20 mW; for a 200-ns cycle, the total power dissipation per chip is below 200 mW. The worst case access time on chip is 65 ns; typical values are in the range of 50 ns.

This paper presents the main features of this chip, the measures, how they were achieved, and gives a typical example of how the chip can be operated in a memory.

II. Assumptions and Design Objective

The design objective was to exploit the potential of a given MOSFET technology with respect to an optimum cost/performance ratio and a minimum power-delay product. In contrast to the prevailing p-channel technologies at that time [1], IBM had decided to take advantage of the favorable electric characteristics of an n-channel MOSFET technology. The gain in power-delay product, however, has to be paid with the need for a thin, well-controlled and clean gate dielectric.

The main features of the given MOSFET technology are the following.

1) n-channel, p-type substrate.
2) Enhancement type (achieved by substrate bias).
3) Gate-oxide thickness 700 Å.
4) Transconductance 32 $\mu A/V^2$.
5) Threshold voltage 0.3 · · · 1.0 V.
6) 5-μm minimum mask dimensions.
7) Junction and gate capacitances are kept low by choice of a sufficiently high substrate bias of −3.0 V.

Furthermore, a hybrid addressing and sensing system has been assumed: the MOSFET array chip is driven by bipolar interface drivers (for the address signals), and bipolar sense amplifiers/bit drivers (for the read/write operations).

The main problems of this MOSFET chip design are related to the large spread of the threshold voltage, the deviations of bias voltages from chip to chip within a hybrid sensing system, and the variations of external signal pulses ("skews") on the memory card. The solution largely takes advantage of the on-chip tracking of device parameters. This will be discussed in detail below.

III. Array Chip Performance

In order to exploit the performance potential of the given MOSFET technology, a dc stable flip-flop type memory cell ("6-device cell") is chosen [2], [3] which avoids time consuming refresh cycles. Fig. 1 shows the addressing and sensing scheme for the memory cell. Only address signals are applied to the array chip.

1) One decoded chip select signal *CS*.
2) A coded word address (five signal pulses).
3) A coded bit address (five signal pulses).
4) Two decoded array select signals *Y*1 and *Y*2.

All auxiliary signals (e.g., restore pulse *R*, decoder clock signal *DCS*) are generated on-chip, thus avoiding external signals and their skews.

The chip access time t_{ACC} consists of two parts (see Fig. 2): the addressing delay t_A until *DCS* starts rising and the sensing delay t_S until the sense current I_S has reached 20 μA. Both are kept short by use of the tracking of device parameters.

A. Addressing Delay

The addressing mechanism is as follows (see Figs. 1 and 2). Word and bit addresses have to be valid before chip select *CS* becomes active. The word and the bit phase splitters, which generate trues and complements out of the address signals, are clocked by chip select *CS*. The decoders have to be clocked by a delayed chip select pulse *DCS* which is generated on-chip

Manuscript received January 26, 1976; revised February 27, 1976.

The authors are with the IBM Laboratories, Boebiingen, West Germany.

Reprinted from *IEEE J. Solid-State Circuits*, vol. SC–11, pp. 352–359, June 1976.

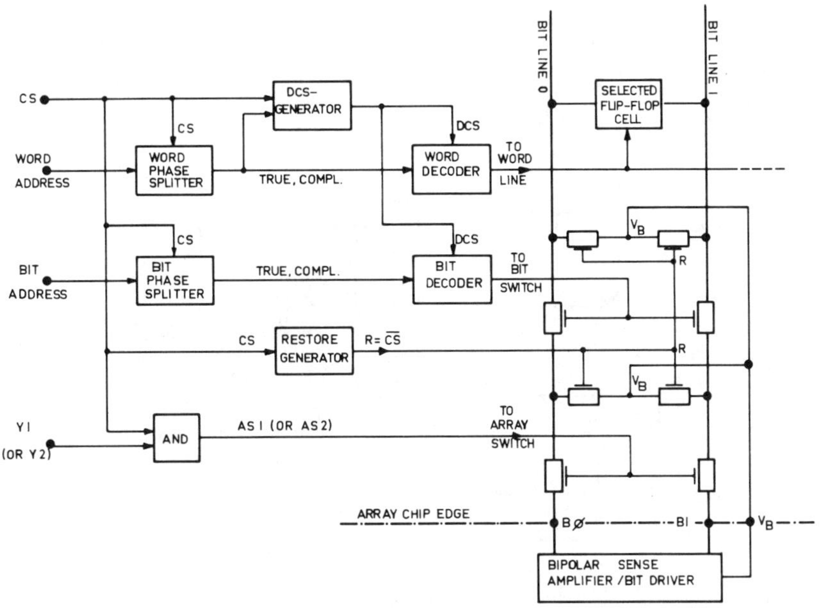

Fig. 1. Addressing and sensing scheme of the array chip. *CS*–chip select; *R*–restore pulse; *DCS*–delayed chip select; *Y*1–array select.

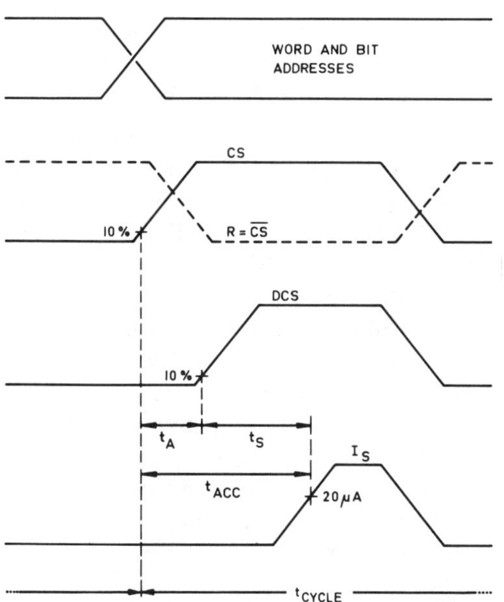

Fig. 2. Simplified timing diagram of a read operation. I_S–sense current; t_{ACC}–chip access time; t_A–addressing delay; t_S–sensing delay.

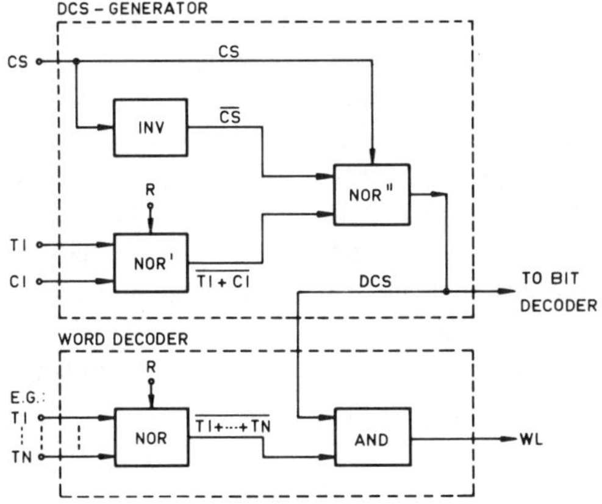

Fig. 3. Decoder and delayed chip select block diagram. *CS*–chip select; *DCS*–delayed chip select; *WL*–selected wordline; *T*1, *C*1–true/complement output of one phase splitter; *T*1 ⋯ *TN*–personalization of decoder; *R*–restore pulse.

by the *DCS* generator. The required delay is equal to the sum of the phase splitter delay plus the decoder delay in order to avoid unwanted selections. Fig. 3 shows this in more detail.

Circuit NOR′ gets the true as well as the complement (*T*1 and *C*1) out of one phase splitter and OR's them. Thus, the phase splitter delay is already included. *T*1 or *C*1 will switch on the decoder clock signal *DCS* after the delay of circuit NOR′. Circuit NOR″ is very fast, but circuit NOR′ simulates the slow circuit NOR within the decoder and therefore the delays of both are tracking. Thus, *DCS* opens the AND gate to the selected wordline *WL* at the same instant when the NOR outputs of the decoders become valid. *DCS* is switched off by $\overline{CS}$, which is generated by an inverter circuit INV and fed into circuit NOR″. Circuit NOR″ is clocked by *CS* to avoid power dissipation during standby.

By these measures, the delay of *DCS* tracks with the phase splitter delay and the decoder delay as required. Thus, a shorter addressing delay is reached for most of the array chips than would be the case with an externally delayed signal pulse *DCS* which has to wait for the worst case array chip.

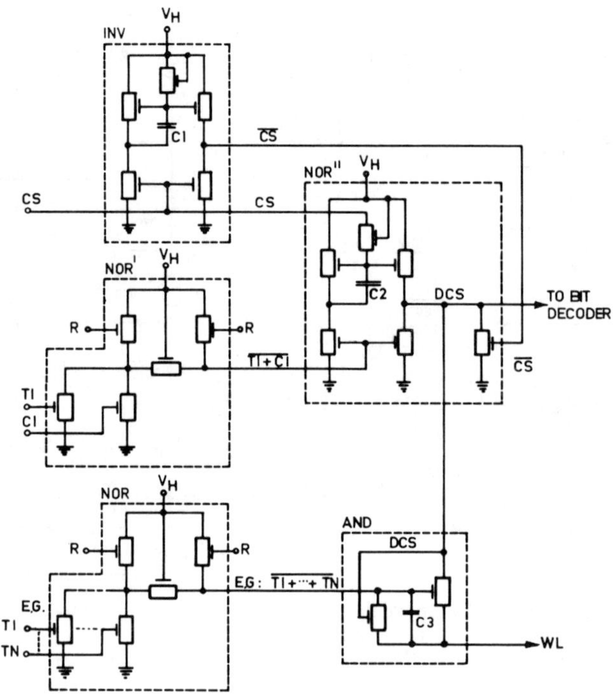

Fig. 4. Typical ac-peripheral circuits: the decoder and delayed chip select circuits.

Fig. 4 shows the corresponding circuits. Their concept is representative for all the on-chip peripheral circuits. The extensive use of feedback capacitors [4] can be seen ($C1$, $C2$, $C3$), as well as the use of fast inverter circuits where the feedback capacitor is not attached to the highly capacitive output, but to a duplication of it with low parasitic capacitance.

During standby, all the feedback and stray capacitors within the decoders are charged. This is controlled by a restore pulse R, which logically is the complement of chip select CS and which is also generated on-chip by the restore generator. This is done since discharging of unselected feedback capacitors during selection is less time consuming than charging of the selected ones.

B. Sensing Delay

The sensing mechanism is as follows (see Figs. 1 and 2). During standby, all the bit lines across the array chip, i.e., the bit line pairs between the cells and the bit switches, as well as between the bit switches and the array switches, are biased to the voltage V_B. This is also controlled by the restore pulse R. The voltage V_B is generated on the bipolar sense amplifier/bit driver chip and fed into the array chip. Both chips are mounted on different modules, but on the same memory card. The tracking of V_B results in a homogeneous bias of the bit lines not only on the array chip, but also on the modules, on the memory card, and on the sense amplifier/bit driver chip. Thus, compensating currents are avoided when the cell is sensed and the differential sense current I_S is not affected by spikes into the wrong direction. This leads to a shorter worst case sensing delay. More details about the read/write operations will be given in Section VI-B.

IV. Array Chip Power Dissipation

The power dissipation of the array chip is kept low by the use of clocked on-chip peripheral circuits which dissipate only ac power (refer to Fig. 4). Thus, the total chip power dissipation is determined by the ac power of the on-chip peripheral circuits and the dc power of the memory cells.

A dc stable, flip-flop type memory cell (6-device cell) has been chosen for performance reasons. Its dc power dissipation does not contribute to the power-delay product, i.e., an increase of this dc power would not decrease the access time. Therefore, it can be kept as low as the cell stability allows it without performance impact. But both the power dissipation and the cell stability are a function of threshold voltage which suffers from a large spread. Therefore, an on-chip gate voltage driver [5] is provided for the memory cell which will be discussed below.

A. Memory Cell Stability

The circuits of the memory cell and the gate driver are shown in Fig. 5. Let us assume that cell transistor $T1$ is off, whereas cell transistor $T2$ is on. A sufficiently high gate voltage V_G is required to maintain the cell stability:

$$V_G = V_{TH2} + \Delta V_2 + V_{TH3} + \Delta V_3$$
$$= V_{TH2} + V_{TH3} + \Delta V. \qquad (1)$$

$\Delta V \equiv \Delta V_2 + \Delta V_3$ is required for current flows through $T2$ and $T3$. Then $T3$ will compensate for the leakage current of the stray capacitance at the gate node of $T2$, and $T2$ will be kept on.

The following voltage V'_G is generated by the gate voltage driver:

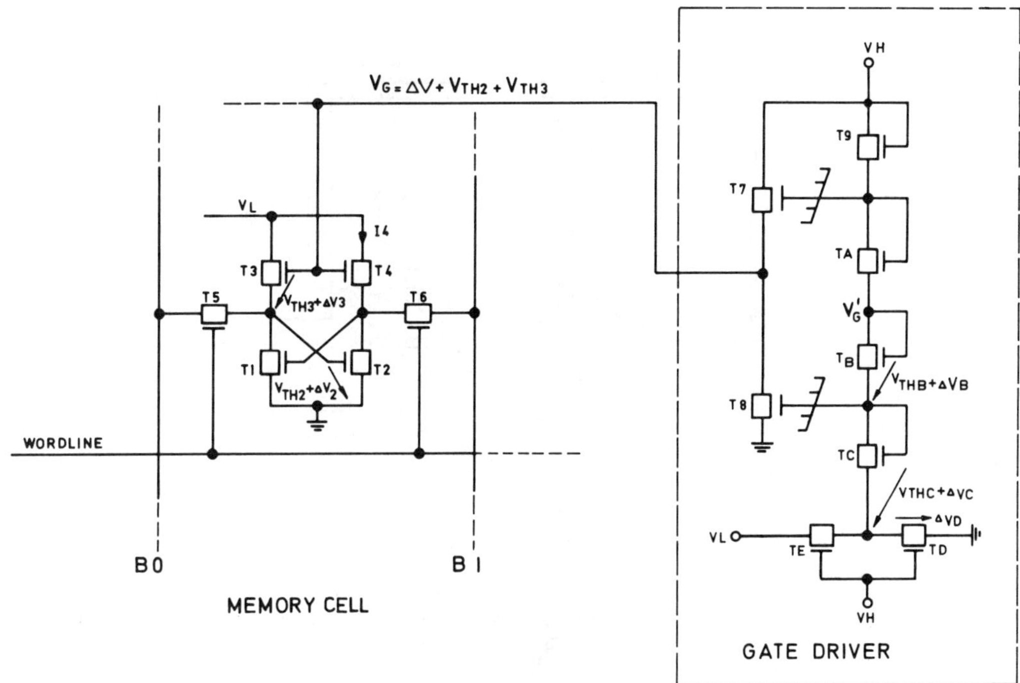

Fig. 5. DC circuits on the chip: gate voltage driver and memory cell.

$$V'_G = V_{THB} + \Delta V_B + V_{THC} + \Delta V_C + \Delta V_D$$
$$= V_{THB} + V_{THC} + \Delta V. \tag{2}$$

We set $\Delta V \equiv \Delta V_B + \Delta V_C + \Delta V_D = \Delta V_2 + \Delta V_3$ by appropriate dimensioning of the driver circuit.

By comparison of (1) and (2) we see that the driver circuit generates the required gate voltage even for a large threshold voltage spread if driver device TC simulates the cell device $T2$, and device TB simulates device $T3$. This is achieved by analogous layouts for the corresponding devices. Then, the gate voltage for the cell's load devices $T3$ and $T4$ will track with the threshold voltage and cell stability is guaranteed. The source followers $T7$-$T8$ are required to drive the large capacitance of the load device gates at power-on.

B. DC Power per Cell

If cell device $T2$ is on, most of the dc power is dissipated within load device $T4$:

$$P_{dc} \approx I_4 V_L$$
$$\approx (V_G - V_{TH4} - V_L/2)\, V_L^2 \gamma_m W_4/L_4$$
$$\sim (V_G - V_{TH4} - V_L/2). \tag{3}$$

Conventionally, a constant power supply V_G would be designed according to (1) for maximum threshold voltages to guarantee cell stability. According to (3), a chip with maximum threshold voltage V_{TH4} dissipates minimum power. But the power dissipation would significantly increase for a chip with low threshold voltage.

In our case, however, V_G tracks with threshold voltage. Therefore, we get from (1) and (3):

$$P_{dc} \sim \Delta V + V_{TH2} + V_{TH3} - V_{TH4} - V_L/2$$
$$\sim \Delta V + V_{TH2} - V_L/2. \tag{4}$$

For a chip with maximum threshold voltage the power dissipation will be equal to the minimum value in the conventional case. If the threshold voltage (i.e., V_{TH2}) assumes low values, the power dissipation will further be decreased according to (4). Thus, the chip's dc power will always be below the minimum values of a conventional design with constant external gate voltage V_G.

Furthermore, the additional power supply V_L can be kept as low as the cell stability allows it. For $V_L = 2.0$ V, the nominal dc power dissipation per cell is below 10 μW.

V. Bit Density per Chip

Since costs are directly related to the bit productivity, we have to look for a bit density on the chip which yields the maximum number of good bits per wafer.

One design point is the memory cell area, which results from the utilized memory cell (6-device cell) and the given layout ground rules with 5-μm minimum mask dimensions. The memory cell layout is shown in Fig. 6. Its area is 2.0 × 3.1 square mils (4000 μm^2). Another design point is the given wafer diameter of 2.25 in. The following relations apply:

bit productivity = bits per wafer × yield
bits per wafer = bits per chip × chips per wafer.

The bits per chip can be increased with increasing chip size. But the number of chips per wafer decreases with increasing chip area. Thus, the bits per wafer reach a maximum value for a certain chip size. The yield, however, is not only a function of the chip size, but it is also determined by the memory cell

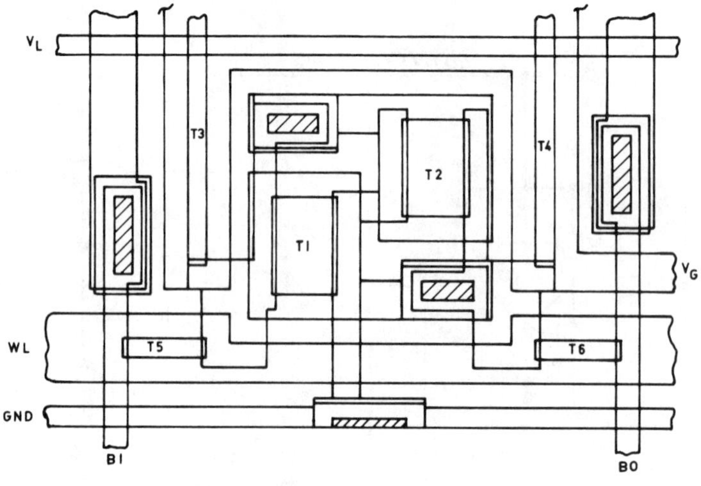

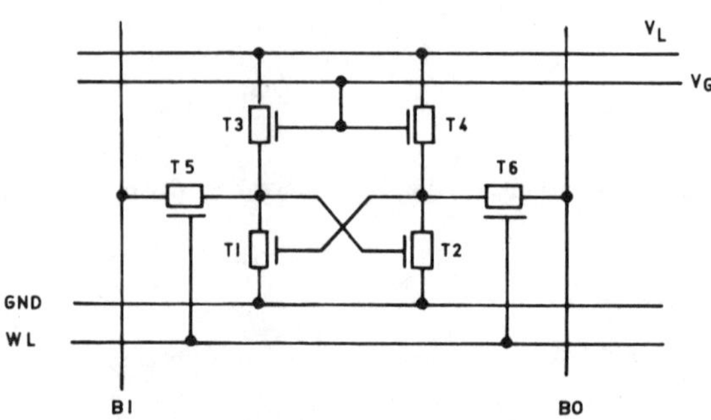

Fig. 6. Layout of the memory cell.

layout, since the memory matrix covers most of the array chip area. Yield has further to be investigated by considering the learning curve of the manufacturing line.

At the time of these investigations, a chip with 2 kbits offered the highest bit productivity for the estimated lifetime of this product. Today, the optimum productivity would rather be with a 4-kbit or 8-kbit chip. In 1972, however, a density of 2 kbits per chip was quite attractive in comparison to the state of the art at that time [8].

To further improve the bit productivity, especially in the early stage of production, the chip has been divided into two identical array halves of 1 kbit each. This allows a built-in half good capability if only one array half is powered. (For more details see Section VI-A.)

VI. Chip Description

A. Chip Characteristics

The chip is organized 2048 × 1 bit. It consists of two 1024-bit array halves. One array half has an area of about 100 × 64 square mils. The total chip size including decoders, other peripheral circuits, and pads is 153 × 178 square mils or 3.88 × 4.52 mm^2 after dicing.

The chip is designed to be operated in a high performance as well as in a low or cost performance mode. Only one power supply has to be changed. The supply voltage for the peripheral circuits V_H is 9.5 V for the high performance and 8.5 V for the cost performance application. The high voltage V_H contributes to the chip performance especially in the peripheral circuitry, whereas the low voltage V_L determines the standby power dissipation of 20 mW. V_L is 2.0 V and the substrate bias voltage V_N is −3.0 V for both modes.

The total power for a selected chip is 120 mW nominal for the cost performance and 150 mW for the high performance application assuming a 200-ns cycle. The maximum power for a selected chip is 200 mW.

The access time of the chip is defined from 10 percent of the rising chip select pulse *CS* to the point in time when the read current I_S out of the sense amplifier has reached a threshold of 20 μA (see timing diagram, Fig. 2). The worst case access time is 75 ns for the cost performance and 65 ns for the high performance mode. Typical measured values are 60 and 50 ns, respectively.

The minimum cycle time is defined from one selection of the chip to the next possible selection. Within this time, a read or a write as well as the necessary restore operation have to be completed (see Fig. 2). The minimum cycle time is 200 ns for the cost performance and 170 ns for the high performance mode.

The chip has a built-in half good capability. Both array halves are supplied by separate power pads. Only the good half will then be powered.

The chip is very flexible with respect to timing requirements.

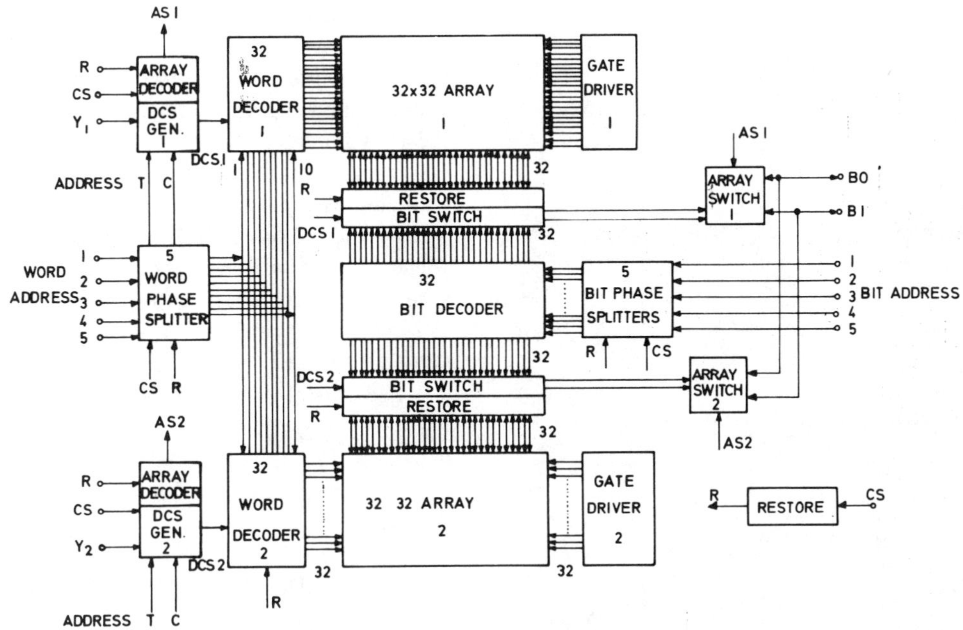

Fig. 7. Block diagram of the chip.

Only the chip select pulse *CS* is a timed pulse. All other address and selection pulses have no specific timing conditions.

B. Block Diagram

The block diagram of the chip is shown in Fig. 7. The two array sections have 32 word lines and 32 pairs of bit lines each. Each half has its own word decoders, whereas the bit decoders are common for both parts. Each section has its own gate voltage driver, delayed chip select generator, and array decoder. The word and the bit phase splitters are common to both.

In order to select a cell, five word and five bit address signals have to be applied. As soon as they are valid, the *CS* pulse may rise and the chip is selected. *CS* drives the phase splitters which generate buffered and inverted address signals. The outputs of five phase splitters supply 2×32 word decoders, whereas the other five phase splitters supply the 32 bit decoders.

The *CS* pulse is delayed in the delayed chip select generators. The outputs of the *DCS* generators (*DCS*1 and *DCS*2) power the outputs of the selected bit and word decoders and drive one word line and one pair of bit-line switches in each array half. Two corresponding cells are therefore selected in each array section.

Since the chip has a one-bit organization, the array decoder has to distinguish between the two cells. It generates the internal array select pulses (*AS*1 and *AS*2) as an AND function of the already decoded address lines *Y*1 or *Y*2, respectively, and *CS*. *AS*1 and *AS*2 control the array switches which connect the appropriate bit-line pair to the output pads *B*0 and *B*1.

After this selection part, the chip is prepared for any read or write operation. The input/output pads *B*0 and *B*1 of the chip are connected to a bipolar sense amplifier/bit driver on the memory card. During a read operation, the sense amplifier maintains the positive voltage V_B at both pads *B*0 and *B*1. Then, different amounts of current flow from these two pads via the bit lines into the selected cell. The current difference between the *B*0 and *B*1 line is the desired information which will be sensed by the sense amplifier.

During a write operation, one bit line remains positive, whereas the other one is pulled down to ground potential by the bipolar bit driver circuit. After some nanoseconds, the cell has changed its state and the lower bit line will be charged up again to standby potential by the bit driver. The restore generator and its function have already been mentioned in Section III.

C. Chip Microphotograph

A microphotograph of the 2-kbit chip is shown in Fig. 8. The two 1-kbit array sections can be seen together with the common bit decoders in between. The word decoders are visible on the left side of each array half. The cross-shaped structures in each array are metal lines for the $V_L = 2.0$ V supply voltage to the memory cells, which is partly supplied by diffused lines across the array. Phase splitters and generators for auxiliary pulses and for the load device gate voltage of the memory cells are located at the chip edge between pads.

VII. Array Module

The first packaging level is the module. A half-inch ceramic substrate can carry two chips. An 8192-bit storage module, therefore, contains 4 chips on two stacked ceramic substrates. Fig. 9 shows a photograph of the upper and lower decks, two stacked substrates, and the encapsulated module [6].

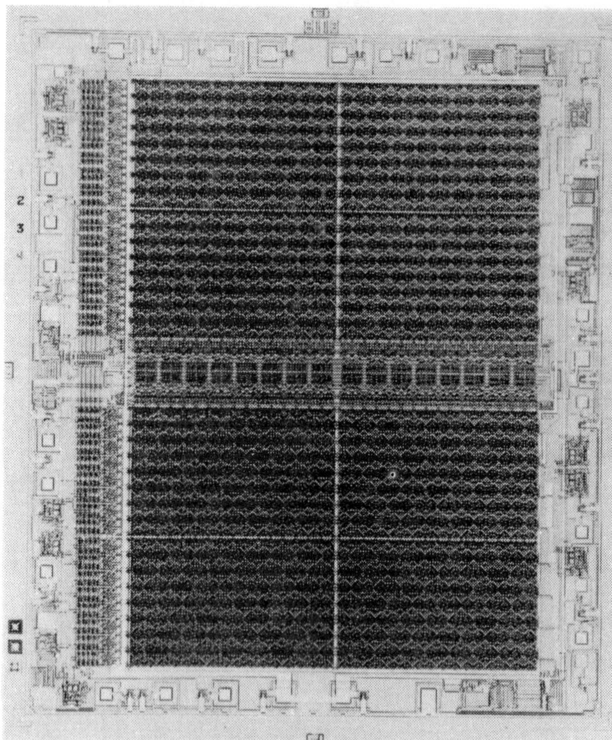

Fig. 8. Microphotograph of the chip.

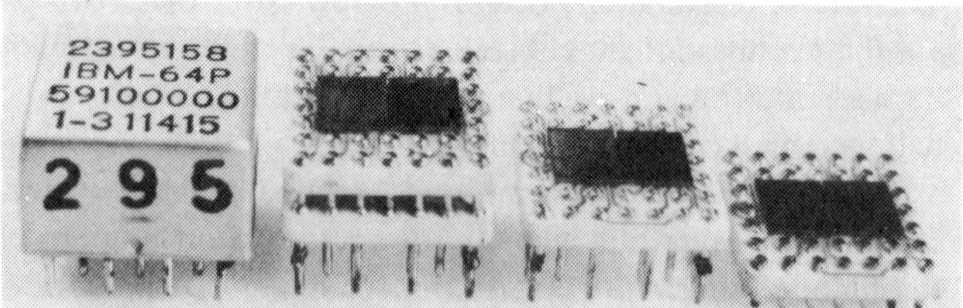

Fig. 9. Photograph of an 8K × 1 module.

One chip per module can be selected by activating one of the four *CS* inputs. All address lines are common for all four chips and all outputs are dotted.

VIII. Memory Card

MOSFET memories with a high performance objective have to use the hybrid memory card approach. MOSFET modules are used to store the information, whereas bipolar support modules are used to drive and to sense the MOSFET storage modules.

A photograph of a 256-kbit card which actually stores 262.144 bits is shown in Fig. 10. It carries 32 array modules (8192 × 1 bit each), four bipolar interface driver modules for the address signals, four bipolar sense amplifier/bit driver modules, and four logic modules. The organization of the 115 × 85 mm^2 large organic card is 32k × 8 bits [7].

The bipolar interface driver circuits are used to convert the logic levels of about half a volt swing into about 8-V swings required by the MOSFET array modules. They have to drive large capacitive loads within short rise times.

The bipolar sense amplifier/bit driver circuits are used to sense the low differential read current of the MOSFET chip, detect the information, and convert it into said logic levels of about half a volt. They are also used to write information into the array modules.

The logic modules are necessary to generate already decoded chip address input signals such as chip select *CS* and array select $Y1$ and $Y2$ out of high order address signals.

The 32k × 8 bit card has a typical performance of 165 ns access/280 ns cycle time with cost performance power supplies (V_H = 8.5 V, V_L = 2.0 V, V_N = -3.0 V) and a power of 8.5 W (selected mode).

A 128-kbit high performance card (V_H = 9.5 V, V_L = 2.0 V, V_N = -3.0 V), which has been built, offers a typical performance of 115 ns access/200 ns cycle and a power dissipation below 10 W. Both card data are without error correction and detection.

IX. Functional Memory Unit

Thirty-six memory cards which store approximately 1 Mbyte can be placed on one memory board. Six boards (four memory boards and two control logic boards) are packed into one frame of a 4-Mbyte memory which has a mechanical size of about 1 × 1 × 0.3 m^3.

It might be interesting to mention that the bit density of approximately 3 × 10^5 bits/cm^3 on the chip level reduces to about 150 bits/cm^3 on the frame level (including control logic, blowers, etc.). This shows that the present packaging technology is by no means exploiting the density potential of the silicon chip technology.

X. Summary and Outlook

A 2048-bit read/write memory chip has been described. It uses a modified 6-device memory cell in an n-channel MOSFET technology. To exploit the potential of the given MOSFET technology with respect to the cost/performance ratio and the power-delay product, special provisions were taken.

The power was kept low by the gate driver concept as well as by clocked peripheral circuits. High performance was achieved with fast peripheral circuits, the delayed chip select concept, and a bipolar sense amplifier which also supplies the bit-line restore voltage. Circuits have been presented which successfully utilize the on-chip tracking to reduce the impact of device parameter tolerances on worst case power and performance. The high reliability of this chip has mainly been achieved by an extensive computer analysis of the on-chip circuits, together with careful layout studies. This analysis took not only the absolute values and tolerances of all important device parameters into account, but of all parasitic devices as well. These data were the result of a statistical evaluation of device measurements over a long period of time. It has been shown how the memory chip is packaged on modules, cards, and boards to build up functional memory units.

When the design was started, the goal was to come up with a chip which offered some real improvements in comparison to available products within the company and on the open market. This goal, to be better with respect to performance,

Fig. 10. Photograph of a 32K × 8 memory card.

power, and density, has been successfully achieved. Even if we look at the present market or at [8], which gives a comprehensive overview on available chips, one can easily see that this design is still attractive from a performance and power point of view. The density, of course, would be considerably higher if the design would have been started this year.

Acknowledgment

The MOSFET memory chip described in this paper has been designed in the IBM Laboratories, Boeblingen, West Germany. The first engineering hardware has also been processed in the Boeblingen pilotline. The success of this chip design was only possible by the close cooperation between a team of circuit and device designers in the laboratories and the pilotline engineers in the IBM Manufacturing Locations, Sindelfingen, West Germany, and Burlington, VT, USA.

References

[1] G. Cheroff, D. L. Critchlow, R. H. Dennard, and L. M. Terman, "IGFET circuit performance–n-channel versus p-channel," *IEEE J. Solid-State Circuits*, vol. SC-4, pp. 267–271, Oct. 1969.

[2] J. S. Schmidt, "Integrated MOS random-access memory," *Solid-State Design*, pp. 21–25, 1965.

[3] L. M. Terman, "MOSFET memory circuits," *Proc. IEEE*, vol. 59, no. 7, July 1971.

[4] R. W. Polkinghorn *et al.*, "FET driver using capacitor feedback," U.S. Patent 3.506.851, 1970.

[5] W. O. Haug *et al.*, "Halbleiter-Schaltungs-Anordnung," Offenlegungsschrift 2.232.274, Deutsches Patentamt, 1974.

[6] C. A. Harper, *Handbook of Thick Film Hybrid Microelectronics*. New York: McGraw Hill, 1974, p. 996.

[7] W. K. Liebmann, "Monolithic memories in IBM Systems/370-135 and 145," Czechoslovak Scientific and Technical Society, Pisek, Czechoslovakia, Apr. 1972.

[8] R. W. Mitterer, "A review on random access MOS memories," invited paper presented at the European Solid-State Circuits Conf., Canterbury, England, 1975.

A High Performance 4K Static RAM Fabricated with an Advanced MOS Technology

Richard D. Pashley, William H. Owen III, Kim R. Kokkonen, Robert M. Jecmen, Anne V. Ebel, C. Norman Ahlquist and Peter Schoen

Intel Corp.

Santa Clara, CA

RECENT TECHNOLOGICAL advances have allowed N-channel MOS designs to achieve bipolar performance at MOS power levels[1,2]. Using advanced MOS technology, a 5-V, 4096-bit static RAM has been designed with a typical access time and power dissipation of 45ns and 500mW, respectively. The memory is fully static and offers a 40mW powerdown mode.

The high performance of the MOS memory was achieved by combining MOS device scaling[1] with on chip substrate bias generation[2]. By reducing the physical parameters of the MOS device by a fixed scaling factor, circuit density and performance were increased while decreasing active circuit power. The advanced technology uses polysilicon gate lengths under 4μ and a gate oxide thickness less than 1000Å. Shallow junctions ($<1\mu$) are obtained by using arsenic as the source-drain diffusant. In addition, oxide isolation and depletion load processing are employed to improve further circuit performance and density. Substrate bias is used to reduce device body effect and parasitic junction capacitance. The back bias voltage is generated on board the memory to eliminate the requirement for an additional pin and power supply. The technology figure of merit, the speed-power product, was measured to be 1pJ using an 11-stage ring oscillator with stage fanout of 3. For comparison conventional 6μ gate N-channel MOS has a speed-power-product of 4pJ.

A photomicrograph of the 4096-bit MOS RAM is shown in Figure 1. The memory is organized as a 4096 x 1 bit RAM and fits in a standard 18 pin package. The die size measures 25,004 mils^2. All pins are TTL compatible and the RAM operates from a single 5V supply. The memory is fully static and requires no clocks or internal refreshing; i.e., a multiple read operation can occur during a single chip enable cycle. As a result of using simple static circuitry in the periphery, over 60% of the chip area is memory array.

Like its forerunners, the MOS RAM uses the basic 6-transistor cross-coupled flip-flop as its memory element. Layout area is 3.75 square mils. Internally, the cell uses depletion load transistors to obtain full supply voltage while maintaining a typical cell current of 1μA.

The schematic of the cell, column and output sense circuitry is illustrated in Figure 2. The low diffusion capacitance allows the memory cell to drive the output sense amplifier directly, without the aid of a column sense amplifier. The output sense circuit is a simple differential amplifier with dc feedback to provide for process and temperature compensation.

The powerdown mode is controlled by chip enable. During powerdown ($\overline{CE}$ high), the memory array is completely deselected and the column and I/O buss is reset to a threshold below supply voltage. By balancing the internal circuitry during powerdown, it is possible to overcome the additional chip enable powerup delay and obtain a powerup access time equal to the address access time; Figure 3.

Typically, the RAM accesses in 45ns and has an active power dissipation of 500mW. Powerup does not display current spikes typical of dynamic circuitry and powerdown takes less than 30ns. A summary of the device characteristics is presented in Table 1.

The standby power dissipation is independent of temperature and supply voltage. In Figure 4, the chip access time and power dissipation are plotted as a function of temperature. The 7mA standby current is divided among the memory array (80%), the substrate bias generator (10%), and the chip enable buffer (10%).

In summary, an advanced technology based on MOS device scaling has yielded a 158 mil square 4K static RAM. A nominal 45ns memory access and 500mW power dissipation were observed and a 40mW powerdown mode was attained without an access time penalty.

DC Characteristics	
Supply voltage	5V
Active power dissipation	500mW
Standby power dissipation	35mW
I/O levels	TTL
Output sink current (Vo = 0.45V)	25mA
Output source current (Vo = 2.4V)	15mA
AC Characteristics	
Address access time	45ns
Chip select access time	45ns
Powerdown time	30ns
Read cycle time	45ns
Write cycle time	30ns
Write pulse width	7ns

TABLE 1—Summary of the device characteristics.

[1] Dennard, R.H., et al., "Design of Ion-Implanted MOSFET's with Very Small Physical Dimensions", *IEEE J. of Solid State Circuits*, p. 31-37; Oct., 1974.

[2] Pashley, R.D. and McCormick, G.A., "A 70ns 1K MOS RAM", *ISSCC Digest of Technical Papers*, p. 138-139; Feb., 1976.

Reprinted from *IEEE Int. Solid State Circuits Conf.*, pp. 22–23 and p. 231, 1977.

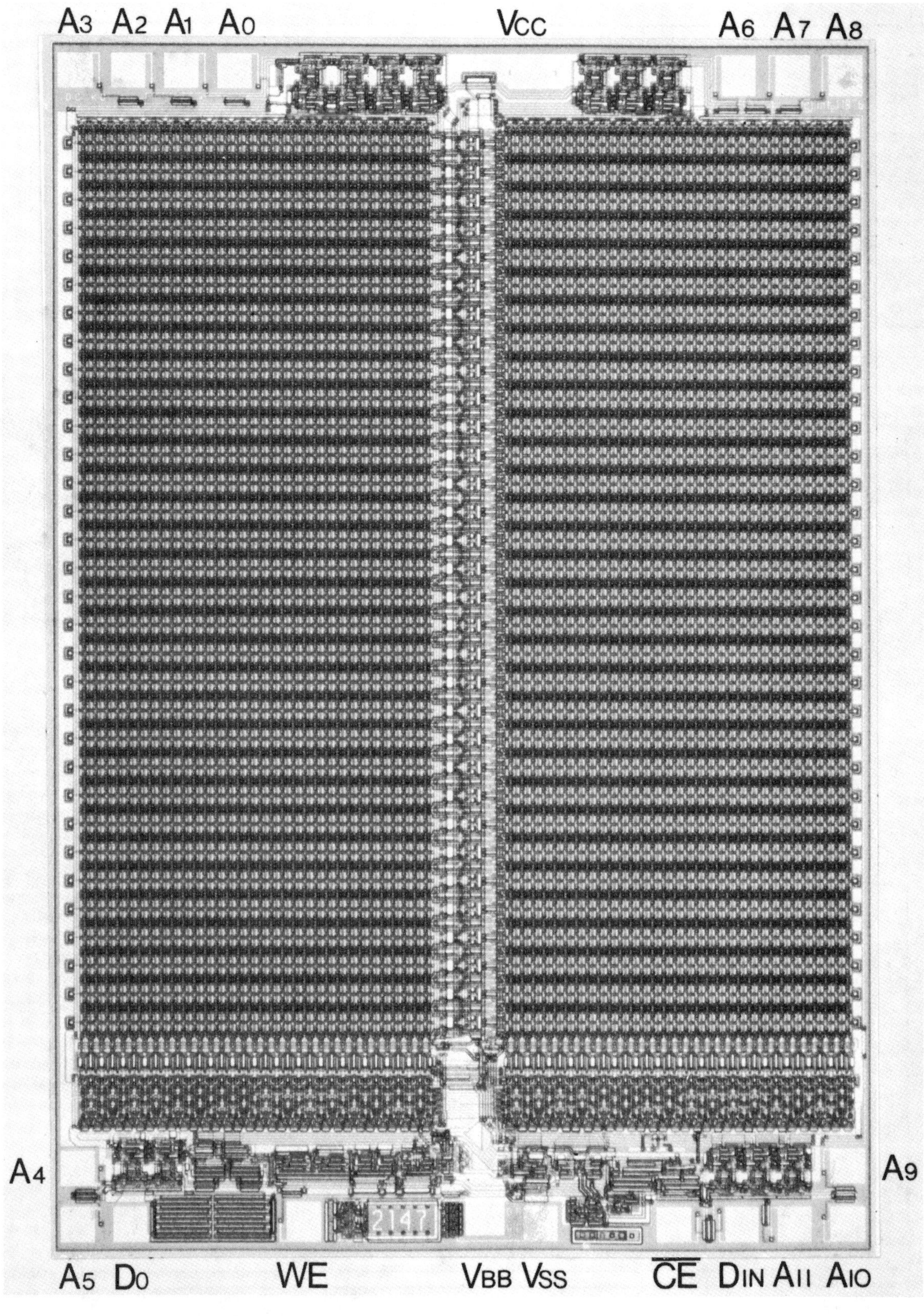

FIGURE 1 – Photomicrograph of the 133 x 188 mil MOS RAM. The pads vias are labeled on the 4096 bit RAM.

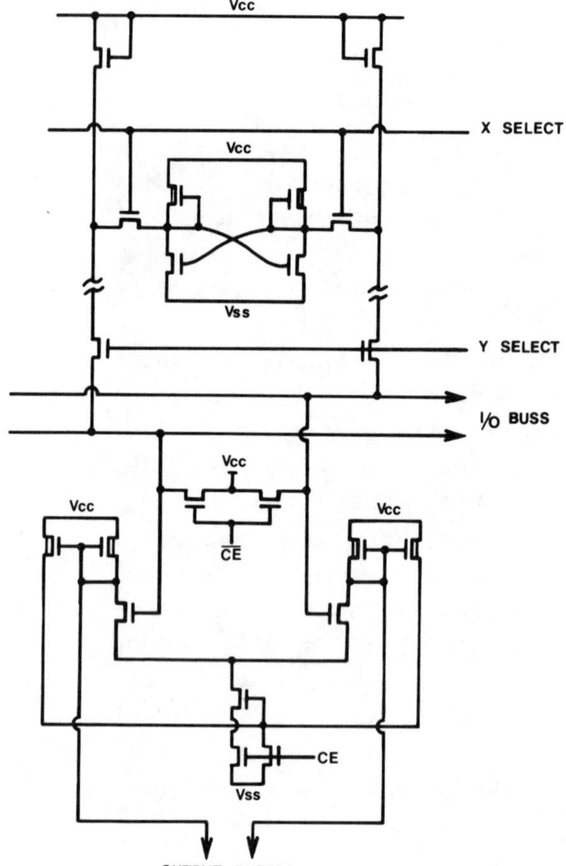

FIGURE 2 – Partial schematic of the RAM cell, column and output sense amplifier circuitry.

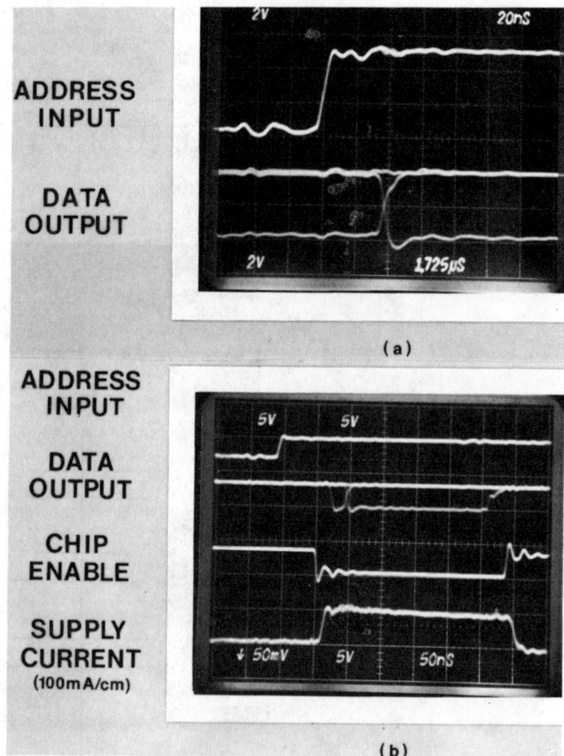

FIGURE 3 – Oscillograph of memory access time *(a)* from address transition with the chip previously enabled; *(b)* from chip select with the addresses previously defined. Operating conditions are T = 23°C and V_{CC} = 5V for the read-modify-write cycle.

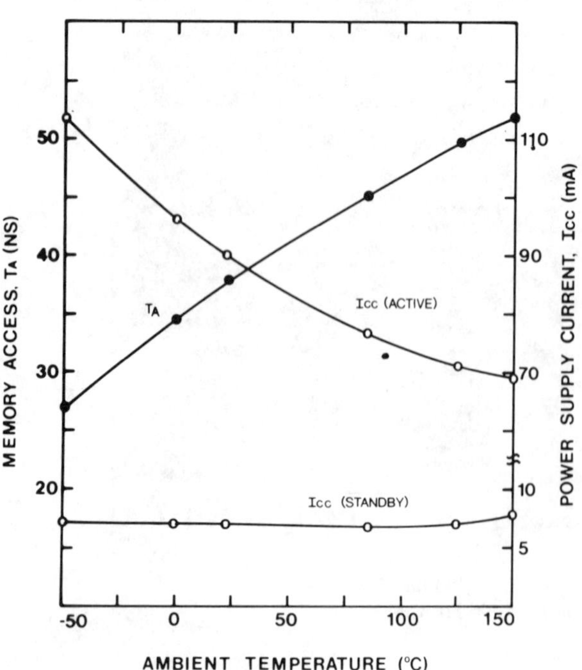

FIGURE 4 – The temperature dependence of the memory access time and power supply current (both active and standby) with V_{CC} = 5V.

A 5 V-Only 4-K Static RAM

Vernon G. McKenny

Mostek Corp.

Carrollton, TX

HISTORICALLY, 5V static MOS RAMs have been slow, or have had high operating power and high standby power, or have been some compromise thereof.

The RAM to be described, operating at + 5V ± 10%, has a typical access time of 150 ns, READ/MODIFY/WRITE (R/M/W) cycle time of 260 ns, operating power of 80 mW, and standby power of 8 mW.

The photo of Figure 1 shows the 4K x 1 RAM chip with memory matrix, decoders, clock generators, and sense amp outlined. The relatively small chip size (136 x 184 mils, or 3.45 x 4.67 mm) and the extremely low standby power are attributable to the use of a new type of static cell in the matrix and dynamic circuit techniques in the clock generators, row and column decoders and output buffers.

The negative going edge of $\overline{CE}$ triggers a sequence of internal clock edges which activate the address buffers, discharge the precharge clock, transfer true and complement address data to the inputs of the row and column decoders, and transfer the decoded row and column addresses to the proper word line and column select line. After these events the static input address buffers are turned off so that they no longer consume power. After a delay to allow time for the cell to transfer data to the differential output sense circuitry, additional clocks activate the output sense circuitry and finally the output buffer.

The positive going edge of $\overline{CE}$ causes the precharge clocks to go high, discharging all other clocks, and open-circuiting the output. The entire chip remains in the precharge mode, which is also the low-power standby mode, on a completely static basis. There is no maximum time limitation for $\overline{CE}$ to remain high.

The cell, shown in the schematic diagram of Figure 2 consists of two high-impedance polysilicon load resistors between V_{DD} and the two storage nodes. There is also a cross-coupled pair of transistors and a pair of address transistors with their gates connected to the poly word line.

This cell, which occupies only 2.75 mil^2 (1775 μ^2) of area, is shown in the photo of Figure 3. The high-impedance load devices are fabricated using a simple modification of a standard Si-gate process. The high-impedance poly regions lend themselves to a compact layout arrangement, resulting in a cell size about half that of previous static NMOS cells. These load resistors conduct typically less than 1 nA each, making possible a total matrix standby power of less than 20 μW. In addition, load resistor current levels are adjustable from less than 0.1 nA to more than 1 μA with ion implant. Because of the very low current levels of the load resistors, the cell will retain data with a V_{DD} as low as a few hundred mV above transistor threshold voltage (typically 1V). However, the peripheral circuitry requires slightly more voltage. With V_{DD} at + 2.0V the chip will retain data properly and will typically dissipate 0.8 mW permitting convenient battery backup.

Figure 4 shows the typical timing requirements under nominal operating conditions for a chip having 150 ns access time. Each READ, WRITE, or R/M/W operation must be preceded by a minimum precharge time of 75 ns and is initiated by the negative going edge of $\overline{CE}$. The input addresses must remain valid for only 70 ns past the negative edge of $\overline{CE}$. In the case of a READ cycle (not shown), $\overline{CE}$ may be returned to a high level as soon as Data Out becomes valid or may be held low for as long as 100 μs. Data Out goes open circuit approximately 25 ns past the positive going edge of $\overline{CE}$. If the cycle is to be a R/M/W cycle, then $\overline{CE}$ must be held low until the WRITE operation is also complete. This is accomplished by holding both $\overline{WE}$ and $\overline{CE}$ low for at least 35 ns. Input data must be valid within 10 ns after the negative edge of $\overline{WE}$ and must remain valid 10 ns past the positive edge of either $\overline{WE}$ or $\overline{CE}$, whichever comes first. A WRITE cycle (not shown) is accomplished by bringing $\overline{WE}$ low no later than 80 ns past the negative going edge of $\overline{CE}$. Data Out will then remain OPEN throughout the entire cycle permitting straightforward common I/O memory systems. The timing requirements of $\overline{CE}$, $\overline{WE}$ and D_{in} are otherwise the same as in the R/M/W cycle.

The graph in Figure 5 illustrates the power levels of a typical RAM at 25°C in three different modes of operation. In the active mode at 4 MHz the RAM will dissipate 80 mW average power at the maximum V_{DD} of 5.5 V. In the standby mode, with $\overline{CE}$ held continuously at a high and with V_{DD} still at its maximum value the chip power drops to only 8 mW. The chip is put into the battery backup mode of operation by dropping V_{DD} to about 2V while maintaining $\overline{CE}$ at V_{DD}. Under these conditions the chip power is only 0.8 mW.

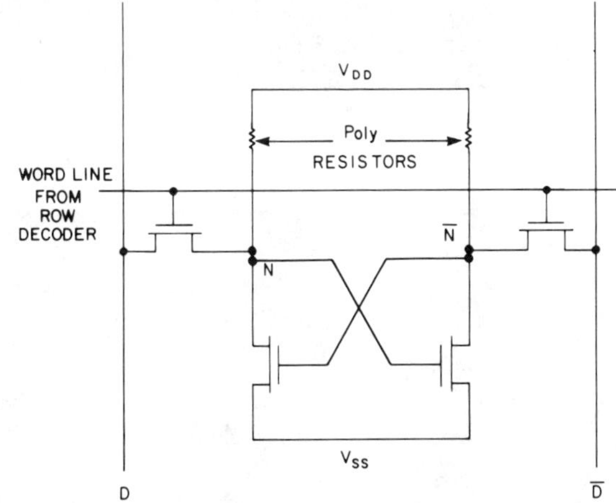

FIGURE 2 – Schematic of static memory cell.

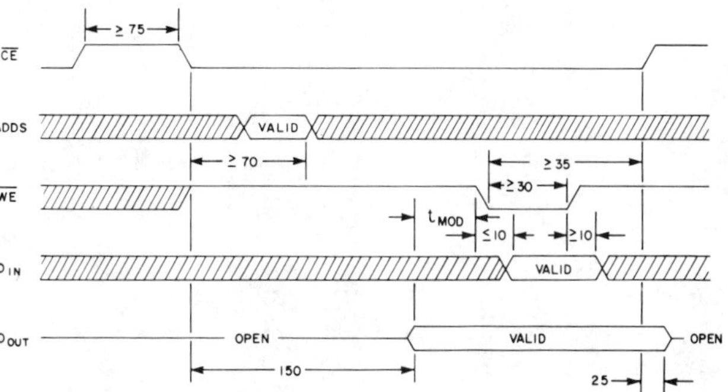

FIGURE 4 – READ/MODIFY/WRITE timing diagram. Values (in ns) shown are for a 150 ns access time chip under nominal operating conditions.

Reprinted from *IEEE Int. Solid State Circuits Conf.*, pp. 16–17, 1977.

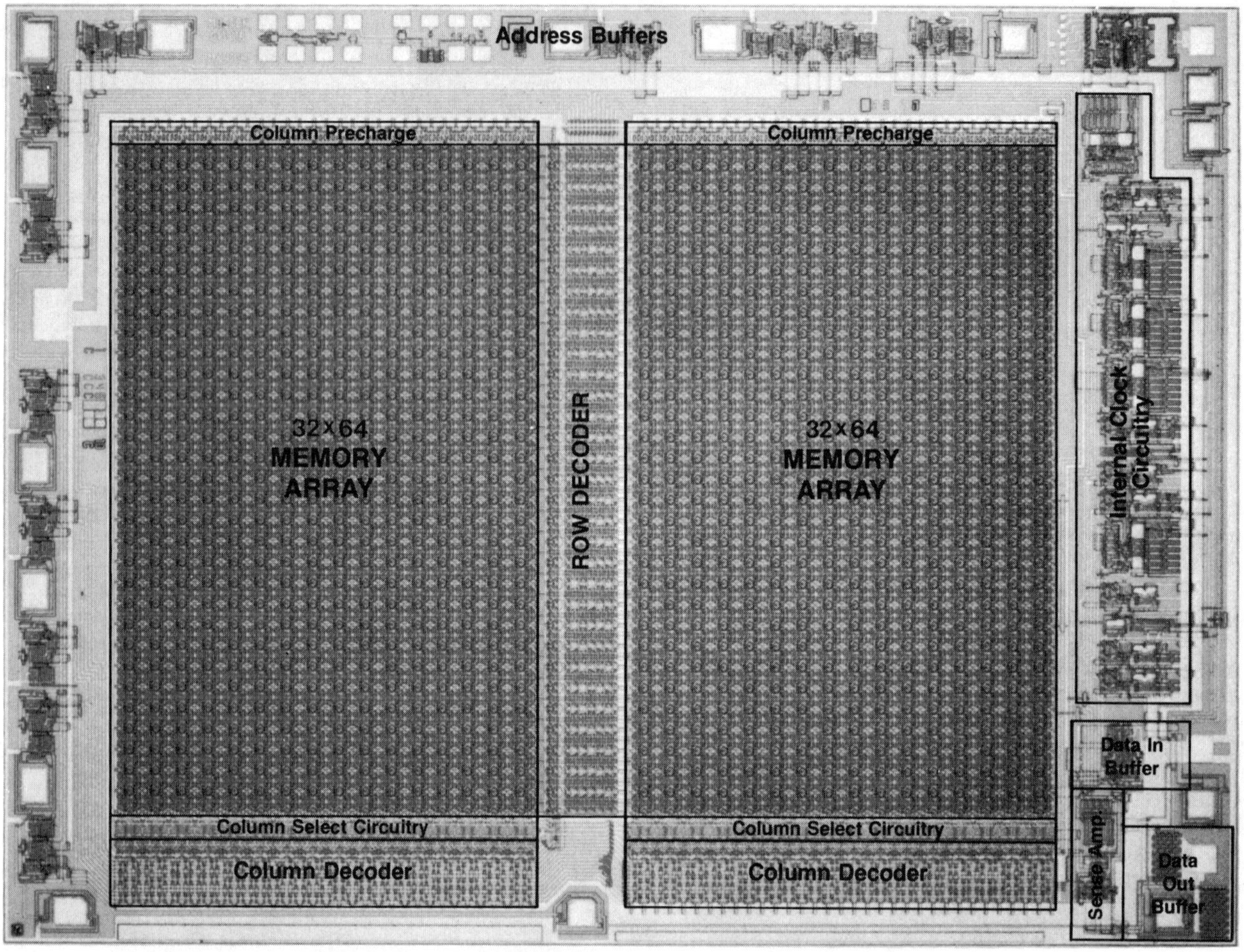

FIGURE 1 – 4K static RAM photo with major sections outlined.

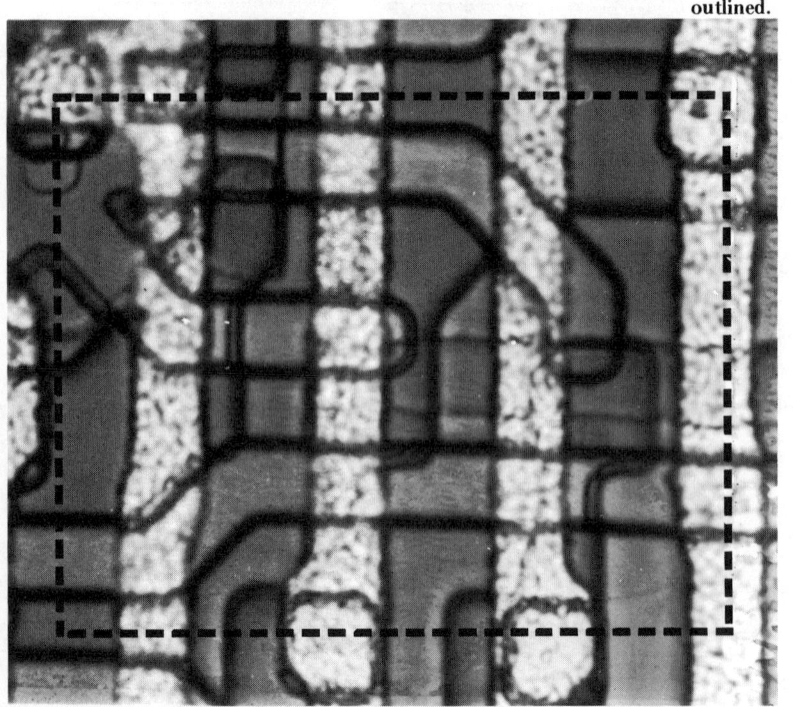

FIGURE 3 – Cell photo. Four transistors and two high impedance poly resistors are contained in 2.75 mil^2.

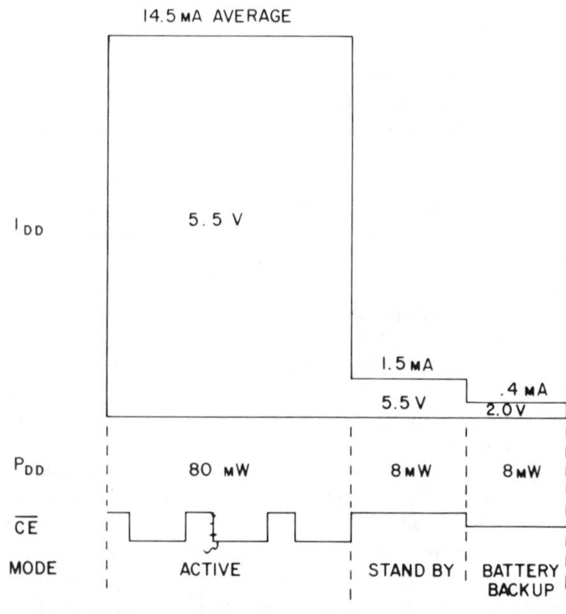

FIGURE 5 – Typical power levels for various operating modes.

A 25ns 4K Static RAM

Robert M. Jecmen, Anne V. Ebel, Ronald J. Smith, Virgil Kynett, Chi-Hung Hui and Richard D. Pashley

Intel Corporation

Santa Clara, CA

THE PERFORMANCE OF STATE-OF-THE-ART static RAMs has improved significantly with the introduction of device scaling to N-channel MOS technologies. By selectively using some of the features of scaling theory, it has been possible to develop a technology which reduces many of the critical physical parameters without the necessity of reducing the power supply voltage.

Table 1 summarizes the details of the technology. The 2μ channel lengths and 400Å gate thickness dimensions represent a scaling factor of 3 compared to typical 1976 MOS technologies. By scaling the MOS devices, high drive currents can be maintained while reducing parasitic capacitances. The lower capacitance allows improved gate delays with no increase in power consumption. A minimum gate delay of 400ps and a speed power product of 0.5pJ has been achieved. This is an order of magnitude better than the performance of a typical 6μ technology.

This performance did not come at the expense of process complexity. A single poly technology with standard positive resist photolithography was used. Shallow junctions were obtained by using arsenic as the source-drain dopant. The technology also features depletion loads and an on chip V_{BB} generator.

A 1024 bit static RAM was designed to be a yield and development vehicle for the technology. The device is organized as a 1024 x 1 bit RAM and has a die size of 10816 mils^2. All pins are TTL compatible and the RAM operates from a single 5V supply. Typical address access time is 15ns with a power dissipation of 370mW. The access time represents an improvement of N-channel MOS speed; Figure 1.

In addition, a 4096 bit RAM was designed with performance as its key goal. A photomicrograph of the RAM is shown in Figure 2. The memory is organized as a 4096 x 1 bit RAM with the array split into two 32 x 64 planes separated by a common row decoder. Conservative 4μ design rules were used in layout. A 6 transistor cross coupled flipflop cell 3.0 mils^2 in size was used in the memory array. The entire chip measures 21240 mils^2 and fits into a standard 18-pin package.

A typical address access time of 22ns was achieved with a nominal power consumption of 500mW. The 4K RAM features a 45mW powerdown mode controlled by chip select. Typical output sourcing and sinking currents are 33mA at 2.4V and 31mA at 0.45V respectively. The design is fully static and operates from a single 5V supply. All I/O levels are TTL compatible. A summary of the device characteristics of both the 1K and 4K RAM is listed in Table 2.

The 45mW powerdown mode causes no slow down when accessing from the deselected state. Figure 3 shows typical oscillographs of address access and chip select access times. During powerdown ($\overline{CS}$ HIGH), the memory is deselected and the I/O buss is reset to a threshold below V_{CC}. Equivalent chip select and address access times are achieved by balancing the internal circuitry during powerdown which compensates for the additional delay due to chip select powerup. Previous designs[1] have exhibited access time pushouts of more than 10ns if the circuit is deselected for very short times (<20ns). The pushout occurred as a result of insufficient time for balancing of the columns and buss lines. Modification in the chip select buffer and powerdown design, however, have eliminated this problem. The chip select buffer generates an additional signal to powerdown the X decoder rapidly while the address buffers powerdown more slowly (Figure 4). This allows for the address buffers to remain powered up and the columns and buss lines to reset quickly during a short deselect time.

In conclusion, static RAMs using scaled MOS technology, afford typical access times of 15ns and 22ns, respectively for 1K and 4K RAMs. A 45mW powerdown mode is available on the 4K RAM with equivalent chip select and address access times independent of deselect time.

Parameter	*1K*	*4K*
Physical Characteristics		
Die size	10816 mils^2	21240 mils^2
Organization	1024 x 1	4096 x 1
DC Characteristics		
Supply voltage	5V	5V
Active power dissipation	330mW	500mW
Standby power dissipation	—	45mW
I/O levels	TTL	TTL
Output sink current (V_0=0.45V)	26mA	31mA
Output source current (V_0=2.4V)	31mA	33mA
AC Characteristics		
Address access time	15ns	22ns
Chip select access time	6ns	22ns
Powerdown time	—	10ns
Read cycle time	15ns	22ns

TABLE 2—Typical device characteristics.

[1] Pashley, R.D., et al., "A High Performance 4K Static RAM Fabricated with an Advanced MOS Technology", *ISSCC DIGEST OF TECHNICAL PAPERS*, p. 22-23; Feb., 1977.

Reprinted from *IEEE Int. Solid State Circuits Conf.*, pp. 100–101 and p. 285, 1979.

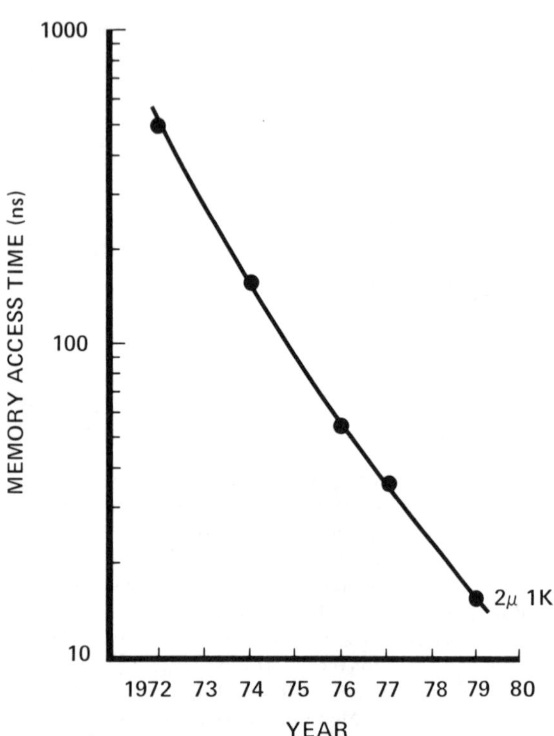

FIGURE 1–1K MOS static RAM performance.

Channel length ℓ (μ)	2.0
Gate oxide thickness Å	400
Power supply voltage	5V
Minimum gate delay	400ps
Speed power product	0.5pJ

TABLE 1–Key features of the MOS technology project.

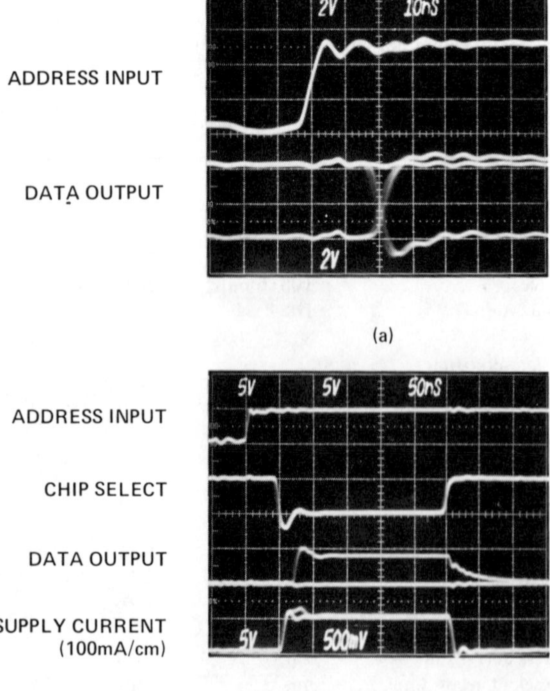

FIGURE 3–Oscillograph of memory access time; (*a*)–from address transition with chip previously selected; (*b*)–from chip select with address previously defined. Operating conditions T = 23° C at V_{CC} = 5V.

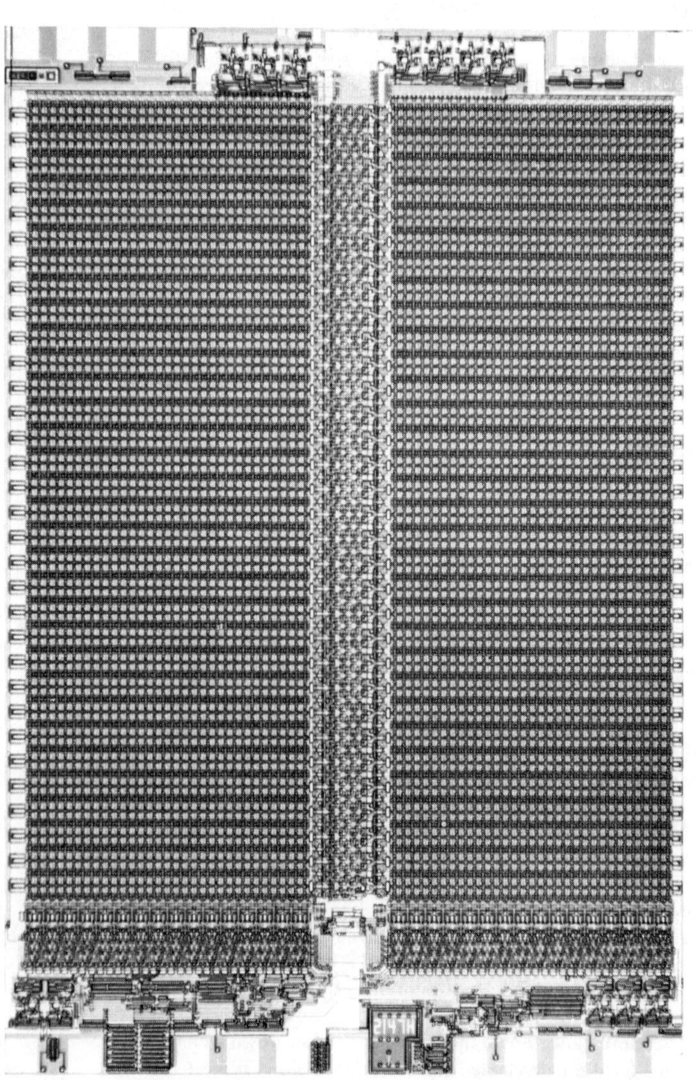

FIGURE 2–Photomicrograph of the 4K static RAM.

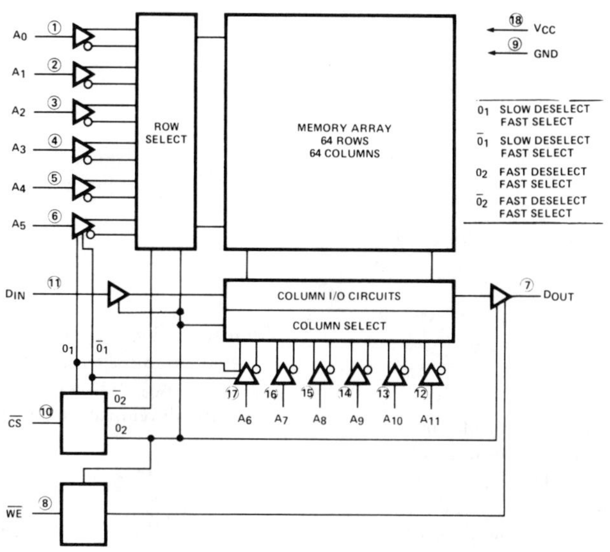

FIGURE 4—Block diagram of 4K RAM powerdown circuitry.

A 1Kx8-Bit 5V-Only Static RAM

George S. Leach, John M. Hartman, Ken L. Clark and Tim R. O'Connell

EMM-SEMI, Inc.

Phoenix, AZ

OVER THE YEARS there has emerged a large family of nonvolatile 1Kx8 and 2Kx8 memory devices for microprocessor applications. These include EPROMs, PROMs, and ROMs. To compliment this microprocessor *by-eight* memory family, a 1Kx8-bit static RAM has been developed. Chip timing matches the 2MHz microprocessor requirement and the chip function matches the common I/O and three-state requirements of data bus systems. Special consideration was given to chip organization and pinouts for socket compatibility to the popular 8K and 16K EPROM, PROM and ROM devices. The photomicrograph of Figure 1 shows the chip organization and Figure 2 the pinouts.

Three concepts were used to meet the performance characteristics shown in Table 1. First, clocked peripheral chip circuitry was used to reduce power, increase speed, and prevent race problems[1]. Second, very high value polysilicon resistors were used to decrease memory cell size and power. Finally, a high performance silicon gate process was developed to further increase density and performance.

Internally-generated clock signals are used throughout the chip to synchronize the address and data signals. Figure 3 shows their use in an input latch. When the chip is enabled, $\overline{CE}'$ goes low activating the input stage while CE′ strobes the data in. Next, CED (chip enable delayed) goes high to latch the data. CED^2 then goes high and the data is bootstrapped and transferred to the decoders shown in Figure 4. After one of the X and one of the Y decoders are selected, CED^3 goes high causing the selected X and Y lines to bootstrap high and select the intended memory cell.

The memory cell has been designed to pull down one of the sense lines previously set high by $\overline{CE}$. The 50MΩ polysilicon memory load resistors, like all the resistors on this chip, are only present to sustain against junction leakage current. Each memory resistor occupies an area of only .04 mil^2 and typically draws only .01μA. A depletion load, six transistor memory cell was ruled out due to the larger memory cell size, higher current and difficulty in controlling this current due to the square law dependence on the depletion threshold.

Operation of this 1Kx8 RAM can be seen in Figure 5. Read one and read zero are illustrated with typical access times of 250ns driving a TTL load. Illustrated also is the very low I_{CC}.

The process uses a single polysilicon deposition resulting in continuous poly runs having both low resistance for the interconnects and gates as well as 50MΩ per square resistance for the resistors. Conservative 5μ micron photolithography was used in the layout, but special substrate doping profiles, thin gate oxide, and shallow junction depths make this process similar to the recently developed silicon gate process[2].

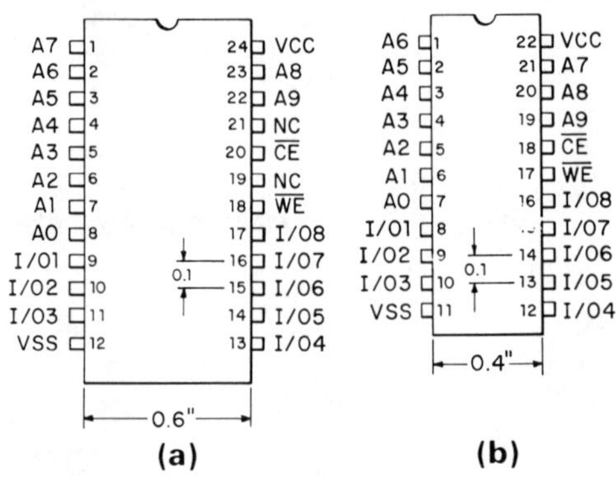

FIGURE 2—Industry standard pinouts*: 24-pin (*a*) is compatible to popular EPROM, PROM and ROM pinout; 22-pin (*b*) has the same pinout sequence.

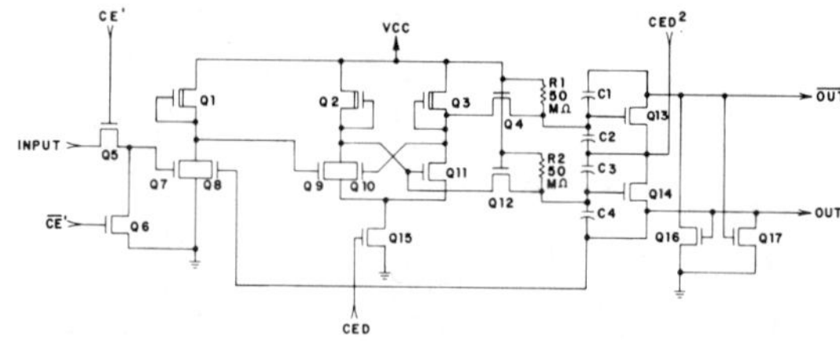

FIGURE 3—Address and $\overline{WE}$ latch circuitry. This circuitry dissipates no power when the chip is deselected.

PARAMETERS	8108/8308
ORGANIZATION	1K x 8
SUPPLY VOLTAGE	+5V
INTERFACE	TTL (THREE STATE I/O)
ACCESS TIME	300 ns
CHIP ENABLE WIDTH	300 ns to ∞
CYCLE TIME	450 ns
SELECTED CURRENT	16 mA
DESELECTED CURRENT	6 mA
CHIP SIZE	40,000 mil^2
PACKAGE	22/24 pin

TABLE 1—**Summary of the device characteristics. Parameters were chosen for a broad range of microprocessor applications.**

[1] O'Connell, T.R., et. al., "A 4K Static Clocked and Non-Clocked RAM Design", *ISSCC DIGEST OF TECHNICAL PAPERS*, p. 14-15, Feb., 1977.

[2] Pashley, R.D., et. al., "A High Performance 4K Static RAM Fabricated with an Advanced MOS Technology",*ISSCC DIGEST OF TECHNICAL PAPERS*, p. 22-23; Feb., 77.

*Pinouts: (a) = 8308; (b) = 8108.

Reprinted from *IEEE Int. Solid State Circuits Conf.*, pp. 104–105, 1978.

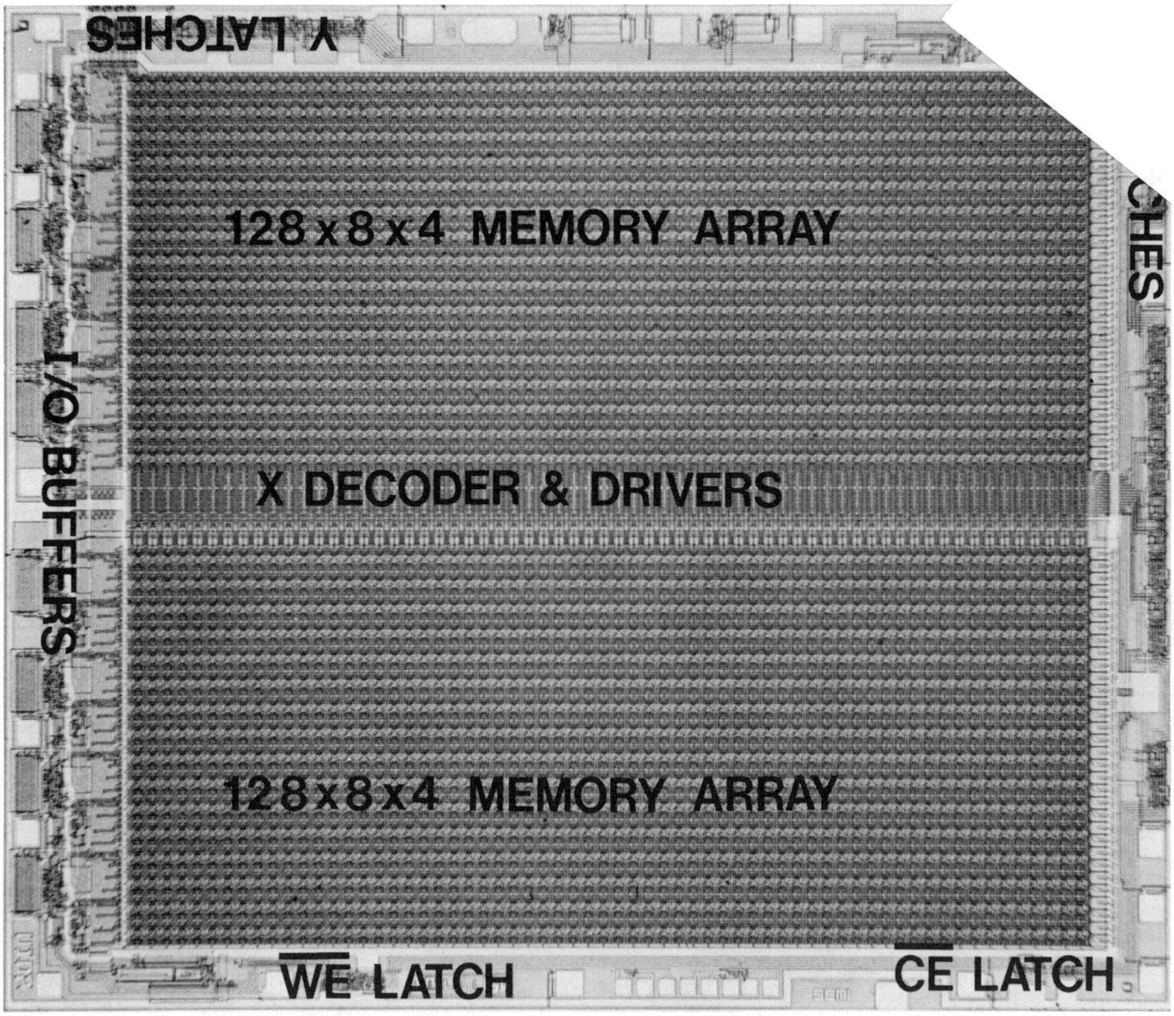

FIGURE 1—Photomicrograph of the 8192 bit MOS static RAM. Chip size is 182x219 mil.

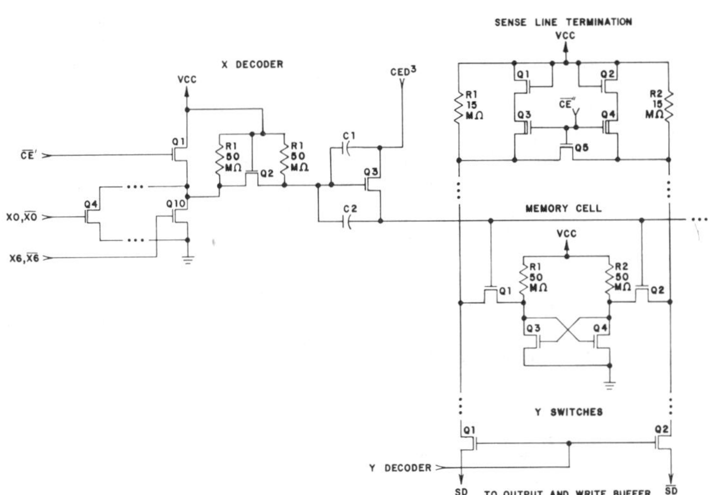

[Left]

FIGURE 4—Memory cell and peripheral circuitry. The memory cell dissipates only 0.5μW per bit.

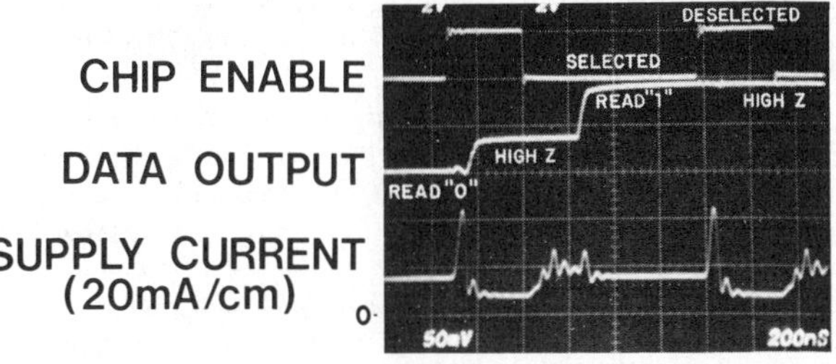

FIGURE 5—Oscillograph of memory read operation driving a TTL load. Address and write enable (not shown) are latched by chip enable going low. Outputs remain valid for entire chip enable pulse width.

A 16Kx1b Static RAM

Richard D. Pashley, Samuel S. Liu, William H. Owen, III, Judy M. Owen, Joseph Shappir, Ronald J. Smith and Robert M. Jecmen

Intel Corporation

Santa Clara, CA

RECENT TECHNOLOGICAL ADVANCES have allowed static RAMs to become mainframe memories[1,2]. Using an advanced double poly MOS technology, a 16,384 bit static RAM has been designed with a 40ns typical access time and 500mW active power dissipation. The memory is fully static and offers a 75mW powerdown mode.

The high density of the MOS memory was achieved by combining double poly MOS technology with poly load devices. The second layer of poly silicon serves two functions. By implanting this layer, high resistance poly is created which is patterned to form the memory cell load devices. In addition, selective doping is used to convert regions of this layer into a low resistance interconnect. Together, these features make this technology twice as dense as conventional single poly NMOS.

The density of the double poly technology is best demonstrated in the 16K memory cell. The memory cell is a basic 4-transistor cross-coupled flipflop with two poly load devices used to maintain data storage. Four MOS transistors are fabricated from the first poly layer with the poly load devices overlayed in poly 2. The power supplies for the cell are bussed in diffusion and poly, while the column lines are carried in metal. Using conservative 4μ design rules, the memory cell is layed out in 1.5 square mils ($24 \times 41\mu$). Typically, the cell draws less than $0.1\mu A$.

A 4,096 x 1 bit static RAM was chosen as a test vehicle to develop the double poly technology. The 4K die size is 12,792 $mils^2$ (82 x 156 mil) and the memory accesses typically in 35ns. The nominal active power is 200mW with a 50mW standby mode.

A photomicrograph of the 16,384 bit MOS RAM is shown in Figure 1. The die measures 37,697 mil^2 and is narrow enough to fit in a standard 0.3" wide 20 pin package. The 16,384 x 1 bit RAM is internally split into two 64 by 128 bit subarrays with a common row decoder separating them. Due to the tight memory column pitch, two input/output busses serve the memory array in an interleaved fashion. The device contains all the buffers, decoders, and write circuitry needed for fully static operation. A back bias generator is included to reduce device body effect and parasitic junction capacitance. As a result of using simple static circuitry in the periphery, over 67% of the chip is memory array.

The memory employs a novel buffered NOR X-decoder circuit; Figure 2. By using a buffer, the NOR device sizes can be shrunk, hence reducing the loading on the input buffers and also cutting the X-decoder active power in half. In addition, the buffered NOR is faster than the standard NOR decoder and can be easily powered down.

Typically, the 16,384 bit RAM accesses in 40ns and consumes 500mW with a 75mW standby mode; Table I. All pins are TTL compatible and the RAM operates from a single 5V supply. The output typically sinks 25mA at 0.45V and sources 30mA at 2.4V. The temperature dependence of the memory access time and the power supply current are shown in Figure 3. The memory is fully static and requires no clocks or internal refreshing; i.e., a multiple read operation can occur during a single chip select cycle.

The memory features two distinctly different read cycles; the address access cycle and the chip select access cycle. In the address access cycle, the chip is selected previous to address change. Circuit operation in this mode is identical to that of a conventional fully static RAM; Figure 4*a*. However, the chip select access cycle is unique. In a chip select access cycle, the address inputs are valid before or coincident with chip select. Chip select not only initiates a read operation, but it also controls device power dissipation; Figure 4*b*. When the memory is deselected it typically dissipates one-seventh its active power. Access from chip select is equivalent to that of an address access.

In summary, a 194-mil square 16K static RAM has been designed using a double poly MOS technology. A nominal 40ns memory access time and 500mW power dissipation were observed and a 75mW powerdown mode was attained without an access time penalty.

DC characteristics	
Supply voltage	5V
Active power dissipation	500mW
Standby power dissipation	75mW
I/O levels	TTL
Output sink current (V_o = 0.45V)	25mA
Output source current (V_o = 2.4V)	30mA
AC characteristics	
Address access time	40ns
Chip select access time	40ns
Powerdown time	30ns
Read cycle time	40ns
Write cycle time	30ns
Write pulsewidth	7ns

TABLE I—Summary of the typical device characteristics.

[1] Pashley, R.D., et al., "A High Performance 4K Static RAM Fabricated with an Advanced MOS Technology", *ISSCC DIGEST OF TECHNICAL PAPERS*, p. 22-23; Feb., 1977.

[2] Jecmen, R.M., et al., "A 25ns 4K Static RAM", *ISSCC DIGEST OF TECHNICAL PAPERS;* this issue p. 100-101.

Reprinted from *IEEE Int. Solid State Circuits Conf.*, pp. 106–107 and p. 287, 1979.

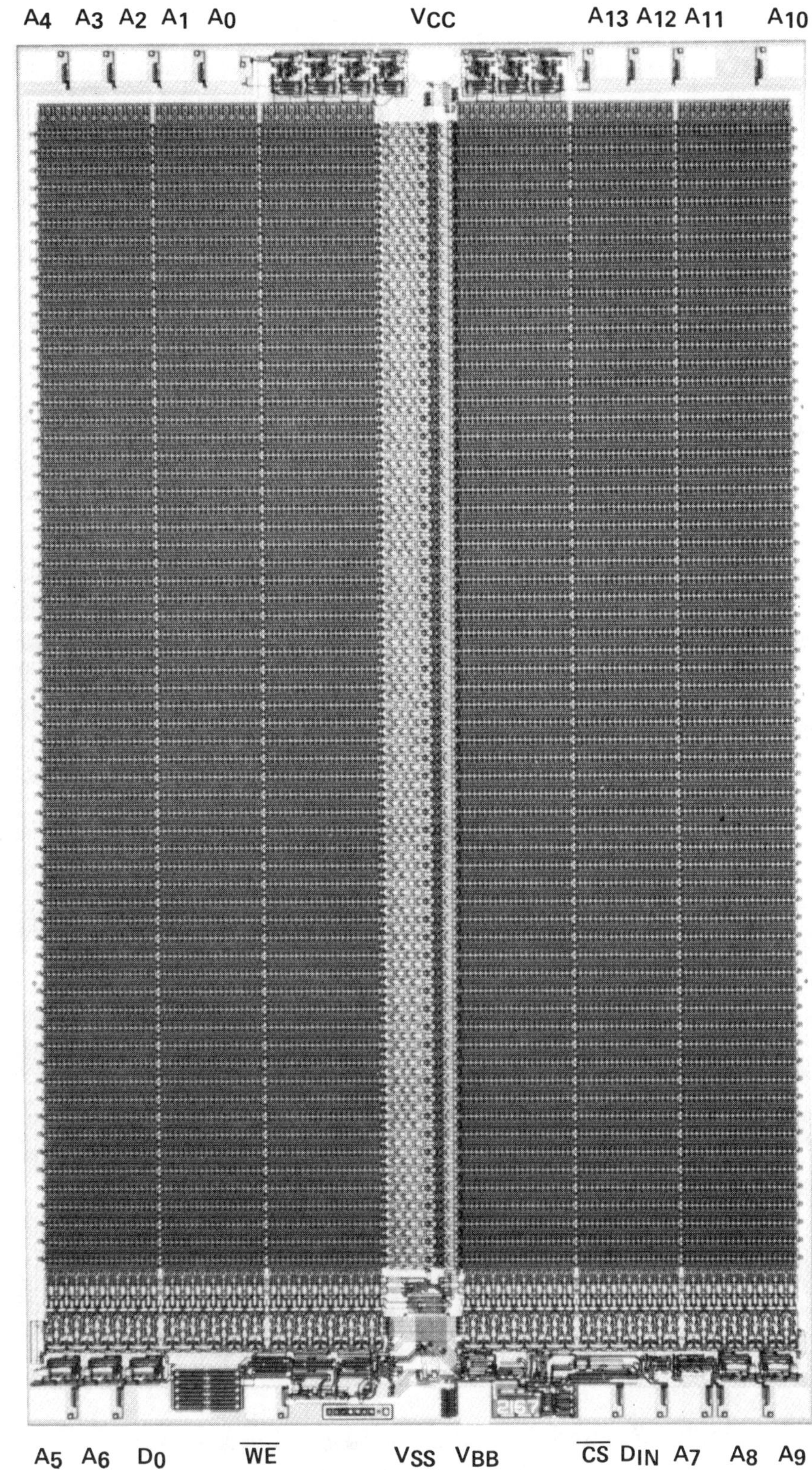

FIGURE 1–Photomicrograph of the 149x253 mil 16K static RAM.

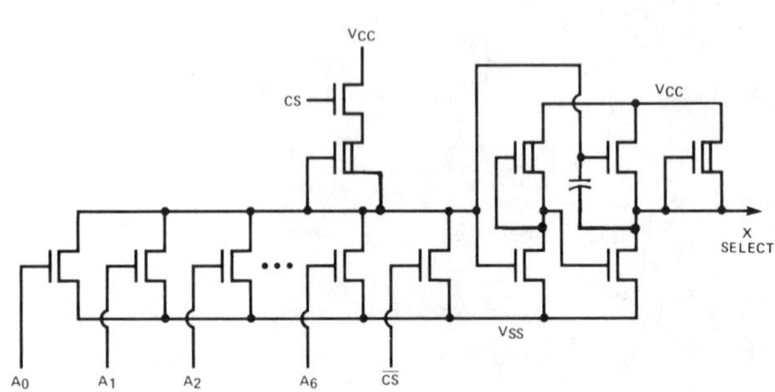

FIGURE 2—Schematic of the 16K row decoder (X select) circuit.

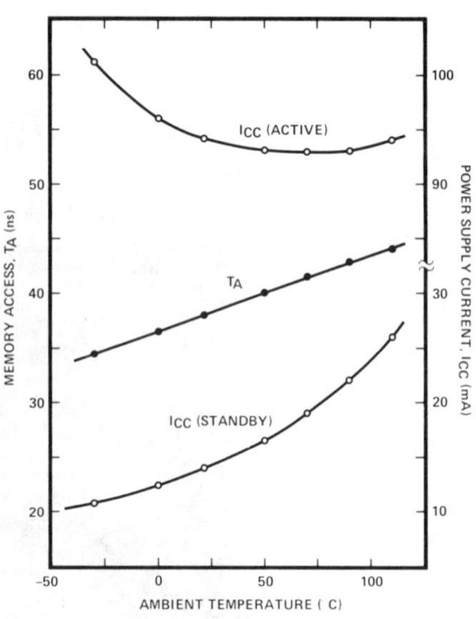

FIGURE 3—The temperature dependence of the memory access time and power supply current (both active and standby) with $V_{CC} = 5V$.

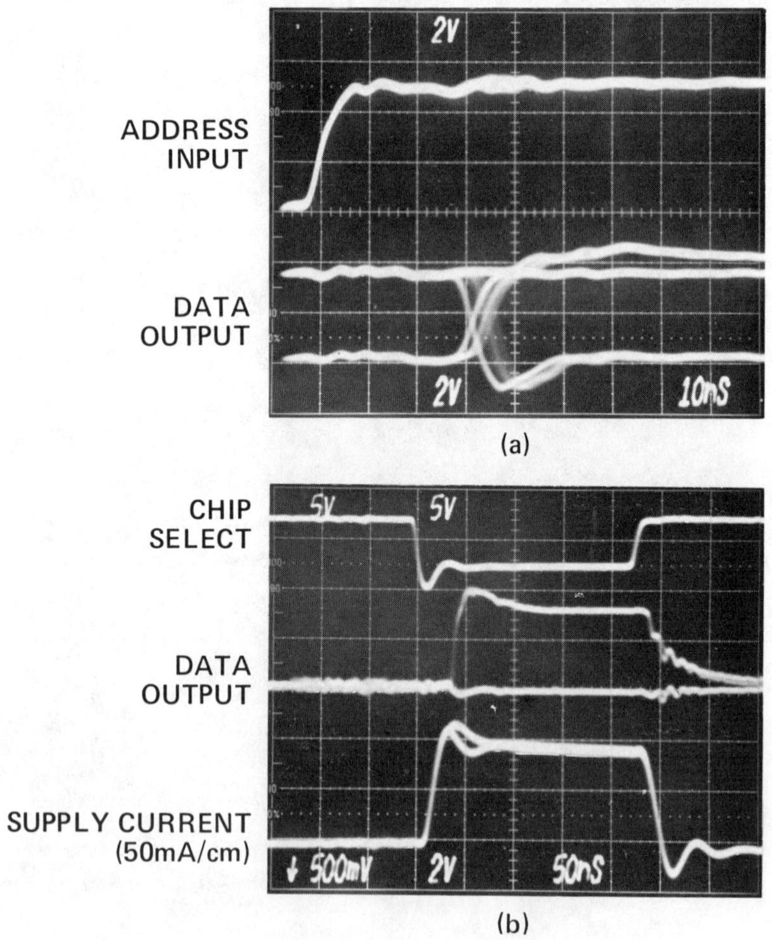

FIGURE 4—Oscillograph of memory access time: (*a*)—from address transition with chip previously selected; (*b*)—from chip select with the addresses previously defined. Operating conditions: T = 23° C and $V_{CC} = 5V$ for read-modify-write cycle.

A HIGH-PERFORMANCE MOS TECHNOLOGY FOR 16K STATIC RAM

S.S. Liu, R.J. Smith, R.D. Pashley, J. Shappir, C.H. Fu, K.R. Kokkonen

Intel Corp., 3065 Bowers Ave., Santa Clara, Calif. 95051

ABSTRACT

A scaled double-poly MOS technology has been developed which features a static memory cell size of 1.5 mil^2 with 4μ design rules using conventional photolithographic techniques. The technology scales the gate oxide thickness to 400Å and poly-Si channel length to 2.1μ with arsenic source-drain and self-aligned poly-poly via contact. Four different types of transistors are implemented to enhance circuit design versatility. Hot electron failures and soft errors do not limit the applicability of the technology.

INTRODUCTION

The density of Static RAMs has improved dramatically over the years, from the 1K level in 1972, to the 4K in 1976, and now to the 16K level. Major technological advances in bulk NMOS have allowed this to occur. Depletion loads, device scaling and projection printing were utilized to achieve the 4K density (1), (2). Now a second layer of polysilicon has been added for RAM cell pullups and interconnect. Even with conservative design rules, this reduces the cell size to 1.5 mil^2, a factor of two over its 1979 single-poly counterpart. The density aspect of the 16K technology can be illustrated best by comparison of the photomicrographs shown in Figure 1.

SCALED DOUBLE-POLY STATIC RAM TECHNOLOGY

The high density of the MOS memory was achieved primarily by combining double poly MOS technology with poly load devices. The second layer of poly serves two purposes. By implanting this layer with arsenic at a dose of $\sim 1.0 \times 10^{14} cm^{-2}$, high resistance poly is created which is patterned to form the memory cell load devices. In addition, selective doping is used to convert regions of this layer into a low resistance interconnect. Further density improvement is realized through the use of a self-aligned poly-poly via contact scheme. This contact provides a direct connection between the two poly-Si layers without any penalty for misalignment sensitivity. Together, these features make the technology at least twice as dense as the conventional single poly NMOS.

To achieve high performance as well, the technology also features a scaled poly channel length of 2.1μ and gate oxide thickness of 400Å. This results in a speed-power product of 0.6pJ at a fan-out of three, nearly doubling that of the 1977 technology. A comparison between this technology and its single-poly predecessors is summarized in Table 1.

TABLE 1: COMPARISON OF HIGH-PERFORMANCE STATIC RAM TECHNOLOGIES

	1979 Double Poly	1979 Single Poly	1977 Single Poly
No. of Poly-Si layers	2	1	1
Load Device	Poly resistor	Depletion	Depletion
Memory Cell size (mil^2)	1.5	3.0	3.75
4K die size (mil □)	113	146	158
16K die size (mil □)	194	---	---
Poly Channel length (μ)	2.1	2.1	3.5
Gate Oxide Thickness (Å)	400	400	700
Speed-Power Product (pJ)	0.6	0.5	1.0

The conventional projection printer with a 2μ misalignment tolerance is used throughout the process. The design rules for some of the key photomasking layers are listed in Table 2. The front-end isolation is achieved with the conventional local

Reprinted from *IEEE Int. Electron Devices Meeting*, pp. 352–354, 1979.

oxidation approach. An arsenic source-drain doping scheme is applied to achieve shallow junctions consistent with device scaling. The back-end of the technology utilizes a standard contact process involving the reflow of a thick (∿2μ) phosphosilicate glass for the improved step coverage of Al-metallization.

TABLE 2: SUMMARY OF KEY DESIGN RULES

Layer	Minimum Final Line Width (μ)	Minimum Final Spacing (μ)
Diffusion	3.5	5.5μ
Poly 1 (Gate)	2.1	4.9μ
Contact	7.0	---
Metal	5.0	6.0μ

THE 16K MEMORY DESIGN

The 16,384 bit MOS RAM measures 37,697 mil^2 and is narrow enough to fit in a standard 0.3" wide 20 pin package. Typically, the memory accesses in 40ns with a nominal power consumption of 500mW. All pins are TTL compatible and the RAM operates from a single 5V supply. Using a novel approach, chip select is used to control device power dissipation. When the RAM is deselected, power is switched off to all non-essential circuitry. Typically, the deselected power is one-seventh the active power. No access time penalty is paid for this special feature. Access from chip select is equivalent to that of an address access. The memory is fully static and requires no clocks or internal refreshing; i.e., a multiple read operation can occur during a single chip select cycle.

To achieve the special circuit design features, such as power-down, four different types of active transistors have been incorporated into the technology (Table 3). The four unique transistors are fabricated by the selective use of two threshold adjust implants. The key to powerdown is the availability of the zero threshold switching transistor. The chip select buffer is used to drive these power switches that have been selectively placed in each circuit block. In addition to the standard enhancement/depletion pair, a second depletion device is offered for low power applications.

TABLE 3: MOS DEVICE DESCRIPTION

Device Type	Channel Implant	Threshold Voltage	Circuit Application
Enhancement	B_{11}	0.7	Pulldown Device
Depletion	As	-3.0	High Performance Load
Depletion	As, B_{11}	-1.5	Low Power Load
Zero Threshold	None	-0.2	Powerdown Device

RELIABILITY

By selectively following device scaling theory without proportionately reducing the supply voltage, substantially higher electric fields are created within the MOS device. This increases the probability of hot electron generation and trapping, which may degrade performance by causing threshold voltage shifts. An accelerated testing scheme, which stresses devices at 6-9V and -70°C, has been used to simulate the long term effect under standard conditions. Extrapolations indicate that almost 60 years would be required to cause a 5mV threshold shift for a minimum channel length device. Similar accelerated testing of the 4K Static RAM fabricated with this technology shows less than a 0.5ns shift in access time for 10 years of normal operation.

Very dense Static RAM memories fabricated with bulk NMOS can be sensitive to α-particle-generated soft errors. As shown schematically in Figure 2, the cell may flip if the charge collected from the α-particle trajectory is greater than the charge stored capacitvely on the cell node and greater than the charge supplied through the cell pullup resistor. Previous generations of depletion load RAM cells had two advantages over the present poly load cell, as shown in Table 4. First, the effective load resistance was much less, since the array standby current requirement for the 4K density level was less stringent. Second, the cell node capacitance was higher, in part due to the gate oxide capacitance of the depletion load itself. Accelerated testing of the depletion load cell shows it to be totally immune to α-particles. While the poly resistor load cell is not totally immune, the soft error rate for the 16K RAM has been kept to less than .05%/khr, which is comparable to the projected hard failure rate. This required careful layout to maximize node capacitance, and simulation to enhance the circuit stability of the cell flip-flop.

TABLE 4: SOFT ERROR DATA SUMMARY

	1979 Single Poly Depletion Load	1979 Double Poly Resistor Load
Soft Error Rate*	0%/khr	<0.05%/khr
Cell Size	3.0 mil^2	1.5 mil^2
Cell Node Capacitance	∿120fF	∿50fF
Range Of Load Resistance	5-10MΩ	50-200MΩ

* Soft error rate valid for commercial spec range.

ACKNOWLEDGEMENT

We appreciate the support of Frank Louie and Isao Nojima for circuit design, and Russ Reininger and Steve Jacobs for reliability data.

REFERENCES

(1) Pashley, R.D., et al., "A High Performance 4K Static RAM Fabricated With An Advanced MOS Technology", ISSCC DIGEST OF TECHNICAL PAPERS, pp. 22-23, Feb. 1977.

(2) Jecmen, R.M., et al., "A 25ns 4K Static RAM", ISSCC DIGEST OF TECHNICAL PAPERS, pp. 100-101, Feb. 1979.

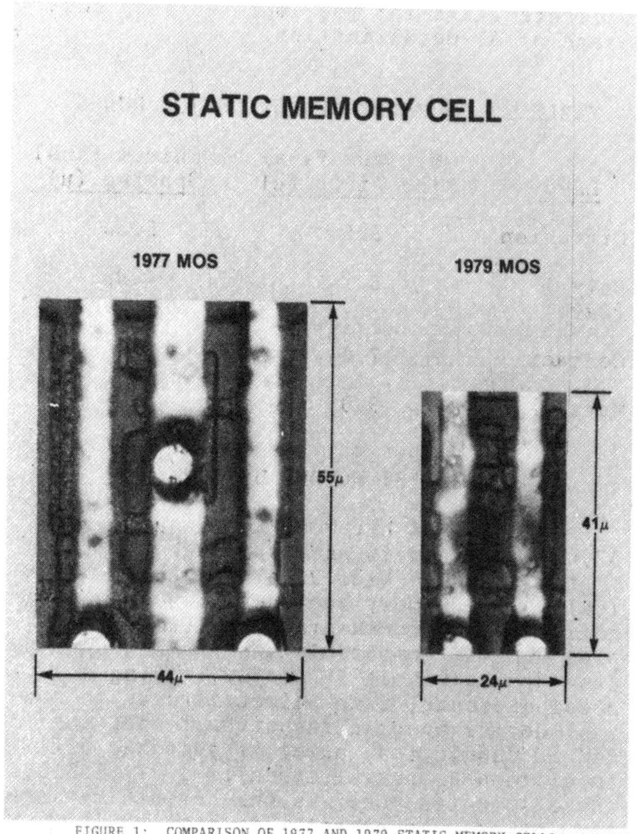

FIGURE 1: COMPARISON OF 1977 AND 1979 STATIC MEMORY CELLS

STATIC RAM SOFT ERROR SENSITIVITY

- CELL FLIPPING CAUSED BY Q_α INJECTION (I_α)
- SOFT ERROR DESIGN CONSIDERATION

$$I > I_\alpha \text{ OR } Q_C > Q_\alpha$$

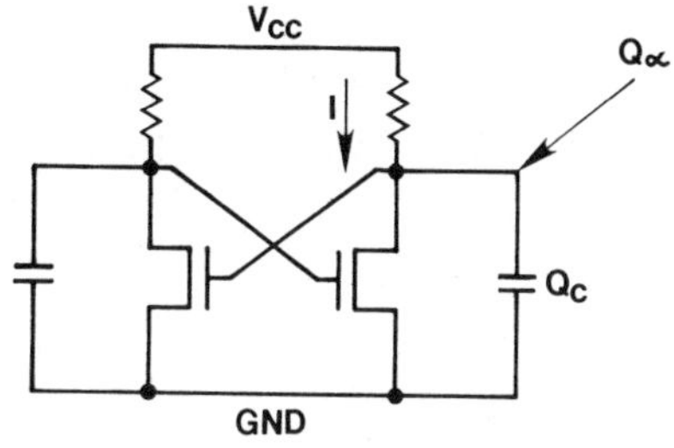

FIGURE 2: STATIC RAM SOFT ERROR SENSITIVITY

2Kx8b HCMOS Static RAMs

Toshiaki Masuhara, Osamu Minato, Toshio Sasaki, Hideaki Nakamura and Yoshio Sakai

Hitachi Central Research Laboratory

Tokyo, Japan

Tokumasa Yasui and Kiyofumi Uchibori

Hitachi Musashi Works

Tokyo, Japan

ADVANCES IN MEMORY SYSTEMS in large and microcomputers and peripheral equipment have accelerated the developments of 16K static RAMs based on double-poly NMOS technologies[1,2,3]. However, difficult technological problems exist in large capacity static RAMs, such as high operating power, relatively complex processes, and soft errors due to alpha particles.

This paper will report on 16K static RAMs based on HCMOS technology previously described[4,5]. The cell layout and a cross section are shown in Figure 1. Current to the high resistivity loads for data retention is fed through the buried JFET. The JFET powered cell[6] eliminates the supply line and provides flexibility of layout. It also permits the use of single poly technology and reduces processing costs. Cell area is 28x32 microns.

One advantage of using such a memory cell structure is that the existence of a P-well and optimum design of its doping profile give considerable immunity to alpha-particle induced soft errors. Experimental data shown in Figure 2 were obtained using 4K NMOS, 4K and 16K HCMOS arrays and a 1μCurie Americum source. It is seen that the soft errors in HCMOS arrays are significantly smaller than in NMOS arrays. At normal operating voltage of 5V, soft errors in HCMOS arrays are undetectable, while 4K NMOS arrays produce some soft errors. The estimated error rate of the present 16K RAMs at 5V is less than 0.1 FIT (Failure in Time, i.e., 1 Failure in 10^9 Hours), taking into account the alpha sources contained in the package. This value is several orders of magnitude better than those for static NMOS and dynamic NMOS arrays. The difference between NMOS and HCMOS can be explained by the existence of a potential barrier between the N-substrate and the P-well in the HCMOS case. This potential barrier keeps generated electrons away from the N^+ memory storage node.

Two RAMs having the pin functions shown in Figure 3 were designed. One has JEDEC standard EPROM-compatible pinouts. The other has CS_2 (true chip select) function instead of an $\overline{OE}$ (output disable) function for ease of system design in battery backup operation. Since both RAMs were fabricated by metal layer masterslice techniques, they have almost identical performance characteristics; therefore this paper focuses on the JEDEC standard version.

Figure 4 shows a microphotograph of the chip. The chip measures 4.76 by 5.5mm^2 and fits into a plastic 24-pin package. To obtain high speed and low power characteristics, CMOS peripheral circuits are used. Column and row decoders, word drivers and sense amplifiers are shown in Figure 5. Sixty-four row decoders and word driver/multiplexers choose one of 128-word lines. Since the resistance of the word line and the corresponding signal delay is large, the word line signal is buffered and amplified in the middle portion of the word line. This enables a delay of approximately 25ns from address input to the rise of the word line signal.

After a word line is selected, 350mV of common data line voltage appears at the sense amp inputs. The use of a single NMOS device for the level shift in the common data line load avoids threshold voltage offset that may occur when two NMOS transistors are used. This signal is amplified by a CMOS sense amplifier having a power switched current source. The sense amp has a gain of 6.2, which provides enough voltage to drive the output buffers. The output buffers use a bipolar-CMOS configuration to assure fast risetime and large V_{OH} (output-high voltage), typically $V_{CC}-0.5V$. The output waveforms are shown in Figure 6, and Table 1 summarizes the typical features of the RAM.

The low power characteristics and large immunity to alpha particles that are inherent in HCMOS configurations appear to be quite advantageous for future VLSI RAM and logic designs.

Acknowledgments

The authors wish to thank Dr. Makimoto and Dr. Kubo, Messrs. Tomozawa, Kosa and Megro for process arrangements and supervising.

---

[1]Pashley, R.D., et al., "A 16K x 1 Bit Static RAM", *ISSCC DIGEST OF TECHNICAL PAPERS*, p. 106-107; Feb., 1979.

[2]Electronics Newsletter, Vol. 15, No. 41, p. 33; July 6, 1978.

[3]Ohzone, T., et al., "A 2K x 8 Bit Static RAM", *IEDM Digest of Technical Papers*, p. 360-363; Dec., 1978.

[4]Masuhara, T., et al., "A High Speed, Low Power HCMOS 4K Static RAM", *ISSCC DIGEST OF TECHNICAL PAPERS*, p. 110-111; Feb., 1978: also Minato, O., *IEEE Ed. Trans.*; June, 1979.

[5]Sakai, Y., et al., "High Density, High Speed CMOS (Hi-CMOS) Device Technology", *Proc. 10th Conf. Solid-State Devices*, Tokyo; 1978.

[6]Minato, O., et al., "Buried JFET Powered Static RAM Cell", to be published in *Proc. 11th Conf. Solid-State Devices*, Tokyo.

Reprinted from *IEEE Int. Solid State Circuits Conf.*, pp. 224–225 and p. 277, 1980.

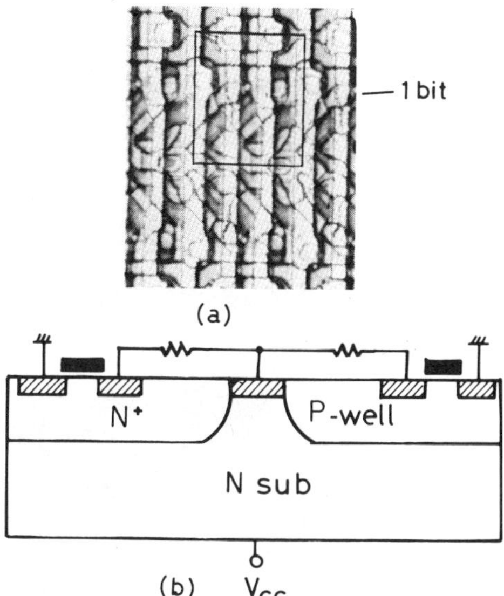

FIGURE 1—Cell layout and cross section.

[Below]
FIGURE 2—Comparison of soft error rate due to alpha particles. Data are obtained using high resistivity load cells.

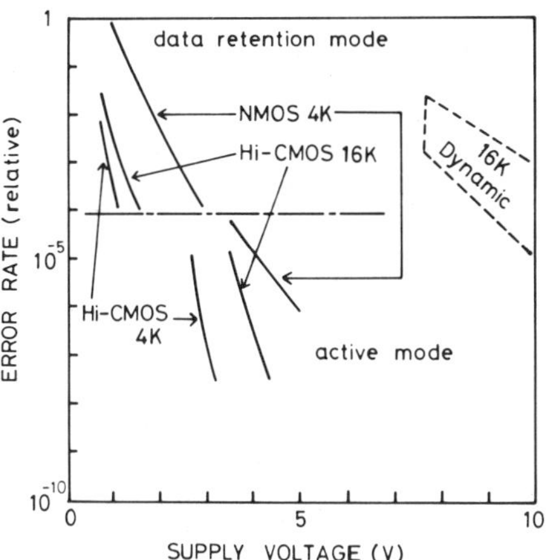

[Below]
FIGURE 4—Microphotograph of the chip.

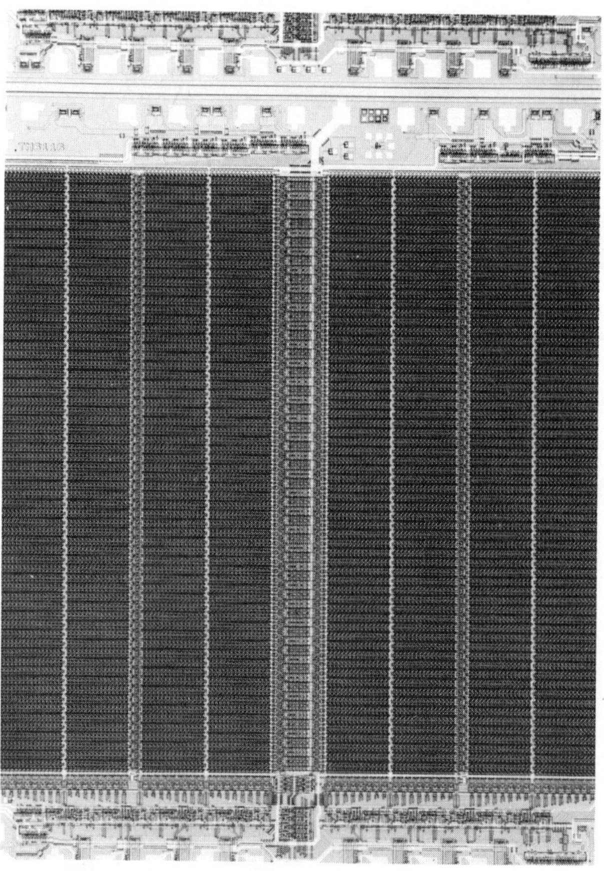

[Below]
FIGURE 3—Two types of pinouts made by the masterslice of metal layer.

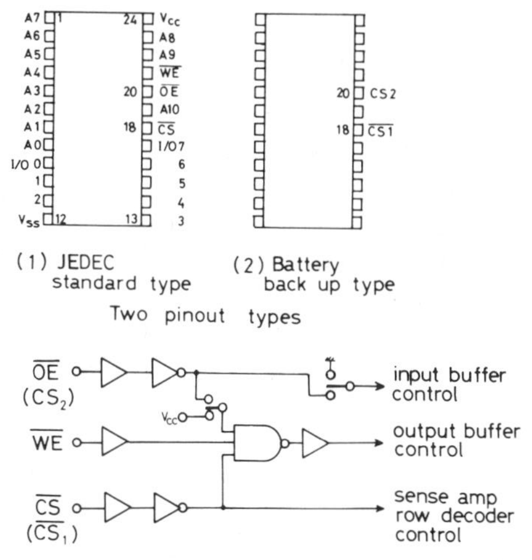

[Right]
TABLE 1—Features of 16K HCMOS static RAM.

Address access	74 ns	$= t_C$
CS access	60 ns	
OE access	42 ns	
Active current	38 mA	$\overline{CS} = 0.8$ V
Standby current 1	4.8 mA	$V_{IN} = V_{IH}$
Standby current 2	5 μA	$V_{IN} = V_{CC}$
Output sink	7.4 mA	$V_{OL} = 0.4$ V
Output source	8.6 mA	$V_{OH} = 2.4$ V
Input level	TTL	
Write width	26 ns	
Address setup	-12 ns	

At $V_{CC} = 5$ V, $T_a = 25$°C, C=100 pF

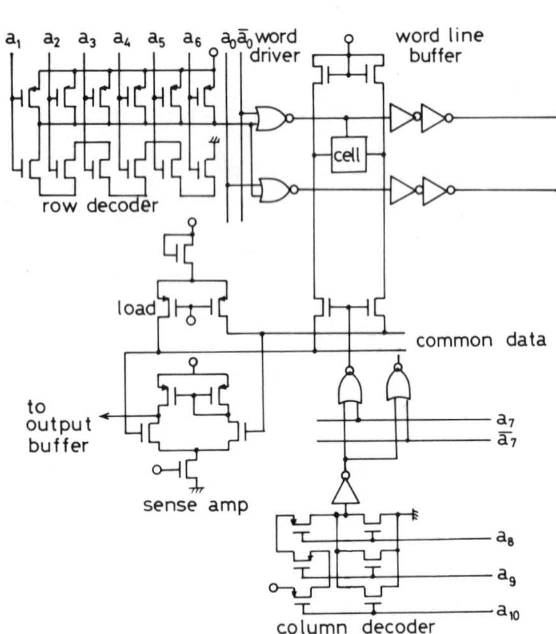

FIGURE 5—16K HCMOS static RAM circuit schematic.

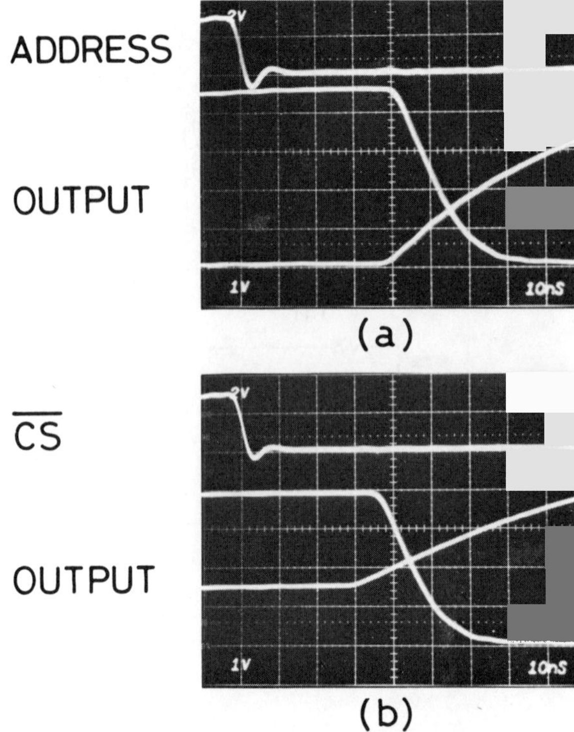

FIGURE 6—Output waveforms of the RAM.

Fully Static 16Kb Bulk CMOS RAM

Tetsuya Iizuka, Kiyofumi Ochii, Takayuki Ohtani, Takeo Kondo and Susumu Kohyama
Toshiba Corp.
Kawasaki, Japan

A FULLY STATIC 16K CMOS RAM using a high density Si-gate bulk CMOS process and a circuit with a basic six-transistor CMOS RAM cell will be reported. The memory offers a 95ns typical access time, 200mW active power dissipation and standby power of less than 1μW.

Double polysilicon MOS technology has allowed static RAMs to reach 16K chips with polysilicon load devices. However, their standby current should be relatively high, since the load resistance value must be kept low to compensate for process variations. On the other hand, a six-transistor CMOS RAM cell has many advantages, especially in wide operational margin and low standby power. But, the cell area tends to be large, since the cell consists of four NMOS transistor cross-coupled flipflops with two PMOS load transistors. Therefore, an extremely tight layout rule must be used to achieve a 16K CMOS RAM for the desired device performance.

High density of the CMOS memory has been achieved by selective scaling of device parameters and fully utilized dry etching processes[1]. Typically, the gate oxide thickness and the effective channel length are 700Å and 2.4μm, respectively, for both P and NMOS transistors. The minimum contact hole width is 2μm being formed by reactive ion etching technology. The complete 16,384b CMOS RAM* (Figure 1) contains 1.03×10^5 transistors. The memory cell is layed out in 1122μm^2 (33 x 34μ), and the die measures 5.06 x 5.77mm (199 x 227mils) which fits into a standard 24-pin plastic package.

Table 1 summarizes typical characteristics. The device is organized as a 2048 word x 8b RAM. All I/O levels are TTL compatible and the RAM operates from a single 5V supply. The device is pin compatible with standard 16K EPROMs*, providing another board design flexibility.

The memory block diagram is shown in Figure 2. The device has two chip enables $\overline{CE_1}$, $\overline{CE_2}$ and write enable $\overline{WE}$. Data input/output buffers are controlled by these signals. $\overline{CE_2}$ selects active and standby modes. In write cycles, $\overline{WE}$ signal need not be a clock pulse, provided that either $\overline{CE_1}$ or $\overline{CE_2}$ is clocked. In other words, the write operation can be performed in at least three different modes.

A fast access, typically 95ns, was achieved by a predecoded address circuit and a high-speed sense amplifier. Figure 3 shows the predecoding circuit for a pair of row address signals. The circuit operates with the same number of address inputs as a conventional one-step decoding, but with much higher speed resulting from its larger transistor conductance for the final decoding. The high speed sense amplifier, shown in Figure 4, is connected to a pair of bit lines through a preamplifier. With feedback paths to the sources of the cross-coupled NMOS transistors in the NAND-type differential circuit, a sensitive and fast static sense amplifier was achieved.

A plot of memory access time vs supply voltage is shown in Figure 5. Typical access time, t_{ACC}, ranges from 95ns at 5V to 75ns at 8V. The address access time t_{ACC} is equivalent to chip select access time t_{CO2} which is measured from $\overline{CE_2}$. Access time t_{CO1} measured from $\overline{CE_1}$ is 35ns provided that the address set up time with respect to $\overline{CE_1}$ is longer than, or equal to 60ns. The oscillographs of the memory access time, t_{ACC} and t_{CO1} are shown in Figure 6.

Read and write operations show a quite large margin for the supply voltage V_{CC}, ranging from less than 1.8V to higher than 8V with data retention down to 1.3V. In a standby mode with $\overline{CE_2}$ high and all input levels higher than $V_{CC} - 0.3$V or lower than 0.3V, the device dissipates typically 1μW standby power, sufficiently low for the battery backup use.

Acknowledgments

The authors are grateful for the cooperative efforts of many people who contributed to this project, especially for their process development support.

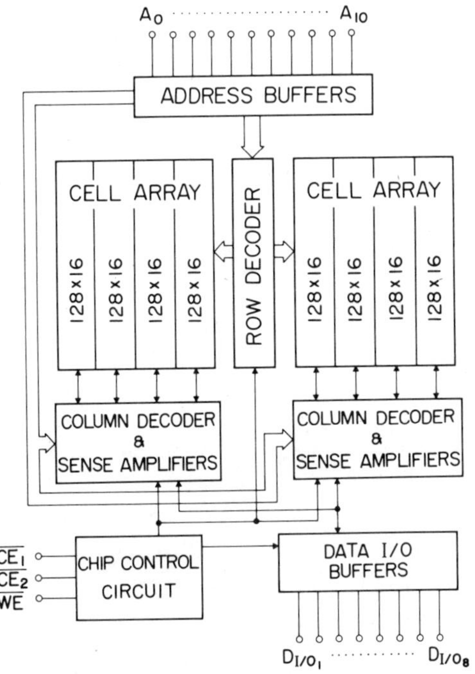

FIGURE 2–16K CMOS RAM memory organization.

*2716.

[1]Nozawa, H., Nishimura, S., Horiike, Y., Okumura, K., Iizuka, H. and Kohyama, S., "High Density CMOS Processing for a 16-Kbit RAM", *IEEE IEDM Digest;* Dec., 1979.

Reprinted from *IEEE Int. Solid State Circuits Conf.*, pp. 226–227 and p. 277, 1980.

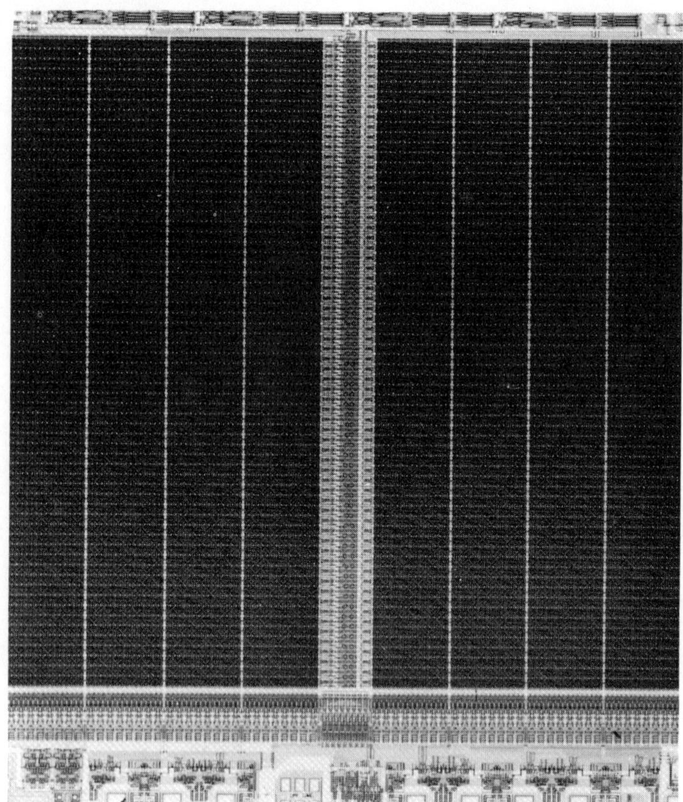

FIGURE 1—Photomicrograph of the 16K bulk CMOS static RAM.

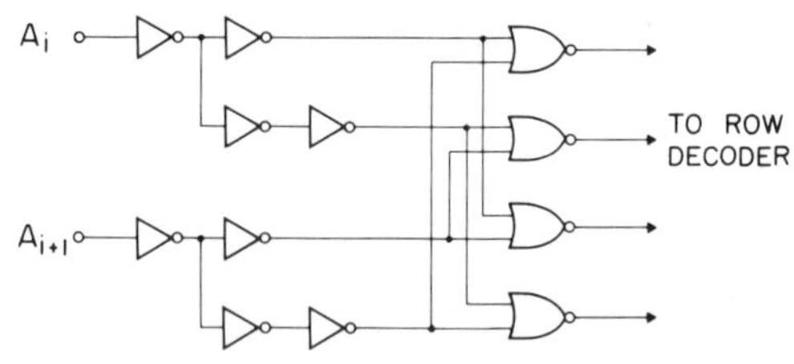

FIGURE 3—Predecoding circuit of a pair of row address signals.

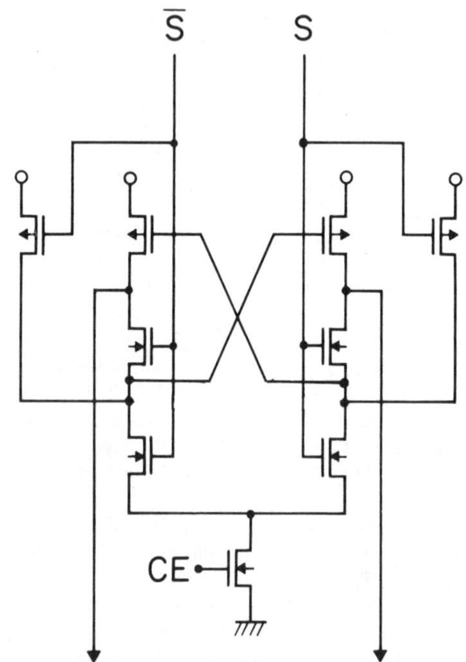

FIGURE 4—Schematic of sense amplifier.

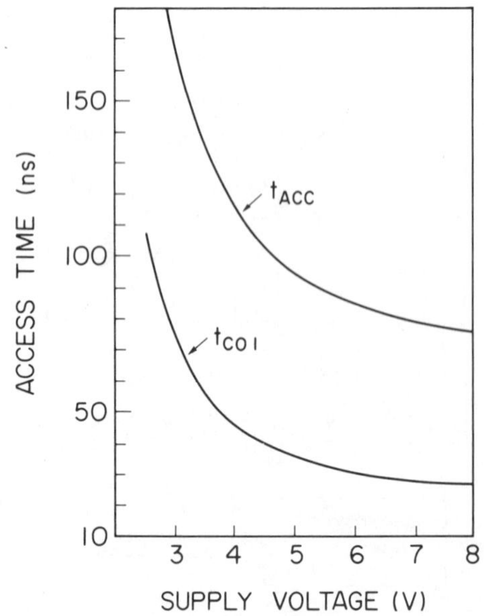

FIGURE 5—Typical memory access time as a function of supply voltage: t_{ACC}, measured from address transition; t_{CO1}, from $\overline{CE_1}$ signal.

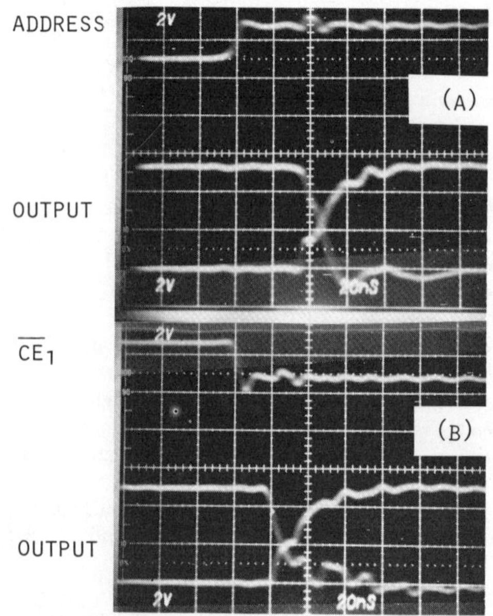

FIGURE 6—Oscillograph of memory access time: (*a*) — from address transition (t_{ACC}); (*b*) from $\overline{CE_1}$ (t_{CO1}).

Technology	Advanced Si gate CMOS process
Chip Size	5.06 x 5.77mm
Organization	2048 x 8
Pinout	24 pin standard
Supply Voltage	5V
I/O Levels	TTL compatible
Access Time	
from address transition	95ns
from CE_1	35ns
from CE_2	95ns
Active Power Dissipation	200mW
Standby Power Dissipation	1μW

TABLE 1—Summary of the typical device characteristics.

A 64Kb Static RAM

Takashi Ohzone, Shuji Kondo, Kazuhiko Tsuji, Tsuyoshi Shiragasawa, Takeshi Ishihara and Shiro Horiuchi

Matsushita Semiconductor Research Laboratory

Osaka, Japan

THIS PAPER WILL REPORT on the application of double-level polysilicon[1] and NMOS/CMOS process technologies to the design of a 64Kb fully static RAM, with 80ns typical access time. The RAM dissipates 300mW and 75mW in active and standby mode, respectively.

The RAM utilizes N-well CMOS technology[3] with N^+-doped polysilicon-gates in both N- and P-MOSFETs. Boron doping into polysilicon-gates of P-MOSFETs in the process step of boron implantation to form source/drain is avoided by a two-step photolithography technique. As a result, boron penetration through the thin gate oxide of 40nm resulting in threshold voltage shift of P-MOSFETs is also bypassed. The memory cells are fabricated on P-type substrate by NMOS technology. Peripheral circuits such as row and column decoders, I/O circuits and sense amplifiers consist of N-well CMOS circuits.

The memory cell is a basic cross-coupled flipflop with four N-MOSFETs and two polysilicon load resistors. The memory cell size of $304\mu m^2$ ($16x19\mu m$) is realized by adopting $2\mu m$ design rules and the double-level polysilicon technology in which two load resistors are fabricated with the second-level polysilicon films above driver MOSFETs[1]. Figures 1 and 2 show a schematic cross sectional view of the RAM and a photomicrograph of memory cells, respectively.

A photomicrograph of the RAM is shown in Figure 3. The chip size is $31.6mm^2$ (5.44x5.80mm). The memory cell array occupies about 63% of the chip area. The 64Kb RAM with a memory cell array of 256 rows and 256 columns is organized as 8Kx8b for 8b and 16b microprocessors. The RAM also has socket compatibility to that of 16Kb static RAMs and 64Kb ROMs/PROMs.

A schematic of memory cell and peripheral circuits are shown in Figure 4. Row driver and sense amplifier circuits are controlled by $CE \cdot CS_1 \cdot CS_2$ signal generated in the chip select control circuit to reduce power dissipation at standby mode operation. The memory cells are completely deselected and currents flowing in pull-up MOSFETs of data lines are cut off at standby mode, because row decoder outputs become unconditionally *low*. The dc current that passes in peripheral circuits is also completely cut off; thus the power dissipation at standby mode is determined by the resistance of the polysilicon load resistors. The cell in the RAM draws about $0.2\mu A$ resulting in standby current of about 15mA. The data signals from a memory cell are amplified by the CMOS differential amplifier and the NMOS cross-coupled amplifier to adjust the amplified output voltage to the input level of the next CMOS inverters. Address access time and chip select access time are designed to be nearly equivalent by using a circuit analysis program. The low load capacitance of $CE \cdot CS_1 \cdot CS_2$ signal line which drives only 8 of the row drivers and 8 of the sense amplifiers can permit high speed chip select access time and low active power dissipation.

The RAM is fully static and requires no clocks or internal refreshing. Typically, the RAM accesses in 80ns and consumes 300mW which is reduced to one fourth at standby mode. All pins are TTL compatible and the RAM operates from a single 5V supply. The output typically sinks 15mA at 0.45V and sources 20mA at 2.4V.

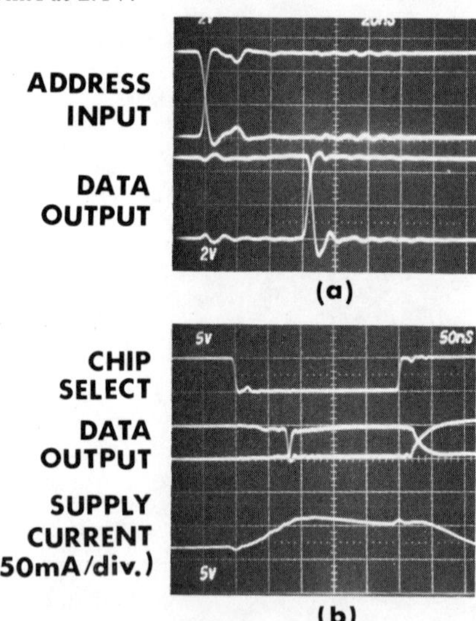

FIGURE 5—Oscillograph of typical memory access time: (*a*) address access time, (*b*) chip select access time.

PARAMETERS	64K STATIC RAM
ORGANIZATION	8K×8
SUPPLY VOLTAGE	5V
INTERFACE	TTL
ADDRESS ACCESS TIME	80ns
CHIP SELECT ACCESS TIME	80ns
ACTIVE POWER DISSIPATION	300mW
STANDBY POWER DISSIPATION	75mW
CHIP SIZE	5.44×5.80mm
MEMORY CELL SIZE	16×19μm
PROCESS	DOUBLE-POLYSILICON n-MOS/CMOS
PACKAGE	28PIN

TABLE 1—Summary of the 64Kb RAM characteristics.

[1] Ohzone, T., Hirao, T., Tsuji, K., Horiuchi, S. & Takayanagi, S., "A 2Kx8-Bit Static RAM", *Tech. Digest of Int. Electron Devices Meeting*, p. 360-363; Dec., 1978.

[2] Masuhara, T., Minato, O., Sasaki, T., Kubo, M. and Yasui, T., "A High-Speed, Low-Power Hi-CMOS 4K Static RAM", *ISSCC DIGEST OF TECHNICAL PAPERS*, p. 110-111; Feb., 1978.

[3] Black, Jr., W.C., McCharles, R.H. and Hodges, D.A., "CMOS Process For High-Performance Analog LSI", *Tech. Digest of Int. Electron Devices Meeting*, p. 331-334; Dec., 1976.

Reprinted from *IEEE Int. Solid State Circuits Conf.*, pp. 236–237, 1980.

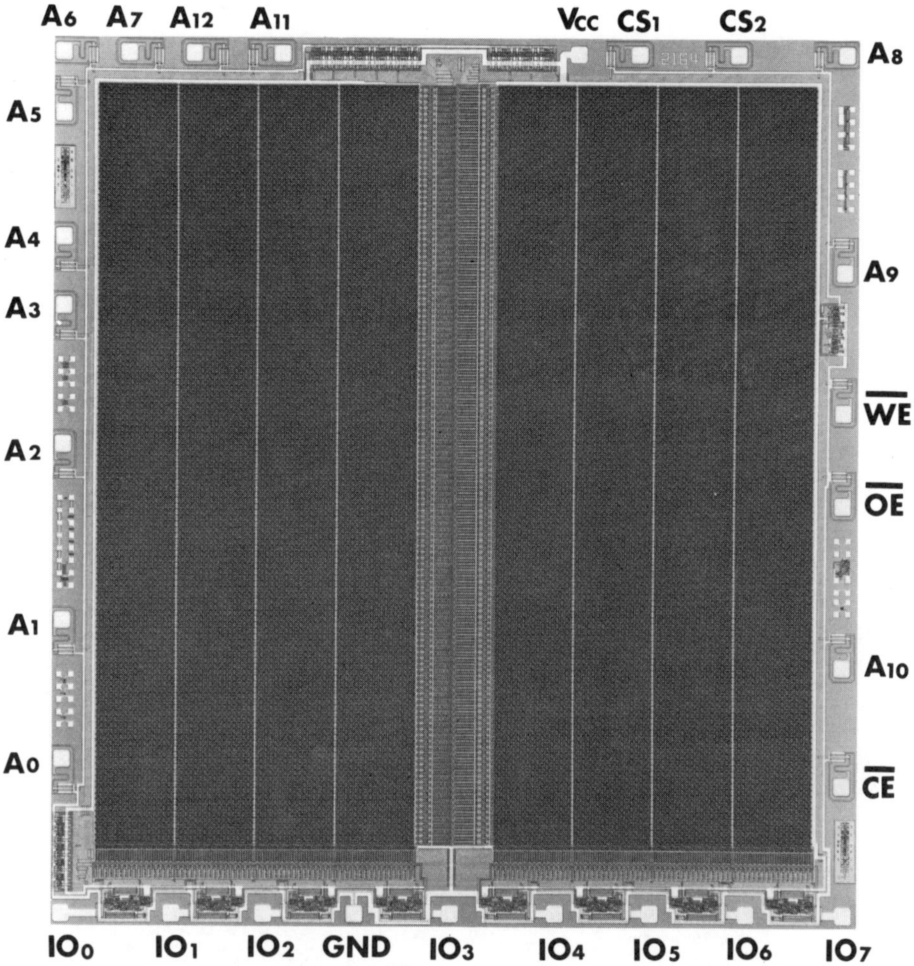

FIGURE 2—Photomicrograph of memory cells before aluminum metalization. Cell size is 16x19μm.

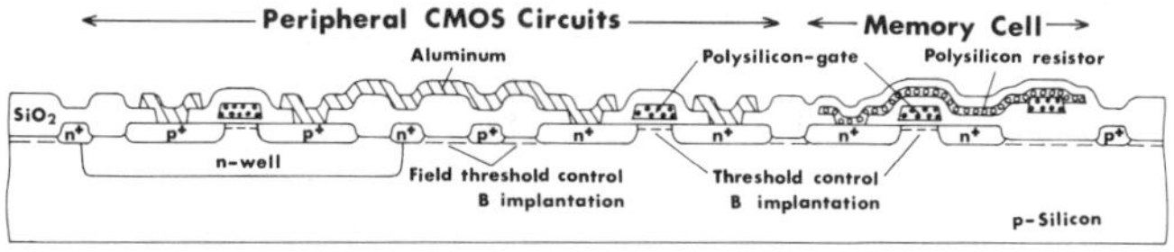

FIGURE 1—Cross sectional view of the RAM.

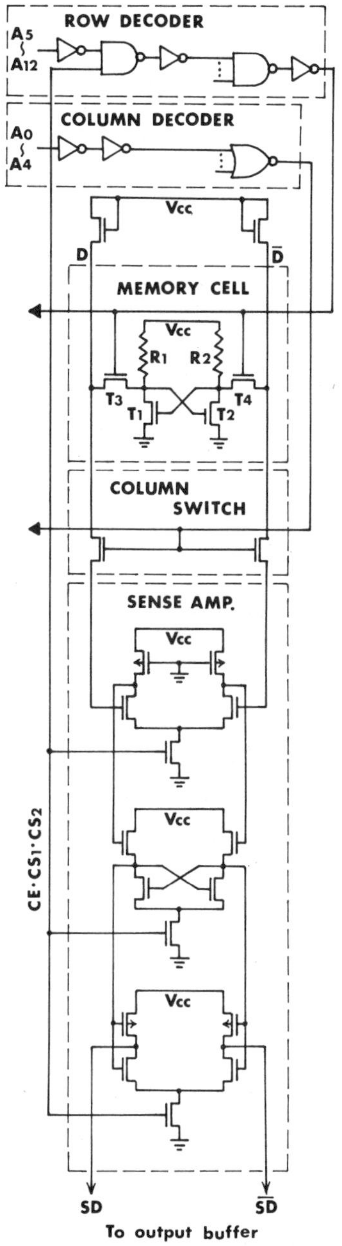

FIGURE 4—Schematic of memory cell, row and column decoder and sense amplifier circuits.

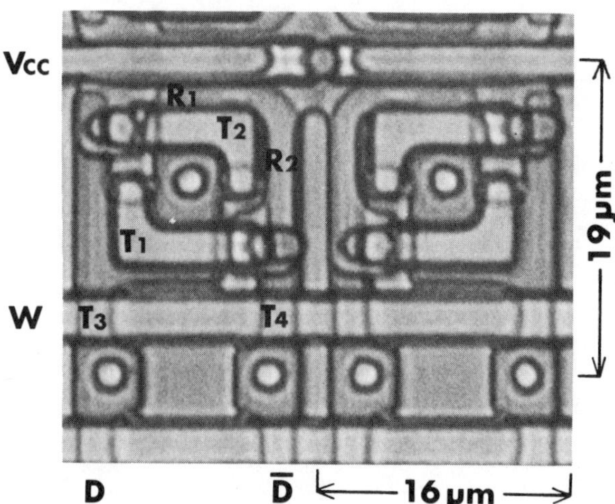

[Left]

FIGURE 3—Photomicrograph of the 64Kb RAM. Chip size is 5.44x5.80mm.

Section 4.5
Dynamic RAMs

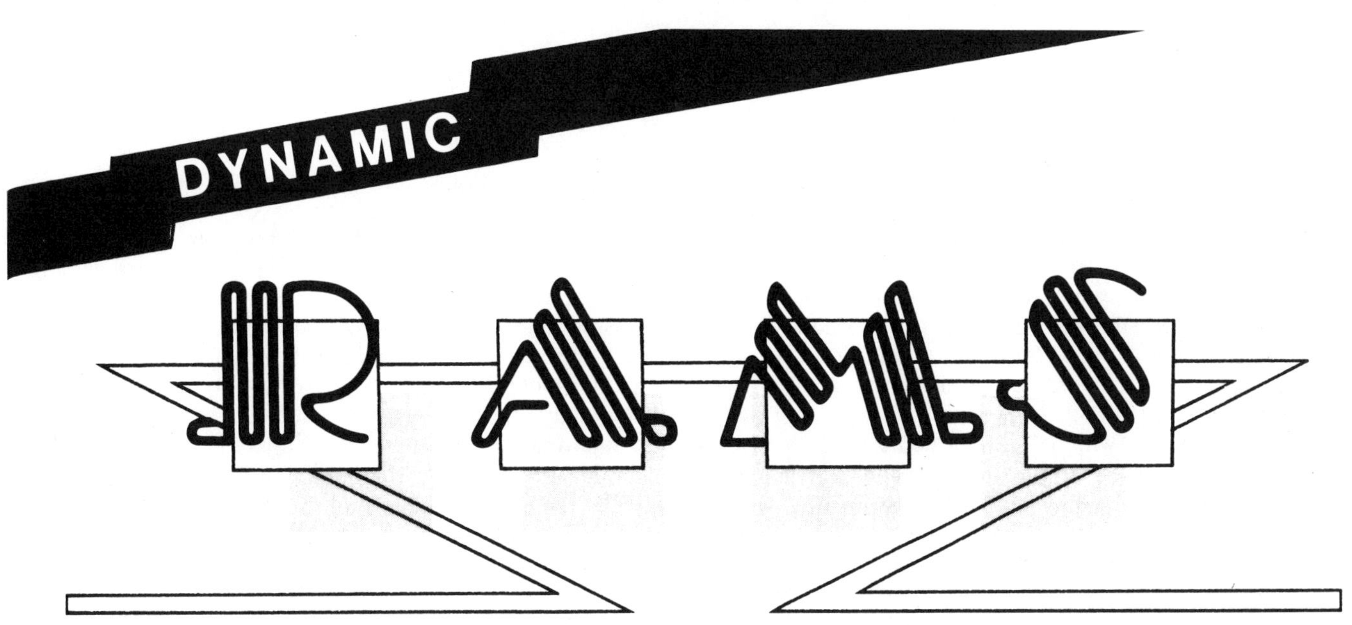

What to expect next: a special report

64-K and larger dynamic memories struggle toward the market, trusting in a variety of technologies

by John G. Posa

☐ Early cost-per-bit studies projected that 64-K random-access memories would be competitive with 16-K RAMs in 1981. However, this prediction was predicated on a bad assumption: that semiconductor manufacturers possessed the resources and technical prowess necessary to mass-produce the parts. For this reason and others, that crossover point has been pushed back two years. While memory users will be denied their bits, this lull in volume production affords an excellent opportunity to compare and contrast 64-K and bigger dynamic RAMs in the offing.

Although the 16-K RAM demanded a second level of polysilicon, its device geometries were not significantly reduced from 5 micrometers, so in-place projection lithography equipment that exposed 4-K RAMs could be used for the new generation. In contrast, the 64-K RAM needs linewidths of 3.5 μm or less, so the contestants must all learn the art of scaling. This minimum feature also taxes present lithography machines, yet the alternatives—deep-ultraviolet and direct-step-on-wafer exposure systems—are back-ordered.

To make matters worse, it was established that 64-K RAMs should generate their substrate bias internally for operation from a single 5-volt supply. This, in conjunction with roughly half-sized cells, lowered internal operating margins while at the same time increasing susceptibility to alpha radiation. Undeterred, at least 18 U. S., Japanese, and European chip makers say they will make 64-K RAMs (see table). The carrot being held in front of them is a market exceeding $1 billion by 1983, according to some market research firms (see "A $1 billion 64-K market by 1983," p. 121).

Many choices

With so many manufacturers poised to crowd the market, it is reasonable to expect that some or most of the chip designs will be identical or at least similar. Nothing could be further from the truth, however; indeed, the most fascinating aspect of the upcoming dynamic RAMs is the variation in their design. These differences—some subtle, others striking—are no longer just being debated at circuits conferences, but are being put into silicon. And each manufacturer feels strongly justified in choosing the architecture and manufacturing process that it will put into practice.

RAM storage areas are being partitioned into two, four, and eight array sections. Open and folded bit-sense lines will both be used, as will a unique sense amplifier

Reprinted with permission from *Electronics*, vol. 53, pp. 119–129, May 22, 1980.
Copyright © 1980 by McGraw-Hill, Inc. All rights reserved.

fed by four bit-sense lines—double the usual number. The chips will be refreshed in 2 milliseconds with 128 cycles or in 4 ms with 256 cycles, and at least three 64-K memories have or will be given counting circuitry for automatic refreshing, done on chip.

Redundancy will be used in some cases to improve yield, while new materials and implants are being tried to up the capacitance of the storage cells. Refractory silicides and laser annealing are being experimented with to lower the resistance of polysilicon wiring, and various coatings are being prepared as shields against ionizing alpha radiation. As a result of this diversity, access times and power dissipations for the latest generation of dynamic RAMs, too, will span a wide range.

A bit of history

The design of 64-K dynamic RAMs got off to an early start in Japan through an adjunct program of its recently concluded four-year, government-sponsored program for research and development of very large-scale integration. But at present the Japanese appear no closer than U. S. chip makers to volume production of 64-K RAMs, although they are regarded as the ultimate threat in the domestic and world dynamic RAM markets—Nippon Electric Corp. was second only to Mostek Corp. in global 16-K RAM shipments for 1979.

Specifically, Japan's initial 64-K RAM designs were targeted for Nippon Telegraph and Telephone Public Corp. equipment. NTT has a research arm—its Musashino Electrical Communication Laboratory—but no real production facilities. At the 1978 International Solid State Circuits Conference, NTT described a 64-K RAM that was partitioned into 16 4-K arrays; later, in a paper coauthored by Nippon Electric Co., a 16-K-by-4-bit dynamic RAM was presented. Last year, it reported a 64-K chip with a 1-μm molybdenum gates. None of these designs were slated for production.

Some more recent 64-K RAMs originally intended for NTT were, however, manufactured by NEC, Fujitsu Ltd., and Hitachi Ltd. All were two-supply parts. Between shipments to NTT, Fujitsu and NEC stock their own computers with these devices. Fujitsu also offers its part, the MB8164, commercially; if fact, the company claims to be the only company that can, today, supply 64-K RAMs "by the thousands per month." In the light of the single-supply precedent set by the U. S., Fujitsu plans to introduce a 5-V-only device this month, the MB8264. The fate of its older +7- and −2.5-V RAM depends on demand, says Fujitsu.

Fujitsu's 8164, considered by some to be the first 64-K RAM, was announced in 1978 along with devices from Texas Instruments Inc., International Business Machines Corp., and Motorola Inc., in that order. In 1979, Bell Laboratories and Mitsubishi Electric Corp. followed suit, as did Hitachi, now with a 5-V-only device. Since then, a great many other chip makers have promised 64-K RAMs. Also, 256-K memories have been described by NEC and the Musashino Lab. And the now defunct Kawasaki Cooperative Laboratories of Japan's VLSI Technology Research Association has laid the groundwork for half-megabit and even larger monolithic dynamic RAMs [*Electronics*, Feb. 14, p. 138].

It is interesting to note that two big names in the memory business—Intel Corp. and NEC—have so far been very close-mouthed about their 64-K devices. NEC will introduce a single-supply device this summer; Intel will do so shortly thereafter. In previous generations, NEC took pride in being the last to announce a device,

A SURVEY OF 64-K DYNAMIC RANDOM-ACCESS MEMORIES

Manufacturer	Part number	Die size[1] (mil^2)	Access time[1] (ns)	Power dissipation[1] (mW)	Voltages (V)	Refresh (cycles/period)	B[2]	W[2]	32-K partial[7]	5-V 16-K[7]
Fujitsu, Tokyo, Japan	MB8164[3]	34,250	150/200	385/n.a.	+7[3], −2.5	128/2	FM	P	N	M
Texas Instruments, Dallas, Texas	TMS4164	33,000	150/200	125/17.5	+5	256/4	D	M	N	Y
IBM, Essex Junction, Vt.	internal	62,500	330–440	360/20	+8.5, +4.25, −2.2	256/2–3	D	M	Y[4]	N
Motorola, Phoenix, Ariz.	MCM6664[5]	39,000	150/200	275/30	+5	128/2	FM	P	Y	Y
Bells Labs, Murray Hill, N.J.	internal	61,800	170	440/n.a.	+8, −5	128/4	P	M	N	N
Hitachi, Tokyo, Japan	HM4864	45,460	150/200	330/20	+5	128/2	FM	P	M	Y
Mostek, Carrollton, Texas	MK4164	40,750	100/120	300/20	+5	128/2	P	M	Y[6]	Y
Mitsubishi, Tokyo, Japan	M58764S	41,750	150/200	250/27.5	+5	256/4	D	M	N	Y
National, Santa Clara, Calif.	NMC4164	31,000	120/150/200	200/20	+5	256/4	M	P	Y	Y
Toshiba, Tokyo, Japan	TMM4164C	38,600	120/150	250/20	+5	128/2	D	M	M	N
NEC, Tokyo, Japan	μPD4164	50,650	200	250/28	+5	128/2	D	M	N	Y
Intel, Santa Clara, Calif.	2164	n.a.	100/150/200	n.a.	+5	128/2	n.a.	n.a.	Y	Y
Siemens, Munich, West Germany	HYB4164	39,000	150	250/n.a.	+5	256/4	n.a.	M	n.a.	n.a.
ITT, Freiburg, West Germany	ITT4564	36,000	150	250/25	+5	128/2	D	M	Y	n.a.
AMD, Sunnyvale, Calif.	Am9064	< 40,000	100/150/200	200/20	+5	128/2	n.a.	n.a.	M	Y
Fairchild, Mountain View, Calif.	F64K	36,450	120	< 200	+5	256/4	M	P	n.a.	n.a.
Inmos, Colorado Springs, Colo.	n.a.	< 40,000	n.a.	n.a.	+5	256/4	n.a.	n.a.	N	Y
Signetics, Sunnyvale, Calif.	2164	40,700	60/80/120	300/15	+5	256/4	n.a.	n.a.	Y	n.a.

1. Actual and speculative values are intermixed. 2. B = bit-line material, W = word-line material, M = metal, D = diffused (ion-implanted), P = polysilicon, F = folded bit line. 3. Newer 8246 is 5-V-only. 4. Not a partial. 5. Newer 6665 has no pin-1 refresh. 6. 4332 contains 2 16-K RAMS; 4532 is a 64-K partial. 7. Y = yes, N = no, M = maybe.

A $1 billion 64-K market by 1983

Updating its outlook for the dynamic RAM marketplace, Dataquest Inc. now foresees 64-K RAMs crossing the $1 billion threshold by 1983. As shown in the graph on the left, the Cupertino, Calif., research firm expects the market for 64-K chips to start a steep upward climb in 1981, gaining nearly $4.5 million in market size per year at least to 1984, leaving the other device types in the dust just after 1982's onset.

The data it has compiled on the single-supply 16-K RAM, too, is optimistic, indicating that a linear upward ramping has already commenced, shooting to hit $400 million by 1984. But, as underscored by current fluctuations in the cost of triple-supply RAMs due to a softening in demand, RAM pricing and market size are particularly sensitive to industry capacity and day-to-day economics. "If the market goes soft for the 16-K, it will provide the incentive to push wafer starts," states Dataquest's Daniel Klesken. This may close the window on the single-supply 16-K RAM, he cautions.

Based on Dataquest's average selling price curves (center graph), the single- and triple-supply 16-K RAMs will not compete on a cost-per-bit basis until the second half of 1981. The curve for the 64-K RAM crosses that for the three-supply 16-K in the second half of 1982 and that for the one-supply 16-K RAM in mid-1983 (right graph).

In a market study done by Hitachi Ltd., growth curves for the 16- and 64-K parts are more conservative; but for the 256-K RAM, it forecasts a $0.5 billion market by 1985. Hitachi sees the same peak year for the 16-K RAM—1983—and although its curves resemble those of Dataquest's, Hitachi's combined total for both 16-K device types comes within only 60% of Dataquest's, on the average. With the 64-K RAM, Hitachi closely tracks Dataquest until 1983, at which point it predicts a market of only $700 million, followed by a wait until 1985 to reach $1 billion from a more moderate slope.

These market estimates are for worldwide consumption in noninflated, or constant, dollars. Dataquest's Klesken adds that of the total, the U. S. consumes about 55%, Europe about 25%, and Japan, about 20%. He feels that Japan might pick up 5 to 8 percentage points in the next five years for its own computers, subtracting from both European and U. S. shares. But much of this equipment will "get purchased in Europe and the U. S. anyway."

In terms of production, Dataquest says that about 16,000 64-RAMs were shipped in 1979, of which about 10,000 came from Motorola, about 2,400 from TI, and the rest from Fujitsu. Motorola does not repudiate these estimates; in fact it adds that though Dataquest quotes Hitachi as merely supplying samples of its 64-K RAM in 1979, it has "heard rumors that Hitachi may have shipped as many as 1,000 64-Ks last year." IBM and Western Electric (for Bell Labs) both claim to be in volume production of their devices, albeit for captive consumption.

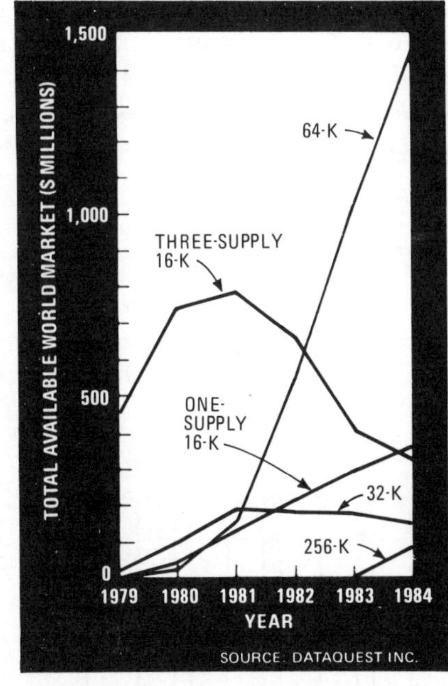

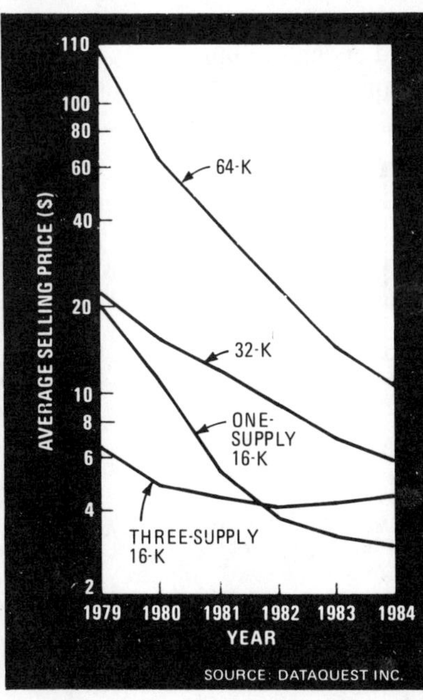

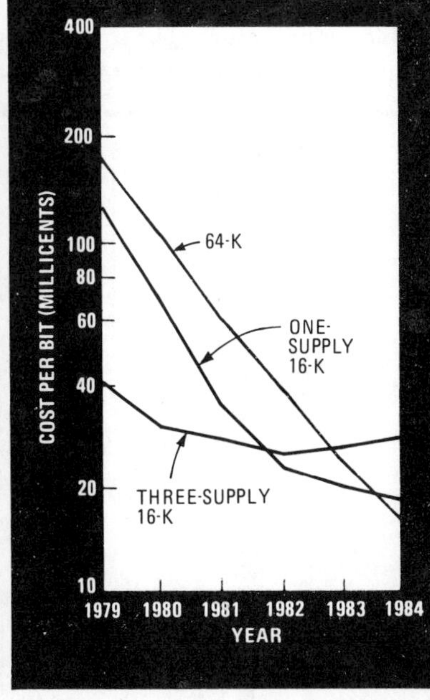

but afterwards began production with a vengeance and quickly forged its way to the top of the pack. With the materialization of the market so distant, these two companies feel no compulsion to rush. After all, each is profiting from 16-K dynamic RAM sales—NEC from its three-supply device and Intel from its new, expensive, but fast single-supply 2118.

As the table shows, more than half of the companies planning 64-K RAMs are also considering single-supply 16-K memories. There will be diversity in these designs too. Some of the manufacturers will first build 64-K RAMs, then offer tiny 16-K chips incorporating the same scaled-down design rules. Others, like Intel, to beat the competition to the market, will first introduce 5-V-only 16-K parts with relaxed geometries. Single-supply 16-K RAMs will not be competitive with three-supply devices for at least another year, especially when 64-K RAM features are used. The parts therefore must—and do—

have something else to offer: speed. Intel's 2118 is twice as fast as the slower versions of its 64-K RAM.

The single-device cell used in modern dynamic RAMs actually contains a MOS FET in series with a storage capacitor. The drain of the transistor connects to a bit line that in turn feeds a sense amplifier for that column of cells. The gate of the transistor connects to a word (or row) line. The bit lines are perpendicular to the sense amplifiers. The word lines are parallel; thus, their number settles how many cells will hang on a sense amp, as well as the number of refreshing cycles.

Dynamic organizations

The most daring way to organize a dynamic RAM is to divide up the array the fewest number of times consonant with the requirements of such peripheral circuits as the sense amps and decoders. Large, solid arrays mean long, unbroken bit and column lines, and since metal is rarely used for both, the nonmetallic set of interconnections may exhibit long RC time delays and bog down access time. In addition, if large numbers of cells are attached to the bit lines, more sense amp sensitivity might be required or operating margins may suffer. Also, partitioned arrays may be more conducive to use as partial devices, and it is possible to shut down unused array sections to conserve active power.

No manufacturer has so far been bold enough to build a high-density dynamic RAM and not split up the array at least once. The degree to which 64-K and denser parts are divided is shown in Fig. 1. At the 64-K level, Texas Instruments, Mitsubishi Electric Corp., and Siemens AG begin with a 256-by-256-bit matrix and split it down the middle into two 32-K arrays. It is believed that Signetics Corp. is adopting the same plan for its 64-K chip.

With two 128-by-256-bit arrays, there are 256 sense amps that connect to 256 cells each—128 on either of the two arms that emanate from every amplifier. Since in general the number of cycles required to refresh the array equals the number of cells serviced by each sense amp, TI, Mitsubishi, Siemens, and Signetics all specify a 256-cycle refresh.

Although every 16-K RAM is refreshed with 128 cycles, this 64-K departure from precedent has become a non-issue. As the 128 cycles must be supplied in 2 ms, 256-cycle RAM makers simply specify a 4-ms period. This means that the overhead—the percentage of time wasted on refreshing—is the same in both instances. A common method of refreshing 128-cycle devices is with 7 bits from an external binary counter. But counters have 8 bits if they have 7, so the previously unconnected line is simply brought over to the eighth address line—A_7—of a 256-cycle RAM.

However, with 256 cells attached to each sense amp and with 4 ms elapsing between refreshes, companies like Texas Instruments must take added precautions against leakage or the charge stored on the cells will fade away. Data loss is caused by a buildup of minority carriers underneath and around the storage region, degrading a stored 1 to a 0. Expressing minority carrier buildup mathematically, TI found that leakage currents

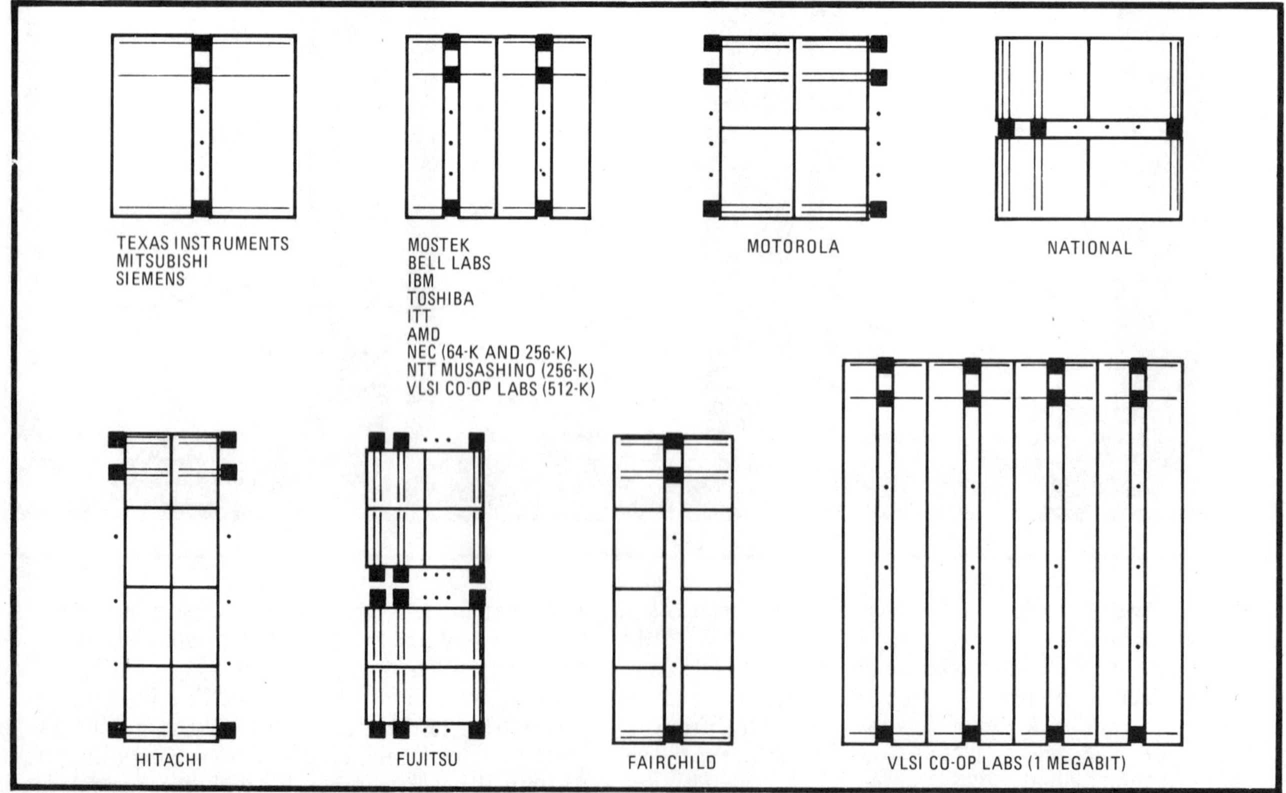

1. Array of arrays. Dynamic RAMs are partitioned into two, four, or eight subsections in accordance with sense amplifier and cell design. The sense amps (the small tinted boxes) usually have two bit-sense lines emanating from them. Folded bit-sense lines are adjacent.

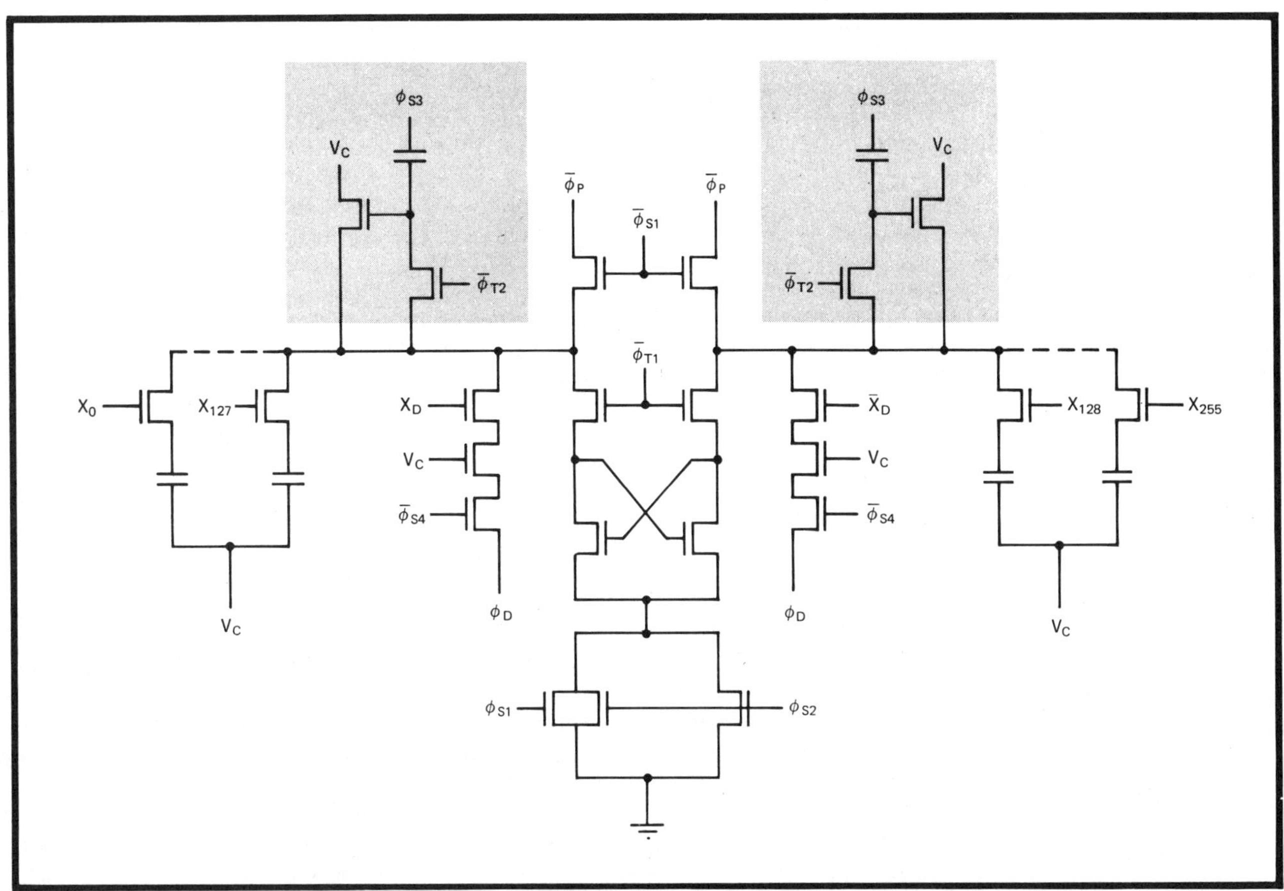

2. TI's sense amp. This sense amplifier is used by Texas Instruments in its 64-K RAM. The word lines, x_0–x_{255} are bootstrapped so full V_{DD} potentials are written into the cells. The active load devices (shown tinted) restore this level after reading and refreshing.

are aggravated by increasing the negative substrate voltage, V_{BB}, so the Dallas, Texas, company straps the substrate of its 64-K RAM to the cold-water pipe—in other words, to ground, V_{SS}.

However, all other domestic 64-K RAM suppliers generate a negative substrate bias on chip—with the exception of IBM and Bell Labs, which forgo 5-V-only operation and bias the substrate externally. So TI's practice of making V_{BB} equal to 0 V certainly has given the rest of the industry something to talk about. For instance, the competition cannot fathom how TI achieves workable operating margins since the loss of V_{BB} truncates internal signal swings by at least 2 V.

Enough margin

To keep margins up in the 64-K RAM, most chip makers—TI included—bootstrap their word lines to a high voltage so that a full V_{DD} logical 1 level can be written into the cells. This bootstrapping offsets the threshold voltage of the cell's selection transistor, which must otherwise be subtracted from the potential stored on the cell. In addition, after a cell is written, state-of-the-art sense amps keep it at full V_{DD} level after read and refresh operations.

TI's sense amp is shown in Fig. 2. V_C is a regulated version of V_{DD}. The active loads (shown tinted) keep 0s equal to V_{SS} and 1s equal to V_{DD}. Until those pull-ups are clocked, however, operation is more or less as in 16-K parts. With a high-going row-address strobe, $\overline{RAS}$, indicating a precharge mode, precharge clock ϕ_P is set to V_{DD} and sense amp clock $\overline{\phi}_{S4}$ is pulsed to establish a dummy-cell reference between V_{SS} and V_{DD}.

Whether to read it or refresh it, the desired cell is selected with an appropriate word line (x_0 through x_{255}) and, simultaneously, a dummy cell is selected on the opposite side of the sense amp. At this point the cross-couple flip-flop in the sense amp goes through its decision-making process on the basis of signals presented to it by the dummy cell and the memory cell. With clock $\overline{\phi}_{T1}$ high, ϕ_{S1} and ϕ_{S2} are sequenced to amplify these voltages, now latched on opposite sides of the flip-flop.

Those active loads now swing into play. First, $\overline{0}_{T2}$ is raised; on the side of the sense amp that reads 0, this discharges the gate of the load transistor (the device across V_{DD} and the bit-sense line). On the high side of the sense amp, though, raising $\overline{\phi}_{T2}$ charges up the gate of that load device. Now ϕ_{S3} is brought higher than V_{DD}—this time to avoid the threshold of the load device—and a full V_{DD} level is restored to the cell. Had a cell been selected on the other side of the sense amp—the zero side—current would have been unable to flow between V_{DD} and the bit-sense line so that the cell would remain near ground.

Active loads and extra clock lines, in addition to bootstrapped lines—are they worth it? TI gives an unequivocal "yes." With the exception of National and Fairchild, for a reason that will be explained shortly, all of the designs with 128-cycle, 2-ms refreshing need double TI's number of sense amplifiers, or 512. "About 80% of the power dissipation is in the sense amps," explains Dick Gossen, manager of MOS memory development at TI. He and A. C. D'Augustine, dynamic-RAM marketing manager, feel that the schemes using 512 sense amps "are going to have a tough time matching the TMS 4164's 200-mW specification" and parts now coming off the assembly line consume even less, they claim. The TI officials also like to observe that "every successful dynamic RAM to date—including the 1-K 1103, 4-K 4060, 4-K 4027, and 16-K 4116—has had a square organization with a single rail of sense amps running down the middle."

Double strength

In all other 64-K dynamic RAMs, the sense amps are loaded down with only 128 cells, essentially doubling the signal strength riding on the bit lines. This camp of manufacturers believes their almost doubled margins yield a more mass-producible part; after all, if the 64-K RAM cannot be manufactured, who cares about the 256-K RAM anyway? The only drawback with the 128-cycle refresh is that a slightly larger die area is required.

Mostek, Bell Labs, Toshiba, and the others listed in Fig. 1 divvy up the main array lengthwise into a pair of 128-by-256-bit subarrays, each with a row of sense amps running up the middle. They get 128-cycle refreshing, but with the extra row of sense amps. Toshiba feels that two 32-K arrays are just right in light of package restraints and 16-K compatability. It says that "further division [into more arrays] would only increase the amount of on-chip wiring." Also, while TI makes claims about low power consumption, Bell Labs interjects that with two arrays, active power and peak current are both minimized because only one of the arrays need be selected at a time—in the other block, only row decoding and refreshing occur.

As mentioned briefly already, National and Fairchild use sense amps with double the refreshing power. In their 64-K RAMs, each sense amp is shared between two pairs of bit lines. Both chips use a 256-cycle, 4-ms refresh, need only 128 sense amps, and connect each bit line to only 64 cells.

National's sense amp is shown in Fig. 3 (Fairchild's is similar in principle). Note that it is symmetrical about the sense amp enable line, $\overline{\phi}_{SE}$. Bit lines 1 and 4 are balanced, as are bit lines 2 and 3. Clocks ϕ_{T1} and ϕ_{T2} select one of these pairs, while a memory cell is singled out with the appropriate word line, say X_1. A dummy cell is also selected, but on the same side of the sense amp as the chosen memory cell.

If the memory capacitor is charged to store a 1, the added charge from the dummy cell causes bit line 1 to be slightly more positive than bit line 4. If a zero is stored, the imbalance will go the other way. The difference is sensed and amplified as $\overline{\phi}_{SE}$ is lowered.

John Barnes, a senior staff member in Fairchild's dynamic-memory department, points to another distinct advantage of this scheme: "It allows a full-sized dummy-cell capacitor." The charge on such a capacitor can be divided between two bit lines, presenting each with a midpoint reference; this is exactly what a sense amp wants to see for its comparison. Older dynamic RAMs allowed half-sized dummy capacitors to be fashioned for this purpose, but new RAMs practically forbid it. "How can you make something with half the minimum feature?" asks Barnes.

The sense amps of National and Fairchild are optimally laid out with metal bit (not word) lines. This makes polysilicon the logical choice for the word lines, though now a greater distance must be traversed, forcing a further division of the array to circumvent the speed

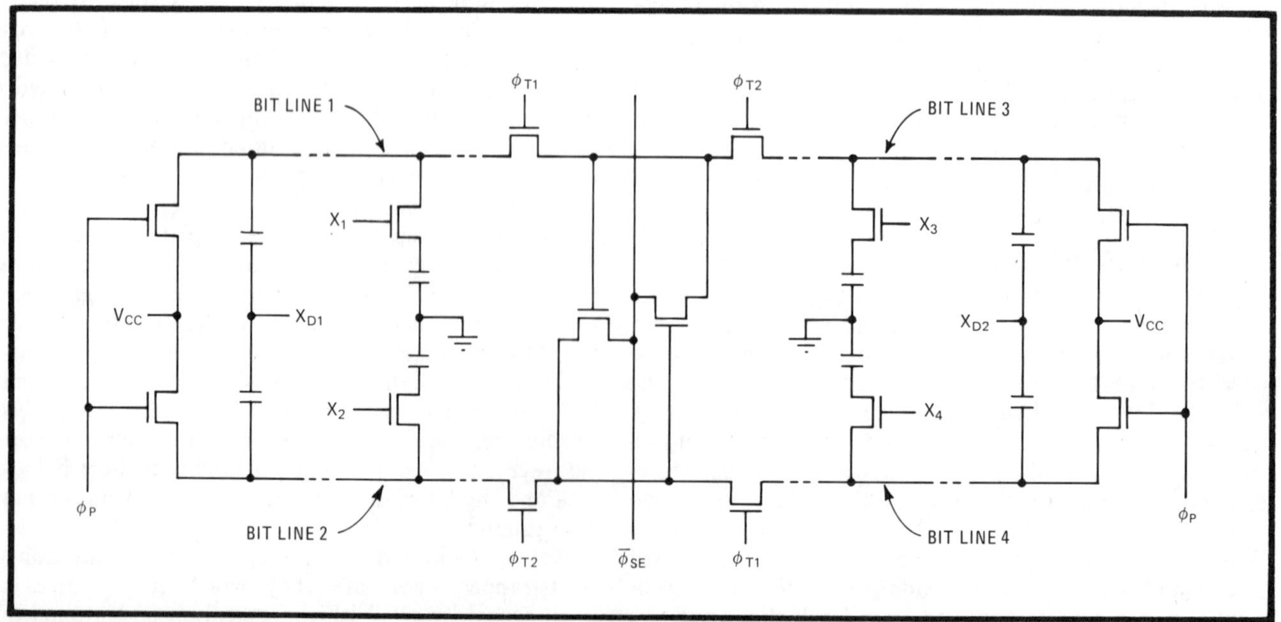

3. Four for one. National uses this sense amp in its 64-K RAM and Fairchild will use a similar version. Each amplifier is responsible for four bit lines—twice the usual number—so these two companies are able to achieve 256-cycle refreshing with only 256 sense amps.

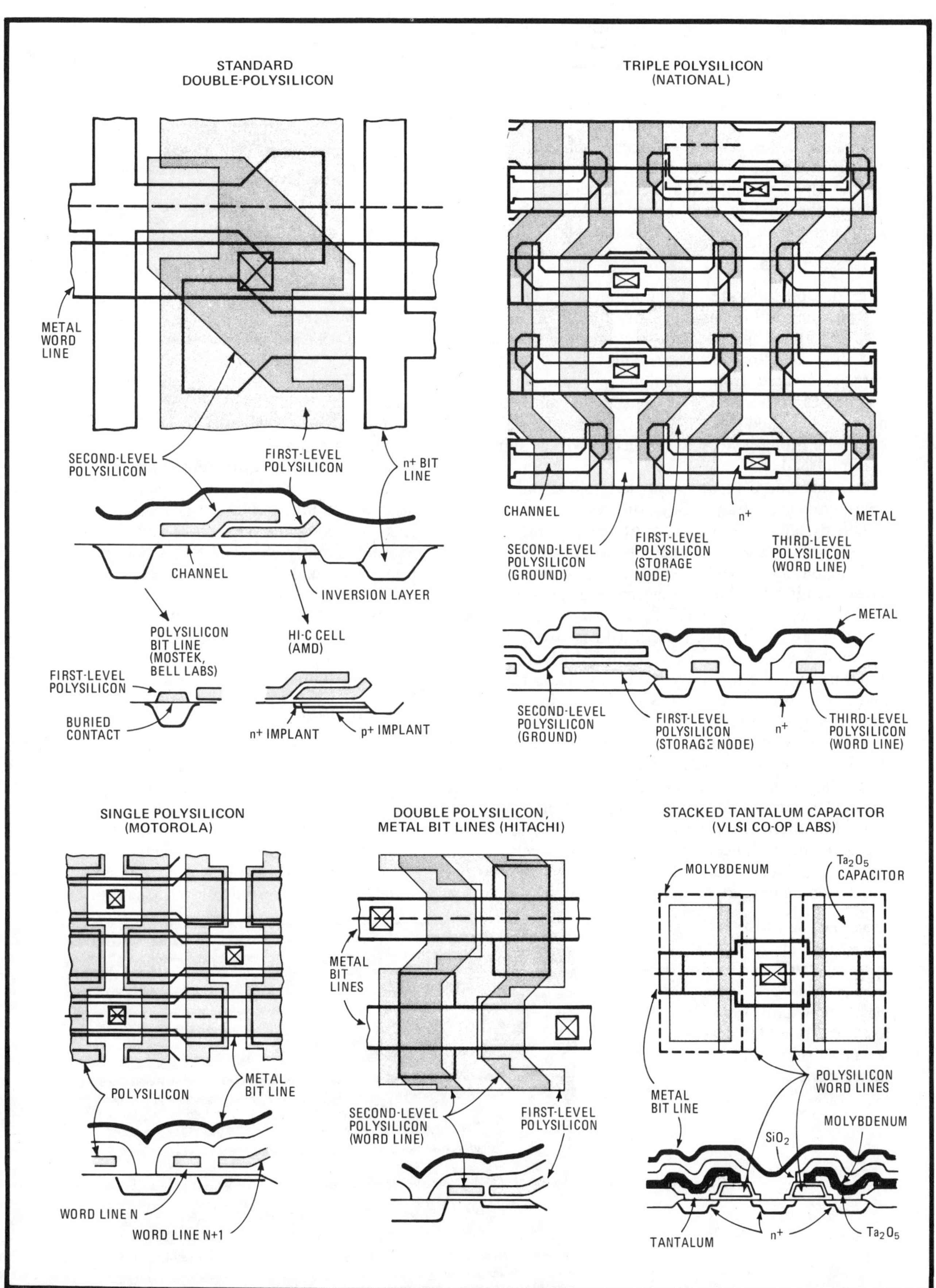

4. Cells for sale. Mostek and Bell Labs give polysilicon bit lines to the standard double-polysilicon cell. AMD is giving it high-capacity storage; Motorola has a single-poly process; National's cells have three; Hitachi folds its bit lines; and the VLSI Co-op Labs use tantalum.

problems inherent in polysilicon's high sheet resistance.

Metal bit lines are also helpful against alpha radiation, since diffused bit lines appear even better than the storage nodes at collecting the excess charge generated by the alpha particles. Further shielding is realized by folding the bit lines, which is what Motorola, Hitachi, and Fujitsu have done in their 64-K RAMs.

A twofold plus

Folded bit lines are nothing magical. Each sense amp is still connected to only one pair of bit lines, but instead of being aimed in opposite directions, the lines are laid out right next to each other. The rationale is that the carriers created from the alpha particle will now be coupled to both sides of the sense amp. Since the sense amp is designed to amplify a difference signal, the chance of alpha-generated soft errors will be significantly diminished.

At least one company says that folded bit lines also give layout advantages. Says Bill Martino, a Motorola circuit designer who helped on its 64-K RAM, "You can put the sense amps on one end of the pair of bit lines and you can put a decoder with an I/O section on the other. It saves running the bit lines across the decoder," which can foul up the signal. But, as with the designs of National and Fairchild, metal bit lines strongly suggest polysilicon word lines. As a result, Motorola, Hitachi, and Fujitsu were similarly forced to divide their array and place column decoders within it to decrease word-line propagation delay.

In sum, then, for the same performance that metal word lines provide, polysilicon word lines ask for a somewhat larger die. In addition, Mostek claims that folded bit lines do not permit bootstrapping of the word lines. But there is reason to believe that metal bit lines are a winning choice. Aside from some thick, organic coatings, folded metal bit lines seem to be the best protection against alpha particles. No U. S. 16-K RAMs feature folded bit lines, but Fujitsu's 16-K RAM does. "Ask any user, and he'll tell you that the most reliable 16-K RAM is Fujitsu's. Its alpha particle error rate is practically three orders of magnitude less than Mostek's device's," says a senior memory designer at Inmos. "Folded bit lines are the only way to go."

It is no secret that the smart RAM makers are investigating methods to lower polysilicon's sheet resistance. This, in the industry, is referred to as "the low sheet rho problem," the Greek letter ρ symbolizing resistivity. Whereas some IC manufacturers think that the problem can be put off until the 256-K level, Mosaid Inc., the MOS memory analysts in Ottawa, Canada, maintain that low sheet ρ will be needed for the 64-K RAM.

At the present time there are three techniques to heighten polysilicon's conductivity. These include the use of a second metal layer, refractory metal silicides, and laser annealing of the polysilicon itself. All three schemes are being tried. IBM uses two levels of metal in its 64-K RAM, NTT uses molybdenum disilicide word lines in its 256-K device, and memory makers are buying up laser annealing equipment at a fast pace.

As yet, no manufacturer will admit that it is using laser annealing, but there is reason to believe that at least one company—NEC—is using it in its 64-K RAM. Mosaid recently observed NEC's polysilicon interconnections and found them to exhibit large grains and a sheet resistance of about 22 ohms per square. Heavily doped polysilicon has a resistance of over double that. It has also been rumored that Intel Corp. intends to solve the low sheet ρ problem on its 64-K RAM; this decision may have contributed to the tardiness of its chip.

Cells on offer

Besides the variety of architectures and interconnection schemes in the new dynamic RAMs, there is variety in their cell designs. These are based on compact layout, to be sure, but because of the reduced stored charge resulting from scaled geometries, the primary focus is how to achieve more capacitance for the micrometer.

Commercial 16-K RAMs and some 64-K chips use the standard double-polysilicon cell (see Fig. 4). Bit lines are

5. Burned out. IBM, Bell Labs, and the Musashino Lab of NTT have designed dynamic RAMs with redundant elements to improve yield. Each concern has a unique method of swapping in the extra circuitry. In Bell Labs' 64-K RAM, spare rows and columns are inserted with a laser at the time of wafer probing.

diffused and staggered so that their hammerhead-shaped appendages, sometimes referred to as spades, interlock. Cell capacitors reside at the tips of these spades. First-level polysilicon field-plate lines meander between each bit line, forming the top capacitor plates and connecting them to V_{DD}. Upper-level polysilicon is used as gate material, controlling current between bit lines and storage capacitors. To save room, this second polysilicon layer with its single contact via is shared between two cells from adjacent bit lines. Although two layers will be most common, dynamic RAM cells have been also given one or three layers of polysilicon.

Inversion layers

Actually the bit lines of modern RAMs are ion-implanted and not diffused, but the terminology has held on from the old days. Also, the polysilicon field-plate line has another role. Besides connecting upper capacitor plates to V_{DD}, it also inverts the surface of the silicon underneath it, and the resulting collection of charge becomes the bottom plate of a capacitor.

A logical 0 is represented by the electrons trapped in this inversion layer, and a 1 is established through the removal of some of these electrons via the MOS FET switch. The inversion layer can be augmented with a diffusion or implant and, if p-type, the field-plate line can be grounded yet retain electrons.

Evidently Mostek added such a p-type ion implantation (and its mask step) because the capacitors in its 64-K RAM are grounded and not attached to the supply. Sam Young, Mostek's strategic marketing manager of memory products, points out that this configuration eliminates the signal loss due to power supply excursions, commonly known as voltage bumps. Other companies, like TI, circumvent this problem by regulating V_{DD} right on the chip.

Mostek also switched from diffused to polysilicon bit lines for its 64-K RAM. This adds a mask for the buried contact between the diffused and polysilicon regions, but Young explains why the tradeoff is worthwhile: "It allows a larger cell without enlarging the die size. Diffused bit lines sit on the same physical plane as the capacitor, which means that a 4-μm-wide bit line has to be 7 μm away from the capacitor on each side.

"With the polysilicon bit line," Young continues, "the entire distance between both capacitors—with the 4-μm-wide bit line in between—can be reduced to 7 μm, thus saving 11 μm" between the two capacitors. According to Bell Labs, which also chose polysilicon bit lines, the resulting ratio of storage cell to bit-line capacitance is 0.08 compared with 0.05 for diffused bit lines and the same layout rules.

To up the capacitance in their 64-K RAMs, Advanced Micro Devices Inc. and a major Japanese chip maker are going to use the high-capacity or Hi-C RAM cell. In this cell, first described by TI in late 1977, a deep p-type implant dramatically increases the otherwise negligible depletion-region component of the storage cell capacitance. Unfortunately the implant also raises the threshold necessary to form the inversion layer, so a second, shallow n-type implant is used to counteract this unwanted side-effect. Aside from the two implants and

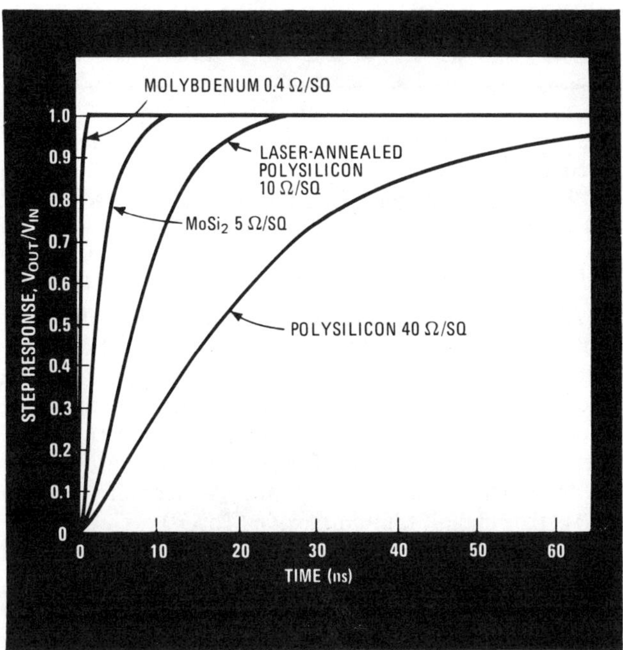

6. Good, better, best. If polysilicon is to be used for long, unbroken interconnection paths in dynamic RAMs, its resistance will have to be lowered. This graph, from TI, shows the combined effects of laser annealing, molybdenum disilicide, and pure molybdenum.

their associated masking steps, the Hi-C cell need not be different from a standard double-polysilicon cell.

It takes guts to use the Hi-C cell, though, because alignment is of the essence. If the shallow n implant encroaches too far into the MOS FET's channel region, undesirable short-channel effects may occur. Worse still, if the p implant is allowed to completely engulf the n implant, a potential barrier might arise and prevent reading of the cell capacitor. Nonetheless, "we have taken care of that with our cell structure," boasts Jeff Schlageter, product manager of MOS dynamic RAMs at AMD. "Alignment [of the implants] is no more critical than anything else in the circuit." TI originally predicted that the storage capacity per unit area could be 50% to 100% greater with the Hi-C cell; in practice, AMD expects a 30% increase.

Motorola is the company that gets by with a single level of polysilicon in its 64-K RAM cells; the resulting six-mask process probably did not adversely affect the chip's manufacturability. Using a cell first discussed by Teletype Corp., it also makes every word line double as a field plate line for an adjacent row, as shown in the bottom-left drawing in Fig. 4. This space-saving trick has, however, been criticized from a reliability standpoint. Under certain test procedures and operating conditions such as refreshing, a capacitor's field plate line, being a word line, may be rapidly pulsed. This, say some, may induce built-in voltage-bump problems.

National's 64-K RAM cell adds a third level of polysilicon, allowing both capacitor plates to be made of polysilicon. This layering "allows us to double the amount of charge that can be stored," according to Gene Miles, director of memory components marketing for National. The capacitor is also of higher quality, with only one fifth of the storage node's total area subject to substrate leakage. Although the third polysilicon level is said to be second in complexity only to epitaxy and the formation of buried n^+ regions, Miles contends that National's 64-K RAM will use eight or fewer mask steps.

A better dielectric

All of the increases in cell capacitance described thus far have been achieved with silicon dioxide as the dielectric material. But capacitance is directly proportional to the dielectric constant of the insulator, so a change in this material provides another degree of freedom. At last February's ISSCC, Japan's Cooperative Laboratories presented experimental 512-K and 1-megabit dynamic RAMs that exploit tantalum oxide (Ta_2O_5).

Combining the stacked-capacitor RAM cells first described by Hitachi in 1978 with their own quadruply self-aligned MOS process, the lab members refer to their creation as the stacked-high capacitor RAM. With a basic design rule of 2 μm, the team's 512-K RAM—at about 71,000 square mils—is roughly twice the size of an ordinary 64-K RAM. To build a megabit RAM, it essentially puts two 512-K RAMs onto a single 140,000-mil^2 die. The designers also state that with a 1-μm process, chips of "several megabits" are possible.

If the area of the storage capacitor in a standard double-polysilicon cell were to be reduced to the dimensions of the ones in the Co-op Labs' megabit RAM, stored charge would drop from about 250 femtocoulombs to below 30 fC, assuming that cell voltages are restored to full V_{DD} levels. This works out to fewer than 200,000 electrons. Such a minute charge packet would demand almost constant replenishing, and an alpha particle would wreak havoc.

So the researchers opted for tantalum oxide, which has a dielectric constant of 22; SiO_2's value, at 3.9, is less than a fifth of that. As shown in the cross section in Fig. 4, the tantalum makes direct contact to diffused regions. Next, to form Ta_2O_5, the tantalum is anodically oxidized, then covered with molybdenum.

The process requires 10 masks, but the reward is twofold. One benefit is more stored charge than in conventional double-polysilicon 64-K RAM cells. The second boon is low leakage through the Ta_2O_5: it takes 3.7×10^4 seconds for a 5-V stored level to decay to 4 V—if the Ta_2O_5 plate is the only escape path, that is.

Adding extras

Tough as it is to squeeze thousands of cells and hundreds of sense amps and decoders onto one substrate, some companies are adding extra circuitry. Bell Labs, IBM, and the Musashino Lab of NTT add redundant cells to improve yield. Motorola and Mostek add to their 64-K RAMs self-refreshing logic, activated with a low signal applied to pin 1. AMD is studying the approaches taken by these two companies as it prepares to pick one of the techniques for a version of its upcoming 64-K RAM. And up Inmos' sleeve is a way to get refreshing without dedicating a pin to the function.

As the logistics of on-chip refreshing are ironed out, there will be a fusion of static and dynamic RAM technology. This will not really affect by-1-bit memory organizations, but it will have a profound impact on byte-organized pseudostatic RAMs, as they are often called. A majority of the 64-K RAM makers also have a self-refreshing 8-K by 8 bit version in the works. If on-chip refreshing can be perfected to the point where dynamic RAMs appear to be truly static—and many feel this probable—it may signal the demise of fully static RAMs beyond the 16-K level, says one TI memory designer.

Interestingly, the three approaches to fault-tolerant yield are unique. NTT's 256-K RAM (probably another research vehicle) has four 128-by-512-bit sections, each with one spare word line and four spare bit lines, for a total of 4,096 spare bits; the superfluous cells are substituted with 15-V programming pulses applied at wafer probing. Bell Labs provides two spare rows and two spare columns for each of the four 64-by-256-bit arrays in its 64-K RAM, for a total of over 2,560 bits. Programming here, however, is done by opening 3-μm-wide polysilicon links with a laser (see Fig. 5).

On IBM's 64-K chip, another device intended just for in-house use, redundant lines pinch-hit for cells, rows or columns that fail functional testing. Bad addresses are stored in an on-chip ROM programmed with the second metalization level; incoming addresses are compared and routed accordingly. IBM's chip contains over 2,000 bits of built-in redundancy, says Nicholas M. Donofrio, manager of systems and test at IBM's General Technology division's development laboratory in Essex Junction, Vt.

In these three examples, neither the percentage of redundant storage nor the method of swapping the extra circuitry is the same. Obviously, a standard form for dynamic RAM redundancy does not exist. Although opinions vary, the consensus is that spare circuitry will not be put into commercially available RAMs, even at the 256-K level. Even though Bell claims that a fault-tolerant memory occupying 62,000 mil^2 (the size of its chip) will yield better than a memory half that size (slightly smaller than all the others), semiconductor manufacturers are still too proud to anticipate imperfection. And besides, the sale of partially good devices is going well.

Even though on-chip refreshing techniques have been endorsed by some major chip manufacturers, it is the important users that have given the concept a lukewarm welcome. David Ford, Motorola's strategic marketing manager of MOS memories, estimates that "about 50% of our customers want it," but concedes that those customers are in the minority when it comes to sales. "The mainframe guys don't want to refresh," he admits. "That's why we're offering a part [the 6665] that doesn't have it."

Motorola's 6664, the version with refresh, features two internal modes initiated with a low-going signal applied to pin 1. These are self-refresh and automatic refresh. Mostek's pin-1 refresh cycle is a perfect subset of the latter, though there are two minor differences. One is that Mostek specifies that the refresh line be inactive (brought high) for a minimum of 125 nanoseconds within the refreshing cycle. And Motorola puts an upper bound of 2 microseconds on pin 1's low state.

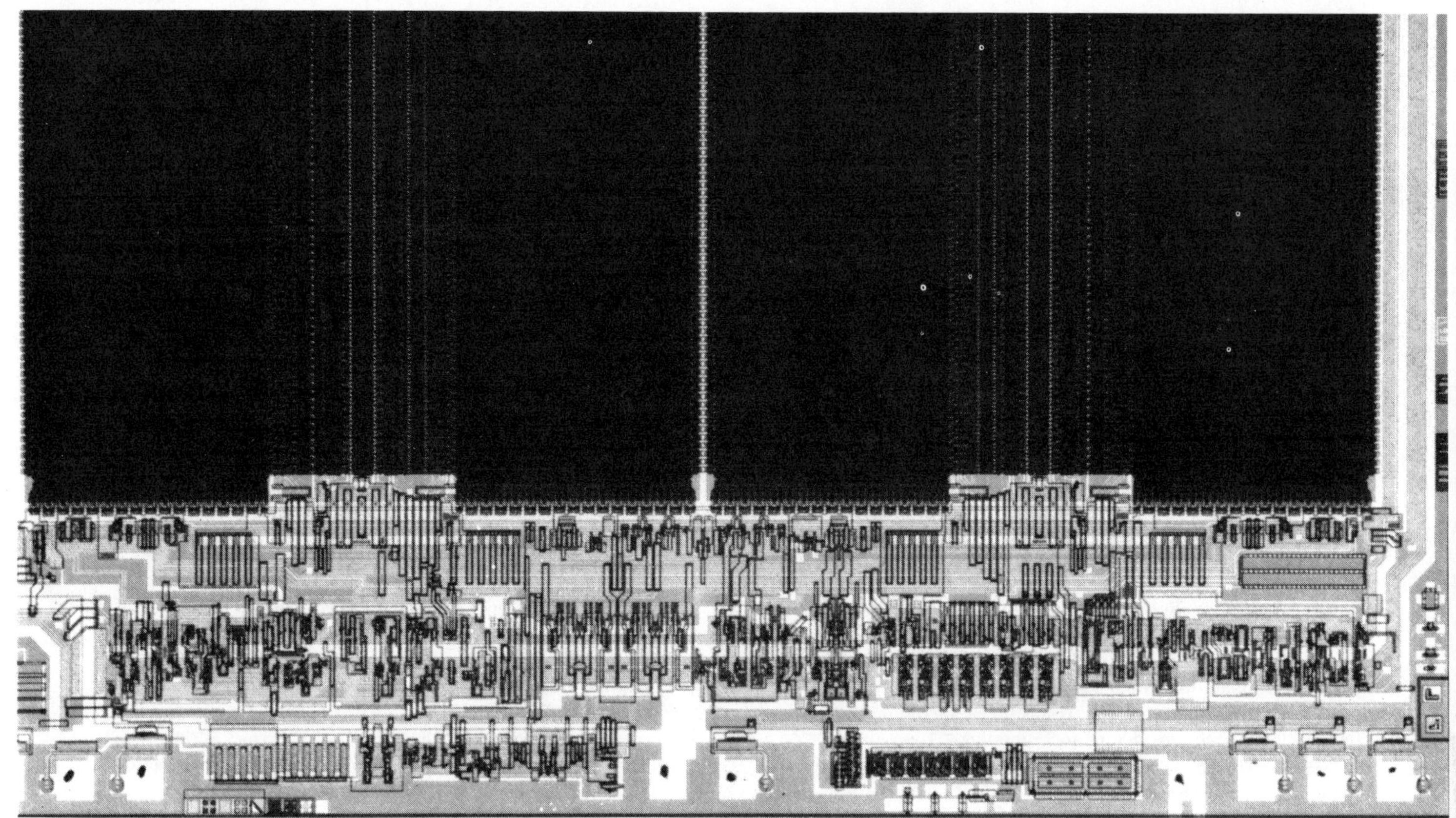

7. New kid in town. It is nowhere near volume production, but the Nippon Electric Co. is actually fabricating this 256-K RAM with wafer steppers from GCA Corp. The chip is only about twice the size of 64-K devices; NEC fit it into a standard 16-pin DIP.

Motorola limits how long pin 1 can be low because after about 13 μs the chip enters the self-refresh mode, a condition unique to Motorola's 64-K RAM. In this state, a new row is refreshed every 12 to 14 μs; thus, even in the worst case, the entire memory will be refreshed in less than the 2 ms specified. Motorola says this mode is mainly intended for battery-backup applications.

Packaging problems

There is reason to believe that pin 1 will be used for the ninth address line, A_8, for the 256-K RAM. Such a decision would forgo pin-1 refreshing. This has not yet been standardized by the Joint Electron Device Engineering Council's JC-42 committee, but Intel for one has already announced that it will use this pin for that purpose.

One solution to this dilemma is being proposed by Inmos. When the column address strobe, $\overline{\text{CAS}}$, is pulled low before $\overline{\text{RAS}}$, the row address strobe, an internal refreshing sequence will be activated in its 64-K design. This should not conflict with normal read and write operations since all manufacturers specify that the row address be latched before the column address.

Another solution, being looked at by both Motorola and Mostek, is a package with more pins. Mostek, for example, through a so-called bit-wide concept, will use the same 18-pin package for its 32- and 128-K products. The pin designations have actually been established already with the MK4332, a 32-K RAM built with two 16-K chips. Next, when the 32-K partial of the 64-K RAM becomes available, it too will be put in this package, as will two fully functional 64-K chips for a 128-K device. One reason why Motorola and Mostek want to salvage dedicated-pin refreshing is that the newer microprocessors have refresh pins that, in cases, can be directly interfaced to pin 1 on their parts.

More pins are only one of the bitter pills that will be swallowed as higher-density random-access memories draw near; the medicine is being tasted already at the 64-K level. To make the 256-K RAM, IC manufacturers will want to increase sense amplifier sensitivity. For optimum performance and alpha particle hardening, respectively, capacitance will have to be stolen from on-chip wiring and given to the storage nodes while decreasing cell size. A routine method of lowering polysilicon's resistance is anxiously awaited—perhaps only perfection (see Fig. 6). Cells exploiting Hi-C-like concepts will tend to prevail; maybe the use of a higher-dielectric material such as tantalum oxide is the answer.

Alphas revisited

Many of these problems will have to be solved to confound alpha particles. Hitachi has been coating its chips with a proprietary version of the organic material polymide it calls PIQ. A thickness of 40 to 55 μm diminishes soft errors by a factor of 1,000. Although invisible, alpha particles will still be heard from. But chip coatings, cells with high capacitance, and folded metal bit lines will sufficiently frustrate them.

There exists an entire other class of dynamic RAM cells that combine transfer and storage functions into a single unit. The taper-isolated cell and the stratified-charge memory are 2 of the 10 or so approaches that come to mind. Maybe the next generation of dynamic RAMs will be graced with the enormous density advantages that such concepts have the potential of offering. □

A 16K x 1 Bit Dynamic RAM

Paul R. Schroeder and Robert J. Proebsting

Mostek Corp.

Carrollton, TX

A 16K x 1 BIT dynamic RAM capable of 150-ns access time has been developed using a two-level N-channel polysilicon gate process and a single transistor cell. Utilizing the standard 16-pin package configuration, seven address bits are multiplexed. All clocks and other inputs are TTL compatible. Maximum user flexibility has been provided by incorporating ±10% supplies, a nonlatched tri-state data output controlled by $\overline{CAS}$, a wide multiplex timing window, page mode capability, and $\overline{RAS}$-only refresh.

A block diagram of the circuit is shown in Figure 1 and a photograph of a fabricated device appears in Figure 2. The chip is organized internally as a single 128 x 128 balanced array with both column decoders and sense amplifiers located in a row through the center of the array. To maintain a balanced configuration, each column decode circuit is divided into two parts with one half on either side of the sense amplifiers. These column decoders provide 1 of 64 selection. The final 1 of 128 column decoding is accomplished by selection of one of two pairs of data, data buses which also run through the center, and which are used for I/O coupling to the selected digit circuits. Since access is provided to both the true and complement sense lines associated with each amplifier, no digit pullup transistors are required. This permits completely dynamic flipflop type detectors to be used, resulting in very low power consumption.

The basic digit circuit – Figure 3 – consists of sense amplifier, memory cells, reference cell, and input-output coupling. Each sense amplifier is shared by 128 cells, 64 on each side (plus reference cell). Dimensions of the double-poly cell[1,2] are approximately 14.5 μm x 30 μm. Cell and digit line capacitances are estimated to be 0.04 pF and 0.8 pF, respectively.

A single set of seven address buffers is used for both row and column addresses in a multiplexed mode. A set of switches connects the address and address complement lines running through the row decoder to corresponding lines in the column decoders. During row address decoding time, these switches are left in the open circuit condition so that signals generated by the input buffers are coupled onto the row decode address lines only. Once row decoding is completed, row select information is trapped dynamically in the row decoder circuits, the address input buffers are reset, and the switches are closed in preparation for receiving column address information. At column address time the address lines, going now to both row and column decode circuits, are activated with column address signals. Column decoding takes place in the usual fashion. The row decoders, however, are effectively disabled at this time so that the previously completed row selection is undisturbed. A schematic of the row decoder circuit is shown in Figure 4.

This decoder architecture is a logical modification of earlier work implemented in a 4K RAM where both the input buffers and decoders are multiplexed. The higher density memory array used in the present 16K design, however, makes the use of a single multiplexed decoder for both row and column selection impractical.

To provide wide operating margins and noise immunity desired by users, a special input stage was designed to detect the TTL input levels. A circuit schematic of this stage is shown in Figure 5. Differential detection with a 1.5-V reference level is employed to maximize noise margin and avoid dependence on device threshold and other process parameters.

In the Figure 5 circuit, a positive common mode voltage boost is capacitively coupled to the gates of transistors T3 and T4 to assure that at least one of these is turned on at latch time, even though both the input and reference voltages may be less than the device threshold voltage. The addition of T1 and C1 in the V_{IN} path helps to increase the amount of negative undershoot on V_{IN} which can be tolerated between the time TA goes low and the time latching takes place. This is necessary to avoid a long row address hold time which would otherwise be required.

Key device characteristics are summarized in Figure 6.

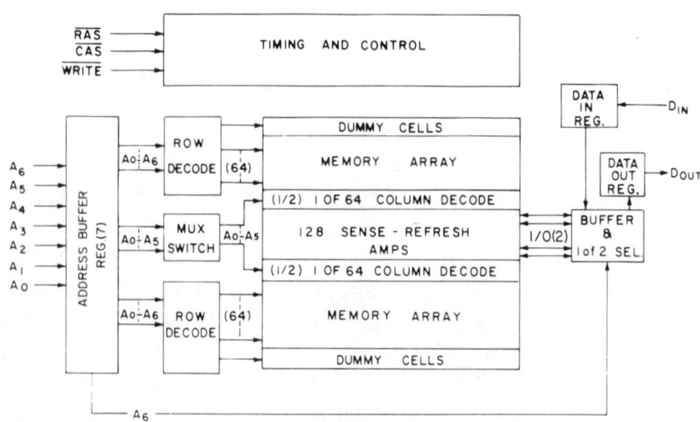

FIGURE 1 – Block diagram.

[1] *Electronics*, Vol. 48, No. 26, p. 29; December 25, 1975.

[2] Ahlquist, C.N., Breivogel, J.R., Koo, J.T., McCollum, J.L., Oldham, W.G., and Renninger, A.L., "A 16K Dynamic RAM", *ISSCC Digest of Technical Papers*, p. 128, 129; Feb., 1976.

Reprinted from *IEEE Int. Solid State Circuits Conf.*, pp. 12–13, 1977.

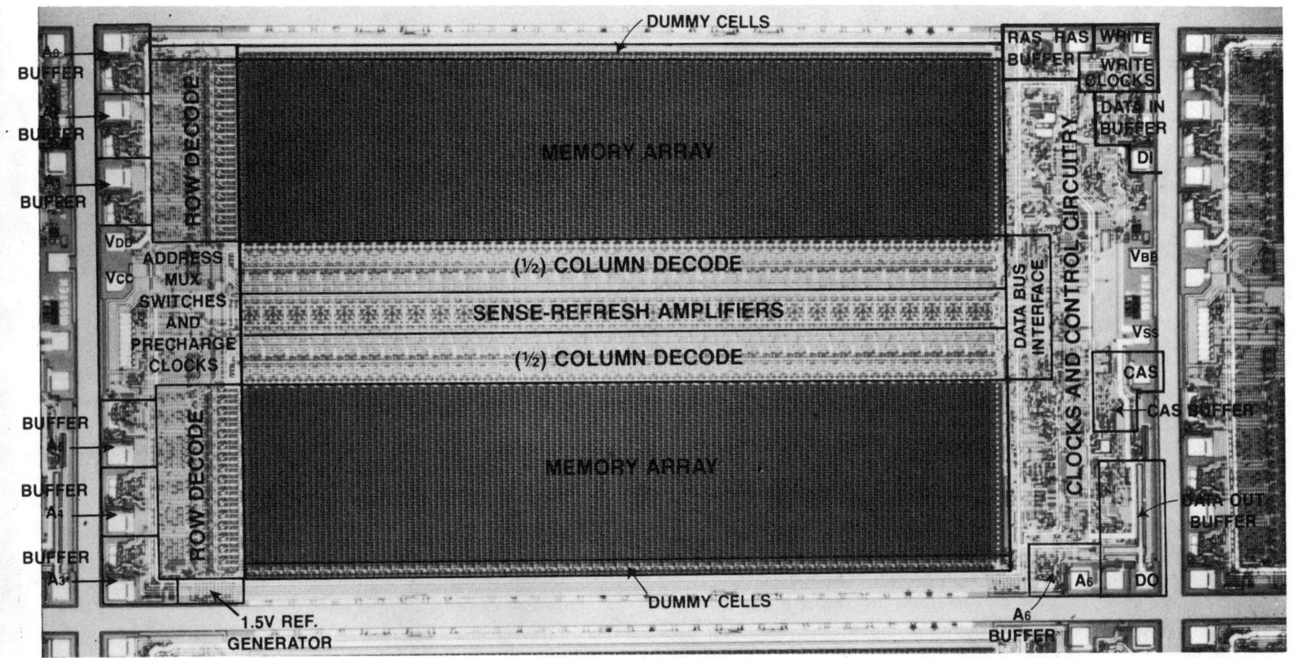

FIGURE 2 – Photograph of a 16K die showing location of important circuit blocks.

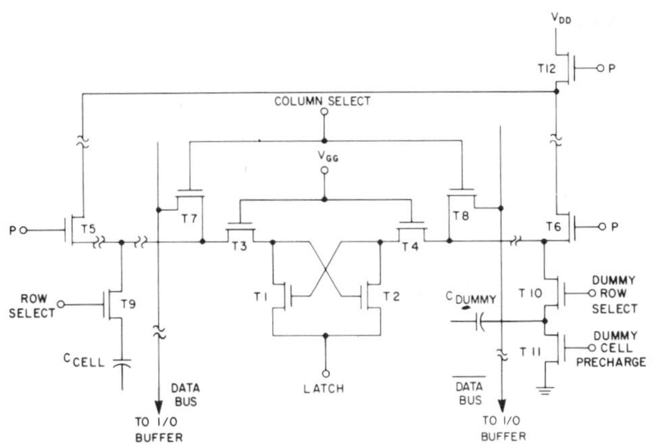

FIGURE 3 – Digit and sense circuit schematic.

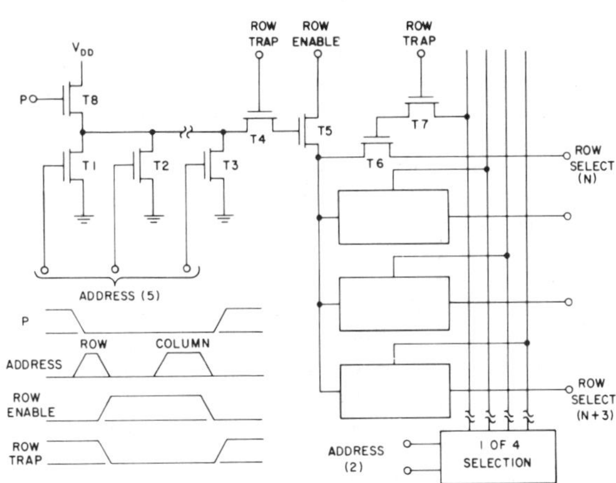

FIGURE 4 – Row decode circuit.

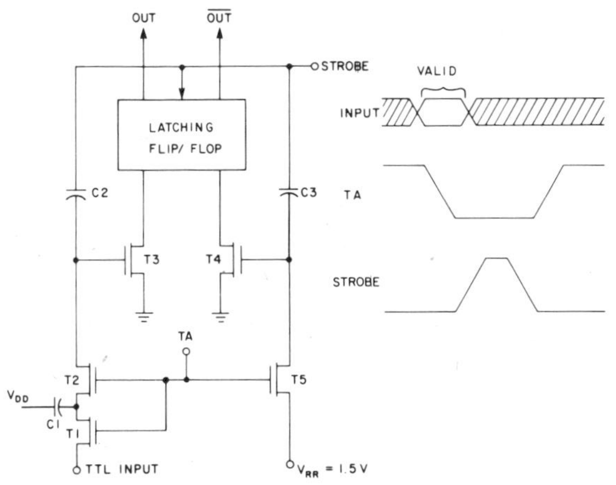

FIGURE 5 – Address buffer showing operation of input stage.

TECHNOLOGY	2 LEVEL POLY N SI GATE
CELL SIZE	0.7 MIL^2
DIE SIZE	0.122" x 0.227" (27,700 MIL^2)
ACCESS TIME	150 NS
CYCLE TIME	250 NS
SUPPLIES	+12, +5, -5 (ALL ±10% TOLER.)
ACTIVE IDD CURRENT	20 MA (@ 500 NS CYCLE)
STANDBY IDD CURRENT	0.8 MA
REFRESH	128 CYCLES/2 MS.

FIGURE 6 – Summary of typical characteristics of the 16K RAM.

A 5V-Only 64K Dynamic RAM

Lionel S. White, Jr., Ngai H. Hong, Donald J. Redwine and G. R. Mohan Rao

Texas Instruments, Inc.

Houston, TX

A 65,635b X 1 WORD, dynamic RAM for use in mainframes and minis will be described.

Operating from a single 5V power supply, the device (16 pin) is fully TTL compatible and can accept dc input levels of –1V and +7V with ac transients beyond these limits. The system ground is used for both the VSS supply and the substrate bias. The RAM has an access time of 100-150ns and a worst case power dissipation <200mW at a cycle time of 250ns.

The device is <35Kmil^2 in area. The memory cells are optimally arranged as a square array of 256 columns (sense amp) and 256 rows. The minimum geometry size (typically 2.5μ) is printed on the first level to provide maximum dimension control and reproducibility. The minimum transistor length is 3μ with 4μ used on all booted or otherwise critical nodes to minimize short channel problems such as subthreshold leakage, impact ionization and related phenomena. The minimum transistor length in the array is 4μ to insure maximum charge retention in both store and access modes. Multiplexed address inputs with non-multiplexed address buffers are used to simplify clock design and circuit operation and to provide optimum set up and hold times to facilitate memory system design.

A dynamic sense amplifier with active loads (Figure 1) which restores a full V_{DD} level for a *1* in the cell is used to minimize power dissipation and maximize refresh time. In Figure 1, $\overline{\phi}_P$ is clocked to speed equalization of the bit lines. ϕ_D is clocked to provide a grounded dummy cell voltage level for sensing and to prevent injection of minority carriers from the dummy cell ground line during precharge. $\overline{\phi_{T1}}$, a bilevel signal, provides isolation of the bit line from the sensing nodes. $\overline{\phi_{T2}}$, a bilevel signal, provides both maximum precharge for the gates of the load devices and reduced loading of the bit line during sensing. The gate of the load device on the *0* side of the sense amplifier will be discharged prior to activating the load devices. Three transistors are used to activate the sense amps. The two transistors driven by ϕ_{S2} have different widths and threshold voltages to optimize the sensing sequence.

A high speed NOR decoder (Figure 2) which is immune to short channel leakage is used to speed the selection of the X-word line and to reduce the die size by eliminating the ground line in the decoder circuit. The address lines, are connected to both the gate and the source of the NOR gate and are precharged high. Selection occurs by grounding at least one source (address line) of an unselected decoder input.

A standardized design, Figure 3, is used for the clock generators to provide optimum tracking of the generators as the internal timing varies over the process and operation windows. The overlap capacitance of transistor T8 boots the level of node 5 to ensure that T6 remains off while charging capacitor C1. The delay of the stage is controlled by the size of T11 and the negative feedback to node 7 produced by C2. T8 and T10 are relatively large to provide a sharp discharge rate for node 5.

In order to maximize voltage and process margins an interlocked clock scheme is used to eliminate internal race conditions; Figure 4. For example X1, which activates the X-word line, cannot be generated until decoding is complete as indicated by one of a pair of address lines reaching ground potential. Another example is the interlocking of the X-dummy line (X2) with the precharge clocks to insure that the bit line precharge sequence does not start until the storage cell gating device is turned off.

In addition to providing full TTL compatibility for the device, the grounded substrate reduces the noise level in the substrate for better sensing and increases the differential signal to the sense amps by increasing the capacitance of a stored *0* level. Minority carrier injection in the periphery is minimized by preventing any circuit node from dropping below ground potential and by clocking a V_{SS} buss line that may be forward biased by capacitive coupling in the substrate. Minority carrier injection from the device inputs is limited with a series MOS filter network. Those carriers that are injected are collected by either a guard ring at V_{DD} potential or by a low lifetime region in close proximity to the injecting source. In addition, the cell array is surrounded by a guard ring at V_{DD} potential to prevent minority carrier drift from the periphery to the storage cells.

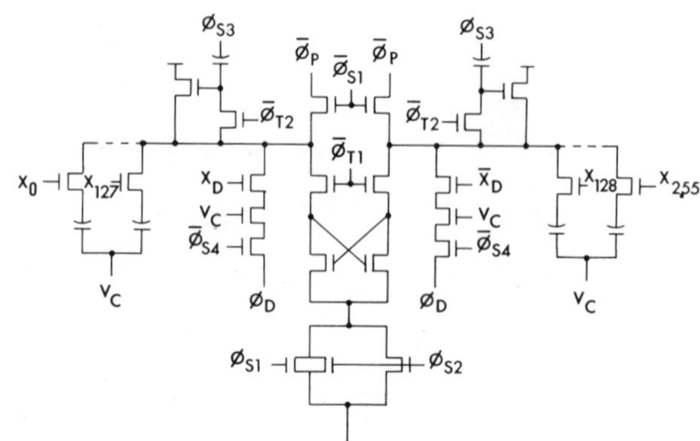

FIGURE 1–Dynamic sense amplifier circuit with active loads.

Reprinted from *IEEE Int. Solid State Circuits Conf.*, pp. 230–231, 1980.

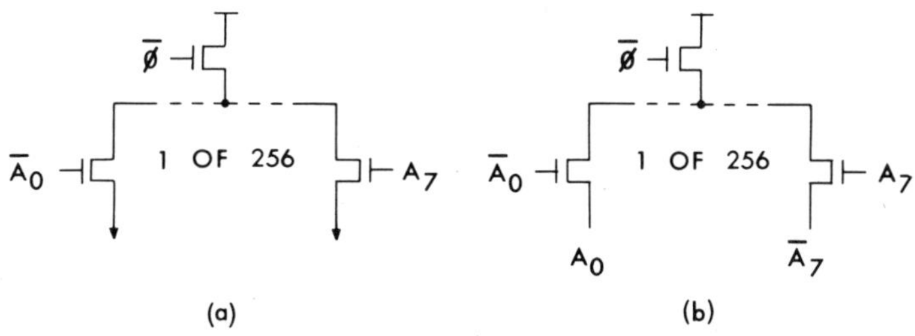

FIGURE 2—Standard NOR decoder gate, with low to high inputs (*a*); high-speed NOR decoder which is immune to short channel effects, with high to low inputs (*b*).

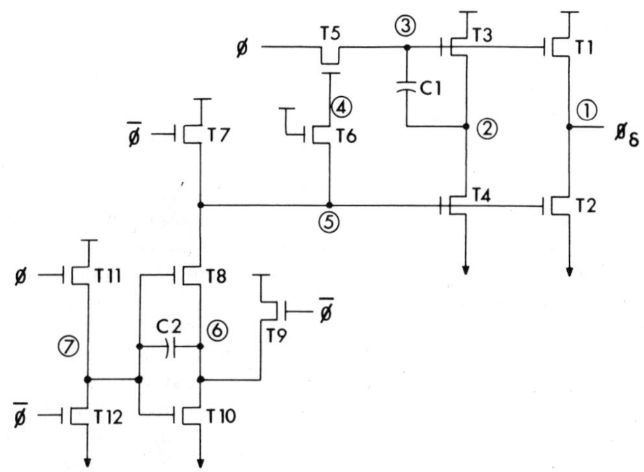

FIGURE 3—Dynamic clock circuit with negative feedback delay circuit.

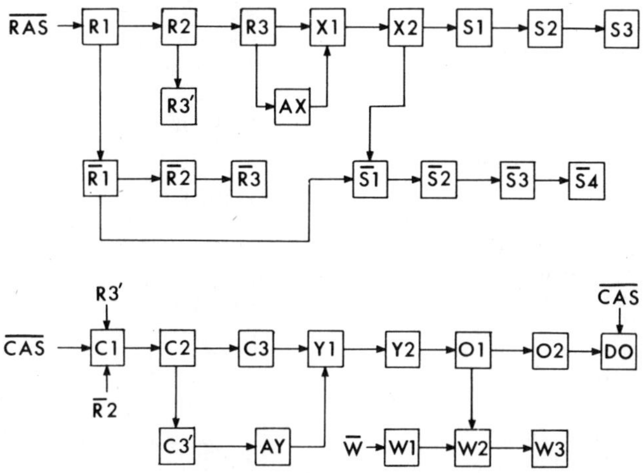

FIGURE 4—Interlocked clock scheme: row clocks (R), column clocks (C), address line (A), X-select (X), Y-select (Y), sense amp clocks (S), output clocks (O), write clocks (W).

A Single 5V 64K Dynamic RAM

Kiyoo Itoh, Ryoichi Hori, Hiroo Masuda and Yoshiaki Kamigaki

Hitachi Central Research Laboratory

Tokyo, Japan

Hiroshi Kawamoto

Hitachi Device Development Center

Tokyo, Japan

Hisao Katto

Hitachi Musashi Works

Tokyo, Japan

THIS PAPER WILL DESCRIBE a single 5V, 64K dynamic RAM with a substrate-bias generator, typical power didsipation of 170mW at 300ns cycle time, typical access time of 120ns and 25.8mm^2 chip area, using chip coating techniques to prevent soft errors.

Three sense configurations, Table 1, were investigated in terms of signal-to-noise ratio and substrate coupling noise ΔV_{BB}, essential to stable memory operation. As a result, a folded data line configuration[2] shown in Figure 1 was chosen. The design reduces substrate coupling noise from data lines through junction capacitance, dominant among substrate noise sources. Additionally, small data line capacitance and excellent common mode noise rejection are afforded. Furthermore, the layout features a self-aligned contact hole to the diffused area and a modified cell arrangement. This facilitates the small data line capacitance, especially junction capacitance, and large storage cell capacitance, which also results in a large signal-to-noise ratio. Peripheral circuits were also carefully laid out to reduce junction capacitance and to cancel coupling noise from the substrate to differential type circuits such as the sense amplifiers. Table 1 shows the estimated ΔV_{BB}.

The substrate-bias generator is composed of a conventional three-stage E/E ring oscillator. V_{BB} is set to about −3V.

Inverters having two kinds of threshold voltage, i.e., a smaller one, VthL (typically 0.4V for V_{BB}=−3V) for the load MOST, and a larger one VthH (typically 0.6V) for driver MOST, were used to obtain a higher speed by reducing the threshold voltage loss. This approach produces a speed about 20% higher than that of conventional Enhancement/Enhancement (E/E) inverters. However, minimum VthL must be carefully chosen to insure that current flow does not occur even until the V_{BB} generator starts oscillating (i.e., V_{BB}=0). This is because a large surge current flow I_{DC} is built up during power-on if VthL is a large negative value for V_{BB}=0 as shown in Figure 2. The 0.4V VthL was chosen, as shown in the plot, considering that the total W/L of transistors which contribute to this current is 3000, and the tolerable maximum peak current is 2mA.

The memory array is divided into eight 8K arrays to reduce word line delay. Each 8K array is organized as 128x64b array with 64 sense amplifiers; Figure 3. The entire memory is refreshed by the 128 Row Address Strobe ($\overline{RAS}$) cycle.

A single set of eight address buffers is used for both row and column addresses to reduce chip area. The circuit shown in Figure 3 is proposed to realize this configuration. The circuit features a combination of address switches with Y decoder control signal ϕ_{dy}. This is suitable for an organization whose X decoders are located in the center of memory arrays as shown in the diagram. After X decoding takes place through address switches, these switches are turned off (ϕ_{xy} off). Then Y decoders are set by application of Y addresses and ϕ_{dy}.

A microphotograph of the 64K RAM chip fabricated by a two-level poly silicon process is shown in Figure 4. Waveforms of a memory chip, having an access time from $\overline{RAS}$ low of 120ns, are shown in Figure 5. Typical operating and standby power dissipation for the nominal operating condition (5V, 25° C) are 170mW at 300ns cycle and 8mW, respectively. A V_{BB} of −2.9V and substrate noise ΔV_{BB} of about 1V without detrimental effects were measured as expected. No switch-on power surge current was observed.

Acknowledgments

The authors would like to thank N. Hashimoto and Y. Kosa for preparing samples, and H. Yoshimura, T. Asaoka and N. Ieda of the NTT Musashino Electrical Communication Laboratory for their continuing guidance.

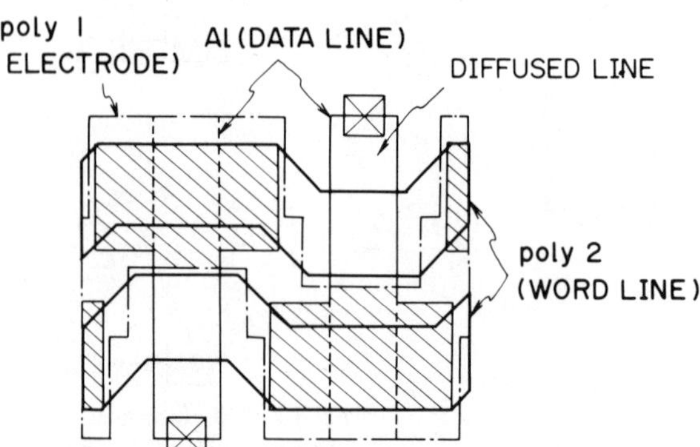

FIGURE 1—Memory cell layout. Area is 8 x 18μm^2: C_S = 38fF, C_D = 515fF.

[1] Itoh, K., et al., *1978 ESSCIRC Dig. Tech. Papers*, p. 103; Sept., 1978.

[2] USP 4044340.

Reprinted from *IEEE Int. Solid State Circuits Conf.*, pp. 228–229, 1980.

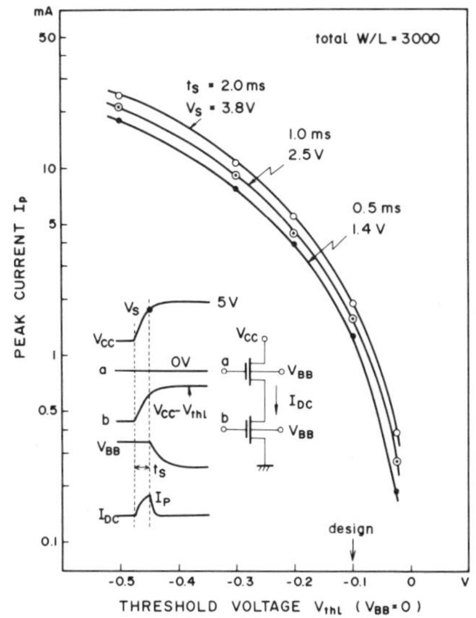

FIGURE 2—Threshold voltage vs calculated surge current.

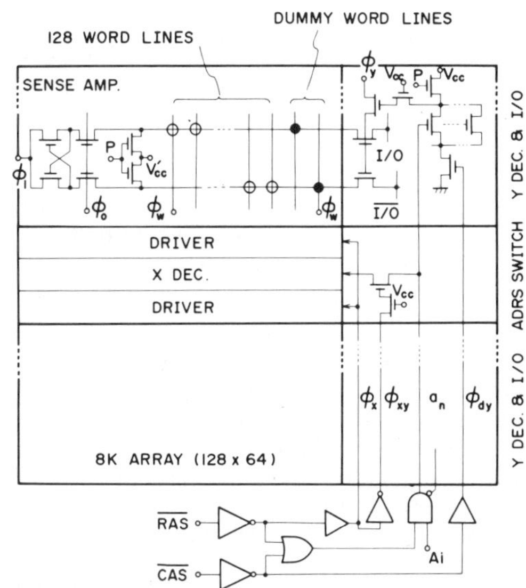

FIGURE 3—Decoding scheme of 64Kb RAM.

FIGURE 4—Photograph of 64Kb RAM.

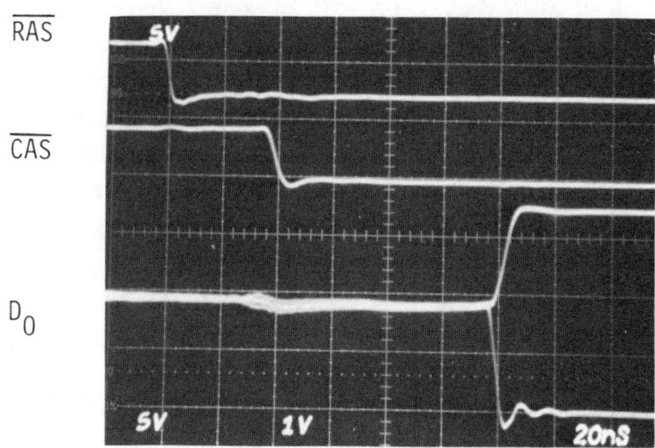

FIGURE 5—Operating waveform of 64Kb RAM. V_{cc} = 4.5V, 70° C; loading capacitance of D_O = 100pF.

Memory Cell	Sense Configuration	Chip Area	Signal	Total Substrate Capacitance	Substrate Coupling Noise ΔV_{BB}
		mm²	mV	pF	
Folded Data Line Al data line poly Si word line 8 x 18 μm²	SA SA 128 refresh	25.5	106	960	X Dec. Others data lines Y Dec. 0.5V 1.0V
Conventional diffused data line Al word line 8 x 18 μm²	128 refresh	25.9	55	980	1.0 1.5
	256 refresh	22.0	37	830	1.0 1.4

TABLE 1—Estimated signal and noise for typical memory cells.

A Fault-Tolerant 64K Dynamic Random-Access Memory

RONALD P. CENKER, DONALD G. CLEMONS, WILLIAM R. HUBER, MEMBER, IEEE, JOSEPH B. PETRIZZI, FRANK J. PROCYK, AND GEORGE M. TROUT

Abstract—**A 64K dynamic MOS RAM with features and performance fully compatible with current 16K RAM's has been designed and characterized. The memory cell is a one-transistor-one-capacitor structure, standard except for a polysilicon bit line. A dual-32K architecture, along with partial selection and stepped recovery, holds power and peak current values below those of 16K parts. Spare rows and columns, which can be substituted for defective elements by the laser opening of polysilicon links, enhance yield. Worst case column enable access time of the memory is 100 ns, row enable access time is 170 ns, and only 128 cycles within 4 ms are needed to refresh the device.**

I. INTRODUCTION

USER ACCEPTANCE of a new generation of MOS dynamic memory depends on several factors beyond mere availability. Such aspects as compatibility with the previous generation, cost, reliability, and the existence of second-source suppliers tend to dominate purchase decisions once the sample evaluation phase is complete. With these factors in mind, a 64K dynamic RAM has been designed. This paper describes the chip design with special emphasis on unique features including spare elements for yield enhancement. Characteristics of working chips are included.

II. ORGANIZATION AND ARCHITECTURE

Table I indicates three potential organizations for a 64K memory and their influence on the number of circuit functions and refresh cycles, sensing signal level, and chip length. The 2 X 128 X 256 organization was chosen over a 256 X 256 alternative because: 1) the available signal for sensing is larger (half as many cells load each column line); and 2) only 128 refresh cycles are required, thus improving compatibility with 16K parts. The 128 X 512 organization was eliminated because of the excessive chip length required. Hence the 64K chip is organized in two 32K arrays, one above the other, with each containing 128 rows by 256 columns. In this organization row decoders, column decoders, and sense amplifiers are provided within each array.

By organizing the memory as two arrays, active power and peak currents can be reduced because only one array need be fully selected [1], [2].[1] In the fully selected array, both row and column decoding are performed. Reading and/or writing of a cell, as well as refreshing of the selected row of cells, take place only in that array. In the partially selected array, row decoding and refreshing take place. Column decoders in the partially selected array remain in their standby condition, thus reducing both average and peak currents. Furthermore, sense amplifier latching in the partially selected array is delayed and recovery is advanced relative to the fully selected array, thus staggering current peaks.

TABLE I
POTENTIAL 64K ORGANIZATIONS

	256×256	128×512	2×128×256
SENSE AMPLIFIERS	256	512	512
COLUMN DECODERS	64	128	128
RELATIVE SENSE SIGNAL	0.5	1	1
REFRESH CYCLES	256	128	128
ROW DECODERS	64	32	64
CHIP LENGTH IN mm	~8.6	~14	~8.6

The present design also employs "stepped recovery" of all circuits to the precharge condition once their function is complete. This technique distributes transient currents throughout the cycle and prevents them from occurring simultaneously as in other memories.

A photograph of the memory chip with an overlay indicating the locations of major circuit blocks is shown in Fig. 1. Dimensions of the chip are 4300 μm X 9350 μm (approximately 169 mils X 368 mils). The left end of the chip contains the row decoders and all row related clocks ($\overline{RE}$-activated). Eight $\overline{RE}$-activated address buffers are also included on this end. Dual 32K arrays, each bisected by sense amplifiers and column buffer/decoders, span the central part of the chip. All column enable ($\overline{CE}$) activated clocks and data input/output circuitry are positioned at the right end. Eight column address buffers are situated here to accept address levels from the multiplexed address terminals. Address buffers are not multiplexed, thus simplifying the design and permitting an alternate future design of a nonmultiplexed part for high-speed applications.

III. OPERATION

Overall memory operation can be understood by referring to the functional block diagram of Fig. 2. A read cycle will be described.

Eight address buffers are strobed by the first enable pulse, $\overline{RE}$, to provide double-rail row addresses $RA0$ through $RA6$ and column address $CA8$. The row addresses are decoded to control selection of 1 of 128 rows as well as a reference row in each array. Details of row decoding are discussed in Section

Manuscript received November 13, 1978; revised February 26, 1979.
The authors are with Bell Laboratories, Inc., Allentown, PA 18103.

[1] In [1] and [2] the writers report similar multiple array organization but more than the minimum number of refresh cycles and/or action by the user to define a special "refresh" cycle are required.

Reprinted from *IEEE Trans. Electron Devices*, vol. ED-26, pp. 853–860, June 1979.

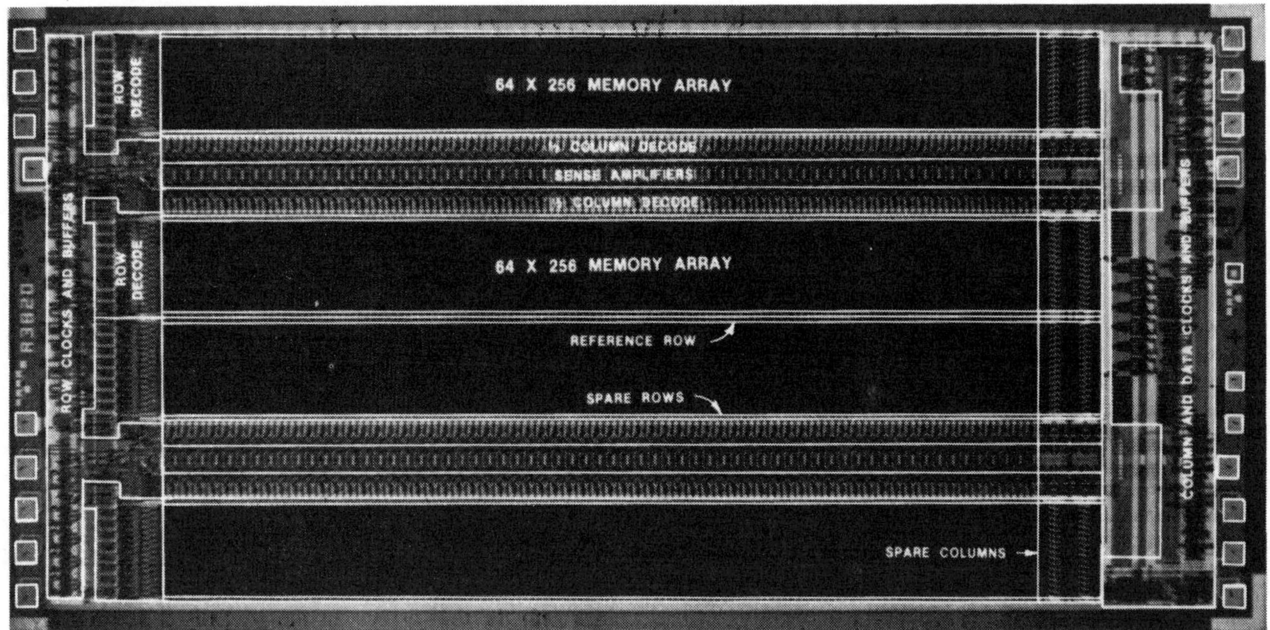

Fig. 1. 64K dynamic random-access memory chip with map of major circuit blocks. Dimensions are 4.3 mm × 9.35 mm.

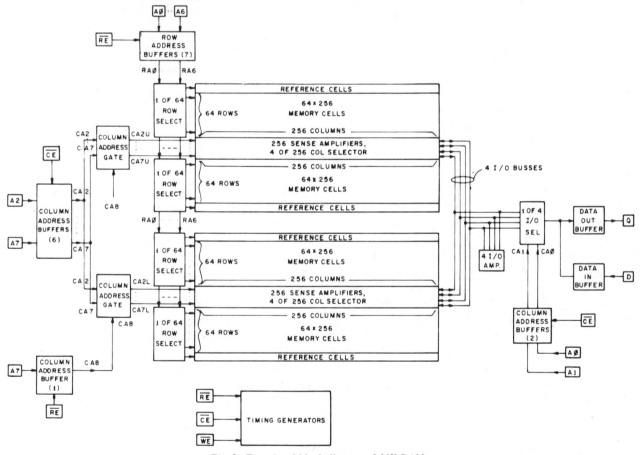

Fig. 2. Functional block diagram of 64K RAM.

IV-A. The *CA*8 address is used for various steering and enabling functions to determine which 32K array, upper or lower, will be fully selected for reading or writing.

After the selected rows are activated, data are transferred from the accessed cells and reference cells via column lines to the sense amplifiers. The resulting small differential signal is amplified by latching the sense amplifiers. Further details of the sense amplifier operation are described in Section IV-C.

Meanwhile, just after $\overline{RE}$ occurs, column addresses can be established at the address pins. The second enable pulse, $\overline{CE}$, transfers these inputs to buffers where double-rail column addresses $CA0$ through $CA7$ are generated. After sense amplifier latching, column addresses $CA2$ through $CA7$ are transmitted, under control of $CA8$, to the column decoders of the fully selected 32K array; these addresses are blocked from the column decoders of the partially selected array. When column decoding is complete, the signals from four selected sense amplifiers are transferred onto four double-rail input/output (I/O) lines. Each column decoder serves four columns, primarily because of layout constraints. The I/O signals are then amplified, and one pair is selected by column addresses $CA0$ and $CA1$ for transmission to the data out buffer where a single-rail TTL-compatible output is generated.

IV. Specific Circuit Descriptions

A. Row Decoder/Driver

Fig. 3 shows a row decoder/driver circuit. This block serves 4 row lines and is replicated 32 times in each half of the memory. The 5 transistors at the left provide a 1 of 32 decoding function which, together with a 1 of 4 decoding of the row clock ($CR0$ through $CR3$), accomplishes a 1 of 128 selection in each 32K array. The arrangement shown here differs from conventional practice in modern dynamic RAM's in three ways.

The first, and most obvious difference, is the laser-programmable link in series with each row line. This link is opened by a laser, as described in more detail in Section V-C, to disconnect a faulty row line.

The second difference is the precharge level of the decode node and the gates of the row driver transistors. Row decoder precharge, *PRDB*, and row decoder interrupt clock, *CRDIB*, are both boosted above $V_{DD} + V_T$ (where V_T is the device threshold voltage) in the standby state. Therefore, the decode node and row driver gates are precharged to V_{DD}. This provides an extra degree of row line driving capability which is especially important at low supply voltages and high threshold voltages.

The third difference is the recovery sequence of the nonselected row decoders. After the selected row has been driven to V_{DD} by the selected row clock, the row decoder interrupt is lowered to ground. Then the row address buffers are recovered to their standby state, thus resetting all internal row address lines to ground. Finally, *PRDB* recovers to its high-voltage state and precharges all row decoders. This entire row address buffer/row decoder recovery sequence occurs during the active part of the memory cycle, independent of the termination of $\overline{RE}$.

B. Memory Cell

The memory cell is a one-transistor-one-capacitor double-polysilicon cell [1], [3], [4] with a polysilicon column line. Cell layout and vertical geometry are shown in Fig. 4. The cell has a 9.5-μm row dimension and a 25-μm column dimension, thus utilizing 237.5 μm² of silicon area. Columns are Poly II lines which contact the source (drain) diffusion region of the access transistors via polysilicon-diffusion contacts. The polysilicon column replaces the more conventional diffused

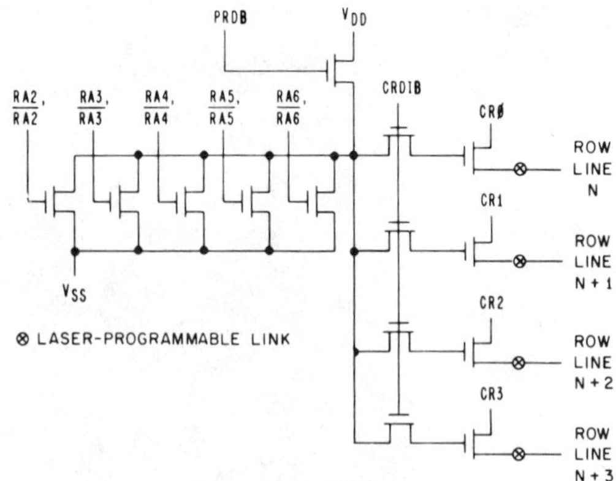

Fig. 3. Row decoder/driver circuit diagram. A single decoder serves 4 row lines.

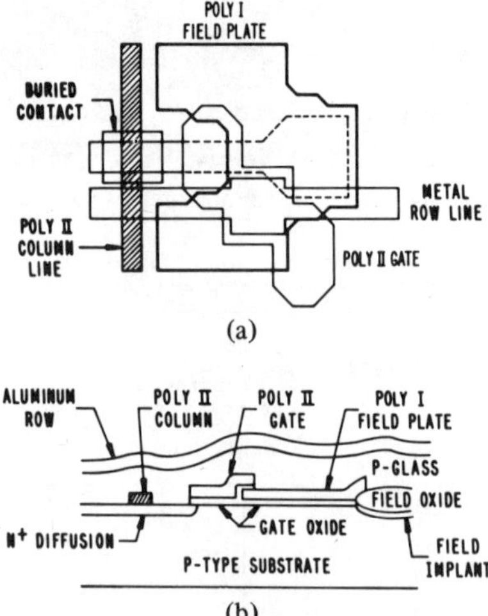

Fig. 4. Double-polysilicon, one-transistor-one-capacitor memory cell with polysilicon column line. (a) Layout. (b) Vertical geometry.

column to reduce area and sidewall p-n junction contributions to column capacitance and to permit a larger storage capacitor. The resulting ratio of storage cell to column capacitance is 0.08 (excluding sense amplifier and column buffer loading) as compared to 0.05 for a diffused column cell of the same dimensions.

C. Sense Amplifier/Column Buffer

The sense amplifier/column buffer circuits [4], [5] and associated waveforms of this memory are shown in Fig. 5. Two elements particularly critical to the performance of this sense amplifier are interrupt transistors *M*209 and *M*219. Although these devices act as a relatively high impedance, they introduce little delay in coupling the signal from the high-capacitance column lines to the low-capacitance sense amplifier nodes. However during latching, the high impedance of these devices provides two important benefits. First, the capacitance of the column line is partially decoupled from the sense amplifier thereby allowing the low-going sense amplifier node to be discharged quickly. On the selected column, this rapidly developed signal is then coupled directly to the I/O lines via devices *M*207 or *M*217. Second, the rate of discharge of the low-going column line is limited thereby reducing current peaks. Thus data are available on the I/O lines while

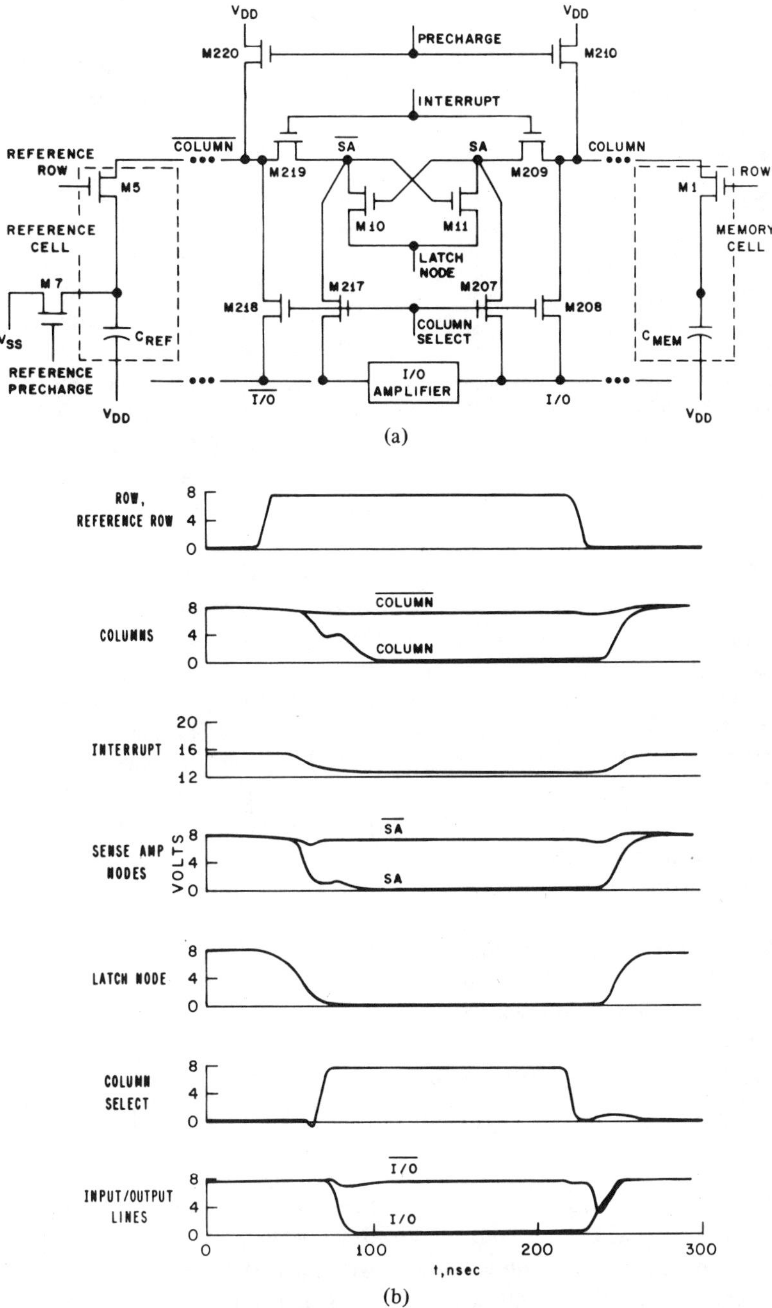

Fig. 5. Sense amplifier/column buffer. (a) Circuit diagram. (b) Important waveforms. Note that the I/O line reaches ground significantly before the column line.

the cells are still refreshing, and fast access time is combined with low current transients.

Other aspects of the sensing function [6], such as the geometrical reference cell [4], dual-slope latching [5], [7], [8], and I/O differential amplifier [2], [4], [7], [9] are similar to previous designs.

V. Spare Elements [10]-[13]

Evaluation of previous smaller memory chips showed that a large percentage of functional failures occurs because of localized defects which affect single bits, rows, or columns of the array and that substitution of a small number of spare elements (rows and columns) for defective elements would have a major impact on the yield of functional chips. Based on these data, a mathematical model was constructed to predict memory yield as a function of the number and type of spare elements. When applied to a 64K design, this model predicted that the minimum cost per good chip would occur with 16 spare elements, 8 rows and 8 columns. The predicted relative yields for a chip with 16 spare elements and for a smaller but otherwise identical nonredundant design are plotted as a function of defect density in Fig. 6. The Price defect density distribution with 5 critical levels [14] was used in generating these curves. The leverage due to the use of spare elements is

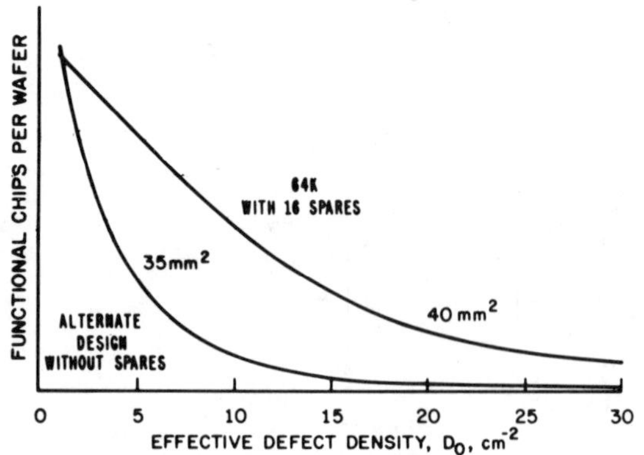

Fig. 6. Predicted relative number of functional chips on a wafer as a function of defect density. Equivalent 64K designs with and without fault tolerance are plotted.

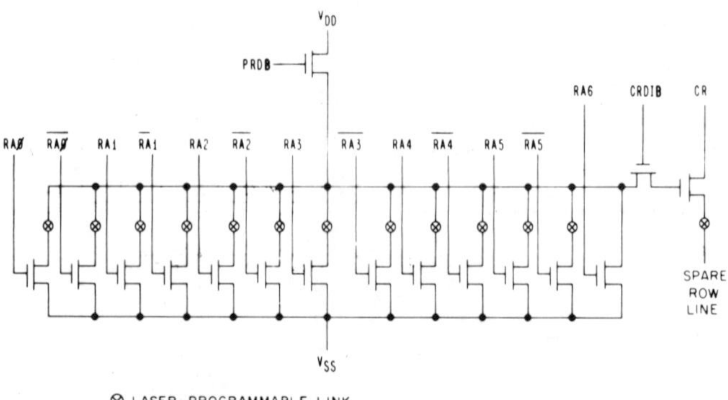

Fig. 7. Spare row decoder/driver circuit diagram. Each spare row has a dedicated spare row decoder/driver.

considerable for practically achieveable defect densities; and in fact for $D_0 > 7\ \text{cm}^{-2}$, a fault-tolerant memory occupying 40 mm^2 is predicted to have more good chips than a non-redundant design of half that area.

The circuits and technology used to delete defective elements are described in the following sections.

A. Spare Row Decoder/Driver Circuit

For each spare row, a spare row decoder/driver is used as shown in Fig. 7. The decoder portion at the left consists of dual devices with gates connected to each row address (RA_n, $n = 0, \cdots, 5$) and its complement ($\overline{RA_n}$), and with a laser-programmable link between each drain and the common decode node. Prior to laser opening, each spare decoder is deselected during every memory cycle. The address of a faulty row is programmed into the spare decoder by opening the proper links. By locating the link in the drain of the deselecting device, the capacitive loading on the decode node is made similar to that of a standard decoder. Therefore, there is no significant difference in deselection times between standard and spare decoders. The defective row is disabled by opening the polysilicon link at the output of the row driver devices, as described earlier.

Note that row addresses $RA0$ and $RA1$ (and their complements), which are used to decode the *CR* pulse for standard row decoders, appear as inputs to this spare decoder. Also, the row driving pulse is a nondecoded *CR* pulse. With this arrangement, a spare row has the decoding flexibility to replace any one of 64 standard rows, yet requires only one row driver transistor. There are a total of eight spare rows on the chip, two for each 16K segment.

B. Column and Spare Column Decoder/Buffer Circuits

Standard column circuitry is shown in Fig. 8. A defective column is electrically removed from the array by opening two polysilicon links, one to the I/O_n ($n = 0, 1, 2, 3$) line and one to the $\overline{I/O_n}$ line. Once removed, the defective column continues to be latched in the normal manner but can no longer influence the I/O_n lines.

A spare column decoder/buffer/sense amplifier is shown in Fig. 9. Again, dual devices with gates connected to each column address ($CA_n, n = 2, \cdots, 7$) and its complement ($\overline{CA_n}$) constitute the decoder. Each spare column is connected through transmission devices (M207S, M208S, M217S, and M218S) to all four pairs of I/O_n lines. Prior to laser opening, the spare column decoder is deselected on every memory cycle, and the transmission devices are, therefore, not activated. To replace a defective column, the desired address is programmed into the spare decoder by opening the proper links and the spare column is disconnected from all but the desired I/O_n-$\overline{I/O_n}$ pair by opening the links to the other I/O_n-$\overline{I/O_n}$ lines. Thus a spare column can replace any standard column within the same 32K array, regardless of which I/O_n pair the defective column was connected to. There are eight spare columns on the chip, four for each 32K half.

If a spare row or column has been substituted for a defective element and is itself found to be defective, the spare can be removed in the same way and another spare activated.

C. Repair Technology

A constraint on the circuit design was that deletion of defective elements and incorporation of spares would require only the opening of conductive links. An "open" link is defined as one having an impedance of $>10\ \text{M}\Omega$, and this requirement is easily accomplished in practice. The links are 3-μm wide polysilicon lines, deposited and patterned along with all active transistor gates and covered with phosphorus glass, as is the balance of the chip prior to metallization. No separate processing steps are associated with the polysilicon links.

Link opening is done on a commercially available laser trimmer which has been modified to include improved positioning accuracy and a TV camera for visual monitoring and alignment. Functional testing and laser programming are fully automatic and require no additional wafer handling or manual intervention. Replacement of each defective row or column takes about 1 s. A chip with no defective bits requires no laser opening.

An SEM of a spare column decoder-I/O_n line region, including 3 opened and 1 intact links is shown in Fig. 10(a). Progressive enlargements of the intact and one of the opened links are shown in Fig. 10(b)-(e). All of these SEM's were taken prior to the application of a top protective layer.

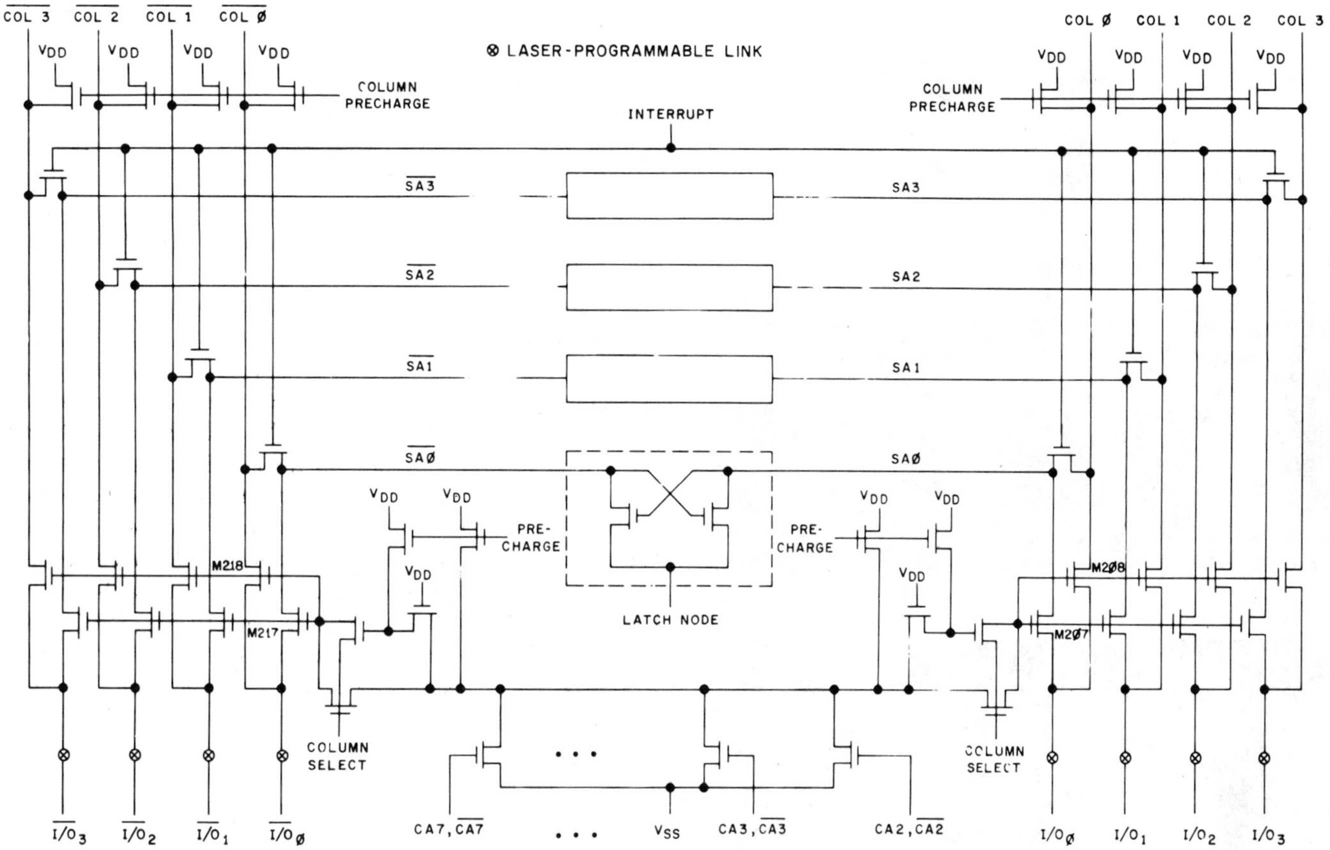

Fig. 8. Diagram of a standard column circuit. The column decoder connects 4 columns at a time to the 4 I/O pairs.

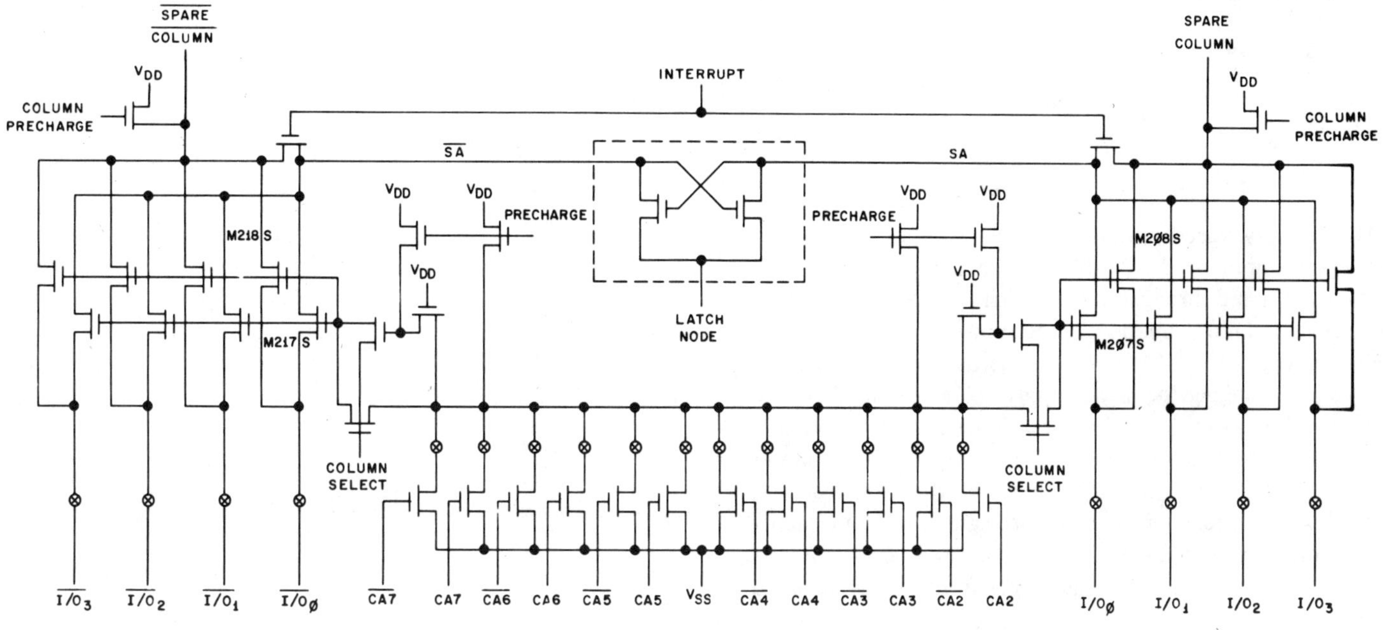

Fig. 9. Diagram of a spare column circuit. Each spare column has a dedicated spare column decoder and can be connected to any of the 4 I/O pairs.

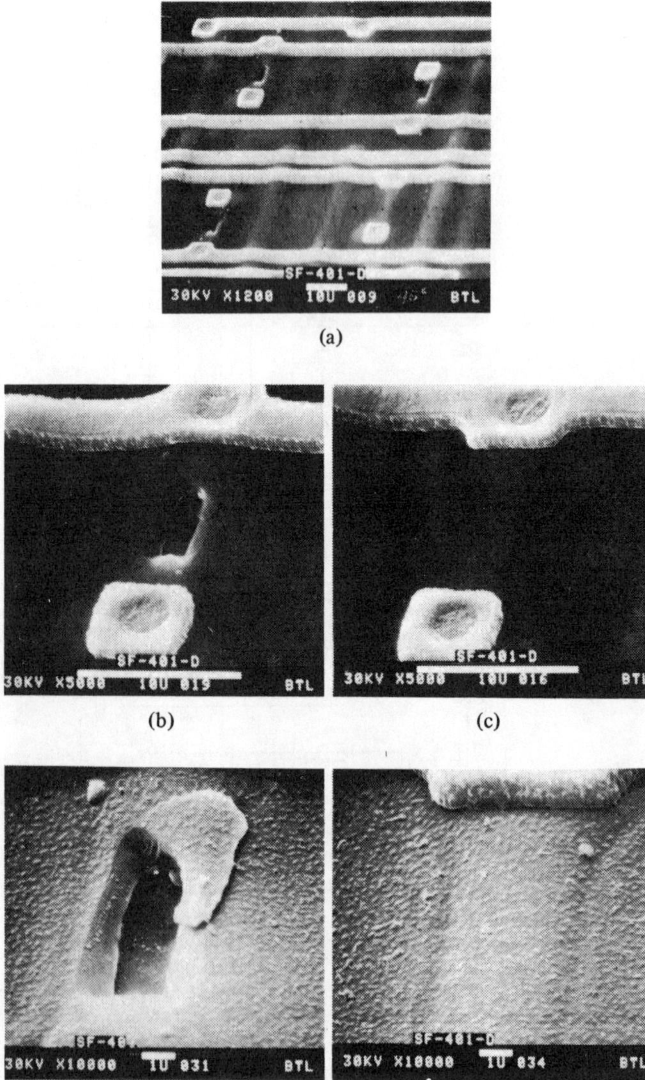

(d) (e)

Fig. 10. SEM view of a spare column decoder-I/O_n line region. (a) 3 opened and 1 intact links, ~900X. (b), (c) ~3750X of 1 opened and 1 intact link. (d), (e) ~7500X of the same links.

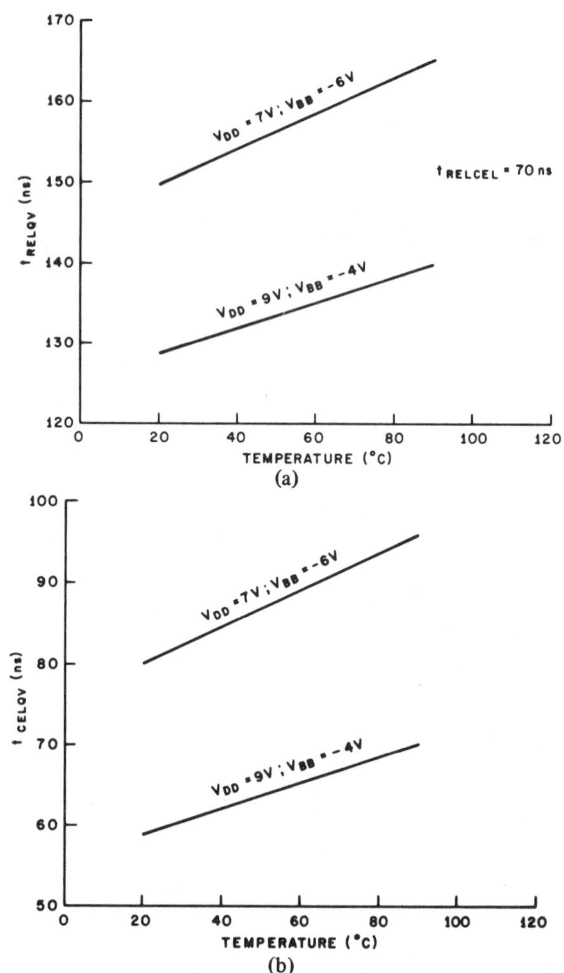

(b)

Fig. 11. Access times as a function of temperature at power supply extremes. (a) $\overline{RE}$ access times. (b) $\overline{CE}$ access time.

TABLE II
CHARACTERISTICS OF 64K RAM

PACKAGE	16 PIN, 300 MIL DIP 16K RAM COMPATIBLE
CASE TEMPERATURE	0-80°C
POWER SUPPLIES	+8V ± 10%, -5V ± 10%
ACTIVE CURRENT	50mA MAX @ 375ns CYCLE
STANDBY CURRENT	1.5mA MAX
RE ACCESS TIME	170ns MAX
CE ACCESS TIME	100ns MAX
CYCLE TIMES READ, WRITE, RMW PAGE MODE (READ, WRITE, RMW)	 375ns MIN 205ns MIN
REFRESH (LATCHED OR HIGH-Z OUTPUT)	128 CYCLES/ 4ms
DIE SIZE	4.3mm x 9.4mm
CELL SIZE	9.5μm x 25μm
TECHNOLOGY	N-CHANNEL, SILICON GATE, DOUBLE POLY

VI. DEVICE CHARACTERISTICS

The primary specifications and characteristics of this 64K RAM are summarized in Table II. Compatibility with 16K parts was stressed throughout the design and has been achieved in package, pinout, function, speed, power, and peak current specifications. This 64K part can be used in 16K memory boards by changing the V_{DD} supply voltage from 12 to 8 V and providing a multiplexed address rather than V_{CC} on pin 9.

Fig. 11 shows access times versus temperature at power supply extremes for an early model of the 64K memory. This chip was programmed by replacing 3 rows in the upper 32K array and 4 columns in the lower 32K array. Access time of spare cells is indistinguishable from that of standard cells.

Average power supply current I_{DD} is plotted as a function of operating frequency in Fig. 12. At a 375-ns cycle time, the average active current is 39 mA with a 9.0-V power supply. Peak I_{DD} current is below 200 mA for even the fastest parts operated with V_{DD} = 9.0 V.

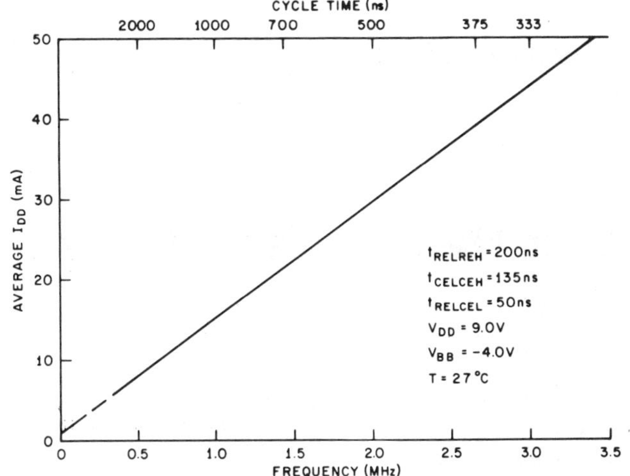

Fig. 12. Average power supply current as a function of operating frequency.

VII. Summary

A 64K MOS dynamic RAM, pin and speed compatible with 16K parts and including spare elements to provide fault tolerance, has been designed and fabricated. The technology and memory cell are the same as those used for 16K memories, except that a polysilicon column line has been substituted for a diffused column.

A dual-32K architecture with partial selection and stepped recovery result in active power and peak supply current levels comparable to those of 16K devices. All standard modes of memory operation including normal and page mode read, early write, and read-modify-write, along with $\overline{RE}$-only refreshing with either latched or high-impedance output are provided.

The spare rows and columns are incorporated, and defective ones deleted during wafer testing by use of a computer-controlled laser.

Working models have verified both the chip design and the laser-programming capability.

Acknowledgment

The authors gratefully acknowledge the many contributions by others in the area of technology and process development, chip layout, computer simulation methods, mask making, laser opening hardware and software design, and package design. They also appreciate the support and encouragement given by their management to the previously untried concept of placing spare elements on an RAM chip.

References

[1] C. N. Ahlquist *et al.*, "A 16 384-bit dynamic RAM," *IEEE J. Solid State Circuits*, vol. SC-11, pp. 570–574, Oct. 1976.

[2] K. Itoh *et al.*, "A high-speed 16kbit n-MOS random-access memory," *IEEE J. Solid-State Circuits*, vol. SC-11, pp. 585–590, Oct. 1976.

[3] L. Altman, "Specifications of 16-k RAM memories beginning to emerge," *Electron.*, vol. 48, pp. 29–31, Dec. 25, 1975.

[4] P. R. Schroeder and R. J. Proebsting, "A 16K × 1 bit dynamic RAM," in *ISSCC Dig. Tech. Papers*, pp. 12–13, Feb. 1977.

[5] E. Arai and N. Ieda, "A 64-kbit dynamic MOS RAM," *IEEE J. Solid-State Circuits*, vol. SC-13, pp. 333–338, June 1978.

[6] K. U. Stein *et al.*, "Storage array and sense refresh circuits for single transistor cells," *IEEE J. Solid-State Circuits*, vol. SC-7, pp. 336–340, Oct. 1972.

[7] C. Kuo *et al.*, "16-k RAM built with proven process may offer high start-up reliability," *Electron.*, pp. 81–86, May 13, 1976.

[8] W. T. Lynch and H. J. Boll, "Optimization of the latching pulse for dynamic flip-flop sensors," *IEEE J. Solid-State Circuits*, vol. SC-9, pp. 49–55, Apr. 1974.

[9] R. C. Foss and R. Harland, "Peripheral circuits for one-transistor cell MOS RAM's," *IEEE J. Solid-State Circuits*, vol. SC-10, pp. 255–261, Oct. 1975.

[10] J. W. Lathrop *et al.*, "A discretionary wiring system as the interface between design automation and semiconductor array manufacture," *Proc. IEEE*, vol. 55, pp. 1988–1997, Nov. 1967.

[11] B. R. Elmer *et al.*, "Fault tolerant 92 160 bit multiphase CCD memory," in *ISSCC Dig. Tech. Papers*, pp. 116–117, Feb. 1977.

[12] R. Aubusson and I. Catt, "Wafer-scale integration—A fault-tolerant procedure," *IEEE J. Solid-State Circuits*, vol. SC-13, pp. 339–344, June 1978.

[13] S. E. Schuster, "Multiple word/bit line redundancy for semiconductor memories," *IEEE J. Solid-State Circuits*, vol. SC-13, pp. 698–703, Oct. 1978.

[14] J. E. Price, "A new look at yield of integrated circuits," *Proc. IEEE* (Lett.), vol. 58, pp. 1290–1291, Aug. 1970.

Richard A. Larsen

A Silicon and Aluminum Dynamic Memory Technology

The Silicon and Aluminum Metal Oxide Semiconductor (SAMOS) technology is presented as a high-yield, low-cost process to make one-device-cell random access memories. The characteristics of the process are a multilayer dielectric gate insulator (oxide-nitride), a p-type polysilicon field shield, and a doped oxide diffusion source. Added yield-enhancing features are backside ion implant gettering, dual dielectric insulators between metal layers, and circuit redundancy. A family of chips is produced using SAMOS, ranging from 18K bits to 64K bits. System features such as on-chip data registers are designed on some chips. The chip technology is merged with "flip-chip" packaging to provide one-inch-square modules from 72K bits through 512K bits, with typical access times from 90 ns to 300 ns.

Introduction

In October 1978, a new semiconductor memory technology was introduced by IBM Corporation's General Technology Division. This new technology is used to produce a family of chips with densities of 18K-, 32K-, 36K-, and 64K-bits per chip [1]. The Silicon and Aluminum Metal Oxide Semiconductor (SAMOS) process is a metal gate technology which provides a distinct productivity leap over previous IBM 2K- and 4K-bit products through the combination of one-device memory cells [2, 3] and new process concepts. Among these are 1) backside ion implant for leakage control, 2) doped oxide self-aligned diffusion source, 3) multidielectric gate insulator, 4) p-type polysilicon field shield for isolation and cell capacitance, 5) lift-off aluminum metallurgy, and 6) quartz-polyimide passivation between metal layers. The use of new processes poses new challenges in device physics. In particular, the use of a nitride layer in the gate dielectric prevents further oxidation of the gate during polysilicon oxidation and provides low defect densities due to the dual dielectric. At the same time, the hot electron [4] effects were intensified by the use of nitride, and they had to be understood, characterized and brought under routine process control. These effects are not unique to SAMOS, however, and will be encountered by all technologies of small dimensions.

Since the objective of the SAMOS technology is to provide large-volume, low-cost memory bits suitable for use in computing systems, the capabilities of the semiconductor process must be merged with the needs of the systems. A number of tradeoffs can be made during process and chip design among yield, performance, density, function, flexibility, and manufacturability. In SAMOS, a design philosophy is adopted to optimize yield and reliability, and circuits are added on the chips to further enhance yield (redundancy [5]) and provide systems functions (on-chip register). Different requirements for performance and density are met by the family of chips.

In order to cover the above topics, this paper is divided into a number of sections. First, the process is shown in a skeletal outline, and the development history is reviewed. Next, the process is presented in detail, divided into sections through and after first metallization, while the third section is devoted to the technology challenges associated with SAMOS, and their solutions. The final section discusses the tradeoffs made in SAMOS to maximize reliability and productivity, with specific discussion of redundancy, on-chip register, and the chip family.

SAMOS process overview

The SAMOS process and the related technology issues will be covered in the sections that follow. For reference, a skeletal outline of the process through first-level metallization will be given here. Figure 1 provides a pictorial summary.

Copyright 1980 by International Business Machines Corporation. Copying is permitted without payment of royalty provided that (1) each reproduction is done without alteration and (2) the *Journal* reference and IBM copyright notice are included on the first page. The title and abstract may be used without further permission in computer-based and other information-service systems. Permission to *republish* other excerpts should be obtained from the Editor.

Reprinted with permission from *IBM J. Res. and Develop.*, vol. 24, pp. 268–282, May 1980.
Copyright © 1980 by International Business Machines Corporation

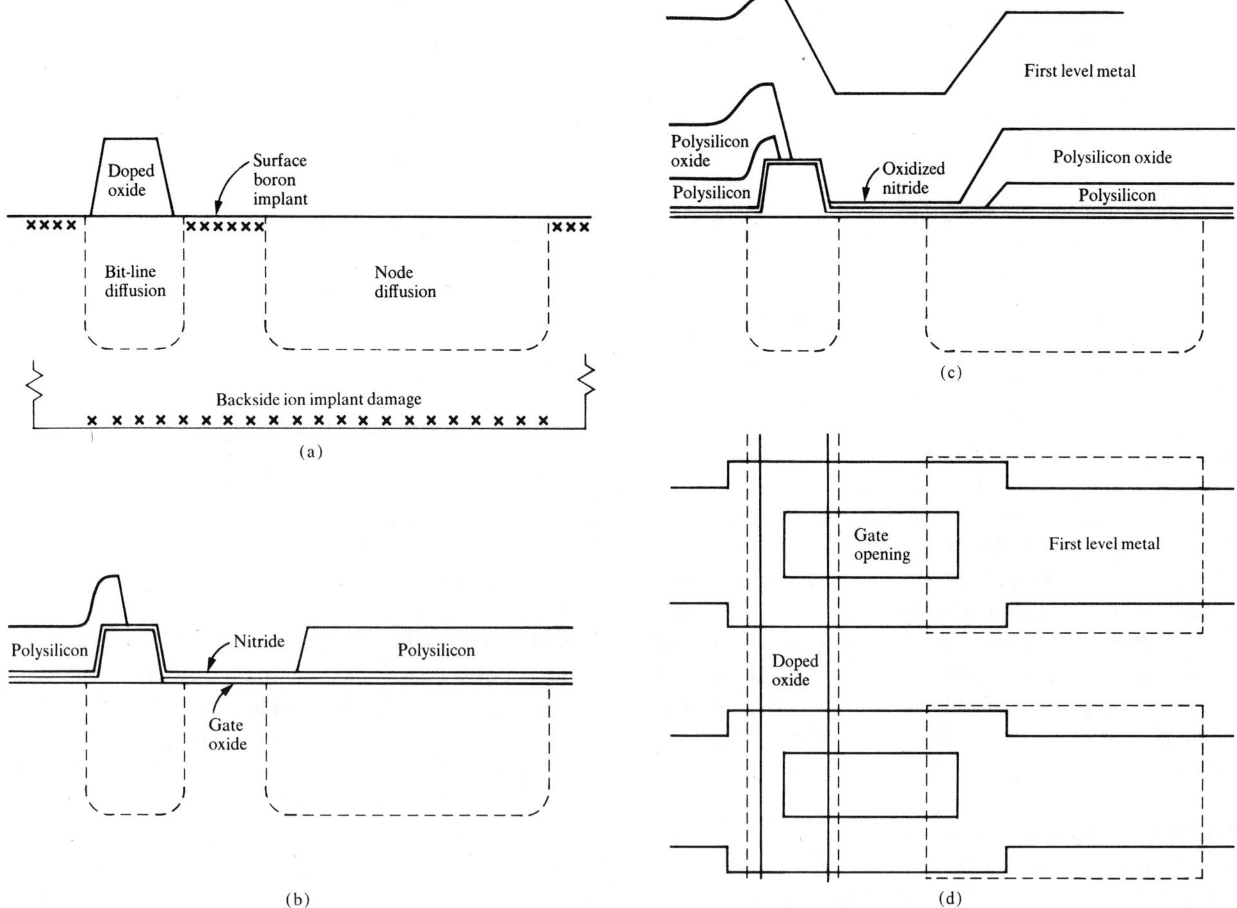

Figure 1 Views of the SAMOS memory cell. Figure (a) shows a cross section immediately prior to gate oxidation, while (b) is the same cross section after the polysilicon patterning mask step. The structure after first-level metallization is shown in (c). A top view of two nodes on a bit line is shown in (d), with the extent of n^+ diffused areas being shown by dashed lines.

1. Ion implant argon (wafer backside)
2. Deposit arsenic-doped oxide/cap oxide
3. Pattern doped oxide
4. Drive in arsenic diffusions
5. Implant boron for surface tailoring
6. Remove doped oxide on nodes [see Fig. 1(a)]
7. Oxidize gate silicon (gate dielectric)
8. Deposit nitride/polysilicon
9. Pattern polysilicon [see Fig. 1(b)]
10. Oxidize polysilicon
11. Open contact holes
12. Deposit and pattern first metal [see Figs. 1(c) and (d)]

Historical background

The SAMOS technology was developed at the IBM Burlington laboratory, Essex Junction, Vermont. The physical structures needed for this field effect transistor memory were proposed by W. Smith [6], with a suitable fabrication process provided by W. Smith and R. Garnache [7]. As proposed, the process used four mask steps to first metallization and could produce a chip of $\approx$200 μm^2/bit with an access time of 1800 ns. The process was basically similar to the presently used process, with one clear difference in concept. After doped oxide was patterned on the wafer and diffusions driven in, all doped oxide was stripped from the wafer. The result was that the diffused bit lines were separated from the polysilicon field shield by thin oxide and therefore exhibited a large bit-line capacitance which limited performance. The process was developed in a piloting facility, and a 32K-bit, 4.09-mm × 5.1-mm chip was designed with the above performance and density. Redundant lines were used on this chip, as on future chips. The first functional 32K-bit chip, fixable by redundancy, was obtained in November 1972. The first perfect chip followed in April 1973.

In order to meet more aggressive density/performance goals, SAMOS evolved into a five-mask version. The fifth

Table 1 Leakage data—diffused monitors on product wafers.

Time period	Percentage of defective sites	
	Argon BSII	Nongettered
Period 1	5	20
Period 2	0.4	0.5
Period 3	1.2	19.6

mask protected the bit-line doped oxide, while that over the storage node was etched away. Using the five-mask process, a family of product offerings ranging from 18K-bit, 90-ns access to 64K-bit, 300-ns was designed. The 18K-bit chip was designed in IBM Deutschland Lab, Boeblingen, Germany, while three other designs originated in the Burlington laboratory. The first functional 64K-bit chip was produced in the pilot facility in August 1976, and volume production on a manufacturing line started in January 1978. Computer systems using the SAMOS technology were first announced in October 1978.

Process through first metallization

The SAMOS process begins with an argon backside ion implantation of dose and energy sufficient to form an amorphous silicon layer. Backside ion implantation [8-12] provides a particularly simple and clean process for leakage control, an important aspect of VLSI technology, since the charge stored on a cell is on the order of only 200-300 $\times 10^{-15}$ coulombs. Implantation gettering provides a convenient method to ensure low leakage levels on a large-volume manufacturing line. Table 1 shows typical leakage data for diffused monitors on product wafers. The monitors accurately predict leakage-limited yield through a modeling technique [13]. The data illustrate the general SAMOS experience that, in times of optimum initial wafer quality and process cleanliness, gettering does not improve yield, but that when substrate or process problems do occur the backside gettering provides a protection against major yield falloff. The gettering effect results from the formation of $1/2\langle 110\rangle$ dislocations during the regrowth of the amorphous damage region [11, 12]. Metallic impurities precipitate at the dislocation and do not end up near diffusion junctions on the wafer frontside. Initially the SAMOS backside implantation was done using boron, but a switch was made to argon since it is as effective as boron, does not require as high a dose [11], and can be produced with higher flux in the implanter.

Backside ion implantation is followed by three process steps which, taken together, constitute the SAMOS diffusion technology. An arsenic-doped oxide and an undoped capping oxide are deposited in a continuous chemical vapor deposition reactor. The process uses a mixture of silane, arsine and oxygen to produce an As_2O_3-SiO_2 glass as the doped layer. This blanket film is patterned by the first mask level, then driven in. A thin thermal oxide is grown during the drive-in cycle.

Solid state arsenic diffusion sources have been studied for a number of years [14-17]. A blanket doped oxide layer can be applied to the wafer using either arsine-silane oxidation or a spin-on arsenosilicate glass. If a doped oxide is deposited after a masking nitride or undoped oxide has been deposited and patterned, the resulting diffusion line width can be characterized by

$$W_T = W_p + 2 \times 0.7X_j + 2B,$$

where W_p is the photo mask image width, B the etch bias of the masking layer, and X_j the junction depth. A similar equation is obtained if a diffusion is produced by capsule diffusion or by an arsenic ion implantation. In contrast, the SAMOS doped oxide is applied directly to the entire wafer, then patterned and removed subtractively at the first mask level. The etch bias decreases the line diffusion width. In addition, the edge of the doped oxide does not make an efficient source for arsenic, so the apparent edge for diffusion is back under the doped oxide by some apparent amount (δ). The line width becomes

$$W_T = W_p + 2 \times 0.7X_j - 2B - \delta.$$

For the SAMOS process, the empirical result is that the diffusion line width is essentially equal to the photo mask image width. Narrow diffused lines can be made without using very small lithographic lines. A second advantage of the subtractive-etch doped-oxide process is that a thick oxide layer is left self-aligned to the diffusions. Depending on whether this doped oxide is removed or left intact in later processing, the diffusion is selected to exhibit either high or low capacitive coupling to the overlaying conductors. In order to utilize the advantages offered by the doped oxide diffusion source, the doped oxide deposition, patterning, and drive-in steps must be integrated to prevent doping of the exposed silicon areas by arsenic counterdoping and to provide proper sheet resistance (R_s) and junction depth under the doped oxide.

Arsenic counterdoping is controlled by use of 1) low mole percent arsenic in the doped glass ($\approx$2%), 2) an undoped capping oxide over doped oxide, 3) HCl in the drive-in process to react with free arsenic, and 4) an oxidizing atmosphere in the first phase of drive-in to oxidize the bare silicon. In addition, the use of arsenic instead of phosphorus in the doped glass is in part based on the assumption that arsenic has a lower vapor pressure at drive-in temperature. Even with these steps, careful monitoring must be maintained to detect possible counterdoped conditions and allow early process correction. The monitoring techniques utilized are discussed in a later section.

The junction depth for SAMOS is 0.8 μm, which represents a tradeoff between competing effects. A shallower junction would mean less threshold reduction at short channel lengths and smaller overlap capacitance of the diffused bit line to polysilicon field shield. A deeper junction would have a lower injection rate of channel hot electrons into the dielectric, and would have a lower incidence of metallurgy spiking through the diffusions at contact holes. In order to achieve the 0.8-μm value for X_j, arsenic is preferred, since it will not undergo appreciable further diffusion later in the process. A value of 25 Ω/□ is chosen for diffusion sheet resistance as the optimum tradeoff between process capability and design requirements. The R_s and X_j values are obtained by using a sequential drive-in O_2/N_2 ambient followed by N_2. During the drive-in the As_2O_3 in the oxide diffuses to the silicon and the arsenic is reduced by

$$2\ As_2O_3 + 3\ Si \rightarrow 4\ As + 3\ SiO_2.$$

This reaction in a nonoxidizing atmosphere would lead to formation of an arsenic layer at the oxide-silicon interface [18], which would impede further reaction. Oxygen is used to prevent the formation of the arsenic layer. The relative amounts of O_2/N_2 in the initial zone strongly affect R_s, as shown in Fig. 2 [19]. The R_s is high with low O_2 percentage because of arsenic buildup, and rises again at high O_2 percentage because of the oxidation of the silicon surface under the doped glass. After the proper amount of arsenic is introduced into the silicon in the O_2/N_2 cycle, a pure N_2 ambient is used to drive in the arsenic to the proper depth.

During the drive-in oxidation an oxide is formed on the wafer surface. This oxide is used as a screen for a boron implant of $\approx 1 \times 10^{12}$ ions/cm^2. As discussed in a companion paper [20], the dopant control inherent in implantation is far superior to the intrinsic doping variability of the wafer itself. In addition, the implant leads to a final doping profile of boron $\approx 1.8 \times 10^{16}$ atoms/cm^3 at the wafer surface, but only $\approx 1.1 \times 10^{15}$ atoms/cm^3 in the silicon bulk. Threshold voltages with substrate bias (V_{SUB}) of -2.2 V are then around 1.3 V, high enough to limit subthreshold leakage of array devices with the gate off. The rise of threshold as V_{SUB} becomes more negative is minimized by the low background doping, allowing more signal to be written into the cell, which operates in a source follower mode. Within limits, the implant can be used to maintain constant threshold voltage, being raised or lowered to counter long-term trends in flatband voltage. The implant

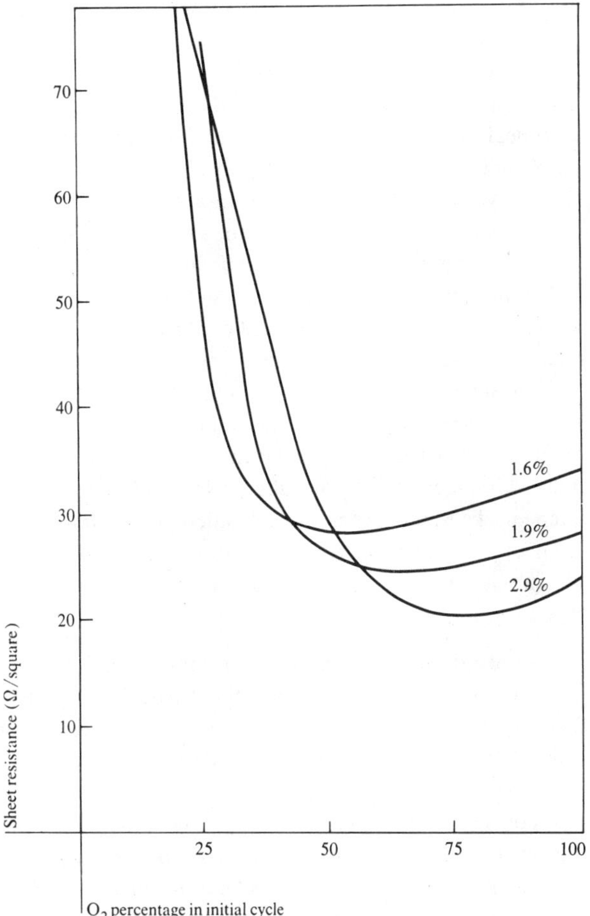

Figure 2 Sheet resistance as a function of O_2 percentage in the oxidizing phase of drive-in, for various mole percentages As_2O_3 in the doped oxide (from Ref. [19]).

level is restricted on the high side by substrate hot electrons, a phenomenon which will be discussed in a later section.

Following implantation, the wafer is masked for a second mask level, the step added in five-mask SAMOS. This photolithographic step protects the doped oxide over the bit line from etchant, but allows the doped oxide to be removed from the storage node. Following photoresist removal, a dip etch is performed to remove the thin drive-in oxide. At this point the cell is as shown in Fig. 1(a). The result is that the storage node will eventually have only thin dielectric between the diffusion and field shield for maximum capacitance, while the doped oxide remains over bit lines to minimize the parasitic capacitance of diffused line to field shield.

At this point, the silicon doping is complete. The next series of steps defines the insulators and conductors used to control the state of the silicon surface. First, a thermal oxide is grown on the wafer, resulting in a thickness of 31 nm over lightly doped p regions and 38 nm over the n^+ diffusion pockets. The gate oxidation is followed by a chemical vapor deposition step which provides 20 nm of Si_3N_4 and a layer of p-doped polysilicon, sequentially. The polysilicon is then removed in areas to be used for gates and for contacts to the silicon, as shown in Fig. 1(b). Next, the wafer is oxidized, producing a layer of oxide $\approx$300 nm thick on the polysilicon, and converting $\approx$7 nm of nitride to oxide in the gate and contact openings. Contact holes are then simultaneously etched to polysilicon, silicon substrate, and diffused lines. The simultaneous etch of thick polysilicon oxide and thin oxide-nitride-oxide is achieved by adjusting the temperature and the relative concentrations of buffered HF and water in the etchant. The etch opens the polysilicon oxide first, with contacts opening shortly thereafter. The first metallization layer is then applied and patterned.

The nitride layer in conjunction with polysilicon provides the most distinctive characteristic of SAMOS. Except for bit lines, the entire chip surface is covered by thin dielectric. The nitride provides an oxidation barrier such that when a thick thermal oxide is formed to insulate the polysilicon from metal, no appreciable oxide growth occurs in the gates. The nitride also provides enhanced dielectric integrity. Where polysilicon is not etched from the wafer, the surface characteristics are determined by a silicon-nitride-oxide-silicon (SNOS) structure. Where polysilicon is removed, a metal-oxide-nitride-oxide-silicon (MONOS) structure controls the surface. The understanding and control of SNOS and MONOS properties are crucial to the successful implementation of SAMOS. Items relative to SNOS behavior are discussed here, while the crucial technology challenges relative to MONOS are presented in a later section.

The p-type polysilicon layer serves a twofold purpose—to form a ground plane above the storage node capacitor, and to act as a field shield and shut off surface leakage. The polysilicon layer is shorted to the p-doped substrate using first-level metal. The p-doped polysilicon has somewhat higher resistivity than n-doped, but it provides the important advantage of higher SNOS threshold voltage and therefore, for a given charge level in the dielectric, shuts off the silicon surface more completely [21]. In addition, the intentional shorting of polysilicon to silicon substrate makes any possible SNOS pinholes in this field region inconsequential, and prevents any voltage stressing of the SNOS structure. Potential SNOS threshold instability [22] is of no concern, since SAMOS does not use any SNOS switching devices.

Over the diffused nodes, the SNOS structure provides $\approx$85% of the capacitance for cell charge storage; near the bit line, however, the SNOS structure results in a parasitic capacitance. The region of thin dielectric capacitance is seen in Fig. 1(b). The diffusion extends out from under the doped oxide and in this region is separated from either polysilicon or metal by only the gate oxide/nitride. A major portion of the total bit-line capacitance results from this region of thin dielectric, and as such it represents an important factor in SAMOS performance.

Dielectric integrity is required over the storage nodes, since a defect will short the diffusion to the polysilicon and therefore to the substrate. The dual dielectric structure can be superior to oxide in defect density, since defects must be coincident in both layers to cause a short. When defects are random due to poor oxide growth or nitride deposition, the likelihood of coincident defects in the layers will still be low, and dielectric fails should not occur. The nitride covers up possible holes in the oxide, and it also can prevent their formation. Areas of weak oxide would normally begin to conduct under high electric field, leading to heating, increased conduction, and eventual breakdown of the oxide in a thermal runaway condition. With the nitride trap density, however, any electrons which start to flow are trapped above the localized problem area, lowering the electric field across the oxide and shutting down the conduction before it can run away.

The dual dielectric clearly offers advantages over oxide alone if the oxide has pinholes or weak areas. SNOS failure can also be caused by particles with dimensions on the order of tenths of microns to microns. The particles cause coincident disruption of both layers in the same spot, so the oxide-nitride structure offers no advantage over a single oxide against particle-caused defects. If an SNOS short should occur over an array storage node, however, the SAMOS structure minimizes any adverse consequences. Since the field shield is at substrate potential, no current flows through the pinhole and the polysilicon plate/field shield usefulness is not impaired; only an individual node is rendered inoperative. With the polysilicon plate operation unaffected by the defect, the defective cell can be straightforwardly replaced by word line/bit line redundancy.

As noted previously, after the SNOS structure is formed, the polysilicon is patterned and then oxidized. Contact holes are opened, and the wafer is given first-level metallization. This is done by forming a "lift-off" structure on the wafer, followed by metal evaporation. The use of lift-off as opposed to subtractive etch results in improved ground rules, as the desire is to produce minimum spacing (W_w) between metal lines. The difference is shown in Fig. 3. With subtractive etch, metal is evaporated on the entire wafer and covered with photoresist. The minimum developed image in the photoresist is given by W_p. When the metal spaces are created by subtractive etch, appreciable over-etch must be ensured to clean out the space and eliminate shorts. The spacing on the wafer becomes

$$W_w = W_p + 2B,$$

where B, the bias, is typically 0.6 μm for metal 700 nm thick.

In a lift-off metallization [23a], a stencil structure is produced before metal evaporation. The stencil is typically a resistant material, either a metal film [23b–d] or a photoresist layer [24a, b] on top of an organic polymer or photoresist layer. Once the stencil is patterned and the underlying, less resistant layer developed, a characteristic lift-off structure results. In general, there will be an overhanging lip of stencil material with the photoresist removed under the lip, as shown in Fig. 3(b). The spacing between the overhanging edges of adjacent lift-off lands is essentially the photolithographic image spacing W_p. Next, the metal is evaporated onto the wafer at low pressure, providing metal coverage on top of the silicon layer and within the wells. Because of the overhang, the walls of the lift-off structure are not covered with metal. When the photoresist is stripped, the metal on top of the photoresist lifts cleanly from the wafer. Note from the figure that the bias which occurs during metal evaporation leads to wider metal lines, and therefore smaller spaces. The minimum metal space obtainable with lift-off metal is given by

$$W_w = W_p - 2B,$$

where B for SAMOS is approximately 0.3 μm.

The metallurgy used must be compatible with the lift-off process, in that it must be applied at normal incidence without overheating the photoresist on the wafer. The metallurgy must give low contact resistance to the diffusions without junction penetration, must be amenable to deposition by rf heating, since electron-beam evaporation could cause large V_{FB} shifts due to radiation damage in the nitride, and must resist electromigration [25], the thinning and possible opening of current-carrying lines. All of these requirements are met by using a thin layer of aluminum, a layer of copper, and a thick aluminum layer [26]. The thin aluminum layer is needed for bonding to the silicon. It must be thick enough for good process control, but thin enough so that Cu diffusion can occur quickly throughout the entire layer. A barrier intermetallic layer of Al_2Cu is formed as the wafer is sintered, retarding the migration of Si into Al and Al into Si. The Al_2Cu layer also serves to provide added resistance to electromigration. A possible alternative to Al-Cu-Al would be Al-Cu-Si, which was tried on SAMOS. The silicon should provide the solid solution of Al-Si and prevent the upward migration of silicon from the substrate. This technique was found to be less acceptable, however, since the solid solubility temperature dependence caused aggregates of silicon to precipitate from the alloy as the wafer temperature was changed, causing erratic and high resistance at diffusion contacts [27].

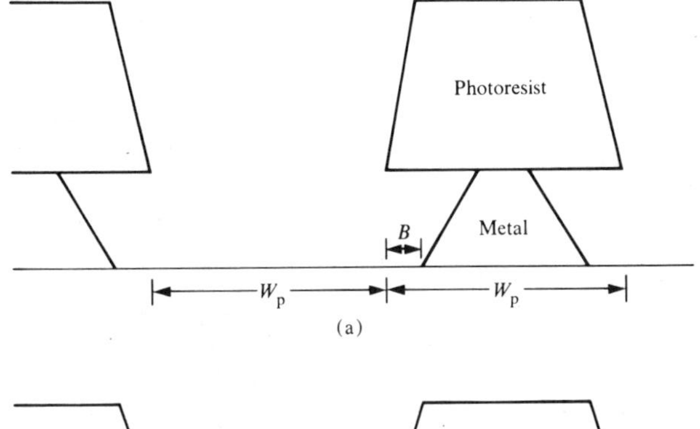

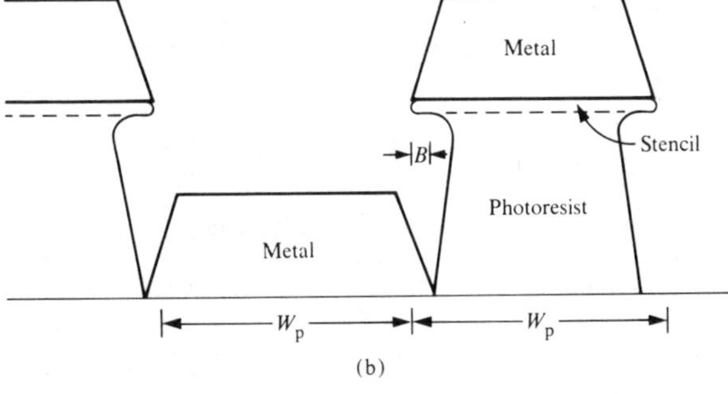

Figure 3 Relative metal line width and space for sub-etch (a) and lift-off (b) aluminum. In both cases equal printed image widths and spaces (W_p) have been used. For lift-off, the bias B enhances the metal line width, while for sub-etch it reduces the metal line.

Process through module level

The SAMOS process after first-level metallization is designed to passivate the first-level metallurgy, insulate it from second-level metal, and protect the entire chip surface from the outside environment. The ideal passivation/insulation layer should provide an environment for semiconductor device and interconnection metallurgy which protects them from degradation in their useful life. It should provide good coverage for all edges and steps in topology, dielectric strength and freedom from pinholes, and protection against chemical contamination. For SAMOS, this is accomplished by a dual layer consisting of sputtered quartz covered by polyimide [28]. The dual layer provides distinct advantages in defect densities and in mechanical properties.

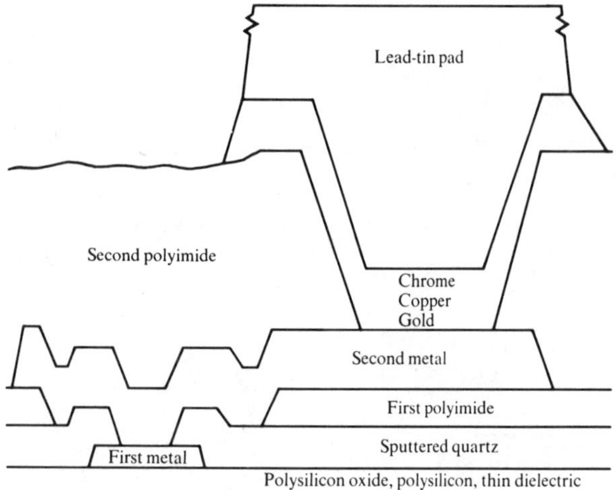

Figure 4 General view of metallization and passivation layers used in SAMOS. The structures are roughly to scale, with the exception of the much-reduced lead-tin pad height.

In the case of a single-layer insulator, a defect in the insulator itself (quartz flakes, polyimide nonhomogeneity) or in the photoresist layer during insulator etch can lead to at least three potential problems. Yield can be reduced by interlayer shorting, or reliability can be impacted by either of two problems. Ionic contamination can reach the dielectric under the first-level metal, leading to threshold instability, or leakage-induced metal migration can occur, resulting in metallic "whisker" growth and eventual shorting. With the dual layer, both quartz and polyimide are put down as blanket films over the entire wafer. Via holes are etched in the polyimide using one mask level. The photoresist developer additionally serves as the polyimide etch. After photoresist strip, a second photoresist layer is applied, and vias are etched through the quartz within the polyimide vias. Through use of two dielectrics and two mask steps, an extraneous hole will occur only in the unlikely event that dielectric or photoresist random defects are coincident. The use of the polyimide cushion on the rigid quartz layer also provides improved mechanical properties, resulting in better integrity of metal lines and metal-metal contacts.

The via etching is followed by a co-deposited aluminum-copper layer, again using rf evaporation to avoid potential radiation damage to the nitride. During evaporation the wafer is kept heated to desorb organics and provide lower contact resistance between first and second metal layers. As in first metal, the copper in second metal inhibits electromigration. Second-level metal serves a number of distinct functions in SAMOS. It is used to bring the first-level metal pads out to terminals, and it provides an extra wiring capacity to carry signals within the chip. The second-level metal is also patterned to form the fuses for SAMOS redundancy [29].

After second metal the wafer is tested for functionality. Chips which are non-perfect but fixable have the failing addresses written into the second-level metal by blowing the redundancy fuses. Next, the final chip seal is provided by a second polyimide layer, the thickness of which is sufficient to cover all metal exposed during the fuse-blowing operation. The polyimide is removed from the wafer only between chips and above the second-level metal pads. A molybdenum mask is aligned to the polyimide vias and the wafer is dc sputter-cleaned for good contact resistance. Next, five metal layers are evaporated through the mask sequentially to provide 1) sealing of via holes, 2) good conductivity, 3) corrosion resistance, and 4) a strong, reliable seal to a solder connection.

A thin chromium layer is evaporated first to provide complete sealing of the via holes by virtue of good adhesion to both aluminum and polyimide. The chromium also protects the underlying aluminum metallurgy from solder. Before chromium evaporation ends, evaporation of a thick copper layer is initiated. Copper provides an inexpensive, highly conductive layer. Gold is used to cover the copper and protect it from oxidation. The basic rationale of the sputter clean and Cr-Cu-Au layer has been discussed previously by Totta and Sopher [30]. The chrome-copper-gold evaporation is followed by a lead-tin evaporation for solder connections. After the molybdenum mask is removed, the structure is heated to reflow the solder [31]. During reflow, the Sn-Cu layers form an intermetallic compound. The mechanical mixing of copper and chromium prevents this intermetallic compound from breaking away from the chromium. The structure resulting from these processes is shown in Fig. 4.

After this terminal metallization, the wafers are diced and the individual chips tested. Usable chips are mounted to one-inch-square ceramic substrates by the IBM "flip-chip" method with a maximum of four chips mounted on each substrate. In the case of the 64K-bit chip, modules with as many as 524 288 bits are produced through use of stacked substrates with a total of eight chips. The ceramics have a basic array of 9 × 9 pins. For any given application, all pins under the chips are removed. Typical modules have 40–60 usable I/O pins.

SAMOS technology challenges

In any semiconductor technology, potential problem areas must be recognized and understood, and the process and products must be developed either to prevent the problem occurrence or to reduce it to an inconsequential level. For the doped oxide and nitride SAMOS process, the major technology challenges are listed below, along with a discussion of the appropriate solutions.

1. Movement of dielectric charge when gate is stressed positively (stability).
2. Injection of channel electrons or leakage-generated electrons into the dielectric under stress conditions (channel and substrate hot electrons).
3. Parasitic leakage from source to drain with gate off (sidewalk).
4. Control of fixed charge in dielectric (flatband voltage).
5. Prevention of arsenic doping into gate regions from the doped oxide (counterdoping).

The stability, hot electron, and sidewalk effects are all reliability-oriented, since the device characteristic changes in use and can lead to failure of an initially good chip. The flatband voltage and counterdoping impact the threshold voltage at the time of initial test, and as such are potential yield detractors.

- *Stability*

Threshold instability under positive gate bias results from movement of charges within the insulator. Instability can occur in MOS structures due to dielectric contamination with mobile ions, usually alkali ions [32]. This mechanism could occur on SAMOS due to contamination of either oxide layer in the MONOS structure, but it is essentially eliminated by the usual precautions of line cleanliness coupled with the use of HCl in the oxidizing ambients during gate growth and polysilicon oxidation. In addition, any mobile contamination which may be present in the oxidized nitride layer is prevented from moving appreciable distances, since the nitride layer acts as a barrier to alkali ions [33].

While mobile ion migration is reduced by the nitride, electron conduction is enhanced, resulting in a second possible instability mechanism which must be understood. In any multilayer dielectric, the differences in conduction between the layers will lead to charging of the interfaces between the dielectrics [34]. For the MONOS dielectric at the gate voltages used in SAMOS, the 31-nm oxide is essentially nonconductive, while electrons move through the nitride by a number of mechanisms, with Frenkel-Poole conduction predominating [35]. The electrons move across the upper oxide by tunneling. The result is an apparent positive charging of the lower oxide-nitride interface. In SAMOS, these problems were solved by developing a suitable nitride process. The process is hot (925°C), uses an H_2 carrier gas, and uses a large excess of ammonia in the ammonia-silane reaction. The H_2 carrier is thought to inhibit gas phase decomposition of NH_3 or SiH_4 by forcing the reverse reaction. With this process the MONOS dielectric is quite stable under positive gate stress, with data provided by J. Franz showing an expected V_T shift of only ≈20 mV at 100 kh at 125°C with 10-V gate stress.

- *Channel hot electrons*

Channel hot electrons present a second mechanism for threshold shift under stress. During a strongly "on" condition with gate and drain voltages high, electrons flowing from source to drain can be scattered by the lattice and injected over the potential energy barrier at the oxide-silicon interface [4, 36, 37]. This problem will be present in all VLSI technologies as shorter channels are approached, although it will lessen with lower power supplies. The problem is exacerbated in a nitride technology, however, since the nitride acts as a nearly perfect trap for the injected electrons [38]. The amount of V_T shift can be reduced by keeping the nitride thin to minimize charge imaging in the silicon, and by keeping the boron doping low and the drain junctions deep to minimize the vertical fields near the drain. These factors all had to be considered in the design of the process. Once the process was adjusted to minimize hot electrons, the residual effects were carefully characterized and modeled for various use conditions and included as part of the SAMOS design criteria [20].

- *Substrate hot electrons*

Hot electrons can also be generated by leakage current, the generation of electrons within the depletion region of an "on" gate, or the drift of electrons into that region. This mechanism is known as leakage-induced threshold shift (LITS), or as "substrate hot electrons" [4, 39–41]. The effect will also be present in any technology, but again it is intensified in SAMOS due to the nitride trap efficiency. Substrate hot electron injection occurs if the electric field near the semiconductor surface is strong enough so that electron energy within a mean free path of the surface is comparable to the oxide-silicon potential barrier [42] (see Fig. 5). LITS is controlled on SAMOS by keeping the electric fields low. A high-resistivity wafer is used and the ion implant doping is strictly maintained below certain levels. Added protection is provided by keeping wafer leakage as low as possible and by operating the chips in the dark.

- *Sidewalk*

A fourth reliability mechanism (sidewalk) exists, which, unlike the mechanisms discussed earlier, does not involve vertical charge movement within or into the gate dielectric, but rather the development of a parasitic channel between source and drain after positive gate stress. Sidewalk is caused by mobile charged contaminants near the

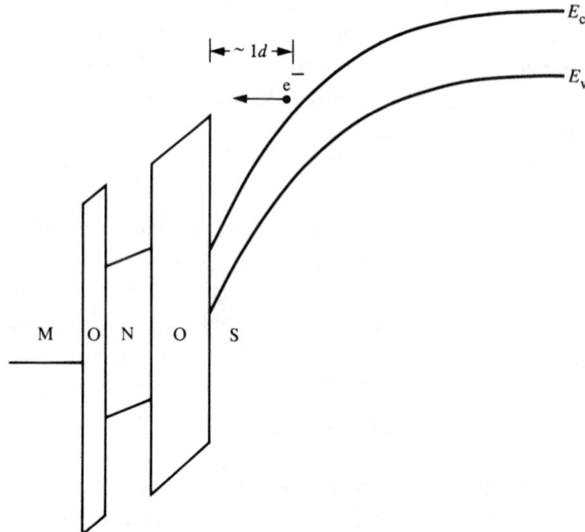

Figure 5 Band diagram for triple dielectric metal-oxide-nitride-oxide-semiconductor (MONOS) structure depicting electrons most likely to be injected over the oxide barrier and into nitride traps.

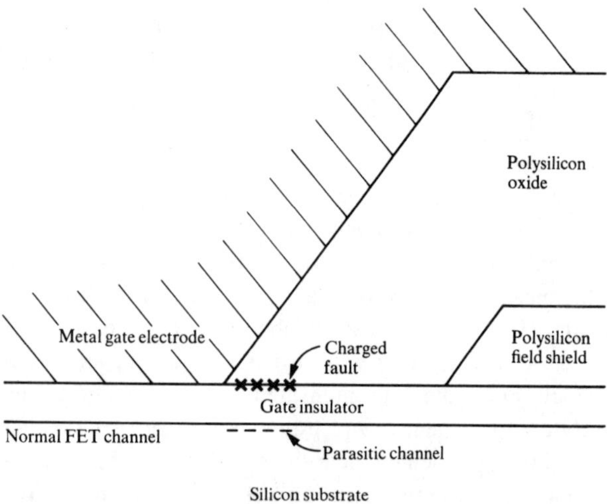

Figure 6 View of the gate sidewall, showing the region into which charged contaminants could be forced, resulting in a parasitic sidewalk current (from Ref. [43]).

edge of the metal gate, in conjunction with recessed areas into which the contamination can be driven. Repeated positive bias on the gate forces the charged ions into the region between the metal gate and field shield. The situation shown in Fig. 6 can develop, where the ions are not in contact with either conductor. Some of the charge is imaged in the silicon, resulting in a parallel FET not controlled by the metal gate. The device will then exhibit subthreshold current characteristics, as shown in Fig. 7. With the lift-off aluminum technology it has proven difficult to eliminate the ions, so the recesses have been eliminated. The polysilicon oxidation temperature was adjusted to eliminate lifting of the polysilicon oxide, and the etched polysilicon edges have shallow slopes to prevent the formation of cusps at the polysilicon oxide edge. Most important, SAMOS was changed from an MNOS gate to a MONOS gate. Originally, the oxidized nitride was removed from the gate region by a brief dip-etch. This etch created or aggravated crevices at the polysilicon oxide-nitride interface, providing a site for contamination. By leaving the oxidized nitride intact, this mechanism was eliminated [43].

• *Threshold voltage control and monitoring*

The foregoing represented reliability mechanisms which needed to be understood and controlled by SAMOS processing. A yield-related challenge, threshold voltage (V_T) control, also arose due to 1) charges in the multilayer insulator (V_{FB}) and 2) arsenic contamination of the gates affecting surface doping (counterdoping). On SAMOS product wafers, the first problem is sorting V_{FB} from doping effects, since both impact V_T. Troutman [44] has provided analytic solutions for the SAMOS gaussian doping profile, giving V_T as a function of V_{FB}, oxide thickness, and doping magnitude. J. Coady has demonstrated that, by measuring device FET characteristics to give oxide thickness and to give V_T as a function of substrate bias, V_{FB} and counterdoping effects can be individually extracted and used for large-scale SAMOS line characterization.

The actual V_{FB} behavior found for MONOS is much more complex than that of simple oxides, due to the existence of three layers and two interior interfaces for possible charge buildup. The amount of charge is influenced by oxidation precleans, oxidation anneals, nitride conditions and metallization conditions. (For example, electron-beam-evaporated aluminum is found to be unacceptable for SAMOS due to radiation damage of the nitride.) The fixed charge level of the MONOS gate is even affected by processing after first metallization, as quartzing anneals some of the charge. An interesting observation in SAMOS is that certain metallic impurities can "ride" on top of the growing oxide. No effect is seen on MOS V_{FB}, since the charge is all imaged in the metal gate. Once nitride is deposited, however, the charge is separated from the gate and alters V_{FB}.

The doping behavior is equally complex, since arsenic can be deposited in the bare silicon surface either during drive-in, during doped oxide etch, or during chemical cleaning steps. The problem occurrence can be limited by frequent changes of etchants and cleans, use of HCl during oxidation, and control of temperature profile for quick oxidation at drive-in. If counterdoping does occur, it can be quickly detected using electrical measurements capable of detecting arsenic contamination in the 1×10^{10} atoms/cm^2 range. The techniques are employed on MOS capacitor monitor wafers processed with product through drive-in. A measurement of surface potential as a function of capacitor "gate" voltage is made [45], from which arsenic contamination level can be deduced [46]. Alternatively, a measurement of the slope of the usual capacitance-voltage curve can be made near the flatband voltage, with the slope becoming steeper in a quantitative manner as counterdoping occurs.

The various facets of threshold are controlled by in-line MOS monitoring. Additional process leverage in controlling V_{FB} and doping is obtained on product wafers themselves by pulsed capacitance measurements immediately after polysilicon patterning on capacitors etched in the polysilicon. The wafer doping and flatband voltage can be accurately predicted, providing process feedback without waiting for measurements after first metallization.

Yield-density-performance tradeoffs

While the description thus far has been of the semiconductor process, the ultimate goal is a semiconductor product which can meet system needs for performance and reliability, doing so at the highest possible productivity and lowest possible cost. A number of decisions must be made to determine the appropriate technology, the general design philosophy, and the possibility of added on-chip functions. An optimum tradeoff is then selected among yield, reliability, density, and performance.

The SAMOS technology was chosen for 1) high reliability, and 2) yielded bits per wafer. SAMOS is basically a simple, manufacturable process, producing 64K-bit chips with only five masks through first metallization. As will happen with any new technology, certain challenges were raised by the SAMOS process. Phenomena related to the use of nitride in the gate dielectric required learning and careful characterization, but they are not fundamental problems. Hot electrons, stability, and sidewalk are cleanly overcome through routine process control.

The second decision is the design philosophy relative to horizontal layout ground rules and parametric assumptions. Each layout ground rule is characterized by a standard deviation σ which is based on the statistical variations of the components which contribute to the ground rule. For each ground rule, a limit is set at the wafer dimension which results in a yield or reliability exposure to the chip. A guard band, measured by $n\sigma$, is set between the wafer nominal dimension and the ground rule limit. A

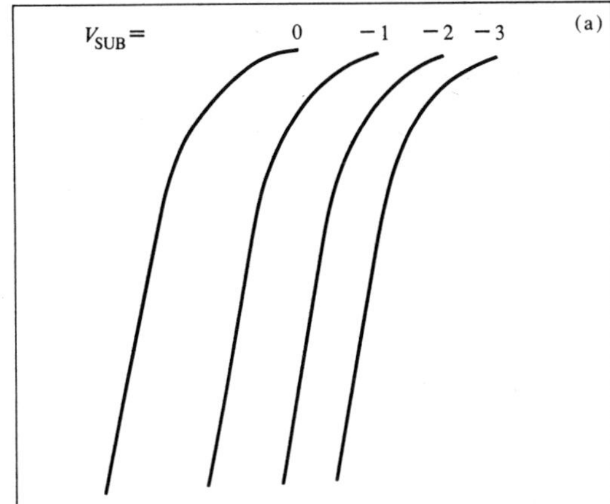

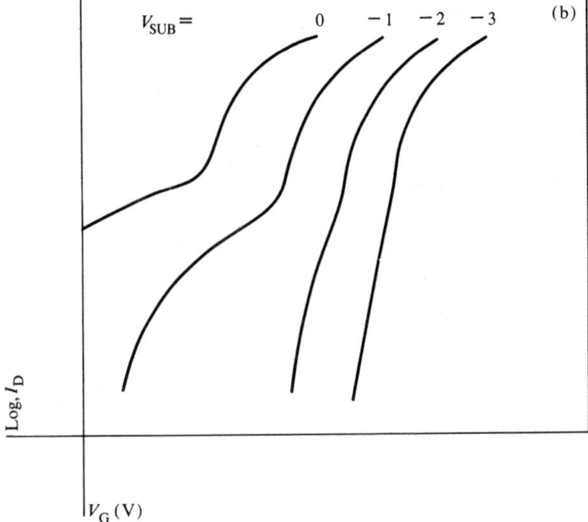

Figure 7 Subthreshold leakage resulting from sidewalk contamination. The drain current I_D is shown as a function of gate-source voltage V_G for a number of source-substrate voltages V_{SUB}, (a) prior to stressing and (b) post-stressing (from Ref. [43]).

large value of n reduces the probability that the limit will be exceeded but results in a penalty in chip area. Yield and reliability are traded directly against density. Similar considerations apply to parametric assumptions. A chip can be designed to function at large variations in threshold, transconductance, channel length, etc., but a density/performance penalty must be paid in such a design. For SAMOS, both layout and parametric rules are highly weighted to maximize yield and reliability.

The process description and design ground rules define one set of inputs to chip design. Another input must be the system needs in terms of performance, data organization, and off-chip supports. The chip designer must merge these capabilities and needs in order to maximize the number of usable bits per wafer. In SAMOS, the needs of

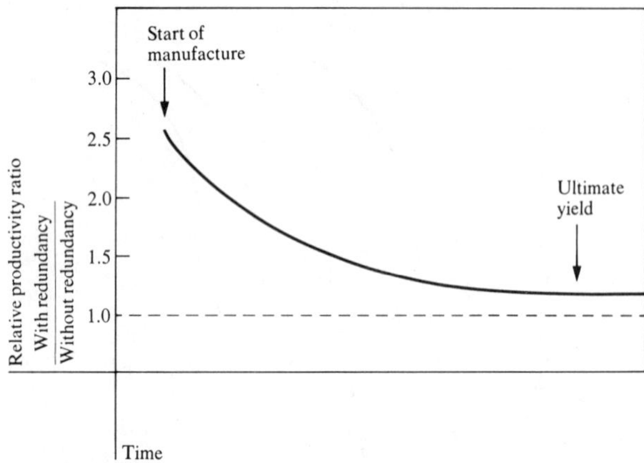

Figure 8 Yield improvement with redundancy, modeled for the 64K-bit chip (from Ref. [47]).

different systems and applications are met by a family of chips, each trading performance against density in a different manner, varying from a chip of 18K-bit, 90-ns typical access to 64K-bit, 300-ns typical access. Each member of the chip family also contains (in addition to the normal array, timing chain, decoders and I/O circuits) specialized circuits to enhance productivity or provide system flexibility. Two examples will be discussed here: the use of redundancy and the use of an on-chip register. The chip family will be discussed in the final section.

Redundancy

Redundancy to increase yield is presently used on all SAMOS chips. The redundancy actually exists in two levels. The first is the use of two-island chips. For instance, the 64K-bit chip has two 32K-bit islands, each capable of standing alone should the other be nonfunctional. The second level is the use of redundant bit lines and word lines within each island. The two-island approach and redundant lines both require extra circuits and result in increased chip size. The 64K-bit chip pays a penalty of ≈20% in chip area due to the two-island approach, and another 10% for word and bit redundancy [47]. The use of redundancy, either as dual islands or as fixable word and bit lines, is always based on an optimization of productivity. For each chip design, critical areas and defect densities are input to the yield model [13], and the projected number of usable bits per wafer calculated with and without redundancy. For all four chip designs thus far, some word or bit redundancy has resulted in a higher modeled productivity, while the dual-island approach has been incorporated on both the 64K-bit and 32K-bit chips. Any of the redundancy techniques will result in smaller improvements as manufacturing experience is gained and defect densities reduced. For dual islands, a crossover point will be reached eventually when the yield improvement does not compensate for the area penalty. Similarly, word or bit redundancy will become less important. Figure 8 shows the productivity improvement obtained by redundancy as a function of time, reflecting the real and projected SAMOS experience.

Even though the array represents less than 50% of the chip area, array redundancy is especially important because the cell node charge is so small and the array is so tightly packed. Defects which are of no consequence in support circuits will cause node failures. An example is leakage, for which a typical support will still function at more than 10× the level sufficient to cause node failure. Typical SAMOS history is that the large majority of defects on leakage monitors are of the "cell node fail" type and are not of a sufficiently high leakage level to cause a fail in a support circuit. Most leakage defects are therefore fixable by redundancy if they occur in the array and are inconsequential if they occur in other areas.

SAMOS array redundancy is implemented using what can be described as a "write-once read-only memory." Fusible links in the second-level metallurgy are used in a scheme which has minimum impact on chip performance. Redundancy is provided in both the bit-line and word-line directions. After second-level metal testing, the failing addresses of "fixable" chips are stored for fuse blowing. When the fuses are blown electrically, the address of a failing line is written into the fuses, and an additional enable fuse is blown to activate the redundant line. The circuit details of how the redundant lines are used are treated in a companion paper [48]. Whenever any redundancy is used in SAMOS, the chips are mounted into modules such that the redundancy is transparent to the user. A module made of "single-island good" chips will have twice as many chips inside as one made from perfect parts, but all module inputs and outputs will be identical.

On-chip register

The on-chip register is used on the 64K-bit chip to provide extra flexibility to the system. It is included at a penalty in chip area of ≈7%. The chip is organized in two islands, each with 128 word lines and 256 bit lines. When the ith bit line ($i = 1, 32$) is addressed, eight bit lines $i + 32n$, where $n = 0$ through 7, are decoded. All eight bits are read into the register in parallel. Eight input pins called data gates are available, and any number of these (1-8) may be sequentially addressed in any desired order at a 10-MHz rate. The stored bits are brought off the chip on a single pair of output pins. This chip organization has been used at the card level to achieve data rates higher than the cycle time of the chip. For example, the card used in the IBM 4300 processors is capable of reading a 4-

Table 2 Summary of chip characteristics.

	18K-bit	*32K-bit*	*36K-bit*	*64K-bit*
Chip organization	2K by 9	8K by 4	4K by 9	64K by 1
Cell type	Twin-cell	Single	Single	Single
Cell size (μm)	9.3 × 42	9.3 × 32.7	11.5 × 22	9.3 × 17.9
Chip size (mm)	4.46 × 5.52	5.9 × 6.1	5.0 × 5.0	5.95 × 6.15
Redundant word lines	2	8	4	8
Redundant bit lines	0	8	4	4
Typical access (ns)	90	190	900	300
W.C. access/cycle (ns)	140/256	285/470	1500/2000	440/980
Power; stdby/sel (mW)	10/690	12/612	10/220	40/360
No. I/O	45	31	30	38
Bits/cycle	9	1, 2, or 4	9	8

Table 3 Summary of module characteristics.

	18K-bit	*32K-bit*	*36K-bit*	*64K-bit*
Module organization (max)	8K by 9	32K by 4	16K by 18	128K by 4
Inputs	Hi-level FET	Hi-level FET	Hi-level FET & TTL	Hi-level FET
Data out	Differential current sense	Current sense	TTL	Current sense
No. I/O	59	45	46	51
Supplies	+8.5 V ± 10% +5.0 V ± 10% −2.2 V ± 15%	+8.5 V ± 10% −2.2 V ± 15%	+8.5 V ± 10% +1.5 V ± 15% −1.5 V ± 15%	+8.5 V ± 10% +4.25 V ± 10% −2.2 V ± 15%
Bits/cycle	9	1, 2, or 4	18	32

byte word (40 bits) at a sustained data rate of 150 ns per word, rather than at the chip cycle time specification. With a conventional design approach, this would have required a chip with a 150-ns cycle time.

It should be noted that the 64K-bit chip is used predominantly in large systems that use a single-bit-correction, double-bit-detection error correction code, typically with a 39-bit word. Since each chip supplies only one bit of the word, a chip fail in the system causes only a single-bit error and is hence correctable at the system level.

Chip family

The SAMOS process is used to meet the needs of a multitude of users through a family of four chips, ranging from 18K-bit, 90-ns typical access through 64K-bit, 300-ns access. By design, the different chips are all made identically in the process, with the differences being determined only by the photolithographic masks used. A summary of chip characteristics is given in Table 2 [1]. The 18K-, 32K-, and 64K-bit chips show directly the tradeoff of performance against density among the different designs. The 36K-bit chip appears to be anomalous in this progression, in that it is the slowest chip but not the densest. It was, however, an earlier-vintage, more conservatively designed chip used for early manufacturing learning. The high-performance chips are characterized by larger storage nodes and shorter bit lines resulting in larger signals and simpler sense detection schemes [49]. All chips can be used to provide multiple bits in each cycle, either simultaneously (18K, 32K, 36K) or sequentially (64K). The 18K- and 36K-bit chips are typically used in byte-organized applications where each 9-bit output will be an 8-bit byte plus a parity bit for error detection. The 32K- and 64K-bit chips are bit-organized. Figures 9 and 10 show the 18K-bit and 64K-bit chips, respectively, with areas labeled as to function.

The characteristics of the various chips after they are mounted into modules are given in Table 3, with a stacked module of 64K-bit chips shown in Fig. 11. At the module level, the full capability and flexibility of the overall tech-

Figure 9 The 18K-bit chip, with areas labeled as to function. Typical access time is 90 ns, worst-case access is 140 ns.

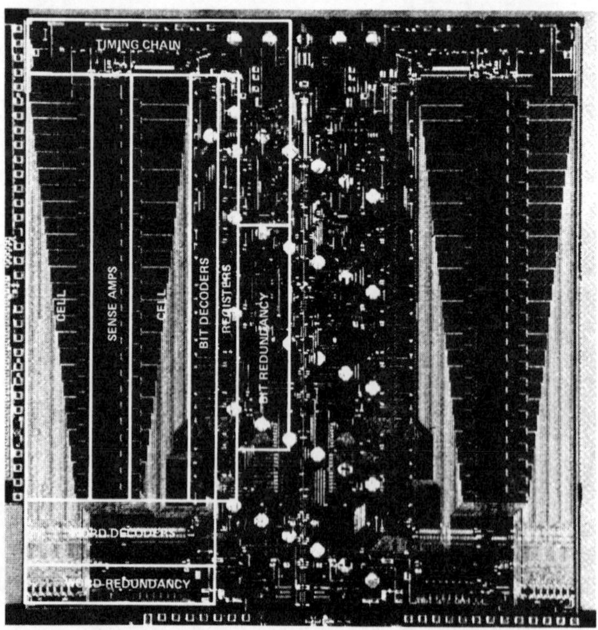

Figure 10 The 64K-bit chip, showing the on-chip shift register. Typical access time is 300 ns, worst-case access is 440 ns.

nology becomes apparent. For high-performance applications a 2.54-cm (one-inch)-square module with 72K-bit storage can provide nine bits of simultaneous output in a 256-ns worst-case cycle. When high density is required, a different 2.54-cm (one-inch)-square module with more than one-half megabit capacity can provide, in a cycle of $\approx$1000 ns, four parallel channels of output, each channel eight bits deep.

Summary

The SAMOS process, the motivation behind the process steps, and the merger of process capabilities and system needs have been discussed in this paper. SAMOS combines the one-device-cell concept and a number of unique process steps, which can be summarized as follows.

1. Backside ion implantation provides a simple, clean technique for leakage control.
2. Diffusions are driven in from a doped oxide layer which was applied to the bare wafer and removed subtractively. The technique allows narrow diffused lines to be made, and the doped oxide can be left above the diffusions where desired to provide a self-aligned oxide for low capacitance to conductive layers.
3. A thin oxide-nitride dual dielectric covers the entire wafer with the exception of contact holes and some diffused areas. The dual dielectric provides low defect density, and the nitride performs the crucial role of preventing oxidation of gate regions in later processing.
4. A conductive polysilicon layer is used as a field shield to shut off surface leakage, and forms the plate of the diffused storage node capacitors.
5. Lift-off aluminum metallurgy is used to provide minimum spaces between aluminum lines.
6. A dual layer of quartz and polyimide separates first and second levels of metallization, providing passivation and insulation with very low defect density.

Because of the use of the nitride in the gate dielectric, a number of yield- and reliability-related phenomena had to be overcome. Potential problem areas included threshold voltage control, threshold stability, hot carrier injection (channel or substrate), and parasitic device leakage. The general technique to overcome these items has been to understand the physics and eliminate processing causes where possible. When the problem was inherent in VLSI devices, it was carefully characterized, and circuits were designed to tolerate the changes expected with time.

The process was merged with a design philosophy aimed at optimal reliability and yield. Guard bands were used so that devices still function at large excursions of the process from nominal. A family of chips was designed for different applications, ranging from high performance (18K-bit, 90-ns typical access) to high density (64K-bit, 300-ns typical access). All chips are produced by the same process, with the only difference being the photolithographic patterns. The 32K-bit and 64K-bit chips use a dual-island approach, and all chips use some word or bit redundancy for enhanced yield. A penalty is paid in chip size in order to optimize the number of usable bits per wafer, and features such as an on-chip register are included where appropriate to enhance system performance. The chips are mounted on one-inch-square substrates with up to four chips on a substrate. Using stacked substrates, a maximum module density of 524 288 bits is obtained.

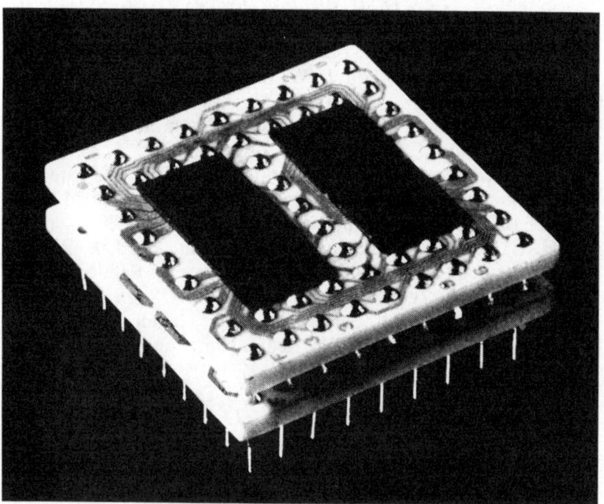

Figure 11 Uncapped view of a module with two decks, each deck having four 64K-bit chips. This module contains 524 288 bits of random access memory in a 2.54-cm × 2.54-cm-square area.

Acknowledgments

Sincere appreciation must be expressed for the efforts of the large number of colleagues at the IBM facilities in Essex Junction, Vermont, and in Sindelfingen/Boeblingen, West Germany, who developed the SAMOS process and product set, overcame the obstacles of a new technology, and successfully brought the process into manufacturing. In addition, many people made helpful suggestions on this manuscript. The assistance of G. S. Alberts, R. R. Troutman, V. L. Rideout, R. H. Kruggel, R. H. Linton, P. A. Farrar, D. R. Weed, E. P. Thoma, G. H. Parikh, R. M. Quinn, R. R. DeSimone, and others is appreciated.

References and notes

1. R. R. DeSimone, N. M. Donofrio, B. L. Flur, R. H. Kruggel, H. H. Leung, and R. Schnadt, "FET RAMs," *1979 IEEE ISSCC Digest of Technical Papers* **22,** 154-155 (1979).
2. R. H. Dennard, "Field Effect Transistor Memory," U.S. Patent 3,387,286, 1968.
3. V. L. Rideout, "One Device Cells for Dynamic Random Access Memories—A Tutorial," *IEEE Trans. Electron Devices* **ED-26,** 839-852 (1979).
4. P. E. Cottrell, R. R. Troutman, and T. H. Ning, "Hot-Electron Emission in N-Channel IGFET's," *IEEE J. Solid-State Circuits* **SC-14,** 442-455 (1979).
5. S. E. Schuster, "Multiple Word/Bit Line Redundancy for Semiconductor Memories," *IEEE J. Solid-State Circuits* **SC-13,** 698-703 (1978).
6. W. M. Smith, Jr., "Field Effect Transistor Integrated Circuit and Memory," U.S. Patent 3,811,076, 1974.
7. R. R. Garnache and W. M. Smith, Jr., "Integrated Circuit Fabrication Process," U.S. Patent 3,841,926, 1974.
8. B. Masters, J. Fairfield, and B. Crowder, *Ion Implantation*, F. Eisen, Ed., Gordon and Breach Science Publishers, New York, 1971.
9. T. M. Buck, K. A. Pickar, J. M. Poate, and C. M. Hsieh, "Gettering Rates of Various Fast Diffusion Metal Impurities at Ion-damaged Layers on Silicon," *Appl. Phys. Lett.* **21,** 485 (1972).
10. T. E. Seidel, R. L. Meek, and A. G. Cullis, "Direct Comparison of Ion Damage Gettering and Phosphorus Diffusion Gettering of Au in Si," *J. Appl. Phys.* **46,** 600 (1975).
11. H. J. Geipel and W. K. Tice, "Reduction of Leakage by Implantation Gettering in VLSI Circuits," *IBM J. Res. Develop.* **24,** 310-317 (1980, this issue).
12. H. J. Geipel and W. K. Tice, "Critical Microstructure for Ion-Implantation Gettering Effects in Silicon," *Appl. Phys. Lett.* **30,** 325 (1977).
13. C. H. Stapper, A. N. McLaren, and M. Dreckmann, "Yield Model for Productivity Optimization of VLSI Memory Chips with Redundancy and Partially Good Product," *IBM J. Res. Develop.* **24,** 398-409 (1980, this issue).
14. J. Scott and J. Olmstead, "A Solid-to-Solid Diffusion Technique," *RCA Rev.* **26,** 357 (1965).
15. A. W. Fisher, J. A. Amick, H. Hyman, and J. Scott, "Diffusion Characteristics and Application of Doped Silicon Dioxide Layers Deposited from Silicon (SiH_4)," *RCA Rev.* **29,** 533 (1968).
16. M. L. Barry and P. Olofsen, "Doped Oxides as Diffusion Sources," *J. Electrochem. Soc.* **116,** 854 (1969).
17. M. Ghezzo and D. M. Brown, "Arsenic Glass Source Diffusion in Si and SiO_2," *J. Electrochem. Soc.* **120,** 110 (1973).
18. P. C. Parekh, D. R. Goldstein, and T. C. Chan, "The Influence of the Reaction Kinetics of O_2 and Source Flow Rates on the Uniformity of Boron and Arsenic Diffusions," *Solid-State Electron.* **14,** 281 (1971).
19. This work is attributed to A. S. Bergendahl, D. W. Rakowski, and P. Hazelton, IBM General Technology Division, Essex Junction, VT.
20. R. R. Troutman, "VLSI Device Phenomena in Dynamic Memory and Their Application to Technology Development and Device Design," *IBM J. Res. Develop.* **24,** 299-309 (1980, this issue).
21. S. A. Abbas, C. A. Barile, and R. C. Dockerty, "Low Leakage, N-channel Silicon Gate FET with Self Aligned Field Shield," *IEDM Tech. Digest*, 371-373 (1973).
22. T. L. Chu, J. R. Szedon, and C. H. Lee, "The Preparation and *C-V* Characteristics of Si-Si_3N_4 and Si-SiO_2-Si_3N_4," *Solid-State Electron.* **10,** 897-905 (1967).
23. (a) M. Hatzakis, "Electron Resists for Microcircuit and Mask Productions," *J. Electrochem. Soc.* **116,** 1033 (1969).
(b) G. Bergasse, "Two-Resist Layers Lift-Off Process," *IBM Tech. Disclosure Bull.* **16,** 2110-2111 (1973).
(c) E. C. Fredericks, G. C. Schwartz, and L. B. Zielindi, "Polysulfone Lift-Off Masking Technique," *IBM Tech. Disclosure Bull.* **20,** 989 (1977).
(d) Y. Hom-ma, H. Nozawa, and S. Harada, "A New Lift-Off Metallization Technique for High Speed Bipolar LSI's," *IEDM Tech. Digest*, 54 (1979).
24. (a) B. J. Canavello, M. Hatzakis, and J. M. Shaw, "Process for Obtaining Undercutting of a Photoresist to Facilitate Lift-Off," *IBM Tech. Disclosure Bull.* **19,** 4048 (1977).
(b) W. D. Grobman, H. E. Luhn, T. P. Donohue, A. J.

Speth, A. Wilson, M. Hatzakis, and T. H. P. Chang, "1 μm MOSFET VLSI Technology: Part VI—Electron-beam Lithography," *IEEE Trans. Electron Devices* **ED-26**, 360 (1979).

25. F. M. d'Heurle and P. S. Ho, "Electromigration in Thin Films," *Thin Films: Interdiffusion and Reactions*, J. M. Poate, K. N. Tu, and J. W. Meyer, Eds., John Wiley & Sons, Inc., New York, 1978.
26. Paul A. Farrar, "Method for Making Integrated Circuit Contact Structure," U.S. Patent 3,830,657, 1974.
27. R. M. Geffken, "Effect of Various Thin Film and Interface Phenomena on Al-Si Contact Resistance," presented at the IEEE VLSI Workshop, New York, May 4, 1979.
28. H. C. Cook, P. A. Farrar, R. R. Uttecht, and J. P. Wilson, "Structure for Improving the Passivation of Semiconductor Chips," *IBM Tech. Disclosure Bull.* **16**, 728 (1973).
29. G. S. Alberts, P. A. Farrar, and R. L. Hallen, "Method for Constructing a ROM for Redundancy and Other Application," U.S. Patent 3,959,047, 1966.
30. P. A. Totta and R. P. Sopher, "SLT Device Metallurgy and its Monolithic Extension," *IBM J. Res. Develop.* **13**, 226 (1969).
31. L. F. Miller, "Controlled Collapse Reflow Chip Joining," *IBM J. Res. Develop.* **13**, 239 (1969).
32. E. H. Snow, A. S. Grove, B. E. Deal, and C. T. Sah, "Ion Transport Phenomena in Insulating Films," *J. Appl. Phys.* **36**, 1664 (1965).
33. J. V. Dalton, "Sodium Drift and Diffusion in Silicon Nitride Films," *J. Electrochem. Soc.* **113**, 165C (1966).
34. D. Frohman-Bentchkowsky and M. Lenzlinger, "Charge Transport and Storage in Metal-Nitride-Oxide-Silicon (MNOS) Structures," *J. Appl. Phys.* **40**, 3307 (1969).
35. P. K. Chaudhari, J. M. Franz, and C. P. Acker, "Electrical Properties of Vapor Deposited Silicon Nitride Films Measured in Strong Electric Fields," *J. Electrochem. Soc.* **120**, 991 (1973).
36. S. A. Abbas and R. C. Dockerty, "Hot Carriers Instability in IGFET's," *Appl. Phys. Lett.* **27**, 147 (1975).
37. T. H. Ning, C. M. Osburn, and H. N. Yu, "Effect of Electron Trapping on IGFET Characteristics," *J. Electron. Mater.* **6**, 65-76 (1977).
38. P. C. Arnett and B. H. Yun, "Silicon Nitride Trap Properties as Revealed by Charge-centroid Measurements on MNOS Devices," *Appl. Phys. Lett.* **26**, 94 (1975).
39. T. H. Ning, C. M. Osburn, and H. N. Yu, "Threshold Instability in IGFETS due to Emission of Leakage Electrons from Silicon Substrate into Silicon Dioxide," *Appl. Phys. Lett.* **29**, 198-200 (1976).
40. R. R. Troutman, "Silicon Surface Emission of Hot Electrons," *Solid-State Electron.* **21**, 283-289 (1978).
41. T. H. Ning, C. M. Osburn, and H. N. Yu, "Emission Probability of Hot Electrons into Silicon Dioxide," *J. Appl. Phys.* **48**, 286-293 (1977).
42. J. F. Verwey, "Nonavalanche Injection of Hot Carriers into SiO_2," *J. Appl. Phys.* **44**, 2681 (1973).
43. This work is attributed to J. P. Wilson, M. D. Potter, R. A. Powlus, R. R. Uttecht, J. P. Stinson, W. J. Ayer, and A. J. Wager, IBM General Technology Division, Essex Junction, VT.
44. R. R. Troutman, "Ion Implanted Threshold Tailoring for Insulator Gate Field-Effect Transistors," *IEEE Trans. Electron Devices* **ED-24**, 182-192 (1977).
45. B. H. Yun, "Inspecting Impurity Concentrations in Semiconductors," *IBM Tech. Disclosure Bull.* **18**, 4226 (1976).
46. This work is attributed to B. H. Yun (IBM Data Systems Division, East Fishkill, NY) and to R. A. Corcoran, W. A. Keenan, A. Kaloustian, and D. Michaelides (IBM General Technology Division, Essex Junction, VT).
47. R. H. Kruggel, presented at the IEEE Computer Elements Committee Workshop, Vail, Colorado, June 24-27, 1979.
48. B. F. Fitzgerald and E. P. Thoma, "Circuit Implementation of Fusible Redundant Addresses on RAMs for Productivity Enhancement," *IBM J. Res. Develop.* **24**, 291-298 (1980, this issue).
49. Kenneth S. Gray, "Cross-Coupled Charge-Transfer Sense Amplifier and Latch Sense Scheme for High-Density FET Memories," *IBM J. Res. Develop.* **24**, 283-290 (1980, this issue).

The author is located at the IBM General Technology Division laboratory, Essex Junction, Vermont 05452.

A 256 K Dynamic RAM

Shigeki Matsue, Hirohiko Yamamoto, Keizo Kobayashi, Toshio Wada, Masato Tameda, Takashi Okuda and Yasaburo Inagaki

NEC-Toshiba Information Systems, Inc.

Tokyo, Japan

IN A CONTINUING EFFORT to lower the cost, and increase the density, a 256K x 1b single transistor cell RAM has been designed, and assembled in a standard 300mil 16pin DIP.

The RAM is organized to be compatible with existing 16pin 16K RAMs and 16pin 64K RAMs. The pin configuration and the photo are shown in Figure 1. The chip is arranged as a 256 rows x 1.024 columns matrix and is organized internally as two 128K RAMs. The location of important circuit blocks on the chip is shown in Figure 2.

The memory cell layout is shown in Figure 3. The cell measures 5.7 x 12.5μm and has a storage capacitance of 0.035pF by decreasing the cell capacitor oxide thickness to 200Å.

To reduce the ratio of digit line to cell capacitance, the digit line is formed in the second polysilicon layer. The resulting capacitance ratio is 20:1. To reduce dynamic noise on the digit line caused by the substrate current ransients, the digit lines are sheltered by the first polysilicon ground plane.

To make the higher density RAM practical, several steps were taken to provide immunity from alpha-particles. The memory cell capacitance was made large enough for the soft error caused by one alpha-particle. The critical areas of digit lines were made small by the use of transfer gates and precise timing. The chip surface was covered by a silicone coating, and a cold seam welding method used for package sealing. The calculated MTBF due to the soft error is 30,000 device hours.

To accomplish 1.5μ photolithography, fabrication of the wafer was with a one-tenth optical step-and-repeat system directly on the wafer, with only dry etching and ion-implantation processes.

The design target for the device was: access time 250ns, cycle time 410ns, and power dissipation 300mW. These objectives have been met. Figure 4 shows the performance of a typical device. A summary of the die characteristic is given in Table 1.

Acknowledgment

The authors wish to thank Y. Matsukura, T. Matsumura, T. Kurosawa, T. Odada for their contribution to this project.

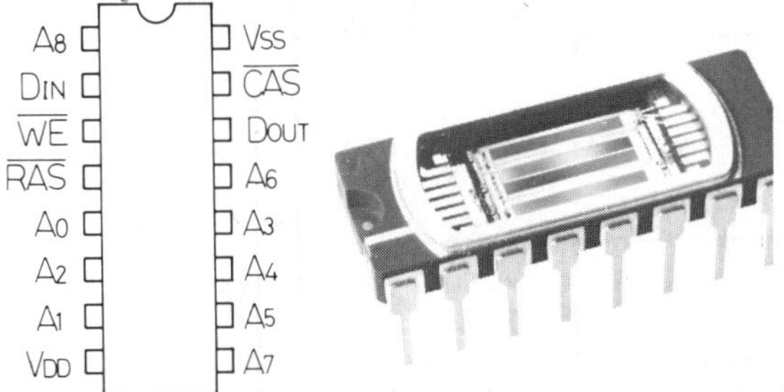

[Left]

FIGURE 1—The 256K RAM in a 16-pin DIP and pin configuration.

FIGURE 3—Photograph of the memory cell layout.

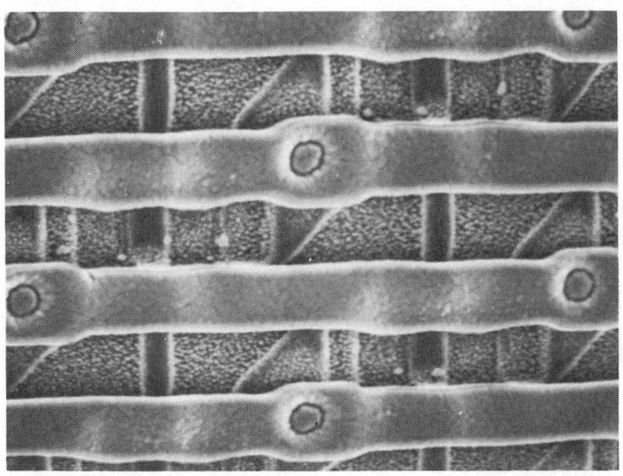

[Below]

FIGURE 4—Performance of a typical device in the read mode. The conditions are T=25° C and V_{DD}=5.0V.

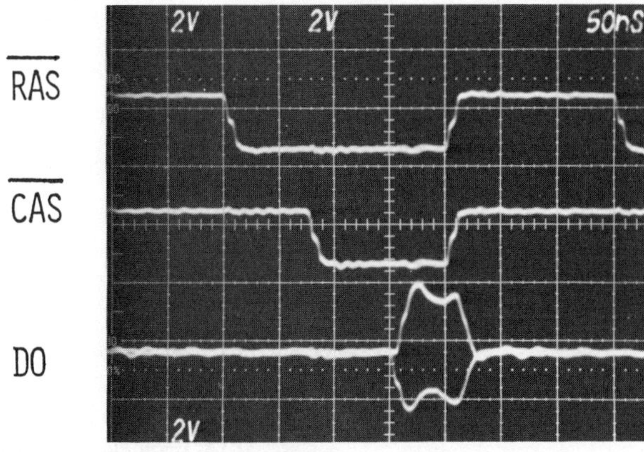

Reprinted from *IEEE Int. Solid State Circuits Conf.*, pp. 232–233, 1980.

(a)

(b)

R/W, I/O CIRCUITS
TIMING CIRCUITS

128 X 512 CELL ARRAY

ROW DEC.

512 SENSE AMPLIFIERS
COLUMN DECODER I/O CKTS

128 X 512 CELL ARRAY

ROW DEC.

128 X 512 CELL ARRAY

ROW DEC.

512 SENSE AMPLIFIERS
COLUMN DECODER I/O CKTS

128 X 512 CELL ARRAY

ROW DEC.

ADDRESS BUFFERS

FIGURE 2—The 256K RAM layout: (*a*) photo of the chip whose overall dimensions are 8.59x4.84mm; (*b*) location of important circuits.

Package	16pin, 300mil DIP
Technology	2 level poly N-Si Gate
Channel Length	1.5μ
Gate Oxide	400Å (cell 200Å)
Cell Size	5.7μ x 12.5μ (71.25μ^2)
Chip Size	4.84m x 8.59m (41.58mm^2)
Access Time	160ns
Cycle Time	350ns
Power Supply	5V ± 5%
Active Current	45mA
Standby Current	5mA
Refresh	256 cycles at 4ms intervals
Interface	TTL compatible

TABLE 1—Summary of typical characteristics of the 256K RAM.

Automatic Refresh Dynamic Memory

Harry J. Boll, Ellis N. Fuls, James T. Nelson and Leopold D. Yau

Bell Laboratories

Murray Hill, NJ

AN AUTOMATIC REFRESH random access memory cell has been derived from the single transistor cell with a modest increase in cell complexity and size. Advantages are:

(1)– Refresh operation is asynchronous so read and write cycles can be initiated at any time.

(2)– All cells are refreshed simultaneously so the refresh interval can be very short, allowing high temperature operation.

(3)– Refresh power is much lower than in standard dynamic memory because addressing and timing clocks are not involved in refresh.

(4)– Existing single transistor designs can be easily modified to include automatic refresh.

The cell shown in Figure 1 includes the usual word (W) and bit (B) lines connected to the single transistor cell T_1 and C_S. Refresh is accomplished by the added components T_2, T_3, C_1, and refresh line R. The added circuit elements require little additional space, because T_3 is a part of C_S, C_1 is the natural overlap capacitance between R and the gate of T_2, and R can be shared between two cells. In addition, because the cell when empty remains completely empty, C_S can be smaller than in a comparable single transistor cell. Capacitances C_2, C_3 and C_4 are unwanted and are to be minimized.

With N-channel devices and with a constant voltage +V on the counter-electrode CE, operation is as follows:

Empty Cell: When capacitor C_S is nearly empty (no inversion layer of electrons), T_3 is off. By way of C_1 a peak-to-peak alternating voltage, V_R, applied to R drives the floating node, F, through a peak-to-peak voltage V_F. The equation in Figure 1 relates V_F to V_R. On the negative-going excursion of V_F, excess electrons which may have collected on node F, flow through T_3 into C_S. F is thereby clamped to be more positive than $+ V - V_{T3}$, where V_{T3} is the threshold voltage of T_3. The following positive peak of V_F turns on T_2 which transfers electrons from C_S to R. To prevent electron injection into an empty C_S, R must always be more positive than $+ V - V_{T3} - V_{T2}$. It is advantageous for V_{T3} to be greater than V_{T2}. It is advantageous for V_{T3} to be greater than V_{T2}. Otherwise, when T_2 conducts electrons from C_S to R, T_3 also conducts from C_S to F. The T_3 conduction reduces the positive excursion of V_F reducing refresh efficiency. The threshold difference can be achieved in a number of ways including ion implantation, oxide thickness difference, and short channel effects.

If a full cell is rewritten to an empty state during the positive peak of V_R, the subsequent negative-going transition of V_R injects electrons into C_S via C_1 and T_3. This produces a partially filled cell which can prevent T_2 from turning on during the subsequent positive peaks of V_R. This problem can be avoided in two ways: First, T_3 threshold can be made sufficiently higher than that of C_S and T_2 so that it remains off even when C_S is partially filled. Second, V_R can be actively pulled down to its negative peak whenever the chip is accessed.

Full Cell: When C_S is full of electrons, T_2 remains off because T_3 effectively shorts F to C_S. Full cells remain full by themselves because leakage to the substrate exceeds leakage to the positive electrodes.

Experimental Results: Figure 2 is a photo of four individual cells fabricated in P-channel silicon gate technology. To simplify testing, a voltage sensing transistor T_S was attached to each cell as shown in Figure 3. By monitoring the dc conduction of T_S, it was easy to determine the charge state of C_S, thus avoiding the need for the usual strobed, balanced detector circuits.

In the top two cells of Figure 2, transistors T_3 and T_S were ion implanted to increase their threshold voltages by approximately 1-V. The nonimplanted transistors had thresholds of approximately –2 V.

Experiments with these cells showed that automatic refresh action could be obtained with a 6 to 8 V peak-to-peak voltage on R, over a frequency range, f, from 100 Hz to 1 MHz. Both ion-implanted and non-ion implanted cells operated satisfactorily with the latter requiring somewhat higher V_R. Auto refresh could be obtained with a variety of wave-shapes on V_R including sinusoids, square waves and pulses.

By illuminating the cell it was possible to simulate the effects of PN junction leakage current at elevated temperatures. With $V_R = 0$, the cell operates as a standard single transistor cell. The light brightness could be adjusted to yield a wide range of storage times. These experiments showed that for automatic refresh there was an inverse relationship between f and the storage time in the absence of V_R. For a storage time of 0.1 ms, which corresponds to a temperature of approximately 130°C, the required f was approximately 100 kHz.

Figure 4 shows an N-channel, silicon gate[1] 4096-bit memory chip of the single-transistor design that was modified to include the automatic refresh feature. To minimize the design effort, the modifications were introduced in such a way that the overall circuit layout and chip size were unchanged. This required a reduction of 35% for C_S; the reference cell capacitance was also reduced accordingly. The resulting margin loss was minimal, because as explained previously, C_S can be smaller with automatic refresh. The contact between the source of T_3 and the gate of T_2 was made by direct polysilicon-to-silicon contact which allowed the metal word lines to pass over the top of the contact. The refresh lines were interleaved between adjacent cells parallel with the bit lines.

Masks were made so that three types of devices could be made on each silicon slice, the unaltered design, and the automatic refresh design with and without ion implantation of T_3. All three types operated successfully as single transistor memories in the normal refresh mode. The auto-refresh designs operated properly for V_R greater than about 8 V.

[1] Clemens, J. T., Doklan, R. H., and Nolen, J. J., "An N-Channel Si-Gate Integrated Circuit Technology," *International Electron Devices Meeting*, Dec., 1975.

Reprinted from *IEEE Int. Solid State Circuits Conf.*, pp. 132–133 and p. 237, 1976.

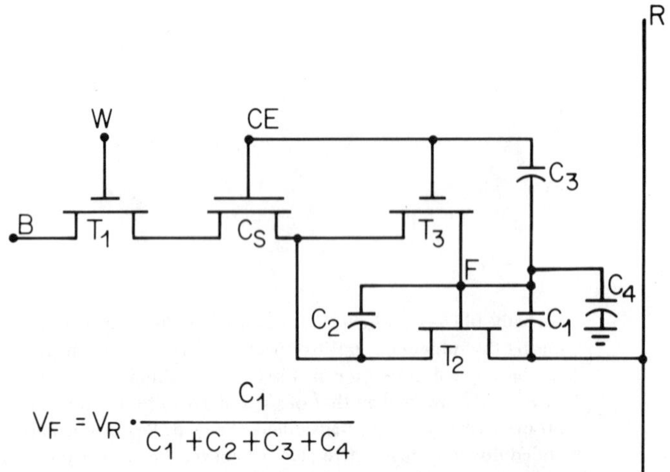

$$V_F = V_R \cdot \frac{C_1}{C_1 + C_2 + C_3 + C_4}$$

FIGURE 1—The automatic refresh random access memory cell.

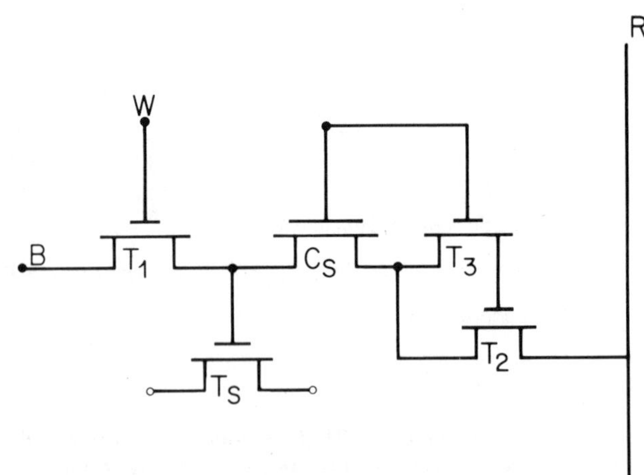

FIGURE 3—Circuit diagram of cells in Figure 2.

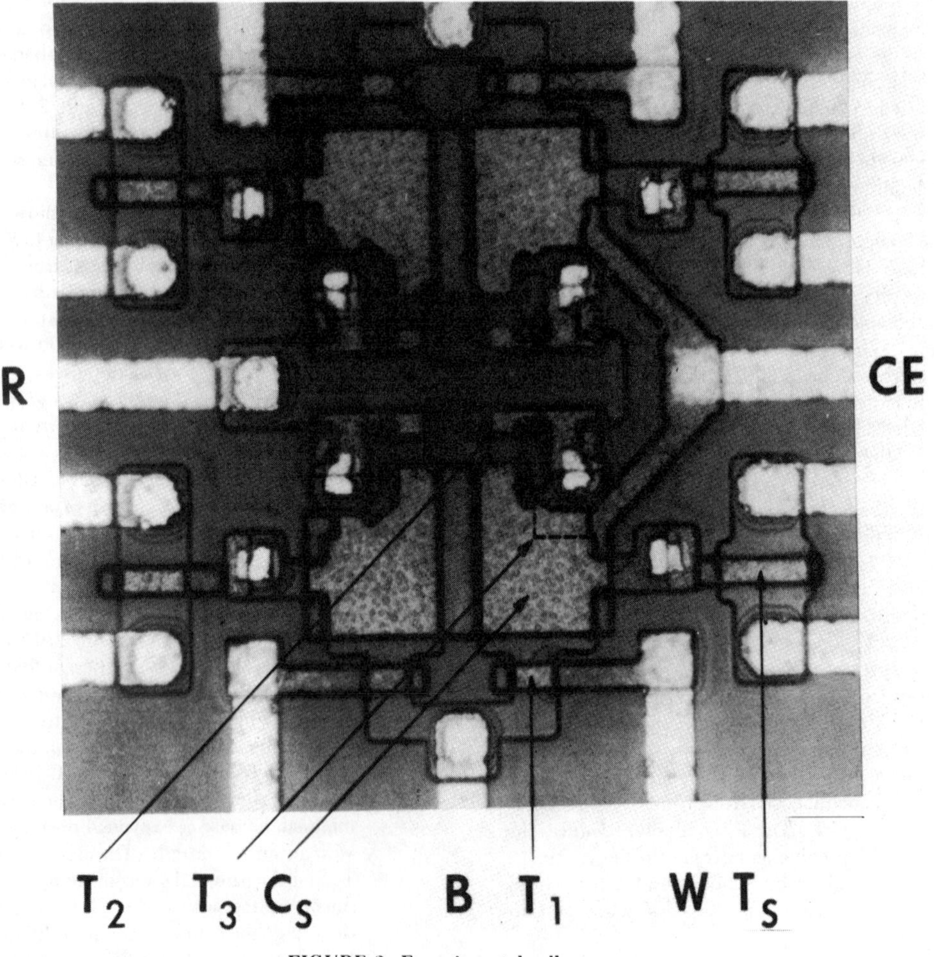

FIGURE 2—Experimental cells.

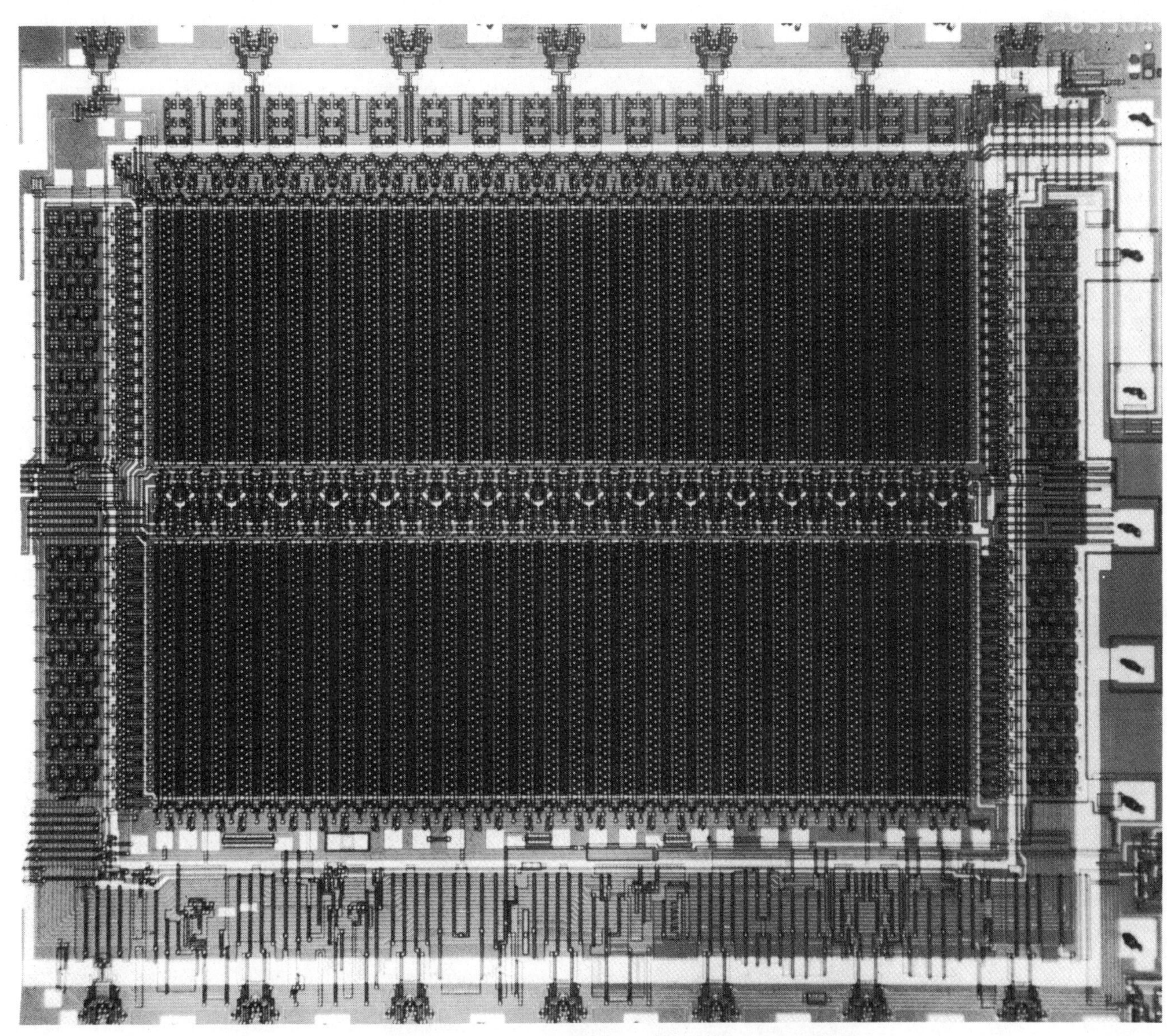

FIGURE 4—An N-channel silicon-gate 4096-bit cell memory chip.

A Self-Refreshing 4K RAM with Sub-mW Standby Power

John M. Caywood, Jagdish C. Pathak, Greenic L. VanBuren and

Scott W. Owen

Intel Corporation

Santa Clara, CA

MEMORY APPLICATIONS in which extremely low standby power is required because of battery backup or battery operation are becoming increasingly common as distributed processing becomes more widespread. CMOS is traditionally the technology preferred for this application, but CMOS RAMs have a high cost penalty resulting from their large die size relative to NMOS RAMs[1,2]. The RAM to be reported uses NMOS technology to serve these applications and possesses a die size comparable to NMOS static RAMs. The RAM draws typically only 40μW in standby and 30mW active, while occupying 2.9mm x 5.2mm, and offering a typical access time of less than 200ns. The standby power of the new RAM is two orders of magnitude less than that reported for earlier NMOS RAMs[3], and the active speed power product is half that of existing 4K RAMs, CMOS or NMOS.

This performance was accomplished by combining dynamic peripheral circuitry with a modification of a self-refreshing cell first proposed in 1976[4]. This modified cell, shown in Figure 1, occupies 1400μ^2. In operation, if the storage capacitor, Q_2, of the refresh cell is depleted of electrons (or more precisely if the quasi-Fermi level in Q_2 is more than a few kT below the inversion level of Q_3), when the refresh line, R, goes from low to high, the floating node, N, is capacitively coupled high. This activates transistor Q_4 and allows electrons which have leaked onto Q_2 to flow through Q_4 to R. If Q_2 is full of electrons (i.e., the quasi Fermi level of Q_2 is high enough, so that Q_3 is inverted) the source of Q_4 is connected to its gate and it never turns on. Moreover, in this case, the voltage swing on R is capacitively divided between the gate capacitance of Q_5 and that of Q_2, rather than between Q_5 and the parasitic capacitance of N, as is the case when Q_3 is depleted. This results in a much smaller swing on N in the case that Q_2 is full of electrons than when it is devoid of electrons. Moreover, since Q_5 is a nonlinear capacitor, the charge attracted to N when R goes high with Q_3 inverted, is much less than if Q_5 were a linear capacitor. This is significant, for if a write operation occurs to change Q_2 from a charged to discharged state while R is high, the charge attracted onto N is injected into Q_2 when R goes from high to low. If this charge is large enough to bring the quasi-Fermi level of Q_2 to within several kT of the inversion level of Q_3, the cell will not refresh and leakage current will gradually completely fill Q_2.

Figure 2 shows test chip data for the new cell. It can be seen that the voltage swing resulting from charge attracted to node N by R swinging high is only 10% of the swing resulting from a cell charged full of electrons. Because of a charge level of 10% is much too small to inhibit refresh, this new cell can be refreshed completely asynchronously from read or write operations. This RAM takes advantage of this property by using a planar refresh clock generated on chip which is completely invisible to the user. This clock has very slow rise and fall times and operates at ~200μs cycle time; this rate allows minimal power to be used in refreshing the cells, while significantly relaxing the cell leakage current requirement from that of dynamic RAMs which commonly utilize 2ms refresh cycles. Thus, the device functions as a clocked static RAM.

Figure 3 shows a photograph of a 5V-only 1Kx4RAM with self-refresh cell. From the viewpoint of peripheral circuits, the cell is a one-transistor cell; thus the chip is organized like a dynamic RAM with sense amplifiers and column decoders down the middle. The address buffers are latching which allows multiplexing of address and I/O lines for use with microprocessors without the necessity of external latches. The data input buffers and read/write control circuitry are static with data being latched into memory on the trailing edge of the write pulse. All inputs and outputs are TTL compatible.

The design of the CE buffer had to meet a number of conflicting requirements. The buffer must be static, must operate from TTL levels, must be fast enough to allow the design of 200ns access time parts, and must draw so little power in standby that the part can compete with CMOS; e.g., I_{CC} ~10μA. The simplest static buffer is a simple inverter as is shown in Figure 4*a*. For this circuit, I_{CC} and propagation delay are inversely propotional. For example, if the circuit is to draw 10μA with CE high and the circuit must drive an internal load of 10pF, the propagation delay is several μs which is clearly incompatible with the stated speed goal. If the part is defined with CE low in standby and high when active, the circuit in Figure 4*a* can be designed to meet the requirements, but the problem is merely passed on to the next stage.

The solution found for these requirements is shown schematically in Figure 4*b*. When the external CE signal is low, the AND gate output is low and the output of the first stage inverter supplies drive to keep the internal CE signal, CE_{INT}, clamped low. Since Q_1 and Q_3 are both off, no current is drawn in this circuit in standby. When the CE input goes high, there is a time interval determined by the delay, τ, during which the output of the AND gate is high. During this time, τ, Q_3 and Q_5 are both on and both sides of the capacitor are clamped to ground. After the signal from the input inverter propagates through the delay element, both Q_3 and Q_5 turn off and Q_4 pulls CE_{INT} up capacitively. The MOS level signal can now be buffered with conventional circuitry. This circuitry thus provides TTL to MOS translation while drawing no power during standby.

Figure 5 is a photograph of waveforms for a typical read cycle. The cycle is initiated when CE, trace A, goes high. The addresses, trace B, are presented to the memory at the beginning of the cycle and may then be changed since they are latched internally. After 150ns, data becomes available at the output as is seen in trace C. The I_{CC} trace at the bottom of the photograph illustrates the real performance advantage of this part. As can be readily seen, the largest single current drawn is that required to charge the external capacitive loads when reading "1" 's. Table I gives the typical values of some major ac and dc parameters.

---

[1] Ochii, K. et al, "C²MOS 4K Static RAM", *ISSCC DIGEST OF TECHNICAL PAPERS*, p. 18-19; Feb., 1977.

[2] Diamond, S.L. and Kappor, U.K., "Application and Design of a Static CMOS 4096-bit RAM", *IEEE Computer Society International Conference Digest of Papers*; Feb., 1977.

[3] McKenny, V.G., "A 5V-Only 4K Static RAM", *ISSCC DIGEST OF TECHNICAL PAPERS*, p. 16-17; Feb., 1977.

[4] Boll, H.J. et al, "Automatic Refresh Dynamic Memory", *ISSCC DIGEST OF TECHNICAL PAPERS*, p. 132-133; Feb., 1976. Boll, H.J., "Self-Refreshed Capacitor Memory Cell", *U.S. Patent No. 4,030,083*.

Reprinted from *IEEE Int. Solid State Circuits Conf.*, pp. 16–17 and p. 272, 1979.

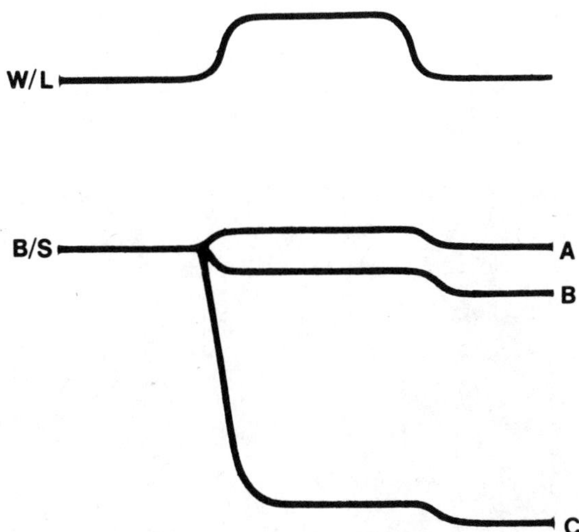

FIGURE 2—Bit/sense line voltage during Read comparing "1" written with R low, A, "1" written with R high, B and "0", C.

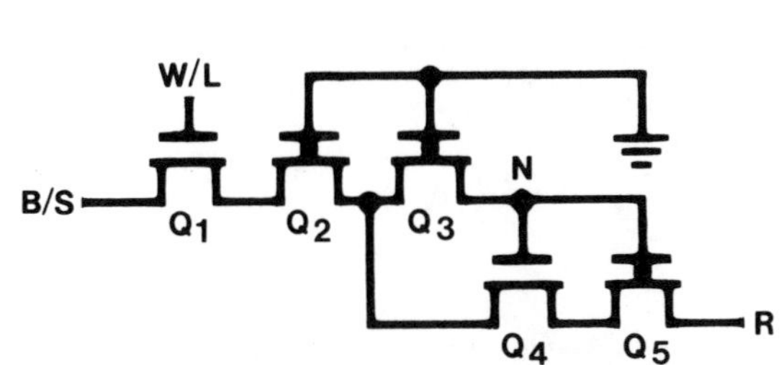

FIGURE 1—Schematic diagram of the memory cell used in RAM.

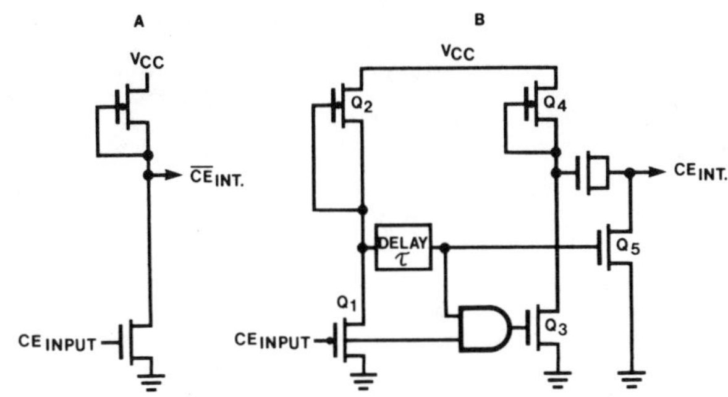

FIGURE 4—Comparison of classic static inverter (*a*); schematic of CE buffer employed on chip (*b*).

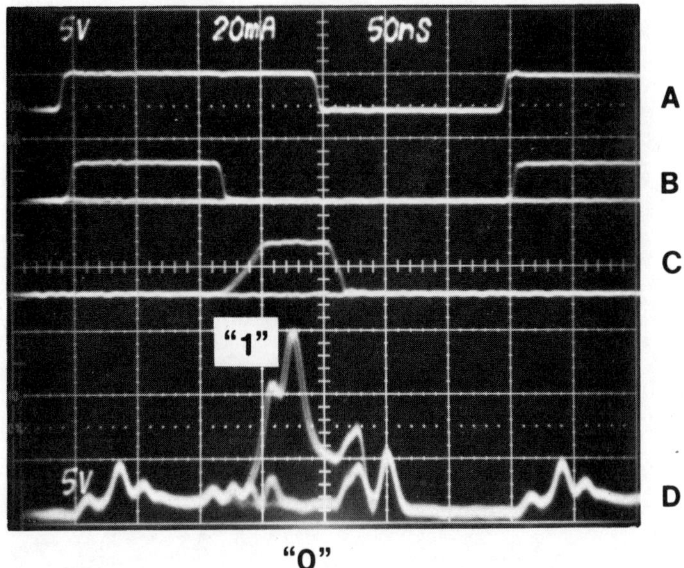

FIGURE 5—Photograph of waveforms for typical Read cycles showing CE input, trace A, address inputs, trace B, data out, trace C, and I_{CC}, trace D.

I_{CC}, active	5mA (300ns cycle time)
I_{CC}, standby	8μA
Read Access Time	200ns
Read Cycle Time	300ns
Address Setup Time	–20ns
Address Hold Time	60ns
Write Pulsewidth	110ns
Data to Write Overlap	50ns
Data Hold From Write	0ns

TABLE I—Typical operating characteristics: test conditions: T = 25° C, V_{CC} = 5V

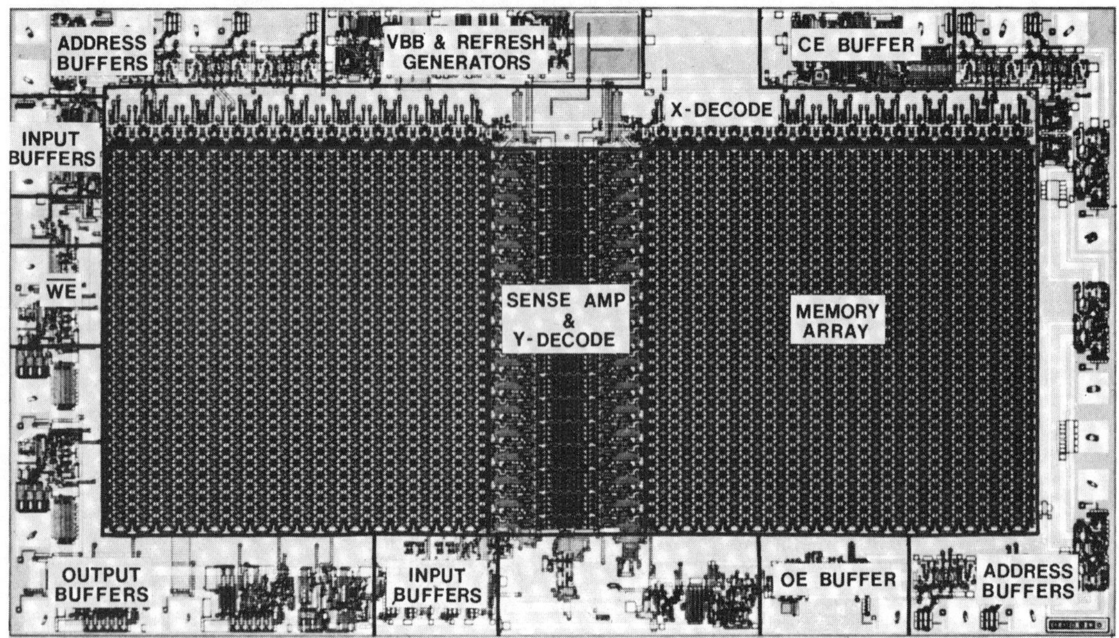

FIGURE 3—Photomicrograph of die with major functional blocks.

Section 4.6
ROMs, PROMs, and EPROMs

High-Density CMOS ROM Arrays

ROGER G. STEWART, MEMBER, IEEE

Abstract–A single transistor cell and a precharge signal are used to reduce the memory cell area in bulk CMOS ROM arrays to 1.12 mil²/bit. Use of SOS/CMOS technology further reduces the memory cell area to 0.38 mil²/bit and makes possible CMOS ROM's of up to 32 768 bits. Operation of both the array and the decoders is controlled by a precharge signal which is generated internally in a way which is transparent to the user. The CMOS ROM's thus produced are competitive with NMOS ROM's in both density and speed, yet retain all of the advantages of static CMOS circuits such as 1-μW power dissipation, full 2.8-15 V voltage operating range, and full -55°C-125°C temperature range.

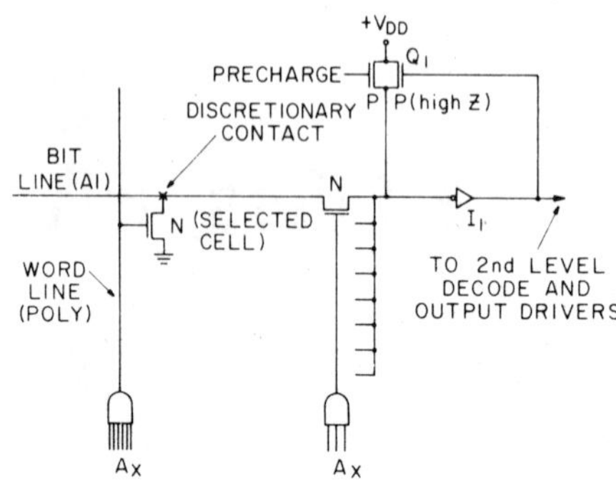

Fig. 1. ROM storage cell and sense amplifier connected together by an n-channel transistor to form a 1 of 8 predecoder.

I. Introduction

The use of static CMOS circuitry has become increasingly important to users concerned about low power dissipation, wide temperature extremes, or noisy environments. By reducing the cost and size of the system, the use of LSI technology has accelerated the trend toward putting sophisticated electronic systems in mobile applications such as calculators, watches, and cars where power dissipation and survival in harsh environments are critically important. Static CMOS technology is ideally suited for such applications since it offers power dissipation of typically only 1 μW @ 5 V, 2.8-15 V voltage operating range, -55°C-125°C temperature operating range, better than 30 percent noise immunity, etc. However, extensive use of CMOS technology in these applications has been limited by a lower chip capacity and higher cost compared to competitive PMOS and NMOS technologies.

The problem of matching NMOS performance, cost, and density has been particularly apparent in read only memories (ROM's). In the past, CMOS ROM's have always been slower, provided less capacity, and cost many times more than comparable NMOS ROM's on a cost/bit basis [1]-[3]. This paper describes how a single transistor cell, a high density process, and use of an internally generated precharge signal can be combined to achieve array densities competitive with NMOS without compromising the attractive features of static CMOS technology.

II. Structure of ROM Array

The new memory structure includes a single transistor cell in the array which then operates together with opposite conductivity-type transistors in the sense amplifier to perform a function similar to that of a CMOS NOR gate. The array consists of n-channel transistors fabricated with silicon-gate CMOS processing and arranged with metal bit lines and polysilicon word lines (see Fig. 1). The ground supply is bussed on metal between each group of eight bit lines. Programming is done by means of the contact mask, which controls whether or not the selected transistor is connected to the bit line.

During a read operation, the word decoder is first disabled and all bit lines and sense amplifiers are precharged to V_{DD}. The word decoder is then enabled, driving the gates of the n devices in the selected word line to V_{DD}. If the drain contact is absent at the location determined by the selected word and bit lines, then the bit line and sense amplifier input are held high by the high-impedance p transistor Q_1. However, if a drain contact does exist, the selected transistor overdrives the high-impedance p device and the bit line and sense amplifier input are pulled to ground. This causes the output of inverter I_1 to be driven high, turning Q_1 off, thereby eliminating quiescent current flow. Once discharged, the bit line will be held at ground indefinitely by the selected n transistor in the array.

Fig. 2 shows the layout for the memory cell using C²L technology. In C²L (closed COS/MOS logic), the self-aligned silicon gate completely surrounds the drain region. This fully enclosed structure is therefore self-guardbanding. This technique not only saves area, but increases the operating speed to typically 4 to 5 times that of standard CMOS because of reduced drain area and increased output drive current [4]. When used in the ROM array, the C²L topology simplifies, as shown in Fig. 2, to a dense ladder structure ideal for high density arrays. The area of the cell shown in Fig. 2 is only 1.12 mil²/bit despite use of conservative design rules such as 0.3-mil metal width, 0.3-mil metal spacing, and contacts 0.25 × 0.30 mil.

In this array, density is limited as much by the pitch of the

Manuscript received May 2, 1977; revised June 20, 1977.
The author is with the Solid State Technology Center, RCA Corporation, Somerville, NJ 08876.

Reprinted from *IEEE J. Solid-State Circuits*, vol. SC-12, pp. 502-506, Oct. 1977.

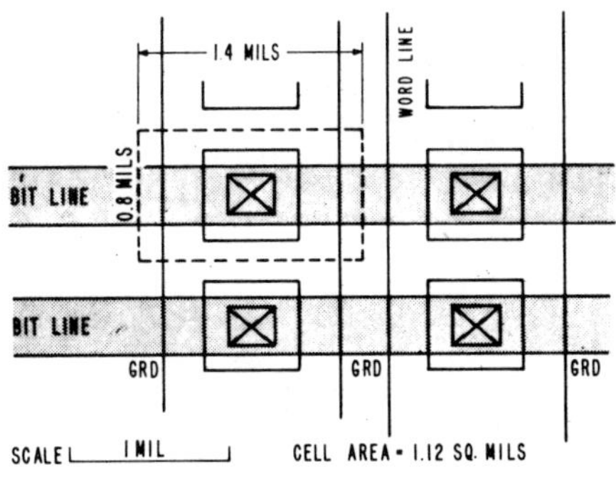

Fig. 2. ROM memory cell using C^2L technology.

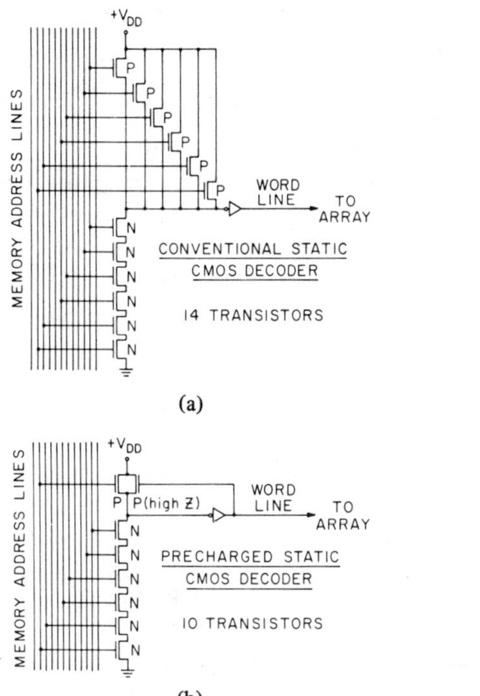

Fig. 3. Comparison between a conventional CMOS decoder and a simplified static CMOS decoder using precharge.

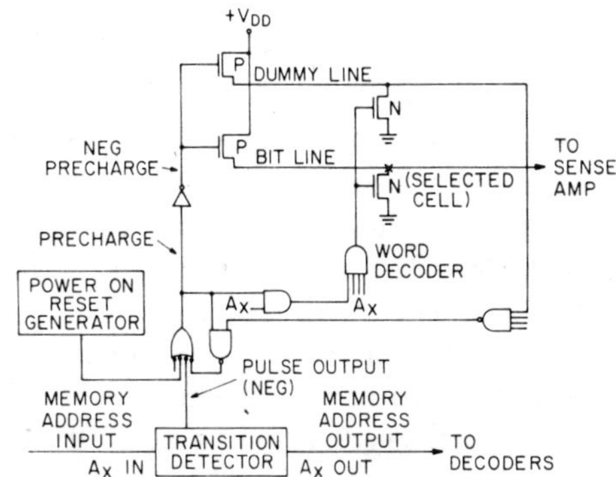

Fig. 4. Circuits used to generate and control the duration of the internal precharge cycle.

decoders as by layout of the memory cell itself. The bulk CMOS ROM requires a pitch of 1.4 mils in the word decoders and 0.8 mils in the bit line decoder which is too tight for a conventional CMOS design. The 0.8-mil pitch in the bit line decoder was achieved by using a 3-bit decoder located off pitch to control simple n-transistor gates located on pitch as shown in Fig. 1. However, this form of "predecoding" was not practical for the word decoder, so the 6-bit CMOS decoder was modified, as shown in Fig. 3, to simplify the design and achieve a tighter layout. A precharge device and positive feedback across the buffer inverter are used to eliminate the six parallel connected p transistors normally used in static CMOS decoders.

III. Precharge Generation and Control

While a precharge signal is useful for increasing the speed and density of CMOS memory arrays, the requirement to generate such a precharge signal externally is unacceptable in many applications. It is necessary to generate the precharge signal internally in a way that is totally transparent to the user. Fig. 4 shows how such a precharge signal can be generated. Proper operation of the word decoders and sense amplifiers requires that a precharge cycle must occur every time new data are accessed. Since access to new data will always necessitate a change in at least one memory address input line, it is sufficient to monitor the memory address lines and automatically initiate a precharge in response to a change or transition on any one of them. Each transition detector shown in Fig. 4 produces a negative pulse output in response to any change in its memory address. The pulse outputs of all transition detectors are ORed together to provide the precharge signal which in turn disables and precharges the word decoders, the sense amplifiers, and the array itself. Once started, the ROM is held in the precharge mode by the feedback gate.

Duration of precharge is controlled by the array itself. Dummy bit lines in the array sense the point when each of the polysilicon word lines has been discharged to ground along its entire length, and all bit lines have been precharged to V_{DD}. As soon as a complete precharge is sensed by the dummy lines, the latch on the precharge pulse is interrupted, thus terminating the precharge and allowing data to be read out of the memory.

The precharge control circuits therefore generate a pulse just wide enough to fully charge the array. Variations in polysilicon sheet resistance, word line capacitance, bit line capac-

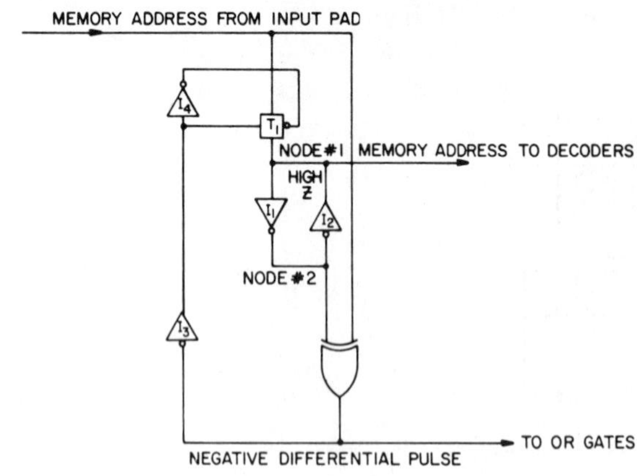

Fig. 5. Circuit diagram for transition detection using self-clocking latch.

itance, etc., are corrected by the feedback path through the dummy bit lines. Most importantly, the user is not hampered by any restrictions on the timing of memory address transitions. For example, address transitions occurring when precharge is complete will simply extend the precharge until addresses are firm. The ROM dissipates virtually no power in either the precharge or access mode of operation so the memory can continue to operate in either mode indefinitely if required by the user's system. The data on the outputs of the ROM are always valid one access time after addresses are firm, as is the case with other fully static memory devices. No timing signals of any kind are required.

IV. Transition Detectors

Conventional transition detectors based on delay networks are not adequate for the present application because their performance varies according to the rise time and fall time of the input signals. A new type of transition detector was developed, based on digital storage instead of a delay network. This detector, shown in Fig. 5, consists of inverters I_1 and I_2 that form a static latch along with a transmission gate T_1 connecting it to the address line. During any quiescent state, T_1 is off and the transition detector output is high. However, consider the situation where the address changes from a logic 0 to a logic 1 state. Since T_1 is off, node #1 will remain in a logic 0 state, and node #2 remains in a logic 1 state. Both inputs to the exclusive OR gate are now the same, so the output of the exclusive OR gate [labeled as the negative differential pulse (NDP)] drops to a logic 0. The internal memory precharge is then triggered off this signal. In addition, the logic 0 signal on NDP is fed back through I_3 and I_4 to turn on transmission gate T_1. With T_1 on, the logic 1 on the address line will be written into the latch formed by I_1 and I_2. This leaves the two exclusive OR gate inputs in opposite states which restores NDP to a logic 1 state thereby ending the timing pulse. Finally, the logic 1 on NDP is fed back through I_3 and I_4 to return transmission gate T_1 to an off state, thereby completing the cycle. The circuit is now ready to detect the next transition; i.e., a change from logic 1 to a logic 0. Operation of the circuit with a 1 to 0 transition will be similar to the 0 to 1 transition already described. Note that since the enable signal for the latch comes from the NDP itself, the presence of the timing pulse is guaranteed regardless of the input signal waveform or relative gate delays in this circuit.

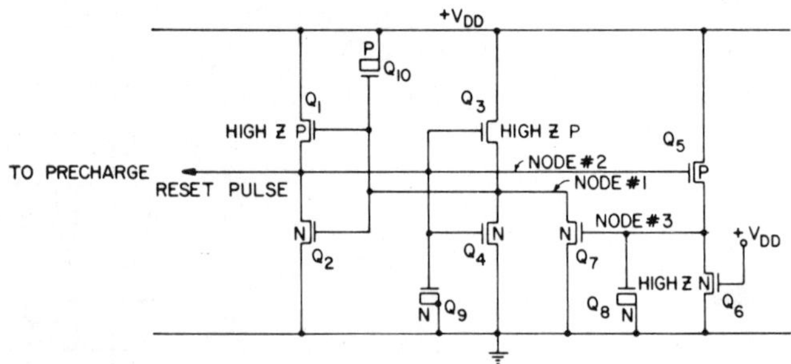

Fig. 6. Circuit diagram for the reset generator.

V. Reset Generator

The precharge generation circuits discussed above are adequate for normal operation of the ROM; however, during power-up conditions, a special situation may develop. The latches in the transition detectors, sense amplifiers, and word decoders may come up in a nonprecharged state without triggering the necessary precharge cycle. In order to guarantee that data on the outputs are valid prior to the first address transition, it is necessary to reset or precharge the ROM every time the ROM is powered up–in effect detecting transitions on the power supply pin.

Fig. 6 shows the circuit used in the power-up reset generator. Transistors Q_1, Q_2, Q_3, and Q_4 together form a latch biased to power up in a preferred state where node #1 = V_{DD} and node #2 = ground. Biasing of the latch is accomplished with capacitors formed by Q_8, Q_9, and Q_{10} and by modifying the structure of the latch transistors to ensure that the leakage of Q_3 is greater than Q_1 and the leakage of Q_2 is greater than Q_4. A precharge cycle in the ROM will then be started in response to the ground on node #2.

However, once the precharge has been started, the precharge triggering signal from the reset generator must be terminated to allow the ROM to return to its normal mode of operation. This is done by a pair of threshold sensing inverters, which perform a sequential AND function. The output of this AND gate will be used to terminate the precharge triggering signal. The circuit initially powers up with the reset generator latch in the preferred state. This leaves the input to Q_5 low. The circuit remains stable until $V_{DD} > V_{TP}$, at which point Q_5 turns on and starts to pull up node #3 against the load represented by Q_6. The scaling ratio between Q_5 and Q_6 is such that the switching of node #3 to a high level will occur when $V_{DD} \gtrsim V_{TP} + 0.4$ V.

The second and complementary threshold sensing inverter uses Q_7 as the driving device and the latch itself as a load. Assuming node #3 goes to V_{DD}, then the latch will be reset to its nonpreferred stable state when $V_{DD} \gtrsim V_{TN} + 0.4$ V. The circuit formed by Q_5, Q_6, Q_7, and the latch itself provide the logical AND function:

$$(V_{DD} \gtrsim V_{TP} + 0.4) \cdot (V_{DD} \gtrsim V_{TN} + 0.4) \Longrightarrow \text{End Precharge.}$$

In other words, the circuit will end the precharge triggering pulse only when the supply voltage is higher than both the p

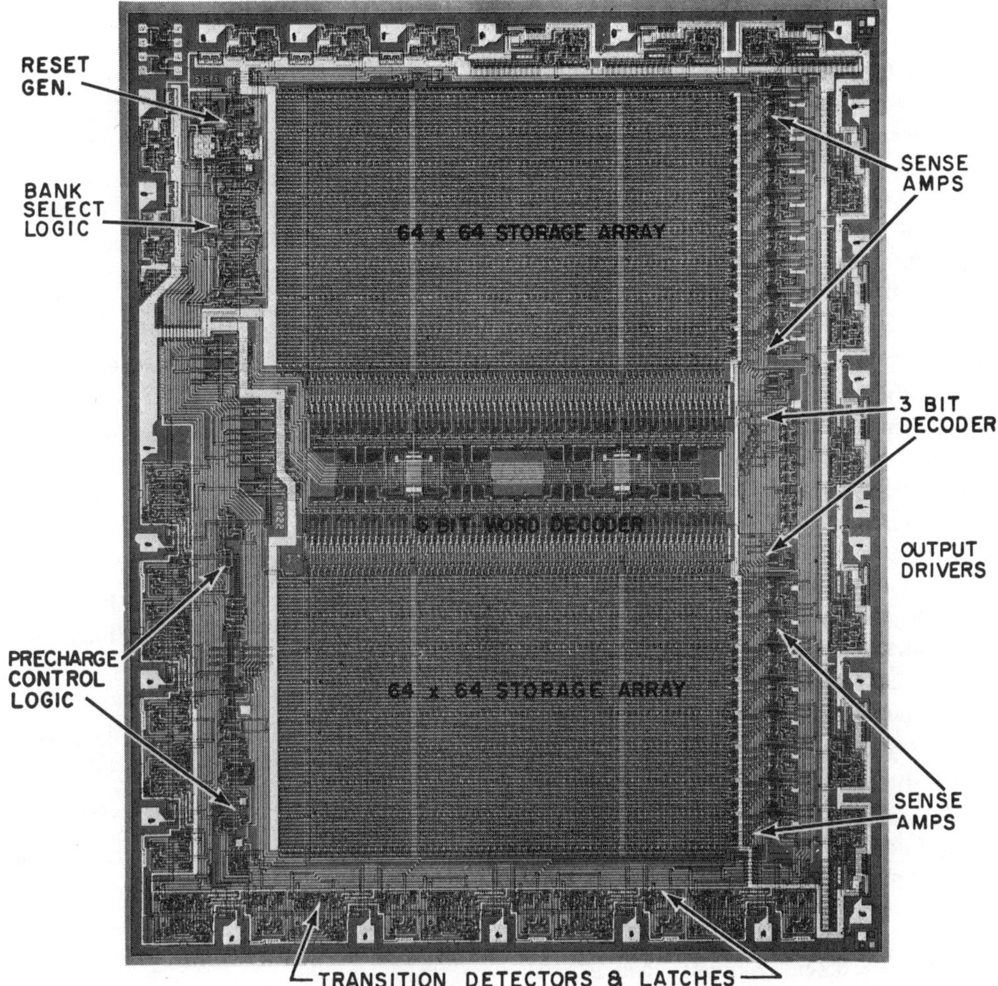

Fig. 7. Photomicrograph of 8192-bit CMOS ROM (170 × 206 mils).

and n thresholds by at least 0.4 V. This is the same condition necessary for propagation of the precharge pulse through a CMOS circuit and guarantees that this circuit is operational and can respond to the precharge pulse.

Note that only one precharge pulse will be generated each time the circuit is turned on. Once the latch is driven to the nonpreferred state, Q_5 and Q_7 will be turned off and the circuit will remain dormant until the power supply is turned off and then on again. Also, in its dormant state, there are no current paths to ground so the power dissipation is extremely low. The circuit can tolerate wide variations in either p or n thresholds and gain, and will always provide a reset signal during a small but reliable window occurring in the range between the highest of the p or n thresholds and a point 0.4 V higher than this (typically 1.0–2.0 V). The circuit has proved highly insensitive to the rise time of the power-up transient and preserves the "zero quiescent power" dissipation features of CMOS circuits.

TABLE I
TYPICAL CHARACTERISTICS OF 8192-BIT CMOS ROM

	CDP 1834
CHIP SIZE	170 x 206 MILS
ORGANIZATION	1,024 8-BIT WORDS
OPERATION	FULLY STATIC, NO CHIP ENABLE STROBING OR OTHER TIMING SIGNALS NEEDED
READ ACCESS TIME	300 nsec @ 10 V 700 nsec @ 5 V
MEMORY CYCLE TIME	250 nsec @ 10 V 600 nsec @ 5 V
QUIESCENT POWER DISSIPATION	.01 mW @ 10 V .001 mW @ 5 V
DYNAMIC POWER DISSIPATION	100 mW @ 10 V, 1 MHz 25 mW @ 5 V, 1 MHz
VOLTAGE OPERATING RANGE	2-17 V (2.8-15 V TESTED RANGE)
TEMPERATURE OPERATING RANGE	–55°C TO 125°C
NOISE IMMUNITY	40% (30% TESTED)
OUTPUT DRIVERS	2 T^2L LOADS (1 T^2L LOAD TESTED)
PROGRAMMING	CONTACT MASK PROGRAMMABLE
PROCESSING TECHNOLOGY	C^2L (CLOSED COS/MOS LOGIC)
ARRAY DENSITY	1.12 SQ MILS/BIT

VI. RESULTS

A family of high density ROM's has been developed based on the circuit techniques described in this paper. The first memory was a 4096-bit CMOS ROM using C^2L technology and measuring 151 × 167 mils [5]. Next, a larger, faster, and more efficient 8192-bit CMOS ROM was developed which also used C^2L bulk technology. A chip photograph of the 8K CMOS ROM is shown in Fig. 7 and characteristics of this chip are summarized in Table I. The chip measures 170 × 206 mils with an array density of 1.12 mil^2/bit. The

8K ROM uses four forward-conduction-optimized diodes on each input to protect the circuit from transients of up to 4000 V [6] (192 pF, 560 Ω). The outputs use conventional symmetrical CMOS tristate buffers scaled to drive a single T^2L load under worst case conditions. Note that the quiescent power is typically so low as to be negligible in most applications. For a random bit pattern, the dynamic power dissipation follows the classical relation:

$$P = 1/2 f C_T V^2$$

where f is the number of memory access cycles, or more precisely, the number of complete precharge cycles. C_T is the total capacitance in the system which equals the sum of 2000 pF plus all capacitances driven by the output lines.

Access time is typically 300 ns at 10 V where about 150 ns is used for the precharge cycle and the remaining 150 ns used for memory access cycle. Due to overlap of the precharge cycle, the ROM can operate with a memory cycle time equal to or less than the memory access time. Chip selects on the 8K ROM can be used to disable the precharge cycle, as well as the output drivers, thereby reducing dynamic power dissipation by approximately 80 percent. Memory access time measured from a chip select input is typically 250 ns @ 10 V.

More recently it has been shown that use of silicon-on-sapphire (SOS) processing technology can yield further improvement in both the speed and density of CMOS ROM arrays. SOS memory cells using 0.3-mil metal width, 0.25-mil metal spacing, and 0.2 × 0.2-mil contacts, yield an array with a density of 0.38 mil^2/bit. Use of this array leads to a 16 384-bit CMOS ROM on a chip measuring only 124 × 164 mils. The projected chip size for a 32 768-bit CMOS ROM is 160 × 196 mils.

VII. Conclusions

The use of an internally generated precharge signal has made it possible to design CMOS ROM arrays with a density equal to that of NMOS ROM's, but with the added CMOS features such as 1-μW power dissipation, full 2.8-15 V operating range, full -55°C to +125°C temperature range, easy to use static operation, and higher speed performance than could be achieved with passive loads. Arrays of up to 8K bits have already been fabricated and arrays of 32K bits or more have been shown to be feasible with existing technology. This technique for generating user transparent timing signals could also be used to increase density or improve the speed of other circuits such as RAM's, EAROM's, UART's, and microprocessors.

Acknowledgment

The author would like to thank T. Loscuito for his help in layout of the arrays, K. Phelps for his help in breadboarding and evaluation, and J. Oberman for many hours of invaluable consultation.

References

[1] R. M. Greene, "A 32K ROM using differential ramp techniques," in *1976 Int. Solid-State Circuits Conf., Dig. Tech. Papers*, Philadelphia, PA, Feb. 1976, pp. 186, 187.

[2] S. Davis, "ROM's push microprocessor applications," *Electron. Eng. Times*, pp. 18, 32, Nov. 3, 1975.

[3] S. Davis, "Mostek, T. I. introduce 32K ROM's using single supply," *Electron. Eng. Times*, p. 8, Feb. 7, 1977.

[4] A. G. F. Dingwall and R. E. Stricker, "C^2L: A new high-speed, high density bulk CMOS technology," in *1976 Int. Electron Devices Meeting Tech. Dig.*, Washington, DC, Dec. 1976, pp. 188-191.

[5] R. G. Stewart, "High density CMOS ROM arrays," in *1977 Int. Solid-State Circuits Conf., Dig. Tech. Papers*, Philadelphia, PA, Feb. 1977, pp. 21, 22, 230.

[6] R. G. Stewart and D. Hampel, "EMP hardened CMOS circuits," *IEEE Trans. Nuc. Sci.*, vol. NS-21, pp. 332-339, Dec. 1974.

A 4Mb Full Wafer ROM

Yoshitaka Kitano, Shigeto Kohda, Hideo Kikuchi and Shigenobu Sakai

NTT Musashino Electrical Communication Laboratory

Tokyo, Japan

THE MEMORY ORGANIZATION, memory cell, defect tolerant technology and operation of a full wafer mask programmable ROM will be described. The full wafer ROM was designed for a Chinese ideograph character generator.

The memory capacity of the ROM is 4Mb, and is composed of four 1Mb modules and two module select circuits on a 3" wafer; Figure 1. The full wafer ROM can store 15,040 characters of a 16 X 18 matrix. It has 16 bit address inputs, 16 bit data outputs and 4 control timing signal lines. All of the signals have TTL interface.

If address signals and an address enable signal are supplied to one of the modules, its timing circuit is driven and the module outputs the accessed 16 X 18 bit character data. When the accessed data have been latched into the latch circuit in the module, a data valid signal is output. After that, 16b width data are transferred 18 times by an internal counter synchronized with an external 1MHz clock. The access time is 12μs and the data transfer rate is 16Mb. Although the access time is rather long, it is enough for printer and CRT uses. The long access time is caused primarily by the charging and discharging of the long polysilicon word lines and the long channel of the cells. The power supply voltage is +5V and the power dissipation is 2W.

The memory cell is a multi-gate MOS transistor whose structure is similar to a CCD; Figure 2. The channel region under each gate electrode which corresponds to a memory cell is made either depleted or enhanced depending on whether the information it is storing is *0* or *1*. In the complete design – a Multi-Gate transistor ROM (MUGROM) – a single array has 52 gate electrodes, 47 for memory cells and word lines (W lines), 4 for channel select signal lines (C lines), and 1 for a control timing signal line (T line). Four MUGROM arrays are connected to a common sense amplifier; Figure 3. The cell area is 99μm^2.

Normally, all the lines but the T line are kept at the high level, so the drain is charged to the high level. In read operations, one C line and one W line are grounded. The T line is raised to the high level. At that time, the arrays that have the depletion channel under the grounded C line are selected. The drain current flows when the cell under the selected word line has a depletion channel (storing *0*), whereas no conduction occurs when it has an enhancement channel (storing *1*).

For yield enhancement, the full wafer ROM makes use of a defect tolerant technology incorporating a duplicated cell block configuration; Figure 4. Each pair of duplicated cell blocks stores the same information. Even if there are defects in one side of a duplicated cell block, the output of the cell block including defects is changed to a fail safe data *0* by a defect correcting control signal (S_A or S_B) which is generated in each cell block. As a result, normal output is obtained through the *OR* circuit.

If, for example, there is an open circuit defect on a bit line, as shown in Figure 5, the input of the left side latch circuit is kept at the high level. Therefore, a *1* data is latched into the data latch circuit when the ϕ_L timing pulse is applied to it. The *1* data is always corrected to the fail safe data *0*, when the low to high transition of the ϕ_R timing occurs.

This defect tolerant technology is effective for dealing with open or short circuit defects, but ineffective for defects in which a stored *0* data is changed to a *1*. Such defects are expected to be very rare in the MUGROM fabrication procedure.

An example of output character data is shown in Figure 6, where (*a*) is normal output data from duplicated cell blocks (blocks A and B) after correction by the defect tolerant technology; and (*b*) and (*c*) are before correction.

Acknowledgments

The authors wish to thank M. Terajima and T. Suzuki and K. Hasegawa for useful suggestions and discussions, M. Yamamoto for simulation and layout, T. Wada for process techniques, and T. Tanaka for DA system use.

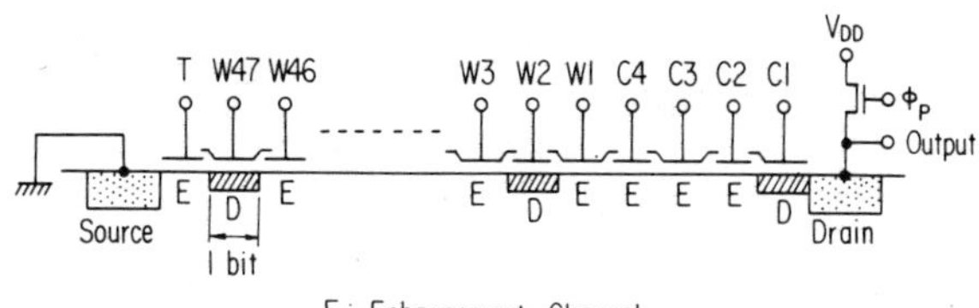

FIGURE 2–Schematic structure of a single MUGROM array.

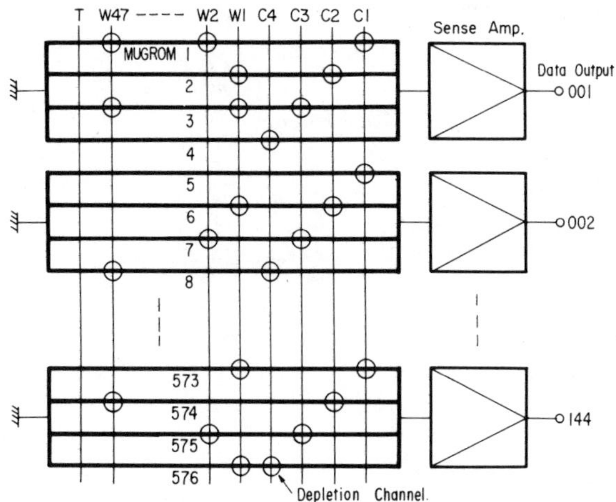

FIGURE 3–Cell array configuration.

Reprinted from *IEEE Int. Solid State Circuits Conf.*, pp. 150–151, 1980.

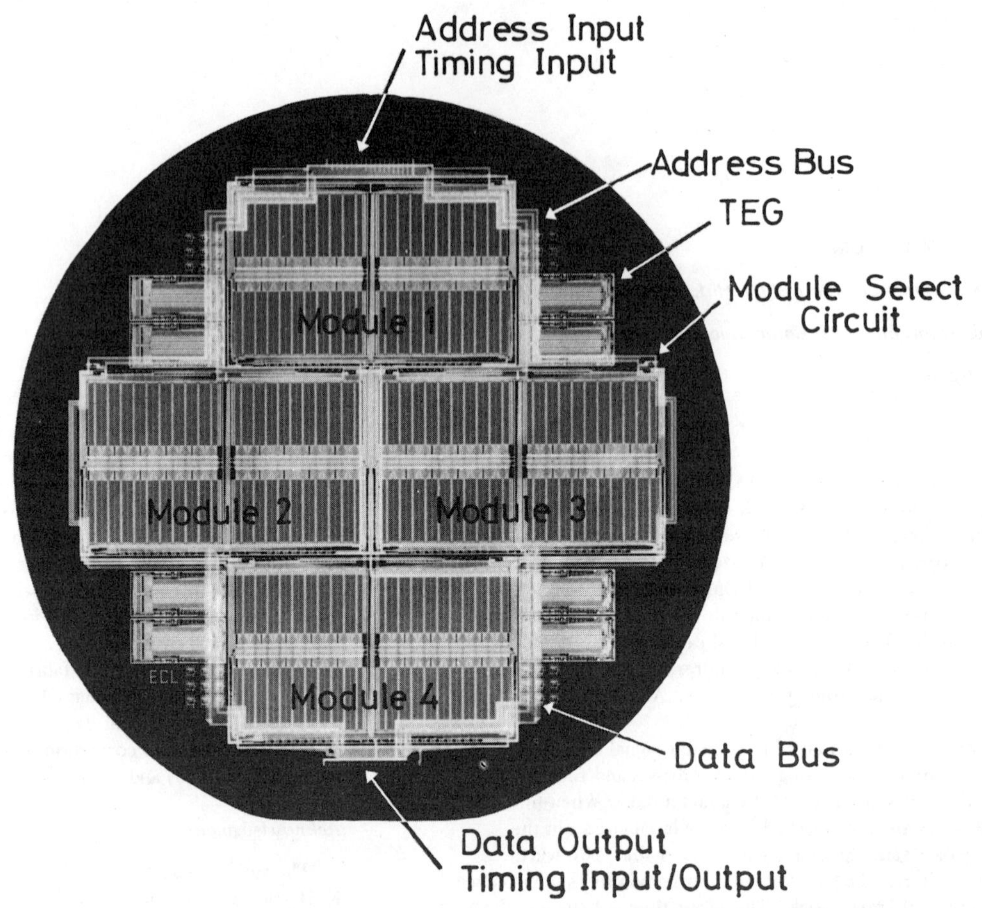

FIGURE 1—4Mb full wafer ROM configuration.

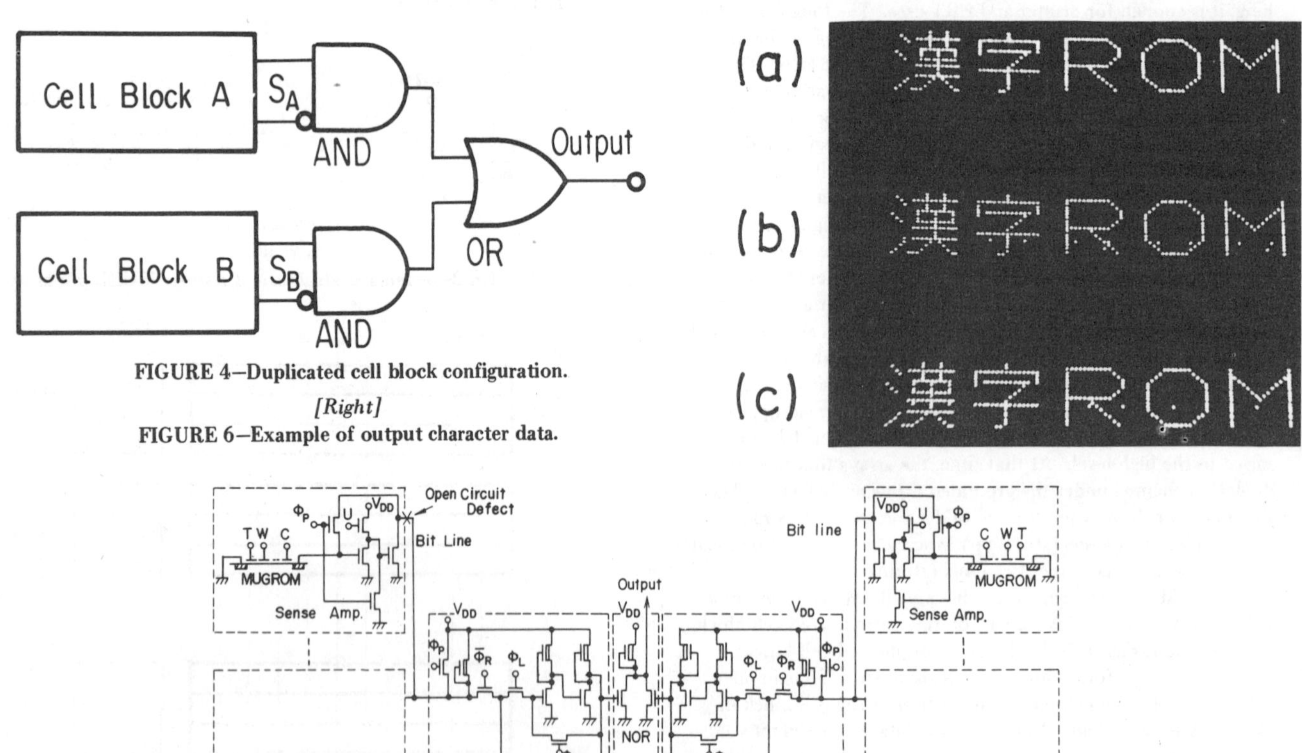

FIGURE 4—Duplicated cell block configuration.

[Right]

FIGURE 6—Example of output character data.

FIGURE 5—Example of defect tolerant circuit.

A 16Kb Electrically Erasable Nonvolatile Memory

William S. Johnson, George Perlegos, Alan Renninger, Greg Kuhn and T. R. Ranganath[†]

Intel Corp.

Santa Clara, CA

FLOATING GATE STRUCTURES have been highly successful as nonvolatile devices because of their compatibility with silicon gate processing and their excellent charge retentivity with applied voltage at operating temperature. The accepted method of erasure in the commercial marketplace is ultra-violet light (EPROM)[1], although proposals have been made to erase electrically by avalanche injection of holes[2], electron tunneling[3,4], or a combination of both[5]. These methods, however, have typically suffered from poor reproducibility and very fast wearout during program/erase cycling.

To realize nonvolatile devices which can be erased electrically with high program/erase endurance, many have resorted to MNOS structures[6] which are programmed and erased by direct tunneling through a thin oxide. In this approach, charge is stored in traps within the nitride dielectric. A major problem with this approach is that the properties of the nitride/oxide dielectric are difficult to control and are adversely affected by normal silicon gate processing. Furthermore, the threshold voltages of these structures are vulnerable to disturbance by even small applied voltages and data retention is not easily guaranteed for long periods (years).

The device reported (FLOTOX, for *f*loating gate *t*unnel *ox*ide) retains the processing and the retention advantages of floating gate over MNOS while solving the traditional endurance problem. This is accomplished by utilizing an oxide less than 200Å thick between a floating poly gate and an N^+ region, as shown in Figure 1. In FLOTOX both program and erase are accomplished by tunneling[7] of electrons through the tunnel oxide using voltages of less than 25V. A typical endurance plot for a single cell appears in Figure 2. This shows that the threshold window remains open beyond 100,000 cycles. Also by keeping voltages low during read, this structure can retain charge over 10 years under full power, at operating temperatures. There is no refresh requirement no matter how many read accesses are made.

The FLOTOX cell configuration, shown in Figure 3, uses two devices, a select transistor and a memory transistor. Cell area is 0.85mil^2. Clearing of the memory is accomplished by programming every device in a row. This is done by selecting a row and raising the program line to VPP, which attracts electrons to the floating gate. Writing is accomplished by erasing selected bits within a word. This is done by again selecting a row, but now the program line is held at zero volts while selected columns go to VPP. Electrons are thus removed from the floating gates of the selected devices.

Figure 4 shows the 16K chip, which is arranged as 2K/8b words. It is packaged with 24 leads with a pinout identical to the 16K EPROM*. The chip is automatically powered down until selected ($\overline{\text{CE}}$ low). Read is accomplished by selecting the part and enabling the output buffers ($\overline{\text{OE}}$ low). On the other hand, selecting the part and taking VPP to 20V for 10ms puts the chip in write mode and writes a word. If the incoming data are all 1's, then the chip automatically goes into clear mode and clears the addressed word. Thus, a clear-write sequence requires merely two 10ms writes, first all 1s, then the data desired. If clearing of the entire chip is desired, this can be accomplished with one 10ms pulse by applying VPP to $\overline{\text{OE}}$ as well as the VPP pin with the chip selected. This approach allows a wide variety of functions while maintaining simple control and complete EPROM compatibility.

FLOTOX utilizes a new high performance N-channel two-level-poly silicon gate technology with channel lengths of 3.5μ. Access times for the 16K FLOTOX E^2PROM are below 200ns as shown in Figure 5. This allows use of the device with the newer microprocessors which operate in the 5-8MHz range without wait states. Other features of the 16K E^2PROM are listed in the table.

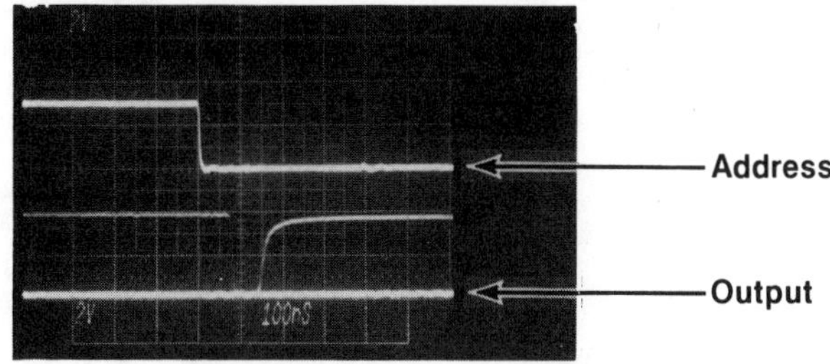

FIGURE 5—Access time for E^2PROM.

[†]Current Address: Hughes Research, Malibu, CA

*2716.

[1]Salsbury, P.J., Morgan, W.L., Perlegos, G. and Simko, R.T., "High Performance MOS EPROMs Using A Stacked Gate Cell", *ISSCC DIGEST OF TECHNICAL PAPERS*, p. 186; Feb., 1977.

[2]Gosney, W.M., "DIFMOS — A Floating-Gate Electrically Erasable Nonvolatile Semiconductor Memory Technology", *IEEE Transactions on Electron Devices*, ED-24, p. 594; May, 1977.

[3]Gulterman, D.C., Rimari, I.H., Halvorson, R.D., McElroy, D.J. and Chan, W.W., "Electrically Alterable Hot-Electron Injection Floating Gate MOS Memory Cell With Series Enhancement", *IEDM Technical Digest*, p. 340; Dec., 1978.

[4]Harari, E., Schmitz, L., Troutman, B. and Wang, S., "A 256-Bit Nonvolatile Static RAM", *ISSCC DIGEST OF TECHNICAL PAPERS*, p. 108; Feb., 1978.

[5]Scheibe, A. and Schulte, H., "Technology of a New N-Channel One-Transistor EAROM Cell Called SIMOS", *IEEE Transactions on Electron Devices*, ED-24, p. 600; May, 1977.

[6]Hagiwara, T., Kondo, R., Yatusuda, Y., Minami, S. and Itoh, Y., "A 16Kb Electrically Erasable Programmable ROM", *ISSCC DIGEST OF TECHNICAL PAPERS*, p. 50; Feb., 1979.

[7]Lenzlinger, M. and Snow, E.H., "Fowler-Nordheim Tunnelling into Thermally Grown SiO_2", *J. of Applied Physics*, 40, p. 278-283; Jan., 1969.

Reprinted from *IEEE Int. Solid State Circuits Conf.*, pp. 152–153 and pp. 271, 1980.

	16K E^2PROM	*16K EPROM*
Configuration	2K X 8	2K X 8
Package	24 pin	24 pin
Power Supplies		
read mode	+5	+5
clear/write	+5, +20	+5, +25
Write		
method	tunnel injection	hot electron injection
time/word	10ms	50ms
Clear		
method	tunnel ejection	UV light
time/word	10ms	–
time/chip	10ms	30 min
Access Time	200ns	450ns
Power Dissipation		
active	500mW	550mW
standby	100mW	100mW
Data Retention	10 years	10 years
Refresh Requirement	None	None

TABLE 1

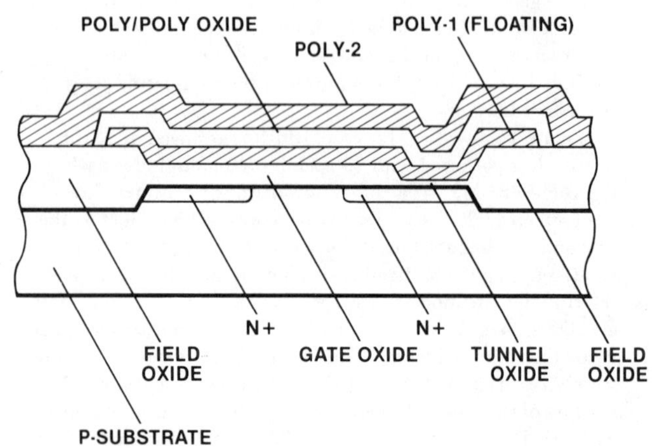

FIGURE 1—Cross section of memory transistor.

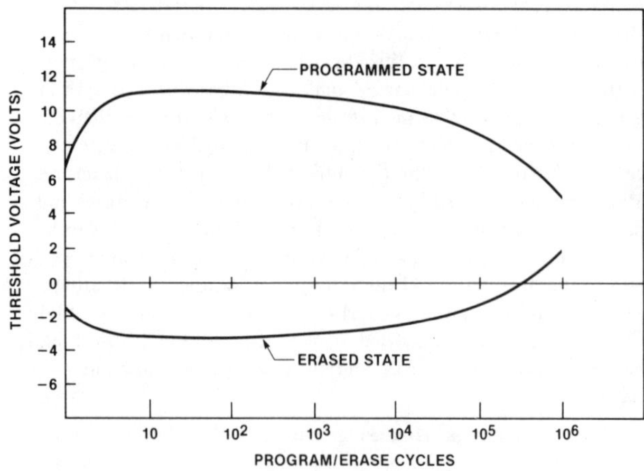

FIGURE 2—Program/erase endurance for single cell.

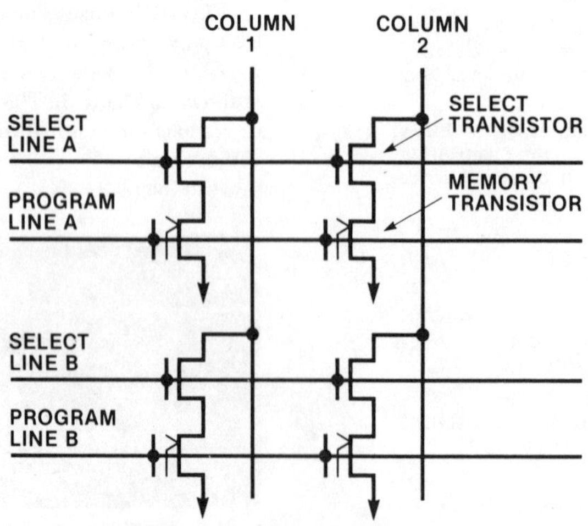

FIGURE 3—Schematic of memory cells.

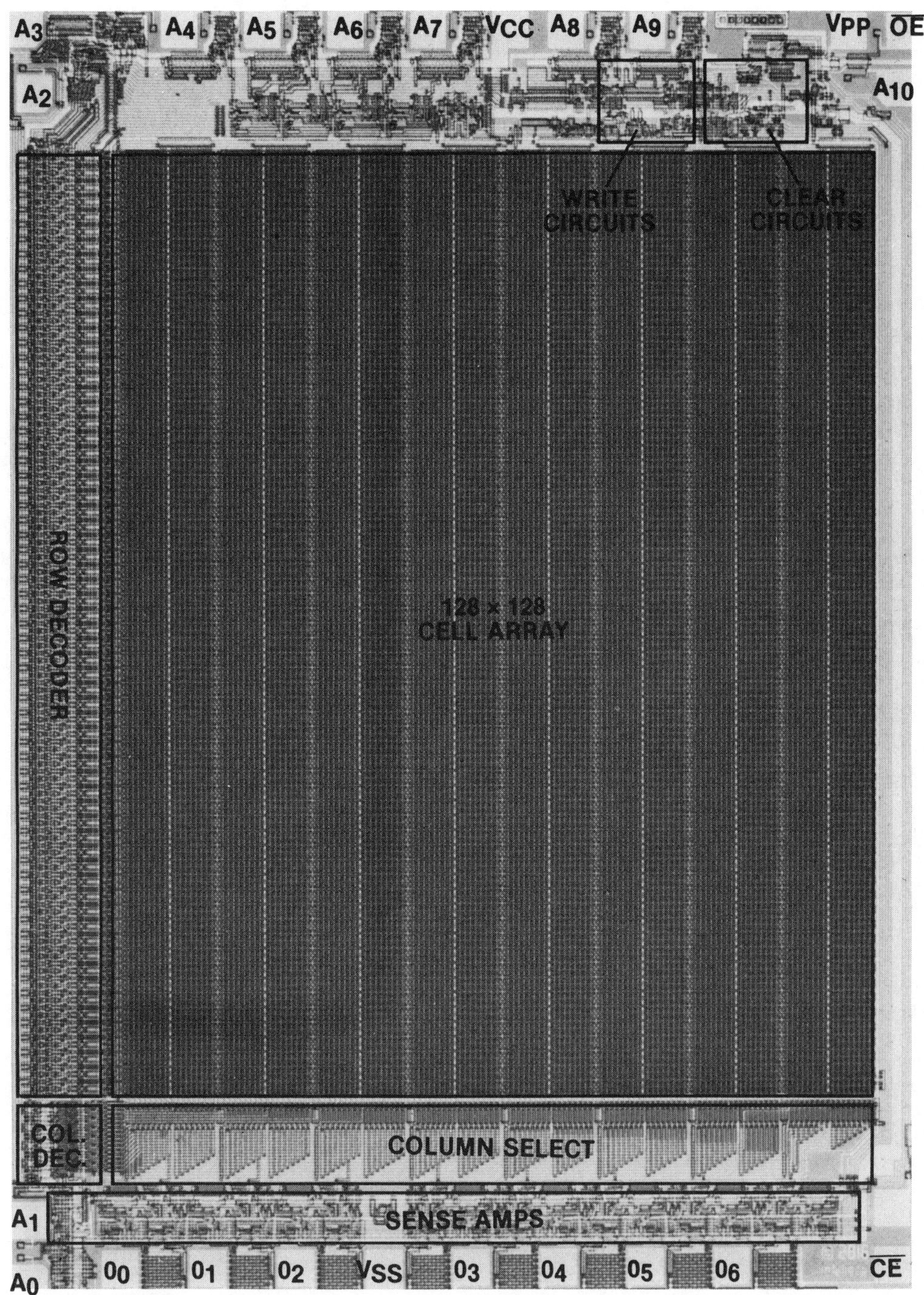

FIGURE 4—Photograph of 16Kb E^2PROM.

A 64K EPROM using Scaled MOS Technology

George Perlegos, Saroj Pathak, Alan Renninger, William Johnson, Mark Holler, Joseph Skupnak, Michael Reitsma and Greg Kuhn

Intel Corp.

Santa Clara, CA

THE CONTINUED NEED for higher density, higher performance erasable proms (EPROMs) has been established by the evolution of faster, more dense microprocessors, and their dependence on convenient program storage memories. This need was first served by the 2Kb FAMOS P-channel floating gate EPROM[1,2], implemented by a two-transistor cell. The second generation N-channel microprocessors were served by the 8Kb and 16Kb[3,4], N-channel MOS stacked gate EPROMs which used a one transistor cell.

With the arrival of another generation of microprocessors*, the need for yet higher density and higher performance EPROMs has again become critical. In response to this need, a third-generation 64K EPROM has been developed featuring a scaled stacked cell (cell area = $0.25mil^2$), t_{access} <200ns, fully static operation and single 20V pulse programming. Advances in both technology and circuitry were utilized in realizing these characteristics.

The cell, illustrated in Figure 1, is a self-aligned structure fabricated by a dual-layer polysilicon gate process. The first layer of poly (POLY 1) forms the floating gate and the second layer of poly (POLY 2) forms the top select gate.

A cell size of $159\mu m^2$ ($0.25mil^2$) is achieved through the use of a scaled EPROM technology. Channel lengths of ~3.5μm are obtained in the array and periphery with better Critical Dimension (CD) control and less undercutting. Increased coupling for lower programming voltages and smaller programming times is available by scaling down the first and second gate oxide thickness to approximately 700Å and 800Å, respectively. Additional geometry changes in the cell and periphery are the result of scaling, optimized to account for special EPROM requirements. As demonstrated in Figure 2, the chip size for a 32K density changes from $200mil^2$ on a standard EPROM technology to $145mil^2$ on a scaled EPROM technology.

The memory cell is programmed by means of hot electrons injected through the oxide to the floating gate[3]. The charge retention characteristics have not changed and are similar to the original FAMOS cell. The cell is 13μmX12μm and uses 3.5μm gate lengths.

Circuit innovations contributing to the performance of the memory include a differential sensing technique and the use of transfer gates within the x-decoder, as shown in Figure 3. The differential sense amplifier, in conjunction with a special reference circuit, provides increased sensing margin. The transfer gate between x-DECODER and x-SELECT localizes the high voltage during programming, leading to a compact, high speed select design. The 64Kb EPROM shown in Figure 4, is organized 8KX8, and measures $179X181mil^2$. The chip is packaged in a 28-lead package, allowing the use of separate $\overline{OE}$ and $\overline{CE}$ control. The chip automatically powers down to a standby power of <100mW when deselected via $\overline{CE}$. Active power is <500mW, and active read access time <200ns.

The evolution of EPROM devices is summarized in Table 1. The 64K memory does not only achieve a breakthrough in speed and power but new trends in programming voltages, programming speed, and packaging. Higher density and speed were achieved with the use of a scaled MOS technology. The trend to lower programming voltages was adopted with the introduction of arsenic junctions to overcome the lower breakdown voltages.

Acknowledgments

The authors wish to thank W. Morgan and G. Korsh for their technical contributions, P. Salsbury for direction and support and C. Scott for processing support.

EPROM Evolution	02	08	16	32	64
• Voltages	+5, −9V	±5, +12	+5	+5	+5
• Program Supplies	−50	+27	+25	+25	+20
• Density	256 × 8	1k × 8	2k × 8	3k × 8	4k × 8
• Access	1ms	450ns	450ns	450ns	200ns
• Devices	P-Channel	N-Channel Enhancement	N-Channel Enhancement Depletion	N-Channel Enhancement Depletion	N-Channel Enhancement Depletion Zero V_T Devices
• High Voltages	Bootstraps	Bootstraps	Depletion Devices	Depletion and Bootstraps OE/V_{PP} Circuits	Depletion Devices
• Programming	1ms-Pulses	100-1ms Pulse/Word	1-50ms Pulse/Word	1-50ms Pulse/Word	1-25ms Pulse/Word
• Power	750mW	1 watt	500mW 50mW (Power Down)	750mW 50mW (Power Down)	500mW 50mW (Power Down)
• Package	24 Pins	24 Pins	24 Pins	24 Pins	28 Pins

TABLE 1—Evolution of EPROM devices.

---

*8086.

[1] Frohman-Bentchkowsky, D., "A Fully Decoded 2048-Bit Electrically-Programmable MOS-ROM", *ISSCC DIGEST OF TECHNICAL PAPERS*, p. 80-81; Feb., 1971.

[2] Frohman-Bentchowsky, D., "FAMOS — A New Semiconductor Charge Storage Device", *Solid-State Electronics*, Vol. 17, p. 517-529; 1974.

[3] Salsbury, P.J., Morgan, W.L., Perlegos, G. and Simko, R.T., "High Performance MOS EPROMs Using a Stacked Gate Cell", *ISSCC DIGEST OF TECHNICAL PAPERS*, p. 186-187; Feb., 1977.

[4] Stamm, D., Buddy, D. and Morgan, W., "A Single Chip, Highly Integrated, User Programmable Microcomputer", *ISSCC DIGEST OF TECHNICAL PAPERS*, p. 142-143; Feb., 1977.

Reprinted from *IEEE Int. Solid State Circuits Conf.*, pp. 142–143 and p. 269, 1980.

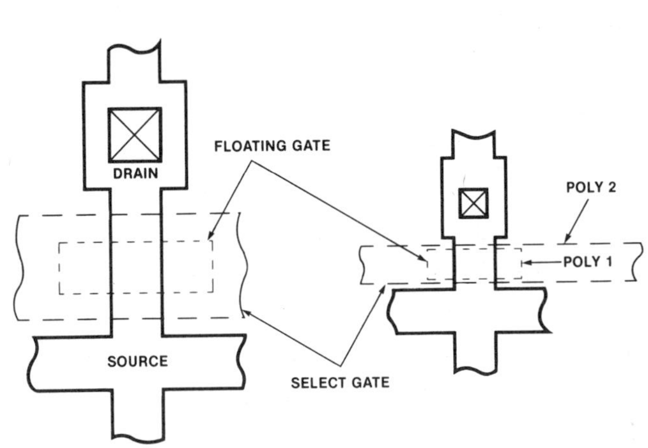

FIGURE 1—Comparison of original and scaled stacked gate cell.

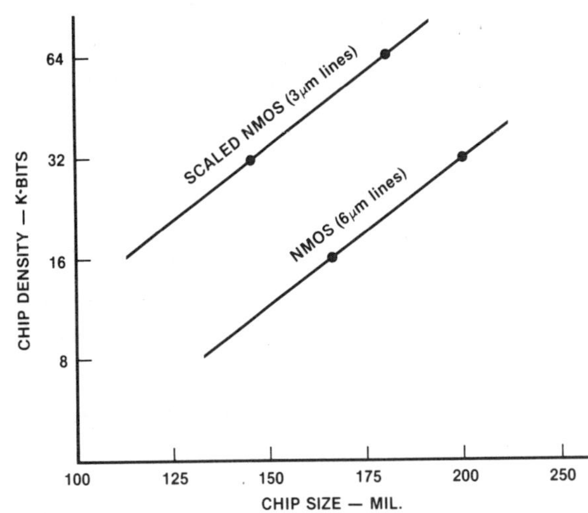

FIGURE 2—Advances in EPROM technology.

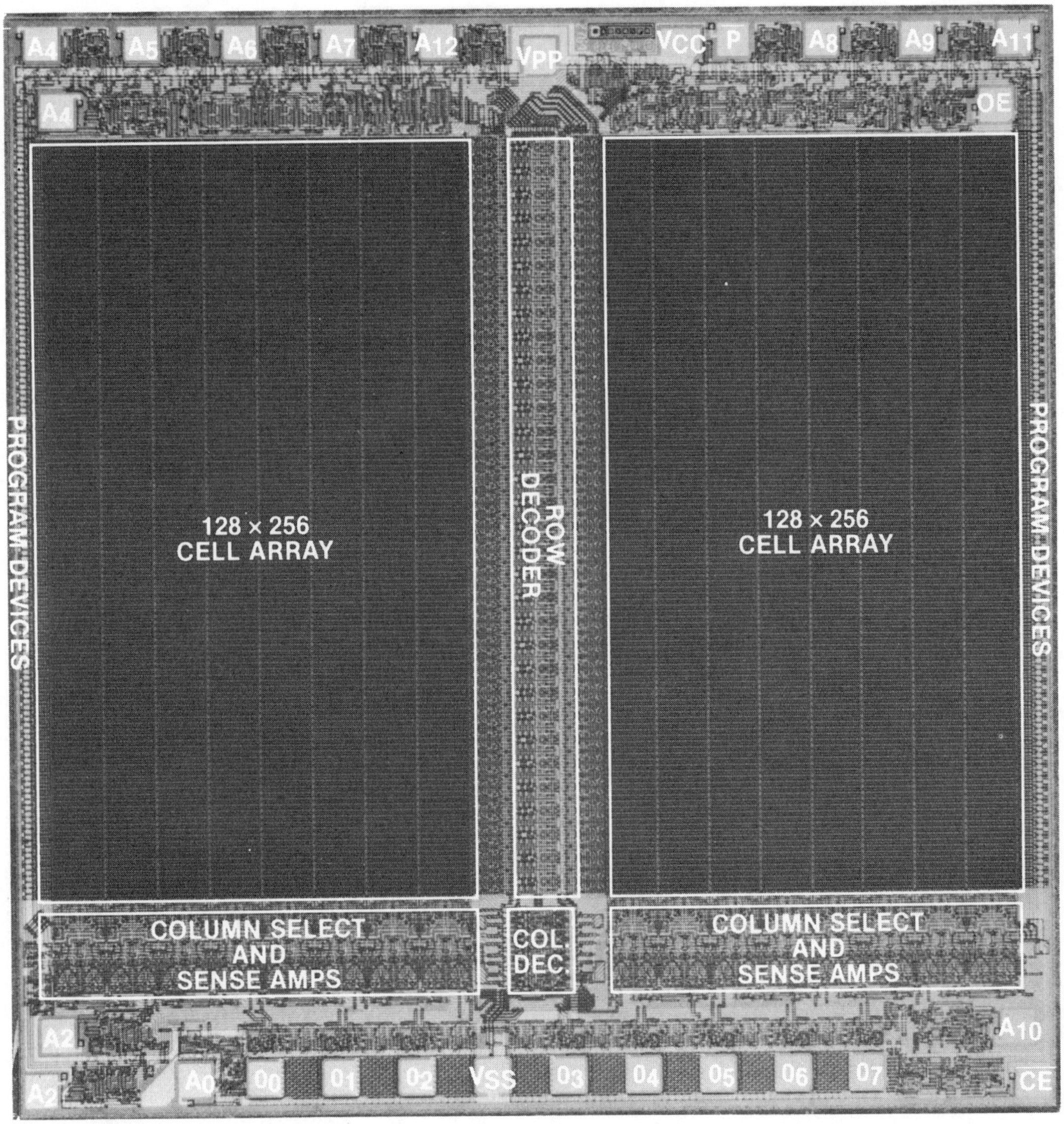

FIGURE 4—Chip photo for 64K EPROM.

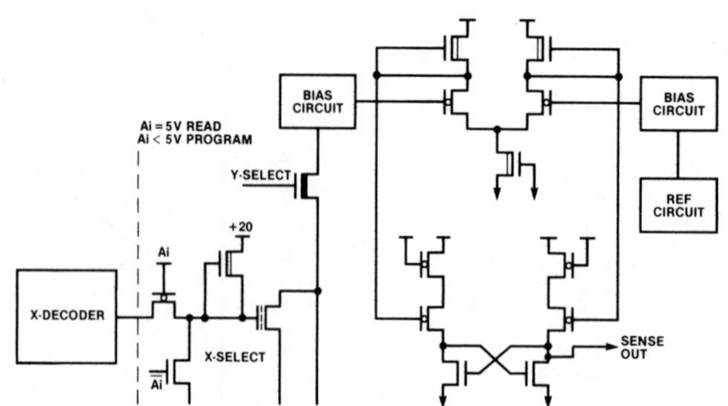

FIGURE 3—Circuit schematic of memory array organization.

Bibliography

Note: Most of the recent work on MOSFETs and MOSFET related areas are reported in the current issues of:

1. The IEEE Journal of Solid-State Circuits.
2. The IEEE Transactions on Electron Devices.
3. The Digests of Technical Papers of the IEEE Solid-State Circuits Conferences.
4. The Digests of the IEEE International Electron Devices Meetings.
5. The IEEE Electron Devices Letters.
6. Solid State Electronics
7. Electronics.
8. Solid State Technology.
9. The IEEE Spectrum.
10. The IEEE Proceedings.
11. The IEEE Transactions on Components, Hybrids and Manufacturing Technology.
12. The IEEE Transactions on Nuclear Sciences.
13. The Proceedings of the IEEE International Symposium on Circuits and Systems.
14. The Proceedings of the European Solid State Circuits Conferences.
15. The Proceedings of the European Solid State Devices Conferences.
16. Microelectronics Journal.

1—MOSFETs in Digital Circuit Design

1. M. Fisher and A. Young, "CMOS Technology Can Do It All in Digital and Linear Systems", EDN, June 1979, pp. 106-14.
2. M. Kawashima et al., "Depletion-Type M.O.S.F.E.T.s for Low-Temperature Operation", Electron. Lett., Nov., 1979, pp. 759-60.
3. S. Young, "Evolution of MOS Technology", 1978 Wescon Technical Papers, Sept., 1978, pp. 1-7.
4. H. Lilen, "The Synthesis of Advanced Technologies For Digital Integrated Circuits and Memories. HMOS, VMOS, SOS and 12L, ALS and MEM-Which to Choose?", Electron and Appl. Ind., March, 1979, pp. 23-9.
5. B.G. Bosch, "Gigabit Electronics - A Review", Proc. IEEE, March, 1979, pp. 340-79.
6. A.C. Ipri, "Impact of Design Rule Reduction on Size, Yield, and Cost of Integrated Circuits", Solid State Technol., Feb., 1979, pp. 85-9.
7. K.-H. Diener et al, "Contributions to the Design of Highly Integrated MOS Circuits", Nachrichtentiech. Elektron., 1979, pp. 57-62.
8. A. Kawamata, "Research and Development on LSI Memory Systems", Electr. Commun. Lab. Tech. J., 1978, pp. 1905-9.
9. J.P. Moreau and G. Dubois, "MOS Silicon Gate Technology Present Technics Review", Onde Electr., Dec., 1978, pp. 805-11.
10. R.W. Knepper, "Dynamic Depletion Mode. An E/D MOSFET Circuit Method for Improved Performance", IEEE J. Solid-State Circuits, Oct. 1978, pp. 542-8.
11. J. Bula et al, "Substrate Voltage Transient Reduction Circuit", IBM Tech. Disclosure Bull., Jan., 1978, pp. 3214-15.
12. D. Sharma et al, "Negative Dynamic Resistance in MOS Devices", IEEE J. Solid-State Circuits, June, 1978, pp. 378-80.
13. D. Ritchie and S. Sato, "Merging Technologies: Bipolar and MOS", Jpn. J. Appl. Phys., 1977, p. 287.
14. R.L. Wadsack, "Fault Coverage in Digital Integrated Circuits", Bell Syst. Tech. J., May-June, 1978, pp. 1475-88.
15. R.L. Wadsack, "Fault Modelling and Logic Simulation of CMOS and MOS Integrated Circuits", Bell Syst. Tech. J., May-June, 1978, pp. 1449-74.
16. W.H. Schroen, "Physical MOS Models", Proceedings of the NATO Advanced Study Inst. on Process and Device Modelling for Integrated Circuit Design, July, 1977, pp. 689-704.
17. G. Merckel, "Ion Implanted MOS Transistors-Depletion Mode Devices", Proceedings of the NATO Advanced Study Inst. on Process and Device Modelling for Integrated Circuit Design, 1977, pp. 677-88.
18. F.M. Klaassen, "Characterization and Measurements of Most Devices", Proceedings of the NATO Advanced Study Inst. on Process and Device Modelling for Integrated Circuit Design, 1977, pp. 573-88.
19. F.M. Klaasen, "Review of Physical Models for MOS Transistors", Proceedings of the NATO Advanced Study Inst. on Process and Device Modelling for Integrated Circuit Design, 1977, pp. 541-71.
20. H. Martinot and P. Rossel, "Hierarchy of MOS Transistor Models", Modelling Semiconductor Devices, 1977, pp. 253-84.
21. R.A. Bishop, "LSI CMOS Applications", Microelectron and Reliab., 1977, pp. 461-75.
22. I.R. Sinclair, "Beginner's Guide to Integrated Circuits", Newnes Technical Books, 1977.
23. A. Marcelius, "Interfacing Logic Circuits and Inductive Loads", Autom. and Strum., June, 1977, pp. 311-15.
24. N. Akamatsu, "A High-Speed MOS-FET Logic Circuit with Negative Resistance", Trans. Inst. Electron. and Commun. Eng. Jpn., March, 1977, pg. 150.
25. A.C. Ipri, "Lambda Diodes Utilizing an Enhancement Depletion CMOS/SOS Process", IEEE Trans. Electron Devices, June, 1977, pp. 751-6.
26. A. Masaki et al., "Comparison of MOS Basic Logic Circuits", Syst. Comput. Control, July-Aug.,1975, pp. 11-19.
27. J. McDermott, "Semiconductor Memories", Electron. Des.", June, 1976, pp. 78-82.
28. P.W.J. Verhofstadt, "Evaluation of Technology Options for LSI Processing Elements", Proc. IEEE, June, 1976, pp. 842-51.
29. A.D. Odell and K.A.M. Arton, "A System of Synchronous MOS Logic Using a Single Phase Clock", IEE. Assoc. Elletrotecnica and Elletronica Italiana, et al., 1975, pp. 62-63.
30. M.E. Homan, "Fet Depletion Load Push-Pull Logical Circuit", IBM Tech. Disclosure Bull., Aug., 1975, pp. 910-11.
31. N.C. De Troye, "Digital Integrated Circuits with Low Dissipation", Philips Tech. Rev., 1975, pp. 212-20.
32. J.P. Ellul et al., "MOS Capacitor Pull-up Circuits for High-speed Dynamic Logic", IEEE J. Solid-State Circuits, Oct., 1975, pp. 298-307.
33. F.F. Fang and H.S. Ruprecht, "High Performance MOS Integrated Circuit Using the Ion Implantation Technique", IEEE J. Solid-State Circuits, Aug., 1975, pp. 205-11.
34. J. Kroeger and B. Threewitt, "Review the Basics of MOS Logic", Electron. Des., March, 1974, pp. 98-105.
35. W. Walker, "Examining Worst-Case Fan-Out of Standard C-MOS Buffers", Electronics, June, 1974, p. 125.
36. C. Crook, "Comparing the Power of C-MOS with TTL", Electronics, May, 1974, pp. 132-3.
37. M.I. Elmasry, "An Optimal Two-Phase M.O.S.-LSI Logic System", IEEE, 1973, pp. 136-7.
38. A. Wilnai, "Eliminating Clock Waveform Imperfections in MOS Dynamic Circuits", Comput. Des., Sept.

1973, pp. 94, 96.
39. Y. Hayashi et al., "Design of ED-MOS Buffer", Electron. and Commun. Jap., Oct., 1972, pp. 107-14.
40. R.B. Seeds and R. Badertscher, "N Versus P Channel For Single-Supply TTL Compatibility", IEEE, Feb., 1973, pp. 32-3.
41. R.A. Bishop, "Complementary M.O.S. Offers Many Advantages to the Digital-Systems Designer", Electron. Engineering, Nov., 1972, pp. 67-70.
42. M.P. Forrer, "Survey of Circuitry For Wristwatches", Proc. IEEE, Sept., 1972, pp. 1047-54.
43. "Discussing Complementary MOS", Microelectronics, Summer, 1972, pp. 20-8.
44. B. Crawford, "Implanted Depletion Loads Boost MOS Array Performance", Electronics, April, 1972, pp. 85-90.
45. I.H. Williams, "4-Phase and Other Ratioless MOS Circuit Forms", Joint IEE/Inst. Phys., Dec., 1971, pp. 1.
46. H. Dirilten, "On the Mathematical Models Characterizing Faulty Four-Phase MOS Logic Arrays", IEEE Trans. Comput., March, 1972, pp. 301-5.
47. J.W. Foltz, "Silicon Gate CMOS in Micropower Digital Systems", IEEE, Aug., 1971, 10 pp.
48. R.R. Burgess and R.G. Daniels, "C/MOS Unites with Silicon Gate to Yield Micropower Technology", Electronics, Aug., 1971, pp. 38-43.
49. T.E. O'Brien, "Monolithic Level Shifter Lets MOS, TTL Share Same Network", Electronics, July, 1971, pp. 70-2.
50. C.E. Marvin, "MOS/LSI Throughout", 1971 IEEE Int. Convention Digest, Mar., 1971, N.Y., pp. 74-5.

2—MOSFET Characterization and Device/Circuit Modeling

1. L.A. Akers, "A Model of the Temperature-Dependent Operation of a MOSFET", Simulation, Jan., 1980, pp. 1-9.
2. N. Sasaki and M. Nakano, "Anomalous Leakage Current of MOSFETs Under BT Stress", Jpn. J. Appl. Phys., Feb., 1980, pp. 325-30.
3. V.P. Sidorenko et al., "Modelling of Narrow-Channel MOS Transistors", IZV. Vuz Radioelektron, Jan., 1980, pp. 80-2.
4. M. Matsumura and K. Sakamoto, "A Simple Model for Short-Channel MOS FETS", Trans. Inst. Electron. and Commun. Eng. Jpn. Sect. E., Oct., 1979, pp. 720.
5. G.G. Kiruthi et al., "MOSFET Model Algorithms for Pocket Calculator Nonlinear Circuit Analysis", IEEE, July, 1979, pp. 951-4.
6. H.C. Lin et al., "Modeling a Depletion Mode MOSFET", IEEE, July, 1979, pp. 778-81.
7. K.-H. Diener et al., "Modelling of Integrated MOS Gates and Determination of the Network Analysis Parameters from the Layout", Nachrichtentech. Elektron., 1979, pp. 408-11.
8. S.P. Li and J. Meserjian, "Prediction of Field-Time-Dependent Gate-Oxide Breakdown in MOS Devices", Solid-State Electron., Nov., 1979, pp. 939-42.
9. J. Yamada, "A New Method for the Transient Analysis of MOS LSI", Trans. Inst. Electron. and Comm. Eng. Jpn. Sect. E., June, 1979, pg. 437.
10. J.M. Brice et al., "Behavior of the Floating Substrate of SOS/CMOS Transistors in Transient Operation", IEE, Sept., 1979, pp. 163-5.
11. R. Hofmann et al., "Calculation and Measurement of the Sense Signal of Dynamic MOS RAM", IEE, Sept., 1979, pp. 107-9.
12. R.C. Foss et al., "An MOS Transistor Model for a Micro-Mini Computer Based Circuit Analysis System", IEE, 1979, pp. 56-7.
13. W.P. Noble, Jr., "Short Channel Effects in Dual Gate Field Effect Transistors (LSI Design)", IEEE, Dec., 1978, pp. 483-6.
14. E. Sun et al., "Breakdown Mechanism in Short-Channel MOS Transistors", IEEE, Dec., 1978, pp. 478-82.
15. G. Merckel and J. Gautier, "A Model of Punchthrough Current in Short-Channel MOSFETs, From Low to High Injection Levels", IEEE, Dec., 1978, pp. 476-7.
16. M.W. Powell and L.F. Jelsma, "A Precise Model of the Transient Response of MNOS Memory Capacitors", IEEE, Dec., 1978, pp. 38-41.
17. R. Kasai and T. Kimura, "Two-Dimensional Structure Analysis of Short-Channel MOS Transistors", Trans. Inst. Electron. and Commun. Eng. Jpn. Sect. E., June, 1979, pp. 430-1.
18. H. Sibbert et al., "An Analytic Model for the Power Handling Capacity and Scaling of the Smallest MOSTS for VLSI Digital Circuits", NTG-Fachber, 1979, pp. 128-34.
19. G.R. Mohan Rao, "Sub-Threshold Leakage Currents in Weakly Inverted Short Channel IGFETS", Solid-State Electron., Aug., 1979, pp. 729-34.
20. G.W. Taylor, "The Effects of Two-Dimensional Charge Sharing on the Above-Threshold Characteristics of Short-Channel IGFETS", Solid-State Electron., Aug., 1979, pp. 701-17.
21. A.K. Owczarek, "Potential and Carrier Concentration Distributions in MOS Transistors at Punch-Through", Phys. Status Solidi A., Aug., 1979, pp. 761-71.
22. M. Nishida, "Depletion Approximation Analysis of the Differential Capacitance-Voltage Characteristics of an MOS Structure with Nonuniformly Doped Semiconductors", IEEE Trans. Electron Devices, July, 1979, pp. 1081-5.
23. T. Arnborg, "A Finite Element Method for Semiconductor Device Computations", 21st Midwest Symposium on Circuits and Systems, 1978, pp. 526-30.
24. G. Posdziech, "A Model of the Depletion Transistor", Nachrichtentech. Elektron., 1979, pp. 236-9.
25. K. Yamaguchi, "Field-Dependent Mobility Model for Two-Dimensional Numerical Analysis of MOSFETs", IEEE Trans. Electron Devices, July, 1979, pp. 1068-74.
26. D.B. Scott and S.G. Chamberlain, "A Calibrated Model for the Subthreshold Operation of a Short Channel MOSFET Including Surface States", IEEE J. Solid-State Circuits, June, 1979, pp. 633-44.
27. S.F. Johnson and K.E. Lonngren, "Transient Response of an Inhomogeneous MOS Transmission Line", Solid-State Electron., July, 1979, pp. 671-5.
28. B. Hoefflinger et al., "Model and Performance of Hot-Electron MOS Transistors for VLSI", IEEE J. Solid-State Circuits, April, 197 , pp. 435-4.
29. A. Moschwitzer, "A Simple Threshold Model for Depletion MOST", Phys. Status Solidi A., May, 1979, pp. K43-5.
30. C.T. Kirk, Jr., "Valence Alternation Pair Model of Charge Storage in MNOS Memory Devices", J. Appl. Phys., June, 1979, pp. 4190-5.
31. H.J. Geipel, Jr. and A.G. Fortino, "Process Modeling and Design Procedure for IGFET Thresholds", IEEE J. Solid-State Circuits, April, 1979, pp. 430-5.
32. R.C. Jaeger and F.H. Gaensslen, "Simple Analytical Models for the Temperature Dependent Threshold Behavior of Depletion-Mode Devices", IEEE J. Solid-State Circuits, April, 1979, pp. 423-9.
33. Dang Luong Mo, "A Simple Current Model for Short-Channel IGFET and Its Application to Circuit Simulation", IEEE J. Solid-State Circuits, April, 1979, pp. 358-67.
34. E. Sun, "Short Channel MOS Modeling for CAD", Conf. Record of the Twelfth Asilomar Conf. on Circuits, Systems and Computers, 1978, pp. 493-9.
35. D.B. Estreich and R.W. Dutton, "Modeling Latch-Up in CMOS Integrated Circuits", Conf. Record of the Twelfth Asilomar Conf. on Circuits, Systems and Computers, 1978, pp. 489-92.

36. G.G. Kibuthi et al., "A MOSFET Model with Substrate Bias for the Pocket Calculator", Conf. Record of the Twelfth Asilomar Conf. on Circuits, Systems and Computers, 1978, pp. 55-8.
37. D.J. Coe and H.E. Brockman, "Corner Breakdown in MOS Transistors With Lightly-Doped Drains", Solid-State Electron., April, 1979, pp. 444-6.
38. N. Sasaki and R. Togei, "Effect of Silicon Film Thickness on Threshold Voltage of SOS-MOSFETs", Solid-State Electron., April, 1979, pp. 417-21.
39. W. Link and H. May, "Low Temperature Characteristics of MOS Single-Transistor Memory Cells", Arch. Elektron and Uebertragungstech., June, 1979, pp. 229-35.
40. N. Kotani and S. Kawazu, "Computer Analysis of Punch-Through in MOSFETs", Solid-State Electron., Jan., 1979, pp. 63-70.
41. W. Schemmert, "Charge Transport in Ion Implanted Buried Channel MOS Transistors", Arch. Elektron. and Uebertragungstech., Jan., 1979, pp. 23-31.
42. D.L. Lile, "The Effect of Surface States on the Characteristics of MIS Field Effect Transistors", Solid-State Electron., Oct., 1978, pp. 1199-207.
43. P. Gentil, "A Model of the Leakage Current in N-Channel Silicon-on-Sapphire MOST's", Rev. Phys. Appl., Dec., 1978, pp. 609-13.
44. U. Kumar, "Accurate Two-Port Model of the Metal-Oxide Semiconductor Transistor", Microelectron. and Reliab., 1978, pp. 427-32.
45. J.R. Davis, "Discharge Mechanisms in Floating-Gate E.P.R.O.M. Cells", Electron. Lett., Jan., 1979, pp. 20-1.
46. Y. Omura and K. Ohwada, "Theoretical Analysis of Short-Channel MOS FET Based on Surface Channel Charge Neutralization", Trans. Inst. Electron. and Commun. Eng. Jpn. Sect. E., Oct., 1978, pp. 858-9.
47. H.P. Hertzschel, "Reduction of Current Consumption in CMOS Devices", Microelectronics., June, 1978, pp. 16-17.
48. H. Feltl, "Threshold Voltage of M.O.S. Transistors Doped Nonuniformly Near the Surface", IEE J. Solid-State and Electron Devices, Nov., 1978, pp. 191-8.
49. D.E. Ward and R.W. Dutton, "A Charge-Oriented Model for MOS Transistor Capacitances", IEEE J. Solid-State Circuits, Oct., 1978, pp. 703-8.
50. R.M. Barsan, "Free Charge Propagation in a Resistive-Gate MOS Transmission Line", IEEE Trans. Electron Devices, Sept., 1978, pp. 1109-19.
51. G. Arnout and H.J. De Man, "The Use of Threshold Functions and Boolean-Controlled Network Elements for Macromodeling of LSI Circuits", IEEE J. Solid State Circuits, June, 1978, pp. 326-32.
52. S.P. Li et al., "Model for MOS Field-Time-Dependent Breakdown", IEEE Reliability Physics 16th Annual Proceedings, 1978, pp. 132-6.
53. R.T. Jerdonek and W.R. Bandy, "Modeling the Operation of the N-Channel Deep-Depletion SOS/MOSFET", IEEE Trans. Electron Devices, Aug., 1978, pp. 899-907.
54. D. Kranzer et al., "Theshold Voltage Model of ESFI-SOS-MOS Transistors", IEEE Trans. Electron Devices, Aug., 1978, pp. 890-4.
55. P.G. Cottin and J.M. Pinel, "CMOS/SOS Transistor Model Under Ionizing Irradiation Environment", IEEE Proceedings of the 1978 IEEE International Symposium on Circuits and Systems, 1978, pp. 113-18.
56. H. Masuda, "Electrical Measurement of Channel Length in MOS FETS", Trans. Inst. Electron. and Commun. Eng. Jpn. Sect. E., March, 1978, pg. 264.
57. G. Merckel, "CAD Models of MOSFET's", Proc. of the NATO Advanced Study Inst. on Process and Device Modelling for Integrated Circuit Design, 1977, pp. 751-64.
58. F.M. Klaasen, "A MOST Model for CAD with Automated Parameter Determination", Proc. of the NATO Advanced Study Inst. on Process and Device Modelling for Integrated Circuit Design, 1977, pp. 739-50.
59. O. Kudoh et al., "Influence of Substrate Current on Hold-Time Characteristics of Dynamic MOS IC's", IEEE J. Solid-State Circuits, April, 1978, pp. 235-9.
60. T. Toyabe et al., "A Numerical Model of Avalanche Breakdown in MOSFET's", IEEE Trans. Electron Devices, July, 1978, pp. 825-32.
61. P.P. Wang, "Device Characteristics of Short-Channel and Narrow-Width MOSFET's", IEEE Trans. Electron Devices, July, 1978, pp. 779-86.
62. D.E. Ward and R.W. Dutton, "A Charge-Oriented Model for MOS Transistor Capacitances", 1978 Eleventh Annual Asilomar Conf. on Circuits Systems and Computers, 1978, pp. 23-8
63. R.A. Haken, "Analysis of the Deep Depletion MOSFET and the Use of the D.C. Characteristics for Determining Bulk-Channel Charge-Coupled Device Parameters", Solid-State Electron., March., 1978, pp. 753-61.
64. G.R. Mohan Rao, "An Accurate Model for a Depletion Mode IGFET Used as a Load Device", Solid-State Electron., March, 1978, pp. 711-14.
65. R.T. Jerdonek et al., "Weak Accumulation Operation of the N-Channel Deep-Depletion SOS/MOSFET", IEEE 1977 International Electron Devices Meeting, Dec., 1977, pp. 525-8.
66. F.H. Gaensslen et al., "Low Temperature Threshold Behavior of Depletion Mode Devices-Characterization and Simulation", IEEE 1977 International Electron Devices Meeting, Dec., 1977, pp. 520-4.
67. T. Toyabe et al., "A Two-Dimensional Avalanche Breakdown Model of Submicron MOSFETs", IEEE 1977 International Electron Devices Meeting, Dec., 1977, pp. 432-5.
68. N. Akamatsu, "FET-Device Modeling for Computer Aided Design and Its Applications", Trans. Inst. Electron. and Commun. Eng. Jpn. Sect. E., Jan., 1978, pp. 27-8.
69. U. Kumat and A.B. Bhattacharyya, "Modified Charge-Control Model for MOS Transistors", Solid-State Electron., March, 1978, pp. 593-4.
70. T. Agatsuma and S. Ishii, "An Analysis of Equivalent Circuit with Gate Protection and MOS Devices", IEEE Trans. Electron Devices, April, 1978, pp. 491-2.
71. K. Natori et al., "An Analysis of the Concave MOSFET", IEEE Trans. Electron Devices, April, 1978, pp. 448-56.
72. T.E. Hendrickson, "A Simplified Model for Subpinch-off Conduction in Depletion-Mode IGFET's", IEEE Trans. Electron Devices, April, 1978, pp. 435-41.
73. C. Trullemans and F. Van de Wiele, "Bulk Lifetime Determination of MOS Structures by a Voltage Step Response Method", Solid-State Electron., March, 1978, pp. 561-4.
74. J.R. Brews, "A Charge-Sheet Model of the MOSFET", Solid-State Electron., Feb., 1978, pp. 345-55.
75. G. Baccarani et al., "Analytical I.G.F.E.T. Model Including Drift and Diffusion Currents", IEE J. Solid-State and Electron Devices, March, 1978, pp. 62-8.
76. W. Fichtner, "Two-Dimensional Modelling of S.O.S. Transistors", IEE J. Solid-State and Electron Devices, March, 1978, pp. 47-51.
77. G.W. Taylor, "Subthreshold Conduction in MOSFETs", IEEE Trans. Electron Devices, March, 1978, pp. 337-50.
78. G. Merckel et al., "Model of a Micro-MOS Transistor in Weak and Strong Inversion, Effect of Very Low Temperature on Parameters", Modelling Semiconductor Devices, 1977, pp. 349-62.

79. F. Van De Wiele et al., "Models for Implanted MOS Transistors", Modelling Semiconductor Devices, 1977, pp. 325-38.
80. E. Gonauser, "Modelling Complementary ESFI-SOS MOS Transistors", Modelling Semiconductor Devices, 1977, pp. 339-48.
81. J. Tihanyi, "Subthreshold Model for N-Channel MOS Devices", Modelling Semiconductor Devices, 1977, pp. 303-13.
82. T. Poorter et al., "A Simple and Accurate Model for an MOS-Transistor in the Triode and Saturation Regions", Modelling Semiconductor Devices, 1977, pp. 285-301.
83. H.C. Lin et al., "Modeling of Short Channel MOS Transistors", Modeling and Simulation, 1976, pp. 567-71.
84. U. Kumar and S.C. Dutta Roy, "A Simple Small-Signal Two-Port MOST Model for the Pre-Pinchoff Region" Solid-State Electron., Dec., 1977, pp. 1021-2.
85. D.J. Coe et al., "A Comparison of Simple and Numerical Two-Dimensional Models for the Threshold Voltage of Short Channel MOSTS", Solid-State Electron., Dec., 1977, pp. 993-8.
86. M.I. Elmasry and A.G. Eldin, "Functional Modelling of Floating Substrate MOS Structures", Int. J. Electron., Nov., 1977, pp. 433-44.
87. E.R. Worley, "On the Characteristic of the Deep-Depletion SOS Transistor", IEEE Trans. Electron. Devices, Dec., 1977, pp. 1342-5.
88. N. Miyahara et al., "Design and Characteristics of Short-Channel MOS FETS for LSI RAM", Elect. Commun. Lab. Tech. J., 1977, pp. 1061-80.
89. R.R. Troutman and A.G. Fortino, "Simple Model for Threshold Voltage in a Short-Channel IGFET", IEEE Trans. Electron Devices, Oct., 1977, pp. 1266-8.
90. H. Masuda et al., "Device Design of Short Channel MOS-FETS Based on Two Dimensional Numerical Analysis Program", Trans. Inst. Electron. and Commun. Eng. Jpn. Sec. E., April, 1977, pp. 213-14.
91. Y.A. El-Mansy and D.M. Caughey, "Characterization of Silicon-on-Sapphire IGFET Transistors", IEEE Trans. Electron Devices, Sept., 1977, pp. 1148-53.
92. V.I. Il'in et al., "Analysis of Methods of Simulation of MOS Transistor Characteristics for Computer-Aided Design of Integrated Circuits", Autom. and Remote Control, Feb., 1977, pp. 291-7.
93. B.K. Ahuja and A.R. Boothroyd, "Modelling of V-Channel MOS Transistor", IEEE Internat. Electron Devices Meeting, 1976, pp. 573-6.
94. S.R. Combs et al., "Characterization and Modeling of Simultaneously Fabricated DMOS and VMOS Transistors", IEEE Internat. Electron Devices Meeting, 1976, pp. 569-72.
95. Dang Luong Mo, "A One-Dimensional Theory on the Effects of Diffusion Current and Carrier Velocity Saturation on E-Type IGFET Current-Voltage Characteristics", Solid-State Electron., Sept., 1977, pp. 781-8.
96. W.R. Bandy and D.P. Kokalis, "A Simple Approach for Accurately Modeling the Threshold Voltage of Short-Channel MOSTS", Solid-State Electron., Aug., 1977, pp. 675-80.
97. H.N. Kotecha et al., "Characterization of Short and Narrow Channel Effects for CAD-IGFET Model", IEEE 1977 Internat. Solid-State Circuits Conf., 1977, pp. 42-3.
98. M. Fukuma and M. Matsumura, "A Simple Model for Short Channel MOSFETS", Proc. IEEE, Aug., 1977, pp. 1212-13.
99. H. Nielinger and W. Schneider, "Network Analysis Program for Integrated MOSFET Inverters", Elektronik, April, 1977, pp. 109-12.
100. J. Compeers et al., "A Process and Layout-Oriented Short-Channel MOST Model for Circuit-Analysis Programs", IEEE Trans. Electron Devices, June, 1977, pp. 739-46.
101. K. Lehovek, "Transient Charge and Current Distributions in the Nitride of MNOS Models", IEEE Trans. Electron Devices, May, 1977, pp. 536-40.
102. J.E. Brewer, "MNOS Density Parameters", IEEE Trans. Electron Devices, May, 1977, pp. 618-25.
103. Y.A. El-Mansy and A.R. Boothroyd, "A Simple Two-Dimensional Model for IGFET Operation in the Saturation Region", IEEE Trans. Electron Devices, March, 1977, pp. 254-61.
104. Y.A. El-Mansy and A.R. Boothroyd, "A New Approach to the Theory and Modeling of Insulated Gate Field-Effect Transistors", IEEE Trans. Electron Devices, March, 1977, pp. 241-53.
105. H.C. Card and M.I. Elmasry, "Functional Modelling of Non-Volatile MOS Memory Devices for Computer-Aided Design", IEEE, 1975 Internat. Electron Devices Meeting, 1975, pp. 565-8.
106. "Limitations on the Maximum Operating Voltage of CMOS Integrated Circuits", IEEE, 1975 Internat. Electron Devices Meeting, 1975, pp. 551-4.
107. T.K. Young and R.W. Dutton, "Mini-MSINC-A Minicomputer Simulator for MOS Circuits with Modular Built-in Model", IEEE J. Solid-State Circuits, Oct., 1976, pp. 730-2.
108. M.B. Bandali and T.C. Lo, "On Modeling of the Self-Aligned Field Implanted MOS Devices with Narrow Widths", IEEE, 1975 Internat. Electron Devices Meeting, 1975, pp. 573-6.
109. B.R. Chawla et al., "An MOS Circuit Simulator for Integrated Circuit Design", 1975, IEEE Internat. Symposium on Circuits and Systems, 1975, pp. 228-30.
110. H.C. Card and E.L. Heasell, "Modelling of Channel Enhancement Effects on the Write Characteristics of FAMOS Devices", Solid-State Electron., Nov., 1976, pp. 965-8.
111. H.C. Card and M.I. Elmasry, "Functional Modelling of Non-Volatile MOS Memory Devices", Solid-State Electron., Oct., 1976, pp. 863-70.
112. P.E. Cottrell and E.M. Buturla, "Steady State Analysis of Field Effect Transistors Via the Finite Element Method", IEEE, 1975 Internat. Electron Devices Meeting, 1975, pp. 51-4.
113. A. Phillips et al., "IGFET Hot Electron Emission Model", IEEE, 1975 Internat. Electron Devices Meeting, 1975, pp. 39-42.
114. F.M. Klaassen, "A MOS Model for Computer-Aided Design", Philips Res. Rep., 1976, pp. 71-83.
115. D.R. Alexander and R.M. Turfler, "An MOS Modeling Hierarchy Including Radiation Effects", IEEE Trans. Nucl. Sci., Dec., 1975, pp. 2611-16.
116. R.R. Troutman, "Low-Level Avalanche Multiplication in IGFET's", IEEE Trans. Electron Devices, Apr., 1976, pp. 419-25.
117. P. Rossel et al., "Accurate Two Sections Model for MOS Transistor in Saturation", Solid-State Electron., Jan., 1976, pp. 51-6.
118. J.S.T. Huang and G.W. Taylor, "Modeling of an Ion-Implanted Silicon-Gate Depletion-Mode IGFET", IEEE Trans. Electron Devices, Nov., 1975, pp. 995-1001.
119. H. Runge, "Threshold Voltage Shift of MOS Transistors by Ion Implantation", Electron. Engin., Jan., 1976, pp. 41-3.
120. B.R. Chawla et al., "Motis-An MOS Timing Simulator", IEEE Trans. Circuits and Syst., Dec., 1975, pp. 901-110.
121. J. Verjans and R. Van Overstraeten, "Electrical Characteristics of Boron-Implanted N-Channel MOS Transistors for Use in Logic Circuits", IEEE Trans. Electron Devices, Oct., 1975, pp. 862-8.
122. T.J. Rodgers et al., "An Experimental and Theoretical Analysis of Double-Diffused MOS Transistors", IEEE J. Solid-State Circuits, Oct., 1975, pp. 322-31.
123. T.K. Young and R.W. Dutton, "Extraction and Sensitivity of Parameters for Higher Order MOS Models", 8th Asilomar Conf. on Circuits, Systems and Comp.,

1975, pp. 518-23.
124. T. Masuhara et al., "MOS-FET Model Including Low-Current Region Near Threshold", Electron. and Commun. Jap., Aug., 1973, pp. 125-32.
125. D.J. Breed, "A New Model for the Negative Voltage Instability in MOS Devices", Appl. Phys. Lett., Feb., 1975, pp. 116-18.
126. J. Tihanyi and H. Schlotterer, "Influence of the Floating Substrate Potential on the Characteristics of ESFI MOS Transistors", Solid-State Electron., April, 1975, pp. 309-14.
127. T.W. Collins and J.N. Churchill, "Exact Modeling of the Transient Response of an MOS Capacitor", IEEE Trans. Electron Devices, 1975, pp. 90-101.
128. H. Katto and Y. Itoh, "Analytical Expressions for the Static MOS Transistor Characteristics Based on the Gradual Channel Model", Solid-State Electron., Dec., 1974, pp. 1283-92.
129. T. Masuhara et al., "A Precise MOSFET Model for Low-Voltage Circuits", IEEE Trans. Electron Devices, June, 1974, pp. 363-71.
130. T.W. Collins, "Exact Modeling of Time-Dependent Phenomena in an MOS Structure", IEEE, 1973 Int. Electron Devices Meeting Tech. Digest, 1973, pp. 342-5.
131. R.R. Troutman, "Subthreshold Design Considerations for Insulated Gate Field-Effect Transistors ", IEEE J. Solid-State Circuits, April, 1974, pp. 55-60.
132. A.W. Lo and J.J. Gibson, "Simple MOSFET Modeling for Digital Applications", IEEE J. Solid-State Circuits, Oct., 1973, pp. 391-3.
133. D.J. Pilling and J.G. Skalnik, "A Circuit Model for Predicting Transient Delays in LSI Logic Circuits", 6th Asilomar Conf. on Circuits and Systems, 1973, pp. 424-8.
134. R.R. Troutman, "Subthreshold Design Considerations for Insulated-Gate Field-Effect Transistors", IEEE Internat. Solid State Circuits Conference, 1973, pp. 108-9.
135. J. Borel et al., "A Connection Between Technology and Models using a Computer Analysis", IEEE Int. Solid State Circuits Conf., 1973, pp. 102-3,205.
136. G.D. Hachtel and M.H. Mack, "A Graphical Study of the Current Distributions in Short-Channel IGFETS ", IEEE Internat. Solid State Circuits Conf., 1973, pp. 110-11, 206.
137. M.S. Mock, "A Two-Dimensional Mathematical Model of the Insulated-Gate Field-Effect Transistor", Solid-State Electron., May, 1973, pp. 601-9.
138. J.S.T. Huang, "Characteristics of a Depletion-type IGFET", IEEE Trans. Electron Devices, May, 1973, pp. 513-14.
139. J.J. Kalinowski, "A Compact MOS Model for Design Analysis", Proc. IEEE, Aug., 1972, pp. 1000-1.
140. J. Foltz and F. Musa, "Computer Helps Design of Complementary MOS Logic", Electronics, June, 1972, pp. 85-9.
141. D.P. Smith and J.G. Linvill, "An Accurate Short-Channel IGFET Model for Computer-Aided Circuit Design", 1971 Internat. Solid State Circuits Conf., 1971, pp. 40-1.

3—MOSFET Processing Technologies

1. P.I. Suciu et al., "High-Speed NMOS Circuits Made with X-Ray Lithography and Reactive Sputter Etching", IEEE Electron Device Lett., Jan., 1980, pp. 10-11.
2. S. Muramoto et al., "A New Self-Aligning Contact Process for MOS LSI", IEEE, 1978 Internat. Electron Devices Meeting, 1978, pp. 185-8.
3. G.F. Derbenwick and W.C. Black, Jr., "Radiation-Tolerant High-Voltage CMOS/MNOS Technology", IEEE, 1978 Internat. Electron Devices Meeting, 1978, pp. 226-9.
4. G.W. Hughes and G.J. Brucker, "Radiation Hardened MOS Technology", Solid State Technol., July, 1979, pp. 70-6.
5. N. Tsubouchi et al., "The Applications of the High-Pressure Oxidation Process to The Fabrication of MOS LSI", IEEE Trans. Electron Devices, April, 1979, pp. 618-22.
6. L. Baldi et al., "The Role of Point-Like and Extended Defects in MOS Processing", Surf. Technol., Feb., 1979, pp. 161-70.
7. P.L. Shah, "Refractory Metal Gate Processes for VLSI Applications", IEEE Trans. Electron Devices, April, 1979, pp. 631-40.
8. E. Arai et al., "High Integration MOS Process Technology", Rev. Electr. Commun. Lab., Jan.-Feb., 1979, pp. 18-32.
9. T. Araki et al., "Device Fabrication Process Technology for High Density MOS LSI", Electr. Commun. Lab Tech. J., 1978, pp. 1975-94.
10. M. Hirai et al., "Development of Fabrication Process for 64 K MOS RAM", Electr. Commun. Lab. Tech. J., 1978, pp. 1957-73.
11. M. Kondo et al., "A High Speed Molybdenum Gate MOS RAM", IEEE J. Solid-State Circuits, Oct., 1978, pp. 611-16.
12. K. Ohwada et al., "Design and Process for High Speed Short Channel CMOS IC", Trans. Inst. Electron, and Commun. Eng. Jpn. Sec. E., Aug., 1978, pp. 699-70.
13. H.I. Stoller, "Recessed Dielectric Isolation Defined IGFET Having a Gate Formed at Lower Position than the Source and Drain Surface", IBM Tech. Disclosure Bull., March, 1978, pp. 3883.
14. K. Hoffmann and R. Losehand, "VMOS Technology Applied to Dynamic RAMS", IEEE J. Solid-State Circuits, Oct., 1978, pp. 617-22.
15. J. Sakurai, "A New Buried-Oxide Isolation for High-Speed High-Density MOS Integrated Circuits", IEEE J. Solid-State Circuits, Aug., 1978, pp. 468-71.
16. T. Mochizuki et al., "A New MOS Process Using MOSI/SUB 2/ As a Gate Material", Jpn. J. Appl. Phys., 1977, pp. 37-42.
17. J.E. Deweese and T.R. Ligon, "An NMOS Process for High-Performance LSI Circuits", Hewlett-Packard J., Nov., 1977, pp. 26-9.
18. S. Fukunaga et al., "FA-CMOS Process for Low Power Prom With Low Avalanche Injection Voltage", IEEE 1977 Internat. Electron Devices Meeting, 1977, pp. 291-3.
19. Y. Wada et al., "Evaluation of Arsenic Implanted Layers by Means of MOS Memory Characteristics", Solid-State Electron., March, 1978, pp. 513-18.
20. C.H. Stapper and P.B. Hwang, "Simulation of FET Device Parameters for LSI Manufacturing", Electrochemical Soc. Spring Meeting, 1977, pp. 595-7.
21. A.G. Fortino and R. Silverman, "Polysilicon Drain MOSFET Memory Cell", IBM Tech. Disclosure Bull., July, 1977, pp. 539-40.
22. R. Mitterer and H. Schulte, "MOS-RAM Storage Cells Using Double Pilysilicon Technique", Elektron Anz., July, 1977, pp. 19-22.
23. E. Adler, "High Density Silicon Gate Field-Effect Transistor Fabrication Process", IBM Tech. Disclosure Bull., April, 1977, pp. 4094-6.
24. S. Aymeloglu et al., "Freeze-Out Effects in Ion-Implanted MOSFET's", Electrochemical Soc. Spring Meeting, 1977, pp. 471-2.
25. T.J. Rodgers et al., "VMOS Memory Technology", IEEE J. Solid-State Circuits, Oct., 1977, pp. 515-24.
26. D.L. Critchlow, "High Resolution Lithograph and its Impact on High Performance MOSFET Logic and Memory" , IEEE 14th IEEE Computer Soc. Internat. Conference, 1977, pp. 110-13.
27. E. Adler and R.M. Quinn, "Double-Level Polysilicon Memory Cells Process", IBM Tech. Dis. Bull., Dec., 1976, pp. 2478-9.

28. B. El-Kareh et al., "Electron Beam Fabricated IGFETS", IEEE Inter. Electron Devices Meeting, 1976, pp. 443-5.
29. H. Oikawa et al., "Molybdenum Metallization System for Large Scale Integrated Circuits", Rev. Electr. Commun. Lab., May-June, 1976, pp. 407-17.
30. E.C. Douglas and A.G.F. Dingwall, "Surface Doping Using Ion Implantation for Optimum Guard Layer Design in COS/MOS Structures", IEEE Trans. Electron Devices, Oct., 1975, pp. 849-57.
31. P.J. Krick, "The Implanted Stepped-Oxide MNOSFET", IEEE Trans. Electron Devices, Feb., 1975, pp. 62-3.
32. G. Marr and G.L. Mowery, "A Depletion-Load, P-Channel, Bipolar-IGFET Technology", Bell Syst. Tech. J., Jan., 1975, pp. 69-79.
33. T.G. Athanas, "Development of COS/MOS Technology", Solid State Technol., June, 1974, pp. 54-9.
34. E.C. Douglas and A.G.F. Dingwall, "Ion Implantation for Threshold Control in COSMOS Circuits", IEEE Trans. Electron Devices, June, 1974, pp. 324-31.
35. B.B.M. Brandt et al., "LOCMOS, A New Technology for Complementary MOS Circuits", Philips Tech. Rev., 1974, pp. 19-23.
36. V.L. Rideout et al., "Device Design Considerations for Ion Implanted MOSFETS", IEEE, 1973 Internat. Electron Devices Meeting, 1973, pp. 148-51.
37. J. Borel et al., "A Depletion Load Self-Aligned Technology", Solid-State Electron., Dec., 1973, pp. 1377-81.

4—MOSFET Digital VLSI

1. K.N. Ratnakumar et al., "Performance Limits of E/D NMOS VLSI (Most Analytic Model)", 1980, IEEE Internat. Solid-State Circuits Conf. Digest of Tech. Papers, 1980, pp. 72-3.
2. J.R. Brews et al., "Generalized Guide for MOSFET Miniaturization", IEEE Electron Device Lett., Jan., 1980, pp. 2-4.
3. F.H. Gaensslen, "Geometry Effects of Small MOSFET Devices", IBM J. Res. and Dev., Nov., 1979, pp. 682-8.
4. T.H. Ning et al., "Hot-Electron Design Constraints for One-Micron IGFET", IEEE, 1978 Internat. Electron Devices Meeting, 1978, pp. 472-5.
5. K.W. Yeh et al., "Optimum Short-Channel MOS Device Design for High Performance VLSI", IEEE, 1978 Internat. Electron Devices Meeting, 1978, pp. 468-71.
6. B. Hoefflinger et al., "Model and Performance of Hot-Electron MOS Transistors for High-Speed, Low Power LSI", IEEE, 1978 Internat. Electron Devices Meeting, 1978, pp. 463-7.
7. T. Yamaguchi et al., "A New Submicrometer Channel/High-Speed MOS-LSI Technology", IEEE Trans. Electron Devices, April, 1979, pp. 611-18.
8. R.R. Troutman, "VLSI Limitations from Drain-Induced Barrier Lowering", IEEE J. Solid-State Circuits, April, 1979, pp. 383-91.
9. J.J. Barnes et al., "Short-Channel MOSFETS in the Punchthrough Current Mode", IEEE J. Solid-State Circuits, April, 1979, pp. 368-75.
10. P. Antognetti et al., "Considerations and Simulation of Scaled MOS Circuits", IEE Internat. Conf. on Computer Aided Design and Manufacture of Electronic Components, Circuits and Systems, 1979, pp. 26-7.
11. N. Miyahara et al., "Design and Characteristics of Short-Channel MOS FETS for LSI RAM", Rev. Electr. Commun. Lab., Jan.-Feb., 1979, pp. 137-50.
12. N. Miyahara and K. Miura, "Design of Short-Channel MOS FETS for VLSI RAM", Electr. Commun. Lab. Tech. J., 1978, pp. 1945-56.
13. F. Faggin, "The Influence of VLSI on Computer Structures, II, Elektronik, Nov., 1978 pp. 57-61.
14. E.A. Valsamakis, "A Short Channel MOSFET Model", IEEE, 1977 Internat. Electron. Devices Meeting, 1977, pp. 516-19.
15. F.H. Gaensslen, "Geometry Effects of Small MOSFET Devices", IEEE, 1977 Internat. Electron Devices Meeting, 1977, pp. 512-15.
16. F.H. Gaensslen et al., "Very Small MOSFET'S for Low-Temperature Operation", IEEE Trans. Electron Devices, March, 1977, pp. 218-29.
17. H.N. Kotecha and K.E. Beilstein, "Currents and Capacitances in Narrow Width MOSFET Structures", IEEE, 1975 Internat. Electron Devices Meeting, 1975, pp. 47-50.
18. F.H. Gaensslen et al., "Design and Characterisation of Very Small MOSFETS for Low Temperature Operation", IEEE, 1975 Internat. Electron Devices Meeting, 1975, pp. 43-6.
19. A.D. Odell and K.A.M. Arton, "Operation of Single-Channel MOS LSI At Low Supply Voltages", IEE, 1st European Solid State Circuits Conf.-ESSCIRC (Extended Abstracts Only), 1975, pp. 99-100.
20. K.E. Kroell and G.K. Ackermann, "Threshold Voltage of Narrow Channel Field Effect Transistors", Solid-State Electron., Jan., 1976, pp. 77-81.
21. H.C. Poon et al., "DC Model for Short-Channel IGFET'S", IEEE, 1973 Internat. Electron Devices Meeting Tech. Digest, 1973, pp. 156-9.

5—MOSFET Digital Signal Processors

1. R. Milton, "The Outlook for CMOS Technology in Communication Systems", Nachr. Elektron., Jan., 1979, pp. 10-11.
2. H.J. De Man et al., "High-Speed NMOS Circuits for ROM-Accumulator and Multiplier Type Digital Filters", IEEE J. Solid-State Circuits, Oct., 1978, pp. 565-72.
3. G. Zeidler and D. Becker, "MOS LSI Custom Circuits Offer New Prospects for Communciations Equipment Design", Electr. Commun., 1974, pp. 88-93.
4. L. Winner, ed., "Monolithic Modular Digital Filters", Digest of Tech. Papers of the 1973 IEEE Internat. Solid State Circuits Conf., 1973, pp. 60-1.

6—MOSFET Logic Circuits and Microprocessors

1. H. Hinkel et al., "Reprogrammable MOSFET Structure", IBM Tech. Disclosure Bull., Sept., 1978, pp. 1500.
2. C.R. Briggs, "A 20 MHZ C.M.O.S.-On-Sapphire Microprocessor", New Electron., June, 1978, pp. 87, 90, 94, 96.
3. G. Katz et al., "A MOS LSI Capacitive Keyboard Interface Chip", IEEE J. Solid-State Circuits, Oct., 1978, pp. 561-5.
4. D.L. Fraser, Jr. and S.W. Director, "Multiple Objective Function Optimization of Digital MOSFET Circuits", IEEE, Proc. of the 1978 IEEE Internat. Symposium on Circuits and Systems, 1978, pp. 1114-15.
5. T. Nakashima et al., "D10 High Speed Central Processor' Semiconductor Devices", Electr. Commun. Lab. Tech. J., 1977, pp. 3321-30.
6. N. Ohnishi et al., D10 High Speed Central Processor' Main Memory", Electr. Commun. Lab. Tech. J., 1977, pp. 3281-92.
7. R. Greene, "Dense, Interchangeable ROMS Work With Fast Microprocessors", Electronics, March, 1978, pp. 104-7.
8. J.T. Easterbrook and R.G. Bennetts, "Failure Mechanisms in Logic Circuits and Their Related Fault Effects", New Developments in Automatic Testing, 1977, pp. 44-7.
9. D.C. Rollenhagen et al., "LSI Multiplier-Divider

9. cont'd.
for 8080", IEEE, Proc. of the IEEE 1977 National Aerospace and Electronics Conf., Naecon '77, 1977, pp. 887-92.
10. L.W. Martinson and J.A. Lunsford, "A CMOS/SOS Pipeline FFT Processor-Construction, Performance and Applications", IEEE, Proc. of the IEEE 1977 National Aerospace and Electronics Conf., Naecon '77, 1977, pp. 574-9.
11. H. Blume et al., "A Universal Peripheral Interface Chip for Microprocessor Systems", IEEE, 14th IEEE Comp. Sci. Internat. Conf., 1977, pp. 107-9.
12. C.R. Hewes and M. De Wit, "NMOS Tone Generator", IEEE, 1977 Internat. Solid-State Circuits Conf., 1977, pp. 30-1.
13. J.R. Verjans, "A Serial-Parallel Multiplier Using the NENDEP Technology", IEEE J. Solid-State Circuits, June, 1977, pp. 323-5.
14. I. Bromme et al., "A High-Speed 4-Bit Microprocessor in N-Channel Silicon Gate Technology", Siemens Forsch.- and Entwicklungsber, 1976, pp. 319-23.
15. K. Yoshida et al., "A 16-Bit LSI Minicomputer", IEEE J. Solid-State Circuits, Oct., 1976, pp. 696-702.
16. C.A. Mead et al., "128-Bit Multicomparator", IEEE J. Solid-State Circuits, Oct., 1976, pp. 692-5.
17. L. Altman, "Memory Types Multiply, Microprocessor Families Grow", Electronics, Oct., 1976, pp. 76-8, 81-82.
18. G. Peppiette, "Memory Architecture and the Influence of the Microprocessor", Microelectron. and Reliab., 1976, pp. 307-13.
19. G. Nash, "The MOS Implementation of Low Speed Modems", IEEE, 1976 Internat. Conf. on Communications, 1976, pp. 48/13-15.
20. K. Horninger, "A High-Speed ESFI SOS Programmable Logic Array with an MNOS Version", IEEE J. Solid-State Circuits, Oct., 1975, pp. 331-6.
21. J.R. Verjans and R.J. Van Overstraeten, "NENDEP-A Simple N-Channel MOS Technology for Logic Circuits", IEEE J. Solid-State Circuits, Aug., 1975, pp. 212-18.
22. M. Mizuno et al., "An N-Channel 16-Bit Variable Architecture Microprocessor", 6th Internat. Congress on Microelectronics, 1974, 5 pp.
23. M.E. Hoff, "Microprocessors", 6th Internat. Congress on Microelectronics, 1974, 6 pp.
24. D. Chung, "Four-Chip Microprocessor Family Reduces System Parts Counts", Electronics, March, 1975, pp. 87-93.
25. D.P. Martin and K.S. Berland, "ICS Interface Keyboard to Microprocessor", Electronics, March, 1975, pp. 83-4.
26. C. Masson and J. Michard, "Design of an LSI-MOS Programmable Logic Array", Internat. Conf. on Large Scale Integrated Circuits, 1974, pp. 242-3.
27. W.F. Gehweiler et al., "CMOS/SOS Correlator and Multiplier", IEEE Aerospace and Electronic Systems Soc., Proc. of the IEEE 1974 National Aerospace and Electronics Conf., 1974, pp. 252-9.
28. K. Horninger, "Fully Decoded MNOS Storage Arrays in ESFI MOS Technology", IEEE J. Solid-State Circuits, Dec., 1974, pp. 444-6.
29. M. Shima and F. Faggin, "In Switch to N-MOS Microprocessor Gets a 2-MUS Cycle Time", Electronics, April, 1974, pp. 95-100.
30. L. Young et al., "N-Channel MOS Technology Yields New Generation of Microprocessors", Electronics, April, 1974, pp. 88-95.
31. E. Gibson, "Adaptive High Speed Data MODEMS", IEEE, 1973 IEEE Conf. on Decision and Control Including 12th Symposium on Adaptive Processes, 1973, pp. 227-31.
32. J.P. Klosky and R.J. Paluck, "Custom MOS LSI Development for a Data Communications Terminal", IEEE, 1973 National Telecommunications Conf., 1973, 41D/1-5.
33. D.R. Lewis, "Microprocessor or Random Logic?", Electron. Des., Sept., 1973, pp. 106-10.
34. H. Sakamoto and L. Forbes, "Grounded Load Complementary FET Circuits' Sceptre Analysis", IEEE J. Solid-State Circuits, Aug., 1973, pp. 282-4.
35. W.F. Kalin, "Using Complementary MOS Circuits for Control Instrumentation", Instrum. and Control Syst., Sept., 1972, pp. 75-8.
36. T.M. Whitney and R.J. Paluck, "MOS Circuit Development for the HP-35 (Calculator)", IEEE Digest of Papers on the Six Annual IEEE Computer Society Internat. Conf., 1972, pp. 73-6.
37. P.J. Coppen et al., "A Complementary MOS 1.2 Volt Watch Circuit Using Ion Implantation", Solid-State Electron., Feb., 1972, pp. 165-75.
38. D.G. Schweikert, "Computer-Generated IGFET Layout Using a Vertically-Packed Weinberger Arrangement", IEEE, Digest of Technical Papers of the 1971 Internat. Solid State Circuits Conf., 1971, pp. 118-19.
39. A.A. Alaspa and A.G.F. Dingwall, "COS/MOS Parallel Processor Array", 1970 IEEE Internat. Solid State Circuits Conf., 1970, pp. 118-19.

7—MOSFET Static RAMs

1. T. Ohzone et al., "A 64KB Static RAM", 1980 IEEE Internat. Solid-State Circuits Conf. Digest of Tech. Paper, 1980, pp. 236-
2. T. Iizuka et al., "Fully Static 16KB Bulk CMOS RAM", 1980 IEEE Internat. Solid-State Circuits Conf. Digest of Tech. Papers, 1980, pp. 226-7.
3. T. Masuhara et al., "2K*8B HCMOS Static RAMs", 1980 IEEE Internat. Solid-State Circuits Conf. Digest of Tech. Papers, 1980, pp. 224-
4. A.C. Graham et al., "Battery Backup Circuits for Memories (NMOS RAMs)", 1980 IEEE Internat. Solid-State Circuits Conf. Digest of Tech. Papers, 1980, pp. 58-9.
5. K.D. Beyer and M.R. Poponiak, "Reduction of Bit Line Capacitance in Memory Cells", IBM Tech. Disclosure Bull., Nov., 1979, pp. 2347.
6. T. Ohzone et al., "A 2K*8-Bit Static RAM", IEEE, 1978 Internat. Electron Devices Meeting, 1978, pp. 360-3.
7. T. Iizuka, "Substrate-FED CMOS Memory Device", IEEE 1978 Internat. Electron Devices Meeting, 1978, pp. 222-5.
8. A.G.F. Dingwall et al., "High-Density, Buried-Contact CMOS/SOS Static RAM", IEEE 1978 Internat. Electron Devices Meeting, 1978, pp. 193-6.
9. D.W. Kemerer, "Decoder with Tri-state Output", IBM Tech. Disclosure Bull., June, 1979, pp. 53-4.
10. O. Minato et al., "A High-Speed Low-Power Hi-CMOS 4K Static RAM", IEEE Trans. Electron Devices, June, 1979, pp. 882-5.
11. J.M. Caywood et al., "A Novel 4K Static RAM With Submilliwatt Standby Power", IEEE Trans. Electron Devices, June, 1979, pp. 861-4.
12. U. Cilingiroglu, "A Charge-Pumping-Loop Concept for Static MOS/RAM Cells", IEEE J. Solid-State Circuits, June, 1979, pp. 599-603.
13. M. Akiya and M. Ohara, "Design for CMOS Static RAM", Trans. Inst. Electron. and Commun. Eng. Jpn. Sect E., April, 1979, pp. 286.
14. I. Zarkov and P. Volkov, "Static Random Access Memories in MOS Technique with Reduced Power Requirements", Nachrichtentech. Elektron., 1979, pp. 206-7.
15. W. Chu et al., "A 5 V 4k*8 Quasi Static RAM", 1979 IEEE Internat. Solid-State Circuits Conf. (Digest of Tech. Papers), 1979, pp. 156-7.
16. R.R. Desimone et al., "FET RAMs", 1979 IEEE Internat. Solid-State Circuits Conf. (Digest of Tech. Papers), 1979, pp. 154-5.

17. R.G. Stewart and A.G.F. Dingwall, "16 K CMOS/SOS Asynchronous Static RAM", 1979 IEEE Internat. Solid-State Circuits Conf. (Digest of Tech. Papers), 1979, pp. 104-5.
18. R.M. Jecmen et al., "A 25 NS 4K Static RAM", 1979 IEEE Internat. Solid-State Circuits Conf. (Digest of Tech. Papers), 1979, pp. 100-1.
19. T. Mimoto et al., "Five-Transistor CMOS Memory Cell", Trans. Inst. Electron. and Commun. Eng. Jpn. Sect. E., Jan., 1979, pp. 63.
20. L. Arzubi, "Duffusionless Memory Array", IBM. Tech. Disclosure Bull., Sept., 1978, pp. 1381-3.
21. G.S. Leach et al., "A 1K*8-Bit 5 V-Only Static RAM" , IEEE J. Solid-State Circuits, Oct., 1978, pp. 711-15.
22. R.J. Hollingsworth et al., "A CMOS/SOS 4K Static RAM", IEEE J. Solid-State Circuits, Oct., 1978, pp. 664-9.
23. Y. Torimaru et al., "DSA 4K Static RAM", IEEE J. Solid-State Circuits, Oct., 1978, pp. 647-50.
24. K. Shimotori et al., "A 50 NS 4K Static DSA MOS RAM", IEEE J. Solid-State Circuits, Oct., 1978, pp. 639-46.
25. T. Wada et al., "A 15-NS 1024-Bit Fully Static MOS RAM", IEEE J. Solid-State Circuits, Oct., 1978, pp. 635-9.
26. J. Nishizawa et al., "High Speed and High Density Static Induction Transistor Memory" IEEE J. Solid-State Circuits, Oct., 1978, pp. 622-34.
27. L. Schrader and G. Meusburger, "A New Circuit Configuration for a Static Memory Cell with an Area of 880 MUM/SUP 2/", IEEE J. Solid-State Circuits, June, 1978, pp. 345-51.
28. T. Masuhara et al., "A High-Speed, Low-Power Hi-CMOS 4K Static RAM", 1978 IEEE Internat. Solid-State Circuits Conf. (Digest of Tech. Papers), 1978, pp. 110-11.
29. G.S. Leach et al., "A 15K*8-Bit 5 V-Only Static RAM", 1978 IEEE Internat. Solid-State Circuits Conf. (Digest of Tech. Papers), 1978, pp. 104-5.
30. W.J. Fischer, "Technology and Circuit Technique of Static MOS Memories", Nachrichtentech. Elektron., 1978, pp. 279-83.
31. L.G. Walker et al., "Four-Transistor Static CMOS Memory Cells", 1977 Internat. Electron Devices Meeting, 1977, pp. 402-5.
32. D. Huffman et al., "Substrate Bias Generator Optimizes Military MOS Memories", Mil. Electron./ Countermeas., Sept., 1977, pp. 62, 64, 76.
33. G.J. Brucker, "Characteristics of CMOS/Bulk and SOS Memories in a Transient Environment", IEEE Trans. Nucl. Sci., Dec., 1977, pp. 2209-12.
34. J.H. Kroeger, "New Directions in 4K Static R/W RAMs", 1977 Electro Conf. Record, 1977, pp. 1-4.
35. H. Takagi and G. Kano, "Dual Depletion CMOS (D/Sup 2/CMOS) Static Memory Cell", IEEE J. Solid-State Circuits, Aug., 1977, pp. 424-6.
36. A. Onoyama et al., "CMOS 4K Static RAM", Toshiba Rev., July-Aug., 1977, pp. 23-9.
37. F.H. De la Moneda, "Bipolar-IGFET Memory Cell and Array", IBM Tech. Disclosure Bull., March, 1977, pp. 3780-1.
38. T.R. O'Connell et al., Two Static 4K Clocked and Nonclocked RAM Designs", IEEE J. Solid-State Circuits, Oct., 1977, pp. 497-501.
39. R. Pashley et al., "Speedy RAM Runs Cool With Power-Down Circuitry", Electronics, Aug., 1977, pp. 103-7.
40. R.D. Pashley et al., "A High Performance 4K Static RAM Fabricated with an Advanced MOS Technology", IEEE, 1977 Internat. Solid-State Circuits Conf., (Digest of Tech. Papers), 1977, pp. 22-3.
41. V.G. McKenny, "A 5 V-Only 4-K Static RAM", IEEE, 1977 Internat. Solid-State Circuits Conf. (Digest of Tech. Papers), 1977, pp. 16-17.
42. T.R. O'Connell et al., "A 4K Static Clocked and Nonclocked RAM Design", IEEE, 1977 Internat. Solid-State Circuits Conf. (Digest of Tech. Papers), 1977, pp. 14-15.
43. T. O'Connell et al., "An 80 NS Low Power MOS Static 4K RAM For the System 370/168 Computer", 1977 IEEE Internat. Symposium on Circuits and Systems Proc., 1977, pp. 114-17.
44. K. Shiga et al., "A Mono-Stable 4-Transistor CMOS RAM", Natl. Tech. Rep., Oct., 1976, pp. 607-12.
45. J.M. Schlageter et al., "Two 4K Static 5-V RAM's", IEEE J. Solid-State Circuits, Oct., 1976, pp. 602-9.
46. R.D. Pashley and G.A. McCormick, "A 70-NS 1K MOS RAM", 1976 IEEE Internat. Solid-State Circuits Conf. (Digest of Tech. Papers), 1976, pp. 138-9., 238.
47. J.M. Schlageter et al., "A 4K Static 5-V RAM", 1976 IEEE Internat. Solid-State Circuits Conf. (Digest of Tech. Papers), 1976, pp. 136-7.
48. S. Koike et al., "New Two-Terminal C-MNOS Memory Cells", IEEE Trans. Electron Devices, Sept., 1976, pp. 1036-41.
49. R.C. Henderson et al., "A High-Speed P-Channel Random Access 1024-Bit Memory Made with Electron Lithography", IEEE J. Solid-State Circuits, Apr., 1975, pp. 92-6.
50. A. Dingwall et al., "Hi-Speed SOS COS/MOS Random-Access Memories", RCA Eng., Dec. 1973-Jan. 1974, pp. 70-4.
51. K. Goser and M. Pomper, "Five-Transistor Memory Cells in ESFI MOS Technology", IEEE J. Solid-State Circuits, Oct., 1973, pp. 324-6.

8—MOSFET Dynamic RAMs

1. T. Mano et al., "A 256K RAM Fabricated Molybdenum-Polysilicon Technology", 1980 Internat. Solid-State Circuits Conf Digest of Tech. Papers, 1980, pp. 234 -5.
2. S. Matsue et al., "A 250K Dynamic RAM", 1980 IEEE Internat. Solid-State Circuits Conf Digest of Tech. Paper, 1980, pp. 232-
3. L.S. White et al., "A 5 V-Only 64K Dynamic RAM", 1980 IEEE Internat. Solid-State Circuits Conf. Digest of Tech. Papers, 1980, pp. 230-
4. K. Itoh et al., "A Single 5 V 64K Dynamic RAM", 1980 IEEE Internat. Solid-State Circuits Conf. Digest of Tech. Paper, 1980, pp. 228-
5. K. Ohta et al., "A Stacked High Capacitor RAM", 1980 IEEE Internat. Solid-State Circuits Conf. Digest of Tech. Papers, 1980, pp. 66-7.
6. K.L. Anderson, "Bit Line Charge Pump", IBM Tech. Disclosure Bull., Dec., 1979, pp. 2687-8.
7. R.C. Dockerty, "Two-Device Memory Cell", IBM Tech. Disclosure Bull., Nov., 1979, pp. 2299-3000.
8. J.M. Gaworecki and N.G. Thoma, "Memory Sense Amplifier Circuit", IBM Tech. Disclosure Bull., Sept., 1979, pp. 1411-12.
9. K. Shimotori et al., "A 64K-Bit Dynamic MOS RAM", Mitsubishi Denki Giho, July, 1979, pp. 491-4.
10. A. Troll, "Refresh Logic Realised for the Operation of Dynamic RAMs in Microcomputers", Radio Fernsehen Elektron., 1979, pp. 159-62.
11. P.K. Chatterjee et al., "Taper Isolated Dynamic Gain RAM Cell", IEEE 1978 Internat. Electron Devices Meeting, 1978, pp. 1-2.
12. M. Koyanagi et al., "Novel High Density, Stacked Capacitor MOS RAM", IEEE 1978 Internat. Electron Devices Meeting, 1978, pp. 348-51.
13. J.J. Fatula, Jr. and P.L. Garbarino, "Buried Diffusion Storage Node Memory Cell", IBM Tech. Disclosure Bull., Aug., 1979, pp. 1000-1.
14. G.W. Taylor et al., "A Punch-Through Isolated Dynamic RAM Cell", IEEE 1978 Internat. Electron Devices Meeting, 1978, pp. 352-5.
15. J. Sakurai, "The BO-MOS RAM Cell", IEEE 1978

15. cont'd.
Internat. Electron Devices Meeting, 1978, pp. 197-200.
16. M. Takada et al., "A 65K Dynamic RAM Using Short Channel MOSFETS", Trans. Inst. Electron. and Commun. Eng. Jpn. Sect. E., July, 1979, pp. 484-5.
17. K.S. Gray and S.C. Lewis, "Sense Amplifier Signal Margin Circuit", IBM Tech. Disclosure Bull., June, 1979, pp. 56-7.
18. A.L. Roberts, "Dynamic Memory Cell Layout Using Double Level Metallurgy", IBM Tech. Disclosure Bull. , June, 1979, pp. 51-2.
19. B. Cassidy and G. Rugila, "Dynamic MOSFET Logic Clock Driver", IBM Tech. Disclosure Bull., Aug., 1979, pp. 1093-4.
20. G.W. Leehan, "Charge Shuttle Clock Driver", IBM Tech. Disclosure Bull., June, 1979, pp. 214-16.
21. P.K. Chatterjee et al., "Charge-Coupled Device Structures for VLSI Memories", IEEE Trans. Electron Devices, June, 1979, pp. 871-81.
22. F. Jones and D. Wooten, "The Impact of MOS Dynamic Memories on System Architecture", 1978 WESCON Technical Papers, 1978, pp. 1-3.
23. P.K. Chatterjee et al., "Leakage Studies in High-Density Dynamic MOS Memory Devices", IEEE J. Solid-State Circuits, April, 1979, pp. 486-97.
24. K. Natori et al., "A 64 KBit MOS Dynamic Random Access Memory", IEEE J. Solid-State Circuits, Apr., 1979, pp. 482-5.
25. J.M. Gaworecki et al., "Sense Signal Characterization and Test Aid for One-Device Dynamic Memory Arrays", IBM Tech. Disclosure Bull., Jan., 1979, pp. 3107-8.
26. I. Lee et al., "A 64 KB MOS Dynamic RAM", 1979 IEEE Internat. Solid-State Circuits Conf. (Digest of Tech. Papers), 1979, pp. 146-7.
27. J.M. Lee et al., "A 80 NS 5 V-Only Dynamic RAM", 1979 IEEE Internat. Solid-State Circuits Conf. (Digest of Tech. Papers), 1979, pp. 142-3.
28. P.K. Chatterjee et al., "Circuit Optimization of the Taper Isolated Dynamic Gain RAM Cell for VLSI Memories", 1979 IEEE Internat. Solid-State Circuits Conf. (Digest of Tech. Papers), 1979, pp. 22-3.
29. H. Strack et al., "The Detrimental Influence of Stacking Faults on the Refresh Time of MOS Memories" , Solid-State Electron., Feb., 1979, pp. 135-40.
30. T. Yano et al., "Highly Sensitive Sense Circuit for Single Transistor MOS RAM", Rev. Electr. Commun. Lab., Jan.-Feb., 1979, pp. 10-17.
31. L.A. Gladstein and L.C. Martin, "Elimination of Bit Line Charging Through a Thick Oxide FET Read-Only Storage Device", IBM Tech. Disclosure Bull., Nov., 1978, pp. 2593-4.
32. R.M. Geffken et al., "Process for High-Capacitance Single-Device Memory Cell", IBM Tech. Disclosure Bull., Nov., 1978, pp. 2257-9.
33. N. Ieda et al., "64 K-Bit MOS RAM Design", Electr. Commun. Lab. Tech. J., 1978, pp. 1915-32.
34. E.G. Crabtree et al., "Bit Lines Having Integral Inversion Pull-up Capacitor", IBM Tech. Disclosure Bull., Sept., 1978, pp. 1545-6.
35. S.N. Chakravarti et al., "Injected Charge Capacitor Memory with Improved Signal", IBM Tech. Disclosure Bull., Aug., 1978, pp. 944-5.
36. G. Meusburger et al., "An 8 MM/SUP 2/, 5 V 16K Dynamic RAM Using a New Memory Cell", IEEE J. Solid-State Circuits, Oct., 1978, pp. 708-11.
37. T. Wada et al., "A 150 NS, 150 MW, 64K Dynamic MOS RAM", IEEE J. Solid-State Circuits, Oct., 1978, pp. 607-11.
38. G.R. Mohan Rao and J. Hewkin, "64-K Dynamic RAM Needs Only One 5-Volt Supply to Outstrip 16-K Parts", Electronics, Sept., 1978, pp. 109-16.
39. T. Yano et al., "Highly Sensitive Sense Circuit for Single Transistor (Cell) MOS RAM", Trans. Inst. Electron. and Commun. Eng. Jpn. Sect. E., May, 1978,
39. cont'd.
pp. 410-11.
40. E. Arai and N. Ieda, "A 64-KBit Dynamic MOS RAM", IEEE J. Solid-State Circuits, June, 1978, pp. 333-8.
41. K. Shimotori et al., "Sensitivity Analysis of Sense Amplifier Used for Dynamic MOS RAM", Trans. Inst. Electron. and Commun. Eng. Jpn. Sect. E., June, 1978, pp. 495.
42. H. Yoshimura et al., "A 64 KBit MOS RAM", 1978 IEEE Internat. Solid-State Circuits Conf. (Digest of Tech. Papers), 1978, pp. 148-9.
43. O. Minato et al., "High Performance 4K Dynamic RAM Fabricated with Short Channel MOS Technology", Jpn. J. Appl. Phys., 1977, pp. 65-9.
44. N. Ieda et al., "A 64K MOS RAM Design", Jpn. J. Appl. Phys., 1977, pp. 57-63.
45. R.C. Varshney and K. Venkateswaran, "Characterization of an MOS Sense Amplifier", IEEE J. Solid-State Circuits, April, 1978, pp. 268-71.
46. N. Ieda et al., "Single Transistor MOS RAM Using a Short-Channel MOS Transistor", IEEE J. Solid-State Circuits, April, 1978, pp. 218-24.
47. A.F. Tasch et al., "The NI-C RAM Cell Concept", IEEE, 1977 Internat. Electron Devices Meeting, 1977, pp. 287-90.
48. V.L. Rideout et al., "A One-Device Memory Cell Using a Single Layer of Polysilicon and a Self-Registering Metal-to-Polysilicon Contact", IEEE, 1977 Internat. Electron Devices Meeting, 1977, pp. 258-61.
49. H.S. Lee, "Analysis of the Merged Charge Memory (MCM) Cell", IBM J.Res. and Dev., Sept., 1977, pp. 402-14.
50. A. Tasch, Jr., et al., "The HI-C RAM Cell Concept", IEEE Trans. Electron Devices, Jan., 1978, pp. 33-41.
51. D. Coker, "16K - The New Generation Dynamic RAM", 1977 Electro Conf. Record, 1977, pp. 1-6.
52. P.R. Schroeder, "Prospects for the 64K-An Outline of the Problem", 14th IEEE Computer Soc. Internat. Conf., 1977, pp. 114-15.
53. R. Proebsting, "Dynamic MOS RAMs", IEEE, 1977 Internat. Conf. on Commun., 1977, pp. 147-50.
54. G. Meusburger, "A New Circuit Configuration for a Single-Transistor Cell Using AL-Gate Technology with Reduced Dimensions", IEEE J. Solid-State Circuits, June, 1977, pp. 253-7.
55. K. Itoh et al., "A High-Speed 16-KBit N-MOS Random-Access Memory", IEEE J. Solid-State Circuits, Oct., 1976, pp. 585-90.
56. K. Itoh et al., "A High-Speed 16K-Bit NMOS RAM", 1976 IEEE Internat. Solid-State Circuits Conf. (Digest of Tech. Papers), 1976, pp. 140-1.
57. A.F. Tasch et al., "The Charge-Coupled RAM Cell Concept", IEEE J. Solid-State Circuits, Feb., 1976, pp. 58-63.
58. L.M. Terman and L.G. Heller, "Overview of CCD Memory", IEEE J. Solid-State Circuits, Feb., 1976, pp. 4-10.
59. H.J. Boll and W.T. Lynch, "Design of a High-Performance 1024-B Switched Capacitor P-Channel IGFET Memory Chip", IEEE J. Solid-State Circuits", Oct., 1973, pp. 310-18.
60. L. Boonstra et al., "A 4096-B One-Transistor Per Bit Random-Access Memory with Internal Timing and Low Dissipation", IEEE J. Solid-State Circuits, Oct., 1973, pp. 305-10.
61. R.A. Abbott et al., "A 4K MOS Dynamic Random-Access Memory", IEEE J. Solid-State Circuits, Oct., 1973, pp. 292-8.
62. R. Proebsting and R. Green, "A TTL Compatible 4096-Bit N-Channel RAM", Digest of Tech. Papers of the 1973 IEEE Internat. Solid State Circuits Conf., 1973, pp. 28-9.
63. C.W. Lambrechtse et al., "A-4096 Bit One-Transistor Per-Bit RAM with Internal Timing and Low Dissipa-

63. cont'd.
tion", Digest of Tech. Papers of the 1973 IEEE Internat. Solid State Circuits Conf., 1973, pp. 26-7, 194.

9—MOSFET ROMs, PROMs, and EPROMs

1. D.C. Guterman et al., "X-Series Approach to High Density 128K and High Speed 32K EPROMs", 1980 IEEE Internat. Solid-State Circuits Conf. Digest of Tech. Paper, 1980, pp. 154-
2. C.R. Hoffman, "Floating Gate Nonvolatile Memory Cell", IBM Tech. Disclosure Bull., Nov., 1979, pp. 2403-4.
3. H. Harima et al., "A 16K-Bit Uv-erasable and -Programmable ROM", Mitsubishi Denki Giho, July, 1979, pp. 487-90.
4. R.G. Stewart, "A CMOS/SOS Electrically Alterable Read Only Memory", IEEE, 1978 Internat. Electron Devices Meeting, 1978, pp. 344-7.
5. D.C. Guterman et al., "Electrically Alterable Hot-Electron Injection Floating Gate MOS Memory Cell with Series Enhancement", IEEE, 1978 Internat. Electron. Devices Meeting, 1978, pp. 340-3.
6. M. Horiuchi and H. Katto, "A Low Voltage, High-Speed Alterable N-Channel Nonvolatile Memory", IEEE, 1978 Internat. Electron Devices Meeting, 1978, pp. 336-9.
7. M. Kikuchi et al., "A New Technique to Minimize the EPROM Cell", IEEE, 1978 Internat. Electron Devices Meeting, 1978, pp. 181-4.
8. M. Kyomasu et al., "A Low-Power 8K-Bit CMOS EPROM", Mitsubishi Denki Giho, May, 1979, pp. 359-63.
9. H. Wanka, "Advances in Nonvolatile Semiconductor Memories (RAM)", Elektronik, Oct., 1979, pp. 43-6.
10. R. Klein et al., "5-Volt-Only, Nonvolatile RAM Owes it all to Polysilicon", Electronics, Oct., 1979, pp. 111-16.
11. M. Horiuchi and H. Katto, "FCAT-A Low-Voltage High-Speed Alterable N-Channel Nonvolatile Memory Device", IEEE Trans. Electron Devices, June, 1979, pp. 914-18.
12. T. Ito et al., "Low-Voltage Alterable EAROM Cells with Nitride-Barrier Avalanche-Injection MIS (NAMIS)", IEEE Trans. Electron Devices, June, 1979, pp. 906-13.
13. C.A. Neugebauer and M.M. Barnicle, "Characteristics of Interface-Doped NMOS Memory Devices", IEEE Trans. Electron Devices, June, 1979, pp. 893-8.
14. D.C. Young, "Non Volatile RAMs in CMOS", Electron. and Appl. Ind., June, 1979, pp. 37-9.
15. J. De Montaigne, "DIFMOS Memories' Nonvolatile, Erasable and Electrically Reprogrammable", Electron. and Appl. Ind., April, 1979, pp. 36-9.
16. W.D. Brown, "MNOS Technology-Will it Survive?", Solid State Technol., July, 1979, pp. 77-83.
17. J.L. West, "The NOVRAM - A New Concept in Electrically Alterable Memories", Microelectron. J., March-April, 1979, pp. 13-15.
18. D. Vatjeva, "MOS Read Only Memory Store", Nachrichtentech. Elektron., 1979, pp. 204-6.
19. D.C. Guterman et al., "An Electrically Alterable Nonvolatile Memory Cell Using a Floating-Gate Structure", IEEE J. Solid-State Circuits, April, 1979, pp. 498-508.
20. Y. Egawa et al., "A 1 MB Full Wafer MOS RAM", 1979 IEEE Internat. Solid-State Circuits Conf. (Digest of Tech. Papers), 1979, pp. 18-19.
21. K. Kiuchi et al., "A 65 MW 128K EB-ROM", 1979 IEEE Internat. Solid-State Circuits Conf. (Digest of Tech. Papers), 1979, pp. 12-13.
22. R. Zinniker, "Random Access Memory Semiconductor Stores Produced by NMOS Techniques", Elektroniker, 1979, pp. 13-22.
23. D.C. Young, "Designing Non-Volatile Memory Arrays With CMOS RAMs", Electron. Eng., Apr.,1979, pp.71, 73, 77-8, 81, 84.
23. cont'd.
24. Y. Egawa et al., "Design of Full Wafer MOS Memory", Rev. Electr. Commun. Lab., Jan.-Feb., 1979, pp. 82-91.
25. T. Mochizuki and K. Ohuchi, "A High-Speed MOSI/SUB 2/-Gate 8-KBit Read-Only Memory Made with Silicon -Gate Compatible Processing", IEEE Trans. Electron Devices, Dec., 1978, pp. 1409-11.
26. A.W. Young and L. Thurlow, "Programmable Memories", Electron, Dec., 1978, pp. 27-8, 30.
27. Y. Egawa et al., "Design of Full Wafer MOS Memory", Electr. Commun. Lab. Tech. J., 1978, pp. 2049-61.
28. L.I. Popova et al., "Discharge of M.N.O.S. Structures", IEE J. Solid-State And Electron Devices, Jan., 1979, pp. 17-20.
29. R.R. Troutman, "FET Programmable Read-Only Memory", IBM Tech. Disclosure Bull., Sept., 1978, pp. 1374-6.
30. U. Hartmann, "Status of Development of Non-Volatile Floating-Gate-Transistor Base Semiconductor Memories", Nachrichtentech. Elektron., 1978, pp. 409-11.
31. Y.-F. Chan, "A 4K CMOS Erasable PROM", IEEE J. Solid-State Circuits, Oct., 1978, pp. 677-80.
32. J.-M. Brice et al., "A Nonvolatile Eight-Bit Asynchronous Counter and its Applications", IEEE J. Solid-State Circuits, June, 1978, pp. 355-62.
33. D.R. Wilson and P.R. Schroeder, "A 100 NS 150 MW 64 KBIT ROM", 1978 IEEE Internat. Solid-State Circuits Conf. (Digest of Tech. Papers), 1978, pp. 152-3.
34. E. Harari et al., "A 256-Bit Nonvolatile Static RAM", 1978 IEEE Internat. Solid-State Circuits Conf. (Digest of Tech. Papers), 1978, pp. 108-9.
35. Chan Yiu-Fai, "A 4K CMOS Erasable PROM", 1978 IEEE Internat. Solid-State Circuits Conf. (Digest of Tech. Papers), 1978, pp. 106-7.
36. E. Suzuki, "Nonvolatile Semiconductor Memory", J. Inst. Electron. and Commun. Eng. Jpn., Feb., 1978, pp. 189-92.
37. M. Kikuchi et al., "A DSA-Type Non-Volatile Memory Transistor with Self-Aligned Gates", Jpn. J. Appl. Phys., 1977, pp. 49-54.
38. G. Ramachandran, "Single-Supply Erasable PROM Saves Power with C-MOS Process", Electronics, July, 1978, pp. 106-11.
39. T. Ito et al., "10 V Write/Erase, EAROM Cells with Directly Nitrided Silicon Nitride Films as First Insulating Layers", IEEE, 1977 Internat. Electron Devices Meeting, 1977, pp. 284-6.
40. J.J. Barnes et al., "Operation and Characterization of N-Channel EPROM Cells", Solid-State Electron., March, 1978, pp. 521-9.
41. D.R. Wilson, "Cell Layout Boosts Speed of Low-Power 64-K ROM", Electronics, March, 1978, pp. 96-9.
42. R.G. Muller, "Electrically Reprogrammable MOS Semiconductor Fixed Memories, In Particular with Floating Gate", Digitale Speicher. (Digital Stores) , March, 1977, pp. 22-24.
43. P.A. Ernst, "Pulsing a PROM's Supply Voltage Greatly Reduces the Energy Used", Electron. Des., Aug., 1977, pp. 102.
44. L.B. Medwin and A.C. Ipri, "FACMOS EAROM", RCA Tech. Not., June, 1977, pp. 1-4.
45. T. Yamaga, "1K-Bit Non-Volatile Static RAM", JEE, Feb., 1977, pp. 38-9.
46. P.S. Smith, "AROM' A 4K Electrically Alterable Read Only Memory", Proc. of the IEEE 1977 Nat. Aerospace and Electronics Conf., NAECON '77, 1977, pp. 633-6.
47. M.L. Lonky et al., "VINRAM-An MOS/MNOS RAM", Proc. of the IEEE 1977 Nat. Aerospace and Electronics Conf., NAECON '77, 1977, pp. 628-32.

48. M.A. Horne and B.A. Brillhart, "A Military Grade 1024-Bit Nonvolatile Semiconductor RAM", Proc. of the IEEE 1977 Nat. Aerospace and Electronics Conf., NAECON '77, 1977, pp. 627.
49. J.E. Brewer et al., "Low Cost MNOS BORAM", Proc. of the IEEE 1977 Nat. Aerospace and Electronics Conf., NAECON '77, 1977, pp. 624-6.
50. L.F. Howard, "Nonvolatile Memory Structure", IBM Tech. Disclosure Bull., March, 1977, pp. 3675-6.
51. R.G. Stewart, "High-Density CMOS ROM Arrays", IEEE J. Solid-State Circuits, Oct., 1977, pp. 502-6.
52. R.G. Muller et al., "An 8192-Bit Electrically Alterable ROM Employing a One-Transistor Cell with Floating Gate", IEEE J. Solid-State Circuits, Oct., 1977, pp. 507-14.
53. P. Mars and B.J. Adamson, "Design of a Read-Only-Memory Programmer", Int. J. Electron, July, 1977, pp. 1-18.
54. J.L. Fagan et al., "A High Density Nonvolatile Charge-Addressed Memory (NOVCAM)", Proc. of the IEEE 1976 Nat. Aerospace and Electronics Conf., 1976, pp. 767-70.
55. C.A. Beltz and R. Fedorak, "MNOS Block Organized Random Access Memory System Development", Proc. of the IEEE 1976 Nat. Aerospace and Electronics Conf., 1976, pp. 751-5.
56. C.E. Collum and R.L. Wiker, "The Evolution of the MNOS EAROM and Its Application to Avionics and Other Military Systems", Proc. of the IEEE 1976 Nat. Aerospace and Electronics Conf., 1976, pp. 730-50.
57. J.I. Raffel and J.A. Yasaitis, "A Selection System for MNOS Capacitor Memories", IEEE, 1977 Nat. Solid-State Circuits Conf. (Digest of Tech. Papers), 1977, pp. 192-3.
58. J.E. Schroeder and R.L. Goslin, "A 1024-Bit, Fused-Link CMOS PROM", IEEE, 1977 Internat. Solid-State Circuits Conf. (Digest of Tech. Papers), 1977, pp. 190-1.
59. R.G. Muller et al., "Electrically Alterable 8192 Bit N-Channel MOS PROM", IEEE, 1977 Internat. Solid-State Circuits Conf. (Digest of Tech. Papers), 1977, pp. 188-9.
60. P.J. Salsbury et al., "High Performance MOS EPROMS Using a Stacked-Gate Cell", IEEE, 1977 Internat. Solid-State Circuits Conf. (Digest of Tech. Papers), 1977, pp. 186-7.
61. C.A. Neugebauer and J.F. Burgess, "Electrically Erasable Buried Gate PROM", IEEE, 1977 Internat. Solid-State Circuits Conf. (Digest of Tech. Papers), 1977, pp. 184-5.
62. W.H. Dodson and J.D. Heightley, "Bootstrap-Pumped Control Circuitry for an MNOS EAROM", IEEE, 1977 Internat. Solid-State Circuits Conf. (Digest of Tech. Papers), 1977, pp. 182-3.
63. W. Spence et al., "A Word Alterable ROM", IEEE, 1977 Internat. Solid-State Circuits Conf. (Digest of Tech. Papers), 1977, pp. 180-1.
64. J. Barnes et al., "Operation and Characterization of N-Channel EPROM Cells", IEEE, Internat. Electron Devices Meeting (Tech. Digest), 1976, pp. 173-7.
65. R.M. McLouski, "Interface Modification to Enhance DC and Pulse Response of MNOS Memory Transistors", Electrochemical Soc. Fall Meeting, 1976, pp. 805-7.
66. T. Matsuo et al., "1 K-Bit Nonvolatile Semiconductor RAM", Toshiba Rev., March-April, 1977, pp. 25-8.
67. T. Wada, "Electrically Reprogrammable ROM Using N-Channel Memory Transistors with Floating Gate", Solid-State Electron., July, 1977, pp. 623-7.
68. T. Hagiwara et al., "Analysis and Experimentation on FIMOS (N-Channel FAMOS) Devices", 1976 Internat. Conf. on Solid State Devices, Sept., 1976, pp. 1-3.
69. S. Koike et al., "A New Two-Terminal C-MNOS Memory Cell", 1976 Internat. Conf. on Solid State Devices, Sept., 1976, pp. 1-3.
70. S. Koike, "Nonvolatile Static Read/Write Memory Cell Using CMNOS Structure", IEEE Trans. Electron Devices, Aug., 1977, pp. 1098-102.
71. B. Rossler, "Electrically Erasable and Reprogrammable Read-Only Memory Using the N-Channel SIMOS One-Transistor Cell", IEEE Trans. Electron Devices, May, 1977, pp. 606-10.
72. D. Kahng et al., "Avalanche Punch-Through Erase (APTE) Mode in Dual-Dielectric Charge-Storage (DDC) Cells", IEEE Trans. Electron Devices, May, 1977, pp. 531-5.
73. J.J. Chang, "Theory of MNOS Memory Transistor", IEEE Trans. Electron Devices, May, 1977, pp. 511-18.
74. C.A. Neugebauer, "Electrically Erasable Buried-Gate Nonvolatile Read-Only Memory", IEEE Trans. Electron Devices, May, 1977, pp. 613-18.
75. W. Spence et al., "A 4096-Bit Word-Alterable ROM", IEEE Trans. Electron Devices, May, 1977, pp. 610-13.
76. W.M. Gosney, "DIFMOS-A Floating-Gate Electrically Erasable Nonvolatile Semiconductor Memory Technology", IEEE Trans. Electron Devices, May, 1977, pp. 594-9.
77. Y. Hsia, "MNOS LSI Memory Device Data Retention Measurements and Projections", IEEE Trans. Electron Devices, May, 1977, pp. 568-77.
78. Y. Uchida, "Avalanche-Tunnel Injection in MNOS Transistor", IEEE Trans. Electron Devices, June, 1977, pp. 688-93.
79. A. Scheibe and H. Schulte, "Technology of a New N-Channel One-Transistor EAROM Cell Called SIMOS", IEEE Trans. Electron Devices, May, 1977, pp. 600-6.
80. A.V. Ferris-Prabhu, "Charge Transfer by Direct Tunneling in Thin-Oxide Memory Transistors", IEEE Trans. Electron Devices, May, 1977, pp. 524-30.
81. J.I. Raffel and J.A. Yasaitis, "Storage Experiments With Ultra-High Density MNOS Capacitors", Proc. IEEE, Nov., 1976, pp. 1629-30.
82. R. Greene et al.,"The Biggest Erasable PROM Yet Puts 16384 Bits on a Chip", Electronics, March, 1977, pp. 108-11.
83. J.W. Kelley and D.F. Millet, "An Electrically Alterable ROM-And It Doesn't Use Nitride", Electronics, Dec., 1976, pp. 101-4.
84. Y. Rai et al., "Electrically Reprogrammable Nonvolatile Semiconductor Memory with MNMOOS (metal-Nitride-Molybdenum-Oxide-Silicon) Structure", IEEE, 1975 Internat. Electron Devices Meeting (Tech. Digest), 1975, pp. 313-16.
85. R.J. Lodi et al., "MNOS-BORAM Memory Characteristics", IEEE J. Solid-State Circuits, Oct., 1976, pp. 622-30.
86. R.M. Greene, "A 32K ROM Using Differential RAMP Techniques", IEEE, 1976 IEEE Internat. Solid-State Circuits Conf. (Digest of Tech. Papers), 1976, pp. 186-7.
87. T.J. Rodgers et al., "VMOS ROM", 1976 IEEE Internat. Solid-State Circuits Conf. (Digest of Tech. Papers), 1976, pp. 60-1, 232.
88. J.R. Cricchi et al., "Space Charge Effects in MNOS Memory Devices and Endurance Measurements", IEEE, 1975 Ieternat. Electron Devices Meeting (Tech. Digest), 1975, pp. 459-62.
89. T.H. Ning et al., "Threshold Instability in IGFET's Due to Emission of Leakage Electrons from Silicon Substrate into Silicon Dioxide", Appl. Phys. Lett., Aug., 1976, pp. 198-200.
90. H. Kawagoe and N. Tsuji, "Minimum Size ROM Structure Compatible with Silicon-Gate E/D MOS LSI", IEEE J. Solid-State Circuits, June, 1976, pp. 360-4.
91. J.F. Dickson, "On-Chip High-Voltage Generation in

91. cont'd.
MNOS Integrated Circuits Using an Improved Voltage Multiplier Technique", IEEE J. Solid-State Circuits, June, 1976, pp. 374-8.
92. H. Iizuka et al., "Electrically Alterable Avalanche-Injection-Type MOS Read-Only Memory with Stacked-Gate Structure (SAMOS)", IEEE Trans. Electron Devices, April, 1976, pp. 379-87.
93. Y. Uchida et al., "A 1024-Bit MNOS RAM Using Avalanche-Tunnel Injection", IEEE J. Solid-State Circuits, Oct., 1975, pp. 288-93.
94. R.A. Kenyon and B.H. Yun, "Density Improvement in MNOS Array by Overlapping Gate Electrodes", IBM Tech. Disclosure Bull., June, 1975, pp. 68-9.
95. G. Carlstedt et al., "A Content-Addressable Memory Cell With MNOS Transistors", IEEE J. Solid-State Circuits, Oct., 1973, pp. 338-43.

10—MOSFET Device/Circuit Reliability and Testing

1. S.W. Levine, "Alpha Emission Measurement of Lids and Solder Preforms on Semiconductor Packages", IEEE Trans. Components, Hybrids and Manuf. Tech., Dec., 1979, pp. 391-5.
2. J.A. Woolley et al., "Low Alpha-Particle-Emitting Ceramics' What's the Lower Limit? (For Dynamic RAM and CCD Memories Encapsulation)", IEEE Trans. Hybrids and Manuf. Technol., Dec., 1979, pp. 388-91.
3. T.C. May, "Soft Errors in VLSI' Present and Future" , IEEE Trans. Components, Hybrids and Manuf. Technol., Dec., 1979, pp. 377-87.
4. P.W. Peterson, "The Performance of Plastic-Encapsulated CMOS Microcircuits in a Humid Environment", IEEE Trans. Components, Hybrids and Manuf. Technol., Dec., 197 , pp. 422-.
5. E.E. King, "Radiation-Hardening Static NMOS RAMs", IEEE Trans. Nucl. Sci., Dec., 1975, pp. 5060-4.
6. C.S. Guenzer et al., "Single Event Upset of Dynamic RAMs by Neutrons and Protons", IEEE Trans. Nucl. Sci., Dec., 1975, pp. 5048-52.
7. L.L. Sivo et al., "Cosmic Ray-Induced Soft Errors in Static MOS Memory Cells", IEEE Trans. Nucl. Sci., Dec., 1975, pp. 5042-7.
8. G.J. Brucker, "Application of Simple Hardening Techniques in System Design and Verification of Survival by EMP and Gamma Tests (CMOS/SOS Memory Circuits)", IEEE Trans. Nucl. Sci., Dec., 197 , pp. 4949-52.
9. J.T. Nelson et al., "Alpha Particle Tracks in Silicon and Their Effect on Dynamic MOS RAM Reliability", IEEE, 1978 Internat. Electron Devices Meeting, 197 , Session 2/1.
10. W. Nasswetter, "Failure Analysis on a 65K MOS RAM With a New Type of Memory Display", IEE, Fifth European Solid State Circuits Conf. - ESSCIRC 79, 1979, pp. 113-15.
11. D.J.W. Noorlag et al., "The Effect of Alpha-Particle-Induced Soft Errors on Memory Systems with Error Correction", IEE, Fifth European Solid State Circuits Conf. - ESSCIRC 79, 1979, pp. 86-8.
12. R.W. Stevens and J.R. Brailsford, "Cost Effective Semiconductor Memory Testing", IEE, Fifth European Solid State Circuits conf. - ESSCIRC 79, 1979, pp. 82-5.
13. D.L. Crook, "Techniques of Evaluating Long Term Oxide Reliability at Wafer Level (MOS Memory Devices)", IEEE, 1978 Internat. Electron Devices Meeting, 1978, pp. 444-8.
14. R. Kondo, "Test Patterns for EPROMS", IEEE J. Solid-State Circuits, Aug., 1979, pp. 730-4.
15. K.O. Jeppson and C.M. Svensson, "Retention Testing of MNOS LSI Memories", IEEE J. Solid-State Circuits, Aug., 1979, pp. 723-9.
16. C.W. Green, "PMOS Dynamic RAM Reliability = A Case Study", IEEE, 17th Annual Proceedings Reliability Physics, 1979, pp. 213-19.
17. G. Schindlbeck, "Analysis of Dynamic RAMs By Use of Alpha Irradiation", IEEE, 17th Annual Proc. Reliability Physics, 1979, pp. 30-4.
18. C.C. Huang et al., "Component/System Correlation of Alpha Induced Dynamic RAM Soft Failure Rates", IEEE, 17th Annual Proc. Reliability Physics, 1979, pp. 23-9.
19. H.P. Gibbons and J.D. Pittman, "Alpha Particle Emissions of Some Materials in Electronic Packages", IEEE, Proc. of the 29th Electronic Components Conf., 1979, pp. 257-60.
20. T.C. May, "Soft Errors in VLSI-Present and Future", IEEE, Proc. of the 29th Electronics Components Conf., 1979, pp. 247-56.
21. J.W. Peeples, "Electrical Bias Level Influence on the Results of Plastic Encapsulated NMOS 4K RAMs", IEEE Trans. Electron Devices, Jan., 1979, pp. 72-7.
22. H.A. Batdorf et al., "Reliability Program and Results for a 4K Dynamic RAM", IEEE Trans. Electron Devices, Jan., 1979, pp. 52-6.
23. D.S. Yaney et al., "Alpha-Particle Tracks in Silicon and their Effect on Dynamic MOS RAM Reliability" , IEEE Trans. Electron Devices, Jan., 1979, pp. 10-16.
24. J.M. Waddell, "Achieving Quality and Reliability in Memories", New Electron, March, 1979, pp. 30, 32, 35, 37, 39-40.
25. H. Roder, "Quality Test of Semiconductor Memories by Jitter Measurement", Electron. Lett., July, 1979, pp. 428-9.
26. J.A. Roberts, "A Design Review Approach Toward Dynamic RAM Reliability", Microelectron. and Reliab., Jan.-Feb., 1979, pp. 97-105.
27. G.J. Brucker and L. Thurlow, "Memory Behaviour in a Radiation Environment", Electron. Eng., Jan., 1979, pp. 67, 70-1.
28. J.E. Arsenault and D.C. Roberts, "MOS Semiconductor Random Access Memory Failure Rate", Microelectron. and Reliab., Jan.-Feb., 1979, pp. 81-8.
29. L.J. Gallace and H.L. Pujol, "Improving COS/MOS Reliability", Electron, Nov., 1978, pp. 27.
30. R. Freeman and A. Holmes-Siedle, "A Simple Model for Predicting Radiation Effects in MOS Devices", IEEE Trans. Nucl. Sci., Dec., 1978, pp. 1216-25.
31. M. Schlenther et al., "'In Situ' Radiation Tolerance Tests of MOS RAMs", IEEE Trans. Nucl. Sci., Dec., 1978, pp. 1209-15.
32. P.J. Vail, "A Survey of Radiation Hardened Microelectronic Memory Technology", IEEE Trans. Nucl. Sci., Dec., 1978, pp. 1196-204.
33. T.P. Haraszti, "Radiation Hardened CMOS/SOS Memory Circuits", IEEE Trans. Nucl. Sci., Dec., 1978, pp. 1187-95.
34. R.W. Tallon, "Ionizing Radiation Effects on the Sperry Rand Nonvolatile 256-Bit MNOS RAM Array (SR2256)", IEEE Trans. Nucl. Sci., Dec., 1978, pp. 1176-80.
35. A. London and R.C. Wang, "Dose Rate and Extended Dose Characterization of Radiation Hardened Metal Gate CMOS Integrated Circuits", IEEE Trans. Nucl. Sci., Dec., 1978, pp. 1172-5.
36. J.C. Pickel and J.T. Blandford, Jr., "Cosmic Ray Induced Errors in MOS Memory Cells", IEEE Trans. Nucl. Sci., Dec., 1978, pp. 1166-71.
37. J.H. Fusselman, "Memory Tester Correlation", IEEE, 1978 Semiconductor Test Conf., 1978, pp. 240-2.
38. R. O'Keefe et al., "Test Patterns for Static RAMs", IEEE, 1978 Semiconductor Test Conf., 1978, pp. 86-8.
39. T.P. Haraszti, "CMOS/SOS Memory Circuits for Radiation Environments", IEEE J. Solid-State Circuits, Oct., 1978, pp. 669-76.
40. L.J. Gallace, "Reliability of CMOS Circuits", New Electron., April, 1978, pp. 48, 50, 53, 56, 58, 60, 62.

41. J.W. Peeples, "Influence of Electrical Bias Level on 85/85 Test Results of Plastic Encapsulated 4K RAMs", IEEE, Reliability Physics 16th Annual Proc. 1978, 1978, pp. 154-60.
42. H.P. Feuerbaum et al., "Quantitative Measurement with High Time Resolution of Internal Waveforms on MOS RAMs Using a Modified Scanning Electron Microscope", IEEE J. Solid-State Circuits, June, 1978, pp. 319-25.
43. R.M. Alexander, "Accelerated Testing in Famos Devices-8K EPROM", IEEE, Reliability Physics 16th Annual Proc., 1978, 1978, pp. 229-32.
44. H.A. Batdorf et al., "Reliability Evaluation Program and Results for a 4K Dynamic RAM", IEEE, Reliability Physics 16th Annual Proc., 1978, 1978, pp. 14-18.
45. R.C. Foss, "Electrical Testing for Design Verification and Operating Margins (MOS Dynamic RAM)", IEEE, Reliability Physics 16th Annual Proc. 1978, 1978, pp. 75.
46. A.J. Gonzales and M.W. Powell, "Resolution of MOS One-Transistor, Dynamic RAM Bit Failures Using SEM Stroboscopic Techniques", J. Vac. Sci. and Technol., May-June, 1978, pp. 1043-6.
47. A. Aitken and P. Kung, "The Influence of Design and Process Parameters on the Reliability of CMOS Integrated Circuits", Microelectron. and Reliab., Jan., 1978, pp. 201-10.
48. R.V. Pappu et al., "Screening Methods and Experience with MOS Memory (Reliability)", Microelectron. and Reliab., Jan., 1978, pp. 193-9.
49. D.D. Rinerson and A. Tuszynski, "Identification of Causes of Pattern Sensitivity (RAMs Testing)", IEEE, 1977 Semiconductor Test Symposium, 1977, pp. 166-70.
50. J.G. Taylor, "Test Implications of Higher Speed 16K RAMs", IEEE, 1977 Semiconductor Test Symposium, 1977, pp. 171-5.
51. L.L. Morgan, "Testing 4K RAMs For the Minicomputer Manufacturer", IEEE, 1977 Semiconductor Test Symposium, 1977, pp. 158-65.
52. J.M. Patterson, "Failures Due to Pinholes in Polysilicon Conductors in CMOS Memory Devices", IEEE, ATFA 77, 1977, pp. 60-3.
53. J.R. Cricchi et al., "Radiation Hardened CMNOS/SOS Programmable ROM and General Processor Unit", IEEE Trans. Nucl. Sci., Dec., 1977, pp. 2236-43.
54. J.R. Cricchi et al., "Hardened MNOS/SOS Electrically Reprogrammable Nonvolatile Memory", IEEE Trans. Nucl. Sci., Dec., 1977, pp. 2185-9.
55. T.C. Lo and M.R. Guidry, "An Integrated Test Concept and Switched-Capacitor Dynamic MOS RAM's", IEEE J. Solid-State Circuits, Dec., 1977, pp. 693-703.
56. G.P. Nelson and E.E. King, "Methods for Radiation Testing Random Access Memories and LSI Circuits", IEEE Trans. Nucl. Sci., Dec., 1977, pp. 2341-6.
57. L.L. Sivo and P.R. Measel, "Radiation Hardness of CMOS LSI Circuits", IEEE Trans. Nucl. Sci., Dec., 1977, pp. 2219-25.
58. C.R. Barrett and R.C. Smith, "Failure Modes and Reliability of Dynamic RAMs", 14th IEEE Computer Soc. Internat. Conf., 1977, pp. 179-82.
59. R.W. Owen, "Optimized Testing of 16K RAMs", 14th IEEE Computer Soc. Internat. Conf., 1977, pp. 183-5.
60. J.C. McDonald and P.T. McCracken, "Testing For High Reliability (Digital ICS)", 14th IEEE Computer Soc. Internat. Conf., 1977, pp. 190-1.
61. M.J. Fox, "A Comparison of the Performance of Plastic and Ceramic Encapsulations Based on Evaluation of CMOS Integrated Circuits", Microelectron. and Reliab., 1977, pp. 251-4.
62. C.H. Sie et al., "Soft Failure Modes in MOS RAMs", IEEE, 15th Annual Proc. Reliability Physics, 1977, pp. 27-32.
63. M.L. Malwah et al., "Hot Carrier Injection in the Dual Polysilicon Gate Structure and its Related Reliability Effects on Dynamic RAM Refresh Time", IEEE, 15th Annual Proc. Reliability Physics, 1977, pp. 23-6.
64. S. Shabde et al., "Moisture Induced Failure Mode in a Plastic Encapsulated Dynamic Timing Circuit", IEEE, 15th Annual Proc. Reliability Physics, 1977, pp. 33-6.
65. W.R. Ortner and J.T. Clemens, "A Reliability Failure Mode in Dynamic MOS Circuits - The Unopened Metal to Polysilicon Contact Window and the Floating Gate Transistors", IEEE, 15th Annual Proc. Reliability Physics, 1977, pp. 16-22.
66. B. Euzent, "Hot Electron Injection Efficiency in IGFET Structures", IEEE, 15th Annual Proc. Reliab. Physics, 1977, pp. 1-4.
67. C.R. Barrett and R.C. Smith, "Failure Modes and Reliability of Dynamic RAMs", IEEE, Internat. Electron Devices Meeting (Tech. Digest), 1976, pp. 319-22.
68. G. Gear, "FAMOS PROM Reliability Studies", IEEE, 14th Annual Proc. Reliability Physics, 1976, pp. 198-201.
69. F.L. Schuermeyer, "Test Results on an MNOS Memory Array", IEEE Trans. Electron Devices, May, 1977, pp. 564-8.
70. S.A. Abbas and R.C. Dockerty, "Hot Electron Induced Degradation of N-Channel IGFETS", IEEE, 14th Annual Proc. Reliability Physics, 1976, pp. 38-41.
71. S.A. Abbas and E.E. Davidson, "Reliability Implications of Hot Electron Generation and Parasitic Bipolar Action in an IGFET Device", IEEE, 14th Annual Proc. Reliability Physics, 1976, pp. 18-22.
72. D.C. Kliment et al., "Architecture an Performance of Radiation-Hardened 64-Bit SOS/MNOS Memory", IEEE Trans. Nucl. Sci., Dec., 1976, pp. 1749-55.
73. D.K. Myers, "Radiation Effects on Commerical 4-Kilobit NMOS Memories", IEEE Trans. Nucl. Sci., Dec., 1976, pp. 1732-7.
74. R.A. Kjar et al., "Radiation Hardened 64-Bit CMOS/SOS RAM", IEEE Trans. Nucl. Sci., Dec., 1976, pp. 1728-31.
75. T.M. Madzy, "FET Circuit Destruction Caused by Electrostatic Discharge", IEEE Trans. Electron Devices, Sept., 1976, pp. 1099-103.
76. W.S. Richardson, "Diagnostic Testing of MOS Random Access Memories", Solid State Technol., March, 1975, pp. 31-4.
77. E.D. Colbourne et al., "Reliability of MOS LSI Circuits", Proc. IEEE, Feb., 1974, pp. 244-59.

Author Index

A

Ahlquist, C. N., 382
Aitken, A., 160
Asai, S., 97

B

Baitinger, U. G., 374
Bartelink, D. J., 115
Bassous, E., 77
Blaser, E. M., 62
Boddie, J. R., 348
Boll, H. J., 315, 449
Brews, J. R., 112
Burgess, J. F., 47

C

Caywood, J. M., 452
Cenker, R. P., 424
Chatterjee, P. K., 258
Clark, K. L., 390
Clemons, D. G., 424
Conrad, D. A., 62
Cook, P. W., 65, 89, 218, 331
Critchlow, D. L., 65, 164

D

Daryanani, G. T., 348
Davis, R. E., 149
Dennard, R. H., 77, 89
Di Lonardo, V., 218
Doering, E., 310
Doken, M., 339

E

Easley, R. L., 258
Ebel, A. V., 136, 382, 387
Eldumiati, I. I., 348
El-Mansy, Y. A., 37, 118, 172
Elmasry, M. I., 4, 172

F

Fichtner, W., 112
Field, R. L., 149
Foss, R. C., 301, 303
Foster, M. J., 204
Freedman, D. R., 218
Fu, C. H., 395
Fu, H-S., 258
Fuls, E. N., 449

G

Gadenz, R. N., 348
Gaensslen, F. H., 77, 89
Gibbons, J. F., 184
Gunter, T., 364

H

Hamdy, E. Z., 172
Harland, R., 303
Hartman, J. M., 390
Hashimoto, N., 29, 182
Heller, L. G., 321
Hirao, T., 153, 285
Ho, C. W., 331
Holler, M., 466
Hong, N. H., 420
Hori, R., 422
Horiuchi, S., 285, 404
Huber, W. R., 424
Hui, C-H., 136, 387

I

Ieda, N., 296
Iizuka, T., 290, 401
Inagaki, Y., 447
Ishihara, T., 404
Itoh, K., 422

J

Jecmen, R. M., 136, 382, 387, 392
Johnson, W. S., 463, 466
Joynson, R. E., 47

K

Kamigaki, Y., 422
Kaneko, H., 290
Katto, H., 422
Kawakami, Y., 346
Kawamoto, H., 422
Keyes, R. W., 187
Kikuchi, H., 461
Kimura, T., 339
Kitano, Y., 461
Kobayashi, K., 447
Kohda, S., 461
Kohyama, S., 290, 401
Kokkonen, K. R., 382, 395
Kondo, S., 404
Kondo, T., 401
Koomen, J., 55
Kubo, M., 105
Kuhn, G., 463, 466
Kung, H. T., 204
Kynett, V., 136, 387

L

Larsen, R. A., 432
Leach, G. S., 390
LeBlanc, A. R., 77
Lee, K. F., 184
Liu, S. S., 392, 395
Lyman, J., 124
Lynch, W. T., 315

M

Mahan Rao, G. R., 420
Masuda, H., 105, 422
Masuhara, T., 29, 182, 398
Matsue, S., 447
May, P., 326
McKenny, V. G., 385
Mead, C. A., 196, 231
Meindl, J. D., 115
Minato, O., 182, 398
Mizutani, Y., 290
Mohsen, A. M., 231
Morgan, W. L., 294
Morse, S. P., 355
Mundy, J. L., 47
Murota, J., 296

N

Nagata, M., 29
Nakai, M., 105

Nakamura, H., 398
Nelson, J. T., 449
Neugebauer, C., 47
Nicollian, E. H., 112
Nishitani, T., 346
Nozawa, H., 290

O

Ochii, K., 401
O'Connell, T. R., 390
Ohmori, Y., 296
Ohta, K., 178
Ohtani, T., 401
Ohwada, N., 339
Ohzone, T., 153, 285, 404
Okuda, T., 447
Osburn, C. M., 164
Owen, J. M., 392
Owen, S. W., 452
Owen, W. H., III, 382, 392

P

Parrillo, L. C., 149
Parrish, J. T., 218
Pashley, R. D., 382, 387, 392, 395
Pathak, J. C., 452
Pathak, S., 466
Payne, R. S., 149
Pedersen, R. A., 348
Perlegos, G., 294, 463, 466
Petrizzi, J. B., 424
Pohlman, W. B., 355
Posa, J. G., 407
Procyk, F. J., 424
Proebsting, R. J., 418

Q

Queyssac, D., 351

R

Ranganath, T. R., 463
Ratnakumar, K. N., 115
Ravenel, B. W., 355
Redwine, D. J., 420
Reisman, A., 164
Reitsma, M., 466
Rem, M., 196
Remshardt, R., 374
Renninger, A., 463, 466
Reutlinger, G. W., 149
Rideout, V. L., 77, 271

S

Sakai, S., 461
Sakai, Y., 182, 398
Salsbury, P. J., 294
Sasaki, T., 398
Schiereck, F. C., 326
Schoen, P., 382
Schroeder, P. R., 418
Schuster, S. E., 218, 331
Shappir, J., 392, 395
Shimizu, K., 178
Shimura, H., 153
Shiragasawa, T., 404
Sihling, A., 310
Simko, R. T., 294
Skupnjak, J. A., 466
Smith, R. J., 136, 387, 392, 395
Stein, K. U., 310
Stewart, R. G., 456
Stritter, E., 364
Sugimoto, E., 346
Suzuki, M., 346
Sze, S. M., 112

T

Takayanagi, S., 285
Tameda, M., 447
Tanimoto, M., 296
Tarui, Y., 178
Tasch, A. F., Jr., 258
Taylor, G. W., 258
Terman, L. M., 65, 243
Thompson, J. S., 348
Toyabe, T., 97
Trout, G. M., 424
Tsuji, K., 153, 285, 404

U

Uchibori, K., 398

V

Van Buren, G. L., 452
Van den Akker, J., 55

W

Wada, T., 447
Walker, E. J., 89
Walters, S. M., 348
White, L. S., Jr., 420
Wollesen, D. L., 141

Y

Yamada, K., 178
Yamamoto, H., 447
Yamauchi, E., 346
Yasui, T., 398
Yau, L. D., 449
Yu, H-N., 77, 164

Subject Index

A

Address buffers, 294, 418
Advanced MOS technology
  for 4K statis RAM, 382
Amplifiers
  sense, 241, 294, 301, 303, 321, 404, 420
Architecture
  dynamic RAM, 424
  Motorola 68000, 364
  16-bit microprocessor, 355
Automatic refresh dynamic memory
  random access, 449

B

Bibliographies
  comprehensive, 469
Biography
  author (M. I. Elmasry), 489
Bootstrapping, xi, i
  in MOS circuits, 47
  loads, 4
Bulk CMOS RAM
  fully static 16 Kb, 401
Bulk silicon
  for CMOS inverter, 184
  for VLSI CMOS, 160
Buried load logic
  MOS, 182

C

Canned software
  single-chip microcomputer, 351
Charge-transfer sense amplifiers, 321
Clock generators, 218
Clock sequencing, 303
CMOS, 1, 4, 326
  inverters, 184
  LSI, 141, 339
  RAM, 290, 401
  ROM, 456
  SDW, 172
  silicon-gate, 153
  twin-tub, 149
  VLSI circuits, 149, 160
Comparators, 204
Coupling systems
  general-purpose computers, 204
  IBM, 374
  microprocessors, 218, 294, 331, 355, 364
  use of VLSI, 196
Content-addressable memory
  VLSI, 196
Cross-coupled charge-transfer sense amplifiers, 321

D

Data I/O buffers, 401
Data processing, 323
Decoder gates
  standard NOR, 420
Decoders
  CMOS, 456
  column, 404
  row, 294, 392, 404, 418, 424
Depletion-mode FET, 62
Depletion-mode IGFET, 37
Depletion-type load elements, 29
  MOSFET logic circuits, 65
DFT, 339
Digital circuits
  MOS, 1, 47
Digital electronics
  evolution towards VLSI, 187
Digital filters, 339
Digital integrated circuits
  bibliography, 469
  CMOS, 153, 160
  extrapolation through remainder of this century, 187
  MOS, 323
  MOSFET, 77, 469
  SDW, 172
  tutorial, 4
  VLSI, 73, 160
Digital signal processing
  bibliography, 469
  for voiceband applications, 346
  for telecommunication applications, 348
  programmable, 348
  use of LSI, 339
Double-poly MOS technology
  scaled, 395
dRAM (dynamic RAM), 258
  one-device cells, 271
DSP *see* Digital signal processing

Dynamic flip-flop sensors
  optimization of latching pulse, 315
Dynamic memories
  automatic refresh, 449
  bibliography, 469
  fault-tolerant, 424
  SAMOS, 432
  5-V only, 420, 422
  16-K × 1 bit, 418
  64-K and larger, 407, 420, 422, 424
  256-K, 447

E

E/D NMOS VLSI
  performance limits, 115
Electrically erasable nonvolatile memory
  16-Kb, 463
Elmasry, Dr. M. I.
  author, 489
English language programming
  single-chip microcomputer, 351
Enhancement devices *see* E/D NMOS VLSI
EPROM's, 390, 463
  bibliography, 469
  MOS, 294
  use of scaled MOS technology, 466
Erasable nonvolatile memory
  16-Kb, 463
Etching, 124

F

Fault-tolerant 64-K dynamic RAM, 424
FET (field effect transistors)
  depletion-mode IGFET, 37
  logic configuration, 62
  VMOS, 271
FFT, 339
Flip-flops, 301, 303
  dynamic sensors, 315
  gated, 310
  NMOS, 4
  optimum latchup, 315
  static, 4
Fourier transforms, 339
Full wafer ROM
  4-Mb, 461

G

Gettering, 124, 432

H

HCMOS
  statis RAM's, 398, 401
HMOS fabrication 136

I

IGFET, 315
  depletion-mode, 37
Integrated circuits
  beam processing, 124
  computer systems, 196
  development trends, xi
  etching, 124
  highly miniaturized, 77
  lithography, 124, 164
  LSI, xi, 29, 141, 339
  medium scale, xi
  MOS, 4, 29, 73
  silicides, 124
  small scale, xi
  VLSI, xi, 1, 73
Intel 8086 microprocessors, 355
Inverters, 182
  CMOS, 184
  depletion-load, 29, 231
  E/D, 115
  MOST, 55
  NMOS, 4
  SOS/CMOS, 160
  static, 4, 452
Ion-beam milling, 124
Ion implantation, 432
  Si-gate n-well CMOS, 153
Ion-implanted MOSFET's
  with small dimensions, 77

J

JFET, 182

L

Large capacitor lines
  driving and sensing signals, 231
Laser-recrystallized polysilicon, 184
Latching pulse
  for dynamic flip-flop sensors, 315
LATV (logic and array test vehicle) devices, 164
Lithography, 124, 164
LOCMOS, 326
Logic arrays, 164, 331
  in LOCMOS, 326
Logic circuits
  bibliographies, 469
  FET, 62
  MOS buried load, 182
  MOSFET, 65, 218, 469
Logic gates
  static, 4
LSI (large scale integration)
  early development, xi
  for digital signal processing, 339

M

Memories
  associative system, 196
  C-MOS processes, 141
  content-addressable, 196
  dynamic, 407
  Intel 8086 microprocessor, 355
  MOS cells and circuits, 241, 296, 301
  MOSFET, 243, 374
  nonvolatile, 463
  one-transistor, 310
  RAM, 136, 178, 196, 258, 271, 285, 301, 382, 385, 387, 390, 392, 395
  read-only, 29
  ROM, 456, 461
  TTL-compatible, 29
Microprocessors and microcomputers
  architecture, 355, 364
  bibliography, 469
  Intel 8080, 355
  Intel 8086, 355
  Motorola, 364
  projection of VLSI impact, 351
  single-chip, 351
  third-generation, 351
  world market, 351
Miniaturization
  MOSFET, 112
  NMOS, 243

MOS, 4, 73
buried load logic, 182
device characteristics, 4
digital circuits, 1, 323
EPROM, 466
memory cells and circuits, 241, 285, 294, 382, 385, 395, 424
n-channel, 29
PROM, 296
QSA, 178
scaling, 118
MOS circuits
dynamic, 4, 301
EPROM, 294
threshold losses, 47
VLSI, 73
MOS/CMOS, 153
MOSFET, 1, 73, 153
bibliography, 469
ion-implanted, 77
logic circuits, 65
memory circuits, 243, 285, 310, 374
miniaturization, 112
scaled-down, 105
short-channel, 97, 105
single-device-well, 172
VLSI, 89, 164, 178, 218
MOST inverters
with improved switching speed, 55
Motorola 68000 mincroprocessors, 364
MSI (medium scale integration), xi
Multiple resists, 124
Multiplier LSI
CMOS, 339

N

NMOS, 1, 4
SDW, 172
source follower, 4
static inverters, 4
transmission gates, 4
VLSI, 115
NMOS/CMOS technology
for static RAM, 404
Nonvolatile memories
electrically erasable, 463
NOR circuits, 89, 218
decoder gate, 420

O

On-chip registers, 432
One-device cells
for dynamic RAM, 271
One-gate-wide CMOS inverters
on laser-recrystallized polysilicon, 184
One-transistor cell MOS RAM
peripheral circuits, 303

P

Packaging problems
of memories, 407
Pattern matching chips, 204
Peripheral circuits
for one-transistor cell MOS RAM's, 303
Phase locked loops
digital, 339
PLA (programmed logic array), 164, 218
in LOCMOS, 326
macros, 331
PLL *see* Phase locked loops
Polysilicon, 407, 418, 432
for CMOS RAM, 290
laser-recrystallized, 184
plasma-etched, 124
processing, 149
resistors, 296
variable resistance, 290
Polysilicon transistors, 290
PROM, 241, 390
bibliography, 469
MOS, 296
Push-pull drivers, 4

Q

Quadruply self-aligned MOS, 178

R

RAM, 243
automatic refresh dynamic, 449
bibliography, 469
CMOS, 290, 401
dynamic, 258, 271, 301, 407, 418, 420, 422, 424, 447, 469
fault-tolerant, 424
fully static, 401
high-density, 258
MOS, 178, 301, 303, 382, 385, 395, 424
SAMOS, 432
self-refreshing, 452
static, 136, 241, 285, 382, 385, 387, 390, 392, 395, 398, 404
VLSI, 196
Read-only memories, 29, 331
bibliography, 469
CMOS, 456
4-Mb full wafer, 461
Read/write memory chips
2048-bit, 374
Register macros, 218, 331
ROM *see* Read-only memories
ROS (read only storage) *see* Read-only memories
Row decoders, 294, 392, 418, 424

S

SAMOS (Si and Al MOS) technology
for dynamic memories, 432
Scaled-down devices, 77
MOSFET, 105
Scaling
MOS, 118, 136, 466
MOSFET, 77, 97
VLSI, 124
Self-refreshing 4-K RAM
with sub-mW standby power, 452
Sense amplifiers, 241, 294, 301, 303, 404
charge transfer, 321
dynamic, 420
Sense/refresh circuits
for single-transistor memory cells, 310
Sensors
flip-flop, 315
Shift registers, 243
on-chip, 432
variable length, 339
Short-channel MOSFET, 105
analytical models, 97
Signal processing, 323
digital, 339, 346, 348, 469
Signals
driving and sensing, 231
Silicides, 124
Silicon-gate MOSFET, 89
Single-device-well MOSFET's,

CAD simulation, 172
SOS
for VLSI CMOS, 160
SOS/CMOS technology
for CMOS ROM arrays, 456
Source followers
NMOS, 4
SSI (small scale integration) bipolar chips, xi
Static inverters, 452
NMOS, 4
Static RAM's
bibliography, 469
HCMOS, 398, 401
64-Kb, 404
Storage arrays
for single-transistor memory cells, 310
Substrate-bias generators, 4
for single 5-V, 64-K dynamic RAM, 422

T

Telecommunications
use of digital signal processors, 348
TTL-compatible ROM, 29
Tutorial papers
on digital MOS integrated circuits, 4
Twin-tub CMOS
for VLSI circuits, 149

V

Varactor coupling, 47
VLSI (very large scale integrated circuits)
bibliography, 469
CMOS, 160
computing structures, 196
development trends, xi
digital, 73, 323
digital electronics, 187
impact on microprocessors, 351
MOSFET, 89, 164, 178, 218, 469
NMOS, 112
QSA, MOS, 178
scaling, 118, 124
signal transmission, 231
special-purpose chips, 204
twin-tub CMOS, 149
VMOS, 258
FET, 271
Voiceband applications
single-chip digital signal processors, 346

W

Weinberger image, 218

Editor's Biography

Mohamed I. Elmasry was born in Cairo, Egypt on December 24, 1943. He received the B.Sc. degree from Cairo University and the M.A. Sc. and the Ph.D. degrees from the University of Ottawa, Ottawa, Ontario, Canada in 1965, 1970, and 1974, all in Electrical Engineering.

Dr. Elmasry has worked in the area of integrated circuits design for the last fifteen years. He was with the Department of Electrical Engineering, Cairo University from 1965 to 1968 as an instructor and research assistant, and was with the Department of Electrical Engineering, University of Ottawa, from 1968 to 1971 as a teaching and research assistant. As a member of the scientific staff of Bell-Northern Research, Ottawa, from 1971 to 1974, he designed communications LSI chips using bipolar, NMOS, and CMOS technologies. Since 1974 he has been with the Department of Electrical Engineering, University of Waterloo, Waterloo, Ontario, Canada, where he is an Associate Professor. He has served as a consultant in the area of LSI/VLSI functional modeling and circuit/subsystem design for R & D Laboratories in Canada and the U.S., including Bell Laboratories, Linear Technology, Xerox, and Bell-Northern Research. During 1980–1981 he was at the Micro-components Organization, Burroughs Corporation in San Diego, California, on leave from the University of Waterloo.

Dr. Elmasry has authored or coauthored over thirty papers on LSI circuits, including contributions to emitter-function-logic (EFL), I^2L, and single-device-well (SDW) MOSFETs. He is a member of the Association of Professional Engineers of Ontario and a senior member of the Institute of Electrical and Electronics Engineers.